Welcome

It seems that people the world over are having to tighten their pockets. The aftermath of the credit crunch is still being felt, and in the UK in particular, the mixture of tax rises and spending cuts means that more and more people are looking for a fresh way to bring in some extra cash.

That's where eBay comes in. With over £1,000 per second changing hands on eBay across the world, it's become a favoured shopping destination of many. For buyers, it's a chance to snap up some great deals, and save valuable pounds on items against the high-street price. Furthermore, it's a treasure trove of items you simply wouldn't be able to get anywhere else.

For sellers? Where else would you be able to offer your wares to over 230 million people through just one website? Not for nothing have many people gone on to base successful businesses around the eBay service.

And yet it's not quite as simple as it seems. Is that bargain as good as it looks? Are you about to get scammed? How do you make your auctions more appealing to buyers? And what are the pitfalls that you need to avoid?

That's where we come in. Across the jam-packed pages of this guide, we're going to look at the secrets of being a successful buyer and seller on eBay. There's no lashing of gloss paint here; we're going to look as much at the cons as the pros. However, with some common sense, the advice we've got to offer and perhaps even the assistance of one of the many eBay aids reviewed in this book, you can get the deals you've been hoping for, and perhaps do your bank balance a bit of good too.

Happy bidding!

Simon Brew
simon_brew@dennis.co.uk

Contents

Chapter 1
Why Use eBay?

If you're brand new to eBay, then start right here, as we look at just what it can do for you, and how things have changed...

Chapter 2
What You Need To Get Started

So you're ready to take the plunge? Here's what you need to get up and running on eBay

Chapter 3
Introductory Selling

It's not tricky to get an item on eBay, but making a successful sale is another matter. It pays to get your listing right, and we've got lots of help right here

Chapter 4
Advanced Selling

If you're looking to do more than just sell a few items through eBay, then there's added help at hand, and a few tips and tricks worth knowing...

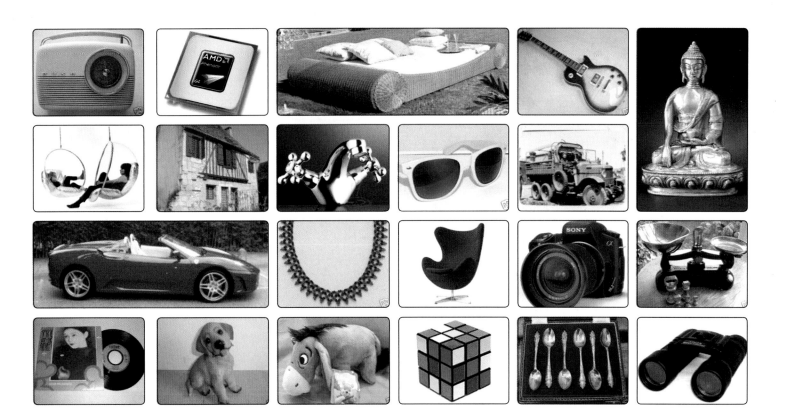

Chapter 5
Buying Through eBay

It's easy to pay over the odds on eBay, but armed with our advice there are great deals to be had

Chapter 6
PayPal

What is PayPal and how much is it going to cost you to use?

Chapter 7
eBay Alternatives

eBay doesn't have the monopoly on buying and selling. Here are some other places for your to promote your wares…

Chapter 8
Reviews

Lots of eBay services, programs, websites and more put to the test!

Case Studies

Chapter 1
Why Use eBay?

Why Use eBay?

It's the world's most successful auction website by far. So what makes it so special and how does it differ from its competitors?

When it comes to buying and selling online, there's still only one name that springs to mind: eBay. Like Google, eBay has managed to make a nonsense word familiar simply by being the best at what it does. It's a name that's always in the news for one reason or another - perhaps because of someone's astounding success story, or thanks to something weird, wonderful or controversial turning up for sale. But what is it about this online auction site that draws so many people in?

WORLDWIDE CAR-BOOT SALE

The popularity of eBay brought about possibly the most socially significant change to the way people buy and sell things since credit cards were invented. Sure, in the past people might have gone to jumble sales and picked up a few second-hand bargains, but even the biggest car-boot sale pales into insignificance when compared with eBay. Imagine having access to everything that anyone in the world might want to sell, whenever you want, from the comfort of your computer.

When you log into the site, you might not have any idea what you want to buy, or you might have something specific in mind. Either way, you're likely to be able to find something to bid on. It's worth bearing in mind, however, that the sale of certain items is prohibited, and eBay removes contentious sales pretty quickly. The current list of prohibited items includes plane tickets, alcohol, franking machines, fireworks, human parts and used cosmetics (you can find the full list at **pages.ebay.co.uk/help/policies-ov.html**) For most of us, though, all of that is no great loss. And for pretty much anything else, eBay's still your best bet, warts and all.

ONLINE DEPARTMENT STORE

Not everything on sold on eBay is second-hand. Retailers increasingly have an eBay arm to their business (and the increasing number of high-street stores on eBay has been a source of complaint in recent times), or will pass excess stock on to traders to sell on eBay, so the products won't have been used, or even taken out of their boxes. A PowerSeller logo beside an eBay trader's name indicates that this is someone who takes eBay seriously, sometimes running their entire business through the site.

eBay is also great fun just to browse around. Half the fun of shopping is browsing, and eBay has enough on offer to fill hours and hours of your life. It's all too easy to get drawn into a never-ending cycle of finding something you like, clicking through to the seller's shop to see what else they've got, then browsing through categories. Because any search is likely to bring up a variety of different options, it's easy to get carried away, looking at things that you never knew you wanted, and perhaps even buying a few.

◄ All kinds of things you didn't know you wanted are for sale

12 cornflake crispies

Item condition: **New**

Time left: 18d 20h (11 Aug, 2010 15:43:05 BST)

Quantity: 1   2 available

Price: **£4.00**   Buy It Now

Watch this item

Postage: £3.00 Royal Mail 1st Class Standard See disco
See all details
Estimated delivery within 2-3 business days.

Payments: **PayPal**, Postal order or Banker's draft, Credi
See details

Returns: Returns accepted | Read details

eBay Buyer Protection

Zoom unavailable   Enlarge

OPOSSUM TAXIDERMY ARM GAG GIFT WEIRD

Item condition: --

Ended: May 14, 2010 19:32:25 PDT

Bid history: 3 bids

Winning bid: **US $11.50**

Shipping: **FREE shipping** US Postal Service Parcel Post | See all details
Estimated delivery within 3-10 business days.

Returns: 7 day money back, buyer pays return shipping | Read details

eBay Buyer Protection
eBay will cover your purchase price plus original shipping.
Learn more

◄ Enlarge

◄ One of the more bizarre items you can bid on

GET RICH QUICK

Of course, the biggest attraction for many people is the promise of a quick and easy way to make money. Something about eBay appeals to the same part of our brains as TV programmes like *Antiques Roadshow* and *Cash In The Attic*; the idea that we might be sitting on a fortune is irresistible to most of us. Whereas once upon a time, people just held on to their valuables in order to pass them down to their children, nowadays we just have to know: is it worth much? And if it is, who might want to buy it?

In the past, some truly bizarre and often worthless items have been sold for enormous amounts of money on eBay, which can only be encouraging to would-be salespeople. One of the biggest items ever sold was a dismantled US Navy fighter jet, which sold for around $1 million on the US site. But that seems downright conventional when you consider that some people have managed to flog empty jars containing 'ghosts' (or even their own souls) on eBay. It's hard to argue with that kind of creativity.

It's much more enterprising, in any case, than those who've sold toenail clippings, a place at the birth of their child, or even their virginity. All of these are testament to the possibilities of eBay. Many of these items, of course, contravene eBay's terms and conditions, but that doesn't mean they still don't manage to turn up from time to time.

SOCIAL NETWORKING

As social networks go, eBay is never going to match up to the likes of Facebook and Twitter, but there is, nevertheless, a social side to the auction website. Buying something from an online store is usually a pretty impersonal experience; on eBay, you'll find yourself not only bidding against other people - and some auctions can get pretty frenzied - but you're also buying from a real person. The seller's screen name and feedback ratings are right there in front of

▲ eBay's social side has even led to marriage

you, and new eBay users might find that monitoring their feedback quickly becomes an obsession.

And the social aspect goes beyond trading messages with fellow eBayers. Some people have even met their future spouses on the site. One man, who was bidding on an ornamental eagle, ended up meeting the seller and falling in love with her. Another couple who met on the auction site actually ended up getting married at eBay's Annual User Conference in New Orleans in 2004. So while a relationship might be the last thing you're looking for on eBay, stories like this prove it's not beyond the realms of possibility.

DON'T BE SCARED!

As overwhelming as eBay might seem at first glance, it's easy to get around once you know how. That said, it's far from a perfect beast, and it pays to have advice and help in your corner. With that in mind, coming up, you'll find comprehensive advice from some of the UK's eBay experts, and plenty of case studies to show you how it should (and shouldn't) be done.

What Can It Do For You?

Whether you're just doing a spot of shopping or looking to set up your own business, eBay has something for everyone

eBay can be used for a variety of different purposes, and not everyone uses it in exactly the same way. You may never use all of eBay's features and functions, or you might use one now, and a different one later. Chances are, though, there's at least one way that eBay can be useful to you.

The three most obvious reasons for signing up to the site, and their relative advantages compared with the alternatives, are examined here.

CLEARING OUT THE GARAGE

Most people have a sizeable amount of 'stuff' that just sits in their house, taking up space. Over the years, unwanted gifts, impulse buys, and gadgets of all kinds fail to find their place in your life, and end up finding their place in the back of a cupboard, or in the attic or garage. You could round it all up and take it to a local charity shop, but some of it might be valuable, and wouldn't it be nice to make some money from it?

eBay obviously isn't the only solution, but it's a lot easier than placing an advert in the paper, or even going to a car-boot sale. Instead of having to drive to a field at 6am on a drizzly weekend morning, you can just log into a website, sit back, and wait for people to buy your items. There's also less haggling, and more structure; you're less likely to get ripped off using eBay because of the various procedures put in place.

eBay's rules make sure both buyers and sellers know where they stand legally right off the bat.

The other advantage is that you'll be reaching a much wider audience. Even if you're only willing to pay the postage on sending items out to bidders located in the UK, you'll be able to offer your items to people across the country, not just those who read your paper or attend your markets. That means you're more likely to find someone who's interested and, perhaps even more importantly, someone who's willing to pay you a price you're happy with.

MOVING YOUR BUSINESS ONLINE

Almost all businesses now have websites; the Internet is an important, if not a necessary, part of most business strategies. However, getting started can be quite daunting; websites can be expensive, difficult and time-consuming to set up, and if you want to be able to sell your products through your website, that adds an extra dimension of difficulty. It's easier, not to mention cheaper and quicker, to set up an eBay shop instead. Yes, you'll have to pay a fee to eBay in order to trade in this way, but it's likely to be a much smaller sum than you would otherwise spend on web development and maintenance.

There's also the fact that eBay has a built-in audience. People will already be logging into the site to shop, and might choose to look there before they'd

▶ **eBay provides a way for sellers to keep overheads low, so even low-cost items can be profitably sold**

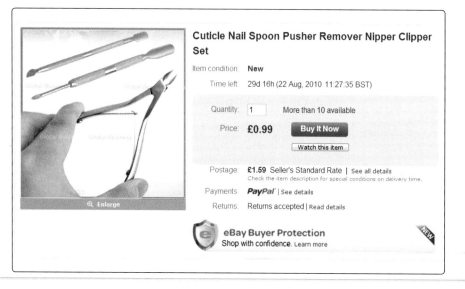

Cuticle Nail Spoon Pusher Remover Nipper Clipper Set

Item condition:	**New**
Time left:	29d 16h (22 Aug, 2010 11:27:35 BST)
Quantity:	1 More than 10 available
Price:	**£0.99** Buy It Now
	Watch this item
Postage:	**£1.59** Seller's Standard Rate	See all details
	Check the item description for special conditions on delivery time.
Payments:	**PayPal**	See details
Returns:	Returns accepted	Read details

eBay Buyer Protection
Shop with confidence. Learn more

DID YOU KNOW?

At the time of writing, every minute four mobile phones, ten books and 20 items of women's clothing are sold on eBay.

UK Coca Cola Cherry Coke 150ml 'picnic' can 1998, empty

Item condition: **New**

Quantity: | 1 | 4 available

Price: **£4.00** | **Buy It Now**

Watch this item

Postage: £1.25 Royal Mail 2nd Class Standard | **See all details**
Estimated delivery within 4-6 business days.

Payments: *PayPal*, Postal Order or Banker's Draft, Personal cheque, Credit card | See details

Returns: Returns accepted | Read details

eBay Buyer Protection
Shop with confidence. Learn more

🔍 Enlarge

▲ Even things normally reserved for the dustbin can end up on eBay

look at individual websites. For existing customers, or people who have already heard of your business, you can link from a main site to your eBay auctions (and vice versa), so they won't have to look very far to find what they're after either.

The most difficult part of moving a business online is probably finding a way to handle payments. With eBay, that's already taken care of: eBay's associated payment system, PayPal, is easy to use, reliable, and trusted by most web users. It's often more secure than other payment methods, with a much smaller margin for error.

FINDING A BARGAIN
As previously discussed, eBay is a prime location for finding pretty much anything, from antiques to records, from books to imaginary friends. It's a marketplace on an almost unimaginable scale. Because a lot of eBay

sales come from individuals selling things they no longer want (although the service is used more and more by big name business now), much of it will be a lot cheaper than you'd expect to pay if you found the item in a shop. Similarly, sellers who run most of their business through eBay will have lower overheads than traders who work from shops, so again the price you pay will probably be lower. And if not many other bidders are interested in the item you want, you could nab some real bargains.

There are any number of tricks and tips that can help you find the best deals, some of which will be covered later in this book. There's also a huge amount of satisfaction to be found in winning an auction and carrying off your prize, especially if it's something that's no longer on general sale, or something you've wanted for a long time and have never been able to find.

The fact that you can search auctions based all over the country - or even the world - widens your net and increases your chances of bagging a bargain. You can set your highest bid level at a price you're willing to pay, which means you can ensure you don't spend more than you're comfortable with, and you'll soon learn that even if you lose one auction, another one will be along shortly.

GETTING STARTED
By now, you should have some idea why people love eBay so much (and you may be drawing up plans of your own to buy and sell). The rest of this book, then, will explain exactly how to use the site, and warn you of any pitfalls you might encounter on your travels.

The Pros & Cons Of eBay

There are a number of advantages and disadvantages to using eBay. Here, we take a look at what they are

It's difficult to imagine the Internet without eBay now. For many people, it's a tool without which they couldn't run a business; for others, it's a last chance to find a must-have item not available on the high street. Many users will evangelise for hours on end about how brilliant it is, even those left cold by some of the increasing number of changes to the service over the past few years. But eBay isn't without its flaws. As with any service or marketplace, you'll need to keep your wits about you.

COMMUNITY SPIRIT

There are five 'fundamental values' that underpinned eBay, which used to be published on the site, although they've been removed in recent times. However, the guiding philosophy always used to be:

- We believe people are basically good.
- We believe everyone has something to contribute.
- We believe that an honest, open environment can bring out the best in people.
- We recognise and respect everyone as a unique individual.
- We encourage you to treat others the way you want to be treated.

The removal of these values from the site doesn't necessary mean that eBay no longer works to them, it's just it seems shyer about telling you so. That said, while it was never the case that eBay's founders didn't mean what they said, not everyone is always well-intentioned, and not everyone is trustworthy. Even if you assume that eBay employees adhere to these principles, that doesn't mean every single person doing business on the site will.

For every story about someone finding a treasure on eBay, there's a counter-story where someone got caught out by a hoax. Both are, of course, as rare as each other. A once common hoax is for sellers to pretend to sell some new and expensive consumer electronic item, but in fact only be offering the box; the photograph may well depict the real equipment, but somewhere buried in the listings will be a mention that only the box is up for auction. Fake Apple iPhones were listed on eBay before the real thing was available in the shops, and though these types of auctions are usually removed posthaste, you can't rely on eBay to catch all the fakes immediately. A few years ago, a schoolboy hit the headlines when a PlayStation 2 he bought on eBay turned up in a box stuffed with £44,000 worth of Euros. Quite rightly, his parents turned the money over to the police; there was clearly something suspicious going on.

Fast forward to the summer of 2009, meanwhile, and English 20 pence coins were attracting opportunists en masse. A small batch of said coins were minted without the date, and some eBay sellers grabbed the headlines when they tried to charge up to £5,000 - with free postage! - for collectors looking to pick up such a rarity.

NEWS ▶ LIVE BBC NEWS CHANNEL

News Front Page
World
UK
England
Northern Ireland
Scotland
Wales
Business
Politics
Health
Education
Science/Nature
Technology
Entertainment
Also in the news

Video and Audio
Have Your Say
Magazine
In Pictures
Country Profiles
Special Reports

Related BBC sites

Page last updated at 11:05 GMT, Wednesday, 27 August 2008 12:05 UK

✉ E-mail this to a friend   🖶 Printable version

Taxpayers' details found on eBay

A Leicestershire council is investigating a report that a computer containing taxpayers' personal details was sold on auction website eBay.

Bank account numbers and sort codes of people in the Charnwood Borough Council area were reportedly found after the equipment was sold for £6.99.

The authority said it was urgently investigating the matter.

The security scare comes a day after it was revealed a computer which held data on bank customers was sold on eBay.

An investigation is under way in that case after IT manager Andrew Chapman bought a computer on eBay, not knowing that the hard drive contained personal information relating to bank customers.

Information including bank account numbers, telephone numbers...

Charnwood Borough Council is investigating the report

" No hardware is ever resold.

▲ Sometimes you can get more than you bargained for

▲ Bob Geldof wasn't happy when Live 8 tickets appeared on eBay

BAD EGGS

Those were extraordinary cases; a more common eBay issue is a seller who just doesn't produce the promised item, or sends something in worse condition than they'd originally indicated. There are measures that can be taken against these people, but it's discouraging nonetheless. And, of course, it works both ways: sometimes, people bid on items but never pay for them, forcing the seller to relist the item and start all over again.

Some eBay sales might not seem illegal, but still fall foul of the rules and regulations. Tickets for the Live 8 charity concerts a few years ago, for example, popped up all over the auction site. Because these tickets were supposed to be free, the auctions were removed (and replaced with a vocal condemnation from Bob Geldof, you may remember). More recently, tickets for Michael Jackson's memorial concert were to be found on eBay at one point. Tickets for other concerts or events are listed for sale on eBay all the time (aside from football tickets, which eBay prohibits), and though these are perfectly fair game and have often been put on sale by genuine fans who can't attend the event for one reason or another, sometimes they're scalped or counterfeit tickets. It's important to think about what you're buying when you use eBay.

RINGING THE CHANGES

Another problem with eBay is that the rules can change at any time. For example, one of its policy changes meant that UK listings didn't automatically show up in searches performed on the US site. American customers could still browse UK listings, but they'd have to click through to the advanced search functions.

Obviously, this had a massive effect on UK traders who regularly sold to Stateside customers, and although eBay publicly apologised, it didn't change the policy back. According to eBay, this system made the listings more relevant to customers, and it was happy with its decision. After all, UK customers hadn't been prevented from using the US site; they'd just have to pay an additional listing fee to make sure that US bidders saw their items. This isn't a reason not to use eBay, but it might be a reason to avoid depending on it too heavily.

More recently, eBay introduced a policy that meant UK sellers weren't allowed to charge postage and packaging for DVDs. For those already on tight margins, not being able to charge postage has been a controversial move, which has been popular with buyers, but has led to some sellers moving away from eBay altogether, no longer able to compete with the big-name sellers. Fortunately, said policy has since been reversed, although limits are still in place.

▲ For all its advantages, it pays to exercise caution on eBay

Not all policy changes are so controversial. For example, a policy change to the jewellery section of the site meant that sellers could only describe their wares as diamonds if they met certain criteria - in other words, if they really were diamonds. Other look-alike gems, such as cubic zirconia, had to be clearly labelled; if the word 'diamond' was used in the listing, 'imitation' or 'simulated' had to precede it. Undoubtedly, this change would have upset some sellers, but it's clearly for the good of the customer.

Price changes originally introduced during the autumn of 2008 incited some discussion and debate, as eBay introduced changes for fixed-price sellers that led to complaints of favouring businesses over individuals. Changes since then have led to complaints along similar lines, and the alterations to the feedback system in the past years have moved more power into the hands of buyers, leading to outrage among sellers. This is covered in more detail elsewhere in this book.

BUSINESS SENSE

It's important to take into account the fact that eBay is, ultimately, a business, and it's a hugely successful one at that (in spite of the growing criticisms that it's faced in recent times). People often talk about eBay as if it's a purely altruistic organisation, but it's not. Yes, it's an exciting service with potentially a lot to offer, but before you do anything else, you should make sure you've read the terms and conditions.

eBay By The Numbers

Not all eBay auctions are successful. More than half end without a single bid. What are people after? We check out the top searches

Financially, eBay is huge. However, it hasn't been immune to the credit crunch and recession of recent times. According to the Wall Street Journal, it suffered a year-on-year quarterly decline of 9%, taking revenue down to just under the $2 billion mark. Despite seeing a string of consecutive drops in earnings, its share price nevertheless climbed, so it's obvious that the site which tells you to "Buy It, Sell It, Love It" has persuaded a lot of people to do those exact three things, with investors remaining confident about the world's largest auction website.

By mid-2009, eBay was reporting 233 million members, with around half that number in the US (which is one of 37 markets in which eBay has a presence). In the UK there are 14 million active users, 40.62% of whom visit eBay.co.uk at least once a month. Recent figures estimate that 178,000 users in the UK use eBay to run a business or as their primary or secondary source of income, posting items in 13,000 categories (there are 50,000 categories worldwide). Across the world more than $60 billion worth of merchandise is traded and $1,900 (approx £1,155) is spent via eBay every second.

WHAT WORKS?

So what kind of items are most popular, and what are buyers looking for? The largest stores tend to sell books, DVDs and car parts, but a glance at eBay's 'Pulse' data (which you can find at **pulse.ebay.co.uk**) reveals that it's technology that's still being actively hunted down; mobiles phones, games consoles, iPods, and laptops continually dominate the top ten, with only clothes and cars regularly making in-roads in the chart. In fact, the 'Collectables' category is the most used, accounting for about 15% of all auctions where Hornby items, Pokemon, postcards, flags, medals, Betty Boop, enamel signs and Guinness figure highly. It's not the most lucrative, however. It's eighth overall, with motor vehicles coming top. Then again, they do cost more to actually buy on the whole!

The total number of 'collectable' items actually increases when you take into account other categories being used to advertise them. In the 'Cars, Motorcycles & Vehicles' category, for example, classic cars are the fourth most popular search term. Not for nothing is one of the key terms most used when listing products on eBay the word 'vintage'.

Given eBay's past reputation as a place to get items stupidly cheap, these statistics aren't surprising, but the situation is very different now that the world has latched on. Whereas it used to be possible to sneak in at the last second and put in a winning bid, or find an auction that nobody else had stumbled on, it's getting increasingly hard to find genuine bargains on the most popular and top-selling products. Also, most sales tend to be Buy It Now only, sadly, which has taken some of the fun away too.

What eBay's popularity boom has done, however, is make far more items available than ever before. Not only are there a lot more auctions based in a lot more places, the range of items has widened as people realise that there's a market for just about anything. Some of the stranger auctions (and eBay.co.uk has broken the barrier for having had ten million items available at any one time) include a single cornflake (which, incredibly, sold for £1.20), positive energy, squirrel underpants, a flexy straw (which went for $60.98) and a log shaped like the Mercedes Benz insignia. You can be certain that in the ten years of eBay.co.uk and more in the US, there have been some strange old auctions.

If all this sounds like the whole set-up is somewhat strange, then that would be an understandable conclusion to reach, but it's one of the reasons why eBay is one of the best places for selling anything from anywhere. Whatever's in the

▲ **eBay Pulse gives access to a wide source of information**

Categories

Most popular eBay categories by revenue:

eBay Motors	$16.5 billion
Consumer Electronics	$4.9 billion
Clothing & Accessories	$4.5 billion
Computers	$4 billion
Books/Movies/Music	$3.1 billion
Home & Garden	$3.6 billion
Sports	$2.6 billion
Collectibles	$2.7 billion
Business & Industrial	$2.2 billion
Toys	$2.1 billion
Jewellery & Watches	$2 billion
Cameras & Photo	$1.5 billion
Antiques & Art	$1.4 billion
Coins & Stamps	$1.3 billion

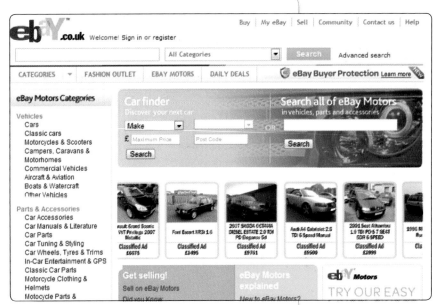

▲ **eBay Motors has grown year on year**

loft, or whatever someone has a desire to put in the loft, it's almost guaranteed to be on eBay. Sometimes, the more obscure the better.

In that sense, it's not hard to see why so many people choose eBay over other auction sites such as CQOut (**www.cqout.com**). Although there was initially some competition when the idea of Internet auctions appeared (names such as QXL, Yahoo! Auctions and Amazon Auctions have all fallen by the wayside), it was eBay that out-muscled every other name. This was pretty surprising in the case of Yahoo! Auctions, which was a free service and has now closed completely in the UK. The sheer scale of eBay, which makes other sites look positively minuscule in comparison, means that using those other sites is a bit like going to a small-town local market with a handful of stalls, rather than a county-advertised car-boot sale that fills an entire field.

SUCCESS OR FAILURE

This, of course, isn't without its problems. Around 54% of all listings on eBay end without getting a single bid. Putting an item up for sale doesn't necessarily mean that the ideal buyer is going to find it within the allotted time, or pay the price demanded, or that they haven't found an alternative lot in better condition or closer to where they live. In car-boot terms, it's like being stuck on a wallpapering table in the furthest corner from the entrance, half-an-hour from the burger van and in a large puddle. And if this happens, you still have to pay for your listing - unlike Amazon, for example, where advertising an item only incurs a fee if it sells. The exception comes if you're a private eBay seller and you list your item in an eligible category in the auction-style format with a

starting price of up to 99p. In those cases, insertion is free.

Some eBay users prefer Amazon when it comes to selling books, CDs and DVDs. Amazon user James said, "The great thing about Amazon is that you get far longer to sell the item, and if you don't manage to find a buyer, you haven't lost anything. You can pay quite a lot of money to eBay for an unsuccessful ten-day listing, whereas on Amazon you get 60 days for free. Although Amazon does take a hefty fee on completion of a sale, you tend to make it back on the postage. Sometimes you can sell a book for a penny and still get more for it overall than you would have done on eBay - had you sold it at all."

However, with Amazon, you are generally - although not always - at the mercy of which products it already currently sells. "Amazon is no good for more obscure things, and sometimes I haven't been able to list modern titles with ISBN codes. That's frustrating for both the seller and any potential buyers, especially if it's something you could get from Waterstone's or HMV. Amazon is fantastic if you're dealing with specific and reasonably easily available items, but eBay wins when it comes to rare or just downright odd."

BIG MONEY

eBay Motors is arguably the greatest success story from the site as a whole. It has 12 million monthly unique visitors and, once the site had established a level of trust, sales rose from $1.5bn (£760m) in 2002 to $18bn (approx. £10bn) in 2008. A staggering 34% of all online automotive minutes are spent on eBay Motors, making eBay the top online automotive site based on the percentage of minutes users are surfing

DID YOU KNOW?

A Shropshire businessman who had been burgled spotted some of his possessions on eBay. As a result, police raided three addresses in Shrewsbury, recovering goods worth up to £7,500.

▶ AuctionSniper: another of the many sniping tools available to download from the web

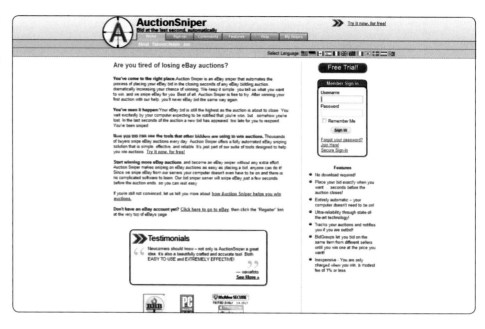

auto listings. eBay used to have an attached feeling of paying your money and taking your chances, but little by little it became the weapon of choice for those having no luck in the classified ads. Ironically, eBay now does classifieds of its own, as well as auctions, and, given the weight of traffic flowing, it seems a more attractive prospect than the local paper (or even some of the bigger ones, such as Loot).

This counts even more so if the item that contains a motor isn't necessarily a car. If you ever fancy buying an aeroplane, there's no shortage here. Helicopters, fighter jets and even a Russian space shuttle have appeared over the years, along with the necessary consumables, simulators and ejector seats. The most expensive item ever sold was a private business jet for $4.9 million. Is eBay unique? Certainly.

EASY TO USE?
But just how easy is it to use? Is buying really that simple? If someone's only got a few items to sell, is it worth them even signing up? What if they have a whole shop full of stuff and would like an Internet-based outlet as well?

Signing up is easy enough. You provide a username and password, exactly like registering with any other site, and then some personal details. The one 'detail' you might balk at providing is a credit or debit card, but this is a standard procedure, which has been in place for years to help combat fraud and misuse of the service. Verify your account by checking your e-mail for the automated message, and the process is complete and you can start bidding. It's that fast.

Bidding is equally easy, which has been the downfall of some addicted users. You read the item description, put the maximum amount you're willing

to pay into the box and confirm your bid. You don't even have to worry about going back and bidding again, as the proxy system means that eBay will do it for you.

"I was long attracted by eBay, and one day decided to take the plunge," said Bill Dove, who lives near Falmouth, Cornwall. "I began selling some of my old board games that I had stored in my loft and cupboards for years. That was in 2000. I had a large collection and really needed to downsize to create more space, and the extra income proved very useful. But I remember buying as well and having to wait at the computer while an auction was ending, eager not to miss out."

These days, 'sniper' software will ensure that you aren't outbid at the last second, and there are various auction management programs and websites that will help to keep track of multiple auctions (you'll find a round-up of some of your options at the back of this book). eBay's own interface is detailed enough to keep any user up to date with all their activity, and

▲ The Bidnapper sniping tool

DID YOU KNOW?

As eBay rarely intervenes in disputes between traders, an alternative is the small claims court. It can deal with claims of up to £5,000 in England and Wales or up to £3,000 in Scotland, and you can take the case there yourself without a solicitor. As journalist and eBay user Stuart Campbell said, "People don't know how simple and inexpensive the small claims court is."

you can even have warnings sent to your mobile phone if you're in danger of losing an item.

Paying for things is a lot easier than it used to be. Years ago, when you won an auction, you usually had to pay by cash or postal order, which was not good if you were buying from the States. International money orders are expensive, so if there was something you really wanted from over the pond, you'd hide some cash in a letter or padded envelope.

Thankfully, the days of putting bank notes in the post and hoping the mail sorters were honest are over. eBay introduced the PayPal system as a means of payment, and then liked it so much it bought it. Completing a transaction is now as straightforward as pressing 'Pay Now', entering the relevant amount and hitting 'Send'. If the seller's on the ball, it's possible to get the item as early as the next day. And it's not just auctions; hundreds of thousands of eBay Shops are online, allowing you to purchase directly as from any other Internet store, and often delivering much quicker.

SELLING WORK

Selling is a different matter, of course, and requires some work. You'll have to choose a category, write up a description, include a photograph (which increases your chances of success), decide starting prices and which payment methods you'll accept. eBay seller James said that this has got easier: "You can put in your item title now and eBay will try to identify a category that's relevant. If it can't, and to be honest it often doesn't, you just choose from a list and then some subcategories. It can take a while to put a page

▲ eBay has become the number one way for people to get rid of their old belongings

together, but sometimes the simplest ones are the best anyway. People hate having to wade through loads of unnecessary detail when all they really want is a photograph and a price."

It's then a case of sitting back and watching the bids roll in - or not, if the 54% is anything to go by. Common advice states that waiting for an appropriate time to list an item can really help, as does Jenny's experience from when she sold a copy of a Derren Brown book for three figures. "I saw some copies a while back and knew that they were already quite rare, so I bought one with the intention of reading it and then reselling it when his new series started. I did exactly that and sold it for more than twice what I paid for it. Looking at prices now, I got in at exactly the right time. He went off the TV and nobody has sold one for that amount since."

James agrees: "Sporting goods can be a real balancing act. Do you just sell them, or wait for the team or player to start doing well? What if they get injured? What if you miss that window of opportunity? Selling things can be very difficult if you don't know all the ins and outs. That's fine if you want to attempt getting rid of some junk or you don't care about getting the maximum possible amount for your items, but tough if you're dealing with Collectables - which, of course, is what eBay's all about."

If you want to give eBay a try, you have nothing to lose; just stay sensible and alert and follow some simple rules. If you manage to keep your head, then you're far likely to be successful using eBay than someone who gets caught up in the moment, and puts common sense aside.

Facts & Figures

1995: The year eBay was founded in the US

233 million: The number of registered users worldwide

49%: The amount of revenue eBay pulls in from America alone

$1,839: The sum, per second, eBay users worldwide trade on the site

6.4 million: The number of new listings added each day

39%: The amount of goods now sold at a fixed price

632,000: The number of worldwide stores

Five billion: The number of feedback comments left

MEMORABLE EBAY AUCTIONS

TREASURE TROVE

The British Museum is keen to point out that treasure hunters who find valuables such as gold and silver coins or Roman jewellery and sell them on eBay are breaking the law. Items found in this way should be reported to the authorities as treasure trove, and the Museum has set up the Portable Antiquities Scheme (PAS) to police eBay for such items.

The Evolution Of eBay

How did a computer programmer's home page grow into the world's biggest online auction site, and arguably the dot-com boom's greatest success story? Let's take a look...

Like many web users in the mid-90s, Baltimore-based Franco-Iranian computer programmer Pierre Omidyar had a home page. And like many home pages, it was pretty trivial. It even included a tongue-in-cheek 'tribute' section dedicated to the Ebola virus. But it was soon to grow into something massive. The 28-year-old coder became interested in the technical issues involved in setting up an online auction site, where sellers and buyers could interact independently of the facilitator. He added a test-of-concept feature, which he called AuctionWeb, to his website and went live with it on America's Labor Day weekend in 1995.

The very first item sold on AuctionWeb was a broken laser pointer, listed for sale by Omidyar himself. His expectations for the auction were low, believing it would only make a few cents, if it sold at all. This first, trivial listing was intended to test how his new subsite performed with a live auction rather than to sell the product. But to his astonishment, it went for $14.83. "You do realise it's broken?" Omidyar e-mailed to the winning bidder. "I'm a collector of broken laser pointers," he replied.

Omidyar had never intended AuctionWeb to take off to any great degree. He was more interested in the

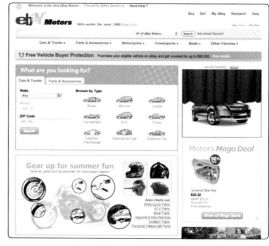

▲ eBay Motors was launched in 1999

technical side of things than running it as a business. Yet as the laser pointer auction proved, he was onto something big. Sellers began listing all manner of items on AuctionWeb, which soon took over his entire domain. When it became too big even for this, he moved the site to a new, more expensive business domain. He tried to register www.echobay.com, after his consultancy firm, Echo Bay Technologies, but the URL was already taken, so he chose a shortened version; ebay.com was born!

According to eBay, "from day one, Omidyar built eBay around what remain the company's core values" that people are basically good, that everyone has something to contribute and an open environment brings out the best in people. According to the website, "The success of eBay underscores the truth of these values, and is at the heart of eBay's continuing success."

EARLY GROWTH

The budding auction site grew and grew. In early 1996, Omidyar started charging a fee based on the final sale price. He wasn't sure whether the users would accept this, but the money soon came rolling in. Monthly profits reached $10,000 by June, having doubled for four consecutive months. It was time to quit his day job and devote his full-time attentions to eBay, which took on its first employee around now, a

▲ eBay's head office in San Jose, California

Popular eBay Items

The most popular items sold each year, by category and item, are as follows:

2000 Toys & games: TV and film character toys, including Pokémon trading cards
2001 Sports memorabilia: football programmes
2002 Music: pop CDs
2003 Music: pop CDs
2004 Music: pop CDs
2005 DVDs: action/adventure movies
2006 Mobile & home phones: mobile phones
2007 Clothing, shoes & accessories: women's clothing
2008 Clothing, shoes & accessories: women's clothing
2009 Clothing, shoes & accessories: women's clothing

part-timer called Chris Agarpao. He was soon joined by the company's first president, Canadian-born businessman Jeff Skoll. By the end of the year, eBay boasted 41,000 registered users, and a Gross Merchandise Volume (the total value of all goods sold on the site) of $7.2 million. eBay soon entered its first third-party licensing deal, licensing its SmartMarket Technology to a company called Electronic Travel Auction, which sold plane tickets and other such travel products.

By 1997, aided by an investment of $5,000,000 from a venture capital firm, the company had grown to 41 employees. It's said that in the early days they sat on folding chairs, and used self-assembly desks they had to screw together themselves. Unlike other hungry dot-com start-ups, Omidyar was keeping costs as low as possible, even though business was growing at a phenomenal rate. eBay was hosting over 200,000 auctions a month, compared to 250,000 auctions for the whole of 1996. Collectors found the site especially useful, with the market for Beanie Babies alone surpassing $500,000 a year. Registered users crossed the 341,000 mark, and gross sales exceeded $95 million. Feedback stars made an appearance too, joining the feedback forum introduced the previous year. In September, the AuctionWeb name was dropped and the entire site branded under the name 'eBay'.

In March 1998, Harvard Business School graduate Margaret Whitman joined eBay as CEO to further develop and expand the business, which she went on to do with a series of shrewdly planned buyouts. The personalisation tool, My eBay, was launched to make it easier for both buyers and sellers to manage their accounts, and the eBay Foundation was set up as a charitable institution. In September, just three years after selling that broken laser pointer on his home page, eBay went public. Omidyar and Skoll became instant billionaires. By now the company boasted 138 employees, 2.1 million registered users and had a Gross Merchandise Volume of $740 million.

INTERNATIONAL REACH

1999 saw some major changes to the online auction site. First of all, it went international, with local versions of eBay launching in several countries. Germany was first, with www.ebay.de launching in June. The UK and Australia got their own eBay sites in October. The march towards world domination had begun. eBay Motors was also launched that year. This specialist site, found at www.motors.ebay.com, offers an online marketplace for cars, vans, motorcycles, boats, collectables and other vehicles, as well as parts and accessories. The 'Buy It Now' option was introduced, enabling sellers to sell at a fixed price instead of going through the auction process, and a partnership with AOL was launched. eBay paid $75 million to become AOL's official auction site for four years, giving it prominent placement on several sites owned by the ISP, including AOL.com, Compuserve, instant messaging service ICQ and the newly acquired Netcenter Web portal of Netscape Communications Corporation. By now the auction site, which was still only four years old, had 640 employees and ten million registered users.

eBay started the year 2000 as the net's number one e-commerce site, a position it cemented with a series of new international launches. In April, the auction site opened a Canadian branch, with France following in October and Austria in December. eBay Taiwan

▲ PayPal introduced Buyer Protection in 2003

▲ eBay's front page in April 2000

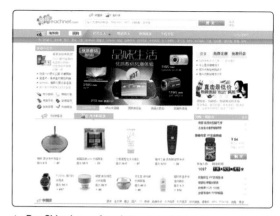

▲ eBay China is now found at www.eachnet.com

▲ By 2006, the categories list began to show the range and diversity we know today

▲ eBay UK, as it is today. Easily navigable, with lots of categories to choose from

launched this year too. But one wing of the company which wasn't doing so well was Billpoint. An online payment system bought by eBay in May 1999, Billpoint was intended to take some of the risk out of paying for goods won on eBay. By February 2000, it was processing 4,000 payments a day, but start-up company PayPal was getting through 200,000 daily transactions. Ironically, most of these were generated by eBay sales. Yet this was a minor glitch in an otherwise unqualified success story. By the end of the year, the auction site had around 1,900 employees, which was triple its 1999 workforce, and 22 million registered users.

In another charitable move, eBay launched Auction for America on 17th September 2001, to raise money for the victims of the terrorist attacks on the Pentagon and the World Trade Center six days earlier. eBay Stores was also launched that year, as were new international marketplaces in Ireland, Italy, Korea, New Zealand, Singapore and Switzerland. eBay was going from strength to strength. In the past year, its registered users had almost doubled to 42 million, and its employees swelled to 2,500.

The phishing scam that hit the site in 2001 was much less welcome. A spam e-mail claiming to be from eBay encouraged users to follow a link and enter their registration details into what was a fake version of eBay's home page. eBay issued a warning.

PAYPAL

By the summer of 2002, eBay had already acquired and swallowed up eight companies, mostly rival online auction sites. But its most significant acquisition came in October of that year. PayPal, by now a near monopoly in the independent online payments market, was bought by eBay for $1.5 billion. By the time of the buyout, PayPal was already the payment system of choice for around 50% of eBay users and, under the eBay umbrella, it continued to grow. Competing services such as Citibank's c2it and Yahoo!'s PayDirect soon closed as PayPal became as dominant in the online payments market as eBay was in online auctions. In 2008 it processed transactions of $60 billion in total, an increase of 27% over the previous year. Naturally, PayPal's position as the de rigueur payment method for eBay made life easier for eBayers. Sellers could get away with offering only one payment type without risking their auction prices, and buyers knew their PayPal accounts were valid anywhere on eBay

eBay Facts & Figures

Here are some things you may not know about eBay:

- A women's dress is sold every 18 seconds, a mobile phone every six seconds and a major appliance every minute.
- eBay currently enjoys approximately 84 million active users worldwide.
- More than $1,900-worth of goods are traded on the site every second.
- eBay UK currently has over 15 million users, with over 70 million items listed at any one time.
- 45% of active UK Internet users visit eBay.co. uk at least once a month.
- eBay has localised websites in 30 countries.
- Since 2005, there have been over 1.5 million charity auctions on eBay, raising more than £18.3 million.
- In 2008, the last year for which we have complete figures, the company had a turnover of $8.46 billion and a net income of $348 million.
- You can buy just about anything on eBay, which today has over 13,000 product categories, but a few items are prohibited. These include live animals, bootleg or pirated movies and music,

By 2003, eBay had topped 5,700 employees, up from 4,000 the previous year. There were around 95 million registered users, and 40 million people with PayPal accounts. And still the company continued to grow, opening a Hong Kong site in December. PayPal introduced Buyer Protection in this year. Now, if you bought an item on eBay and it didn't arrive or was significantly different to how it was described in the auction, you could appeal to PayPal and possibly get your money back (including the postage), subject to adjudication by PayPal. The maximum amount covered was boosted to $1,000 the following year. eBay UK reached a major milestone in 2003 too. Come December, it crossed the 100 million listings barrier.

2004 was another year of expansion and acquisitions, as eBay opened local sites in Malaysia and the Philippines and bought out the Bazee marketplace in India, and Rent.com closer to home. eBay also opened its China Development Center in Shanghai to accelerate technology innovation. By now it employed 8,100 staff worldwide, and enjoyed 135 million registered users.

The following year, eBay made its biggest purchase to date, paying $2.6 billion in cash and stock for Internet telephony leader Skype. Other acquisitions included Verisign Merchant Gateway and Shopping. com, and there were launches in Poland and Sweden. eBay was growing at such an incredible rate that in 2006, the company boasted 222 million users and 13,200 employees. The following year, the UK site reached another milestone, crossing the one billion listings mark. Also in 2006, eBay made available some of its programming interfaces, allowing third-party developers to build applications that work with eBay.

CHANGES

Two changes made in 2008 got a mixed reception from eBay users. At the beginning of the year, the feedback system was changed so sellers could no longer give negative feedback on buyers. The move was made due to complaints from buyers that they couldn't leave deservedly negative feedback without risking a retaliatory strike, but sellers complained they now had no recourse against a miscreant buyer. In December, the site abandoned its live auctions, which had been run in association with an auction house and allowed eBay users to bid through eBay, just as they would if they were at the venue. According to Jim Ambach, vice president of Seller Experience, live auctions were no longer part of eBay's immediate focus and were therefore retired.

While users might gripe and groan about changes in the rules and alleged lack of support when there's a problem, almost everyone agrees the site has grown in user-friendliness over the years. As Pennsylvanian eBayer Colleen Allison put it, "I've sold more on eBay in the last four months than I did in the previous three years combined, and it has definitely become more user-friendly."

And the site is growing in popularity on this side of the pond too. eBay UK, which celebrated its tenth anniversary in the autumn of 2009, today offers more than 17 million live listings at any one time. 45% of active UK Internet users visit eBay.co.uk at least once a month, and it's been estimated that 178,000 users run a business as a primary or secondary source of income. And with 13,000 categories to choose from, there's an excellent chance you'll find what you're looking for.

It seems eBay has come on a long way since it sold that broken laser pointer over a decade ago...

Chapter 2
What You Need To Get Started

Your eBay Toolkit

You've decided to give eBay a try, but don't know where to begin. In this chapter, we show you what you need to get started

Given that eBay's an online service, the place to start with your toolkit is a computer with Internet access. Broadband isn't essential but is certainly desirable, because browsing a dynamic e-commerce site like eBay using dial-up is like walking down the street while wearing concrete boots. You'll manage it, but not very quickly.

You'll also need a web browser like Microsoft Internet Explorer or Mozilla Firefox so you can access eBay and the wider web. It's also advisable to have some kind of anti-virus protection and firewall installed on your computer. eBay ensures that all your personal details are encrypted using secure communication software, but it's always a good idea to protect your interests at your end.

BRING AND BUY

In addition to a computer to sit behind, a potential eBay buyer also needs a roof over their head, or at least a front door with a number or name on it. A postal address is required to receive the items you buy. To purchase said items, you'll also need a

suitable form of payment, which is not as blindingly obvious as it may sound, because it depends entirely on the seller's preferences. Some sellers will happily accept traditional forms of payment such as cash (how quaint!), postal orders and cheques. However, the vast majority of sellers prefer to receive online payments, because they're processed much more quickly and securely. Some sellers will only accept online payments using services like PayPal or Nochex.

What does this mean? Well, eBay policy now states that all sellers must offer PayPal as a payment method, so you can easily pay for any item online, although you will need a credit card or bank account to facilitate the payment. If you don't already have a PayPal account, one will be created for you. All you need to do is specify whether you want to draw the funds from a credit or debit account. It's simple, and because the transaction is completed immediately, you can be sure that your items are winging their way towards you much more quickly.

▲ Pictures play an important part when selling goods

▲ A computer is obviously one of the key requirements for any potential eBay user

THE HARD SELL

If you intend to sell items on eBay, then you also need a PayPal (or similar) account. Again, you'll need to link your online account to a credit card or bank account. As a seller, it's recommended that you verify your account. There's more information on PayPal at the end of this chapter.

An essential piece of equipment for every seller is a digital camera, as it enables you to take photographs of your items and use them to illustrate your listings. After all, people like to see exactly what they're buying. When eBay was in its infancy and digital cameras were still very much a luxury item, very few sellers uploaded images, but these days you'd be committing commercial suicide if you didn't provide at least one image. If you don't have a digital camera, then it's almost essential to get or borrow one. You'll also need some means of transferring the photos from your camera to your computer - check your camera's documentation for further details.

eBay charges you for uploading multiple pictures (only one photo per listing is free), so if you'd like to display more than one picture it's a good idea to acquire some personal web space and host the images yourself. If you're planning to sell regularly, then this will work out cheaper than having to continually pay eBay's image fees (and you won't be limited to the default 400 x 300 dimensions that eBay rather stingily resizes your images to). Check with your Internet service provider; you may find that you've been supplied with some free web space,

which will be useful for image-hosting purposes. We'll be coming back to images in more detail later in this book.

CHECK IT OUT

You should now have everything you need to start wheeling and dealing on eBay. An Internet-enabled computer? Check. A postal address? Check. A bank account and/or credit card? Check. A digital camera? Check. There's just one thing missing: an eBay account. Registering for an account is free and easy. Just follow our step-by-step guide and you'll become a member of the world's largest marketplace in a matter of minutes.

What's In A Name?

When you register with eBay, you must enter a User ID. This is your unique username that's displayed (rather than your real name) when you buy and sell on eBay. If you use eBay casually, your choice of User ID isn't overly important. It just needs to be something that a) you're not going to forget, and b) doesn't put people off. However, if you're planning on specialising in a particular area and bulk-selling a certain type of product, you should choose a User ID that reflects your business. If you're not happy with your chosen ID, eBay lets you change it at any time (but not more than once a month).

MEMORABLE EBAY AUCTIONS

FLYING SAUCER

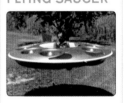

According to inventor Paul Moller, "the M200X was the first VTOL aircraft of its kind (flying car) to fly successfully and did so repeatedly during the 1980s." He planned to put the vehicle into production, but sold the original prototype on eBay. Some experts doubted the veracity of Moller's claims for the device.

How To... Set Up Your eBay Account

Whatever your reason for going to eBay, you'll need to get registered and set up your account. Here's how:

1 There are two types of eBay account: private and business. This guide covers the registration process for a private account. If the volume of items you sell increases, you can always switch to a business account later.

2 The eBay home page bombards you with links and featured items. You can ignore all of this for now. Look at the top-left corner of the page and you'll see the welcome line, which reads, 'Welcome! Sign in or register.' You can browse eBay without becoming a member, but to buy and sell you must sign up to the site, so click 'Register'.

3 If it says 'Hello' followed by a username, then someone else uses eBay on the same computer, and they've asked for eBay to remember their login details for them. You must never use someone else's membership, so click the 'Sign Out' option to exit their account. You can now click the 'Register' option.

4 You're prompted to enter your details, but before you begin filling in the boxes, click on the 'Privacy Policy' link. As you'll shortly be submitting personal information, including bank account details, you should be aware of how eBay stores and uses this.

5 Don't get too hung up on the details; it's all pretty standard. When you get to the bottom of the page, click the 'eBay User Agreement' link. This page displays eBay's terms and conditions, which all users have to

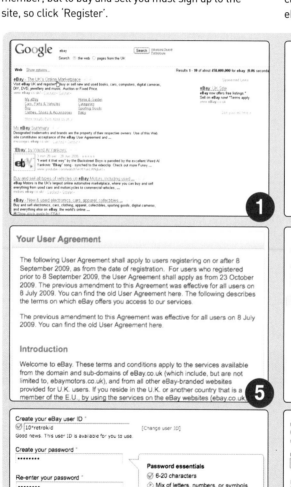

accept. Read through the details so you know where you stand as a user.

6 Okay, now you've got your head around all the legal stuff, you can return to the registration page and enter your details. The form should be familiar, as it's very similar to other online forms that you've no doubt completed in the past. All fields marked with an asterisk need to be completed.

7 Next, enter your name, address and telephone details. You must enter your primary phone number. There's no need to worry about receiving unsolicited calls, because eBay will only contact you by telephone in the event of there being a problem with your account. Similarly, you're also required to enter a working e-mail address.

8 The next step is to enter your User ID (see the previous information about suitable usernames). Enter your User ID and wait while the site checks it. If the username you've opted for has already been taken by another user, the site will suggest several alternatives that you can choose from instead.

9 Once your User ID has been accepted, you then have to create a password to go with it. To ensure your chosen password is secure, a number of rules are imposed: it must be at least six characters in length; include a mixture of numbers, letters and symbols; not be similar to your username or e-mail address; and not easily guessable.

10 When you enter a password, eBay will instantly assess it and let you know if it satisfies all of the rules. If any red flags appear, you must tweak your password until four green flags are displayed. When eBay is happy with your password, you must re-enter it in the box below for verification purposes.

11 In case you forget your password later, you must enter the answer to one of the secret questions. If

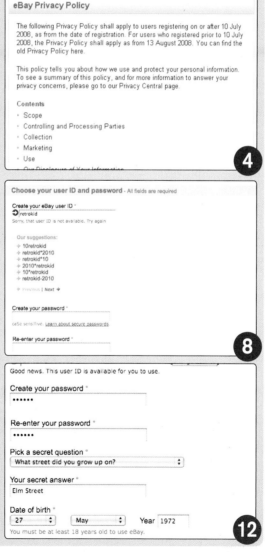

you then request for your password to be sent to you, eBay will ask you your chosen secret question and will only supply the password if the correct answer is given.

12 Next, enter your date of birth using the day and month drop-down menus, then tap the year into the final box. This step checks that you're 18 or over. If you're under 18, then you're not legally allowed to buy and sell on eBay. Sorry, kids!

13 To ensure you're a real flesh-and-blood person and not an evil account-registering robot, you must enter the numeric verification code in the box. If you're struggling to decipher the jumble of numbers, click the 'Refresh this image' link until a clear code appears.

14 Tick the box at the bottom to confirm you've read the User Agreement and the Privacy Policy, and understood the terms of use, then click the 'Register' button at the bottom of the page. eBay will then send a confirmation e-mail to your chosen e-mail address.

15 Open your e-mail application and wait for the message to land in your inbox (it may take a short while to arrive, so don't worry if it doesn't appear immediately). When it does, click on the 'Confirm Now' button on the e-mail to confirm that your e-mail address is correct.

16 If for some reason nothing happens when you click on the link, you'll notice that a Confirmation Code is also included in the e-mail. Copy this code and then click the link displayed below. You'll be taken to a screen where you can paste the code and confirm your e-mail address. Click 'Register' when done.

17 Once your e-mail address has been confirmed, you will be automatically signed in under your User ID. You can now begin to browse, bid for and buy items. However, if you wish to sell items on eBay you must follow some additional steps, in order to create a seller's account.

18 As a new eBay user, before you can list your first item, you'll be prompted to register as a seller. You will incur fees every time you sell an item, so you have to select a method of payment from the three available options: PayPal, credit/debit card, or direct debit.

19 If you choose to put your debit or credit card on record, carefully enter the card details, making sure all the fields are filled in. The billing address for the card must match the address you registered with. If you need to amend the address, click the 'Change' link.

20 As an extra security measure, eBay will confirm your landline telephone number with an automated call in which you're given a confirmation code. Click the 'Call Me' button, then answer the call and jot down the four-digit code. Enter the code on screen to continue.

21 Once you've chosen how you wish to pay for your eBay selling fees, you will become a registered seller and be returned to the selling screen. All fees you now incur will be paid automatically on a monthly basis.

22 It's important you keep your personal details up to date. If you need to make a change, click the 'My eBay' option found at the top of every eBay page. Here you can monitor items you're watching or selling, view messages, change preferences and update your details.

23 Open the 'Account' tab at the top of the page and click the 'Personal Information' link. You'll see all the information you entered when you registered. To make a change, click the 'Edit' link to the right of the detail you wish to amend. You will be prompted to re-enter your password for each change.

24 If you should forget either your User ID or password, go to the Register screen and you'll see links that you can use to request a reminder. For your password, you'll need to answer your secret question and enter various personal details.

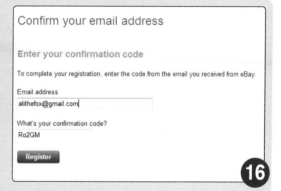

Get To Grips With PayPal

If you're going to be a good eBayer, it's worth getting yourself an account with its most popular payment system

PayPal is eBay's own online payment system that enables you to send and receive funds via the Internet. Essentially, it acts as a monetary middleman between the buyer and the seller, ensuring that the transaction is both speedy and secure (neither party has access to the other's personal banking details). It should come as no surprise, then, that it has become phenomenally popular as a payment method on eBay, with reports suggesting that more than 90% of all

eBay purchases are handled through the service that PayPal offers.

No longer must buyers post off cheques or postal orders and then be forced to wait for the funds to clear at the other end before receiving the item. No longer must sellers trudge into town to cash these bothersome bits of paper at their local bank. Instead, the funds are transferred between parties in less time than it takes to simply click a mouse button.

How To... Set Up A PayPal Account

As well as being a convenient way to pay for goods on eBay, PayPal is also used by many other sites to transfer money. And if you want to be an eBay Seller, it's compulsory to offer it to your buyers. To set up an account, just follow these six simple steps, and you'll be ready before you know it.

1 To begin, simply go to **www.paypal.co.uk** and click the orange 'Sign Up' button on the left of the page. Choose your country from the drop-down menu and select the type of account you wish to open; this example shows you how to open a Personal account, which is ideal for buying and selling online.

2 Begin by entering your e-mail address. In PayPal, your e-mail address is the equivalent of your eBay User ID. Whenever you sign into the

site, you will have to enter your e-mail address and password, and during all transactions your e-mail address is displayed. Your password must be at least eight characters long.

3 Fill in the rest of the form (all fields are mandatory). Your address must match the billing address of the debit or credit card you plan to link your PayPal account to. A telephone number is required so that PayPal can contact you quickly should a problem arise with your account.

4 Carefully enter the details of your credit or debit card. The CSC is the identification number usually found on the back of your card. Browse the PayPal Service Description, User Agreement and Privacy Policy pages, and when you're happy, click 'Agree and Create Account'.

COUNTING THE COST

For the buyer, PayPal is a completely free service. It costs nothing to open an account and nothing to send money to other users. You simply link your PayPal account to your bank account or debit/credit card and PayPal will automatically withdraw and transfer funds when you wish to make a payment.

The seller, however, must pay a fee each time they receive a credit or debit card funded payment. This fee is typically around 3% of the total amount. Some users begrudge paying these charges, particularly as PayPal is owned by eBay, and eBay already charges sellers a listing and final percentage fee. The way they see it, they're getting hit in the pocket twice. However, the majority of people don't mind paying a bit extra, as PayPal really does take the hassle out of receiving payments, and the service's added security is also a valuable asset.

HELD TO ACCOUNT

PayPal offers three different types of account: Personal, Premier and Business. Business is self-explanatory, but what's the difference between Personal and Premier? In short, a Personal account is ideal for those who'll be shopping more than selling. You can accept payments from other users, but there's a monthly volume limit. A Premier account is essentially the same, but there's no limit, so if you plan to sell regularly on eBay, a Premier account is recommended. If you're not sure, begin by opening a Personal account, and you can upgrade to either a Premier or Business account later.

It should be pointed out that while PayPal is preferred by most eBay users, alternative online payment systems such as WorldPay and Nochex are available. The alternatives are covered elsewhere in this guide.

5 PayPal will validate your credit or debit card details and, provided everything is okay, you will see this success screen. Your PayPal account is now active and you can use it to pay for items online and send money to other PayPal users. The final step is to get your account verified.

6 By verifying your account you will lift the spending limits imposed on unverified accounts. It's easy to do and basically involves adding a bank account and supplying additional business information. To do this, sign into your account and click the 'Get Verified' link, then follow the steps.

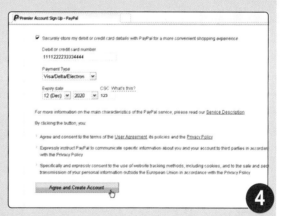

Case Study: **Tiny Tags**

Can the beautiful game inspire a beautiful eBay business?

If there's one thing people love about eBay, it's the personal touch. That's brilliant news for Natalie Capaldi who's built her entire online business on just such a premise.

Natalie runs Tiny Tags (**stores.ebay.co.uk/ TinyTagsBaby**), a visually stunning store that sells T-shirts for babies, emblazoned not only with their name but a loving nickname too. She has a long list of the most popular names as well as a facility for people to design their own.

The idea came after Natalie had a baby, George, and noticed that other mums in her post-natal group were always calling their babies by cute nicknames. "There was a 'Gorgeous George' and a 'Chilled-out Charlie', she laughed. "I thought other parents might do this so thought up nicknames for the most popular baby names and learned how to print T-shirts."

Since then, she's added designs for aunties, uncles, grandmas and granddads. "They seemed to be the people buying the babygrows as a present for family," she said. But that's not all; local sports teams have approached her to produce tailor-made T-shirts. Business is booming.

Natalie has been an eBay member since 2003, but she'd used it to buy and sell personal items. The birth of her son meant she was looking around for a way of making money that would fit around the demands of looking after a baby.

Before taking the plunge, she checked out the competition. "There wasn't much at the time," she said. "Also I was printing in flock and the only big competitors were using embroidery. There are pros and cons to each method, so I used the pros of mine to an advantage, basically being able to create bright, bold designs. Most customers would have a clear preference for one style or the other, modern versus traditional, so I pressed on at that point, confident that I'd found a niche for my items."

Natalie also worked on the design of the shop. The front page is very professional and emphasises Tiny Tags' clear brand. The attractive logo and use of a cute teddy bear immediately projects a child-friendly image and also inspires confidence in the business. There's also a large splash graphic, which includes sample T-shirts. Further down, Natalie details the quality of the clothes and she also prominently places her e-mail address on the site, which makes it easy for people to contact her - all things to consider when setting up a shop on eBay.

So how does she spread the word? "I only advertise within eBay," she said. "Google searches link to eBay, so your listings can come up in Google results if you get the wording right on your description."

Natalie works on the business alone but said her son is her business partner. Well, he did inspire her. Customers tend to be friends or family of someone who has had a baby, although the business is aimed at soon-to-be parents too. And Natalie must be doing well, given her 100% feedback.

"Feedback is crucial," she stressed. "It gives potential customers confidence that they won't be disappointed in your service and the quality of your item. As most of my sales are gifts for new parents, it's an important purchase for the customer and usually something they will be excited to give or receive.

"Therefore they want to know they're buying from the right place, because who wants to hand over a gift that looks low quality or poorly made. Also, when you're working hard and putting a lot of care and effort into your work, good feedback can give you a little boost and make you feel proud of what you're doing. It's needed sometimes to keep you going."

But not everything has run smoothly for Natalie. At first she didn't calculate profits and losses. She would buy stock and guess the sale price without working out her profit margins. This could prove to be disastrous, and it's essential to have a plan from the start if you're serious about setting up an eBay business.

"You need to have a business plan and know exactly how many items you need to sell in order to cover the eBay fees," she said. You need to account for the listing fee, store and subscription fees, PayPal fees and so on. "Your selling price needs to reflect a profit after the price of producing and posting the item," she adds. "You need to ensure it covers all the other fees and price your item accordingly."

Natalie realised she was making a mistake. So she closed the store for a few months, did a bit of research, and then opened up again, having learnt a bit more about how things needed to be done. "This problem has now gone away, as it's just something I had to learn. It wasn't an issue with the site itself," she said.

So does that mean she is 100% happy with eBay? "Well, when I first set up the store on eBay there was the facility to use something called Featured First. You paid something like £40 a month and your listing (just one listing) would appear at the top of search results in its own special 'featured first' area. Using this for a general listing designed solely to lead people to the rest of the store worked wonders, as the visibility was huge. This was around August 2009.

"When I recently reopened the store for business a few months later I was sorry to see that the feature had been discontinued (unless you're a PowerSeller, in which case you're already doing pretty well and on the front page) This makes it hard for small sellers who start up to get any visibility at all. If your item is any more than five pages into the search results, then it's pretty much guaranteed no one will see it. So you could be selling the perfect product for someone's needs, but that person may not ever come across it. Views of my listings dropped sharply."

She also takes issue with eBay's listings and she discusses the auction versus fixed price debate. "It's hard for Buy It Now listings to get on the front page," she said. "Auction style listings ending that same day still seemed to show on the first page of search results. Time left is one of the many factors contributing to where your item shows on the 'best match' placement of listings, so it's hard therefore when your items are fixed price listings (which most business will have) to get on that front page."

To get around this problem, Natalie has a few listings in auction style on a one-day auction. It

means she has some listings present on the first page each day due to being in the 'auction style' format with less than 24 hours remaining.

"Those listings only cost 25p a day, so a few of those every day pretty much equates to the featured first cost of £40 per month that I previously paid," she said.

For all of that, however, Natalie said eBay is a brilliant way to get into business. She believes it's impossible to get such visibility for your venture anywhere else, although she feels the fees and competition makes it a difficult market. The recession has, she argues, caused a surge in eBay businesses with people looking to supplement their income. "I can only see it getting worse before it gets better unfortunately," she said. "There are probably ten times more people doing what I do compared to this time last year."

But she also believes that eBay can be a good gauge of whether your idea is a good one and whether people like your products. "This can be extremely useful for a start-up business to test the water before they fork out for expensive websites, marketing, perhaps a physical shop or market stall and so on, plus all the other costs involved in selling. You will find out pretty quickly whether your idea will sell and what people think of it."

Natalie is set to add more designs to Tiny Tags and expand the range of clothing she offers. She's also looking into setting up a stand-alone, non-eBay website which she will cross-promote from her eBay store and she is set to approach local stores in the hope of selling her products on a sale or return basis.

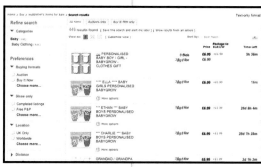

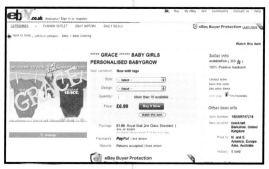

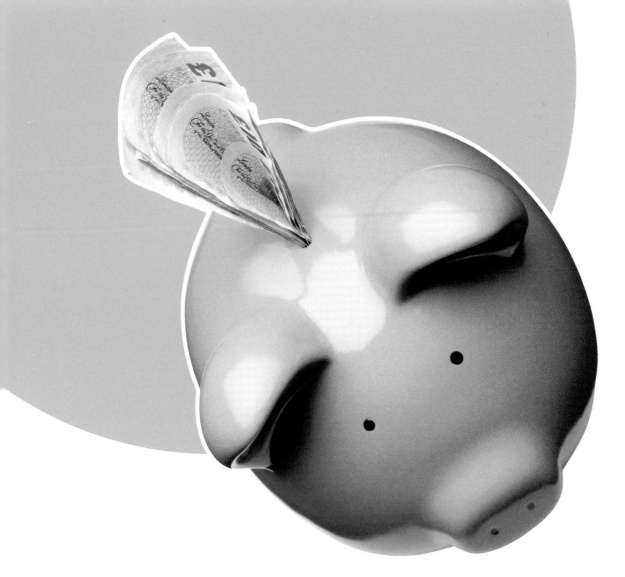

Chapter 3
Introductory Selling

Let's Start Selling

Your listing is your virtual shop window, so if you want to draw in the punters, it pays to spend some time making it look good

It's easy to start selling on eBay: just click 'Sell' in the menu bar (the menu bar appears in the top-right corner of almost every page, so you'll seldom have trouble finding it). There's no messing about; you're whisked immediately into the listing wizard. Jump right in, using the steps below to guide you through the various options and stages. You don't need to be signed into your account in order to begin a listing, but sooner or later in the process it'll become essential, so you might as well log in before you start.

CHOOSE A CATEGORY

First, you need to choose the category in which your item will appear. There are more than 30 main categories and several thousand subcategories, so it's essential to take your time and choose carefully. If you list your item in anything but the most appropriate category, untold numbers of potential bidders might never find it.

Pinpointing the right category for your item can be achieved in one of two ways. One method is to type some keywords into the text box. Maybe you've been clearing out your cupboards and you've unearthed a still unopened model kit. Your keywords in that case might be 'knight rider model car' (unless it's a Lancaster bomber, of course). When you're done, click 'Start selling'. You're now taken to a 'hit list' of likely categories. Tick the box beside the one you think fits the bill (very often this isn't the one at the top). Once you're happy with your choice, click 'Continue'.

The second method of choosing a category is to browse for it manually. To do that, click 'Browse categories' (available on both the initial selling page and the 'hit list' page). Now you can explore every single main category and every single subcategory. Drill down through the lists until you reach what seems most appropriate. Click 'Continue' when you're done.

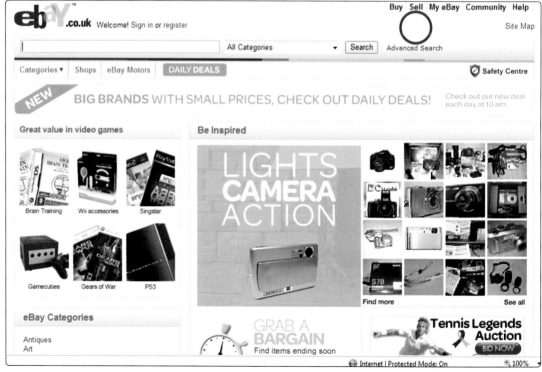

▲ Click 'Sell' in the menu bar to launch the listing wizard

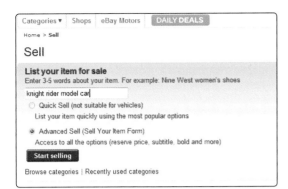

▲ One way to select a category is to enter some keywords

▲ Tick the most appropriate category

▲ You can list your item in two categories

It's a good idea to satisfy yourself that you've chosen your category wisely. To do that, click 'See sample listings', a link that appears near the bottom of the page once you've made your selection. A list of recently completed auctions then pops into view. Does your item sit well with what else is on offer? Are other people with listings in Toys & Games > Model Kits > Models selling vehicles from 1980s TV shows? If not, a rethink is probably in order.

Tip: When starting a listing, you'll probably notice there are two approaches: Quick Sell and Advanced Sell. Advanced Sell, the default, is the traditional approach, and the one shown throughout this guide. Quick Sell is a relatively new approach, where the listing process is semi-automated and you're offered only a limited set of options and upgrades. It's best used only for very simple listings.

ADD A SECOND CATEGORY

Sometimes the item you're selling might be appropriate for two different categories. When that happens, you can list it in both. Take the Knight Rider model, for instance. Examples of this item can regularly be found not only in Toys & Games > Model Kits > Models but also in Toys & Games > Diecast & Vehicles > Other Diecast & Vehicles. That might seem a pretty poor choice, but who cares? If this is where people are looking for such things, it's as valid a category as any.

If you use the keyword method to select a category, adding a second one is as simple as putting ticks in two different boxes. If you use the browsing method, you need to click 'Add a second category and reach more buyers', a link near the bottom of the page. You can then drill down through the categories and subcategories again.

The snag with listing in two categories - and it's a big one - is that most of your listing fees get doubled (but not your selling fees). Usually, you pay the same as you would for listing two separate

items. The only fee that remains single-rated is the one charged for scheduling (an option covered later in the chapter).

COMPOSE YOUR TITLE

Now it's time to look at one of the most important aspects of selling on eBay: the task of building up your actual listing. The first job is to compose a title. This is the heading that buyers will see when they're looking through lists of items.

Imagine a shopper called Mr Browser. He wants to buy a music CD. He walks into a record shop, wanders up and down the aisles, flicks through the racks, and sooner or later finds the title he's looking for. It's as good a method as any, and Mr Browser uses just the same technique when shopping on eBay. He picks a category that looks appropriate, roots through the subcategories, peruses the pages of auction headings, and eventually finds an example of the item he wants to bid on. Mr Browser is why listing your item in the right category is critical.

Then there's Mrs Specific. When she wants a music CD, she walks into a record shop, heads immediately for the counter, asks the assistant for the location of the desired title, and plucks it straight off the shelf. On eBay, Mrs Specific doesn't bother with categories. Instead, she enters some keywords into the search box. The only auctions

▲ For the title and subtitle, you get just 55 characters apiece

▲ Item specifics can help your item appear in more searches

she's then given to look through are those with titles that contain her keywords (and such auctions might be spread across a dozen different categories). Mrs Specific is why your auction title needs to be just right.

You've only got 55 characters to play with, so think carefully about what you write. The art of creating a solid title is covered in 'What Makes A Good eBay Listing?' elsewhere in this book.

ADD A SUBTITLE

Adding a subtitle is optional. It costs £0.35. You get a further 55 characters, but bear in mind that they're only scanned in searches if a buyer elects to search both titles and descriptions (one of many optional search criteria). Most buyers don't bother. Don't worry too much about keywords, then; be free and loose. As with your title, the art of a good subtitle is covered elsewhere in this eBay guide.

SELECT ITEM SPECIFICS

Next you need to complete the item specifics. These are presented in the form of drop-down menus, the headings for which depend on the category in which you're listing your item. For Toys & Games > Model Kits > Models, the headings are Type, Subtype, Model, Scale, Brand, and Condition. The Condition menu, which offers choices of New and Used, is common to all categories (even Antiques, oddly enough).

Often the choices in a menu aren't suitable. For example, in the Brand menu for Toys & Games >

Model Kits > Models, there's no Aoshima. That's bad luck if you're listing a plastic K.I.T.T. from one of Japan's top model makers! When this happens, though, you can select 'Other'. This opens up a free-form text box in which you can enter anything you like. Alternatively, you can opt to specify nothing; just leave the menu on '-'.

Tip: Many sellers don't bother with item specifics, preferring instead to leave them all blank. However, when buyers perform searches, they can opt to only see results that fulfil certain criteria. One of those criteria is whether or not an item is new or not. If yours is, then be sure to say so under the Condition heading. Do that at the very least, because if you don't, your item could easily be missed unwittingly by thousands of potential buyers.

UPLOAD A PICTURE

They say a picture is worth a thousand words. Nowhere is that more true than in the world of eBay. An item illustrated with at least one good image will receive hugely more interest - and perhaps higher bids - than an otherwise identical item described by words alone.

Your first picture is free. To get started, click 'Add pictures'. This opens a new window, and you're presented with three tabs: Basic, Enhanced, and Self Hosting. The Enhanced tab is your best bet (and the one used in this guide). The Basic tab is similar but it lacks the handy editing tools that allow you to alter a picture's size, rotation, contrast, and brightness.

In the new window, under '1', click 'Add Pictures'. This will bring up a dialogue box that enables you to leaf through the folders on your hard drive and other storage devices. Once you've located your chosen picture, double-click the filename or highlight it and click 'Open'. You can add up to a further 11 pictures (under '2', '3', '4', and so on), though each one after the first carries a price of £0.12. When you've added all you want, click 'Upload'.

▲ Examples of listings with and without subtitles

Bring your item to life with pictures   Add or remove options |

The first picture is free. Each additional picture is £0.12.

Add pictures   Remove all pictures

▲ To add an image, click 'Add pictures'

If you prefer, your free picture can be one that's hosted on the web. This is useful if your Internet account comes with free web space or if you're signed up with a photo-sharing site such as Photobucket (**photobucket.com**) or Flickr (**www. flickr.com**). To use this service, click 'Add pictures' and then use the Self Hosting tab. In the text box, enter the full URL (web address) of where your picture is located. To finish, click 'Insert Picture'.

Sadly, the Self Hosting option is a mere shadow of what it once was. Until recently, you could add up to six pictures, but now you can only add one (the free one). Don't go thinking you can add one picture via Self Hosting and then several others by uploading them from your hard drive; it's either one method or the other. It's a great shame. The mind boggles at why eBay has crippled what used to be such a valuable service.

Tip: The maximum picture size is 4MB if you use the Basic tab and 8MB if you use the Enhanced tab (there's no limit if you use Self Hosting). To help them load quickly in bidders' browsers, pictures are automatically compressed when they appear in your actual listing (though this doesn't apply to Self Hosting, so be careful). You can use any of the following formats: JPG, BMP, GIF (both static and animated), TIF/TIFF, PCX, and PNG.

DECIDE ON PICTURE UPGRADES

As standard, your first picture appears in small form at the top of your listing and in larger form near the bottom. Additional pictures appear near

▲ If you prefer, you can host your free picture on the web

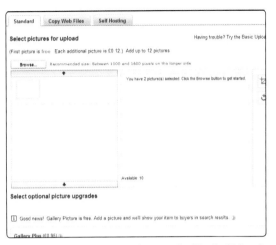

▲ If your image is on your hard drive, use the Standard tab and click 'Browse'

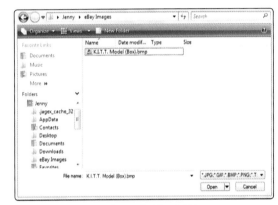

▲ Leaf through your folders to find the right image

the bottom in a cluster of clickable thumbnails. If you'd like more control and sophistication, you need to use one or more of eBay's picture upgrades. These are described below.

Gallery: With the Gallery upgrade, a thumbnail of your item gets shown beside your title on search results pages. Buyers can then see what you're selling without actually having to open up the full listing. Until last year, Gallery used to cost £0.15, but now - hallelujah! - it's free. Previously, without it, all that appeared against your title was a camera icon (so long as your listing actually contained a picture at all).

£0.95 Gallery Plus: Gallery Plus is essentially the Gallery option gone large. As with Gallery, a thumbnail image of your item gets shown beside your listing's title on search results pages, but there's a big difference -quite literally. If an interested eBay user hovers over the Enlarge link, the image pops up in its own box,

▲ Multiple images are shown below your main image as an interactive slideshow

▲ You can choose to enlarge the image to take a closer look as well

▲ Go large with Gallery Plus

greatly magnified - up to 400 x 400 pixels. Additional pictures in the listing are shown in the box as thumbnails, and the buyer can also magnify those as well.

£0.60 **Supersize:** If you want any potential bidders to see your item in greater detail, you can pay for the Supersize upgrade. When they click on a picture (perhaps a thumbnail in the cluster at the bottom of your listing page), it will then display at up to 800 x 800 pixels (assuming your pictures are at least that size

to begin with). The standard size is only up to 400 x 400, so the result it truly impressive. Be aware, however, that Supersize isn't available if you're also using the Self Hosting option.

FREE **Picture Show:** As with Gallery, the Picture Show upgrade used to cost £0.15, but now you get it automatically for free if you're including at least two pictures. It replaces the item image at the top of your listing with an interactive slideshow. This cycles through your images one by one, and buyers can stop it, start it, move forward, and move back. If you also buy the Supersize upgrade, buyers can view the slideshow in a separate window, where the images are displayed at up to 800 x 800 pixels. Note that Picture Show isn't available if you're using the Self Hosting option.

£0.90 **Picture Pack:** Normally, if you bought five extra pictures and the Supersize option, you'd pay £1.20. With the Picture Pack upgrade, you pay just £0.90. With eleven extra pictures and Supersize, Picture Pack costs £1.35, whereas buying the upgrades separately would set you back £1.92. If you really believe your listing can't survive without every picture upgrade going, Picture Pack can save you a fair few pennies. Note that Picture Pack isn't available if you're using the Self Hosting option.

▲ The Standard window provides basic formatting tools

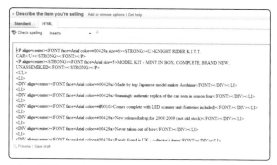

▲ Use HTML to truly customise your listing

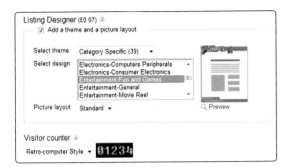

▲ £0.07 buys you a theme

▲ Themes can really help spruce up a listing...

▲ ...but be sure to choose one that's appropriate!

COMPOSE YOUR DESCRIPTION

Next up is the main attraction: your item description. A poor description can mean low bids and even no sale. A fabulous description can send the bidding through the roof. The lowdown on putting together something perfect is covered in greater detail towards the end of this chapter.

You can enter your description using either the Standard window or the HTML window (click the tabs to switch between the two). Private sellers usually use the Standard window. To help bolster and brighten your text, there's a toolbar giving you basic word-processing functions - font, size, colour, bold, centre, and so on. You can also insert bullet points and give your spelling the once over.

The HTML window allows you to build up your description like a web page. This is the approach often taken by business sellers; it requires some effort and a little bit of skill, but the results tend to be more professional. You don't get any editing facilities, however, so your best bet is to use a separate website designer and then copy and paste your HTML from there. A simple but workable solution (and it's free!) is the Composer applet built into the Mozilla SeaMonkey suite (**www. seamonkey-project.org**).

Tip: With some simple HTML, you can adorn your description with as many (web-hosted) pictures as you care to include - any size, any position, and all for free. Why not run a Google search and track down an introductory HTML tutorial?

ENHANCE YOUR LAYOUT

Does your listing look drab or boring? If you think so, you can apply a theme. This gets you a fancy border, a background and some clipart. You can also specify where your pictures go - top, bottom, left, or right. The price is £0.07. It's an upgrade that works best on a Standard description, but you can also use it if you've gone down the HTML route.

There are dozens and dozens of themes to choose from. If you're selling a kettle, for example, you could use In The Home-Kitchen. For a model of

Michael Knight's K.I.T.T., it might be fun to go for Entertainment-Fun and Games. There's a preview link, so you can see what your choices look like in the flesh. Have a play!

PICK A VISITOR COUNTER

A visitor counter - otherwise known as a hit counter - indicates how many buyers have checked your listing out. Only unique visits are recorded; if the same buyer visits multiple times, you get just the one hit. The counter, if you choose one, appears at the bottom of your description.

There are three types to choose from: Basic Style, Retro-computer Style, and Hidden. The Hidden counter is visible only to you; buyers never see it. Sometimes an auction with a lot of hits (several hundred) can pull in the bids, because buyers get the impression your item is something

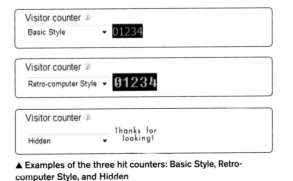

▲ Examples of the three hit counters: Basic Style, Retro-computer Style, and Hidden

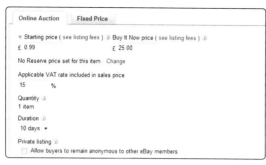

▲ Fill in your auction's starting price...

▲ ...or choose to sell at a fixed price

▲ A standard auction in action (with the Buy It Now option)

▲ A fixed-price 'auction' in action (with the Best Offer option)

special. Conversely, an auction with scarcely a handful of hits (half a dozen) can put buyers off (perhaps your item has something wrong with it?). If in doubt, choose Hidden.

Always have a counter of some sort; it's good to know what interest your auction's attracting. Indeed, a counter is such a useful feature it's a miracle eBay doesn't charge for it!

THE STANDARD AUCTION

There are two sorts of listing: auction and fixed-price. Select the one you want by simply clicking on the appropriate tab. This section deals with auction listings.

An auction is exactly what you'd expect: people bid against each other over a set period of time and the person who bids the highest in that time wins the item. First, then, you need to enter your item's starting price. The figure you enter here can determine the 'insertion fee' eBay will take for hosting your auction. This fee is also dependent on what you're selling.

For mobile phones with contracts, the insertion fee is a flat £7.95, regardless of your starting price. It's a similar story for property; the flat fee there is £35. For media items (books, magazines, CDs, DVDs, videogames, and the like), there's no insertion fee at all if your starting price is £0.99 or lower (except if you're a business seller, where it's £0.05). For media items starting at £1 or higher, the fee is £0.10. For every other type of item (including mobile phones without contracts), the

insertion fee rises with the starting price, as listed in the scale below.

- £0.01-£0.99 = Free (or £0.10 if you're a business seller)
- £1-£4.99 = £0.15
- £5-£14.99 = £0.25
- £15-£29.99 = £0.50
- £30-£99.99 = £1
- £100+ = £1.30

If you're worried your item might sell for below its worth, you can specify a reserve price. To do that, click the 'Change' link, which opens a separate window that allows you to enter the desired amount (£50 is the minimum). If the bids on your item fail to reach this figure, the item remains unsold. Of course, there's a fee for this upgrade (in addition to the insertion fee). For property, it's a flat £2. For everything else, it depends on the reserve's size:

- £50-£4,999.99 = 2% of reserve
- £5,000+ = £100

If you want, you can also specify a Buy It Now price (though to do so you need a verified PayPal account and a feedback rating of ten or higher). This enables a buyer to cut out the bidding process altogether and click a button to purchase your item immediately (thus ending the auction). As soon as someone makes an opening bid, however, the Buy It Now button disappears; your listing continues as

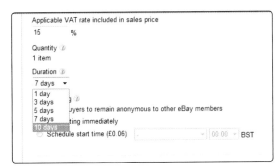

▲ Choose your auction's duration

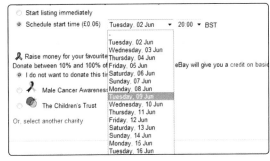

▲ Specify when you'd like your auction to begin

a standard auction. If you've set a reserve, the Buy It Now button will remain in place until the reserve's been met. There's a fee for all this, naturally, and the amount you'll pay depends on your Buy It Now price (which must be at least £0.99). The rates are listed below.

- £0.99-£4.99 = £0.05
- £5-£14.99 = £0.10
- £15-£29.99 = £0.15
- £30+ = £0.25

Tip: If your item is a road vehicle, caravan, boat, or aircraft, it falls under the umbrella of eBay Motors (this applies equally to fixed-price listings, covered next). The fee structure in that case is somewhat different to that outlined above. For more detail, see **pages.ebay.co.uk/help/sell/motorfees.html**.

THE FIXED-PRICE 'AUCTION'

A fixed-price auction, also known as a Buy It Now (or BIN) auction, really isn't an auction at all. You see, there's no bidding. None at all. It works similarly to the Buy It Now option in a standard auction (and, like there, you need a verified PayPal account and a feedback rating of ten or higher). Basically, you set your price (£0.99 is the minimum) and then a buyer, if he or she likes what's on offer, simply clicks a button to 'win' your item. The insertion fee is always a flat amount, regardless of your selling price, but, as shown below, there are different figures for different types of item.

- Mobile phones with contracts = £7.95
- Property = £35
- Media = £0.20
- Everything else = £0.40

With a fixed-price auction, there's also the option to adorn your listing with a Best Offer mark. With this, if a buyer likes your item but doesn't want to pay the full price, he or she can click 'Make Offer' and submit a suggested figure. It's a bargaining tool. eBay forwards you an e-mail with the offer

and you have 48 hours to accept or decline (unless the auction finishes sooner). The best thing about this upgrade is that there's no fee!

Tip: You should only alter the VAT rate from the default if you're a VAT-registered business selling an item at net price (this applies equally to standard-auction listings). Private sellers sometimes erroneously alter the rate to 0%, believing VAT isn't relevant. Don't make this mistake; potential buyers might get confused and think VAT will be slapped on to the final price!

THE LONG AND THE SHORT OF IT

Your listing can run for three days, five days, seven days, or ten days. For standard auctions (but not fixed-price ones), a one-day option is also available (so long as you've got a feedback rating of five or higher). For fixed-price auctions (but not standard ones), there's a 30-day option too. The snag with that, though, is that it trebles every listing fee except the insertion fee. The default length is seven days, but if you'd like to change that, simply make your choice from the Duration drop-down box.

Ordinarily, your auction begins immediately after you submit your listing. That means it'll finish at the same time of day it begins and one, three, five, seven, ten, or 30 days later (depending on what duration you've chosen). If you prefer, you can set up a schedule. For £0.06 (and as long as you have a credit or debit card linked to your account for billing purposes), you can have your auction start at any time you choose and on any day up to three weeks into the future. Simple use the relevant drop-down boxes to do so.

KEEPING THINGS PRIVATE

At this stage, there's an option to make matters private. Ordinarily, the User IDs of all bidders and

▲ If necessary, you can hide bidders' identities

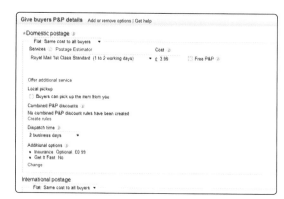

▲ Charity begins at eBay

▲Decide how your item will be delivered

buyers are available for everyone to see. If you tick the appropriate box, however, only you, as the auction's 'owner', will be able to see these IDs. Be aware, though, that doing this can attract suspicion, because people might wonder what you're hiding. Use this option only if you've got a genuine reason to keep your bidders' and buyers' identities a secret.

WANT TO GIVE GENEROUSLY?

If you're feeling particularly generous, you have the option of giving a portion of your sale's proceeds to charity. You can either choose one of the charities featured by eBay or, alternatively, you can click the link to choose your own. Doing the latter opens up a new window, from where you can select from over 3,500 institutions. The percentage you decide to give can be between 10% and 100% (in 5% increments), but the minimum amount is £1. By default, all donations are collected via the same payment method used to collect your eBay fees (in practice, PayPal or a debit or credit card), but you have the option to change this from within your account settings.

As an incentive, eBay reduces your insertion fee and final value fee by the same percentage as you donate. For example, if you donate 10% and your

▲ Do you want to ship abroad?

insertion fee and final value fee total £1, you'll only be charged £0.90. Bonus!

MONEY, MONEY, MONEY

Next, you need to decide how the winner of your item will pay. This is a simple section to complete; you just tick the relevant boxes. PayPal used to be optional but, with the exception of listings for property, services, and eBay Motors, it's now compulsory. Be sure to enter the correct e-mail address here; you wouldn't be the first to discover payment has been made to someone else's account!

If you're running a listing with a Buy It Now price (either a fixed-price listing or a standard auction),

▲ How will your buyer pay you?

▲ What's your returns policy?

▲ Preview your listing and make final edits before putting it up

▲ Time to groan: see how much it's all going to cost

you can choose to display a message informing buyers that you require immediate payment (via PayPal). Tick the relevant box to enable this feature. If you do, when a buyer 'buys' your item, it'll remain unsold and available to everyone else until that buyer makes payment.

SHIPPING AND STUFF

Next come the shipping options. You need to decide what delivery service you're going to use, how much you'll charge your buyer for it, whether or not you're going to offer insurance, when you'll dispatch, and what countries or territories you're prepared to ship to. This section is another point-and-shoot affair.Simply tick the boxes, select from the menus, and enter your figures. If you're willing to dispatch your item within one business day of the sale and use an overnight delivery service, you can also choose to have a Get It Fast logo appended to your listing.

Rounding off this part of the process are a couple of free-form text boxes in which you can give potential buyers information not covered elsewhere. Declare your returns policy (will you accept unwanted items back for a full refund?) and maybe state the time-frame in which you expect to be paid after your item's sold.

LAST-CHANCE EXTRAS

Your listing is now nearly complete! Once you've filled in all the blanks detailed in the sections above, click 'Continue'. You're then given one last chance to take up some of the upgrades you've already been offered (eBay really, really wants you to take them!).

This is also the point when eBay sellers used to be offered a batch of new upgrades, such as Bold, Highlight and Featured Plus. However, these are no longer offered, and all that remains is Featured First, which is only available if you've been an eBay seller for some time and are able to meet certain criteria in terms of sales and feedback.

£44.95 **Featured First:** With this, your item really can move up the pecking order. When a buyer makes a search, Featured First auctions within the relevant category are randomly selected to appear on page one (in the Featured Items section), regardless of how long they've got left to run. In some categories, Featured First auctions are so few and far between that yours could be virtually guaranteed a page-one position for its entire duration. For your money, you get Gallery Plus thrown in, too.

Unfortunately, this powerful upgrade is only available to Top-rated Sellers. These are sellers that have opted into the PowerSeller program, and who meet a number of requirements laid down by eBay. These include at least 100 transactions and £2,000 in sales in the last 12 months and a positive feedback score of at least 98%.

As well as access to the Featured First option, Top-rated sellers receive the following privileges and benefits:

- Priority customer service
- Up to a 30% discount on final value fees
- Unpaid item protection
- Expanded seller protection from PayPal
- A badge on listing pages
- Increased visibility in Best Match search results

PREVIEW AND GO!

That's it. You're all done! You're now given the opportunity to preview your listing - to see exactly how it'll look to potential buyers - and also the chance to make any last-minute edits. Crucially, you're also shown the total amount of your hard-earned cash eBay will take in listing fees. If you've chosen a fixed-price listing, you're also shown how much you'll be charged as a selling fee (if your item sells). When you're happy, click 'List your item'!

What Makes A Good eBay Listing?

Getting your listing right is essential, so what can you do to make yours stand out from the crowd?

If eBay gave statistics of those items that sell well, they'd show that the impression presented by the listing is crucial in making sales and in attracting bids. Creating listings that give your items the very best chance is a vital skill that any successful seller needs to master. The listing performs a number of crucial functions, including:

- Giving clear and concise information about what's being offered
- Outlining under what conditions sale is offered
- Providing confidence that the seller is a good eBayer
- Giving buyers an opportunity to ask questions
- Initiating the mechanism to buy or bid

If your listing succeeds in this respect, then the chance of your item selling for what you want, or more, is dramatically increased.

MIXING A PERFECT EBAY CAKE

For a successful listing to meet all the requirements of the checklist above, it's worth comparing it to making a cake: if you leave out even a single important ingredient, then the flavour of the cake is impaired. With that in mind, before you start to create and edit a listing on eBay, it's worth collecting together all the information you need to sell your

item, putting most of it in a document, which you can easily cut and paste from in order to save time. You'll need to have handy:

- The title of your item
- The category it falls into (maybe more than one)
- The condition of the item - new or used
- A full description, telling the prospective buyer what they'll get for their money
- A listing template
- A picture, showing the item
- A starting price
- Planned duration of the sale
- Shipping cost details
- Accepted payment types
- Returns policy

You need to consider each of these things before listing an item, as they can all have an impact on how much money you get and the number of people that are likely to be interested. It may look an exhausting list, but it's actually quite straightforward, and much of it revolves around simple common sense. Let's go through it in a bit more detail.

TITLE

This is the single most important decision you need to make about any listing, as the title is the reason most

 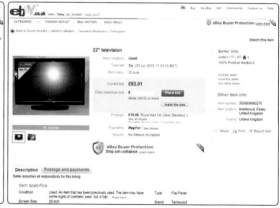

▲ The title is a valuable means to hook a customer. Which of these two listings is trying to give the most information?

◀ This listing is for Nokia phone products. Not that many people will find it, because, for whatever reason, it's listed under the category of 'Bears'

potential customers will take a closer look at your item. A vague, incorrectly spelled or confusing title can easily get overlooked.

If other people are selling the same item, see what they're doing and follow the lead. You have 55 characters to play with in your title, so make the most of them.

For example, let's say the item is a golf club. In the title you need to get across the brand, model, style and condition, if you can fit that in. It's now common to use upper case, as it makes the title stand out more (although some potential buyers may equate this to shouting, and thus give your listing a miss). eBay also allows for a subtitle, but relatively few people use this feature, relying instead on the full description to provide any secondary information.

CATEGORY

As we've discussed, buyers that actively search eBay do it in two distinct ways. Some know exactly what they're looking for, and search for that item specifically (for instance, a 30GB Apple iPod).

Others know they want a type of item, but are unsure what brand/make they'd like (so they might, perhaps, search for an MP3 player instead of specifically requesting an iPod).

The second type of search is often category-based, and attracting those people requires that you put your listing in the right category for your item. If you're unsure, then try searching yourself, and see where similar items to the one you're looking to list have been placed.

eBay allows you to place the listing against multiple categories, at an extra cost, with an increased viewing count likely if you choose to do so. For most people,

though, just getting the category right is enough to attract interest.

There is a peculiar reverse logic that can also apply here. For whatever reason, items that appear in the wrong category can also get more attention. This is a risky strategy, as your item might be ignored, and you might seem an inept seller, but it can work. As a rule, research the correct category and use that one.

CONDITION

New is good, and used is less so. However, don't be tempted to suggest that an item is new when it isn't. You'll rightly upset the buyer who might be tempted to ask for a refund or to complain. Unless an item is new, never mark it as such. What you can do to help promote a used item is to mention in the title or description a few more details; for example, 'as new' or 'perfect condition'.

Unless it's an item where the age is actually a selling point, most people want new or at least new-looking purchases.

DESCRIPTION

If the item that you're selling is one that eBay recognises (such as a DVD or CD), then a short description of it will automatically appear at the top of the listing. However, this information on its own is rarely enough to answer all of a buyer's questions.

Getting all the relevant information in this section will help the potential bidder decide if they want your item, so it's worth taking the time to make it clear exactly what you're selling. In general, the more information you provide, the better the listing will be, but keep it relevant to the customer. They might not want to know that you've ended a relationship using that phone, or that you're selling an item to pay a parking fine. A good source of information to use in this section can be found on the brand or manufacturer's website, if one exists. A bit of rapid highlighting, copying and pasting could save you plenty of typing. And unless you've got the wrong product, the details should be totally correct.

Please take note: eBay holds you responsible for making sure the information is accurate. Therefore, it's of real importance to get the description right and to not mislead people, otherwise there could be recriminations further down the line.

LISTING TEMPLATE

Built into eBay are a range of HTML listing template formats, which fall under the banner of the 'Listing Designer'. Although you're charged a small amount extra for choosing one of these templates, the overall impact it will have on your listing can be very positive, and thus worthwhile.

Templates give the layout of the listing more structure, colour, and the impression you've put more effort into presenting your product. The only problem with the eBay templates is that frequent users will have seen them all, and recognise them as such. But even then, it's hard to argue that they do any harm.

Third-party templates are an alternative, and they're available from a wide range of online locations. One of the biggest free suppliers is **www. auctioninsights.com**, where you'll find a free template creation tool. There are plenty of companies offering such templates, and other popular options are **www. auctionsupplies.com/templates**, **www. foamtemplates.com**, and **www.auctiva.com**.

Alternatively, a large number of software tools are available that allow you to create a listing away from

eBay, and then post it to the site in a single operation. These all have their own template designs from which you can choose. Some of these, such as The Seller Sourcebook (**www.sellersourcebook.com**), are online tools for which a subscription is payable for use.

Others, like eBaitor (**www.ebaitor.com**), Auction Ad Designer Pro (**www.freeauctionhelp.com**) and Auction Lizard (**www.auction-lizard.com**) provide a separate installable Windows application that creates the listing offline. The beauty of these tools is that you can work on a listing to the point where you're entirely happy with it before committing to upload it and make it live on the eBay site. It also allows you to reload old listings and tweak them for repeat use, which can save lots of time.

If you intend to build a business through eBay, or you plan on selling in significant quantities, then investing in a listings design tool might be a worthwhile exercise.

THE PICTURE

This one feature can be a real sale maker or breaker. A good picture can say a thousand words, and convince a buyer that it's exactly what they want to bid on. Conversely, a poor image can confuse matters and persuade people not to bid or buy. It's why we touch on images so much in this book, and we'll be going into pictures in a lot more detail shortly.

Included in the basic cost of an eBay listing is one picture, and you can add more for, of course, a fee. Extra pictures can enable your listing to show specific details of your item, and can be a necessity when selling something like a car or antique.

For low-cost items, using multiple pictures probably isn't particularly worthwhile, but for high-value items they can be invaluable in interesting your customers. A cheap way to get extra pictures and higher-resolution images into your listing is, as we've seen, to place them on a picture-hosting service and to provide a link in your description, so bidders can access those images.

Two sites that specialise in providing this service are AuctionPix (**www.auctionpix.co.uk**) and Vendio (**www.vendio.com**), but you can also use the general photography-hosting sites such as those run by Google, Yahoo! and Flickr.

If your sale item is new and unused, the best pictures can usually be sourced from online shops or the manufacturer's website, but if those aren't available you can take your own using any serviceable digital camera.

The maximum picture size that eBay will allow you to post is 800 x 800 pixels, so uploading anything bigger than that is pointless and time consuming. Ideally, take the images into a photo-editing application (such as Adobe Photoshop Elements or

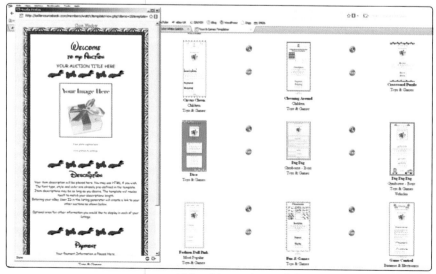

▲ A template can give your listing a more professional touch

▲ Given the choice between these two watches, regardless of price, which one would you be more interested in?

Corel Paint Shop Pro) and first crop out the superfluous parts of the image, and then scale the end product to get as close as possible to eBay's maximum size, without damaging the quality of your picture. After you've done this, save the image (usually in JPEG format) for uploading.

Adding a decent picture is one of the skills that many eBayers lack, and putting a good one on your listing could make a major difference. Try to follow these pointers:

- If you take the picture yourself, think about how it will look at a very small size alongside your item's title in a listings search.
- Close-up shots can easily be out of focus if your camera doesn't have a 'macro' feature, or you don't use it properly.
- Try finding a simple location to shoot, where the background won't distract the viewer. A blank wall or hardwood floor is ideal.
- If the item is small, like a coin, then put some other well-known object or a ruler in the shot so that the bidder can get an idea of scale.
- eBay has image-adjustment tools for picture brightness and contrast, but it's better to get these things right in a photo-editing application before uploading the picture.
- Camera flash can make some items difficult to see correctly. The best pictures are taken outside in natural light where possible.
- If it's important that the item you're selling is functional, you should show it working properly in a picture.
- Defects like scratches and marks can be shown in a photo to explain how minor or not they are.
- Never post a tiny or blurry picture. It only makes people suspicious.

These are merely a few simple pointers regarding how to use images in your eBay listings. We'll go into this topic of pictures in greater detail elsewhere in this book.

OTHER LISTING HINTS

If there's one single message for anyone creating a listing, it's simply this: don't put barriers between the item and the potential customer. It only takes one reason for them to click away to something else, so try not to give it to them.

The most common problem with any given listing is not providing sufficient information, leading the eBayer to assume it's either not the item they want or something they need. For example, if you offer Collection Only as a postage option, it's a good idea to explain why. Maybe the item is just too heavy or large to practically ship, but don't assume the potential bidder knows this; say it.

The other sticking point is with any limitations that you've set. These could be countries that you'll post to, payment types you'll accept, or a dozen other things. The more flexible you are in terms of these factors, the larger your potential audience will be. So only apply these restrictions if you must - if you don't feel comfortable with cheques, for example.

SUMMARY

Simple, common-sense rules apply. Present your sale item in the best possible light without exaggerating. Give as much information as possible and even encourage people to ask questions. Place the item in the correct category and be flexible about postage, international mailing and types of payments that you'll accept.

In short, give your items the best possible chance to sell, at the best price you can get.

Which Extras Are Worth Paying For?

eBay provides several optional add-ons to improve your listing, but which ones are you likely to need?

As a business, eBay needs to make a profit and will always look for ways to do so. One way it does it is to provide sellers with a range of optional extras for their listings.

The number of extras available was cut quite dramatically as of 30th September 2009. Previously, sellers could add effects like bold text and highlighting to their listings for a small fee. There was also an extra called Featured Plus, which has also been discontinued under these changes.

According to eBay itself, its reasons for doing so are as follows: "eBay buyers want an improved and consistent shopping experience that delivers a quick and satisfying result. These changes will eliminate buyer confusion and cut unnecessary costs for you." As odd as that sounds for a profit making company, it certainly makes for a more streamlined experience for both sellers and buyers.

In spite of this scaled back approach, there are still a number of extras and upgrades on offer, and they can dramatically expand the possibility of getting a sale or the amount you ultimately receive for an item. However, some of them are likely to be more suitable for you than others, so which ones should you choose and which ones you should leave alone?

THE STANDARD EXTRAS

£0.35 **Subtitle:** The subtitle provides key selling points about your item (benefits, accessories, etc.). You get 55 characters for anything that won't fit in the Title section.

The Pros: According to eBay, listings with a subtitle typically sell for 20% more, which would suggest, statistically, that if your product is worth more than a few pounds, it's a worthwhile exercise.

The Cons: Subtitles are not included in the results when somebody does a basic search. The only time subtitles will show up is when a bidder does a search by title and description. Also, it's not cheap for high-volume sellers.

Bottom Line: If the subtitle were referenced in a basic search, then using it would make more sense, but because it isn't, the subtitle probably isn't worth it for simple or low-cost items. Obviously, if you didn't fill the title line up, then adding a subtitle is a complete waste of time and money.

 COST VARIES **Listing In Two Categories Or More:** Beware! This is an exceptionally dangerous feature, which eBay encourages sellers to use without them fully understanding the consequences. The problem with multiple categories is that each additional one multiplies the total cost for the listing. Two categories will double it, and three will treble it. That's not only the listing fee, but any extras you decide to take into the bargain.

Let's say your fees are £5. Selecting another category increases that to £10. With increases like that, your fees can rapidly spiral out of control.

The Pros: More people will see the item, which should drive up the number of bidders.

The Cons: The cost of the listing fee can negate what you make when you sell.

Bottom Line: A person listing a single low-to-medium-cost item should never use this feature. It's far better to list an item in one carefully chosen category and spend a little on extras than double or more the total fee. The only situation where it has any value is when you're listing multiples of the same items, with ten or more of them to sell. Then it might be worth placing it in more than one category, but only if you're supremely confident that it will help you sell more.

£44.95 **Featured First:** With a cost of £44.95 per item this isn't a feature for the faint-hearted or low-cost items. However, it's only available to Top-rated Sellers - an accolade that takes quite some time and effort to earn.

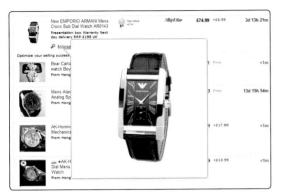

▲ With the Supersize picture feature, buyers can get a better look at your item without entering your listing

▲ The Highlight option which, along with Bold, was discontinued by eBay in favour of a simpler approach

The Pros: Puts you product above the rest, occasionally. Includes Gallery Plus!

The Cons: This isn't a guarantee of being 'first'. What it actually offers is the chance that it will appear on the first page in the featured items. It will be randomly cycled with other items listed with this feature. Also, it's only relevant when users sort by Best Match, so it's a clearly limited extra. As part of eBay's new Top-rated Seller scheme, it's an extra that you're unlikely to be using unless you're truly serious about selling through eBay.

Bottom Line: How useful this option is depends entirely on how many items a typical search for your item returns. The question you need to ask yourself is whether cutting the cost of your item by £44.95 will have a bigger impact on your profit than taking a chance on this.

Note: Items listed in the 'media' section can have this option for just £11.95.

GRAPHICS: PICTURES ON YOUR LISTING

A picture is, indeed, worth a thousand words, and takes much less time for an eBay customer to absorb. You get a single picture for free, which you should always take advantage of. But beyond that, what are the options?

Pictures: In addition to the free picture eBay gives you as standard, you can add a further 11, each costing you another £0.12. These pictures will be presented as 'Standard' with a maximum resolution of 400 pixels along the longest edge.

FREE
Gallery Picture: Shows a small preview of the first picture loaded in the search listing. Size is 64 x 64 pixels, from whatever size it originally was. This

option originally cost extra money, but it's now a standard eBay feature.

Gallery Plus: This option displays a larger picture (standard resolution) in search results when a buyer's mouse hovers over the hyperlinked word 'Enlarge' under the gallery picture.

FROM £0.90
Picture Pack: (£0.90 for six pictures or £1.35 for seven to 12 pictures) This is a slightly confusing option, and the extra amount isn't just for the volume of pictures added. What it gives you is six or 12 pictures, plus Gallery and Supersize on those pictures you've uploaded.

For six pictures, that means you get Gallery listing and Supersize functionality for just £0.30. Inherently this then includes Picture Show for viewing all the item pictures at the top of your item page.

£0.60
Supersize Pictures: This will display the uploaded pictures to a maximum resolution of 800 x 800, which is more than twice the size of the standard resolution for £0.60.

EXTRA ENHANCEMENTS

£0.07
Listing Designer: A range of themed templates, providing layouts and graphics that enhance your listing. Simply select the one you like and preview its impact on your listing.

The Pros: Makes your listing more interesting.

The Cons: The eBay templates are well known, so things looking better may not fool anyone.

Bottom Line: Free templates are available elsewhere, so use them instead and save the money. They're not suitable for eBay businesses, where you

need to create a unique identity and not use an off-the-shelf one.

£0.06 **Schedule Start Time:** Starting your auction the moment you finish the listing can often be a bad plan. For a little extra you can delay the start, which will correspondingly delay the finish. The best time for an auction to end is Sunday, while people are using the Internet at home. The worst days are Friday and Saturday. However, a bidding war isn't likely to break out if your item ends at 3am in the morning. The best time is between 9pm and 11pm in the evening. If you can't arrange for the item to be posted to fit with that time-scale, then spending a small amount of money to delay the start is almost certainly worth it.

Also, if you're selling something on the US eBay site, or which would be of interest to people in a specific country, think about the time differences that apply.

This isn't an advantage that helps a specific type of seller; everyone should be conscious of their timing, and schedule the best point to end an auction when they can. It could possibly be argued that this isn't relevant to those running Buy It Now listings, but many people do Ending Soon searches, so it can play a part even there.

The Pros: Allows your listing to start and end at the best times. It's a cheap option.

The Cons: You could save this small amount by being more organised.

Bottom Line: This is one extra you that should always use, unless you always post your auctions at the perfect time. As you can now save your listings before releasing them, this isn't the issue it once

▲ Featured First is a particularly expensive extra, so think carefully before you opt for it

was. If you have lots of items, the 6p this costs might eventually be significant, though.

PLAYING THE PERCENTAGES

If the advantages presented by eBay were guaranteed, using every extra would be a no-brainer. Alas, these numbers are only averages, and extras are most often used for selling high-value items, which can distort their benefits.

For someone starting out on eBay, it's a good plan to use extras sparingly, and only when you think they'll deliver a real benefit. Those running a business can experiment to find their true worth by selling the same things with and without the help of an extra. They'll be able to better judge if using them is a cost-effective investment, or merely filling eBay's pockets.

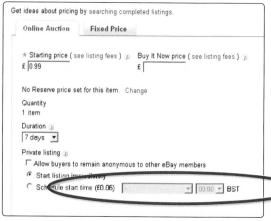

▲ For very little cost, you can choose when to start your auction. In most cases, this is worth paying for

▲ Setting up the options for a picture on eBay

Standard Picture Sizes On eBay

Picture Types	Resolution	File Size
List View	64 x 64 pixels	1-3KB
Thumbnail	92 x 76 pixels	2-5KB
Preview	200 x 150 pixels	10-20KB
Standard	400 x 300 pixels	30-40KB
Supersize	Up to 800 x 800 pixels	>50KB

Getting The Right Picture

A good picture can be an invaluable asset for an eBay listing. It could be the difference between a passing interest and a sale

The quality of your eBay listing and how you handle enquiries and fulfill orders builds confidence among your buyers - confidence in you. The photos that accompany your listings build up buyers' confidence in the item you're hoping to sell.

Great images can come out of inexpensive cameras. As long as you stick to a few rules, time spent on photos will pay off in increased sales. People may be put off by wordy or scant descriptions. If you're not the eBay poet you'd like to be, let your pictures speak for you.

BUYER FOCUS

Always have the buyers in mind as you snap your shots. Be sure they're properly lit from all sides so no area is obscured, and avoid harsh shadows on or around the item. Flash photography rarely improves shots, and glare can be a problem on reflective surfaces, so use ambient light when possible. It may be tricky in areas where it rains a lot, so plan photo shoots for sunnier days. Shoot outdoors if possible or indoors with lamps.

If the scale of an item is hard to judge, it's a good idea to put a recognisable object next to it. Coins are often used beside small items, and rulers and yardsticks can be placed with large items. Text descriptions of size are hard to visualise, and international buyers may not want to do conversions. Even if you think it spoils your photos, these types of visual aids are always appreciated.

IMAGE BASICS

Buyers want to identify merchandise at a glance. Remember, it takes them far less time to click away

from your page than to stop and find their glasses, so make your images stand out. Arrange and focus each shot so the item fills the available space, or crop it later, leaving a border of roughly 10% around the item.

Use the macro setting, if your camera has one, for very small items or close-ups of details in larger pieces, but be sure to use it properly. Choose high-contrast, solid, seamless, clutter-free backgrounds. Use light-coloured backgrounds for dark items, and darker shades for light items.

Include as much detail in each photo as possible, especially if there's a problem. Buyers need to know if an item is cracked, stained, torn or chipped. Sellers who post a zoomed image of a small flaw often get feedback comments of 'better than expected', when the item with its petite imperfection arrives. Those who try to hide or disguise damage in photos risk receiving negative feedback from buyers, which will reduce confidence from future potential buyers.

Be considerate of buyers' time and bandwidth. If your photos are slow to load, they'll move on. File sizes should be the smallest achievable without sacrificing quality. Keep in mind there are people who still have computer display desktop settings of 800 x 600 pixels, which is why eBay recommends dimensions of 400 pixels along the longest edge of your image.

Be aware, if you host your images outside of eBay's services, you'll be given an option to 'standardise your images' when you set up your page, meaning eBay will rescale each image to its recommended size. This can have disastrous effects on pictures you've worked hard

◄ A matchbox reveals this item's size instantly

◄ This seller brands their tattoo equipment photos with their name

◀ Near identical images from two completely different sellers

on. Resized images may contain unattractive moire patterns (wavy lines). Always preview your images at reduced dimensions before you approve any resizing.

REAL SELLERS' PICTURES

While you're learning to improve your photos, don't be tempted to copy images from other sellers. Not only will buyers notice, but you could lose your eBay account and face legal action. Have faith in yourself and your abilities, and buyers will too.

To protect your own pictures from being used by other sellers, add identifying text (like your account name or store address) to your photo with an image-editing program. Make it semi-transparent if you've got the expertise to do so (many image-editing programs make this easy) and place it where it's either impossible

or too much trouble to remove, being sure not to obscure an important feature of your item. If it's stolen and altered, it'll be obvious which is the original and which was tampered with.

For example, the two rubber ducks above are from different sellers, yet the images are identical. However, the one on the right didn't bother to copy the entire shadow. If you're reselling new goods, manufacturers and wholesalers often have professional, free product shots available through their sites or on request.

USEFUL LESSONS

The best lessons are learned from other people's mistakes and successes. The examples on the following pages of eBay seller images demonstrate more right and wrong ways to photograph your wares.

Additional Tips

Take additional, high-resolution images of your items, even if you won't be posting them. They can be supplied to interested buyers on request to clinch sales, or kept as insurance and proof if the quality or condition of an item is challenged after the sale.

Be aware that newer web browsers and available add-ons and extensions make it possible for buyers to enlarge not only the text in web pages, but images as well. That enables sellers to post smaller pictures, and viewers can choose to enlarge them when they need to. This works to everyone's advantage, as long as the image quality is high enough. Test your images by resizing in a zoom-enabled Internet browser (such as Firefox or Opera) before uploading or linking them to your pages (you can simply drag and drop JPEGs onto an open browser window).

Don't become an urban legend! Be sure you're not capturing your own image in any reflective surfaces of your items or in the room. Photos have been forwarded through e-mails and put on sites over the years featuring alleged auction site sellers in the nude, caught in

glass-doored china cabinets and gleaming steel kettles. Whether legitimate, intentional, accidental, or faked, they're a great reminder to scrutinise your pictures carefully before posting in public places.

In spite of the prior paragraph, remember that your photos always reflect on you. If you post haphazard, sloppy shots, buyers will assume you treat customers in the same way. Lazy photography can be just as damaging as negative feedback.

◀ This picture exposes more than any buyer needs to know

Picture Rights And Wrongs

▲ This ladies' top, clamped and stretched across a hanger, and shot on the back of a door, doesn't look very attractive, or instil confidence that its buyer has any chance of looking attractive in it.

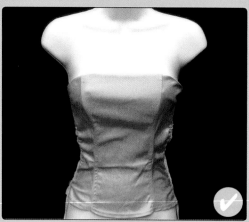

▲ Compare the first pink top to this seller's photo. This person has invested in a mannequin and shot against a high-contrast background, revealing the potential of the garment when worn.

If you don't sell enough to justify the expense of a mannequin or dress form, ask a same-sized friend to model the clothes. You don't have to include more than the torso, so your model can remain anonymous.

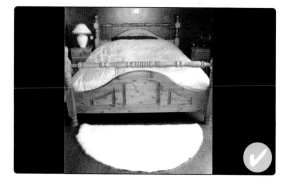

▲ Some items warrant breaking the rules. While most should be shot against plain backgrounds free from clutter or distracting elements, other items are more impressive in a setting, like this rug. It's a 'lifestyle' shot that demonstrates how it looks when used.

On its own, it would look like a non-descript semi-circular smudge of white. Here, it's accentuated against the dark wood and complements a tidy, attractive bedroom, so a buyer can picture it in their own home.

▲ Some items are more of a challenge to show at their best, like this 'original and trendy' cork picture frame. When there's little to work with, don't fail to adequately depict what is there. Nowhere in the description are dimensions mentioned or what hardware is included to stand or hang this 'envy of all your friends' frame.

◄ Part of eBay's advice is to photograph items 'at an angle'. That doesn't mean 'don't bother rotating images'. No one appreciates risking neck pain to view merchandise. This snap of a gargoyle ornament suffers from being on its side, and the damage is doubled by a muddled background. The cloth colour is too similar to the item colour, especially in shadowed areas. Buyers will struggle to tell where the ornament ends and the background begins. Its description includes 'sits on edge of shelf'. That's exactly where the photo should be shot.

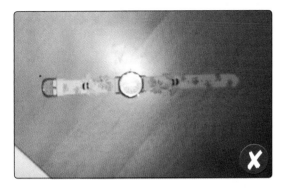

▲ This photo of a child's watch has multiple problems working against it. The glare from the camera's flash wipes out any detail on the glass face and strap design. It's impossible to tell the size or condition of the watch, and there's far too much space around the item, with distracting corners left in. It should be shot on a non-reflective surface like cloth, in natural light, without a flash and cropped much more tightly. Including a ruler in the shot would indicate length at a glance.

▲ This low-resolution rectangle of dingy brown is actually a 'caramel cream' shaggy chenille bathroom rug. It's been heavily compressed and pixelated, and smeared around the edges. It looks more like a coarse fabric doormat designed to strip mud off boots than the soft, luxurious surface a buyer would want to step on with bare wet feet. This picture would benefit from a 'lifestyle' setting like the rug opposite, with a high-resolution close-up of the velvety tufted pile as an inset.

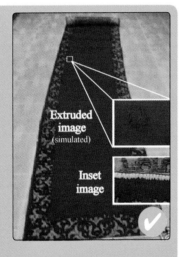

Extruded
image
(simulated)

Inset
image

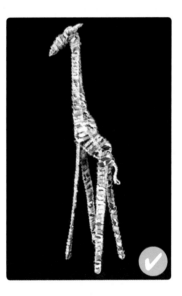

▲ The appeal and value of many items, like 'semi-antique' Persian rugs, are determined by original workmanship and present condition. This long, blurry shot doesn't show any detail whatsoever, only a vague indication of colour and pattern. Buyers need to know the exact condition of this item. They expect wear and tear on older, used items and, with certain things, this is even preferable to 'like new' condition.

▲ This seller wisely includes additional close-up shots of the pattern, weave, and worn areas, giving the buyer plenty to examine to make an informed purchase. If you're limited to displaying a single shot, by space or budget, you can include inset or 'extruded' images (zoomed or more detailed parts pulled from the main image) of a portion or section of a large item, like this revised image made from two of the seller's additional shots.

▲ This giraffe made from a soft-drink can is an ideal image for display. The high-contrast background and high resolution are perfect. It can be enlarged in a browser to full-screen dimensions without losing detail, is expertly lit, properly cropped with sharp focus, and shot at an interesting angle. As unique as the item is, the flawless photographic treatment makes it even more attractive.

Why Ratings And Feedback Matter

The rating system built into the eBay service is an important barometer of how trustworthy a trader is. Here's why

Quick reality check: when you use eBay you're trading with a complete stranger. Whether selling or buying, it's absolutely essential to get some measure of how reliable the other eBay member is. In short, will the goods/money arrive? This is why trading history is part of your eBay profile; it's used to determine whether or not to do business with you.

This might be something of a catch-22 situation if everyone required their buyer or seller to be experienced before trading, since it would not be possible to accumulate a rating without first having a good trading history. However, in practice, sellers of items under £100 are likely to accept business from almost anyone, allowing rookie users to build up their score. It's probably a good idea to start out buying smaller things on eBay to get the hang of it before taking the plunge and going for more expensive items.

As of mid-2008 an eBay member's reliability is scored only on the basis of buyer's feedback; you do not get ratings points for any purchases you make. However, you can read a member's feedback comments to get a measure of how good they are as a buyer.

HOW IT WORKS

Generally speaking, feedback - and thus, a rating - is given when a transaction is complete, the money has been cleared, the goods are delivered and both sides are happy. If the buyer is paying through PayPal, the seller might give them their feedback straight away, since there's very little else required of the buyer, and receiving a thank you comment can encourage the buyer to reply in kind.

If something goes wrong with the transaction, then the feedback system is one way of informing other eBay users about the reality of dealing with this particular user. It should be pointed out that leaving negative feedback is not the first course of action to take if there's a problem. It's best for everyone to resolve matters with a positive attitude, rather than by resorting to 'revenge feedback'. Recent changes to the feedback system also include a three-day delay before you can give non-positive feedback, which can be time enough to cool off and maybe talk it over some more.

Feedback is an important part of the pseudo-gaming aspect of eBay. It's no coincidence that eBay describes a successful purchase as a 'winning bid', and awards a score to its members. Winning auctions and good feedback ratings are an important part of the eBay experience; it keeps people using the system and also provides a threat against misusing the service.

RATINGS

A feedback rating is composed of a choice of 'positive', 'negative' or 'neutral', along with a comment on the transaction. Generally speaking, a transaction should end with a positive result. Only very poorly managed transactions should be classed as neutral, and only in cases where there has been a complete failure, coupled with some sort of material loss on one side or another, should the transaction be rated as negative. Negative basically describes the other party as totally impossible to work with.

The comment in the feedback usually falls into one of two categories. It is either a stock 'thank you', which many people adorn with their own brand of hyperbole, or it's a description of what went wrong or, indeed, right with the transaction.

It is important, on the rare occasions where you need to deliver negative feedback, to make it

▲ Feedback profiles are central to the workings of eBay

absolutely clear why you're doing it. For example, you might write 'The seller sent me three poor excuses and then stopped replying to e-mails', which would clearly explain why no other person should deal with them. Conversely, writing 'This guy is a moron and needs help!', while it may be cathartic, is missing the point somewhat.

Some people seem to use the opportunity of giving feedback to wax lyrical about how much they enjoy using eBay. With some sellers, this can almost be an incentive to buy further items, just to see what they will write next.

THE RATING NUMBER

The ratings are compiled into a single 'score'. For every positive rating you get, your score is increased by one. For every negative rating, the score is reduced by one. Neutral, predictably, has no effect. However, an extra detail is that your score cannot be affected by more than a total of one by any individual eBay user in a given week. So, if you sold one hundred items to the same user and received all positive feedback, your feedback rating will still be one. Conversely, if you sold one item per week for a year to the same person and received positive feedback, you would score 52. To make things more complex, if the same user, in the same week, gives a variety of positive and negative ratings to the same seller, the overall positive or negative effect on that seller's feedback score will be determined by the balance of different ratings - a bit like the 'swing-ometer' showing how election results affect the political parties.

When reading a user's rating, do not just rely on the points total; there's also a description of the overall total percentage of positive feedback. A new feature of eBay is also the DSR (Detailed Seller Rating), which shows a star-based scoring system in terms of item description, communication, delivery time and how reasonable the postage charges were.

eBay sellers who trade in high volume and continue to receive a high percentage of positive feedback are designated as PowerSellers. This is a hard rating to achieve, but the confidence a buyer can feel with a PowerSeller is often reflected in increased sales. In addition, once you're a PowerSeller, it's harder for a buyer to leave you negative feedback.

IDEAL FEEDBACK RATINGS FOR BUYERS

As a buyer, if you have a choice of seller, you should prefer one with a long trading history and a large number and high percentage of positive feedback ratings. Ideally, you should find no negative feedback for your seller. If there has been negative feedback, it would be best if that transaction happened a while ago (you can see a breakdown of ratings received in the last one, six and 12 months).

Feedback Icons

You will notice an icon next to an eBay User ID. This icon represents how good that user's trading history has been. This table shows what they all mean.

Number of points	Icon
10 - 49	Yellow star ☆
50 - 99	Blue star ★
100 - 499	Turquoise star ☆
500 - 999	Purple star ★
1,000 - 4,999	Red star ★
5,000 - 9,999	Green star ☆
10,000 - 24,999	Yellow shooting star 🌠
25,000 - 49,999	Turquoise shooting star 🌠
50,000 - 99,999	Purple shooting star 🌠
100,000 - 499,000	Red shooting star 🌠
500,000 - 999,999	Green shooting star ☆
Over 1,000,000	Silver shooting star ☆

You should also read the last few feedback descriptions, as they appear on the ticker on the profile page, to see what else buyers have to say about dealing with the seller. The Detailed Seller Ratings should be an honest appraisal of the seller, because they're left anonymously.

Look for comments and DSRs that describe items arriving rapidly and in excellent condition. If there has been any negative feedback, it might be worth trying to find out exactly what happened. It's possible that the cause of the negative rating was a particularly unreasonable buyer, and the seller's reply to the feedback, explaining their side of things, may give you a more balanced view of what happened and also how that seller treats their buyers.

Overall, though, it's in the interest of a seller to make sure that they get a satisfactory rating of their conduct on eBay. Feedback ratings are the primary way that a prospective trading partner gets to decide whether you look reliable, so every negative rating counts heavily.

RECEIVING NEGATIVE FEEDBACK

Having described the importance of a clean record on eBay, it's still almost inevitable that a transaction will go wrong, especially if you're dealing with countless members of the general public, not all of whom know how to use eBay properly. Should you receive negative feedback, there are two possible things you can do to deal with it.

Leave Feedback

Your Feedback counts - share your trading experience with the eBay Community. Other members learn from your overall ratings, and buyers can leave specific Feedback about the item description, the seller's communication, and postage. Learn more

⊘ Sellers can no longer leave negative or neutral Feedback for buyers.
Buyers should leave honest Feedback without the fear of receiving negative or neutral ratings. Read more

Show items: All | Bought | Sold   Find a transaction   Search

Leave Feedback for 1 (viewing 1-1)

Pair of GUITAR STRAP BUTTON & END PINS PEGS spares parts - [View item summary]   Item # 120271289840

Seller ████████ (14448 ☆) ⚡Power me 📋
Ended: 20-Jun-08 12 37 32 BST

Rate this transaction. This Feedback helps other buyers and sellers ⓘ
◉ Positive   ○ Neutral   ○ Negative   ○ I will leave Feedback later

Please explain Item arrived as described, in perfect condition and on time | 20 characters left

Click on the stars to rate more details of the transaction. These ratings will not be seen by the seller. ⓘ

How accurate was the item description?   ★ ★ ★ ★ ★
How satisfied were you with the seller's communication?   ★ ★ ★ ★ ★   ⓘ Remember – these Detailed Seller Ratings are
How quickly did the seller dispatch the item?   ★ ★ ★ ★ ★   anonymous, so please feel free to leave honest
How reasonable were the P&P charges?   ★ ★ ★ ★ ★   ratings about your buying experience

◀ In the majority of cases, you'll be leaving positive feedback. Only in the worst possible scenario would you consider leaving negative feedback

First and foremost, you should respond. Your response will be listed alongside the complaint and allows you to give a more balanced view of what happened. It's not necessary to give your opinion of the other person involved. You need to portray yourself as a reasonable person to trade with.

If necessary, you may be able to appeal to eBay to have the feedback removed. It has very strict rules governing the removal of feedback and will only do so if there's a breach of those rules. See **pages.ebay. co.uk/help/policies/feedback-abuse-withdrawal. html** for the exact terms of feedback removal. In a nutshell, it will remove abusive or libelous feedback, along with feedback resulting from clearly malicious behaviour - like winning an auction purely for the chance to give negative feedback, rather than to buy the item.

AVOIDING NEGATIVE FEEDBACK

Prevention is the best cure. Even with the best will in the world, things can go wrong during the course of completing a transaction. If you keep the other party informed every step of the way, they're less likely to consider your service to be poor. This is not a recommendation to spam them with hourly updates (once every two hours is more than enough). However, if there are going to be delays, it's a good idea to keep the other person informed as you work through the problem.

Generally speaking, people are quite reasonable and respond well to being kept informed, even if it's bad news you're delivering. When you've completed your side of the transaction, contact the other person to make sure that they're happy and to offer assistance if they require it.

Leaving negative feedback is really a last resort for dealing with problems. If you're proactive, friendly and helpful throughout your dealings with other eBay users, the chances are that they'll give you a positive feedback rating, even if there were problems.

TIT FOR TAT

Amid some controversy, eBay changed its feedback system in 2008. Originally, the idea of allowing people to give mutual feedback made eBay seem like a self-policing community. However, the ability for a seller to reward a disgruntled customer with negative feedback, alongside the facility to mutually withdraw feedback, had resulted in a couple of phenomena. Firstly, there was a tit-for-tat effect when a buyer gave a negative rating and the seller immediately responded in kind. This discouraged some buyers from being honest, lest they get smeared in the process.

Secondly, the fact that a rating could be withdrawn had the possible effect of encouraging some people to bully their reviewer into agreeing to withdraw the feedback. One aspect of dealing with the general public over the Internet is that there are some crazies out there, and they may have nothing better to do with their time than annoy you on eBay.

The changes, which include anonymous Detailed Seller Ratings, are a big step forward; they recognize that the person risking the most on eBay is the buyer; ultimately it's the buyer who sends the funds and risks receiving nothing, or something they didn't bargain for.

POSITIVE FEEDBACK

Though there's much to say on the subject of dealing with negative feedback, it's worth remembering that part of being a good eBay trader is the accumulation of positive feedback from different eBay users in order to aggregate a good overall score. A better score will enable you to deal with more eBay users.

Good communication and prompt payment or delivery are the main sources of positive eBay feedback. If in your communication or item description you under-promise, and then, in reality, over-deliver (for example, claiming you deliver in a week, but you actually turn around delivery in three days), you will make people happy. If, in addition, you contact the other eBay user on completion of the transaction and remind them to leave you feedback, having given them a positive feedback score, then you are more than likely to receive positive feedback in kind. Success on eBay can be as much about good social skills as good business skills.

WHEN TRANSACTIONS GO BAD

Overall, trading on eBay is about as safe as buying something from a stall at your local market. eBay provides a range of services to help you resolve disputes, and the vast majority of transactions go by without a hitch. However, when eBay transactions go wrong, they can do so spectacularly. The fact that most items are bought by mail order is a significant complicating factor, as is the fact that many people on eBay are enthusiastic amateurs, rather than professional businesspeople.

TAKING THE RISK

Although there are risks associated with eBay transactions, and though you may prefer to reduce those risks by dealing only with PowerSellers or those eBay users with huge feedback ratings, it's best for the eBay community as a whole to give people the benefit of the doubt. There are ways of dealing with failed transactions and, assuming that the other person is in the UK, normal trading laws govern the sale. Although some eBay users are unreliable, it is better to play the game rather than miss out on good deals 'just in case'.

Conversely, when buying something from an eBay user with a low feedback rating, you should consider the value of the transaction. Could you afford to lose this money? Although you might, ultimately, be able to recover the funds or replace a faulty item bought at that price, would it be worth the hassle?

Generally speaking, the average eBay user should expect to have some sort of problem with an eBay transaction around 5% of the time, usually with low-value items where the seller isn't making enough of a profit to be able to do much to rectify any problems that occur.

▲ If your item arrives looking like this, negative feedback might be in order, but try to resolve the situation amicably first

NOT RECEIVING THE GOODS

Sometimes eBay items do not arrive. In this situation, the first thing to do is check that the seller has received the funds and ask them for the date when the item was sent. If the seller has proof of mailing, then they should be able to chase the matter up with the post office. If they've sent the item via Special Delivery, it's possible to track the item through the post office's system.

In order to bring costs down, many items are sent via normal mail. This makes them difficult to track and they may end up permanently lost in the mail. Given that many eBay sellers are selling unique items, possibly from their own personal house clearance, the chances of getting a replacement for that exact item are low.

If you're concerned about the possibility of the item being lost in the mail, ask whether the seller is prepared to add postal insurance to their delivery service, which should offer some guarantee of arrival or a refund if the item is lost.

BUYER COMPLAINING OF NON-RECEIPT

When considering how a seller might respond to your complaint about non-receipt of an item, think how you

A Tale Of Two Problems

In one eBay transaction, a particular seller had specified that they would only deal with damaged goods if the buyer paid postal insurance. The item in question, a CD, was shipped without its jewel case in a padded envelope. It arrived at the buyer's snapped in two. The buyer complained and was told that nothing could be done. This resulted in a heated e-mail exchange, with various insults traded, and negative feedback. All that fuss over a £5 CD.

In a different eBay transaction, the seller had specified a refund or replacement on computer hard disk sales. One of the hard disks, retailing for about £40, was found to be faulty, so was duly returned and a replacement was received a day or so later. This too was found to be faulty. The seller again agreed to replace it and sent another through. This third disk was also faulty. The buyer complained again to the seller, who offered a refund, concerned that perhaps something about the buyer's usage of the disks was the problem. Eventually, the seller was persuaded to send another disk, which worked perfectly. Positive feedback all around. Cooperation really works.

would react if one of your buyers contacted you, claiming they haven't received the goods. On one hand, it's quite possible that the postal system has failed, or that you incorrectly addressed the package. On the other hand, there are going to be some people who receive their items perfectly, and then contact you complaining of non-receipt in an attempt to get a refund on top of the goods.

You have to take the buyer's claims at face value. Therefore, it's recommended that for any item of value, you use Royal Mail's special delivery service or an equivalent (even getting a simple certificate of posting for low-value items). Postal or courier tracking on an item, and the insurance to replace it if it's lost, is a good way to resolve any complaints. For items worth more money than you can afford to lose, consider tracking and insurance to be an absolute must.

RECEIVING DAMAGED GOODS

If an item arrives damaged or faulty, it's easier to convince a seller that there's a problem. You can take digital photographs or even return the item to them. It's important that you're fully aware of the seller's returns policy before you agree to bid on the item. Most sellers will expect you to pay for the return postage. Some sellers may stipulate that they will only deal with damaged items in situations where postal insurance has been bought. In any case, the first thing to do is contact the seller, explain the problem and ask them what they can do.

NOT RECEIVING PAYMENT

It's best not to send an item to your buyer until their payment has already cleared. Receiving a check is all very well, but checks can easily bounce. PayPal, despite charging a transaction fee for sellers, is an instant method of payment and it also simplifies things greatly.

If you haven't received any form of payment, you can prompt the other user with an eBay invoice, for which there's a link on the e-mail confirming the sale. After that, you can contact them directly, perhaps offering them an alternative means of payment (PayPal, check, money order, bank transfer and so on).

If you've sent the item out before cleared payment, or if a check bounces, then you're in a very weak negotiating position. Don't do this; it's really not worth the stress. If you've sent the item on trust and have received no payment, then you can send an invoice to the buyer's delivery address and could, ultimately, proceed to the small claims court. This is much better avoided by withholding the item until cleared funds are received. The overwhelming majority of buyers will have no problem with you doing so. If a buyer is putting pressure on you to deliver before you receive the check, consider it a warning sign; there's seldom a good reason for this sort of behavior.

NEGOTIATING WITH THE OTHER PERSON

eBay users are, in general, reasonable people who are worried about their feedback rating. Putting aside all the things that can go wrong, people generally go onto eBay to trade honestly, rather than con each other. Wherever there has been a problem, the best step to take first is to contact the other user and discuss it. You shouldn't storm in with threats about negative feedback, because although it means something, it's also a fairly limited 'punishment'. If you're polite and reasonable with the other person, there's a high chance you'll be able to come to an agreement over how to solve the problems blighting a transaction.

EBAY COMPLAINTS PROCEDURE

If negotiation fails, then eBay has a Dispute Console. You can use this to ask eBay to step in to help resolve the problem. eBay will not refund your money. Indeed, the worst eBay can do to a buyer or seller is suspend their account until they have either resolved the problem or, more likely, set up a new account in a different name and continued trading regardless.

In some cases, the threat of an account suspension, or even the more official nature of disputes taken up through eBay's Dispute Console, will break a stalemate in negotiations, so it's worth

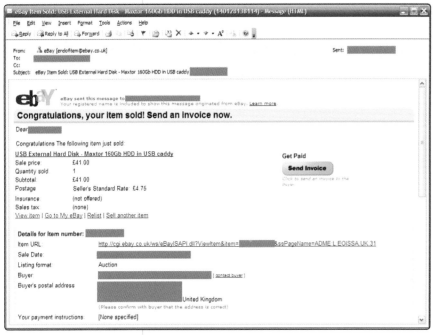

▲ You should keep careful records of your transactions, and make sure the other party has a copy too

following this course of action if you can't resolve things amicably directly with the other person.

PAYPAL PROTECTION

PayPal was acquired by eBay in order to provide financial services for its customers. Along with the ability to manage credit cards and virtual funds in multiple currencies, protecting those vital personal details, rather than revealing them to the other person, PayPal also provides insurance on every purchase you make. This insurance will cover you up to 100% of the value of an item that never arrives, or arrives but proves to be significantly different from the item description. Given that this is an insurance policy, however, PayPal will be as keen to follow the small print of the original item description as the seller was.

It is certainly confidence-inspiring to think that if an expensive item does not arrive, there's the possibility of PayPal refunding its worth. PayPal's service extends to sellers as well, offering insurance against chargebacks. A chargeback is when someone asks their credit card company to reverse a transaction for some reason. If this were to happen against an eBay sale you were involved with, you would be obliged to return the funds. However, PayPal insures you against this.

Overall, using PayPal is a good way to protect your interests on eBay, even though its disputes team and complaints process can be quite hard work.

CREDIT CARD PROTECTION

Many credit cards offer protection against fraudulent transactions. If you've bought something and paid by credit card, and this includes your credit card being debited by PayPal for an auction item, you can contact your credit card company for its assistance in reversing a transaction, or at least putting pressure on the merchant to resolve the matter. At the very least, it may put a hold on the transaction so you neither have to pay it off, nor pay any interest on it until the matter is resolved.

THE LAW

If you've paid for services and they haven't been provided, or if the items sent to you are counterfeit or unfit for purpose, then you have the support of UK law. This is more complicated when dealing with overseas eBay users. Within the UK though, you can contact your lawyer, Citizen's Advice Bureau, local Trading Standards office, or even the police, in order to get help dealing with your problem.

In particular, if you've been provided with counterfeit goods, your complaint to the authorities may help them to deal with an organised counterfeiting group.

Caveat Emptor

The eBay item description will show you what you might be getting should you choose to bid. It can be an excellent sales pitch. However, it also represents a contract between the seller and buyer. Read the description in its entirety and do not bid if you're uncertain about exactly what is being sold. Ask questions of the seller before bidding if you're still not sure. A small phrase in the description might well be used retrospectively to justify why the item turns out to be something other than expected. Likewise, a few words in the seller's returns policy might make it difficult to get any after-sales service if something goes wrong.

Although you have statutory rights dealing with traders in the UK, bear in mind that not all eBay traders are based in the UK (this may be in the small print), and it may simply not be worth your while to pursue a claim.

The 'Resolved' Dispute

A particular eBay purchase of some apparently end-of-line DVDs with boxes missing resulted in the delivery of some illegal DVD copies. The buyer contacted the Resolution Center. The Resolution Center went through its procedure until the seller terminated their eBay account.

At this point, the dispute was marked as resolved. There was nothing further that eBay would do. The buyer could have taken the matter further with external agencies, including FACT (the Federation Against Copyright Theft), but seemingly thought it not worth the effort for the few pounds that the item cost.

THE REALITY

Thankfully, trading on eBay seldom results in a complaint, claim, or lawsuit. The reason eBay works as well as it does is that there are huge numbers of honest people out there. Likewise, selling on eBay is a relatively straightforward process, especially if you go into it with the right attitude.

You need to recognize the difference between an eBay PowerSeller, from whom you might expect the same guarantee of service as many dedicated online stores (and many PowerSellers have their own sites outside of eBay as well), and an individual trader, who won't be selling on eBay full time, so might need longer to complete the transaction, and is less able to provide after-sales support. eBay is as its best when buyers and sellers work together to make the transactions succeed.

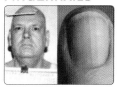

Ten eBay Con Tricks To Watch Out For

What are the most common tricks used by the less scrupulous eBayers, and how can you go about protecting yourself?

1 PHOTOS OR HOW-TO GUIDES

A quick look at the description suggests that you will be buying the item in the picture. Watch out for the small print, though. People commonly sell a picture of or a document about an item, rather than the item itself. The listing may have the same title as others for that item, perhaps with a clone of the item description used in the other auctions. Copy-cat item descriptions do not bode well for the seller.

Some listings suggest you can buy something that will help you get the item you want cheaply. Perhaps they're offering a 'trade secrets' book or CD, which claims to tell you how to get the item at a heavily discounted price - that's after first forking out for the guide, which in turn may simply state something completely obvious.

2 COUNTERFEIT GOODS

Although eBay is proactive about removing fake items from its listings, there's good business in the quick sale of fake designer items, even at a fraction of their high-street price. When buying branded goods, be sure to identify the seller and read their feedback carefully. There are also legal clones of popular items. Beware of descriptions with 'like' in them. The item may well be similar to the real thing, but may be a generic brand, not worth as much as you paid.

3 ILLEGAL IMPORTS

Because eBay is an international market place, you can deal with traders from anywhere in the world. It doesn't follow that listings on the UK site come from UK sellers only. If the item you're buying is usually subject to import duty, you should check that the seller is going to pay this tax. If they're not paying to export the item to the UK, it's possible that you'll end up having to pay duty before Customs & Excise will release the item. This is something that eBay will not protect against.

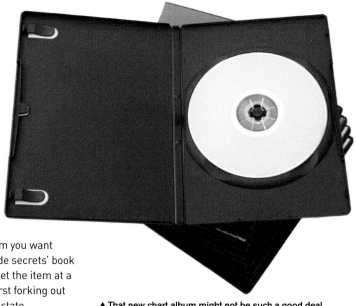

▲ That new chart album might not be such a good deal

4 PRE-BROKEN ITEMS

An old-fashioned auctioneering con is to sell items 'as seen'. This can be used by an unscrupulous seller as a way of selling items that are already broken. Alternatively, if the seller stipulates that they will not be held responsible for breakages during delivery, they could send an already broken item and claim it broke in transit. Watch out for small print in the item description and returns policy. Even an item that claims to be broken may not be much of a deal; the words 'ideal for spares or repair' may actually mean 'totally destroyed and ideal for the bin'.

5 CD-R VERSIONS

With several major retail sites selling brand new chart CDs at around £7, it's fair to say they can't be bought much more cheaply. Older albums may well come out cheaper, sold second-hand, or from surplus stock. However, if you're buying a new album at too cheap a price, be cautious. Some people are happy to buy illegal -copies of CDs, or CD-Rs with MP3 versions of several albums on. These are an infringement of copyright, and no money goes to the artist.

6 MASSIVE STOCK NEW SHOP

A seller with little to no selling history and a huge stock of items might be a genuine person doing a life-laundry. Alternatively, they may be trying to close a large number of bogus deals before being discovered. A bogus seller is unlikely to have as random an assortment of different items as a genuine first-timer with a bunch of their possessions to sell.

7 FAKE MEMORABILIA

Buying memorabilia is always a risky business. How can you be sure that this really is the towel that Amy Winehouse wiped herself on at Glastonbury 2008? Do your research. For instance, with a signed item, try to find out how it was acquired by the seller. Can you see a picture of the signature? Does it match another example of a signed item by the same celebrity? Memorabilia can be cherished greatly, but is far too easy to fake.

8 FAKE RATINGS

You have chosen to deal with a particular seller because they have a 100% positive rating with several happy buyers. Are you sure that these are genuine buyers? Have you looked at what they bought? It's not very difficult to set up several fake eBay accounts and use them to buy very cheap eBay items that were listed by another fake eBay account, thus building up a ratings portfolio paid for with a few hundred eBay listing fees.

This sounds like a lot of effort to go to, but if the seller is selling something expensive, like jewellery or large electrical items, it may be worth building up a fake profile in order to get away with a few bogus sales before cessation of trading. If you're buying something that costs more than a few pounds, perhaps look at the items and other eBay users listed on the seller's feedback profile. It's harder to fake a lot of genuine satisfied customers, buying the same item as you, who have been eBay users for years.

9 THE IMPOSSIBLE TO GET ITEM

A lot of people use eBay to buy something that's not available elsewhere. If you're looking for something that everyone is trying to buy, where genuine stocks are in short supply, the chances are that you'll risk rubbing shoulders with some dodgy sellers. Whether it's the latest videogames console, or tickets to a sold-out music festival, the season's hot properties are going to appear on eBay, and not all of the listings are going to be genuine. Even with the genuine article, the chances are that you might be dealing with a trader who's bought from the limited stock in order to tout the item at an inflated price to make a profit. It is up to you whether you wish to line this person's pockets.

If you're buying sold-out festival tickets, you're advised to check whether those tickets are genuinely transferable. Go to the festival's website and find out about the security measures. Many festivals have learned from the over-touting of Glastonbury tickets in previous years and now have strict policies regarding ticket transfers.

10 TOO GOOD TO BE TRUE

There are some excellent deals to be had on eBay, but the fundamental concepts of trading still apply to eBay sellers. In other words, although you can get a huge discount buying something directly from an eBay seller, who may be running without the overheads of a larger business, they still have to source the goods from somewhere and pay something similar to the usual trade price. If anything is discounted too much, or seems to be too good a deal, you need to question exactly why. How sure can you be that you're buying what you expect? How sure can you be that the goods are legitimate?

If something looks too good to be true...

11 THE JOKE ITEM/DO NOT USE EBAY WHILE DRUNK!

At number 11 in the list of ten, this is definitely the joker in the pack. Sometimes people make bizarre things and put them on eBay. Sometimes, in the spirit of adventure, or under the influence of alcohol, some items seem like a good purchase. A joke item may have been listed on eBay to make people laugh and raise a couple of pounds. A serious item, like, say, a wheelchair, may also seem like a hilarious purchase when you're drunk. Beware the joke item; it will only seem like a good idea until it arrives. Strangely, the novelty wears off and you're left with the eBay equivalent of a hangover.

Dishonourable Mentions

Don't forget to avoid:

- DVDs with the same name as a famous film, but which happen to be the non-famous film-adaptation of the story.
- Revenge items - the disgruntled husband trying to sell his estranged wife by putting her personal details on eBay. Don't ring her; for all you know, the whole thing is a scam. Anyway, someone else probably beat you to asking her out.
- Dodgy photos. Don't look in the reflections in photos of furniture or ceramics; some men forget to wear clothes while photographing their items.
- The 'question about your eBay item' scam. Spam e-mails, possibly snuck through eBay's system, inviting you to look at particular eBay items you've never heard of. If you wanted to look at an eBay item, you'd search for it.

Case Study: **Miss Shoes**

Shoes are big business, especially so for Martin Lott, and his online store, Miss Shoes...

Studies show that one in two British women now own more than 30 pairs of shoes and one in ten women spend more than £1,000 on footwear each year. Given that one in four women would rather buy a pair of shoes than pay a bill, there will be many men out there staring at credit card statements in despair. For Martin Lott, though, these statistics make for happy reading.

Martin started selling items on the Internet in 2001, flogging computer components on QXL and Dabsexchange, and building up a fledgling business in the process. This stopped when he went to university for three years, but in 2005 he met his future wife, Monica, and the pair decided to take a plunge into online selling together.

Monica had always wanted to set up her own business, and she knew a friend in Norwich who worked as a shoe distributor. "We tested the water with about 100 pairs and they sold okay," said Martin.

But things didn't go according to plan in those early days. "Times were tough," he confessed. "Monica's friend and our other main supplier went out of business in our first year of trading."

Undeterred, Monica and Martin, who both live in Norwich, ploughed on, and they've built up a successful eBay company called Miss Shoes (**stores. shop.ebay.co.uk/Miss-Shoes**). It sells a range of footwear for men, women, boys and girls and has thousands of items on sale at any one time. All of the items are sold on a Buy It Now basis rather than an auction and there are variable postage and packing costs depending on the weight of shoes that are being sold.

The main reason the couple sell at a set price is due to the flexibility it provides. Budget brands are sometimes sold with a narrow profit margin, making auctions more risky, while premium brands, whose owners can be more insistent on achieving the recommended retail price, are given at least 30 days' listing time in which to sell.

"The average pair of shoes sells for around £10 to £15 and that's including postage and packing," said Martin. "And we sell around 6,000 pairs each month. Like most large eBay sellers, our profit margins on some items are so narrow it has led some suppliers to question our prices, but we want to offer value to customers above all."

FULL TIME

While Martin juggles the business with his work as a researcher in the School of Computing Sciences at the University of East Anglia - a busy job that entails him providing computing expertise to biologists - his wife operates the company full time. It was Martin, however, who suggested that they use eBay. "By 2005, we found eBay had become the dominant online marketplace while rivals had pretty much disappeared," he said. "We didn't test the water with Miss Shoes anywhere else - we went straight to eBay - but we did have a quick look at what some other big sellers were doing. We once tried a car boot sale, sold one pair all morning and never went back."

Each listing at Miss Shoes is packed with information, and it makes good use of large photographs, which are vital in order to help customers see exactly what they're buying. Monica uses large text, which makes it easy to see at a glance the size of each shoe. This information also contains the title of each item for sale. Delivery information is clear and concise, and the couple invite potential customers to ask questions.

For Martin, it's all about trust, and it's for this reason that he takes the unusual step of not only allowing customers who make a purchase up to 14 days to pay for them, but also has a 14-day returns policy and a guarantee for any shoes that, on those very rare occasions, end up lost in the post.

▲ **The happy couple**

▲ The Miss Shoes eBay store run by Martin and Monica Lott

"Actually, items being lost in the post is an ongoing issue," said Martin. "But the majority of buyers are understanding. In fact, a lot of it comes down to trust. I believe a good reputation is a major advantage not just for our business, but for any company on eBay. Nowhere else can people see unbiased opinions from past customers at the click of a button."

POWERSELLER

Miss Shoes is a PowerSeller. Around 90,000 items have been sold and the company has 99.9% positive feedback - a staggering number for such high-volume sales. The number of customers is also surprising given that Miss Shoes never advertises ("We've never felt the need to; we offer great prices and service so the business advertises itself," said Martin) and it has become such a worthwhile venture that it employs several workers. The company has also recently moved to new premises and it may look to diversify into other types of goods in the future.

"Good feedback is one thing that makes us stand out from the crowd on eBay," said Martin. "We hope to sell to anyone who buys online, and this typically people in their 20s, 30s and 40s. We do our best to offer outstanding prices and service and that's why people keep coming back."

Miss Shoes has About Me page, giving a postal address and telling visitors about the firm's business partners. An About Me page is vital because, if it includes transparent information, it gives shoppers greater confidence. It's a chance to sell your company to a visitor and cement your brand - using humour and an informal style can also work well.

▲ Miss Shoes has a generous returns policy

But is it hard work interacting with customers? "Right from the start, the sheer volume of messages we received from customers presented a challenge," said Martin. "We still get about one message for every three sales. Each customer needs a personalised response, indicating when their order was sent, for example, so it is time consuming. It's a situation we will always face. I think eBay is working on a new system that will help deal with customer queries, but selling shoes presents unique challenges due to the number of different styles and problems when they don't fit."

So does Martin have any helpful advice for would-be eBay sellers? "Of course," he said. "Be prepared to work hard! Anyone can sell a few bits and pieces on eBay, just as anyone can kick a football around a field... but not so many people can play in the Premier League."

Chapter 4
Advanced Selling

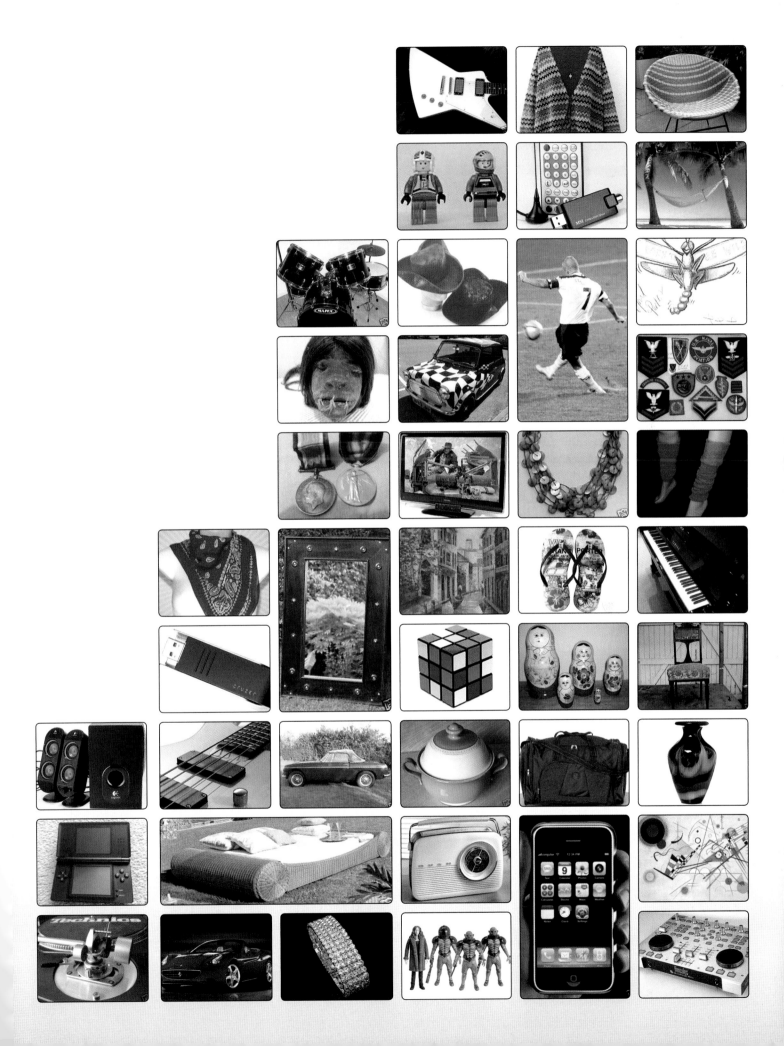

Setting Up An eBay shop

If you have lots of regular stock to sell, then you may want to consider setting up your own shop. We look at getting a store up and running

After you've dipped your toes into the eBay waters, you'll have gained a good feel for the buying and selling process. However, if you want to take your selling to higher level, then it's worth setting up an eBay shop.

By doing so, you're not limited to one-off auctions or short-term advertisements of your goods. You will be able to get yourself noticed, work on a larger scale and sell to your heart's content. In this chapter, we're going to explain what a shop actually is, and how it will benefit you, the eBay seller. We'll explore just how you go about setting up your shop and, more importantly, whether or not it's worth doing.

OPEN ALL HOURS

Using eBay to sell the odd item is a great way to make some extra cash, but if you're planning on using eBay to make a living, then you'll need a good way to make your auctions stand out from the crowd, and make a name for yourself in the eBay community. Selling items and providing a great service is a good way of doing this, but feedback alone won't get your merchandise the coverage you need.

One of the most effective methods to get this wide coverage and high profile is to set up an eBay shop, granting access to a whole heap of benefits. If all goes well, you'll shift more stock than ever before - a fact that eBay is proud to state, with a claim that "75% of eBay Shops sellers surveyed said that opening an eBay shop increased their sales."

An eBay shop is your own personal virtual storefront on the eBay site. Whereas selling individual items with a normal eBay auction account lets you put items up for sale that can then be searched for among all other items currently listed on the site, having a shop means

you have your very own marketplace. In this shop you can list and sell as many items as you like, with no one else's listings cluttering up the place.

The shop comes with your own customised header (shop name and/or logo), as well as your own search feature (to search through all of the items you sell), promotional sections and even the option to include a newsletter, among many other things. This all adds up to your own personalised area of commerce, and is a fantastic way to get your business up and running. You can enjoy some of the benefits of a bricks and mortar business, without the overheads. There's no shop floor to rent, and no staff or utility bills to pay - just the monthly subscription.

REQUIREMENTS

Before you consider setting up your own shop you'll need to meet the minimum demands laid down by eBay. You obviously need to be a registered eBay user, so if you've never sold anything on eBay before, you'll be unable to jump right in and set up shop. Even with an established account set up, you'll need to have a feedback rating of at least ten or be PayPal verified to open a basic shop. To run a featured shop you also need to be a registered business seller on eBay and maintain a 12-month average detailed sellers ratings score of 4.4 or above in each of the four areas. Those running Anchor shops must have an average score of 4.6.

EBAY SHOP FEATURES

The additional features available to eBay shop owners are many and varied. Some are basic extensions of current eBay features, and others are in-depth options geared towards larger-scale e-commerce. Let's look at some of the benefits you can expect.

To start with, your shop will be enveloped in your own store branding and will have a custom web address. This includes your own shop header featuring your own design and logos. Although the full eBay header still remains at the top for users on the Basic package (with the header being greatly reduced for Featured and Anchored shops), your own identity is still clear.

In the header, you can also enter your shop description. This includes your eBay rating, along with a description of your shop and the types of items you sell. By entering keywords into the shop description that accurately describe your shop, people looking for the types of goods you sell will find you far easier.

▲ You should take time to customise the e-mail that bidders will receive if they win your auction

▲ Using the List View option means you can display more products on screen at once

The Basic package used to be limited when it came to the header, and you could only select from available templates. Now, just as with the Featured or Anchored packages, you're able to fully customise your header (with HTML), forming a truly unique banner that can be used not only on your shop, but in other advertising too. This banner can include links to self-hosted pictures, text, and details of highlighted items and offers.

It's also possible to create and customise your own store-front pages. This grants your shop even more distinction. These pages, like the header, are created using HTML, so if you have the skills, you can let your imagination run wild, or you could pay someone to design it for you. Depending on the package you choose, you're limited to a number of custom pages, with those opting for the Basic subscription having the ability to make use of up to five custom pages in their shop.

TAGS
This customised content is all handled via the HTML builder tool eBay supplies, as well as some useful wizards. To help users get the most out of this user-defined content, eBay has also created special tags which, when combined with the right HTML code, can quickly add useful information to your shop.

These tags include {eBayUserID}, which will display your eBay User ID, along with your feedback score (including any relevant icons), {eBayFeedback}, which can display detailed feedback information in various configurations, and {StoreItemShowcase}, which is a very useful bit of code that, when used with your own settings, displays some of the items you're selling in your promotional boxes.

These tags eliminate the need to type out whole reams of code, and let users of all HTML abilities build their stores with ease. However, eBay has restricted the use of some shop tags (specifically the item specific shops tags) in the eBay Shops header. Using these restricted shops tags in the header will result in the shop tag appearing as text and eBay asks people not to use {eBayStoresItemList}, {eBayStoresItemShowcase}, eBayStoresItem}, {eBayStoresItemDetail} and {eBayPromo}.

eBay Shop Insertion Fees For Buy It Now Listings (Three, Five, Seven, Ten, 30 Days)

Insertion Price	Basic Shop	Featured Shop	Anchor Shop
All categories (excluding media - generally books, comics, magazines, DVDs, film and TV, games, music)	£0.20	£0.05	£0.01
Media products (single item)	£0.10	£0.05	£0.01
Media products (multiple items)	£0.10	£0.05	£0.01

eBay Shop Listings Final Value Fees For Buy It Now Listings

Final Sale Price (Excluding Technology And Media)	Final Value Fee
Item not sold	No fee
£0.99 to £49.99	9.9% of the amount of the final selling price up to £49.99
£50 to £599.99	9.9% of the initial £49.99 (£4.95), plus 5.9% of the remaining balance of the final selling price
£600 or more	9.9% of the initial £49.99 (£4.95), plus 5.9% of the initial £50 to £599.99 (£32.45), plus 1.9% of the remaining balance of the final selling price

Technology eBay Shop Listings Final Value Fees For Buy It Now Listings

Final Sale Price for technology (generally Mobile and Home Phones, Computing, Consumer Electronics, Photography)	Final Value Fee
Item not sold	No fee
£0.99 to £29.99	5.25% of the final selling price, up to £29.99
£30 to £99.99	5.25% of the initial £29.99 (£1.57) plus 3% of the remaining balance of the final selling price
£100 to £199.99	5.25% of the initial £29.99 (£1.57) plus 3% of the initial £30 to £99.99 (£2.10) plus 2.50% of the remaining balance of the final selling price
£200 to £299.99	5.25% of the initial £29.99 (£1.57), plus 3% of the initial £30 to £99.99 (£2.10), plus 2.50% of the initial £100 to £199.99 (£2.50) plus 2% of the remaining balance of the final selling price
£300 to £599.99	5.25% of the initial £29.99 (£1.57), plus 3% of the initial £30 to £99.99 (£2.10), plus 2.50% of the initial £100 to £199.99 (£2.50) 2% of the initial £200 to £299.99 (£2.00) plus 1.50% of the remaining balance of the final selling price
£600 or more	5.25% of the initial £29.99 (£1.57), plus 3% of the initial £30 to £99.99 (£2.10), plus 2.50% of the initial £100 to £199.99 (£2.50), plus 2% of the initial £200 to £299.99 (£2.00) plus 1.50% of the initial £300 to £599.99 (£4.50), plus 1% of the remaining balance of the final selling price

Media eBay Shop Listings Final Value Fees For Buy It Now Listings

Final Sale Price For Media	Final Value Fee
Item not sold	No fee
Item sold	9.9% of the amount of the closing balance

For a listing of these useful tags, along with the available settings to be used with them, visit **pages.ebay.co.uk/help/sell/stores-tags.html**.

SEARCH AND CATEGORIES

Along with the personalised header and custom page design, you'll get some staple additions, such as your own search and category boxes. Using the categories system, you can split the items you want to sell into different sections. For example, you could have a clothes section, a section for electronic goods, and a special section for collector's items.

You can have up to 300 categories at once, and all your categories can be changed and updated when you like. Changing names will not affect the item listings found within. You can also use subcategories too, further enhancing your browsing functions.

For people wishing to sell a lot of merchandise, this use of categories is a bonus, and enables the quick and easy browsing of your items. Couple this with the search facility, and all your items will be within easy reach.

Several promotion boxes are available to all subscription types. These are used to highlight different items being sold on special offer, or just to announce new stock, complete with links that take the customer to the item's own page.

Of course, no shop is complete without the main gallery page, where customers can scroll through the items on sale, and the main portion of your shop is taken up by this window.

That's the basic visual make-up of an eBay shop, but that's not all. As with the rest of eBay, when an item is clicked by a user, the product is opened up in a listing frame, which contains all the information associated with the item, along with a larger picture. This function is expanded in an eBay shop, and you have access to a custom listing frame. This is a special frame that allows customised headers and sidebars, thus giving you your own listing windows for your products. Not only does this look more professional, but it's also a great way to advertise your shop, because you have effectively branded your item, which can be discovered by any eBay user, whether they're in your shop or not.

SHOP INVENTORY

You will, no doubt, already be familiar with eBay's two main methods of selling items: auction style and fixed price. However, when you open an eBay shop you'll have access to a third sale type: Shop Inventory.

This is a special sale-type that lists items at a set price with no bidding. The fee structure for the listings is different to normal options, however. Up-front fee listings are lower, costing you less to place items up for sale, but the final value fees if a sale is successful are higher. Your listings have an unlimited duration, as you can choose whether you want a listing to end after 30 days or continue beyond that.

There's also the option of a Good Till Cancelled (GTC) listing. This is a special option, which lets you list an item and have it automatically renewed every 30 days (as long as stock is available). This renewal will occur every month, until you decide to cancel it (with each 30-day cycle incurring a new listing charge).

MARKETING TOOLS

No self-respecting shop owner would go into business and simply wait for customers to come rolling in. After all, if people don't know your shop exists, they're not likely to visit and buy anything. This is just as true with eBay as it is in the real world, and it's here where the eBay Shops marketing features come into play.

Along with your shop, you'll have access to a range of marketing tools, designed to help you get noticed. One of the most useful is the e-mail marketing tool. Using this you can fire off e-mails to potential and existing customers, advertising new items or special offers.

As with most of the shop design process, you set up these e-mails using a step-by-step wizard in which you select the e-mail design and content. You can even include item galleries that users can click on to visit the shop. Feedback can be included, giving your customers peace of mind from the off.

As well as the e-mail service, eBay Shops lets you create promotional flyers that can be posted or packaged with items you sell. You'll also have access to a custom listing frame, and listing feeds (such as RSS). Shop comparisons are also an option, making your listings available to third-party search engines and product-comparison sites.

A range of item-based promotional functions are featured too, letting you cross-promote stock, advertise top picks, and point users to similar items. You can even customise the e-mail footers and invoices with your own logos. All this marketing muscle should be a very welcome aid for anyone trying to increase their sales.

IS IT WORTH IT?

Setting up an eBay shop certainly sounds like a good idea on paper, but will setting up your own shop help increase your sales? Can the extra costs be justified?

DID YOU KNOW?

eBay no longer includes digitally delivered items such as e-books in its feedback system. This is because some users made multiple purchases of such items, which often go for pennies with no postal costs, to artificially inflate their feedback score.

▲ Increase your shop's profile with the 'Email Marketing' tool

How To... Set Up Custom Pages

While the standard eBay pages aren't bad, if you really want to look professional, you'll want to add some extra personality. Here's how:

1 Custom Pages can be used to give your shop a more personalised look. Creating one is easy. Select the Custom Pages link from the Shop Manager menu and you'll see this screen. Select the layout from the range of templates, and click 'Continue' to go the next step.

2 Now you can tweak and refine your page. You'll need to give the page a title, and you can then start to add in the required text. At various points in this section you can also use eBay's HTML Builder, to further customise your page.

3 Custom pages also let you employ promotion boxes for various uses, such as advertising new items, or linking to other sections of the shop. You can also design your own promo boxes if you wish.

4 You can now add some more custom text to the page (again, with the help of the HTML Builder, if needed), and you can specify the item display type. To emphasise your items, you can also opt to hide the left-hand navigation bar, giving prime real-estate solely to your stock.

Would some users be better off staying with one-off auctions? The only people who can really answer these questions are actual shop owners.

Given the amount of extra coverage and space an eBay shop provides, it's no surprise that many shop owners are glad that they decided to set one up. Cathy Grant, owner of Aromabar (**stores.ebay.co.uk/ Aromabar**) is very happy with her featured eBay shop but would like more power and custom control. "I'm happy with my eBay store on the whole but would prefer to have more free, easy-to-use tools provided by eBay to allow me to make the design and layout better, as I feel it could look more professional."

Like many eBay shop owners, Cathy runs her eBay shop in parallel to her own website, and sees distinct benefits in running a stand-alone site: "I've made more profit on sales through my own site due to no fees. I paid a total of £40 for my site template with hosting and have done all the hard work myself." So eBay shops may be easy to set up, but having your own site is still the way to go for many users.

Other eBay shop owners don't necessarily open a shop for the profits alone, and instead use it as a glorified advert for their real shop. Peter, of Genki Video Games (**stores.ebay.co.uk/Genki-Video-Games**) is one example. He appreciates the extra coverage that an

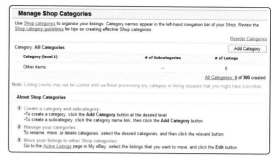

▲ Creating promotional displays

▲ Sort your goods out with the shop categories

▲ The shop summary page

▲ Keywords help potential customers find you

eBay shop grants, but doesn't welcome the additional costs. "The main reason we use eBay is to try to get some additional coverage for our website. To be honest, I'm not sure we even break even once the listing fee, subscription fee, percentage of sale fee and PayPal fee is taken," he said.

Having a store doesn't guarantee extra visits either. "We do use auctions, but only to get attention for our store, as it seems surfers on eBay are far more drawn to auctions."

It's clear that having an eBay shop can be beneficial to setting up a business online, if only for the expanded audience and the extra advertising it generates. The costs are scalable, thanks to the three subscription options, and as long as you have the stock to keep your shop up and running, you'll have a constant outlet for your merchandise that gives you access to a range of extra features not as readily available to many stand-alone web stores.

But many eBay shops have come and gone and many people have become disillusioned with the service. Julie Stamp ran Lolli Dollies on eBay but has since closed it in favour of a stand-alone store. "For me, one of the drawbacks of running an eBay shop is that customers seem to think you're there to answer any enquiries they have, in my case with regards to doll collecting or a doll already in their collection, rather than sticking to questions about items in your eBay shop."

She said the amount of admin time and space required for packaging material is off-putting but the advantage is having your items sold to a worldwide customer base. "If you sell to a niche market, eBay is ideal, as it tends to be the first stop for collectors," she

said. "Search engine optimisation is a given with eBay, and listing items and uploading photos is easy."

Mark Withers, who used to actively sell pictures on eBay, now uses his stand-alone site **www.studioworx. co.uk**, but said, "What eBay does is help you build your own unique brand, and it's an easy point of contact and bookmark. You can organise products into custom categories, making it easier for the customer to find products. There's a buyer confidence with eBay, and while I don't actively sell on eBay any more, I do pursue other business interests associated with it, helping other sellers get started."

SHOP MAINTENANCE

When your shop is built, you can manage it from the Shop Management screen. You'll find a raft of options that cater for every facet of your new trading empire. A good place to start is by organising your stock.

Select Shop Categories from the left-hand menu and you'll be taken to the category screen. Click the 'Add Category' button to create your sections. Enter them into the boxes provided and then click 'Save'. Your categories will be added. You can add more if you like, and can also create subcategories.

Click the 'Promotion Boxes' link to customise these useful features and create more. You can move boxes around, change the box type, content text and name. You can view boxes by category and can edit, remove, or duplicate existing ones.

Just as with any website, search keywords are invaluable. Without them your shop would be very hard to find - not good for sales.

Subscription Types And Fees

BASIC SHOP
The starter pack of the shop system. This is the option for most users, and is great for first-time sellers or those who want to see if a shop is the right option for them before advancing further.

FEATURED SHOP
Has more options for tracking sales and performance, and has more advertising tools. Good for users who want to begin their business growth.

ANCHOR SHOP
The high-end option for advanced eBay sellers who need to get as much coverage as possible and who need to manage their business on a daily basis. Has the most advertising options.

eBay Shops Tariffs

	Basic	Featured	Anchor
Monthly subscription fee	£14.99	£49.99	£349.99
One-time set-up fee	£0	£0	£0
Sales management tools	N/A	£0 (Selling Management Pro)	£0 (Selling Management Pro)

Build Your Shop	Basic	Featured	Anchor
Shop home page and unlimited product pages	Yes	Yes	Yes
Custom pages	Five pages	Ten pages	15 pages
Custom web address	Yes	Yes	Yes
Promotion boxes	Yes	Yes	Yes
Shop categories	300	300	300
Custom shop header	Yes	Yes	Yes
eBay header reduction	No	Yes	Yes
Sales Management			
Access to shop inventory listing format	Yes	Yes	Yes
Free sales management tools	Selling Manager	Selling Manager Pro	Selling Manager Pro
Vacation/holiday	Yes	Yes	Yes
Picture manager (hosting images)	1MB free	1MB free and reduced subscription fees	50MB free and reduced subscription fees

Promote Your Shop	Basic	Featured	Anchor
On eBay			
Increased Exposure On eBay			
Shops logo appears next to your shop name in listings	Yes	Yes	Yes
All listings include additional 'See All Items Listed in Your Shop' link	Yes	Yes	Yes
Listings displayed in eBay Shops gateway search and results browser	Yes	Yes	Yes
Shop name appears in 'Related Shops' search results	Occasionally	Sometimes	Frequently
Rotating promotional space on the eBay Shops gateway	None	Text link at centre of page	Shop logo at top of page
Cross-promotions	Yes	Yes	Yes
Custom listing frame	Yes	Yes	Yes
HTML builder	Yes	Yes	Yes
Off eBay			
E-mail marketing	5,000 e-mails per month	7,500 e-mails per month	10,000 e-mails per month
Promotional flyers	Yes	Yes	Yes
Shop-branded business materials	Yes	Yes	Yes
Search engine keyword management	Yes	Yes	Yes
Listing feeds	Yes	Yes	Yes
Track Your Success			
Traffic reports	Yes	Yes (advanced info)	Yes (advanced info)

How To... Set Up An eBay Shop

If you're serious about selling on eBay, and want to shift a large quantity of goods, then you may want to consider setting up your very own eBay shop. It takes a little bit more work to get going, compared to setting up a normal eBay account, but it stands a real chance of getting noticed and bringing in more business for you. Also, more and more buyers are used to the idea of buying direct from an eBay shop, rather than going through the traditional bidding process. So if you want to get cracking, here's what you need to do. Just follow this step-by-step guide, and you'll have your new shop ready for business in no time at all.

1 The first thing you need to do is to select the subscription level you require. Obviously, you pay more for the advanced services, but for now, the Basic package will suffice. If you feel you need the extra features at a later date, you can always upgrade easily enough. For now, choose 'Basic Shop' and then click 'Continue'.

2 As you'd expect, you'll need to read through a user agreement before you can proceed. Although you may skip this for most products, it's worth having a good read through, as it's a business you're setting up, not just a software package. Accept and then click 'Subscribe' to fire up your account. Remember, you must keep your shop open for a minimum of 30 days and will be billed for a month even if you cancel within that period.

3 Okay, now you've set up your shop account and you're ready to begin. You're now offered the chance to use the Quick Shop Setup. This is a process that will build and design your shop in just a few minutes. However, you can also refine and enhance your shop at any time later.

4 The Quick Shop Setup screen. Here you lay the foundation of your shop. As you scroll down through the page, you build the various aspects of your shop, and can personalise the template to suit your preferences.

5 First up is the shop colour and theme. Click the 'Edit' link under the 'Shop colour and theme' section and you'll see a box containing the options that are available to you. Simply browse through these and click the radio button next to your selection. Click 'Save' when you're done.

6 Now you need to give your shop a description. This is the text that will appear in search results for eBay shops, next to the shop logo. You'll want to make this as welcoming and descriptive as possible, but keep it short. Buyers don't want to read an essay to find out what your shop is all about.

7 Next, decide how you want your items to be displayed to your customers. You can choose Picture Gallery or List view. Gallery is the most descriptive option, but List view lets you fit more on screen. You can also choose the order in which items will appear.

8 Promotion boxes are important, because they help to draw a shopper's attention to certain items. Here you can choose to have four promotion boxes, or none at all. Depending on how much stock you have, you may or may not need these now. You can change this at a later date, so don't worry too much about your choice at this point.

9 Listing frames can be customised by shop owners, and in the next step you choose the template you wish to make use of. Header & Navigation is the best template, as it's the most flexible, but you may want to opt for the other layouts.

10 With the basic building blocks of your shop complete, you can now preview it. Although it's going to look a little sparse at the moment, you can see the general layout and feel of it. And there you have it; your shop is created. However, there are far more options to play around with, so don't be afraid to experiment.

DID YOU KNOW?

A common eBay con is to buy a new gadget, and then recoup some of the money by selling the empty box on eBay, hoping buyers misread the auction and think they're bidding for the product itself rather than the packaging. It's especially common with newly released technology where demand outstrips supply, such as freshly launched games consoles or the mobile phones.

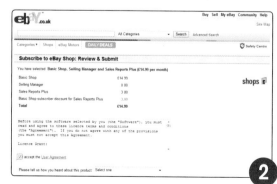

3

4

Change Shop Colour and Theme

Select a color and theme for your Shop that is visually appealing and complements your product offerings.

If you decide to change your Shop colour and theme later, you can choose from a variety of additional colours and themes using Manage My Shop in My eBay.

- Navy
- Emerald
- Green
- Lavender

Recommended Recommended Recommended Recommended

- Slate
- Coral
- Khaki
- Coffee

Save Cancel

5

Change Shop Description

Enter a brief description that tells buyers what you're selling.

This description will appear when buyers search for Shops on eBay.

To increase the chances that your Shop will appear in Internet search engines, use key words in your description that you think people might enter when searching for a product.

Welcome to my eBay Shop. Please add me to your list of favourite sellers and come again. Thank you for your business.

183 characters remaining

Save Cancel

6

Change Item Display

Specify how you'd like to display your items to buyers when they browse or search in your eBay Store.

- **Picture Gallery** showcases each item using small picture to give your Shop a professional look that resembles that of many online businesses
- **List view** is useful for showing long lists of items - each item takes up less space, making more items immediately viewable.

Layout

- Picture Gallery
- List View

Recommended

Sort order

Select the order in which items should appear.
Recommended: Ending soonest

Ending soonest ▼

Save Cancel

7

Change Promotion Boxes

Specify whether you'd like to activate four promotion boxes.

Promotion boxes appear on various pages in your Shop and can be customised to highlight featured items, announce specials, or provide alternative ways for buyers to browse in your Shop.

If you decide to change your promotion boxes later, you'll have access to additional types of promotion boxes using Manage My Shop in My eBay.

- Four promotion boxes
- None

1 Newly Listed
2 Ending Soon
3 Postage & Payment
4 Newsletter Sign-up

Recommended

Save Cancel

8

Change Custom Listing Frame

Select a listing frame to customize all of your item pages with key navigation elements that will drive more traffic to your eBay Store.

You can select layouts that include a Shop listing header with links to your eBay Shop and a left-navigation bar with links to your Shop categories.

- Header & Navigation
- Header
- None

Recommended

9

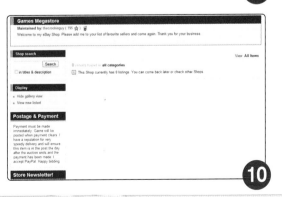

10

Increasing Your Share Of eBay Sales

So you're up and selling on the eBay site, but what's the best way to sell more items?

With an established, organised eBay shop, you're well situated to grow your business. And the most obvious way to do that is to offer more for sale. Expanding your selection of merchandise and adding new categories of goods can drive your small shop toward the medium or high sales leagues.

But is that always a good idea? Are there any pitfalls to avoid? And is there help available to aid in expanding your shop listings?

THE PROS

Exposure: The main advantage of listing lots of items is the increased exposure it grants. The wider the range of products you have on offer, the greater the chance of catching a potential buyer's attention.

For example, you may enjoy a thriving business in men's ties, with your best-selling item being 100% silk styles, although in limited colour choices and a few traditional patterns. Anyone searching for 'ties', or 'silk', or even 'menswear' or 'men's accessories' is likely to find you. However, run out of your leading product one month, and sales slump, leaving you struggling to recover in following months. If you add socks, belts and wallets to your inventory, you'll reach a much wider audience seeking those items. When they click into your shop, they'll see your

popular silk-tie line and may add to their sock order. Even if they only buy socks, you're still ahead. A new customer has put that all-important, albeit virtual, first foot through your door.

Discounts: Widen the variety of items in your shop through wholesale purchases with the same supplier, and you'll likely be entitled to volume discounts. Check your supplier's discount schedules and ask about lower rates to evaluate new merchandise in addition to your usual orders, and watch for any special offer items you can audition. Deeply discounted sale items added to your shop listings will earn you maximum extra profits with minimal risk.

THE CONS

Space: More inventory requires more space. If you're selling 'virtual' goods (electronic books and the like) or services, floor space isn't a consideration. For anything else, you'll need room to store your inventory until it's sold. If your current shop is under-utilising existing space, you'll be able to stock more items without worry. But if you're already encroaching into non-work areas, and the dining room table, chairs and half a settee are overflowing with items, space - or the lack of it - is a high priority.

Capital: More items in your inventory requires more money. The more items you offer for sale, the more you'll pay or owe your suppliers. Also, more fees will be due to eBay. Increasing stock is always a gamble; you'll have the potential to sell and earn more, but it's never guaranteed.

Expanding listings in a shop that's already floundering may doom it to failure. You could easily over-extend yourself financially, and the damage may be difficult to recover from.

Workload: The main goal of more stock is, ultimately, more sales. However, with it comes an increase in the time and effort required to reach that end.

Any successful business needs a fair bit of work in pre-sales areas like marketing and post-sales labours like bookkeeping and banking - all the while

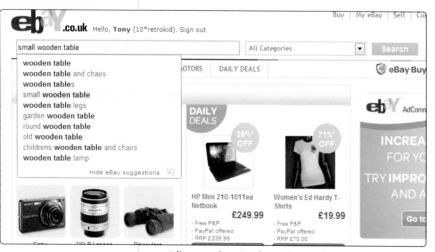

▲ Item searches steer buyers to your shop

keeping an eye on everything else in between. Adding many listings to a flourishing small business may be the act that ruins it, with too much time taken from family or personal pleasures and the added stresses of bigger business worries.

THE BALANCE

It looks as though the cons outweigh the pros. Surely there's a happy medium, or no one would start or grow a business.

The key is in balance, finding ways to recognise and minimise the downsides. And the best way to prevent problems is with planning.

Measuring Up: When you opened your eBay shop you probably thought about how and where you'd store things. Now, in considering listing even more things, you need to take a closer look at the space you have available. Will it be adequate? At what point will it become insufficient? Do you have family or friends nearby that can share for free or at low cost, clean, secure, always accessible space to store your stock? Would travelling there be more hassle than any added sales are worth?

Renting commercial, contracted space is a move that should only be considered by shops and sellers who've enjoyed substantial profits for well over a year or two. All others should be like goldfish, limiting their growth to the physical space they possess. Committing to a long-term expense in untested waters is a sink-or-swim affair, best avoided until it becomes the only option.

Controlling Cash: Everyone's familiar with the entrepreneurial edict 'It takes money to make money', and there's no arguing with that. There is great potential in offering more items to increase sales and profits, but how do you know just how big a leap to take into unknown territory? A good, established method is to stock about a month's worth of goods at a time. Research what amount of products similar eBay shops sell in a week and order roughly four times that much.

That gives you a few weeks grace period to reorder if sales are faster than you expected, while your out-of-pocket outlay is a maximum of a few weeks' worth of inventory if sales are sluggish.

For this to work, you need to be very familiar with your suppliers and know they're reliable and can supply stock quickly.

If your shop has never enjoyed brisk sales, and you suspect you'd do better selling entirely different items, replace your current items rather than add to unpopular products. Shove your slow-moving items into auctions to clear unwanted inventory and make room for new goods.

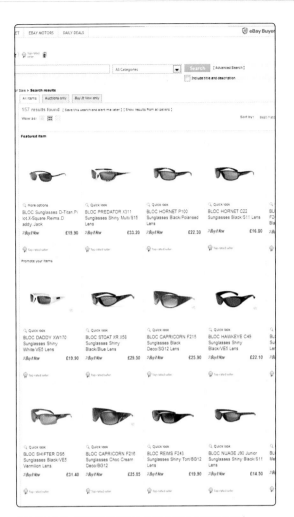

▲ Listing lots of items requires more pages, pictures and category classifications

Be prepared for the added incidental expenses of per-item listing fees and extra packaging materials should your newly listed items prove popular. Be realistic, rather than begrudging, about fees. For many sellers, listing fees will be comparable to the cost of other advertising avenues such as Google AdWords. Consider the cost of listing fees a form of advertising investment and they become a much more tolerable business expense.

Taking Stock Of Yourself: When deciding if expanding your product line will be worth the added time and work, take a good look at yourself, as much as anywhere else. Are you the type who excels under stress? Or do you want a business that takes 40 hours per week of your time and not a minute more? Will adding 50 new items and the potential e-mail enquiries, order fulfilment, feedback activity, and possible complaints or returns for each, make you 50 times happier or 50 times more likely to hide away in a dark room with your regrets?

MEMORABLE EBAY AUCTIONS

A CURIOUS KETTLE

A picture of a kettle sold on an Australian auction site showed a reflection of the photographer's naked body. The picture kicked off a craze for getting naked and semi-naked pics on other people's websites, including several on eBay. It's known as 'reflectoporn', and is a sort of hi-tech streaking.

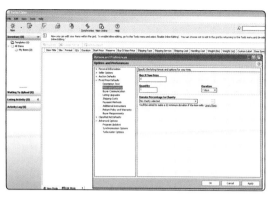

▲ A free multiple listings tool, Turbo Lister is available for Windows users

If you welcome the extra work, how much are you willing to do before needing to hire help? That could be the solution to reclaiming your leisure life, if you can trust someone else to do the work the way you want it done. If not, you'll be more stressed than if you did it yourself in the 70th hour of the week.

Whether you decide to work alone, or with assistance, and in or out of 'normal' hours, there are programs and tools that can help.

TOOLS TO GROW ON

One of the advantages of building your business through an eBay shop is easy access to the seller tools eBay makes available.

When you first set up shop, you probably used the Sell Your Item form to list each of your products. If you're adding many listings, that will quickly become a frustrating, time-consuming process. Turbo Lister (**pages.ebay.co.uk/turbo_lister**) is a free Windows-only tool you can use to upload lots of listings all at the same time. You simply enter all the information for your items offline and then upload everything in one go. You can add thousands of items to your shop, previewing each of them before they're added. An online tour with step-by-step instructions is available,

which will help you learn to use this customisable bulk-listing tool.

If you prefer to use your own inventory software, and you've been registered for 90 days or more and have at least 50 active listings per month for two months running, then you qualify for eBay's free File Exchange (**pages.ebay.co.uk/file_exchange**). It's a high-volume seller's tool for multiple listings from CSV (Comma Separated Values) files via Excel and other spreadsheet and database programs on all platforms.

Another free tool from eBay is Selling Manager (**pages.ebay.co.uk/selling_manager**). This tool is used online exclusively, so it's available to help sellers on all operating systems manage their listings and fees. The more listings you have, the more you'll need a tool of this type to keep track of what's pending, active and sold, generate feedback, and print invoices and labels. eBay identifies Selling Manager as a medium-volume tool and recommends Selling Manager Pro (**pages.ebay.co.uk/selling_manager_pro**), which automates some of the features and provides restock alerts to high-volume sellers, for £4.99 per month.

You can also use the eBay Seller Tools Finder (**pages.ebay.co.uk/seller_tools_finder**) to pick the right tool for the job based on the volume of sales you want to achieve in a month and what area you need help with - sales, shipping, repeat listings, and other categories.

Finally, eBay lists third-party software that can help with volume listings and the extra management they require.

You have an alternative choice in another free mega listing tool, an eBay-compatible program called The Poster Toaster (**www.brothersoft.com/the-poster-toaster-65312.html**). It allows the creation of templates for categories of items you sell on a regular basis and includes a picture manager to automate FTP (File Transfer Protocol) uploads of item

▲ File Exchange works with your existing software on any platform

▲ Use Selling Manager to keep track of more listings, fees and feedback - all for free

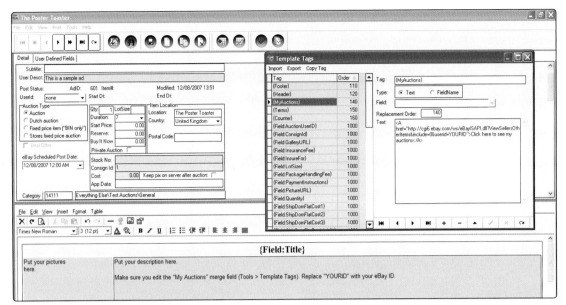

▲ The Poster Toaster is another free bulk-listing tool

images. You can verify your listings and fees before posting, and it accepts ads from Turbo Lister.

A more fully featured option at a reasonable price is SDN Store (**www.sysdatanet.com**), which is an automated content-management system. For a one-off fee of about £50 you can build a shop-front website, complete with support for forums and e-mail, which you can integrate with an eBay shop. Mid- and high-volume sellers may benefit from the dual exposure, or use the eBay module on its own and synchronise it to their existing eBay shop. Both allow bulk listings you can verify before uploading.

Those are a few of the available tools to help list lots of items at a time and broaden your sales potential. New tools and options may be added, so check in the Solutions Directory under 'Listings Management' (**tinyurl.com/637y23**) for current information on companies, site (country) support, prices, and user ratings.

TO GROW OR NOT TO GROW

Put as much thought into each step you take in growing your shop as you did in deciding to sell in the first place, and this should lead you down the road to success with a minimum of potholes along the way. Review your original research and revisit other eBay sellers' shops, auctions, and completed listings (**search-completed.ebay.co.uk**) to get the most up-to-date information before deciding to expand.

Remember, the larger the inventory the higher the risk, both to your finances and stress levels. Limit risk to a degree of loss you can recover from. Weigh up the risks, the benefits, and work involved before you take each step in building your eBay empire.

If a leap forward leaves you less than sure-footed, scale back, and reconsider your next growth spurt for another time. There's no rule that states you need to keep growing. Take small steps and you'll find the ideal shop inventory size for you.

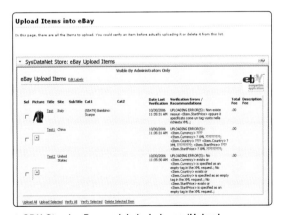

▲ Seller resources and tools are stored in eBay's Solutions Directory

▲ SDN Store's eBay module includes an 'Upload Items' tool

Keeping On Top Of Business

Building up sales is part of the challenge for the serious eBay user. However, it can be a stressful business, so be prepared

If you've been selling items on eBay for a while and want to ramp up the amount of goods you sell, then you'll need to become more organised. At the basic level, when you sell one or a handful of items, you have to list your goods, respond to queries, complete the sale, take payment and ship the goods. And all you need is the main eBay website, the My eBay account section, a consumer PayPal account and a cheap digital camera to photograph the goods with.

However, as the volume of products you sell on eBay increases, it will become clear very quickly that you need to keep a closer eye on a fair few other things. For example, how do you keep on top of money? Or of tracking payments? Of stock? Of postage? Of storage? Some people find the basic eBay sales tools aren't really up to the job of volume sales or, if you go a step further, running an eBay business. It is easy to very quickly get yourself into an administrative, organisational and logistical mess that will do nothing for your reputation, seller rating or finances.

As many of you will know, the popularity of eBay means it's an obvious business opportunity, and with the downturn in the economy leaving more people without steady employment, being able to make extra cash buying and selling will be welcomed. As anyone who's started a business will tell you, however, you do need to be aware of tax, accounting and legalities. If you end up selling online in order to subsidise your income, then such regular activity will mean you may come to the attention of the Inland Revenue.

Within three months of starting your business, you need to contact the Inland Revenue (it also has a handy guide to getting things off the ground at **www.hmrc.gov.uk/startingup/index.htm**) and decide whether or not you're going to be self-employed or a limited company. You will also want to set up a bank account separate from your personal one in order to keep a better check on your finances.

We're not going to delve too deeply in the accounting side of running a company, because it could fill an entire book in itself. There are, however, computer programs available that can help you to manage an increased customer base and ensure that your cash flow is properly accounted for.

PAYMENTS

Most eBay users who move up a scale into volume selling may struggle to keep a check on payments, however. It's easy to lose track of payments and work out when an item is ready to ship. Some people may pay by PayPal immediately, while others may opt for a cheque that takes a week to arrive. All the while, you need to keep on top of this and ensure orders don't get missed or that items aren't shipped before a payment has cleared.

Before we look at how to do this, let's look at the core parts of a transaction. This way it's easier to work out what kind of applications or services you'll need to help you out, and you can develop systems to help you keep on top of things.

The basics of an eBay transaction from start to finish roughly goes like this:

- Identify product to sell
- Write product description
- Determine starting price (along with reserve price or Buy It Now pricing, if applicable)
- Source/take photography
- Determine postal costs
- Assemble/publish auction page
- Respond to pre-sales queries
- Conclude sale
- Generate invoice for winning bidder
- Send reminders as necessary
- Collect payment via electronic payment service or physical payment method (cheque, postal order, cash, etc.)
- Dispatch goods
- Leave and receive feedback

The basic start-to-finish process can become more complicated by multiple-item sales to the same buyer, requests for combined or overseas

▲ Selling Manager is a free tool

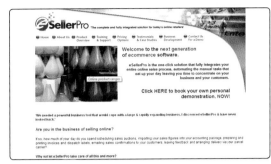

▲ eSellerPro isn't restricted to eBay

postage quotes, items returned as faulty, items not received at all, requests to collect items in person and requests to pay by other means (cheque, cash, postal orders, other electronic payment services). So if someone is going to sell in volume on eBay, they need tools and software in place to manage and automate as much of the process as possible. The option that many eBay home and small businesses opt for is the web-based all-in-one eBay management system.

SINGLE MANAGEMENT SYSTEMS

As you start to sell in volume, you begin to realise that the workload becomes so vast that without software to help you, it's likely you will struggle. But before you take the plunge, you need to know what you'll need the software for; if you are struggling to keep track of your items, unsure who should be sent what or whether a bidder has paid or not, then you will require an auction management package.

These programs act like a big toolbox, offering you everything you need to get your listings up and running, keeping a check of the stock that you have and aiding you with labelling your items, working out payments and allowing you to work with e-mail templates, which come in handy when dealing with your buyers.

You could start with eBay's own Turbo Lister, a package that lets you upload in bulk. What it doesn't do, though, is allow you to get a grip on payment management, and that's where the free eBay tool Selling Manager comes in.

Working online, it allows for better listings management. It lets you track your shipping, payment and feedback status more easily than within eBay itself but it doesn't allow you to create listings (although you can relist sold and unsold items). So anyone using Selling Manager would probably want to use Turbo Lister alongside it, allowing the former to manage the listings created by the latter.

By using Selling Manager you will also be able to cut down on the amount of time you spend sending

e-mails, since it has customisable templates that you can use. The program also allows for the printing of smart-looking labels and invoices, and it even lets you tap in a selection of feedback comments that you'll be able to quickly add to buyers' accounts, thereby greatly reducing the time needed to type them in one by one.

If you're serious about your business, you may want to try eBay's Selling Manager Pro, which costs £4.99 a month. It allows you to create listings and it also has facilities for automatic listing and relisting, automated payment and shipping status. Usefully, you can create monthly profit and loss reports, discover your products' success ratio and average selling price and download your sales history as a .csv file.

THIRD-PARTY HELP

Of course, you don't have to use eBay's own auction management tools. Depending on the extent to which you want to grow your eBay activities, you can choose a third-party tool. eSellerPro (**www.esellerpro.com**) has many fans and it not only allows you to work with eBay, but it also integrates with sites such as Amazon, and it comes with a complete stock management system that even covers ordering from suppliers. It has designs that can be used for the website too.

Marketplaces (**www.channeladvisor.co.uk/marketplaces**) is the most popular single solution for managing an entire eBay business, but it can be

▲ Marketplaces is popular but can be expensive

expensive and it's really aimed at heavy auction business. It makes it easier to deal with bulk purchases, with the software allowing you to take full advantage of eBay, delivering a level of operational automation, and helping you sell more. It claims to lower costs and enhance customer service, in short making dealing with bulk items easier for the seller.

One of the benefits of Marketplaces is being able to manage an entire eBay transaction from start to finish. It can handle the initial creation and uploading of an auction item, including creating pages in advance and presetting future start times for auctions, thus automating the replenishment of active auctions. Marketplaces can also host product images (you get between 100MB and 500MB of space), dispensing with the need for a separate image-hosting service such as Flickr, or even paying eBay to use images in an auction. While the auction is running, it can help you keep track of the number of watchers, the number of visitors to each auction page, the number of bids in a single view and it can automate most communications with the buyer.

Aside from automating the eBay sales process, Marketplaces also provides tools for postage management and integrates it with PayPal for payment collection. The problem is that it's geared up more for heavy business. If you're after a simpler system of keeping track of eBay's comings and goings, you may well want something else.

NetSuite (**www.netsuite.com/portal/industries/ ecommerce/ebay-integration.shtml**) is a popular hosted business application suite. It is designed for small businesses, and integrates with eBay as one of several ways to sell goods. It offers many of the same features as Marketplaces, such as

integration with postal services, and payment management, and can combine an existing web-based shop (created and hosted in NetSuite) with eBay auctions. Therefore, the items a seller has listed on eBay can be taken from an existing online store, and auctions shown in the same store. This is useful if you're using eBay for fixed-price Buy It Now sales rather than traditional auctions.

STORAGE

As your business grows, so too will the space you need to keep the items you're selling. And once you've taken up the garage, shed and children's bedrooms, you may be forced to look elsewhere in order to keep your stock in one place and your family from screaming at you.

Companies such as Safestore Self Storage (**www. safestore.co.uk**) have premises all across Britain. Annoyingly, there are no prices on the Safestore website, but many customers comment on its low cost, and how much you will pay is determined by the space you will need. There are many similar storage companies across the country, however, so it's worth doing a search online for a solution that suits you.

One thing worth factoring in, whether at home or in a storage facility, is a small area dedicated to packing and shipping. When you put an item up for sale, make sure it's located within your storage area, to prevent you having to search around for it. Indeed, it's important to organise your items well, and if you stack them, you can optimise your space.

Use plastic bags to help prevent items from developing smells or becoming musty. Bags also ensure items don't rub together and cause damage. Label each item and place them in boxes that are labelled alphabetically, which means you can get at them with greater ease and, if possible, buy transparent boxes so you can easily keep an eye on stock levels and know exactly what's in each container. If you develop good storage habits, you'll save lots of time.

An alternative to storage that's worth exploring is drop shipping. Essentially, this will mean the goods that you sell aren't kept in stock by you. Your orders are transferred to a manufacturer or a wholesaler, which then dispatches the item directly to the customer on your behalf. You take the difference in price between the amount you've sold at and the wholesale cost.

Some research online is needed, and you also need to understand the potential pitfalls (if an item isn't in stock at the warehouse, you'll be one receiving the hassle from a customer, and it becomes your job to find out if enough stock is available and that the price hasn't changed).

▲ NetSuite is designed for small businesses

▲ Self storage is an option worth thinking about

▲ Print your own stamps from the Royal Mail website

▲ There's a range of options available from Royal Mail

LOGISTICS AND SHIPPING

Depending on the size of your item, you may opt to use the standard postal service or you might decide to try out a courier. Using Royal Mail for postage has got much easier for the eBay seller, because you can now buy postage online and print it yourself (**tinyurl.com/38ebzk**). Online prepaid postage is the closest thing to having your own franking machine, without the costs and complexity of actually owning one. It also means that postage can be applied in the seller's own time, with the prepaid, pre-labelled packages dropped off, rather than the user having to queue to weigh and pay for postage for each individual item. For example, the cost of a first class stamp via home printing is exactly the same as a traditional stamp (£0.41), so online stamps are cheaper than a franking machine as well.

Royal Mail can also supply a post office box (PO Box) for your incoming mail in the same way as commercial services like Mail Boxes Etc. A Royal Mail PO Box costs £95 a year or £60 for six months, and is usually hosted at a local sorting office, or a large main post office. A seller can either collect the mail themselves or, for an additional fee, have it delivered with the regular post. Either option means a seller doesn't have to reveal their address to strangers, and can handle returns and payment by post.

The two essential purchases you'll need to make are a set of scales and a tape measure. With Royal Mail postal prices (**tinyurl.com/postprice**) now based on size as well as weight, it's important that these metrics can be measured accurately, so that the correct postage is applied. Failure to apply the right postage will result in the buyer being hit with a surcharge from the postman before they can receive the goods.

High-street shipping specialists such as Mail Boxes Etc (**www.mbe.com**) have branches all over the UK and can offer specialist services to eBay sellers trying to tackle posting and package management. As well as providing packaging supplies and space to package goods, stores such as these can also help with the weighing and pricing of packages (particularly heavy and awkward-shaped goods) for conventional posting via Royal Mail (**www.royalmail.com**) or its parcel arm ParcelForce (**www.parcelforce.com**). In addition, these stores can tackle the more complex task of sending goods via a courier company such as FedEx (**www.fedex.com/gb**), UPS (**www.ups.com/content/gb/en/index/jsx**) or DHL (**www.dhl.co.uk**) on a per-item basis, without the seller having to set up their own account with the courier company. These stores can also provide a seller with a mailbox to receive incoming mail such as cheque payments, if they don't want the hassle or potential risk of distributing their home address to unknown customers.

Some buyers, particularly overseas customers, will prefer the security of a branded and traceable courier service delivering their goods purchased from an unknown seller. Courier companies can also offer competitive prices for international insured shipping compared to traditional postal services such as Royal Mail. Also, they provide an important alternative to bypass delays caused by strikes, national holidays and the restrictive opening hours of a post office.

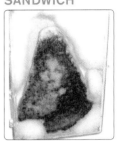

Keeping On Top Of Communications

Bad communication as a seller can potentially cause a lot of problems. How do you make sure this doesn't happen to you?

If there's one thing the Internet has done for mankind, it's aid communication. Whether we're letting people know what we were up to last night on Facebook or Twitter, or filing a quick e-mail to the boss to inform them of the progress of a project, keeping folk in the loop and divulging snippets of information has been made much easier with a keyboard at our fingertips.

So why do so many eBayers go wrong when it comes to communications? Bad communication is at the heart of most disputes, which means it's vital that you keep people up to date when they're buying your items on eBay. If you keep people informed at every opportunity, they're not only far less likely to leave you negative feedback, but they may well be encouraged to buy something else from you in the future, which is great if you decide to move up the ladder of eBay selling and shift items in greater volume.

STARTING POINT

Communication starts from the moment you begin to create your eBay listing. It's important that your descriptions are incredibly clear, because you're trying to give people a feel for an item without them actually being able to get their hands on it before they make a purchase. Go to Amazon.co.uk, Play.com or any number of other top websites and see how they produce listings but essentially give as much information as possible. Indeed, why not go the whole hog; if something needs instructions, maybe put those up as part of your listings so that buyers will be able to see just what they need to do after they make their purchases. Less is not more in the case of eBay, but lay out your listing so that it doesn't overwhelm.

Secondly, make sure everything that's included in your package is listed and, if something that a buyer will believe to be in the box is missing, let them know at this stage so you don't encounter problems later

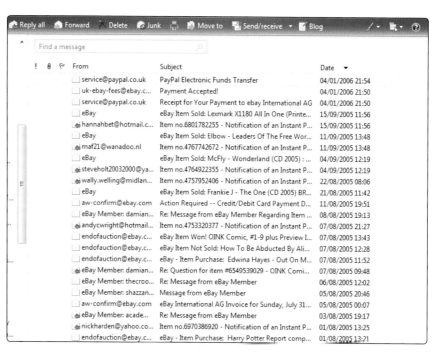

◀ Make sure you keep on top of your e-mails, otherwise you could end up with some unhappy buyers

on. And do make this information prominent; if, for example, you're selling a computer and you're not shipping it with a mouse, keyboard or monitor, it would be good for your reputation and prove less hassle in the long run to make this absolutely clear up front.

Also, it goes without saying that you will pack that listing with good-quality images and state very clearly exactly how long a buyer will expect to have to wait to receive the item you're selling. The clearer you are about this right from the start, the greater the chance of avoiding any hassle from somebody who believed you would be shipping the item that very same day. Add in a returns policy that's properly spelled out, and a buyer will be less inclined to take issue further down the line should a problem become apparent.

While your listing is running its course, you may receive countless messages from potential buyers asking questions about your item (although a good FAQ, an About Me page and a solid description should limit the numbers). Questions that go unanswered will result in customers taking their bids elsewhere, because they'll see you as unreliable, perhaps rude and disorganised.

It is vital that you answer every query politely, courteously and with as much information as you can. Don't lie - be honest if you're not sure about something - and answer as quickly as possible. You may have bad news or you may need time to find an answer, but by letting people know straight away, you'll reap the rewards. Even an immediate and simple "I'm not sure - let me find out and I'll get back to you asap" is better than not replying or taking days

to do so. Above all, be friendly. People are more likely to buy something from you if you come across as being pleasant.

AFTER SALES

Communication, however, must continue when somebody actually makes a purchase. This is the stage where many eBay sellers fall short. Countless buyers can tell you about sellers who take your money and then cut off communication, leaving you wondering what's happening with your purchase until the moment it suddenly arrives on your doorstep.

This points to one of the biggest problems eBay users face: staying on top of the barrage of messages associated with trading. Even someone selling the occasional item will quickly find that a single act of selling on eBay can generate an enormous amount of e-mail.

To put the volume of mail generated by a single item into perspective, here's what a seller can expect to see arrive in their inbox. There are confirmations of a listing, daily updates on the progress of the auction item or multiple items, questions from potential buyers, replies to those queries, confirmation of the final selling price or confirmation that the item didn't sell, any reminders sent to the buyer seeking payment, PayPal payment confirmation, and the invoice from eBay requesting payment for the initial listing. It can, at first glance, be overwhelming but, as with most things, some common sense and good organisation really pays off.

Many eBay sellers swear by Google Mail (**gmail. com**), with many opting for it because of the large

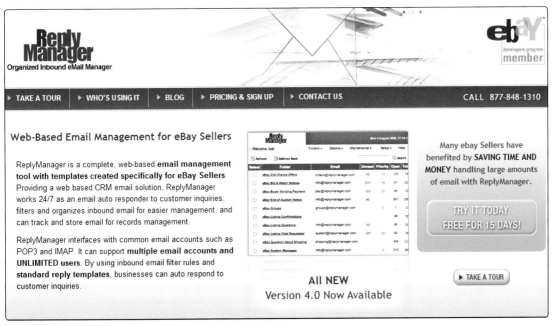

▲ ReplyManager can take some of the hard work out of communicating with your customers

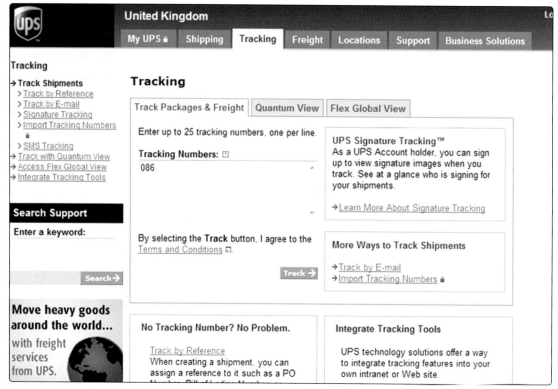

▲ If you have a tracking number for an item, make sure you pass it to your customer, so they can track their purchase

storage space (more than 7GB), good anti-spam features and a powerful search which, as Google itself claims, means you never have to delete anything to stay on top of your e-mail.

Of course, you can use other e-mail providers such as Hotmail (**hotmail.co.uk**) or Yahoo! (**mail.yahoo.com**). And if you're serious about selling, why not try Reply Manager (**replymanager.com**), which is free to try for 15 days and is a web-based e-mail management tool? It will send automatic replies to customer inquiries as well as organise your inbound e-mails, working with accounts such as Google Mail and Yahoo!. It can be expensive, however, with prices starting at $50 a month (roughly £30) and for that you only get 50MB of storage. There's also a one-off fee of $150 to get you started.

No matter what system you choose, it's how you use it that matters. We've already stated the importance of responding; if you send people e-mails and never get a reply, odds are you will feel quite disgruntled and so will your customers. You need to be proactive too; if you have an item ready to ship but you're having a problem getting it to the Post Office within the promised time, let your customer know. If you've sold an item that you don't have available at that time, then give them an estimated time of arrival. Don't leave them hanging and wondering where their item is.

Indeed, if you use a courier to ship an item and are able to get a tracking number, let your customer

know what it is. This way they can quickly find out when their package is set to arrive, and it takes away some of the pressure on you.

Of course, you don't want to ship out an item until it has been paid for, so if a buyer is late with his or her payment, then contact them, politely asking if they still intend to pay. If you don't hear back, write again, asking if they would like to mutually cancel the transaction. If they do, then you can file an Unpaid Item Dispute (UID) with eBay and receive a refund on your fees. Sometimes you won't get a reply from the buyer at all, in which case you can go ahead and file the UID, but don't file one without having tried to contact the buyer first, because that could lead to negative feedback.

Sometimes it pays to be generous, however, especially if you're serious about setting up an eBay business. A small card apologising for a late delivery or a simple, inexpensive gift thrown in to make up for a delay can go a long way to appeasing an otherwise annoyed customer. If you have other stock, you could think about throwing in a discount on their next purchase. This will encourage them to buy something else from you, and it also shows them the value of their custom.

One thing you also want to do is offer good after-sales service. People want to feel secure in the knowledge that, even after they've received an item, they can still go back to you if they have a problem, so

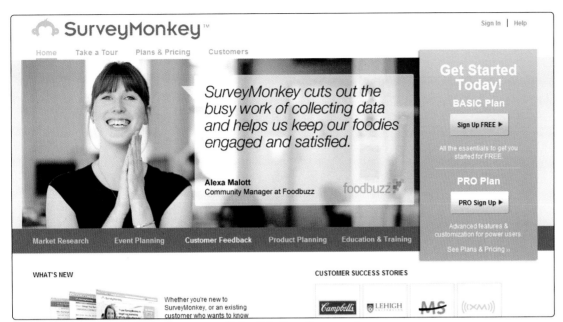

▲ Consider sending surveys to your buyers to gauge their satisfaction with your service

◀ If a buyer doesn't pay you, then you can open a dispute with eBay, but make sure you try to contact the other party first to get their side of the story

have a set of cards or letters printed that include your telephone number or e-mail address, and include them with every order. Make them as personal as possible so that buyers will feel they're dealing with a real person, and include on these cards or letters a pleasant note asking them to get in touch without hesitation if they have an issue. This shows that communication is both ways, and will hopefully prevent a buyer from posting a negative comment without having contacted you first.

Indeed, you may want to actively encourage buyers to post feedback. One good thing about this is that when a buyer leaves positive feedback, you can effectively tick off that particular transaction. Feedback also allows you to improve; you may even want to go beyond eBay and send buyers a survey (try SurveyMonkey.com). This will inspire confidence and trust in you from purchasers, since they will see you as someone that's keen to improve their service. If you place a link to the survey on your eBay listing page, you'll be able to hammer that message home right from the start.

FEEDBACK

Finally, hang fire on leaving feedback. Although you're unable to post negative feedback against poor buyers, you can withhold positives. Therefore, wait until you get positive feedback. Most buyers will want to boost their feedback numbers, so will be more inclined to try to get good feedback from you by posting a positive account of your transaction rather than risk not getting any feedback from you at all.

Making Extra Money

There are ways to squeeze every penny out of an eBay transaction. However, some of them are rightly frowned upon

When you're selling items online, the aim is to make as much money as possible. Luckily, there are many ways in which you can maximise your revenue using a few neat tricks. However, beware, not all of them are entirely fair, and you run a serious risk of receiving potentially damaging negative feedback.

POSTAGE FEES

While searching for items on eBay, you might notice how much the costs of postage often differ widely, even if identical products are being sold. It's a fair bet that the more expensive postage fees include extra revenue for the seller. Although eBay policy states sellers may charge reasonable postage and packaging charges to cover the costs of posting, packaging, and handling, many people add on a little more and pocket the difference.

That's because the term 'handling' is vague and open to interpretation, so those who appear to charge more than others can justify it by calling the extra cost a 'handling charge'. The key is not to get carried away; charge too much and you will inevitably attract negative feedback. Also, if the buyer reports you, further action could be taken by eBay, with your

account put in jeopardy. It's really about what you can get away with, but it's essential to have morals in a community-based site on which feedback is everything. Otherwise it can badly backfire on you (see **pages.ebay.co.uk/help/policies/listing-shipping.html**).

It's worth noting that you're also banned from listing postage, packaging and handling charges as a percentage of the final sale price. This is for obvious reasons. If an item sells unexpectedly for £100 and you were charging 10% for postage, then you would pick up an extra £10. If it sold for £20, you would receive an extra £2. The actual cost of sending the parcel would remain the same, however, so you would, in effect, be ripping off your customer on goods that sold for higher prices.

For fixed-cost sales, there are sellers who try to be a little cleverer. They use a low price for their item and then use the postage fees to make up for it. For example, you may see a memory stick retailing for £1 and decide, because it's so inexpensive, it's worth getting. Only when you read the listing properly do you see the postage costs are £10, yet the seller has achieved the aim of at least getting you to look at the listing. Of course, with postage fees now listed alongside the cost of an item, it's becoming easier to spot this 'scam'.

eBay did for a while make it compulsory for you to offer free shipping on a selection of categories. This was not a popular move among sellers, but in 39 categories, they had no choice. However, after a backlash from users, it subsequently revised this policy in 2010 to apply maximum shipping costs instead. This applies on certain, but not all product lines. You are still able to charge extra for premium postage services, such as guaranteed delivery or extra insurance.

POSTAGE COSTS

There is nothing wrong in trying to cut costs when posting items, however. One top tip is to keep any padded envelopes or boxes that you may come across. You can reuse these to send items of your own, not only saving you the cost of buying a new padded envelope or box but also helping to save the environment. All you need to do is pop a fresh label over the old one. Even if you've torn open a padded envelope in the excitement of getting your hands on

▲ Some sellers set high postage prices to get more money

▲ Be wary of trying to inflate insurance prices

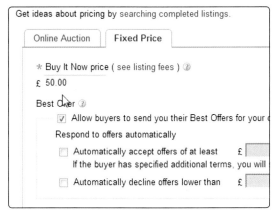

By using the Buy It Now option, you can decide on an actual price and boost your profit

Changing the duration of your auction can impact on your sales and the amount you can earn

the goodies inside, you could place it inside a normal envelope and still save cash. Do buyers mind? Not at all; the main point is their purchases arrive in one piece and few care about the funny-looking wrapper.

INSURANCE

Another way sellers have been known in the past to make money is by upping the insurance cost by a small amount. This is forbidden by eBay, which says sellers offering insurance may only charge the actual fee for insurance. No additional amount may be added, such as 'self-insurance', and sellers who don't use a licensed third-party insurance company may not ask buyers to purchase insurance. It's easy for buyers to check if the insurance charge is over the top, so if you're selling, you need to be aware of that.

PENALTIES

If eBay feels you have breached its policy, it can take a range of actions, including cancelling your listing, limiting your account privileges, suspending your account, forcing you to forfeit your eBay fees and stripping you of PowerSeller status, if applicable.

SECOND CHANCE OFFERS

When an auction ends, you can offer non-winning bidders the chance to buy your item. Of course, you will need to have more stock of the item in question, and it must be exactly the same product as the one you have just sold.

It works by allowing sellers to make an offer to a non-winning bidder under certain conditions. The offer contains a Buy It Now price equal to the non-winning bidder's bid amount. You can offer the second chance immediately after a listing ends and for 60 days afterwards.

Second Chance Offers can be sent for a one-, three- or seven-day duration. They come in handy if your winning bidder fails to pay you or if your reserve

price has not been met. In the latter scenario, you may decide that a non-winning bidder's offer is acceptable. The price at which you can offer your product is equal to their last-showing bid amount.

By offering a second chance, you can increase your revenue without all the hassle of going through the whole eBay process again. If you have multiple stock of an item, this is a great way to offload it, and because there are no fees associated with making a Second Chance Offer, you're saving money too. All you have to do is pay the final value fee when the offer is accepted.

Some sellers try to make offers via the Ask Question facility, which sends an e-mail to a buyer with the subject line 'Question from eBay Member'. This is outlawed by eBay, because it's not a legitimate way to offer a second chance, and if you use it, you can be banned. The transaction will certainly not be supported by eBay.

Feedback can still be placed with Second Chance Offers, so you still need to take the utmost care when dealing with your buyer, otherwise you may receive a negative in the process.

BUY IT NOW

Offering a Buy It Now means you're in control of the price. It's the best way to maximise profits in the shortest possible time. However, set the price too high and you won't sell; you need to look at other listings for an indication of how much your item is going for and set it accordingly.

Buy It Now options can also run alongside an auction to give a buyer the chance to snap up the item without bidding. As soon as a bid is made, the option is removed. If it's a Reserve Price Auction, the option disappears as soon as the reserve is met.

What's good about Buy It Now is that it helps you to use some neat advertising tricks. The whole Buy It Now concept creates a sense of urgency, so why not build on that by creating added impetus to buy your product? It's far more popular than running a straight auction on eBay now.

One way of adding urgency is to add a subtitle to your listing. In this subtitle you can add some pushy statements such as 'Buy now while stocks last', 'Buy now or lose it forever', or 'Only two in stock - buy now'. Then in the listing itself, continue to push the urgent line without being rude or over the top. You want to create a feeling that the buyer shouldn't wait, just in case someone else comes in, without alienating that person with over-the-top claims.

You're appealing to impulse buyers, and you can speed up your profit-making. Rather than wait for a seven-day auction to end, you could, if your product and selling approach is right, sell items every day.

So to maximise the amount of money you can make from your sale, you have to be canny. Don't list a videogame such as Grand Theft Auto IV as 'Buy now - only two in stock' because there are so many copies of this title being sold elsewhere that you'll simply end up losing credibility. If your price is competitive, however, you could perhaps write 'Last chance to buy at this price'.

Similarly, there's no point in putting a DVD on eBay with a starting price of 99p and a Buy It Now of £50. That £50 is more than you would expect to pay in a high-street shop. What you need to do is pitch the Buy It Now so that it attracts an inpatient buyer and doesn't encourage someone to bid just to get rid of the option.

DIFFERENT-LENGTH LISTINGS

By opting for a ten-day option and paying the small additional listing costs, it means that your item can be on eBay for a longer period of time, therefore increasing the likelihood of it being seen. Although most bids come in the dying moments of an auction, it doesn't hurt to have the item on display for a few days longer.

For Buy It Now options, you may find a shorter time frame is better; after all, you'll be looking for a speedier sale and you'll want it to be shown on the front page of the listings as soon as possible. A three- or five-day option could be ideal, but you should gauge this according to how popular you feel your item will be and how many other listings of a similar nature are out there.

USE ABBREVIATIONS IN TITLE

You're only given a limited number of characters in an eBay title, so you need to make good use of the space available. Using abbreviations is one effective way of doing so. Useful ones include BNIB (Brand New, In Box), NBW (Never Been Worn), NR (No Reserve). The eBay savvy will notice them and be more likely to be drawn in. See **pages.ebay.com/help/account/acronyms.html** for a good list.

SHOPS

Having a shop can also maximise your profits, particularly if you use effective links in your listings. You could pop a product into auction for ten days and also make it available from your eBay shop. All you need to do then is place a link saying 'Click here to buy this item now from my shop'.

This also drives traffic to your shop. If they decide they don't want the item any more, they may be persuaded to have a quick browse around your store and pick up something else.

GENERATING SALES

What if you're able to get hold of lots of stock, yet a buyer has ended up on your listing and then realised your product is not the perfect match for their requirements? Simple. Just ask buyers to contact you through your About Me page with their requirements. Promise them you will have a look around for the right product to suit their needs.

Beware of trying to conduct sales outside of the eBay service, however. Although you save on listing and final value fees, you can incur the auction house's wrath if the buyer reports you.

CREATE A BIDDING WAR

There's nothing more exciting than watching two or three people battling it out for your item, pushing the

you're selling Add or remove options | Get help

A▾ B I U ≡≡≡ ≡≡ ≡≡ 🛇 Check spelling Inserts

Grand Theft Auto IV

Hurry - only two copies left

▲ By having a sense of urgency, you can push people into buying

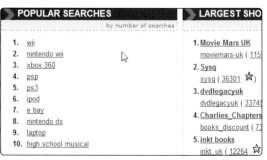

POPULAR SEARCHES	LARGEST SHO
by number of searches	
1. wii	1. Movie Mars UK
2. nintendo wii	moviemars-uk (115
3. xbox 360	2. Sysq
4. psp	sysq (36301 ☆)
5. ps3	3. dvdlegacyuk
6. ipod	dvdlegacyuk (3374
7. e bay	4. Charlies_Chapters
8. nintendo ds	books_discount (73
9. laptop	5. inkt books
10. high school musical	inkt_uk (12264 ☆

▲ eBay Pulse is the place to go to see the trends, including top keywords

price skywards. All you need are a couple of enthusiasts and your bank balance will start to look much healthier.

One thing you could do is bundle two items together. For example, you may have a mint condition Superman comic and a signed Star Wars photograph. Even better, you could pop unrelated items into one lot - a Shakespeare book with an old Beano, maybe. Now what you have done is made your listing attractive to two different types of buyer. Pop a listing under 'books', for instance, and create another under 'comics' and you're further widening the scope. If your items are desirable enough, you may get one person dying to get hold of your Shakespeare book and another itching for the comic. They'll battle it out, raising your price. This won't work if one item is so common that no one will bother bidding anyway. Also, by its nature, it's a risky strategy.

USE KEYWORDS

Using popular keywords is a great way to ensure that people are being drawn to your listings. This can also create a bidding war or may simply result in a quicker sale.

The eBay Pulse pages are a perfect source of keywords. See what the most common search terms are and pop them in (without losing the gist of what your product is all about, of course). You can find eBay Pulse at **pulse.ebay.co.uk**.

OFFER FREEBIES

You need to make your listing more attractive to potential buyers than the competition. So you could offer full after-sales support, have free postage (which you may be able to absorb into a Buy It Now price), and add extra bits and bobs into the package that add value to the overall sale (a nice box or a free badge, for example).

Offer free gifts and bonuses to attract interest away from people selling similar items. For example, offer

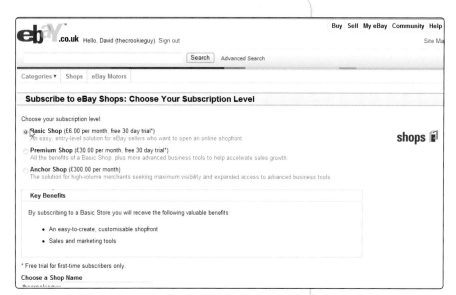

▲ Put your goods on sale in an eBay Shop

three cufflinks where most offer two (emphasise these things get damaged, lost, stolen); ship items postage free; add complementary items such as a matching tie pin (free or otherwise) with cufflinks, free presentation boxes with every batch of wholesale necklaces, and so on. If you make your free gift even more valuable than the actual product for sale, you can not only create a bidding war, but offload less saleable products.

You just need to make sure that the bonus is available to the buyer no matter what the outcome of the auction and that, if using Multiple Item Listings, the bonus will be sent out to all winners.

BIDDING ON YOUR OWN ITEM

Artificially inflating the price by bidding on your own item or getting friends and family to bid is morally wrong, but it does happen. Such shill bidding is forbidden on eBay and it's not something we would ever recommend.

▲ Allowing as many payment options as possible can increase the chance of a sale

▲ Using abbreviations such as BNIB (Brand New, In Box) can save space in your title

DID YOU KNOW?

'Mystery' auctions, where buyers bid for a sealed box containing a mystery item, or an envelope stuffed with an unspecified amount of cash, are often fraudulent. Because there are no checks on these type of auctions, sellers can manipulate the results according to the final price. It's been estimated that on average, a 'winner' in an envelope auction only receives 20% to 30% of his or her outlay.

Chapter 5
Buying Through eBay

Finding Your Dream Item On eBay

Let's take a look at eBay from a buyer's perspective now. What should you do if you're looking to pick up a bargain or two?

To bag an eBay bargain, you first have to find it. The ubiquitous eBay 'Search' box can yield an impractically long and unfocused list of results. Filtering out inappropriate auctions - and sellers - is essential to good eBaying...

SEARCHING BY TITLE AND DESCRIPTION

By default, eBay searches only in the short title description of auction items. Therefore, if the search word you enter only exists in the description of an auction, that auction will not appear in your search results - and it could, of course, be just the item you're looking for.

However, you can click on Advanced Search at the top of the screen, and then you can tick the 'Include title and description' box and repeat the search.

With descriptions included, search results may multiply alarmingly, frequently on account of sellers who practice keyword spamming (we'll be talking about that a little later) in their listings.

You can narrow down your search by adding extra keywords (such as 'walnut cupboard' instead of 'cupboard'), but this may remove as many interesting and valid auctions as 'spam' auctions. A better approach is to use the search commands that eBay provides in its search facility.

USING CATEGORIES

One obvious way to streamline bloated search-results is to select an appropriate category from the drop-down menu next to the search box, at the top of your results page.

Unfortunately, many eBay listings remain miscategorised; a very rare and sought-after DVD, for instance, may end up being put in Entertainment Memorabilia instead of the DVD category. Adding extra categories to an auction listing costs the seller more, so they may not bother to do so. The item might also comprise part of a lot of diverse items, or be miscategorised by mistake, so you should use this feature with care.

LOCAL VERSUS GLOBAL

More than 150 countries participate in eBay, but search results from ebay.co.uk will not automatically include listings from non-UK auctions (unless the sellers have specifically included the UK as a target market for their item).

There are good reasons to begin your search 'locally': items won may arrive quicker, affordable courier services are available for larger items and you may be able to pay for your win by cheque, postal order or Nochex as well as PayPal. You can also search for items within a certain distance from where you live, which means you can pick them up in person if the seller agrees.

However, the UK is a relatively small marketplace, with a price levy often reflected in eBay auctions, and associated postal costs that can often dwarf overseas shipping tariffs for smaller items. Even with international shipping, your item may be available cheaper abroad, or may never have been available here (such as rare editions in the fields of music, movies, books and magazines).

▲ Searching in the description can reward you with more results

▲ The categories can help narrow down results

BIDDING ON ITEMS FROM NON-UK SELLERS

You can include worldwide sellers in your eBay searches, but there are special considerations to take into account when bidding on non-UK auctions.

Delivery: Will the seller deliver to the United Kingdom? Check the item's 'Postage and packaging' section; if you can click on 'United Kingdom' in the drop-down list, the seller will ship here and has provided a price. If not, check the listing itself; it may provide information as to where the seller is willing to ship their item. Otherwise, you can use the 'Ask a question' link to ask about the possibility and cost of shipping to the UK.

Payment: If the seller doesn't accept or you don't use PayPal, how can an item you've won be paid for? Wire transfer services such as Western Union and Moneygram are not permitted at eBay, while international money orders can be costly and might not be acceptable to the seller in question. Sending currency-exchanged cash in the post is against eBay regulations, and is unwise anyway, because it leaves you with no redress in disputes over payment and

▲ Remember to check the shipping costs if buying from abroad

delivery. Shortly, we'll see how to limit worldwide eBay search results to sellers that accept PayPal.

The Language Barrier: eBay will warn you if you're sending a question to a seller from a non-English-speaking part of eBay. Unless you speak the seller's language, try to keep all communications brief; the responsibility rests with you if you fall foul of terms, conditions or information that were explained in a listing (or correspondence) you couldn't understand.

eBay Search Commands

Aim	Method	Example
Exclude several keywords from a search	Put a minus sign after your keyword and then a list of comma-separated words in brackets. There must be no space after each comma OR Add each excluded word after your search term preceded by a dash (-) There must be a space between each 'excluded' term and no space between the dash and the word it is excluding	Genesis -(sega,bible,trek,manga,snorkel) OR Genesis -sega -bible -trek -manga -snorkel
Find an exact phrase	Put the words in full quotes (")	"New Order"
Find at least one of two (or more) words	Group the comma-separated words in parentheses (no spaces after the comma)	(hammer,nails,screwdriver) Will return search results containing any of the above words.
Find auctions containing words that begin with a certain sequence of letters	Append an asterisk (*) to the search-term	record* Will find auctions containing 'record', 'records', 'recorder', 'recording', etc.
Find auctions with a specific spelling of a search term	Enclose the word in quotations (")	"record" Will exclude auctions containing 'records' in title or description.
Find two (or more) words without 'auto-expanding' search results	Enclose a possible category word in quotations (")	If one of your keywords is recognised by eBay as pertaining to an eBay category, your search may be 'automatically expanded' to search for the remaining words in that category. For example, the search 'Bruce Willis DVD' may 'auto-include' irrelevant results in the DVD category that contain 'Bruce' or 'Willis' - e.g. Bruce Almighty. The search 'Bruce Willis "DVD"' will only return pertinent results that actually contain the word 'DVD'.

▲ Seek out misspelled bargains at fatfingers.co.uk

▲ Saved searches remember all your custom search options, and results can be e-mailed to you daily

Online translation services such as Babelfish (**babelfish.yahoo.com**) and Google Translate (**translate.google.com**) can help when dealing with foreign sellers, but they don't cover all possible languages. They're also best used for short and simple phrases, because they often produce muddled results that could make matters worse.

Mindful of these caveats, foreign-language eBay auctions can be a good opportunity to find sought-after items with fewer competing bidders: simply run your translated keyword through an online translation service and do a 'rest of the world' search.

TYPO BARGAINS

Sometimes sellers mistype (or just don't know how to spell) a word when placing a listing on eBay; the resultant 'nonsense' word (for example, 'cuboard' instead of 'cupboard') will probably never end up in a bidding war - or even in search results. You can take advantage of the low visibility of auctions such as this by hunting out typos and misspelt words when searching for items.

Many sites offer eBay typo searches, where you can search eBay directly for a wide range of possible misspellings. Two of the most popular are **www.fatfingers.co.uk** and **www.typozay.co.uk** (which even offers search plug-ins for users of the Firefox web browser). Check out the reviews from page 146 for more examples.

ADVANCED SEARCH

Power bidders and buyers belong on the 'Advanced Search' page, where you can broaden your search results to include sellers worldwide, and specify many other options to focus your search and zero in on a potential bargain.

To get started, click on the 'Advanced Search' link to the right of the search box at the top of your results, or go to **search.ebay.co.uk** and click on the 'Advanced Search' link.

SEARCH COMMANDS

At the top of Advanced Search, you can apply some of the search commands that we came across earlier without needing to use any of the special formatting (see 'eBay Search Commands' table).

View Ended Auctions: The 'completed listings' checkbox enables you to search for auctions that have finished. This is a useful indicator of prices you can expect to pay for items you're currently seeking. It's also a good way to locate sellers who are suitable for you but may not currently be offering any items.

▲ The 'Advanced Search' link

▲ Apply search commands naturally

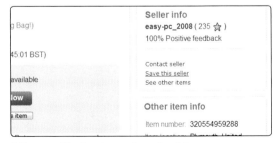

▲ You can add sellers to your favourites list

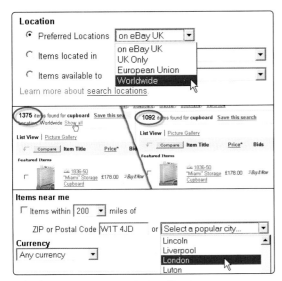

▲ (Top) Search the whole world if you like
▲ (Middle) Before and after clicking the deceptive 'Show all' link
▲ (Bottom) Find a local bargain on eBay with Advanced Search

▲ Want It Now enables you to tell sellers exactly what you're looking for

Save The Search: Saved searches are a useful way of repeating an advanced search at a later date. You can save your custom search by ticking the 'Save this search to My eBay' option in Advanced Search, or with the 'Save this search' link near the top of your results.

Saved searches have their own section in My eBay, and you can subscribe to them, receiving the initial ten results from any saved search by daily e-mail.

Specify A Price Range: In the 'Items Priced' boxes you can put minimum and maximum prices for item listings. The 'minimum price' option is particularly useful for excluding the thousands of worthless 'one cent' auctions that some unscrupulous sellers employ to boost their own reputations.

Specify Sellers: If you're looking for items from a particular eBay seller, you can type in their eBay User ID here (you'll need to know exactly what it is). You can also use the 'Exclude' option in the drop-down box to make sure that a particular seller's items don't appear in your results. Currently, you can only 'blacklist' one seller per search in this way.

If you've built up a list of favourite sellers (see 'Other search methods'), you can also specify to search their auctions only.

Include The World!: Here, finally, we can search beyond the UK by selecting 'Worldwide' from the drop-down list in the 'Location' section. Be warned, results pages using this option have a misleading 'Show All' link attached to them. Press it, and the number of items actually shrinks! The link reduces the scope of your search back to UK-only.

The 'Items located in' section lets you specify a geographical location for the item. You can choose any country that eBay deals with from the drop-down list, but this is most useful when seeking UK-based items.

▲ Check out the latest listings via Google Reader or any RSS aggregator
◀ Look for this icon to add an RSS feed for a search

◀▲ Customising your search

▲ Your Saved Sellers list

▲ Custom search options will narrow down results

If you want to include foreign listings from only those sellers who explicitly ship to the UK, leave the 'Items available to' drop-down list at 'United Kingdom', but be aware that you exclude many UK-friendly foreign sellers by doing so.

OTHER OPTIONS IN ADVANCED SEARCH
- Find PayPal-listed items only.
- Find Buy It Now items only (no bidding necessary).
- Find items that are located near you (UK version - you gave eBay your postcode when you signed up).
- Find items with free postage and packaging.
- Find items that have a minimum and/or maximum number of existing bids.

THE SIDEBAR
eBay displays a yellow Search Options sidebar to the left of search results; here you can toggle advanced options and further refine your search. You can customise the sidebar to include only the parts of Advanced Search that you want to use regularly by clicking the 'Customise' link.

TRACK LISTINGS VIA RSS
You can subscribe to an RSS feed for any search, and keep track of new listings via Google Reader, Live Bookmarks in Firefox, the RSS features in Internet Explorer or any other RSS aggregator. You can set a

feed to be updated as often as you like; it's a good way to keep on top of new Buy It Now offers, which can close within minutes of first being listed.

OTHER SEARCH METHODS
Want It Now: At **pages.ebay.co.uk/wantitnow** you can let eBay sellers know about items you're looking for, and optionally post a picture as a guideline.

Favourite Sellers: You can add any seller or eBay shop to your Favourite Sellers list simply by clicking the 'Add to favourite sellers' link in their profile. eBay can optionally send you regular e-mails with new listings from your favourite sellers, who also have their own page in My eBay where you can find them again easily and even add notes about them.

Seller Communication: Whether you've won or lost an auction at eBay, why not get in touch with the seller and let them know if you're looking for something specific? Serious sellers will be glad to have a ready-made potential buyer for new listings.

IS IT CHEAPER ELSEWHERE?
Check the regular commercial outlets for your item before going to eBay. Are you sure that special edition DVD you're after isn't available on Play or Amazon, brand new and cheaper than the lowest eBay price?

▲ The feedback system has been a vital part of eBay's success

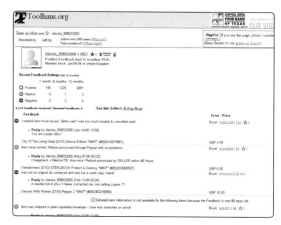

▲ Check out all of a seller's negative feedback at a glance at Toolhaus.org

CHECKING SELLER FEEDBACK BEFORE BIDDING

Every time an item sells, people have the chance to leave feedback about a seller. Feedback can be positive, negative or neutral, and can also be withdrawn by mutual agreement. We've covered it in more depth elsewhere in this guide. The total number of items sold and bought by the seller is displayed in brackets next to their name in the item's listing - click on it to go to their Feedback Profile.

The Positive Feedback percentage is the seller's reputation. If it's below 98%, then it's worth considering whether you want to do business with them. However, this is modified by how many total sales and purchases are represented. There is no way of checking only negative feedback at eBay itself, but you can input the user's ID at **www.toolhaus.org** to see a full listing of their negatives.

QUALITY OF FEEDBACK

Check one or two of the 'View Item' links in the seller's Feedback Profile. Many eBayers boost their reputation by buying 'one cent' lots that automatically grant positive feedback; such auctions are selling good reputation in volume. Certain sellers also manage to maintain more than one eBay account with the intention of 'selling' feedback to themselves. This trick is easy to spot with a little investigation of a Feedback Profile: look for numerous low-value items from the same seller, often digital goods such as 'guides' in PDF and Microsoft Word format. Some of these practices have been clamped down on by eBay, however.

CHANGED IDENTITY

eBay users can change their User ID, and if your seller has done this, then a symbol will appear next to their name.

Feedback is carried over from the old ID, but an auction where the seller is in the process of switching identity could mean that they're trying to start over at eBay. Why? Tucked away in the 'View more options'

drop-down menu in the Feedback Profile screen is the 'View ID History' option, which will quickly reveal any identity changes.

THE REAL DEAL

There is no pervasively useful method to identify fake goods across all listings in eBay, since signs of bad faith vary greatly across types of items. However, here are some considerations:

- If it's too good to be true, then it probably isn't true, particularly for Buy It Now items. Maybe a cuckolded wife really is selling her husband's Porsche for a dollar, but avoid items listed at significantly below market value.

- Does the listing have a generic picture that you've seen before? eBay supplies stock images for DVDs, CDs and certain other types of listings to sellers, but a 'domestic' picture of the item listed is a more encouraging sign, although it's not an infallible mark of authenticity.

- Does the listing explicitly state what the item is? You could be bidding on the very picture you're examining, rather than the item it displays! The devil is in the details, and nothing protects you better than a careful reading of the listing.

Boosting profits by overcharging for postage is known as 'scalping', and the 'Postage and packaging' section in each item listing should state clearly what you'll pay to have the item sent to you. If it doesn't, check the listing, and use the 'Ask a question' link to ascertain exact postal charges if necessary. If the seller is vague in response, pin them down, and if they won't specify an exact cost, don't bid.

Use the 'Customise view' link in your search results to add 'Shipping costs' to your search results (although they should be displayed by default). While not all items will be able to display their cost in the shipping costs column, it will help you eliminate most scalpers at a glance.

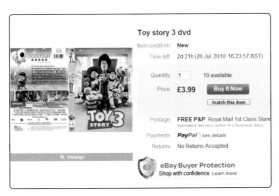

▲ At the time, Toy Story 3 was barely into cinemas. Pirated goods like this are likely to be poor quality

▲ Check the ID History of an eBayer to see how many times they've changed their name

Smart Bidding And Good Buying

When and how you bid on an item can make all the difference. We look at how you can increase your chances

So you've found your item; now it's time to bid and win it. However, there are some tricks to master before the item is in your hands and all parties are leaving positive feedback for each other.

SNIPING
Waiting until the last few minutes - or seconds - of an auction to place your bid is known as 'sniping'. Last-minute bidding gives your rivals no chance to bid higher, but this technique cannot defeat a bidder whose secret top-bid is higher than yours. The best way to ensure a win is to bid as much as you're willing to pay for the item. If you lose, it will usually be by a much higher margin than it appears, as eBay augments bids in small increments, and all top-bids are secret until outbid. The top-bid of a winner is known only to them.

ODD BIDS
Most eBayers place bids in rounded-off amounts, but sometimes you really can win an auction by a margin of a few pennies, so make your bids in odd amounts such as £11.67 or £7.89.

SILENT RUNNING
The more attention an auction receives, the more likely a costly bidding war is - great for the seller, not so great for you. A listing has three possible 'attracting forces': a bidder, a hit counter (if the seller has put one in the listing) and the number of

people who add the listing to their 'watch' list in order to monitor the auction's progress.

The hit counter is usually visible to all, but only the seller knows how many people are 'watching' the item; if sufficient 'watchers' gather, the seller may be encouraged to augment the listing and attempt to attract further buyers. The only safe way to track a listing without hiking up the hit counter or adding to the number of 'watchers', is to chase it through the ever-shifting pages of the search results through which you found the item in the first place. If you bookmark the listing and check it regularly, your own 'hit' is counted once a day.

However, nothing can turn an unnoticed listing into a frantic bidding war more effectively than when it's bid on very early in its run. Many eBayers search for items based on the existing number of bids, so even if you're not planning to 'snipe', don't bid on an item too early.

EBAY FEVER
When an item you've been seeking for years suddenly shows up on eBay, it's surprisingly easy to ignore all preceding advice and get caught up in the excitement. If you bid (or buy) recklessly, you can end up with an overseas item that you're unable to pay for due to the seller's payment methods or for other practical reasons. The only recourse then is to contact the seller via the 'Ask a question' link, explain what happened, and offer to pay the cost of a relisting. The seller remains entitled to wait 30 days and open a dispute for non-payment, so examine alternative payment methods if possible and keep it courteous, since the fault is with you.

Retracting a bid is rarely permitted, and you're only usually allowed to withdraw substantially mistyped amounts bid (i.e. entering £1,010 instead of £10.10). A bid on eBay is a binding contract. For an overview of eBay's policy, see **pages.ebay.co.uk/ help/buy/bid-retract.html**.

CORRESPONDING VIA EBAY
Corresponding with sellers outside of the eBay messaging system is ill-advised; if all your

> **DID YOU KNOW?**
>
> eBay UK overtook Amazon UK to become the country's top online shopping site in the spring of 2003.

▲ Choose the right option when corresponding with sellers

Congratulations You committed to buy the following item:

THE ENTITY (1981) Uncut | +Extras | Anchor Bay | R1 DVD

Sale price: £8.99
Quantity: 1
Subtotal: £8.99
Postage Royal Mail 1st Class £2.00
Standard:
Royal Mail Airmail £3.00
(Small Packets):

Insurance: (not offered)

View item | Go to My eBay

Get Your Item

Pay Now

Click to confirm postage, get total price and arrange payment.

▲ eBay's 'Pay Now' button

correspondence remains within eBay, you have a clear history to present in the event of dispute arbitration. Take it to e-mail, and you're on your own. The 'Ask a question' message form has a tick-box that lets you choose to hide your e-mail address from the recipient. This is the easiest way to keep your messages in eBay itself.

The form also has four options in a drop-down list to indicate whether your enquiry concerns payment, combined shipping for multiple items, shipping, or is a general enquiry. Since you have to choose one of these options to send a message, choose the right one; a busy seller may respond more quickly if you do so.

SIDE-STEPPING EBAY

Do not approach sellers with offers outside eBay's listings system. It's against the rules, and auctions can only be ended early in unusual circumstances. If you're interested in buying similar items 'off-site' from the seller in future, they may be interested in dealing with you, but they can't cancel an auction in progress, can't privately offer you the safeguards that eBay does, and would probably prefer to see someone as enthusiastic as you bidding hard against others users in a regular eBay auction!

DUPLICATE BIDDING

Do not place bids on multiple listings of the same item in the hope of winning one of them. If you win them all, you'll have to pay for them all.

UNWELCOME BIDS

Do you qualify to bid for an item? If you can't meet the seller's terms for a listing, they have the power to cancel your bid and bring down penalties on you from eBay administration. These can include account suspension and loss of PowerSeller status.

Sellers can refuse bids from buyers on their 'blocked bidder' list, and for many other reasons. As long as these are clearly stated in the listing itself, you'll have to respect them. Sellers may choose to 'ban' bidders who:

Select a payment method (seller accepts the following)

PayPal

MasterCard VISA AMEX DISCOVER eCHECK

○ **Other accepted payment methods**
(Money order / Cashier's check; Personal check)

Continue >

About eBay | Announcements | Security Center | Policies | Site Map | Help

▲ Select a method of payment from those available

- Have negative feedback comments.
- Have a 'non-domestic' shipping address.
- Have received Unpaid Item Strikes in an after-sales dispute.
- Don't have a PayPal account (although this doesn't oblige the seller to use PayPal as the payment method for their listing).

'Malicious buying' is deemed by eBay to occur when a buyer:

- Bids far beyond an item's value to 'prevent' serious bids and block the sale.
- Bids on multiple items from one seller with no real intent to buy.
- Bids on a seller's item after being placed on their 'blocked bidder' list.

Review payment details

Seller: ★ Power Seller

Item Title			Qty.	Price	Subtotal
THE ENTITY (1981) Uncut	+Extras	Anchor Bay	R1 DVD (280128288110)	1	£8.99	£8.99

Payment Instructions
PAYMENT METHODS FOR UK BUYERS - Credit/Debit Card, Personal Cheque, Postal Order & Bank Transfer.
PAYMENT METHODS FOR BUYERS OUTSIDE THE UK - Credit Cards, International Bank Transfer, International Money Orders/Bank Drafts provided they are made out in Sterling (GBP) & Moneybookers.

Postage and packing via Royal Mail 1st Class Standard: £2.00
Postal insurance:(not offered) --
Seller discounts (-) or charges (+): 2
Seller Total: £12.99
recalculate

Questions about the total? Request total from seller

▲ Add the correct postage, if it's not already included in the total

PAYING FOR YOUR WIN

When you finally win an auction listing, you will receive two notification e-mails from eBay: one to confirm your win, and one soliciting payment on behalf of the seller. Both will contain a big 'Pay Now' button, as will the item listing and the 'Won' page in My eBay.

Press it, and you'll be asked to select a method of payment (the methods available will be in accordance with those of the original listing).

You'll be asked to confirm shipping details and to add postage to the invoice if this hasn't automatically been done. Take care to input the correct postage. Postage is usually charged in the seller's native currency, but you may need to translate the agreed postage amount in order to input it (try the Universal Currency Converter at **www.xe.com/ucc**). You can also add an optional note to the seller at this point, and change the

▲ Pay for your win directly from the PayPal site

▲ Check all the details again before finalising the payment

shipping address by selecting another from your eBay Saved Addresses or adding a new one.

PAYING DIRECT FROM PAYPAL

In certain circumstances - usually when you've arranged unusual terms with a foreign seller - you may find that your only options for inputting postage are inappropriate drop-down lists of 'domestic' packing rates. In this case, you'll need to contact the seller and ask them to change the automated payment procedure from their end. If this proves problematic, and PayPal is acceptable to your seller, you can still use PayPal's Send Money feature to conclude the auction, without losing the security of an eBay acknowledgement that you've paid for your win. However, you'll need the seller's e-mail address. The process is as follows:

- Log into your PayPal account and click the 'Send Money' tab.
- Click on 'eBay item' in the 'For...?' section and type your eBay User ID and the auction number.
- Enter the seller's e-mail address in the 'To' field, or, if you've previously dealt with the seller, select it from the drop-down list underneath.
- Enter the winning amount including postage, click 'Continue, and then confirm on the next page. The item will be acknowledged as 'paid' in My eBay.

PAYING WITHOUT PAYPAL

PayPal is an eBay subsidiary company, and using it to pay for an eBay win means that you're covered for up to £500 through the PayPal Buyer Protection Program (see 'Damage Limitation'). Since no other eBay payment method carries this kind of guarantee, PayPal is arguably the best choice to complete auctions, and eBay is at times borderline insistent that you use it.

However, PayPal has many detractors, and if you need to complete a deal by other means, the options allowed (but not necessarily endorsed) by eBay are:

- **Personal cheque:** Convenient, can be stopped if necessary (for varying fees) and is traceable.
- **Credit/debit card:** The seller may have their own checkout system, integrated (often poorly) into eBay's own payment procedures. Credit card payments additionally have varying - and limited - liability insurance for physical items. Be sure that your auction payment is acknowledged by eBay afterwards, as this fails to happen more often through bad coding than ill intent.
- **Postal orders:** Convenient, but almost as transparent as cash

- **Bank transfer:** A favourite in European transactions, but involves sharing banking information with a third party. Refunds can be very problematic.
- **Banker's draft:** For higher value items; fees for issue may exceed the item's value.
- **E-cheque:** Slightly faster clearing than physical cheques, but if you're able to send one, you might as well use PayPal.
- **Escrow:** Only practical for higher amounts. Both parties have to be happy with the transaction before money is released - **www.escrow.com**.
- **Cash:** Caveat emptor - if you must use it, send the package well wrapped (with opaque lining) and by a method whereby the receiver must sign for it.

INTERNATIONAL MONEY ORDERS

Some transnational banks used to make international money orders a relatively easy option. These days, the term has little meaning, and generally sellers are actually talking about cheques from international banks that are to be specified in the seller's native currency (usually dollars). Such services are far too expensive to be practical for small wins.

LEAVING FEEDBACK

Many sections of My eBay will ask you to leave feedback on transacted auctions (and the seller will remind you if no one else does!). eBay is regularly reviewing its feedback policy, and it's covered in more detail elsewhere in this book.

DAMAGE LIMITATION

If you don't receive your item, or the item is significantly different from its listing description, contact the seller about the matter in the first instance. An amicable solution is often possible, retaining goodwill and avoiding bad feedback for either party.

One of the top causes of disputes is non-delivery, usually due to items being lost or stolen in the post. The only way to avoid this is to have them sent insured at greater expense, thus protecting both buyer and seller. Unfortunately, this can negate the 'bargain' value of eBay and, in practice, an enormous number of eBay items are consigned to the basic postal system (often of more than one country) every day. Nonetheless, verify the address used and date of actual posting from the seller, and ensure that adequate time has been allowed for the item to arrive.

For items covered by PayPal's Buyer Protection Program, the advantage is with the buyer if an uninsured item doesn't arrive or doesn't match its

listing description; you can open a dispute from My eBay within ten to 60 days of payment.

As ever, maintain any correspondence via eBay rather than e-mail. The seller has ten days to respond, but if no satisfactory agreement is reached, you can elevate your dispute to a claim. The seller's account may be limited or even suspended if a claim is granted, and funds are usually recovered and then credited back to your PayPal account.

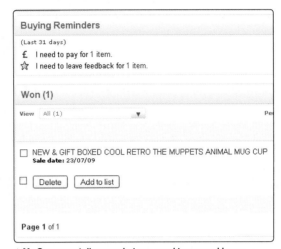

▲ My Summary tells you what you need to pay and leave feedback for

▲ Feedback allows you to rate and comment on other eBayers, either positively or negatively

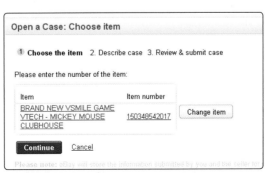

▲ If the seller won't help you, you can open a dispute about your missing or misdescribed item

MEMORABLE EBAY AUCTIONS

LUNCH WITH MURDOCH

Media tycoon Rupert Murdoch offered lunch with himself at News Corporation's New York headquarters, in a charity eBay auction. Bidding started at $25,000, and the money went to a Jerusalem technology college.

Combining Purchases From One Seller

If you're buying several items from the same seller, you could save a bundle on postage costs. Here's how

Should you purchase more than one item from a single trader, you may find that you can combine said purchases into one shipment, thus saving yourself a few pounds in the process - at least in theory! There are various different approaches to doing this, but in all likelihood, eBay auctions that offer discounts on shipping for multiple items will continue to require a measure of personal correspondence between buyer and seller, and this is easy enough with the 'Ask a question' link. Simply select 'Question about combined shipping for multiple items' from the drop-down list and make your enquiry.

NO 'SHOPPING BASKET'

The problems begin to surface when the seller attempts to automate the process or let eBay do it on their behalf, and this is particularly true with North American sellers, who have the widest range of postage-calculating tools built into their listing templates. Many of these tools can auto-calculate combined shipping to the UK, usually via the UPS shipping service, but all of them require deviations from standard eBay practice regarding paying for items. As things stand, Bay has no ubiquitous 'shopping basket' - a la Amazon - and when you win an item or 'Commit To Buy' it, there is no consideration given for other items that you might have bought or wish to buy from the same seller.

However, while it's currently therefore impossible to combine purchases in one basket, eBay is at last experimenting with a basket system. There's no date as yet for when it plans to fully roll this out, however.

CUSTOM SOLUTIONS

Many PowerSellers invest in software solutions that provide a 'shopping basket' for you behind the scenes; when eBay informs them of a new sale of one of their items, they will invite you to pay for the item, but inform you that you may take advantage of shipping discounts for multiple items purchased. Committing to further items from that seller will add your deliveries to the seller's own Amazon-style list, with combined shipping calculated, and the final payment procedure may take place via eBay checkout (if the seller has integrated their system directly into it) or at the seller's site (if the seller has their own checkout software).

Sellers who offer such services will usually also mention them in their listings, along with (often tedious) instructions on how to proceed in order to not lose the combined shipping. Read and follow these carefully, because they vary widely from seller to seller.

Any custom checkout should send eBay an acknowledgement of payment for all your items automatically, but make sure this is done shortly after payment for your multiple items, and contact the seller otherwise.

COMBINED SHIPPING - GUIDELINES

If you intend to take advantage of any combined shipping deals a seller is offering, do not pay for any single item from them until you have 'claimed' all the items from their listings or store that you intend to buy (to 'claim' means to secure an item by either winning it in an auction or pressing 'Commit To Buy' on a Buy It Now listing).

• Read carefully what terms the seller is offering on combined postage for an item you intend to buy - if any automatic postage calculations should fall short after you've won or committed to buy the

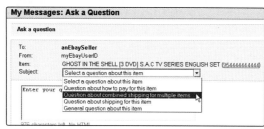

▲ The best bet is always to ask the seller first

▲ Check the seller's listings to see if they give details about combining postage

▲ Several items all from one seller, but what's the best way to buy more than one of them?

item, the seller will have to honour the postage that they offered - by other means if necessary - and you're likely to win any eventual dispute on the matter.

• Ensure that shipping terms are consistent across all the same-seller listings that you intend to bid on or buy. Calculate the combined postage based on the listing's stated rates and 'claim' your items. If you're bidding on multiple or sequential auctions and hoping to combine postage on successive wins, be aware that the first item won is payable within 30 days of a winning bid or a commitment to buy.

• You're likely to receive more than one (usually automated) e-mail from eBay requesting payment for each item as you win (or Commit To Buy) it. If you do so before all the items are 'in the basket', you risk losing some or all of your combined shipping discount.

• When all your items are claimed, check out the most recent automated e-mail from the seller for details of how to combine shipping. If the calculation is to be done through eBay Checkout itself, make sure that eBay's combined estimate corresponds with the seller's advertised deal. Verify also that the rates are appropriately UK or international, depending on the seller's location.

PAYPAL ITEMS FROM DIFFERENT SELLERS

Be careful not to confuse combined shipping with combined payment. If you've won several eBay items from different sellers, but haven't paid yet, you can click the 'Pay For All PayPal Items' link in My eBay.

Any items not listed with PayPal won't be included in the combined payment. If there are multiple items in the list from one seller from whom you wish to obtain a shipping discount, remove them from the list before making your combined payment; they will need to be dealt with separately.

▲ 'Pay For All PayPal Items' is not the same as a combined order

Case Study: **Ex-eBay Shop Owner**

Sometimes sellers decide to turn away from eBay, for a variety of reasons...

Not every eBay business will last forever, but it can inspire you and give you confidence. That's what Julie Stamp took away from her eBay business, Lolli Dollies, which she began on the auction site in 2003. Although she closed her eBay shop in 2006, she went on to set up her own successful stand-alone business called Lolli Dollies Online. Ill health and a desire to concentrate on her writing and degree caused Julie to close that business last year, but she's determined her six years of selling over the Internet will not go to waste. "It gives you great enthusiasm and it shows you that you can do anything if you put your mind to it," she said.

Julie is a great lover of Sindy dolls, which for more than 30 years was one of Britain's best selling toys. Along with Sindy came boyfriend Paul, sister Patch and huge wardrobe of fashionable clothes, which reflected UK fashion from 1963 - when the doll was launched as a rival to Barbie - through the 1980s. They were manufactured by Pedigree Toys in Canterbury, 15 miles from Julie's home. So when, in the winter of 2003, she saw a few Sindy dolls for sale on eBay, she began to collect them, purely as a nostalgia thing.

From that grew a hobby that led to her collecting all types of teenage vintage dolls, including the American rival, Barbie. It rapidly became a business, expanding from a corner of the dining room into the spare bedroom. Eventually it took over the main bedroom, which became a workshop with storage tubs, shelves and more computers.

The reason for this rapid expansion was eBay. Yet Julie only discovered it by accident. She said, "I was bought a Ghost skirt from eBay in the autumn of 2003. I asked what eBay was and was shown it, and from then on I was hooked."

It was while searching for obscure items that she came across 40 listings for a Tressy doll. She was amazed; at a traditional auction it could takes years to find just one. She then turned her attention to Sindy and ended up making her first purchase: a 1960s doll for around £9. She began to realise there was a huge market out there for vintage dolls, and thousands of collectors - or potential buyers.

Julie's business began two months later in February 2004 when she bought a doll that required some tender loving care. After washing, conditioning and teasing Sindy's hair into a 1960s flick style and then dressing her in a genuine Sindy outfit, she sold it for £7. Since she had bought the doll and the clothes for £4.50, she had made a tidy profit.

Four months later, she set up the eBay shop Lolli Dollies and it soon had an established customer base in the UK and across Europe, America, Japan, Korea, Australia and Hong Kong.

Julie did everything right. The shop was well laid out. It had the Lolli Dollies logo nice and bold in the top-left corner and to the right was an explanation of the shop and what it sold. Just above the description, and easily accessible, was the all-important feedback link and next to that was the 'About Me' option, which customers could click on to find out more about the shop.

The About Me page remains important, particularly if you want to make a serious go of your business. Julie used her page to describe in greater detail what her shop was about, spelling out that it sells gently renovated dolls, which were only listed when she was 100% happy with them. She said she aimed to keep the dolls affordable and informed buyers they were kept in a smoke and pet-free environment. Finally, she made a note that she was a UK seller, so prices

were in sterling and postage costs were based on posting within and from Britain.

A nice touch at Lolli Dollies was a collection of links under the heading 'Shop Pages'. Julie added greater depth to her store's shopping experience by allowing buyers to glimpse behind the scenes at her company. She included pictures and words on how her dolls were restored and gave buyers a look at her workshop in action. And she also linked to a self-written article about why she got into collecting and what she collected, again accompanied by pictures. Straight away, it added a personal touch to what can sometimes be a faceless medium. Buyers knew they were dealing with a genuine person whose face they could put to a name. And they knew that person was an avid collector who cared for her customers and dolls.

But not everything ran smoothly. "For me, one of the drawbacks of running an eBay shop is that customers seem to think you are there to answer any enquires they may have (in my case, with regards to doll collecting, or about a doll already in their collection), rather than sticking to questions about items in your eBay shop," she recalls. "They also seem to think - more so these days than in 2005 -

that you are a big high-street shop and can therefore 'get something in for me' if they do not see it listed. [All credit to eBay though, for enabling sellers to give this impression.]"

One of the reasons she gave the shop up was time. If you're going to set up an eBay shop, you need to ensure you're not going to be incredibly busy with other things. "Admin takes up an incredible amount of time," she said. "And then you have to consider the amount of space you'll need too. The wrapping and actual posting of items can be very time consuming, unless you have someone to help you and a post office that's geared up to take your packages. Do not underestimate the amount of 'behind the scenes' time required to run an eBay shop."

But there were lots of things that Julie loved, and she said eBay is a perfect place on which to start a business and build a reputation. "Advantages include an easy-to-set-up and professional store front, a worldwide customer base [although you can choose to post UK only, which is good for heavy, bulky or very fragile items], and the ability to place a reserve on higher-value items, although I was disappointed when eBay set a minimum reserve rate of £50 - not fair to smaller shop owners."

Lolli Dollies was aimed at the average collector with an average income. It was for this reason she didn't sell boxed or mint condition dolls, which commanded higher prices. To keep prices low, she sometimes dressed dolls in just part of an original outfit such as the skirt and blouse to which the buyer could add at a later date when finances allowed. That kind of strategy encouraged repeat buyers.

"If you're selling to a niche market, as I was with vintage dolls, then eBay is the ideal retail outlet, as it tends to be the first stop for collectors, and eBay purchases/shops are discussed frequently on collector and enthusiast online forums," Julie said. "Search engine optimisation is a given with eBay, so you have no worries about paying expensive hosting fees and extra SEO fees for minimal hits/conversions."

She said listing an item and uploading photos is easy, as eBay guides you through every step and, if you're selling the same or similar items often, you can even use one of your existing listing templates. "Return and refund policies can be set up, and you can create an enhanced ME page in which you can tell your customers more about yourself and/or your shop," she added. "Navigation within an eBay store is a simple process for your buyers, and a seller can access past sales records, feedback scores, seller account, PayPal account and so on very easily."

So any more tips? "My advice to other people wanting to set up on eBay is to choose a field you are an expert in, or that you at least enjoy, and are willing to put the time and money into learning more about."

Chapter 6
PayPal

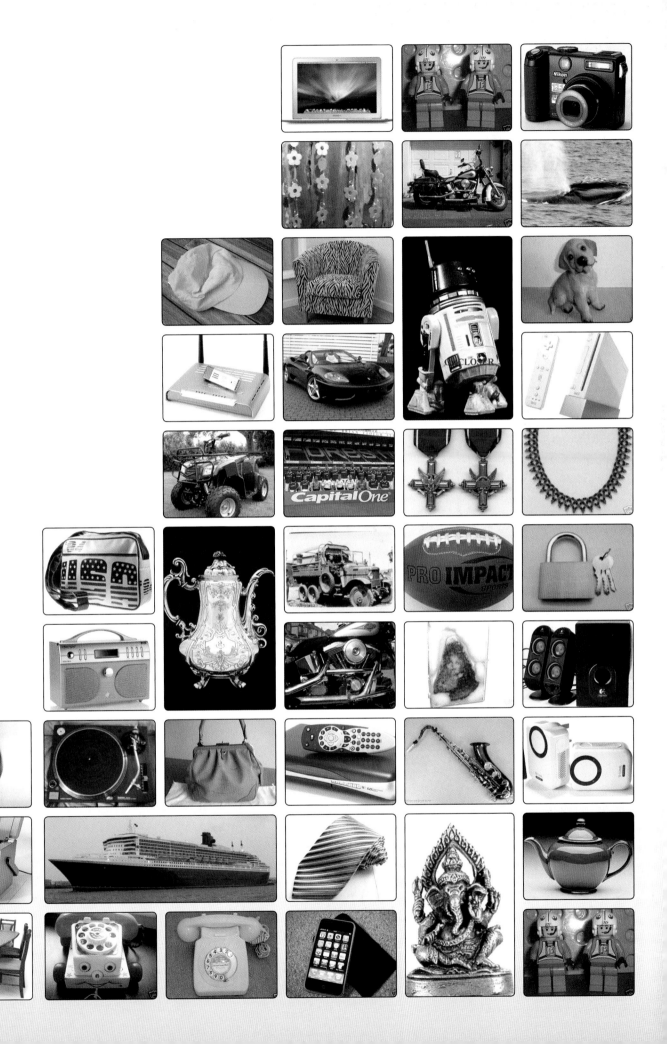

What Is PayPal?

It's now an essential part of the eBay experience, so here's your crash course on what this payment system is all about

You'll have seen PayPal mentioned many times throughout this guide, but what exactly is it, and how does it work? Well, while PayPal isn't really a bank, you won't go far wrong if you think of your PayPal account as being like a bank account. Ordinarily, you can't use it to set up direct debits for your energy bills, though; almost all your transactions will be manual and one time only. PayPal is also entirely virtual: you can't nip to your local branch on a Saturday morning to make a deposit or withdrawal. Everything occurs over the Internet.

On eBay, a PayPal account is vital. About 90% of all eBay sales are concluded with PayPal, and worldwide there are over 180 million accounts. For buyers, PayPal is simply the most convenient way to pay. For sellers, allowing PayPal as a payment method is pretty much compulsory (you can only get away with not offering it on items listed in property, services, or eBay Motors).

One of PayPal's big advantages over traditional payment methods is its speed. You can pay for an item via your PayPal balance or a credit or debit card (and, with some caveats, direct from your bank account), and in most cases the seller receives the money instantly. Neither party has to mess about with cheques, waiting for them to clear. For the seller, it's like having a professional merchant system, the sort of thing used by large retailers.

Another big advantage is security. When you buy something off eBay, you're usually dealing with strangers or unknown businesses. Only a fool wouldn't be cautious about handing over debit- or credit-card information. With PayPal, though, there are no worries. You see, PayPal acts as an intermediary, a broker, so you don't actually pay the seller directly. Your financial details are locked up safe in your PayPal account, and the seller never sees them.

HOW IT WORKS

As a buyer, having just won an auction, you're given several opportunities to pay. First, you'll see a big Pay Now button at the top of your browser window. Second, there'll be a new entry, and a 'Pay now' link, in the Won section of your Activity tab in the all-seeing eye that is My eBay. Third, you'll receive two eBay-generated e-mails: a win confirmation and an invoice. Both will feature Pay Now buttons. You might receive an e-mail directly from the seller too.

Whichever path you take, you'll soon enough find yourself at the screen where you need to choose your payment method. PayPal is usually the default, but if the seller also takes cheques and so on, there'll be an option for 'Other accepted payment methods'. Taking the PayPal route, just type in your PayPal password (your PayPal e-mail address will normally already be displayed) and click 'Log in'.

PayPal and eBay are parts of the same organisation, so naturally they're very tightly integrated. The beauty of this is that the PayPal payment process occurs within eBay itself; you won't get whisked away to the actual PayPal website. What you'll see now is the review screen. If your PayPal account has sufficient funds in it, payment will be sourced entirely from your balance. However, if there's not enough (or none at all), the amount not covered (or, where your balance is £0, the full cost) will be sourced from your bank account

▲ If you haven't yet signed up, what are you waiting for?

▲ Around 90% of all eBay purchases are paid for with PayPal

▲ After a win, click the Pay Now button in the browser window…

▲…or click the Pay now link in My eBay…

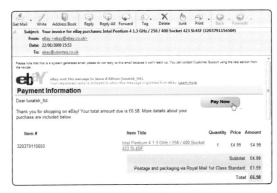

▲…or the Pay Now button in either of the sale-generated e-mails

or credit or debit card (depending on what you've got registered). If you want to change anything here, just click 'More funding options'.

As a seller, having just achieved a spectacular price for your first-edition copy of Casino Royale, the PayPal process is even simpler. Basically, you don't need to lift a finger. When the buyer makes payment, you'll receive confirmation by e-mail. If you then log into your account, you'll find the money ready and waiting. A receipt is e-mailed to the buyer automatically, but in the name of good feedback and communication, you'd do well to also send a personal thank you.

Tip: Be aware that a payment made from your bank account - an e-cheque - will usually take between seven and nine days to clear. Don't expect despatch of your purchase until the money finally drops into the seller's PayPal account. You're much better using your PayPal balance or a credit or debit card.

ACCOUNT TYPES

Setting up PayPal is a subject covered in chapter two, but here it's worthwhile going into more detail about the different types of account. Basically, there are three: Personal, Premier, and Business. All of them are free, and there are no start-up costs or monthly administration fees.

A Personal account is intended for eBayers who are chiefly interested in buying. If you sell, any

PayPal payments you receive must be funded from a PayPal balance or a bank account (although your buyers won't be aware of that). If someone pays for an item via a card - a scenario that'll happen sooner rather than later - your confirmation e-mail will inform you that you need to upgrade. Until you do, the money will remain unavailable, and if you haven't upgraded after 30 days, it'll be returned to the buyer.

You can upgrade at any time; after logging into your account, just click the Upgrade link at the top of the Overview page. If you intend to sell, however, you might as well forgo a Personal account altogether and just sign up for a Premier account. This will lift the limitation on card payments right from the start. Most people who begin as buyers quickly end up as sellers, so save yourself the hassle. Once the eBay bug bites, you'll want to start making some cash from all that stuff in your attic.

A Business account differs from a Premier account in that it can be held in the name of a company (Dealz4U Ltd, for example) - the other account types can only be held in the name of an individual. Transactions and e-mails will therefore look more professional. Furthermore, if you've got co-workers, they can be assigned different access rights. For instance, you might want someone to be able to view transactions but not spend or withdraw. To set this up, go to your account's Overview page, click

▲ You can change the funding source that PayPal will use

▲ There are three account types to choose from

▲ A Personal account is great for buyers but not sellers

▲ If you've got a Business account, you can configure different access rights for different users

'Profile', select 'Manage Users', then click 'Add User'. Choose a User ID and password, which will then be the co-worker's login (instead of the usual e-mail address and password), and tick the required rights.

Tip: Officially, you're allowed one Personal account and one Premier or Business account. In practice, though, there's no way for that restriction to be enforced, so you can actually set up as many accounts as you want or need. However, every account must have its own e-mail address and financial details. You can't register the same credit card to two different accounts, for example.

STANDARD FEES

They say it's better to give than to receive, and that's certainly true where PayPal's concerned. While sending money (to a seller, say) is free, getting paid (by a buyer, for instance) is anything but. There are nasty, nasty fees.

In most cases, the commission you pay to PayPal is 3.4% of the transaction amount plus an extra £0.20. For example, if a buyer pays you £100, you'll be charged £3.60 - that's £3.40 (3.4%) plus £0.20. In your PayPal account, you'll receive £96.40.

Matters are worse if the buyer pays in a currency other than British pounds. For that, there's a 2.5% conversion fee. Furthermore, if the buyer doesn't live in the UK, there's a 0.5% cross-border fee. It all

adds up! Imagine you've just sold an item to someone in the USA. Payment will be made in dollars. When the money hits your account, it'll be automatically converted into pounds (for PayPal's current exchange rates, visit **tinyurl.com/47rsl**). Your total commission will be a whopping 6.4%. And then there's the old £0.20 to be added on top. To check in advance what fees will be payable on any given transaction, have a look at PPCalc at **tinyurl. com/d5golw**.

Sadly, PayPal fees are levied in addition to eBay fees: you're charged twice. That's a situation that makes most eBay sellers quite, quite mad. After all, as PayPal and eBay are really one and the same, it's a case of double-dipping. Most categories on eBay attract a 10% selling fee, so when everything's combined (don't forget there are usually listing fees too), you're likely to be coughing up about 15% in commission - even more if the transaction involves an extra currency and a border crossing. Small wonder that Pierre Omidyar, eBay's founder, is the 156th richest person in the world!

Tip: Don't try to reclaim your PayPal fees from your buyers. It's against eBay's rules. If you adorn your listings with something like 'PayPal payments incur a 3.5% surcharge', they're likely to get pulled, and for repeated offences your eBay account could even be suspended. It's not fair, of course. Other retail outlets

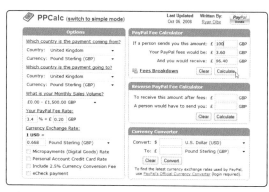

▲ For working out what it's all going to cost, try PPCalc, the online fee calculator

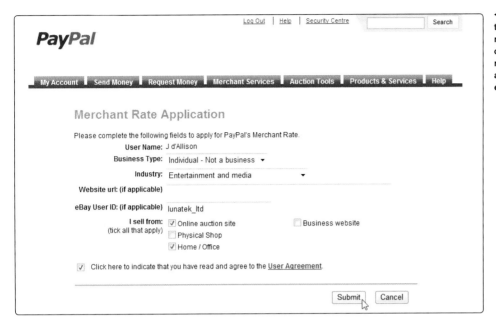

◀ Don't forget to apply for merchant commission rates as soon as you're eligible

regularly charge for using a credit card, so why can't eBay sellers charge for using PayPal?

MERCHANT FEES

As illustrated above, PayPal's standard commission rate is 3.4%. However, if you become a really successful seller and your monthly receipts exceed £1,500, you're entitled to a lower, merchant rate. The rate comes down as your income goes up. The full set of tariffs is shown below.

- £0 to £1,500 = 3.4%
- £1,500.01 to £6,000 = 2.9%
- £6,000.01 to £15,000 = 2.4%
- £15,000.01 to £55,000 = 1.9%
- £55,000.01 or more = 1.4%

The rate for the current month is decided by your income for the previous month. For instance, if you have a great January and receive £7,000, your rate in February will be 2.4%. If February is terrible and you receive only £1,200, your rate in March will be 2.9%.

To be eligible for these lower rates, you must have held your PayPal account for at least 90 days. Also, you need to submit an application. Once this is accepted, you'll be moved up and down the tariffs automatically as appropriate. There's no need to reapply if you slip back to the standard 3.4% from time to time. Note that the rates aren't back-dated, however, so don't mess about; send in your application as soon as possible.

To do that, log into your account, click 'Fees' at the bottom of any page, click '1.4% to 3.4% + £0.20 GBP', then click 'Are you eligible for lower rates?'

Read through the introductory spiel and then click the 'Apply now' link. Finally, fill out the form, accept the user agreement, and click 'Submit'. Don't apply before your 90 days are up or before you've clocked up £1,500 or more in the previous month, because the application will be immediately refused (though you can reapply later, of course).

PERSONAL TRANSFERS

Not all PayPal receipts attract a fee. Personal transfers - payments between friends and family - can in fact be free. That's only true if they're funded from a PayPal balance or a bank account, though. If they're funded by a card, that old 3.4% commission applies (regardless of the sum involved).

To make such a transfer, click 'Send Money' at the top of any page and then select the Personal tab. Enter the amount to be sent and also the recipient's PayPal-linked e-mail address. Next, click 'Continue'. You'll now be shown a summary, and if there are any fees, this is where you'll need to

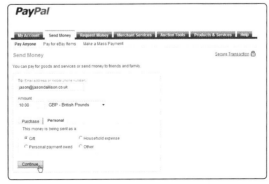

▲ Payments between friends and family are usually free

▲ Where have all the fees gone?

decide who pays them - you or the recipient. Once you're all done, just click 'Send Money'.

ACCOUNT WITHDRAWALS

Often you'll want to spend your PayPal money right out of your PayPal account, particularly as an ever-increasing number of websites are offering PayPal as a payment method (it's not just an eBay thing). Just as often, though, you'll want to withdraw your PayPal money to your regular current- or savings account - especially as PayPal doesn't pay interest. Until recently, there was a £0.50 charge for withdrawing less than £50, but now there's no charge at all, but the minimum withdrawal amount is £6.

To get the ball rolling, go to your account's Overview page, hover your mouse over the Withdraw menu, then select 'Transfer to Bank Account'. On the next screen, enter the amount to withdraw and also the bank account you want to withdraw it to (if you've got more than one bank account registered).

After clicking 'Continue', you'll get a confirmation screen. Click 'Submit' and you're done. Within a few seconds you'll also get a confirmation e-mail. Note that it'll take up to five working days for the money to arrive.

VERIFYING YOUR FINANCIAL DETAILS

When you first open your PayPal account, its status will be Unverified. This means that you've yet to establish ownership of the associated bank account - assuming you've registered one. If you haven't yet registered one (during the initial PayPal set-up, it's possible to get away with registering just a credit or debit card), you'll need to do so. On your account's Overview page, hover your mouse over the Profile menu and select 'Add or Remove Bank Account'.

But what's the big deal? Well, until you upgrade your status from Unverified to Verified, there'll be limits on the amount of money you can spend, receive, and withdraw. These are listed below.

- Sending limit per transaction = £900
- Sending limit per year = £1,000
- Withdrawal limit per month = £500
- Withdrawal limit per year = £650
- Receiving limit per year = £1,700

The limits are there so that PayPal can conform to EU anti-money-laundering laws. They also help to fight fraud. To see how much you've currently eaten into them, click the 'View limits' link on your account's Overview page.

To lift the limits, and thus become Verified, there are a couple of hoops you need to jump through first.

▶ Withdrawing your PayPal money to your regular bank account really couldn't be easier

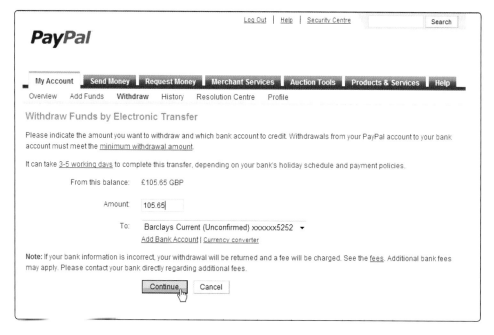

▲ Until you become Verified, your PayPal account will be somewhat limited

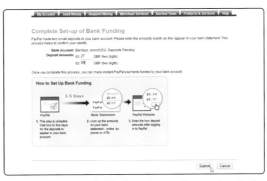

▲ Keep your eyes peeled for those two small sums deposited into your bank account

When you registered your bank account, PayPal will have dropped two small deposits into it, each less than £1. You'll need to wait between two and five days for these to appear; keep checking your statement online or use the mini-statement facility at your bank's cash machines. With the figures to hand, log into PayPal, click the 'Get verified' link on the Overview page, and type them into the text boxes. Finally, click 'Submit'. Job done - and you even get to keep the deposits!

CONFIRMING YOUR ADDRESS

Another form of security PayPal employs is address confirmation. This usually occurs automatically as soon as you register a credit or debit card. PayPal checks that the address you gave when setting up your account matches the one held by the card issuer. Unfortunately, if you've only registered a bank account (and have no card you can register), your address will probably remain forever Unconfirmed.

That could arouse suspicion. Imagine your PayPal login details have somehow been stolen. A fraudster could change your address, go on a spending spree, and attempt to clean you out. However, the supplied address would then show as Unconfirmed, and for many sellers that would be grounds enough to refuse shipment (and reverse payment). Indeed, if a seller ships an item to an address that isn't Confirmed, the transaction ceases to be eligible for Seller Protection. As a genuine buyer, you could find that no one will take your money!

All these security measures are, of course, designed to make PayPal safe. They also facilitate the aforementioned Seller Protection - and Buyer Protection too. Details on those areas are covered in chapter five, and for the latest policies and eligibility requirements, visit the PayPal Security Centre (**tinyurl.com/3abeq8k**). Is PayPal as perfect as it's cracked up to be, though? Is it 100% secure and problem-free? Well, you're about to find out...

▶ Does your address show as confirmed?

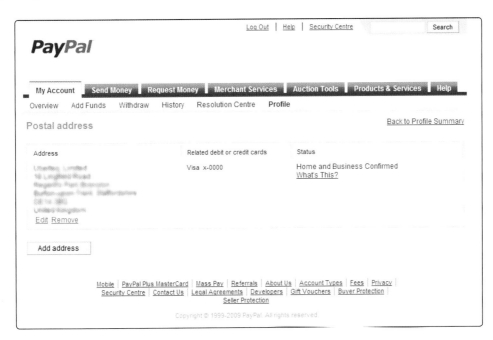

Problems With PayPal

It may be the most popular payment system on eBay, but don't be fooled by the hype; it's far from perfect...

PayPal has been with us for roughly ten years now, and as time has gone by, it has come to dominate online auction transactions the world over. These days, it's almost impossible to trade on eBay without holding such an account, thanks to the increasing tightening of eBay regulations in that area. But is it really all it's made out to be? Are there any chinks in its armour that you should be aware of?

Firstly, it would only be fair to point out that the vast majority of PayPal's millions of customers have never had a problem with the service. They find it both a convenient and reliable means for trading on eBay. For them, PayPal works exactly as it should, providing a means of transferring money from one account into another securely and without fuss. It's a free service for the buyer, and sellers don't mind paying a little bit extra in charges if it takes away the hassle of receiving payments.

However, the picture isn't quite as rosy as you might first think. There are countless horror stories of people having their accounts locked out, and being unable to access their money. Every day, millions of hoax e-mails get sent pretending to be from PayPal, and people have fallen for scams like this in the past. There are also plenty of users who feel hard done by when it comes to paying the charges set by both eBay and PayPal when selling an item. And, of course, there's the lack of choice presented to those consumers who wish to avoid the service altogether. They view PayPal's share of the market and lack of viable alternatives as being both anti-competitive and negative.

ACCOUNT FREEZES

It's important to remember that PayPal, despite handling some extremely large financial transactions, is not actually a bank. As such, it's not governed by the same rules and regulations that banks and similar organisations are. For this reason, it can attract money launderers and other criminal elements looking to transfer substantial sums of money without raising too many eyebrows. This was particularly rife in PayPal's early days, but since then, stricter security measures have been put in place, and there are now more regular audits and checks on people's accounts. The upshot of all this is that PayPal is now more a lot more careful and stringent with how it deals with potential cases.

One of the first things PayPal does when it notices discrepancies is to place a freeze on the account in question. This means that while an account is being investigated, all money is blocked from entering or leaving. In some cases, perfectly innocent people have had a lock placed on their account, and have had to wait months until the restriction was lifted and they could use their account again. As you can

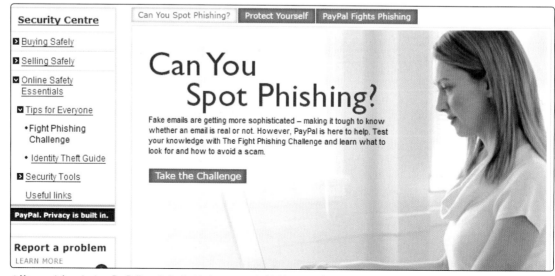

▲ You can take a test on PayPal's website that helps you spot phishing e-mails

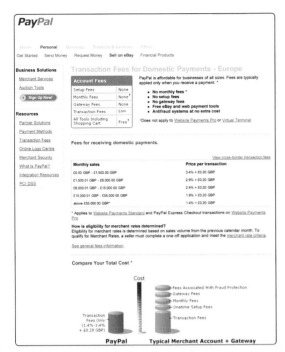

▲ PayPal's fees can soon add up, especially when you consider they come on top of the standard eBay charges

▲ PayPal has had its fair share of hackers and fraudsters over the years

imagine, this has left a fair few people unhappy, particularly as many of them rely on PayPal as a source of income.

The most practical advice here is to make sure that there's never a large sum of money resident in your PayPal account. It could be potentially disastrous if you can't get access to several thousand pounds, but not so if there's less money involved.

It's very rare for this to happen to anyone, but if you're worried that you may fall victim to this one day, the best thing to do is look at alternative payment systems to use instead. Unfortunately, for eBay users, however, they don't really have much choice in the matter.

It's notoriously easy to open a PayPal account, so it can be open to abuse, but just be careful with who you trade with, apply some common sense, and the problem can be minimised.

PHISHING AND HOAX E-MAILS

Hoax e-mails have been a problem that has plagued PayPal for a number of years now. If you ever receive a message purporting to be from PayPal, but something doesn't seem right (for example, you may be told that an item has been purchased from your account that you previously weren't aware of, or money has left your account that you didn't authorise), the safest thing to do is log into PayPal yourself to check. It always pays to be far too cautious than far too little. By clicking on the link in one of these hoax e-mails, you'll usually be redirected to

another website, which requests your bank details and other personal information. This is known as a phishing scam.

These e-mails look almost identical to official e-mails sent out by both PayPal and eBay, which can fool some people if they're not careful. The e-mail normally instructs the person to follow a link to a website, which again looks very similar to a legitimate site, whereupon they're asked to enter their bank details in order to verify the account.

It goes without saying that you shouldn't do this, because you're handing over all your personal information to a stranger. You should always be very wary when asked via e-mail to send any personal information. A little bit of common sense is required to spot these e-mails, but some scams are less obvious than others.

One of the biggest giveaways is the address in the browser. The link may say www.paypal.com, but when you click on it and actually visit the site, you'll find that you've been redirected somewhere else. It's best to always play safe.

If you're worried about falling victim to fraudsters and hackers, there are a few simple precautions that you can take in order to keep your account safe. These are all sensible procedures that you should follow for any online accounts involving finances or personal details.

Firstly, make sure you choose a good password that other people can't guess easily. Having your surname or part of your address as a password is a

▲ Phishing is one of the many scams PayPal users have to contend with

▲ Credit card fraud is one of the biggest problems facing the Internet today

risky move. Try to keep it as ambiguous as possible - nothing that a potential hacker will be able to easily guess. If you're worried that your details may still be in danger of falling into the wrong hands, then change it regularly.

Do not share your account details with anyone who isn't connected with PayPal itself. Certain hoax e-mails ask for this information, but you should always bypass these and log into your PayPal account by typing the web address in your browser. Never follow a link sent via e-mail, because this could be rerouted to another website.

When accessing your PayPal information, make sure the site is accessed through a secure connection. You can tell if it is by looking at the address bar. It should read 'https' rather than 'http' before the actual web address.

Keep on top of things too. Check your PayPal account regularly, in order to know exactly how much money is in there at any given time. It will show all your recent transactions, and if there's any unexpected activity on your account, you should be able to catch it as soon as possible.

DOUBLE CHARGES

PayPal sellers on eBay are hit with two sets of charges - something that has irked many users for some time now. When you decide to sell an item on eBay, you're charged an insertion fee, based on either the starting or reserve price. You may also be charged optional fees for various features that can be incorporated into the listing (such as a picture). The fees don't end there, though; when you make a sale, eBay then charges you a fee based on the final selling price. All well and good, but then if you make a sale using PayPal, you will also get charged an additional fee for the transaction (normally 3.4% plus £0.20). That's two sets of fees: one for eBay and the other for PayPal. This is particularly annoying when you consider that eBay owns PayPal, so you're pretty much paying the same company twice.

As a case in point, let's have a look at how much selling an item for £10 would cost you, with the list price starting at £0.01.

Item value: £10
eBay insertion fee: £0
eBay sale completion: £1
PayPal charge: £0.54
Total returned to you: £8.46

The more expensive the product, the more charges increase in value. For example:

Item value: £50
eBay insertion fee: £0
eBay sale completion: £5
PayPal charge: £1.90
Total returned to you: £43.10

Many sellers offset these fees by including them in the list price. The buyer will cover any charges in their purchase, as a consequence leaving the seller with more profit. As mentioned previously, you can

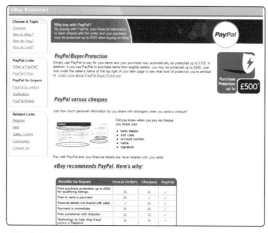

▲ PayPal and eBay - there's no escaping them!

use the online calculator at **www.ppcalc.com** to find out exactly how much charges will come to.

POOR CUSTOMER SERVICE

PayPal's customer service has also come under attack in some quarters, with the majority of complaints being centered around its support guarantee. Because PayPal doesn't operate under the same laws as a bank or financial organisation, many people are left disappointed when it comes to trying to claim money back. PayPal, it has be said, is almost a law unto itself.

If your claim is rejected by PayPal, and you feel that justice hasn't been done, apart from the police, there's nowhere else really that you can turn, short of something like the small claims court. It may offer guarantees, but these are only set by an extremely strict criteria that a seller must follow if they're to have any chance of winning their money back. Even then, if everything possible is done to follow the conditions set (all records and proof of postage have been kept, and the claim is within the period of response), PayPal can still decide to reject the claim.

Matters are only made worse with the lack of customer contact numbers on its website. If you wish to make a complaint, then you have to e-mail customer services and wait for a reply, which is hardly the swift response you need in a crisis.

So what can you do? If you're unhappy with your complaint to PayPal, you must obtain a letter from it that's known legally as a 'stalemate letter', confirming that there's a dispute. Once you receive that, you the have the right to complain to the Financial Ombudsman. A long, drawn out and rather painful process.

Like many things in life, PayPal is fine when it's working for you, but a complete pain when something goes wrong. Poor response times, unsatisfactory solutions and, most importantly, no way of legally challenging its decisions have resulted in some people losing a lot of money.

MARKET DOMINATION

PayPal has such a grip on eBay that buyers and sellers are almost forced to use it if they wish to trade. For more than two years now, it has been a compulsory ruling for new sellers on eBay's UK site to offer PayPal as a payment method in their listings. The rules are simple: if you don't use PayPal, you can't list your item. It argues that PayPal is the safest way of trading on the auction site, but this has still riled many people, who may have wished to avoid using it.

As it stands, the only category where PayPal isn't a must-have is in Motors, where by its very nature the

▲ It's hard to find any mention of rival payment services on eBay

collection and payment part of the transaction is normally dealt with in person.

The same ruling has been applied in other countries as well. That said, in Australia, eBay had to backtrack on its PayPal-only crusade. The ruling conflicted with the Australian Consumer Competition Commission, which forced eBay to delay making such widespread changes.

The PayPal-only plan effectively blocks other payment systems from use on eBay and, as such, many rival services are missing out on their share of any profits to be made. Buyers too, who may not wish to use PayPal, are equally left with no alternative options. Unfortunately, with eBay being as established as it is, there aren't many alternative auction sites to use either.

▲ In the early days, PayPal was no stranger to courts of law...

PayPal Alternatives

It's not just about PayPal when it comes to eBay. Here are some of the other web-based payment methods available

Without doubt PayPal is the king of web-based payment methods. Indeed, such is its dominance that you'd be forgiven for thinking it's the *only* web-based payment method, but it isn't - far from it. Of course, as an eBay seller, offering PayPal is in most cases compulsory. And as an eBay buyer, PayPal is undeniably quick and convenient.

It's always good to have a back-up plan, though. As a seller, you'll sometimes encounter buyers for whom PayPal is a no-no. Maybe they've had their fingers burnt in the past. If you're able to offer an alternative, you could swing deals in your favour. And as a buyer, what if you get tangled up in a claim or dispute and your PayPal account becomes temporarily frozen? Being signed up with a different payment system could be a life-saver.

Generally, PayPal alternatives fall into two categories. First, there are those that eBay specifically permits: sellers are allowed to offer them. Second, there are those that eBay specifically forbids: sellers who offer them are likely get their listings pulled (and maybe even their eBay accounts suspended as well).

EBAY-COMPATIBLE PAYMENT SYSTEMS

The PayPal alternatives that eBay allows are sadly few and far between. Here's the list: allpay, Cash 2 India (now part of Xoom), Fiserv (previously CheckFree), hyperWALLET, Interac (previously CertaPay), Moneybookers, Nochex, Ozpay (now defunct), Paymate, ProPay, and Xoom. All but two can be discounted; they're either heavyweight merchant solutions or intended simply for person-to-person transfers. Some also unavailable in the UK. The only systems of interest are Moneybookers and Nochex.

MONEYBOOKERS
www.moneybookers.com

The Moneybookers website immediately inspires confidence. It's a very polished affair - more helpful and better organised than PayPal's. If there's safety in numbers, the 13 million account holders should inspire confidence too. Sure, 13 million is small potatoes compared to PayPal's 150 million, but it's a respectable figure nonetheless.

There are three types of account: basic, 'Email Pay' merchant, and 'Gateway' merchant. Only the basic account is really relevant to eBay users. The nuts and bolts of the fee structure are shown below:

- Sending money = 1% (maximum £0.50)
- Receiving money = Free
- Funding = Free by bank transfer, cheque, Maestro, and Solo; 1.9% by credit card
- Withdrawals = £1.49 by bank transfer and credit card, £2.89 by cheque

▲ Moneybookers: one of only a handful of PayPal alternatives

▲ Moneybookers' fees are generally very competitive

▲ Nochex: a worthy PayPal rival

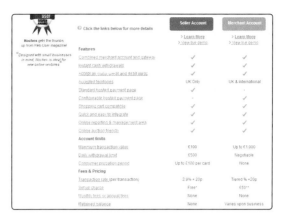

		Seller Account	Merchant Account
Click the links below for more details			
		> Learn More	> Learn More
		> View live demo	> View live demo
Features			
Combined merchant account and gateway			✓
Instant cash withdrawals		✓	
Accept all major credit and debit cards		✓	✓
Accepted territories		UK Only	UK & International
Standard hosted payment page		✓	
Configurable hosted payment page		-	✓
Shopping cart compatible		✓	✓
Quick and easy to integrate		✓	✓
Online reporting & management area		✓	✓
Online auction friendly		✓	✓
Account limits			
Maximum transaction value		£100	Up to £1,000
Daily withdrawal limit		£500	Negotiable
Consumer protection period		Up to £100 per card	None
Fees & Pricing			
Transaction rate (per transaction)		2.9% + 20p	Tiered % +20p
Set up charge		Free*	£50**
Monthly fees, or annual fees		None	None
Retained balance		None	Varies upon business

▲ The Nochex fee structure can be a little hard to understand

- Currency conversions = 1.99%
- Border crossings = Free

Unlike PayPal, it's the buyer, not the seller, who gets stung for the fees. But just look at those fees; they're so low they make PayPal look positively greedy. The snag, of course, is that buyers are never going to make payment via a service that charges them, not when they can use PayPal for free. Sellers can get round this, perhaps, by reducing the initial amount that buyers need to pay. The fees, once added on, will bring the total up to the full and proper purchase price.

Unfortunately, as a buyer, you have to fund your account in advance (the methods and fees for doing so are listed above). That means that if the cupboard's bare, you can't buy anything. With PayPal, of course, it's perfectly okay to keep your balance permanently at £0; purchases just get charged directly to your bank account or credit or debit card. By comparison, then, the Moneybookers approach is a hassle.

Even so, Moneybookers is a worthy PayPal rival. In some ways it's superior - look at the options for withdrawals, for example. As a buyer, though, the choker is finding auctions that actually offer it. And as a seller, how do you persuade buyers away from PayPal? The chief issue there is that Moneybookers and eBay aren't integrated, so buyers will always have to visit the Moneybookers website and enter the transaction details themselves. First, they'll have to sign up for an account too.

If you have your own website and want a payment system for a shopping cart, the picture looks somewhat brighter, however. The Moneybookers 'Gateway' merchant account comes with no set-up fees, allows full site integration, offers competitive rates (often lower than PayPal's), and lets you take card payments directly (without buyers needing to have an account). You'd be a fool not to at least give it consideration.

NOCHEX

www.nochex.com

Nochex, like Moneybookers, is based in the UK. Once again too, its website is polished and intuitive. There's no hint of how many account holders there are, but the company has had a presence on auction sites since 2001. Its name is also probably better known than Moneybookers'.

There are three account types: Personal, Seller, and Merchant. Broadly, these are aligned with PayPal's Personal, Premium, and Business accounts. The first of the bunch can be pretty much ignored, because it has some ludicrous restrictions. For example, you're not allowed to hold an account balance of more than £90 - a total deal-breaker for most people. All in all, the Seller account is the one for eBayers. The core features of this are:

- Sending money = Free
- Receiving money = 2.9% + £0.20 (regardless of your monthly receipts)
- Withdrawals = Free (£0.25 for less than £50)
- Maximum transaction value = £100
- Daily withdrawal limit = £500

An advantage over Moneybookers is that sellers pay the fees - just like PayPal. Also, there's no requirement for buyers to pre-fund their accounts - again, just like PayPal. One nasty downside to the service, though, is the maximum-transaction amount, which at a stroke renders Nochex unsuitable for sellers trading in items of high value. Also, the Seller account is UK-only; there's no facility to take payments from abroad or in foreign currencies. You should be aware too that inactive accounts - those not used for six months or more - can be charged an administration fee of up to £5 per quarter (unless the balance is £0). Ouch.

Interestingly, and stealing a march on both Moneybookers and PayPal, buyers can make payment via Nochex even if they don't hold an account.

However, such buyers can only spend up to £100 with any one card (in either a single transaction or several). Once that limit's reached, any further payments require a different card (with the same proviso). However, when 75 days have elapsed since a card's first use (the 'probation period'), this restriction is lifted.

Like Moneybookers, Nochex is a worthy rival to PayPal, and, like Moneybookers again, it's managed to pick up a good reputation for customer service (PayPal could learn a thing or two there). Also, there are some great features, not least of which for low-volume sellers is the cracking 2.9% fee rate (compared to PayPal's 3.4%). As ever, though, the big downer is lack of eBay integration.

Of course, if you've got your own retail website, take a good look at the Nochex Merchant account. There's a £50 set-up fee, but it's definitely a big hitter - you even get a dedicated account manager. In terms of services, it's a system that operates in a similar fashion to Moneybookers' 'Gateway' affair.

NON-EBAY-COMPATIBLE PAYMENT SERVICES

Now it's time for the PayPal alternatives that eBay forbids. The list is long, but there's little point in printing it, because if a payment system isn't specifically permitted, you can assume it's banned. Nonetheless, if you really want to, you can view it here: **tinyurl.com/yhw6sw**.

Why would you need a payment system that isn't accepted on eBay, anyway? Well, as shown in Chapter 7, eBay isn't the only auction site in town. On these rival sites, PayPal doesn't have the same stranglehold. Being signed up to a PayPal alternative could be useful for buying and selling via classified ads as well, and also for sending monetary gifts to friends and family. Which systems are worth considering, though? Below is an overview of some of the better ones.

PAYPAY
www.paypay.com
PayPay, a US-based outfit, offers a set of services similar to PayPal's. One advantage, though, is the two-level fee scheme for receiving: it's free for payments funded from another PayPay account (2.99% plus £0.30 for businesses); and it's a flat 4.99% plus £0.30 for payments funded by card (2.99% plus £0.30 for businesses). That's a refreshing change from PayPal's one-size-fits-all 3.4%, but it's a shame the card fee is so high. Sadly, there's also a charge for withdrawals: £0.99 to verified bank accounts and 2.99% plus £0.30 to unverified bank accounts.

Overall, PayPay is solid, safe, and deserving of recommendation. However, be careful: in some

▲ There's more to PayPay than the one-letter difference to PayPal might suggest

▲ PPPay is popular on eBay rival eBid

situations PayPal could be cheaper (as hard as that is to believe).

PPPAY
www.pppay.com
According to eBay, it only permits payment systems that are safe, easy to use, and able to offer strong protection. However, like all four of the services detailed here, PPPay, a UK company, meets every one of those requirements. For a start, it's the official payment method of eBay's increasingly popular rival eBid, and people are more than happy with the service there.

Could it be, then, that eBay's real reason for disliking PPPay is that it poses a serious threat to its own service, PayPal? Certainly the fees are competitive. Like PayPay, there's a two-level scheme for receiving: payments from another PPPay account are free; payments via card attract a 3.3% commission. A slight downer, however, is that sending or buying costs £0.49, and unfortunately there's also a 1% withdrawal fee (£0.75 minimum). Even so, use PPPay with confidence, especially as it's almost a must-join if you're planning to buy or sell on the UK's second most popular auction site (eBid).

NETELLER
www.neteller.com

Neteller might sound like a brand of chocolate spread, but there's definitely nothing nutty about it. As with PPPay, though, it's not clear why eBay feels justified in banning it - it's been around since 1999, has a solid UK foundation, and is even listed on the London Stock Exchange. It's true that Neteller is often the payment system of choice for funding accounts on gambling sites, so maybe it's felt this somehow tarnishes it.

Like Moneybookers, Neteller accounts have to be pre-funded. Doing that is free by bank transfer but 1.75% by card. Unlike Moneybookers, though, sending money costs nothing - in a more traditional manner, the recipient gets charged 1.9%. What really sets Neteller above the rest, however, is the Net+ debit card. You can use this to spend your account's funds at any online or high-street retailer that accepts MasterCard (no charge), and you can also use it for instant withdrawals at virtually any cash machine (£3 a time). It's a winning trick by any standard.

GOOGLE CHECKOUT
checkout.google.com

Google: now there's a name to be reckoned with. When the company's Checkout system launched in 2006 (2007 in the UK), it was regarded by many pundits as a being full-on challenger to PayPal. However, in reality it's always been intended as a cheap, simple, competition-busting merchant process for online retailers looking for shopping-cart

▲ Neteller's Net+ card is a serious incentive for signing up

functionality. For example, there's no virtual bank account, so you can't store funds anywhere. All purchases must be done directly via card, and all receipts are deposited automatically to your registered bank account (typically taking up to five working days).

Until February 2008, the fee for receiving was as low as mathematically possible: there wasn't one. And until May 2009, it was just 1.4% plus £0.20. Now, though, Checkout employs a tiered structure, with fees effectively identical to PayPal's. Even so, as a merchant system, it's got PayPal beat, both in user-friendliness and in popularity. If you've got your own website and want to start selling, you need a very good reason not to use it.

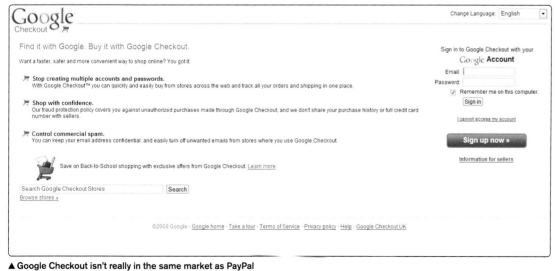

▲ Google Checkout isn't really in the same market as PayPal

Case Study: **Rel8 Media Football Memorabilia**

Can the beautiful game inspire a beautiful eBay business?

It's interesting to see how far football programmes have come over the years. From a mere team sheet to the revamped official offerings of the 1970s to the glossy magazines today, they've gone beyond a printed volume of information and features about various football clubs to become true collectors items.

One company scoring highly in this marketplace is Rel8 Media Football Memorabilia (**stores.shop.ebay.ie/ Rel8-Media-Football-Memorabilia**), an eBay PowerSeller from Scotland. Run by Andy McGregor from Fife, it specialises in Scottish programmes but it also has thousands of publications from the English leagues as well as hundreds and hundreds more non-league, international, reserve and FA Cup matches. There are many rare items among this little lot too.

ORIGINS

Andy has been a member of eBay since October 2006. He began by using the website as a hobby, to buy and sell various items to make some extra cash. Within a short space of time, however, he became increasingly attracted by the immediate access to a global market. "I soon realised that if I was going to set up a company, then the professional web presence of eBay would give my company a head start from the outset. The eBay interface also allows for easy record-keeping, which is important when accounts have to be compiled."

Andy's eBay shop makes great use of the website's facilities. The shop's header contains immediate information about the store, spelling out that the company specialises in football programmes and other soccer-related items and that new categories are added regularly. This means collectors are likely to make the shop one of their favourites and come back time and time again just in case something of interest appears.

The New Arrivals and Ending Soon boxes immediately below the header allow Andy to promote his new stock and help ensure that any items with a few minutes left get maximum exposure in order for them to sell. Andy doesn't need shoppers to bump up the auction price in these last moments, however; most of his stock is sold on a Buy It Now basis.

"I sell rarer items on auction," said Andy, "but the vast majority of sales are fixed price 'Buy It Now' items. Auctions can produce excellent prices if more than one person is 'chasing' an item, but you have to know which items will attract bids and which will not. Fixed-price listings are a much cheaper option for business sellers; unsold auction items are a drain on finances for business sellers."

COMPETITION

Before Andy began selling as a business on eBay, he checked out the competition, which is a wise move for anyone starting a company. "I was aware of other sellers using eBay to sell similar items to those I intended to promote," he said. "Many of them also sell through other avenues, including postal catalogues. I had bought from other eBay sellers and had made a mental note of aspects of their service that I was impressed with, and any aspects that I was less impressed with."

Andy understands his market well, so each match programme is clearly pictured so that any wear and tear – if indeed there is any - can soon be spotted. He also has a system of grading his programmes: excellent, good, fair and writing, and he explains on each listing exactly what this means. By having this information as a template, it cuts down on the time it takes to upload each programme.

The most vital information for each listing is contained in the title of each item, and Andy doesn't repeat this in the copy. Again, this is a way of speeding

Magazines (720)		FA Cup 81/2 West Ham United v Everton Jan 2	Buy It Now	£1.00 +£1.02	58m
Non League in the FA Cup (494)					
Foreign Programmes (341)					
Friendly Games (324)		FA Cup 8183/4 /2 West Ham United v Crystal Palace Repla	Buy It Now	£1.00 +£1.02	58m
Irish Programmes (316)					
Trade Cards (274)					
Non Football items (271)					
Books (243)		League 68/9 West Ham United v Coventry City Mar 14	Buy It Now	£1.00 +£1.02	58m
Badges (236)					
FA Cup (224)					
Tickets (209)					
Postcards (200)		League 68/9 West Ham United v Everton Aug 19	Buy It Now	£1.00 +£1.02	58m
European Competitions (152)					
Reserves / Youths (145)					
Scottish League Clubs (121)					
Internationals (67)		League 68/9 West Ham United v QPR Nov 2	Buy It Now	£1.00 +£1.02	59m
Aston Villa (50)					
Testimonials (48)					
Arsenal (35)					

▲ Andy puts the most important information in the title

up the uploading process, and although some customers may want more information in the listing itself, it does prevent quick browsers from being overwhelmed by information.

Although most items sell for around £1, with around 20,000 to 25,000 listings at any one time, the ability to generate revenue is stark. By being such a high-volume seller, it also negates the need to advertise. "I don't really see the need to advertise widely," he asserted. "The eBay brand is well enough known and because of the number of listings I have at any given time, people can easily find my eBay shop."

DIVERSITY

As with many businesses, Rel8's customer base is diverse. "There's a large community of collectors who have different wants," said Andy. "Some collect items related to their favourite team; some specialise in particular types of football match such as Internationals or European ties. I also find custom from people who used to be involved with football but didn't keep any souvenirs of their playing days. I've also sold to local historians who are seeking material related to a particular locality."

With so many items for sale, you'd think Andy would be overwhelmed, and yet he's still a sole trader. Although he is considering employing someone to deal with all the dispatching, he's also thinking about widening the range of memorabilia that he sells beyond just football-related items. Such a workload underlines the need for swift uploading of his listings, but there's still lots of work to be done in keeping up with eBay's changes and with postage costs. It's important for any eBay business to keep an eye on postage and packing so as not to be out of pocket when it comes to a sale.

"It took a while to fully understand the postal options that are available, particularly when sending items outside the UK," said Andy. "Royal Mail generally provides a superb service, but there are all sorts of anomalies and quirks in its pricing policy. Sometimes it can be cheaper to send an order in three separate packages than all together. This is a problem I face every year. I have to relearn the pricing system when Royal Mail implements its annual 'price review'."

STATS

Although football is hot on stats, Andy has some of his own, not least the fact that he has a 100% record over the past 12 months. By running his business efficiently and answering questions from members quickly, he has built a strong reputation for customer service. The lesson is obvious: no matter what you sell, you won't be able to build a long-standing business if you fail to be reliable and trustworthy.

"It's not that I don't come across problems," Andy explained. "Sometimes buyers offer to purchase items 'outside eBay', for instance. However, sellers must remember that eBay monitors the messaging system, and accepting such invitations is a breach of its policies. Therefore, I always decline. It makes life simpler for accounting purposes if all transactions are carried out through eBay.

However, feedback is very important for Andy. "I aim to maintain very high standards in terms of posting items out quickly and with appropriate packaging," he said. "The vast majority of customers appreciate this. I always try to resolve any problems as quickly as possible; like anyone, I can make mistakes, and the postal system can occasionally let me and my customers down."

Of course, in 2008 eBay changed its feedback rules, and sellers are unable to leave negative feedback for buyers. This led to much anger among many sellers, and Andy responded by changing the way he operates. "I have altered my policy on leaving feedback for buyers; I only do so once they have left feedback for me. However, I've set my automation preferences to ensure they receive feedback as soon as they leave theirs."

By stocking many items that aren't available elsewhere, he is helping to ensure people return to his shop regardless of feedback. But is eBay as geared up for businesses as it used to be? "Any business seller must be prepared to constantly evaluate what they're doing," he said. "In 2008 eBay made changes that were to the benefit of business sellers like me. In 2009 it made further changes, which made things more difficult for me and favoured private sellers. Things are always changing, and you have to keep on top of eBay's announcements and policies."

Chapter 7
eBay
Alternatives

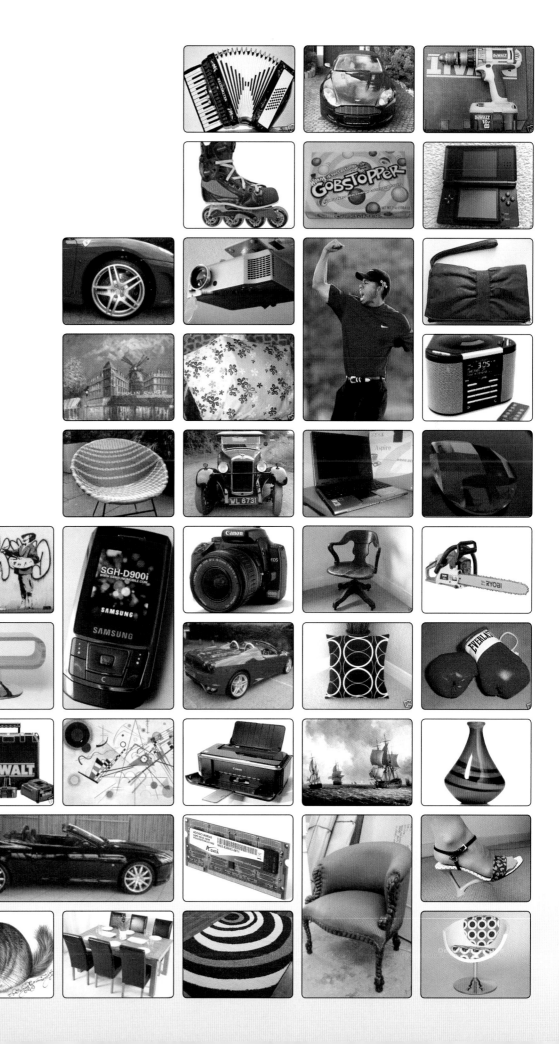

Using PlayTrade

A comparably new service that's proving something of a rival to eBay and Amazon Marketplace...

One of the biggest online retailers in the UK is Play.com. Relatively recently, the firm launched its own attempt to muscle in on the likes of eBay and Amazon Marketplace in early 2007, entitled PlayTrade.

PlayTrade is a service through which sellers can put up items for sale at Play.com. A link to PlayTrade sellers then appears on virtually every item description page. This works in a similar manner to Amazon Marketplace, in that Play's own price for a product is prominently displayed, followed a little further down the screen by PlayTrade's best price.

The obvious limitation is that you can only sell items that Play.com itself stocks, and even then, you can't sell mobile content, clothing or accessories. A further restriction is that the sale of certain electronics and

gadgets is limited to what Play.com calls ProTraders. That said, there are still tens of thousands of products you can list as a standard user of PlayTrade. Furthermore, it also specifically allows you to list collectable versions of a product. Amazon Marketplace didn't use to do this, but has caught up since PlayTrade introduced the feature. As such, you can highlight a book signed by its author, or a very rare limited-edition DVD, for example.

PROS AND CONS

There are certain pros and cons to using the PlayTrade service, and the biggest advantage is price. Play.com charges a £0.50 fee per completed sale, and then a commission of 10% on the final item price (the

How To... Sell On PlayTrade

1 The first thing you need to do is find the item you want to sell. In our example, we've got an *Iron Man* 2 game we'd like to list, so we choose the Sell Your Stuff option on the top menu bar.

2 This then brings you to a search box. We choose Games from the drop-down menu, type in 'Iron Man 2', and hit 'Search'. If we had an ISBN, UPC or EAN number, then that could be entered directly.

3 That brings us to this screen. We're selling the Xbox 360 edition of the game, because we don't really like it very much (it really isn't very good, sadly). Thus, all we need to do here is click on the 'Sell This Item' button to the right of it.

4 That brings you here, to a screen that looks very similar to its Amazon equivalent. Here, we fill in details regarding the condition of our item, and any extra information. Use the Comments box to elaborate regarding the item's condition, if necessary (particularly useful if it's a collectable item you're selling!), and you can select delivery region by scrolling to the bottom of the screen.

5 Now it's time to set a price. Remember, the amount has to include delivery costs! Use the Play.com price and the current lowest price on PlayTrade as a guideline. Go over those amounts too much, and you'll have little chance of attracting a sale.

exception to the rule is with tickets, where Play.com pockets 15% of the sale price, on top of the £0.50 completion fee). That's keenly competitive with its major rivals, and may be tantalising enough to tempt a few sellers, who are fed up with the service that other e-tailers are offering. As with Amazon Marketplace, there's no listing fee, and you only pay a fee should you sell a product.

However, in line with Play.com's policy of offering free shipping across the board, the price that you sell your item for must include postage and packing, so an allowance needs to be made for that. It's a great feature for a buyer, but may prove a headache for a seller. Furthermore, compared to Amazon Marketplace and eBay, PlayTrade is a service that's still comparably in its infancy. Thus, its userbase is smaller, although that could, conversely, make it easier to be noticed. That said, PlayTrade has been growing at speed for the past three years, and this is less of a problem than it was.

Do note, however, that PlayTrade has slightly different delivery demands from the likes of Amazon. Firstly, there's the aforementioned inability to add a shipping charge. Secondly, Play.com requires you to post out

ProTrader

Sellers who intend to move a reasonable number of items through PlayTrade may want to consider the ProTrader option. ProTraders don't have to pay the £0.50 fee on each of their listings, instead paying a £19.99 monthly subscription. This makes it a worthwhile option for those selling more than 20 individual items.

Further benefits include being able to list more than 100 items at once, and the ability to list items in otherwise restricted categories. Furthermore, special volume selling tools are also made available.

However, not all applications to become a ProTrader are successful, as Play.com has extra security checks for those who apply.

your item within 24 hours of a sale taking place. That's a little quicker than the one to two days you're given by Amazon, and this needs to be taken into consideration.

Most other features are broadly in line with what you'd expect. Funds, for instance, are deposited in a PlayFunds account, which incurs a 5% transfer fee when you withdraw money. There's no fee if you use these funds as credit towards a Play.com purchase, however. PlayTrade also works on a similar feedback system to its rivals, where positive and negative scores can be applied.

6 Further down the same screen, here you need to state what country you'll be posting the item from (usually UK), how many you have to sell (one in our case) and an optional reference code. The latter would be useful if you have lots of listings to manage! All done? Hit 'Continue'.

7 At this stage, you'll either have to sign in if you haven't already, or create an account if you don't have one. Both are straightforward enough. You ultimately end up at the item confirmation screen where, if you're happy with everything, you can press the 'Confirm Listing' button. That's it!

Should You Use Amazon Instead?

eBay isn't the only place you can buy from, and there are a lot of good alternatives, including one very familiar name

If you dig out the list of the UK's 50 most popular online retailers, compiled by IMRG-Hitwise and published regularly, you'll discover that it managed to include the same company twice in its top ten released in July 2009. And no, this wasn't a mistake, or some kind of typo. Instead, this was testament to the global reach and power of one of e-tailing's biggest names.

Leading the chart, as it pretty much always does and has done since the list first came about, was Amazon.co.uk. It's held this position for some time, and sits ahead of the likes of Argos, Play.com and Tesco. But number six in the list is the firm's American arm, Amazon.com. Granted, it's down from fourth place 12 months ago, but it still leads the likes of Marks & Spencer and Tesco Direct. It's staggering to think that so many UK residents favour shopping at an American-based site - with high postage charges and customs fees to consider - over the thousands of UK alternatives. Such is the power of Amazon.

It's worth noting that said list excludes online auction houses, or else no doubt eBay would march straight into the top slot (or at least put up a mighty fight for it), but it does also highlight the fact that there's a potent alternative if you decide eBay is not for you.

THE AMAZON ROUTE

For many years now, Amazon has run its Marketplace service, which allows small traders to offer their products on the site. Marketplace's big advantage is that it potentially lists your price alongside Amazon's on the same single product screen. So should a buyer search for a paperback copy of Dan Brown's The Lost Symbol, the product screen offers the choice to pay Amazon's price, but underneath that is a box labeled 'More Buying Choices', listing the lowest available price from new and second-hand alternatives. Clicking on that box will bring up a list of sellers and the prices they're charging.

Inevitably, this makes the Amazon Marketplace service even more price-focused than eBay, and the lowest price nearly always wins here. Even if you're only a few pence over the current lowest price, yours inevitably won't be the listing that buyers will be clicking on, unless there's a distinct positive difference in the condition of your item. On the upside, it does get your listing on the world's biggest online retailer, and gives it surprising prominence too.

Yet there's a hefty downside: Amazon takes a sizeable amount of your purchase price as a result. Considering it handles the entire transaction for you - processing the credit card payment, generating a packing slip, providing e-mail communication - you

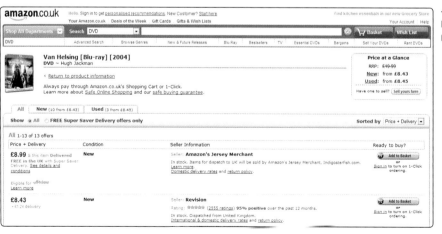

◄ Amazon Marketplace listings are increasingly popular

£0.01   Used - Good
- £2.75 shipping
⊘ LOW ITEM PRICE

£0.01   Used - Acceptable
- £2.75 shipping
⊘ LOW ITEM PRICE

£0.01   Used - Good
- £2.75 shipping
⊘ LOW ITEM PRICE

▲ Traders can sell books for just a penny, and make the money back on postage charges

Buy Used
Used - Very Good See details
Price: £2.01
Fulfilled by Amazon

[🛒 Add to Basket]
or
Sign in to turn on 1-Click ordering.

More Buying Choices
106 used & new from £0.49
Have one to sell? [Sell yours here]

Available to Download Now
Buy the MP3 album for £4.76

◀ Here, Marketplace sellers are offering a music CD for over £4 less than the official Amazon download version costs!

get a bit more for your money. Amazon charges an £0.86 fee on completion of every purchase, in addition to 17.25% of the selling price (an amount that decreases to 11.5% if it's an item in the electronics or photo categories).

HARRY POTTER
Imagine you sold a copy of Harry Potter And The Deathly Hallows for £5. Out of that money, for starters, would come that £0.86 charge, so we're down to £4.14. Take away 17.25% of £5 as well, which knocks a further £0.86 out of your takings, and the money that you're credited with from the sale is £3.28.

Only it isn't, because on top of that - and this is a bonus - Amazon also allows you a generous domestic postage allowance, which varies depending on what item you're sending. You have no variance on postage costs, because Amazon rigidly applies a uniform amount, so for a DVD it's £1.24, while for a videogame £1.99 is allowed. Books have a generous £2.75 allowance, and what's more, Amazon doesn't support postage discounts for multiple purchase. So for two slim paperbacks, Amazon automatically charges your buyer two lots of £2.75. However, there's a slight hit here, as Amazon also charges an administration fee on said delivery charges. On books, the admin fee - which is in addition to the large slice that Amazon already takes - is £0.49, leaving the postage credit at £2.26. Incidentally, the prices on VAT-chargeable items are set to increase from 1st January 2010, when UK VAT goes from 17.5% to 20%.

Let's go back to our (VAT-exempt) Harry Potter book. When we left it, we had £3.28 of our £5 sale price left. When we add the £2.75 to it, Amazon is now giving us £6.03 for the sale, and is taking the aforementioned £0.49 administration charge off. The total to us, therefore, is £5.54, and Amazon transfers our money every fortnight directly into our bank account. If ever you wonder why Amazon sellers sell books for £0.01, it's down to the generosity of this postage allowance, presumably calculated with a

good hardback in mind. A paperback book, in reality, would cost less than £0.50 to post. For certain items, then, the Amazon service is well worth using.

There's no listing fee, and your item remains on the site for 60 days. You pay nothing unless your items sells. For items that people go to Amazon for regularly - books and DVDs being prime examples - there's a hefty procession of potential customers likely to see your listing. If you're a Pro-Merchant seller (a status designed for those selling more than 30 items a month), then items stay on the site until sold.

However, there's a further fly in the ointment where Amazon is concerned: you can only place Marketplace listings alongside items that the site already sells. Therefore, if you have a DVD for sale that Amazon doesn't, you simply can't add it. Furthermore, if you have 50 copies of a new major book release coming in, you can't list them until it

Selling Toys

Given the large number of individuals who look to sell toys and games in the run-up to Christmas, and presumably given the corresponding increase in fraudulent sellers at that time of year, Amazon places strict criteria in place for this category at certain points of the year.

Amazon generally stops accepting new sellers into the Toys & Games category from September of each year. Furthermore, for a seller to list toys or games between mid-November and early January, Amazon asks that they've shipped at least 25 orders using Marketplace, and that they have a defect rate of at most 1%. These are restrictions to the Toys & Games category only, and it means that sellers looking to do business in this sector at the most lucrative time of the year need to plan ahead to be able to do so. If you fail to do so, you won't be allowed to sell your wares.

How To... List An Item On Amazon Marketplace

Assuming you already have an account with Amazon - which you will have if you've ever bought anything from the site before - it's not too tricky to get yourself selling on Amazon Marketplace. Here's how:

1 Here, we're halfway down the front page of the Amazon site. See that 'Sell Your Stuff' option on the left of the screen? That's where we're going to start. Give it a click.

2 From here, you need to choose what you want to sell. For this example, we're going to sell a copy of Jamie's Dinners by Jamie Oliver in hardback. So we've chosen 'books' from the drop-down menu, and typed the name of the book into the search box. Then we just click 'Start Selling'.

3 With books, you can also search by the likes of ISBN number, but seeing as it's a very popular title we're selling, it's unsurprisingly popped up at the top of the list. We're selling the 2004 hardback edition, which is first in the list, so we're going to click the 'Sell Yours Here' button to the right of it.

4 Check that you've picked the right item, and then enter the condition of the item from the drop-down menu. Our Jamie's Dinners had never been read and was in very good condition,. So we're choosing 'Used - Very Good'.

5 On the same screen, there's the option to add extra comments to your listing. In the same way you would with an eBay listing, this is where you should declare anything particular about the product. How damaged is it? Is it signed? Is it shrink-wrapped? Here's the place to let people know.

6 Hit 'Continue' and then it's time to set your price. Amazon tells you its own price, and the cheapest alternative already available from Marketplace sellers.

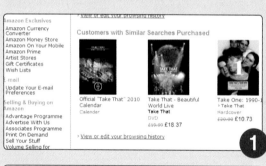

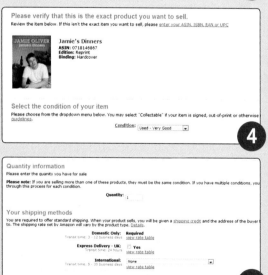

You can click on the list on the right to see if the low price is one seller or the general consensus, and then set your price accordingly. It's a good idea to at least undercut Amazon's price!

7 Scroll down the screen, and you then need to indicate how many copies you have to sell, where you're willing to ship to, and if you offer express delivery. We've only got one, and are only selling within the UK. And we've no express delivery, either. Once you've made your choices, click 'Continue'.

8 If you aren't already, you need to be logged in. First-time sellers now have to set up a selling account. If you haven't done this already, then you need to do so. If you have, then you'll end up at the confirmation screen.

9 That's it! Your listing is ready to go. Carefully check all the information that you're about to list, and hit the 'Submit Your Listing' button. You'll also find on this screen a breakdown of the fees and what Amazon will pay you if the item sells. Well done; you've listed your first item on Amazon!

has been released; you won't be able to try to attract preorders, even if Amazon has a listing page up for the product concerned.

Amazon used to try to compensate for this with its own Auctions and zShops services, but both of these seem to have been quietly closed down. The latter has migrated into the Marketplace services, while the former was simply unable to compete with the might of eBay. However, for the determined seller, there are still a couple of other tools at Amazon worth exploring.

AMAZON ADVANTAGE

Amazon Advantage is a scheme aimed at small publishers that are looking to get their products listed on the main Amazon site. It's available in the Books, Music and DVD & Video categories at Amazon, and allows you to manually add a new product into the site's catalogue, ready to be sold (although Amazon will review it before uploading it, a process that takes several working days).

Amazon Advantage is not a service that lends itself to someone clearing out the contents of their loft or garage, however, and is firmly targeted at those publishing their own works. That means certain requirements are in place. For instance, all books must have an ISBN number and scannable barcode, while a DVD must be shrink-wrapped and also fulfill the barcode criteria.

Furthermore, you have to formally apply for an account with the service, and pay an annual membership fee of £23.50. On top of that, you'll be expected to cover the cost of delivering your products to Amazon's warehouse, and of any returns to you.

Yet therein lies the key to Amazon Advantage. Whereas using Marketplace you may be holding your stock in a spare room or in a cupboard (unless you have a business account and pay for Amazon to handle fulfilment for you), with Amazon Advantage, everything is fulfilled by Amazon itself. Thus, should you be trying to publish a book, Amazon will initially take a copy off you, and if it sells, will order a few more. If sales continue to increase, then more will be ordered. Amazon expects a (large) discount on the product you're looking to sell, so it can make its own mark-up on the product, yet Advantage remains a potent and useful way for smaller media producers to break onto the site.

Seller Account

To set up an Amazon Seller account, you need a credit card, bank account, address and phone number ready. Amazon makes an automated phone call to you as part of the process, where you need to input a supplied PIN number. From there, you'll set up your financial information so Amazon can send you money from your sales.

Further Alternatives

Determined to find somewhere other than eBay or Amazon to do business? Here are some further options

According to some, it's the second most popular UK online auction site, but eBid nonetheless trails eBay by some way. However, unlike many of its other auction rivals, there's enough business done over on eBid to warrant at least taking a look. Certainly it manages to bring in a reasonable number of page views and item bids (it boasted over 2 million auctions when we were visiting), and it might be worth trying if you're struggling to find a niche on eBay.

Its big selling point is the fact that it doesn't take listing fees up front, instead charging you based on a final value fee, so there's no fee if you don't sell your item. Furthermore, you can pay a subscription, or a one-off charge, to quality for Seller+ status. The price for this ranges from £1.99 for a week, through to £74.99 for a lifetime. The big advantage is that you won't have to pay a final value fee ever again.

CQOUT (WWW.CQOUT.CO.UK)
CQOut - or Seek You Out - used to claim to be the UK's second largest marketplace, and it too is an online auction site that's existing in eBay's slipstream. It does boast a reasonable number of auctions, though, even though a heavy proportion of them appear to be Instant Buy auctions, eschewing bids in favour of an immediate outright sale.

When you sign up for selling, you're charged a £2 admin fee, and after that, there's no listing fee (unless you opt for extras such as second category listing or extra images), as CQOut charges a percentage of the item sale. It boasts too that its fees are less than eBay's, and presents a comparison on its site for your perusal.

CQOut has endured for many years, although it seems to offer little threat to eBay's dominance in the auction website business. However, if you don't mind paying the initial administration fee, you might find that you attract a new buyer or two by giving it a try (even if

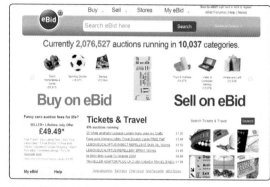

▲ The eBid site claims to be second only to eBay

▲ CQOut is a popular alternative

the business you get through the site is likely to be moderate compared to eBay).

WINNIT (WWW.WINNIT.CO.UK)
Formerly known as Auctions-United, Winnit is a UK auction site that's again trying to move in on eBay's market. It charges a listing fee, starting at just a penny, as well as a final commission of 1% on listings. However, there doesn't seem to be much traffic at all heading towards the site, and lower footfall means less chance of a sale. One of the most popular areas of the site is its adult listings, so it clearly serves a niche audience in that respect. But even then, the numbers are low.

FLOGITALL (WWW.FLOGITALL.COM)
FlogItAll appears to enjoy an even smaller audience than the sites already mentioned, but this one isn't the work of an international conglomerate. Instead, it's one

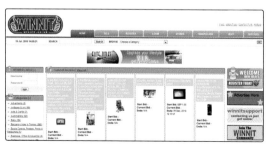

▲ Another alternative is Winnit

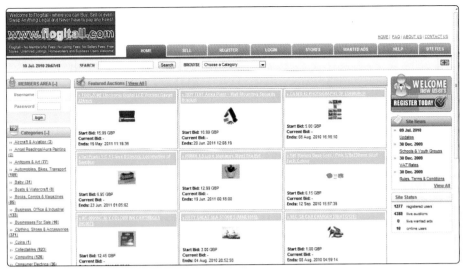

◄ Tazbar was successful for a while, but shut up shop in July 2009

man's hobby, which he funds himself and, as such, it doesn't charge listing fees. It's entirely free to use.

MICRO MART (WWW.MICROMART.CO.UK)

Some magazines still offer classified ad services through their publications and websites. If you're buying and selling computer equipment, a specialist publication such as Micro Mart can help. It'll put you in front of less buyers than eBay, but the upside is your items will be read by a targeted niche audience.

The Micro Mart service is free of charge, which is a welcome bonus. Other listings publications such as Loot and Bargain Pages also offer broader classified services, but with certain charges attached.

YAHOO! AUCTIONS, QXL & TAZBAR

After many years of trying to unsuccessfully compete with eBay and Amazon, Yahoo! opted to 'retire' its American auction service in June 2007. In territories where Yahoo! Auctions are still popular - namely Hong Kong, Singapore and Taiwan - the service continues to exist, and thrive.

The British arm of Yahoo! Auctions was closed down even earlier, in 2002, with a holding page still in place that directs users to eBay in its place.

Long-time eBay competitor QXL also shut its doors a while back, after many years of trading. It wasn't making any dents in the eBay business, though, and its closure wasn't unexpected.

The most recent eBay rival that's shut up shop is Tazbar. Tazbar was originally set up as an alternative to eBay back in 2006, in an attempt to snare less-than-happy eBay customers. It had some success too, and was certainly one of the busier eBay alternative sites in the market. However, the strength of the competition it was up against couldn't be ignored, and the decision to pull the plug was taken in June 2009. Tazbar's site was taken down for good one month later.

▲ Classifieds are a good way to reach a niche audience

▲ Yahoo! gave up trying to compete with eBay in America

Specialist

If you have a particular niche hobby, then it's always worth doing an Internet search to see if you can find a selling community specific to that interest. After all, while eBay brings in great quantities of buyers, there's little guarantee that it'll attract people specifically concerned with the type of items you're selling.

The same applies if you're buying; for instance, you'll find travel agents with auction modules as part of their service, offering late deals. It's an idea that's replicated in many sectors, so it's well worth hunting around.

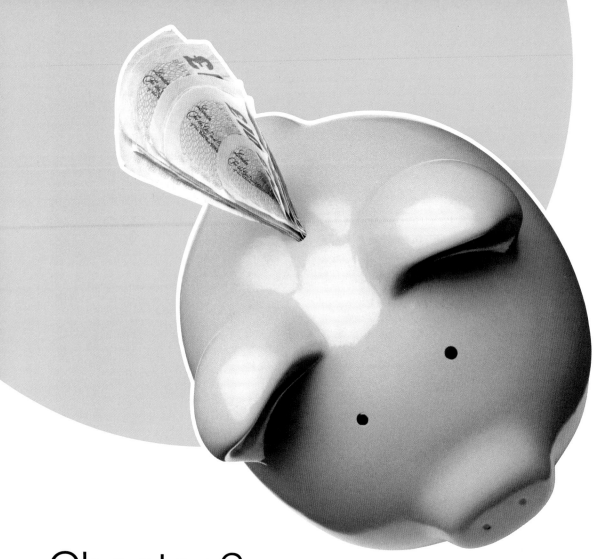

Chapter 9
Reviews Directory

Reviews Directory

Over the following pages, we've tested a collection of products to help you with eBay, starting with buying & searching tools...

AUCTION DESKTOP
www.auction-desktop.com

★★★☆☆

Free
PC - Windows

Auction Desktop puts the search step of eBay within a small, unobtrusive box on your desktop, allowing you to easily browse for items in a fraction of the space a web browser demands.

▲ Browse through a tiny box, but login and bidding is standard web browser stuff

Open the tiny program and you're directed to log into eBay's site and returned to the program to browse. Entering a search term returns mini displays of items that can be expanded to show more information.

If you spot anything worth bidding on, you're taken back to the eBay website where you bid as usual. Desktop notifications advise when auction end times are nearing and if you're the highest bidder.

Desktop space is precious, so anything that helps save it will be welcome, but the program requires you to launch your browser at least twice, limiting the gains. A small portion of the window updates with a list of what other searches are ongoing, letting you know what's popular at the moment, which may add to its appeal. And, with it being completely free, you certainly can't fault the price.

AUCTION INTELLIGENCE
www.auctionintelligence.com

★★☆☆☆

Free
Online service

▲ Some great deals can be found on eBay, even if the seller's typing skills leave a lot to be desired

Searching eBay is easy enough, but one thing you can't control are other people's typing or spelling abilities. For example, searching for 'PlayStation' will yield plenty of results, but you'll miss listings for such incorrect entries as 'Plastation' or 'Playtation', possibly losing out on some great bargains.

Auction Intelligence tries to address this problem, and using the service you can return incorrectly typed results for the item you're looking for. Simply type in the correct item name, and then click the search button, and

AUCTIONFINAL
www.auctionfinal.com

★★★☆☆

Free
Online service

Gazumping other eBay bidders at the last second is one of the best ways to get the items you desire on the world's biggest auction site, but this can be tricky at the best of times. Another way to get a good deal is to seek out auctions with no interest, and making a token bid before it closes.

AuctionFinal is an Internet tool that gives you this ability. Using the search engine provided on the

website, you can choose any eBay site (from all the global eBay outlets), choose the time left before the auction finishes and select a specific category (including 'all'). The engine will then return a list of auctions matching your criteria that are about to close, giving you the chance to win auctions for next to nothing.

Results include item descriptions, end time, time left and the asking price, and you can click on any results to go straight to the eBay page.

This is a very useful tool for snooping out bargains but unfortunately, you can't manually

▲ Use AuctionFinal to root out auctions with no bidders

type in actual product criteria, and can only search via eBay categories. Still, it's a handy trick to have up your sleeve, even with this limitation.

you'll see a list of incorrectly typed entries and, hopefully, some good deals.

A great little tool, the service would score higher if it let you enter search criteria with more than one word, but it's still a handy trick to employ.

AUCTION LOTWATCH
www.auctionlotwatch.co.uk

★★★☆☆

Free
Online service

▲ Auction Lotwatch lets you browse eBay as well as other auction sites for bargains

Saving precious time is paramount these days, and while some things can't be rushed, checking for the latest bargains on eBay needn't be a long and arduous task. In fact, you can search for items without even going to the website or downloading any new software.

A quick visit to Auction Lotwatch will grant you access to a speedy and easy search tool that can scour eBay, as well as a few other auction sites, in seconds, returning with a list of applicable items. Once the list has been retrieved, you can then view the items, prices and time left, and you can also click the direct link to the eBay page itself.

This is a great way to quickly view and compare auctions, and there's even an option to show common misspellings for the item you've searched for, so you

AUCTIONPIXIE SEARCH
www.auctionpixie.co.uk/search

★☆☆☆☆

Free
Online service

AuctionPixie produces a few eBay tools, and this particular applicaton enables eBay browsers to search for misspelled items.

▲Oh dear. Unreliable results don't bode well for AuctionPixie

To use the tool, all you need to do is enter your search terms and click the Search button.

can widen the search and include items you may usually miss due to typos.

As Auction Lotwatch is a website-based service, you don't need any extra software, and can access it from anywhere. But, although useful, the search results aren't as in-depth as a dedicated program, and the difference between searching this way and using eBay itself isn't that great. However, if you want to compare auctions on eBay to similar additions on other auction sites, you should find this useful. It's free too.

AUCTION REMIND
www.auctionremind.com

★★★☆☆

Free
Online service

If you fancy using your e-mail inbox to gather search results, Auction Remind may be for you. This is search automation of a different type. Register on the site, then log in and launch a search and the service does the virtual legwork for you.

Whenever it turns up items that meet your criteria, it'll fire off an e-mail with the details.

The benefit of this is that you can retrieve finds from anywhere you can access your e-mail, and don't need to be at

▲ Have search results delivered by e-mail to collect from anywhere you can access your inbox

your own desk to learn of bargains. The downside, of course, is that you have to access your mail to receive results, but if you're an on-the-go type and frequently download e-mail anyway, this may suit.

The Auction Remind site states a very firm privacy policy but, nevertheless, a web-based disposable e-mail account may be in order. It also says you can cancel your account at any time, and it's an interesting free option to consider.

AUCTION SIDEBAR TOOL VERSION 2.91
www.auctionsidebar.com/download.htm

★★★★☆

Free
PC - Vista or Windows 7

AuctionPixie will then turn up any results for you. Options are very limited, with only the search box and a listing of recently searched for items.

Sadly, AuctionPixie just isn't very good, and several searches we ran turned up no results, despite competing tools finding plenty. And the description for this tool still contains a typo, which doesn't instil confidence.

▲ Attractive and informative, Auction Sidebar Tool is a great eBay helper

Certainly one of the most visually pleasing eBay sidebars around, the Auction Sidebar Tool provides at-a-glance information about all of your current eBay bids, sales or watches. With product images, prices, number of bids and time left, this little tool can keep you on top of things at all times.

Also included is an eBay search bar, your own feedback and the ability to send notification pop-ups to you, making sure you're in the know. For more information, you can activate flyout windows simply by clicking on each item.

This is a very popular tool for eBay users, and deservedly so. It's small, easy to use and can provide all the info you need to stay on top of your eBay account.

BUYING & SEARCHING TOOLS

LISTING TOOLS

SNIPING TOOLS

SELLER TOOLS

MANAGEMENT SOFTWARE

MISCELLANEOUS SOFTWARE

AUCTIONSLEUTH

www.auction-sleuth.com

★★★★☆

15-day free trial; $19.95 (£12.33 approx) and $11.95 (£7.39 approx) licence renewal per year
PC - Windows XP or later

Finding items interesting enough to part you from your cash can take a long time using eBay's standard search. Yes, it does the job, but it can be a laborious process at times. Luckily, AuctionSleuth can help improve this whole system.

The core of the program is made up of a powerful, user-configured search engine. This allows custom searches throughout eBay based on the criteria you put in. This can be very specific, showing you results that meet your conditions to the letter, and you can also use the program to list auctions that are only a short time from ending, giving you a chance to jump in.

A very useful feature of AuctionSleuth is its ability to search for any new Buy It Now items that meet your criteria, and it includes being able to perform automatic refreshes at set times, so you can stay on top of new items without having to manually search for them.

Also included in the program is a fully integrated sniping tool. This isn't an online service, but runs from the installed program, and can make sure you're able to grab that last successful bid.

Other features include e-mail notifications, pop-up alerts, SMS text alerts and support for multiple users. And, as this isn't a

▲ Powerful searching and integrated sniping await users of AuctionSleuth

AUCTIONSIEVE 2.50

www.auctionsieve.com

★★★☆☆

Free
PC/Mac

As the author of this tool states, searching eBay can be a very hit-and-miss affair, and also a time-consuming one. Finding the best items and weeding out those you're not interested in is a pain. With this program, you'll be able to filter the results, separating the wheat from the chaff.

To use the tool, you first need to build your preferences and individual searches. This is done by choosing categories to create your 'sieves', and then using these to filter out the first level of unwanted items. You can then add 'catch words' to your searches to further trim down results to items

▲ Use word-based filters to eliminate unwanted search results

that contain these words. To ditch items you're not interested in, you add words to the 'Trash Words' list, and any items that contain words in this list will be removed from your results.

This is a simple system, but one that, if handled correctly, can make finding items you're looking for much easier. However, it can also hint at sledgehammer tactics and, if you're not careful, you can filter out too many results with the wrong word filters.

pay per auction service, there are no extra bid costs, or winning auction charges.

This is a great buying tool that contains a wealth of valuable options and, for the relatively meagre price, it's certainly worth a punt.

AUCTION TYPO

www.auction-typo.com

★★★☆☆

Free
Online service

As with many similar services offered online, Auction Typo can help find eBay sales where the seller has misspelled the item description, usually meaning that you'd never see the result in your listings.

By typing in the correct spelling and then clicking the search button, the search engine will scour eBay for any similar, misspelled results, and will then take you to the

corresponding eBay search results page. All correctly spelled results can be excluded, so you can browse through just the items you might not normally see.

You can filter results by choosing PayPal or Buy It Now items only, and you can elect to exclude words to further limit the results.

EBAY BUDDY UK

addons.mozilla.org/en-US/firefox/addon/11398

★★★☆☆

Free
Firefox

▲ Right-click Firefox to quickly access a range of eBay pages and services with eBay Buddy

With eBay Buddy installed, you'll be able to use the Firefox right-click context menu to access all sorts of eBay functions and screens, regardless of the website you're currently on. There are quick links to selling and buying items, your 'My eBay' page, and the eBay community. Within these sections are further menus, including links to the usual buying and selling tools, as well as web stores. You can even highlight text on a page and then double-click eBay Buddy to search the auction site, all without ever touching the keyboard.

Any extra ways to access your tools or services above and beyond the norm are welcome, and integrating eBay with the Firefox browser so seamlessly here is a good thing indeed. Sadly, at the time of writing, eBay Buddy doesn't work with the latest version of Firefox (3.0), but this should be remedied in due course.

EBAY ON IPHONE
pages.ebay.com/mobile/iphone.html
★★★★☆
Free
Mobile service

eBay has officially created a tailored eBay experience for the iPhone via a custom iPhone application.

Available from the iTunes store, the official eBay application grants iPhone users full, touch-screen-controlled access to the site and all its features. Thanks to the specially designed

▲ Get access to eBay pages on your iPhone

interface, which makes the most of Apple's sleek UI design, the eBay site is delivered with the touch controls in mind. You can easily glide your finger around the site, scrolling up and down to view items, and bidding on any items you wish using your standard eBay account. Best of all, it's completely free.

Before you use the software, you should ensure your iPhone is fully updated to the latest version. Once done, simply download the app from the iTunes store and then log on. The interface is simple and easy to use, with three main tabs - Home, Search and My eBay - at the bottom of the screen. The Home screen quickly shows a summary of items you're currently watching, bidding on and other stats. Other features, such as full-screen image previews, help further enhance the mobile eBay experience.

INVISIBLE AUCTIONS
www.invisible-auctions.com
★★★☆☆
Free
Online service

▲ Route out incorrectly spelled items with Invisible Auctions

Being able to find auctions with misspelled titles can be a very good way to uncover some great deals among the thousands upon thousands of items on eBay, and using Invisible Auctions you'll be able to get the upper hand. The Invisible Auctions website allows you to search for particular items, such as a brand name or specific product, on the global eBay sites, and the results supplied include the misspelled versions for the item you're looking for.

Additional options in the search include the ability to view Buy It Now items only, eBay Shops only and completed auctions. You can also search in both the title and description. You can filter results to wrong spelling, right spelling or both right and wrong, but the wrong spelling option is the best one to use to find better deals.

There are plenty of similar tools on the Internet, and Invisible Auctions is comparable to many of them. However, it's still a useful service to have when you're planning to purchase any items from the world's biggest auction, so take a look.

EBAY DESKTOP
desktop.ebay.com
★★★☆☆
Free
PC - Windows XP or later/Mac OS X 10.4 or 10.5

eBay desktop is a stand-alone web browser. It replaces the usual browser with a custom eBay front end. The package includes all the tools buyers need to browse and search the site, all wrapped up in an attractive interface.

From the main page you can select from any of the standard eBay categories, which can be drilled down further, and you can also initiate your own searches. These searches can be further refined by a useful search-shaping tool that allows you to add or remove certain criteria to

fine-tune your selections, and the displayed listings include thumbnail images, descriptions, prices and even a real-time clock that shows how much time is left in the auction.

Once you've found items you're interested in, you can add these items to your own watch list (with a single click on the results listings). This is found under the

▲ Serious about eBay? A dedicated browser is a great aid

My Items tab. Here all of your watched items will be listed, along with other useful additions such as messages, reminders and any notes you've taken. You can also filter items to recent additions only.

The Bid/Buy tab is very useful, and it's here where you'll keep track of items you're actively bidding on, along with the auction status. A list of your previous transactions is also available.

The Feeds tab lets you add RRS news feeds, which can be viewed through the program. All these features contained in a stand-alone application should make browsing and shopping on eBay easier for many users, not to mention more convenient. It's just a pity it's not been updated in quite a long time now.

MUNNIN-LIGHT

www.munnin.com/en/
home_thing.php

★★☆☆☆

Free

PC - Windows 98 or later

Rather than being a separate widget or application that partially replaces your web browser for eBay searches or watched items, Munnin is an eBay-specific browser. It's designed to work better for all you hope to accomplish with auctions - sales and shopping - with improved layout and functionality that your usual browser just can't match.

▲Munnin is a dedicated eBay browser with plenty of benefits

It uses a tree structure and tabs to organise categories of criteria, improving search results, and can be customised to show more or less windows. Munnin can even help with shipping costs, flagging high prices in red. Background scanning can monitor for

searched items at timed intervals, and notify you with an audible alert or by sending you an e-mail.

It includes an integrated database so results from all your activity can be stored, saved and retrieved at any time, as well as the ability to add your comments to each item, leaving helpful notes for yourself when debating between items to purchase.

The Light version is intended as an unlimited trial of the $14.95 (£9.24 approx) program, but check the website for details of requirements on older versions of Windows to see if additional files need to be installed.

MYTIMEZONE FOR EBAY

addons.mozilla.org/en-US/firefox/
addon/5497

★★★☆☆

Free

FireFox

This is an interesting Firefox add-on for eBay, which provides a selection of useful tools, chief among them being the date and time formatting tool. Once installed, the program can apply the date format you choose to eBay's pages. So even if you're looking around eBay US from the UK, you can still use UK format dates. The tool can also synchronise with eBay's own clocks, and you can choose from a 12- or 24-hour clock format.

Additional features of MyTimeZone For eBay include an automatic currency calculator for instant conversions to British pounds, as well as the ability to automatically update to current conversion rates, an auction-ending alarm and a range of extra tools designed to make using eBay more enjoyable, getting rid of such annoyances as eBay ads (it will skip them automatically). It also includes

the option of hiding 'featured' items in results, which is nice.

NABIT

us.nabit.com

★★★☆☆

Free

PC - Windows XP

▲ Nabit's developer claims "Winning is good" - true enough

Nabit is a handy, free application that aims to take all the extraneous effort out of eBay by providing a simple, automatically updating overview of your account. Without the need to open your browser, you can monitor current auctions, place new bids and search all eBay sites for potential bargains.

Results of the search include item descriptions, images,

current highest bid and the time remaining. You can search by name, item number and ISBN or UPC codes. Results can be filtered and sorted, and you can save searches for future use.

Nabit is able to send out alerts for any important events, such as a new highest bid, and anything you do in Nabit (such as adding or removing items), is automatically synchronised with your eBay account.

With a simple but attractive interface and a focused set of tools, Nabit may not be the most versatile application around, but it's a good quality helper all the same.

OS X DASHBOARD WIDGET

auctionmonitor.net/widget.php

★★★☆☆

Free

Mac OS X

Designed for the Apple Mac, this widget doubles up as both an eBay search bar and an auction monitor. When collapsed, the search bar functions like any

▲ OS X owners can stay informed with this widget

other, and you can quickly brows eBay for any items of interest. By clicking the expand arrow, you can unveil a full list of any items that you're currently bidding on or watching, as well as those you're selling on the site. This information includes the prices and remaining time. The program also links to your 'My eBay' page, and is updated automatically.

Very similar to the Vista Sidebar Gadget (produced by the same team), this is a simple tool that provides simplified information. There's no advanced features as such, but for speedy updates of your eBay activities, this is a good tool to have.

SEARCH GNOME
www.searchgnome.com

★★★★★

Free
PC

With awards from many respectable software sites, Search Gnome is a powerful and popular eBay search tool that contains many advanced search features not usually available to eBay users.

The program, once downloaded and installed, allows you to search through eBay as you'd expect, but also has a few nice extras. You can add searches to the application and save them, getting rid of the need to set up searches each time you need them, and you can quickly see any items

SHORTSHIP
shortship.com/firefox.html

★★★☆☆

Free
Firefox

▲ See exactly what items cost, with shipping, by using ShortShip

It's an age-old problem. You think you've found a bargain, only to get hit by tax or other unseen costs. Shopping the eBay way isn't immune to this, and you'll often see a great deal, then reel back as the shipping cost offsets this 'bargain'.

ShortShip is a free Firefox add-on that will add an extra sortable column to the end of eBay search results. This will automatically total together the sale price and the shipping, so you can see exactly what the whole cost of an item is.

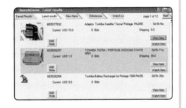

▲ When it comes to searching, Search Gnome has it all

that were added to eBay since the last time you searched. Even items that have been updated are clearly identified by the program, so you're always up to date. The program also makes it easy to search for items where the seller has spelled item names incorrectly. All this is handled via a single application window, and buttons will link instantly to the item pages that you wish to view.

SportShip also performs currency conversion, so if you're browsing for items on the American version of eBay, then you'll be able to see what the items cost in British currency.

YAHOO! MOBILE EBAY WIDGET
mobile.yahoo.com/ebay

★★★☆☆

Free
Mobile service

Yahoo!'s eBay widget for mobiles is a simple web link that takes users to a specially designed eBay portal created by the search engine company.

The portal enables the tracking of watch lists, bids and full eBay searches. You can bid for items from your phone and keep in touch with potential buyers or sellers on the go.

To use the widget, you need a phone that's Yahoo! Go 3.0 compatible (info available via the site) or have an iPhone, Windows Mobile device or a Nokia S60 handset. If you have one of the latter three phones, point your browser to **beta.m.yahoo.com**.

Listing Tools

ALIENFILES
www.alienfiles.net

★★★★☆

$69.95 (£43.24 approx);
free trial
PC - Windows 95 or later

Ask any kind of seller, whether a shopkeeper, market trader or eBay merchant, and they'll all agree that one of the most important things to consider when selling items is appearance. This applies to both the item you're selling and yourself (or your

shop). People are far more likely to buy a product that looks good, is presented well and is sold by someone who clearly knows what they're doing. Therefore, investing in a tool that can improve the look of your listings is a good idea.

Enter AlienFiles. No, this isn't a secret FBI department investigating extraterrestrial occurrences, but is instead a suite of tools that can give your item's listing a helping of sale bling. Using this program, you can change listings from simple text and images, to advertisements that feature image galleries, feedback displays, scrolling banners, Flash adverts and even embedded video clips. These listings are formatted in attractive templates, which can look far better than the usual white background, blocks of text and small images.

The program doesn't require any knowledge of HTML or other coding, and uses a simple interface that looks similar to a word processor, and even includes a spell-checker, so you can nail those ever present typos before committing anything to eBay. Most sections of the tool use a similarly straightforward interface, with plenty of guidance and tabbed options. Even adding a map to your location is easy.

There are no image-hosting costs, and you can also add other files, such as Microsoft Office documents (.doc, .xls, etc.), and video clips use the now familiar YouTube Flash player embedded into your listings. All of your creations can be saved, so you can use them or edit them later for additional items.

AlienFiles is an accomplished and intuitive tool, and using it should be a cakewalk for even the most inexperienced computer or eBay user. More advanced users with HTML knowledge won't get much from the program, though, as they'll be able to achieve the same results for free.

CHAPTER 8

REVIEWS DIRECTORY

BUYING & SEARCHING TOOLS

LISTING TOOLS

SNIPING TOOLS

SELLER TOOLS

MANAGEMENT SOFTWARE

MISCELLANEOUS SOFTWARE

EBAITOR

www.ebaitor.com

★★★☆☆

£14.95; 14-day trial
PC - Windows XP or later

Creating a good eBay listing can take a lot of effort, and if you're careful, you can come up with an ad that will pull in the bids. However, you could just as easily create an ad that fails to generate any interest. eBaitor, as its name suggests, is designed to help you reel in those bids and get more than a few tentative nibbles on your hook.

What we have here is an approachable and flexible listing creator that uses an attractive interface, along with a good deal of layout tools and even rudimentary image editing to output some very impressive product adverts.

The main thrust of the program is all down to layout. You can apply your text and images (by browsing to and importing them) to the listing, and can then move and resize them by simply dragging and dropping. Text can be formatted, fonts can be changed and colour schemes can be altered. All items can be easily aligned too.

▲ If you're struggling with listing layouts, eBaitor may be able to help

Images can be rotated, resized and cropped, and you can easily add hyperlinks to most items and apply effects, such as blur, sharpness and noise, as well as a range of 3D, artistic and geometric effects. There are also some other quite useful image tools above and beyond these effects, including red-eye removal and transparency support.

There are some templates included to get you going, and image hosting is free (although images will be deleted after 90 days).

Overall, eBaitor is good at what it sets out to do. It's certainly not the most creative tool around, and is more about actual layout than adding extra special features to your ads, but if you want to spruce up your haphazard clutter of text and images, then this may fit the bill.

LISTING FACTORY 2009

www.auctionlistingcreator.com

★★★★☆

$34.95 (£21.60 approx) Standard, $49.95 (£30.87 approx) Pro; 30-day trial
PC - Windows XP or later

▲ Some of Listing Factory 2008's templates are very impressive

Listing Factory 2009 is a step-by-step system to creating eBay listings. Like many other listing applications, the program is designed to make creating listings easier than using eBay's standard set of tools. It does this by letting users enter text and import images, to then tweak and arrange them into an attractive ad.

The program comes with a range of templates, and these can be tailored to your own needs, with images, galleries and other customisable content being available.

The interface is clean and efficient, and all the options are clearly displayed, rather than

GARAGESALE

www.iwascoding.com

★★★★☆

$39.99 (£26 approx) single user, $59.99 (£39 approx)
Mac OSX 10.5 or 10.6

GarageSale 6 offers an alternative to eBay's own, often slow, listing tool and is tailored for eBay users who access the site on Macs. Versions are also available too for iPad and iPhone/iPod Touch.

The program itself makes full use of the usual, attractive Mac-style interface, and

within this you can easily put together appealing ads for your items. Text can be added and formatted, font styles can be changed and images can be placed and manipulated.

The program features free image-hosting, 140 included templates, a built-in scheduler for automatically starting auctions, and compatibility with iPhoto, so you can access your photos directly from the service for use in your listings. There's also a messaging system and full support for eBay stores. Newly added Twitter support, embedding of YouTube videos

and Bonjour network sharing are also among the features.

GarageSale is a slick program with excellent support, including tutorial videos, FAQs and PDF manual resources, and the newest improvements make it an even

▲ If you've got a Mac and need a boost on eBay, GarageSale could be your knight in shining armour

hidden away in awkward menus. Also, some of the supplied templates are well designed and implemented, offering some of the best examples seen in any listing app.

Along with the easy-to-use editor, the program offers free image-hosting (100MB with Standard and 400MB for Pro), no image dimension restrictions, no monthly fees, and one licence can be used on two PCs.

Listing Factory 2009 is a great little tool, and one that's been thought out well. All the tools included are useful, and the templates (and the ability to edit them so easily) are a welcome resource. It's a little expensive for this type of application, though, especially for the Pro version, which doesn't really offer all that much more than the Standard package.

more useful sales tool for Mac owners.

MISTER POSTER

classic.auctiva.com/products/
MisterPoster.aspx

★★★★★

Free
PC

Larger-scale eBay sellers will know that posting batches of items onto eBay through the default site tools can be a chore, taking up a ton of precious time. Mister Poster is a tool designed to alleviate this problem and can make the process far easier and, more importantly, faster.

Mister Poster lets you quickly create and preview item entries, and is able to create whole batches of items to be added to your eBay account. Items can be scheduled to be added at certain times and you can also import old batches from eBay's Mr Lister.

Mister Poster has been designed with bulk sellers in mind, so any users who have plenty of merchandise to list should find this a very useful tool indeed.

This is a great little program that really should save plenty of time. Adding hundreds of items in a day is made far, far easier and the addition of scheduled listings means you can even set items up ahead of time and the program will add them automatically at the specified moment. This is great if you need to be somewhere and can't wait around.

Sniping Tools

AUCTION SENTRY

www.auction-sentry.com

★★★★★

$9.65 per year (£5.96 approx) for three-year licence; ten-day trial

PC - Windows 95 or later

According to the program vendor, Auction Sentry is "the #1 eBay Auction Sniper", and to go along with this claim, the program has plenty of awards.

In practice, the program stands up well too. Instead of the usual online service, Auction Sentry is an installed program that works in conjunction with the actual sniping tool provider, using its servers.

Once installed, the program uses a clear, colour-coded list to show you the status of any items that you're bidding on. Red entries mean that you've been outbid, green indicates that you're the highest bidder and yellow is used to notify you that Auction

AUCTIONRAPTOR

www.auctionraptor.com

★★★★★

$4.95 (£3.06 approx) per month, $52.95 (£32.73 approx) per year; one month free

Online service

▲ Hunt down bargains in the dying seconds of an auction with AuctionRaptor

AuctionRaptor is a nicely put together service that aims to be simple and user friendly. The service, which is free for the first month, offers unlimited bids on as many items as you like at once and e-mail notifications to let you know

if your bid is too low to win the auctions, giving you the chance to raise your game.

You can utilise item grouping to bid on the same item from a number of sellers (with the other bids being cancelled if you win one of them), and you can add items to your AuctionRaptor account while browsing eBay. Best of all, AuctionRaptor can place bids as little as two seconds away from the closing time, giving you a great chance of winning (Internet traffic permitting).

While the subscription price is a little more than many competing services, AuctionRaptor's simple but effective features are usually worth it, and the last-second sniping is a real bonus that beats most other services hands down.

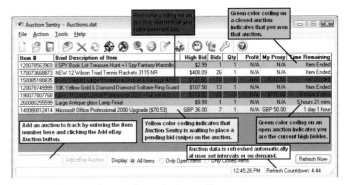

▲ Auction Sentry makes good use of colour coding

Sentry is waiting to snipe the corresponding auction.

The tabbed interface makes it easy to view your auctions, and you can filter listings to make things even easier. To snipe auctions, select the item you're vying for, and specify the maximum bid you're willing to make for it, as well as the time and date before the end of the auction. The program will then do the rest.

Notifications are displayed to keep you up to date, and there's a built-in browser that you can use to peruse eBay (or anywhere else).

There's no denying the power available in this bidding tool, and the actual program installation means you always have access to your current activity, without the need to visit a website. As it boasts on its website, "set it and forget it".

BIDNAPPER

www.bidnapper.com

★★★★☆

£7.99 per month standard subscription; £19.99 (ten snipes)
£36.99 (25 snipes).
Online service

Bidnapper is a flexible and powerful online bidding service that supports not only eBay, but a wide variety of other auction websites (more than 40 in total). As you'd expect, the service allows you to place bids automatically during the last few seconds of an auction, and you can specify your maximum bid amount and also protect your username from searches, to stop your competition from locating you.

Bids can be changed or cancelled at any time, and using the tabbed interface of the service, as well as the included searches, makes it easy to stay on top of things, regardless of how many auctions you're taking part in. The service's interface relays plenty of information about each bid, along with the product image, and you can make notes as well, should you need to.

Bidnapper has won plenty of praise for it successes, and is a good service for users of multiple auction types. The payment methods are flexible too, and you don't need to be tied down to a subscription, which is a bonus.

▲ **Bidnapper works with eBay, and over 40 other auction sites**

EZ SNIPER

www.ezsniper.com

★★★☆☆

$11.99 (£7.90 approx) per month subscription, ten snipes for $21.99 (£14.50 approx).
Online service

Billing itself as one of the cheapest sniping tools around, EZ Sniper features a flexible pricing plan, with last-second sniping for as little as £0.05 per go. Although it charges 1% of your winning bid on top of that, it isn't too bad, and should you be unsuccessful, you don't pay a thing.

All bids can be changed or cancelled as you see fit, and all transactions are totally secure, with your privacy guaranteed.

After a simple registration process, you can use the online applet to add snipes and monitor the status of your auctions, and you can bid on as many items as you like.

▲ **If you recommend it to a friend, you'll get a free month of sniping with EZ Sniper**

EZ Sniper has a free trial that grants you three snipes, and if you register and then recommend the service to your friends, you'll be eligible for the free service, with a whole month of free bids on offer.

GIXEN

www.gixen.com

★★★★☆

Free
Online service

Sniping services, by their very design, usually have a lot in

▲ **Gixen is a totally free sniping tool**

common, and similar features, as well as a price. Using them usually requires a subscription. Not so with Gixen. This is a totally free sniping tool that offers the same features as many paid-for options.

Using Gixen you can snipe auctions in the last few seconds and are able to use groups bids to make sure you grab that elusive item. The number of bids you can place at any one time using Gixen is ten, which is less than most other services. Considering it's free, though, you can't complain.

The developer claims that bids using Gixen are 99.5% reliable, which is a high level indeed and, should you wish to, you can pay for a Gixen 'mirror', which sends two snipes at the same time, effectively doubling your chances of getting that bid in at the last possible second. A downloadable desktop management Gixen tool is now available too, incidentally, also free of charge.

MYIBAY

www.myibay.com

★★★☆☆

Free web-based; $12.95 (£8.00 approx) PC, 30-day trial
Online service and PC (Mac version in beta)

Bid sniping is, of course, a very popular method of nailing that elusive deal on auction sites. Many eBay users now make the most of services that offer this essential trick for snagging items, and if you want to ensure that you stand a chance of winning some of the more hotly pursued deals,

▲ Sniping options in three browser flavours or installed

then tools like Myibay are very useful indeed.

Myibay is a bid sniping and auction management tool. Using it, you can manage and organise your current auction activity, keeping track of time left, current prices and more. Integrated into the service is a sniping tool that can be set to increase your bid on an item automatically should you be outbid. Simply set your maximum bid, and the program will do the rest and attempt to sneak that all-important last-minute bid in for you.

Myibay is available as a free (donations are welcome) service, using extensions, shortcuts and custom buttons for Firefox, Internet Explorer and Opera browsers. If you'd rather use the service locally as a client application, however, you can. You can download a Windows application that includes all the web service's features and free updates. The local version has the benefit of speedier performance, as it's installed on your PC, and may be a good choice for heavy eBay users.

POWERSNIPE

www.powersnipe.com

★★★★☆

$45.99 (£28.43 approx) per year
Online service

PowerSnipe has won awards from various websites for its

reliability, and is an accessible online service that comes with a 30-day money-back guarantee, so sure is its developer that it will help you win eBay auctions.

As is standard, the program only needs an auction number and maximum amount (as well as your user details, of course) and it will then attempt to outbid other users by sniping at the last possible second.

Daily updates are sent to you by the service, and you can also use it to snipe multiple auctions, including group bids.

You can view your full order history via the Auction Manager, and bids can be altered or cancelled should you wish (up to two minutes before the end of the auction).

For under £30 per year, and unlimited snipes, PowerSnipe is a good service to try if you do a lot of eBay bidding. However, occasional users may do best with a token-based service.

Seller Tools

AEROLISTER

www.aerolister.com

★★★☆☆

$24.99 (£15.45 approx) for 30-day licence; $124.99 (£77.26 approx) 180 days, 14-day trial
PC - Windows XP or later

Some of the most time-consuming aspects of selling on eBay include sending buyer feedback, relisting items and other clerical tasks like sending out invoices and order confirmations. These can be tiresome chores, unless you simplify the process, and this is just what Aerolister does.

Once installed on your PC, Aerolister is able to automate a

▲ Aerolister automates the more tedious eBay tasks

whole range of tedious tasks, including sending positive buyer feedback (after payment is received), invoicing and removing items from your lists. The

program also makes relisting expired items that haven't sold effortless, as it can automate this as well.

Since the program runs on your PC, it's faster and more reliable than the eBay online interfaces, and you can set up bulk jobs to handle masses of items at once.

This is a great program, especially for large-scale sellers, but the high monthly price is a bit steep for most. Casual sellers won't benefit from the software at all.

AUCTIONPIX

www.auctionpix.co.uk

★★★★☆

Free
Online service

AuctionPix is a long-running (since 1999) image-hosting service for eBay users. The service offers free image-hosting for all your item shots, and also offers a watermark function on uploaded images (to stop other people pinching your pictures), thumbnail slideshows, templates (both prebuilt and user-created) and image descriptions.

Because this is an online service, there's no software needed to make use of the abilities on offer, and users of any platform can take advantage of it, including Apple Mac and Linux.

There's more to the service than simple image-hosting, though. Indeed, you can actually edit and touch up your images online, and perform such functions as resizing, cropping and adjusting colours.

There are also some forms of protection. As already mentioned, you can

▲ Image hosting and a whole lot more are provided by AuctionPix

watermark your images, therefore ensuring your photographs stay yours, and you can also use the HTML encryption function to protect your descriptions, so other users can't simply copy them and then use them on their own listings.

Other new features offered by AuctionPix include a hosted image that can be used as an eBay auction counter, and a user-customisable cross-promotion slideshow, which can be added to all of your listings to advertise your other items to potential customers.

AuctionPix offers a good level of service, and is one of the better image-hosting services around at the moment. As well as auction image help, the site also features a selection of other eBay tools and template creation facilities that should be checked out.

AUCTIONPIXIE GALLERY

www.auctionpixie.co.uk

★★☆☆☆

Free
Online service

Scrolling galleries can help give your eBay sales potential a boost, as they look more impressive than a simple list of images, and can usually be inserted into any web page, including your own personal website or blog. This activates another route to your eBay items, meaning people can discover your wares without even being on eBay.

AuctionPixie is a free, Flash-based scrolling gallery that, although very simple in appearance, looks attractive and impressive nonetheless. Once you set it up, the gallery will scroll through your current items, and potential buyers can click an image and be taken straight to your eBay pages. The gallery also contains item descriptions, current bid prices and time left, and you can change the colour to your liking.

AuctionPixie enables nice, clean-looking galleries, but when it comes to advanced features, it's a little lacking, so it loses some marks when compared against other similar options. Still, it's a nice addition to traditional eBay selling tactics.

AUTOMATIC EBAY FEEDBACK

www.auctionpixie.co.uk/
automatic-feedback.aspx

★★★★☆

Free
Online service

Paying attention to feedback is crucial to any seller's success. Although it often seems the least fair area of doing business on eBay, it still needs to be dealt with daily.

AuctionPixie has another tool up its online sleeve in the form of feedback management for its members. Join up for free, and set the service to automatically respond to praise from your customers with like-minded good comments for them.

The way it works is you build up a bank of complimentary, generic comments (up to ten per eBay account) that can be applied to any successful sales scenario to be cycled randomly in reply to feedback received.

By using template tags, detailed on the site, you can customise feedback to include the eBay ID of the buyer, or item title, number, or price, for a more unique reply.

You'll also be advised by e-mail of any neutral or negative feedback that's been left for you, so you can quickly try to repair deals that have gone badly.

Automating feedback is fine, but it's advisable to keep an eye on things to know it's being handled professionally. With that caveat, this is a very good resource for sellers at no cost and a huge time savings.

BAYTOGO

www.baytogo.com

★★★★☆

Free (basic service)
PC

BayToGo is a small eBay tool that can keep you informed of auction status wherever you happen to be, even if you're in another country. It does this by sending text messages of any changes in your auctions to your phone.

▲ BayToGo provides a wealth of information about your eBay stats

As well as text notifications, the BayToGo widget can provide a range of information, such as total sales in a period of time, customer information and more.

The service is fully compatible with wireless devices with e-mail/SMS capabilities and can be tailored to your needs, sending messages at any time, or only between times you specify (so you don't get bothered at night or when out with friends, for example). You can also choose which events you wish to be notified about, such as new bids, first placed bid and so on.

This is a great little tool, and with its free option, there's no reason not to give it a go. If you travel around a lot, and need to stay up to date with your eBay auctions, it's a must.

BOLDCHAT

www.boldchat.com

★★★☆☆

$29 (£17.92 approx) per month Basic; $49 (£30.29 approx) per month Pro; $99 (£61.19 approx) per month Premier; free trial
PC - Windows

The best eBay sellers know that customer service goes beyond packaging and a thank you e-mail. Anything you can do to build confidence in your products and services will go a long way towards a successful business.

E-mail contact is fine and marketing tools like newsletters can add a professional touch.

Although those options can be fast, though, they're not nearly as instant and accessible as being able to chat live with potential buyers.

Adding a chat feature to your eBay store you can quickly answer questions, confirm details and firm up sales that may be lost in the slower to and fro of typed communications. Boldchat offers a wide range of seller solutions from less than $300 (approximately £185.43) per year for infrequent sellers to over $1,000 (roughly £618) per year for serious sellers.

If you have the resources to have someone available to chat about your items and terms, you may also want to add Boldchat to your sales team.

DISPATCH LABELS
www.dispatch-labels.com

★★★☆☆

Free
PC

It's often the small things that can take time, and the more tedious the task, the more you'd like to see a computer do it for you. When selling goods via eBay, few things are as tedious as writing out reams of shipping labels for sold items.

Dispatch Labels can help alleviate this tedium, and using it you can enter full details of all your customers, and create a list of mailing labels, which the program can print out for you onto your own sticky labels.

As well as printing the usual shipping labels, the software can also print out warnings (such as "DO NOT BEND") and you can access a full history of previous labels, so you can reprint existing customer labels for repeat buyers.

This is a very useful application that should save you plenty of time. Label designs and customisation are minimal, though, so more professional sellers may need to look elsewhere.

EBAY MARKETPLACE
www.facebook.com/apps/application.php?id=2554599077

★★★☆☆

Free
Online service

Facebook has become a huge, unstoppable juggernaut of social networking, and people can spend all day sharing their thoughts with friends. It stands to reason, then, that with so much coverage, advertising and linking to items you're selling on eBay through your Facebook profile is a good idea.

Using eBay Marketplace is one way of doing this. Available from Facebook itself, this service, once you've signed up for it, allows you to share your eBay listing with others on the social networking service.

You can share items you're selling with others, and you can also show people what you're bidding on. However, this may not be something you wish to advertise, so you can use the tool's settings to restrict what others can see, hiding your secret bids from everyone or a select few.

Once you link your Facebook account to eBay (by simply clicking a link), you'll be able to not only share your eBay info with others, but you'll also be able to view your friends' items using the built-in interface. All items can link back to the main eBay site, and listings found on the Facebook page include the usual assortment of information, such as images, descriptions and price.

A less useful feature, but one that some may find entertaining, is the ability to place a 'wacky' item into your friend's watch lists. This isn't all that valuable, granted, and is obviously intended solely for practical jokes. However, it could be used for subtly hinting at birthday gifts.

EBAY UK FEE CALCULATOR
auctionfeecalculator.com/uk_ebay_fee_calc.html

★★★★★

Free
Online service

The eBay UK Fee Calculator is an always-ready resource that you can access from anywhere. It will help you figure in the total cost of selling any item by working out both eBay and PayPal fees for the transaction, revealing what you can expect to retain and allowing you to adjust options or prices accordingly.

Simply tick the listing options, including upgrades, image details (hosting, Supersize, and volume discounts) and any promotional extras such as Gallery and Featured listings and the costs will be calculated for you.

There's even a handy eBay Breakeven Calculator to help you determine the absolute minimum sale price you need to charge to net your costs back - great for when you need to quickly clear merchandise without taking a beating on the sale.

▲ The eBay UK Fee Calculator is a fantastic tool for sellers

ECAL AUCTION FEE CALCULATOR (FOR EBAY UK AND PAYPAL)
ecal.altervista.org/en/fee_calculator/ebay.co.uk

★★★★☆

Free
Online service

This online service provides free calculators to compute and compare listing fees and costs on many eBay sites. The UK page is dedicated to the fee structures for users in the United Kingdom, and has you choose from Auction, Buy It Now and eBay Store format tabs. It also includes a special facility to add or change VAT for European Union countries.

Simply enter the details of the intended sale item, (or Multi-item Dutch Auctions), and tick the listing upgrades and picture services you're interested in, such as Gallery, or scheduled, highlighted or bold listings, and the costs will be tallied up for you.

If they seem too high to get the profit you're hoping for, you can make changes that alter the features of your listing and affect your bottom line. Having this info in advance helps you plan for the cost of every item and to control each sale.

Frequent sellers should be using fee calculators on a regular basis. This is a good, up-to-date choice for the infrequent seller or if you're working away from your desk and need access to a service to plan sales strategies away from home or the office.

FAST PHOTOS

www.pixby.com

★★★★★

$24.95 (£15.42 approx); 21-day free trial

PC - Windows XP or later

This image editing program is as streamlined as they come and concentrates on the improvements that matter, helping users make good, clear, colourful, correctly cropped images at files sizes that won't slow shoppers down.

It includes an extremely handy watermarking feature for identifying your unique shots as yours, and a one-click thumbnail creator for building nearly instantaneous galleries.

An instant browser preview lets you test your images as they'll be seen. Once you've got your shots perfected, a built-in

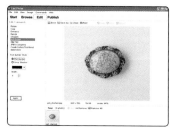

▲ **Picture perfect results without extra, unused options**

FTP feature delivers them to where they'll be stored.

The idea of an image editor made specifically for the needs of busy eBay sellers with many other chores to accomplish during their days is extremely appealing. The price is perfect, and it's easily recommended, even for those who own more fully featured image editors, where too many options may get in the way of good, quick, fuss-free item photo creation.

INSTANTFEEDBACK

www.merlinsoftware.com/instantfeedback

★★★★☆

$19.95 (£12.33 approx); 15-day trial

PC

Feedback management is undeniably a major admin headache for eBay sellers and InstantFeedback may be the pill for the job.

It's a small and simple program that sits in the Windows System Tray waiting and watching for feedback activity on your eBay account. When positive feedback is found, it can automatically generate positive feedback in return, reciprocating the actions of your buyers as well as sending along a thank you e-mail message.

If you have a lot of feedback to catch up on, the program can help with that too by producing

a list of those needing your comments and can also request feedback from customers who have yet to give their opinions.

InstantFeedback will also alert you to any neutral or negative feedback received, so you can make amends should you need to.

Feedback tools are very welcome, yet surprisingly few are to be found considering the value and cost of good and bad comments. InstantFeedback is recommended to those who prefer an installed tool that's updated often by its creator.

▲ **Catch up and keep up-to-date with InstantFeedback**

JUST SHIP IT

www.justshipit.co.uk

★★☆☆☆

Subscription - £29.99 monthly, £249.99 one year; 15-day trial

PC - Windows XP or later

Taking care of shipping labels is just a small part of the after-sales tasks you need to perform when using eBay and running your own business. There are invoices, posting items and keeping an audited list of all your sold items. This can be a headache, but a program like Just Ship IT could help.

This app aims to take care of everything, from producing shipping labels (which you can customise), to invoices and keeping tabs on previous sales. It'll even download your listing information from eBay, storing it in one easy-to-access place.

Shipping labels can include images, such as your company logo, as well as postage paid impressions, should you use this for easy posting. Likewise, invoices are fully customisable, and you can use existing templates or create your own.

The history of sold items is a big help to anyone wishing for an easier time keeping track of orders, and all details can be printed off for archiving.

Just Ship IT is a very useful tool, but at £249.99 per year to use the service, the price is very steep, especially as there are both cheaper and free alternatives that accomplish the same thing.

▲ **Just Ship IT takes care of after-sales tasks, but at a heavy price for light use**

KYOZOU WIDGET

www.kyozou.com/widget.html

★★☆☆☆

Price available on request
Online service

▲ Direct traffic to your sales from any web page that allows Flash

The coverage that can be gleaned from a presence on social networking sites is invaluable, so if you're planning on reaching the maximum amount of possible buyers, then finding a way to advertise your wares on these well-trodden avenues is vital.

This is where Kyozou Widget comes in. It's a specially designed Flash-powered listing box that can be slotted into any site that allows custom content. By pasting the required code into your page, you'll publish an interactive panel that contains all your current listings.

The information contained in the widget includes a thumbnail image of the item, description, price and end time. The panel can also include your own company logo and description.

The widget can be customised by the user, and different layouts can be set up.

Sadly, the widget isn't free, and you'll need to contact Kyozou for pricing, which makes it a lot less attractive for casual users. However, if you're interested in the widget, you can try it out by entering your eBay ID into the online demonstration. This will then show you a fully working widget, complete with your own current listings.

LABEL WIZARD

www.ledset.com/labwiz

★★★★☆

$19.95 (£12.33 approx); 45-day trial
PC

▲ Add company logos to your shipping labels with Label Wizard

Printing your own shipping labels via a dedicated label-making program doesn't just save time, it also adds an element of professionalism to your sales. It also gives you the chance to include details of any other websites or stores you that may run, further extending the potential for sales.

Label Wizard, like many label-making programs, enables you to create your own custom labels for use on your packages to be shipped. All you need to do is enter the customer's details and you're away. Using the more advanced features, though, you can also add images to labels, as well as business-card-like footers, containing your company logo and any other details.

Using the program is easy, and adding extra info and images is a breeze. Printing works with all the most popular label formats, and you can perform a search for any previous labels, so you can quickly print off labels for repeat customers.

Label Wizard isn't free, but it does provide some great label customisation, and the ability to advertise your services with every sale.

MERCHANTRUN GLOBALLINK 3.0

www.merchantrun.com/MerchantRun/

★★★☆☆

From $29.99 to $374.99 (£18.54 to £231.78 approx) plus 1% of sales, which reduces with plan scales and volume
Online service

While most casual eBay users will be content with selling the odd item once in a while through their country's eBay incarnation, more advanced, larger-scale sellers may not be so easily pleased. For some, an adequate portion of the market isn't simply with their native eBay, and getting their listings placed internationally is key. This is where MerchantRun GlobalLink comes in.

With this service you can simultaneously upload listings to

▲ Become an international seller with MerchantRun

21 eBay sites all over the world. This process includes category translations, currency conversion, cross promotions, prebuilt templates, and image-hosting. The translation services alone will make the it essential to many, making this a very interesting selling application to consider.

MerchantRun can also automatically relist items (including relist to store), and it can also keep a fixed number of listings active, and list according to a predefined schedule.

The ability to list items to 21 different international eBay sites is a huge bonus to anyone wishing to expand beyond their borders, and for sellers with truly international aspirations, this is a great tool to have close to hand.

Commissions are based on the item sale price only and don't include shipping, unlike other percentage-based offers - a detail often overlooked when choosing services.

PAYLOADZ

www.payloadz.com

★★★☆☆

Free Basic account (1GB storage), various Premium accounts
Online service

Not everything sold on eBay takes the form of physical objects such as collectable figurines, cars, clothes and CDs. More and more people have opted to use the auction site to sell downloadable software. With eBay being so popular, you're almost guaranteed extra coverage compared to an independent website.

Payloadz is a service that aims to make the sale of electronically distributable items easier for both the seller and the buyer. It works in conjunction with eBay and PayPal, and once payment has been received, will send a thank you e-mail to the buyer, along with details of where and how to download the software.

Payloadz is a welcome service for small-scale software developers and distributors who need a simple, effective way of peddling their wares. Providing secure file storage using its servers, you can opt to supply downloads or even provide CD copies. The free account can help test the waters for the sale of e-books and other digital files without long-term commitment.

PAYPAL FEE CALCULATOR

www.rolbe.com/paypal.htm

★★★☆☆

Free
Online service

▲ **Reverse calculate payment processing fees and more with this simple and effective online tool**

With this PayPal calculator you can check the impact and effect of payment processing fees on your sales. It will quickly do the math for you and save your brainpower for other tasks.

This calculator has the added attraction of a 'reverse' feature to effortlessly arrive at the net amount you want to receive for items you sell. Enter the desired amount and it calculates the exact amount a person would need to send you. Of course, there's the more traditional, straightforward method of figuring fees as well.

With a handy percentage-to-decimal conversion feature for 18 different countries, including a Cross Border Payment function, and links to other equally useful calculation tools, this is definitely a site worth bookmarking for frequent use.

RELIABID BID ASSURE

www.reliabid.com

★☆☆☆☆

0.25% of total sale (including shipping), minimum $5 (£3.09 approx) per month; 30-day trial
Online service

Non-payment is a frustrating experience for sellers. Too many bad debtors and your plans for successful selling fall apart. The ReliaBid program's aim is to eliminate non-paying bidders. It does this with a warning sign (seal) that states that payment is expected. Then it claims to follow up on the threat with action from a collections agency (for US buyers only).

This international seal service isn't recommended because, as any experienced seller can tell you, the chance of non-payers exists in any business, and you need to develop your own way of professionally handling it.

Plastering your pages with warnings is hardly welcoming to the trustworthy, and those bad bidders in the midst of collection proceedings are fobbed off with ReliaBid's website statement that it isn't responsible in any way. A poor choice for a solution to a common selling concern.

SOURCE CODE PROTECTOR

www.auctionpixie.co.uk/source-code-protector.aspx

★★★★★

Free
Online service

You work hard to stand out from the crowd of other sellers. Imagine the frustration of someone coming along and stealing your perfectly colour co-ordinated pages and poetic descriptions of your wares.

If you'd like to keep your hard work yours alone, stop by the Source Code Protector, enter your listing's HTML, press Encrypt and voila! Your code is transformed and written in a manner that's impossible to edit without decrypting, yet you can paste it, as is, into your listing and it will display as perfectly as the original.

If you're exceedingly proud of your work or have developed an above average look that you'd like to maintain as exclusive, this free service from AuctionPixie may appeal. It's only practical for infrequent use but, together with watermarked photos, helps keep your brand and style unique among the throngs of lazy sellers only too willing to copy and paste their way to success. Dedicated thieves can, of course, duplicate your look with some effort. Copying is done to save time and trouble, and this service could discourage those types.

SUPREME GALLERY

www.supreme-gallery.com

★★★☆☆

Free
Online service

Cross-selling is an all-important method of making yourself an eBay hit, and a popular way of achieving this is to use an integrated scrolling gallery, which can be placed on any website, creating further links to your eBay sales. Supreme Gallery is one of many options to achieve this.

Using the free service you can create your own basic scrolling gallery, made up of multiple product shots, with descriptions, time left, current bids and how many total bids each item has had, all in less space than a single shot would otherwise occupy.

Creating a gallery is about as easy as it gets. All you need to do is enter your eBay details, colour choices and other gallery settings into the site's form, and once you've agreed to the terms and conditions, you're ready to roll. Supreme Gallery will e-mail you the HTML for the gallery, which you can place where you like, including your eBay pages.

Supreme Gallery states that the gallery should improve your sales by up to 30%, and the product is 100% eBay compatible, so you should have no problems implementing it into your eBay account and, with a bit of luck, your items should start to attract more bids than ever. Also, as it's free, there's no real risk involved.

This is a good solid tool, and the gallery the service produces is clean and tidy, but it's also fairly limited in the information it can provide, and the actual basic design choices are restricted to simple colours and backgrounds, meaning that you can't really tailor it to your own tastes all that much.

More advanced users may be able to play around with the HTML code if they're feeling adventurous, but as this is a Flash-based tool, the possibilities are very limited. In the end, it's the functionality that's important, and the service does its intended job well enough to attract more buyers to your wares.

T-HUB

www.atandra.com/Prod_THub.htm

★★★☆☆

$300 (£196 approx) Standard; $500 (£327 approx) Professional; $700 (£458 approx) Advanced; set-up and training ($200 to $300, £130 to £196 approx) and annual support ($200 to $300, £130 to £196 approx) additional; 15-day trial
PC (MS Access and QuickBooks software required)

If you're running a serious business, either solely through eBay or with eBay making up a part of your operation, then you'll no doubt need to keep track of your orders, including sales figures, card payments, shipping costs and so on. Doing this manually is no small task,

Management Software

AUCTIONBLOX
auctionblox.com

★★★☆☆

$99 ($61.19 approx) per month plus 1.0% transaction fee for Merchant account; prices available on request for Enterprise account (no transaction fees)
Online service (server-based)

AuctionBlox isn't a stand-alone solution for selling items on eBay. Instead, it integrates with osCommerce shopping carts, as a means of selling through eBay and a store or website.

All of the standard, must-have capabilities common among seller tools are present such as invoicing, e-mailing, and shipping help.

AuctionBlox automates listing chores like relisting of unsold items and immediate listing of new items

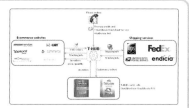

▲ T-Hub offers many benefits for advanced sellers

and even if with accounting software, getting your eBay info into it can be tricky.

T-Hub is a special tool that's designed to effortlessly transport data from your online store into the popular QuickBooks software. It'll handle order management, credit card processing and shipping   with just a few clicks, and should help to streamline the whole process.

T-Hub is a very useful tool for advanced, larger-scale sellers, but it's not for most eBay sellers. It's expensive and, of course, requires QuickBooks to function.

on the close of successful sales. Also, the notification process for winning bids, feedback, and other communication is streamlined as well.

More advanced features are available in the form of Checkout Redirect, which can generate 'upselling' opportunities by enabling sellers to view additional items you have for sale, as they're stepped through the payment process. This has obvious benefits to sellers, but also offers buyers savings on shipping of their combined purchases. An Inventory Management feature monitors stock, cancelling eBay auctions when items are depleted in shops to avoid overselling.

There's a wealth of help available for installing and getting to grips with the software, including a wiki, a community forum, and even a Feature Request Form via the website. But, at last visit, AuctionBlox has discontinued free trials (although they may be started again at any time) and the software looks complex enough to warrant a no-fee dry run before a long-term investment, especially as hosting services (for online storage of the software) aren't included in the Standard price package, but only with the Gold, Platinum and Enterprise editions.

AUCTION HAWK
www.auctionhawk.com

★★★★☆

$12.99 to $19.99 (£8.03 to £12.30 approx) per month; 21-day free trial
Online service (server-based)

Auction management starts on day one of deciding to be an eBay seller. If you haven't had any tools in place from the first sale, it can be more difficult to make the move after the fact. Auction Hawk imports up to two months of

listings "within ten minutes of sign-up". From then on you can continue with improved bulk relisting, scheduling and feedback tasks and get alerts on bad feedback.

You can produce, customise and track customers' e-mails (using an 'exclusive E-mail Ping feature'), and integrate bidder notifications with delivery tracking to streamline purchase through fulfilment stages. Sales, fees and full customer history reports are always at hand through popular financial and banking tools or Excel charts and graphs and can be searched easily on any criteria.

Listing duties are simplified through Auction Hawk's 1-Page Lister, which suits beginners as well as experienced sellers using professional templates, Item Specifics, and creation of customised shipping and payment profiles.

Its image hosting service, a substantial part of the pricing levels, includes scrolling showcases and galleries.

Flat-fee plans range from Basic with 220 listings, 50MB of space and 2,000 images to Unlimited listings, 500MB of storage and 20,000 images, with no percentage of sales due on any price or service category .

Auction Hawk throws an hourly hit tracker into the package so you have an instant, visual indication of the number of page visits your auctions are achieving. A 21-day free trial is more than enough time to see if it's worth the monthly cost to carry on.

▲ Auction Hawk's 1-Page Lister places everything you need in one convenient form

AUCTIONSPLASH
www.auctionsplash.com

★★★★★

Free
PC

AuctionSplash is a simpler sellers' tool than many of the others available, but it comes free of charge and can help sellers of all levels stay informed about their auctions.

It uses the free Microsoft .NET Framework 2.0, used by many freeware and shareware applications, to notify you of eBay events while you work on other tasks throughout the day. It monitors your auctions, advising you of bids and informing you about the number of prospective buyers who've chosen to watch your items.

You can put it to use creating templates for listings, which you can preview and refine, as well as finding out all the costs associated with selling the item. A single-page listing-creation tool steps you through ten stages to creating your listing, with free picture hosting, including supersize images. And it offers advanced selling tools such as scheduled listings, to launch your auctions on set dates and times, and a selling summary.

The software also follows sales, keeping track of payment status and producing labels to get merchandise to buyers along with handling automatic feedback.

▲ Auction Splash's listing tool is only a part of what's included, and all for free form

Additional tools aid buyers as well, with an auto login function that makes accessing eBay areas instantly from the desktop a cinch. Or use it to issue e-mail alerts before the close of an auction and use configurable desktop alerts, including optional audible signals, for up-to-the-minute news on auctions.

An intelligent search function, including misspelled words and a buying summary rounds out the program. There's a full User Guide with precise details of every aspect of the program and excellent full-colour accompanying images in addition to over 100 auction templates. And if that weren't generous enough, an interactive tutorial is also available on the website, with more planned, making AuctionSplash easy to recommend for both buyers and sellers without reservation.

AUCTION WIZARD 2000
www.auctionwizard2000.com

★★★★★

$100 (£61.81 approx) first year, $50 (£30.90 approx) per year thereafter; 60-day free trial
PC - Windows XP, Vista or 7

Some of the best software was developed to fill a need, rather than as a commercial effort, and if it's especially good it often reaches other customers by knowing just what the user wants to accomplish firsthand.

Such is the case with Auction Wizard 2000, a very fully featured seller management package that was originally designed by the owners to sell estate assets through eBay, and it includes the tools that proved to be the most helpful.

Choose from among dozens of included customisable listing templates, for professional pages without any previous experience of HTML, and select, resize, upload and remove images, all from within the same program.

A powerful database doesn't just sit there, holding onto your figures. You can generate equally powerful and useful reports for full control over financial decisions and directions. A built-in ledger tracks income and expenses, and data can be imported or exported in CSV format for use in numerous software titles. You can import data from any supported auction site, and back-up and restore tools - essential to your peace of mind - are included as well as a purge and archive utility to keep all your vital records relevant and tidy.

Inventory management and invoicing are covered, and there's unlimited support for multiple User IDs. E-mail is produced automatically at each stage of the auction process and a spell checker will help maintain a professional presence.

With built-in image-editing capabilities and e-mail, FTP and HTML modules, it's an all-inclusive package that goes beyond typical management software and more than justifies the price, eliminating the need for separate software to handle those tasks, and consolidating work into one program rather than across many.

The maker claims owners recoup the cost of the software through the quick relisting feature alone, with reduced fees for second-shot listings of unsold items.

Multiple users working across a network are supported, although each workstation requires a separate licence, but it's good to know the software can grow with you as you grow your business. With 60 days to trial the package, there's plenty of time to have a good root around.

Miscellaneous Software

FEEDBACK ANALYSER PRO 2

www.feedbackanalyzer.com

★★★☆☆

$37 (£22.87 approx)

PC - Windows 98 or later

▲ Make greater use of eBay feedback with this helpful tool

eBay feedback is one of the most useful ratings for anyone using the site. Knowing if the person you're buying from is reputable, or likely to take your money and run is important. It's also just as important for sellers to check out their potential buyers.

This research tool is able to provide you with full feedback information on eBay users, both buyers and sellers, and can split this feedback into neutral, good and bad, so you can quickly gauge the kind of feedback a particular person has received. These lists can then be saved out to several formats including text, CSV and HTML.

As well as this, the software can produce feedback ads for your own page. By using this HTML code, good feedback can be clearly seen on your page so people can see that you're a highly rated seller, and hopefully will be far more confident in buying from you. The program currently comes with ten free templates for these ads, all of which can easily be implemented in your page.

Seeing feedback ahead of time is useful, and this app makes this much easier by gathering details into one place.

FIREFOX EBAY-EDITION

pages.ebay.co.uk/firefox/

★★★★★

Free

PC - Windows XP, Vista or 7

Few would dispute that Firefox is the most popular alternative to Microsoft's Internet Explorer. One of the reasons for this popularity is its ability to accept plug-ins that augment its functionality. And yes, there are plug-ins for eBay too, such as this eBay helper add-on.

Billed more as a special version of Firefox (the download now includes the browser itself), this package adds an eBay sidebar that lets you stay in the know at all times while you're browsing the Internet.

The side panel includes a built-in eBay button, and pressing this opens up a menu with quick access to eBay's search, as well as links to buy and sell items, your My eBay page and feedback tools.

The actual eBay Companion Sidebar displays full details of current auctions and watched items, as well as feedback status. The eBay Alert Box does just that, and alerts you to any changes right away. Less intrusive 'Glow Alerts' can also be used, and if anything changes, the eBay logo in the browser will glow silently to signify an event.

There's a wide range of settings that let you take full control of the Companion, and automatic updates are included. Security is also given attention, and will show when you're on a real eBay or PayPal site, so you can avoid any dodgy fakes.

There are more accomplished tools available out there that feature a wider range of abilities, but few are as polished and as well integrated as this one, which is also free. A definite recommendation, and an essential tool for any Firefox and eBay fans.

GET4IT

www.get4it.co.uk

★★★☆☆

Free

Online service

A major question on both eBay buyers' and sellers' lips is, 'How much is it worth?' When you're looking to buy, you want to find the best price for the item you're looking for, and if you're planning to sell on the site, you don't want to price yourself out of the market by putting too high a reserve on your wares.

To help with this dilemma, you could visit Get4It. This website features a search function that lets you enter search criteria in

▲ Get4It can give you a good idea of reasonable prices when buying or selling on eBay

order to see what specific items have sold for on eBay before, as well as the most popular results. You'll see a graph that shows at a glance the price bracket similar items fall into, and you'll also get the minimum and maximum amounts people have paid.

You can narrow searches down by entering more detailed search criteria, and the engine even shows the maximum number of bids received for the item. A very useful research tool whether you're buying or selling.

RSS AUCTION

www.rssauction.com

★★★★★

Free

Online service

RSS (Really Simple Syndication) feeds are a fantastic way to be automatically notified of updates and additions to your favourite sites. And eBay pages can be treated to the same techie touches.

The RSS Auction page holds an online form that makes creating custom RSS searches simple by selecting categories and key words and choosing the length of time until the feed expires. Have your feeds fade after one month or up to a year, or never expire at all.

More advanced options include limiting item searches to your localation, setting minimum and maximum prices,

selecting currencies and sorting by a number of factors such as price, distance and auction time remaining.

Buyers can be fed information about collectable items all year round, and sellers can keep up to date with competition selling the same or similar items. Receive and read feeds in the traditional way, through an RSS reader, or by having them sent directly to any e-mail address.

This is a brilliant, free resource that can be used in many creative ways by anyone with an eBay business or buying habit.

▲ Have RSS feeds of custom searches delivered to you

The eBay FAQ

To finish off, a recap of some of the most asked questions surrounding eBay

And so we round off with a look at some of the common questions that emerge regarding eBay. Many of these were covered in more detail earlier on, but the following four pages are a useful quick reference guide nonetheless to some of the more common questions that pop up...

BUYER TIPS

Is eBay safe, and will I get a good deal?

Yes, it's generally safe to buy on eBay, but it pays to employ a bit of common sense. Something that's too good to be true is generally too good to be true, and sellers with lots of negative feedback tend to have that for a reason. Sellers, too, who try to circumnavigate the eBay system and approach you directly should be treated with a degree of caution.

Yet the truth remains that millions of transactions are conducted on eBay every year, the vast majority of which go without a hitch. Are you going to get a good deal? Again, that depends on how good a shopper you are! It certainly pays not to get carried away with the euphoria of bidding, which often ends up with you feeling like you've won something, rather than bought something, at the end of a furious bidding war. Compare the eBay price to other outlets, set yourself a strict bidding limit, observe it, and you should be able to seek out some very fine deals.

Do watch out for the likes of postage charges, though, and remember to factor them in.

Should I bid on an item if someone has a poor feedback rating?

It's not a good idea, in general, and should absolutely be avoided on high-value items. If you can't afford to potentially lose the money on the item, then don't bid.

If it's a low-value item that you're keen on, then by all means read the specific feedback and make a judgement based on that. Also, if the seller is local, it might be worth seeing if you can pick an item up in person, which will get round potential problems.

Ultimately, though, the feedback system is there for a reason, and while all eBay purchases have an implicit level of risk, bidding with a low-rated seller enhances the chances that something will go wrong.

Can I trust a high seller rating?

You can certainly take confidence from it, but again, for high-value items, it's worth doing just a bit more

How can I be sure a seller will receive the item I send?

Short of putting it in their hands yourself, you can't. However, there are some precautions you can take.

Firstly, for higher-value items, use a trackable form of postage, one that has insurance built into it to cover any potential losses should your item go astray. Also, if it's trackable, your delivery company will be able to tell you if an item has been signed for or not. Royal Mail offers tracking services, as do other courier firms, whose fees may not be as prohibitive as you may at first assume.

Even for low-ticket items, it's worth getting a certificate of postage from your local Post Office, which at least gives you some small comeback should your item go missing.

The onus is firmly on you to ensure that the item concerned arrives with the buyer, and if it fails to do so, you will have to issue a refund

Should I pay with PayPal?

It certainly gives you a level of protection, yes, although it's far from perfect. On bigger items, it certainly makes sense to use the PayPal service, as in the event of a problem, its own dispute channel is generally the most effective way to get your money back.

You should certainly avoid payment methods such as cash and bank transfer (both of which leave you no recourse if something goes wrong, and are regularly exploited by fraudsters), and Western Union transfers too should be setting off loud alarm bells in your head.

work. If, for instance, somebody is selling a £2,000 television, but all that seller's feedback is from people who have bought 1p e-books, then that should instantly raise alarm bells. The more homework you do (and you can click through and find out recent transactions that a seller has been involved in), the safer you will be.

That said, there's always a chance that things will go wrong. However, sellers with very high ratings, and large quantities of transactions, are invariably the safest to go with.

An item has arrived, and it's not as the seller described. What should I do?

Contact the seller immediately, but do so through eBay's communication channels, rather than private e-mail. That way, there's a communication trail which, should you need to escalate the dispute, can be easily referred to. Most problems are easily resolved this way.

You need to detail exactly how the item differs from the description, and take photographs to back up your claims. Do not start using the item. Tell the seller you want a refund, or a part refund if you still want to hang on to the item. If you don't hear back from them within 72 hours, then start a dispute with eBay and PayPal (if you paid with the latter). Again, keep the details clear, and include photographic evidence where appropriate. Tell eBay that the item was Significantly Not As Described.

I've won an auction, but the seller won't sell the item. What should I do?

This sometimes happens if an item, for instance, has

sold for less than the seller had hoped for, but it's still a clear breach of eBay's terms and conditions. Send the seller an e-mail asking them to supply the item, or else you'll have no option but to report them to eBay.

Should you not receive a satisfactory response, or any reply at all, then raise a dispute with eBay for non-supplying of goods. You should also leave them negative feedback. However, if someone doesn't want to sell you something, then no matter how hard you push them, you won't ultimately be able to get it. It's best, once feedback has been left and the matter reported, to chalk it up to experience and move on.

Someone has approached me about an item, and asked if I want to buy it outside of the eBay system. What should I do?

There's a clear advantage to conducting a transaction outside of eBay, given that it would save on both eBay and PayPal fees, which can ultimately be to the benefit of both parties. However, not only is this a practice that eBay frowns upon, it's a case of the risks far outweighing the advantages.

You lose the protection that eBay and PayPal offer on transactions, and should something go wrong with

a deal, then you're likely to be left high and dry. Clearly, eBay will not intervene in a problematic transaction that's taken place outside of its walls. It's thus recommended to refuse any such offer that a seller may approach you with.

SELLER TIPS

My auction has ended, but I haven't heard from the buyer. What should I do?

As soon as an auction ends, it's a good idea to send an invoice through the eBay system as soon as possible. If you don't hear from your buyer after a week or so, then something clearly has gone wrong. As usual, try the common-sense approach first: try to contact the buyer again and, if necessary, inform them that you'll have to go through eBay's reporting channels.

After seven days, you can file a report for a non-paying bidder with eBay (or you can do it instantly if the buyer has since left the eBay service and no longer has an account). If you still hear nothing back after a further seven days, you can at least claim your final value fees back (although you'll still be liable for any listing extras you bought, as well as the listing fee itself). To do this, you need to close your case with eBay within 60 days of the end of the auction. If you fail to do this, then eBay will not refund you.

Sadly, the eBay system doesn't allow you to leave negative feedback for the buyer concerned, thanks to controversial changes in the feedback system that were implemented in 2008.

I've sold an item, but the buyer has left me negative feedback unfairly. What can I do?

Feedback can be mutually withdrawn if both parties agree, yet if your buyer steadfastly refuses to do so, then, unfortunately, you're stuck with it. At the very least, though, it's worth replying to the feedback to state your case. This will appear alongside the feedback on your transaction that future bidders will see, so you at least get to state your side of the story.

It seems to cost a lot of money to sell my item. What am I doing wrong?

Quite possibly nothing. However, it's important not to get carried away when putting together your listing. Only choose the extras that will genuinely help and enhance your listing, for instance, and be wary of overspending on low-ticket items. Be aware of the final value fee eBay will take at the end of your auction, and adjust your pricing accordingly. There's little point allowing bids to start at 1p, when it's an item that you won't feel the financial benefit of until bidding reaches £20.

Don't discount using specialised alternatives to eBay, either, depending on the item you're looking to sell. For example, with a second-hand car, there are many outlets through which you might get a better ultimate price, once charges have been taken.

However, the best tip is this: be aware of what it's costing you to list your item, choose your listing enhancements with care, and set your pricing at a realistic level. You are, after all, getting your item in front of millions of potential buyers by listing it on eBay!

I've sold an item, and the buyer has now revealed that their address is outside of Europe. What should I do?

If you didn't list worldwide shipping in your listing, then you can refuse the sale. You should certainly do so if your buyer is located in one of the many hotspots for online scams - Nigerian, Thai and Indonesian addresses are notorious, for instance. If in doubt, it's best in these instances to not send your item out, as your chances of getting payment that won't bounce are much lower than usual, and also the chance of hearing from your buyer once a problem arises is virtually non-existent.

However, as noted earlier, you can't leave a reciprocal piece of negative feedback. Not surprisingly, this is not one of eBay's most popular policies, and you may end up having to simply dust yourself down and move on.

When should I post an item?

The ideal answer is when payment has cleared. With the likes of PayPal, that's straightforward, as you're informed when a payment has been made. If you must proceed with a bank transfer - and this is only recommended for traders you have some trust in - then again, allow three to four working days.

Cheques are trickier. When payment clears in this case varies from bank to bank, and even from cheque to cheque! Even when funds appear on a bank statement, that doesn't necessarily mean that a cheque has fully cleared, and said funds can still potentially be pulled. You can ring your bank if it's a

high-value cheque for guidance, but it's likely to recommend four working days at least, or perhaps even a couple of weeks.

Depending on your own financial situation, you might find it good practice to ship before this process is complete on lower-value items. At the very least, you need to advise your buyer throughout the process, and ideally list in your original auction that you will require a cheque to have cleared before you'll ship the goods.

SECURITY

I've had an e-mail from eBay asking me to confirm my account details. What should I do?

Ignore it. This is what's known as a phishing scam, where unscrupulous criminals will try to direct you to a plausible-looking eBay site. The problem? It's more than likely a fake designed to get your login details and password. Once a phisher has those, then they can log into your account, and potentially get access to your financial details too, as well as conduct fraudulent activity.

If in any doubt, don't click on the links in such an e-mail, and send it directly to eBay for analysis. It generally comes back to you quite quickly to let you know whether it's a fake or not.

AND FINALLY

eBay isn't the be all and end all, but used properly and intelligently, it can be a great source of bargains, and a good way to make some pocket money. Keep your expectations realistic, know when to walk away, and keep an eye on all the hidden costs. Happy bidding!

Reviews Index

THE INDEPENDENT UK GUIDE TO EBAY 2011

Editors:
Anthony Enticknap
Simon Brew

Writers:
Martin Anderson, Aaron Birch, Gaye Birch, Martyn Carroll, David Crookes, Jason D'Allison, Sarah Dobbs, Ashley Frieze, Ian Osborne, Mark Pickavance, Mark Pilkington, Kevin Pocock, Jenny Sanders

Design & Layout:
Laura Passmore, Heather Reeves

Digital Production Manager:
Nicky Baker

Bookazine Manager: Dharmesh Mistry

Production Director: Robin Ryan

Managing Director of Advertising:
Julian Lloyd-Evans

Newstrade Director: Martin Belson

Chief Operating Officer: Brett Reynolds

Group Finance Director: Ian Leggett

Chief Executive: James Tye

Chairman: Felix Dennis

MAGBOOK™

MAGBOOK
The Magbook brand is a trademark of Dennis Publishing Ltd.
30 Cleveland St, London W1T 4JD.
Company registered in England. All material © Dennis Publishing Ltd, licensed by Felden 2010, and may not be reproduced in whole or part without the consent of the publishers.
The Independent UK Guide To eBay 2011
ISBN 1-907232-30-3

LICENSING
To license this product, please contact Winnie Liesenfeld on +44 (0) 20 7907 6134 or e-mail winnie_liesenfeld@dennis.co.uk

HARRISONS OF LIVERPOOL

A chronicle of ships and men 1830-2002

Inanda in the roads at Port of Spain, Trinidad. Painted by Colin Verity RSMA for Harrison Line in 1986.

HARRISONS OF LIVERPOOL

A chronicle of ships and men 1830-2002

Graeme Cubbin

World Ship Society
Ships in Focus Publications

Published in the UK in 2003 jointly by
The World Ship Society, PO Box 706, Gravesend, Kent DA12 5UB, UK
Ships in Focus Publications, 18 Franklands, Longton, Preston PR4 5PD, UK

Printed by Amadeus Press Ltd., Cleckheaton.
Typeset by Highlight Type Bureau, Bradford
ISBN 1 901703 48 7

This page: *Craftsman* (275) in Liverpool. *[Malcolm Donnelly]*
Front endpapers: *Defender* (296) berthed in the West Float, Birkenhead on 5th September 1970. *[Paul Boot]*
Rear Endpapers: *Cap Vilano*, ex-*Adviser* (326) on the Elbe, 28th May 1997. *[Jim McFaul]*

To the memory of my dear wife Alice,

who with patience and forbearance lent steadfast support during the lengthy gestation

of this book but who sadly did not survive to see it brought to fruition,

I dedicate this work.

CONTENTS

Crofter (290) discharging in Avonmouth, 19th February, 1971.   *[Malcolm Cranfield]*

Charente Limited

Port of Liverpool Building, 2nd Floor, Pier Head, Liverpool, L3 1BY
Telephone: 0151-236 5611 Facsimile: 0151-236 1200

I feel very honoured to have been asked by Rear Admiral Roger Morris of the World Ship Society to make a brief Foreword to this detailed and illuminating account of the Harrison Line fleet history.

The author, Graeme Cubbin, joined the Company as a cadet in 1940, was promoted to Master in 1964, and subsequently became a Marine Superintendent in 1973. Captain Cubbin retired in 1986, at which time, so he tells me, he started researching this book. I should add that during his retirement he assiduously looked after all the archives in the museum in Mersey Chambers, until they were handed over to the Merseyside Maritime Museum to be retained for posterity.

This book is a monumental work, which has taken an immense amount of research. It is not just any old tome of a company's long and distinguished history, it is brim-full of anecdotes and incidents which could so easily have been overlooked and passed unnoticed and forgotten. This is what brings the book so alive. From the very beginning, from brigs and schooners, from steamers to diesel-driven cargo liners, to the bulk carriers and container ships of recent years, it is all here. Historical episodes and major incidents are described in detail; it is a complete record of the life of the Company from start to finish, in good times and bad. Naturally this includes all the details of the part played by the Company's vessels in the two World Wars, and I appreciate this opportunity to pay tribute to the grievous losses which were suffered - 27 ships and 130 lives in the First and 31 ships and 422 lives in the Second.

It has been sad for all those involved with the Company to witness the gradual decline of the fleet. This became inevitable as a result of the apparently limitless capital available to the global container operators, combined with their policy of never-ending rate cutting, which signalled the end for virtually all the well-known old British liner companies. However, it has been of some comfort that the Company was able to sell its long-standing liner trade to and from the Caribbean and South and Central America, South Africa and East Africa to the one remaining British liner company of any substance - P.&O.

It is also pleasing to know that Charente Ltd., the holding Company which owned the ships operated as the Harrison Line, still continues to operate in various maritime fields, in particular as a provider of charts and nautical instruments.

All who read this book in the years to come owe a great debt to Graeme Cubbin for the vast amount of work he has put into producing such a definitive account of a most distinguished Company with a long and proud history.

Sir Thomas Pilkington
Chairman of Charente Limited
June 2003

PREFACE

The question has been put to me many times. "Why on earth are you writing this history?"

Why, indeed! It is a fair question, and merits an answer, perhaps the easiest being because the story is there, waiting to be chronicled, like a mountain waiting to be climbed. But of course the answer is more complex than that.

The Victorian era was an age designed for entrepreneurs. Almost anyone with a good idea, a full reservoir of energy, a minimum of capital, and a modicum of luck could build up a thriving business, and amass a fortune. Labour was plentiful and comparatively cheap; regulation and red tape were in many respects immature; new types of powered machinery were replacing the ox and the horse; fuel to drive the new machines was readily available in vast quantities. The expanding British Empire was an inexhaustible source of raw materials, and the world market for British exports had never been greater. Liverpool and the Mersey lay at the hub of all this commercial activity, and the city quickly became the cradle for hundreds of new businesses connected with shipping, most of them family orientated. The firm of Thos. and Jas. Harrison began as such, the brothers Thomas and James, typical troopers in this entrepreneurial army of shipbrokers, shipowners, shipbuilders, shiprepairers, shipchandlers, shippers of cargo, and master porters. The growth of the Harrison fleet under the direction of the two brothers is proof of their success, an achievement which enabled their descendants to prosper well into the 20th century. It was during this latter period that my contemporaries and I, as ships' officers and masters, were privileged to play a small but not insignificant part for most of our working lives. It is chiefly on their behalf that I set about this task.

My own career with the Harrison Line began in 1940, when I joined the SCIENTIST as a cadet. My first voyage ended in misfortune, when my ship was captured and sunk by the German raider, ATLANTIS. However, I survived, and over the years obtained the obligatory certificates of competency, progressing steadily up the promotional ladder to reach the rank of Master in 1964. However, in 1973 I was invited to come ashore to assist the Marine Superintendent until my retirement in 1986. Which was when I began my research for this project.

I soon became aware of my limitations in the field, which is probably why this work is more of a fleet history than a company history. Ships and seamen have been my life; board meetings and balance sheets hazards on an ill-charted shore

close to leeward. For those who wish to study the overall policies and fluctuating financial structures of mid-Victorian shipping companies I would unhesitatingly recommend the works of the late Professor Francis Hyde of Liverpool University, of which *Shipping Enterprise and Management, 1830-1939; Harrisons of Liverpool* (Liverpool University Press, 1967) is a prime example. Professor Hyde has spared no pains to describe the development of trades, the founding of shipping conferences, and the disciplined marketing practices of those days, and his research, as might be expected of such a distinguished academic, is meticulous.

However, the main theme of this work concerns the ships and some of the men who sailed in them. The matters under discussion have been the subject of a great deal of original research, much of which has been, to say the least, fascinating, and all of it rewarding.

One of my early problems was to sort out the identity of one "T. Harrison", the nominated owner of certain ships listed in mid-nineteenth century copies of *Lloyd's Register*. Sometimes he was referred to as "T. Harrison & Co.", the "Co." usually turning out to be a motley collection of merchants, widows, farmers and clergymen, all of whom owned shares in a particular ship, and who had appointed "T. Harrison" as their managing owner.

However, it quickly became obvious that there was more than one "T. Harrison" owning and managing Liverpool ships in those days, and the problem was to isolate the Thomas Harrison of our history, and assign his ships to their proper ownership. Our Thomas Harrison was associated with Samuel Brown and Son from the earliest days, later with Richard Williamson and his son. These names, together with those of his brothers, James, Richard, John and Edward Hodgson, provided vital clues within the *Liverpool Register Books,* which, prior to incorporation in 1884, listed individual shareholders. However, it was not always that easy, for Thomas was often listed as a minority shareholder among others outside the family. One such example was the ship, PEVERIL OF THE PEAK (1860-1869), in which T. Harrison held only eight shares, and a certain Charles Barnes and James Laing held 28 each. Such a line-up may have prompted some doubt about the identity of T. Harrison, but the fact that the ship's passage details are recorded in the Voyage Books indicate that Thomas Harrison was indeed manager of the ship, as well as being part-owner.

Another Thomas Harrison owned a ship called the GOLCONDA in 1864. This Thomas also had a brother called James, and a nephew of the same name, while another relative called James Burgess Harrison also had shares in the ship. Their place of business was in the Clarendon Building, Liverpool. But the ship is not mentioned in the Voyage Books, and consequently was dismissed as an alien.

Yet another contemporary Thomas Harrison had offices in Wapping, Orange Court off Castle Street, and Dale Street at various times. His main interests lay in West Africa, but he was also associated with James Baines and the Black Ball clippers. He also had a son named Thomas, and the firm was known as Thomas Harrison and Son. Confusion over his identity led to two of his vessels, the NINA (1842-48) and LIGHTNING (1854-69), being erroneously assigned to our Thomas Harrison's ownership at one time. There were other shipowners called Harrison in other ports, notably London, Glasgow and Whitby, whose ships had to be carefully scrutinised in order to be identified correctly.

Having thus established ships as being owned, or part owned, by members of the Harrison family and associates, it was my task to seek out the vessels' individual histories, noting the salient points and incidents. To this end, the various publications issued by Lloyd's Register, the shipping columns of the London *Times,* and such of the company's records which have survived, proved invaluable.

No doubt there are those who will complain that this work is no more than a chapter of accidents. Alas, to some extent, the accusation is only too true. Mishaps, accidents, and disasters tend to be recorded for posterity, whereas smooth, humdrum voyages, which occupy some 90% of a ship's life, tend to go unheeded. Even during the several wars of the period, in which Harrison ships and men never failed to contribute significantly to the cause of the nation, encounters with the enemy were generally too one-sided to yield the essence of a good story, but the reader, nevertheless, will find several shining examples to lighten the general gloom.

Finally, the question arises, is the history complete? This, of course, can never be. No sailor ever told a tale that could not be capped by another sailor, and I cannot claim to have recorded every incident of importance or non-importance to have occurred in the past, and there are indeed many anecdotes which still remain to be chronicled. The theme is endless; my task is ended. I just hope that in this work I have contributed something to perpetuate the story of Thomas and James Harrison Ltd., shipowners.

Author (298) being assisted through the Liverpool dock system in October 1963.   *[Eddie Jackson]*

INTRODUCTION

When I first considered the prospect before me, I confess the task seemed huge and daunting. Over three hundred and thirty ships spread over a period of more than 160 years of incident-crammed history! I decided to arrange the work in intervals of about one generation - 25 to 30 years. This approach seemed to fit in with the way points mapped out during the firm's career, and suggested a book divided into six parts, each part describing the ships launched or acquired in that period, and preceded by an introduction outlining the company's aspirations, activities, and achievements during those years.

Part 1 From brigs and schooners to full-rigged ships 1836-1860 (ships 1-36) deals with Thomas Harrison's introduction to the shipping world through the medium of his early employers, Samuel Brown and Son, shipbrokers of Liverpool; the meeting with his patron, Richard Williamson; the arrival on the scene of his brother James; the development of the coal-out and brandy-home trade with the Charente ports of western France; and a description of the many brigs and schooners in which the brothers bought shares.

Part 2 The transition years - from sail to steam 1860-1884 (ships 37-90) is concerned with the advent of steam, and the Harrisons' first tentative moves in the ownership of steamers. Their trading interests were to expand world-wide, especially to Brazil and India, where their position in the emigrant trade to the West Indies became prominent.

Part 3 The years of expansion 1884-1914 (ships 91-166) covers the company's most expansionist period, from its metamorphosis in December 1884 as managers of the registered parent company, the Charente Steam-Ship Co. Ltd., to the outbreak of the First World War; taking in the early conference lines; the purchase of four ships from Rathbone's Star Line in 1889, and seven from the Rennie Line in 1911.

Part 4 The years of conflict 1914-1945 (ships 167-267) depicts the destructive effects of two world wars linked by a severe economic depression; the grievous losses of ships and men, and the valiant attempts to replace lost tonnage, to revive former trades and establish new ones. This part is by far the longest, but does not divide neatly into two smaller ones, as ships continued in service during both world wars.

Part 5 The innovatory years 1946-1977 (ships 268-324) highlights the measures taken to repair the ravages of the Second World War, and to rebuild the fleet. For the first time, the company laid down diesel-driven ships, and initiated the introduction of specialist heavy-lift equipment. After a late start, the latest new technical devices, such as true-motion radar and electronically controlled auto-steering gear, became standard fittings in all the ships.

Part 6 The ebbing tide 1977-2000 (ships 325 - 334) follows the swift decline of British shipping generally, and the company's fortunes in particular, leading to a rapid depletion of the fleet, flagging out, offshore manning, and the eventual disbandment and redundancy of the company's long-standing pool of experienced officers and ratings. During this period of orderly retreat, and despite sanguine efforts to combine with former rivals in the trades in order to combat the threat from the east and elsewhere, Harrisons' grip on the so-called niche trades was gradually loosened, releasing one after the other, until by October 2000 none remained, and Thos. and Jas. Harrison Ltd. ceased to exist.

There is an introduction to each part, in which I have endeavoured to describe the company's development (and latterly, alas, its decline) during the relevant period. I have also included some details regarding the Harrison family and their partners in business which I feel will be of interest to readers. But the overriding theme must concern the ships, and some of the men who sailed in them. Their story, I hope, will take you, the reader, on a venturesome voyage of discovery.

Two small notes concerning the convention used throughout: When referring to Harrisons I have used "the company", without further explanation. And except when quoting directly from a report or letter, all times have been expressed in the twenty-four hour clock even when this is strictly anachronistic, and refer to the local time at the position under review except when an alternative is expressly mentioned.

Graeme Cubbin, September 2003

ACKNOWLEDGEMENTS

The writing of a history of this nature could not be undertaken without a great deal of help from a variety of people and sources. I am grateful to the late W.M. Graham, former Director and Vice-Chairman of the company, for allowing me to consult his private papers. Moreover, it was due to an early initiative of his that I ventured to embark on this voyage of discovery. During the late 1950s he persuaded many serving and retired seafarers to write down their experiences in peace and war, and send them to him. There was a good response, and each item was punctiliously acknowledged and filed. And there the matter rested until someone could find the time to collate and edit them, a veritable gold mine of anecdotes and reminiscences - the very ingredients of historical research, as I discovered.

A most reliable source of encouragement and enlightenment was Nigel Hollebone, also a Director until recently. He has laboured long and earnestly to foster my work and keep it on the rails. As Editor of the company's *Newsletter* for nineteen years, he was instrumental in collecting and disseminating a great deal of material information which I have found extremely useful.

I also gladly express my thanks to the late Eric Carter Braine, erstwhile Director and Manager of the London Office. He exuded a lively enthusiasm for the old days, and was a source of much wisdom and experience.

Of course, I am extremely grateful to Sir Thomas Pilkington, the present Chairman of the Charente Group, and his fellow Directors collectively for allowing me free access to company records, and providing stationery, word-processing, and copying facilities. Knowing and understanding my purpose in hovering about the office precincts long after my retirement, they were always quick to further my aims with a brief word of encouragement at every opportunity. In this regard, I owe a large debt to C.D. Johnson, a former Director, and to his Secretary at the time, Hilda Dixon, whose early work in establishing the company's museum and archives provided such a firm foundation for my research.

My thanks are also due to Captains Michael Jones and Ian Mathison, and all my former colleagues in the Marine Department for assisting me with charts and sailing directions whenever I needed them. Nor can I forget the kindness of my friends in the Superintendent Engineer's Department for occasionally putting me right on technical matters beyond my ken.

Beyond the confines of Harrison's office, I would like to thank my friends and colleagues in the Liverpool Nautical Research Society for their help and encouragement, and for leading by example. My thanks is especially directed to Professor Valerie Burton, now of Halifax, Nova Scotia, whose timely intervention brought to my notice the unique *Liverpool Shipping Registers,* and made them available to me at the Merseyside Maritime Museum's Library and Archives Centre. My thanks, too, to the staff of that oasis of research, who on frequent occasions graciously trundled large volumes to and fro for my inspection.

I am grateful also, to my friends and mentors at the World Ship Society; to Rear Admiral R.O. Morris and Roy Fenton of the Publications Committee; to Kevin O'Donoghue and John Bartlett who patiently edited the text; to Michael Crowdy who first decided the work had merit, and to Louis Loughran for his help in tracing obscure house flag and funnel designs, and generating the artwork which illustrates these. My thanks are also due to John Clarkson for his close attention to illustrative material and page layout. Further afield, at the Ministry of Defence in London, a special word of thanks goes to R.M. Coppock of the Foreign Documents Section. His meticulous and detailed replies to my queries about wartime losses of ships did much to facilitate my research. I am sure I took up a great deal of his time, but he never failed to produce answers. My thanks, too, to Dr. Ian Buxton, Clive Guthrie, Brian Hillsdon, the late Rowan Hackman, Captain John Landels and William Schell, who provided details. A general thank you to photographers, photograph collectors, past and present throughout the world. Without them there would be no photographic record of Harrison's ships. Photographs not otherwise credited are from Harrison Line's collection, now lodged with the Merseyside Maritime Museum.

Across the Channel, my thoughts and my thanks go to Jean-Marie Williamson of Nantes, a direct descendent of the Yorkshire Williamsons incarcerated in France during most of the Napoleonic Wars, and who, twenty years or so after their release and repatriation, became early patrons, friends, and partners of the young Harrison brothers. Jean-Marie's unrivalled knowledge of his family's history was placed at my disposal, enabling me to cast new light on the important "French Connection".

On a more personal note, I cannot overlook the contribution to my efforts made by Betty Warburton, a well-respected Harrison Line secretary, whose warm-hearted enthusiasm for all things connected with the company's history provided a much-needed prop, and a constant source of inspiration. I am grateful to Michael Hunton, also a former Director, who thoughtfully shared with me the skills of his talented Secretary, Ann Toner. As to the lady herself, I acknowledge a debt I can never repay. For she it was who stoically typed out the entire manuscript, complete with tables and appendices, in her spare time! Effortlessly, or so it seemed, the text was absorbed into her word processor and recorded on disk to be recalled at will. It was a remarkable process, but there were times when Ann and her machine were taxed to the limits by my obsession for making amendments, and my tendency to add extra paragraphs to inconvenient text areas. Ann took it all in her stride, however, and even began to take a proprietary interest in the work itself. Thank you, Ann, for turning an unlikely liaison into a sound working relationship. I hope you have enjoyed it as much as I.

There were, of course, many other contributors, present and past, to whom I have cause to be grateful, but whose names are too numerous to mention here. They are acknowledged in the textual notes, but if I have inadvertently omitted anyone, I beg his or her forgiveness.

Finally, a word of thanks to my patient wife, whose support and encouragement never wavered, despite the seemingly endless nature of the task which inevitably weaned me away from chores of a more domestic nature. It is sad to reflect that she did not live to see the culmination of this work, but it cannot be denied that she is still a significant part of it.

BIBLIOGRAPHY

Bryant, Arthur *Years of Victory, 1802-1812*, William Collins, 1944.

Bulfinch, Thomas *Myths of Greece and Rome*, Allen Lane, 1979.

Chandler, George *Liverpool Shipping - A Short History*, Phoenix House, 1960.

Chatterton, E. Keble *Q-Ships and their Story*, Sidgwick and Jackson, 1923.

Churchill, Winston S. *The Second World War*, Cassell, 1952.

College, J.J. *Ships of the Royal Navy Volume 2*, David and Charles, Newton Abbot, 1970.

Cowden, J.E. and Duffy, J.O.C. *The Elder Dempster Fleet History, 1852-1985*, Mallett and Bell Publications, 1986.

Davidson, A.S. *Marine Art and Liverpool*, Waine Research Publications, Wolverhampton, 1986.

Dent, G.R. and Nyembezi, C.L.S. *The Scholar's Zulu Dictionary*, Shuter and Shooter, Pietermaritzburg, 1969.

Detmers, Captain Theodor *The Raider KORMORAN*, William Kimber, 1959.

Eddy, P. and Linklater, M. *The Falklands War*, William Collins, Glasgow, and Times Newspapers,1982.

Fisk, Robert *Pity the Nation*, Andre-Deutsch Ltd, 1990.

Gilmour, David *Lebanon: The Fractured Country*, M. Robertson, 1983.

Graham, Gerald S. *The Ascendancy of the Sailing Ship, 1850-1885*, Economic History Review, Volume 9, 1956/57.

Harrison Line Newsletters Editors: Graham W.M. (1973-1981), and Hollebone N. J. (1981-2000)

Grant, Robert M. *U-Boats Destroyed 1914-18*, Putnam, 1964.

Haws, Duncan *Merchant Fleets, Volume 15 - Thos. and Jas. Harrison*, T.C.L. Publications, Hereford, 1988.

H.M.S.O. *British Vessels Lost at Sea, 1914-1918*, Reprinted by Patrick Stephens, Cambridge, 1977.

H.M.S.O. *British Vessels Lost at Sea, 1939-1945*, Reprinted by Patrick Stephens, Cambridge, 1976.

Hope, Ronald *A New History of British Shipping*, John Murray, 1990.

Hoyt, Edwin P. *The U-Boat Wars*, Robert Hale,1984.

Humble, Richard *Hitler's High Seas Fleet*, Ballantine, 1972.

Hurd, Archibald *The Merchant Navy*, John Murray, 1924.

Hyde, Francis E. *Liverpool and the Mersey*, David and Charles, Newton Abbot, 1971.

Hyde, Francis E. *Shipping Enterprise and Management, 1830-1939: Harrisons of Liverpool*, Liverpool University Press, Liverpool, 1967.

Infield, Glen B. *Disaster at Bari*, Robert Hale and Co., 1974.

Irving, David *The Destruction of Convoy PQ17*, William Kimber, 1980.

Lecky, S.T.S. *Wrinkles in Practical Navigation*, 15th Edition George Philip, 1910.

Lewis, F.M. and Gnosspelius, J. *An Outline History of the Grange Hotel, Holmefield Road, Aigburth*, The Gateacre Society, Liverpool, 1989.

Liverpool Registry of Merchant Ships, and Transaction Books, from 1739, Merseyside Maritime Museum Records Centre, and the Liverpool Custom House.

Lloyd's List Law Reports, Lloyd's, London.

Lloyd's Register of Shipping, Lloyd's Register.

Lloyd's Weekly List of Casualties, Lloyd's, London.

Lubbock, Basil *The Blackwall Frigates*, Brown, Son, and Ferguson, Glasgow.

Macdougall, Philip *Mysteries on the High Seas*, David and Charles, Newton Abbot, 1984.

Marine News, World Ship Society, Kendal and Gravesend, 1947-date

Mohr, Ulrich, and Sellwood, A.V. *ATLANTIS: The Story of a Germany Surface Raider*, Werner Laurie, 1955.

Moore, Arthur R. *A Careless Word...A Needless Sinking*, American Merchant Marine Museum, King's Point, New York, 1983.

Mountfield, Stuart, *Western Gateway*, Liverpool University Press, Liverpool, 1965.

Munro, D.J. *Convoys, Blockades, and Mystery Towers*, Sampson Low, Marston.

Murray, Marischal *Ships and South Africa*, Oxford University Press, 1933.

Murray, William *Atlantic Rendezvous*, Nautical Publishing Co., Lymington, 1970.

Nepveux, Ethel S. *George Alfred Trenholm, and the Company That Went to War, 1861-1865*, Published privately, Charleston, South Carolina, 1973.

Norie, J.W. *Norie's Nautical Tables*, Imray, Laurie, Norie and Wilson, 1938.

Orchard, B. Guinness, *Liverpool's Legion of Honour*, 1893.

Pemsell, Helmut translated by Smith, D.G, *Atlas of Naval Warfare*, Arms and Armour Press, 1977.

Purnell, *History of the 20th Century*, B.P.C. Publishing, 1968.

Rabson, Stephen and O'Donoghue, Kevin, *P. and O. - A Fleet History*, World Ship Society, Kendal, 1988.

Reed, Thomas, *Reed's Tables of Distances*, Thomas Reed and Co. Ltd., Sunderland. (12th Edn., 1953).

Richie, Carson I.A. *Q-Ships*, Terence Dalton, 1985.

Ritchie-Noakes, Nancy, *Liverpool's Historic Waterfront*, H.M.S.O., 1984.

Rogge, Bernhard *Under Ten Flags*, Weidenfeld and Nicholson, 1957.

Sawyer, L.A. and Mitchell, W.H. *The Liberty Ships*, David and Charles, Newton Abbot, 1970.

Sea Breezes, various editions

Sieff, Marcus *Don't Ask the Price*, Weidenfeld and Nicholson, 1986.

Slader, John *The Red Duster at War*, William Kimber, 1988.

Stapleton, M. *The Cambridge Guide to English Literature*, Cambridge University Press, 1983.

Swinson, Arthur *Scotch on the Rocks*, Peter Davies,1963.

Syrett, David, The Operations of the Drossel U-Boats, *Mariner's Mirror*, 1993, 79, No. 3

United States Navy, *Civil War Chronology, 1861-1865*, Washington, USA, 1971.

Van der Vat, Dan *The Last Corsair: the Story of the EMDEN*, Hodder and Stoughton, 1983.

Whale, Derek M. *The Liners of Liverpool* (in three volumes), Countryvise, Birkenhead, 1986/1988.

Williamson, Jean-Mari *Captain Richard-Pierre Williamson 1813-1874*, Published privately, Nantes May 1991.

Winchester, Clarence, Editor, *Shipping Wonders of the World*, Fleetway House,1937.

Woodward, David *The Secret Raiders*, William Kimber, 1955.

Notes on the ships' histories

Ships' histories are presented in the format developed and refined by the World Ship Society, close to that used in Ships in Focus publications.

On the first line, the number in brackets following the ship's name indicates how many times that name has been used in the fleet. The dates are those of entering and leaving the company's ownership or management. Next is indicated the hull material and, for sailing vessels or auxiliaries, the rig. Brigs and brigantines are all two-masted, whilst full-rigged ships are all three-masted. Barques are three-masted unless otherwise indicated. All steam and motor ships are screw propelled. Then follows a brief description of the vessel, its figurehead, number of decks and holds.

On the second line is given the ship's official number (O.N.) in the British Register; then her tonnages at acquisition, gross (g), net (n), and in many cases deadweight (d), followed by dimensions: overall length x breadth x draft in feet or metres. Next is cargo capacity and/or number of passengers and for later ships details of cargo gear. For any substantial rebuild, new dimensions are given in a subsequent line. Dimensions and descriptions of vessels, and any changes thereto, are derived from three main sources: Liverpool Shipping Registers, Lloyd's Register of Shipping and/or company archives. Where there is a conflict of opinion (and there are many) the Liverpool Shipping Register is accepted as the final arbiter.

On the next line are given signal letters. Marryat's Code of Recognition Signals are as listed in Davidson, A.S.

Marine Art and Liverpool, Waine Research Publications, Albrighton, 1986.

On the following line is a description of the engine(s) fitted and the name of their builder. Steam engines may be single cylinder (1-cyl.), two-cylinder simple (2-cyl.), two cylinder compound (C. 2-cyl.), three-cylinder triple-expansion (T. 3-cyl.), or quadruple expansion four cylinder (Q. 4-cyl.). For oil engines are given the type (e.g. Sulzer, Burmeister & Wain), the number of cylinders, whether two stroke (2SC) or four stroke (4SC) cycle, single acting (SA) or double acting (DA). Next come cylinder dimensions for steam engines, given as the diameter of the cylinders in decreasing order of size by stroke, followed by the ship's speed. Any changes of engine are listed, with dates, on subsequent lines.

Subsequent lines give the details of builder and the ship's full career, with acquisition and sale prices being quoted where known. The transfer of shares, and ship sales are as recorded in the Liverpool Shipping Registers and Transaction Books kept at the Merseyside Maritime Museum. The port indicated after the title of the owning company is the port in which the owners are domiciled, not necessarily that where the ship is registered. For ships sold to operators using flags of convenience, efforts have been made to indicate the actual owners and the managers (not always the same body). For these vessels, the flag can be taken to be the same as the domicile of the shipowning company unless otherwise stated.

Diplomat (293) sailing from Eastham.   *[Eddie Jackson]*

Novelist (311) on 5th October 1969.   *[Les Ring collection, World Ship Photo Library 26534]*

PART 1

FROM BRIGS AND SCHOONERS TO FULL-RIGGED SHIPS
1836 - 1860

The links

The brothers Thomas and James Harrison were, at the outset of their careers, closely linked commercially to two other families: Samuel Brown and his son, George; and Richard Williamson and his son, Richard-Pierre. It is perhaps questionable whether Thomas and James, deprived of the Browns' commercial wisdom and the Williamsons' maritime expertise, would ever have become shipowners of world renown, although it is safe to assume that, whatever, their chosen field, they would have succeeded, for clearly they were well-endowed with those qualities of energy and enterprise essential to success.

To draw an analogy, the firm of Samuel Brown and Son, shipbrokers of Liverpool, was the shackle in the chain which joined the links of Williamson and Harrison. Other links became attached and detached from time to time; for example, Henry Smith, an associate of the Browns; Cornelius Glaves, a friend of the Williamsons; and fellow siblings of the Harrison family - Richard, John and Edward Hodgson Harrison.

Starting with the Browns: we know that they were established in Liverpool in the early part of the 19th century, first as merchants, and later as ship brokers and shipping agents.[1] Although their shipping interests extended worldwide, the firm had a particular interest in chartering tonnage for the brandy trade from Charente in Western France, and acting as agents to masters engaged in that trade. On 17th July 1820 the brigantine JUBILEE, 101 tons, registered at Scarborough, berthed at Liverpool with a cargo of brandy consigned to Samuel Brown and Co. Her master was Richard Williamson. Thus we find here the first connection between the Williamsons and the Browns as being that between master and agent.[2] Like the Browns, the Williamsons had a substantial interest in the Charente brandy trade, and their parallel interests helped to forge a lasting relationship.

That relationship developed naturally into partnership, and in June 1823 the brig MARGARET was registered in Liverpool, the declared owners being Samuel

and George Brown, Richard Williamson and his son, also Richard, and one Cornelius Glaves, a farmer of Scarborough. The younger Richard Williamson was also master of the vessel.[3] He had, at this time, been residing in Liverpool for some years with his French wife, Lucie, and their two young sons, Richard-Pierre and Francis. The elder boy had been baptised in St. Matthew's Church Liverpool on 14th February 1819, when he was six years old.[4]

The partners

The Williamson family's links with France had an inauspicious beginning, when the brig EAGLE, with the elder Richard Williamson in command and his 14-year old son, also named Richard, were captured by a French privateer on 18th October 1803.[5] Richard and his son were interned, and billetted with a French family in the town of Verdun. During their long internment - it would last 10½ years - they were allowed a generous amount of freedom, and made many friends. It was, perhaps, inevitable that young Richard, grown to manhood, should meet, fall in love, and marry a local girl, Lucie Pierre. A son, Richard-Pierre Williamson, was born to them on 1st March 1813. At this time the war was going badly for Napoleon, and the internees were moved west, first to Blois, and then to Gueret in La Marche. Whilst there, they learned that Napoleon had abdicated, and the war was over. Shortly afterwards Richard Williamson and his extended family were repatriated to England through the port of Bordeaux.[6] The men returned to seafaring, but young Richard's most formative years had been spent in France; he had married a young French woman, and had developed a deep affection for the country, even choosing to retire to Tonnay-Charente in his later years. Thus the link with France had been forged, and the foundation for the Harrisons' involvement firmly laid through joint investment in ships, and partnership in business.

In 1814 Richard Williamson the elder subscribed to the fitting out of a brig, the JUBILEE, in which young

Thomas Harrison
1815 - 1888

Richard Williamson
1787 - 1861

James Harrison
1821 - 1891

13

The brig *Tom Tough (2)*. The brig is sailing closehauled under close-reefed topsails off the Skerries, Anglesey.

[Attributed to Joseph Heard. Bonhams, London]

Richard sailed, at first as an officer and later as master until in July 1820, as we have seen, we find him with his ship in Liverpool, entered into Samuel Brown and Son.

In 1821 Richard bought a house in Charente doubtless partly to please his wife and partly to give himself a shrewd foothold amid the fertile vineyards and prolific distilleries which provided much of the lucrative trade on which they all depended.

The Williamson family now suffered a series of grievous blows. On 7th September 1825 the elder Richard died at Scarborough. He was 65-years old and had led a richly varied life. Three years later Lucie became ill and died on 3rd August 1828. She was only 35. Her death was closely followed by that of her small son, Francis, who died on 28th August 1828. They now lie together in Walton Churchyard, Liverpool.[7]

Meanwhile, Richard-Pierre, under the tutelage of his father, was eagerly following the family tradition. He undoubtedly sailed in many ships part-owned and commanded by his father, and their voyages brought them frequently into Liverpool where Samuel Brown and Son acted as their agents. In due course, Browns and Williamsons became partners, sharing ownership of several fine vessels, notably the brig MARGARET (1823), the brigantine MARIOTE (1825), and the brig TOM TOUGH (1829).

The triumvirate
The Harrisons, like so many embryo Liverpool shipowners - Brocklebanks, Ismays and Inmans - sprang from farming and land-owning stock dwelling in that north west corner of England which lies between the Fylde and the Solway Firth. In December 1812 one James Harrison, farmer, married Ann Hodgson at Cockerham. James and Ann were to have eight children, one of whom (the first James) died in infancy. Thomas, the second son, was born in 1815, when Richard-Pierre Williamson was already two years old. James, the fifth son and second to bear that name was born in 1821. When Thomas was 15 in 1830, he travelled to Liverpool following in the footsteps of his elder brother, Richard, who was already established in a shipping office there. Thomas was apprenticed to the firm of Samuel Brown and Son,

shipping agents and brokers, with premises at 27 King Street, off Paradise Street, demolished in the bombing raids of May 1941, and now the site of a multi-storey car park.

We know very little about Thomas's early apprenticeship, but can safely assume that he did well and rose in the esteem of his masters. We may also be sure that he made the acquaintance of many shipowners and captains who called to discuss business with the Browns. Among them, of course, were Richard Williamson and his son, Richard-Pierre, a youth of Thomas's own generation. We can imagine that they became firm friends and, being mainly in the short-sea trades, the Williamsons would be frequent visitors. The musty, counting-house atmosphere of the agent's office, bleakly furnished with sloping desks and high stools, would come to life when the shipowner and his son breezed in, recounting their tales of peril on the high seas and adventure in foreign parts. It was enough to capture the young man's imagination and convince him that his future lay in shipping and in the dynamic port of Liverpool. In June 1834, the brig TOM TOUGH, then owned by Richard Williamson, Jeremiah Hudson and Henry Smith, arrived from the Charente with Richard-Pierre Williamson in command. It must have been an occasion for congratulation and celebration, but Richard-Pierre's new-found eminence was short-lived. In his own words "As she was finishing loading, I had a few words with the owners, so I took my discharge."

He then went to Scarborough to visit his friends and relations. Some weeks later a letter from Samuel Brown and Son (who by that time had moved their premises to 14 South John Street) recalled him to Liverpool, where he was given a berth as mate of the brig MARIOTE. In November of that same year, 1834, however, he was again in command, this time in Richard Williamson's schooner LETITIA also trading to Charente.[8]

Meanwhile, young Thomas was approaching the end of his apprenticeship, and in 1835 Samuel Brown retired to his home in Litherland confident that the business he had founded was safe in the hands of George and his young assistant. By 1836 Thomas had grown in stature and confidence and when Richard Williamson offered him a quarter share in the brig JANE and a third share in the brig

TOM TOUGH, Thomas seized the opportunity with enthusiasm. The deal was set up and Thomas Harrison took his first tentative step in the enterprise of shipowning, the two vessels being duly registered in Liverpool in the names of Richard Williamson and Thomas Harrison, as sole owners, on 16th and 23rd August 1836 respectively.[9] At this time, Richard-Pierre Williamson was again master of the brig TOM TOUGH. This young man was also approaching a landmark in his life for on 1st November 1836 he married Jane Allen of Ormskirk; he was 23 and Jane was 19 years of age. Eight days later he sailed for Whitehaven and the Charente, taking his bride with him, "to commence a sailor's life".[10]

In 1837 the schooner CRESCENT was acquired by Richard Williamson (43/64) and Thomas Harrison (21/64). Later that year, however, Thomas sold his interest to his elder brother, Richard Harrison, who was at that time a shipbroker in his own right, and also occasionally referred to in the registers as a "ship's bread-baker". For in 1840 Richard founded a firm to manufacture and distribute ships' biscuits under the style of Richard Harrison and Co. The plan was to supply biscuits with a long shelf-life to Liverpool ships, especially those in which his brothers were interested. The company's primary products, which were known locally as "Liverpool Pantiles", maintained their

Richard-Pierre Williamson 1813 - 1874

pristine condition for long periods, but eventually tended to become infested with weevils. Consequently, quantities of weevily biscuits were returned to the home port unconsumed, but a ready market for these rejects was quickly found in the kennels of the neighbouring shires.

In about 1855, Richard Harrison sold his interest to one of his partners, Henry Wright, who established the firm of flour, cereal and biscuit suppliers known as Wright and Co. (Liverpool) Ltd., which was still trading for many years after the Second World War.[11]

On 1st January, 1838, James Harrison, at the age of 16, left his father's farm to seek a career in Liverpool buoyed up no doubt by stories of his brothers' continuing success. He too began his career as an apprentice at Samuel Brown and Son, there to learn all he could about the shipping business, just like brother Thomas, now a rather serious young man of 23. That year Thomas invested in a fourth ship, the brig EUPHEMIA, his only partner again being Richard Williamson.

The year 1839 saw a further significant change when George Brown offered Thomas Harrison a partnership in his shipbroking and agency business. This was entirely separate from the individual shipowning proclivities of the several partners and associates, although undoubtedly the booking of cargo and all agency matters were undertaken by the firm. Thomas accepted the offer and the firm changed its style to George Brown and Harrison, with premises at 25 South John Street. It continued to flourish as the port developed, Thomas still pursuing his interest in shipowning. That year he acquired a quarter share in the brig SIR COLIN CAMPBELL, the remaining 48 shares being equally divided between his brother Richard and his old patron Richard Williamson. Here, for the first time, we see members of the Harrison family holding the majority interest in a vessel. It must not be imagined, however, that a partner's interest remained fixed and immutable. In fact, shares changed hands with bewildering rapidity, but invariably within the same close-knit group. By 1842, James too, was admitted to the shipowning fraternity when Thomas sold him 11 shares

in TOM TOUGH and 8 in JANE. Three years later, Richard-Pierre Williamson joined the club, sharing ownership in the brig ROBERT PRESTON, 115 tons - which he subsequently commanded [12] - with George Brown, James Harrison and Richard Williamson, his father, who had just retired from active seafaring at the age of 56.

The brothers
In 1840, another Harrison sibling appeared on the Liverpool shipping scene: young Edward Hodgson Harrison then 15, ten years younger than Thomas and the baby of the family. He too went into shipping, but not with George Brown and Harrison. Instead, he entered the firm of brokers known as Whitaker, Whitehead and Co., becoming a full partner in 1852. Nevertheless, he was keen to maintain the family connection and, shortly after completing his apprenticeship in 1845, we find him buying shares in his brothers' ships, acquiring a quarter share in the schooner CHARLES SOUCHAY, brother James and Richard Williamson holding the remaining interest. Doubtless Thomas and James received their kid brother's intrusion into their world with the indulgent air assumed by elders everywhere. This fraternal relationship was also demonstrated by his elders' willingness to lend their young brother money on occasion, as manifested in Edward Hodgson's own note-book, where every such transaction is meticulously recorded.[13]

Old Samuel Brown died in 1841, but it was not until 1849 that James Harrison became a partner in the old man's firm. This meant that the firm's style had to be changed yet again to Brown and Harrisons, and taking over new premises at 18 Chapel Street. That year the brig MAZEPPA joined the fleet of Harrison-related vessels, the Harrisons and Williamsons owning equal shares between them.

Three years later, the name of the remaining Harrison brother appears in the registers, that of John Harrison, born in 1819. Unlike his brothers, John did not go to Liverpool, but was evidently destined by his father to succeed to the farm. For there he remained working the family estates and perhaps thinking wistfully of his brothers' independence down in the big city. Still, if he could not join them in person, he could perhaps join in their enterprises and with this end in view he bought in 1852 a one-eighth interest in the schooner INVINCIBLE. That vessel, unfortunately, was wrecked the following year but this misfortune did not deter John from making further modest investments in his brothers' ships from time to time.

George Brown, Thomas's friend and partner for 23 years, died on 22nd March 1853 at the comparatively early age of 54. It is believed that he died intestate and a widower. His only son, Samuel George Brown, had no interest in his father's business and so the name Brown disappeared from the firm's title, changing for the last time, as events proved, to Thomas and James Harrison. This, of course, was the shipbroking and agency business only and did not at that time include the shipowning enterprises pursued by the brothers.

Meanwhile, Edward Hodgson Harrison was prospering in the brokerage business. On 10th September 1856 he married Elizabeth Harpin of Holmfirth. In 1883, at the age of 58, he established his own firm as a foreign produce broker under the style of E.H. Harrison and Co., with premises in 9 Rumford Street. By this time, Edward was also a justice of the peace for the County of Chester (his home was in Eastham, Cheshire), Deputy Chairman of the

Bank of Liverpool, and Deputy Chairman of the London and Lancashire Fire Insurance Co. He also became Honorary Secretary and Treasurer of the New Brighton Convalescent Institution, one of many local charities in which he was interested.[14]

Although a good deal is known and much can be deduced from the records of the business activities of the Harrison brothers, little is known of their private lives, their outside interests, family life, or personal characters. They were content, it seems, to conduct their business affairs with a minimum of limelight and publicity. It was noted in one work of reference dedicated to Liverpool's leading citizens that: "The members of this family [Harrisons]...have little of

the oratorical faculty and avoid public life, so that they are comparatively unknown beyond a narrow business circle where the present, like the last generation, is held in the highest esteem."[15]

Thus, with the advent of the firm of Thos. and Jas. Harrison, shipbrokers, on 1st July 1853, our introduction is complete. The future stretched before the brothers Harrison like a map of the world - the Crimean War; the Suez Canal; trade routes to India, Brazil, Mexico and of course Charente; absorbing and surviving a succession of booms and slumps right up to the closing years of the century.

FLEET LIST Part 1

1. JANE 1836-1849 Wooden brig. One deck. Female bust figurehead.
115 tons 69.3 x 20.0 x 11.5 feet.
Marryat's Code First Distinguishing Pennant: 2479 (pre-1840), 5842 (post-1840).

1833: Built by Thomas Barker, South Shields for Thomas Burnett, South Shields as a snow. *31.3.1833:* Sold to Robert Porritt, Whitby. *27.11.1833:* Sold to Joseph Fearon, Liverpool. *16.8.1836:* Acquired by Richard Williamson (48 shares) and Thomas Harrison (16 shares), Liverpool from the executors of Joseph Fearon. *1.5.1837:* Richard-Pierre Williamson, son of the senior partner, appointed master. *1838:* Made two voyages to Brazil, the first Harrison-interest vessel to visit that country, which was later to become a source of regular trade. *4.2.1839:* Reported to have ridden

out severe westerly gales in the Irish Sea during which a "great many vessels had been lost". *15.3.1839:* Called at Stromness, Orkney, to take the cargo salvaged from the wreck of the barque ETHIOPE of Hull, wrecked 7.1.1839 in a great storm. *8.12.1849:* Sold to Henry Curry, Liverpool. *10.11.1850:* Sold to William McCready, Douglas, Isle of Man. *24.1.1851:* Registered at Douglas. *5.1.1852:* Registered at Belfast in the ownership of Thomas Keenan, Belfast. *12.1859:* Lost. *23.6.1864:* Register closed.

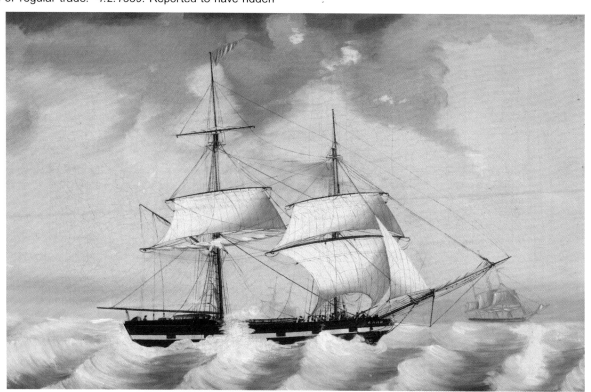

Brig *Jane*.

[W. Whitham (c.1840. Bonhams, London]

2. TOM TOUGH 1836-1845 Wooden brig. One deck. Male bust figurehead.
114 tons 63.9 x 20.25 x 11.0 feet.
Marryat's Code Second Distinguishing Pennant: 1829 (Post-1840).

7.7.1829: Launched by George Woodhouse Porritt, Scarborough, and later delivered to John Dale and William Henry, Scarborough. *20.7.1830:* Sold to Richard Williamson and his partners Henry Smith and Jeremiah Hudson. *1.6.1834:* Richard-Pierre Williamson appointed master. *9.7.1834:* Richard Williamson became sole owner. *23.8.1836:* Thomas Harrison purchased 21 shares from Richard Williamson. *5.3.1837:* Sailed for Liverpool with a cargo of brandy from Charente. Subsequently "experienced

strong easterly gales and sprung the mainmast above deck off Scilly. Sent down topgallant mast and secured the mast".[16] *18.1.1842:* Thomas Harrison sold 11 shares to his brother James. *1.2.1843:* Sold his remaining 10 shares to James. *10.1845:* Sold to William Smith (22 shares), William Corner (21 shares), London and Francis Hudson, Whitby (21 shares) and registered in London. *31.11.1847:* Register closed after vessel sank.

3. CRESCENT 1837-1862 Wooden two-masted schooner. One deck. Female bust figurehead.
O.N. 4914 123 tons (93 tons under old measurement) 62.2 x 20.1 x 12.7 feet.
1847: 147 tons 83.4 x 19.6 x 13.1 feet.
Marryat's Code First Distinguishing Pennant: 2438. Commercial Code: JFMP.

1818: Built at Plymouth, Devon. *24.5.1837:* Acquired by Richard Williamson (43 shares) and Thomas Harrison (21 shares), Liverpool from mortgagees Holmes and Heyworth and owner Robert Wise. *19.8.1837:* Thomas Harrison transferred his shares to his brother, Richard Harrison. *21.3.1842:* Richard Harrison transferred his shares to Richard Williamson. *20.1.1844:* Richard Williamson transferred 8 shares to James Harrison and 8 shares to Francis Williams, Liverpool. *1847:* Rebuilt, lengthened and re-rigged as a three-masted schooner with one deck and a poop. *19.10.1847:* Registered in the ownership of Richard Williamson (48 shares), James Harrison (8 shares) and Francis Williams (8 shares), Liverpool. The master named on this register was James Harrison, although he was superseded at Irvine four days later by Francis Williams. *1862:* Sold. *1863:* Deleted from the Register and probably broken up.

Schooner *Crescent* and brig *Jane* passing off Holyhead.

[Joseph Heard (1799-1859). Bonhams, London]

4. EUPHEMIA 1838-1840 Wooden brig. One deck. Female bust figurehead.
145 tons 71.5 x 22.2 x 13.5 feet.
Marryat's Code First Distinguishing Pennant: 1506 (pre-1840), 3659 (post-1840).

1828: Built at South Shields. *10.4.1838:* Acquired by Richard Williamson (40 shares) and Thomas Harrison (24 shares), Liverpool from Hunter and Co., Greenock, for whom she had been a Newfoundland trader. *22.1.1840:* Stranded and lost off Flamborough Head. The first marine loss sustained by the Harrison/Williamson partnership.

5. SIR COLIN CAMPBELL 1838-1845 Wooden brig. One deck. Male bust figurehead.
160 tons 80.6 x 19.5 x 12.3 feet.
Marryat's Code Second Distinguishing Pennant: 851.

1838: Built at Bridgetown, Nova Scotia for Isaac Willet and Co., Nova Scotia. *27.12.1838:* Acquired by Thomas Harrison (16 shares), Richard Harrison (24 shares) and Richard Williamson (24 shares), Liverpool. *6.3.1841:* While anchored at Cabane Carre, Rochefort, swung to the flood tide, fell foul of a lugger loaded with salt and sank her. *1.1.1842:* Thomas Harrison transferred 8 shares to James Harrison. *19.3.1842:* Richard Harrison transferred 16 shares to Richard-Pierre Williamson and 8 shares to Elizabeth Pritchard, Scarborough. *17.8.1842:* Ran aground on the Isle of Ruhnu in the Gulf of Riga when on passage from Liverpool to Parnu, Estonia. She was refloated after 24 hours following the jettisoning of 65 tons of cargo. *8.11.1842:* Shortly after sailing from Elsinore she was caught in a gale on a lee shore. The captain was forced to carry more sail than was prudent in an effort to clear the land, but even so she struck bottom five times in the process.

8.12.1842: Upon arrival at St. Helier, Jersey it was found that the scarf of the keel had been split. She remained at St. Helier for ten weeks obtaining and fitting a new keel.[17] *15.2.1845:* Sold to Thomas Rigby, Runcorn and resold to J. Sedman, Liverpool. *9.1848:* Sold to William Dale, Whitby. *4.1859:* Sold to John Groves, Whitby. *1.1861:* Sold to John Wilkinson senior (22 shares), John Wilkinson junior (21 shares) and Joseph Wilkinson (21 shares), Whitby. *27.12.1866:* Lost on North Foreland.

Sir Colin Campbell was a distinguished soldier who had seen service in the field against Napoleon's armies, and later in India and the Crimea. As Commander-in-Chief, India, newly appointed in 1857, the year of the Indian Mutiny, his forces of British and loyal Indian troops raised the sieges of Cawnpore and Lucknow in 1857-58, and quelled the rebellion.

6. TEMPLAR 1842-1855 Wooden full-rigged ship. Two decks. Male figurehead.
565 tons 115.8 x 26.1 x 20.0 feet.
Marryat's Code Second Distinguishing Pennant: 3741.

1842: Built by Francis Oliver and Co., Monkwearmouth, Sunderland for Ingleby and Co., Liverpool. *29.8.1842:* Acquired by Thomas Harrison (8 shares), Richard Harrison (8 shares), George Brown (16 shares), James Browne (16 shares) and Patrick William Byrnes (16 shares), Liverpool. *3.5.1845:* Richard Harrison transferred 8 shares to Thomas Harrison. *1847:* The first Harrison-interest vessel to make a voyage to India, later a regular source of trade. *9.11.1848:* Marcella Byrnes (widow of Patrick William Byrnes) transferred 16 shares to John Fenwick, Newcastle. *9.8.1853:* Ann Clay, Bootle, administratrix of George Brown, transferred 8 shares to Richard Harrison and 8 shares to James Browne. *15.9.1853:* Re-registered and the master's name was recorded as Richard Harrison. However, he was superseded by Reginald Barrett at London on 26.10.1853. *27.11.1855:* Foundered in the Bay of Maranham, Brazil, while under the command of Reginald Barrett.

A misconception associates the name TEMPLAR with Malta,

and it is said that this relationship inspired Harrisons to adopt the Maltese Cross as their house flag. This confuses the Templars, the Poor Knights of the Temple of Solomon, founded in 1118, suppressed in 1312, and never having any connection with the island of Malta, with the Knights of Malta, the Knights of the Hospital of St. John of Jerusalem, founded c.1100, who occupied Malta in 1530. The cross patee used by the Harrisons, though often known as a Maltese Cross, is in fact misnamed, as the true Maltese Cross is a forked cross of eight points, and the flag of the Knights was (and still is) a plain white cross on a red field. The Harrisons' house flag, with its red 'Maltese'. cross, seems to be simply a legacy in part from Samuel Brown and Son, their early employers and partners, whose flag, according to contemporary paintings, depicted a blue 'Maltese' cross. The Harrisons apparently decided to keep the emblem, but changed the colour to reflect the new regime which came about in 1853, when George Brown died, and the firm of Thos. and Jas. Harrison was born.

7. ROBERT PRESTON 1845-1858 Wooden brig. One deck.
O.N. 25726 115 tons 71.0 x 17.5 x 11.0 feet.
Marryat's Code Second Distinguishing Pennant: 4821. Commercial Code: PHFB.

1.6.1844: Launched by Isaac Middleton, Maryport. *16.2.1845:* Acquired by Richard Williamson (24 shares), George Brown (10 shares), James Harrison (14 shares) and Richard Pierre Williamson (16 shares), Liverpool for £1,300. Captain Richard-Pierre Williamson, master. *24.12.1847:* From R.P. Williamson's diary: "Took a pilot for Marans and took the ground going up the River, (River Serre, northern Charente Inferieure) and remained until springs. Got two lighters down from town to lighten the vessel. I went to Charente and spent Christmas week at my father's. Returned to ship at Marans, 8th January 1848." *13.12.1849:* "At 4 a.m. John Small, Mate ... fell from the maintop and was

drowned". *28.12.1849:* On arrival at Cadiz on the vessel was put in quarantine for ten days "for losing the Mate overboard". Port Health Authorities, aware of the convenient means of disposal of suspicious fatalities, played safe! *29.10.1850:* "Arrived in Liverpool (from Cadiz) after the extraordinary passage of 46 days, after having been given up for lost. The only damage the ship received was that she ran into the Landing Stage on arrival!" *4.6.1858:* Sold to Thomas Curwen, Maryport for £587. *1896:* Sold to Henry Palmer, Maryport. *22.1.1897:* Wrecked near Seascale, Cumberland, while on a voyage from Belfast to Maryport.

8. CHARLES SOUCHAY 1845-1861 Wooden two-masted schooner. One deck.
O.N. 1265 118 tons 70.1 x 17.3 x 11.6 feet.
Marryat's Code Second Distinguishing Pennant: 4823. Commercial Code: HJGK.

1844: Built by H. Fellows and Co., Southtown, Yarmouth. *2.10.1845:* Delivered to Richard Williamson (32 shares), James Harrison (16 shares) and Edward Hodgson Harrison (16 shares), Liverpool for £1,075. *1855:* Re-rigged as a

brigantine. *22.4.1861:* Sold for £450. *14.3.1862:* Sold to J. Mulreany and R. Walsh, Liverpool. *11.6.1863:* Sold to John Timothy, Portmadoc. *1868:* Wrecked.

Charles Souchay seen entering the Mersey with the Rock Lighhouse under her bowsprit.

[Attributed to W. K. McMinn]

9. URGENT 1845-1848 Wooden full-rigged ship. One deck.
O.N. 2506 622 tons 126.4 x 28.4 x 21.0 feet.
Marryat's Code Second Distinguishing Pennant: 2076. Commercial Code: HPLB.

1839: Built by Andrew Neilson, Quebec. *1845:* Acquired by Thomas Harrison (24 shares), George Brown (8 shares), James Browne (16 shares), and Christopher Pilkington (16 shares), Liverpool. *14.11.1845:* Registered at Liverpool. *12.9.1848:* Sold to John Low and Neil Boag, Belfast.

11.1853: Sold to Hugh Wardlaw, Belfast. *2.1855:* Sold to Robert Corry and Neil Boag, Belfast. *5.1855:* Sold to Thomas H. Woods and Joseph Spence, Sunderland. *1857:* Sold to foreign owners.

10. REDBREAST 1846-1857 Wooden two-masted schooner. One deck. Female bust figurehead.
O.N. 14044 132 tons 73.8 x 20.2 x 12.4 feet.
1852: 110 tons 71.3 x 17.7 x 12.1 feet.
Marryat's Code Second Distinguishing Pennant: 83. Commercial Code: LKNF.

1833: Built at North Hylton, Durham. *1.1840:* Owners were Edward Cox, Liverpool and Edward Grace, Leeds. *5.1841:* Owners restyled Cox, Grace and Hinton. *5.1843:* Sold to Robert Davidson and Wallace Gilfillan, Liverpool, and resold to George Mackern, Liverpool. *9.4.1846:* Acquired by Richard Williamson (32 shares), James Harrison (16 shares) and Edward Hodgson Harrison (16 shares), Liverpool for £550. *13.4.1846:* Registered. *1848:* Richard-Pierre Williamson records that on 27.3.1848, while his brig ROBERT PRESTON was loading at Liverpool, he was sent down to Fowey to inspect REDBREAST, which had put into that port in a waterlogged condition. The temporary repairs he put in train lasted over three years, but by late 1851 rather more elaborate renovations were necessary. *2.11.1851:* Captain Williamson arrived at the yard of Barr and Shearer, Ardrossan to superintend the rebuilding of the schooner. *30.12.1851:* Richard-Pierre Williamson was transferred 21 shares by Thomas Harrison (5 shares), Edward Hodgson Harrison (5 shares) and Richard Williamson (11 shares). *2.1.1852:* Re-launched. *5.1.1852:* Re-registered. *7.2.1852:* Sailed for Charente after being windbound for five weeks. *16.12.1852:* Again sailed from Ardrossan and was once again assailed by bad weather. By the end of the year she was sheltering in Belfast Lough making repairs to heavy weather damage and by 19.1.1853, still on a voyage to Charente, had only got as far as Dublin Bay. There the Captain was relieved at his own request and returned to Liverpool by steam packet where, as he remarks rather pointedly, "I arrived the same day!" *10.2.1857:* Lost off Faro, Portugal.

11. GOOD INTENT 1846-1858 Wooden brigantine. One deck. Female bust figurehead.
O.N. 1984 138 tons 78.8 x 18.9 x 10.75 feet.
Marryat's Code 1st Distinguishing Pennant: 4608. Commercial Code: HMGF.

1829: Built by Tyrrell, Wells-next-the-Sea, Norfolk. *1846:* Acquired by Thomas Harrison (32 shares) and Gilbert Pennington (32 shares), Liverpool for £900. *11.2.1850:* Thomas Harrison transferred 21 shares to James Harrison, and 11 shares to Edward H. Harrison. *13.7.1858:* Sold to Thomas Bartlett, Weymouth for £650. *19.10.1862:* Lost. *24.11.1862:* Register closed.

12. DAUNTLESS 1846-1850 Wooden full-rigged ship. One deck. Male bust figurehead.
O.N. 26070 698 tons. 134.8 x 26.8 x 20.6 feet.
Marryat's Code 1st Distinguishing Pennant: 2581. Commercial Code: PJNW.

1837: Built by Jardine at Richibucto, New Brunswick. *16.12.1846:* Acquired from Isaac Jackson, Lancaster by James Harrison (16 shares), John Browne (8 shares), Christopher Pilkington (16 shares), Thomas Rogers (16 shares) and Elizabeth Johnson (8 shares), Liverpool. *1847:* Inaugurated a regular trade with Brazil. *24.9.1850:* Sold to Thomas Curry, Liverpool. *1855:* Sold to Thomas H. Holderness. *26.10.1856:* Wrecked on the coast of Gibraltar.

13. CITY OF LINCOLN 1848-1850 Wooden full-rigged ship. One deck.
O.N. 2394 891 tons 150.6 x 28.2 x 22.1 feet.
Marryat's Code Second Distinguishing Pennant: 5793. Commercial Code: HNWM.

14.5.1847: Launched by J.J. Jeffrey and Son, Quebec for George Symes and David Young, Quebec. *22.2.1848:* Acquired by James Harrison (8 shares), Edward Hodgson Harrison (8 shares), Henry Jumpe (32 shares) and William Wittleton (16 shares), Liverpool for £5,494. *1848:* Became the first Harrison-interest vessel to trade to US Gulf ports. *27.9.1850:* Sold to H. Holland and Co., Liverpool. *16.8.1852:* Sold to Edward Bates, Liverpool. *3.4.1854:* Sold to John Starr de Wolf and Co., Liverpool. *11.4.1854:* Shares transferred to Edward Oliver, Liverpool. *8.3.1855:* Edward Oliver sold 16 shares to H.W. Wood and 16 shares to J. Alexander. *1856:* Sold to Owen and Co., Cardiff. *7.11.1860:* Sailed from Quebec for Penarth. *12.12.1860:* Found waterlogged and abandoned by the steamship CITY OF BALTIMORE.

Brig *Hero* (see over).   *[Joseph Heard (1799-1859]*

14. HERO 1849-1858 Wooden brig. One deck. Male bust figurehead.
O.N. 24387 173 tons 77.0 x 20.0 x 14.0 feet.
Marryat's Code First Distinguishing Pennant: 5180. Commercial Code: NWMR.

26.6.1841: Launched by Edward Esrouf, St. Helier, Jersey for Tupper and Co., Guernsey. *5.3.1849:* Acquired from Richard Rostron, Liverpool by Thomas Harrison (16 shares), James Harrison (16 shares), Richard Williamson (24 shares) and

Richard-Pierre Williamson (8 shares), Liverpool. *6.6.1851:* Thomas Harrison transferred 16 shares to Richard Harrison. *27.3.1858:* Sold to John Beeby, Whitehaven. *1861:* Lost.

15. AMERICA 1849-1854 Wooden snow. One deck.
O.N. 25826 162 tons 85.7 x 19.2 x 12.0 feet.
Marryat's Code 1st Distinguishing Pennant: 297. Commercial Code: PHNR.

1848: Built at Prince Edward Island for Matthew H. Warren and Charles S. Warren, St. John's, Newfoundland. *21.5.1849:* Sold to William Ford the younger, Liverpool. *18.8.1849:* Acquired by James Harrison (16 shares), Edward Hodgson Harrison (16 shares), Richard Williamson (21

shares) and Richard-Pierre Williamson (11 shares), Liverpool for £850. Employed in the brandy trade between Charente and the United Kingdom. *5.4.1854:* Sold to H. Cross and Co., Sunderland for £772. *30.12.1854:* Register cancelled, vessel lost.

16. ANLABY 1849-1850 Wooden two masted schooner. One deck.
130 tons 75.9 x 17.9 x 11.4 feet.
Marryat's Code First Distinguishing Pennant: 361.

1819: Built at Sculcoates, Hull for W. Voase, Hull. *1846:* Sold to Jones and Co., Liverpool. *1848:* Sold to Saul and Co., Liverpool. *28.9.1849:* Acquired by Thomas Harrison (16 shares), James Harrison (16 shares) and Richard

Williamson (32 shares), Liverpool. *2.1.1850:* Vessel not heard of after this date and presumed lost.

The name is that of a village near Hull.

17. MAZEPPA 1849-1860 Wooden brig. One deck. Billet figurehead.
O.N. 2891 134 tons 78.1 x 20.0 x 12.3 feet.
Marryat's Code First Distinguishing Pennant: 8269.
Commercial Code: HRBQ.

6.8.1831: Launched by Brocklebank, Whitehaven for whom she traded to the Baltic. *15.12.1849:* Acquired by James Harrison (32 shares), Richard Williamson (24 shares) and Richard-Pierre Williamson (8 shares), Liverpool from Tasker Fairie and Co., Liverpool for £694. *1858:* Richard-Pierre Williamson records that 8.9.1858 MAZEPPA carried two of his sons, two daughters and himself from Ardrossan into semi-retirement in Charente. The family arrived 27.9.1858 "after a very rough passage". His wife and the rest of the family arrived 8.10.1858 in the brig DARING. *15.8.1860:*

Sold for £403. *7.1.1862:* Registered in the ownership of Henry Harrison (48 shares) and James S. Moffatt (16 shares), West Hartlepool. *3.1862:* Lost.

The name is from a Polish folk-hero, Ivan Stepanovitch Mazeppa, a Cossack leader who fought against Russia on the side of the Swedes. He shared in the downfall of the Swedish Army, defeated by Peter the Great at Poltava in 1709.[18]

18. LAUREL 1850-1860 Wooden brig. One deck. Female bust figurehead.
O.N. 12002 150 tons 72.0 x 20.2 x 13.7 feet.
Marryat's Code First Distinguishing Pennant: 7015. Commercial Code: KWBD.

1.6.1848: Launched at Miramichi, New Brunswick. *15.3.1850:* Registered in the ownership of Edwin Hughes, Liverpool. *5.7.1850:* Sold to John Barr and James Shearer, Ardrossan. *21.8.1850:* Acquired by James Harrison (16 shares), Edward Hodgson Harrison (16 shares) and Richard Williamson (32 shares), Liverpool for £850. James Harrison is recorded as being the master 27.8.1850 but was

superseded at Irvine 30.8.1850 by Owen J. Williams. *10.11.1860:* Sold for £684. *2.8.1861:* Registered in the ownership of John Beeby, Whitehaven. *20.12.1869:* Owners became John Beeby (16/62), John G. Nicholson (8/64), and others, Whitehaven. *12.11.1875:* Register closed, vessel broken up.

19. HEBE 1851-1860 Wooden two-masted schooner. One deck.
O.N. 24161 100 tons 68.9 x 17.5 x 11.5 feet.
Marryat's Code 1st Distinguishing Pennant: 4970. Commercial Code: NVPQ.

10.8.1835: Launched at Turnchapel Dockyard, Plymouth. *21.11.1835:* Registered in the ownership of William Ford and Samuel V. Thompson, Liverpool. *21.2.1851:* Acquired by James Harrison (16 shares), Edward Hodgson Harrison (16 shares) and Richard Williamson (32 shares), Liverpool. *15.10.1860:* Sold James Coffey, Youghal for £520. *24.3.1862:* Sold to Michael Veale, Youghal. *28.7.1866:* Owned by James Murphy, Waterford. *16.3.1867:* Peter

Shallow, Waterford. *13.12.1873:* Sold to Richard Power, Waterford. *14.9.1874:* Sold to William Lawlor, Mount Misery, County Waterford. *11.2.1878:* Resold to Richard Power, Waterford. *15.7.1881:* Register closed after being run into and sunk in the Bristol Channel.

The name derives from the Greek goddess of youth and spring, daughter of Zeus, wife of Hercules.[19]

20. MONARCHY 1851-1875 Wooden full-rigged ship. Two decks. Female figurehead.
O.N. 15876 776 tons 137.5 x 28.6 x 21.1 feet.
Marryat's Code Second Distinguishing Pennant: 7152. Commercial Code: LVDJ.

1851: Built by P. Chaloner and Sons, Liverpool. *13.3.1851:* Registered in the ownership of Thomas Harrison (16 shares), John Browne (24 shares), John Fenwick (8 shares), Hugh Taylor (12 shares) and C.F. Jackson (4 shares), Liverpool. *25.9.1855:* Richard-Pierre Williamson reported in his diary that MONARCHY and the company's vessels ADMIRAL GRENFELL, COLUMBIA and LANCASHIRE were

together in Balaclava harbour during the Crimean War. *6.1.1875:* Sold to William M. and William E. Corner, London for £1,150. *22.4.1875:* Sold to William Wright, London. *23.12.1878:* Sold to Thomas W. Sweet, London. *8.7.1880:* Sold to Robert Hellyer, Hull. *6.10.1886:* Register closed, in use as a coal hulk.

21. GEM 1851-1854 Wooden snow. One deck. Scroll figurehead.
216 tons 87.4 x 20.2 x 14.0 feet.
Marryat's Code 1st Distinguishing Pennant: 4215.

1848: Built at Prince Edward Island, New Brunswick for Richard Hutchison, Miramichi, New Brunswick. *1849:* Sold to Mary Ann Rennards, Birkenhead. *29.1.1850:* Mortgaged to Robert Rankin, of Rankin, Gilmour and Co. "for seven hundred and seventy-five pounds, seven shillings and fourpence and interest, and in default to sell". *8.12.1851:* Acquired by James Harrison (32 shares), Richard Williamson (24 shares) and Richard-Pierre Williamson (8 shares), Liverpool. *25.7.1854:* Sold to foreign buyers.

22. INVINCIBLE 1852-1853 Wooden two-masted schooner. One deck.
133 tons 79.2 x 18.8 x 12.4 feet.
Marryat's Code Second Distinguishing Pennant: 5640.

1841: Built at Ipswich for Richard Thornton, London. *1852:* Acquired by James Harrison (20 shares), Edward Hodgson Harrison (8 shares), John Harrison (8 shares) and Gilbert Pennington (28 shares), Liverpool for £960. *5.12.1853:* Wrecked on a reef off Isla Verde near Algeciras in Gibraltar Bay. The loss was reported in a statement dated 30.1.1854 by Gilbert Pennington, master and part-owner.

23. EDWARD BOUSTEAD 1852-1864 Wooden barque. One deck. Male figurehead.
O.N. 24657 443 tons 108.5 x 25.7 x 18.8 feet.
Marryat's Code Second Distinguishing Pennant: 3671. Commercial Code: PBRS.

5.1842: Built by J. Challoner and Co., Liverpool for John Dugdale and Co., Manchester. *9.11.1852:* Acquired by Thomas Harrison (32 shares), James Browne (16 shares), Edward Hodgson Harrison (6 shares), John Fenwick (6 shares) and John Browne (4 shares), Liverpool. *13.4.1864:* Sold to William Wallace Bruce, Liverpool. *3.1865:* Sold to Joseph Thompson, Whitby. *1870:* Sold to T. Turnbull and others, Whitby. *1.1871:* Struck Long Sand whilst on a voyage from Grimsby for Spain. Came off but sank. Crew saved by a Belgian smack.

24. LANCASHIRE 1853-1864 Wooden full-rigged ship. Two decks. Male figurehead.
O.N. 16351 855 tons 143.6 x 29.2 x 21.0 feet.
Marryat's Code Second Distinguishing Pennant: 3764. Commercial Code: MBFC.

26.2.1853: Launched by Peter Challoner, Sons and Co., Liverpool. *6.4.1853:* Delivered to Thomas Harrison (8 shares), James Harrison (16 shares), James Browne (16 shares), John Browne (8 shares), Henry Jumpe (8 shares), John Fenwick (4 shares) and Collingwood F. Jackson (4 shares), Liverpool. *1864:* Lost. The loss was reported in a letter dated 12.3.1864 from the managing owner.

Lancashire off South Stack, Anglesey. The crew are reefing in the lower main topsail in a stiff westerly breeze.
[Attributed to Joseph Heard (1799-1859) or Thomas Dove (1812-1886).]

25. DEVONPORT 1853-1854 Wooden full-rigged ship. One deck. Scroll figurehead.
767 tons 130.3 x 29.4 x 21.6 feet.
Marryat's Code 1st Distinguishing Pennant: 2687.

2.5.1840: Launched by James Jeffrey and Co., Quebec for Benn and Co., Liverpool. *1853:* Acquired by Thomas Harrison (16 shares), James Harrison (20 shares), James Browne (20 shares) and John Browne (8 shares), Liverpool for £3,200. *10.1854:* Foundered. *21.4.1855:* Register closed.

26. COLUMBIA 1854-1859 Wooden full-rigged ship. Two decks.
O.N. 24369 1,291 tons 180.0 x 35.0 x 22.5 feet.
Marryat's Code 1st Distinguishing Pennant: 2095. Commercial Code: NWLM.

1853: Built by White and Connor, Belfast, Maine, USA for Ralph C., H.H. and Alfred Johnson, Belfast, Maine as RALPH C. JOHNSON. *18.4.1854:* Acquired by Thomas Harrison (24 shares), James Harrison (8 shares), John Browne (6 shares), James Browne (10 shares) and Richard Lyon Jones (16 shares), Liverpool for £1,834. *15.3.1859:* Foundered.

27. ORKNEY LASS 1854-1857 Wooden barque. One and half decks. Female figurehead.
O.N. 1610 327 tons 109.2 x 26.2 x 16.2 feet.
Marryat's Code Second Distinguishing Pennant: 5812. Commercial Code: HKRG.

1848: Built by John Stanger, Stromness, Orkney. *4.4.1849:* Sold to Pryde and Jones, Liverpool. *31.10.1851:* Sold to Imrie and Tomlinson, Liverpool. *3.8.1854:* Acquired by Thomas Harrison (12 shares), James Harrison (20 shares), Richard Harrison (10 shares) and Gilbert Pennington (20 shares), Liverpool. *17.10.1857:* The Harrison brothers sold all their shares to Joseph Haycock and John Plowditch, Wells-next-the-Sea, Norfolk. *1869:* Lost.

Orkney Lass painted from two different angles in the River Mersey by William Kimmins McMinn (1818-1898). To the left she is shown changing tack and to the right after tacking and now heading for Princes Dock. In the left background can be seen the dome of St Pauls, between the main and foremasts the terminus of the Holyhead to Liverpool semaphore mounted on the roof of a warehouse. The church of St Nicholas is forward of the mainmast of the left hand view of the *Orkney Lass*. The Custom House is on the right.   *[Bonhams, London]*

28. ADMIRAL GRENFELL 1854-1858 Wooden barque. One and half decks. Male bust figurehead.
O.N. 14770 324 tons 127.1 x 23.0 x 13.0 feet.
Marryat's Code Second Distinguishing Pennant: 7159. Commercial Code: LPMQ.

3.1851: Built by George Cox and Co., Bideford. *11.4.1851:* Delivered to Millers and Thompson and Co., Liverpool. *17.10.1854:* Acquired by Thomas Harrison (16 shares), James Harrison (12 shares), Edward Hodgson Harrison (8 shares), Richard Williamson (20 shares) and Richard-Pierre Williamson (8 shares), Liverpool. *20.10.1854:* Thomas Harrison sold 8 shares for £500 to Edward Binnington, Scarborough. Richard-Pierre Williamson was appointed master. *17.6.1858:* Sold to John H. Hamilton, Le Havre for £2,931. *1863:* Reported lost, but by 1886 listed in the Universal Register as CLORINDA owned by Sanchez and Cardenas, Valparaiso, Chile. *1892:* Wrecked.

Captain Richard-Pierre Williamson and the ADMIRAL GRENFELL

Most of what we know of ADMIRAL GRENFELL has been handed down in the notebooks and diaries of Captain Richard-Pierre Williamson, the ship's master. He records, on 4th November 1854, that he, his father and Messrs. Harrison, "having bought the barque...laying at London, went up to London to see that all was delivered right to the Owners, according to inventory."

Their first undertaking came in the form of a charter voyage to Pernambuco. The ship sailed from Liverpool on 19th December 1854, and arrived at her destination on 30th January 1855. There she discharged her consignment of goods (we are not told what they consisted of, but R-P.W. records ruefully that he "found much of the cargo damaged", probably due to the "ship making a good sup of water through her topsides" on the outward passage.) However, the ship subsequently loaded sugar and hides at Pernambuco and Paraiba for another charter voyage, this time to the Piedmontese port of Genoa, presumably after the Captain had initiated a sustained caulking session throughout her "topsides"! Piedmont at that time was part of the Kingdom of Sardinia. R-P.W. records: "July 1 1855. Fixed the vessel to load for the Sardinian Government for the Crimea." (The Kingdom of Sardinia had declared war on Russia in January 1855, and her troops had joined the Allies in the Crimea). ADMIRAL GRENFELL finished loading her cargo of hay and bread and sailed on 27 July. On September 10, the ship passed through the Dardanelles into the Sea of Marmara and on 21st: "came to an anchor in

Balaklava Roads. Lay there for orders until 25th, when we proceeded into the harbour. The COLUMBIA, the LANCASHIRE and MONARCHY - all three ships belonging to the same employ in Balaklava Harbour. Got discharged."

ADMIRAL GRENFELL sailed on 14th October bound for Constantinople. There she loaded "400 tons of live shell" for Malta. To minimise the risk of any accidents to her dangerous cargo in those narrow waters the ship was towed as far as the exit from the Dardanelles, where she anchored and waited a few days for a favourable wind before proceeding on her voyage to Malta. That mission safely accomplished, she made her way to Alexandria to load for Liverpool, where she arrived on 4th April 1856 after being away for about 16 months.

After a month or so in Liverpool, the ship was fixed and loaded for a voyage round Cape Horn to the Pacific coast of Guatemala, a voyage likely to be beset with problems. Accompanied by his wife, R-P.W. sailed on 8th May 1856, passing the Canary Islands on 28th May.

Three months later the ship was rounding Cape Horn. "Aug 25 1856. The furthest south that we were was 61°35', and west longitude 73°30'. " This position is 210° and 388 miles from the Horn. "We were 32 days under close-reefed topsails from that day until we let them out." On 15th October 1856, ADMIRAL GRENFELL put into Callao to land two sick seamen. They were admitted to the local hospital on the 16th. R-P.W. continues: "Oct. 17 1856. At 1 a.m. heard noise on deck. Went up the companion, found that we were fastened down below and that one of the quarter boats some of the crew were lowering into the water. Could not get on deck to give the alarm. Found our way up through the skylight which was also secured. On gaining the deck found that three of the hands had run off with the boat. Had to give £4. 10/- to get the boat back. Shipped four extra hands, and proceeded to La Union (Honduras) where we arrived on 7 November."

Discharging his cargo in several Central American ports, R-P.W. set sail across the Pacific Ocean on 22nd January 1857, bound for Shanghai. He called at Molokai in the Sandwich (Hawaiian) Islands for fresh provisions, and arrived at Shanghai on 1st May, "after a pleasant passage." He then appears to have taken his ship 530 miles up the Yangtse River to Qingshan to load a cargo of alum for Hong Kong.

It was on the return voyage, with a general cargo for Shanghai, that the ship ran into very bad weather, and R-P.W. faced his most daunting task: "July 22 1857. Made the Barren Isles and at 8.15 my wife was confined of a fine boy, which we named Grenfell after the ship."

Three days later the ship was berthed at Shanghai. Once again the reader is left to fill in the dramatic detail for himself, but it is doubtless partly due to R-P.W.'s skill as a midwife and nurse that both Mrs. Williamson and little Grenfell lived to a ripe old age.

It was now time to go home, and the ship was chartered to load a cargo of tea for home ports. However, during the time spent on the China Coast, cargoes of sugar had been carried, and the rich, syrupy smell lingered on. "The vessel had to lay 10 days to sweeten. Could not get the smell out of the ship. The tea-tasters came on board, but would not give orders to commence loading until they thought all the smell of the sugar was off."

At last, on 1st September, the chests of tea were brought alongside. Further delays were incurred by the inclement weather, heavy rain disrupting the loading. At last, all was completed, and the ADMIRAL GRENFELL sailed on 22nd September 1857, and anchored for four days off Woosung Island to await favourable weather.

ADMIRAL GRENFELL crossed the South China Sea, and entered the Indian Ocean via the Sunda Straits on 8th November, stopping at Anjer, Java, to buy poultry, eggs, fish and vegetables. She rounded the Cape of Good Hope on 7th January 1858, after a passage of light winds and fine weather.

On 17th January, the barque came to anchor in St. James' Bay, St. Helena, where she watered, and more provisions were bought. Captain Williamson also took the opportunity to send up a new main topmast, the old one having been sprung. On the 19th, they set sail for England, passing close to Ascension Island on the 23rd, where they saw several vessels at anchor, but did not stop. Instead, Captain Williamson "signalized" the Fort to report his ship at home.

They passed the Tuskar Rock on 13th March in rather rough weather; failed to get into Kingstown (Dun Laoghaire) owing to the strong westerly winds, and bore away for Belfast Lough. On the 17th the ship docked in Belfast and discharged a small consignment of tea, then made sail to cross the Irish Sea to Liverpool. Finally, the ship berthed in the Albert Dock on 27th March 1858, and discharged her precious cargo of tea "in good order." It was about this time that Richard-Pierre decided to retire, and make a new life in France. At the same time the partners decided to put ADMIRAL GRENFELL up for sale.

This remarkable voyage, which lasted 22 months and 19 days, covered at least 37,500 miles on straight courses. But sailing vessels seldom steered a straight course, and this figure should be increased by at least fifty per cent. One would like to think the venture produced a handsome profit for the partners, but it is sad to record that ADMIRAL GRENFELL was not a profitable ship.[20] Nevertheless, thanks to Jane Williamson, the Captain was able to bring home a very handsome bonus!

Admiral Grenfell anchored in Hong Kong harbour. The tricolour burgee of the Williamsons flies at the main.
[From a painting by an unknown Chinese artist. Courtesy of the Williamson family of Nantes]

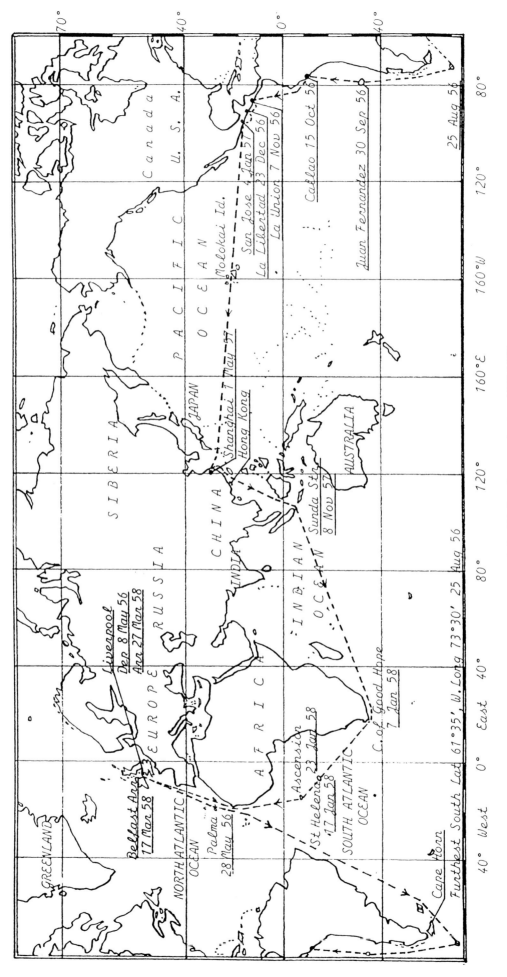

GREENLAND

NORTH ATLANTIC
OCEAN

EUROPE

<u>Belfast Arr.
17 Mar 58</u>

Palma
28 May 56

<u>Liverpool
Dep. 8 May 56
Arr. 27 Mar 58</u>

RUSSIA

SIBERIA

Canada

U.S.A.

JAPAN

CHINA

INDIA

AFRICA

<u>St Helena
17 Jan 58</u>

Ascension
23 Jan 58

SOUTH ATLANTIC
OCEAN

<u>C. of Good Hope
7 Jan 58</u>

INDIAN
OCEAN

AUSTRALIA

<u>Sunda Str.
8 Nov 57</u>

<u>Shanghai 7 May 57</u>
<u>Hong Kong</u>

PACIFIC
OCEAN

Molokai Id.

<u>San Jose 4 Jan 57</u>
<u>La Libertad 23 Dec 56</u>
<u>La Union 7 Nov 56</u>

<u>Callao 15 Oct 56</u>

<u>Juan Fernandez 30 Sep 56</u>

<u>25 Aug 56</u>

Cape Horn

Furthest South Lat 61°35', W. Long 73°30' 25 Aug 56

40° West   0° East   40°   80°   120°   160°E   160°W   120°   80°

70°   40°   0°   40°

Admiral Grenfell's 688-day circumnavigation, 1856-1858.

29. DARING 1855-1861 Wooden brig. One deck. Female figurehead.
O.N. 1177 168 tons 80.0 x 20.0 x 13.5 feet.
Marryat's Code First Distinguishing Pennant: 2567. Commercial Code: HGVL.

1844: Built at Cardiff. *21.4.1855:* Acquired by James Harrison (42 shares), Edward Hodgson Harrison (11 shares) and John Harrison (11 shares), Liverpool for £1,454.

10.1861: Sold to R.H. Bay, Whitby for £713, John Harrison retaining his shares. *2.1873:* Wrecked on S.W. Patch, Cross Sands, off Yarmouth whilst on a voyage from Leith to London.

30. WEST DERBY 1855-1876 Wooden full-rigged ship. One deck.
O.N. 1350 821 tons 155.6 x 30.4 x 21.9 feet.
Commercial Code: HJPW.

19.3.1855: Launched by Peter Challoner, Sons and Co., Liverpool. *28.4.1855:* Delivered to James Browne (24 shares), John Browne (16 shares), John Fenwick (4 shares), Thomas Harrison (12 shares) and Collingwood F. Jackson (8 shares), Liverpool. *17.7.1873:* Reported re-rigged as a barque. *26.4.1874:* Sailed from Charente with a cargo of 997 tons of brandy, an unusual assignment for a fairly large sailing vessel. To assist her departure she was towed to sea by the company's steamer FRANKFORT (47). *11.6.1874:* Arrived at her destination, Bic, Quebec. *23.6.1876:* Sold to Friend Lamb, Sunderland. *1876:* Sold to L. Larsen, Kragero, Norway and renamed OCEAN. *1885:* Deleted from *Lloyd's Register.*

The name derives from a village (now a suburb) near Liverpool.
It is interesting to note that WEST DERBY was the first Harrison-interest ship to serve as a voluntary observing ship for the Meteorological Office. Log books in the possession of that organisation show that Captain J. Sergeant and his officers recorded regular observations from 11th December 1857 to 26th February 1859 during a

voyage to Whampoa. On 12th July 1860, the Meteorological Office agent in Liverpool placed a set of their own instruments on board and, on the next voyage to Calcutta, a record of observations was kept from 20th July 1860 to 20th April 1861.[21]
The master's log of a voyage beginning on 21st July 1870 at London, the ship bound for Quebec and Montreal, records that the owners agreed to provide each member of the crew, each day, with 1lb of bread, 1/2 ounce of coffee, 1/8 ounce of tea, and 3 quarts of water. Beef and pork was to be provided on alternate days, on a scale of 1 1/2 lbs and 1 1/4 lbs respectively. Issued on a weekly basis, the men would receive 1/2 lb of rice and 14 ounces of sugar. On Sundays, Tuesdays and Thursdays, they would each be allowed 8 ozs. of flour and on Mondays, Wednesdays and Fridays, 1/3 pint of peas. Wages varied, according to service and experience, between £7 and £9 per month. At Quebec eight men deserted; and the voyage ended in Liverpool on 22nd November 1870.

West Derby anchoring in the Mersey off Egremont from a painting by Thomas Dove (1812-1886). The steam tug has cast off, the yards have been backed and the ship is drifting astern to take the strain on the anchor cable.

31. PRINCE OF ORANGE 1855-1858 Wooden barque. One deck.
O.N. 26045 526 tons 122.8 x 30.0 x 22.0 feet.
Marryat's Code 1st Distinguishing Pennant: 9782. Commercial Code: PJMG.

1814: Built at Sunderland. *12.12.1855:* Acquired by Thomas Harrison (20 shares), James Harrison (8 shares), Henry

Jumpe (12 shares) and Roger Lyon Jones (24 shares), Liverpool. *29.4.1858:* Foundered near Mauritius.

32. TIMANDRA 1856-1861 Wooden full-rigged ship. Two decks.
O.N. 25226 1030 tons 178.9 x 36.6 x 21.8 feet.
Marryat's Code Second Distinguishing Pennant: 1783.

1853: Built by Harris and Co., Monkton, St. John, New Brunswick. *23.3.1854:* Sold to Edward Oliver, Liverpool. *24.3.1854:* Sold to Henry Ellis, Liverpool. *17.10.1856:* Acquired by Thomas Harrison (16 shares), James Harrison (8 shares), James Browne (12 shares), John Browne (8 shares), Henry Jumpe (12 shares) and Roger Lyon Jones (8 shares), Liverpool. *20.9.1861:* Wrecked off Itaparica, Brazil, on a voyage from Cardiff with a cargo of coal. *26.9.1861:* Hull sold for £230 after being stripped of fittings.

TIMANDRA is a minor character in Shakespeare's "Timon of Athens". She is a mistress of Alcibiades, a soldier and friend of Timon. When Timon, in a fit of bitterness and grief, insults the lady, Alcibiades intercedes, saying "Pardon him, sweet Timandra, for his wits are drown'd and lost in his calamities..." [22]

33. PHILOSOPHER (1) 1857-1879 Iron full-rigged ship. Two decks. Male figurehead.
O.N. 14686 1,059 tons 189.0 x 34.7 x 21.9 feet.
1875: 1,330g, 1281n 230.0 x 34.7 x 21.9 feet.
Commercial Code: LPFB.

1857: Built by Thomas Vernon and Sons, Liverpool. *4.6.1857:* Delivered to Thomas Harrison (8 shares), James Harrison (8 shares), James Browne (8 shares), Henry Jumpe (8 shares), John Browne (4 shares), John Fenwick (4 shares), William J. Cookson (12 shares), John Liddell (8 shares) and Collingwood F. Jackson (4 shares), Liverpool. *23.6.1869:* Sailed from Melbourne for Calcutta with a consignment of 120 horses, of which 33 died on the passage which lasted 55 days. *1875:* Lengthened. *26.9.1879:* Wrecked at the mouth of the Daya River, near Puri, on the coast of Orissa, India whilst on a voyage from Calcutta to Boston, Mass. with general cargo. Half of her crew were lost. Her Captain was F. J. Evans.

The first vessel ordered by the Harrisons and their partners to be built of iron, and also the first vessel to be named for a trade or profession, the start of a tradition which was to become a hallmark of the company.
    During the period from 1870 to 1879, PHILOSOPHER was occasionally employed in the Coolie trade, carrying indentured labourers from Calcutta to the sugar plantations of Demerara, Surinam and the West Indies. On one such voyage, the ship sailed from Calcutta on 21st February 1878 with 473½ adults on board. She arrived at Demerara, via St. Helena on 24th May. Two coolies died on the voyage. The ship returned to Liverpool via New York. [22]

Joseph Heard's depiction of *Philosopher* off Anglesey, close hauled on the port tack.   *[Bonhams, London]*

34. GEOLOGIST (1) 1859-1872 Wooden full-rigged ship. Two decks. Male torso figurehead.
O.N. 27939 854 tons 164.5 x 33.2 x 21.5 feet.
Marryat's Code Third Distinguishing Pennant: 5713. Commercial Code: PTJM.

30.8.1859: Launched by J. Challoner and Co., Liverpool. *18.10.1859:* Delivered to Thomas Harrison (8 shares), James Harrison (8 shares), Edward Hodgson Harrison (4 shares), James Browne (12 shares), Henry Jumpe (12 shares), John Browne (8 shares), John Fenwick (4 shares), Collingwood F. Jackson (4 shares) and George Fenwick (4 shares), Liverpool at a cost of £1,620. *12.1868:* Reported aground at Banjuwangi, Java, and refloated only after the crow had jettisoned 100 tons of her rice cargo. *12.2.1872:*

Sold to John William Ford, London for £5,600. *1876:* Sold to H. Ravot and Co., Havre, France and renamed ONCLE FELIX. *12.1881:* Abandoned.

GEOLOGIST's figurehead was said to be in the likeness of Hugh Miller, a well-known geologist. It was carved by the firm of Allen and Clotworthy, who created most of the figureheads for Harrison ships. [23]

35. ASTRONOMER (I) 1860-1883 Iron full-rigged ship. Two decks. Male figurehead.
O.N. 28181. 1,119 tons 191.0 x 34.2 x 23.0 feet.
Marryat's Code 3rd Distinguishing Pennant: 5712. Commercial Code: PVJQ.

11.1859: Launched by Thomas Vernon and Sons, Liverpool.
1.2.1860: Delivered to Thomas Harrison (8 shares), James Harrison (10 shares), Edward Hodgson Harrison (8 shares), Richard Harrison (4 shares), James Browne (8 shares), John Browne (8 shares), Henry Jumpe (8 shares), John Fenwick (2 shares), Collingwood F. Jackson (4 shares) and George Fenwick (4 shares), Liverpool at a cost of £19,000.
5.10.1864: Dismasted in the Calcutta cyclone. It was

reported that nearly 200 ships parted their moorings that day. *26.10.1875:* Thomas Harrison appointed managing owner. *28.3.1883:* Sold to J. Browne and Co., Liverpool (one of the original shareholders) and rerigged as a barque. *21.3.1886:* Struck Pole Rock in Freshwater Bay, Pembrokeshire, and became a total loss. She was on passage from Port Pirie to Dublin with a cargo of wheat. *3.4.1886:* Register closed.

Astronomer sailing under forecourse and lower topsails before a westerly gale.

36. PEVERIL OF THE PEAK 1860-1869 Wooden full-rigged ship.
O.N. 15029. 713 tons 151.2 x 31.1 x 20.6 feet.
1879: 734g 704n 161.6 feet.
Marryat's Code Third Distinguishing Pennant: 1923. Commercial Code: LQNV.

1856: Built at Liverpool. *9.4.1860:* Registered in the ownership of Charles Barnes (28 shares), Thomas Harrison (8 shares) and James Laing (28 shares). *1.10.1868:* Called at Madeira when on passage from Liverpool to Karachi to land the crew of MARGARATHE GEORGINA; presumed to be the survivors of a vessel lost at sea. *20.10.1869:* Sold to

W.J. Hunter and Co., Glasgow for £2,100. *1879:* Lengthened. *1879:* Sold to Dhan Mull Pulcham, Rangoon, Burma. No subsequent information.

Named after a romantic character in a novel by Sir Walter Scott.

PART 2

THE TRANSITION YEARS – FROM SAIL TO STEAM
1860 - 1884

The Harrison brothers began their early ventures in shipping exclusively in sail. Steam ships were at sea in the 1830s and early 1840s, but they were invariably paddle steamers and the firm of Geo. Brown and Harrison showed little interest in them. Besides, their experienced seafaring partners, the Williamsons, being sailing men born and bred, probably had a built-in prejudice against the noisy, smoky, coal-consuming steamers, and were understandably disinclined to invest in them, or recommend them to their shore-based partners. Certainly, the early steamers, with their ungainly sponsons and rotary paddles powered by inadequate and unreliable steam engines were indifferent sea-boats, prone to breakdowns, and even the best of them at that stage could not compete with the splendid ocean-going sailing ships of the day. The steamer's principal advantage, of course, lay in her ability to steam directly to windward and to keep on going when there was no wind at all. Despite this, the Harrisons and their partners were content to trade in sail, at least for the time being, but doubtless keeping a wary eye on developments.

Thus, when screw-propelled steamers began to appear in the 1840s it is reasonable to suppose that an interest in steam was rekindled. A screw-propelled vessel was a different proposition altogether. The initial cost of a single cast-iron propeller was far less than the cost of a pair of enormous paddle wheels and it soon became apparent that a propeller gave more thrust per unit of power than a brace of paddle-wheels. These factors encouraged shipowners to believe that running a steamship could be an economical and profitable enterprise, although the problems associated with finding a supply of coal in the right place at the right time still gave rise to caution. However, in the event of a breakdown, a screw steamer could be sailed more readily out of trouble, since the drag of a propeller would affect the ship's sailing qualities much less than that generated by a pair of paddle wheels. This was a matter of prime importance to a generation - almost the last generation - of seamen raised in sail.

Consequently, interest in the steam engine and screw-propulsion quickened. Insofar as the Harrisons were concerned it is said that the younger brother, James, was the first disciple and principal advocate of steam. Shipping men of the day must have awaited the result of the Royal Navy's famous experiment in April 1845, a contest between a paddle steamer and a screw steamer, with keen interest. Two steam sloops were selected for the contest, both of similar tonnage and fitted with steam engines of similar horse-power. HMS RATTLER, screw-propelled, and HMS ALECTO, paddle-powered, were secured stern to stern, and each tried to tow the other backwards. When HMS RATTLER succeeded in towing her opponent astern at a rate of three knots, it must have decided the issue in many minds despite the obvious crudity of the experiment.[24] However, another fifteen years were to elapse before the Harrisons would feel the time was ripe to lay down their first steamers - the GLADIATOR and COGNAC in 1860 - and they, of course, would be screw-propelled.

In a letter dated March 1860, and circulated to shippers in the Charente region of France with whom, up to this juncture, Harrisons had conducted almost 90% of their business, the brothers announced their plan to introduce two screw steamers into the brandy trade:

"We think the time has arrived when the trade must, for the most part, be carried on by screw-steamers. We beg to inform you that we are making arrangements in conjunction with our friend Mr. Williamson of Charente, to place two new and powerful boats on the berth, which we expect to have running before next season's brandies are ready for shipment."[25]

From that time onwards, the steamer side of the fleet expanded rapidly, but the Harrisons, in conjunction with their partners and associates, still continued to build sailing vessels, full-rigged ships and barques, until 1874. These fine ships were employed mainly on the oceanic routes, especially on the long hauls round the Cape to India and the Far East, or round the Horn to the West Coasts of South and North America. The steamers, for the most part, were retained on the short-sea trades to the Charente and Cadiz, with occasional sorties into the Baltic, Mediterranean and even the Black Sea. The main exception to this general rule was the regular service to Brazil, which began in 1864, and

Olinda (45), passing the Tuskar Rock inward bound, the artist is not known.
[Bonhams, London]

was maintained by the steamers GLADIATOR, OLINDA and AMAZON.

The early years of the period covered by this section were dominated by the American Civil War which inevitably affected the fortunes of shippers and importers trading with that unhappy nation. Despite some romantic claims in certain latter-day press accounts of a Southern persuasion, there is no evidence that Harrison ships as such were ever directly involved in running the Federal blockade to bring succour to beleaguered rebel ports. Nevertheless, there was undoubtedly a great deal of sympathy for the Southern cause in cotton-hungry Lancashire, and grounds for believing that the sympathies of the Harrison brothers lay with the Confederates. The evidence lies in the inclusion of the firm's name in a Federal "black list" of Liverpool merchants trading with the "enemy" compiled by the US Consul in Liverpool, Thomas Haines Dudley, for the State Department in Washington. The list also records such household names as Cunard, Lamport and Holt, Bahr Behrend, and Henry Fernie.[26] However, one early Harrison steamer, the GLADIATOR, did indeed play a part in the war, but only after she had been

John William Hughes
died 1917

sold and passed through several hands, before becoming, in 1861, a Confederate blockade runner. Eventually, she was returned to her original owners in April 1864, and spent a long and useful life serving the Harrison trade routes.

It was around 1860 that a young man, still in his teens, joined the firm of Thos. and Jas. Harrison as a book-keeper. His name was John William Hughes. His ability and presence evidently impressed his employers, for in 1866 he was permitted to purchase two shares in the FIRE QUEEN and, in 1867, two shares in the PANTHEON. From this small beginning John Hughes was able to accumulate a considerable holding, usually in steamships. For it did, in fact, become a "steam-ship" company, all shares in the steamers eventually becoming concentrated in the hands of six people, the three surviving Harrison brothers (Richard having died in 1862, and John in 1867); Richard-Pierre Williamson; John W. Hughes and his brother, Thomas Hughes, who had lately joined the firm. The fleet's sailing ships, of which there were 21 trading between 1860 and 1888, were not included in this "family" arrangement, with the majority of shares in these ships tending to remain in the hands of "outsiders", although the ships were still managed and operated by Thos. and Jas. Harrison.

By the seventies, the large sailing ships like ARTIST, PHILOSOPHER and KING ARTHUR were finding fairly regular employment in the emigrant trade from Calcutta to Demerara and the West Indies, the so-called coolie-trade. The emigrant ships were commissioned by the Government Emigration Board and selected by tender. If hired they were obliged to conform to certain standards which were strictly enforced. A press cutting dated 10th March 1870 invited tenders for one or more ships to transport Indian emigrants from Calcutta to British

Guiana. It specified:
"For each adult of 10 years (sic) the space required is 12 superficial feet, and for each child between the ages of two and 10, eight superficial feet. The ship must be fitted with an apparatus, to be approved by the Emigration Agent, for distilling fresh from salt water in a quantity not less than 500 gallons in 24 hours, and must take out and land in Calcutta, without additional charge, any coolie clothing and stores that the Commissioners may wish to send out."[27]

One can readily imagine what a difficult trade this must have been. The ships carried between 400 and 500 men, women and children, all under the statutory care of a Surgeon-Commissioner. The emigrants were conveyed to their new life at the rate of £10 to £12 per adult, according to the state of the market. The voyage from Calcutta to the Guianas was a tedious one lasting fully three months. Climatic conditions varied from violent storms rounding the Cape of Good Hope to the exhausting heat and glassy calms of the doldrums, as the ship crossed and re-crossed the tropics. The problems of feeding such a multitude, of sanitation and hygiene, and of maintaining discipline, were formidable, and called for organisation of a high order.

Thomas Hughes
died 1912

Nevertheless, to learn that a number of emigrants failed, on occasion, to survive the voyage is hardly surprising. What is even more surprising is the fact that large-scale epidemics were avoided, and it is on record that Harrison vessels, their captains and crews, received a good press for their professionalism and humane treatment of the travellers in their care.[28]

At around this time there was a move to co-ordinate the shipowning enterprises in which the partners and associates of Thos. and Jas. Harrison were involved. Members still continued to buy and sell shares in individual ships on a casual, almost haphazard basis.

Sometimes individuals bonded together to form informal groups, and it seemed sensible to appoint one of the senior partners (usually Thomas Harrison) as managing owner, the shareholding groups paying a commission to the management. The rudimentary company thus formed in 1871 became known as The Charente Steam-Ship Company. Details of its structure are sparse, but it was unlikely to be registered under the existing Companies' Acts of 1862 and 1867. For the time being it remained as an informal group of family and friends, its capital linked to personal share ownership in individual ships. Nevertheless, there must have been a capital structure of some kind, if only to govern the value of shares and dividends. It is known, for instance, that in 1871 John William Hughes purchased shares equivalent to three sixty-fourths of the total capital value of the company for the sum of £6,750. This indicates that the company's declared capital at that time was £144,000. Three years later the price paid by J. W. Hughes for a further three sixty-fourths was £17,500, implying a capital of about

29

£373,300 - a considerable appreciation in so short a period.[29]

In 1871 the main assets of the Charente Steam-Ship Company consisted of 15 screw-steamers with an aggregate gross tonnage of 18,660 tons. The nine sailing vessels still in service at the time were owned by several shareholders other than the Harrisons, Williamsons and Hugheses (who alone by this time shared ownership of the steamers) and sail continued to be operated outside the group under the old system, managed by Thos. and Jas. Harrison.

During the 1870s a second generation of Harrisons had begun to take an active interest in the firm: Thomas Fenwick Harrison, son of Thomas; Frederick James Harrison and Heath Harrison, sons of James. Towards the end of the decade, as the founders grew older, the management of the firm tended to be left more and more in the hands of John W. Hughes and his brother, Thomas, at least until the younger generation of Harrisons attained maturity.

One of the more significant international events to occur during this period was the opening of the Suez Canal by the Empress Eugenie of France in 1869. James Harrison was a particularly enthusiastic supporter of the canal enterprise, and made it his business to meet and cultivate the friendship of de Lesseps, the engineer in charge of the project. James Harrison foresaw a great future for the new waterway, and was the instigator of a Harrison Line steam ship service to India within weeks of its inauguration. The first Harrison vessel to navigate the Canal was the FIRE QUEEN, which left Liverpool on 13th January 1870, passed through the Canal (becoming the 27th vessel to make the transit) on 4th February, and arrived at Bombay on 25th.

One evening in 1873, Richard-Pierre Williamson, the intrepid master mariner who had pioneered so many of the company's trade routes, the friend and partner of the Harrison brothers since they first met in George Brown's counting-house in the 1830s, was returning in his carriage from Rochefort to his home in Tonnay-Charente, when he was suddenly struck blind. He died a year later, on 11th March 1874, at the age of 61.[30] He left a sizeable fortune of which his interests in the Charente Steam-Ship Company formed a considerable part. In a codicil to his will dated six weeks before his death, Richard-Pierre gave instructions for his shares in the Charente Steam-Ship Company to be realised by his executors and trustees, James Harrison and J. W. Hughes, and the proceeds to be paid into his estate.[31] However, the elder sons of Richard-Pierre, Captain R. R. Williamson and Thomas Williamson, each retained one share in the company, thus maintaining the Williamson connection.

The company now faced the challenge of the future with younger men at the helm - the Harrison sons, Frederick, Heath and Thomas Fenwick and the more mature Hughes brothers. Of the founders, James had virtually retired in 1880 to live on his country estate at Dorden near Tunbridge Wells. Thomas still remained in overall command, though in indifferent health, happy that his son, his nephews and his protégés should see to the day-to-day running of the firm, while keeping himself available to advise and direct as circumstances demanded. It was to prove a fruitful arrangement.

FLEET LIST Part 2

37. GLADIATOR (1) 1860-1861, 1864-1878 Iron steamship rigged as three masted schooner. One deck and four holds.
O.N. 29018 592g 460n 192.8 x 27.8 x 15.7 feet. Cargo capacity: approx. 32,000 cubic feet. Certificate for 15 passengers.
International Code: QCVL.
Two x 2-cyl. by Hackworth and Co., Stockton-on-Tees; each 36 x 26 inches, 9 knots.
1881: C.2-cyl. by Dunsmuir and Jackson, Glasgow; 23, 42 x 30 inches.

29.10.1860: Launched by M. Pearse and Co., Stockton-on-Tees (Yard No. 28) for T. and J. Harrison and Partners, Liverpool at a cost of £11,800. *12.1860:* Delivered. *1861:* Sold to Peninsular and North African Steam Navigation Co.[32] *24.10.1861:* Sold to Melchior G. Klinginder, Liverpool, agent for the Galway Line to the U.S.A. and a dealer in armaments. The vessel was then fitted out as a blockade runner in the service of the Confederate States. Upon completion, sold to C.K. Prioleau, financial agent to the Confederacy and a partner in Fraser, Trenholm and Co. of Charleston, South Carolina and Liverpool. *10.11.1861:* Cleared Gravesend with a cargo of munitions and equipment destined for the Confederate Army of Virginia. *9.12.1861:* Arrived at Nassau, Bahamas, and transferred her cargo to KATE and other vessels. *3.1862:* Sold to John Fraser and Co. *18.6.1862:* Registered at Liverpool in the ownership of Melchor G. Klinginder and mortgaged to C.K. Prioleau. *10.11.1863:* Mortgage discharged and sold to C.K. Prioleau. *4.1864:* Reacquired by T. and J. Harrison for £11,540. *13.5.1864:* Cleared outwards from Liverpool for Charente on

her first commercial voyage. *23.9.1864:* Registered in the names of Thomas Harrison (22 shares), James Harrison (20 shares), Edward Hodgson Harrison (8 shares), John Harrison (6 shares) and Richard-Pierre Williamson (8 shares). *1.10.1864:* Sailed for Pernambuco, inaugurating Harrison's regular service to Brazil. This service was to continue until just prior to the outbreak of the Second World War. *10.1869:* Sank the brig ANDRONIKOS in a collision off Tulchai (Tulcea) on the Danube in Romania. *7.3.1873:* Put back to Liverpool after being run down by the steamer MORAVIAN (2,481/64) and spent six weeks under repair in dry dock at Clover, Clayton and Co., Liverpool. *4.1877:* Laid up at Liverpool for extensive repairs and structural repairs to forecastle plates and bulkheads. *25.7.1878:* Sold to M.C. de Pothonier, Liverpool for £3,800. *1881:* Fitted with a new engine. *1883:* Sold to Layborn and Legge, Liverpool. *1.12.1887:* Sold to David MacBrayne and Co., Glasgow. *12.12.1893:* Wrecked at Zabara, Cadiz, when on passage from Mauritius to Liverpool with a cargo of sugar.

GLADIATOR and the American Civil War
The GLADIATOR plied for two-and-a-half years between Liverpool, Nassau and ports in the rebel Southern States carrying military stores outwards and badly needed cotton homewards. The risks were high, but so were freights and wages. It is recorded that shipmasters who ran the gauntlet between Nassau and Wilmington could earn as much as £1,000, seamen and firemen £50 - princely sums in those days for a couple of weeks' work.
She is mentioned twice in the US Navy's Official History of the Civil War.[33]
17-18.12.1861 "By making herself a target of chase, she (the Confederate steamship THEODORA) unsuccessfully attempted to lure U.S.S. FLAMBEAU away from Nassau, hoping to allow opportunity for the British steamer GLADIATOR to escape from that port with her cargo of

munitions, said to be sufficient to arm 25,000 Confederates."[34] Again, in February 1862 the Confederate steamer CATAWHA "arrived at Nassau bearing a cargo of cotton and rice, and took on arms and powder from the British s.s. GLADIATOR."[35]
Further light is shed on these incidents by Ethel S. Nepveux who writes, "By the time FINGAL (another blockade runner) had reached Savannah (in November 1861), Major Caleb Huse was loading a screw-steamer, the GLADIATOR, with a million dollars worth of supplies. She was slow, but the best ship the Confederates could get. Her cargo included 22,240 Enfield rifles. Captain Bird, formerly Captain of the Fraser, Trenholm ship ADELAIDE, took the GLADIATOR to Nassau". Bird had intended leaving Nassau the same day, but a Yankee gunboat, the FLAMBEAU,

Commander William G. Temple USN, had also arrived. Captain Bird then considered it imprudent to leave, in case FLAMBEAU gave chase, because GLADIATOR was the slower ship. In fact, when Commander Temple heard the nature of GLADIATOR's cargo, "he kept the fires banked under his boilers so that he could follow the GLADIATOR out at any moment, even without a Pilot if necessary".[36]

The Confederate authorities, and particularly General Lee, were desperate for GLADIATOR's cargo. Various expedients were suggested and rejected under the watchful eye of Commander Temple. He himself believed that two small Confederate ships, the THEODORA and ELLA WARLEY, would attempt to lure him out of the harbour to enable the GLADIATOR to escape, but he determined to sit tight, despite the ostentatious and provocative displays of defiance put on by the rebels. When they eventually sailed he ignored them.

On 18th January 1862, the Confederate ship CAROLINA came into Nassau. She had just been purchased by John Fraser and Co., a subsidiary of Fraser, Trenholm, with an office in Nassau. She was renamed KATE. US Consul Whiting was furious with Commander Temple for failing to apprehend the rebel ships, which were slipping in and out of Nassau, and re-appearing at enemy ports with something approaching regularity. Commander Temple was unimpressed, however.

It was now KATE's turn to discharge her cargo of 250 bales of cotton, and clandestinely to load what remained of GLADIATOR's arms cargo. She sailed unmolested, and turned up at Fernandina, Florida on 15th February 1862.

Meanwhile, Commander Temple reported ruefully that "the GLADIATOR was now drawing three-and-a-half feet less water". In March, the GLADIATOR was sold to John Fraser and Co. because she was "a marked vessel, watched by the enemy", but she entered Liverpool with a cargo of cotton and rosin on 25th May, and continued to serve the rebel cause for another two years.

By 1864 the Federal Navy had grown in strength, and interceptions became more frequent. In desperation, the Confederate agencies in Britain and elsewhere sought out the fastest vessels they could find - usually river or cross-channel paddle steamers with low freeboard and light draft for negotiating the shallow creeks and rivers. Some of these vessels were capable of speeds up to 18 knots, and could out-run any Federal gunboat. Obviously GLADIATOR was not in this class, but she was cleared from Liverpool to Nassau on at least two other occasions, on 27th November 1862 and again on 25th April 1863, commanded by a Captain A. Hora. At Nassau, a Captain Wallace took command, and on 25th May she cleared for Matamoras, a Mexican town just across the Rio Grande from Brownsville, Texas. Then in October 1863, and January 1864, GLADIATOR apparently made two voyages to Alexandria, a town on the Potomac near Washington, under the command of Captain V. Caster.[37] These must have been forlorn ventures for, after Gettysburg in July 1863, Lee's Army of Northern Virginia had been forced to retreat south to defend Richmond, the Confederate capital. Consequently, even if GLADIATOR had been able to elude the Federal blockade, she would be entering territory overrun by hostile Union troops.

38. COGNAC (1) 1860-1898 Iron steamship rigged as three-masted schooner. Two decks and two holds.
O.N. 29159 490g 376n 770d 170.0 x 25.1 x 16.3 feet. Cubic capacity: 29,472 cubic feet.
International Code: QDLV.
C.2-cyl. by Lees, Anderson and Co., Glasgow; 17, 32 x 27 inches.
1882: C. 2-cyl. by Lees, Anderson and Co., Glasgow; 17, 32 x 27 inches.

31.10.1860: Launched by Thomas Vernon and Son, Liverpool. *12.1860:* Delivered to Thomas Harrison (16 shares), James Harrison (16 shares), Edward Hodgson Harrison (8 shares) and Richard-Pierre Williamson (16 shares), Liverpool for £11,450. *18.10.1862:* Put into Milford Haven after the cargo of steel pipes and pig iron had shifted in heavy weather during a voyage from Greenock to Lisbon. *8.1868:* Whilst anchored off Ardrossan was forced to slip her anchor and chain and was driven ashore. Refloated three days later after lightening. *18.9.1875:* In collision with the Spanish steamer BEATRIZ (731/64) which was on passage from Cork to Liverpool. Spent three weeks under repair in dry dock at Clover, Clayton and Co., Liverpool. *11.1876:* In collision with the Glasgow steamer COPELAND (798/74) when on passage from Ardrossan to Charente. *11.11.1876:* Put into Fishguard for repairs and subsequently resumed her voyage. *18.5.1882:* Laid up at Aitken Slip, Glasgow and subsequently fitted with a new engine at a cost of £5,200. The mizzen mast was removed. *2.11.1882:* Returned to service. *12.8.1884:* Sailed from Troon for Charente and ran aground on Ailsa Craig. Refloated after five hours and resumed her voyage. *18.12.1884:* All the partners

transferred their shares to The Charente Steam-Ship Co. Ltd. *22.8.1896:* In collision with the company's steamer EDITOR off the North West Lightship in Liverpool Bay. Captain E. Clegg and Second Officer W.P. Bevan of the EDITOR were dismissed following an internal enquiry. *11.11.1898:* Sank in the Irish Sea following a collision with the Belfast steamer VOLTAIC (612/67) off the Skerries, Anglesey. The crew took to the boats and all were saved. She was on passage from Charente to Liverpool with a cargo of brandy and general.

One of two iron screw steamers built for the Charente brandy trade in 1860, COGNAC was classed under Bureau Veritas rules. She was destined to ply the route in the company of sailing ships for the next two years since her slightly larger consort, GLADIATOR, was taken over for service in the American Civil War. Her primary trading pattern lay between the Mersey and the Charente - coal and manufactured iron products outwards, brandies homewards. Later, Scottish and Irish ports were worked into the schedule and the route was extended to include the wine ports of Spain and Portugal.

Cognac was Harrison's second steamer; the *Gladiator* having been launched two days earlier.
[From a painting by Clarles Leduc].

39. DRAGON 1862-1866 Iron steamship rigged as three-masted schooner. One deck. Dragon figurehead (subsequently lost at sea).
O.N. 42642 315g, 257n 160.0 x 22.6 x 12.8 feet.
Commercial Code: TKPR.

8.1861: Launched by Jones, Quiggin and Co., Liverpool (Yard No. 113) and delivered to Peter Eaton Hinde, Liverpool. *1862:* Acquired by Thomas Harrison (26 shares), James Harrison (20 shares), Edward Hodgson Harrison (8 shares) and Richard-Pierre Williamson (10 shares), Liverpool for £7,500. Designated to open a direct service between London and Charente, but after four voyages in the face of keen opposition, reverted to the West Coast trade with her sisters CHARENTE and COGNAC. *24.3.1866:* Sold to John Shaw, Liverpool for £6,075 and mortgaged to James Stirling, Dublin. *6.1.1868:* James Stirling became sole owner and registered at Dublin. *5.3.1868:* Registered in Glasgow in the ownership of John Bell of Edinburgh. *6.3.1868:* Register closed, sold foreign.

40. CHARENTE 1862-1863 Iron steamship rigged as three-masted schooner. Two decks.
O.N. 44638 565g 441n 176.8 x 27.2 x 16.1 feet.
C. 2-cyl.

15.2.1862: Launched by James Laing, Sunderland (Yard No. 248). *4.4.1862:* Delivered to Thomas Harrison (36 shares), James Harrison (20 shares) and Edward Hodgson Harrison (8 shares), Liverpool for £12,500. *6.1863:* Sold to the Secretary of State for India for £12,012, renamed AMBERWITCH and refitted as a cable ship at North Woolwich. *11.1863:* Sailed for Bombay via Cape of Good Hope. Subsequently employed laying and repairing telegraph cables in the Persian Gulf. *4.1873:* Withdrawn to Aden for picket duties. *1887:* Relegated to Royal Indian Navy Reserve. *1888:* Sold for Rupees 21,000, presumably for scrap.

CHARENTE's alter ego
Between April 1862 and June 1863, the CHARENTE made several round voyages to the brandy ports of the Charente region of Western France. Occasionally, trade would take her further afield to such ports as Lisbon, Cadiz and Alicante. In September 1862 she steamed as far as Patras in the Gulf of Corinth to load 520 tons of currants. She returned to London, via Gibraltar for bunkers, on 16th October 1862.

In the following year, on 12th June 1863, the vessel arrived in London after a voyage from Cadiz only to be sold to the Secretary of State for India, for £12,012, "for employment in the service of the Government of India", according to a letter to the Liverpool Customs Register from the India Office dated 7th July 1863. That the sale was sanctioned with some reluctance is revealed in the wistful comment, written in James Harrison's bold hand: "Sic transit Gloria Mundi..."

The purchase had been negotiated on behalf of the Indian Government by Colonel Patrick Stewart of the Bengal Engineers. His was the task of converting the ship for cable-laying and repair duties in the Persian Gulf in accordance with plans to lay a telegraph cable from Basrah to Karachi, completing a direct link between London and India.

Later that month, the ship's name was changed to AMBERWITCH, and early in July she went to North Woolwich to be fitted out for her new rôle under the command of Lieutenant Arthur Stiffe, RIN.

In November 1863, armed with two brass cannon, and loaded with submarine cable, she sailed for Bombay, and a completely new life.

Charente is a river in western France flowing into the Bay of Biscay. It also gave its name to the Charente Steamship Company.

Charente outward bound in the English Channel.   *[From a painting attributed to Frederick Tudgay and at present in the British Mercantile Marine Memorial Collection].*

41. BOTANIST (1) 1863-1881 Iron full-rigged ship. Two decks. Three-quarter man figurehead.
O.N. 45852 1,160g 1,127n 215.5 x 33.7 x 23.0 feet.
Commercial Code: VGBR.

19.1.1863: Launched by James Laing, Sunderland (Yard No. 256). *24.2.1863:* Delivered to Thomas Harrison (16 shares), Edward Hodgson Harrison (4 shares), John Fenwick (4 shares), Collingwood F. Jackson (4 shares), Francis W. Reynolds (16 shares), Charles Barnes (12 shares) and Horatio Nelson Hughes (8 shares), Liverpool for £18,565. *1863:* Inaugurated a service to India, anchoring 1.7.1863 in Madras Roads and berthing 27.8.1863 at Calcutta. *3.1879:* Converted to barque rig at Liverpool. *10.8.1881:* Sold to Hermann Conrad Johannes Folsch and Co., Hamburg, Germany and renamed PAPOSO. *10.1883:* Reaching the final stage of a voyage from Iquique to Hamburg, she came to an anchor off Gluckstadt on the River Elbe. Hours later she was struck by the Newcastle steamer CRAMLINGTON (859/72) and was so badly damaged that she sank. Eighty-four years later the wreck was discovered, completely silted up, during dredging operations in 1967. Among artefacts recovered were a sextant and a brass nameplate. These form part of the Baltes Collection, now preserved in the Wreck Museum at Cuxhaven.

A versatile trader - the sailing vessel BOTANIST, 1863-1881

Prior to setting out on the inaugural voyage to India in 1863 the owners gave the master a long letter full of instructions to guide him throughout the new venture. It included a list of agents to be employed in the several ports he might visit, and advice on the securing of homeward freight. Liverpool was the port preferred to London "even at the sacrifice of about £400 in freight".[38] Looking on the dark side, and weighing the possibility of an accident, the master was advised to "make the expenses as small as possible, for under any circumstances the underwriters are liable for only two-thirds of the actual damages arising from the accident, and not, as is by many supposed, for all sorts of things that a master may choose to get done".

The master was forbidden to take his ship "through the Torres Straits, unless under absolute necessity, and then advise the owners, before you start, of your intentions". And curiously "calling at the Cape of Good Hope or at St. Helena is strictly forbidden, except under special and extreme necessity, which will be strictly investigated on arrival. Care must be taken before sailing to provide against any such calls being required". This was, presumably, a temporary injunction, though the reasons for it are obscure.

The advice on heavy lifts is as appropriate today as it was 125 years ago: "When you have any heavy article to discharge or take on board, be careful to have sufficient tackle, and also that no damage is done to the other goods in removing the heavy package".

A call at Mauritius during the southern summer months was fraught with anxiety and apt to stir up apprehension in the stoutest heart: "Vessels arriving in Mauritius from November to April during the hurricane season ought to be well-supplied with coir rope fenders, and the Captain of the Port recommends ships in tiers to be lashed together, with good stout fenders to prevent chafes. Most of the damage done to vessels in a hurricane in this port is from ships breaking adrift, and falling down on the next tiers. If lashed together and well-fendered it would prevent a good deal of damage. The holding ground is not good..."

During the 1870s the BOTANIST, along with several other Harrison square riggers, was engaged in the coolie trade between Calcutta and the West Indies. This enterprise was strictly regulated by Act of Parliament, and ships engaged in the trade had to comply with certain standards of accommodation, sanitation, ventilation, and culinary arrangements. On 29th August 1875 BOTANIST, under the command of Captain Longridge, sailed from Calcutta with 421$^1/_2$ "adult" coolies on board. This is a composite figure which includes adult men and women, children (i.e. half-adults) and infants. It was the count on which the freight of £12 per head was paid; infants travelled free, and children under 11 at half-adult fare. On this particular voyage there were in fact 454 "souls" on board. The ship arrived at Demerara on 3rd December, and landed 416 "adults", 5$^1/_2$ having died on the voyage. Actually, BOTANIST landed 452 "souls", having had eight deaths, and six births among the passengers.[39]

Two years later, on 21st August 1877, the ship again sailed from Calcutta with 426 "adults" (438 "souls") on board, plus her crew of 38. The ship was engaged on a French Government charter to carry her human freight to Guadeloupe. The ship called at Capetown on 16th October, and sailed again on 18th, having taken fresh stores and water. According to Captain Edgar's notes, the ship arrived off the harbour of Pointe-a-Pitre, Guadeloupe, on 27th November, and "was visited by a health officer and interpreter, who did not come on board so we were not allowed to correspond with the shore." On 29th the pilot came out and got the ship underway and anchored close to the coolie depot. The coolies were landed soon after in the depot, 442 (sic) souls, 13 adults and eight infants having died, and having had nine births during the voyage.

Fragments of notes and diaries on many of the BOTANIST's voyages are still in existence, at least in transcript form. A few of the more interesting features of those voyages are reproduced here:

"Voyage 9. Hauled out of East India Dock on 13 October 1871, and anchored at Gravesend. 14 October, towed to Beachy Head. 16 October. Put into Spithead, crew refusing duty. I proceeded again on Friday 20. Draught 17'. Arrived at the Sandheads 7 February 1872, 109 days out". (What happened to the recalcitrant crew is not recorded).

"Voyage 10. Liverpool to Sydney. Tuesday 22 October 1872; hauled out of Princes Basin and anchored in River. 23 October; proceeded to sea in tow of steam tug RETRIEVER. Arrived in Sydney on 11 February 1873 111 days... Sailed from Sydney for London on 21st April 1873. Cargo consisted principally of tin ore, tallow, preserved meats, and 383 bales of wool. Sum total of freight £6,050. Arrived and docked in London on 28 August after a long passage of 124 days".[40]

A more detailed inventory of cargo than that provided above by Captain Longridge is listed in a press item pasted into one of the Voyage Books. In addition to two passengers, the ship carried: "3818 (sic) bales of wool, 21 bales cotton, 333 casks tallow, 2218 cases meat, 18 bales skins, 12654 ingots copper, 1839 cakes copper, 1282 hides, 50 bales leather, 1327 packages tin ore, 331 packages tin, 228 bags copra, 44 hogsheads molasses, 180 cases gum, 14 cases wine, 15 packages sundries, and a quantity of bones and horns." An excellent cargo by any standards!

Voyage 14. This was the voyage which began at Liverpool on 26th February 1877, and went to Guadeloupe with coolies on the French Government charter. From Guadeloupe, the ship sailed for Baltimore, Maryland in ballast, the ballast consisting of 113 tons of stones, and 67 tanks (the coolies' water tanks) filled with salt water. "Arrived at Pilot Station on 25 December 1877. Reached town (Baltimore) on 1 January 1878. Towage from 8 miles inside the Capes U.S.$150. Tug MARY SHAW Pilot Adams". Her cargo consisted of grain, flour, tallow and timber. "Lower hold full of grain and from part of after hatch to one stanchion before main hatch. Flour from grain towards foremast. Tallow and cornel wood in after tween decks, with a quantity of flour, and one tween deck empty. Under the grain oak planks, and a quantity under the tween deck cargo. Thinnest planks used for shifting boards in lower hold, four feet from deck. Arrived Liverpool on 17 February 1878 after a rough passage."

Voyage 15. After arriving at Calcutta on 1st July 1878 the ship loaded 2,209 tons of general cargo for New York, and sailed on 13th September. "Full ship. After leaving found the ship very tender. Sent royal yards down on deck. After crossing the Equator (in the Atlantic) sent them up again; ship was then stiffened. Carried them the remainder of the passage. 18 January 1879. Arrived, and anchored at Sandy Hook after a passage of 125 days; all well". The ship left New York on 9th February 1879 with a cargo of corn and cotton for Liverpool, berthing in the Albert Dock on 6 March.

"Voyage 16. (First voyage as a barque). Sailed from Liverpool on 10 April 1879. Put back from Crosby Lightship - jibboom carried away, and Mate (Mr. Black) fell overboard. Mate picked up by Lightship's boat all but dead. Got medical advice and new boom fitted. Sailed again on 12 April, Mate recovered". The ship continued her voyage to Rangoon, arrived on 6th August 1879, and discharged her cargo of 1,591 tons of salt. She was then chartered to load a cargo of rice for "U.K. or Continent, Channel for orders". The freight per ton payable was 27/6d to U.K. or 30/- to Continent. As Harrisons always preferred their ships in Liverpool a "special offer" of 25/- was made as an inducement to charterers to direct the ship to that port. In the event, the ship went to London.

Voyage 17, master, Captain Black, Cardiff to Valparaiso. The vessel sailed from Cardiff on 7th April 1880, towed by the tugs ROYAL TUSCAN and TWEED, and loaded with a cargo of 1,099 tons of gas coal, and 450 tons of patent foundry coke. She rounded the Horn without incident and arrived at Valparaiso on 22nd July, after 104 days on passage. "Received Custom House papers on 27 and proceeded to sea that night bound for Totorabillo. Arrived on 3 August and anchored in the Bay in 12 fathoms of water and commenced to discharge on the 9. Put out all the coke, and 500 tons of coal. Left Totorabillo on 9 September bound for Pina Blanca ... arrived on the 17 and commenced to discharge (the balance of coal) on the 21.

Totorabillo and Pina Blanca are two inhospitable ports to go to; the westerly swell sets in so heavily it makes landing bad, and consequently keeps you from discharging. There is no fresh water to be got at either port fit for use, and no supplies of any kind, but fresh beef, and that you have to pay a very high price for. I recommend a ship to get all her supplies at Valparaiso if going north of Coquimbo".

Left Pina Blanca with 600 tons sand ballast on October 23, bound for San Francisco". There, the ship loaded a cargo of wheat for Queenstown for orders. She arrived at Queenstown after a passage lasting 163 days, "ship very foul and sluggish in the water". She was then ordered to Hull, and arrived in the Humber on 24th July 1881 after a total voyage lasting 16 months and 14 days. Once her cargo was discharged, the ship was sold to German owners on 10th August 1881 and renamed PAPOSO, of Hamburg.

42. NATURALIST (1) 1863-1879 Iron full-rigged ship. Two decks. Half man figurehead.
O.N. 45853 1,165g, 1,093n 211.4 x 33.8 x 22.7 feet.
Commercial Code: VGBS.

1863: Launched by Thomas Vernon and Sons, Liverpool. *2.1863:* Delivered to Thomas Harrison (20 shares), Edward Hodgson Harrison (4 shares), John Harrison (4 shares), John Fenwick (4 shares), Charles Barnes (12 shares), Horatio Nelson Hughes (8 shares), Collingwood F. Jackson (4 shares) and John Vernon (8 shares), Liverpool for £20,016. *14.11.1864 - 2.12.1864:* Participated in meteorological observations under Captain Arthur Hyde on a voyage from the Equator to Sandheads. *1877:* Made one voyage in the coolie trade out of Calcutta, carrying 414 adult coolies to Demerara at £12 per head. *2.2.1879:* Sailed from Calcutta with a cargo of 2,033 tons of gunnies and jute and not seen again. *22.10.1879:* Posted missing at Lloyd's. Customs at Liverpool were notified of the ship's loss in a letter dated 1.11.1879 from Thos. and Jas. Harrison.

Naturalist of 1863 under storm canvas in a full gale. *[Artist unknown]*

43. GREYHOUND 1864-1871 Wooden full-rigged ship. Three decks.
O.N. 14632 1,411g 199.2 x 39.4 x 21.4 feet.
Marryat's Code: First Distinguishing Pennant: 4713. Commercial Code: LNWJ.

1853: Launched by W. and J. Gardner, Baltimore for Hancock and Dawson, Philadelphia, USA as EUROCLYDON. Employed mainly in the tea trade from India to the United Kingdom. *5.12.1864:* Acquired by Thomas Harrison (24 shares), Hoskins Brothers (8 shares), John Davies (8 shares), James Jackson (24 shares), Liverpool and renamed GREYHOUND. (Edward H. Harrison held three shares in the ship in 1857, but sold them in 1862, before Thomas and his partners purchased the ship). *20.2.1871:* Sold to George Dryden Dale and William Crighton, North Shields. *9.9.1873:* Sold to Henry Nelson, South Shields, George Fenwick, North Shields and S. H. Frazer, London. *6.10.1884:* Sold to William Clay and partners, South Shields. *1886:* Reduced to barque rig. *6.6.1888:* Sold to S. Svenson, Arendal, Norway and renamed EBBA. *21.2.1889:* Wrecked on Breton Island whilst on a voyage from Algoa Bay to Ship Island, New Orleans in ballast. The crew were landed at New Orleans.

44. ARTIST (1) 1864-1886 Iron full-rigged ship. Two decks. Male figurehead.
O.N. 51040 1,371g 222.6 x 36.45 x 23.3 feet.
Marryat's Code 2nd Distinguishing Pennant: 6437. Commercial Code: JLQS.

18.10.1864: Launched by Humber Iron Works and Shipbuilding Co., Hull. *6.12.1864:* Delivered to Thomas Harrison, Liverpool. Shares were then disposed of as follows: Thomas Harrison (6 shares), James Harrison (4 shares), John Liddell (4 shares), Collingwood F. Jackson (4 shares), Charles Barnes (4 shares), John Fenwick (6 shares), Horatio Nelson Hughes (8 shares), Joseph Straker (4 shares), John Straker (4 shares), William J. Cookson (4 shares), William Crosfield (8 shares) and Francis William Reynolds (8 shares). Shares changed hands fairly frequently over the next twenty years, most of them coming into the hands of the sons of the Harrison brothers, Fenwick (son of Thomas), Frederick James and Heath (sons of James). *25.3.1878:* Coasting from London to Liverpool could be a tiresome and costly operation in adverse winds, as demonstrated by the following itinerary. The ship left London in tow of the tug RESCUE and at 16.00 on 26.3.1878 she was reported off the Isle of Wight. On 28.3.1878 she was reported off the Lizard, and only parted with the tug on 30.3.1878 fifty miles north by east of the Longships. *2.4.1878:* Arrived at Milford Haven at 10.30 and sailed next day at 07.00, again towed by the tug RESCUE. She arrived at Liverpool on 4.4.1878. *6.1881:* In collision with the French fishing schooner EMILE ERNESTINE, which sank. Six crew from the schooner were lost.[41] *10.1884:* Chartered by P.& O. Steam Navigation Co. for a cargo of 1,864 tons coal to Bombay at 17/6d per ton, a total of £1,631. *27.2.1886:* Sold to R.H. Dixon and Sons, Liverpool. *5.11.1887:* Destroyed by fire in the South Pacific when on passage from Liverpool to Wilmington, California. The crew were rescued by the Newcastle steamer SILVERDALE (2,249/81). *17.1.1888:* Register closed.

Harrison Line's involvement in the coolie trade

Between 1874 and 1880, the ARTIST was employed regularly in the coolie trade - carrying immigrant workers from Calcutta to the West Indies. Details of the following voyages have survived:

Sailed from Calcutta	Arrived at Demerara	No. of days on passage	No. of adult coolies	Freight	Return
4. 8.1874	8.11.1874	96	471¹/₂	£7,000	Via New York
18. 8.1875	10.11.1875	89	481¹/₂	£5,778	Via Demerara
26. 8.1876	23.11.1876	89	481¹/₂	£5,778	Via New York
30. 9.1877	2.1.1878	94	475	£5,700	Via Demerara
1.11.1878	25. 1.1879*	85	476¹/₂	£4,765	In ballast
9.12.1879	9. 3.1880**	91	479	£4,790	In ballast
Totals			2,865	£33,811	
Averages		90²/₃	477¹/₂	£5,635 = £11.16s/coolie	

* Arrived Trinidad   **Arrived Guadeloupe

The average cost of fittings, food and water for the passengers was recorded as 23/4d per adult. The voyages tended to follow a regular pattern - out from Liverpool to Calcutta with a full load of salt; embark the emigrants and ship them across two oceans to the West Indies. The ships would then hope to pick up a cargo of sugar and rum for Liverpool; if not, then a similar cargo for New York. If the incentive was there, they would even ballast up to New York to load a cargo of cereals, timber, cotton and tobacco for Liverpool, the entire round voyage occupying about twelve months.

The following extract from a Georgetown newspaper, written on the occasion of the ARTIST's second voyage in the trade, is perhaps typical: *"The Coolie ship ARTIST, which arrived at the Light Vessel on the 10th November (1875), crossed the bar on Sunday the 14th, and came to her moorings off the Kingston Stelling, where the immigrants were partly examined by the Immigration*

Authorities. The ship proceeded the next morning to the Stelling of Messrs. Sandbach Parker and Co., the consignees, where the people were landed at 3 p.m. and the inspection was concluded at the Immigration Depot next morning. The Immigration Agent-General, and Medical

Officer to the Department were much pleased with the appearance of the immigrants, and pronounced them an even finer body of people than those introduced in the LINGUIST (which had arrived off the port on 6 November 1875, and must have seen ARTIST arrive before she got under way on 11th). They were under the medical care of Richard Rivers Esq., an old and experienced medical gentleman. The ship is commanded by Mr Sergent, and the Immigration Agent-General was pleased to express his entire satisfaction with the ship, her fittings and stores, as well as with the conduct of the Commander and others of the ship. The Surgeon, Mr Rivers, spoke highly of the discipline on board, and the care and attention displayed by the Commander and officers for the care and comfort of the Coolies. There were landed 383 men, 81 women, 17 boys, 10 girls and 19 infants. "[42] As this makes a roll-call of 477¹/₂, it would appear that four passengers died during the voyage.

Artist shortening sail and backing the main yards to make a lee for the pilot. Probably depicted on the East Coast as the artist, H.S. Wilson was Hull based.
[Peabody Museum, Salem, Mass.]

45. OLINDA 1865-1872 Iron steamship rigged as two-masted schooner. One deck. Female bust figurehead.
O.N. 51420 632g 512n 207.5 x 25.25 x 16.8 feet.
2-cyl. by Charles and William Earle, Hull; 34, 34 x 30 inches.
3.1882: C. 2-cyl. by David Rollo, Liverpool; 23, 46 x 36 inches.
Commercial Code: JLQD.

3.1.1865: Launched by Charles and William Earle, Hull (Yard No.88). *2.1865:* Delivered to Thomas Harrison, Liverpool for £13,190. *11.2.1865:* Sailed at 18.30 from Hull for Sunderland and her maiden voyage for Charente under Captain F. Williams. *22.3.1865:* Thomas Harrison sold 42 shares thus: James Harrison (20 shares), Edward Hodgson Harrison (8 shares), John Harrison (6 shares) and Richard-Pierre Williamson (8 shares). *26.12.1872:* Sold to Moss Steamship Co. Ltd. (James Moss and Co., managers),

Liverpool. *3.1882:* Re-engined. *11.1898:* Sold to Carl Eriksen (Harald Pedersen, manager), Christiania, Norway and renamed DUDLEY. *21.11.1898:* British Registry closed. *6.2.1902:* Wrecked on a reef near Vera Cruz, Mexico whilst on a voyage from Port Arthur to Vera Cruz with a cargo of lumber.

The name is that of a Brazilian resort near Pernambuco (Recife).

46. AMAZON 1865-1872 Iron steamship rigged as three masted schooner. Two decks.
O.N. 51492 673g 528n 200.0 x 28.5 x 15.6 feet. Certificated for 33 passengers.
2-cyl. by Fossick and Hackworth, Stockton-on-Tees; 38, 38 x 26 inches.
Commercial Code: JLQB.

29.3.1865: Launched by M. Pearse and Co., Stockton-on-Tees (Yard No. 61) as AMAZON. She had been laid down as GERTRUDE ELLEN. *29.5.1865:* Delivered to Thomas Harrison, Liverpool for £14,000. Maiden voyage from Liverpool to Cadiz under Captain R.R. Williamson. *24.3.1866:* Thomas Harrison sold 42 shares thus: James Harrison (20 shares), Edward Hodgson Harrison (8 shares), John Harrison (6 shares) and Richard-Pierre Williamson (8 shares). *5.1868:* Whilst on passage from Syria to Constantinople, the propeller 'slipped', necessitating a tow which cost £200. *19.4.1870:* Lost propeller and was towed into Queenstown by the tug ROYAL ARCH for a fee of £90. *1.2.1872:* Sold to George P. Forwood, Liverpool and registered under the Mersey Steam Ship Co. Ltd. *1.1.1878:* Lost off Pointe d'Azemmour, 11 miles east north east from Mazagan, Morocco. *30.2.1878:* Register closed.

47 FRANKFORT 1865-1874 Iron steamer rigged as a brig. One deck plus quarter deck. Shield figurehead.
O.N. 1677 658g 414n 190.0 x 26.6 x 16.8 feet.
Commercial Code: HKWR.
2-cyl. by John Reid and Co., Port Glasgow; 40 x 33 inches.

16.5.1851: Launched by John Reid and Co., Port Glasgow. *26.7.1851:* Delivered to Frederick Chapple, Liverpool. Later sold to H.E. Moss and Co., Liverpool. *9.11.1865:* Chartered by T. and J. Harrison at the cost of £1,500 for six month's trading to Charente. *13.11.1865:* Detained in Newport, Monmouthshire by Admiralty writ, possibly in connection with financial claims against the owners. *16.11.1865:* Released. *17.11.1865:* In collision with a local tug. Harrisons paid £12 to the tug owners to repair the damage. *11.1865:* 48 shares mortgaged to Thomas Harrison. *3.1866:* This mortgage discharged, whereupon Moss sold his shares in the ship to Thomas Harrison and six months later his partners sold out to the brothers James and Edward Hodgson Harrison. Total purchase price was £7,643. *26.3.1867:* Sailed from Huelva and spent several days searching for a derelict, the GLENLEE, without success, arriving 8.4.1867 at Liverpool. *1.1868:* Encountered heavy weather when on passage from Liverpool to Gibraltar, which caused considerable damage to lifeboats, funnel casing and bulwarks. The pumps became choked and she was forced to put into Falmouth on 23.1.1868. The Second Mate, Mr. Moore, was lost overboard in the storm. *2.9.1874:* Sold for £3,600 to P. McGuffie and Co., Liverpool. Thomas Harrison held a mortgage on 48 shares which was discharged 24.3.1876. *8.4.1878:* Sold to R.C. Macnaughton and Co., Liverpool. *4.9.1880:* Stranded four miles west of Skerryvore whilst on a voyage from Liverpool to Stockholm with general cargo. The 16 crew and one passenger were saved.

48. FIRE QUEEN 1866-1879 Iron steamship rigged as a two-masted schooner. Three decks. Shield figurehead.
O.N. 49805 1,172g 797n 248.5 x 29.6 x 14.1 feet.
Marryat's Code 2nd Distinguishing Pennant: 4329. International Code: WFMH.
C. 2-cyl. by Randolph Elder and Co., Glasgow; 25, 50 x 36 inches.
1872: C. 2-cyl. by J. Jones and Co., Liverpool; 25, 50 x 36 inches.

1.10.1864: Launched by T.H. Pile and Co., West Hartlepool (Yard No. 2). *10.1864:* Delivered to J. Pile and J. Spence, West Hartlepool. *3.1866:* Acquired by Thomas Harrison, Liverpool for £20,000. *12.1868:* Thomas Harrison sold 42 shares thus: James Harrison (20 shares), Edward Hodgson Harrison (8 shares), James Harrison and Edward Hodgson Harrison (6 shares), Richard-Pierre Williamson (6 shares) and John William Hughes (2 shares). *8.7.1866:* Sailed from Liverpool to inaugurate a regular service to New Orleans in the name of the Southern Line. *8.8.1866:* Arrived at New Orleans with 499 tons deadweight of cargo, 42 tons measurement and 4 passengers. *21.3.1867:* Happened across the disabled French brig DIOSMA when bound from New Orleans to Liverpool. The French vessel, bound from Belize to Nantes, was in obvious distress and foundering after being dismasted during a severe storm. The entire crew was taken off by FIRE QUEEN leaving the vessel to sink some time later off Brandon Point, County Kerry. *13.1.1870:* Sailed from Liverpool to inaugurate a new regular service to India via Suez. *4.2.1870:* Passed through the Suez Canal, the first Harrison vessel to do so, and the 27th of all vessels to make the transit. *25.2.1870:* Arrived at Bombay. *4.8.1872:* Laid up at Liverpool while a new engine was installed by J. Jones and Co. *2.8.1872:* Successful trials were carried out in Liverpool Bay. *7.1878:* Towed the company's disabled steamer CORDOVA (59) into Liverpool, arriving 9.7.1878. *25.8.1878:* Disabled when her propeller shaft fractured during a voyage from New Orleans to Liverpool. The incident occurred in position 37.34N, 69.00W, about 335 miles and 122 degrees from Sandy Hook, New Jersey. *31.8.1878:* Taken in tow by the German steamer BALTIMORE (2,344/68) and arrived at New York 2.9.1878. *29.8.1879:* Sold for £7,500 to John Clark, Barcelona and Henry Swan, Newcastle-upon-Tyne in part payment for the steamer AUTHOR then building at Charles Mitchell and Co., Newcastle-upon-Tyne. *10.1.1880:* Sold to William Banks, London. *7.4.1884:* Mortgaged to Henri Germain Hermet, Paris, for the sum of £4,800 at 6%. *26.5.1885:* Since the debt was not repaid, the vessel was arrested at Le Havre and a French court ordered her to be sold at public auction. *1887:* Sold to R. Beveridge, London. *1888:* Sold to Christopher Furness, West Hartlepool. *1890:* Sold to W.F. Conner, London, resold to F. Auquetil et Fils, Rouen, France, and renamed FERDINAND A. *11.12.1894:* Wrecked at the mouth of the River Seine whilst on passage from Spain to Rouen.

Fire Queen loading cotton at a New Orleans wharf, circa 1866.

49. ALHAMBRA 1866-1871 Iron steamship rigged as a brigantine. Two decks and two holds.
O.N. 51464 789g 537n 219.0 x 28.0 x 15.9 feet. Cargo capacity: 68,464 cubic feet.
2-cyl. by John Jones and Co., Liverpool; 42 and 30 inches.
Commercial Code: JLNF.

25.2.1865: Launched by Preston Iron Ship Building Co., Preston as ADA WILSON. *31.8.1866:* Acquired by Thomas Harrison (32 shares) and Daniel James (32 shares), Liverpool for £10,500 and renamed ALHAMBRA. *17.8.1867:* Sailed from Liverpool bound for New Orleans. *9.9.1867:* Lost her propeller when the shaft fractured whilst off Great Isaac Lighthouse in the Florida Straits. *19.9.1867:* Taken in tow by the wooden paddle sloop HMS BARRACOUTA and towed into Nassau the following day. *20.10.1867:* Sailed from Nassau in tow of the US tug AMERICA and arrived 27.10.1867 at New Orleans. A new shaft, propeller and

bearings, which had been shipped out from Liverpool, were fitted and she sailed 3.12.1867 for Liverpool. The towage from Nassau to New Orleans lasted 7 days 10 hours and cost $10,000. *18.7.1869:* Ran aground on Loggerheads Cay, Florida, when on passage from New Orleans to Liverpool. Refloated three days later, continued the voyage and was dry docked at Liverpool to make repairs to the rudder. *30.3.1871:* Sold to Quebec and Gulf Ports Steam Ship Co. Ltd., Quebec. *1889:* Reported broken up.

The name is that of a Moorish palace in Granada, Spain.

50. ALICE 1866-1886 Iron steamship rigged as a brig, later a schooner. One deck.
O.N. 29954 881g 599n 217.0 x 30.0 x 18.3 feet.
1868: 1182g 889n 264.2 x 30.5 x 18.5 feet.
Commercial Code: JLND.
2-cyl. by Fossick and Hackworth, Stockton-on-Tees; 44, 44 x 36 inches.
1873: C. 2-cyl. by Thompson, Boyd and Co., Newcastle-upon-Tyne; 29, 58 x 63 inches.

12.5.1865: Launched by Backhouse and Dixon, Middlesbrough (Yard No. 14). *1.10.1866:* Acquired by Thomas Harrison, Liverpool for £17,500 and sailed on her maiden voyage from London to Charente. *23.7.1868:* Arrived at Belfast and work commenced to fit a second deck, poop and a third mast. She was lengthened and certified to carry 70 passengers. *1.10.1868:* Thomas Harrison sold 42 shares as follows - James Harrison (20 shares), Edward Hodgson Harrison (8 shares), James Harrison and Edward Hodgson Harrison (6 shares), Richard-Pierre Williamson (6

shares) and John William Hughes (2 shares). *24.6.1873:* Arrived at Newcastle-upon-Tyne to be re-engined. *10.9.1873:* Sailed on completion of work. *18.12.1884:* All partners transferred their shares to The Charente Steam-Ship Co. Ltd. *10.5.1886:* Sold to Raylton Dixon and Co., Middlesbrough for £4,500 and resold to John Livingstone (H. Smith, manager), Middlesbrough. *19.9.1887:* Sailed from Riga for London with a cargo of sleepers and disappeared with her crew of 18.

Alice standing off the Skerries with the Liverpool pilot schooner No.5 *Victoria and Albert*, in the offing.
[Attributed to an unknown Liverpool Chinese artist]

51. SAPPHIRE 1866-1870 Iron steamship rigged as two-masted schooner. One deck.
O.N. 29951 672g 436n 189.3 x 28.1 x 16.7 feet.
2-cyl. by Fossick and Hackworth, Stockton-on-Tees; 40, 40 x 30 inches.
Commercial Code: JLNP.

1865: Launched by Candlish, Fox and Co., Middlesbrough (Yard No. 9) for the British and American Steam Navigation Co. Ltd. (Henry Fernie, manager), Liverpool. *10.1866:* Acquired by Thomas Harrison, Liverpool for £11,500 and sailed on her maiden voyage from Liverpool to Charente. *31.1.1868:* Thomas Harrison sold 42 shares as follows: James Harrison (20 shares), Edward Hodgson Harrison (8 shares), James Harrison and Edward Hodgson Harrison (6

shares), Richard-Pierre Williamson (6 shares) and John William Hughes (2 shares). *15.9.1870:* Sailed from Liverpool under the command of Captain Gill, bound for Havana and New Orleans. *6.10.1870:* Struck a reef off Florida and abandoned in a sinking condition. *22.4.1871:* Derelict was reported off Key West and again 12.5.1871 off Havana.

The name is that of a blue corundum gemstone.

52. PANTHEON 1867-1869 Iron steamship rigged as a brigantine. Three decks.
O.N. 55069 998g 679n 205.8 x 28.0 x 15.8 feet.
2-cyl. by Forrester and Co., Vauxhall; 38, 38 x 30 inches.

5.2.1867: Launched by Preston Iron Ship Building Co., Preston. *25.3.1867:* Delivered to Thomas Harrison (22 shares), James Harrison (20 shares), Edward Hodgson Harrison (8 shares), Richard-Pierre Williamson (6 shares), James Harrison (6 shares) and John William Hughes (2 shares), Liverpool for £16,700. Subsequently sailed from Liverpool for St. John, New Brunswick on her maiden voyage. *26.11.1868:* Sailed from New Orleans and encountered heavy weather on the eastbound voyage. The lifeboats, spars and sails were washed away. *13.12.1868:* Captain Beeley was washed overboard and drowned. *22.12.1868:* Put into Queenstown to make repairs and Captain John Corbishley was sent across to take command. *28.2.1869:* Sailed from New Orleans. *5.3.1869:* Collided with the tug HEROINE outside the Southwest Pass and sank

with her cargo of 17,000 bushels of wheat and 555 bales of cotton. *25.5.1869:* Wreck sold for $1,950.

The ship's certificate of registry is normally a jealously guarded document, but this ship's was an exception. The original was "lost", and a new certificate was issued on 30th October 1867. That was "destroyed by rats" and renewed on 28th August 1868. That one was "mislaid" and renewed on 10th October 1868. However, when the vessel foundered in 1869, her certificate was very properly rescued, "delivered and cancelled" at New Orleans.

The name derives from a temple to all the gods in classical literature.

53. CHRYSOLITE 1867-1886 Steel steamship rigged as two-masted schooner. One deck.
O.N. 29934 702g 478n 189.7 x 28.4 x 17.2 feet.
Commercial Code: JLPR.
2-cyl. by T. Richardson and Sons, Hartlepool; 40, 40 x 27 inches.
1874: C. 2-cyl. by J. Jones and Co., Liverpool; 23, 46 x 30 inches.

5.8.1865: Launched by Candlish, Fox and Co., Middlesbrough for the British and American Steam Navigation Co. Ltd. (Henry Fernie, manager), Liverpool. *16.10.1866:* Chartered to Thos. and Jas. Harrison Ltd. for three round voyages to Lisbon and Brazil. *15.4.1867:* Towards the end of the third charter voyage acquired for £12,000 by Thomas Harrison, becoming the first steel-hulled ship to join the fleet. *21.4.1868:* Ran on to rocks off Cape Angelo, Morea, Greece. One hundred tons of coal were jettisoned in efforts to lighten her and she was eventually towed off by the Newcastle steamer MAGNA CARTA at the cost of £500. A subsequent survey showed no damage to the hull. *16.7.1868:* On the following voyage, she ran ashore again, this time in the Dardanelles. Once again there was no report of damage and the towage fee was only £80. *8.1.1869:* Thomas Harrison sold 42 shares as follows - James Harrison (20 shares), Edward Hodgson Harrison (8 shares), James Harrison and Edward Hodgson Harrison (6

shares), Richard-Pierre Williamson (6 shares) and John William Hughes (2 shares). *1.1874:* An explosion on board killed one man and injured another and she put into Penarth Roads for assistance. *5.1874:* Laid up at Liverpool, during which period a new engine was installed. *9.1874:* Returned to service. *6.6.1878:* Suffered a further explosion whilst lying in Penarth Roads and ten members of the crew were injured. *1.1883:* New main deck fitted at Liverpool. *18.12.1884:* All partners transferred their shares to The Charente Steam-Ship Co. Ltd. *1886:* Sold to J. Ramos, Cette, France for £1,929, renamed JUAN RAMOS and registered in Alicante, Spain. *1888:* Sold to J.J. Casanova, Benejama, Spain. *1890:* Sold to J. Faes, Alicante, Spain and renamed ADOLFO. *28.3.1894:* Lost off Mauritius with the loss of eleven crew.

The name is that of a gemstone, a yellow-green olivine of magnesium iron silicate.

54. CASTILLA 1869- 1870 Iron steamship rigged as three-masted barque. Two decks and poop. Billet figurehead.
O.N. 45950 1,980g 1,569n 281.1 x 38.1 x 22.0 feet.
1864: 2,245g 1713n.
Commercial Code: JLPF.
2-cyl. by Fossick and Hackworth, Stockton-on-Tees; 60, 60 x 36 inches.

1863: Launched by M. Pearse and Co., Stockton-on-Tees (Yard No. 45) for J.A.K. Wilson, Liverpool as THE SOUTHERNER. *11.6.1863:* Delivered. *17.11.1863:* Sold to C.K. Prioleau, Liverpool, a Confederate agent. *8.12.1863:* Sold to W.J. Fernie, Liverpool. *11.2.1864:* Sold to foreign owners, probably as a way of effecting a name change, and renamed WESTMINSTER. *22.2.1864:* Returned to the British Register. *27.8.1864:* Sold again to foreign owners and renamed PERUVIAN. *6.9.1864:* Sold to British and American Steam Navigation Co., Liverpool. An extra deck was fitted and she was re-measured. *21.4.1868:* Sold to Merchant Trading Co., Liverpool and mortgaged to Horatio Nelson Hughes for £6,500. *6.7.1868:* Mortgage discharged. *30.1.1869:* Sold to foreign owners and renamed CASTILLA. *3.1869:* Chartered by Alfred Le Blanc, on behalf of the company, to take the place of PANTHEON (51) which had sunk in a collision. *29.3.1869:* Sailed from New Orleans to Liverpool with a cargo of cotton, oil cake and staves.

19.5.1869: Acquired by Thomas Harrison, Liverpool. *9.6.1869:* Sailed from Liverpool for New York with 200 passengers, picking up a further 60 at Queenstown. *29.3.1870:* Sold to Compania Catalana de Vapores Transatlantica, Barcelona, Spain. *1890:* Sold to Stefano Repetto, Genoa, Italy and renamed AMERICA. *1898:* Broken up at Genoa.

CASTILLA was the largest vessel to join the Harrison fleet up to this juncture. She was probably too big for their purposes, certainly too big for the Charente and the shallow Brazilian ports. She was not particularly fast for a heavy consumption of fuel and was evidently not suitable for the Suez Canal or the service to India, hence the rather precipitate sale.

The name is the Spanish spelling of a former kingdom within what is now Spain - Castille.

55. STATESMAN (1) 1869-1891 Iron steamship rigged as a brig. Two decks and three holds.
O.N. 63219 1,851g 1,210n 310.6 x 33.0 x 24.1 feet. Cargo capacity: 120,450 cubic feet. Berths for 12 first class and 50 second class passengers.
Commercial Code: JLNV.
C. 2-cyl. by C. and W. Earle and Co., Hull; 35, 70 x 42 inches.

9.9.1869: Launched by C. and W. Earle and Co., Hull (Yard No.126). *24.11.1869:* Ran trials. *5.12.1869:* Delivered to Thomas Harrison (22 shares), James Harrison (20 shares), Edward Hodgson Harrison (8 shares), Edward Hodgson Harrison and James Harrison (6 shares), Richard-Pierre Williamson (6 shares) and John William Hughes (2 shares), Liverpool for £36,385. *2.1876:* Entered dry-dock at Liverpool

following a collision with the steamer MERCIA. *7.1.1880:* When on passage from Palermo to New Orleans with a cargo of oranges, broke her main shaft when about 350 miles south of the Azores in position 32.44N, 28.55W. *11.1.1880:* After drifting for four days taken in tow by the steamer ACTON (1,646/74). *15.1.1880:* Arrived off Funchal, Madeira, but a strong wind and heavy sea prevented them from anchoring. She was therefore towed round to the lee side of the island and a safe anchorage was found the following day after a tow of 480 miles. A new shaft was shipped to Funchal and fitted. *10.2.1880:* Sailed for New Orleans. Watts, Watts, the owners of ACTON, were awarded £1,800 for their efforts at the subsequent Admiralty Court hearing. *18.12.1884:* All the partners transferred their shares to The Charente Steam-Ship Co. Ltd. *25.8.1891:* Sold to Christopher Furness, West Hartlepool for £7,920. *14.9.1891:* Sold to Benchimol and Sobrinho, Lisbon, Portugal and renamed ALICE. *1896:* Sold to Empreza de Navegaçao Cruzeiro do Sul, Lisbon and renamed TEJO. *1897:* Sold to J.T. Barbosa Vianna, Rio de Janeiro, Brazil and renamed TRINIDADE. *1898:* Sold to G. Elysio & Co., Rio de Janeiro and renamed AMAZONAS. *1900:* Sold to Empreza de Sal e Navegaçao, Rio de Janeiro. *1907:* Sold to Compania Commercio e Navegaçao, Rio de Janeiro and renamed MOSSORO. *1922:* Owners became Pereira, Carneiro & Cia. Ltda. Compania (Commercio e Navegaçao), Rio de Janeiro. *1925:* Dismantled.

The STATESMAN was the first of a new class of vessel designed for the prestigious services to India and the Far East via the Suez Canal, with passengers and cargo. They were larger, more powerful, and faster than their predecessors. A typical voyage from China has been recorded thus: *20.7.1871:* Sailed from Foochow at 13.00 with a cargo of tea - 2,826 measured tons at 90/- per ton - Captain R.R. Williamson in command. Vessel called at Singapore and Aden for bunkers. *10.9.1871:* Arrived at Victoria Dock, London, at 10.00, 52¼ days out of Foochow. As a result of this fast passage the ship was awarded the annual premium for bringing in the first teas of the season.

Statesman, in a stiff breeze passing Point Lynas outward bound from Liverpool. Artist unknown.

56. HISTORIAN (1) 1870-1891 Iron steamship rigged as a barque. Two decks and four holds.
O.N. 63238 1,830g 1,202n 2,565d 323.5 x 33.4 x 24.0 feet. Cargo capacity: 115,680 cubic feet. Berths for 16 first class and 24 second class passengers.
Commercial Code: KJNF.
C. 2-cyl. by J. Jack and Co., Liverpool; 35, 70 x 42 inches.

5.1.1870: Launched by Harland and Wolff, Belfast (Yard No. 69). *9.3.1870:* Delivered to Thomas Harrison, Liverpool for £35,953. *15.3.1870:* Thomas Harrison sold 20 shares to James Harrison. *17.3.1870:* Thomas Harrison sold 22 shares thus: Edward Hodgson Harrison (8 shares), James Harrison and Edward Hodgson Harrison (3 shares), Richard-Pierre Williamson (6 shares) and John William Hughes (5 shares). *30.8.1870:* Sailed from Liverpool and made a record passage out to Colombo, arriving 30.9.1870, having spent one day in Malta and two in the Suez Canal area. *17.2.1876:* Sailed from Aden bound for the Suez Canal and a few days later ran aground on Ashrafi Reef in the Straits of Gubal at the entrance to the Gulf of Suez. 1,500 bales of Indian cotton were jettisoned during the operation to refloat the vessel. She was then able to continue the voyage to Liverpool where the bottom plating was repaired in dry dock and a new propeller fitted. *9.1.1884:* Came across the steamer HORACE (1,634/78), disabled with a broken main shaft, when bound from New Orleans to Liverpool. HORACE was bound from Baltimore for Sharpness with a cargo of wheat, and the total value of ship and cargo was estimated as £32,300. HISTORIAN towed her 138 miles to Bermuda and was awarded £2,400 for the service. The award was apportioned as

follows: £1,900 to the owners and £500 to the Captain and crew of which the Captain received one third. *18.12.1884:* All of the partners transferred their shares to The Charente Steam-Ship Co. Ltd. *13.7.1891:* Sold to Christopher Furness, West Hartlepool for £7,920. *14.1.1892:* Sold to William Williamson, West Hartlepool. *25.1.1892:* Sold to Henry Withy, West Hartlepool. *4.2.1892:* Sold to Benchimol and Sobrinho, Lisbon, Portugal and renamed CIDADE DO PORTO. *1895:* Sold to Empreza Navegaçao Cruzeira do Sul, San Francisco do Sul, Brazil and renamed DOURO but registered in Lisbon, Portugal. *19.12.1896:* Abandoned off Ushant whilst on a voyage from Antwerp to the River Plate.

Historian off Holyhead, Anglesey

57. ATALANTA 1870-1873 Iron steamship rigged as a four-masted barque. Two decks.
O.N. 45360 2,299g 1,479n 341.9 x 34.2 x 30.9 feet. Berths for up to 50 passengers.
Commercial Code: VCWT.
Two C. 2-cyl. Smith and Rodgers, Govan; 60, 16 x 48 inches.

28.11.1863: Launched by Smith and Rodgers, Govan (Yard No. 90) as IOWA but completed for William Malcolmson, Waterford as ATALANTA. *31.5.1870:* Acquired for £50,000 by Thomas Harrison, Liverpool together with BELLONA (No.58) and CELLA (No. 60). *20.7.1871:* Thomas Harrison sold 42 shares thus: James Harrison (20 shares), Edward Hodgson Harrison (8 shares), James Harrison and Edward Hodgson Harrison (3 shares), Richard-Pierre Williamson (6 shares) and John William Hughes (5 shares). *5.3.1872:* In collision with the steamer LUMLEY CASTLE (1,670/70) in the Straits of Gibraltar between Tarifa and Cape Trafalgar. At the subsequent court of enquiry, both ships were found

equally to blame. *1.4.1873:* Sold to Horatio Nelson Hughes, Liverpool for £24,150. *1880:* Sold to G.W. Palmer, Liverpool. *1881:* Sold to the Bristol Steam Navigation Co. Ltd., Bristol and renamed CLIFTON. *1886:* Sold to North Atlantic Steam Ship Co. Ltd., London. *1887:* Sold to Clarence R. Gillchrest, Liverpool. *1890:* Sold to Rederibolaget 'Ocean' (Adolph Meyer), Gothenburg, Sweden, and renamed OCEAN. *15.7.1897:* Put ashore at Knarsalo after striking submerged rock. Refloated, taken to Gothenburg and condemned.

The name is that of an Arcadian princess whose hand was won by Hippomenes in a foot race.[43]

Atalanta off Gravesend 2nd March 1878 in the ownership of H.N. Hughes, here seen schooner rigged and reduced to three masts.
[National Maritime Museum G1502]

58. BELLONA 1870-1875 Iron steamship rigged as four-masted barque. Two decks.
O.N. 29549 1,914g 1,430n 300.3 x 34.2 x 24.1 feet.
Commercial Code: QGCV.
Two C. 2-cyl. by Smith and Rodgers, Govan; 50, 14 x 48 inches.

1862: Launched by Smith and Rodgers, Govan for William Malcolmson, Waterford. *1870:* Acquired for £50,000 by Thomas Harrison (44 shares) and James Harrison (20 shares), Liverpool together with ATALANTA (No. 57) and CELLA (No. 60). *7.1870:* Ran ashore off Mocha when on passage from Suez for Aden and refloated after ten hours. She continued the voyage and was dry docked at Bombay some three months later. *20.7.1871:* Thomas Harrison sold 22 shares thus: Edward Hodgson Harrison (8 shares), James Harrison and Edward Hodgson Harrison (3 shares), Richard-Pierre Williamson (6 shares) and John William Hughes (5 shares). *20.11.1871:* Sailed from Savannah and became disabled when her shaft fractured. *7.12.1871:*

Sighted in position 45N, 50W and reported. *25.12.1871:* Arrived Cuxhaven, having completed the voyage under sail. *27.12.1871:* Left Cuxhaven under tow of the tug RATTLER and one other. *29.12.1871:* Arrived at Liverpool.[44] *9.3.1875:* Sold to Horatio Nelson Hughes, Liverpool. *19.9.1879:* Sold to Joseph Hoult, Liverpool and renamed BENBRACK. *10.11.1882:* Sold to Steam Ship Benbrack Co. Ltd. (Arthur C. Hay, manager), Liverpool. *23.1.1889:* Stranded on the island of Texel whilst on a voyage from Savannah to Bremerhaven with a cargo of cotton. *14.6.1889:* Register closed.

Bellona was the Roman goddess of war.

59. CORDOVA 1870-1880 Iron steamship rigged as three-masted schooner. Three decks.
O.N. 49732 1,417g 1,064n 245.5 x 30.3 x 23.0 feet.
Commercial Code: HBRG
2-cyl. by Greenock Foundry Ltd., Greenock.
1874: C. 2-cyl. by J. Jones and Co., Liverpool; 30, 56 x 36 inches.

1864: Launched by John Horn and Co., Waterford for Benjamin Sproule, Liverpool. *12.7.1870:* Acquired by Thomas Harrison, Liverpool for £15,310. *6.2.1873:* Sailed from Bremen for Newport, Monmouthshire and disabled whilst off Cape Cornwall with a loose screw. Taken in tow, repaired and returned to service. *25.2.1874:* Laid up at Liverpool and fitted with new engine, mast and decks. *9.6.1874:* Returned to service. *9.6.1878:* Left New Orleans for Liverpool and broke her crankshaft on the voyage. The company's FIRE QUEEN (No. 48) which had left New

Orleans a week later, sighted her and took her in tow. *9.7.1878:* Both vessels arrived Liverpool. *27.9.1880:* Sold for £7,700 to S.S. Coen fu D., Leghorn, Italy and renamed ELISA ANNA. *1891:* Sold to Pietro Tassi, Leghorn, Italy. 1903: Sold to G.B. Mavroleon, Piraeus, Greece and renamed KILIKIA. *1922:* Deleted from Lloyd's Register.

Cordova is the anglicised spelling of Cordoba, a Moorish city in Spain.

40

60. CELLA 1870-1874 Iron steamship rigged as four-masted barque. Two decks.
O.N. 45351 2,048g 1,538n 297.4 x 34.4 x 24.0 feet.
Commercial Code: VCWJ.
Two C. 2-cyl. by Smith and Rodger, Glasgow; 50, 14 x 48 inches.
1876: C. 2-cyl. by J. Jack and Co., Liverpool; 40,71 x 36 inches.

1862: Launched by Neptune Iron Works, Waterford for William Malcolmson, Waterford. *8.8.1870:* Acquired for £50,000 by Thomas Harrison (64 shares) together with ATALANTA (57) and BELLONA (58). *21.8.1870:* Sailed from London with 500 tons of general cargo and 1,750 tons of submarine cable for Hong Kong. *25.10.1870:* Arrived Hong Kong and proceeded to lay the cable between that colony and Singapore. *29.3.1871:* Cable laying completed. The Master was Captain R.R. Williamson, son of Richard-Pierre Williamson, one of the partners. *3.3.1874:* Sold to Horatio Nelson Hughes, Liverpool. *1876:* Fitted with new engines.

1883: Sold to 'Cella' Steamship Co. Ltd. (F.A. Jaques), Newcastle-upon-Tyne. *1884:* Sold to Stevens, Griffiths and Co., Chepstow. *22.10.1885:* Mortgaged to Wood, Jacobs and Forwood, London, and operated by William Stevens, Chepstow. *3.8.1886:* Condemned and sold by order of the Tribunal Premier Justice at Antwerp to Idare-i Mahsusa, Istanbul, Turkey and renamed SARK (SHARKI). *1890:* Laid up at Istanbul. *1891:* Out of the Register. *1892:* Sold for demolition at Istanbul.
The name refers to the principal room in a Greek or Roman temple.

61. WARRIOR (1) 1870-1872 Iron steamer rigged as a brig. Two decks. Shield figurehead.
O.N. 56837 1,502g 956n 264.7 x 32.2 x 21.0 feet.
Commercial Code: JSRK.
C. 2-cyl. by Randolph, Elder and Co., Glasgow; 22, 50 x 36 inches.
1874: C.2-cyl. by J. Jones and Sons, Liverpool; 22, 50 x 36 inches.

10.1867: Launched by Randolph, Elder and Co., Glasgow (Yard No. 39) for Tait and Co., London (later to become the London, Belgium, Brazil and River Plate Steamship Co.) as CITY OF LIMERICK. *29.9.1870:* Sold to foreign owners. *4.10.1870:* Acquired through Tait and Co., London by James Harrison, Liverpool for £16,510. *12.10.1870:* James Harrison sold 44 shares to Thomas Harrison. *15.10.1870:* Renamed WARRIOR. *22.10.1870:* Sailed from the Thames for India with troops numbering 18 officers and their ladies,

412 men, 29 women and 41 children. Called at Malta, Port Said, Aden and Galle before berthing 4.12.1870 at Calcutta. *9.1871:* Ran aground off Mocha in the Red Sea when on passage from Suez to Singapore. Refloated after ten hours and resumed voyage. *4.7.1872:* Sold to Liverpool, Brazil and River Plate Steam Navigation Co. (Lamport and Holt, managers), Liverpool for £17,000. *5.11.1873:* Renamed VANDYCK. *1874:* New engines fitted. *1892:* Reduced to a coal hulk at Rio de Janeiro.

62. CITY OF BRUSSELS 1870-1871 Iron steamship rigged as a brig. Two decks. Scroll figurehead.
O.N. 56918 1,427g 916n 271.3 x 32.5 x 21.0 feet.
Commercial Code: JHGB.
C. 2-cyl. by Randolph, Elder and Co., Glasgow; 39½, 71 x 36 inches.

5.3.1868: Launched by Randolph, Elder and Co., Glasgow (Yard No. 41) for Tait and Co., London. *11.1870:* Acquired by T. and J. Harrison, Liverpool. *21.8.1871:* Sold to Compagnie Générale Transatlantique, Paris, France, and renamed

DÉSIRADE. *28.12.1887:* Assisted the stranded brig ENTREPRENEUR near Malaga. *12.8.1889:* Disabled and towed into Gibraltar by SAINT AUGUSTIN. *1.1906:* Sold to shipbreakers at Marseilles.

63. KING ARTHUR 1871-1878 Iron full-rigged ship. Two decks. Shield figurehead.
O.N. 29783 1,275g 1,211n 230.5 x 35.4 x 21.9 feet.
Commercial Code: QHCM.

4.1861: Launched by Pile, Spence and Co., West Hartlepool (Yard No. 34). *12.4.1871:* Acquired by Thomas Harrison, Liverpool, who sold 16 shares to Robert Heath, 8 shares to William Crosfield, 8 shares to James E. Reynolds, and 8 shares to Francis W. Reynolds. *30.4.1873:* Thomas Harrison sold 12 shares to Thomas A. Lowe and Henry Davison. *15.6.1878:* Letter of complaint against Captain Rickwood from father of two apprentices (see below). *6.10.1878:*

Sailed from Charleston, South Carolina, with a cargo of 4,226 bales of cotton for Liverpool. *31.12.1878:* Ran aground on rocks in Bannow Bay, County Wexford, and became a total loss. Local tugs managed to salvage some 1,700 bales of cotton and, at the subsequent court of inquiry, it was found that the ship "was navigated improperly, and in an unreasonable manner". Captain Nelson's certificate of competency was suspended for six months.

Sinister allegations of cruelty
KING ARTHUR was one of the last square-riggers to join the Harrison fleet. Like her sister sailing-ships, she was employed on long oceanic hauls, mainly to India round the Cape of Good Hope. Between November 1875 and March 1878 the ship made three voyages in the coolie trade from Calcutta to Demerara. On each of these voyages, under Captain Rickwood, she transported more than 420 indentured emigrants to work in the plantations. It was during the last of these voyages that Captain Rickwood became the focus of a scandal with regard to his treatment of the young apprentices in his care. In letters dated 4th May 1878 at New York two boys named Fuller complained bitterly to their parents about Captain Rickwood's cruelty, upon which their father, resident in Calcutta, sent a terse letter to the management with copies of his sons' letters.

In the first, which was a hand-written copy of the original, Frank Fuller informs his mother that his brother, Barry, "has run away".
"*New York, 4th May 1878.*
Dear Mother,
I write these few lines in hopes of finding you and the rest of the family in good health. I am going to inform you that Barry has run away, the reason is because he was ill-used by the Captain. He was caught smoking, and the Captn. made him eat an oz. of tobacco and drink a quart of hot water and

scrape the trysel mast down. He went to tell the Captain he was sick, and to forgive him. The Captain flogged him, and he has often struck me. Here you will find a letter that Barry sent with mine. We are bound for Liverpool, and we are underway today, the 4th of May. Dear Mother, do not fret about me. I will be home soon by your side again once more. I am going to leave her when I get back, and that will be for good. Captain Rickwood flogged three apprentices, they have run away. I got no more news at present. Goodbye,
Your sincere son,
F. Fuller. "
The second copy quotes Barry's story, as follows:
"*New York.*
Dear Mother,
I write these few lines in hopes that they will find you and all the family are enjoying good health as it leaves me, and Frank the same, at present. We have been sadly disappointed in not received (sic) your letter in either port. Frank is getting on pretty well with his seamanship but I am sorry to say that he has not taken to Navigation at present but I hope to see him take to it after we leave Liverpool. As for myself I am in the blue books of the skipper just because he caught me smoking once and he wanted me to eat an oz. of honeydew tobacco and I refused to do it. He knocked me down on my back and put it down my throat and made me drink a quart of water and

then scrape the masts down. When I felt sick he licked me with a rope. I forgot to tell you that two of the apprentices ran away from her in Demerara. I think you know them Rix is one and Pitney is the other. He struck them with his fist most unmercifully. Remind me to all the young ones.
Goodbye, dear Mother and Father.
Barry.
I am in a hurry, so you must excuse all mistakes."

The relevant Voyage Book does not name the Fuller brothers among the apprentices, but this could perhaps be because the boys joined the ship in Calcutta, where apparently their father had his place of business, and therefore their

home. Clearly, these youngsters had a bad time, but nevertheless it would have been interesting, and perhaps instructive to hear Captain Rickwood's version of events. It is not known whether the boys' family brought suit against him or his employers although the letters were copied to the family solicitor. However, it is perhaps significant that when KING ARTHUR sailed again from Liverpool on 27th August, she sailed with the half-deck empty of apprentices, and without Captain Rickwood. He, unhappy man, had changed places with Captain Nelson of the NATURALIST (42), which disappeared after leaving Calcutta on 2nd February 1879.

64. STUDENT (1) 1871-1877 Iron steamship rigged as two-masted schooner. Two decks and poop.
O.N. 65902 727g 461n 204.7 x 26.1 x 16.65 feet.
Commercial Code: KSDM.
C. 2-cyl.by James Taylor and Co., Birkenhead; 25, 50 x 30 inches, 9 knots.

31.10.1871: Launched by Bowdler, Chaffer and Co., Seacombe (Yard No. 79). *18.12.1871:* Ran trials. *21.12.1871:* Registered in the ownership of Thomas Harrison (22 shares), James Harrison (20 shares), Edward Hodgson Harrison (8 shares), James Harrison and Edward Hodgson Harrison (3 shares), Richard-Pierre Williamson (6 shares) and John William Hughes (5 shares), Liverpool, cost £13,149. *9.9.1872:* Ashore at Pernambuco. *15.9.1872:* Refloated. *22.1.1874:* Sailed from Liverpool bound for the Black Sea. *26.1.1874:* A boiler furnace exploded when off Cape Finisterre. Three crew were killed in the blast and considerable damage was caused. *28.1.1874:* Arrived at Lisbon for repairs. *7.3.1874:* Repairs completed and voyage

resumed. *23.2.1875:* Arrived at Pernambuco and, whilst loading for home, one of the holds was pierced when she sat on her anchor in the shallow waters off the port. Some 509 tons of sugar and ten bales of cotton were landed, much of it ruined, and a claim for £960 was submitted to the underwriters. She was then pumped dry and patched and sailed 2.4.1875 for Liverpool by way of Paraiba and Madeira. *24.5.1877:* Sold to Società Navigazione à Vapore Puglia, Bari, Italy for £9,750 and renamed MESSAPO. *16.4.1887:* Beached at Punta Alice, Gulf of Taranto, after springing a leak whilst on a voyage from Adriatic ports to Genoa and Marseilles with a cargo of wine and oil.

65. JURIST 1872-1873 Iron steamship rigged as two-masted schooner. Two decks and poop.
O.N. 65908 727g 464n 204.7 x 26.1 x 16.65 feet.
C. 2-cyl. by Jas. Taylor and Co., Birkenhead; 25, 50 x 30 inches.

28.11.1871: Launched by Bowdler, Chaffer and Co., Seacombe (Yard No. 80). *17.1.1872:* Delivered to Thomas Harrison (22 shares), James Harrison (20 shares), Edward Hodgson Harrison (8 shares), James Harrison and Edward Hodgson Harrison (3 shares), Richard Pierre Williamson (6 shares) and John William Hughes (5 shares), Liverpool for

£13,163. *16.1.1873:* Sailed from Liverpool for Lisbon on the Pernambuco route on which she had been employed for the past year. She was not seen or heard of again and it is presumed that she foundered in the Bay of Biscay in the Great Gale of January 1873.

66. ARBITRATOR (1) 1872-1876 Iron steamship rigged as two-masted schooner. One deck.
O.N. 65972 1,262g 814n 249.7 x 32.0 x 17.55 feet.
Commercial Code: LKJR.
C. 2-cyl. by Ouseburn Engineering Co., Newcastle-upon-Tyne; $29\frac{1}{2}$, $57\frac{3}{4}$ x 36 inches, 9 knots.

23.3.1872: Launched by Davison and Stokoe, Sunderland (Yard No. 20). *30.9.1872:* Delivered to Thomas Harrison (22 shares), James Harrison (20 shares), Edward Hodgson Harrison (8 shares), James Harrison and Edward Hodgson Harrison (3 shares), Richard-Pierre Williamson (6 shares) and John William Hughes (5 shares), Liverpool for £24,124. *23.8.1876:* At 01.20, 12 days out of New Orleans for Liverpool, struck a low edge of ice about 10 feet high about 236 miles east south est of Cape Race. The forward holds

and stokehold flooded and she sank within 20 minutes in position 45.30N, 47.40W. The crew safely abandoned ship and were picked up at 08.00 by the brigantine BALTIC to be disembarked 8.9.1876 at Dublin. It was probably as a result of this unhappy incident that the so-called Harrison's Buoy was "established" in position 40N, 40W. Harrison Line masters bound from the Gulf of Mexico were instructed to steer for this waypoint before setting a course for the British Isles and so avoid the southern encroachment of ice.

67. AMBASSADOR 1872-1876 Iron steamship rigged as a brig. Two decks.
O.N. 65975 1,951g 1,258n 300.9 x 34.1 x 23.6 feet.
Commercial Code: LKJV.
C. 2-cyl. by Maudslay, Sons and Field, East Greenwich, London; 38, 70 x 48 inches.

22.7.1872: Launched by James Laing, Sunderland (Yard No. 348). *3.10.1872:* Delivered to Thomas Harrison (44 shares), James Harrison (20 shares), Liverpool for £37,326. Thomas Harrison subsequently sold 22 shares, thus: Edward Hodgson Harrison (8 shares), James Harrison and Edward Hodgson Harrison (3 shares), Richard-Pierre Williamson (6 shares) and John William Hughes (5 shares). *17.2.1874:* Sailed from London for Brazil with 540 miles of submarine cable. *16.3.1874:* Arrived at Rio de Janeiro and proceeded to lay cable to Santos. Captain R.R. Williamson, eldest son of Richard-Pierre Williamson, was master at this time. In recognition of his services to the nation, Dom Pedro II, Emperor of Brazil, invested Captain Williamson as a Knight

of the Order of the Rose. *25.12.1876:* Sank in the Arabian Sea following a collision with the US ship GEORGE F. MANSON in position 15.06N, 73.27E, about 30 miles south west of Goa, whilst on a voyage from Calcutta to Bombay. The story of the incident handed down to the family claims there were only two survivors of the disaster, a young cabin boy and the Captain R.R. Williamson. According to Captain Williamson's granddaughter, the AMBASSADOR was cut clean in half by the impact and sank immediately. It was said that Captain Williamson could not swim but while struggling in the water he managed to seize a goose, one of several kept in pens on deck. The bird kept him afloat until he was eventually picked up by the ship which had run them down.

68. LEGISLATOR (1) 1873-1887 Iron steamship rigged as a brig. Two decks.
O.N. 65995 2,126g 1,375n 310.5 x 34.1 x 24.4 feet.
Code: LVBQ.
C. 2-cyl. by Maudslay, Sons and Field, East Greenwich, 42, 72 x 48 inches, 9 knots.

19.10.1872: Launched by Maudslay, Sons and Field, East Greenwich. *1.1.1873:* Delivered to Thomas Harrison (44

shares) and James Harrison (20 shares), Liverpool for £38,000. *7.3.1873:* Thomas Harrison sold 22 shares, thus:

James Harrison and Edward Hodgson Harrison (3 shares), Richard Harrison (8 shares), Richard-Pierre Williamson (6 shares) and John William Hughes (5 shares). *12.5.1874:* Chartered at Hong Kong for a series of voyages to Foo Chow, Singapore, Bushire, Sydney, Melbourne, Brisbane, Saigon and other ports. *23.4.1875:* Returned to Liverpool with boiler leaking badly. It was said that the ship was "never the same again".[45] *18.12.1884:* All the partners transferred their shares to The Charente Steam-Ship Co. Ltd. *12.5.1887:* Sold to Raylton Dixon and Co., Middlesbrough for £8,000. *7.6.1887:* Resold to Marques de Campo, Cadiz, Spain and renamed HONDURAS. *1890:* Sold to M. M. de

Arrotegui, Bilbao, Spain and renamed CASTELLANO. *1893:* Sold to G. Tweedy and Co., London and renamed KASHGAR. *1893:* Owners became London Steamers Ltd., London. *1894:* Sold to Macbeth and Gray, Glasgow. *1895:* Sold to Röed McNair and Co., Tönsberg, Norway. *1895:* Owner became Hjalmar Röed, Tönsberg. *1898:* Sold to Société Anonyme de Transports Miniers, Antwerp, Belgium and renamed MARIA. *1901:* Sold to J. Espina Galofre, Barcelona, Spain and registered in Montevideo, Uruguay. *1905:* Renamed IGNACIO ROCA. *5.3.1905:* Left West Hartlepool for Barcelona with a cargo of coal and disappeared.

69. OBERON 1872-1879 Iron steamship rigged as two-masted schooner. One deck and poop.
O.N. 65280 1,207g 786n 247.0 x 32.1 x 17.4 feet.
Commercial Code: KSQL.
C. 2-cyl. by Humphreys and Pearson, Hull; 56, 30 x 33 inches, 10 knots.

2.12.1871: Launched by Humphreys and Pearson, Hull (Yard No. 22) for their own account. *2.12.1872:* Acquired by T. and J. Harrison, Liverpool for £22,000. *12.2.1873:* Registered in the ownership of James Harrison (64 shares), Liverpool. *10.1876:* A serious fire broke out in the cargo of cotton when on passage from New Orleans to Liverpool. Captain Burnett was injured while attempting to extinguish the fire. *24.10.1876:* Put into Norfolk, Virginia, and lay there six days putting out the fire and discharging damaged cotton. *30.10.1876:* Sailed under the command of Mr. Campbell, the

First Mate. *20.1.1879:* Ran aground in Queenstown Harbour when calling on a voyage from New Orleans to Liverpool. *5.2.1879:* Refloated. *26.2.1879:* Following temporary repairs, sailed for Liverpool in tow of a tug. *28.2.1879:* Arrived Liverpool. *7.3.1879:* Dry docked. *2.4.1879:* Sold to George R. Clover and Co., Liverpool. *12.11.1879:* Sold to Compagnie du Sénégal et de la Côte Occidentale d'Afrique, Marseilles, France and renamed MANDINGUE. *1895:* Broken up during third quarter.

70. CHANCELLOR (1) 1873-1886 Iron steamship rigged as a brig. Two decks.
O.N. 69232 2,052g 1,329n 310.4 x 34.2 x 23.9 feet.
Commercial Code LQMK.
C. 2-cyl by Thompson, Boyd and Co., Newcastle-upon-Tyne; 38, 70 x 42 inches, 10 knots.

30.11.1872: Launched by James Laing, Sunderland (Yard No. 192) for Thomas Harrison (22 shares), James Harrison (20 shares), Edward Hodgson Harrison (8 shares), Richard-Pierre Williamson (6 shares) and John William Hughes (5 shares), Liverpool for £37,032. James Harrison and Edward H. Harrison also held a joint interest in 3 shares. *13.3.1873:* Delivered and sailed from Sunderland for Liverpool. *8.1876:* When on passage from Galle to Suez, encountered the Spanish steamer YRURAC BAT (2,037/71) in the Red Sea and towed her to Suez. The ship was awarded £1,500 and the crew £350 by the underwriters. *8.9.1876:* Sailed from Hamburg for Liverpool and broke her main shaft off Anglesey. *12.9.1876:* Assisted into Holyhead, she was then

towed to Liverpool by the tugs RESCUE (127/57) and TOILER (75/74), arriving the following day. *22.1.1879:* Captain Valiant defies Consul sailing from New Orleans (see below). *18.12.1884:* All the partners transferred their shares to The Charente Steam-Ship Co. Ltd. *12.11.1886:* Sold to James Laing (J.W. Squance, manager), Sunderland for £8,000 and renamed ETTRICKDALE. *1891:* Sold to the Plate Steam Ship Co. Ltd. (Gellatly, Hankey Sewell and Co., managers), London and renamed OCAMPO. *1904:* Sold to Yazaki Tsunesaburo, Kobe, Japan and renamed KYOYEI MARU No. 1. *7.12.1907:* Wrecked near Hokkaido whilst on a voyage from Katami to Kobe with a cargo of timber.

Valiant tactics
On 22nd January 1879, at about 20.00, Captain James Valiant took the unprecedented step of sailing his ship from New Orleans without papers or clearance, and risked arrest by a US gunboat. All the papers, including the ship's articles and register, had been retained by the British Consul, with whom there had been an altercation earlier in the day. It arose thus. A disaffected fireman, one Peter Kelly, had made a complaint to the Consul regarding his treatment on board the CHANCELLOR, and alleged that both the Master and Chief Engineer had made threats against his safety. (Kelly, apparently, liked to sleep in of a morning, and the Chief in exasperation had perhaps voiced a desire to "have his guts for garters!" or used a similar colourful expression.) Mr. A. de G. de Fonblanque, the British Consul, thereupon summoned the Master and Chief Engineer to appear at his office to hear the

complaint, but when they arrived Kelly was not there. The Consul declined to proceed in the absence of the plaintiff, and adjourned the hearing until the morrow. In vain, Captain Valiant protested that the ship was due to complete and sail that night, and demanded his papers. The Consul was adamant, however, and refused to hand them over. By now the Captain was very angry. He resolved to sail, come what may, and left the Consulate in high dudgeon. Later that evening, when Kelly staggered aboard in his cups, he was seized by a couple of trusty sailors and locked up until the ship was well clear of the port. The incident led to a good deal of frosty correspondence between the Board of Trade and Harrisons, but no further action was taken. And Mr. Kelly, despite all so-called threats, arrived safely in the United Kingdom, but his future employment in Harrison vessels was no doubt severely jeopardised.[46]

71. VANGUARD 1873-1881 Iron steamship rigged as two-masted schooner. Three decks. Three-quarter man figurehead.
O.N. 60573 1,405g 913n 253.0 x 34.0 x 24.1 feet.
Commercial Code: JTLB.
C. 2-cyl. by Thomas Clark and Co., Newcastle-upon-Tyne; 30, 60 x 36 inches, 10 knots.

18.12.1870: Launched by W. Pile and Co., Sunderland (Yard No. 193) for the River Parana Steam Ship Co. Ltd., Liverpool. *1871:* Completed. *11.11.1873:* Acquired by Thomas Harrison (22 shares), James Harrison (20 shares), Edward Hodgson Harrison (8 shares), James Harrison and Edward Hodgson Harrison (3 shares), Richard-Pierre Williamson (6 shares) and John William Hughes (5 shares), Liverpool for £24,000. *28.2.1877:* Arrived in the River Mersey from New

Orleans and grounded on the Pluckington Bank while docking. Sustained substantial bottom damage and spent nearly two months in dry-dock making repairs. *28.5.1881:* Sold to Pinkney and Sons Steam Ship Co. Ltd. (D.G. and T. Pinkney, managers), Sunderland for £12,000 and renamed SOLANO. *6.5.1885:* Wrecked on Venedick Rash Rocks, near Heraclea, Turkey whilst on a voyage from the Tyne to Constantinople with a cargo of coal.

72. WARRIOR (2) 1874-1888 Iron steamship rigged as two-masted schooner. Two decks and two holds.
O.N. 69347 1,231g 797n 1,660d 241.7 x 30.2 x 22.4 feet. Cargo capacity: 77,428 cubic feet.
C. 2-cyl. by Ouseburn Engine Works Co., Newcastle-upon-Tyne; 29½, 56 x 36 inches, 10 knots.
Commercial Code: NVBK.

20.1.1874: Launched by Davison and Stokoe, Sunderland (Yard No. 29) for Thomas Harrison (22 shares) and James Harrison (42 shares), Liverpool for £26,477. Later James Harrison transferred 22 shares to the remaining partners, Edward Hodgson Harrison (8 shares), Richard-Pierre Williamson (6 shares), John William Hughes (5 shares) and James Harrison and Edward Hodgson Harrison (3 shares). *24.3.1874:* Delivered. *28.3.1874:* Sailed from Sunderland after delivery, but returned due to engine trouble. *1.4.1874:* Sailed again following adjustments. *18.10.1878:* Rescued 240 of the 500 coolies (the rest swam or scrambled ashore) aboard the sailing vessel PANDORA, stranded in the Boca de Huevos, Gulf of Paria, Trinidad. The PANDORA had sailed the previous day from Port of Spain for Calcutta with some 500 coolies and had been swept on to a reef in the Boca de Huevos by strong currents. She eventually broke her back and was impaled on the reef for many years afterwards. *7.3.1881:* When in a position about 178 miles southwest by west of Funchal, Madeira, on passage from Pernambuco to Liverpool with a cargo of cotton and sugar,

fire was discovered in the cotton cargo in the starboard 'tween decks. It was a serious outbreak and defied all efforts of Captain Jones and his crew to extinguish it. The vessel put into Funchal the following day and the fire was eventually extinguished, but not before Captain Charles Newman, Lloyd's Surveyor and Salvage Agent, had been seriously injured in the process. *12.3.1881:* Sailed from Funchal. *19.3.1881:* Arrived at Liverpool where repairs took eleven weeks. Captain Newman was subsequently awarded £400 compensation. *18.12.1884:* All the partners transferred their shares to The Charente Steam-Ship Co. Ltd. *9.1886:* Sailed for Belize to initiate a new service carrying fruit to New Orleans. The service was not a success as she was too slow to compete with other vessels in the trade and the venture was abandoned within a year. *29.2.1888:* Sold to John Dent Junior, Newcastle-upon-Tyne for £4,316. *1889:* Sold to G.W. Allen and Co., South Shields. *12.5.1890:* Sold to Essayan Sirketi, Istanbul, Turkey and renamed TARSUS. *1895:* Sold to Idare-i Mahsusa, Istanbul. *1909:* Laid up at Istanbul. *1912:* Sold for demolition at Istanbul.

73. SENATOR (1) 1874-1889 Iron full-rigged ship. Two decks. Male figurehead.
O.N. 69375 1,768g 1,695n 2,053d 256.2 x 41.1 x 23.6 feet.
International Code: NDJB.

16.5.1874: Launched by Mounsey and Foster, South Dock, Sunderland (Yard No. 67) for Thomas Harrison (32 shares) and James Harrison (32 shares), Liverpool. *18.6.1874:* Delivered. *20.6.1874:* Sailed from Sunderland and towed to London for a fee of £100. *21.1.1878:* Sailed from Calcutta for Demerara with 550 adult coolies on board at £12 per head. In fact, there were 650 aboard,* besides the crew, on this her only voyage in the coolie trade. It was a record "lift". *15.4.1878:* Arrived after a good passage of 84 days. *26.2.1879:* Sailed from Liverpool and collided with the French barque VANQUELAIN which necessitated a return to the Mersey for repairs. Arrived 1.3.1879 and sailed 8.3.1879 for Rangoon. *8.4.1889:* All 64 shares transferred to Heath Harrison. *12.4.1889:* Ownership transferred to Sailing Ship Senator Co. Ltd. (Walter de Wolf, later C.E. de Wolf and Co., managers), Liverpool. *8.5.1900:* When on passage from British Columbia to Liverpool, came upon the hulk of the Norwegian sailing vessel SUPERB, dismasted and abandoned in position 36N, 32W, about 1,300 miles west of the Straits of Gibraltar. The crew had been taken off by the British barque SEAFARER (2,211/88) and landed in the United Kingdom. Chief Officer J.H. Wilson of the SENATOR volunteered to salvage the derelict with five men. The captain agreed and a quantity of sails and provisions were put on board. She made good headway and when 70 miles west of Cape Trafalgar an offer from the Spanish steamer JULIO (1,848/88) to tow to Gibraltar for a fee of £100 was accepted. *22.6.1900:* Arrived safely at Gibraltar. *1910:* Sold

for £2,000 to Brazilian interests. *3.1911:* Towed to Manaos for use as a hulk by Booth Line. Reported still at Manaos in 1956. A report dated 9.5.1989[47] reveals that the hulk was moored in the Rio Negro, before Manaos, in 1960, and was being used as an ammunition store, presumably by the Brazilian forces. In 1965 the hulk was beached near Manaos in a sinking condition and was reported submerged during the high river season. Shortly afterwards she was broken up.

* The number includes children ("halves"), and infants, who travelled free.

Corrective note
It has long been assumed that SENATOR was the proud holder of a record 89-day passage to San Francisco, set in 1889 after her transfer to Walter de Wolf. This assumption was based on a passage in 'The Last of the Windjammers' by Basil Lubbock, describing SENATOR's feat, and the celebratory "high jinks" in San Francisco which marked the achievement. Alas, Mr Lubbock seems to have got hold of the wrong name and date, and the whole episode apparently refers to the MERIONETH, which completed a record passage in the winter of 1887/1888. This amendment to the record is the outcome of research carried out by Herbert H. Beckwith, Catalogue Librarian of the National Maritime Museum at Fort Mason, San Francisco in 1981. He could find no reference to SENATOR being in San Francisco in 1889, either in shipping records, or the press, but the success of the MERIONETH is well documented.

Senator, Harrisons last sailing ship, possibly at Penarth early in 1911 after her sale to Brazilian buyers.
[National Maritime Museum N.21926]

74. LINGUIST (1) 1874-1879 Iron full-rigged ship. Two decks. Male figurehead.
O.N. 70890 1,601g 1,534n 250.1 x 38.25 x 22.9 feet.
International Code: WSVG.

26.10.1874: Launched by Mounsey and Foster, South Dock, Sunderland (Yard No. 69) for Thomas Harrison (14 shares), Edward Hodgson Harrison (4 shares), James Harrison (2 shares), Thomas Fenwick Harrison (4 shares), Frederick James Harrison (4 shares), John William Hughes (4 shares) and others (32 shares), Liverpool. *8.12.1874:* Delivered. *24.12.1874:* Sailed from Sunderland on her maiden voyage bound for Calcutta loaded with 2,228 tons of railway iron and sleepers. *28.4.1875:* Arrived at Calcutta, after a lengthy passage of 125 days, and discharged her cargo. *8.1.1879:* Sailed from Liverpool under the command of Captain Thomas and loaded with 2,069 tons of salt for Rangoon. *11.1.1879:* Foundered in a severe gale, some 70 miles south east of Cape Clear.

LINGUIST's first and last voyages

After LINGUIST's arrival at Calcutta on 28th April 1875, it was not until July that a quota of emigrants was ready to come on board whereupon she embarked 546½ adult coolies bound for Demerara and loaded 1,122 tons of linseed for Liverpool, generating a total freight of nearly £9,000. *1.8.1875:* Sailed and arrived 6.11.1875 at Demerara. Her draft was too deep to permit her to enter the port, so she anchored near the lightship to await arrival of a tender. The following account appeared in a local newspaper:

"Mr. Crosby, the Immigration Agent General, accompanied by Dr. Watt, the Medical Officer to the Department and Mr. Forster, the first clerk, went out to the ship LINGUIST in the steamer BERBICE yesterday morning to inspect the Coolies on board that ship, she being unable to cross the Bar. The immigrants and ship were inspected and the immigrants, 362 men, 148 women, 33 boys, 23 girls and 31 infants were then transferred from the ship to the BERBICE and brought into port. The ship was found in admirable order and the Coolies, under the medical charge of Dr. George Stuart, in a fine and healthy condition. Two immigrants, both men, jumped overboard during the voyage and committed suicide; and one woman gave birth to a child in one of the closets and tried to thrust it through the shoot into the ocean, but the infant's cries were heard and it was rescued. The LINGUIST is a fine new ship (1,534 tons), this being her first voyage, under the command of Mr. Charles M. Curry. The Immigrant Agent-General was much pleased with the cleanliness and discipline of the ship and paid a high compliment to her Commander and Officers."[48]

It will be noted that the "out-turn", if the term can be used with respect, was the equivalent of 538 adults, indicating that 8½ adults had died on the passage.

LINGUIST's second voyage also found her on the coolie run to Demerara, embarking on this occasion 549½ adults. She completed the passage in the remarkable time of 79 days, but with the loss of three immigrants. This, incidentally was to be her final appearance in the trade.

The LINGUIST last sailed from the Mersey on Wednesday 8th January 1879, attended by a steam tug. The winds must have been very contrary, for the tug's services were retained until the following morning when the ship was off St. David's Head, Pembrokeshire. Casting off the tug, the ship headed southwards into a rising westerly gale, close-hauled under a press of canvas. The gale moderated to some extent on the morning of the 10th January, but it was only a brief respite. Sea and swell were very heavy and the ship tended to roll violently as she struggled southwards.

Later during the day some heavy spars, secured with chain-lashings, broke adrift. The crew managed to re-secure them, but that night, as the weather worsened, they broke loose again. While the ship was sailing at about six knots, close-hauled on the starboard tack under reefed topsails, the ship began to list heavily to leeward. Fearing for the safety of his ship, Captain Thomas decided to put about, and return to Liverpool. The lee braces were cut away in an attempt to haul the yards round and head the ship on to the other tack, but it was an impossible manoeuvre against the list. In an effort to trim the ship, all hands were sent below to shift cargo, shovelling salt up into the high side of the dimly-lit hold. But the main hatch-coaming had been breached and with each wave that broke on board, tons of sea water cascaded into the hold, to be absorbed by the salt, which quickly became a deliquescent sludge. The pumps were useless, and the ship's stability was rapidly eroded.

At some time between midnight and 01.00 on 11th January, in a position about 70 miles south east of Cape Clear, the LINGUIST heeled over on to her beam ends in a sinking condition. A few seamen managed to scramble out of the hold; several attempted to cut away the boats; more were trapped below, or were washed overboard. Somehow, a boat was cleared and splashed into the sea right way up. A seaman and an apprentice clambered aboard, but the boat was swamped by a huge sea which swept over the dying vessel. The next boat to be released miraculously survived the turmoil and two seamen, William Pritchard and James Coleman, clambered aboard. They kept their heads and at once set to work baling out their waterlogged craft. The ship now had green seas breaking over her, her yards tossing and dipping into the water. Pritchard and Coleman, displaying gallantry of a high order, guided their cockleshell through the combing seas and the wreckage to rescue their mates, all of whom were now floundering in the water. By the time LINGUIST finally sank, twelve men had been rescued by these very able seamen and the boat remained on the scene until daylight. Captain Thomas stayed by his ship and perished with her. The survivors bent to their oars and headed eastwards.

At noon, hope flared when they sighted a brig, but their efforts to attract attention were ignored and soon she disappeared below the horizon. However, in the busy St. George's Channel it was not long before another ship was sighted. This time the castaways were seen and the ship put about to investigate. She was the French vessel EQUATEUR, bound for Pwllheli. The Frenchman picked up the survivors and their boat and resumed course. The French seamen shared bedding, blankets and food in an open-hearted manner which was warmly appreciated by the shipwrecked seamen. But alas, the LINGUIST's survivors were still far from seeing the end of their ordeal. On 13th January, running into Cardigan Bay before a south east gale in poor visibility, EQUATEUR made too much easting and ran ashore on the reef of Sarn Badrig, some 10 miles south of Pwllheli. The ship, grievously wounded, slipped off the reef and sank in deep water, all hands taking to the boats. Once more the survivors from the LINGUIST launched their own trusty boat and eventually, after five hours of strenuous pulling at the oars, reached the town of Pwllheli. They, together with their French rescuers, were again greeted with warm hospitality.

Fourteen seamen out of a crew of twenty-nine survived the double disaster.

Joseph K. Thompson, Third Officer	Robert Headon, Bosun
George Clarke, Apprentice	Frederick. B Holland,Apprentice
Robert Sprague, Apprentice	Harold D. Wilkinson, Apprentice
H. Clements, AB	James Coleman, AB
Edwin Grant, AB	David Hughes, AB
William Pritchard, AB	William Sharrard, AB
Patrick Sloan, AB	Richard Watson, AB

Third Officer J. K. Thompson, the only officer to survive, continued to serve in the company until he died in Calcutta in 1900, at the age of 40 and with the rank of Chief Officer.

75. MEDIATOR 1876-1884 Iron steamship rigged as two-masted schooner. Three decks and three holds.
O.N. 65961 2,011g 1,304n 300.3 x 34.7 x 25.2 feet. Cargo capacity: 139,088 cubic feet.
International Code: LGWT.
Two C.2-cyl. by George Forrester and Co., Liverpool; 2 x 21, 2 x 47 x 39 inches, 11 knots.

8.5.1872: Launched by R. and J. Evans and Co., Liverpool (Yard No. 48) for Hargrove, Ferguson and Co., Liverpool as DAHLIA. *17.8.1876:* Acquired by T. and J. Harrison, Liverpool for £25,000. *26.9.1876:* Renamed MEDIATOR.

18.8.1883: Returned to Liverpool following a collision with the Norwegian barque AGAT off the Tuskar Rock. *23.8.1883:* Sailed again following repairs costing £450. *5.7.1884:* Run down and sunk by the German steamer THURINGIA (1,964/80) whilst berthed in Willemstad Harbour, Curaçao having arrived from Liverpool with general cargo.

76. DISCOVERER (1) 1877-1893 Iron steamship rigged as three-masted schooner. Two decks and four holds.
O.N. 76484 2,218g 1,455n 2,290d 311.3 x 34.05 x 25.65 feet. Cargo capacity: 128,500 cubic feet.
International Code: QNKT.
C. 2-cyl. by J. and J. Thomson, Glasgow; 35, 70 x 48 inches.

15.2.1877: Launched by Aitken and Mansel, Whiteinch, Glasgow (Yard No. 89) for T. and J. Harrison, Liverpool for £38,900. *21.4.1877:* Delivered. *28.1.1878:* Ashore at Budge Budge in the Hooghly River, India. *30.1.1878:* Refloated. *18.12.1884:* The partners transferred their shares to The Charente Steam-Ship Co. Ltd. *8.8.1893:* Sold to Francis Vivian Japp, Liverpool for £5,095. *16.8.1893:* Resold to Paolo Viale di G.B., Genoa, Italy and renamed VITTORIA V. *1896:* Renamed BALAKLAVA. *1899:* Broken up at Naples during the second quarter.

77. COUNSELLOR (1) 1877-1893 Iron steamship rigged as three-masted schooner. Two decks and four holds.
O.N. 76504 2,217g 1,456n 2,990d 311.0 x 34.1 x 25.65 feet. Cargo capacity: 128,500 cubic feet.
International Code: QRFC.
C. 2-cyl. by J. and J. Thomson, Glasgow; 35, 70 x 48 inches.

17.4.1877: Launched by Aitken and Mansel, Whiteinch, Glasgow (Yard No. 90) for Thomas Harrison (20 shares), James Harrison (20 shares), Edward Hodgson Harrison (8 shares), John William Hughes (8 shares), Thomas Fenwick Harrison (2 shares), Thomas Hughes (2 shares), Richard Robert Williamson (2 shares) and Thomas Williamson (2 shares), Liverpool for £39,000. *1.6.1877:* Delivered. *4.1878:* Measured at Calcutta and authorised to carry 538 coolies. *28.2.1883:* Broke her tail shaft at 21.00 when in position 45.20N, 35.30W, on passage from New Orleans to Liverpool. She made sail but was eventually taken in tow 12.3.1883 in position 44.35N, 29.19W by the French steamer CHATEAU LAFITE (3,462/81), having sailed just 267 miles in about 12 days. *19.3.1883:* The two vessels reached Ile d'Aix, about 1,180 miles away. *18.5.1883:* Delivered 50 Jersey cows and 10 calves at New Orleans, after transporting them safely from Liverpool. The freight was £4 per head (£2 for calves) and the vessel was 22 days on passage. *18.12.1884:* The partners transferred their shares to The Charente Steam-Ship Co. Ltd. *7.11.1893:* Sold to the shipbuilders C.S. Swan and Hunter, Newcastle-upon-Tyne for £5,445, in part-payment for the newbuilding MUSICIAN (112). Registered in the ownership of George B. Hunter. *23.8.1894:* Sold to Giuseppe fu Domenico Zino, Savona, Italy, and renamed ALACRITA. *4.1904:* Broken up at Genoa.

78. EXPLORER (1) 1877-1906 Iron steamship rigged as brig and later two-masted schooner. Three decks and three holds.
O.N. 69243 2,011g 1,298n 2,875d 300.3 x 34.7 x 25.2 feet. Cargo capacity: 138,330 cubic feet.
International Code: LSFQ.
C. 2-cyl. by G. Forrester and Co., Liverpool; 24, 47 x 39 inches.
1887: T. 3-cyl. by Blair and Co. Ltd., Stockton-on-Tees; 20, 33, 54 x 36 inches.

2.1.1873: Launched by R. and J. Evans and Co., Liverpool (Yard No. 51) for Hargrove, Ferguson and Co., Liverpool as CROCUS. *1873:* Completed. *23.8.1877:* Acquired by Thomas Harrison (39 shares) and James Harrison (25 shares), Liverpool for £27,500. *21.11.1877:* Renamed EXPLORER. *18.12.1884:* The partners transferred their shares to The Charente Steam-Ship Co. Ltd. *1887:* Fitted with new engine. *13.10.1894:* Suffered a violent explosion in No.2 hold when loading ocean coal at Alfred Dock, Birkenhead. One coal heaver was killed outright and four others died of their injuries during the next fortnight. *9.1902:* Ran aground on Old Providence Island, Colombia, when on passage from Colon to Belize. She was ashore for three days and only refloated after jettisoning 500 tons of cargo and 125 tons of coal. *12.3.1906:* Run down by the Brazilian steamer GONCALVES DIAZ (1,859/02) whilst at anchor off Cardiff. *23.8.1906:* Sold to Pacific Steam Navigation Co., Liverpool for £3,826 for use as a coal hulk. Stationed first at Panama and later at Valparaiso. *1919:* Reported abandoned at Valparaiso.

79. COMMANDER 1877-1884 Iron steamship rigged as three-masted schooner. Two decks.
O.N. 76550 1,580g 1,039n 265.1 x 32.0 x 23.8 feet.
International Code: RCGB.
C. 2-cyl. by Barrow Shipbuilding Co. Ltd., Barrow; 32, 60 x 42 inches, 10 knots.

27.9.1877: Launched by Barrow Shipbuilding Co. Ltd., Barrow (Yard No. 38) for Thomas Harrison (32 shares) and James Harrison (32 shares), Liverpool for £28,000. *3.11.1877:* Delivered. Share ownership subsequently redistributed to Thomas Harrison (20 shares), James Harrison (20 shares), Edward Hodgson Harrison (8 shares), John William Hughes (8 shares), Thomas Fenwick Harrison (2 shares), Thomas Hughes (2 shares), Richard Robert Williamson (2 shares) and Thomas Williamson (2 shares). *4.9.1881:* When on passage from New Orleans to Liverpool, shed one or more propeller blades. The voyage continued under sail and she was spoken to by several vessels: on 6.9.1881, the steamer MORAY (2,185/77) and the barque ESTHER (280/54); the ship McDOUGALL 8.9.1881 and the barque KORSFARER 12.9.1881 in position 42.20N, 43.45W. *29.9.1881:* Taken in tow by the steamer CORONILLA (1,361/79) in position 40.11N, 27.00W and the two ships arrived at 18.00 on 30.9.1881 at St. Michaels in the Azores. For a tow lasting just over 32 hours, CORONILLA received an award of £2,000. *14.6.1884:* Sailed at 18.45 from Maceio, Brazil for Liverpool, with 1,696 tons of sugar and 1,377 bales of cotton. About five hours later she ran ashore at Barragrande, Cape San Antonio and was wrecked.

80. ORATOR (1) 1878-1889 Iron steamship rigged as two-masted schooner. One deck, poop and two holds.
O.N. 78743 1,342g 850n 1,877d 250.0 x 32.0 x 20.15 feet. Cargo capacity: 82,460 cubic feet.
International Code: RCPS.
C. 2-cyl. by Thompson and Co., Newcastle-upon-Tyne; 30, 60 x 36 inches, 10¹/₂ knots.

21.11.1877: Launched by Charles Mitchell and Co., Newcastle-upon-Tyne (Yard No. 353) for Thomas Harrison (32 shares) and James Harrison (32 shares), Liverpool for £24,600. *18.1.1878:* Delivered. Share ownership subsequently redistributed to Thomas Harrison (20 shares), James Harrison (20 shares), Edward Hodgson Harrison (8 shares), John William Hughes (8 shares), Thomas Fenwick Harrison (2 shares), Thomas Hughes (2 shares), Richard Robert Williamson (2 shares) and Thomas Williamson (2 shares). *26.2.1880:* Collided with and sank the brigantine RINGLEADER (181/53) in the River Mersey just south of Albert Dock, Liverpool, when inward bound to Brunswick Dock. *10.1.1884:* Serious fire broke out in the cotton cargo when homeward bound from Brazilian ports for Liverpool in position 00.40S, 30.50W. It was decided to put back to Pernambuco, a distance of 480 miles. *13.1.1884:* Arrived Pernambuco whereupon the fire was extinguished, the damaged cargo discharged and a new shipment loaded.

18.12.1884: The partners transferred their shares to The Charente Steam-Ship Co. Ltd. 17.10.1888: Joint ownership assumed with Edward Asher Cohan (T. Fenwick Harrison, manager), Liverpool. 1.5.1889: Sold to Edward Asher Cohan, Liverpool for £8,750. 21.12.1890: Wrecked on South Briggs Rock, off Groomsport, County Down, at the entrance to Belfast Lough whilst on a voyage from the Clyde to Sicily with a cargo of coal.

ORATOR swings into trouble

The incident of 26th February 1880, in which ORATOR collided with and sank the brigantine RINGLEADER, is documented in a statement made by Captain John Corbishley to the company's lawyers. The statement is interesting in several respects, not least in the listing and composition of the crew of this quite small steamer: "29 hands all told - Self, 2 Mates, Carpenter, Boatswain, Lamptrimmer, 2 Stewards, Cook and 9 seamen, 3 Engineers, 7 Fireman and 1 Engineers' Steward".

Captain Corbishley 1841 - 1892

Captain Corbishley then goes on to explain how the ship sailed from New Orleans on 6th February, with a cargo of cotton and grain and arrived off Point Lynas on 26th to pick up a licensed pilot, John Walters, from No. 3 Pilot Cutter. The ship was fairly light, drawing 14' 5" forward and 16' 8" aft, but even so had to wait over an hour for sufficient water to cross the Bar. This she did at 20.40, though the weather was bad, blowing a gale from the north north west with gusty squalls of rain and hail. The spring tide was at the flood, with high water expected two minutes after midnight. The conditions were such that Captain Corbishley was rather reluctant to go up the river that night.

"Before we entered the River I told the Pilot I was in no hurry to get up and that I was quite willing to wait until daylight. He said there was no danger in coming up then. I left the matter entirely to his discretion".

The ship passed the Rock Light at 21.40 and reduced speed, awaiting an opportunity to swing, in order to stem the flood and drop down to the Brunswick entrance. Traffic was heavy, however, and visibility was frequently impaired by the squalls and the ship had reached the Wallasey (Seacombe) Landing Stage before an opportunity occurred. There were no passing vessels in the vicinity at that time: the lights of several vessels at anchor could be seen over against the southern end of the Albert Dock, but they seemed well clear.

"The Pilot gave me the order to stop the engines and himself ordered the helmsman to put the helm hard-a-starboard. When the helm was got hard-a-starboard the Pilot gave the order to go ahead full-speed to turn the vessel. As we began to turn we could see a number of lights on the Liverpool side of the River, close inshore, opposite the south end of the Albert Dock. A heavy hail and rain squall then came on which obscured the lights and it was very dark. The wind was blowing a moderate gale and acting on the steamer's port bow. It prevented her from coming round on

her starboard helm as quickly as she otherwise would. The flood tide was at this time running about 4 or 5 knots. The steamer payed off under the starboard helm and in about 2 or 3 minutes, when the vessel's head was about east, or a point or two to the northward, the Mate (who was forward) reported a vessel on the starboard bow and in a second or two I could see her. She was about 2 cables length distant on our starboard bow. I thought we should clear her, but in about a minute we could see that we could not do so by going ahead as the wind prevented our vessel coming round on her starboard helm and the tide was carrying us up the River. So the Pilot gave the order to reverse full-speed and to stand by the anchor… In about a minute the Pilot gave the order to let go the Port anchor… The anchor did not hold at first although It checked her a little and before the ship's way was stopped she was carried by the force of the wind and the strength of the tide against the RINGLEADER, the bluff of our starboard bow taking her just between the masts. The blow was very slight. We payed out a little chain and our steamer brought up astern of the brigantine… She was one of those vessels whose lights we had seen before we began to turn round. We hailed her and those on board her said she was sinking. We instantly swung out a boat and hove up our anchor. We intended to tow our boat ahead of her and then let it drop down to her as the tide was too strong for the crew to pull the boat against it. Before we got the anchor up, however, a tug came alongside the brigantine, and she slipped the chain. The boatman who was going to assist us in docking had by this time come from the shore and I sent him to the brigantine to render assistance. Seeing that the brigantine had plenty of assistance and that we could do nothing for her we hove up the anchor and went into the Brunswick Dock".

The Inquiry was held in Liverpool on 28th May 1880 and after making another voyage to Brazil, Captain Corbishley was taken out of his ship to attend it. Unfortunately, the outcome is not recorded, but subsequent events confirm that, happily, and despite the shadow cast by an earlier serious misfortune (see PANTHEON, 51) Captain Corbishley still retained the confidence of his employers. He continued to command their vessels until his death from heart disease on 20th November 1892, whilst his ship, which at that time was VESTA, lay at New Orleans. He was only 50 years of age.

---

81. INVENTOR (1) 1878-1905 Iron steamship rigged as two-masted schooner. Two decks and four holds.
O.N. 78801 2,291g 1,536n 3,139d 325.8 x 34.05 x 25.8 feet.
International Code: RVGS.
C. 2-cyl. by J. and J. Thomson, Glasgow; 35, 70 x 48 inches.

17.7.1878: Launched by Aitken and Mansel, Whiteinch (Yard No. 98). *22.8.1878:* Delivered after sea trials to Thomas Harrison (20 shares), James Harrison (20 shares), Edward Hodgson Harrison (8 shares), John William Hughes (8 shares), Thomas Hughes (2 shares), Richard Robert Williamson (2 shares) and Thomas Williamson (2 shares), Liverpool for £40,000. *18.12.1884:* All the partners transferred their shares to The Charente Steam-Ship Co. Ltd. *8.1896:* Developed a fault in the steering gear after leaving New Orleans and ran ashore in the South Pass. Refloated after seven hours. *12.7.1902:* The main engines were said to have "stuck" while leaving Liverpool, causing the vessel to strike and damage the Spanish steamer INGENIERO. *9.1904:* In collision with the British steamer

GOOLISTAN (2,756/98) off Oporto, Portugal, while on passage from Liverpool and Barry for Pernambuco. The GOOLISTAN, on passage from Karachi to Plymouth with grain, sank with the loss of the Third Officer and six crew. INVENTOR put into Lisbon badly damaged and at the subsequent inquiry was held to blame, with a liability estimated at £20,500. *14.10.1905:* Sold to Lamport and Holt, Liverpool for £3,937, for use as a hulk. *1920:* Returned to service for D. Escobar y Compania, Buenos Aires, Argentina, but registered in Valparaiso, Chile. *1923:* Sold to D. Pedretti, Buenos Aires. *1923:* Sold to E. Ross y Compania., Valparaiso, Chile and renamed ADRIANA. *21.11.1925:* Beached after springing a leak at Canical whilst on a voyage from Valparaiso to Genoa with a cargo of scrap

82. AUTHOR (1) 1880-1890 Iron steamship rigged as two-masted schooner. Two decks and two holds.
O.N. 81327 1,393g 885n 2,035d 250.8 x 32.1 x 21.25 feet. Cargo capacity: 94,577 cubic feet.
International Code: TBKP.
C. 2-cyl by Wallsend Slipway and Engineering Co. Ltd., Wallsend; 28, 56 x 39 inches, 10 knots.

15.1.1880: Launched by Charles Mitchell and Co., Newcastle-upon-Tyne (Yard No.393). *2.3.1880:* Delivered to Thomas Harrison (16 shares), Frederick James Harrison (20 shares), Thomas Fenwick Harrison (16 shares), and John William Hughes (12 shares), Liverpool for £21,039. Employed in the Western Ocean trade to Brazil, the Caribbean and U.S. Ports. *18.12.1884:* All the partners transferred their shares to The Charente Steam-Ship Co. Ltd. *28.10.1890:* Sold to Corinthia Steam Ship Co. Ltd. (James Henry Goodyear and Co., managers), Liverpool for £8,970 and renamed CORINTHIA. *7.6.1903:* Wrecked on Stroma Island in the Pentland Firth when on passage from Danzig to Liverpool with a cargo of railway sleepers.

83. ARCHITECT (1) 1880-1897 Iron steamship rigged as two-masted schooner. Two decks, poop and three holds.
O.N. 84044 1,934g 1,236n 2,681d 302.05 x 34.5 x 23.1 feet. Cargo capacity: 108,600 cubic feet.
International Code: TPCS.
C. 2-cyl. by Cunliffe and Dunlop, Port Glasgow; 34, 68 x 42 inches, 10 knots.

22.10.1880: Launched by Cunliffe and Dunlop, Port Glasgow (Yard No.142) and delivered to Thomas Harrison (16 shares), Frederick James Harrison (20 shares), Thomas Fenwick Harrison (16 shares), and John William Hughes (12 shares), Liverpool for £30,500. *24.12.1881:* Sailed from Liverpool and subsequently came across a disabled vessel, the PODOR, which she towed into Belle Ile, earning £300 for the service. *30.4.1883:* In collision with the company's EXPLORER which was berthed alongside at New Orleans. Damage was slight and both vessels sailed soon afterwards. *18.12.1884:* The partners transferred their shares to The Charente Steam-Ship Co. Ltd. *21.6.1897:* Sold to M. Louis Guette of E. Bories, Bordeaux, France for £4,500, and renamed ISABELLE. There was some dispute over the state of the stern frame which was eventually amicably settled and 29.7.1897 the sale was concluded. *1905:* Sold to A. Magnano fu B., Genoa, Italy. *10.1905:* Broken up at Genoa.

84. MARINER 1881-1896 Iron steamship rigged as brigantine. Two decks and two holds.
O.N. 84089 1,443g 917n 2,050d 250.1 x 32.05 x 21.2 feet. Cargo capacity: 94,577 cubic feet.
International Code: VLPW.
C. 2-cyl. by Blair and Co. Ltd., Stockton-on-Tees; 30, 55 x 36 inches, 10 knots.

1.3.1881: Launched by M. Pearse and Co., Stockton-on-Tees (Yard No.183). *1.4.1881:* Delivered to Thomas Harrison (16 shares), Frederick James Harrison (10 shares), Thomas Fenwick Harrison (16 shares), John William Hughes (12 shares), and Heath Harrison (10 shares), Liverpool for £21,500. *25.2.1882:* Sailed from Liverpool and two miles west north west of the Bar Lightvessel collided with the Liverpool Pilot Cutter No.9, the GUIDE. The schooner sank and one pilot was lost. The claim was settled in the sum of £1,112.15s.10d. *18.12.1884:* The partners transferred their shares to The Charente Steam-Ship Co. Ltd. *18.4.1896:* Sold to Mossgiel Steam Ship Co. Ltd. (J. Bruce and Co., managers), Glasgow. *1910:* Sold to Galbraith Brothers, Glasgow. *1913:* Sold to S. Galbraith, Glasgow and resold to J.J. King and Sons Ltd. to be dismantled.

85. MERCHANT (1) 1881-1897 Iron steamship rigged as two-masted schooner. Two decks and two holds.
O.N. 84094 1,401g 896n 2,050d 250.8 x 32.1 x 21.3 feet. Cargo capacity: 94,577 cubic feet.
International Code: VLRG.
C. 2-cyl. by Wallsend Slipway and Engineering Co. Ltd., Wallsend; 28, 56 x 39 inches, 10 knots.

19.2.1881: Launched by Charles Mitchell and Co., Low Walker (Yard No.415). *14.4.1881:* Delivered to Thomas Harrison (16 shares), Thomas Fenwick Harrison (8 shares), John William Hughes (12 shares), Heath Harrison (20 shares) and Edward Hodgson Harrison (8 shares), Liverpool for £22,000. *16.4.1881:* Sailed from the Tyne for Liverpool, a ballast voyage that took five days due to bad weather and fog. *28.4.1883:* Arrived at Reval on a charter voyage from Brazil to the Baltic. After discharge of her cotton cargo, found to be trapped fast in the ice and was not freed for four days. *18.12.1884:* The partners transferred their shares to The Charente Steam-Ship Co. Ltd. *11.5.1897:* Sold through Bahr, Behrend and Ross to Linea de Vapores Serra, Bilbao, Spain for £4,400 and renamed CECILIA. *1910:* Sold to Ajuria & Cia., Bilbao. *1911:* Broken up at Bilbao during the fourth quarter.

86. GOVERNOR (1) 1881-1900 Iron steamship rigged as three-masted schooner. Two decks and four holds.
O.N. 84098 2,623g 1,717n 3,600d 347.0 x 37.0 x 25.5 feet. Cargo capacity: 191,400 cubic feet.
International Code: VMND.
C. 2-cyl. by J. and J. Thomson, Glasgow; 38, 75 x 54 inches, 10.5 knots.

15.3.1881: Launched by Aitken and Mansel, Glasgow (Yard No.108). *2.5.1881:* Delivered to Thomas Harrison (35 shares), Frederick James Harrison (10 shares), Richard Robert Williamson (1 share), Edward Hodgson Harrison (8 shares) and Heath Harrison (10 shares), Liverpool for £43,500. *2.8.1882:* Ran ashore at Fultah in the Hooghly River and refloated after nine days. *11.8.1882:* Arrived Calcutta where she was dry-docked. *18.12.1884:* The partners transferred their shares to The Charente Steam-Ship Co. Ltd. *11.1897:* A serious fire on board whilst at Newport News gutted part of the accommodation and took two days to bring under control. *15.1.1900:* Sold to John White and Co. and registered at Genoa. *1902:* Sold to Società Anonima Genovese di Navigazione à Vapore (John White, manager), Genoa, Italy. *15.5.1902:* Left Genoa, Palermo and Naples for New York with 13 cabin and 335 steerage passengers, chartered by Vincenzo Finizio as an emigrant carrier for this and later voyages. *1911:* Broken up at Messina during the second quarter.

Governor in Brunswick Dock, Liverpool. Note the sails, furled and triced to the masts.

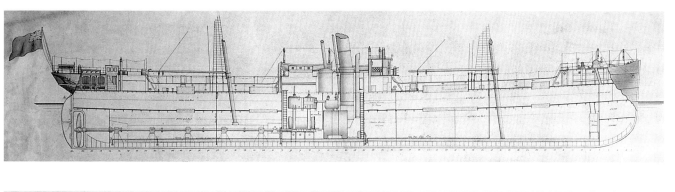

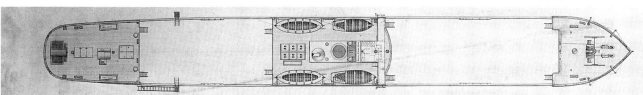

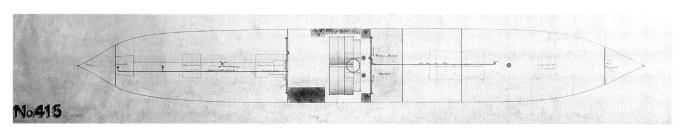

No. 415

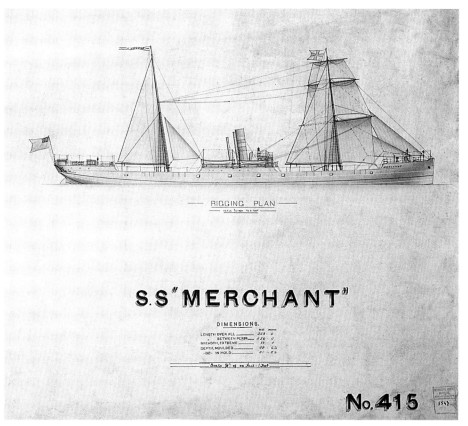

RIGGING PLAN

S.S "MERCHANT"

DIMENSIONS.

LENGTH OVER ALL
" BETWEEN PERPS.
BREADTH, EXTREME
DEPTH, MOULDED
-DO- IN HOLD

No. 415

Merchant (85).

87. PROFESSOR (1) 1881-1895 Iron steamship rigged as three-masted schooner. Two decks
O.N. 84181 2,593g 1,697n 3,434d 352.3 x 37.15 x 25.5 feet. Berths for 24 first class and 579 third class passengers.
International Code: WFKD.
C. 2-cyl. by Greenock Foundry Co., Greenock; 38, 75 x 54 inches.

8.10.1881: Launched by Scott and Co., Greenock (Yard No.204). *19.12.1881:* Delivered to Thomas Harrison (20 shares), Edward Hodgson Harrison (8 shares), Frederick James Harrison (20 shares), Thomas Hughes (2 shares) and John William Hughes (4 shares), Liverpool for £46,000. *18.12.1884:* The partners transferred their shares to The Charente Steam-Ship Co. Ltd. *5.1885:* Replacement stern-tube and bush were fitted while at Colombo by John Walker and Co., Engineers. She was trimmed by the head to raise the stern. *23.2.1895:* Believed to be the first Harrison vessel, loaded with cotton from the US Gulf, to transit the Ship Canal to Manchester. *28.7.1895:* Sold to the Steamship Professor Co. Ltd. (George Windram, manager), Liverpool. *17.12.1895:* Sold to G.B. Lavarello fu P., Genoa, Italy. *1900:* Sold to Luigi Pittaluga, Genoa, Italy. *28.7.1904:* Put into Almeria damaged by an explosion of gas in her cargo of coal, whilst on a voyage from Newport, Monmouthshire to Savona. After temporary repairs, proceeded to Savona, but subsequently broken up at Genoa.

Professor in Colombo Harbour in May 1885, trimmed by the head to allow access to the stern tube.

88. ENGINEER (1) 1882-1899 Iron steamship rigged as three-masted schooner. Two decks.
O.N. 86175 2,667g 1,743n 3,518d 350.2 x 38.0 x 25.3 feet. Berths for 20 first and 100 third class passengers.
International Code: WJRQ.
C. 2-cyl. by J. and J. Thomson, Glasgow; 38, 75 x 54 inches.

18.3.1882: Launched by Aitken and Mansel, Glasgow (Yard No.111). *11.5.1882:* Delivered to Thomas Harrison (16 shares), Frederick James Harrison (10 shares), Heath Harrison (10 shares), Thomas Fenwick Harrison (6 shares), John William Hughes (12 shares), Thomas Hughes (2 shares) and Edward Hodgson Harrison (8 shares), Liverpool for £45,282. *12.5.1882:* Thomas Harrison transferred one share each to Richard Robert Williamson and Thomas Williamson. *27.10.1884:* Sailed from New Orleans and arrived at Liverpool 13.11.1884 - 16 days 13 hours from bar to bar, a company record to that date. *18.12.1884:* The partners transferred their shares to The Charente Steam- Ship Co. Ltd. *31.12.1895:* Arrived at Tampico with the cargo on fire. The outbreak was contained and extinguished and she sailed 5.1.1896. *10.1898:* Carried a diver and surveyor out to Santo Domingo to survey the wreck of VESTA (No.101), aground in Catalinita Bay since 25.9.1898. *10.1899:* 86 head of cattle consigned to Havana were lost due to a stampede. *11.1899:* Fitted with a new funnel at Liverpool. *12.12.1899:* Sold to John White and Co., for £7,000 and registered at Genoa. *23.3.1900:* Whilst leaving dock at Penarth on her delivery voyage with a cargo of coal for Savona, she grounded and broke in two. Subsequently refloated and beached at Penarth Head for breaking up.

Engineer aground at Penarth.   *[Nigel Farrell collection]*

89. SCULPTOR (1) 1882-1889 Iron steamer rigged as brigantine. Two decks.
O.N. 86262 1,400g 894n 1,920d 250.0 x 33.25 x 20.2 feet. Berths for 23 passengers.
C. 2-cyl. by Blair and Co. Ltd., Stockton-on-Tees; 30, 55 x 36 inches.
International Code: WPRT.

28.10.1882: Launched by Raylton Dixon and Co., Middlesbrough (Yard No. 203). *13.12.1882:* Delivered to Thomas Harrison (10 shares), Heath Harrison (10 shares), Edward Hodgson Harrison (8 shares), Frederick James Harrison (12 shares), Thomas Fenwick Harrison (12 shares) and John William Hughes (12 shares), Liverpool for £23,800. *18.12.1884:* The partners transferred their shares to The Charente Steam-Ship Co. Ltd. *20.6.1889:* Sold to Andrew John McDonald, London for £13,000 and subsequently resold to the Bombay and Persia Steam Navigation and Co. Ltd., Bombay and renamed NASERI. *1912:* Sold to C. Matsumura, Nishinomiya, Japan and renamed MATSUYOSHI MARU. *16.5.1914:* Wrecked off Innami.

90. ASTRONOMER (2) 1884-1903 Iron steamship rigged as two-masted schooner. Two decks and four holds.
O.N. 87923 3,075g 2,029n 4,057d 365.2 x 40.0 x 26.6 feet. Cargo capacity: 204,000 cubic feet. Berths for 24 passengers.
C. 2-cyl. by J. and J. Thomson, Glasgow; 38, 75 x 54 inches, 10.5 knots.
International Code: JCVL.

27.11.1883: Launched by Aitken and Mansel, Glasgow (Yard No. 125). *10.1.1884:* Delivered to Thomas Harrison (16 shares), Thomas Fenwick Harrison (12 shares), Frederick James Harrison (12 shares), Heath Harrison (12 shares) and John William Hughes (12 shares), Liverpool for £52,750. *18.12.1884:* The partners transferred their shares to The Charente Steam-Ship Co. Ltd. *8.1886:* Berthed alongside the East Quay at the newly-opened Toxteth Dock, Liverpool to discharge a general cargo from Calcutta. She took full advantage of the new double-storey sheds and modern equipment available, such as the new hydraulic travelling roof-cranes and 3,643 tons of cargo were landed in 25 hours.[49] *7.1895:* Aground at Pensacola, remaining in port for nearly four weeks to effect repairs. *10.1897:* Serious illness was reported on board when homeward bound from New Orleans, two men dying at sea. *5.6.1903:* Grounded in Bahia Bay, Brazil, and the Master informed the board that the engine room and No .3 hold were flooded and the bulkheads were leaking into Nos. 2 and 4 holds. *23.6.1903:* Refloated but in danger of sinking in deep water. *15.7.1903:* Beached. Salvage seemed out of the question and the company, who carried their own insurance in those days, instructed the Salvage Officer, Captain McLellan, to advertise the vessel for sale "as is and in situ". *10.8.1903:* Sold at auction to Empreza Maritima Brazileira, Rio de Janeiro, Brazil for £1,200 and renamed S. LUIZ. *1907:* Sold to Companhia Comercio e Navegação, Rio de Janeiro and renamed ARAGUARY. *1928:* Owners became Pereira Carneiro e Companhia Ltda. (Companhia Comercio e Navegação, managers), Rio de Janeiro. *1930:* Dismantled during the fourth quarter.

Astronomer approaching South Stack, with Holyhead Mountain on the horizon.

THE YEARS OF EXPANSION
1884 - 1914

It was becoming increasingly clear as the 1880s advanced that further rationalisation and re-organisation of the company's structure and capital was advisable. The founders were anxious to ensure that a well-organised corporate body, fully supported by the law of the land, would survive them and sustain their children and their children's children in positions of power and influence. The decision was taken to register the firm under the new Companies' Act of 1880. There were several advantages in this, amongst them the power to regulate and restrict the sale of shares to the original members and their descendants, rather like an entailed estate, and also the right to claim limitation of liability which, though enshrined in shipping law since 1734,[50] had not been written into previous successive Companies' Acts.

The work of re-structuring fell mainly to Frederick J. Harrison and John W. Hughes and it was thanks to their efforts that the new company was incorporated on 16th December 1884, with a registered capital of £512,000, divided into 512 shares of £1,000 each, and a fleet of 22 steam-ships.[51] The remaining sailing ships, ARTIST (44) and SENATOR (73), were again left out of the arrangement; they soldiered on until ARTIST was sold in 1886 and SENATOR in 1889. After some earnest discussion it was decided to retain the former name and style and the Company's Common Seal was engraved with the title, "Charente Steam-Ship Company, Limited". The new company's fleet and its business transactions were to be managed by the private firm of Thos. and Jas. Harrison.

Holders of shares in the Harrison steam ships were now obliged to transfer those shares to the new company and this was done under a series of bills of sale dated 18th December 1884. For the record, the ships concerned are listed below with their gross tonnages.

ALICE	881	GOVERNOR (1)	2,623
ARCHITECT (1)	1,934	HISTORIAN (1)	1,830
ASTRONOMER (2)	3,075	INVENTOR (1)	2,291
AUTHOR (1)	1,393	LEGISLATOR (1)	2,126
CHANCELLOR (1)	2,052	MARINER	1,443
CHRYSOLITE	702	MERCHANT (1)	1,401
COGNAC	490	ORATOR (1)	1,342
COUNSELLOR (1)	2,217	PROFESSOR (1)	2,593
DISCOVERER (1)	2,218	SCULPTOR (1)	1,400
ENGINEER (1)	2,667	STATESMAN (1)	1,851
EXPLORER (1)	2,011	WARRIOR (2)	1,231
Total : 22 steam-vessels; aggregate gross tonnage 39,771.			

The list of original shareholders and the distribution of shares on incorporation appears below.

Thomas Harrison	Mersey Chambers, Liverpool.	Shipowner	128 shares
Thomas Fenwick Harrison	Mersey Chambers, Liverpool	Shipowner	32 shares
Frederick James Harrison	Mersey Chambers, Liverpool	Shipowner	80 shares
Heath Harrison	Mersey Chambers, Liverpool	Shipowner	80 shares
Edward Hodgson Harrison	Mersey Chambers, Liverpool	Shipowner	64 shares
John William Hughes	Mersey Chambers, Liverpool	Shipowner	96 shares
Thomas Hughes	Mersey Chambers, Liverpool	Shipowner	16 shares
Thomas Williamson	Mersey Chambers, Liverpool	Shipowner	8 shares
Richard Robert Williamson	The Hawthorns, Great Crosby	Master mariner	8 shares
Total			**512 shares**

The name of James Harrison does not feature in the list. Though still nominally a partner in the firm of Thomas and James Harrison, James was living in quiet retirement on his Dorden estate and did not seek further involvement in the new limited company, transferring his right to shares to his two sons, Frederick and Heath. He did, however, retain a watching brief and maintained a lively correspondence with his sons and John W. Hughes for the rest of his life. As late as 1887 he was expressing his sincere wish that the old firm should one day become known as "Harrison and Hughes".[52] This wish was never to be fulfilled, but his expression of intent serves to emphasise the high esteem enjoyed by the Hughes brothers in their patron's regard.

Thomas Harrison, though in failing health, remained in overall charge of both companies until his death on 22nd April 1888 at the age of 73. Some 15 months before he died, Thomas Harrison, already a governor of Liverpool University College by virtue of earlier gifts, donated on 17th January 1887 a further £10,000 to endow in perpetuity a chair of engineering, known today as the Harrison Chair of Mechanical Engineering. He lived long enough to see the companies he had established and developed well adapted to their respective roles and his son and two nephews installed at the head of a considerable shipping enterprise. It was fitting that his death should precede by one year, almost to the day, the passing of the company's last sailing ship, the SENATOR, sold to another Liverpool shipowner in April 1889.

He was buried in the old churchyard of St. Anne Stanley in Liverpool. His son, Thomas Fenwick Harrison, built the new parish church of St. Anne Stanley in accordance with his wishes to replace the crumbling old church, and the new church was consecrated by the first Anglican Bishop of Liverpool on 27th September 1890.

James Harrison survived his brother by three years and, under the terms of his will, each and every one of his employees, ashore and afloat, received a bequest in cash. The amounts may seem trivial compared to today's currency but in many cases they corresponded to almost a month's wages.

Frederick James Harrison (1853-1915), eldest son of James Harrison.

Like many Victorians who had, by their own enterprise and business acumen, succeeded in accumulating substantial personal fortunes, the Harrison and Hughes families always seemed to be aware of the debt they owed to society. Their acts of philanthropy were usually anonymous during their lifetime but they were invariably significant, practical and in direct response to a public need.

Between them they founded the Harrison-Hughes Engineering Laboratories at Liverpool University, which were opened in 1912 at a cost of £40,000. They provided substantial sums for the building of the Church of St. Nicholas in Wallasey; and laid out the gardens of St. Nicholas parish church in Liverpool. An unusual benefit bestowed by Mr. Frederick James Harrison in a somewhat flamboyant gesture, but one in keeping with the patriotic euphoria of the times - Christmas 1914 - was the presentation of over 275,000 books to the Royal Navy. There was a parcel for each and every ship, each parcel varying according to size of ship and complement - and it was a very large navy in those days. The average weight of a parcel was 55lbs., and there were altogether 2,478 parcels - about 60 tons of books.

Further evidence of Frederick Harrison's patriotism and his desire to contribute usefully to the war effort is found in the voluntary cession of his yacht CLEMENTINA to the Admiralty, free of hire, for service as a hospital tender. CLEMENTINA had been built by Ramage and Ferguson of Leith for the Principe di Sirignano di Napoli, and had been launched in January 1887 as the RONDINE. With a registered tonnage of 250 nett (625 tons Thames Measurement) the yacht was 193.0 feet in length, 26.8 feet in breadth, and 15.0 feet in depth, and was powered by a triple-expansion engine rated at 143 NHP. In 1893, following a local change of ownership, her name was changed to SULTANA. Five years later she was switched to British registry after being sold to Little and Johnston, London. They changed her name to

CLEMENTINA (Official Number 105571, international call-sign PKGL), and installed a refrigeration plant before selling her to a Darison Dalziel, also of London, in 1900.

In 1903, Frederick Harrison bought the yacht from Dalziel, and was in 1909 elected to the Royal Yacht Squadron. In his hands, CLEMENTINA was not just a pretty toy, for she appeared from time to time at various Harrison Line ports of call, and many a master and crew had cause to look to their laurels whenever the trim vessel was seen slipping between the breakwaters of some distant harbour, for they knew well that the owner would be on board within the hour. It was during one of her wartime missions, in wintry conditions in the North Sea, that Frederick Harrison, who still perceived it as his duty to sail in the vessel whenever possible, caught a severe chill which brought on the pneumonia from which he died on 7th April 1915, at the age of 62. CLEMENTINA outlived her owner by only a few months, being involved in a collision in Plymouth Sound on 5th August. She was beached in a sinking condition near Torpoint, Cornwall, with her foredeck submerged at high water. The records hold no further trace of her, and it is assumed that she became a total loss as a result of this incident.

In contrast, Frederick's cousin, Thomas Fenwick Harrison, chose to donate an organ to his church of St. Anne Stanley as a memorial to those who volunteered for military service in the First World War. Earlier that year, he had laid the foundation stone of a new school to be built near the church, contributing upwards of £8,000 for its construction. It was opened on 10th July 1915. After the death of Lord Kitchener at sea on 5th June 1916 Thomas Fenwick purchased his famous recruiting letter for £6,000 with the intention of presenting it to the nation.

Until 1882, Thomas Fenwick had lived with his parents, first at Stanley, Old Swan, and later at Oakfield House, Fulwood Park. In that year he married Florence Emily Edwards of Winchester, and moved into Ivyhurst, a

Frederick Harrison's yacht *Clementina,* photographed in 1907.

large house in Holmefield Road, Liverpool, which is now the Grange Hotel. In 1889, soon after the death of his father, he purchased a large estate at King's Waldon, Hertfordshire, which included no less than seven large villages. As the "fox-hunting squire", he was Master of the Hertfordshire Hunt for many years. One of his many charitable interests was the Bluecoat School for orphaned children. When the school moved to Wavertree in 1906 he built, in memory of his wife, the Octagon Chapel at a cost of £14,000. Thomas Fenwick died at his home in Hertfordshire on 29th December 1916. His estate was valued at over £1.4m.[53]

Sir Heath Harrison, Frederick James's younger brother, and cousin to Thomas Fenwick, was also a partner in their fathers' firm. He is remembered for his generous endowments of scholarships and bursaries at his old school, Malvern College, and to Brasenose College, his Oxford alma mater. In 1915, he donated £10,000 to Liverpool University to endow a chair of organic chemistry and among his many other notable gifts was £5,000 for Portsmouth Grammar School's new playing fields. In 1917, he donated £50,000 towards the extension of the Union Jack Club in London. Heath Harrison married Mary Adelaide Howard of Colchester in 1882 and for many years the couple lived on their estate, Le Court, near Petersfield, in Hampshire, Heath serving the local community as a magistrate and county councillor. He was an alderman from 1913 to 1927, and was High Sheriff in 1916, being created a baronet in 1917.

Later, in July 1931, Sir Heath donated a new motor-lifeboat to the R.N.L.I. station at Ramsey, Isle of Man. It cost £5,000, and was christened LADY HARRISON. After her husband's death, Lady Harrison donated a new lifeboat to the Port St. Mary station, naming it, with irresistible logic, SIR HEATH HARRISON. Sir Heath and his wife had no children, and the title became extinct when he died in May 1934, at the age of 76.[54]

Thus it came about in the 1890s that, following the departure of Thomas Fenwick and Heath Harrison for the shires, the day-to-day management of the company was left mainly in the capable hands of

Sir T. Harrison Hughes, eldest son of John William Hughes, about 1950. He died in 1958.

the Hughes brothers under the chairmanship of Frederick James Harrison. Meanwhile, within six months of the new Charente Steam-Ship Company's incorporation, the first of three unusual ships had been delivered. They were unusual because they were built of steel rather than iron, their boilers were designed to generate steam at twice the pressure contained by their immediate predecessors and they were powered by triple-expansion engines instead of the ubiquitous, two-cylinder compound engine which had been so popular within the company for 20 years. ACTOR (91) was delivered in June 1885, EDITOR (92) in July 1885 and SCHOLAR (93) in May 1886.

The year 1886 saw the brief flowering of what promised to be a lucrative trade carrying tropical fruits from Belize and Mexico to New Orleans. The scheme was the brainchild of one Lucas E. Moore, Harrisons' original agent in New Orleans. The directors in Liverpool were impressed by his prognosis and projected figures and in September the WARRIOR (72) was sent out to start trading. Competition, however, was fierce and speed - the essential ingredient - was missing, for WARRIOR was at least two knots slower than her rivals. To send out a faster ship, and diminish the efficiency of other more attractive trades, did not appeal to the board and the venture was abandoned after about a year. Neither Moore, nor Alfred Le

Above: the *Lady Harrison*, donated by Sir Heath Harrison in 1931, and used on the Ramsey station until 1948, during which time she performed 48 services and saved 93 lives.

Left: the *Sir Heath Harrison* donated by Lady Harrison after Sir Heath's death. Of the same type as *Lady Harrison* she was stationed at Port St. Mary and also retired in 1948 after 19 services during which 31 lives were saved. Heath Harrison had previously presented a lifeboat to the R.N.L.I., the *Mary Adelaide Harrison*, stationed at Campbeltown in 1888.
[Both: G.D. Learoyd]

Blanc, Harrisons' own representative in the Gulf, were blamed for the failure, but the relationship with Lucas E. Moore and Co., was allowed to lapse as Le Blanc increased his power and influence and eventually established his own agency.[55]

Although Harrisons had been signatories to the Calcutta Conference since 1875, competition in the Indian trades was severe, mainly due to an excess of steamer tonnage. To mitigate the effects of unwelcome rivalry Harrisons, in June 1889, purchased the Star Line from Rathbone Brothers for £135,000. With the goodwill came access to the Indian tea trade and certain berthing rights. Two of the four ships involved were sold almost immediately, but three more Rathbone ships were to join the fleet within six months.[56]

Harrison ships were beginning to acquire a distinctive silhouette by this time, a three-island type with a difference. A bulky hull form, the product of voluminous holds and a pronounced tumblehome (a designed "set-in" of ship's sides amidships), bluff bows culminating in a straight stem, a counter stern with extensive overhang, three prominent islands (forecastle, bridge deck and poop), and towering above all the massive tall funnel crowned with its conspicuous cowl and decorated with broad bands of white and red - the "two of fat and one of lean" of Merseyside folklore. Most of the ships carried two masts at this time but in 1895 the first of 20 even more distinctive four-masted vessels was delivered. She was the STATESMAN (113), built at Belfast by Workman Clark Ltd. Not all had the same internal features - some had triple expansion engines, some quadruple, a few were fitted with twin screws - and some were bigger than others, but in each case the outline was unmistakable.

At the turn of the century, the notion of classing the ships by size and power and identifying them with certain trades began to take shape. There were three main classes:

First Class: 10,000 tons deadweight, on the Calcutta or New Orleans trades.

Second Class: 7,600 tons deadweight, to the West Indies, North Pacific and South African trades.

Third Class: 6,300 tons deadweight, to Brazil, the Caribbean and Mexico.

The little "Brandy boats", COGNAC (127) and JARNAC (105) were, of course, in a class by themselves.

This system of classification was important to seafarers since rates of pay varied according to class of ship and promotion was a dignified progression from class to class.

Statesman, first of Harrison's four masters.   *[Roy Fenton collection]*

Smallest of Harrison's ships were the "Brandy boats": *Cognac* is seen in the Avon.
[Roy Fenton collection]

In 1902, Harrisons were invited to join the South African Conference, which at that time consisted of Union-Castle, Ellerman's Bucknall Line, Clan Line, Bullard King and Co., and John T. Rennie, Son and Co. There was also a German company involved. In practice, Harrisons entered a pooling arrangement with Ellerman and Clan, which operated to their mutual benefit.[57] Harrisons were not newcomers to the region. During the Boer War several of their ships had been taken over by the Government to serve as transports, ferrying troops between Britain and South Africa and transporting horses to the Cape from such widely separated places as New Orleans and Sydney, New South Wales

1906 seems to have been a year for taking stock. There were then 39 vessels in the fleet with an aggregate gross tonnage of 197,966 tons. Two ships, the CANDIDATE (139) and COMMODORE (140), were delivered that year. The number of seafarers in employment in December 1906 was quite prodigious:

Masters	39	Lascar seamen	245
Deck officers	122	Lascar firemen	405
Cadets	7	Asian cooks and stewards	55
Engineer officers	158	Pursers	10
Carpenters	37	*Subtotals:*	
Stewards and cooks	141	European officers	336
Able seamen	273	European ratings	835
Ordinary seamen	42	Asian petty officers and ratings	705
Firemen	342		
		Total	**1,876**

Nigh on ten thousand people, men, women and children, were directly dependent upon the success of Harrisons' shipping enterprises for their welfare.

Trade with India - particularly the tea-trade - was becoming an important issue at this time and since London was at the centre of the tea industry, it was decided in 1910 to open an office in the capital. It so happened that a client, the London firm of Gellatly Hankey and Co., had spare accommodation at Dock House, Billiter Street and Harrisons became their tenants. Mr. Frank Ward was put in charge and he and his successors remained in residence until the building was destroyed by a direct hit during an air raid in April 1941.[58]

Meanwhile, the prospects for trading direct to East Africa via Suez and Port Sudan were looking very favourable. Harrisons discussed the scheme with their partners in the South African Conference, Clan and Ellerman Lines, and it was agreed to run a joint service. The new service was inaugurated on 13th August 1910 with the departure from Liverpool of the steamer TRAVELLER (97) bound for Suez, Port Sudan, Mombasa and Zanzibar. Still on the look out for new trade routes, the company sent Mr. T. Harrison Hughes, elder son of John William Hughes, on a fact-finding world tour in 1910. A direct result of this initiative was the establishment of a regular service from the United Kingdom to North Pacific ports via the Straits of Magellan, with calls at South American ports en route.[59] The service was opened on 25th April 1911, when the CENTURION (141) sailed from Swansea bound for San Francisco and Vancouver. In 1914, the Panama Canal was opened and the service, though disrupted by the First World War, was diverted via the Caribbean. It was finally wound up in 1933.

In order to consolidate their position in the South African trades, Harrisons purchased the Aberdeen Direct Line from John T. Rennie, Son and Co. in 1911. The purchase consisted of a fleet of seven small to medium passenger-cargo liners, five of which carried no more than 40 passengers and two as many as 140. They were very distinctive in their dove grey hulls topped by a buff-coloured funnel and smartly raked masts, a livery which they were to retain in the Harrison-Rennie service until the outbreak of war in 1914. They also retained their euphonious, characteristic Zulu names throughout their lifetime, while Rennies themselves were kept on as London loading brokers and as head agents in South Africa.[60]

The Rennie ships and the officers who served in them always seemed a race apart. Administered and operated from the London office, they were somehow shielded from the diversity and hurly-burly of life in Liverpool. Nevertheless, to be known as a "Rennies man" held something of an aura, which in the early 'twenties, following the demise of the Harrison-Rennie passenger service to South Africa, was to be transposed into the later West Indian passenger vessels, INGOMA, INANDA and INKOSI.

Harrison's had displayed considerable business flair in acquiring rival fleets at bargain prices, but they themselves were not altogether immune to predatory strikes by larger companies. Invariably, however, they had enough clout to resist, as the following fragments of correspondence with the Cunard Line illustrate:

1. From A. A. Booth to J. W. Hughes
5th January 1912.

Referring to our conversation the other day about the Cunard Line and the Harrison Line, it occurs to me that you may think that the time is appropriate for putting the shipping property of your firm on a more conveniently realizable and divisible basis, and that you might welcome the co-operation of the Cunard Line in the carrying out of such a scheme of re-organization. I have no figures of your company before me and therefore anything I am now putting down must be taken merely as illustrative. Supposing, however, that a total capitalization of £1,750,000 suited the facts, this might be divided into £750,000 4½% debenture stock, £500,000 5½% preference capital, £500,000 ordinary capital.

If a public issue was made of the debentures and of such portion of the preference capital as your firm might not wish to hold themselves, the ordinary capital might be divided on suitable terms between your firm and the Cunard

Intaba was bought by Harrisons in 1911 as part of the fleet of John T. Rennie. *[A. Duncan]*

Company. The Cunard Company might be represented on the board by T.R., R.B., and myself, and your firm's interest by as many members of your present partnership as you might wish, with yourself of course, as Chairman.

The public issues of such a company would, I am sure, be readily taken up, and the continuity and Liverpool character of your line, to which personally I cannot help attaching great importance, would be secured.

I am writing this entirely "off my own bat", so if these vague suggestions do not appeal to you at all, at any rate no harm will have been done.

2. From J. W. Hughes to A. A. Booth.

Mersey Chambers, LIVERPOOL
11th January 1912
Dear Mr. Booth,

I received your letter of the 5th on my return from France, yesterday.
We have no idea of selling - should our views change I will give you a hint.

By 1914 the old order established in Victoria's reign was drawing to a close. When Bleriot crossed the Channel in his absurd heavier-than-air machine in 1909, no one saw in that flight any threat to the burgeoning passenger liner fleets of the day. True, the disaster which had overtaken the White Star Line's TITANIC on her maiden voyage in April

1912 had doused the euphoric confidence which had built up in the minds of shipping men during the first years of the century. The age-old problems which had always beset seamen and navigators were still very real, despite advances in technology and henceforth the industry was forced to face up to them soberly, painfully applying solutions as best it could. But 1914 began as a good year, and very few citizens basking in that last glorious summer were even vaguely aware of the storm clouds gathering over Europe. Certain ugly events in the Balkans passed almost unnoticed, yet within weeks, the nations of Europe were at each other's throats. It all happened so very suddenly.

At the outbreak of war, Harrisons' fleet had reached its peak: 56 ships totalling 287,000 gross tons. Not until the 1950s would so many vessels, of so great a tonnage,* ply the trade routes under the flag which bore the red Maltese Cross. During the next four years, 27 ships would be sent to the bottom, 26 by enemy action and one by marine peril. The following pages tell the story of these ships: those which survived the war; those which were destroyed by it; and the many which fulfilled their service throughout the years before.

*Moreover, in 1977-78 the advent of bulk-carriers and container ships (including CITY OF DURBAN) brought the aggregate gross tonnage to nearly 350,000 albeit the fleet then comprised little more than a third of the number of ships in service in 1914.

FLEET LIST Part 3

91. ACTOR (1) 1885-1905 Steel steamship rigged as brigantine. Two decks and two holds.
O.N. 91225 1,649g 1,074n 2,123d 250.0 x 34.0 x 22.95 feet. Cargo capacity: 112,600 cubic feet.
International Code: JWNP.
T. 3-cyl. by Blair and Co. Ltd., Stockton-on-Tees; 20, 33, 54 x 36 inches, 10 knots.

1.6.1885: Launched by Raylton Dixon and Co., Middlesbrough (Yard No. 245) for the company for £20,905. *10.7.1885:* Ran trials and proceeded to Liverpool. *19.8.1893:* When approaching Natal, Brazil, grounded on a sandbank inside the reef while entering the Rio Grande del Norte. Refloated the next day without incurring damage, and sailed 28.8.1893 from Pernambuco for Liverpool. *29.1.1905:* Sold to the Plate Steam Ship Co. Ltd. (Gellatly, Hankey and Co., managers), London for £6,000 and renamed OLYMPO. *1911:* Sold to the Atlantic and Eastern Steam Ship Co. Ltd. (J. Glynn and Son, managers), Liverpool. *10.10.1912:* Beached after collision with the Italian steamer IMERA (1,171/70) off Naples whilst on a voyage from Naples to Liverpool with general cargo. Towed off but again driven ashore and became a total loss.

Actor leaving Barry Dock.   *[World Ship Photo Library collection]*

92. EDITOR 1885-1897 Steel steamship rigged as brigantine. Two decks and two holds.
O.N. 91243 1,675g 1,081n 2,123d 250.0 x 33.9 x 23.0 feet. Cargo capacity: 112,600 cubic feet. Berths for 22 passengers.
International Code: KBNF.
T.3-cyl. by Blair and Co. Ltd., Stockton-on-Tees; 20, 33, 54 x 36 inches, 10 knots.

14 .7.1885: Launched by M. Pearse and Co., Stockton-on-Tees (Yard No. 221) for the company for £20,865. *9.3.1896:* Reported on fire at Liverpool, but the blaze was quickly extinguished. *22.8.1896:* Approaching the Mersey, inward bound from Pernambuco, in collision with COGNAC (38), outward bound to Charente. The accident occurred in the vicinity of the Northwest Lightvessel. Both vessels suffered

substantial damage and, at an internal enquiry, EDITOR was found to be at fault. Her master, Captain E. Clegg, and Second Officer, W.P. Bevan, were dismissed shortly afterwards. *22.3.1897:* Wrecked off Penrhyn Mawr, Anglesey, two miles south of the South Stack Lighthouse when on passage from Maceio to Liverpool with a cargo of sugar and cotton.

Wreck of the EDITOR

As with all such maritime accidents, the loss of the steamer EDITOR was the tragic outcome of a series of adverse circumstances - filthy weather, primitive (by modern standards) navigation equipment, fatigue, and misjudgement. At the subsequent Board of Trade Inquiry,[61] it was established that the EDITOR was a well-found and well-equipped ship and, significantly, her compasses were in good order and condition, with a good record of deviation checks. The ship was homeward bound from Pernambuco to Liverpool and for the past twelve hours had been bedevilled by fog. She had passed Tuskar Rock, at the south-eastern corner of Ireland, in dense fog, at 16.00 on 21st March 1897. The fog signal was heard distinctly and when it was judged to be abeam Captain Henry Watterson stopped his ship to take soundings, obtaining a depth of 37 fathoms. Reference to the chart thus placed the ship approximately four miles off the Tuskar and from this fix a course was laid to the Skerries, passing South Stack Lighthouse at about four miles.

The fog persisted, though perhaps drizzle would be a more accurate description. Whatever, it reduced the range of visibility to a matter of yards, demanding Captain Watterson's constant presence on the bridge. The ship's whistle would be sounding incessantly, keeping the watch below constantly uneasy, banishing all thoughts of sleep. The tide ebbed and flowed; from time to time the sirens of other ships in the vicinity were heard and then the ship's engines were stopped until the danger had passed. It was a black night; no lights were seen; the ship rolled nervously to the swell and the watchers on the bridge felt isolated in a cavern of swirling mist. Occasionally a wave more restless than the rest slammed against the ship's side, spilling over the bulwarks and lacing the mist with salt spray.

The distance from Tuskar to the point on Anglesey where the ship ran ashore 9½ hours later is 84 miles. There was therefore no denying that the ship had averaged nearly 9 knots since leaving the Tuskar and the enquiry ruled that this was an excessive speed in the conditions described - another telling point against the unfortunate Captain Watterson. The question of tides arose and the preponderance of ebb over flood, or vice versa, and whether sufficient allowance had been made at the appropriate times. The enquiry found that sufficient allowance had not

been made for the effect of tide on the course steered - probably an inescapable conclusion in view of the outcome. More perplexing was the neglect to make use of the lead as the ship neared her landfall, particularly since it had been used so assiduously and effectively off the Tuskar.

Apparently, Captain Watterson had relied on hearing the South Stack fog signal in good time. In the event no-one on board heard it, although the enquiry proved to its own satisfaction that it had been operating during the relevant period. Now, audio signals in foggy conditions are notoriously capricious and unreliable and Captain Watterson must have been well aware of these aberrations. The enquiry was thus at a loss to understand why more reliance was not placed on the lead? Who knows? Perhaps the ordeal of two days and two nights on the bridge (as reported in the "Times") without proper sleep had clouded the Master's judgement? Whatever the underlying cause, EDITOR, with her valuable cargo of cotton and sugar, pressed on to keep her appointment with an unkind fate and ran hard aground on the rocks beneath Penrhyn Mawr. The engine-room and stokehold were at once flooded, the furnaces extinguished and the ship rendered powerless.

As if to mock them, the mist cleared away, revealing the low cliffs of the headland rising above the breaking seas, underlining the desperate nature of their situation. The Master gave the order to abandon ship, but getting the boats away was a tricky business. The sea was rough and rocks like blackened fangs gaped through the foaming surf, threatening to impale them. The mariners' plight had been observed from ashore, however, and the Holyhead lifeboat was promptly launched and hastened to the scene of the disaster towed by a steam tug. When she appeared the EDITOR'S crew thankfully abandoned their waterlogged boats and clambered aboard the lifeboat which, still towed by the faithful tug, at once returned to Holyhead.

The wreck rapidly broke up and salvage was considered impractical; only a few bales of cotton were saved. The enquiry felt it had no option but to find that, "the loss was caused by the wrongful act and neglect of the Master," and proceeded to suspend his master's certificate for a period of six months. This, in effect, meant that Captain Watterson would never again be given another command.[62]

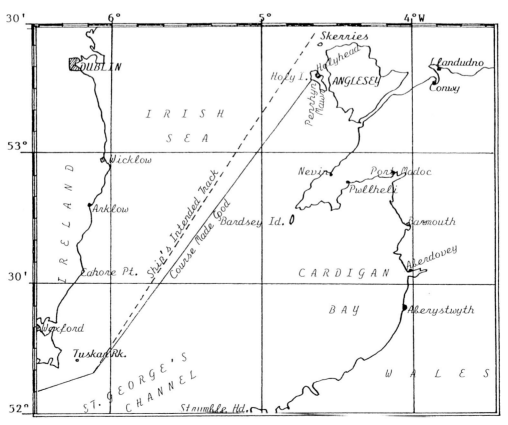

The track of *Editor*, setting towards Penrhyn Mawr, 22nd March 1897.

93. SCHOLAR (1) 1886-1903 Steel steamship rigged as brigantine. Two decks and two holds.
O.N. 93670 1,635g 1,065n 2,100d 250.2 x 34.1 x 22.85 feet. Cargo capacity: 111,400 cubic feet. Berths for 25 passengers.
International Code: KGFJ.
T. 3-cyl. by Blair and Co. Ltd., Stockton-on-Tees; 20, 33, 54 x 36 inches, 10 knots.

4.5.1886: Launched by Raylton Dixon and Co., Middlesbrough (Yard No 270) for the company for £21,000. *30.12.1893:* Sailed from Liverpool for Pernambuco and in collision with the steamer BUENA VENTURA (1,699/71) that had left on the same tide. Both vessels were damaged and returned to Liverpool. *5.1.1894:* SCHOLAR resumed her voyage following repairs. *7.1902:* Took the disabled Belgian steamer BELGENLAND (3,873/78) in tow, arriving 19.7.1902 at Halifax. A salvage award of £3,600 was received for this service. *8.11.1903:* Sold to Atlantic and Eastern Steam Ship Co. Ltd. (J. Glynn and Son, managers), Liverpool for £6,825. *18.5.1918:* Torpedoed and sunk by the German submarine U 55 (Kapitänleutnant Wilhelm Werner) in the Atlantic, 90 miles west by south ¾ south from Bishop Rock. She was on passage, in convoy, from Leghorn to Liverpool with general cargo. Two crew were lost.

With the advent of these three new steel-built vessels, a new disconcerting phrase creeps into the records-books (91,92, 93): "Holds, cross and side bunkers scaled and painted".[63] The first such entry occurs within two years of the ships' delivery - something seldom dreamed about in the former iron-built ships, but which was to develop into a never-ending problem, despite advances in coatings, for the next 100 years. Yet the advantages of steel construction remained paramount; stronger, harder, more flexible than iron, it enabled ships to be built to lighter scantlings (standard dimensions in construction), more cheaply and with greater carrying capacity.

94. NAVIGATOR (1) 1886-1910 Steel steamship rigged as brigantine. Two decks and four holds.
O.N. 93704 2,571g 1,648n 3,500d 301.0 x 37.75 x 27.67 feet. Cargo capacity: 159,920 cubic feet. Berths for 24 passengers.
International Code: KJCQ.
T. 3-cyl. by Blair and Co. Ltd., Stockton-on-Tees; 24, 38, 62 x 42 inches, 10 knots.

28. 9.1886: Launched by James Laing, Sunderland (Yard No.304) for the company for £29,725. *11.3.1897:* In collision with the Hamburg-Amerika steamer VENETIA (2,822/91) at Colon, Panama. Following the incident, the Superintendent Engineer, R.R. Richardson, travelled to Hamburg to inspect the damage to the German vessel. An engineer on

NAVIGATOR was found to have been responsible and the claim was settled for £275. *3.6.1898:* Developed a steering gear fault when leaving New Orleans, collided with a barge and sank it. *1.1910:* Sold for £3,400 to J.J. King and Sons Ltd. for demolition. *11.2.1910:* Delivered at Garston.

95. ELECTRICIAN (1) 1887-1905 Steel steamship rigged as two-masted schooner. Two decks and four holds.
O.N. 93729 2,924g 1,916n 3,995d 325.0 x 40.2 x 28.0 feet. Cargo capacity: 211,890 cubic feet.
International Code: KMNR.
T. 3-cyl. by Blair and Co. Ltd., Stockton-on-Tees; 24, 40, 66 x 45 inches, 10 knots.

25.4.1887: Launched by Raylton Dixon and Co., Middlesbrough (Yard No. 273) for the company for £34,460. *25.6.1887:* Ran trials. *23.9.1905:* Sold to the Britain Steam Ship Co. Ltd. (Watts, Watts and Co., managers), London for £9,400 and renamed WOOLWICH. *3.11.1915:* Captured by the German submarine U 35 (Korvettenkapitan Kophamel) in the Mediterranean, 104 miles south from Cape Sidero, Crete whilst on passage from Safaga Island to Plymouth and Ayr with a cargo of phosphate and tin. She was subsequently sunk by gunfire in position 33.35N, 26.20E.

Electrician in the Suez Canal. This has also been identified as showing the *Engineer* (143), but comparison with a view of her as *Woolwich* leaves little doubt that it is *Electrician*.
[G.R. Scott collection]

96. LEGISLATOR (2) 1888-1898 Steel steamship rigged as brigantine. Two decks and four holds.
O.N. 93795 2,997g 1,900n 4,135d 330.0 x 40.1 x 27.9 feet. Cargo capacity: 205,325 cubic feet. Berths for 35 passengers.
International Code: KTFR.
T. 3-cyl. by George Clark, Sunderland; 24, 40, 66 x 48 inches, 11 knots.

28.5.1988: Launched by Raylton Dixon and Co., Middlesbrough (Yard No.285) for the company for £33,400. *25.7.1888:* Ran trials. *9.1893:* Came upon the US barque E.W. STETSON (1,164/62) in the Western Atlantic when outward bound from Liverpool to the US Gulf. The barque, bound from New York to Havana, had been disabled 25.8.1893 during a hurricane. She had been badly damaged; there was a great hole in her stern, and 16 feet of water in the hold. Three seamen had been swept overboard along with most of her deck cargo. She was taken in tow by LEGISLATOR and delivered at Nassau. *4.1897:* Ran ashore

on Cape Lookout, North Carolina. In order to refloat the vessel, 56 logs of timber were jettisoned. Captain Tennant lost his bonus over this incident. *10.1897:* Homeward bound from the Gulf, many of the crew were prostrated by malaria contracted in Tampico and New Orleans. One seaman died on arrival at Liverpool, 29.10.1897. *16.2.1898:* Abandoned on fire in the North Atlantic in position 31.23N, 44.10W following an explosion amongst the deck cargo of chemicals, during a voyage from Liverpool to Colon with general cargo with the loss of five men.

Fire at sea[64]
The nature of tragedy at sea changes but little over the years, the only significant difference being the speed with which today the whole world is told of the news, with scenes of the drama being flashed live into the living rooms of a remote and wondering populace. Despite modern technology, even in some cases because of it, ships all too frequently still manage to run ashore, collide, founder, or blow up. Crews are lost, and

survivors relate tales of horror, death and privation which match those of their earliest predecessors. The circumstances of the case of the LEGISLATOR have recurred many times, and will continue to recur as long as goods of an ever more volatile nature are carried at sea.

On what turned out to be her last voyage, the LEGISLATOR sailed from Liverpool on 3rd February 1898, bound for Colon, with a crew of 26, two passengers and a valuable general cargo. On deck, stowed securely in sheltered alleyways amidships, was a large consignment of chemicals and combustible substances which included such volatile commodities as ether and benzene (Class 3.1 in the modern I.M.O. Dangerous Goods Code); collodion, spirits of wine and varnish (Class 3.2); phosphorus (Class 4.2); spirits of nitre and chlorate of potash (Class 5.1); carbolic acid (Class 6.1); sulphuric acid and ammonia (Class 8) - as nasty a conglomerate of noxious substances as has ever been carried by sea at any period. The exporting of chemicals was then in its infancy and few seafarers would be aware of the peculiar and lethal properties of some of the substances they lived with. Nevertheless, there was sufficient respect for their pernicious nature to advocate stowage on deck, although, in this case, they were obviously stowed too near the accommodation and the ship's control areas, with too little regard for segregation, to meet the exacting requirements of today's rules.

During the early morning of Sunday 13th February, Chief Officer Peter Arnold, who was on watch, experienced a heart-stopping moment when a flicker of flame illuminated the foredeck, reflecting ominously from masts, ventilators, and deck houses. In the surrounding darkness of that early winter's morning the effect was frightening, for Arnold did not have to be told the reason for this phenomenon. It was obvious to him that the dangerous deck cargo, with all its vicious unknown properties, was ablaze in the alleyways below his position on the bridge.

The Chief Officer hurriedly roused the Master, Captain John Tennant, in command of the LEGISLATOR for the past four years. The time was 04.10. Captain Tennant tried vainly to reach the alleyway where the cargo was stowed, perhaps with the intention of somehow jettisoning the burning packages. But the fire had spread with incredible swiftness and Captain Tennant was driven back by the flames and poisonous fumes, badly burned and gasping for his life. By now the fumes of ammonia and sulphuric acid had enveloped the accommodation amidships, where the officers and engineers had their living quarters, billowing through the ventilators, and driving the sleeping occupants on deck, coughing and choking. Down below, in the engine room and stokeholds, all was confusion as volumes of dense acrid smoke poured in through the great ventilators and open fiddleys. Blinded, their lungs rasping for air, men drove themselves up the iron ladders to the deck, only to be confronted by a wall of explosive, sputtering flame. Somehow they managed to skirt the conflagration and reach the blessed air on the open deck, but five men were badly burned in the process. Another man, who had attempted to escape via the forward stokehold ladder, was fatally overcome, his body found later, collapsed on a grating.

In those desperate moments of escape from below, no attempt had been made to stop the main engine or draw the fires to reduce the head of steam and the ship was still forging ahead at about 11 knots. With the engine room untenable, starting pumps to fight the blaze was out of the question and in those days there was no statutory emergency fire pump situated in a remote part of the ship, which could have been brought into action. Buckets of sea water? Perhaps this expedient was tried but the futility of the exercise in that rapidly worsening situation involving chemicals such as potassium, which reacted violently to the application of water, would soon become apparent. It was therefore becoming increasingly clear that the ship would have to be abandoned. Reluctantly, Captain Tennant reached this conclusion and gave the necessary orders - not without misgivings, for there were serious practical difficulties to contend with.

The ship was still forging ahead and launching a boat from a ship steaming at eleven knots would be a most hazardous, if not impossible, undertaking. Moreover, the boats were situated amidships, directly above the seat of the fire and the boat deck was enveloped in noxious fumes. Trimming the ship's course cleared the weather side of smoke, but launching boats to windward, even in moderate sea conditions, would be an extremely risky operation. They could not wait for the boiler pressure to fall, slowing the ship gradually. The furnaces had been fully charged just prior to the change of watch at 04.00 and might steam the ship for another hour or more, by which time the boats could be consumed by fire.

So the decision was taken to launch the port lifeboat on the weather side whilst the ship was under way. The boat was swung out on the clumsy radial davits and two brave men, Third Officer George Martin and Chief Steward John Gaffney, clambered into it, their brief: to hold the boat alongside whilst the rest of the crew embarked from the ladder. Two able-seamen manned the rope falls whilst others passed the painter forward. The order was given to lower away. One can imagine the terror of the two boatmen as their flimsy craft swung dizzily over the dark water rushing past, apparently rising to engulf them as the boat was lowered. The anxious watchers peering down at the boat, saw it touch the water when it immediately became a wild thing, lurching violently, water spraying from its bows. Somehow, the pair in the boat managed to release the falls simultaneously, narrowly escaping serious injury from the crazily swinging blocks. The Steward crouched in the bow viewing the surging water between boat and ship with wide eyes, while the Third Officer fought the tiller to gain some measure of control. His object was to prevent the boat from smashing itself against the ship's side, yet hold it close enough to enable the crew, some of whom were already clinging to overside rope ladders, to clamber aboard.

For a few hectic moments the boat continued its crazy course, the officers on the boat deck watching helplessly as Third Officer Martin fought to win control. The stresses were overwhelming, however, and something had to give way. Suddenly the painter parted and the boat drifted rapidly astern. The onlookers then realised with horror that the boat was drifting towards the churning propeller. It disappeared under the elliptical stern - and amazingly re-appeared a few moments later, clear of the ship, melting rapidly into the surrounding darkness.

Indeed, it later transpired that the boat's occupants had had a miraculous escape, for their boat had actually been struck by a blade and thrown clear, but badly damaged. The castaways were unhurt and were rescued from their waterlogged boat four days later by a passing ship, the Stockton-registered GLENFIELD (2,159/87) to be landed eventually at Vera Cruz. This was in the days before wireless telegraphy and it was several weeks before news of their deliverance filtered through to head office.

Meanwhile, on board the blazing ship, some efforts were being made to steer towards land. Several members of the crew were now isolated in their living quarters in the forecastle and attempts were made to bring them aft, to the lifeboat stations. One man actually secured a rope round his waist, jumped overboard from the foredeck and was safely picked up aft. This procedure, however, was felt to be too risky by the majority. By this time the engines were slowing down and another attempt was made to launch a boat. It was lowered safely into the water, again on the weather side and Second Officer Thomas Bateman was able to work it forward by means of the painter. The men scrambled into it, but then it capsized, throwing all hands into the sea. Most of them managed to grab trailing ladders and lines and were saved, but Bateman and another man were drowned.

The record is reticent as to how the crew survived the next three days aboard the blazing ship. All her boats had now been lost or destroyed and the only hope left to the men on board was to attract the attention of a passing ship, a hope that had some reasonable chance of fulfilment, thanks to the ugly column of black smoke rising above the wreck. On 16th February she was sighted by Turnbull's steamer FLOWERGATE (1,976/85), which cautiously approached the LEGISLATOR, lowered a boat and took off the survivors.

No attempt was made to take the wreck in tow, and LEGISLATOR was abandoned to her fate. How long did she drift in the North Atlantic, derelict and a menace to navigation, before she sank?

On 4th May 1898 an enquiry into the loss of the LEGISLATOR was held before the Deputy Stipendiary Magistrate at Liverpool, Mr. Kinghorn. It was found that the most likely cause of the fire was spontaneous combustion in the consignment of phosphorous, which ignites on exposure to air. No blame was attributed to the shippers, but the enquiry recommended that, in future, shippers should ensure that all carriers were made aware of the peculiar dangers of their products. It was also observed that the chemicals had been stowed too close to the coal, which had overflowed the coal bunkers onto the deck. A vague reference to the desirability for separate stowage was made, but the enquiry was emphatic that the loss was not due to the wrongful act of the Master or Chief Officer

97. TRAVELLER (1) 1888-1919 Steel steamship rigged as two-masted schooner. Two decks and four holds.
O.N. 93805 3,042g 1,991n 4,210d 330.0 x 40.0 x 29.2 feet. Cargo capacity: 223,080 cubic feet.
International Code: KTRM.
T. 3-cyl. by J. and J. Thomson, Glasgow; 24, 40, 66 x 48 inches, 10 knots.

26.6.1888: Launched by Charles Connell and Co., Scotstoun (Yard No. 153) for the company for £33,650. *3.9.1888:* Delivered. *13.8.1910:* Sailed from Liverpool to inaugurate the new joint service to Port Sudan, Mombasa and Zanzibar. *15.3.1919:* Sold to Limerick Steam Ship Co. Ltd., Limerick for £39,905 and renamed INISHBOFFIN. *13.12.1921:* Ran ashore on Wulff Island in the Gulf of Finland when on passage from Blyth to Petrograd with a cargo of coal. The position was very exposed and salvage appeared extremely doubtful. The Soviet icebreaker LENIN (3,375/17) approached the stranded vessel, but was unable to render assistance on account of the bad weather. The ship was hard aground, with all holds and the engine room flooded and she was given up for lost. *14.12.1921:* The crew abandoned ship; the ice closed in and all salvage attempts were postponed until the spring. *4.5.1922:* Salvage operations were

Traveller believed to be loading at New Orleans.   *[J. and M. Clarkson collection]*

recommenced. In addition to the ravaged bottom plating, it was found that the vessel's side plating had been badly damaged by the ice during the winter months. Incredibly on *19.5.1922* she was refloated and beached in a safe position near Reval. *10.6.1922:* Refloated again and towed to Helsingfors, arriving 12.6.1922 and entering dry dock 30.6.1922. Damage was extensive and, before repairs were complete, 61 plates and adjacent members had been replaced; 57 removed, faired and replaced; and 35 faired in position. *23.8.1922:* Work was completed and the vessel returned to home waters.[65] *5.1923:* Sold to German shipbreakers and demolished at Hamburg.

98. VEGA 1889-1890 Iron steamship rigged as two-masted schooner. Three decks, four holds and poop.
O.N. 81306 3,064g 1,997n 3,480d 361.5 x 38.3 x 27.0 feet. Cargo capacity: 182,400 cubic feet.
International Code: STQM.
C. 2-cyl. by R. Stephenson and Co., Newcastle-upon-Tyne; 33, 70 x 51 inches.

20.8.1879: Launched by Andrew Leslie and Co., Hebburn (Yard No. 202) for Star Navigation Co. Ltd. (Rathbone Brothers and Co. managers), Liverpool. *1879:* Completed. *6.1889:* Acquired by the company for £24,000. *1890:* Sold to Christopher Furness, West Hartlepool for £15,840. *1890:* Sold to Tatham, Bromage and Co., London. *1891:* Sold to Empreza Insulana de Navegacao, Lisbon, Portugal. *1892:* Fitted with new engine. *1899:* Sold to Empreza Nacional de Navegacao a Vapor Para a Africa Portugueza, Lisbon and renamed BENGUELLA. *9.1.1906:* Wrecked south of Mossamedes in Portuguese West Africa.

Vega is a first-magnitude star in the constellation Lyra.

The VEGA was one of four vessels included in Harrisons' purchase for £135,000 of Rathbone's Star Navigation Co., in June 1889. VEGA and CAPELLA (the latter a passenger vessel) were unsuitable for Harrisons' purposes and were quickly sold at a considerable loss. Indeed, it would seem that Harrisons' primary objective in making the purchase was to acquire the goodwill and privileges in the Calcutta tea trade. However, within six months of this purchase three more brand new Rathbone ships would join the fleet. The ships retained their Star Line names.[66]

99. PALLAS 1889-1894 Steel steamer rigged as two-masted schooner. Two decks and four holds.
O.N. 93775 3,175g 2,063n 4,560d 339.8 x 42.2 x 27.2 feet. Cargo capacity: 203,889 cubic feet.
International Code: KRMC.
T. 3-cyl. by George Clark, Sunderland; 28, 44, 72 x 48 inches.

2.2.1888: Launched by Raylton Dixon and Co., Middlesbrough (Yard No. 282) for Star Navigation Co. Ltd. (Rathbone Brothers and Co., managers), Liverpool. *5.1888:* Completed. *6.1889:* Acquired by the company for £50,000. *1894:* Sold to S. Mitsui, Tokyo, Japan for £23,925 and renamed KACHIDATE MARU. *1894:* Sold to J. Prentice, Shanghai and renamed PALLAS. *1895:* Sold to Mitsui Bussan Gomei Kaisha, Nagasaki, Japan and renamed KACHIDATE MARU. *1903:* Deleted from Lloyd's Register, but re-listed 1907 in the ownership of the Government of Korea (Mitsui Bussan Gomei Kaisha, managers), Gensan, Korea as YANG MOO. *1910:* Sold to Harada Shoko Goshi Shosen Kaisha, Tennoji, Japan and renamed KACHIDATE

MARU. *1913:* Sold to Y. Hachiuma, Nishinomiya, Japan. *27.9.1916:* Foundered off Quelpart Island, whilst on a voyage from Hankow to Osaka with a cargo of pig iron.

Pallas is the Greek goddess of wisdom and skill; synonymous with Athene. Also one of the larger asteroids.

PALLAS and her sister VEGA were the first Harrison-owned vessels to be fitted with electric light. In 1891 the facility was installed for the first time in a Harrison-built vessel, the WANDERER (108), but its use was restricted to "cargo work, and the operation of the Suez Canal searchlight".

100. CAPELLA (1) 1889 Steel steamer rigged as two-masted schooner. Two decks and five holds.
O.N. 86166 3,359g 2,189n 4,560d 367.0 x 39.1 x 19.4 feet. Cargo capacity: 231,300 cubic feet.
International Code: WJBK
Two C-2-cyl. by Robert Stephenson and Co., Newcastle-upon-Tyne, driving twin screws; each cylinder 28 and 60 x 64 inches

20.2.1882: Launched by Andrew Leslie and Co., Hebburn (Yard No. 230) for Star Navigation Co. Ltd. (Rathbone Brothers and Co., managers), Liverpool. *6.1889:* Acquired by the company for £34,000. Almost immediately resold "at a slight loss" of £4,435 to Liverpool, Brazil and River Plate Steam Navigation Co. Ltd. (Lamport and Holt, managers), Liverpool and renamed WORDSWORTH. *31.5.1890:* Sold to to Société Anonyme de Navigation Royale Belge Sud-Americaine, Antwerp, Belgium. *4.8.1902:* Wrecked at Assu Torre near Bahia whilst on passage New York for Bahia with general cargo.

CAPELLA is the brightest star in the constellation Auriga, the Charioteer.

HARRISON SHIPS OFF GALVESTON

Two fine views of Harrison ships dating from the late 19th century, both unfortunately unidentified despite the efforts of a number of experts.
[Both: Eric W. Johnson collection]

101. VESTA 1889-1898 Iron steamer rigged as two-masted schooner. Two decks and five holds.
O.N. 84117 3,055g 1,995n 3,710d 367.8 x 39.34 x 27.45 feet. Cubic capacity: 219,341 cubic feet.
International Code: WCVP.
C. 2-cyl. by Scott and Co., Greenock; 33, 76 x 54 inches.

30.4.1881: Launched by Scott and Co., Greenock (Yard No. 201) for Star Navigation Co. Ltd. (Rathbone Brothers and Co., managers), Liverpool. *6.1889:* Acquired by the company for £27,000. *20.11.1892:* Captain John Corbishley died in New Orleans, after being landed 4.11.1892 from the vessel. *2.1897:* Whilst on passage from Liverpool to New Orleans, came across the disabled Canadian barque EDMONTON in the Gulf of Mexico and towed her 250 miles to The Passes in the Mississippi Delta. *25.9.1898:* Wrecked in Catalinita Bay, Santo Domingo whilst on a voyage from Liverpool to Colon and Mexico with general cargo. The vessel was badly holed fore and aft and became a total loss but the cargo in the 'tween decks remained dry and was salvaged. The entire crew was saved and repatriated in the

Royal Mail steamer MEDWAY (3,730/77), arriving 10.11.1898 at Southampton. It has been suggested that the light on Punta Cana, Saona Island (flashing every 10 seconds) was mistaken for the light on Mona Island (flashing every 5 seconds) which may have been temporarily inoperative. Whatever the cause, Captain John Mooney resigned shortly after the accident and was granted a passage to New Orleans in the company's steamer WORKMAN to take up a new job. Henceforth, Harrison Line masters would be instructed to pass east of Mona Island when navigating the Mona Passage.

VESTA is the name of the Roman goddess of hearth and home. Also an asteroid.

Crossing the bar
When the Harrison Line steamer VESTA arrived at Pilottown on 4th November 1892 her Master, Captain John Corbishley, lay dangerously ill, the victim of a heart condition. An urgent message was telegraphed to Alfred Le Blanc, Harrisons' agent and representative in New Orleans, and he at once contacted a Dr. Patton, hired a tug and moved swiftly downstream to meet the incoming VESTA.

A local newspaper reporter takes up the story:[67] "The VESTA arrived at her wharf at 7.30 o'clock, but it soon became apparent that Captain Corbishley was seriously ill, so Dr. Patton advised his removal to Touro Infirmary and accordingly, on Monday Nov. 7, Le Blanc and Stevedore Machray had him conveyed there, where every arrangement had been made for his comfort.

His disease was such that medical skill was of no avail and he gradually grew weaker and weaker and realizing that the shadow of death was over him, the last sacraments and offices of the Catholic Church were administered by Rev. Father J.L. Lambert, of the Church of Our Lady of Good Counsel … and yesterday morning (20th November 1892, at 09.50) he who, it can be truly said, was the most popular of ship captains that visited this port, had joined the silent majority.

On the announcement of his death all the British vessels in port had their flags placed at half-mast in respect to the deceased and Mr. Le Blanc ordered all work suspended until after the funeral. The funeral service will be held at 10 o'clock this morning (21st November) in the parlour of Touro Infirmary. Rev. Father J.L. Lambert will officiate and the remains will be temporarily interred in St. Josephs' cemetery on Washington Street.

Captain Corbishley leaves a widow and three children - one son and two daughters, all at present in Liverpool. The body lay in state last night; a guard of honour consisting of two officers each from the steamships

ENGINEER (88) and COUNSELLOR (78) of the Harrison Line, detailed by the Captains at the request of Mr. Le Blanc, had charge of the remains".

John Corbishley was born at Fleetwood, Lancashire in January 1842 and at the age of 15 was apprenticed to Thos. and Jas. Harrison, his indentures being signed by James Harrison on 10th June 1857. He then joined the new, full-rigged ship PHILOSOPHER (33) in which he served his entire apprenticeship. When the young man had finished his time, in January 1862, James endorsed his copy of his indentures with a glowing testimonial to his "Attentive, industrious and sober conduct during the period of his apprenticeship".

Young Corbishley continued his service with Harrisons, first as able seaman then as Second Mate and First Mate of the COGNAC (38) then, in October 1865, he obtained his master's certificate and was given command of the steamer DRAGON (39) at the remarkably early age of 23. A photograph taken, probably when he was in his thirties, depicts a sturdy, frock-coated figure, with keen eyes, a beard which fails to hide a smiling mouth, and hands like hams. During his career in command, a period which spanned more than half his lifetime, Captain Corbishley suffered his quota of misfortune and disaster. He had been Master of the PANTHEON (51) in February 1869 when she had been rammed and sunk by a tug outside the Southwest Pass; and in the ORATOR (80) eleven years later when she collided with and sank the brigantine RINGLEADER in the Mersey. Despite these setbacks his standing within the company remained high and the esteem in which he was held by his employers never wavered. His death at the untimely age of 50 was a sad loss to his family, his employers and to all his contemporaries.

A splendid view of *Vesta* at New Orleans. *[New Orleans View Company]*

102. MIRA 1889-1909 Steel steamship rigged as two-masted schooner. Two decks and four holds.
O.N. 96387 3,138g 2,039n 4,400d 349.5 x 40.15 x 28.0 feet. Cargo capacity: 228,600 cubic feet.
International Code: LMHD.
T. 3-cyl. by J. and J. Thomson, Glasgow; 24, 40, 66 x 48 inches, 13 knots.

28.9.1889: Launched by Aitken and Mansel, Glasgow (Yard No. 140) for the company. She had been ordered by Rathbone Brothers and Co., Liverpool, and was acquired prior to launch. *12.1889:* Delivered. *29.1.1901:* Sailed from New Orleans and 19.2.1901 was spoken by the Maryport steamer FOREST HOLME (2,407/90), which later reported that MIRA, with her rudder-head fractured was making for Horta in the Azores under her own steam. *1.3.1901:* Arrived at Horta and lay there for over three weeks undergoing repairs. *13.3.1907:* Ran ashore eight miles north of Pernambuco. *15.3.1907:* Refloated and returned to Pernambuco for temporary repairs. *23.3.1907:* Sailed again

and arrived 15.4.1907 at Liverpool. Captain T. Dean and Chief Officer A. Davies were both dismissed shortly afterwards. *13.4.1909:* Sold for £4,250 to Italian shipbreakers "including chronometer, legal fees and 34 tons of coal". *1909:* Resold to Societa Anonima Cantiere di Cardamare, Leghorn, Italy. *1909:* Sold to G.B. Sturlese, Genoa, Italy. *1915:* Sold to F. Felugo, Genoa, Italy and renamed VERTUNNO. *30.10.1916:* Captured and sunk by gunfire from the German submarine U 32, 32 miles west of Cabo S. Vincenzo, Cadiz whilst on a voyage from Brindisi.

MIRA is the binary star Mira Ceti, in Cetus, the Whale.

Rathbone ships were not renamed on acquisition by Harrison. This is *Mira*, anchored in the Mersey awaiting the tide.

103. ORION 1889-1909 Steel steamship rigged as two-masted schooner. Two decks and four holds.
O.N. 96389 3,242g 2,087n 4,448d 350.0 x 40.2 x 27.8 feet. Cargo capacity: 224,272 cubic feet.
International Code: LMHP.
T. 3-cyl. by Blair and Co. Ltd., Stockton-on-Tees; 24, 40, 66 x 45 inches, 10 knots.

27.9.1889: Launched by Raylton Dixon and Co., Middlesbrough (Yard No. 307) for the company. She had been ordered by Rathbone Brothers and Co., Liverpool, and was acquired prior to launch. *12.1889:* Delivered. *29.3.1897:* Ran ashore on the Devil's Bank, Garston Channel in the River Mersey. She was aground for five hours before refloating, losing an anchor and chain in the process. This was recovered two days later and returned for a fee of £60. *19.4.1904:* Collided stern first with the pier head while

undocking at Barry. The rudder was damaged and the vessel was delayed a full week making repairs. *29.3.1909:* Sold for £4,030 to Neugebauer & Co. for demolition. *6.1909:* Broken up at Lemwerder, Germany.

ORION was, according to Greek mythology, a Boeotian giant, a famous hunter, changed into a spectacular constellation on his death.

104. CAPELLA (2) 1890-1910 Steel steamship rigged as two-masted schooner. Two decks and four holds.
O.N. 97741 3,115g 2,036n 4,479d 350.0 x 40.0 x 28.0 feet. Cargo capacity: 231,300 cubic feet.
International Code: LNDM.
T. 3-cyl. by J. and J. Thomson, Glasgow; 24, 40, 66 x 48 inches, 13 knots.

28.10.1889: Launched by Charles Connell and Co., Scotstoun (Yard No. 162) for the company at a cost of £38,000. She had been ordered by Rathbone Brothers and Co., Liverpool, and was acquired prior to launch. *15.1.1890:* Delivered. *16.5.1892:* Struck by lightning, which caused little damage, but seriously affected the vessel's magnetic field. *11.1905:* Towed the disabled steamer LORD DUFFERIN (4,664/98) into Queenstown. *12.6.1908:* Sailed from Savannah, Georgia, and ran aground. She was refloated with tug assistance at a cost of £675 and found to be undamaged. The accident was attributed to pilot error. *2.4.1910:* Sold to Ellerman Lines Ltd., London for £6,229 and renamed ASTURIAN.

Capella in the Bristol Channel. Compared to her sister, *Mira*, her funnel appears to have been extended. *[K. O'Donoghue collection]*

18.2.1917: Attacked by gunfire from the German submarine U 64 in the Mediterranean, 6 degrees and 84 miles from Cape Misurata, Tripolitania, in position 33.48N, 15.15E. She was on passage from Liverpool to Alexandria with 1,500 tons of general cargo. Two men were killed before the submarine was driven off. *1922:* Sold to Olivier and Co. Ltd., London. *7.11.1922:* Reported to be in serious difficulty when her cargo of grain shifted in the Bay of Biscay, in position 47.31N, 06.53W. An emergency call sent by the Master also reported that the vessel was running short of coal and

A striking experience

CAPELLA achieved lasting fame by being mentioned in Captain S. T. S. Lecky's famous "Wrinkles", the late 19th century textbook on navigation and nautical matters.[69] The author, discussing the effect of lightning upon a ship's magnetic field, makes reference to an incident experienced by the CAPELLA in the Indian Ocean:

"On May 16th 1892 … The morning had been squally, with rain, thunder and lightning. About 7.30 the storm seemed to have passed over and the weather showed signs of clearing up, when, after a considerable interval, there was a very vivid flash accompanied by a violent explosion close to the rail near the starboard fore rigging, which seemed as if something had exploded and scattered sparks and fire over the ship. The wooden foretopmast was splintered near the spire and some service torn off the back stay, probably by a branch from the main current. The compass on the upper bridge was deflected from N.72°W to N.45°W and remained that way for a short time. The wheelhouse compass, which had previously shewn WNW, indicated ESE, and the one on the poop was considerably

requested a ship to stand by. The signal was acknowledged by the London steamer ADMIRAL COCHRANE (6,565/17) and on 8.11.1922 she arrived at the scene and stood by the stricken vessel in severe gale conditions. Eventually a tow-line was connected and the two vessels arrived 11.11.1922 at Ferrol. *18.11.1922:* ASTURIAN sailed after trimming the grain cargo and taking in a further supply of bunker coal.[68] *1.1923:* Laid up at Cardiff and subsequently sold to German shipbreakers. *3.9.1923:* Arrived at Wewelsfleth.

affected also. Trial in the wheelhouse of a spare compass card shewed that it and the original card were all right, but the shock had reversed the magnetism of the ship. Later on, the deviation of the upper bridge compass on N.72`W was found to have increased from 9°W to 19°W.

At 4.00 p.m. the same day, the CAPELLA was swung completely round and errors ascertained. They had very much altered. The deviation on North had changed from 6°W to 27°W. After making the circle, the wheelhouse compass regained some of its directive force, as the North point again pointed somewhere towards the North. As the compasses did not go back to their original errors, they had to be entirely re-adjusted."

From this and other similar incidents, Captain Lecky concluded that when an iron or steel vessel was struck by lightning, the compasses retained their directive force intact, but the normal magnetic character of the ship was "completely overwhelmed" by the shock. A wooden vessel, being a poor conductor of electricity, might certainly be set on fire unless protected by lightning conductors.

105. JARNAC 1890-1922 Steel steamship rigged as two-masted schooner. One deck and two holds.
O.N. 97750 618g 370n 920d 185.0 x 28.1 x 15.3 feet. Cargo capacity: 42,373 cubic feet.
International Code: LNTS.
C. 2-cyl. by S. and H. Morton and Co., Leith; 17, 38 x 30 inches, 9 knots.

21.12.1889: Launched by S. and H. Morton and Co., Leith (Yard No.57) for the company. *14.2.1890:* Delivered. *8.9.1912:* When on passage from Liverpool to Glasgow collided with an unknown ship and subsequently dry-docked at Liverpool. *3.1915:* Whilst on passage from Glasgow to Charente in collision with the Glasgow steamer MORION (299/94) which later sank. *26.7.1922:* Sold to Yula Steamers Trading Co. Ltd. (T.B. Stott and Co., managers) Liverpool for £1,930, and renamed STOTTFIELD. *1925:* Sold to Paolo Arzillo fu V., Torre del Greco, Italy and renamed SANTA TERESINA. *22.11.1925:* Abandoned by her crew in a sinking condition off the coast of Yugoslavia whilst on passage from Trieste to Catania with a cargo of wood. The crew was picked up by the Cardiff steamer LEVNET (3,306/14) and landed at Sebenico. *26.11.1925:* Reported to have sunk near the Lucietta Lighthouse, in the vicinity of Zlarin, Yugoslavia.

Jarnac is another brandy town, seven miles above Cognac on the Charente.

The "Brandy boat" *Jarnac* alongside the pier at Tonnay-Charente. The gap between ship and wharf is to allow access for barges.

106. CHANCELLOR (2) 1891-1901 Steel steamship. Two decks and four holds. Three masts. Auxiliary schooner rig.
O.N. 97882 4,753g 3,148n 6,750d 400.0 x 47.0 x 31.5 feet. Cargo capacity: 335,463 cubic feet.
International Code: MGCH.
T. 3-cyl. by Wallsend Slipway and Engineering Co. Ltd., Wallsend; 29, 48, 77 x 51 inches, 11.5 knots.

11.5.1891: Launched by C.S.Swan and Hunter, Newcastle (Yard No. 166) for Christopher Furness, West Hartlepool as CUNDALL. Acquired by the company whilst fitting out for £60,000. *16.7.1891:* Delivered as CHANCELLOR. *5.1900:* Chartered by the British Government for service as a transport during the Boer War and carried 999 mules and two horses from New Orleans to South Africa. Nine mules were lost on the voyage. *3.1901:* Sold to Robert, M. Sloman and

Co., Hamburg, Germany for £38,500. *12.6.1901:* Delivered and renamed PALLANZA. *1903:* Sold to Dampfschiffs Rhederei "Union" A.G., Hamburg. *9.1.1907:* Sold to Hamburg-Amerika Linie, Hamburg. *13.8.1914:* Requisitioned by the German Navy for service as a mine clearance vessel as SPERRBRECHER 4. *4. 11.2.1915:* Ran into a German minefield in dense fog in the Ems estuary, struck a mine and sank in position 53.35N, 06.37E, two miles west of Borkum.

107. DICTATOR (1) 1891-1915 Steel steamer rigged as two-masted schooner. Two decks and five holds.
O.N. 97890 4,116g 2,659n 5,750d 365.0 x 45.1 x 31.25 feet.
Cargo capacity: 282,902 cubic feet.
International Code: MGPV.
T. 3-cyl. by T. Richardson and Sons, Hartlepool; 24, 40, 66 x 51 inches, 10 knots.

8.6.1891: Launched by Sir Raylton Dixon and Co., Middlesbrough (Yard No. 335) for the company. *10.8.1891:* Delivered at a cost of £50,960. *10.1898:* Carried Sir Hugh de Trafford's pack of 50 hounds and 5 ponies to Calcutta. *7.1899:* As a result of an outbreak of plague amongst the crew, the vessel was quarantined at Moses Well, Suez, for eleven days, and 22 crew members were left behind in an isolation hospital when she sailed. On arrival at Liverpool she was delayed a further twelve hours by the Port Health Authority before being allowed to dock. *11.1899:* Chartered for three months by the British Government for service as Transport No.63 carrying troops to South Africa during the Boer War. *6.11.1899:* Sailed from Queenstown with 1,019 troops on board, arriving 7.12.1899 at Capetown. Captain Jeffrey, his ship and his crew evidently created a good impression, testified by the commanding officer in an appreciative letter to the "Daily Mail" published on 29th December 1899. On her second voyage, 876 soldiers were carried. *3.1900:* Carried Lord Chesham and his staff from Capetown to Durban. *15.10.1901:* Captain E. Brown reported an attempted murder on board (see below).

5.9.1915: Intercepted by the German submarine U 20 (Kapitänleutnant Walther Schwieger) whilst on passage from Pernambuco to Liverpool with general cargo. The submarine opened fire and compelled the vessel to stop. The crew were advised to leave and when they were clear the submarine submerged, firing a torpedo which struck the vessel amidships with a violent explosion. The ship took a list and settled by the stern, the submarine then finished her off with gunfire. There is a slight discrepancy between the Admiralty and the German versions of the position of the sinking, the latter recording 49.36N, 08.48W or 164 degrees, 112 miles from the Fastnet Lighthouse; and the former, 49.09N, 08.58W, or 170 degrees, 137 miles from the Fastnet. All the crew escaped safely, and landed at Penzance the following day.

U 20 and Kapitänleutnant Schwieger had already sunk two Harrison ships, the CANDIDATE (139) and CENTURION (141) four months previously, and had achieved absolute notoriety by sinking the LUSITANIA on 7th May. Some small measure of retribution occurred when U 20 was wrecked on the Danish coast on 4.11.1916, and became a total loss.[70]

Dictator approaching a US port.

Mayhem on the high seas

The disturbing incident which took place on 1st October 1901, while the DICTATOR was five days out of Liverpool, bound for Colon, was rare, but not unusual. Fist fights were common enough in the forecastle, and such breaches of discipline were summarily dealt with by the master. It was very seldom that lethal weapons were brought into play and the Captain's concern in this incident is reflected in his report to the management.

s.s. DICTATOR, Colon, 15th October 1901.
Dear Sirs,
I beg to inform you that at 11 p.m. October 1st. the firemen in the forecastle were startled from their sleep by cries of "Murder!" They jumped up and found that Richard Wilson (fireman) had cut the throat of James Murphy, a fellow fireman, who was sleeping in the bunk above him. He then threatened to kill some more of them. The men fled aft, taking the injured man with them. By this time there was quite a commotion and from remarks dropped by the men it was learnt that Richard Wilson had borrowed a razor from one of the firemen at noon and this was seen in his hand immediately after the occurrence. On going forward to the forecastle, [I found] he was standing up looking quite unconcerned. I asked him for the razor and he replied that he had thrown it overboard. Also, when I asked him why he had done such a terrible deed, he said that he did not know why he had done it. The men then begged that he should be locked up, as he was mad and dangerous and one of the most eager for him to be put under arrest was his brother William Wilson [another fireman].
  The man was then handcuffed and on searching him,

the razor was found in his pocket; he remained quite callous and not in the least troubled about what he had done. The wound [in Murphy's throat] was a ghastly one, being very deep, about 5 1/2 inches long and extending from the middle of the throat to just under the left ear. In fact, the windpipe was cut and just escaped being severed. The wound was stitched and bandaged and at the present time he is getting on well. I have just seen the Consul and he says I must keep the culprit under arrest and give him in custody at Belize where he will be charged with Attempted Murder.
I Remain, Yours Obdtly, E. Brown, Master.

At Belize, members of the crew were required to give evidence and the ship was held there for the duration of the trial. The verdict and Wilson's fate, however, are not known.

Captain George Jeffrey (1838-1904) was master of the *Dictator* during her service as a Boer War transport.

108. WANDERER (1) 1891-1922 Steel steamer rigged as two-masted schooner. Two decks and four holds. Isherwood (longitudinal framing) construction.
O.N. 99306 4,086g 2,666n 5,649d 380.0 x 43.85 x 31.75 feet. Cargo capacity: 293,073 cubic feet.
International Code: MGSW.

26.5.1891: Launched by Workman, Clark and Co. Ltd., Belfast (Yard No. 78) for the company at a cost of £51,150. *21.8.1891:* Delivered. *15.12.1895:* Ran aground in the Crosby Channel when entering the River Mersey but soon refloated. *9/10.6.1897:* Three firemen and one able seaman died of cholera at Calcutta. *11.1902:* Sustained considerable damage when ranging heavily alongside the dock at Capetown. *29.8.1908:* Ran aground in the Mobile Channel while leaving port, refloated and sailed 4.9.1908. *27.1.1917:* Picked up survivors from the Brocklebank steamer MATHERAN (7,654/06) which had struck a mine and sunk off the Cape of Good Hope the previous day. *17.10.1920:* In collision with the Norwegian steamer SNEPPE (1,412/02) in the River Scheldt, returning to Antwerp for repairs that lasted over three months. *19.1.1921:* Again in collision at Antwerp. *3.1922:* Sold for £6,188 to Societa Anonima Industrie Navali Edilizie, Genoa, Italy and renamed ENRICHETTA. *1924:* Sold to shipbreakers at Genoa.

Wanderer at Cape Town. The painted-out funnel colours suggest it is during the First World War.   *[Ian Farquhar collection]*

109. BARRISTER (1) 1893-1914 Steel steamship rigged as two-masted schooner. Two decks and four holds.
O.N. 102077 4,750g 3,080n 6,558d 400.0 x 45.2 x 32.16 feet. Cargo capacity: 335,072 cubic feet.
International Code: MWLR.
T. 3-cyl. by T. Richardson and Sons, Hartlepool; 25, 41, 68 x 54 inches, 10.5 knots.

5.11.1892: Launched by Sir Raylton Dixon and Co., Middlesbrough (Yard No. 369) for the company at a cost of £58,375. *2.1893:* Delivered. *21.12.1895:* In collision in the English Channel with an unknown vessel when on passage from London to Calcutta. *2.1907:* Went aground between Alligator Reef and Carysfort Shoal when bound from Liverpool to Mexico via the Florida Straits. Seven hours elapsed before the vessel was refloated. Captain Owen Williams resigned at the end of the voyage. *5.1914:* Sold to the Anglo-Spanish Coaling Co. Ltd., Cardiff for £6,694 and renamed GADITANO. *1915:* Sold to the Admiralty for use as a blockship in the River Medway. Not used as such and in 1916 refitted as an oil storage hulk and sited at Sheerness, Kent. *3.1932:* Sold for breaking up.

Barrister.
[Roy Fenton collection]

110. SENATOR (2) 1893-1914 Steel steamship rigged as two-masted schooner. Two decks and five holds.
O.N. 102078 4,689g 3,049n 6,700d 399.7 x 45.3 x 29.8 feet. Cargo capacity: 364,551 cubic feet.
International Code: MWNK.
T. 3-cyl. by Workman, Clark and Co. Ltd., Belfast; 25, 41, 68 x 54 inches, 10.5 knots.

17.11.1892: Launched by Workman, Clark and Co. Ltd., Belfast (Yard No. 95) for the company. *8.2.1893:* Delivered at a cost of £57,989. *11.5.1898:* In collision with the Bibby liner STAFFORDSHIRE (6,005/94) at Port Said. Damage was slight and she was able to continue her voyage to London. *1.9.1898:* In collision with the steamer HENRY MORTON (922/60) in the River Thames. *6.1914:* Sold to Sociedad Ballenera de Magallanes (P.A. de Bruyne, manager), Punta Arenas, Chile for £13,617 and renamed GOBERNADOR BORIES. Employed carrying whale meat and whale oil between Patagonia and Valparaiso. *1916:*

Sold to Sherman Steam Ship Co. Inc., New York, USA and renamed SHERMAN. *1918:* Requisitioned by the United States Navy and operated by the Naval Overseas Transport Service as USS DURHAM. *1919:* Returned to Sherman Steam Ship Co. Inc. and renamed SHERMAN. *28.2.1923:* The United States Coastguard cutter YAMACRAW was despatched to the aid of SHERMAN, which had called for assistance after running out of fuel southeast of Savannah, when on passage from Antofagasta to Baltimore. *3.3.1923:* Towed into Savannah and allocated bunker fuel. *3.1924:* Sold to shipbreakers for demolition at Genoa.

Senator at Galveston.   *[Eric W. Johnson collection]*

111. LOGICIAN (1) 1894-1923 Steel steamship rigged as two-masted schooner. Two decks and five holds.
O.N. 102160 4,878g 3,162n 7,090d 400.0 x 47.0 x 32.0 feet. Cargo capacity: 370,630 cubic feet.
International Code: NLPH.
T. 3-cyl. by Workman, Clark and Co. Ltd., Belfast; 25, 41, 68 x 54 inches, 12 knots.

22.5.1894: Launched by Workman, Clark and Co. Ltd., Belfast (Yard No. 109) for the company. *31.7.1894:* Ran trials. *8.1894:* Delivered at a cost of £51,175. *6.1912:* Lying at Tampico, Mexico, during the Mexican revolution. The town was the scene of heavy fighting, so much so that the safety of foreign nationals was put in question. There was a British cruiser squadron in the vicinity, under Rear Admiral Cradock flying his flag in HMS GOOD HOPE. He gave orders, through the Consulate, that all British and American women

and children should repair on board the LOGICIAN prepared, if necessary, for evacuation. That night, however, the rebels withdrew, the fighting died down and the refugees were able to return to their homes. *17.8.1914:* Requisitioned by the Shipping Controller whilst at Durban. *14.2.1915:* In collision with the French steamer GANGE (6,876/05) which was moored in dock at Cardiff. *28.5.1923:* Sold to German shipbreakers for £9,113. *9.6.1923:* Left Liverpool in tow for Hamburg.

Logician swinging off Albert Dock, Liverpool with the pilot schooner No. 6 *(Pioneer)* in background.   *[Stewart Bale Ltd.]*

112. MUSICIAN (1) 1894-1923 Steel steamer rigged as two-masted schooner. Two decks and five holds.
O.N. 102177 4,776g 3,055n 6,880d 400.0 x 47.0 x 31.5 feet. Cargo capacity: 353,490 cubic feet.
International Code: NPFV.
T. 3-cyl. by Wallsend Slipway and Engineering Co. Ltd., Wallsend; 27, 44, 71 x 51 inches, 10 knots.

8.5.1894: Launched by C.S. Swan and Hunter, Newcastle-upon-Tyne (Yard No. 192) for the company. *13.11.1894:* Delivered at a cost of £52,700. *18.8.1901:* Ran ashore in Bull Bay, Anglesey, with the pilot still on board. Returned to Liverpool the following day and remained for four weeks renewing the damaged forefoot. *12.9.1905:* Took the disabled French brigantine GENERAL ARCHINARD in tow for Colon, a distance of 23 miles and awarded £20 for the

service. *18.5.1917:* Ran ashore 18 miles south of Cape Spartel, when on passage from Newport, Monmouthshire to Oran with a cargo of coal. *6.6.1917:* Refloated and towed to Gibraltar for repair, arriving the next day. *18.7.1917:* Completed repairs and sailed for Liverpool. *26.5.1921 - 31.12.1921:* Laid up at Preston. *9.1923:* Sold to Antonio Castelli, Genoa, Italy for £9,113. *12.10.1923:* Sailed Liverpool for Barry en route for Genoa for breaking up.

Musician with her crew at lifeboat drill: note boats numbers 1 and 3 in the water. *[Roy Fenton collection]*

113. STATESMAN (2) 1895-1916 Steel steamship rigged as four-masted schooner. Two decks and seven holds.
O.N. 105319 6,322g 4,118n 9,083d 450.0 x 52.5 x 33.7 feet. Cargo capacity: 479,519 cubic feet.
International Code: NWBQ.
T. 3-cyl. by Workman, Clark and Co. Ltd., Belfast; 28.5, 47, 77 x 60 inches, 12 knots.

25.5.1895: Launched by Workman, Clark and Co. Ltd., Belfast (Yard No. 119) for the company. *10.7.1895:* Delivered at a cost of £68,294. *10.1895:* Homeward bound on her maiden voyage, completed a record passage of 29 days from Calcutta to Tilbury, burning 55 tons of coal per day. *6.1897:* In collision with the Dutch steamer CYCLOPS (2,064/80) in the Suez Canal. *22.11.1897:* In collision with the German steamer PRINZ HEINRICH (6,263/94) again in the Suez Canal. *5.1.1898:* In collision with the Italian steamer ADRIATICO (1,154/62) yet again in the Suez Canal. These three incidents, none of which were unduly serious, almost certainly raised doubts about the vessel's handling qualities. *26.5.1902:* Grounded briefly at Moses Well, Suez when homeward bound from Calcutta. *6.1906:* In collision with POLYPHEMUS (4,968/06) in the Suez Canal. *3.1913:* In collision with an un-named sailing ship off San Francisco. The Master, Captain Samuel Bass, was bailed pending the inquiry at a sum equivalent to £15,000. *4.8.1914:* Requisitioned by the Shipping Controller at Plymouth for service as a transport. *3.11.1916:* Attacked by the German submarine UB 43 (Kapitänleutnant Hans von Mellenthin) in the Mediterranean, 200 miles east of Malta. Following an initial torpedo attack, the submarine surfaced and opened fire with her deck gun, but the ship, though badly damaged, did not sink. Six of the crew were killed before the appearance of naval units forced the

Statesman. Of Harrison's four masters, only *Statesman* and *Historian* had their mainmasts stepped forward of the bridge. *[J. and M. Clarkson collection]*

submarine to withdraw, and the survivors were taken off by the Flower-class sloop HMS SNAPDRAGON. A tow line was connected and an attempt made to tow her to Malta, but after 42 hours the line was cast off, as the vessel showed obvious signs of sinking. *5.11.1916:* Sank at 16.30 in position 36.00N, 18.30E. She was on passage from Liverpool to Calcutta with general cargo.[71]

69

STATESMAN at war in Canadian waters

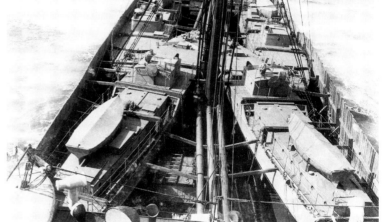

The sequence of four photographs above show Royal Navy motor launches being loaded aboard *Statesman* at Montreal in 1915 and in transit. These comprise a batch of motor launches ordered from Elco of Bayonne, New Jersey through Canadian Vickers which were sent to Montreal for assembly. *[Maritime Photo Library]*.

The photograph to the right was taken by one of her crew and shows *Statesman* coaling at Sydney, Cape Breton on 13th January 1916. *[Nigel Farrell collection]*

114. HISTORIAN (2) 1896-1921 Steel steamship rigged as four-masted schooner. Two decks and seven holds.
O.N. 105364 6,857g 4,455n 9,900d 460.0 x 55.0 x 35.6 feet. Cargo capacity: 504,390 cubic feet.
International Code: PFHG.
T. 3-cyl. by Harland and Wolff Ltd., Belfast; 27.5, 45.5, 75 x 54 inches, 11.5 knots.

7.9.1895: Launched by Harland and Wolff Ltd., Belfast (Yard No. 295) for the company. *29.1.1896:* Delivered at a cost of £70,538. *3.1896:* Picked up 17 survivors from the dismasted barque JANET COURT (1,000/68) when homeward bound from New Orleans on her maiden voyage. *5.9.1899:* Inward bound from Calcutta, the vessel struck and severely damaged the Ovens Buoy in the River Thames. The pilot was reprimanded. *18.2.1913:* Marconi's wireless apparatus installed. *11.2.1920:* Laid-up at Swansea. *2.11.1921:* Sold

to H.M.H. Nemazee, Hong Kong for £16,459. *1923:* Renamed ARABESTAN. *1924:* Sold to Oriental Navigation Co. Ltd., Hong Kong. *1925:* Sold to Societa Anonima Industrie Navali, Genoa, Italy, and renamed DELIA. *1925:* Renamed DELIA TERZO. *19.2.1930:* In collision with the French steamer FORT BINGER (5,250/19) while both vessels were manoeuvring in Rotterdam. *24.12.1930:* Arrived at Savona for demolition, having been sold for £8,200.

Historian did not have the long bridge-deck which was a prominent feature of the *Statesman*.   *[K. O'Donoghue collection]*

115. MAGICIAN (1) 1896-1922 Steel steamship rigged as two-masted schooner. Two decks and five holds.
O.N. 106816 5,065g 3,271n 7,070d 400.0 x 47.0 x 33.1 feet. Cargo capacity: 380,295 cubic feet.
International Code: PMHT.
T. 3-cyl. by Workman, Clark and Co. Ltd., Belfast; 25, 41, 68 x 54 inches, 12 knots.

11.9.1896: Launched by Workman, Clark and Co. Ltd., Belfast (Yard No. 132) for the company. Launching had been planned for 6.9.1896, but a fire in the engine-room 1.8.1896 resulted in a postponement. *30.10.1896:* Delivered at a cost of £52,668 and sailed the same day in ballast for New Orleans to load cotton. *17.6.1897:* Grounded on the Pluckington Bank in the River Mersey but lifted off 40 minutes later by the rising tide virtually undamaged. *18.4.1898:* Towed the disabled steamer BERNARD HALL (2,678/80) into Port Royal, Jamaica. *1.1900:* Chartered by the British Government to make three voyages to South Africa carrying mules and/or horses from New Orleans. On the first voyage she carried 980 mules (losing 25); on the second 768 mules (losing 14); and on the third carrying 999 mules (losing 16). *2.6.1902:* Sailed from Liverpool to inaugurate the new liner service to the Cape of Good

Magician berthed at Willemstad, Curacoa.

Hope. *20.2.1904:* Entering the River Mersey, collided with the Watts, Watts steamer KILBURN (3,271/93) lying at anchor off the Cammell, Laird shipyard. *10.1904:* The claim was settled in the sum of £650 and Captain C.A. Watts of the MAGICIAN was dismissed from the company. *1.12.1914:* Put into Holyhead to repair damage received after colliding with the steamer ELIDIR (398/03). *10.3.1922:* Sold to Hinode Kisen K.K. (Taiyo Kaiun Kabushiki Kaisha,

managers), Dairen, Japan for £10,237 and renamed MAGICIAN MARU. *1922:* Renamed KEIGI MARU. *21.3.1923:* Ran aground on Black Rock, Arena Island in the Sulu Sea whilst on passage from Manila to Fremantle in ballast. *7.4.1923:* A Japanese salvage vessel arrived on the scene but after a week of attempts to refloat her, the wreck was abandoned 14.4.1923 following the removal of deck fittings.

116. CRAFTSMAN (1) 1897-1919 Steel steamship rigged as four-masted schooner. Two decks and seven holds.
O.N. 106865 6,196g 4,030n 9,095d 450.0 x 52.0 x 33.75 feet. Cargo capacity: 503,136 cubic feet.
International Code: PSRB.
T. 3-cyl. by Dunsmuir and Jackson Ltd., Glasgow; 27½, 45½, 75 x 60 inches, 12½ knots.

14.4.1897: Launched by Charles Connell and Co. Ltd., Scotstoun (Yard No. 236) for the company. *13.7.1897:* Delivered at a cost of £70,580. *1900:* Employed as a troop transport (No. 124) during the Boer War. *9.2.1905:* In collision in the harbour at Port Said with the Norwegian steamer CONGAL (1,415/79) which sank. *29.5.1919:* Sold to the Steam Navigation Co. of Canada Ltd. (Japp, Hatch and Co. Ltd., managers), Montreal for £150,109, and renamed HAMPSTEAD HEATH. *29.10.1922:* Arrived off Rotterdam from Wabana, Newfoundland with her steering gear disabled. Towed into port by two tugs. *1923:* Sold to H. A. Christensen, Sandefjord, Norway, converted at Sandefjord to a whale factory ship and renamed KOMMANDØREN 1. *1925:* Owners became Hvalfanger A/S Vega (H. A. Christensen, manager), Sandefjord. *15.10.1926:* Whilst anchored in Morzhovary Bay, Kamchatka, USSR dragged and took the ground. Refloated with assistance from the whaler ANADYR (175/11) and re-anchored in the Bay. Later that same night she again dragged ashore but was refloated without difficulty. Some weeks later, in Todd's Dry Dock at Seattle, it was found that all four propeller blades, the rudder and bilge keel were damaged. The cost of repairs was around $7,000. *1927:* Sold to Compania Argentina de Pesca S.A., Buenos Aires, Argentine, and renamed ERNESTO TORNQUIST. Based on South Georgia and operated as a whale oil tanker. *20.1.1947:* Put into St. Vincent, Cape Verde Islands, to assess damage caused by a fire in No. 1 'tween deck on 13.1.1947, when she was about 190 miles north east of Cape San Roque, Brazil on passage from Buenos Aires to Le Havre. Some wooden fittings had been destroyed, a quantity of ship's stores ruined, and the bulkhead and upper deck in way of the foremast buckled and strained between two frames. *15.10.1950:* Ran aground at 02.15 in Antarctic Bay, South Georgia, when on passage from Sandefjord to Grytviken, South Georgia, with stores. *16.10.1950:* At 07.00, in rapidly deteriorating weather, the crew abandoned the stranded vessel as she lay in a position exposed to the elements. Later that day she broke her back just forward of the bridge. *4.12.1950:* After section sank and, with no prospect of salvage, declared a total loss.

Four views of *Craftsman*.

Top: as a transport, probably during the Boer War: note the number 124 and the awning over the bridge. *[National Maritime Museum P16898]*

Middle left: loading cotton at Westwego on the Mississipi, 16th January 1908. *[K. O'Donoghue collection]*

Middle right: members of the Lascar crew swing out one of the boats. *[National Maritime Museum N478211]*

Left: *Craftsman* as the whale-oil tanker *Ernesto Tornquist*, with prominent neutrality markings. *[Ian Farquhar]*

117. WORKMAN 1898-1912 Steel steamship rigged as four-masted schooner. Two decks and seven holds.
O.N. 109476 6,116g 3,981n 8,986d 450.0 x 52.5 x 33.9 feet. Cargo capacity: 486,960 cubic feet.
International Code: QJLG.
T. 3-cyl. by Workman, Clark and Co. Ltd., Belfast; 27, 45.5, 75 x 60 inches, 12 knots.

4.6.1898: Launched by Workman, Clark and Co. Ltd., Belfast (Yard No. 149) for the company. *10.1898:* Delivered at a cost of £75,000. *23.5.1901:* Ashore briefly on Pluckington Bank in the Mersey when leaving Liverpool for Calcutta. Quickly refloated. *20.4.1908:* Struck by the British steamship VOLGA (4,404/03) in the Suez Canal, both vessels sustaining only minor damage. *2.9.1908:* Once again grounded on the Pluckington Bank and ashore for half an

hour before refloating. The bill for tug assistance was £850. *22.12.1912:* Ashore on Ilha Rasa, 15 miles south of Rio de Janeiro and subsequently declared a total loss. She had sailed 12.12.1912 from Coronel, Chile on passage from Vancouver and San Francisco for London and Liverpool with canned goods, barley and general cargo. The crew was subsequently repatriated in the steamship ORCOMA (11,571/08).

Named as a compliment to her builders, *Workman is* anchored in the Mersey awaiting high water to enter Liverpool docks.

118. POLITICIAN (1) 1899-1922 Steel steamship rigged as four-masted schooner. Two decks and seven holds.
O.N. 110533 7,214g 4,728n 10,475d 469.5 x 56.4 x 35.98 feet. Cargo capacity: 542,300 cubic feet.
International Code: QPSW.
T. 3-cyl. by Wallsend Slipway Co. Ltd., Wallsend; 27.5, 45.5, 75 x 60, 13 knots.

19.10.1898: Launched by C.S. Swan and Hunter Ltd., Wallsend (Yard No. 240) for the company. The launch had in fact been delayed for four days on account of persistent gales. *19.1.1899:* Delivered at a cost of £82,000. *24.2.1899:* When homeward bound from New Orleans on her maiden voyage, ran ashore in the Passes in the Mississippi Delta. Refloated three days later and limped back to New Orleans with a damaged rudder. *2.4.1899:* Sailed from the Mississippi after protracted repairs. *6.1900:* Chartered by the British Government for Boer War service and sailed from New Orleans for the Cape with 1,040 horses. Of these, 121 were lost on passage, leading to complaints from the military against Captain T.A. Chandler. These would not appear to have been sustained as the Captain and all his officers sailed in the vessel on the following voyage. *2.9.1901:* Towed the full-rigged ship CROMARTYSHIRE (1,554/79) into Algoa Bay, after she had been abandoned following an outbreak of fire. *4.1.1911:* Inward bound to London from Calcutta, involved in collision with a barque off Dungeness. Heavy damage was sustained to the port side plating, resulting in a 25-day period in dry-dock.

8.3.1918: Sailed from Dakar in convoy, bound for London, homeward bound from Calcutta. *10.3.1918:* The Australian motor vessel KANGAROO (4,348/15) sheered out of her column and reported that her engines were disabled. The

Politician in a US port.   *[Ian Farquhar collection]*

Commodore signalled Captain J. Gaudie of the POLITICIAN to go to her assistance, and if necessary take her in tow. A bridle of heavy wire was subsequently connected to the KANGAROO's anchor cable, and the two vessels regained and maintained their positions in the convoy. Unfortunately, when off Gibraltar, a west-bound convoy steamed through the columns of the north-bound convoy creating the utmost confusion. One ship careered between POLITICIAN and her tow, carrying away the cable. This was repaired next morning and the tow continued until the English Channel

where a naval tug took over. Captain Gaudie and his crew were subsequently commended for excellent seamanship and competent station keeping in difficult circumstances. *6.1922:* Sold to the South Georgia Co. Ltd. (Chr. Salvesen and Co., managers), Leith for £20,008, renamed CORONDA and converted for the carriage of whale oil in tanks. *11.12.1931:* On passage from South Georgia to Antwerp, diverted to Capetown to bunker and report extensive damage caused by pack ice encountered 24.11.1931. Several plates had been ruptured, and surveyors estimated that 500 barrels of whale oil had been lost, a further 2,035 barrels contaminated by seawater in starboard tank B. Temporary repairs were effected, and the vessel resumed her voyage. *15.9.1940:* Attacked by German aircraft in position 58.07N, 09.24W, or 256 degrees, 102 miles from the Butt of Lewis, while on passage from Iceland to Liverpool with 8,700 tons of herring oil. A bomb exploded near a magazine which caught fire and caused widespread damage. Taken in tow and beached 18.9.1940 in Kames Bay, Firth of Clyde while plans were made for her utilisation as a store ship. *12.1940:* Refloated and moored at Tail of the Bank. *3.1941:* Drydocked at Greenock. *15.10.1945:* Laid up in the Firth of Clyde. *3.1946:* Sold to Van Heyghen Frères for demolition at Ghent. *10.1947:* Demolition began.

Politician in distinguished company: dressed overall and anchored alongside *Mauretania* during a royal visit to Merseyside in July 1913. King George V reviews the ships from the MDHB yacht *Galatea* to the left.

119. COLLEGIAN (1) 1899-1917 Steel steamship rigged as four-masted schooner. Two decks and seven holds.
O.N. 110534 7,237g 4,691n 10,460d 468.8 x 56.25 x 35.98 feet. Cargo capacity: 557,104 cubic feet.
International Code: QPTN.
T. 3-cyl. by Dunsmuir and Jackson, Glasgow; 27.5, 45.5, 75 x 60 inches, 13 knots.

30.11.1898: Launched by Charles Connell and Co., Glasgow (Yard No. 246) for the company. *21.1.1899:* Delivered at a cost of £80,000. *22.1.1899:* Sailed to New Orleans in ballast on her maiden voyage. *22.1.1899:* Put into Moville, at the entrance to Lough Foyle, with over-heated machinery. Resumed the voyage following adjustments and ran into 'fearful gales', which started a few rivets and extended the passage to 30 days. *3.3.1899:* Sailed from New Orleans for Liverpool with a cargo of cotton. *6.3.1899:* Ran ashore on Gun Cay, Bahamas, on the eastern side of the Florida Strait. Floated off six days later and put into Newport News, Virginia, for examination. *1.4.1899:* Arrived at Liverpool whereupon Captain Owen was transferred to another vessel

in the fleet. *23.4.1907:* Outward bound from Liverpool, collided with the British steamer ROSSETTI (6,508/00) and put back to Sandon Basin with severe damage. *6.5.1907 - 22.5.1907:* Dry docked. *20.9.1915:* Arrived at Liverpool with 124 passengers on board, survivors of the French steamer EUPHRATE (6,876/05). *14.6.1917:* Attacked by a German submarine while off the south coast of Ireland. The torpedoes missed their target and the vessel reached her destination safely. *20.10.1917:* Torpedoed and sunk by the German submarine UB 48 (Oberleutnant Zur See Wolfgang Steinbauer) in the Mediterranean 100 miles from Alexandria in position 32.35N, 28.41E. She was on passage from Liverpool to Calcutta in convoy with general cargo and coal.

Collegian. Note the extra long derricks, well seen in the view from her crow's nest. This is probably a wartime shot, as the funnel is grey and the boats are swung out.
[National Maritime Museum P16889 and N47896]

120. CUSTODIAN (1) 1900-1923 Steel twin-screw steamship rigged as four-masted schooner. Three decks and seven holds. O.N. 110635 9,214g 6,023n 12,260d 482.0 x 57.25 x 43.5 feet. Cargo capacity: 671,220 cubic feet. International Code: RMKF.
Two T.3-cyl. by Dunsmuir and Jackson, Glasgow, driving twin screws; each cylinder 21, 35, 58 x 48 inches, 13 knots.

19.12.1899: Launched by Charles Connell and Co., Scotstoun (Yard No. 252) for the company. *19.2.1900:* Delivered at a cost of: £98,000. Immediately chartered by the British Government for service as a transport (No.97) during the Boer War. Sailed on her maiden voyage from Southampton to South Africa with troops and horses. Subsequently made four further voyages between the United Kingdom and South Africa and two between South Africa and Australia. Altogether she ferried 364 officers, 6,142 enlisted men and 4,253 horses to and from the war zone and carried 17,494 tons of stores.[72] *24.3.1903:* Returned to peace-time trading, delayed for nearly six weeks by a dock strike at New Orleans, eventually sailing 1.5.1903. *14.11.1903:* Sailed from New Orleans but put back after 36 hours with a serious cotton fire in number 3 hold. *17.11.1903:* Arrived back on the berth; the fire was extinguished and the damaged cotton subsequently unloaded. *15.3.1910:* Ran aground on soft mud at Port Eads, shortly after sailing from New Orleans. *21.3.1910:* Refloated and sailed for Norfolk, Virginia, for repair. *16.11.1912:* Equipped with the Marconi wireless communication apparatus. *10.1914:* Chartered by the British Government and during the following twelve months made ten round voyages to the United States and Canada carrying up to 955 horses each time to the United Kingdom.[73] *7.6.1916:* Sailed from Liverpool but returned the next day having been in collision with an unknown vessel. *12.6.1916:* Dry docked in No.4 Herculaneum and remained there until 24.6.1916 undergoing repairs. *20.3.1918:* Torpedoed and damaged by the German submarine U 96 in the Irish Sea in position 54.33N, 05.02W. She was on passage from Galveston and New York to Liverpool with a cargo of 9,500 tons of cotton, cereals, minerals, foodstuffs and fuel oil. Three crew were killed but the remaining 62 were taken off by the sloop HMS BUTTERCUP and landed at Belfast. The vessel was then towed to Folly Roads, Belfast Lough, by the armed trawler ELF KING (289/13) and the Admiralty tug MUSGRAVE (220/97). *13.4.1918:* Entered dry dock for repairs which were not completed until 7.6.1918 when she sailed for Liverpool.

13.4.1923: Sold to the Steamship Trust (Cardiff) Ltd. (Henry J. Giffin, manager), Cardiff for £16,909 and renamed POLCEVERA. *5.12.1923:* A heavy item of deck cargo was displaced by a heavy sea and had to be jettisoned in position 44.50N, 08.40W during a voyage from Bahia Blanca to London. Considerable damage was done to deck fittings in the process of getting it over the side. *11.1924:* After taking a severe pounding on a voyage from Bahia Blanca to Antwerp with a cargo of cereals, the vessel put into Portland to carry out repairs in the engine room which had been flooded. *15.11.1924:* Ran aground in the Scheldt between Pipe de Tabac and Buoy 72, remaining there for several hours until refloated with the aid of seven tugs. *1925:* Sold to Hvalfangerselsk. A/S Polaris (Melsom and Melsom, managers), Larvik, Norway, converted to a whale oil factory ship and renamed N.T. NIELSEN-ALONSO. *22.2.1943:* Torpedoed by the German submarine U 92 (Kapitänleutnant Oelrich) in the North Atlantic in position 48.25N, 31.24W. Although seriously damaged, she did not sink until torpedoed by the Polish destroyer BURZA in position 47.50N, 31.10W. She was on passage from the Clyde to New York in ballast.

Two views of the flush-decked *Custodian*, the upper as a Boer War transport: note the soldiers on deck.
[National Maritime Museum P16900 and World Ship Photo Library collection]

75

121. TACTICIAN (1) 1900-1922 Steel steamship rigged as four-masted schooner. Two decks and seven holds.
O.N. 113398 7,281g 4,765n 10,425d 470.0 x 56.25 x 35.98 feet. Cargo capacity: 538,330 cubic feet.
International Code: RTPL.
T. 3-cyl. by Wallsend Slipway and Engineering Co. Ltd., Wallsend; 27.5, 45.5, 75 x 60 inches, 13 knots.

12.7.1900: Launched by C. S. Swan and Hunter Ltd., Newcastle-upon-Tyne (Yard No. 254) for the company. *2.9.1900:* Delivered at a cost of: £106,533 and sailed for New Orleans in ballast on her maiden voyage. *1901:* Chartered by the British Government to carry horses and mules from New Orleans to South Africa during the Boer War. Three voyages were made in 1901 during which she carried a total of 1,970 horses and 1,100 mules, of which only 14 animals failed to survive the journey. *26.12.1901:* Ran ashore outside the South Pass in the Mississippi Delta and remained fast for ten hours before refloating. *25.11.1905:* In collision with the Welsh schooner LEANDER (72/59) off the Nore Lightvessel, following which the

schooner sank. *23.2.1911:* Ran aground when leaving Port Said and refloated three days later. *28.2.1911:* Returned to Port Said and sailed again following examination. *5.3.1914:* In collision with the German steamer MATHILDE (1,260/92) in the River Thames. *29.8.1914:* Requisitioned by the Shipping Controller for service as an Indian Expeditionary Force Transport while at Calcutta. *14-19.7.1916:* Stood by and escorted CRAFTSMAN (116) from Port Sudan to Suez. The latter vessel was having trouble with her main engine. *15.4.1922:* Sold to Taikwa Kisen K.K. (Taiyo Kaiun K.K., managers), Dairen, Japan for £20,008 and renamed YOJIN MARU. *1935:* Sold to shipbreakers at Kobe.

A fine view of a splendid ship: *Tactician,* with steam to spare, presumably on trials; note the number of people on the bridge, with several wearing bowler hats. The hull paint will need to be tidied up before Harrisons take delivery.

122. MECHANICIAN 1900-1918 Steel twin-screw steamship rigged as four-masted schooner. Three decks and seven holds.
O.N. 113414 9,044g 5,892n 12,005d 482.0 x 57.25 x 45.5 feet. Cargo capacity: 670,160 cubic feet.
International Code: RVWG.
Two T. 3-cyl. by Workman, Clark and Co. Ltd., Belfast, driving twin screws; each cylinder 21, 35, 58 x 48 inches, 13 knots.

9.8.1900: Launched by Workman, Clark and Co. Ltd., Belfast (Yard No. 169) for the company. *5.10.1900:* Delivered at a cost of £105,700 and sailed for New Orleans in ballast on her maiden voyage. *2.1901:* Reported to have collided with the company's CHANCELLOR (106) at New Orleans but without significant damage. *2.1901:* Chartered by the British Government to carry horses from New Orleans to South Africa during the Boer War. She completed four round voyages carrying up to 1,100 horses on each trip, the passages occupying 30 to 32 days. Overall the vessel loaded 4,381 horses of which 119 failed to survive the journey. The total gross receipts for this period amounted to £78,832, or nearly £20,000 per trip. In contrast, a cargo of cotton from New Orleans to Liverpool in the following January attracted a freight of £8,375. *10.8.1901:* On one of these voyages, the vessel was loading horses at New Orleans when an attempt was made by persons unknown to blow up the ship. There was a small explosion on board and a search of the vessel revealed a quantity of dynamite. The perpetrators were never caught and the ship continued her

voyage without further disturbance. *1908:* Laid up at Liverpool from early March to late September at a cost of £500. *17.12.1912:* Equipped with the Marconi wireless communication apparatus. *10.1914:* Hired by the British Government for three transatlantic voyages carrying horses from Montreal, St. John, New Brunswick and Newport News respectively. A total of 2,902 horses were carried of which 38 died on passage. *2.1916:* In collision with the steamer LUTETIAN (4,757/08) and spent two weeks in dry dock making repairs which cost approximately £40,000. *6.9.1916:* Requisitioned by the Shipping Controller and served as a transport in the Mediterranean theatre. *29.6.1917:* Commenced service as a Commissioned Escort Ship, serving with North Atlantic convoys. *20.1.1918:* Torpedoed by the German submarine UB 35 (Oberleutnant-zur-see Karl Stoter) in the English Channel, eight miles west of St. Catherine's Point, but beached off the Isle of Wight and became a total loss. She was on passage from Tilbury with a cargo of Government stores. Thirteen crew were killed.[74]

Life and death of the *Mechanician*. The top photograph is in the Mississipi approaching New Orleans, and according to a note on the back was the property of Robert Wilkins who joined her as Sixth Engineer in 1912. The middle photograph shows *Mechanician* during one of her North Atlantic voyages carrying horses: note the canvas wind sails and the stalls built on deck. *[National Maritime Museum P16990]*

The death throes of *Mechanician* are depicted in the lower photographs, taken after she was torpedoed in the English Channel on 20th January 1918. The photograph to the right was probably taken by a Royal Navy airship. *[Maritime Photo Library; National Maritime Museum P16990]*

123. PATRICIAN (1) 1901-1914 Steel steamship rigged as four-masted schooner. Two decks and seven holds.
O.N. 113459 7,474g 4,859n 10,355d 470.0 x 56.3 x 35.2 feet. Cargo capacity: 545,310 cubic feet.
International Code: SGLV.
T. 3-cyl. by Wallsend Slipway and Engineering Co. Ltd., Wallsend; 27.5, 45.5, 75 x 60 inches, 12.25 knots.

22.2.1901: Launched by C.S. Swan and Hunter Ltd., Newcastle-upon-Tyne (Yard No. 261) for the company. *3.4.1901:* Delivered at a cost of £114,221. *2.1906:* In collision with the Nourse sailing vessel FORTH (1,829/94) in the River Mersey. *28.1.1909:* In collision with the steamer STANLEY HALL (4,104/94) in the Suez Canal. *1.1912:* In collision with the French schooner CAPRICIEUSE (156/04) in the Mediterranean, when on passage from Port Said to London. *2.3.1913:* Towed the disabled Hamburg-Amerika steamer BATAVIA (11,464/99) into Cascais Bay, Portugal. *30.11.1914:* Requisitioned by the Admiralty and fitted out as the dummy battle cruiser INVINCIBLE. Following the defeat of Admiral Cradock's cruiser squadron off Coronel in November 1914, the Admiralty decided to reinforce the surviving units with two battle cruisers, INVINCIBLE and INFLEXIBLE, detached from the Home Fleet based at Scapa Flow. To maintain the appearance of the status quo for the benefit of spies known to be operating in the area, the battle cruisers were replaced by dummy warships. *1915:* Purchased for £65,000 by the Admiralty, rebuilt as a naval oiler and renamed TEAKOL. Subsequently operated by the Shipping Controller and managed by Lane and Macandrew Ltd., London. *1917:* Renamed VINELEAF. *12.7.1919:* Sold to the British Tanker Co. Ltd., London and renamed BRITISH

Patrician at lifeboat drill. Numbers 2 and 4 boats, and the quarter boat, are being lowered.
[Ambrose Greenway collection.]

VINE. *3.1.1921:* Towed into Queenstown Harbour after being disabled some days previously with a fractured rudder stock. The broken rudder had also fouled the propeller which had shed its blades. Entered dry-dock and sailed 5.2.1921 for Newport News. *1923:* Sold to A/S Tønsberg Hvalfangerei (H. Borge, manager), Tønsberg, Norway and renamed BUSEN. Employed in the Antarctic whaling trade carrying whale oil to Europe.[75] *29.7.1935:* Arrived at Genoa to be broken up.

124. YEOMAN 1901-1904 Steel steamship rigged as four-masted schooner. Two decks and seven holds.
O.N. 113490 7,379g, 4,784n, 10,300dwt. 470.3 x 56.25 x 36.0 feet. Cargo capacity: 560,030 cubic feet.
International Code: SNKQ.
T. 3-cyl. by Dunsmuir and Jackson, Glasgow; 27.5, 45.5, 75 x 60, 12.25 knots.

4.7.1901: Launched by Charles Connell and Co., Scotstoun (Yard No. 261) as PLEBEIAN for the company. *3.9.1901:* Delivered as YEOMAN at a cost of £107,374. *4.9.1901:* Sailed for Galveston in ballast on her maiden voyage. *24.2.1902:* Towed the disabled Spanish steamer EREZA (4,038/94) to Lewes, Delaware, arriving 26.2.1902. She sailed the following day for Norfolk, Virginia, and ran ashore off Cape Henry. *28.2.1902:* Refloated. *10.2.1904:* Wrecked near Cape Villano, near Corunna, Northern Spain, when on

passage from Liverpool to Calcutta with a cargo of general and salt.

The original name PLEBEIAN was selected as a counterpoise to that of her sister, PATRICIAN. However, it would seem that images of a lowly birth and uneasy reflections on the burgeoning of Karl Marx's militant proletariat prompted a change of heart.

Loss of the YEOMAN[76]
"The YEOMAN, steamship of Liverpool, bound Liverpool to Calcutta, is ashore at entrance to Camelle, North Villano." Such was the message which Lloyd's Agent in Corcubion sent to his principals in London on the morning of 10th February 1904. It was relayed to Mersey Chambers, Liverpool headquarters of Thos. and Jas. Harrison, and one can imagine the dismay and despondency which descended upon staff and management alike. Their worst fears were soon confirmed; the ship was a total loss, but thankfully most of the crew and passengers had been saved. All but four Lascar seamen of the 82 crew members and four passengers were being cared for by the citizens of Camelle. The ship had sailed from Liverpool on 6th February 1904, loaded with about 8,000 tons of general cargo valued at £250,000 destined for Calcutta. She was commanded by a senior master, Captain William Lang, 62, a native of Appledore, Devon, who had served the company since 1867 and as master since 1875. His Chief Officer was Owen Williams from Caernarvon; Second Officer James Hugh Lloyd Richards of Liverpool and Third Officer Clement Wilkie Jones, also of Liverpool. (The latter eventually reached command rank, in 1921 and earned the sobriquet "Mad Wilkie". Captain Lang, on the other hand was held in such deep affection that he was known as "Daddy" Lang.)

From Liverpool, the ship sailed directly into bad weather and it is doubtful whether she had been able to fix her position after rounding the Skerries, off Anglesey. This

would not have been an unusual circumstance at that time of year. Low cloud, driving rain and a restricted, if not invisible, horizon would have obscured the land and prevented the taking of astronomical observations. The officers may not have even had the chance of checking the deviation of the magnetic compass by means of a simple azimuth of sun or star. Whatever the difficulties, the ship - any ship - would press on, navigating by dead reckoning - a blend of knowledge, instinct and experience. There were, of course, no radio aids to assist shipmasters in those days. However, some sources of help were available to which a shrewd shipmaster would often refer, notably the Admiralty Sailing Directions, which included concise information on the nature of climate and currents in a given area. The chart indicated with accuracy how the contours of the seabed rose and fell, and even its composition - sand, shingle, coral, or (a name rolled lovingly round the tongues of articulate candidates for second mate!) globigerina ooze. Consequently, although isolated soundings could not determine precisely the vessel's position they could, in most cases, indicate whether or not a vessel was maintaining a position of safety relative to the land. Consequently, for at least three days YEOMAN pursued an almost blind course in foul weather, with overcast skies and no sure way of knowing how far she had been set off course. Crossing the Bay, the ship had been hove to, riding to severe gales for much of the time in conditions which made it extremely difficult, if not impossible, to arrive at a reliable estimate of drift.

However, on 9th February the weather moderated and the ship resumed her course at full speed. Captain Lang fully expected to sight the light on Cape Villano in the early hours of the next morning. He was right - but not quite.

At 22.00 on the 9th, Captain Lang retired from the bridge to the chartroom to rest, leaving written instructions that he should be called if any light was seen and that a good look out should be kept for the Villano Light. There are three extremely powerful lights on the northwest corner of Spain, Villano, Torinana and Cape Finisterre. All are visible up to 40 miles from seaward in clear weather. Unfortunately, they are perched so high upon the cliff tops, some 400 feet (122m) above sea level, that they become obscured in conditions of low cloud. It was in such conditions that YEOMAN made her fateful landfall in the early hours of 10th February 1904.

At midnight, Second Officer Richards took charge of the watch. At 31, he was an experienced officer and was probably on the threshold of promotion. He noted the night orders, relieved Third Officer Jones and settled down to his vigil. The weather was blustery and squally again, but not as bad as it had been. At about 03.07 he saw what appeared to be a ship's light 2 points on the starboard bow. After watching it closely for some minutes it seemed to take on the characteristics of a shore light. His stomach turned over. A shore light - broad on the starboard bow where no shore-light should be! Hastily he called Captain Lang who emerged on the bridge almost at once, but the light had disappeared. The Captain returned to the chartroom to study the chart and whilst pondering over it he heard the chilling cry, "Breakers ahead!" The Second Officer ordered "hard-a-port" (directing in those days, the ship's head to starboard) and swung the engine room telegraph handle to "full astern". Tragically, it was too late and YEOMAN drove hard and fast aground on the streaming rocks at the entrance to Camelle Bay, about three cables off shore.

The ship began to flood rapidly as water poured in through the ripped up bottom plating and Captain Lang realised that the chances of his ship's survival were nil. His next care was for the safety of the lives of those on board. He ordered the boats to be swung out and lowered, including those on the weather side which were to be brought round under the ship's lee. One of these, into which eight seamen had clambered, was struck by a heavy sea and capsized, throwing the men into the sea. Four of them were rescued, but four disappeared, swallowed up by the angry, broken waters. Eventually the rest of the passengers and crew were brought safely ashore in the remaining lifeboats to be cared for by the good people of Camelle until such time as the authorities were able to take over.

How did YEOMAN come to find herself in such plight? It is easy to be wise after such a tragic event, especially almost 100 years later, when much of the evidence is no longer to hand. But one or two matters call for comment. First, the Master's dead reckoning, which was remarkably accurate, in the circumstances. Suppose that the master's last fix had been obtained passing the Smalls Lighthouse off the Welsh coast. From there to a position 10 miles west of Cape Villano the course is 195½ degrees true

and the distance 531 miles. In all that distance it had not been possible to check the position again. The Master had to rely entirely on dead reckoning, applying successive courses and distances to the position off the Smalls; making due allowance for the Channel tides and the east-going currents which set into the Bay of Biscay, and for leeway and drift in the prevailing gales, especially when hove-to. He expected the watch to sight Villano light early on the morning of the 10th - and so they did, albeit on the wrong bow. The course the ship had made good from the Smalls to Camelle was 194 degrees true - a discrepancy of 1½ degrees - and this was achieved in an era when ships still steered to the nearest ¼ point (about 3 degrees). Perversely, the discrepancy crept in on the wrong side of the course line. Just 1½ degrees the other way and the ship would have passed well clear of all the dangers off northwest Spain.

The other pertinent question is why an experienced shipmaster like Captain Lang did not insist on taking soundings as the time approached for his landfall. An elaborate chain of soundings was not necessary, but a sounding of less than eighty fathoms would have alerted the navigators to the alarming prospect of the ship being too far east, enabling them to adjust the course in plenty of time. The builder's specifications confirm that the ship was equipped with Basnett's Patent Sounding Machine, capable of recording great depths while the ship was moving at speed.*

The enquiry, convened on 15th March 1904 under the chairmanship of Mr. W. J. Stewart, Liverpool Stipendiary, sitting with three assessors, gave judgement on 17th, deciding that "the loss of the vessel was caused by default of the Master," and they were "reluctantly compelled", in view of Captain Lang's long service and good character, to mark their judgement by suspending his certificate for three months. "Daddy" Lang did not go to sea again, and he died a saddened and disillusioned man, twelve months after the enquiry.

YEOMAN was a total loss and Harrisons, who carried their own hull insurance in those days, were faced with a payment of £81,000 from the Insurance Account. Shortly after this tragedy a new rule appeared in the Company's Rules for Navigation instructing masters to steer to pass Cape Finisterre at a distance of not less than forty miles - a wise precaution in the light of this painful episode. There is, on Chart No. 1755, a wreck symbol planted at the rocky entrance to Camelle Bay - a tiny monument, if one were needed to all that remains of the steamer YEOMAN.

*Basnett's Patent Sounding Machine was operated in the same manner and upon the same principles as Lord Kelvin's better known apparatus. As the lead descended, water was forced into a glass tube (sealed at one end) encased in a perforated brass tube which was attached to the line (piano wire in those days), just above the lead. The air in the tube was compressed by water pressure as the depth increased, admitting more water. Unlike the Kelvin tube, in which a chemical coating was discoloured by the sea water, the Basnett tube was designed to trap the water. After striking the sea bed, the tube was retrieved and the amount of water trapped measured against a boxwood scale to give the depth.

125. CHANCELLOR (3) 1902-1915 Steel steamship rigged as two-masted schooner. Two decks and five holds.
O.N. 105336 4,545g, 2,958n 7,015d 400.0 x 47.0 x 32.44 feet. Cargo capacity: 324,200 cubic feet.
International Code: PBSJ.
T. 3-cyl. by Wallsend Slipway and Engineering Co. Ltd., Wallsend; 27, 44, 71 x 51 inches, 12.5 knots.

9.5.1895: Launched by C.S. Swan and Hunter, Newcastle-upon-Tyne (Yard No. 197) for the British and Foreign Steam Ship Co. Ltd. (Rankin, Gilmour and Co., managers), Liverpool as SAINT CUTHBERT. *12.9.1895:* Ran trials. *5.1902:* Acquired by the company for £34,507 and renamed CHANCELLOR. *28.5.1902:* When leaving Liverpool on her first voyage for the company, came in contact with the London steamer AURICULA (815/01). Damage was slight and the voyage was continued. *23.9.1915:* Intercepted by the German submarine U 41 in the

Chancellor.

79

North Atlantic about 86 miles south-by-east from Fastnet Lighthouse. The crew took to the boats and she was sunk by gunfire in position 50.00N, 9.10W. One of the boats, of which Chief Officer R.H. Herbert was in charge, was sighted by the Houston steamer HESIONE (3,363/89) later that evening. HESIONE approached the crowded boat and slowed down, intending to pick up the survivors. Chief Officer Herbert, aware that the submarine was still in the vicinity, and despite the rough weather conditions, waved his rescuers on. The HESIONE veered away at full speed but was shelled by U 41 and, when the crew had abandoned ship, was sunk. The crews of both vessels were rescued by patrol boats shortly afterwards and landed at Queenstown. CHANCELLOR was on passage from Liverpool to New Orleans with general cargo. The submarine, commanded by Kapitänleutnant Klaus Hansen, was sunk the following day in the English Channel by the Q-ship BARALONG. There were only two survivors.[77]

This was the third submarine attack in four months for Robert Whitney, a cabin boy, aged 15, of Birkett Street, Liverpool. The first was CANDIDATE (6.5.1915), next, GLADIATOR (19.8.1915), and then CHANCELLOR (23.9.1915). All three attacks had taken place within one day of leaving a home port. "I am now looking for another ship", he said.

Chief Officer R.H. Herbert was in charge of one of the boats that got away from the *Chancellor*.　　[*E.T. Vanderbilt*]

126. CIVILIAN 1902-1917 Steel steamship rigged as four-masted schooner. Two decks and seven holds.
O.N. 115312 7,100g 4,535n 10,730d 470.0 x 56.1 x 35.98 feet. Cargo capacity: 615,420 cubic feet.
International Code: TPKB.
T. 3-cyl. by Dunsmuir and Jackson, Glasgow; 27.5, 45.5, 75 x 60 inches, 13 knots.

11.7.1902: Launched by Charles Connell and Co., Scotstoun (Yard No. 269) for the company. *2.9.1902:* Delivered at a cost of £96,369. *3.10.1903:* Grounded in the River Mersey when inward bound from Karachi to Liverpool. Refloated on the next tide after lightening 500 tons of cargo. *1-5.1908:* Laid up for 101 days at Galveston, then loaded cotton for Le Havre and Liverpool, only to be laid up a further 69 days at Birkenhead. *8.1910:* In collision with the Norwegian steamer CITY OF MEXICO (1,511/05) at New

Orleans. The Norwegian owners accepted liability and paid all damages. *14.8.1914:* Requisitioned by the Shipping Controller and served as a Squadron Supply Ship. *6.10.1917:* Torpedoed and sunk by the German submarine UC 74 (Kapitänleutnant Wilhelm Marschall) 15 miles north of Alexandria. Two men were killed in the explosion but the survivors landed safely at Alexandria. She was on passage from Liverpool to Calcutta in convoy with general cargo.

Civilian in US waters. Note what appears to be a spark arrester on her funnel.　　[*World Ship Photo Library Isherwood collection*]

127. COGNAC (2) 1902-1935 Steel steamship rigged as two-masted schooner. Two decks and two holds.
O.N. 115320 814g 422n 1,200d 205.4 x 31.45 x 17.99 feet. Cargo capacity: 50,880 cubic feet.
International Code: TQFM (MFMM after 1933)
T. 3-cyl. by Dunsmuir and Jackson, Glasgow; 16, 26, 44 x 30 inches, 10 knots.

22.8.1902: Launched by Charles Connell and Co., Scotstoun (Yard No. 273) for the company. *17.9.1902:* Delivered at a cost of £16,697. Served exclusively in the Charente/UK brandy trade. *16.6.1918:* Damaged in collision with the Norwegian steamer WENDLA (557/93) at Swansea and dry-

docked locally for repairs. WENDLA was found to be solely responsible for the collision but 20.12.1918 her owners successfully appealed to the Admiralty Division of the High Court for their liability to be limited to £3865.18s.5d, based on the statutory limit of £8 per net ton. *19.9.1918:* Attacked in the Bristol Channel by a German submarine, but the torpedo missed. Despite trading exclusively in the immediate war zone, this is the only recorded contact with the enemy by either COGNAC or her consort, the JARNAC, during the First World War. *28.9.1935:* Sailed from Liverpool for the last time in the brandy trade, arriving 4.10.1935 at Tonnay-Charente. *12.10.1935:* At 16.45 made her final departure from the port, bringing a proud era to an end, after nearly 100 years. The company's connection with the brandy trade was not quite over, however, for the steamer ARDGARROCH (964/18) was chartered by Harrison to continue the service for a further 8 months. Thereafter, small parcels of Harrison cargo were carried, by arrangement, in the bottoms of Moss Hutchison vessels. *7.11.1935:* Sold to the Darwen Coal and Mostyn Iron Co. Ltd. for £1,584 for demolition at Mostyn, which took place early in 1936.

Last of the "Brandy boats", *Cognac* at Liverpool. *[J. and M. Clarkson]*

128. COMEDIAN (1) 1903-1917 Steel steamship rigged as two masted schooner. Two decks and five holds.
O.N. 115356 4,889g 3,149n 7,300d 399.5 x 48.5 x 33.82 feet. Cargo capacity: 344,880 cubic feet.
International Code: TVBH.
T. 3-cyl. by Dunsmuir and Jackson, Glasgow; 25, 41, 68 x 54 inches, 13 knots.

30.12.1902: Launched by Charles Connell and Co. Ltd., Scotstoun (Yard No. 274) for the company. *16.2.1903:* Delivered at a cost of £61,324. *8.1904:* When outward bound from Liverpool to Durban, challenged and inspected by the Russian armed merchant cruiser SMOLENSK, but subsequently allowed to proceed. *23.7.1914:* Reported disabled with a damaged rudder off Kinsale. *24.7.1914:* Towed into Queenstown at a cost of £225 and the Liverpool tugs SARAH JOLLIFFE (333/90) and EAST COCK (139/09) were despatched from the Mersey to bring the vessel home. *30.7.1914:* Docked safely at Liverpool, the bill for towage being £217. *12.8.1914-24.8.1914:* In dry dock. *22.2.1915:* Requisitioned by the Shipping Controller and served as a transport for the British Expeditionary Force. *3.1915-12.1915:* Served as a store ship in the Dardanelles, ferrying stores between Alexandria and Gallipoli. When occasion demanded she also served as a troopship or hospital ship. *17.4.1917:* Sailed from St. John, New Brunswick with a cargo of ammunition and war material for Falmouth. *29.4.1917:* Torpedoed by the German submarine U 93 (Kapitänleutnant Freiherr Edgar von Spiegel) in position 48.06N, 10.45W, 200 miles and 238 degrees from Bishop

Rock. The crew abandoned ship, but three men were drowned. The following day U 93 encountered the decoy ship PRIZE and was badly damaged. Her commander was captured, but the submarine was able to limp back to her base under the command of her First Lieutenant.[78]

Comedian. *[Peter Newall collection]*

A COMEDIAN at the Dardanelles[79]
The Dardanelles campaign of 1915 was certainly no laughing matter - but there was a resident COMEDIAN in attendance almost from the start.

In an attempt to break the stalemate on the Western Front, it was decided to create a Southern Front by forcing the Dardanelles with heavy naval units, driving Turkey out of the war, occupying Constantinople, and linking up with the Russians on the Black Sea. The campaign began in earnest on 19th February 1915, when the Mediterranean Fleet under Vice Admiral Carden bombarded the forts in the approaches to the Dardanelles.

It was shortly after this that COMEDIAN, commanded by Captain W.J. Simmonds, sailed from Avonmouth on 9th March for the Mediterranean. Robert Wilkins, O.B.E., who at the time was Fourth Engineer on board COMEDIAN, was an eye witness to the events which followed, events which he faithfully recorded.

COMEDIAN was steaming steadily eastwards through the Mediterranean, having passed Gibraltar on 15th March. Then out of the blue an urgent signal sent her into Malta, there to embark a naval salvage team and load a full

deck cargo of salvage equipment. The battlecruiser INFLEXIBLE, veteran of the Falklands action, was lying at Tenedos in a sinking condition. It was the task of the salvage experts to make her seaworthy again and enable her to return to Malta. Arriving at Tenedos they found the old war horse still afloat on an even keel, but riding low in the water, her upper decks and superstructure still bearing the scars of battle. COMEDIAN laid herself alongside and the work of transferring men, equipment and stores proceeded with the utmost despatch. Eventually, her unexpected mission concluded, COMEDIAN resumed her voyage to Alexandria.

The Navy having been repulsed, it was decided that the Army, under General Sir Ian Hamilton, should attempt a landing, storm the forts and silence the guns with infantry. COMEDIAN once again became a tiny unit in a large armada of ships which sailed from Alexandria in May carrying 70,000 British, French and ANZAC troops, their arms and equipment, towards the Gallipoli Peninsula. The ships called at Mudros on the island of Lemnos to re-group and finalise plans for the assault. The British 29th Division was to land on five small beaches on the southern extremity, Cape

Helles; the ANZACS were to go ashore north of the Gaba Tepe promontory at what was to be known forever as Anzac Cove. The French contingent was assigned to carry out diversionary landings on the Asiatic shore and protect the flank of the 29th Division.

COMEDIAN was among the ships detailed to support the Cape Helles operations and on 24th May 1915, as the sun set over the Aegean Sea, she took her place in the long procession of ships proceeding north to Gallipoli. At dawn on the 25th, COMEDIAN anchored with other store ships on a line south of Cape Helles. The big ships were already pounding the shore defences; close to the headland the Glasgow steamer RIVER CLYDE had been beached and troops were pouring ashore under heavy fire; lifeboats, cutters, pinnaces and other small craft, loaded with troops, were also approaching the beaches, some of which were vigorously defended.

Soon it was time for COMEDIAN to perform her allotted task of unloading her deck cargo of barges to be used in the transport of horses and artillery. This task was carried out under a hail of shrapnel, fortunately without incurring any casualties on board. As the barges were towed away, the ship weighed anchor and proceeded, somewhat reluctantly, for emotions were running high and no one on board wanted to miss anything, back to Alexandria.

It was only after their arrival at Alexandria, when the first hospital ships loaded with wounded began to enter port, that the crew of COMEDIAN came to realise the true cost of the operation and the appalling losses suffered by the Allies. Eventually, COMEDIAN, fully loaded with a cargo of munitions, sailed once more for Cape Helles. She now carried an Army Service Corps unit which would supervise the allocation and distribution of the various types of ammunition which were stowed on board. To the Naval and Army staffs she was now known simply as Storeship S2.

From their position in the now familiar anchorage, the crew had a good view of the beaches. To Bob Wilkins, "The intense activity on the cliff face resembled that of bees in a honeycomb, until, as if by magic, all signs of life instantly disappeared when shells began to fall in the vicinity".

However, the threat of shell fire did not deter younger members of the crew from joining the soldiers on the beaches for a swim. Incongruously, on occasion, the place resembled a holiday resort rather than a battle zone, until the whine of a shell hurtling in their direction "restored the realities" and sent the bathers scurrying for cover under the cliffs

At 06.20 on 27th May, the crew of COMEDIAN were aroused by a shattering explosion, quickly followed by another. Many were convinced that the ship had been hit in one of the ammunition holds and this unnerving impression was seemingly confirmed when Captain Simmond's voice was heard shouting orders for lifeboats to be lowered. Fourth Engineer Wilkins ran to his station where the crew of his boat were already manning the falls. From his vantage point on the boat deck he could see the battleship MAJESTIC, which had anchored nearby late on the previous evening, listing heavily

to port and belching great columns of black smoke. The warship was obviously in serious trouble. As the four lifeboats pulled away from COMEDIAN, Wilkins, in no. 4 boat heard "a sickening rumble and crashing sound, as MAJESTIC turned turtle and all her heavy gear broke loose. There was also a terrible shout of many voices calling in unison, merging into one, like a vast single voice of doom."

Although anti-torpedo nets had been rigged on the anchored battleship as a routine precaution, they had been withdrawn for a brief period in order to launch the Admiral's pinnace. During that fatal interval, the German submarine U 21, under Kapitänleutnant Hersing, had launched two torpedoes which speedily found their target and accomplished the destruction of MAJESTIC in less than seven minutes. That 600 of the 660 men on board survived the disaster was due in no small measure to the valiant efforts of the men of the merchant ships anchored in the vicinity and a tribute to their skill as they promptly launched their boats and hastened to the scene to pick up survivors.

The transports and storeships were by no means immune from attack. Anchored either side of S2 were Alfred Holt's AJAX and Bullard King's UMFULI. Both these vessels were severely damaged by shell-fire and suffered many casualties. S2 survived several near-misses one of which caused slight damage to her propeller. At last, having discharged all her ammunition, S2 returned to Alexandria to find that another Harrison ship, the COMMODORE, had joined the armada.

With the allied armies pinned down on the beaches, the British G.O.C., General Sir Ian Hamilton, decided that

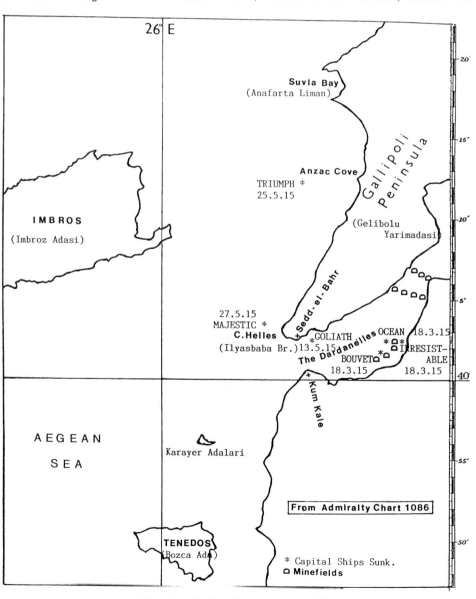

Map of the Dardanelles campaign, 1915.

82

another landing was necessary to surprise the Turks and catch them off balance. Subsequently, S2 found herself in yet another fleet of ships assembling at Imbros, ten miles west of the Gallipoli peninsula. On board was a 50-strong contingent of the feared and hated Leatherheads, the Australian Military Police, whose quaint title was derived from the brown leather hats they wore.

It was with surprise and not a little consternation that the Leatherheads learned that they were to take part in the initial assault. Their apprehension was due mainly to an awareness that they were as likely to be shot by some disaffected Aussie as by a Turk. Wisely, they dispensed with their distinctive headgear for the occasion.

At dusk on 6th August 1915, the assault force sailed from Imbros, traversed the intervening stretch of sea without incident and launched their boats and landing craft into Suvla Bay. Surprisingly, the Turks were caught napping for once and the troops made a virtually unopposed landing. Unfortunately, the landing force at Suvla Bay failed to follow up its initial advantage and priceless wells and dominant hills in the region were left to be occupied by the Turks, who subsequently refused to be dislodged.

It was a long, hot summer; disease was rife and caused more casualties on both sides than the guns. Bloated flies tormented the troops ashore and even the men on the ships. A party of Turkish prisoners received on board S2 were in a filthy and verminous condition, their main preoccupation that of delousing their ragged clothes. A small boat was hoisted on deck, filled with fresh water and the prisoners ordered to bathe - a command which jolted them out of their apathy and filled them with dismay. For it transpired that the Koran stipulates that only running water should be used for cleansing the body. Nevertheless, on this occasion, they bathed.

As time wore on, discipline on board became something of a problem, especially among the fleshpots of Alexandria. Things came to a head one night when all the lights went out while the ship was loading munitions. It quickly became apparent that the boiler had dissipated all its feed water and equally apparent that the erring donkeyman tending it had taken a walk ashore. Other members of the "black gang" were also reported absent without leave and military discipline took over. Early next morning an armed guard of some twenty soldiers with bayonets fixed paraded at the gangway. The Sergeant Major in charge saluted the officer on deck and demanded that the offenders assemble on deck immediately. The glottal accents of a Liverpool voice were heard to exclaim plaintively in protest, "And wot about our bloody breakfast, la'?" The Sergeant Major was in no mood for banter and once he had entered the forecastle the men emerged with alacrity and without breakfast. On the quay they were surrounded by a squad of soldiers on each side and shuffled away sheepishly, vainly trying to keep in step with the soldiers' smart gait and obey the S.M.'s aggressive commands for "left, right - left right"! In the fullness of time, the culprits came before a court martial and were sentenced to brief terms of imprisonment. They were then sent home. Meanwhile, COMEDIAN was provided with Arab replacements who, it is recorded, served the ship faithfully and well.

Back at Gallipoli, COMEDIAN was on one occasion detailed to take in tow an empty hospital lighter which had been stranded during a storm. That night the ship crept inshore, under a low cliff, expecting a hostile artillery barrage at any moment. A towing wire was hauled aboard the lighter and made fast. Just then a series of blinding flashes and deafening explosions made everyone's nerves tense and cringe. "It's all right; they're ours", spoke a relieved voice in the darkness. Sure enough, a New Zealand battery on the low cliff above the salvage operation had opened fire with the intention of keeping the Turks occupied. The lighter, however, despite COMEDIAN'S best endeavours, would not budge and the attempt had to be abandoned.

The onset of winter brought no break in the stalemate, and the Army Staff was ordered to draw up plans for evacuation. As a result, on 19th December, COMEDIAN once again made her way to the crowded beach at Suvla to play her part in embarking the troops and their equipment and carry them to safety. The evacuations of Suvla Bay and Anzac Cove were unqualified successes, achieved without a single casualty. Three weeks later, the evacuation of the Cape Helles beaches was equally successful. The planners had got something right at last, but the Dardanelles remained sealed tight for the remainder of the war.

As the fleet steamed away from the area with its precious burden of weary and exhausted soldiers, feelings on board COMEDIAN were aptly summed up in the final solemn words of Bob Wilkins' detailed account: "As daylight faded we departed sadly from Suvla Bay, leaving our dead to hallow the dust that would be forever British. Gradually, the dim outline of the land receded from our ken. Another imperishable chapter in our history was concluded as we sailed away into the night."

129. WAYFARER (1) 1903-1923 Steel steamship rigged as four-masted schooner. Three decks and seven holds.
O.N. 118002 9,599g 6,222n 12,590d 505.0 x 58.3 x 44.0 feet. Cargo capacity: 693,960 cubic feet.
International Code: TVFC.
Two T. 3-cyl. by Workman, Clark and Co. Ltd., Belfast, driving twin screws; each cylinder 23, 38.5, 66 x 48 inches, 14 knots.

19.12.1902: Launched by Workman, Clark and Co. Ltd., Belfast (Yard No. 195) for the company. *20.2.1903:* Delivered at a cost of £118,704 and sailed for New Orleans in ballast on her maiden voyage under Captain D.A. Wood. *2.4.1906:* A new Load Line Certificate increased draft by 33½ inches, and deadweight to 14,570 tons. These were not exceeded by another Harrison ship until the BENEFACTOR (318) joined the fleet in 1971. *12.5.1908 - 12.9.1908:* Laid up at Liverpool. *7.11.1912:* Marconi wireless apparatus installed. She was the first Harrison vessel to be equipped with the new wireless communication system, about seven months after the TITANIC disaster. *6.1.1913:* Sustained severe damage when she encountered heavy weather when on passage from Liverpool to New Orleans. Two life boats were washed away and two badly damaged, ventilators were crumpled and the funnel swept overboard. *4.7.1914:* Sailed from Liverpool with the first refrigerating plant to be installed in a company vessel, replacing the traditional ice box. *14.7.1914:* Sailed from Cardiff for Rio de Janeiro with a cargo of coal. *5.8.1914:* Approximately eight hours from her destination, intercepted by the cruiser HMS GLASGOW, and ordered to proceed to an anchorage in the Abrolhos Islands, some 300 miles south of Bahia. War had been declared the previous day and the coal cargo was required by the cruiser. *16.3.1915:* Requisitioned by the Shipping Controller for service as a transport. *11.4.1915:* Torpedoed and seriously damaged by the German submarine U 32, 60 miles west north west of the Bishop Rock in position 50.15N, 07.53W. *10.1916:* Loaded biggest single shipment of cotton from Galveston to Liverpool: 36,000 bales. Discharged at Liverpool in 24 hours.[80] *17.8.1918:* In collision with the auxiliary minesweeper VASCO DA GAMA (265/10) in the River Mersey. Returned to dock for repairs, sailing 22.8.1918 for Philadelphia. *5.1.1923:* Sold to Dollar Steamship Lines Ltd. Hong Kong (Robert Dollar Co., San Francisco, managers) for £28,660 and renamed VIRGINIA DOLLAR. *11.2.1924:* Arrived at Honolulu in a critical condition with her sheerstrake split in three places on the starboard side, and one on the port side. *1926:* Sold to Societa Anonima Italiana Prodotti Metallici, Genoa, Italy, and renamed ANGIOLINA R. *4.1.1927:* Arrived at Capetown having run out of coal on a rough weather passage from Dakar, and having burned 28 standards (about 5,000 cubic feet) of her timber deck cargo to keep going. *1927:* Sold to Societa Anonima Fonderie Piemontesi e Impresi Navi, Savona, Italy. *1928:* Sold to Societa Anonima Commerciale Piemontese, Genoa, Italy and renamed SUSA. *21.4.1929:* Aground off Bahia Blanca, Brazil, and 22.4.1929 refloated. *28.5.1929:* In collision in the North Sea with the tanker BRITISH ENSIGN (7,048/17) which was anchored in position 51.31N, 02.18E, about 50 miles west of Flushing. The tanker sustained serious structural damage to shell plating, bridge and accommodation. Numbers 5 and 6 oil tanks were ruptured and began spilling oil into the sea. Despite the damage, she was later able to reach Amsterdam under her own power. SUSA sustained slight damage to her bow-plating. *1932:* Sold to shipbreakers at Genoa for £3,930.

Wayfarer, in her time the largest ship built for Harrisons.

Heavy weather damage

According to the "Liverpool Daily Post and Mercury" dated 15th January 1913: "About 10 o'clock on the morning of the 10th, a sea struck the vessel amidships and wrought fearful destruction. A volume of water calculated to be many tons in weight crashed with terrible force against the funnel and swept it over the starboard side of the ship. The smoke-stack, as it was violently torn from its bed, smashed the steel ventilators on deck and did other damage. Before the crew had time to fully realise the extent of the mischief, another huge wave rose aboard and washed away two of the lifeboats suspended from the davits, besides stoving-in two other lifeboats. This was not all. A large locker containing lifebelts was wrenched from its lashings and driven along by the force of the wind, disabled the steering gear. The vessel was thus in a perilous plight. As one of the men aboard remarked, "Another big wave and she'd have gone". Fortunately, another big wave did not come.

Captain Gaudie promptly took measures to keep his ship under control whilst the steering gear was temporarily repaired. The wireless operator was ordered to signal to any vessels within speaking distance (sic) to stand by in case of need. The White Star liners CELTIC and MEGANTIC and the Allan liner CORSICAN picked up the message, but a few hours later Captain Gaudie cancelled the calls for help. Taking stock of the situation and having ascertained that none of his crew were hurt and that his engines were intact, Captain Gaudie decided to return to Liverpool under the vessel's own steam.

At the time the accident happened, the WAYFARER was upwards of 650 miles from the Fastnet, approximately 1,000 miles from Liverpool. Turning the steamer round, he headed for home. To steam 1,000 miles without a smoke stack was an operation which meant serious discomfort for the men below." Indeed it would and one wonders how the ship was able to generate steam at all. For Harrison ships of those days relied upon the natural draught imparted by their tall funnels to aid combustion in the coal-fired furnaces. Without that draught, steam generation would be a very irksome process. Still, she made it and her entry into the Mersey on 14th January, minus her funnel, but with four tall masts still intact, must have been quite a spectacle.

Ships do not necessarily carry a spare funnel, but a replacement was found or fabricated and fitted somehow, so that the ship was able to resume her delayed voyage to New Orleans on 24th January 1913.

Left: Captain James Gaudie of the *Wayfarer,* and above the ship herself after the loss of her funnel in January 1913.

WAYFARER limps home

In April 1915 WAYFARER was withdrawn from commercial trading, and formally requisitioned by the Government for service in the impending Gallipoli campaign as Transport No. E68. The ship then proceeded to Avonmouth to load army stores, and embark troops and horses for this latest theatre of war.

Subsequently, the ship sailed from Avonmouth on 10th April 1915 carrying 200 soldiers of the Warwickshire Yeomanry, together with their mounts and equipment, bound for Alexandria. Meanwhile, amid all the bustle of departure, a domestic crisis had arisen. One of the cadets, Neil Ian Stewart, a youth of 18, had gone down with sickness and a vile headache. Next morning,11th April, the boy was in a state of high fever, and his condition aroused so much concern that the Master, Captain D.G. Cownie, decided to place him in isolation. Young Stewart's shipmate, Cadet Bob Longster, who was one year his junior, had inevitably been in close contact with the patient, and, consequently, was appointed chief nurse. The two boys were close friends, having served together in the company's GLADIATOR for over six months before being assigned to WAYFARER in the closing days of 1914.

At about two o'clock in the afternoon of the following day, when the ship was about 60 miles west north west of the Scilly Isles, a shattering explosion shook WAYFARER from stem to stern, as a torpedo launched from an unseen submarine found its target amidships. Two men were killed outright by the explosion, which blasted a hole in the ship's port side, flooding three compartments: numbers 3 and 4 holds, and the engine room. Five horses were also among the casualties. The situation looked desperate, but the stoutly built vessel held together and remained afloat. There was no guarantee that this stable situation would continue, and Captain Cownie ordered most of the crew and all his military passengers to take to the boats. An orderly evacuation began, but unfortunately the quarter boat was swamped and capsized by the wash of the ship which was still making headway. Five soldiers were drowned as a result of this incident. Captain Cownie remained on board with a scratch crew of volunteers, hoping the ship might yet be saved.

Meanwhile, the two cadets, the one scarcely able to stand without assistance, were making for their lifeboat stations. Bob Longster saw his charge into a nearby boat (his normal station was the ill-fated quarter boat) and watched as it was lowered away and pulled to safety. He then sought his proper station in the Third Officer's number 4 boat.

In the immediate aftermath of the attack, two steamers had appeared on the scene. One of them, the NEWLYN (4,019/13), picked up most of the men in the lifeboats, and landed them eventually in Falmouth. The other vessel, the FRAMFIELD (2,510/94) of London, after picking up the occupants of number 4 boat, prepared to take WAYFARER in tow. A heavy steel wire hawser, the so-called insurance wire, was paid out to the FRAMFIELD, where it was passed around the poop-house to spread the load before making fast. The eye in the nether end was secured to the WAYFARER's anchor shackle, and thirty fathoms of cable were paid out on the brake

Wayfarer in plain grey during the First World War.
[National Maritime Museum P17038]

(there being no steam to power the windlass). The four-ton anchor thus suspended from the catenary of the towing line made an excellent spring, damping the inevitable stresses like a shock-absorber.

Meanwhile, Bob Longster, who had returned to the WAYFARER with other volunteers, was sent back to the FRAMFIELD where a doctor in the Royal Army Medical Corps ordered him (in his unenviable capacity of one who was most likely to be already infected) to take care of the now desperately ill Stewart. Isolation was re-imposed, and the two boys were confined to a tiny single-berthed cabin, with no facilities, except for one bucket. Presumably food and water were passed into the cabin, but isolation was otherwise strictly enforced, evidently under army discipline.

The two long days which followed were charged with a horror which beggars description. Even today, at the venerable age of 98, Captain Longster remembers his experience with dread. "Worse, far worse, than being torpedoed", he recalls ruefully. The foetid atmosphere of the tiny, airless cabin; the copious diarrhoea symptomatic of the disease; the patient's wild delirium; the gnawing fear of contracting this virulent sickness, the noisome, painful symptoms of which were so cruelly demonstrated to him, all added to feelings of helplessness and dread. What little he could do for his mate he did. He bathed the patient's sweat-stained brow, cleaned him up as best he could with the primitive means available, and restrained him during his wilder bouts of delirium.

The FRAMFIELD, with the helpless, waterlogged WAYFARER in tow, entered Queenstown on the afternoon of 13th April and, their ordeal being partially ended, at least, both cadets were rushed off to hospital. There, young Stewart was given intensive care, while Bob Longster found himself marooned in an isolation ward for three weeks, under observation. By a miracle, the baleful symptoms did not arise, and he showed no signs of having been infected by the disease, quickly confirmed as cerebro-spinal meningitis, or spotted fever. It was a killer in those days, for without the aid of modern antibiotics there could be only one outcome, to which Neil Stewart finally succumbed and died two days later.

Over the next several weeks, WAYFARER was patched up, dried out, and at last sailed under her own steam back to Liverpool, where she lay in dry dock from 19th May to 16th July completing repairs of a more permanent nature.[81]

On 27th May 1915, an Army Order issued by the Secretary of State for War, Lord Kitchener, praised the "gallant conduct and devotion to duty displayed by Major R.A. Richardson and the Officers, NCOs, and men of the 1st Warwickshire Yeomanry on the occasion of a torpedo attack on the transport WAYFARER" Apparently, through their prompt action, 184 men and 763 horses "were brought safely to shore". In what appears to be a hurried afterthought, the Secretary of State insisted that he "could not close this Order without expressing his admiration for the coolness and courage of Captain David G. Cownie, and the Officers and crew of the transport WAYFARER".

Later, in the Admiralty Division of the High Court, Mr. Justice Bargrave Deane awarded the FRAMFIELD £3,000 "for salvage services rendered to the ship WAYFARER".[82]

Wayfarer still in dazzle paint but dressed overall for 'Britain Day', at Galveston on 7th December 1918.
[K. O'Donoghue collection]

130. COLONIAL (1) 1903-1925 Steel screw steamship rigged as two-masted schooner. Two decks and five holds.
O.N. 118005 4,956g 3,174n 7,345d 400.0 x 48.55 x 34.1 feet. Cargo capacity: 367,370 cubic feet.
International Code: TVMS.
T. 3-cyl. by Workman, Clark and Co. Ltd., Belfast; 25, 41, 68 x 54 inches, 12.5 knots.

30.12.1902: Launched by Workman, Clark and Co. Ltd., Belfast (Yard No. 198) for the company. *3.1903:* Delivered at a cost of £61,345. Later sailed from Liverpool to South Africa on her maiden voyage. *5.7.1907:* Arrived at Fremantle with a potentially serious fire on board whilst on an Australian charter voyage for Alfred Holt and Co. The fire was subsequently extinguished. *9.2.1916:* Requisitioned by

the Shipping Controller and placed on French Government Service. *1.7.1924:* Fire broke out in the sugar cargo in No.1 hold whilst berthed at Norfolk, Virginia and was extinguished by injecting steam. Some 200 bags were damaged by fire and 2,100 by injection of steam. *14.4.1925:* Sold to Fratelli Lagorara, Genoa, Italy, for £10,746 and renamed COLOR. *1.1929:* Broken up at Genoa.

Colonial.   *[Peter Newall collection]*

131. COUNSELLOR (2) 1903-1916 Steel steamship rigged as two-masted schooner. Two decks and five holds.
O.N. 118018 4,958g 3,176n 7,300d 400.0 x 48.55 x 34.1 feet. Cargo capacity: 367,370 cubic feet.
International Code: VBLD.
T. 3-cyl. by Workman, Clark and Co. Ltd., Belfast; 25, 41, 68 x 54 feet, 12. 5 knots.

3.4.1903: Launched by Workman, Clark and Co. Ltd., Belfast (Yard No.199) for the company. *8.5.1903:* Delivered at a cost of £61,621 and later sailed from Liverpool to South Africa on her maiden voyage under Captain D.G. Cownie. *19.8.1908:* Arrived at Singapore with a serious fire in the cross bunker. The fire was extinguished and 23.8.1908 sailed. *5.11.1912:* In collision in the Bay of Biscay with the steamer CAMDALE (2,746/95), which later sank. At the subsequent Board of Trade enquiry, COUNSELLOR (Captain W.J. Simmons) was

found to be two thirds to blame, with an estimated liability of £20,000. *14.9.1916:* Struck a mine laid on 17.8.1916 by the German submarine U 79 (Kapitänleutnant Heinrich Jess) and sank in position 51.28N, 09.03W, five miles and 225 degrees from Galley Head. The incident occurred at noon and all crew got away in the lifeboats. She was on passage from San Francisco and Colon for Liverpool with a cargo of barley and timber.

Counsellor on trials.   *[Kevin O'Donoghue collection]*

132. DIRECTOR (1) 1903-1925 Steel steamship rigged as a two-masted schooner. Two decks and five holds.
O.N. 118028 4,931g 3,168n 7,300d 398.5 x 48.5 x 33.67 feet. Cargo capacity: 362,950 cubic feet.
International Code: VCSQ.
T. 3-cyl. by Dunsmuir and Jackson, Glasgow; 25, 41, 68 x 54 inches, 13 knots.

9.6.1903: Launched by Charles Connell and Co. Ltd., Scotstoun (Yard No. 278) for the company. *8.7.1903:* Delivered at a cost of £58,125 and later sailed from Liverpool to South Africa on her maiden voyage under Captain H. Bickerstaff. *20.1.1908:* Grounded on the Pluckington Bank in the River Mersey whilst docking at Liverpool. She was aground for 1½ hours before floating off on the rising tide. *1.1917:* When approaching the port of Willemstad, Curacao, the vessel was refused entry by the neutral Dutch Governor because she carried a gun and her entry might attract German reprisals. During the First World War it was the practice to land guns at a British or Allied port before clearing for a neutral port in order to avoid this sort of

A deep-laden *Director* approaches the locks at Liverpool.

embarrassment. Somehow, the procedure was overlooked in this case. *11.11.1918:* Celebrated Armistice Day in the last convoy out of Gibraltar. *12.3.1925:* Sold to Emmanuel A. Stavroudis, Chania, Greece for £11,284 and renamed EMMANUEL STAVROUDIS. *5.9.1925:* Whilst lying alongside at Santos, Brazil, struck on the port side by the Japanese steamer YEIFUKU MARU (5,861/18). *30.10.1928:* Fire was discovered in number 3 deep tank when passing through the Panama Canal on passage from the west coast of America to Europe with a cargo of nitrate. The cause was unknown and the fire was smothered by the time the vessel arrived at Cristobal. Ship's officers and surveyors found no further signs and the incident was quickly forgotten. When the vessel arrived at Ostend and commenced discharging, the damage was found to be far greater than first believed. Much of the nitrate cargo had to be discharged with the aid of pick axes, as it had solidified. Some 460 tons were either damaged or partially damaged and wholly unsaleable. *1929:* Transferred to Madame A.E. Stavroudis, Chania, Greece. *18.12.1930:* When in position 40.40N, 03.07E, about 60 miles south east of Barcelona, the vessel sent out an S.O.S. message at 02.30 reporting that her steering gear had broken down in heavy weather. However, the next day the steering gear was repaired, the message cancelled, and the vessel resumed her voyage to Genoa. *22.3.1935:* Arrived at Spezia to be broken up.

The price of peace[83]

This anecdote was first related by Captain J.J. Devereux, who joined Harrison Line from Rankin and Gilmour in April 1918. His first appointment was as Chief Officer in DIRECTOR, at that time commanded by Captain R.H. Pugh. After a voyage lasting many months, calling at ports in South Africa and Burma, the ship, homeward bound at last, reached Gibraltar. There, a convoy of 21 ships was being assembled and at the final conference the Convoy Commodore announced his intention of hoisting his flag in the DIRECTOR. Suitably flattered, not to say honoured, Captain Pugh returned to his ship to order the preparations for the proper reception of the Commodore and his entourage of signalmen. Eventually, on 8th November 1918, the convoy sailed, closely shepherded by its escort of destroyers and torpedo boats.

Three days later, when the convoy was entering the Bay of Biscay, a radio message from the Admiralty in London broke the news of the signing of the Armistice with Germany and the cessation of hostilities as from 11.00 that day, 11th November. Convoys at sea were consequently ordered to disperse, their ships to proceed independently to their ports of destination, displaying full navigation lights at night.

There was, naturally, considerable rejoicing throughout the convoy at this welcome news. At the appointed hour the Commodore ordered his yeoman to hoist the signal to disperse. "You won't need me any more, Captain", he said jovially as he left the bridge.

One can readily imagine the intense feelings of relief pervading the minds of all as they realised that the monstrous

Captain Robert H. Pugh (1867-1944), master of *Director* at the time of the Armistice in 1918. *[Medrington's Ltd.]*

killing of the past five years had ended at last; and the profound sense of thankfulness that they at least had survived and had only the normal perils of the sea to face.

That evening, Captain Pugh, described by his contemporaries as a temperate man, invited Mr. Devereux and his Chief Engineer, Ben Johnson, to his cabin for a modest celebratory drink, for if ever there was a cause to celebrate, then this was it. Captain Pugh beamed upon his most senior officers, the epitome of genial host. "Sit down, gentlemen. I've asked Mr. McColl to send up a bottle of Scotch. We cannot let this day pass unmarked!" His guests readily agreed and the three were soon engaged in an animated discussion on the heady prospects for a peaceful future, waiting with anticipatory pleasure for the arrival of the Chief Steward and the Scotch.

Ten minutes later they were still waiting. At last, a chastened Mr. McColl appeared in the doorway, empty handed. "It's that Commodore, sir!" he complained, dismay and indignation sending his voice up an octave. "He has commandeered all the liquor from the bond in the name of the King, and locked himself in his cabin. I can't get a word out of him!"

And in his cabin the Commodore remained, his war over, and quite oblivious to threats and entreaties alike. Only when the ship dropped anchor at the Mersey Bar did he reappear to clamber hazily over the rail and drop into the smart naval launch which had come alongside to collect the Royal Navy contingent.

Perhaps this last act of arbitrary expropriation was but a small price to pay for peace.

133. HUNTSMAN (1) 1904-1917 Steel steamship rigged as a four-masted schooner. Two decks and seven holds.
O.N. 118103 7,460g 4,828n 10,560d 470.0 x 57.25 x 35.98 feet. Cargo capacity: 554,170 cubic feet.
International Code: VTFS.
T. 3-cyl. by Dunsmuir and Jackson, Glasgow; 27¼, 45½, 75 x 60 inches, 13 knots.

19.5.1904: Launched by Charles Connell and Co. Ltd., Glasgow (Yard No. 284) for the company. *4.7.1904:* Delivered at a cost of £83,380 and later sailed from Liverpool to Calcutta on her maiden voyage under Captain H. McKee. *23.9.1910:* In collision with the steamer RAMESES (2,490/93) in the Mediterranean when on passage from Liverpool to Calcutta. The damage sustained was on the starboard side in way of No.2 hold, which was quickly flooded. The situation appeared serious and several boats were lowered while the damage was inspected. The bulkheads appeared to be holding, however, and the boats were recalled. Eventually she made Alexandria where repairs lasting three weeks were undertaken and the voyage to Calcutta was resumed. *20.10.1914:* Requisitioned by the Shipping Controller at Calcutta and served as a transport for the Indian Army. Her first assignment was to transport an Indian Lancer regiment from Bombay to Marseilles. *15.12.1914:* Arrived. *5.11.1915:* Chased and attacked by gunfire in the Mediterranean off Algiers in position 37.26N, 03.00E, by the German submarine U 38 (Kapitänleutnant Max Valentina) which was driven off by her defensive armament. She was on passage from Liverpool to Calcutta with 8,000 tons of general cargo. *2.2.1916:* Entered Gravesend Reach at 08.40, having just left Tilbury for Liverpool in the closing stages of a voyage from Calcutta. Coming up the Reach, bound for Purfleet, was the collier LOCKWOOD (1,142/96) and the weather was fine and clear. The Alfred Holt steamer LYCAON (7,552/13), inward bound from Japan, had anchored in the Reach overnight and was just getting under way, turning to port in order to proceed upstream. Meanwhile, LOCKWOOD and HUNTSMAN had shaped course to pass under LYCAON's stern, to the north side of the river. There was, however, little room for manoeuvre and HUNTSMAN struck LOCKWOOD amidships with her bow causing considerable damage. An enquiry was subsequently held in the Admiralty Court and it was ruled that the pilot, master and officers of HUNTSMAN should have realised earlier that LYCAON was turning, and waited in a position well clear until the latter had completed her manoeuvre. The subsequent claim was in the region of £10,000. *25.2.1917:* Torpedoed and sunk by the German submarine U 50 (Kapitänleutnant Gerhard Berger) in position 53,04N, 13.40W, 180 miles north west by west from the Fastnet. The crew abandoned ship at 05.25 hours and she sank with a loud explosion. Two lives were lost and the survivors were picked up a few hours later by the steamer ANSELM (5,450/05). HUNTSMAN was on passage from Liverpool to Calcutta with general cargo.

Two views of *Huntsman.* The lower shows her in the winter of 1914, transporting a regiment of Indian Army Lancers from Bombay to Marseilles. On the bow she carries the number 125, reminiscent of the Boer War transport numbers. These were briefly applied to requisitioned ships during the First World War, but were painted over as the ships assumed a wartime grey. Note the windsails to provide ventilation to the holds carrying the horses.
[National Maritime Museum P16945 and P16947]

Captain Ernest.A. Brown, master of *Custodian* when she was engaged on Boer War transport work in 1901.

Colonial loading sheep and cased goods at Fremantle in July 1907. Her heavy timber derricks can be seen to advantage.

134. MATADOR (1) 1904-1917 Steel steamship rigged as a two-masted schooner. Two decks and five holds.
O.N. 118124 3,400g 2,197n 5,345d 350.5 x 46.0 x 28.44 feet. Cargo capacity: 251,680 cubic feet.
International Code: HBFC.
T. 3-cyl. by Swan, Hunter and Wigham Richardson Ltd., Newcastle-upon-Tyne; 21, 35, 58 x 48 inches, 11 knots.

28.7.1904: Launched by Swan, Hunter and Wigham Richardson Ltd., Newcastle-upon-Tyne (Yard No. 717) for the company. *9.9.1904:* Delivered at a cost of £39,225 and later sailed from Liverpool to Central America on her maiden voyage under Captain E. Maycock. *3.7.1917:* Torpedoed and sunk by the German submarine UC 31 (Kapitänleutnant Otto von Schrader) in the North Atlantic in position 51.56N, 12.33W, 115 miles west by north half north from the Fastnet Rock. Two seamen lost their lives. She was on passage from New Orleans to Liverpool with general cargo.

Matador. The white line on the hull is unusual.   *[G.R. Scott collection]*

135. GLADIATOR (2) 1904-1915 Steel steamship rigged as a two-masted schooner. Two decks and five holds.
O.N. 118123 3,359g 2,168n 5,370d 349.7 x 46.2 x 28.44 feet Cargo capacity: 258,730 cubic feet.
International Code: HBDW.
T. 3-cyl. by Dunsmuir and Jackson, Glasgow; 24, 50, 65 x 45 inches, 11 knots.

2.8.1904: Launched by Charles Connell and Co. Ltd., Scotstoun (Yard No. 287) for the company. *20.9.1904:* Delivered at a cost of £39,677 and later sailed from Liverpool to South Africa on her maiden voyage under Captain J.T. Falla. *1905:* Became an observing ship for the Meteorological Office, the first company ship to volunteer since the sailing ship NATURALIST in 1864. *27.10.1912:* At Cabadello when STUDENT (146) went aground on English Bank and assisted in towing her clear. *19.8.1915:* Shelled and sunk by the German submarine U 27 (Kapitänleutnant Bernd Wegener) some 75 miles south east of Waterford. The crew took to the boats and were later picked up by patrol boats and landed at Milford Haven. There were no casualties. She was on passage from Liverpool and Cardiff to Pernambuco with general cargo.

At Pernambuco, Brazil in December 1911 when four Harrison ships were in port over the Christmas and New Year periods. Left to right: *Warrior* (136), *Professor* (145), *Matador* (134) and *Gladiator* (135).

136. WARRIOR (3) 1905-1927 Steel steamship rigged as a two-masted schooner. Two decks and four holds plus bridge space.
O.N. 120873. 3,491g 2,265n 5,815d 350.0 x 46.0 x 30.63 feet. Cargo capacity: 270,090 cubic feet.
International Code: HDCR.
T. 3-cyl. by Dunsmuir and Jackson, Glasgow; 24, 40, 65 x 45 inches, 10.5 knots.

5.7.1905: Launched by Charles Connell and Co. Ltd., Scotstoun (Yard No. 297) for the company. *16.8.1905:* Delivered at a cost of £41,020 and later sailed from Liverpool to Brazil on her maiden voyage under Captain W.H. Rushforth. *3.8.1921:* The owners of the barge MARGARET brought a claim against the WARRIOR alleging that the ship had struck and sunk the barge, laden with 50 tons of tin, whilst the ship was manoeuvring off the West India Dock, London. However, Mr. Justice Hill, sitting in the Admiralty Division of the High Court, found the case not proved, and gave judgement in favour of the WARRIOR, with costs. *18.12.1922:* A potentially hazardous fire in the bunkers whilst at Durban was extinguished before any serious damage occurred. *25.9.1923:* Whilst moored at Eston Buoys at Middlesbrough, the vessel parted the flood buoy moorings during a gale and laid athwart the River Tees. She was eventually assisted into dock by tugs. *18.11.1924:* Grounded on the Demerara Bar when outward bound. The vessel's draught at the berth was 18 feet 6 inches, height of tide on the Bar 17 feet 2 inches. Although it was normal to load the ship up to a foot over bar draught (the Bar consisting of soft mud which she could plough through without fear of damage), 16 inches was evidently a bit too much. Some of the sugar cargo was unloaded into lighters and she refloated on the next high tide. *2.2.1927:* Sold to Compagnie des Chargeurs Francaise (Société Auxiliaire des Chargeurs Francais, managers), Rouen, France for £9,702 and renamed NEUILLY. *27.11.1928:* Ran aground on the island of Kascalie, 10 miles from Djibouti. The cargo was discharged into lighters and she refloated next day and returned to Djibouti for survey. Only slight damage was reported. *1929:* Sold to Compagnie des Bateaux à Vapeur du Nord, Dunkirk, France and renamed ORANIE. *11.1931:* Sold to Italian shipbreakers. *11.1.1932:* Arrived at Savona.

Warrior. The square framework around her funnel top may be to support the radio aerials.   *[G.R. Scott collection]*

137. AUTHOR (2) 1905-1916 Steel steamship rigged as a two-masted schooner. Two decks and four holds plus bridge space. O.N. 120877 3,490g 2,248n 5,815d. 350.0 x 46.0 x 30.63 feet. Cargo capacity: 270,090 cubic feet. International Code: HDJV.
T. 3-cyl. by Dunsmuir and Jackson, Glasgow; 24, 40, 65 x 45 inches, 10.5 knots.

15.8.1905: Launched by Charles Connell and Co. Ltd., Scotstoun (Yard No. 298) for the company. *14.9.1905:* Delivered at a cost of £41,022 and later sailed from Liverpool to South Africa on her maiden voyage under Captain T. Dean. *15.1.1906:* Struck the pier at Barry Dock and caused damage amounting to £201. *13.1.1916:* Captured by the German commerce raider MÖWE and scuttled with explosives 225 miles west by half north of Lisbon in position 39.05N, 13.56W. She was on passage from London to Durban with general cargo.[84]

Author.   *[World Ship Photo Library]*

138. ORATOR (2) 1905-1917 Steel steamship rigged as a two-masted schooner. Two decks and five holds. O.N. 120887 3,563g 2,283n 5,945d 350.3 x 46.1 x 30.45 feet. Cargo capacity: 291,680 cubic feet. International Code: HDPN.
T. 3-cyl. by Workman, Clark and Co. Ltd., Belfast; 21, 35, 58 x 48 inches, 11 knots.

1905: Launched by Workman, Clark and Co. Ltd., Belfast (Yard No. 224) for the company. *10.10.1905:* Delivered at a cost of £42,044 and later sailed from Liverpool to Brazil on her maiden voyage under Captain J.S. Henry. *1.7.1906:* Captain J.S. Henry was discharged "for being drunk at Greenock". *10.1909:* While on passage from Savannah to Liverpool, picked up 25 men from the French brigantine JEANNE D'ARC (376/80) of St. Malo. The sailing vessel had foundered about 1,500 miles west of the Fastnet. *28.6.1916:* Encountered the disabled French steamer EDITH CAVELL (1,367/08) when on passage from St. Lucia to Savannah and towed her into Fort de France, Martinique. *8.6.1917:* Torpedoed by the German submarine U 96 (Kapitänleutnant Heinrich Jess) about 84 miles west north west of the Fastnet. The submarine then surfaced and finished the attack with gunfire. Five men died in the attack. She was on passage from Pernambuco for Liverpool with general cargo.

Orator flying light as she enters the Mersey.   *[A.H. Joyce collection]*

139. CANDIDATE (1) 1906-1915 Steel steamship rigged as a two-masted schooner. Three decks and five holds. Shelter-deck type.
O.N. 120950 4,521g 2,917n 7,840d 399.0 x 51.2 x 30.58 feet. Cargo capacity: 416,755 cubic feet.
International Code: HGKF.
T. 3-cyl. by Dunsmuir and Jackson, Glasgow; 25, 41, 68 x 54 inches, 13 knots.

20.4.1906: Launched by Charles Connell and Co. Ltd., Scotstoun (Yard No. 304) for the company. *31.5.1906:* Delivered at a cost of £59,227 and later sailed from Liverpool to South Africa on her maiden voyage under Captain W.M. Booth. *6.5.1915:* Shelled by the German submarine U 20 (Kapitänleutnant Walther Schwieger) off the southern coast of Ireland. CANDIDATE tried to escape but was then torpedoed in the engine room. She did not sink immediately and required several waterline shots before sinking at 10.00 in position 51.47N, 06.27W. All crew survived the attack and were later landed at Milford Haven. She was on passage from Liverpool for Kingston, Jamaica and New Orleans with general cargo. The same day U 20 attacked and sank CENTURION (No.141) and the following day the Cunard liner LUSITANIA (30,396/07).

Candidate in Brunswick Dock, Liverpool with *Warrior*.

140 COMMODORE (1) 1906-1915 Steel steamship rigged as a two-masted schooner. Three decks and five holds. Shelter-deck type.
O.N. 123981 4,521g 2,914n 7,840d 399.0 x 51.2 x 30.58 feet. Cargo capacity: 416,755 cubic feet.
International Code: HGQD.
T. 3-cyl. by Dunsmuir and Jackson Ltd., Glasgow; 25, 41, 68 x 54 inches, 13 knots.

Commodore arriving at Galveston to load cotton for the UK.

Commodore's first master, Captain Sam Bass.   *[Medrington's Ltd.]*

5.6.1906: Launched by Charles Connell and Co. Ltd., Scotstoun (Yard No. 305) for the company. *10.7.1906:* Delivered at a cost of £59,406 and laid up in Clydebank Dock for the rest of the month before sailing from Liverpool to the West Indies on her maiden voyage under Captain Sam Bass. *16.10.1910:* The crew of the schooner FLORENCE LEYLAND (344/82) were rescued before she foundered in position 40.30N, 60.00W, about 200 miles south of Sable Island. For his "praiseworthy services", Captain Sam Bass was awarded the Liverpool Shipwreck and Humane Society's Silver Clasp and an Illuminated Vote of Thanks. *17.4.1912:* Fire broke out in her cargo when on passage from Calcutta to Liverpool and she put into Malta. She struck the breakwater heavily as she entered Valetta Harbour and consequently, what with dealing with the fire and its after effects and making repairs to the contact damage, it was 4.5.1912 before the voyage was resumed. *20.3.1915:* Requisitioned by the Shipping Controller for service as a transport in the Eastern Mediterranean under the command of Captain Herbert Russell. *2.12.1915:* Shelled by the German submarine U 33 (Kapitänleutnant Konrad Gansser) in the Mediterranean, about 160 miles east south east of Malta. The vessel stopped and the crew abandoned ship. Explosive charges were attached to the hull and detonated and she sank in position 35.10N, 17.39E, after further

gunfire. One man was killed and six injured. She was on passage from Salonika to Marseilles in ballast. The survivors were adrift for 28 hours before being rescued by a Belgian ship and landed at Southampton 18.12.1915.

One of the earliest recorded cases of a claim for industrial injury was brought against the company by John Hamilton Barton, Chief Cook on the COMMODORE. Barton alleged that, on 5th October 1907, as the ship was in the North Sea bound for Hull, he scratched a finger of his right hand on a jagged edge while greasing tins for pudding making. He was discharged at Hull on 8th and returned to Liverpool by which time his injury had seriously deteriorated so that he had to undergo medical treatment at a hospital. He was unable to work for weeks and he applied to the court for compensation under the Industrial Injuries Act. His case was heard in Liverpool County Court on 21st February 1908 before Judge Shand. Mr Rigby Swift instructed by Simpson, North and Company, appeared for the respondents. Various witnesses were called from the ship to confirm that nothing was seen or heard of Barton's injury whilst he was on board, the implication being that the injury could have been inflicted anywhere. Judge Shand, however, found for the applicant, and made an award of £1 per week in the claimant's favour.[85]

COMMODORE - transport to Gallipoli, 1915

The following account of one merchant ship's contribution to the ill-fated Dardanelles campaign of 1915 is based on extracts from a diary kept by Captain Herbert Russell, Master of COMMODORE, and reproduced here by kind permission of his family.

Captain Herbert Russell gazed round the crowded harbour of Alexandria, struck with amazement. A bold, amphibious stroke, the forcing of the Dardanelles, was about to begin. Captain Russell's diary reflects the mood of optimism which pervaded the harbour: "The greatness of it all is wonderful! Some ships load up stores for 60,000 men for 10 days, and go off to Lemnos... Tank steamers load up water, for there is no water at the Dardanelles...some steamers are going with fodder, others with coal, motor transport, and pontoon boats to land men and horses...everyone here seems anxious for it to begin, and no one has any fear of us not coming out on top!"

This entry is dated 21st April 1915, and COMMODORE, having sailed from Avonmouth on 9th April, had just arrived at Alexandria with a contingent of 210 officers and men of the Queen's Own Dorset Yeomanry, and a section of Royal Army Medical Corp personnel. Also on board were 623 horses (12 had died on the voyage out), and a vast amount of equipment. At last, the horses stumbled down the inclined gangways, and the troops marched off to their base south of the port to join their units. The landings at Cape Helles and Cape Gaba Tepe began four days later.

Captain Herbert Russell (1874-1936) recorded events at Gallipoli in his diary. *[Priestley and Sons Ltd.]*

COMMODORE, however, was to take no part in the initial landings, and on 4th May she left Alexandria for Port Said, with orders to embark 333 men of the East Lancashire Regiment, their guns, 209 horses, 26 vehicles, and seven days' stores and fodder for a full brigade. She sailed at 17.30 on 6th May, bound for Cape Gaba Tepe. Whilst on passage they met up with what purported to be the battlecruiser INFLEXIBLE, but which in fact turned out to be the former Harrison steamship PATRICIAN in disguise - a sheep in wolf's clothing. Meanwhile, HMS INFLEXIBLE now lay in a Malta dry-dock, repairing extensive damage incurred in the abortive attempt to force the Dardanelles by sea power alone, in March 1915.

On 9th May, COMMODORE arrived off the beaches. The battle was at its height; COMMODORE'S crew could see it all from their position half-a-mile offshore. Obviously, this was to be no walkover, a view sadly reinforced by the melancholy boat loads of wounded being ferried towards the rapidly filling hospital ships. Alexandria seemed a long way away.

Next day, COMMODORE was ordered to close the beaches at Cape Helles, and land her troops there. During the initial landings a merchant ship, the Glasgow steamer RIVER CLYDE, had been beached at Sedd el Bahr as a sort of prototype landing craft. She was then lying hard and fast aground, parallel to the beach, with large square holes cut in her flanks. A pontoon bridge extended from the inshore side to terra firma. It was towards this makeshift harbour that COMMODORE'S laden lifeboats and horse boats were steered, towed by trawlers. They floated over the sill of the hole in the port side, and disappeared into the gaping maw of the ship's hold. Then it was a stirring sight to see the soldiers re-emerge, fully accoutred for war, horses harnessed, guns limbered up, to clatter across the pontoon bridge, and gallop away in a cloud of dust towards the front line. From the time of leaving the ship to opening fire was less than half-an-hour.

Night fell; COMMODORE continued landing troops, stores, and munitions while the fighting went on. To the crew it was all very exciting, but "...every once in a while a boat-load of wounded comes off, and then we think, and forget to joke...everyone seems of the same opinion, and that is that there's a long job ahead, and lots of men will be sacrificed before the Dardanelles are forced."

COMMODORE returned to Alexandria on 14th May, her arrival coinciding with that of three hospital ships thronged with wounded soldiers. Captain Russell made it his business to visit some of them. The ship sailed from Alexandria again on 20th May with a detachment of Australian troops, veterans of the initial landings returning to their units after treatment for minor wounds, and 500 sheep. During the voyage they were chased by an enemy submarine, but managed to elude it among the scattered islands of the Cyclades group. Consequently, the ship arrived at Port Mudros at 10.00 on 23rd May, six hours later than expected.

Two days later, COMMODORE was lying off Cape Gaba Tepe preparing to disembark troops, when, three miles away, the battleship, TRIUMPH, was torpedoed. She sank in 10 minutes with heavy loss of life.

COMMODORE, together with the other transports, returned to base. Another attempt to land troops was carried out two days later, on 27th May, but that was again frustrated when the same submarine, U 21 (Hershing), sank another battleship, MAJESTIC, off Cape Helles, with the loss of 42 men.[86] This time, COMMODORE was ordered back to Kephalo, Imbros Island, there to lie alongside the headquarters ship, ARCADIAN, with the Commander in Chief, General Sir Ian Hamilton, on board. The other side of the Royal Mail liner was flanked by another storeship, the two ships thus forming an effective barrier against any intrusive torpedo attacks directed at G.H.Q.

Thus, with U-boats infesting the area of operations, COMMODORE had to wait until 31st May before it was clear for her to proceed to Cape Gaba Tepe to land her troops at the third attempt. Captain Russell was dismayed, and sadly disappointed, to observe that the front line trenches were no further forward than they had been three weeks earlier. The following entry in his diary reflects his anger and frustration.

"June 1st, 9.00 p.m. There was a night attack, with big guns and rifles going all the time... One of them (a destroyer) flashed his searchlight along the shore, and found some Turks coming up with a gun, so opened fire and all had the pleasure of seeing the Turks wiped out, and the gun blown in the air. They (the naval gunners) found the range very quickly, and soon polished them off."

On the following day, the Turks apparently seized an opportunity to exact revenge: "Suddenly, there was a bang, and we heard a shell coming. It passed between the funnel and bridge, about 10 feet above the deck. The next passed between funnel and mainmast, the third in the same place. They all dropped about 50 feet the other side of the ship, and by the time the fourth came, we were going full speed, out from the land, and clear... The shells fired at us were supposed to be from the GOEBEN..."

COMMODORE then moved south to Cape Helles in order to discharge the 500 live sheep which had been loaded at Alexandria. On the following day, Captain Russell had the opportunity to visit the captured fort at Sedd el Bahr. There, among the ruins, he found a stone inscribed in Arabic, which, when translated, read: "Died suddenly, Abdul Hools, my life went to God in the year 1173" (i.e. 1173 A.H. in the Muslim calendar, or 1795 A.D.). He kept the stone as a souvenir, and eventually brought it back to Liverpool. However, according to his son, R.H. Russell, his wife would not allow it in the house, being convinced it would bring ill fortune. Consequently, Captain Russell was obliged to take it away with him on his next voyage to the Eastern Mediterranean - only to be torpedoed off Malta.

On 4th June, Captain Russell was again on shore when another fierce bombardment signalled yet another attack, this time on the hill position of Achi Baba, a Turkish stronghold. He was forced to take shelter in a bunker, from which vantage point he witnessed "...a grand sight. The shells were passing overhead, and the hill, Achi Baba, was one mass of bursting shells, and the Turks were trying their best to return [fire]".

After an hour or so he was able to retreat to the beach and regain his ship, which was then ordered to Mudros. There she embarked 400 Turkish prisoners-of-war, and set sail for Alexandria at 18.00 on 7th June 1915.

That was the final episode of the COMMODORE'S involvement in the Dardanelles campaign. She was back in the United Kingdom by the end of June, and spent some three months re-fitting and making repairs before returning to the Mediterranean. She was at once involved in the campaign to occupy Salonika, before being sunk by U 33 on 2nd December 1915.

141. CENTURION (1) 1908-1915 Steel steamship rigged as two-masted schooner. Three decks and five holds. Shelter deck type.
O.N. 127927 5,945g 3,854n 9,230d 399.0 x 51.2 x 30.56 feet. Cargo capacity: 419,260 cubic feet.
International Code: HNCV.
T. 3-cyl. by Dunsmuir and Jackson Ltd., Glasgow; 25, 41, 68 x 54 inches, 13 knots.

31.7.1908: Launched by Charles Connell and Co. Ltd., Scotstoun (Yard No. 322) for the company. *9.9.1908:* Delivered at a cost of £65,847. Later sailed from Liverpool to Mexico on her maiden voyage under Captain W. H. Rushforth.
25.4.1911: Sailed from Swansea to inaugurate a new service from United Kingdom to North Pacific ports in the United States and Canada via Brazil and the Straits of Magellan. When the Panama Canal opened in 1914 the service, though seriously curtailed by the exigencies of war, was

Centurion. [*Ambrose Greenway collection*]

redirected via the Caribbean. It was discontinued in 1933. *6.5.1915:* Torpedoed and sunk by the German submarine U 20 (Kapitänleutnant Walther Schwieger) in the St. George's Channel, about 15 miles south of the Barrels Lightvessel. All the crew survived the attack and landed at Rosslare. She was on passage from Birkenhead to South Africa with 8,309 tons of general cargo.[87]

142. MERCHANT (2) 1908-1929 Steel steamship rigged as two-masted schooner. Two decks and five holds.
O.N. 127930 3,682g 2,378n 5,895d 349.3 x 46.05 x 30.63 feet. Cargo capacity: 312,040 cubic feet.
International Code: HNFJ.
T. 3-cyl. by Dunsmuir and Jackson Ltd., Glasgow; 21, 33, 58 x 48 inches, 11 knots.

1.9.1908: Launched by Charles Connell and Co. Ltd., Scotstoun (Yard No. 323) for the company. *30.9.1908:* Delivered at a cost of £43,450. Later sailed from Birkenhead for South Africa on her maiden voyage under Captain A.E. Oxburgh. *29.10.1910:* Ran aground at Natal, Brazil, but refloated 1.11.1910. An adverse situation was compounded by getting a rope round the propeller, which so delayed the vessel further that she was neaped (i.e. unable to sail until the next spring tides gave sufficient water on the bar) until 13.11.1910. *26.10.1913:* Ashore at Kilifi, 35 miles north of Mombasa. *31.10.1913:* Refloated. *12.8.1914:* Requisitioned by the Shipping Controller for service as an Expeditionary Force Transport. *12.8.1918:* Towed the Norwegian barque BA (1,174/84) into Rio Grande, Brazil. *23.9.1926:* While berthed at the wharf in Pernambuco, struck by the incoming French steamer GUARUJA (4,282/21) which then went on to strike the German steamer NIENBURG (4,154/22). The damage to all three vessels was slight. *29.6.1929:* Sold to Societa Anonima Commerciale Italo-Cilena, Genoa, Italy for £12,137 and renamed MILANESE. *1931:* Renamed GABON and owners subsequently reported to be in liquidation. *1933:* Sold to "L'Equatoriale" Societa Anonima Esercizio Armamento e Navigazione, Genoa, Italy. *4.1.1935:* When leaving Marseilles in heavy weather, fell heavily against the quay wall, sustaining a leak on the port side amidships. Sub-

sequently entered dry dock for repairs. *1935:* Sold to Tito Campanella Societa di Navigazione, Genoa, Italy and renamed MIRA. *6.3.1936:* Leaving her berth at Piraeus, the propeller struck and penetrated a lighter containing 65 tons of grain which had just been unloaded from her holds. Two local tugs quickly grappled and supported the lighter, which was thus enabled to discharge at least half of its cargo undamaged. *14.5.1943:* Bombed and sunk during an Allied air attack at Civitavecchia, Italy. Subsequently raised and laid up pending an engine overhaul. *9.1943:* Taken over by German forces. *1.1944:* Again bombed and sunk at Civitavecchia. *2.1947:* Refloated but sold to Italian shipbreakers. *12.10.1948:* Arrived at Savona for demolition.

Merchant in Manchester Docks. [*C. Downs*]

94

143. ENGINEER (2) 1908-1920 Steel steamship rigged as two-masted schooner. Three decks and five holds.
O.N. 127942 5,883g 3,797n 9,190d. 399.0 x 51.0 x 30.52 feet. Cargo capacity 429,600 cubic feet.
International Code: HNJB.
T. 3-cyl. by North Eastern Marine Engineering Co. Ltd., Wallsend; 25, 41, 68 x 54inches, 13 knots.

17.7.1908: Launched by Swan, Hunter and Wigham Richardson Ltd., Newcastle-upon-Tyne (Yard No. 807) for the company. *4.11.1908:* Delivered at a cost of £62,490. Later sailed from the Tyne to Galveston in ballast on her maiden voyage under Captain W. Llewellyn. *3.10.1910:* When homeward bound from Bombay via Genoa there was a severe outbreak of malaria in the vessel, affecting most of the crew. Four able seamen and seven firemen were left behind at Genoa, but they recovered and were repatriated 15.10.1910. *1.1.1911:* Sailed from Liverpool for New Orleans. Whilst on passage, came across the disabled Italian steamer CEREA (4,295/00). She was taken in tow and arrived 15.1.1911 at Bermuda. *14.6.1920:* Arrived at Delagoa Bay, Portuguese East Africa, on a voyage from the United Kingdom to Mauritius via South and East Africa. *18.6.1920:* At 15.45 on an outbreak of fire was discovered in the coal cargo. Efforts to fight the fire were unavailing and by 5.7.1920 it was so much out of control that the vessel was abandoned to the underwriters in a sinking condition, becoming a total loss.

Three views of *Engineer* which span her career. Top is probably a trial's view. Middle was taken by a member of her crew, and shows her dressed overall, possibly in a US port. Bottom shows her well ablaze in Delagoa Bay during June 1920, when a fire in her coal cargo led to *Engineer's* total loss.

[Top: Ian Rae collection]
[Middle: Nigel Farrell collection]
[Bottom: Peter Newall collection]

144. ARTIST (2) 1909-1917 Steel steamship rigged as two-masted schooner. Two decks and five holds.
O.N. 128007 3,570g 2,300n 5,945d 350.1 x 46.05 x 30.62 feet. Cargo capacity: 312,040 cubic feet.
International Code: HQBT.
T. 3-cyl. by Dunsmuir and Jackson Ltd., Glasgow; 20, 34, 58 x 48 inches, 11.5 knots.

26.10.1909: Launched by Charles Connell and Co. Ltd., Scotstoun (Yard No. 330) for the company. *24.11.1909:* Delivered at a cost of £39,600. Later sailed from Liverpool to Colombia on her maiden voyage under Captain W.H. Rushforth. *7.8.1914:* Requisitioned by the Shipping Controller and served as a transport for the British Expeditionary Force. *7.10.1914:* One of 24 transports in the port of Ostend unloading stores for the British 7th Division. *10.10.1914:* Following the fall of Antwerp, orders were issued for Ostend to be evacuated. Every effort was to be made to reload the stores and equipment just landed, the task being made even more difficult by the streams of refugees pouring into the port. Few stevedores were available, and ship's officers and crews,

Artist. [*Nigel Farrell collection*]

assisted by men of the Naval Division and the Marine Brigade, loaded and stowed the cargo themselves.[88] *24.1.1917:* Sailed from Newport, Monmouthshire with a cargo of Welsh coal and railway stock for Alexandria. *27.1.1917:* Whilst still in the St. Georges Channel, hove to in a bitter easterly gale, torpedoed without warning by the German submarine U 55 (Kapitänleutnant Wilhelm Werner) and sank quickly, barely having time to transmit a distress signal. A patrol boat was sent out to search for survivors but

found nothing. At least one boat was successfully launched but when it was found three days later by the steamer LUCHANA (3,051/04) with a young cadet in charge, seven of the twenty-four occupants were dead from wounds and exposure. The remaining 28 members of the crew, including the Master, were never seen again. The position of the loss was recorded as 51.37N, 07.14W, 58 miles west by half south from the Smalls Lighthouse.[89]

145. PROFESSOR (2) 1910-1930 Steel steamship rigged as two-masted schooner. Two decks and five holds.
O.N. 128017 3,581g 2,288n 5,930d. 350.2 x 46.15 x 30.62 feet. Cargo capacity 309,232 cubic feet.
International Code: HQKF.
T. 3-cyl. by Workman, Clark and Co. Ltd., Belfast; 20, 34, 58 x 48 inches, 12 knots.

30.11.1909: Launched by Workman, Clark and Co. Ltd., Belfast (Yard No. 288) for the company. *3.2.1910:* Delivered at a cost of £39,677. Later sailed from Liverpool to the West Indies on her maiden voyage under Captain W.N. Nielson. *13.1.1916:* Requisitioned by the Shipping Controller. *22.1.1916:* Sailed from Liverpool for the Mediterranean. *8.2.1916:* Approaching Alexandria attacked by a German submarine on the surface. She retaliated with her 4.7-inch gun and successfully fought off the challenge. *11.9.1925:* Whilst lying at Durban, coal in the port side 'tween deck bunkers began heating and at the same time a quantity of old coal in the bridge deck alleyways began to emit toxic fumes. Although most of the crew lived forward under the forecastle head, a certain number lived amidships, off the main deck alleyways. Among them were the Bosun, Carpenter, Lamptrimmer, and two Ordinary Seamen. Between their quarters and the bridge deck bunker space was a wooden bulkhead and during the night lethal coal fumes filtered through into the cabins where the men lay sleeping. The Ordinary Seamen, Connolly and Service, and the Lamptrimmer were found dead in their bunks next morning. As a result, 35 tons of heated coal were landed 15.9.1925 and sold. What remained in the bunker was brought up on deck to cool, and then transferred to the bridge space. *17.10.1927:* Grounded on the bar at Puerto Mexico, causing considerable damage. She proceeded to New Orleans where temporary repairs were effected, enabling her to proceed to Manchester where permanent repairs could be carried out. These involved fairing a bent and fractured stern frame, the renewal of 14 bottom plates and the fairing of 30 more along with the associated frames.[90] The vessel was in dry-dock at Manchester from 30.12.1927 to 7.2.1928 and the total cost was in the region of £5,200. *7.4.1930:* Sold to Pentwyn Steam Ship Co. Ltd. (Lambert, Barnett and Co., managers). Cardiff for approximately £12,000 and renamed PENTRENT. *9.1933:* Sold to Italian General Shipping Co. Ltd. for £3,600 for onward sale to Italian shipbreakers. *1934:* Broken up at Monfalcone.

Professor (above) and as *Pentrent* in the colours of Lambert, Barnett and Co. on 8th April 1933 (below)
[*Upper: G.R. Scott collection; lower: World Ship Photo Library*]

First voyage - 1925 style[91]

A Harrison Line shipmaster, Captain H.G. Skelly, made his first voyage to sea in the PROFESSOR in 1925 and penned a brief account of those early days. He retains a vivid recollection of driving from Euston Station to West India Dock in a hansom cab. He was clearly disappointed, however, to find that his first assignment as a cadet was to a "Third Class" ship. Apparently, "The largest and finest vessels were known as "First Class". The (PROFESSOR's) officers and crew were all junior men...commanded by a short, stout shipmaster, Captain Thomas Chapman. He was in his fifties, rotund, red of face and quick of temper, but his seamanship and practical application to the existing order and conditions left no doubt that he managed the sea in all its moods as he managed his officers and crew. He was sailing-ship trained, held an Extra Master's Certificate and under his bluff exterior was a generous, kindly man."

On 2nd August 1925 the ship sailed from London, minus a radio officer, whose union had called a strike. Nevertheless, the company had applied for and been granted a permit to sail the ship without one.

Thirty days later, on 1st September, the ship arrived at Durban. During the long voyage, records Captain Skelly, "We had consumed all the fish, flesh and vegetables from the ice box; half the salt pork and salt beef from the brine casks; and even some of the Steward's very precious tins of meat from his storeroom. We had, incidentally, used all the coal from the bunker spaces and had spent a week hauling up extra coal from No. 4 deep tank to the afterdeck and trundling it through to the side bunker hatches in wheelbarrows.

"Officers, cadets and sailors worked together on this task, the winch drivers being the Chief and Second Engineer and the Chief Officer the hatchman. My reward at 17.00 was an enquiring word from old Tommy Chapman and three tailor-made cigarettes from his little tin box. For those three cigarettes one would have gladly worked a further three hours, as fourpence per day did not allow one the luxury of factory-produced cigarettes and one of those at night was all the luxury one craved."

It was while the ship was at Durban that the crew learned of the impending cut in the wages of all British seamen. A mass meeting of all the crews of British ships in port was called and it was decided to walk ashore in protest and stay ashore. Unaccountably, by modern practices, the cooks and stewards remained loyal and life on board continued much as usual. It was during this period that young Skelly had his first glimpse of life in the longed-for First Class ship. This happened to be the ASTRONOMER (173), also in Durban and his comments are noted elsewhere.

146. STUDENT (2) 1910-1930 Steel steamship rigged as two-masted schooner. Two decks and five holds.
O.N. 128024 3,580g 2,304n 5,988d 350.0 x 46.1 x 30.63 feet. Cargo capacity 316,550 cubic feet.
International Code: HQMG.
T. 3-cyl. by Dunsmuir and Jackson Ltd., Glasgow; 20, 34, 58 x 48 inches, 11 knots.

8.2.1910: Launched by Charles Connell and Co. Ltd., Scotstoun (Yard No. 332) for the company. *10.3.1910:* Delivered at a cost of £39,684. Later sailed from Liverpool to Mexico on her maiden voyage under Captain R. Richards. *7.10.1912:* In collision in the approaches to Cabedelo, Brazil, veered out of the channel and grounded in the shallows of Rio Paraiba. Later refloated, but ran hard again on English Bank. *27.10.1912:* After being lightened by jettisoning cargo was towed into deep water by two tugs, two trawlers and GLADIATOR (135). The cost of these operations and subsequent repairs was estimated at £18,000, borne by the company's own Insurance Account. Captain Evans resigned in the aftermath of these incidents. *4.1.1927:* Whilst loading for the West Indies at Plantation Quay, Glasgow, damaged by the Anchor Liner MASSILIA (5,156/02). The latter vessel was canting off Stobcross Quay across the river when inward bound from New York. She took a sheer, careered heavily into the STUDENT and stove in the plating on the port side in way of No.2 hold which began to make water. The cargo was rapidly discharged and the vessel entered dry dock for repairs. *20.2.1930:* Sold to Compagnie des Bateaux à Vapeurs du Nord (Société Anonyme de Gérance and d'Armement), Dunkirk, France for £13,402 and renamed LILLOIS. *16.8.1934:* Fire broke out in her cargo of nitrate when berthed at Boulogne. Some 280 tons of cargo was destroyed or damaged before the fire was extinguished. *12.9.1934:* Ran ashore off Oran when on passage from Algiers to Antwerp. Refloated after discharging some 150 tons of cargo into barges. *17.12.1942:* Taken over by German forces following their occupation of Vichy France. *28.3.1943:* Torpedoed and sunk by the British submarine TORBAY, two miles south of Cape Scalea, Italy.

Student anchored in the Mersey.

[J. and M. Clarkson]

147. INVENTOR (2) 1910-1932 Steel steamship rigged as four-masted schooner. Two decks and seven holds.
O.N. 131287 7,679g 4,917n 10,825d. 469.5 x 58.0 x 36.04 feet. Cargo capacity: 593,930 cubic feet.
International Code: HRPC.
Q. 4-cyl. by D. and W. Henderson and Co. Ltd., Glasgow; 25$\frac{1}{2}$, 36$\frac{1}{2}$, 52, 74 x 54 inches, 12$\frac{1}{2}$ knots.

4.8.1910: Launched by D. and W. Henderson and Co. Ltd., Glasgow (Yard No. 470) for the company. *9.1910:* Delivered at a cost of: £79,576. Later sailed from Glasgow to Galveston in ballast on her maiden voyage under Captain Robert Owen. *18.10.1910:* When homeward bound on her maiden voyage, rescued the crews of the Spanish schooners MARTA and HUGO. Serious difficulties had to be overcome during the work of rescue as a close approach to the stricken craft was impossible, but thanks to "courage, seamanship, and perseverance the crews were taken aboard without casualty." So read the citation in Captain Owen's Illuminated Vote of Thanks which accompanied the Silver Medal awarded by the Liverpool Shipwreck and Humane Society shortly afterwards. *14.8.1914:* Requisitioned by the Shipping Controller and served as a transport for the British Expeditionary Force. The retreat from Mons triggered an evacuation of the supply ports of Boulogne and Le Havre

and considerable quantities of military supplies had to be moved from Le Havre to the Loire and INVENTOR was one of the transports assigned to this task. In difficult circumstances, she safely navigated the Loire as far as Nantes, the largest ship ever to do so, where she discharged her cargo.[92] *10.1.1917:* Attacked by a German submarine in the Western Approaches, but returned fire so effectively that the attack was broken off. *4.1921:* While on passage from Fremantle to Durban, the coal bunkers were on fire for most of the time, but the fire was extinguished by the crew's own efforts before she arrived 30.4.1921 at Durban. *5.3.1930:* In collision with the motor tanker SHELL MEX 1 (927/15) off Dungeness, Kent. The tanker was on passage from the Hamble to Lynn with a volatile cargo of benzine and fortunately a potentially nasty incident was avoided. *19.5.1932:* Sold to Italian shipbreakers for £3,315. *21.6.1932:* Arrived at Genoa.

Inventor on trials in the Clyde (above) and dressed overall for Armistice Day at Savannah, Georgia (left). *[Upper: Glasgow University Archives DC101/1229]*

148. EXPLORER (2) 1910-1932 Steel steamship rigged as four-masted schooner. Two decks and seven holds.
O.N. 131295 7,608g 4,871n 11,290d 469.5 x 57.25 x 36.42 feet. Cargo capacity: 599,700 cubic feet.
International Code: HRSB.
Q. 4-cyl. by Dunsmuir and Jackson, Glasgow; 25½, 36½, 52, 74 x 54 inches, 13½ knots.

5.9.1910: Launched by Charles Connell and Co. Ltd., Scotstoun (Yard No. 335) for the company. *10.10.1910:* Delivered at a cost of £79,350. Subsequently sailed from Glasgow to New Orleans in ballast on her maiden voyage under Captain G. Goldman. *5.2.1917:* Sailed from Liverpool for Calcutta with general cargo. *6.2.1917:* At 17.05 torpedoed without warning when approximately seven miles south by east of the Fastnet Lighthouse. She was struck in the fore peak, breaching the collision bulkhead and flooding number 1 hold. *7.2.1917:* Arrived, unaided at Queenstown and lay there for about three weeks making temporary repairs. She then proceeded to Liverpool where cargo was discharged and spent four months in dry dock having the bow rebuilt.[93] *27.11.1930:* Laid up at Fowey. *13.5.1932:* Sold for £3,372 to shipbreakers at Genoa where she arrived 12.6.1932.

Above: *Explorer* heading up the Thames. She appears to have been at anchor, as a ladder has been rigged over the quarter for the Third Officer to read the draught. Below: *Explorer* in dazzle paint, with a gun prominent on her stern. *[A. Duncan and Laurence Dunn collection]*

149. SCULPTOR (2) 1911-1917 Steel steamship rigged as two-masted schooner. Two decks and five holds.
O.N. 131391 3,845g 2,470n 6,460d 365.2 x 47.1 x 29.75 feet. Cargo capacity: 323,740 cubic feet.
International Code: HTPG.
T. 3-cyl. by Dunsmuir and Jackson, Glasgow; 22, 37, 62 x 48 inches, 11½ knots.

12.9.1911: Launched by Charles Connell and Co. Ltd., Whiteinch, Glasgow (Yard No. 339) for the company. *20.10.1911:* Delivered at a cost of £45,712. Later sailed from Antwerp for South Africa on her maiden voyage under Captain R.H. Pugh. *26.10.1915:* Requisitioned by the Shipping Controller for the carriage of ammunition to Northern Russia, later serving as an Expeditionary Force Transport and a collier. *24.6.1916:* Ran ashore on Stroma Island in the Pentland Firth when bound north-about from Dundee to Liverpool. Subsequently refloated and 28.6.1916

arrived at Liverpool. *18.4.1917:* Torpedoed without warning by the German submarine U 53 (Kapitänleutnant Hans Rose) when on passage from New Orleans for Liverpool with a cargo of grain, steel and coffee. The vessel was abandoned and then shelled and sunk by the submarine in position 52.30N, 12.18W, 120 miles northwest by west of the Fastnet Rock. Three lifeboats containing 44 survivors were picked up by the naval vessels PEYTON, BLUEBELL and ACTON, and the survivors were landed in Ireland. One man lost his life.[94]

150. INYATI 1911-1912 Steel steamship rigged as two-masted schooner. Two decks and four holds. Two masts.
O.N. 106542 2,516g 1,600n 3,640d 310.7 x 40.2 x 26.75 feet. Cubic capacity: 140,437 cubic feet. Berths for 28 passengers (one class).
International Code: PMHC.
T. 3-cyl. by Hall, Russell and Co. Ltd. Aberdeen; 24½, 40½, 66 x 45 inches, 13 knots.

6.10.1896: Launched by Hall, Russell and Co. Aberdeen (Yard No. 301) for J. T. Rennie and Son, Aberdeen. *31.10.1896:* Ran trials. *1911:* Acquired by the company for £10,060 and employed on the Harrison-Rennie Line. *1912:* Sold to Compania Valenciana de Vapores Correos de Africa, Valencia, Spain for £13,968 and renamed M. BENLLIURE. *25.12.1915:* Sailed from Glasgow for Genoa with a cargo of coal, a crew of 45 and 28 passengers. *27.12.1915:* Distress signals were picked up from the vessel in a position 40 miles north west of the Scilly Isles but nothing further was heard of the ship, passengers or crew. *9.2.1916:* Posted missing.

INYATI was one of seven small passenger-cargo vessels purchased from John T. Rennie, managers of the Aberdeen Direct Line, towards the end of 1911. The service from London to South Africa continued to operate as the Harrison-Rennie Line until 1921. All the ships had Zulu names, retained by Harrisons, and adopted for future passenger vessels. They also retained their Rennie livery: dove-grey hull and buff funnel (except during

Inyati, part of Rennie's fleet acquired in 1911. *[J. and M. Clarkson collection]*

the war years) and Aberdeen remained their port of registry. INYATI means 'a buffalo' or a 'hefty fellow'.

151. INGELI 1911-1914 Steel steamship rigged as brigantine. Two decks and four holds.
O.N. 108651 2,928g 1,864n 4,215d 330.1 x 41.2 x 27.1 feet. Cargo capacity: 158,858 cubic feet. Berths for 38 passengers (one class).
International Code: PVJD.
T. 3-cyl. by Hall, Russell and Co. Ltd. Aberdeen; 25½, 42½, 69¼ x 45 inches, 12 knots.

28.8.1897: Launched by Hall, Russell and Co., Aberdeen (Yard No. 303) for J.T. Rennie and Son, Aberdeen. *5.11.1897:* Ran trials. *10.1911:* Acquired by the company for £14,005 and employed on the Harrison-Rennie Line. *2.1914:* Sold to Vaccaro Brothers and Co., Ceiba, Honduras for £14,971 and renamed TEGUCIGALPA. Subsequently registered under Tegucigalpa Steam Ship Corporation. *1924:* Company acquired by the Standard Fruit and Steamship Corporation, New Orleans. *1933:* Transferred to Standard Navigation Corporation (Standard Fruit and Steamship Corporation, managers), Ceiba, Honduras. *7.1941:* Sold to the Swiss War Transport Office (Honegger and Ascott, managers), Basle, Switzerland and renamed CHASSERAL. Employed, with the agreement of the warring nations, to

carry food and essential supplies for Swiss consumption.[95] *3.1947:* Sold to Nautilus S.A., Basle, Switzerland. *1951:* Sold to Franco Maresca, Genoa, Italy and renamed MAR CORRUSCO. *1953:* Sold to A.R.D.E.M. for demolition and arrived *19.11.1953* at Savona.

The Zulu name INGELI infers cold, snow or sleet.

Ingeli.
[World Ship Photo Library]

152. INSIZWA 1911-1913 Steel steamship rigged as two-masted schooner. Two decks and four holds.
O.N. 108673 2,984g 1,915n 3,965d 330.2 x 41.1 x 28.04 feet. Cargo capacity: 154,130 cubic feet. Berths for 40 first class and 20 second class passengers.
International Code: RJPW.
T. 3-cyl. by Hall, Russell and Co. Ltd. Aberdeen; 25½, 42½, 69¼ x 45 inches, 13 knots.

23.8.1899: Launched by Hall, Russell and Co. Ltd. Aberdeen (Yard No. 317) for J.T. Rennie and Son, Aberdeen. *24.10.1899:* Ran trials. *13.8.1909:* When passing Cape Agulhas signal station westbound, reported that four bodies had been seen off the Bashee River. This was about a fortnight after the Blue Anchor Liner WARATAH mysteriously disappeared between Durban and Capetown with 92 passengers and 119 crew. When interviewed at Capetown the master of INSIZWA was quite positive as to the sighting, describing some of his passengers as being, "in a state of excitement bordering on the hysterical" as the bodies floated past the ship. There was a heavy sea running and it was considered inadvisable to stop. Tugs were immediately despatched from East London, but nothing was ever found.[96] *9.11.1911:* Acquired by the company for £19,552 and employed on the Harrison-Rennie Line. *12.1913:* Sold to Societa Anonima di Navigazione Sicilia, Genoa, Italy for £22,067 and renamed TOLEMAIDE. *1926:* Transferred to Compagnia Italiana Transatlantica, Genoa. *4.1931:* Sold to shipbreakers at Savona. *6.4.1931:* Arrived.

Insizwa. The Zulu name denotes 'a young bachelor'.
[Martin Leendertz collection, Ship Society of South Africa, courtesy Peter Newall]

153. INKONKA 1911-1919 Steel steamship rigged as two-masted schooner. Two decks and four holds.
O.N. 109650 3,430g 2,206n 4,970d 368.0 x 45.1 x 27.75 feet. Cargo capacity: 215,110 cubic feet. Berths for 12 passengers (one class).
International Code: SDBR.
T. 3-cyl. by Central Marine Engine Works, West Hartlepool; 29, 46, 77 x 48 inches, 10 knots.

11.10.1900: Launched by William Gray and Co. Ltd., West Hartlepool (Yard No. 620) for the Anglo-Arabian and Persian Steam Ship Co. Ltd. (F.C. Strick and Co. Ltd., managers), Swansea as TABARISTAN. *11.1900:* Completed. *1902:* Sold to J.T. Rennie and Son, Aberdeen and renamed INKONKA. *12.1911:* Acquired by the company for £29,921 and employed on the Harrison-Rennie Line. *26.2.1915:* Requisitioned by the Shipping Controller and sailed from London carrying a Royal Flying Corp unit to Alexandria. Subsequently served in many theatres of war including the Dardanelles, France and Russia. *17.11.1917:* Ran ashore near Capo San Vito, near Taranto.

Inkonka. *[World Ship Photo Library]*

Italy. Although refloated some time later, repairs were not completed until 2.1918. *19.6.1919:* Sold to David MacIver and Co. Ltd., Liverpool for £75,165 and renamed TUSCANY. *11.7.1923:* Driven ashore on Atlantida Beach, near the mouth of the Solis Chico River, about 30 miles east of Montevideo. *29.1.1924:* Refloated and towed to Montevideo. *16.4.1924:* Temporary repairs completed, seaworthy

certificate issued, and resumed trading. *1929:* Sold to West of Scotland Shipbreaking Co. Ltd. for £7,700 for demolition and arrived 19.6.1929 at Troon.

The Zulu name INKONKA denotes a species of large buck or bush-buck.

A flaw in the terms of war-risk insurance?
On 14th November 1917, INKONKA sailed from Salonika for Taranto loaded with hospital stores, and carrying a few British troops as passengers. In common with most merchant ships on war service, INKONKA was operating on a T99 Charter drawn up with the Admiralty. On 15th she passed through the Corinth Canal, and set out across the Ionian Sea to Taranto. At this stage she was escorted by the destroyer PINCHER. The weather was stormy and overcast, with poor visibility, and the Master was obliged to navigate by dead reckoning until about 18.00 on 17th, when he was able to snap a set of star sights. From the resulting fix, he laid off the course for Taranto, and estimated the time of arrival to be shortly after 21.00. However, by 21.00 no shore lights were visible, leading Captain R.K. Barrow to conclude that they were either obscured by rain or mist, or extinguished to conform with war zone regulations - i.e. they

were only exhibited when ships were expected, and perhaps INKONKA'S imminent arrival had not yet been heralded. Whatever the reason, the situation called for caution, and Captain Barrow's native prudence prompted him to signal the escort Commander that he intended to stop and wait for daylight. But the destroyer Captain would have none of it, and urged him to carry on, following the pilot escort which had just come out to meet them. Much against his better judgment, Captain Barrow did as he was bid, as he was bound to do under the terms of the T99 Charter.

Suddenly, the pale glimmer of the pilot escort's stern light disappeared in a rain squall. Two minutes later a brilliant red light flashed close to on INKONKA'S port bow, and the helm was put hard-a-port to swing the ship clear. The red light was in fact the light on Capo San Vito standing in the approaches to Taranto Harbour, and which had apparently just been switched on. Even so, its characteristics did not conform to those described in the sailing directions given to the Master at Salonika. Meanwhile, though the ship's head was swinging rapidly to starboard, there was no room to escape, and INKONKA grounded on the off-lying rocks. She was eventually refloated and repaired, but it was three months before she was in any condition to put to sea again.

Naturally, the company at once put in a claim under the War Risk Insurance scheme, underwritten by the Government, which covered all those wartime risks not normally covered by a marine policy. However, the Admiralty repudiated the claim, insisting that the accident was due to a "marine risk", and thus covered by marine insurance. As Harrisons carried their own hull insurance in those days, it was important to get the decision reversed, so they took the matter to arbitration, claiming the INKONKA was operating under wartime conditions, and acting under naval orders. The arbitrator, however, took the view that the ship was not engaged in a "warlike operation", but was merely fulfilling her role as a merchant ship carrying cargo from one port to another, and the accident was such as might occur either in war or peace; i.e. it was a normal marine risk. He found the case proved in favour of the Admiralty.

Harrisons then appealed to the High Court, but Mr. Justice McCardie, giving his judgment on 30th July, upheld the arbitrator's ruling, and ordered the owners to pay costs.[97] The case is interesting when compared with that of the INSTRUCTOR, sunk in a war-time collision, normally a marine risk, but from which an opposite ruling in favour of the owners emerged. (See INSTRUCTOR (177)).

154. INKOSI (1) 1911-1918 Steel steamship rigged as two-masted schooner. Two decks and four holds.
O.N. 115582 3,576g 2,266n 4,590d 350.2 x 43.3 x 30.04 feet. Cargo capacity: 207,828 cubic feet. Berths for 80 first class and 50 second class passengers.
International Code: TRSQ.
T. 3-cyl. by Hall, Russell and Co. Ltd., Aberdeen; 26, 43, 70 x 48 inches, 12½ knots.

2.10 .1902: Launched by Hall, Russell and Co. Ltd., Aberdeen (Yard No. 361) for J.T. Rennie and Son, Aberdeen. *27.11.1902:* Ran trials. *1905:* Became the first vessel in the South African services to be fitted with Marconi's wireless-telegraphy. *12.1911:* Acquired by the company for £38,199 and employed on the Harrison-Rennie Line. *26.3.1918:* Sailed from Liverpool bound for Pernambuco with coal and general cargo. *28.3.1918:* Torpedoed by the German submarine U 96 (Kapitänleutnant Heinrich Jess) in the North Channel, approximately 14 miles and 118 degrees from the Mull of Galloway. The vessel remained afloat and was eventually sunk with gunfire. Three crew were lost.

The Zulu name INKOSI means 'a chief'

Inkosi. *[World Ship Photo Library]*

155. INANDA (1) 1911-1920 Steel steamship rigged as two-masted schooner. Two decks and four holds.
O.N. 118187 4,090g 2,607n 5,135d 370.05 x 46.2 x 30.08 feet. Cargo capacity 208,074 cubic feet. Berths for 82 first class and 55 second class passengers.
International Code: HBCL.
T.3-cyl. by Hall, Russell and Co. Ltd., Aberdeen; 26½, 44, 72 x 48 inches, 13½ knots.

5.6.1904: Launched by Hall, Russell and Co. Ltd., Aberdeen (Yard No. 379) for J.T. Rennie and Son, Aberdeen. *8.1904:* Completed. *9.1911:* Acquired by the company for £45,342 and employed on the Harrison-Rennie Line. *9.6.1920:* Sold to Ellerman's Wilson Line Ltd., Hull for £148,354 and renamed ORLANDO. Employed on their service between Hull and Norway. *21.12.1928:* Laid up at Hull. *7.1932:* Sold to T.W. Ward Ltd. for demolition. *11.7.1932:* Left Hull in tow for Briton Ferry. *20.7.1932:* Demolition began.

The Zulu name INANDA means 'a table-topped mountain'.

Inanda on trials. *[Glasgow University Archives DC101/0303]*

156. INTABA 1911-1927 Steel steamship rigged as two-masted schooner. Two decks and four holds. Isherwood construction. O.N. 129345 4,832g 3,063n 6,100d 386.1 x 48.2 x 30.62 feet. Cargo capacity: 244,550 cubic feet. Berths for 84 first class and 54 second class passengers.
International Code: HRTQ.
T. 3-cyl. by Hall, Russell and Co. Ltd., Aberdeen; 27½, 45½, 75 x 48 inches, 13 knots.

6.9.1910: Launched by Hall, Russell and Co. Ltd., Aberdeen (Yard No. 476) for J.T. Rennie and Son. Aberdeen. *10.1910:* Completed. *8.8.1911:* Acquired by the company for £72,073 and employed in the Harrison-Rennie Line. *2.10.1913:* Reported on fire in the English Channel, having left London earlier that day. Returned to London and docked 3.10.1913 but the damage was such that she was unable to sail again before 1.11.1913. *18.7.1915:* Requisitioned by the Shipping Controller and served subsequently in the Caribbean, Falkland Islands, Far East and also as a depot ship for destroyers of the Dover Patrol. *18.4.1916:* Taken over by the Admiralty for service as a decoy ship and given the pendant number Q2. Fitted with one 4-inch breech-loading gun, two 13- and two 12-pounders. She was also given the alias WAITOMO, but as this would have led to

Intaba in Harrison's colours. [Ambrose Greenway collection]

confusion with the Union Steam Ship Company of New Zealand's vessel of that name, the alias was changed to WAITOPPO. The purpose of the Q-ship was to lure an unsuspecting U-boat within range of its guns and then sink it. Success was, however, limited, only 11 submarines being sunk in this manner. A naval crew under a gunnery officer was placed on board, but she remained under the command of her Rennie master, Captain J.W. Watling, R.N.R. who was later awarded an O.B.E. Her career in this role was largely uneventful except for an inconclusive encounter with a U-boat near the Kola Inlet while patrolling the munitions route to Archangel.[98] *11.7.1917:* Decoy service ceased whereupon she resumed the Harrison-Rennie service to South Africa. *21.5.1921:*

Sailed from Capetown, the last Harrison-Rennie liner to leave South Africa. She was transferred to the London-West Indies passenger service which she operated with INGOMA (162). *17.5.1927:* Sold to H.M.H. Nemazee, Hong Kong for £18,414 and renamed ENGLESTAN. *1929:* Sold to Bengal Burma Steam Navigation Co. Ltd. (A.B. Chowdry. manager), Rangoon, Burma. *1950:* Sold to Scindia Steam Navigation Co. Ltd., Bombay, India. *8.1952:* Sold to Etablissements Van Heyghen Fréres, Ghent, Belgium for demolition and arrived 21.1.1953 at Ghent in tow from Vizagapatnam. *26.1.1953:* Demolition commenced.

The Zulu name INTABA means 'a counsellor'

157. BOTANIST (2) 1912-1920 Steel steamship rigged as four-masted schooner. Two decks and seven holds. O.N. 131419 7,688g 4,912n 10,900d 469.5 x 58.0 x 36.04 feet. Cargo capacity: 551,540 cubic feet.
International Code: HVGP.
Q. 4-cyl. by D. and W. Henderson and Co. Ltd., Glasgow; 25½, 36½, 52, 74 x 54 inches, 12½ knots.

When entering the Manchester Ship Canal, four masts meant there was a lot of work to do to remove the topmasts, not to mention the upper section of the funnel. This is *Botanist* in Manchester Docks: note the pole for the paravane. [Peter Newall collection]

7.12.1911: Launched by D. and W. Henderson and Co. Ltd., Glasgow (Yard No. 476) for the company. 1.1912: Delivered at a cost of £83,823. Later sailed from Liverpool to New Orleans on her maiden voyage under Captain G. Goldman. 6.8.1914: Requisitioned by the Shipping Controller. 20.3.1920: Sailed from Calcutta for London via Colombo with 8,909 tons of cargo. 25.3.1920: A fatal miscalculation put the vessel hard aground on Komuriya Reef on the east coast of Ceylon. All efforts to dislodge the vessel ended in failure. The company's DISCOVERER (163) on passage from Mauritius to Calcutta diverted to offer assistance but the wreck was beginning to break up and she resumed her voyage 28.3.1920. The crew had already departed the stricken vessel. 30.3.1920: Abandoned to the underwriters as a total loss. The Master, Captain Henry Bickerstaff, was dismissed upon his return to Liverpool.

Claims on the BOTANIST

In the months and years which followed the loss of the BOTANIST, many claims from ships and organisations which rendered assistance in some way had to be met or contested by management. Perhaps typical of the trend was the claim for salvage by the Henderson liner ARRACAN (5,525/11). Harrisons conceded £1,500 for services rendered, and cargo interests had paid a further £250. But Hendersons felt they deserved more, and took the matter to the High Court. The case was heard before Mr Justice Bailhache on Friday 29th June 1923. The steamer

ARRACAN, bound from Liverpool to Rangoon, responded promptly to a wireless message from BOTANIST calling for assistance. She arrived off the reef at 14.25 on 25th March, and at once made an attempt to tow the vessel off. The attempt failed when the tow rope parted. Captain Bickerstaff then requested ARRACAN to stand by until a tug arrived. On 26th, nine passengers were transferred to ARRACAN and carried to Colombo where preparations were in hand for a major salvage operation. ARRACAN was asked to take labour and equipment out to the reef. However, on 28th word came that BOTANIST was breaking up and all notions of salvage were abandoned. Only then did ARRACAN resume her voyage. Taking all the facts into consideration, including the amounts of cash already paid, the learned judge awarded ARRACAN a further £1,000 to be paid by the cargo underwriters, a disappointing figure from Henderson's point of view.

Botanist settles by the stern on a reef off Colombo, 25th March 1920.

158. BENEFACTOR (1) 1912-1935 Steel steamship rigged as two-masted schooner. Two decks and five holds.
O.N. 131439 5,511g 3,499n 8,440d Cargo capacity 446,475 cubic feet. 410.7 x 52.25 x 33.91 feet.
International Code: HVWQ (GQMZ after 1933).[99]
T. 3-cyl. by D. and W. Henderson and Co. Ltd., Glasgow; 24½, 42½, 72 x 54 inches, 13 knots.

22.4.1912: Launched by D. and W. Henderson and Co. Ltd., Glasgow (Yard No. 478) for the company. 24.5.1912: Delivered at a cost of £70,663. Later sailed from Liverpool

to Calcutta on her maiden voyage under Captain F.B. Atkinson. 4.7.1935: Sold for £9,108 to Italian shipbreakers. 5.9.1935: Arrived at Venice.

Benefactor.   *[A. Duncan]*

159. INTOMBI 1912-1932 Steel steamship rigged as two-masted schooner. Two decks and five holds.
O.N. 131443 3,884g 2,504n 6,437d 365.0 x 47.0 x 30.48 feet. Cargo capacity: 264,235 cubic feet.
International Code: HWGD.
T. 3-cyl. by Dunsmuir and Jackson Ltd., Glasgow; 22, 37, 62 x 48 inches, 11½ knots.

30.5.1912: Launched by William Hamilton and Co. Ltd., Port Glasgow (Yard No. 237) for the company as ACTOR. Renamed INTOMBI whilst fitting out. *4.8.1912:* Delivered at a cost of £46,925 for service on the Harrison-Rennie Line. Subsequently sailed to South Africa on her maiden voyage under Captain P.J. Jackman. *4.8.1914:* Requisitioned by the Shipping Controller and attached initially to the 1st Light Cruiser Squadron as a store ship based at Scapa Flow. *30.5.1930:* Laid up at Preston. *22.1.1932:* Sailed for Birkenhead. *26.1.1932:* Sold to Maris A. Embiricos, Andros, Greece for £4,010 and renamed MALIAKOS. *13.9.1937:* Ran hard aground near Injeh Burnu, Marmara, Turkey, laden with 6,000 tons of grain. *16.9.1937:* Refloated with difficulty, assisted by two salvage tugs, HORA (593/85) and ALEMDAR (362/98). She then proceeded to Gelibolu (Gallipoli) for a survey. *21.12.1938:* Whilst moored at Braila on the Danube, with two lighters and a grain elevator alongside, the pressure of accumulating drift ice caused the vessel to burst her moorings and drift downstream. She lost both anchors and eventually came to rest in the mud of the right bank. Her anchors and chain were recovered 25.12.1938; she was refloated and returned to her berth, apparently none the worse for the experience. Loading resumed the following day and she sailed 29.12.1938 for Belfast. *23.12.1945:* Ran aground in position 55.19N, 13.15E, about four miles east of Trelleborg, Sweden when on passage from Casablanca to Gdynia with a cargo of phosphate. Water was leaking into number 1 hold and 950 tons of phosphate had to be jettisoned before she was refloated 28.12.1945. She made for Malmo where the remaining cargo was discharged, temporary repairs were effected and cargo was reloaded and the vessel sailed 7.2.1946 for Gdynia. *12.4.1946:* Dry docked at Frederickshavn, Denmark to make good the stranding damage. It was estimated that repairs would take 70 days, at a cost of £14,100. Altogether 18 plates were renewed; 41 removed, faired and replaced, and 30 faired in place. *26.7.1946:* Left the dry dock. *5.8.1946:* Sailed for the Tyne. *1949:* Sold to Ibrahim Kalkavan, Istanbul, Turkey and renamed SARAYKÖY. *26.1.1951:* Sailed from Antwerp fully loaded for Tel Aviv and ran aground in the River Scheldt off Oudendijk. *27.1.1951:* Refloated. *28.1.1951:* Returned to Antwerp. Surveyors anticipated extensive bottom damage and insisted on all cargo being discharged before dry docking for inspection and repairs. Following repairs, cargo was reloaded. *4.5.1951:* Sailed for Tel Aviv. *1954:* Sold to Sapanca Vapuru Isletmesi (Sevket Manioglu ve Naci Ucler), Istanbul, Turkey, and renamed SAPANCA. *28.2.1956:* Whilst on passage from Antwerp to Istanbul with a cargo of fertiliser and chalk and still negotiating the River Scheldt, was struck on the starboard side by the outward bound Holland-Amerika liner BLOMMERSDYK (6,855/22). The vessel's side in way of numbers 1 and 2 holds was ruptured; the holds quickly flooded and she sank, with her masts, funnel and upperworks still above the water. The incident occurred at about 15.30 in the Schaar van de Noord, off Bats. Survivors

Three stages in the career of *Intombi*. Top: running trials on the Clyde in Rennie's colours; middle: in Harrison livery arriving at Preston to lay up on 25th May 1930; bottom: revisiting the Mersey in Greek ownership as *Maliakos*.

[Top: Peter Newall collection; others: J. and M. Clarkson]

were picked up by BLOMMERSDYK and also OSIRIS (3,004/55) and landed at Hansweert. Although just outside the channel, the wreck was considered a hindrance to navigation and, since no tenders for salvage were taken up, plans were put in train to dispose of the wreck with explosives.

The Zulu name INTOMBI means 'a young maiden' or 'sweetheart'

160. DIPLOMAT (1) 1912-1914 Steel steamship rigged as four-masted schooner. Two decks and seven holds.
O.N. 131457 7,615g 4,873n 11,290d. 469.7 x 57.25 x 36.5 feet. Cargo capacity: 537,920 cubic feet.
International Code: HWQM.
Q. 4-cyl. by Dunsmuir and Jackson Ltd., Glasgow; 25½, 36½, 52, 74 x 54 inches, 13½ knots.

15.8.1912: Launched by Charles Connell and Co. Ltd., Scotstoun (Yard No. 347) for the company. *2.10.1912:* Delivered at a cost of £89,385. Later sailed from Liverpool for Calcutta on her maiden voyage under Captain R.J. Thomson. *13.9.1914:* Encountered the German commerce raider EMDEN at about 15.30 in the Bay of Bengal. The vessel was captured and after the crew had been taken off and transferred to the prison ship KABINGA (4,657/07), she was blown up with explosive charges and sank in position 17.55N, 86.45E i.e. 86 degrees and 198 miles from Vizagapatnam. DIPLOMAT was the largest and most valuable of the raider's 24 victims, having an insured value of £81,000 and carrying 7,000 tons of cargo estimated to be worth £250,000.[100] Next day, KABINGA was released with her load of prisoners and reached Calcutta safely on 16.9.1914. Eventually Captain Thomson, Chief Officer S.S. Trickey and most of the crew made their way to Colombo to take over the captured German merchant ship FÜRTH (4,229/07) and sail her to London.

161. ARCHITECT (2) 1912-1933 Steel steamship rigged as two-masted schooner. Two decks and five holds.
O.N. 135428 5,421g 3,415n 8,455d. 410.6 x 52.35 x 34.2 feet. Cargo capacity: 366,510 cubic feet.
International Code: JBHG.
T. 3-cyl. by Dunsmuir and Jackson Ltd., Glasgow; 24½, 42½, 72 x 54 inches, 12½ knots.

12.11.1912: Launched by Charles Connell and Co. Ltd., Scotstoun (Yard No. 349) for the company. *20.12.1912:* Delivered at a cost of £71,293. Later sailed from Liverpool to the Spanish Main on her maiden voyage under Captain W.N. Neilson. *16.5.1914:* Sailed from Seattle and arrived at Cardiff 55 days later on 10.7.1914, completing a remarkable non-stop passage round Cape Horn, during which the vessel steamed 14,338 miles and consumed about 2,800 tons of coal. *6.8.1914:* Requisitioned by the Shipping Controller and frequently chartered to the French Government, running between New England and Virginian ports and ports in Western France and the Mediterranean carrying stores for the Allied armies. *6.5.1916:* Grounded in Barry Roads but refloated the same day and dry docked at Newport. Salvage attracted an award of £9,000. *9.3.1918:* Beached in the Tergrieuse Channel, Quiberon Bay, after striking a rock when inward bound for St. Nazaire from New York. Numbers 1 and 4 holds became flooded and at high water the fore deck was awash. The French Naval Command inspected the casualty the next day. *25.3.1918:* Refloated and towed to St. Nazaire for preliminary repairs. *28.4.1918:* Sailed for West Hartlepool. *10.5.1918:* Dry docked and spent the next three weeks there completing repairs. *25.7.1927:* Rendered assistance to the Belgian steamer SCHELDESTAD (4,889/01) which had run out of coal 23.7.1927 some 130 miles east of Aden. ARCHITECT put a towing line aboard and towed the vessel into Aden. *29.10.1933:* Sailed from Brunswick Dock, Liverpool at 07.00 bound for Nassau, Kingston, Belize and Mexico with 3,466 tons of cargo on board, much of it heavy machinery. Still in the care of tugs, and swinging into the fairway, she ran aground on the Pluckington Bank. Initially four tugs failed to refloat the vessel and an inspection at low water when the ship was practically high and dry revealed several badly damaged plates. However, tugs succeeded in refloating the vessel at high water that same evening, but as she was being towed clear, a sudden rush of water into number 3 hold, engine and boiler spaces put her in danger of sinking in deep water and she was hastily grounded on the bank again. The tide was now falling and as the water drained away the ship was found to be supported by sandbanks at bow and stern, and unsupported amidships. Consequently, at 22.00 the ship broke her back and the onset of a period of stormy weather contributed to her destruction.

Architect at Cape Town.

[A. Duncan]

The end of ARCHITECT

At 09.00 on 30th Liverpool dockers began discharging cargo from all hatches of ARCHITECT. Captain Isaac Mowat and his crew were taken off that day, but the work continued - at least during lulls in the persistent bad weather - and by 3rd November, despite the ship physically breaking up, some 900 tons of cargo had been recovered. On 12th December the vessel was officially declared a total loss, but cargo was still being salvaged by Mersey Docks and Harbour Board. Three weeks after the disaster, Captain Mowat, aged 59, was retired on pension. Formerly employed by John T. Rennie, he had been Master since 1918. He died in 1953. The Pilot, a Dock Board man called J. Kirkpatrick, probably bore much of the blame, and was, in fact, reduced to Second Class status for a period of nine months. Finally, the ship was written off in the sum of £2,852 - a sad reflection on the depressed value of ships at that time. The three photographs show stages in her disintegration.

[Two lower photographs: J. and M. Clarkson]

Ingoma running trials in Rennie's colours, but note how the steel bands for Harrison's colours are visible on the funnel.

[Peter Newall collection]

162. INGOMA 1913-1937 Steel steamship rigged as two-masted schooner. Two decks and five holds.
O.N. 135475 5,686g 3,566n 6,910d 400.5 x 52.25 x 32.08 feet. Cargo capacity: 285,520 cubic feet. Berths for 114 passengers (one class).
International Code: JCNL (GQMY after 1933).
T. 3-cyl. by D. and W. Henderson and Co. Ltd., Glasgow; 26½, 46, 76 x 54 inches, 13 knots.

22.4.1913: Launched by D. and W. Henderson and Co. Ltd., Glasgow (Yard No. 483) for the company. *3.7.1913:* Delivered at a cost of £103,888 for service on the Harrison-Rennie Line. Later sailed from London to South Africa on her maiden voyage under Captain F. Baker. *22.8.1914:* Requisitioned by the Shipping Controller and employed on various transport services, including work for the French and Serbian Governments. *30.1.1916:* Engaged in a running fight with a German submarine off Alexandria and thrice mentioned in despatches. *4.5.1921:* When outward bound from London to the West Indies, with a full complement of passengers, fire broke out in number 1 hold. *5.5.1921:* Put into Falmouth where the fire was extinguished 7.5.1921 by flooding the hold. The seat of the fire was in the orlop deck and some deck plating was buckled by the heat. The damaged cargo was unloaded and the ship cleaned up by 15.5.1921 when she sailed for Barbados. *7.1928:* During a voyage from Antigua to London, the Master, Captain R.K. Barrow, became seriously ill, and a call was sent out for

oxygen and acknowledged by the Eagle Oil tanker SAN ZOTICO (5,582/19). The two vessels agreed to a rendezvous and a boat was sent across to receive the oxygen. Unfortunately Captain Barrow failed to recover and died 15.7.1928, aged 51. He was buried at sea. Thereafter, Harrison line passenger ships always carried a cylinder of oxygen amongst the medical stores. *16.10.1937:* Sold to Compania Ligure di Navigazione, Genoa, Italy for £30,096 and renamed SAN GIOVANNI BATTISTA. *31.1.1942:* Torpedoed by British aircraft in position 33.47N, 12.17E whilst on a voyage from Italy to Tripoli. *2.2.1942:* Stranded 2 miles west of Tagiura after towline broke, subsequently refloated and towed to Tripoli. *19.1.1943:* Scuttled by Italian forces in the harbour entrance at Tripoli in order to avoid capture by the advancing British Eighth Army. Refloated by British salvors and subsequently scrapped

The Zulu name INGOMA denotes 'a song' or 'a hymn'

Ingoma, now in Harrison colours, off Tilbury in September 1923.

[Laurence Dunn collection]

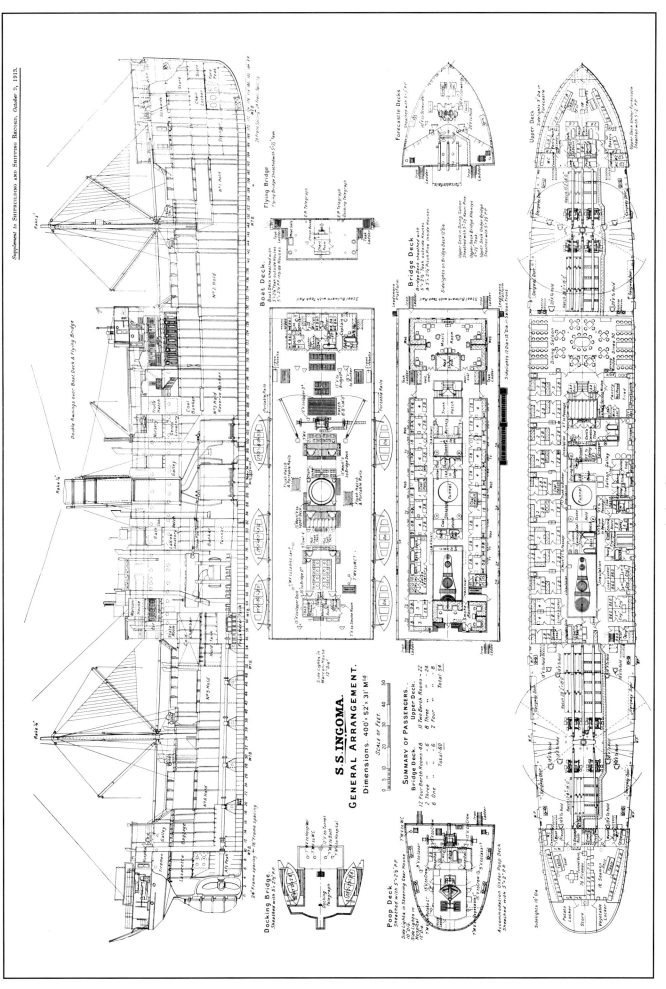

A plan of *Ingoma*.

A fortnight in the life of HM Transport G 1068[101]

In January 1916 INGOMA was serving the Allied cause as HM Transport G 1068 under the command of Captain A.B. Nicholas. A typical voyage began in London when she sailed on 14th January, bound for Plymouth to embark troops. Details of the voyage were recorded in a diary kept by Third Officer Reggie Phillips. After some delay anchored in the Downs, the ship duly arrived in Plymouth Sound at midday on the 16th and later berthed at the Admiralty Wharf, Devonport.

Next day, INGOMA shifted to the Embarkation Wharf, berthing astern of the new battleship ROYAL OAK, which was fitting out and nearing completion. At 07.00 the troops began embarking. Units from the Bedfords and Norfolks followed elements of the Essex Regiment and Royal Army Service Corps up the ship's gangways, loaded with kit and exchanging raucous badinage, dispersing throughout the ship in search of their allotted berths.

At 13.00 the last man was aboard. There were 27 officers and 1,069 other ranks, all under the command of Staff Officer Major Temperley. The mooring gangs appeared, tugs made fast fore and aft, the last lines were cast off. Once clear of the harbour, the pilot clambered over the side into the waiting dinghy and the ship gathered way, swinging through a wide arc onto a course for Ushant. With sirens wailing, two torpedo boats sped past, one on either side, slowing down and taking station on each bow to escort INGOMA down channel.

An oppressive air of dismal reality quickly descended upon the vessel as she headed southwest into the teeth of a rising gale. For the next three days the ship laboured across the Bay of Biscay as a thousand stomachs rebelled violently and a thousand anxious soldiers fervently wished they were back in barracks on Salisbury Plain, or even in the trenches in Flanders' fields - anywhere but in the rolling, heaving, lurching, wretched INGOMA.

On 21st the weather moderated; officers and men trickled back to the saloon and mess decks to show a reviving interest in food. Another day and the discordant sounds of singing and laughter emanating from the soldiers' quarters was a good sign, indicative that morale was being quickly restored. Cape Spartel was sighted at 11.00 on the 23rd and that evening INGOMA passed through the Straits of Gibraltar, cleared for Alexandria, where the troops would disembark.

The next several days were uneventful. The weather was fine and boredom was allayed by several encounters with passing ships of all types: patrolling cruisers and destroyers; hospital ships; sister transports; and on one occasion a barquentine, the ISSALT of Caernarvon, in full sail. Throughout the voyage lifejackets were worn at all times and crew and troops alike slept fully dressed. Submarine warnings came frequently over the wireless and on several occasions Captain Nicholas was obliged to make wide diversions to avoid particularly dangerous areas.

The ship touched in at Malta at noon on the 27th. Some cases of sickness were landed and that evening the troops proved to be an enthusiastic audience at a concert held on the after deck. All hands had a good night's sleep. The ship sailed at dawn steering a zigzag course through the most hazardous waters in the Mediterranean. That night and the following day distress calls from ships shelled or torpedoed by U-boats came over the air waves but INGOMA, under orders, pressed on.

Sunday 30th January 1916 dawned bright and clear. The crew were closed up to action stations, dawn and dusk being favoured times for enemy U-boat attacks. And there she was, at 06.30, bold as brass, sitting on the surface two or three miles away on the port quarter - a U-boat! INGOMA must have presented an excellent target, silhouetted against the lightening eastern sky and the U-boat opened fire, her shots falling short. INGOMA's gun crew, already closed up, quickly loaded and trained their weapon, an ancient Japanese 4.7-inch breech-loader and returned fire with furious enthusiasm.

The Captain demanded more speed - and got it, volunteer soldiers eagerly trimming coal for the firemen labouring at the furnaces. A call for assistance went out on the distress frequency and the running fight continued for at least four hours. At 10.10 the welcome sight of a warship loomed over the horizon and at 10.45 the minesweeping sloop MIMOSA opened fire at extreme range. The U-boat captain evidently decided that the time had come to show discretion and promptly submerged. INGOMA, escorted by MIMOSA, carried on to Alexandria, there to be greeted by the local military hierarchy.

This action, inconclusive though it was, seems to have had an exhilarating effect upon all on board, not one of whom doubted the maxim evolved during the action that, "We'll get the beggar before he gets us!" A gun fight at sea did even out the chances of survival - a stealthy underwater torpedo attack gave no chance at all.

The INGOMA arrived at Alexandria at 10.00 on 31st January and Captain Nicholas duly made his report to the Senior Naval Officer. Reports were also sent to the Director of Trade Division at the Admiralty, which prompted "my Lords Commissioners" to express their approbation of the "skill and devotion to duty displayed by Captain Nicholas and the Officers and men under his command, on the occasion of their encounter with a hostile submarine".

INGOMA was mentioned in despatches on at least two other occasions, once in August 1916, when the French Commander-in-Chief, Mediterranean, had occasion to report to his Minister that INGOMA had "assisted in the most able fashion at the transport of the Serbian Army;" and again in October 1916, when the Commander-in-Chief, East Africa, expressed his appreciation of the "very great assistance rendered by you (Captain Nicholas) and also by the Chief Engineer (James Michie), Third Officer (R.F. Phillips), Fourth Engineer Officer (D. Ritchie) and Carpenter (L. Sanders) on the occasion of the loss of the Transport WISSMAN by fire recently".

The General Officer Commanding Land Forces also conveyed his "admiration of their conduct on that occasion, especially of Mr. Michie, Chief Engineer, who, at great personal risk, revisited the Engine Room".

Sadly, no further details of these incidents have come to light. However, on the vessel's return to the United Kingdom, a more practical token of appreciation - from the crew's point of view - came in the form of an extra month's wages paid to all hands. Whether it was paid by a generous Exchequer, or by a grateful owner, is not recorded, but it came out of the blue with the cautious proviso, "This gesture is not to be considered as establishing a precedent".

---

163. DISCOVERER (2) 1913-1935 Steel steamship rigged as two-masted schooner. Two decks and five holds.
O.N. 135528 5,409g 3,403n 8,415d. 410.0 x 52.45 x 34.21 feet. Cargo capacity: 454,410 cubic feet.
International Code: JDPS (GQNJ after 1933).
T. 3-cyl. by Dunsmuir and Jackson Ltd., Glasgow; 24½, 42½, 72 x 54 inches, 12½ knots.

19.10.1913: Launched by Charles Connell and Co. Ltd., Scotstoun (Yard No. 355) for the company. *11.12.1913:* Delivered at a cost of £80,178. Later sailed in ballast to New Orleans on her maiden voyage under Captain W.H. Rushforth. *10.1915:* When returning from North Pacific ports, transit of the Panama Canal was impeded by a fall of rock in the Culebra Cut. The master, Captain Rushforth, was faced with the dilemma of awaiting clearance or taking the limited bunker coal available and returning via the Straits of Magellan. There was insufficient time to cable the owners for advice and he made the decision to return via the Straits, eventually arriving at Liverpool 27.11.1915, within a few days of the Canal's reopening, his decision vindicated.[102] *18.6.1917:* Commissioned by the Admiralty for service as an Armed Escort Cruiser. The fore and after peak structures were strengthened and the vessel armed with four 6-inch guns and two 11-inch anti-submarine howitzers. Gun trials were conducted in Liverpool Bay from 7 to 11.7.1917 and were declared a success.[103] *11.12.1918:* Ran aground in the outer channel after leaving Brunswick, Georgia. She had been forced to manoeuvre in order to avoid an incoming vessel. *17.12.1918:* Refloated after lightening and sailed 20.12.1918 after reloading. *20.7.1933:* In collision with the steamer LONDON (1,499/21) in Blackwall Reach, River Thames. There were no casualties but DISCOVERER subsequently spent 10 days in dry dock at Middlesbrough for repairs. *1.10.1935:* Sold to Spanish shipbreakers for £6,899. *7.10.1935:* Arrived at Bilbao.

Discoverer in the Mersey.   [J. and M. Clarkson]

Discoverer's first master, W.H. Rushforth.   [Medrington's Ltd.]

164. DRAMATIST (1) 1914-1916 Steel steamship rigged as two-masted schooner. Two decks and five holds.
O.N. 135544 5,415g 3,404n 8,415d 410.1 x 52.35 x 34.21 feet. Cargo capacity 454,410 cubic feet.
International Code: JDVF.
T. 3-cyl. by Dunsmuir and Jackson Ltd., Glasgow; 24½, 42½, 72 x 54 inches, 12½ knots.

11.12.1913: Launched by Charles Connell and Co. Ltd., Scotstoun (Yard No. 356) for the company. *31.1.1914:* Delivered at a cost of £80,178. Later sailed from Liverpool to Mexico on her maiden voyage under Captain W.J. Harris. *7.1914:* The thrust shaft sheared when the vessel was on passage from Liverpool to Barbados. The engineers carried out temporary repairs on board, sails were rigged and she put into Fayal, Azores 7.8.1914. Major repairs were put in hand and 20.9.1914 the voyage was resumed. *18.12.1916:* Intercepted by the German commerce raider MÖWE and sunk with explosive charges 490 miles and 220 degrees from Flores, Azores, in position 33.15N, 37.44W. She was on a voyage from San Francisco via Panama and St. Lucia for the UK with 7,200 tons of foodstuffs.

The short-lived *Dramatist* with her funnel colours painted out.

165. NAVIGATOR (2) 1914-1932 Steel steamship rigged as two-masted schooner. Two decks and five holds.
O.N. 135575 3,798g 2,427n 6,315d 365.2 x 47.1 x 30.91 feet. Cargo capacity: 289,500 cubic feet.
International Code: JFLS.
T. 3-cyl. by Dunsmuir and Jackson Ltd., Glasgow; 23, 38.5, 64 x 48 inches, 11.5 knots.

25.3.1914: Launched by Charles Connell and Co. Ltd., Glasgow (Yard No. 358) for the company. *30.4.1914:* A piston rod overheated during trials and delivery was postponed by 48 hours. *2.5.1914:* Delivered at a cost of £60,375. Later sailed from Liverpool to Brazil on her maiden voyage under Captain J. Gaudie. *26.1.1916:* Requisitioned by the Shipping Controller whilst in Pernambuco, Brazil and employed on transport services. *29.12.1916:* In collision in the Downs when on passage from Dakar to London. Later docked at London but delayed until 11.4.1917 on account of extensive damage. *10.1917:* In collision in the River Thames, put back to London and extensively repaired.

13.2.1918: Returned to service and employed on "experimental work". This was in fact the fitting of anti-torpedo nets, the so-called 'Actaeon' type, devised by Captain Villiers R.N. The nets, which were suspended from the cargo derricks, were streamed in position and were intended to intercept the torpedo which would explode on impact with the mesh. *18.3.1918:* Torpedoed in the English Channel, 10 miles and 294 degrees from Portland Bill, in position 50.35N, 02.41W, by the German submarine UC 75 (Oberleutnant zur See Walter Schmitz). Although the nets stopped the torpedo, the explosion caused severe damage and temporary repairs were effected in Weymouth Roads. She then proceeded to Cardiff where cargo was discharged and she entered dry dock for repairs lasting four months. She was on passage from Middlesbrough and London for South Africa with general cargo. *10.11.1922:* Ran aground in dense fog, two miles south of Tampico, Mexico. Subsequently refloated with the aid of tugs, little damaged. *18.4.1926:* Returned to Liverpool 24 hours after sailing having suffered a broken main stop valve and a fire in the bunker coal. The fire was extinguished and the coal disposed of in three days, but some difficulty was experienced in replacing the stop valve and the voyage resumed 3.5.1926 to the West Indies. *8.11.1931:* Laid up at Fowey. *23.2.1932:* Sold to Maris A. Embiricos, Andros, Greece for £3,267 and renamed LACONICOS. *1933:* Renamed LACONIKOS. *21.4.1935:* When approaching the berth at Zeebrugge for bunkers, collided with the Norwegian steamer HANSI (1,028/21) which was moored at the breakwater. HANSI was badly holed in the starboard bow, while LACONIKOS sustained damage to her stem and bow plating. *2.1.1939:* Reported trapped by ice in the River Danube, near Braila, Romania. Subsequently freed by icebreakers one week later. *7.5.1943:* Torpedoed and sunk by the German submarine U 89

Navigator above at Galveston, and below in Greek ownership as *Laconikos* after 1935.
[Eric W. Johnson collection; A. Duncan, courtesy D. Whiteside]

(Kapitänleutnant Lohmann) in position 41.40N, 18.18W, about 434 miles and 274 degrees from Oporto. She was on passage from Takoradi to Ardrossan with a cargo of manganese ore and sunk in less than one minute. 23 seamen were lost, but 11 others were rescued by the escort vessel SHIPPIGAN.

---

166. SPECTATOR (1) 1914-1917 Steel steamship rigged as two-masted schooner. Two decks and five holds.
O.N. 135585 3,808g 2,435n 6,315d 365.15 x 47.1 x 30.91 feet. Cargo capacity: 289,500 cubic feet.
International Code: JFQP.
T. 3-cyl. by Dunsmuir and Jackson Ltd., Glasgow; 23, 38.5, 64 x 48 inches, 11.5 knots.

30.4.1914: Launched by Charles Connell and Co. Ltd., Scotstoun (Yard No. 359) for the company. *3.6.1914:* Delivered at a cost of £57,843. Later sailed from Liverpool to Brazil on her maiden voyage under Captain C. Netherton. *11.3.1917:* Approaching the waters off the southwest coast of Ireland, attacked by the German submarine U 44 in position 50.59N, 15.53W, whilst on passage from Dakar to Liverpool with 6,000 tons of general cargo. She responded with her defensive armament, several hits were observed and the submarine was later reported sunk. The master and crew were subsequently awarded one month's pay by the company. *19.8.1917:* Torpedoed and sunk by the German submarine UC 33 (Oberleutnant zur See Alfred Arnold), 11 miles south east of Galley Head, County Cork, when on passage from Zanzibar to Liverpool with general cargo. The crew landed safely in Ireland.

The launch of SPECTATOR in April 1914 brought the shipowning enterprise of Thos. and Jas. Harrison to a new peak - 55 vessels of 278,916 gross tons. Thereafter, the devastation of war would reduce the fleet to such

proportions that it would never wholly recover, despite newbuilding and the wholesale acquisition of lesser fleets after the war. However, standards were maintained and progressively improved and overall an air of cautious optimism prevailed.

Salvage
An important constituent of SPECTATOR'S cargo was a large consignment of copper in bars and ingots and in 1934 the Italian salvage company Sorina undertook the salvage of the valuable commodity. In April that year the salvage vessels ARTIGLIO and ARPIONE dragged the sea bed off Galley Head and located the wreck lying in 47 fathoms. ARTIGLIO then returned to the site of the sunken P &O liner EGYPT, where Italian divers had been working since 1930 (and which eventually yielded a treasure worth £1,183,000 in gold bullion), leaving ARPIONE to reap what she could of SPECTATOR'S more mundane harvest of copper.

Between April and October 1934, ARPIONE recovered some 5,000 ingots weighing about 550 tons, worth over £1,000,000 at today's prices.

THE YEARS OF CONFLICT
1914 - 1945

In 1914 the nation's shipping industry was about to enter an extraordinary cycle, beginning with its virtual destruction, followed briefly by restoration, dipping into depression, and touching revival before descending once more into a welter of wanton destruction. This somewhat eccentric circle extended over three decades, and Part 4 will explore and analyse each phase and trace the history of the ships which appeared - and disappeared - during this convulsive period.

Thos. and Jas. Harrison Ltd., as we have seen, entered the First World War with a total of 55 ships amounting to almost 290,000 gross tons. This represented the peak of the company's attainments to date, but during the next four destructive years 27 ships were to be lost, 26 by direct enemy action and one by marine peril brought about by the exigencies of war. At first, human losses within the company were light, only seven lives being lost during the first 28 months of war, despite 11 ships having been sunk by the enemy. In 1917-18, however, after the Kaiser had given the order for unrestricted submarine warfare, 15 ships were sent to the bottom and 107 seafarers died. The most serious losses occurred when the ARTIST (144 - 35 lost) and BARRISTER (183 - 30 lost) were sunk.

From the beginning every effort was made to maintain some sort of service in Harrisons' traditional liner trades, although most of the liner conferences, many of which included German companies, had become disorganised. It was not easy, for the Government needed ships, many ships, to transport troops and supplies overseas, and did not hesitate under the wide emergency powers at its disposal to take over whatever ships were available, some permanently, others on short leases.

At this time, Harrisons' London manager and partner, Mr. Ward, thought he could see a way of maintaining links in East Africa, and late in 1914 he persuaded the company to purchase and register in his name two South American coasters then lying at Cardiff. Frank Ward was a large man, greatly respected throughout the City. He was expansive, with a tendency to leave fine detail to his staff, and had a broad sense of humour. Once, when the Liverpool office asked him to send Eric Carter Braine, his promising young assistant, up north, he replied with some asperity, "Nonsense; Brains are required in Dock House every bit as much as in Mersey Chambers!"[104]

Ward was a great favourite of his patron, John W. Hughes, a fact which was resented somewhat by his sons, Jack and Harry, especially since their father seemed to delight in making unflattering comparisons between them and his protégé. It was Ward's intention to operate a feeder service between Beira and Chinde on behalf of the Clan-Hall-Harrison joint service. Cargo at that time was mainly railway and bridge-building material for Nyasaland, for which Chinde was the port. As ocean-going ships could not get into Chinde, the cargo would be trans-shipped at Beira and carried to Chinde in the coasters, which were named PEMBA (170) and MAFIA (171). Before 1914, the trade had been carried by German coasters, but these had melted away since the outbreak of war, leaving a convenient vacuum to be filled. The service operated until 1921, when the ships were sold, not without feelings of relief all round, for the service had become fraught with problems, mechanical and personal, and the completion of the railway across the Zambesi River made the trade no longer economic.[105]

The close of 1917 saw the fleet reduced to 40 vessels, including the coasters, aggregating 204,000 gross tons. There developed within the company an urge to replace its lost tonnage. Building was not practicable for the yards were overwhelmed with war work, and ships ordered in 1914 were still behind schedule. Besides, prices were escalating dramatically. In 1914 the average cost of building a new Harrison ship was about £15 per gross ton. In 1915 the price remained steady while pre-war contracts were honoured. By 1917, however, the price had increased to around £17.25 and in 1918 to £21 per ton, an increase of 40% on pre-war prices. It was, of course, destined to rise much higher, but 1918 was seen as a crucial year. Harrison then decided to purchase existing tonnage, and towards the end of 1917 entered into negotiations with Rankin, Gilmour for the purchase of 12 Saint Line ships totalling some 61,000 tons, and having an average age of five years. This undertaking proved to be John William Hughes' final major enterprise before his death on 20th November 1917. However, at an average £30 per gross ton, the ships did not come cheaply, and three were lost within a few months of purchase, but at least the surviving ships placed the company on a firmer footing, ready for the post-war boom which everyone expected.

Eric Carter Braine (1898-1998), Director and Vice Chairman. photographed when a young artillery office in January 1919.

For there was a general assumption that a defeated Germany could be made to pay for the ravages wrought by war, rebuild the shattered cities and farms of eastern France, replace the sunken fleets of ships, and renovate depleted industry. These assumptions were given substance by politicians like Sir Eric Geddes who vowed to "squeeze Germany till the pips squeaked".[106] Few people of influence dare suggest that Germany's coffers might be empty and could not be squeezed. So far as shipowners were concerned, the Government compensated them for their losses in quite generous terms. The Harrison Line was granted £3 million, which was more than the purchase value of the ships lost by enemy action. However, it scarcely

Top: Rankin, Gilmour's *Saint George* of 1914, acquired by Harrisons to become the *Statesman* (181). *[G.R. Scott collection]*

Middle: Bought from Prentice, Service and Henderson Ltd. *Crown of Castille* of 1907 became *Candidate* (191). *[Ivor Rooke collection]*

Bottom: Scrutton's *Sargasso* became Harrison's *Scientist* (197). *[Peter Newall collection]*

matched the replacement cost of 27 vessels on which Harrisons were to spend £4.8 million between 1918 and 1920.

After the Armistice, requisitioned ships were returned to their owners, and promptly set about their rightful work, loading exports for India, South Africa, and the West Indies as fast as factories could produce them, and returning with raw material for further production. The boom seemed to be on. To meet the demand Harrison in 1920 augmented their fleet with eight ships acquired from the Crown Line of Glasgow, managed by Prentice, Service and Henderson Ltd., and another five from Scruttons Ltd. Both these companies had been associated with Harrison in the pre-war West Indian Transatlantic Conference, and had extensive trading links in the region which were of vital importance to the new owner. However, these vessels were even more expensive than Rankin, Gilmour's ships, costing £43 per gross ton in the case of Crown Line, and £45 in the case of Scruttons. The ships were older, too, averaging 12³/₄ years and 8¹/₂ years, respectively. A new vessel launched in August 1920, the DRAMATIST (201), cost the company £52 per gross ton.

These were expensive investments, and demonstrated Harrisons' confidence and faith in the future. They were, however, a little misplaced, for to everyone's astonishment the post-war boom faded after little more than a year. During the past four years, while the European industrial powers were settling their differences, the neutral countries of the world had had to fend for themselves, establishing their own industries in mining, textiles, steel, shipbuilding and shipping, while oil was beginning to replace coal, Britain's primary export. Moreover, after Versailles it became clear that German reparations would be nowhere near the fond expectations of their former antagonists. Western statesmen (with the notable exception of the French, who despatched an army to occupy the Ruhr and divert all production westwards into France and Belgium) became worried lest the enforcement of the draconian measures demanded by the treaty would drive the German nation into the Bolshevik camp. So demand fell; factories eased down; coal piled up at the pitheads. Soon, too many ships were chasing too little cargo, for in many countries the inclination - and indeed the ability - to buy in European and American markets had waned. Ships tied up in the docks, sterling plummeted and Western Europe braced itself for a slump. Measures to prevent the devaluation of the pound simply exacerbated the situation.[107]

Consequently, Harrisons, along with many more shipowners, found themselves with more tonnage on their hands than they required and forthwith placed their excess tonnage on the market for whatever price it would fetch, in practice between £2 and £3 per gross ton. Between 1921 and 1923 three small vessels and nine ocean-going ships, most of them more than 20 years old, left the fleet - two of them to the breaker's yard. During the same period four new vessels were delivered from the builders. Even so, for most of the decade, the number of units in the fleet hovered between 48 and 51 and although some were laid up from time to time the rest managed to keep trading regularly. But worse was to come.

In the USA, the stock market crash of October 1929 signalled the onset of worldwide economic depression. Among the means adopted by an almost frantic Washington administration to contain the situation was by raising tariffs on imports to punitive levels. The rest of the world found they could not sell their goods in the huge US market, and raised their own tariffs to keep foreign goods out. The free flow of goods between nations dried up, industry wilted, unemployment rose, and the weakly revival of the last few years relapsed and all but died.[108]

The dire period between 1930 and 1933 saw 15 Harrison vessels sold off, and of the remainder 14 were laid up at various times, a few more than once, for months on end, sometimes years (see diagram below). In all, a total of more than 10,000 ship-days were lost, the equivalent of one ship being laid up for 27¹/₂ years. Seafaring employment was almost impossible to obtain, and many ships' officers who were laid off found they were not eligible for the dole - their earnings when in employment had been slightly above the threshold set to qualify for the National Insurance Scheme. To their credit, Harrisons did all they could to retain their sea-going staff, although the posts on offer were not all an ambitious young officer would wish for. Shipmasters might find themselves serving as ship-keepers aboard the company's vessels laid up at Fowey, Barrow or Preston; certificated ships' officers would return to their old ships to serve as quartermasters; cadets just out of their time and with a brand new Second Mate's Certificate in their pocket, would ship away as able seamen. It was a time of deep anxiety and frustration, but a job was a job, and any job was better than the dole - or no dole and selling matches.

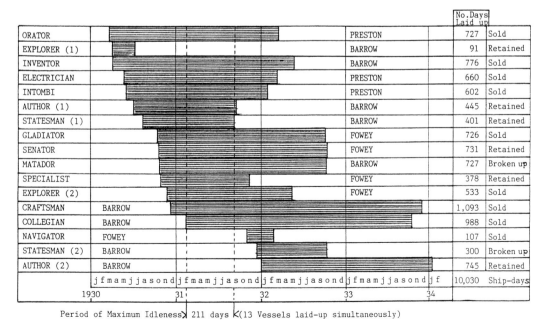

			No.Days Laid up	
ORATOR		PRESTON	727	Sold
EXPLORER (1)		BARROW	91	Retained
INVENTOR		BARROW	776	Sold
ELECTRICIAN		PRESTON	660	Sold
INTOMBI		PRESTON	602	Sold
AUTHOR (1)		BARROW	445	Retained
STATESMAN (1)		BARROW	401	Retained
GLADIATOR		FOWEY	726	Sold
SENATOR		FOWEY	731	Retained
MATADOR		BARROW	727	Broken up
SPECIALIST		FOWEY	378	Retained
EXPLORER (2)		FOWEY	533	Sold
CRAFTSMAN	BARROW		1,093	Sold
COLLEGIAN	BARROW		988	Sold
NAVIGATOR	FOWEY		107	Sold
STATESMAN (2)	BARROW		300	Broken up
AUTHOR (2)	BARROW		745	Retained
	jfmamjjasond jfmamjjasond jfmamjjasond jfmamjjasond jf		10,030	Ship-days
	1930 31 32 33 34			

Period of Maximum Idleness ⟩ 211 days ⟨ (13 Vessels laid-up simultaneously)

Harrison vessels laid up, 1930-1934.

115

Harrisons' traditional trades declined. The export of cotton from the Gulf suffered from tariff restrictions, and the availability of cheaper cotton from Egypt, the Sudan and Brazil. The export of cotton piece goods from Lancashire to India, a staple Harrison cargo, fell to a fraction of its pre-war peak, thanks to a boycott of British goods. To offset these blighted trades, the company plied the comparatively new trades to South and East Africa, to Brazil and the Caribbean, with single-minded determination.

The inauguration of the passenger service to the West Indies in 1921 was a success from the start - popular with passengers, reasonably profitable for the owners, and providing regular employment for the crews. It was also a lucky break. Apparently Royal Mail had withdrawn their traditional service after a disagreement with West Indian associates and a concerned Colonial Office had approached Harrison with a request to bridge the gap. The company complied by transferring the Rennie passenger ships from the South African service to the West Indies.[109]

Competition on all routes was keen and undoubtedly the conference system did provide some defence against ruinous competition, as amply illustrated by the demise of the Thomas Line in 1928. Denied membership of the South African Conference, Sir Robert Thomas operated some of his ships under the imposing title of the British and Continental South African Line. He advertised freight rates well below those charged by the conference lines.[110] By attacking the interests of established Lines like Union Castle, Ellerman, Clan, and Harrison, Sir Robert exceeded his resources. For the lines accepted the challenge, cut their rates, and initiated a freight war which was to last over a year. One of its effects was to disrupt shippers' carefully balanced schedules, particularly in the wool trade, and Sir Robert found his costs mounting when forced to charter tonnage to meet his commitments. He sought to bolster his position by tendering for the mail contract, which was due for renewal in April 1928. However, the South African Government ignored Sir Robert's inducements, and renewed its contract with Union-Castle Line. With the contract came a 10-year freight agreement which applied not only to Union-Castle but also to her partners in the Conference. This development virtually destroyed the Thomas Line's opposition, and their ships were withdrawn.

A similar forlorn adventure in the River Plate trade had also proved disastrous, and in April 1930 Sir Robert Thomas and his company were arraigned before the Bankruptcy Court. By 1932, the "Cambrian" names of the Thomas ships had disappeared from *Lloyd's Register*, but the war had been won at considerable cost, with some lines suffering more than others. In Harrisons' case, for instance, loss of earnings during the freight war had amounted to approximately £20,000.[111]

By 1934 world trade was showing an upturn. Harrison brought their surviving laid-up ships back into

Intombi (159), *Electrician* (180) and *Orator* (178) laid up at Preston.

[*World Ship Photo Library*]

Harrison ships laid up at Fowey in 1931. Farthest away are *Gladiator* (185) and the four-masted *Explorer* (148), in the foreground are *Senator* (172) and *Specialist* (200).

Dorelian (227), still in Leyland Line colours, sailing from Liverpool.

service and looked around for new tonnage. It so happened that J. P. Morgan's grandiose International Mercantile Marine Corporation was divesting itself of some of its less profitable European companies, among them the Leyland Line. Harrison bought seven of the ships at the bargain price of £203,000. With the ships came the goodwill of the Gulf of Mexico trade in which they were involved - a matter of greater import to Harrisons than the ships themselves.

Also in 1934-35 increased competition in the South African trade prompted management to seek out means of combating it. They needed a few bigger and faster ships. Their attention was drawn to four identical Prince Line ships laid up in an Essex backwater since 1930. These vessels were reputably fast, oil-fired, turbine-driven, and capable of lifting 11,000 tons deadweight, ideal for the Cape service. Despite their long sojourn in mothballs, they were said to be in very good condition, although a luxuriant carpet of grass and weed now covered their bottom plating. Some tentative enquiries were put to Furness Withy, the owners.

Statesman (237), the former *British Prince,* in the Mersey on 20th June 1936.

[J. and M. Clarkson]

The story is told how management was prodded towards its decision by Lord Essendon himself, Chairman of Furness Withy. As an inducement, he offered to lend one of the ships for a round voyage to South Africa, provided Harrisons covered her for insurance. It was an offer Sir T. Harrison Hughes could not refuse and on 2nd February 1935 the BRITISH PRINCE sailed on her promotional voyage. She returned to Glasgow in May, where Harrisons bought her and changed her name to STATESMAN. Sir Harry also agreed to buy her three sisters, at a total cost of £123,000. Although dry docking and cleaning added another £55,000 to the bill, it was still a very good bargain. In fact, it was a better bargain than anyone realised, for in 1940, when the ships were requisitioned under the Government's emergency powers, Harrisons were paid the universally agreed fee of 10% of the prime cost which Furness Withy confirmed was in the region of £500,000 for each vessel. Thus a tidy sum was realised, somewhat in excess of the price paid by Harrisons![112]

Throughout the inter-war period, Harrisons had continued to carry their own hull and equipment insurance, regular premiums being paid into a special insurance account on behalf of each ship, usually a percentage of voyage profits. As a rule, the account was quite healthy, so much so that it was often used to finance the purchase of new vessels. As an incentive to avoid incidents which might lead to claims on the Insurance Account, masters and officers were paid a safe navigation bonus at the end of each trouble-free accounting year - a welcome addition to salaries. However, it was a source of much contention at times. For one thing, it was not paid to engineer officers, who were inclined to see it as preferential treatment of deck officers. For another, the bonus was automatically cancelled for all if the slightest mishap causing damage occurred, and the unhappy perpetrator of the misdeed would find he had become enormously unpopular. Many an annual bonus was wiped out on "docking day", when a misplaced fender resulted in a dent in the ship's side.

In October 1935, as the rest of the fleet was slowly recovering from the ravages of the slump, a sad milestone was reached. After 99 years of Harrison involvement in the Charente brandy trade the last of the "brandy-boats", the venerable COGNAC (127), sailed from Tonnay-Charente for the last time. The trade was no longer economic, though Harrison/Williamson brandy would continue to be carried by a chartered steamer, the ARDGARROCH (968/18), for a further eight months. Thereafter, parcels of Harrison cargo would be carried from Charente in Moss Hutchison ships by special arrangement.

From 1937 until the outbreak of war, seven splendid ships were delivered, five of them from Lithgow's new East Yard at Port Glasgow. However, the number of ship sales continued to outstrip deliveries so that when the Second World War broke out on 3rd September 1939 the Harrison Line mustered 45 ships with a total gross tonnage of almost 275,000 tons. The company's first war casualty was the four-masted HUNTSMAN (203), homeward bound from Calcutta. The ship entered the Red Sea on the day Britain declared war on Germany, 3rd September, called at Port Sudan, then instead of heading north for the Suez Canal, a peremptory order from the Admiralty turned her round, sending her home via the Cape of Good Hope. It was while she was on the Durban/Freetown leg of this extended voyage that the ship ran into the formidable arms, or armament, of the German pocket-battleship, ADMIRAL GRAF SPEE on 10th October 1939.[113] HUNTSMAN was destined to be the first of 31 Harrison victims of guns, torpedoes, bombs, mines and marine peril which came to pass during the next five years. Although the number of ships sunk by enemy action - 27 - was just one more than in the First World War, the loss of life was four times greater. During this traumatic period 424 seafarers were to lose their lives in Harrison vessels, a mortality rate of 20%, or one crew member in five. A further 409 (19%) were wounded and/or taken prisoner, so the chances of surviving the war at sea unscathed were a slim three-to-two on, and for those in a ship sunk by the enemy, there was only a slightly better than even chance of escape. Ironically, the odds in the armed forces were rather better, unless one happened to be a Russian or German soldier. (See Appendix 4, Table 4.5).

As in 1914, all merchant vessels quickly came under Government control. Commercial voyages were implemented when and wherever possible, using own or chartered tonnage, but Government cargoes of war supplies and foodstuffs for the home front took priority. At the

The coaster *Ardgarroch* was chartered from P. MacCallum and Sons Ltd. for the brandy trade in 1935.

[J. and M. Clarkson]

117

beginning of the war the Government organised the setting up of a Ministry of Shipping to control maritime affairs by a system of licences. This was scrapped six months later in favour of a Ministry of War Transport established to co-ordinate transport by road, rail and sea. Licensing was discontinued and separate divisions were formed to control tramp and liner shipping. It came to pass that Thomas Harrison Hughes, Chairman of Thos. and Jas. Harrison Ltd., was appointed Director of the Liner Division, but even he was taken aback when the Government announced its decision to requisition the entire British merchant fleet. He was also Vice-President of the Suez Canal Company, having been elected in July 1932, in succession to Lord Inchcape. When France collapsed in the summer of 1940, the French President of the Suez Canal Company sided with the Vichy Government, a circumstance which prompted the British Government to recognise Harrison Hughes as the *de facto* President, an onerous position since the Canal was to remain in British hands throughout the war.

This unexpected honour gave Harry Hughes some cause for alarm. He could visualise endless litigation in French courts after the war if any of his decisions failed to please the French. He therefore demanded and got a form of indemnity from Anthony Eden himself to the effect that the British Government would accept full responsibility for his actions. After a few weeks, however, Harrison Hughes decided he could not carry out both jobs effectively and resigned his position as Director of the Liner Division in favour of Sir William Currie, Chairman of P. & O.[114] He was then free to concentrate on matters relating to the strategically important Suez Canal and, of course, the affairs of Thos. and Jas. Harrison. It was probably no coincidence that Captain S. Fulford, R.N.R., Harrisons' Dock Superintendent in London, was appointed Sea Transport Officer, Port Said, in March 1940.

The convoy system was instituted at first in home waters, but was quickly extended into the eastern Atlantic as a result of U-boat strikes well to the west of the British Isles. While the so-called phoney war was in progress on land and in the air, the war at sea became a grim and desperate struggle from the start, with the sinking of ATHENIA on day one. Between 3rd September 1939 and 9th April 1940 (the day Hitler's armies invaded Denmark and Norway, bringing the phoney war to a violent end) 154 British merchant ships totalling 673,711 gross tons, and 14 Royal Navy vessels were sunk by enemy action.[115]

As hostilities wore on, and maritime casualties mounted, replacement tonnage came down the ways as fast as human ingenuity and industry could produce them. On the British side of the Atlantic the Empire types of freighter were launched; from Canada came the similar Fort and Park type; and later, in US shipyards, the magnificent Liberty ship programme materialised, soon to be supplemented by the faster, larger Victory type. During the war Harrisons operated four Empires and two Liberties for the Ministry of War Transport, the nominal owner. These and many other standard vessels were bought by Harrisons from various sources after the war to help maintain services pending development of the post-war rebuilding programme which was still in the planning stage. Nevertheless, although built only for a specific short-term purpose, at least two Liberty ships served in the fleet for some 20 years.

However, despite these welcome replacements, the Harrison fleet at the end of 1946 stood at only 30 vessels (190,600 gt), its lowest level in peacetime since 1900. No efforts would be spared over the next decade to augment it again to a new peak in 1955 of 43 ships (307,000 gross tons) many of which would be of revolutionary design, far removed from pre-war conservative Harrison tradition.

FLEET LIST Part 4

167. DEFENDER (1) 1915-1952 Steel steamship rigged as four-masted schooner. Two decks and seven holds. O.N. 137459 8,078g 5,176n 11,960d 482.35 x 58.37 x 36.13 feet. Cargo capacity: 591,880 cubic feet. International Code: JLKH (GQNC after 1933).
Q. 4-cyl. by Dunsmuir and Jackson Ltd., Glasgow; 25.5, 36.5, 54.5 x 54 inches, 13.5 knots.

19.3.1915: Launched by Charles Connell and Co. Ltd., Scotstoun (Yard No. 364) for the company. *23.6.1915:* Delivered at a cost of £118,307 and sailed from Liverpool to New Orleans on her maiden voyage under Captain W.W. Bond. *24.7.1918:* Torpedoed and damaged by the German submarine UB 64 about 75 miles and 174 degrees from Queenstown in position 50.36N, 08.04W. She was sailing in convoy from Cardiff and Milford Haven with an Admiralty cargo of 8,600 tons of coal for Gibraltar. Proceeded to Queenstown

Defender in the Mersey.

[J. and M. Clarkson]

where the coal cargo was discharged and temporary repairs were effected in the Haulbowline dry dock, then to Cardiff where permanent repairs were completed in Mount Stewart dry dock.[116] *18.4.1920:* In collision with the Spanish steamer BILBAINO (1,146/77). Both vessels had been anchored in the River Mersey off the Cammell, Laird shipyard and came into contact when swinging to the flood. *12.12.1925:* Driven ashore in Port Louis, Mauritius, after dragging her anchor moorings in a hurricane. Damage was minimal, the ground being soft mud. *18.12.1926:* Attempted rescue of the crew of the US Coastguard schooner LINCOLN, on fire in the

Atlantic. Two men were saved and landed at Fort Lauderdale, Florida. *12.1943:* One of the few vessels to escape from Bari, Italy, following the devastating air strike on 2.12.1943 against Allied shipping in the harbour. *8.6.1952:* Sold to British Iron and Steel Corporation for demolition and allocated to T.W. Ward Ltd., Barrow-in-Furness.

With a continuous period of service of almost 37 years, DEFENDER was the longest serving Harrison vessel, with the exception of the little COGNAC of 1860, which served about 10 months longer.

A very gallant company - DEFENDER, 1926

It was early morning of 18th December 1926, and the small auxiliary schooner LINCOLN was plunging heavily into a northerly gale in the vicinity of Cape Lookout. LINCOLN belonged to the US Coastguard and was used as a supply vessel serving the several coastguard cutters on patrol in the region. For this was the era of prohibition, and bootlegging was a lucrative way of life. At 04.30 there was a violent explosion, and blazing petrol from the ruptured fuel tank sprayed all over the ship, starting fires in several places. Almost at once the ship was an inferno, the flames defying the crew's feeble efforts to douse them. The men gave up and tried to launch their only lifeboat, but the falls carried away and it drifted downwind with one man aboard who was never seen again. As the ship lurched violently in the trough of the seas another hapless sailor was flung overboard. He, too, disappeared to leeward while his mates watched helplessly. The schooner had no wireless but her plight had been observed from the Cape Lookout Light Vessel, a few miles to the northeast. She promptly sent out a call - "CQ: to all ships".

The call was picked up by the Radio Officer on board the DEFENDER, one day out of Newport News bound for Galveston. It gave a position barely ten miles away to the northwest, and Captain Edward Maycock at once altered course towards it. Soon they sighted the stricken vessel, a mass of smoke and flame merging with a misty horizon. At 08.40 the ship hove to and the crew prepared to lower a lifeboat on the port side, the Second Officer, William A. Short, having been detailed to take charge. His account of subsequent events is so moving that it must be quoted in full.[117] "Accordingly, being put in charge of the boat, I called for a volunteer crew, and, as is usual in these cases, every man wanted to come. I could only take six, however, and having chosen them we jumped into the boat and were lowered into the water on the lee side, a distance of about 35 feet. No sooner did we touch the water than we were drenched with spray, and had very hard work to do in order to keep the boat from being smashed against the ship's side. The boat was connected to the ship by means of a stout tow rope with which the Captain was to endeavour to take us nearer the wreck. He started the engines; we gave two or three sickening crashes as the boat plunged into the heavy seas, then - crack! - the rope parted, the ship forged ahead, and we were left exposed to the full force of wind and sea.

Captain Edward Maycock

My feelings as I realised that we must now rely entirely upon ourselves to keep our own boat from disaster, and to save these poor men, can be better imagined than described, but there was no time for such thinking or analysing. Fortunately, we were in a splendid position to windward of the wreck for manoeuvring, but we shipped quite a quantity of water before we managed to turn the boat towards the wreck, about a quarter of a mile away. I felt my heart warm with hope and confidence in our ability to save these poor men, and a sincere sense of gratitude to God who had brought us along in time. Rapidly making my plans as we went along, I informed my crew so that they would know exactly what was in my mind. However, I changed my intentions when I saw the Captain of the doomed ship wave to me to come under his vessel's stern. During all this time we were rolling and tossing about, swept with sprays, drenched to the skin, and chilled through and through, for it was bitterly cold, the temperature being only 42° Fahrenheit.

Still we managed to maintain a good position to windward of the wreck, and arriving to within hailing distance I shouted to them to have a rope ready to throw to us, repeating this several times as we drew nearer. Suddenly - or so it seemed to me - we were very close - ten yards - five yards - and I was looking up into the faces of six anguish-stricken men. Only an instant, this; a straight, steady scrutiny, but in that interval of time volumes of unspoken communication passed between us.

"Where is your rope?" I shouted, and was horrified to find that they did not have one ready. We were only a matter of three yards from them now, and their rescue and safety

depended on the few seconds that I could stay in that position. Hastily catching up a tangle of small rope, one man threw it towards me, but since it was not properly coiled the wind caught it and it fell short. With a sickening consternation at my heart I called on them to throw again, and the same thing happened, the line falling short of my hand by about a yard. They had been too terror-stricken to make even the smallest provision to help me to rescue them. All this happened in a few seconds, and now we began to drift away, unable to stand against the wind and sea. The instant the second line missed I shouted frantically to them to jump for the boat, but not one of them attempted to do so. Five yards away, fighting hard to get back, and shouting to them now, to jump into the water so that I could pick them up, urging my spent crew on to desperate efforts, though they, good fellows, needed no urging. We were now to leeward of the wreck, and this indeed was hell personified. The vessel was heeled to leeward so that we could see right into her and the whole interior for the full extent of her length was a raging inferno. No flames and sparks leaping into the air, but belching straight out horizontally to leeward, the fire roaring and cracking, and emitting dense volumes of smoke and a scorching heat.

For two or three minutes my men pulled for dear life in order to get back to the wreck, but although we maintained a position about 20 yards to leeward we could not progress a foot. During all this time I kept making signs to the men to jump into the water, but to no purpose. One by one, my men became exhausted, and lay spent and haggard on their oars, so that the boat became unmanageable and in danger of being swamped. To prevent our getting into a dangerous position in the trough of the sea, I had the sea-anchor streamed, and we drifted helplessly and rapidly away from the wreck.

We were, I should imagine, about a quarter of a mile away when flames broke out at her stern, within reach of the poor men huddled together there. Hastily throwing several ropes' ends over the stern, they one and all lowered themselves into the water. Too late! Had they done this only five minutes earlier I could have saved them all! But now, even if they had tried to reach me, the life would have been buffeted out of them by the waves long before they could have done so, and our boat was now drifting away much more quickly than they could swim".

DEFENDER was now lying about a mile to windward of the wreck, and weighing up the rapidly deteriorating situation, Captain Maycock decided to steam close to the burning vessel and try to pick up the men in the water. Lines secured to lifebuoys were trailed alongside, and several rope ladders lowered to the water's edge. As the steamer approached the burning vessel's stern two men were sighted clinging to wreckage. Captain Maycock hailed them, his ship passing only three feet from the wreck. A seaman reached out desperately and succeeded in grasping one of the lifebuoys. He was pulled to a ladder and hauled on board, exhausted, but still alive. It was 09.40. Captain Maycock then turned his attention to the lifeboat, drifting helplessly to leeward. Second Officer Short again takes up the story. "We watched these operations from the boat with breathless interest, praying that the Captain might succeed were we had - not ingloriously — failed. After passing the wreck he bore down on us; I cut adrift our sea-anchor, caught the line thrown to us, and hauled up alongside. I sent my exhausted crew on board; called for and obtained another; and the Captain attempted to tow us round to windward again. In doing so, however, we were again in great danger of being smashed against the ship's side, and so threatening did the situation become, that before we were in a good position to windward of the second man in the water, I had to order the boat to be cast adrift. This time we had to row practically right across the wind and sea, and in doing so shipped an enormous quantity of water. Once more we were doomed to bitter disappointment, for as soon as we left the shelter afforded under the lee of DEFENDER, wind and sea caught us, and whisked us away like a feather. My men, fresh as they were, bent strenuously to their work, every nerve and muscle centred on saving this man, but we got, and could get no nearer than 20 yards from him. "Man proposes, but God disposes..."

In our small boat we were opposed to the elements in the proportion of a lamb to a lion. We now had about 18 inches of water in the bottom of the boat and I had two of my men bailing with buckets in order to keep it down. Again observing our helplessness, the Captain again brought DEFENDER along, affording us a lee, and enabling the last survivor to grasp a lifebuoy. We ranged alongside and took him into the boat exhausted, and nearly frozen. I gave him a stiff tot of brandy, put a rope round him, and had him taken on deck.

We still remained in the boat whilst DEFENDER steamed slowly round, all hands looking eagerly for more possible survivors. No hope; not a sign was seen of a body, alive or dead; the wreck had disappeared, and once more, as will ever be the case from year to year, toll had been exacted from "They that go down to the sea in ships, and occupy their business in great waters". With a raging fire on the one hand, and a raging sea on the other, no greater drama of the sea has ever been enacted than this, which, already well unfolded on our arrival, slowly developed in all its horror, and, despite all our efforts, passed on relentlessly to its terrible conclusion".

It was only when he returned on board the DEFENDER that Second Officer Short became aware of his own physical condition. His feet, after being immersed in icy water for two-and-a-half hours, were quite numb; he was shivering uncontrollably both with the cold and emotional stress; his body and limbs were bruised through being tossed about in the boat. But all this was as nothing to the mental anguish he suffered at his failure to save the four men who were lost. Scenes from the drama intruded into his waking thoughts by day, and troubled his sleep at night. If only the men had had a rope ready to throw to him; or if only they had jumped when he passed so close. Captain Maycock did his best to relieve the anguish of his subordinate, commending his handling of the boat, and his devotion to duty, but the Second Officer would not be comforted. However, he concludes his narrative on a more positive note: "Thus, by the Grace of God, we have been instrumental in restoring a son to his mother, a husband to his wife, and I trust and know that God in His great mercy will comfort and strengthen those poor wives and children who this day mourn the loss of their husbands and fathers".

Mr. Short was later to disclaim any personal credit in the rescue of the survivors, asserting that their rescue was a direct consequence of the seamanlike handling of the DEFENDER by Captain Maycock. In a letter addressed to the Secretary of the Mercantile Marine Service Association, who wished to nominate him for the Liverpool Shipwreck and Humane Society's Lifesaving medal, Mr. Short says, "The two survivors were not saved by the lifeboat... It was entirely owing to the skilful handling of the DEFENDER by the Commander, Captain Maycock, that these two men were saved.

Whilst therefore disclaiming any personal consideration to recognition, I feel that to reject your kindly interest and intention would be unjust to the men who manned the lifeboat. I am therefore furnishing you with a résumé of events in connection with the lifeboat operations..."

There follows an account similar to the foregoing, ending "You will see that I cannot claim any distinction for having saved lives in this matter, unfortunately, but on behalf of the boat's crews I am pleased to accept the expressions contained in your letters for the attempts that were made."

However, this disclaimer was rightly ignored, and Mr. Short received the Society's medal, as he deserved. Further recognition came in March 1928 from the US Government which instructed its Ambassador in London to present medals and testimonials to the lifeboat crews on behalf of the President of the United States, Calvin Coolidge. Captain Maycock also received an inscribed gold watch, and Second Officer Short a pair of binoculars.

Retreat from Bari - DEFENDER 1943

Anyone who survived the holocaust which struck the crowded Italian port of Bari on the night of 2nd December 1943 will never forget the experience. (For a full account of the raid and its terrible aftermath see under DIRECTOR, 214) The DEFENDER and her consort, DIRECTOR, were among the few lucky vessels to escape with minor damage. The port was completely disabled, and those ships which could still steam were ordered to leave the port and proceed to Taranto. DEFENDER, however, was instructed to delay her departure in order to embark survivors from the 17 ships which had been blown up or sunk, many of them being walking wounded.

The ship sailed just before sunset on 3rd December, picking her way cautiously through the wreck-littered harbour, past blazing hulks still shuddering with sporadic explosions. Though functioning as a ship, DEFENDER was in a sorry state. Her steel decks were holed and pitted like a dartboard from falling fragments of metal from disintegrating ships, and most of her anti-aircraft guns were bent, or knocked sideways by blast. Overall lay a grisly coating of black oil for, as Captain T.J. Lacey explained almost apologetically to one of his 360 passengers, "It rained fuel oil for quite ten minutes after one explosion last night!" Now, a pall of greasy, black smoke hung over the breakwaters almost obscuring the exit, but at last the ship was clear and heading southeast along the coast.

That night, feeling her way inshore in total darkness, the DEFENDER ran aground on a sandy beach just north of Brindisi. Coming on top of their recent experiences it was a painful moment, jarring the nerves of all on board. However, after a judicious transfer of fresh water and ballast, the ship was refloated a few hours later and resumed her interrupted voyage to Taranto.[118] The ship docked at Taranto next day, and the injured were quickly transferred to military hospitals in the area. On 21st December, her cargo discharged, DEFENDER returned to Alexandria where the ship was dry docked, surveyed and repaired before returning home.

Defender in the Scheldt on 4th November 1945. She is still in wartime rig, although with the Harrison funnel.
[Florent Van Otterdyk]

120

168. GOVERNOR (2) 1915-1917 Steel steamship rigged as two-masted schooner. Two decks and five holds.
O.N. 137483 5,524g 3,493n 8,440d 410.0 x 52.25 x 33.91 feet. Cargo capacity: 441,119 cubic feet.
International Code: JLWN.
T. 3-cyl. by D. and W. Henderson and Co. Ltd., Glasgow; 24.5, 42.5, 72x 54 inches, 12 knots.

13.8.1915: Launched by D. and W. Henderson and Co. Ltd., Glasgow (Yard No. 493) for the company. *13.10.1915:* Delivered at a cost of £85,550. Later sailed from Glasgow and Birkenhead for South Africa on her maiden voyage under Captain M.G. Packe. *19.12.1915:* Requisitioned by the Shipping Controller at Capetown and employed as a transport. *14.3.1917:* Intercepted and sunk by the German raider MÖWE, 930 miles and 267 degrees from Fastnet in an approximate position 50.34N, 34.10W. Four men were killed by gunfire and ten men injured. The latter and the remaining 33 members of the crew were taken prisoner and subsequently interned in Germany.

Captain M.G. Packe, first master of the ill-fated *Governor.*
[Barraud]

169. BARRISTER (2) 1915-1917 Steel steamship rigged as two-masted schooner. Two decks and five holds.
O.N. 137486 3,679g 2,341n 6,170d 353.2 x 47.75 x 30.37 feet Cargo capacity: 276,340 cubic feet.
International Code: JMBT.
T. 3-cyl. by Dunsmuir and Jackson Ltd., Glasgow; 22, 37, 62 x 48 inches, 11.5 knots.

17.8.1915: Launched by Charles Connell and Co. Ltd., Scotstoun (Yard No. 365) for the company. *7.12.1915:* Delivered at a cost of £52,857. Later sailed from Glasgow and Birkenhead for South Africa on her maiden voyage under Captain J. Richards. *6.1916:* Ran aground in Active Pass, near Vancouver, British Columbia, and incurred damage costing £3,700 to repair. *11.5.1917:* Torpedoed and sunk by the German submarine U 49 (Kapitänleutnant Richard Hartmann) seven miles southwest of Mine Head, County Waterford, in position 51.55N, 7.43W. There was no loss of life. She was on passage from Pernambuco to Liverpool with general cargo, sugar and maize.[119]

Barrister, sinking off Mine Head, County Waterford after being torpedoed on 11th May 1917.
[Peter Newall collection]

170. PEMBA 1915-1921 Steel steamship, one deck.
O.N. 139124 533g 212n 161.8 x 24.9 x 11.2 feet.
International Code: JMPC.
C. 2-cyl. by Société des Établissements Bertin Frères, Bezons, France; 17, 30 x 19.5 inches.

1908: Launched by Société des Établissements Bertin Frères, Bezons, France, as ROBERT-SUZANNE for unknown owners. *1908:* Completed. *1912:* Sold to B. Bertucci, Rio de Janeiro, Brazil, and renamed RIO ITAPEMIRIM. *1914:* Sold to Knowles and Foster and renamed PEMBA. *1915:* Acquired by Thos. and Jas. Harrison Ltd. and registered at London in 1916 under the name of Frank Ward, manager and partner. Employed with MAFIA in the coastal trade between Beira and Chinde, Mozambique (the ports respectively for Rhodesia and Nyasaland). They transhipped cargo brought out to Beira by steamers in the Clan-Hall-Harrison service and were managed from Harrison's London office. *1921:* Sold to British and South American Steam Navigation Co. Ltd. (R.P. Houston and Co., managers), London. *1922:* Sold to Thesen Steamship Co. Ltd. (R. P. Houston and Co. also managed Thesen's Steamship Co. Ltd.), Cape Town. *2.2.1923:* Returned to Cape Town after a considerable amount of water was discovered in the after hold. The cargo was discharged, and the after peak bulkhead was found to be leaking badly. Much of the cargo of wheat and salt in the hold was irrevocably damaged and was disposed of. *6.8.1926:* Foundered off the Pondoland Coast, off Port St. Johns, during a gale when on passage from Cape Town to Port Natal with a cargo of guano and empty drums. The lifeboat was launched and all but one seaman survived.

PEMBA is the name of a small island north of Zanzibar, now part of Tanzania.

A sister to *Pemba, Mafia* was photographed in Thesen's colours at Capetown.
[Marin Leendertz, courtesy Peter Newall]

171. MAFIA 1915-1921 Steel steamship. One deck plus awning deck.
O.N. 139125 531g 211n 161.8 x 24.9 x 11.2 feet.
International Code: JMPB.
C. 2-cyl. by Société des Établissements Bertin Frères, Bezons, France; 17, 30 x 19.5 inches.

1907: Launched by Société des Établissements Bertin Frères, Bezons, France for Brazilian owners as OYAC. *1907:* Completed. *1912:* Sold to B. Bertucci, Rio de Janeiro, Brazil and renamed RIO S. MATHEUS. *1914:* Sold to Knowles and Foster and renamed MAFIA. *1915:* Acquired by Thos. and Jas. Harrison Ltd. and registered at London in 1916 under the name of Frank Ward, manager and partner. Employed with her sister PEMBA in the coastal trade between Beira and Chinde, Mozambique. *1921:* Sold to British and South American Steam Navigation Co. Ltd. (R.P. Houston and Co., managers), London. *1922:* Sold to Thesen Steamship Co. Ltd., Cape Town. *11.6.1923:* During a night of severe weather off East London the starboard steering chain parted, causing the vessel to broach to and ship heavy seas. The engine room and stokehold bilges were flooded; deck structures and fittings swept away; doors smashed, and the crew's quarters awash; even the lagging was washed off the tops of the boilers. Surveyed and essential repairs carried out at Port Elizabeth. *1927:* Sold to Massinot and Thery, Diego Suarez. *22.3.1930:* Anchored off Fenerive, Madagascar, a small east coast port some 50 miles north of Tamatave, lying about 1,500 metres offshore loading the final shipments of her cargo of vanilla, coffee, timber, wax, and cloves. Her few passengers had been on board for several hours. Towards midnight, a heavy rain squall struck the vessel, and her anchor cable parted under the strain. She drifted inshore, and struck some submerged rocks broadside on. Eventually the engines were started, but no sooner was she under way than she struck again, and water flooded the engine room. As soon as conditions allowed, steps were taken to land the passengers, and every effort was made by the crew to salvage what they could of the cargo. *31.3.1930:* Abandoned by her owners, and declared a constructive total loss.

MAFIA is the name of a small island south of Zanzibar, now part of Tanzania.

Mafia, again at Capetown. *[National Maritime Museum P811]*

172. SENATOR (3) 1917-1938 Steel steamship rigged as two-masted schooner. Two decks and five holds.
O.N. 137537 3,670g 2,335n 6,170d 352.9 x 47.75 x 30.37 feet. Cargo capacity: 276,340 cubic feet.
International Code: JNWB (GQNM after 1933).
T. 3-cyl. by Dunsmuir and Jackson Ltd., Glasgow; 22, 37, 62 x 48 inches, 11.5 knots.

11.10.1916: Launched by Charles Connell and Co. Ltd., Scotstoun (Yard No. 366) for the company. *19.2.1917:* Delivered at a cost of £53,921. Later sailed from Liverpool to Kingston, Jamaica on her maiden voyage under Captain E. Dunn. *16.4.1921:* Grounded on soft mud on the outer bar when leaving Georgetown, Demerara, but refloated on the next tide. *17.11.1924:* In collision with the US tanker CAPE ANN (7,312/20) in the Houston Ship Channel. Both vessels were damaged above the waterline. *29.5.1926:* Ran ashore off Bolt Head near Salcombe, Devon, when inward bound from St.Lucia to London. A message demanding assistance was transmitted and the Hope Cove lifeboat was launched. The Coastguard assembled a life-saving team and set off for Bolt Head. However, one hour later she signalled that she was afloat again, cancelled assistance and proceeded to London. *31.5.1926:* Arrived at West India Dock, London, and subsequent dry docking revealed that her bottom had been set up, and seven plates had to be removed and faired. This work was carried out in Liverpool between 14.6.1926 and 23.7.1926. The master, Captain W. Walker was dismissed after this incident. *16.10.1930 - 16.10.1932:* Laid up at Fowey. *3.8.1938:* Sold to Kyle Shipping Co. Ltd. (Monroe Brothers, managers), Liverpool, for £11,157 and renamed KYLEGLEN. *14.12.1940:* Torpedoed and sunk by the German submarine U 100 (Kapitänleutnant Schepke) in position 56.25N, 22.50W, 307 miles and 256 degrees from Rockall. She was on passage from Oban for Baltimore and had just dispersed from Convoy OB 256.

In 1938 *Senator* was sold to a company controlled by Monroe Brothers of Liverpool, and as *Kyleglen* became their only deep-sea ship.

[David Whiteside]

Senator. *[Roy Fenton collection]*

Astronomer in the Mersey.
[*J. and M. Clarkson*]

173. ASTRONOMER (3) 1917-1940 Steel steamship rigged as four-masted schooner. Two decks and seven holds.
O.N. 140531 8,681g 5,546n 11,955d 482.7 x 58.25 x 36.1 feet. Cargo capacity: 601,440 cubic feet.
International Code: JQRM (GQNT after 1933).
Q. 4-cyl. by D. and W. Henderson and Co. Ltd., Glasgow; 25, 36.5, 52.5, 75 x 54 inches, 14 knots.

21.4.1917: Launched by D. and W. Henderson and Co. Ltd., Glasgow (Yard No. 494) for the company. *21.8.1917:* Delivered at a cost of £144,786. Later sailed from Liverpool to New Orleans on her maiden voyage under Captain G.W. Goldman. *14.4.1918:* Grounded on the Pluckington Bank in the River Mersey when inward bound from New York. Subsequently refloated by the tug EGERTON (272/11). *27.8.1939:* Taken into Government service delivering anti-submarine boom defence systems to assigned ports and her crew was increased by approximately 50 Royal Navy personnel. *1.6.1940:* Torpedoed by the German submarine U 58 (Kapitänleutnant Herbert Kuppisch) off Kinnaird Head. The torpedo struck in number 7 hold which was demolished, and the propeller shaft was broken. Some three hours later the submarine attacked again, this time hitting number 4 hold and the engine room, blowing a hole in the starboard side. A third torpedo exploded just abaft the bridge. *2.6.1940:* Sank at 04.28 in position 58.02N, 02.12W. She was on passage from Rosyth to Scapa Flow with boom defence equipment. Four men died in the attack and eleven were injured, but 109 survivors were picked up by the escorting trawlers STOKE CITY (422/35) and LEICESTER CITY (422/34).[120]

A question of class

A glimpse of the allure of a "First Class Ship", which so entranced young officers in the 'twenties, is revealed in an article written by Captain H.G. Skelly, who, as a young cadet aboard the lowly third class PROFESSOR (145), saw ASTRONOMER in all her glory when the two ships were berthed alongside each other in Durban harbour in September 1925. He writes "It was decided that ASTRONOMER could load our coastal cargo for Lourenço Marques and Beira, and consequently a Durban tug towed us to the ASTRONOMER and placed us alongside her 500 feet of length. The cargo was thus transferred from one vessel to the other, and for two or three days I was able to see "first class" life close at hand.

Astronomer: 'a First Class Ship'.
[*A. Duncan*]

She was manned by the most senior men of all grades; had a Lascar crew and British quartermasters... [She had] sixteen men on day-work for eight hours a day, six hours on Saturday, and three on Sunday. That gave many man-hours per week to chip and scrape, paint and polish, renew and repair. In consequence she was - and she looked - well cared for and maintained, and in every way "First Class". Her four masts, and multiple derricks, working seven hatches, gave her an excellent loading rate, and soon she was ready for sea. With her fore, main, mizzen and jigger masts cutting the skyline, her teakwood timber work, freshly varnished and reflecting the bright African sunshine, she left harbour to continue her voyage, and I am certain that there were few freighters of her time which could claim to be her equal. She was a First Class Harrison Line steamer of 1925."[121]

174. ACTOR (2) 1917-1939 Steel steamship rigged as two-masted schooner. Two decks and five holds.
O.N. 140541 6,082g 3,830n 8,440d 410.2 x 52.25 x 32.87 feet. Cargo capacity: 425,043 cubic feet.
International Code: JRNV (GMCB after 1933).
T. 3-cyl. by D. and W. Henderson and Co. Ltd., Glasgow; 24.5, 42.5, 72 x 54 inches, 12 knots.

6.8.1917: Launched by D. and W. Henderson and Co. Ltd., Glasgow (Yard No. 495) for the company. *31.10.1917:* Delivered at a cost of £119,021 and promptly requisitioned by the Shipping Controller. Later sailed from Plymouth to India on her maiden voyage under Captain W.J. Simmons. *1.9.1918:* Torpedoed and damaged by the German submarine UB 125 in the Irish Sea in position 51.30N, 06.30W when on passage from Liverpool to Philadelphia in ballast. Taken in tow by the Admiralty dockyard tugs FRANCES BATEY (151/14) and MARGARET HAM (113/13). *2.9.1918:* Arrived at Milford Haven where repairs lasted four months. *1919:* Redelivered to the company and converted along with eleven other vessels to burn oil fuel. This radical step was prompted by the high cost of coal, but was reversed two years later when oil fuel increased significantly in price. *27.7.1922:* The ship's bollards were torn from their beds during a powerful bore tide at Calcutta and she broke adrift. Nine other vessels, including MATADOR (182), were loose in the River Hooghly, but little damage and no casualties were caused. *15.4.1931:* Ran ashore four miles south of Cayo Blanco, Cuba. *16.4.1931:* Refloated following the discharge of 3,000 bags of sugar into lighters. The cargo was subsequently reloaded and she proceeded to Jucaro. *28.4.1933:* Went to the assistance of MAGICIAN (211) which had broken down 1,600 miles north west of Cape Town. She was taken in tow for a few days while repairs progressed on board, thereafter MAGICIAN continued under her own steam, escorted by ACTOR and 9.5.1933 arrived Table Bay. *31.5.1939:* Sold to Nailsea Steamship Co. Ltd. (E.R. Management Co. Ltd., managers), Cardiff for £14,256 and renamed NAILSEA RIVER. *1940:* Sold to Manchester Liners Ltd., Manchester for £55,000 but not renamed because of wartime restrictions. *15.9.1940:* Bombed and sunk by German aircraft about 11 miles, 96 degrees from Montrose in position 56.41N, 02.05W whilst on passage in Convoy SLA 45 from Buenos Aires to the Tyne with wheat.

Actor in the Mersey.   *[J. and M. Clarkson]*

"Reform on ACTOR"

On 26th February 1918, when convoy HE 6 from Port Said to London was attacked by a U-boat in position 49.00N, 04.20W, i.e. about 45 miles north east of Ushant, the Commodore's ship EUMAEUS (6,696/13) was sunk, the Vice-Commodore's, MALTA (6,064/95), disabled by an ill-aimed depth charge from an escort vessel, and, leaderless, the convoy scattered in some disorder. Captain W.J. Simmons of the ACTOR then took it upon himself to signal the ships to "Reform on ACTOR", which they did. Later, from the safe haven of Falmouth where he and the crew of EUMAEUS had landed, the Commodore, Captain D.J. Munro, CMG, RN, warmly commended Captain Simmons in despatches to the Admiralty, upon his initiative.[122]

Captain W.J. Simmons, Master of the *Actor* (seen again left), was commended for his actions when convoy HE 6 was attacked in 1918.

175. AUTHOR (3) 1917-1935 Steel steamship rigged as two-masted schooner. Two decks and five holds.
O.N. 135563 5,596g 3,553n 9,220d 423.2 x 53.0 x 32.64 feet. Cargo capacity: 445,531 cubic feet.
International Code: JFCT (MFCJ after 1933).
T. 3-cyl. by David Rowan and Co., Glasgow; 27.5, 45, 75 x 51 inches, 11.25 knots.

7.2.1914: Launched by Russell and Co., Port Glasgow (Yard No. 661) for the British and Foreign Steam Ship Co. Ltd. (Rankin, Gilmour and Co. Ltd., managers), Liverpool as SAINT EGBERT. *3.1914:* Completed. *26.9.1915:* Requisitioned by the Shipping Controller and employed initially as a collier. *23.12.1917:* Acquired by the company for £177,274. *20.2.1918:* Renamed AUTHOR. *16.3.1918:* Torpedoed and damaged by the German submarine UB 40 in the English Channel in position 50.36N, 00.34W when on passage from North Shields to Genoa with a cargo of 7,400 tons of steel, coke, coal and benzine. *18.3.1918:* Arrived at Plymouth for repair. *11.6.1918:* Chased by the German submarine U 151 (Kapitänleutnant Heinrich von Nostitz und Janckendorff) in the North Atlantic in position 32.10N, 78.20W, but escaped due to her superior speed. She was on passage from Cienfuegos to Hampton Roads with a cargo of sugar. *25.12.1923:* When on passage from San Francisco to Vancouver in a severe northwesterly gale, the air pump developed a fault which immobilised the main engines. The vessel started to drift towards the coast of Washington and the engineers worked frantically to restore power and avoid drifting onto rocks. The vessel was eventually able to work her way out of danger at about three knots and limped into Victoria, British Columbia 28.12.1923 and made a complete repair. *11.1925:* Ashore on Egg Island in the Bahamas and, although quickly refloated, Captain John Williams and Chief Officer Haworth were dismissed on their return to Liverpool. *31.3.1927:* In collision in dense fog about eight miles southeast of Gibraltar with the Spanish floating coal depot JACINTO (1,479/77). AUTHOR was holed in the forepeak but JACINTO foundered in 10 minutes, having been struck on the starboard side. The master and six crew were rescued but eighteen were lost. *28.6.1930 - 16.9.1931:* Laid up at Barrow-in-Furness. *1.1.1932 - 15.1.1934:* Laid up again at Barrow-in-Furness. *24.2.1935:* On her final voyage from Brazil to Liverpool, responded to a call for assistance from the British steamer BEREBY (5,248/19) whose steering gear had broken down in heavy weather. A jury system had been rigged to the winches, but that had been carried away, and AUTHOR was asked to stand by while repairs were carried out. *25.2.1935:* She reached the disabled vessel in position 46.36N, 10.25W, and stood by until repairs were completed. *28.3.1935:* Sold to Italian General Shipping Ltd., London for £9,454. *18.5.1935:* Arrived Venice to be broken up.

Author at anchor in the Mersey. As *Saint Egbert* she was the first of 12 Rankin, Gilmour ships purchased by Harrisons. *[J. and M. Clarkson]*

Strange things happen at sea

No anthology of sea stories would be complete without one or two hinting at the mysteries of the supernatural. A chief engineer, the late Robert Wilkins OBE, relates one such eerie experience which occurred while he was Second Engineer of the AUTHOR in 1926.[123]

"The AUTHOR sailed from Liverpool one day in 1926 fully laden with general cargo for the Gulf and West Indies. The Master was Captain Jackson - "Holy Joe" Jackson - an appellation of which he might have been justly proud. Mr. John Garden was Chief Engineer, whilst I myself was Second; Mr. H.I. Nicholson, Third; and Hughie Macdonald, Fourth. Shortly after breakfast one morning, a few days after our departure, Nick reported to me that there was a stowaway in number 4 hold. This seemed to me so unlikely that I'm afraid his statement was not taken very seriously. You see, number 4 hold was full of cargo, so how could there be a stowaway in there?

"Anyhow, what makes you think there is?" I asked. "Well," replied Nick, "The Fourth called my attention to loud knockings on the steel housing of the shaft tunnel, and furthermore any knocks we made with a hammer were faithfully repeated". With considerable scepticism I proceeded down below and along the shaft tunnel to investigate. Taking up a heavy spanner I gave two raps against the steelwork at the spot indicated. Instantly, from the other side came two answering raps, equally loud. I tapped again and again, and back came the response. At last, I too was convinced that someone must have stowed away, perhaps in a crate which had been swung aboard to the bottom of the hold and which was now overstowed with hundreds of tons of cargo. It would be impossible to reach him let alone release him.

Quickly the situation was reported to Mr. Garden, and I was quite prepared for the look of incredulity which spread over his homely features. However, he accompanied me into the engine room and along the tunnel, to indulge once more in an imaginative sequence of percussive signals which were correctly answered in every case, until Mr. Garden himself was quite satisfied that a living creature was trying to communicate with us from the other side of the tunnel casing.

Make no mistake; these repeated sounds were not light tappings or echoes, but heavy strokes of metal on metal, and came immediately from the opposite side of the steel plate. Here I must confess that a weird sense of disquiet came over me, and I shivered. The claustrophobic but familiar surroundings of the shaft tunnel; the glare from the electric lamps overhead; the steady rhythmic pulse of the shaft revolving in its bearings; even the familiar sight of the donkeyman patiently replenishing his dash-pots with oil, did nothing to dispel the uneasiness which this mystery had aroused. I shivered again.

The reaction of Captain Jackson when told was a blend of amazement, disbelief, and ridicule, for which one could hardly blame him. Nevertheless, he had to satisfy himself, nor was he likely to be easily convinced. So again we went below, in solemn procession, and again the repertoire of knocks was repeated, until finally Captain Jackson tried that familiar percussive phrase, "Tap-tappety-tap-tap...", and back came the traditional reply, "Tap-tap". It was all too much, the matter was settled; someone must be in the hold.

The crew was called out, tarpaulins and hatch covers were removed but the space below was chock-a-block with every kind of crate, case, sack, bale, or package you could think of. We could only bawl down hatches and ventilators, "Is anybody there?" at frequent intervals, punctuated by periods of intent and anxious silence, but every effort of lusty lungs failed to inspire a response.

Reluctantly, the hatches were battened down again, for the weather looked ominous. Everyone felt sure that a rapidly decomposing body would be revealed when the hold was discharged in a couple of weeks time. This gloomy foreboding remained in our conscious thoughts until the compartment was empty, and an intensive search was mounted. But there was nobody (literally, no body) there, nor could we find anything which might account for the weird phenomenon we had experienced. The search for a rational explanation was diligent and ingenious but even now we are still without an answer - although there is a sequel....of sorts.

Some years later, while sailing as Chief Engineer of the WANDERER, I recounted this story at the saloon table to Captain John Bellett, and the Mate, Bill Sawle. I think they considered it a good yarn, but not one to be taken seriously, and who could blame them? It requires hard experience to make a true impression. Nevertheless, believe it or not, there was a similar manifestation on board the WANDERER later that voyage.

Along the shaft tunnel the familiar rigmarole of knocks and answers was repeated, but having heard my tale about the AUTHOR'S visitation the Master and officers were not inclined to give the incident much credence. In fact, I rather thought they were looking at me rather strangely, as if I were playing some sort of sick joke on them.

But if the officers were unmoved, the crew most certainly were not, and, shocked by their officers' apparent callous indifference to the fate of a fellow human being trapped at the bottom of the hold, forthwith they sent a delegation to the Master to seek permission to open the hatch and investigate the matter. To keep the peace, the hatch was opened, but, as in the former case, their anxious calls elicited no reply.

Intrigued and perplexed by this second uncanny experience, and clinging to the conviction that there must be some logical explanation, I again made a thorough search, and again found nothing. My shipmates were looking at me even more strangely as I frantically tossed aside the debris and dunnage which littered the bottom of number 4 hold. For in all these inexplicable happenings there was only one common denominator - me! Did I, perhaps, have my own personal poltergeist in tow, which followed me from ship to ship, and made its presence known on widely separated occasions, without warning? It remains to this day a complete mystery, defying all logic. I leave you to judge - but, listen! What's that loud rapping noise...?"

176. DICTATOR (2) 1918-1932 Steel steamship rigged as two-masted schooner. Two decks and five holds.
O.N. 131408 4,940g 3,149n, 8,300d 404.7 x 52.25 x 30.16 feet Cargo capacity: 402,479 cubic feet.
International Code: HVCP.
T. 3-cyl. by Rankin and Blackmore, Greenock; 26, 42, 70 x 48 inches, 10.5 knots.

4.12.1911: Launched by Russell and Co., Port Glasgow (Yard No. 608) for the British and Foreign Steam Ship Co.Ltd. (Rankin, Gilmour and Co. Ltd., managers), Liverpool as SAINT BEDE. *1.1912:* Completed. *11.1.1918:* Acquired by the company for £141,589. *28.3.1918:* Renamed DICTATOR. *23.3.1928:* Put into Bermuda with a cotton fire in number 3 hold which had been held in check by injecting steam. The cargo was discharged into lighters and by *4.4.1928* the fire was extinguished and the hold was empty. The cargo was restowed and 242 bales of fire-damaged cotton were stowed on deck. About 50 bales had been destroyed and the estimated claim was for £3,000. The vessel was not damaged. *1.7.1932:* Sold for £1,262 through Douglas and Ramsey Ltd. for demolition to Smith and Houston. *4.8.1932:* Arrived at Port Glasgow.

Dictator was the second Harrison ship to carry the name, which was not repeated after the war.
[J. and M. Clarkson]

177. INSTRUCTOR 1918 Steel steamship rigged as two-masted schooner. Two decks and five holds.
O.N. 131441 4,422g 2,807n 7,560d 384.5 x 49.8 x 29.2 feet Cargo capacity: 350,957 cubic feet.
International Code: HWCG.
T. 3-cyl. by Rankin and Blackmore, Greenock; 25, 42, 68 x 48 inches, 10 knots.

30.4.1912: Launched by Russell and Co., Port Glasgow (Yard No. 627) for the British and Foreign Steam Ship Co. Ltd. (Rankin, Gilmour and Co. Ltd., managers), Liverpool as SAINT DUNSTAN. *6.1912:* Completed. *27.2.1916:* Requisitioned by the Shipping Controller for service as a collier and from 24.7.1917 as an Expeditionary Force Transport carrying Canadian stores. *23.1.1918:* Acquired by the company for £131,217. *18.4.1918:* Renamed INSTRUCTOR. *7.7.1918:* Sailed from Plymouth in convoy for Montreal with a cargo of Government stores. The convoy dispersed 13.7.1918 at 02.00 and she proceeded independently towards her destination on prescribed courses. *14.7.1918:* Just before midnight, steaming without lights, ran into a US troop convoy crossing from Halifax to France, also without lights. She was run down by the US transport AMERICA (22,622/05) and sank in approximately 10 minutes in position 43.50N, 34.50W, 306 miles and 328 degrees from Flores, Azores. Sixteen crew members were lost. The AMERICA launched a boat to search for survivors, and picked up two boats from INSTRUCTOR, one with 11 men, the other with 15 men aboard. They were taken on board and eventually landed at Brest.

A war risk, or not a war risk?

Subsequent to the loss of INSTRUCTOR, Harrisons put in a claim for £160,000 under the War Risk Insurance scheme. When it was turned down on the grounds that a collision could only be a marine risk covered by normal marine insurance, the company took the case to court.[124] The point was important, for Harrisons in those days carried their own hull insurance, and so stood to lose a great deal of money.

The case was heard before Mr Justice Roche, sitting with two nautical assessors in the King's Bench Division, on Friday 29th April 1921. In evidence, it was established that the ship was sailing under a T99 Charter, and operated by the Director of Transports. The AMERICA on the other hand, was a unit of the US Navy, Transport Division, manned by a naval crew 1,100 strong, armed with six 6-inch guns, and carrying 6,000 American troops to France. She was leading a convoy of five ships, all steaming at a speed of 16.5 knots, but showing no navigation lights, on a course of north 54 degrees east. INSTRUCTOR's speed was 9.5 knots, her course south 88 degrees west.

Both the Second and Third Officers were on the Harrison ship's bridge, changing the watch, but both were lost, as were most of the engineers. Captain Thomas Jones and the Chief Officer were picked up after being in the water for some time.

According to the helmsman's evidence, the officers on the INSTRUCTOR saw some of the convoy's ships to port, and ordered a slight alteration to starboard. The AMERICA apparently, was not seen, and may have been obscured by a squall.

On the AMERICA's bridge, Lieutenant Bratt saw something dimly, called the Captain, and at last made it out to be a ship half to three-quarters of a mile away. The Captain ordered "Hard right" (i.e. hard-a-port in British ships, swinging the head in those days to starboard). INSTRUCTOR, in those final seconds, also went to starboard, but it was too late to avoid the collision, which occurred at an angle of 45 degrees, AMERICA slicing into INSTRUCTOR's port side between numbers 4 and 5 hatches, shearing away steel plates like so much cardboard.

After one adjournment, judgement was delivered on 29th November 1921. Mr Justice Roche agreed that the Admiralty was not liable for losses due to a "sea risk", but only for those losses normally excluded from an ordinary English Insurance Policy, viz: "Warranted free of capture, seizure and detention and the consequences thereof, or of any attempt, threat, piracy excepted, and also from all consequences of hostilities or warlike operations, whether before or after declaration of war." A merchant ship, navigating without lights on a prescribed course did not in itself constitute a "warlike operation", but a collision involving a vessel forming part of the naval forces of a government, armed, and carrying troops trained for combat, was most certainly a consequence of "hostilities or warlike operations". The judge therefore found the case proved in favour of the suppliants, and that their claim on the War Risk underwriters was a valid one.

The Director of Transports appealed against the judgement on 13th March 1922 on the grounds that, in Mr Justice Roche's summing-up, he implied an element of negligence on the part of either or both vessels on account of "undue delay in taking action". However, Lords Justice Bankes, Warrington and Scrutton agreed there was no negligence, simply a mere error of judgement in appalling circumstances, and the appeal was dismissed.

The case is interesting especially when compared with the case of the INKONKA (153), which ran aground in wartime conditions, but was ruled a marine risk.

---

178. ORATOR (3) 1918-1932 Steel steamship rigged as two-masted schooner. Two decks and five holds.
O.N. 133076 4,622g 2,947n 7,680d 385.5 x 52.0 x 29.16 feet Cargo capacity: 365,855 cubic feet.
International Code: HWRT.
T. 3-cyl. by Rankin and Blackmore, Greenock; 26, 42, 70 x 48 inches, 10.5 knots.

24.8.1912: Launched by Russell and Co., Port Glasgow (Yard No. 638) for Port Line Ltd. (Crawford and Rowat, managers), Glasgow as HAWKHEAD. *10.1912:* Completed. *1916:* Sold to the British and Foreign Steam Ship Co. Ltd. (Rankin, Gilmour and Co. Ltd., managers), Liverpool and renamed SAINT FILLANS. *1.3.1917:* Requisitioned by the Shipping Controller for service initially as a collier, but later on French Government Service carrying steel. *21.10.1917:* Attacked by the German submarine UB 31 in the English Channel, three miles off Berry Head in position 50.27N, 03.29W. She was on passage from Baltimore to Le Havre with a cargo of 5,400 tons of steel billets and 1,000 tons of copper. The torpedo missed. *23.1.1918:* Acquired by the company for £135,589. *10.4.1918:* Renamed ORATOR.

19.3.1930: Laid up at Preston. *9.1931:* Sold to Blue Cross Line (James Russell Ltd., managers), Glasgow. *14.3.1932:* Sold to L.B. Moller (Moller and Co., managers), Shanghai, China and renamed HILDA MOLLER. *1935:* Registered under the ownership of N.E.A. Moller. *1936:* Owners became Moller Line Ltd. *26.8.1937:* Bombed and damaged by Spanish Nationalist aircraft when berthed at Gijon and two crew members were injured. *1.9.1938:* Grounded off Toi Misaki, Japan, and subsequently refloated seriously damaged. Towed to Shanghai for repair. *1947:* Sold to Chinese Maritime Trust Ltd., Shanghai and renamed TANG SHAN. *1949:* Registered at Taiwan. *3.1958:* Sold to Taiwan shipbreakers.

Orator in the Mersey.

[J. and M. Clarkson]

179. SPECTATOR (2) 1918-1927 Steel steamship rigged as two-masted schooner. Two decks and five holds.
O.N. 131349 4,574g 2,860n 7,600d 384.7 x 50.0 x 29.96 feet. Cargo capacity: 363,430 cubic feet.
International Code: HSTR.
T. 3-cyl. by Rankin and Blackmore, Greenock; 26, 42, 70 x 48 inches, 10.5 knots.

11.5.1911: Launched by A. McMillan and Son Ltd., Dumbarton (Yard No. 429) for the British and Foreign Steam Ship Co. Ltd. (Rankin, Gilmour and Co. Ltd., managers), Liverpool as SAINT LEONARDS. *6.1911:* Completed. *15.11.1916:* Struck a mine laid that day by the German submarine UC 26 in the English Channel about 400 yards east south east of Whistling Buoy, Le Havre, and although damaged reached Le Havre safely. She was on passage from Philadelphia to Le Havre with grain. *23.10.1917:* Requisitioned by the Shipping Controller initially for service as a collier. *26.2.1918:* Acquired by the company for £123,419 and later renamed SPECTATOR. *12.9.1923:* Fire broke out in the bunker hatch, when 180 miles east of Kismayu when on passage from Aden to Mombasa. The crew fought

Rankin, Gilmour's *Saint Leonards,* later *Spectator.*

the fire, jettisoning 60 tons of coal in the process. *14.9.1923:* Arrived at Kilindini Harbour with the fire extinguished. *11.1927:* Sold to Carras Brothers, Chios, Greece for £26,408 and renamed YERO CARRAS. *18.2.1929:* In collision off Flushing with the French steamer MEINAM (6,149/07) when nearing the end of a voyage from Mormugao to Antwerp. Two plates on the port side were set in, and part of the upper deck destroyed. *22.2.1929:* When entering Antwerp Docks, fell heavily against the Belgian steamer MONA (475/18) berthed alongside. MONA sustained damage to plating on both sides but was later repaired. *13.11.1930:* Ran hard aground near Cape Pilar in the Strait of Magellan when on passage from Montevideo to Valparaiso in ballast. With most compartments flooded, her position was precarious with a draft of 15 inches forward and 22 feet aft. *16.11.1930:* Abandoned by the crew, straining badly in heavy seas. The salvage vessel ARAUCANIA (624/18) put out from Magallanes (Punta Arenas). *18.11.1930:* ARAUCANIA laid out anchors and installed pumps. *6.12.1930:* Following three unsuccessful attempts she was hauled free of the rocks and beached in Bakers Cove. Temporary repairs were undertaken and by 18.12.1930 she was afloat and able to

reach Magallanes under her own steam. Abandoned there by the owners as a constructive total loss until 5.2.1932 when she broke from her moorings during a gale and drifted out into the Straits. Ten miles west of Magallanes the derelict collided with and sank the Chilean steamer ANTARTICO (605/11). A Chilean naval tug subsequently took YERO CARRAS in tow and returned to Magallanes. *3.1932:* Sociedad Anonima Comercial Braun and Blanchard, Valparaiso commenced repairs and 17.5.1932 she arrived at Montevideo for permanent repair. Registered under Compania Chilena de Navegacion Interoceanica, Valparaiso, Chile and renamed SANTIAGO. *11.2.1933:* Anchored off Punta Mala, about 90 miles south of the Pacific entrance to the Panama Canal, with a serious fire in the reserve bunkers which had ignited the cargo in the adjacent number 2 hold. The blaze spread quickly and when it reached number 1 hold the Master ordered the crew to abandon ship. *13.2.1933:* It was reported by the US Navy tug NOKOMIS that the SANTIAGO had sunk in position 07.25N, 80.02W. She was on passage from Sagua and Mobile for Valparaiso with a cargo of sugar.

Spectator outward bound off the Prince's Landing Stage, Liverpool.

[J. and M. Clarkson]

180. ELECTRICIAN (2) 1918-1932 Steel steamship rigged as two-masted schooner. Two decks and five holds.
O.N. 135460 4,572g 2,884n 7,700d 385.0 x 52.0 x 29.16 feet Cargo capacity: 365,860 cubic feet.
International Code: JCHN.
T. 3-cyl. by J.G. Kincaid and Co.Ltd., Greenock; 25, 41, 68 x 48 inches, 10.5 knots.

22.4.1913: Launched by Russell and Co., Port Glasgow (Yard No. 645) for the British and Foreign Steam Ship Co. Ltd. (Rankin, Gilmour and Co. Ltd., managers), Liverpool as SAINT WINIFRED. *5.1913:* Completed. *14.9.1915:* Requisitioned by the Shipping Controller initially for service as a collier. *25.2.1918:* Acquired by the company for £139,383 and later renamed ELECTRICIAN. *21.11.1926:* In collision in the River Scheldt with the Houston steamer HARMODIUS (5,229/19). Both vessels sustained damage to the bow, above the waterline, but continued their respective voyages. *17.5.1930:* Laid up at Preston. *8.3.1932:* Sold to L.M. Logothetis and M. Fakis, Andros, Greece for £4,436 and renamed AGHIA VARVARA. *24.3.1934:* When anchored in Kiel Harbour waiting for fog to clear, a German torpedo boat crashed into her port side. Damage to the shell plating was repaired at Kiel. *30.9.1937:* When emerging from the Bosphorus into the Black Sea, ran down and sank the Turkish sailing vessel NIMET HUDA. No lives were lost. *22.6.1938:* Ran hard aground at 08.11 in dense fog on Arradic Rocks, two miles south of Ushant, when on passage from Durban to Ghent with a cargo of manganese

Electrician at Preston where she was laid up in the early 1930s. *[J. and M. Clarkson]*

ore. She was leaking badly and at 09.00 the crew abandoned ship. All were saved but she soon sank in deep water and became a total loss.

181. STATESMAN (3) 1918-1932 Steel steamer rigged as two-masted schooner. Two decks and five holds.
O.N. 137419 5,596g 3,553n 9,220d 423.3 x 53.0 x 32.64 feet Cargo capacity: 445,531 cubic feet.
International Code: JHMK.
T. 3-cyl. by David Rowan and Co., Glasgow; 27.5, 45, 75 x 51 inches, 11.25 knots.

17.11.1914: Launched by Russell and Co., Port Glasgow (Yard No. 669) for British and Foreign Steam Ship Co. Ltd. (Rankin, Gilmour and Co. Ltd., managers), Liverpool as SAINT GEORGE. *12.1914:* Completed. *2.1918:* Acquired by the company for £179,947. *18.4.1918:* Renamed STATESMAN. *5.8.1930:* Laid up at Barrow-in-Furness until 10.9.1931 when negotiations for her sale to Blue Cross Line (James Russell Ltd., managers) reached an advanced stage.

She was brought to Birkenhead for a dry dock inspection and the new name BLUE LAGOON was being considered. However, the purchaser was unable to raise sufficient funds and in 12.1931 the sale was cancelled. *16.12.1931:* Returned to Barrow-in-Furness to resume lay-up. *8.10.1932:* Sold to Italian shipbreakers for £3,415. *28.11.1932:* Arrived at Savona.

A victim of the Depression, *Statesman* was broken up at the early age of 18. *[J. and M. Clarkson]*

182. MATADOR (2) 1918-1932 Steel steamer rigged as two-masted schooner. Two decks and four holds.
O.N. 131407 4,761g 2,950n 7,900d 395.7 x 51.5 x 29.58 feet Cargo capacity: 362,221 cubic feet.
International Code: HVBP.
T. 3-cyl. by George Clark Ltd., Sunderland; 25.5, 42, 69 x 48 inches, 10.5 knots.

4.11.1911: Launched by J.L.Thompson and Sons Ltd., Sunderland (Yard No. 485) for the Bedouin Steam Navigation Co. Ltd. (W. and R. Thomson, managers), Liverpool as ARAB. *12.1911:* Completed. *1913:* Sold to British and Foreign Steam Ship Co. Ltd. (Rankin, Gilmour and Co. Ltd., managers), Liverpool and renamed SAINT VERONICA. *8.2.1916:* Requisitioned by the Shipping Controller initially as a timber transport and collier serving North Russia. *11.3.1918:* Acquired by the company for £133,587. *10.8.1918:* Renamed MATADOR. *27.7.1922:* Broke adrift on a strong bore tide while berthed at Calcutta but no damage was reported. (See ACTOR, 174). *17.10.1930:* Laid up at Barrow-in-Furness. *13.10.1932:* Sold to Douglas and Ramsay, Glasgow for demolition. *21.10.1932:* Arrived in the Clyde.

Matador in the Mersey. Note the tall funnel, on which the bead welding for a previous owner's markings can be seen. *[J. and M. Clarkson]*

183. BARRISTER (3) 1918 Steel steamship rigged as two-masted schooner. Two decks and five holds.
O.N. 137498 4,952g 3,143n 8,220d 404.8 x 52.2.x 30.16 feet Cargo capacity: 402,781 cubic feet.
International Code: JMLW.
T. 3-cyl. by J.G.Kincaid and Co. Ltd., Greenock; 26, 42, 70 x 48 inches, 10.5 knots.

12.10.1915: Launched by Russell and Co., Port Glasgow (Yard No. 682) for British and Foreign Steam Ship Co. Ltd. (Rankin, Gilmour and Co. Ltd., managers), Liverpool as SAINT HUGO. *4.1916:* Completed. *8.8.1916:* Requisitioned by the Shipping Controller initially for service with the Commercial Branch for Military Account and employed carrying nitrate. *25.2.1918:* Acquired by the company for £170,840. *6.5.1918:* Renamed BARRISTER. *19.9.1918:*

Torpedoed and sunk by the German submarine UB 64 (Oberleutnant-zur-See Ernst Krieger) in the Irish Sea about 9 miles and 275 degrees from the Chicken Rock, Isle of Man. She was on passage from Glasgow and Liverpool for the West Indies with general cargo and mails. Thirty lives were lost, and among the few survivors was Second Officer James Stocks, who became Marine Superintendent from 1955 to 1962.

184. PATRICIAN (2) 1918-1938 Steel steamship rigged as two-masted schooner. Two decks and five holds.
O.N. 140539 5,742g 3,636n 9,350d 423.0 x 56.0 x 31.46 feet. Cargo capacity: 453,237 cubic feet.
International Code: JRHW (GQNZ after 1933).
T. 3-cyl. by J.G. Kincaid and Co. Ltd., Greenock; 27, 45, 74 x 51 inches, 11 knots.

1917: Launched by Russell and Co., Port Glasgow (Yard No. 692) for British and Foreign Steam Ship Co. Ltd. (Rankin, Gilmour and Co. Ltd., managers), Liverpool as SAINT JEROME. She had been laid down in 1914, but work was delayed by the wartime shortage of steel. *10.1917:* Completed. *7.3.1918:* Requisitioned by the Shipping Controller for service with the Commercial Branch for Military Account and employed carrying nitrate. *12.3.1918:* Acquired by the company for £203,676. *1.1919:* Renamed PATRICIAN. *7.7.1919:* Grounded on the Pluckington Bank in the River Mersey, pulled off by three tugs and docked apparently undamaged. *4.6.1938:* Sold to the Golden Cross Line (Bristol Channel) Ltd., London for £16,929 and renamed MAZIC. Resold some weeks

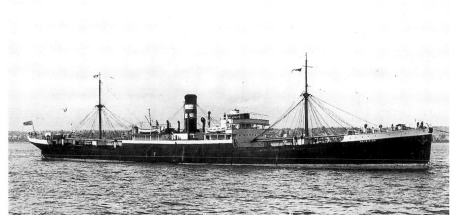

Patrician in the Mersey. *[J. and M. Clarkson]*

later at a profit to Pasquale Mazzella, Naples, Italy and renamed ERMINIA MAZZELLA. *13.2.1941:* Sailed from Kismayu on the eve of its capture by Allied forces and made for occupied Europe via Diego Suarez and the Cape of Good Hope. Intercepted and captured by HMS HAWKINS and units of the South African Navy and escorted to Kilindini Harbour, Mombasa. Renamed IMPALA and transferred to Durban where she was taken over by the Union Government of South Africa for service with the Railways and Harbours Administration. Later renamed AGULHAS. *23.10.1947:*

Diverted to Adelaide on a voyage from Safaga to Newcastle, New South Wales with a cargo of phosphates after sustaining damage during heavy weather. Repairs cost Aus.£3,000 and the Lloyd's Surveyor expressed concern about the condition of the vessel and recommended a thorough examination in dry dock after the cargo was discharged. *1952:* Renamed NOORDEWAAL. *30.5.1954:* Arrived at Hong Kong to be broken up by Pacific Salvage Co. Ltd. *15.6.1954:* Work began.

185. GLADIATOR (3) 1918-1932 Steel steamship rigged as two-masted schooner. Two decks, a shelter-deck and five holds. O.N. 135567 6,372g 4,742n 8,754d 405.1 x 52.0 x 30.22 feet. Cargo capacity: 486,626 cubic feet. International Code: JFHG.

T. 3-cyl. by David Rowan and Co. Ltd., Glasgow; 27, 44, 73 x 48 inches, 10.75 knots.

24.1.1914: Launched by William Hamilton and Co. Ltd., Port Glasgow (Yard No. 295) for British and Foreign Steam Ship Co. Ltd. (Rankin, Gilmour and Co. Ltd., managers), Liverpool as SAINT QUENTIN. *4.1914:* Completed. *15.3.1916:* Requisitioned by the Shipping Controller and initially employed on French and then Italian Government service. *22.3.1918:* Acquired by the company for £164,908 and later renamed GLADIATOR. *2.1919:* Cadet Harold Minshull of Caerwys, Flint, aged 16 and making his first voyage to sea, was "accidentally shot" on board. Captain O.E. Cafferata, on passage from Liverpool to Kingston, put into St. Thomas, but the boy died there 5.3.1919. It cost £40 to bring the body home. *12.3.1923:* Leaving her berth at Number 9 Stuyvesant Dock, New Orleans,

Gladiator laid up at Fowey. [World Ship Photo Library]

she took a sheer while backing off the wharf, and her bow fell down on the Glasgow steamer NORMAN MONARCH (4,997/09) berthed astern at Number 7. Acting on the pilot's advice (and against Captain Herbert Russell's better judgement), GLADIATOR was attempting the manoeuvre in fresh squally weather in a two-knot current without the aid of a tug. The fact that NORMAN MONARCH's port anchor was hanging clear of the hawse-pipe at the point of impact aggravated the damage to both ships, which was substantial. *29.11.1923:* The case was heard in the Admiralty Division of the High Court before Mr Justice Hill sitting with two nautical assessors. Judgement was given in favour of NORMAN MONARCH. *13.10.1930:* Laid up at Fowey. *8.10.1932:* Sold to South Stockton Shipbreaking Co. Ltd. for demolition. *15.10.1932:* Arrived at Stockton-on-Tees.

186. SCULPTOR (3) 1918 Steel steamship rigged as two-masted schooner. Two decks and five holds. O.N. 131459 4,874g 3,054n 8,120d 400.6 x 52.1 x 30.25 feet. International Code: HWRJ.

T. 3-cyl. by David Rowan and Co. Ltd., Glasgow; 27, 44, 73 x 48 inches, 10.75 knots.

27.8.1912: Launched by A. McMillan and Son Ltd., Dumbarton (Yard No. 445) for British and Foreign Steam Ship Co. Ltd. (Rankin, Gilmour and Co. Ltd., managers), Liverpool as SAINT ANDREW. *9.1912:* Completed. *23.10.1915:* Requisitioned by the Shipping Controller and initially employed as a collier. *28.3.1918:* Acquired by the company for £142,751. *18.4.1918:* Renamed SCULPTOR. *17.5.1918:* Torpedoed by the German submarine U 39 (Kapitänleutnant Heinrich Metzger), about 60 miles north west by west a quarter west of Oran, when on passage from Swansea to Salonica with military stores and completely disabled. The Third and Fourth Engineers were killed. The survivors abandoned ship in two lifeboats, which stood by for the rest of the day and most of the night. The Third Officer, W.H. Corlett, and his boat's crew were then picked up by a French trawler and taken to Bizerta. Meanwhile the crew of the other boat, in charge of the Master, Captain S.S. Ward, reboarded the vessel and an attempt was made to put a towing line aboard a Royal Naval vessel and tow the stricken SCULPTOR to Oran. Since she was in imminent danger of sinking, the attempt was abandoned and she was beached near Mers-el-Kebir. Much of her cargo was still intact, and being urgently needed by the army at Salonica, every effort was made to salvage as much as possible using troops stationed locally. Most of the ship's officers still remained with the vessel. A few days later, there was a sudden and tremendous explosion which completely demolished the bridge and adjacent structure, killing everyone in the vicinity. Among the fatalities were Captain Ward, Second Officer M.H. Milestone, the Radio Officer and two crew members. The Chief Officer, W.F. Dowling was seriously injured. The cause of the explosion was believed to have been when acetylene, emitted when a consignment of calcium carbide in number 3 'tween deck came in contact with water, was ignited by a spark from the galley. Unloading of the stores was subsequently resumed and, as some of the holds were flooded, divers were brought in to salvage valuable equipment. The wreck was then abandoned.

The only known photo of the *Sculptor*, taken after the explosion which damaged her bridge whilst beached near Mers-el-Kebir in 1918.

187. GOVERNOR (3) 1918-1950 Steel steamship. Two decks and five holds. One mast.
O.N. 140587 6,152g 3,891n 8,440d 410.3 x 52.25 x 32.85 feet. Cargo capacity: 425,043 cubic feet.
International Code: JTSQ (GQPB after 1933).
T. 3-cyl. by D. and W. Henderson and Co. Ltd., Glasgow; 24.5, 42.5, 72 x 54 inches, 12 knots.

9.5.1918: Launched by D. and W. Henderson and Co. Ltd., Glasgow (Yard No. 500) for the company. *5.7.1918:* Delivered at a cost of £129,184. Later sailed from Liverpool to South Africa on her maiden voyage under Captain W.N. Neilson. *1920:* Converted to oil fuel at a cost of £4,156. *1923:* Reconverted to coal burning. *11.7.1928:* When on passage from Liverpool for Calcutta, encountered thick fog off the Portuguese coast. At 10.40 collided with the starboard quarter of the Royal Mail steamer DEMERARA (11,484/12), tearing a hole above the waterline. GOVERNOR sustained damage to her stem and bow plating, too serious to continue the voyage, and returned to Liverpool for repair. There were no casualties or damage to cargo sustained by either party, but claims for damage exceeded £20,000. *20.1.1941:* Damage to the high-pressure cylinder crankshaft disabled the main engines while in the vicinity of Takoradi on passage from Liverpool to Cape Town. Taken in tow by a Royal Naval vessel and arrived 2.2.1941 at Takoradi. There she was handed over to the tug ATLAS and towed to

Lagos where better repair facilities were available. *18.4.1941:* Sailed for Cape Town following completion of repairs. *1946:* Re-converted to burn fuel oil. *10.9.1949:* Fire broke out in number 4 'tween deck when in position 42.53N, 16.25W, about 360 miles and 286 degrees from Oporto, when on passage from London to the West Indies. She turned and headed for that port at the same time attempting to smother the fire by injecting steam. Meanwhile the company's PROSPECTOR, on passage from Glasgow to Barbados, was instructed to divert from her voyage and stand by the burning vessel. *13.9.1949:* Arrived at Lisbon where the fire was located in the 'tween deck above the deep tank which at that time contained 160 tons of fuel oil. The fire was dealt with using foam and carbon dioxide gas and 15.9.1949 was finally extinguished. *9.1.1950:* Sold to British Iron and Steel Corporation for £11,250 for demolition and allocated to Metal Industries Ltd. *17.1.1950:* Arrived at Rosyth in tow of the tug SEAMAN (369/24) and demolition commenced the same day.

Governor had an unusual rig for a Harrison ship, with only one mast, the main being replaced by a pair of Samson posts. *[J. and M. Clarkson]*

188. COUNSELLOR (3) 1920-1925 Steel steamship rigged as two-masted schooner. Two decks and three holds.
O.N. 115724 2,746g 1,764n 4,270d. 320.0 x 44.0 x 25.48 feet. Cargo capacity: 187,283 cubic feet.
International Code: TRPW.
T. 3-cyl. by Barclay, Curle and Co. Ltd., Whiteinch; 25, 41, 67 x 45 inches, 11.25 knots.

14.10.1902: Launched by Barclay, Curle and Co. Ltd., Whiteinch (Yard No. 435) for the Crown Steam Ship Co. Ltd. (Prentice, Service and Henderson, managers), Glasgow as CROWN OF GRANADA. *11.1902:* Completed. *6.8.1914:* Requisitioned by the Shipping Controller for service as an Expeditionary Force Transport and employed carrying troops across the Channel. *23.3.1917:* Chased and attacked by gunfire from the German submarine U 54 in the Atlantic off south west Ireland in position 49.00N, 15.50W. The submarine was driven off by CROWN OF GRANADA's defensive armament. She was on passage from London to Barbados. *2.3.1920:* Acquired by the company for £94,537. *30.7.1920:* Renamed COUNSELLOR. *20.6.1925:* Sold to P. and W. MacLellan Ltd. for £5,585 for demolition. *2.7.1925:* Arrived at Bo'ness.

Counsellor in the Avon Gorge. As the *Crown of Granada* she was the first of eight ships bought from Prentice, Service and Henderson. *[Roy Fenton collection]*

189. COMMODORE (2) 1920-1925 Steel steamship rigged as two-masted schooner. Two decks and three holds.
O.N. 115715 2,739g 1,762n 4,270d 320.0 x 44.0 x 25.48 feet Cargo capacity: 187,283 cubic feet.
International Code: TQRW.
T. 3-cyl. by Barclay, Curle and Co. Ltd., Whiteinch; 25, 41, 67 x 45 inches, 11.25 knots.

6.9.1902: Launched by Barclay, Curle and Co. Ltd., Whiteinch (Yard No. 434) for Crown Steam Ship Co.Ltd. (Prentice, Service and Henderson, managers), Glasgow as CROWN OF NAVARRE. *10.1902:* Completed. *8.3.1920:* Acquired by the company for £94,537. *2.9.1920:* Renamed COMMODORE. *14.4.1925:* Sold to African and Eastern Trade Corporation Ltd. (W. Nicholl, manager), Liverpool for £7,442 and renamed ETHIOPIAN. *23.2.1928:* Whilst anchored off Freetown, Sierra Leone, a strong wind and spring tide caused the vessel to drag her anchor and collide with the sloop DAFFODIL anchored astern. Her propeller fouled HMS DAFFODIL's cable, forcing the naval vessel to slip. She had also sustained damage to her stem bar and seven shell plates. It took divers, able to work only at slack water, a week to clear the cable from ETHIOPIAN's propeller. *2.3.1928:* Surveyed and pronounced seaworthy. *1930:* Sold to Niger Co. Ltd., Liverpool. *1931:* Owners restyled United Africa Co. Ltd. *1933:* Sold to Bartram and Sons Ltd., Sunderland for demolition. *1.5.1933:* Arrived Sunderland.

Comparing the upper photograph of *Crown of Navarre* in the Avon with the lower view of her as *Commodore* reveals that Harrisons made modifications to her superstructure amidships. Other details were unchanged, including the two-piece masts and what appears to be a heavy derrick on the foremast.

[World Ship Photo Library; Roy Fenton collection]

190. COLLEGIAN (2) 1920-1933 Steel steamship rigged as schooner. Two decks, a shelter deck and four holds. Two twin-masts.
O.N. 133073 7,623g 4,853n 9,900d 455.4 x 56.25 x 39.0 feet Cargo capacity: 547,568 cubic feet.
International Code: HWQN.
T. 3-cyl. by Dunsmuir and Jackson Ltd., Glasgow; 28, 46, 77 x 54 inches, 12.25 knots.

10.8.1912: Launched by Russell and Co., Port Glasgow (Yard No. 635) for Crown Steam Ship Co. Ltd. (Prentice, Service and Henderson, managers), Glasgow as CROWN OF SEVILLE. *9.1912:* Completed. *9.12.1916:* Requisitioned by the Shipping Controller for service as an Expeditionary Force Transport. *1.4.1920:* Acquired by the company for £294,117. *7.1920:* Renamed COLLEGIAN. *22.3.1923:* A fierce fire broke out in number 2 hold whilst berthed in Toxteth Dock, Liverpool, loaded with bales of gunnies from Calcutta. The fire was quickly brought under control but damage was estimated to be about £8,000. *14.11.1925:* In collision with the Thames sailing barge ARTHUR RELF (88/08) in Gravesend Reach. The barge's starboard bow was damaged and she was beached on the north shore by the tug SUN XV (183/25). *21.3.1927:* Put into Vigo with main engines partially disabled. *4.4.1927:* Repairs completed and resumed her voyage to Calcutta. *11.2.1931:* Laid up at Barrow-in-Furness. *26.10.1933:* Sold to W.H.

Arnott Young and Co for £6,002 for demolition. Resold to West of Scotland Shipbreaking Co.Ltd. *13.11.1933:* Arrived at Troon.

Collegian, ex-Crown of Seville, had unusual double masts.   *[J. and M. Clarkson]*

191. CANDIDATE (2) 1920-1928 Steel steamship rigged as schooner. Two decks and five holds. Two twin-masts.
O.N. 124173 4,843g 3,147n 7,990d 400.0 x 52.0 x 29.94 feet Cargo capacity: 392,028 cubic feet.
International Code: HKLR.
T. 3-cyl. by Alexander Stephen and Sons Ltd., Linthouse; 26, 42, 70 x 54 inches, 12 knots.

4.3.1907: Launched by Alexander Stephen and Sons Ltd., Linthouse (Yard No. 417) for Smith and Service, Glasgow as MOUNT SEPHAR. *4.1907:* Completed for the Orm Steam Ship Co. Ltd. (R. and C. Allan, managers), Glasgow as ORMISTON. *1915:* Sold to the Crown Steam Ship Co. Ltd. (Prentice, Service and Henderson, managers), Glasgow. *22.4.1917:* Requisitioned by the Shipping Controller and initially employed on the carriage of Canadian wheat. *7.4.1918:* Attacked with three torpedoes from the German submarine U 53 in the North Atlantic in position 48.17N, 11.20W, some 198 miles 200 degrees from the Fastnet, when on passage from Plymouth to Trinidad in ballast. The torpedoes did not make contact. *12.1918:* Renamed CROWN OF CASTILE. *8.4.1920.* Acquired by the company

for £214,494. *26.7.1920:* Renamed CANDIDATE. *22.10.1928:* Sold to M. Carivalis (Michalinos Maritime and Commercial Co. Ltd., managers), Piraeus, Greece for £19,206 and renamed OKEANIA. *1934:* Transferred to I. Carivalis. *5.12.1936:* In collision in the Kiel Canal at kilometre 43 with the Danish motorship ASNAES (460/21). Both vessels were only slightly damaged and she continued her passage into the North Sea. *8.4.1940:* Struck a mine off Dover, broke in two and sank in position 51.17N, 02.03E, approximately 24 miles, 104 degrees from North Foreland Lighthouse. Twenty nine survivors were landed at Ramsgate but the Chief Engineer was reported missing. She was on passage from Rotterdam for La Plata in ballast and was reported to be travelling outside the swept channel.

Candidate, ex *Ormiston* had twin masts which, unusually, were not joined to make a goalpost mast. *[J. and M. Clarkson]*

192. CHANCELLOR (4) (1920-1939) Steel steamship rigged as two-masted schooner. Two decks and five holds.
O.N. 137822 4,607g 2,942n 7,400d 385.0 x 52.0 x 29.16 feet. Cargo capacity: 363,831 cubic feet.
International Code: JNHR (GQPF after 1933).
T. 3-cyl. by J.G. Kincaid and Co. Ltd., Greenock; 27, 44, 73 x 48 inches, 11.25 knots.

18.5.1916: Launched by Russell and Co., Port Glasgow (Yard No. 688) for Crown Steam Ship Co.Ltd. (Prentice, Service and Henderson, managers), Glasgow as CROWN OF CADIZ. *10.1916:* Delivered. *30.4.1920:* Acquired by the company for £247,374. *26.7.1920:* Renamed CHANCELLOR. *5.1926:* Whilst at Pernambuco there was an outbreak of yellow fever on board. *17.5.1926:* It was decided to fumigate the crew's quarters, but during the disinfecting process there was a violent explosion. Chief Officer Harold Coates was severely burned, Second Officer

W.H. Corlett slightly injured, and both were rushed to hospital. They both eventually made a full recovery. *2.12.1939:* Sank following a collision with the tanker ATHELCHIEF (7,707/25) in position 44.30N, 61.51W, about 70 miles off Halifax in the North Atlantic, while sailing in convoy HXF 11 during dense fog. She was on passage from Belize and New Orleans via Halifax, Nova Scotia for Liverpool and Manchester with general cargo. The crew were rescued by the Pacific Steam Navigation Company's OROPESA (14,118/20).

Crises in convoy
During the afternoon of 2nd December 1939 fourteen ships left Halifax harbour for the open sea. Once clear of the land they deployed into convoy formation of six columns, and although it was difficult to pick out the identification pennants in the uncertain light of a December dusk, there was little confusion. CHANCELLOR, flying numeral pennants "3" and "2", indicating the second ship in the third column, was next astern of the Commodore ship, Furness Withy's NEWFOUNDLAND (6,791/25), whose silhouette was unmistakeable. Over to starboard, leading the fifth column, was another Harrison vessel, the INKOSI, while the Armed Merchant Cruiser ASCANIA took up her station between the centre columns as ocean escort. By the time darkness fell, all ships were in station, the columns three cables apart, while a mere two cables - about three ships' lengths - separated the ships in column.

It was an uneasy setting for merchant shipmasters

to find themselves in. Accustomed as they were to the open sea, where ships passing or crossing within three miles constituted a "close quarters situation", the idea of plunging into the wake of a ship only 400 yards ahead, with little room for manoeuvre on either flank, was most unwelcome. The war was only three months old, and few shipmasters had yet grown accustomed to convoy work. Most of them would have preferred to sail independently, and take their chances with U-boats and surface raiders. The CHANCELLOR's officers were having their first experience of an ocean convoy, and although the younger men were not a little excited by all the signalling and manoeuvres, it was anathema to Captain W.B. Wilford, and totally alien to his settled ways, which were to ring "Full Away" when clear of the port, set a course away from the land; and relax. But now there was no opportunity to relax. Instead, it was necessary to squint continuously through an optical gadget

Two views of *Chancellor,* the lower one being dated 12th July 1934, and of Captain W.B. Wilford OBE, master at the time of *Chancellor's* loss in 1939.   [*J. and M. Clarkson; Starfield and Co.]*

in order to maintain station on the ship ahead; and to whistle down to the engineers every few minutes, and ask them to set the revolutions "up two", or "down four", as the case may be; or to decipher flag signals which inevitably wrapped themselves round the halyards, or fluttered end-on and unreadable in the wind. At night, of course, it was worse. All one could see then was the amorphous shadow of the ship ahead, or sometimes a tiny blue stern light, or perhaps the phosphorescent wash of her wake. And, naturally, the optical station-keeping gadget was quite useless in the dark. Station keeping thus became a matter of guess work, with a tendency to err on the safe side by dropping well astern at night, hoping to get on station before dawn, before the Commodore came on deck (and providing a U-boat did not catch the straggler first).

However, the condition most hated and feared by generations of seamen is fog. And when the ship is in close proximity with other ships, as in convoy, that fear is intensified. Fog disorientates the senses; the soft, clinging cocoon of mist is a treacherous trap, dripping with apprehension, liable to dissipate logical thinking, and impair sound judgement. Such must have been the state of affairs aboard CHANCELLOR and her consorts when, at 19.30, they disappeared abruptly, at a speed of 11 knots, into a bank of thick, blanketing fog. A barrage of sound signals emanated from where the shadowy loom of the Commodore ship had been, but they were misheard or misunderstood by those on the CHANCELLOR. Actually, the whistle blasts

signalled a reduction of speed, a tactic implemented at once by the Commodore.

At 19.42 the officers on CHANCELLOR's bridge observed the stern light of the leading ship perilously close ahead. The helm was ordered hard-a-starboard and the feeble light disappeared as the ship's head swung away some 30 degrees. The immediate danger was past; speed was reduced, and the helm swung the opposite way to resume course. People breathed again - until a few minutes later, when the lookout on the forecastle head tolled the bell, a single knell to warn of the ominous proximity of a ship to starboard. The engines were stopped, but for a few seconds they could see nothing from the bridge. Then at 19.49, according to the report, the bows of a ship were seen darkly looming through the fog, a wreath of white water curling at the waterline. The ship came on with pitiless intent. She buried her stem in the fore part of No. 2 hold, opening up a gaping wound above and below the waterline, admitting a thousand tons of sea water in minutes. With a tortured wrenching of steel, the ships tore themselves apart, and drifted into the fog, out of each other's sight.

CHANCELLOR was mortally wounded, and at 20.05 Captain Wilford broke wireless silence to report the incident, and that his ship was sinking. He ordered the boats to be made ready, and at 20.20 gave the order, "Abandon ship!" The falls were manned, and the boats lowered in good order, for the weather was calm. When all were aboard, they cast off and the ship, still carrying residual way, disappeared into the fog. Three boats kept together, but number 2 boat drifted away, out of sight. There had been a good deal of whistle blowing, as can well be imagined, but the raucous sounds were becoming fainter as the convoy drew away.

Suddenly, a deep bellow sounded close to. The boats' crews answered with some concerted bellows of their own, and out of the fog loomed the stately bulk of Pacific Steam's OROPESA which, as rescue ship designate, had been searching for the castaways. It was little short of a

Chancellor sinking after colliding with the tanker *Athelchief* on 2nd December 1939.

miracle, in the conditions prevailing, that the rescue ship had found them. Moreover, before they were all safely aboard at 22.20 even the missing number 2 boat had turned up. All 42 members of CHANCELLOR'S crew had survived a nerve-wracking ordeal. The mysterious vessel which had been the instrument of CHANCELLOR'S fate was the United Molasses tanker ATHELCHIEF, which limped back to Halifax for repairs.[125]

Meanwhile, OROPESA was doing her best to overtake the convoy. The fog had cleared during the day only to be replaced by a southeast gale. During the graveyard watch on 4th December, the Master, Captain Dunn, was on the bridge with the Second Officer while the ship plunged through gray-bearded combers, barely making nine knots on a course of 089 degrees. Towards 03.00 they sighted the shadowy shape of a ship fine on the port bow. Cautiously, the Second Officer altered course 5 degrees to starboard, and switched on the dimmed side lights. Had they caught up with the convoy at last? Unfortunately, they had not. The stranger was a loner, the Furness Withy steamer MANCHESTER REGIMENT (5,989/22), bound from Manchester to Canadian ports, steering 266 degrees at 12½ knots, on a classic collision course, with the gale on her port quarter. Second Officer Boyce had in turn seen the vague shape of OROPESA fine on the starboard bow, so he altered course 10 degrees to port. The seeds of disaster had been sown. Only when each saw the other's dim lights did the horrifying nature of the situation become apparent, demanding drastic action.

OROPESA put the helm hard-a-starboard -

MANCHESTER REGIMENT went hard-a-port, and a rapidly deteriorating situation became irretrievable. The impact, when it came, was devastating. OROPESA's sharp stem sliced into the MANCHESTER REGIMENT's starboard side, just abaft the bridge. The influx of seawater was overwhelming, flooding number 3 hold, the stokehold, and the engine room. The ship was soon in extremis, and sank shortly afterwards. The crew abandoned her in formidable conditions, and nine men were lost when a lifeboat capsized. Thus OROPESA, only 29 hours after picking up CHANCELLOR's crew, found herself once again in the role of rescue ship, plucking 61 survivors from the sea. Then, with her bows open to the sea, and her fore-peak bulkhead under severe pressure, the injured liner turned about, and headed back to Halifax.[126]

At daybreak on 3rd, CHANCELLOR, her foredeck awash, was still afloat, and the fog having cleared in that vicinity the ocean-going tug, FOUNDATION FRANKLIN (653/18), was sent out from Halifax to make an attempt at salvage. A line was put aboard the drifting hulk, but the ship foundered before the tug could bring her to a safe haven.

In November 1942 the case of the loss of the CHANCELLOR was heard before Mr. Justice Bucknill sitting with two nautical assessors in the Admiralty Court. It was held that the CHANCELLOR alone was to blame for the collision, in that she failed to stop her engines when those in command became aware that she was running up on the Commodore ship, and for altering course to starboard. No blame was attached to the ATHELCHIEF.

193. CRAFTSMAN (2) 1920-1933 Steel steamship rigged as two-masted schooner. Two decks, a shelter-deck and five holds. O.N. 133002 7,619g 4,874n 9,900d 455.4 x 56.25 x 39.0 feet.
International Code: HVCR.
T. 3-cyl. by Dunsmuir and Jackson Ltd., Govan; 28, 46, 77 x 54 inches, 12.25 knots.

22.11.1911: Launched by Russell and Co., Port Glasgow (Yard No. 626) for Crown Steam Ship Co. Ltd. (Prentice, Service and Henderson, managers), Glasgow as CROWN OF TOLEDO. *1.1912:* Completed. *6.8.1914:* Requisitioned by the Shipping Controller and employed as an

Expeditionary Force Transport. *8.4.1920:* Acquired by the company for £287,816. *18.10.1920:* Renamed CRAFTSMAN. *22.12.1930:* Laid up at Barrow-in-Furness. *6.12.1933:* Sold to T.W.Ward Ltd. for demolition. *1934:* Broken up at Barrow-in-Furness.

Craftsman, ex *Crown of Toledo,* with a goalpost foremast.

[*J. and M. Clarkson*]

194. COMEDIAN (2) 1920-1925 Steel steamship rigged as two-masted schooner. Two decks and four holds.
O.N. 112809 3,472g 2,239n 5,720d 345.0 x 46.25 x 26.87 feet Cargo capacity 256,871 cubic feet.
International Code: SFBW.
T. 3-cyl. by North Eastern Marine Engineering Co. Ltd., Wallsend; 24, 40, 64 x 42 inches, 9 knots.

20.12.1900: Launched by William Dobson and Co. Ltd., Low Walker (Yard No.113) for Steam Ship Trafalgar Co. Ltd. (Nye, Clare and Co., managers), London as RODNEY. *2.1901:* Completed. *3.1910:* Sold to Crown Steam Ship Co. Ltd. (Prentice, Service and Henderson, managers), Glasgow and renamed CROWN OF CORDOVA. *18.6.1915:* Requisitioned by the Shipping Controller for service as a collier. *13.5.1920:* Acquired by the company for £128,414. *26.8.1920:* Renamed COMEDIAN. *29.6.1922:* The air pump rod fractured when outward bound from Liverpool to the West Indies and the vessel was disabled off Holyhead. A tug was despatched from Liverpool and she was towed back to the Mersey for repair. *28.2.1925:* The steering gear was disabled off the Mersey Bar Lightvessel and she was towed up river by the tug STORM COCK (215/85). *3.1925:* Sold to Industrie

Comedian, probably in a West Indian anchorage.

Navali Societa Anonima, Genoa, Italy and renamed GRAZIA. Resold to G.B. Schiaffino and Co., Camogli, Italy and later renamed TERESA SCHIAFFINO. *19.1.1927:* Sustained severe damage to her steering gear during heavy weather in the Mediterranean when on passage from Novorossiisk to Falmouth. The Master sent an SOS message giving her position as 12 miles north of Cape Bougaroni and the message was picked up and relayed by stations from Malta to Cadiz and Lands End. Temporary repairs were made by the ship's engineers and she arrived

21.1.1927 at Algiers. *4.1.1932:* The steering gear suffered a further malfunction when bound from Izmir to Genoa with 4,500 tons of fruit and cereals. As a result she ran aground near Aghi Theodori at the eastern entrance to the Corinth Canal. The Matsas Salvage Co. was engaged and she was refloated 10.1.1932 virtually undamaged after discharging some 1,300 tons of cargo. *9.1933:* Sold to shipbreakers at Genoa.

195. CENTURION (2) 1920-1925 Steel steamship. Two decks and five holds. Two twin-masts.
O.N. 124139 4,821g 3,140n 8,020d 400.05 x 52.0 x 29.94 feet. Cargo capacity: 441,835 cubic feet.
International Code: HJGK.
T. 3-cyl. by Alexander Stephen and Sons Ltd., Linthouse; 26, 42, 70 x 54 inches, 12 knots.

17.9.1906: Launched by Alexander Stephen and Sons Ltd., Linthouse (Yard No. 416) for Crown Steam Ship Co. Ltd. (Prentice, Service and Henderson, managers), Glasgow as CROWN OF GALICIA. *10.1906:* Completed. *3.8.1914:* Requisitioned by the Shipping Controller for service as a Squadron Supply Ship. *5.1920:* Acquired by the company for £216,911. *19.11.1920:* Renamed CENTURION. *9.5.1925:* Fire broke out when lying in Toxteth Dock, Liverpool. Extinguished after four hours but many bags of sugar, cotton-seed and bales of cotton in numbers 3 and 4 holds were damaged or destroyed. *25.5.1925:* Sold to Eftikhia Steam Ship Co. Ltd. (P. Wigham Richardson, manager), London and renamed BITO. *25.7.1925:* Struck and seriously damaged by the German steamer SCHEER (8,142/15) whilst lying at buoys in Rotterdam. *19.10.1925:* When outward bound from the River Plate, swung out of the channel near kilometre 68/69 and grounded. Attempts by tugs to refloat her were unsuccessful and work commenced

22.10.1925 to discharge approximately 1,250 tons of her cargo of maize into lighters. On 25.10.1925 the coal bunkers were reported to be on fire but the blaze was kept under control until she was refloated 26.10.1925 and docked at Buenos Aires. The damaged coal was discharged, and the maize re-loaded. *1926:* Sold to Rickmers Rhederei Akt. Ges. (Rickmers Linie), Hamburg, Germany, and renamed ETHA RICKMERS. *19.1.1933:* In collision with the German steamer ELSTER (1,136/22) 10 miles west of Borkum Lightvessel when inward bound from Sabang to Hamburg. The ELSTER was badly damaged on the port side and below the waterline whilst ETHA RICKMERS sustained bow damage. *1938:* Sold to Moller Line Ltd., Shanghai, and renamed GLADYS MOLLER. *7.11.1942:* Wrecked on Baker Rocks on the east coast of Ceylon in position 07.55.50N, 81.35.30E when on passage from Safaga to Vizagapatnam and Calcutta with a cargo of salt.

Centurion, ex *Crown of Galicia,* was a sister of *Candidate* (191).

196. SPEAKER (1) 1920-1926 Steel steamship rigged as two-masted schooner. Two decks and four holds.
O.N. 135278 4,264g 2,688n 6,650d 370.3 x 50.35 x 28.45 feet. Cargo capacity: 386,115 cubic feet.
International Code: JDFV.
T. 3-cyl. by John Readhead and Sons Ltd., South Shields; 28, 46, 75 x 48 inches, 11 knots.

19.8.1913: Launched by John Readhead and Sons Ltd., South Shields (Yard No. 436) for Scrutton, Sons and Co., London as SAVAN. *18.10.1913:* Ran trials and delivered. *12.3.1918:* Torpedoed and damaged by the German submarine UC 71 in the English Channel, 5½ miles east half south from Anvil Point, when on a voyage from London to the West Indies in ballast. The crew of 37 was taken off by the armed trawler TORONTO and landed at Portland. There was one fatality. The master and 10 crew subsequently returned to the vessel and she was taken in tow by the armed trawlers TORONTO, LORD CECIL, ST. CUTHBERT and the tug VULCAIN (200/03) and brought in to Portland Harbour. Repaired and returned to service. *14.4.1920:* Acquired by the company for £194,328. This was to be the first of five Scrutton ships to be bought under an agreement signed 18.2.1920 at which time the company also acquired Scruttons' sugar contracts in the West Indies. The total cost of the deal was £921,800. *23.9.1920:* Sailed from Houston,

Texas to inaugurate a service to Liverpool and Manchester. *27.10.1920:* Renamed SPEAKER. *19.5.1926:* Sold to Société Algérienne de Navigation pour l'Afrique du Nord (Ch. Schiaffino and Cie., managers), Algiers and renamed NICOLE SCHIAFFINO. *16.2.1931:* Arrived at Algiers in tow after having been aground in heavy weather near Bougie. The propeller had shed its blades and the spare was shipped while the vessel remained afloat. *27.12.1932:* In collision with the Finnish steamer BARBRO (2,155/02) at the mouth of the River Seine. Put into Le Havre with bows damaged whilst the BARBRO was beached near Honfleur but was later refloated and towed to Rouen. *1937:* Sold to Francesco Galli fu G., Genoa, Italy and renamed GIOVANNI GALLI. *1939:* Sold to Compania Ligure di Navigazione, Genoa, Italy and renamed SANTA PAOLA. *9.1943:* Seized by German forces at Genoa. *20.3.1945:* Scuttled at Venice to avoid capture by the Allies. Subsequently found to be beyond economic repair and the wreck was broken up.

Savan berthed in the Houston Ship Canal in September 1920 when inaugurating a new service to Texas ports. She was renamed *Speaker* shortly afterwards.

The last drop of blood

To have one's ship taken over by a rival firm, and to be taken over with it to serve new masters, can be a very emotional experience. The late Captain J.J. Devereux, then Chief Officer, and himself but recently acquired by Harrisons from Rankin, Gilmour, has recorded how he was sent down to London in the spring of 1920 to join the Scrutton steamer SAVAN as Chief Officer. He was aware that she was about to become a Harrison ship along with her four sisters. Reaching the ship in the West India Dock he presented his letter of introduction to the Master, Captain Haylett. He was then introduced to Scrutton's Marine Superintendent, Captain Crystal, who was also present. Their manner was somewhat distant, if not exactly hostile, and John Devereux felt as though he was being put through some sort of third degree as he tried to answer a barrage of questions. The frosty atmosphere thawed a little when the Scruttons men learned that he, too, had been "taken over" along with Rankin Gilmour's SAINT WINIFRED only two years previously. However, they were astonished when he admitted that he had never been to the West Indies, knew nothing of the trade, nor of the ways of West Indian crews.

A day or two later, R.R. Richardson, Harrisons' Superintendent Engineer, appeared on the quay and tossed a parcel on board. It was addressed to the Chief Officer, and

contained a brand new Harrison Line house flag. A note in the parcel instructed him to hoist the flag at midday. This directive was duly carried out, and on the stroke of noon down came Scruttons' distinctive sea-blue flag with the crimson red ball in the centre, and up to the masthead went Harrison's red Maltese cross on its white field. It was not long before Captain Haylett noted this significant change.

"Who put that thing there?" he demanded with scant respect. The Chief Officer shrugged. "Orders from the office, sir," he explained sympathetically. The Captain sighed. "Let me have the old one, Mr. Devereux," he said sadly. "I might as well keep that 'last drop of blood' for old times' sake".

"Of course, Captain," said John, starting suddenly, for he had a vivid recollection of an industrious apprentice taking away the 'last drop of blood' with the clear intention of using it for cleaning the brasswork. John hastened away, hoping he would be in time to rescue the old flag from such an unseemly fate.

Meanwhile, Captain Haylett leaned over the rail, and spotted Captain Crystal on the quay. Simultaneously, they pointed incredulously at the fresh, new, red-and-white bunting flying proudly at the main truck. Together they stared, and shook their heads in profound and speechless dismay.

197. SCIENTIST (1) 1920-1925 Steel steamship rigged as two-masted schooner. Two decks and four holds.
O.N. 125734 3,844g 2,434n 5,894d 359.4 x 47.65 x 27.93 feet. Cargo capacity: 349,900 cubic feet.
International Code: HNFM.
T. 3-cyl. by John Readhead and Sons Ltd., South Shields; 26, 43, 71 x 48 inches, 12 knots.

30.7.1908: Launched by John Readhead and Sons Ltd., South Shields (Yard No. 406) for Scrutton, Sons and Co., London as SARGASSO. *10.1908:* Delivered. *7.5.1920:* Acquired by the company for £158,614. *7.8.1920:* Renamed SCIENTIST. *3.9.1925:* Sold to Société Algérienne de Navigation pour l'Afrique du Nord (Charles Schiaffino and Compagnie, managers), Algiers for £18,909 and renamed LAURENT SCHIAFFINO. *4.1937:* Sold to African and Continental Steam Ship Co. Ltd., London and renamed AFRICAN TRADER. *1938:* Owners restyled African and Continental Steamship and Trading Co. Ltd. *5.1939:* Sold to E. Szabados, Venice, Italy and renamed PAOLO. *28.2.1943:* Bombed and set on fire by Allied aircraft at Cagliari, Sardinia and sank at her moorings. *13.3.1943:* Raised. *11.6.1943:* While under repair, a spark from an electric welding torch caused an explosion and fire and she sank again. Subsequently raised and broken up.

Scientist leaving Trinidad on Christmas Day 1921, bound for Georgetown, Demerara.
[World Ship Photo Library collection]

198. SETTLER (1) 1920-1928 Steel steamship rigged as two-masted schooner. Two decks and four holds.
O.N. 135125 4,257g 2,687n 6,670d 370.3 x 50.35 x 28.45 feet. Cargo capacity: 386,839 cubic feet.
International Code: HWMG.
T. 3-cyl. by John Readhead and Sons Ltd., South Shields; 28, 46, 75 x 48 inches, 11 knots.

15.6.1912: Launched by John Readhead and Sons Ltd., South Shields (Yard No. 427) for the Direct Line Shipping Co. Ltd. and the Antilles Shipping Co. Ltd. (Scrutton, Sons and Co., managers), London as SABA. *8.1912:* Delivered. *27.5.1915:* Requisitioned by the Shipping Controller for service as an Expeditionary Force Transport and later employed as an ammunition carrier to Northern Russia and as a collier. *8.3.1918:* Struck a mine one mile west of the Royal Sovereign Lightship in position 50.46N, 00.25E and damaged. The mine had been laid earlier that day by the German submarine UC 71. She was taken in tow by the armed trawlers CHRYSOLITE (251/16) and SCHIEHALLION (225/16) to Stokes Bay and was subsequently repaired and returned to service. She was on a voyage from London to Barbados with seven passengers and general cargo. *7.5.1920:* Acquired by the company for £192,752. *3.9.1920:* Renamed SETTLER. *7.2.1922:* Reported a serious fire in the coal bunkers when in position 10.15N, 27.50W, about 327 miles and 214 degrees from the South Point of Brava, Cape Verde. Extinguished by the crew but considerable damage was inflicted on the steelwork of the starboard lower side bunker. *29.6.1924:* In collision with the British and Continental steamer VANELLUS (1,886/21) in the River Mersey. *1.10.1928:* Sold to Atlanticos Steam Navigation Co. Ltd. (E.G. Culucundis and S.C. Costomeni, managers), Syra, Greece for £18,246 and renamed

ATREUS. *1929:* Sold to E. Marcou, Syra, Greece, and renamed NIKOS-MARCOU. *21.1.1932:* Ran aground in fog near Assens in the Little Belt when inward bound from Rosario to Aabenraa. *25.1.1932:* Refloated with the aid of a tug after discharging over 1,150 tons of her cargo of maize. *1933:* Sold to Bristol Channel and Levant Line Ltd. (Charles Hill and Sons, managers), Bristol and renamed YVONNE under the Panama flag. *26.9.1934:* Fouled a telegraph cable with her anchor off Candia and subsequently drifted ashore in the strong wind. A salvage vessel was employed 29.9.1934 and she was eventually refloated 2.10.1934 when all cargo had been discharged. *1934:* Sold to Metal Industries Ltd. for £5,500 for demolition at Rosyth. *15.11.1934:* Arrived Rosyth and 2.1.1935 work commenced.

Settler, previously Scrutton's *Saba.*
[World Ship Photo Library]

Where angels fear
Inward bound to Liverpool from London in ballast, Captain Thomas Chapman in command, the SETTLER became involved in collision with the British and Continental steamer VANELLUS in the River Mersey on 29th June 1924. The circumstances were rather unusual to say the least. In fact, the judge who tried the case was to use the word "absurd" in reference to them. The "absurd" chain of circumstances began at 21.30 on a summer's evening, when VANELLUS,

which had been anchored in the Sloyne waiting to enter Brunswick Dock, weighed anchor and began approaching the lock entrance. The weather was fine with a moderate west north west breeze, and a flood tide running at 2½ to 3 knots. At this time the SETTLER was observed heading up-river about half a mile away, apparently waiting for tugs.

In those days it was customary for the Dockmaster to hoist the appropriate house flag on the pier head flag pole to signal the ship next in turn. On this occasion, a B. and C. house flag was hoisted above a Harrison flag, signifying that the B. and C. ship should precede the Harrison ship. To complicate matters, and to make nonsense out of the signalling system, another B. and C. ship, the OUSEL, had already entered the lock. SETTLER therefore interpreted the signal to mean that she was next in line. VANELLUS, on the other hand, seeing her flag still in the superior position, assumed *she* was next to enter. The outcome was predictable. The two ships came together violently just off the lock entrance, the VANELLUS caving in her bow against SETTLER's starboard side, severely denting eight plates.

The case was heard before Mr. Justice Roche, sitting in the Admiralty Division of the High Court with two nautical assessors on 5th November 1924. The plaintiffs, British and Continental Ltd., alleged that SETTLER had tried to cut in ahead of their ship, thus causing the accident. Harrisons repudiated the charge, saying that their ship was taking her proper turn after OUSEL. This contention was supported by the Dockmaster, who stated in evidence that it was his intention to admit VANELLUS last. The Judge, however, while finding the signalling system somewhat ambiguous, gave judgement in favour of the VANELLUS, asserting that VANELLUS' intentions should have been obvious to those on the SETTLER, who should not have gone ahead on the engines, in an "obstinate" attempt to cross ahead of the VANELLUS and approach the lock. This was the sole cause of the accident, and SETTLER was found solely to blame.[127]

199. SONGSTER 1920-1926 Steel steamship rigged as two-masted schooner. Two decks and four holds.
O.N. 125621 3,815g 2,426n 5,830d 359.3 x 47.6 x 27.9 feet Cargo capacity: 347,833 cubic feet.
International Code: HLPK.
T. 3-cyl. by John Readhead and Sons Ltd., South Shields; 26, 43, 71 x 48 inches, 12 knots.

13.8.1907: Launched by John Readhead and Sons Ltd., South Shields (Yard No. 403) for Scrutton, Sons and Co., London as SPHEROID. *7.10.1907:* Ran trials and delivered. *5.1920:* Acquired by the company for £156,513. *27.9.1920:* Renamed SONGSTER. *3.5.1926:* Sold to William Thomas Shipping Co. Ltd. (R.J. Thomas and Co. Ltd., managers), Liverpool for £16,493 and renamed CAMBRIAN EMPRESS. *11.1.1929:* Put into Las Palmas with bunkers and the cargo in number 2 hold on fire. The fire was extinguished by 14.1.1929 but 200 tons of cargo was destroyed and a further 900 tons damaged. *31.3.1929:* Grounded at kilometre 108 in the River Plate near Martin Garcia Island. *17.4.1929:* Refloated without damage after much of the cargo had been discharged into lighters. *14.11.1929:* Grounded again in the River Plate, this time at kilometre 80. *25.11.1929:* Refloated. *1931:* Sold to United Africa Co. Ltd., Liverpool and renamed ZARIAN. *1932:* Sold to shipbreakers via Douglas and Ramsey, Glasgow. *29.12.1932:* Arrived on the Clyde.

Songster in a particularly busy Thames. [*World Ship Photo Library collection*]

200. SPECIALIST (1) 1920-1936 Steel steamship rigged as two-masted schooner. Two decks and four holds.
O.N. 140310 4,287g 2,695n 6,610d 370.3 x 50.4 x 28.45 feet Cargo capacity: 386,115 cubic feet.
International Code: JQCN (GQPN after 1933).
T. 3-cyl. by John Readhead and Sons Ltd., South Shields; 28, 46, 75 x 48 inches, 11 knots.

1917: Launched by John Readhead and Sons Ltd., South Shields (Yard No. 453) for Scrutton, Sons and Co., London as SANTILLE. *6.1917:* Delivered. *27.4.1920:* Acquired by the company for £219,593. *28.2.1921:* Renamed SPECIALIST. *29.10.1930 - 11.11.1931:* Laid up at Fowey. *5.2.1932:* In collision with the Thames sailing barge JOHN BAYLY when rounding Blackwall Point on the River Thames, outward bound from London. The barge, loaded with cement, sank at once, but the crew were saved. *19.10.1936:* Sold to Nailsea Steam Ship Co. Ltd. (E.R. Management Co. Ltd., managers), Cardiff for £14,012 and renamed NAILSEA LASS. *6.1.1938:* Bombed by Spanish Nationalist aircraft at Valencia. *12.7.1938:* Bombed again at Cartagena. *24.2.1941:* Torpedoed and sunk by the German submarine U 48 (Kapitänleutnant Herbert Kuppisch) 60 miles southwest of Fastnet. Five crew were killed and two taken prisoner. She was on passage from Calcutta and Table Bay for Oban and London with charcoal, pig iron and general cargo.

Specialist, built as Scrutton's *Santille.*

140

201. DRAMATIST (2) 1920-1949 Steel steamship. Two decks and five holds. Two masts.
O.N. 143695 5,806g 3,670n 8,340d 410.0 x 52.3 x 33.17 feet. Cargo capacity: 453,960 cubic feet.
International Code: KHJL (GDVY after 1933).
Three Brown-Curtiss steam turbines by John Brown and Co. Ltd., Clydebank, double reduction geared to a single screw; 12 knots.

31.8.1920: Launched by Charles Connell and Co. Ltd., Scotstoun (Yard No. 383) for the company. *17.12.1920:* Delivered at a cost of £301,868 and sailed from Glasgow to Kingston, Jamaica on her maiden voyage under Captain W.N. Neilson. *4.1923:* On a voyage from Newport News, Virginia to London, the high-pressure and astern turbines were stripped of their blades, and the vessel proceeded on the low-pressure turbine only. *10.10.1925:* Grounded in the Great Bitter Lake when passing through the Suez Canal, homeward bound from Calcutta. *13.10.1925:* Refloated after the discharge of over 14,000 chests of tea into lighters, proceeded to Ismailia for examination and found to be undamaged. However, a lighter carrying 650 chests of tea sank, blocking the Canal for some 24 hours. *16.10.1925:* Finally cleared Port Said. *5.1945:* One of a fleet of merchant ships supporting operations against the Japanese on the Arakan coast, and took part in the amphibious landings

south east of Rangoon which led to the recapture of that city. *28.6.1947:* Bound for Antigua from London, stopped off the north coast of the island to await daylight before approaching the harbour of St.Johns. Course resumed at 05.25, but at 06.40 she grounded on the northern edge of Diamond Bank, with Sandy Island Light bearing 214 degrees, 4.7 miles. She was not making water and efforts at refloating were made by transferring or pumping out ballast. Bower and stream anchors were laid out, but an attempt to haul off at 15.00 failed when a hawser parted. Two further attempts also failed, but at 20.23 on 1.7.1947 she floated clear and came to an anchor. Subsequently dry docked at Curacao and found to be undamaged. *14.7.1949:* Sold to British Iron and Steel Corporation for £11,000 for demolition and allocated to T.W. Ward Ltd, Briton Ferry where she arrived 24.7.1949.

An early Harrison experiment with turbines, *Dramatist* was photographed by John McRoberts in the Mersey. *[J. and M. Clarkson]*

No fat, and very little lean[128]

On 3rd April 1923, the DRAMATIST under the command of Captain W.E. Harraden sailed from Newport News bound for London. A few days later a "loud roaring explosion" emanating from the engineroom followed by an ominous silence, sent a wave of apprehension throughout the ship. The silence was broken only by a plaintive jangle on the engine room telegraph confirming that all was at "Stop". A quick check ascertained that no one was hurt, but damage to the new steam turbines verged on the catastrophic. The cause of the disaster was attributed to a "lockage of steam between the boilers and the turbine shafts". Apparently, the build-up of steam had suddenly cleared itself with explosive force, stripping the blades off the high-pressure turbine. The blast had also stripped the astern turbine, leaving only the low-pressure turbine as a functional unit.

Captain Harraden was faced with a difficult problem. After consultating the Chief Engineer, W.J. Blease, he had two options - either to call Bermuda and ask for expensive tug assistance into Hamilton, where repair facilities would not be available anyway, or to carry on to London, steaming at three knots on the low-pressure turbine, and praying the weather stayed fine. The latter option was selected, and the ship resumed what had now become a long, slow voyage. The drastic reduction in speed meant that the voyage would be extended by 10 or 12 days, and, although fuel and water would not be a problem, the available quantity of provisions was critical.

The meagre supply of rice was set aside for the East

Captain W.E. Harraden, Master of *Dramatist* in 1923. *[Simpson]*

Indian crew; and what was left of the fresh food had to be consumed before it deteriorated. The rest - meat, potatoes, beans and pulses, condensed milk, butter, tea and coffee - was strictly rationed. The first commodities to disappear were cigarettes and tobacco. Canned meat, butter, milk, and coffee petered out as the ship drifted into the Western Approaches. Nevertheless, the Goanese cook performed miracles with a seemingly inexhaustible supply of weevily oatmeal, dried peas, black beans, curry powder, and spices. By some alchemy he even concocted soups of a sort, but no one ventured to enquire the recipe.

The prayers for fine weather were answered, as the ship drifted along under clear skies through calm waters. The tides in the English Channel, however, all but brought the ship to a standstill until they flowed eastwards again. On 24th April, as DRAMATIST approached Dungeness, six tugs stood out to meet her, and latched on to the ship rather like a party of solicitous stretcher bearers: two ahead, two astern, and one on each flank. One of the tugs had brought out a generous supply of stores and foodstuffs, which the estimable cook at once put to advantage. Despite the efforts of the six tugs, however, the passage through the tide-ripped channels of the Downs and the Thames Estuary was slow and hazardous, but, to the relief of all, the ship nosed safely into her berth at Tilbury late on 25th April, ending a voyage which none of the participants would care to repeat.

202. DIPLOMAT (2) 1921-1940 Steel steamship. Two decks and seven holds. Four masts.
O.N. 145878 8,240g 5,255n 11,960d 482.15 x 58.4 x 37.25 feet. Cargo capacity: 702,350 cubic feet.
International Code KJRF (GFVC after 1933).
Three Brown-Curtiss steam turbines by Dunsmuir and Jackson Ltd., Govan, double reduction geared to a single screw, 13.5 knots.

14.12.1920: Launched by Charles Connell and Co. Ltd., Glasgow (Yard No. 382) for the company. *30.9.1921:* Delivered at a cost of £396,834. Sailed from Liverpool to Calcutta on her maiden voyage under Captain W.N. Rushforth. *8.10.1931:* Captain Rushforth, gravely ill, was landed to hospital in Colombo, where he died of phlebitis on 15.11.1931. *8.2.1940:* Whilst navigating the Southwest Pass of the Mississippi, the main engines seized. The fault was found to lie in the turbine, and after tugs had brought the vessel to a safe berth, three blades were renewed. *26.9.1940:* Damaged by fire during an air raid while lying at Brunswick Dock, Liverpool. *27.11.1940:* Torpedoed by the German submarine U 104 (Kapitänleutnant Harald Jurst) when straggling from Convoy HX88. The crew took to the boats and she was torpedoed a second time, sinking in position 55.42N, 11.37W, about 118 miles bearing 283 degrees from Tory Island. She was on a voyage from New Orleans via Bermuda and Halifax for Manchester with a cargo of steel and cotton. The lifeboats were sighted the following morning by a Sunderland flying boat of Coastal Command and three warships alerted. Later that day 43 survivors were picked up by the destroyer ACTIVE. Fourteen of the crew were lost.

Right: Replacing the top of *Diplomat's* funnel at Eastham after a transit of the Manchester Ship Canal. The rigger atop the funnel would appear to have an exciting job. Her topmasts have also been lowered for the passage to and from Manchester. *Diplomat* is seen below with a complete funnel and a full complement of topmasts.
[Lower: World Ship Photo Library]

142

203. HUNTSMAN (2) 1921-1939 Steel steamship. Two decks and seven holds. Four masts.
O.N. 145895 8,196g 5,241n, 11,960d 482.0 x 58.35 x 37.25 feet. Cargo capacity: 702,350 cubic feet.
International Code KLDJ (GFWS after 1933).
Three Brown-Curtiss steam turbines by Dunsmuir and Jackson Ltd., Govan, double reduction geared to a single screw; 13.3 knots.

5.7.1921: Launched by Charles Connell and Co. Ltd., Scotstoun (Yard No. 385) for the company. *18.11.1921:* Delivered at a cost of £396,614. Sailed from Liverpool to the Gulf of Mexico on her maiden voyage under Captain C.S. Rhodes. *8.4.1922:* Took the ground at Buenos Aires and began to make water in number 3 starboard double-bottom tank. It was later found that the flukes of a stray anchor had pierced the outer skin. The leak was stopped and cemented, but the vessel subsequently spent 19 days in dry dock at Antwerp undergoing repairs. *9.6.1922:* Whilst in dry dock at Antwerp, fire broke out in the stokehold but was extinguished by the fire brigade without significant damage. *16.12.1928:* Rescued 32 members of the crew of the Spanish steamer DELFIN (1,254/85) disabled in heavy seas off the Skerries, Anglesey. *19.12.1936:* When bound from Calcutta for London, broke down with a fractured pump casting shortly after passing through the Straits of Gibraltar. *20.12.1936:*

The Gibraltar-based tug RESCUE (357/04) was able to connect a tow line and commenced towing eastwards making barely half-a-knot against strong head winds. *21.12.1936:* Another tug, the Danish GEIR (323/08) connected and the vessel arrived Admiralty Harbour, Gibraltar, at 17.35 hours. *27.12.1936:* Sailed and resumed her voyage after a new casting had been made in the dockyard. *31.8.1939:* Diverted from Port Sudan for the United Kingdom via the Cape of Good Hope as war was expected. *10.10.1939:* Captured by the German pocket-battleship ADMIRAL GRAF SPEE in the South Atlantic in position 08.30S, 5.15W and the crew were taken prisoner. *17.10.1939:* After some systematic plundering of cargo and fittings, she was sunk by the Germans using explosive charges. She was on a voyage from Calcutta, Mombasa and Durban to London and Liverpool with general cargo, tea, cotton and gunnies.

Huntsman leaving Capetown with the pilot tender standing by.   *[World Ship Photo Library]*

The HUNTSMAN, the hunter, and the hunted

The HUNTSMAN sailed from Colombo on 18th August 1939 bound for London and Liverpool via Port Sudan and the Suez Canal. Having loaded her quota of cotton and cotton seed at Port Sudan the ship sailed on 31st August, and headed north for Suez Bay. Later that night an urgent message from the Admiralty in London turned the ship around, instructing the Master, Captain A.H. Brown, to return to the United Kingdom via the Cape of Good Hope, bunkering at Aden and Durban as necessary. On 3rd September the reason became clear, when it was announced that a state of war existed between the British Empire and Commonwealth, and Germany. The Admiralty believed that the Mediterranean was now a hotbed of German U-boats, and was anxious to keep British shipping out of the way, at least for the time being. Thus the HUNTSMAN became one of many ships diverted to sail round the continent of Africa, eventually clearing the port of Durban on 29th September.

On 10th October HUNTSMAN was heading towards Freetown to join a homeward-bound convoy, and the newly started hostilities seemed very far away. On this placid, sunny afternoon, Chief Officer Alfred Holt Thompson handed over the watch to Third Officer Les Frost, who had come up to the bridge to relieve him for the evening meal. Half-way through the meal, the Third Officer sent word down to his superiors that he had sighted a warship on the starboard bow. Captain "Yankee" Brown (whose nickname derived from the unique distinction of

holding a US Master's Licence in addition to his British Master's Certificate of Competency) at once left the saloon, and Alf Thompson followed him to the bridge. There was no undue alarm, more a lively curiosity, for all on board had complete faith in an omnipresent Royal Navy, and the approaching ship was bound to be "one of ours". Nevertheless, the Radio Officer, A. Taylor, deemed it prudent to leave the saloon, and make his way to the radio shack which was situated abaft the chartroom.

The stranger approached at great speed, and the watchers on the bridge had a brief glimpse of the French tricolor fluttering above the quarter deck. The ship looked lean, powerful, and mean. Suddenly, the tricolor disappeared and the swastika of Nazi Germany took its place. A string of flags swept up to the yardarm quickly followed by another, spelling out the signals for "Heave to", and "Do not use your radio", in the International Code. But "sparks" was already transmitting: "RRRR GFWS - HUNSTMAN - ATTACKED BY UNKNOWN WARSHIP - LAT 8 30 S - LONG 5 15 W", (approximately 195 degrees and 830 miles, from Takoradi), and continued to repeat the message until ordered by Captain Brown to stop, and dump his code books. Unfortunately, it was an off-watch period for the single-operator ships of those early days of the war, and the urgent signal was not picked up.

Meanwhile, Captain Brown had stopped his ship, Alf Thompson was dumping the Admiralty code books in a weighted bag; and a smart motor-launch was already speeding across the water between the two ships. The battleship's two triple eleven-inch gun-turrets were trained on the merchant ship; the approaching launch was crammed with armed sailors. Captain Brown was bitter; there was nothing to do but await events. The boarding-party came over the rails with weapons drawn, and rounded up the crew midships. The officers were sullen and defiant, but under no illusions that resistance would not only be futile, but fatal. Joseph Beazley (until recently Harrisons' resident Superintenent Engineer in Calcutta) later recalled a surrealistic vision of "sparks" backing out of the radio shack with his hands in the air, closely followed by a grim faced German petty officer brandishing a Luger automatic pistol. It was a scene from a film suddenly become mercilessly true. "Your position you have sent?" It was a question, and an accusation. "Of course I have," was the quiet response.

Later, the 40-strong boarding party was replaced by a prize crew of 25 men commanded by a Leutnant-zur-see Schuneman. Obligingly, he gave Captain Brown a receipt from his commanding officer for his ship and cargo, proclaiming that they were now prizes of the ADMIRAL GRAF SPEE, and the lawful property of the German Reich. He also felt it necessary to spell out the consequences of any foolish behaviour on the part of the prisoners, as if the men needed any reminding. Thus it was that HUNTSMAN, with the red-white-and-black swastika ensign flying from her flagstaff, became Harrisons' first casualty of the Second World War, a rich prize for the pocket battleship and her commander Kapitän-zur-See Hans Langsdorff.

This entire episode had lasted a mere 40 minutes, and the warship was again under way, swinging on to a southwesterly course, ordering the HUNTSMAN to follow. Armed guards were stationed throughout the ship, and machine guns mounted in the bridge wings were manned continuously. The crew resumed their normal duties under close supervision, though the officers took no part in the navigation and were denied access to the charts. Thus the ship followed her captor docilely into the South Atlantic, cruising at full speed for almost two days.

At about 14.00 on Thursday 12th October, GRAF SPEE signalled a halt, and, as the two ships lay hove to in the gentle swell, a launch was sent across to pick up Leutnant Schuneman, apparently to receive new orders. The prize officer returned an hour later; the warship gathered way and was soon hull-down on the horizon. It appeared that the ship was to rendezvous with the raider in about four days' time. Meanwhile the ship headed southeast at slow speed.

It was during this period that an absurd situation arose which subsequently enabled the Chief Officer to keep track of their position. At first, it was a rather alarming position in which he found himself, for he was roundly accused of tampering with the compasses and threatened with all the consequences which such an act of sabotage would provoke. Mr. Thompson hotly denied the charge and after some fierce argument it became clear to him what had happened. He offered to check the compass error for his captors, but to do so he would need to know the ship's position by dead reckoning, i.e., estimating course and distance made good. The Germans grudgingly accepted his explanation, and since it was a bit complicated, allowed him thereafter to check the compass error. Thus he was able to keep track of their position, at least for the time being.

The reason behind the confusion was to be found in the different conventions practised by British and German navigators. The latter had long since adopted the new pattern compass, with its card marked in degrees, 0 to 360, in which 0 (or 360) indicated north, 90 east, 180 south, 270 west, and so through to 360 (or zero). Thus the bearing increments regularly in a right-handed or clockwise direction, 90 degrees to a quadrant, in a complete circle. Consequently, when applying variation and deviation (the two errors to which all magnetic compasses are subject) to a magnetic course or bearing, the rule was quite straightforward - ADD if the error was easterly,

SUBTRACT if westerly, reversing the process if working from true to compass. A useful mnemonic "compass to true add east" conveniently shortens into the single word CADET.

HUNTSMAN did not carry a new pattern compass. Hers was a traditional card marked in points, 32 to a complete circle, each point equal to $11\frac{1}{4}$ degrees. Ships using this system normally steered to quarter of a point, or $2\frac{13}{16}$ degrees. This system had persisted since the Middle Ages, but as a sop to progress an outer ring was added to the compass card in the early twentieth century marked in degrees, 90 to the quadrant. But with true British perversity the degrees in each quadrant were marked according to the old notation from the cardinal points, N to E and S to W incrementing clockwise, N to W and S to E incrementing anticlockwise. And it was on this seemingly illogical convention that the German navigators, schooled rigidly in the now pattern system, foundered. For when they applied their add/subtract rule, in two out of the four quadrants they were likely to apply the compass error the wrong way. As long as they steered on southwesterly courses all went well, but on altering to a southeasterly heading the rot set in.

A navigator raised in the old school would neither add nor subtract the error. His practice was to apply it either to LEFT or RIGHT. Thus "compass to truE, easterly to the right (and westerly to the left), truE to compass, easterly to the left (and westerly to the right). Thus when laying off a course in the south west quadrant a compass error of 15 degrees west would be applied to the right (added), and Hans would also be correct. But when the course altered to the south east quadrant, with degrees incrementing anticlockwise, the error would be correctly applied to the right (i.e. subtracted) by Jack, whereas Hans, sticking faithfully to his new pattern rule would again add, thereby setting the ship 30 degrees off her desired true course.

Though this technical difference is irrelevant to the final fate of either HUNTSMAN or GRAF SPEE, the sense of one-up-manship which suffused the British officers involved, and the ability it gave them to keep track of their position as their ship and her predator crossed the wide open spaces of the southern oceans, gave a huge boost to their sagging morale.

Meanwhile the German sailors began taking an interest in the HUNTSMAN'S cargo, peering down hatches, and assessing the contents with acquisitive interest. Eventually, the Lascar seamen were coerced into rigging a derrick or two and hoisting various items on deck for closer inspection.

Sometimes the German officers could be coaxed into conversation, for they all spoke very good English, and during one of these sessions Leutnant Schuneman confided to Joe Beazley that he was a Reserve Officer, and had been a tug master on the East African coast before being called up while on leave. His colleagues on the GRAF SPEE, Leutnants Hertzberg, Holtz, and Ditman were all merchant navy men, not altogether happy with their present lot, since they were invariably given the dirty work to do. "If the tanker fails to show up tomorrow", said Schuneman confidentially, "I have orders to take this ship close to the Brazilian coast, and sink her. Then we'll all go ashore together in the lifeboats at Bahia or Pernambuco". He sighed, adding reflectively, "That will suit me, for I have a brother in Brazil - somewhere to stay until the war is over".

However, it was not to be, for at 07.10 on 16th October the GRAF SPEE was sighted, accompanied by a large oil tanker flying the Norwegian flag, and purporting to be the SOGNE of Oslo. The three ships lay close-to, and motor-launches shuttled rapidly between them, transferring stores from the tanker to the warship, and looted cargo from the HUNTSMAN to both tanker and warship. Fine Indian carpets were in great demand and bales of them were hoisted from the HUNTSMAN'S holds to meet it. Chests of tea were also highly prized.

That night a pipeline was rigged between the warship and the tanker, and the GRAF SPEE topped up her bunkers. Next day, 17th, the storing and looting continued, this time with systematic attention being paid to the HUNTSMAN'S electrical fittings. Fans were stripped out; the saloon Prestcold refrigerator

Captain Albert H. 'Yankee' Brown, master of *Huntsman* when captured by the *Graf Spee*.

cabinet removed; copper piping and small electrical pumps lifted from the engine room. After lunch, clocks, mirrors, glassware and crockery were carefully packed in crates to be ferried across to the tanker along with table and bed linen, and even cushions and pillows. The HUNTSMAN'S crew were ordered to collect their personal effects, but when the officers packed their sextants, chronometers, and binoculars, these were confiscated and formal receipts issued. Later that afternoon all hands were ferried across to the tanker, now identified as the German fleet auxiliary ALTMARK.

Captain Brown was the last man to leave the HUNTSMAN, and after his departure a demolition team went on board to place explosive charges around the ship. She displayed a marked reluctance to sink, so more charges were exploded later. However, it was almost midnight on 17th October before the HUNTSMAN disappeared beneath the waves.

On board ALTMARK living quarters in numbers 3 and 4 'tween decks were allocated to the bulk of the prisoners, but the senior officers and Lascars were housed in a canvas-walled structure under the extended forecastle deck, Officers on the port side, the Lascar seamen on the starboard side. The bare steel deck was liberally covered with gunnies and Indian carpets on which mattresses were laid. A large contingent of prisoners taken from two new victims, the NEWTON BEACH (4,651/25) and the ASHLEA (4,222/29), was transferred from the GRAF

Huntsman with the supply ship *Altmark* in the offing, a photograph taken from the *Graf Spee.* Note the camouflage, designed to give the impression that *Huntsman* is going the other way.

SPEE to the ALTMARK on the following day. During the night the warship disappeared into the darkness to resume her depredations against British and Allied merchant ships, returning nine days later to disgorge more prisoners. This pattern became established over the next six weeks: GRAF SPEE going off on her hunting expeditions; ALTMARK cruising in desultory circles until her aggressive consort returned to transfer more prisoners and take on essential supplies.

Life on the ALTMARK was spartan. Water was a very scarce commodity - barely enough to drink, let alone wash. Food was adequate, but unappetising, consisting mainly of black bread, salt pork, German sausage, sauerkraut, pasta, pulses, and sundry tinned vegetables. Soup, made from whatever ingredients the cooks found to hand, was also a staple constituent of the daily diet. Alf Thompson had managed to salvage four cases of canned milk from the HUNTSMAN'S lifeboats and these had been smuggled aboard ALTMARK carefully concealed amid the baggage. All on board - including the German crew - were thus privileged to have milk in their tea and coffee for at least a few weeks.

Sanitation aboard the ALTMARK was extremely primitive. Number 1 hold was divided horizontally into five orlop decks, each of which was filled with stores, equipment, and boxes which presumably contained ammunition. Access was gained by means of a long vertical ladder, though not all decks were available to the prisoners - only the one which contained the so-called lavatories. In fact, it was obvious that this essential facility had been overlooked during the ship's hurried conversion into a prison ship. Consequently a number of oil drums had been installed by way of improvisation, and of course these convenient receptacles had to be hauled up on deck, emptied, and cleaned several times a day.

Prisoners were allowed on deck for exercise twice a day, three-quarters of an hour in the morning, and half an hour in the afternoon. Smoking was forbidden, and at least one

officer was sentenced to three days' solitary confinement after being caught by the guard having a quick "drag and a draw" in his quarters.* However, after this incident Captain Dau of the ALTMARK relented a little and designated a small compartment deep in the bowels of the ship as a smoking area. There was only one snag. Anyone taking advantage of this concession had to indulge his smoke during exercise periods.

By 11th November, the ALTMARK was believed (by the prisoner navigators) to be somewhere south of Capetown. Cold winds and heavy seas were making the canvas deck house untenable, and, after some forceful complaints, Captain Dau arranged for the senior officers to be accommodated in number 1 hold, in the top flat. The Lascar seamen were transferred to drier quarters in the after hold. These arrangements constituted a turn for the better, and raised morale as only warmth, dry clothes and dry bedding can. However, the uncertainty, the irksome restrictions, and the boredom lived on.

It came as a welcome relief, therefore - at least, for some - to be told on 28th November that all senior officers were to be transferred to the GRAF SPEE. The warship had just returned from a rather fruitless hunting trip, having captured just one small ship, the AFRICA SHELL (706/39)commanded by the doughty Captain Dove, who was to become a leading spokesman for the prisoners and the confidant of Kapitän Hans Langsdorff. At 16.00 that day, 25 rankers said farewell to their erstwhile shipmates, exchanging letters to be posted to families as and when and if occasion arose, and left the ALTMARK to face an uncertain future aboard the GRAF SPEE. The group consisted of masters, officers, engineers, radio officers and, of course, Mr. Beazley, whose status the Germans could not quite make out. They were quartered in a central cabin, about 17 feet by 20 feet, above which was a small galley, the top of which served as the stowage platform for the battleship's Arado reconnaissance aircraft, abaft the funnel. There was a small pantry leading off from the main room, also a washroom with bowls fitted with taps and running water. Above all (in order of priorities, not in elevation) there was a flush toilet.

Diet was as spartan as on the ALTMARK, but for entertainment the prisoners now had a few packs of cards, and several books rescued from a victim's Seamen's Educational Service library before the ship was sent to the bottom. Exercise on deck was limited to an hour in the morning, and an hour in the evening. The men were issued with hammocks which were slung from rods in the deck head at 21.00 each night. There were no portholes in the cabin, just two skylights which were screwed down most of the time.

During the following week the warship captured and sank two more ships, the DORIC STAR (10,086/21) on 2nd December, and the TAIROA (7,983/20) on 3rd. There were now 51 prisoners crammed into the tiny room, and others were housed in a room further aft. To relieve the congestion, longer exercise periods on deck became routine. On 6th December, GRAF SPEE made a rendezvous with her support ship, and more prisoners were transferred, including Captain Brown who expressed a wish to the Kommandant to be with his Indian crew. In return, he gave his parole. (He kept it. On his return to Liverpool he retired on pension aged 64). There were now 29 prisoners in the little room, making it much easier to breathe and move around. On the morning of 7th GRAF SPEE sped away to the southwest. Later that evening the alarm klaxons signalled that another ship had been sighted, and the crew sprang to action stations. The prisoners' quarters were secured and locked. This was always an anxious time, and anyone with tendencies towards claustrophobia suffered dismally. For there was no knowing whether the dreadful urgency of the klaxons heralded the appearance of a harmless merchantman - or a British battle fleet, and the unspoken question in everyone's mind was whether there would be anyone outside to open the steel doors if the ship got the worst of a naval engagement.

On this occasion, however, the intruder turned out to be

*This was Chief Officer Venables of the TREVANION (5,299/37). He was unlucky, for there were many who, watching him being marched off to the brig, inwardly murmured (with John Bradford, the martyr), "But for the Grace of God, there go I".

the British freighter STREONSHALH (3,895/28) of Whitby, and at 21.00 the prisoners were joined by the Captain and Chief Engineer of the ship, who were cordially invited to sling their hammocks.

The next few days passed quietly, with only the crash of the catapult, and the roar of the little recce plane's engine at dawn and dusk disturbing the prisoners' simple routine. Then one morning as the plane was revving up on the catapult, the klaxons blared out stridently and unexpectedly. Once again the prisoners' quarters were tightly secured, and almost immediately the battleship's 11-inch guns opened fire. The prisoners, wide-awake, tumbling from their hammocks, looked at one another anxiously, convinced that this was no sitting duck under the warship's guns. It was 06.10 on 13th December 1939, and the Battle of the River Plate had begun.

Many excellent accounts of the battle have been written, and another would be superfluous. Besides, the prisoners, locked in their quarters, had no idea what was going on, though as the day wore on it was apparent that things were going badly for the raider. In the cramped prison quarters tension was high. The ship was vibrating violently as shaft-revolutions mounted; she heeled over from side to side as helm was applied in strenuous efforts to outmanoeuvre her tormentors. At times, the ship shuddered, as if reacting to direct hits, and the heavy guns roared continuously. About one hour after the battle started, a shell burst in the galley directly above the prisoners' quarters. All the lights went out; the deck-head collapsed, and one of the skylights was shattered. The men were showered with debris and choked with dust, but miraculously, apart from a few superficial scratches, no one was hurt. The prisoners could watch a small facet of the action through a small screw-hole in the steel door to their apartment. They could see the German sailors sweating at the ammunition-hoists just outside. They looked strained and grim, as well they might. During a lull in the shooting, several wounded men were carried past, but no one came to enquire if any prisoners were wounded until nearly 23.00, when a voice from without yelled, "Are you alright, in there?". Captain Dove replied, "We're O.K., but what about something to eat?" Half-an-hour later a dixie full of lime-juice and water and four loaves of black bread were passed inside.

It was a long day, punctuated by occasional salvoes from GRAF SPEE's big guns. The battle had developed into a chase; GRAF SPEE turned westward, heading for the River Plate, and sanctuary. The prisoners knew nothing of this development; even after sunset, the darkness was riven by occasional flashes from the guns. All they knew was that, after more than twelve hours, whatever was chasing the battleship

was still in touch. Thus, their reaction was one of astonishment, quickly followed by relief and jubilation, when at ten minutes to one on the morning of 14th December, they were awakened from fitful slumber by Leutnant Hertzberg, who, standing amid the gently swaying hammocks, gravely announced, "Gentlemen; for you the war is over. We are now anchored in Montevideo harbour, and today you will all be free! Heil Hitler!"

The 34 prisoners in the wrecked cabin looked at each other, dumbfounded. They could not believe it. The engines had stopped, certainly. Someone was hoisted up to peer through the shattered skylight: Yes! There were the harbour lights! No blackout in Montevideo! The tension of the past hours evaporated. The German warship was in neutral waters and, under international law, she could be interned if she did not leave within 24 hours - or was it 48? At any rate, she would have to release her prisoners, wouldn't she? Speculation was rife, and inconclusive, for no one was at all familiar with the niceties of convention between belligerent and neutral states.

At daybreak, the warship weighed anchor and moved into the inner harbour. There was no hot food for anyone that day - both galleys had been blown to pieces. The afternoon came and went, as harbour craft carrying officials shuttled to and fro. A large crowd had gathered on the waterfront - but still the British seamen remained locked up in their cramped quarters. And in a neutral harbour, dammit! Tempers waxed indignant, but at last, at 17.30 they forgot their anger when a depressed-looking Master-at-Arms, Albert Jerichow, told them to be ready to disembark in ten minutes. Quickly, they lined up on the quarter deck, and disembarked aboard a Uruguayan tug, courtesy of the Montevideo Port Authority. Shepherded into the Immigration Office, the erstwhile prisoners, now designated Distressed British Seamen, were handed over into the care of the British Consul. That night there was no peace, thanks to the endless round of interviews with consular officers, naval intelligence, and the attentions of a febrile press. But at least their 65-day period of captivity was now at an end.

Kapitän Dau of the ALTMARK must have listened with dismay to the harrowing details of GRAF SPEE'S demise, broadcast across the world. Ex-prisoners from the GRAF SPEE knew all about the ALTMARK and the 300 British and allied seamen held on board. The subsequent history of the ALTMARK, culminating in the dramatic boarding by Captain Vian in HMS COSSACK in Jossing Fjord on 16th February 1940, is well known.

This account has been based mainly on the reports of Chief Officer A H. Thompson and Superintendent Engineer J. Beazley, supplemented by official material.

204. TRAVELLER (2) 1922-1942 Steel steamship. Two decks and five holds. Two masts.
O.N. 145916 3,963g 2,499n 6,165d 365.0 x 46.9 x 30.0 feet. Cargo capacity: 347,730 cubic feet.
International Code KLRV (GJKM after 1933).
T. 3-cyl. by Dunsmuir and Jackson Ltd., Govan; 23, 38.5, 64 x 48 inches, 11.5 knots.

Traveller in Toxteth Dock, Liverpool.   [J. and M. Clarkson]

14.12.1921: Launched by Charles Connell and Co. Ltd., Scotstoun (Yard No. 393) for the company. *22.3.1922:* Delivered at a cost of £190,555. Sailed from Liverpool to the West Indies on her maiden voyage under Captain W. Gibbings. *17.3.1929:* Ran ashore on Cleats Point, Arran and badly damaged. Refloated several hours later and spent two weeks in dry dock at Glasgow undergoing repairs costing £6,662. *29.3.1929:* Sustained further damage when leaving

dry dock upon striking the jetty at the yard of Harland and Wolff, Govan. *26.1.1942:* Torpedoed and sunk by the German submarine U 106 (Oberleutnant-zur-See Hermann Rasch) in the North Atlantic in position 39.34N, 64.05W, approximately 184 degrees and 306 miles from Halifax. The vessel sank within six minutes and there were no survivors. She was on a voyage from New Orleans to Halifax with general cargo to join a convoy for Liverpool.

205. SCHOLAR (2) 1922-1940 Steel steamship. Two decks and five holds. Two masts.
O.N. 145931 3,940g 2,473n 6,165d 364.9 x 46.9 x 30.0 feet. Cargo capacity: 347,730 cubic feet.
International Code KMDF (GJLV after 1933).
T. 3-cyl. by Dunsmuir and Jackson Ltd., Govan; 23, 38.5, 64 x 48 inches, 11.5 knots.

1.3.1922: Launched by Charles Connell and Co. Ltd., Scotstoun (Yard No. 394) for the company. *30.5.1922:* Delivered at a cost of £185,455. Sailed from Liverpool to South Africa on her maiden voyage under Captain T. O'Connor. *7.9.1929:* Captain A.G. Peterkin landed in hospital at Kingston, Jamaica, with appendicitis. *28.4.1934:* Sailed from Gravesend at 14.00 bound for Middlesbrough in ballast and some twelve hours later ran into thick fog when approaching Cromer Knoll Lightvessel. *29.4.1934:* At 14.30 speed was reduced to half-ahead and occasionally the engines were stopped altogether to allow other traffic to pass clear. A few miles to the north, the Brocklebank steamer MAHOUT (7,880/25) was also cautiously approaching Cromer Knoll, heading south for Antwerp. At 03.08 Second Officer J.L. Curle sighted

Scholar waiting to load in Toxteth Dock.   *[J. and M. Clarkson]*

navigation lights on the port bow and a vain attempt was made to swing the vessel clear. MAHOUT collided with SCHOLAR's port quarter causing extensive damage above the waterline at 03.12 in position 53.10N, 01.17E, about 15 miles north of Cromer. Both vessels then anchored in about 12 fathoms to assess damage. The fog cleared by 10.00 and both vessels proceeded, SCHOLAR arriving 30.4.1934 at Middlesbrough.[129] *21.9.1940:* Attacked twice on the surface by the German submarine U 100 (Kapitänleutnant Joachim Schepke) whilst sailing in convoy. The vessel turned towards the submarine in an attempt to ram, but she crossed the bows at speed and fired a further torpedo from the stern tube. This struck forward of the bridge and

SCHOLAR caught fire; Captain W.R. MacKenzie and three crew members being injured. She was abandoned in a sinking condition in position 55.11N, 17.58W, 332 miles due west of Bloody Foreland, County Donegal. All survivors were picked up by the destroyer SKATE and landed at Londonderry. *23.9.1940:* The derelict, still burning amidships, was taken in tow by the tug MARAUDER in position 55.10N, 17.49W but was found to be too waterlogged to be manageable. The towing cable was slipped the next day in position 54.38N, 16.40W, and she was last seen drifting slowly south. She was on a voyage from Galveston for Manchester with a cargo including cotton, steel and lumber.

Faith or prejudice? A living parable
It is now my task to relate a disagreeable tale of thankless endeavour and human intolerance such as is seldom found in annals of the sea.

It was in the late summer of 1929, and Captain Alfred Gray Peterkin, Master of the SCHOLAR, was completing his first year in command. His Chief Officer, Eric Whitehouse, was making his third voyage as Mate. Doubtless they talked of many things during the voyage, but religion would probably not have been one of them. Seamen, generally, would, if pressed, avow to a simple faith uncomplicated by abstruse theology.

Eric Whitehouse was therefore probably a little surprised but not unduly concerned, to learn that his Captain was a Christian Scientist - or rather, that his wife was a devout disciple of Mary Baker Eddy, the American founder of the religious sect, and that Captain Peterkin professed a nominal interest mainly to please his wife and keep the peace.

The ship had left Liverpool on 17th August 1929, and, after a brief call at Nassau, arrived at Kingston, Jamaica, on 5th September. It was at Kingston that Captain Peterkin began to feel decidedly unwell, with stomach pains, and fits of nausea. He was also running a mild temperature. Reluctantly, for he knew Mrs. P. would disapprove, he allowed Eric Whitehouse to persuade him to see a doctor. After his examination, the doctor offered his diagnosis that the patient could well be suffering from incipient appendicitis. On the other hand, it could be some gastric disorder. Difficult to tell. He advised admittance to hospital for observation. Captain Peterkin exploded. "Impossible, doctor! My ship sails this evening. Besides, I feel much better now".

He left the surgery, and returned to his ship which was

already preparing for sea. It was 7th September, and the ship sailed at 17.00, backing off the wharf, and heading down the harbour channels towards Port Royal. The brief tropical twilight was already waning as the ship disembarked the Pilot in the approach to Plumb Point, and gathered way again. Chief Officer Whitehouse finished securing the anchors, and made his way to the bridge, by which time it was quite dark. The Third Officer was bringing the ship round to the course for Portland Point. There was no sign of the Captain.

"Where's the Old Man?" asked Mr. Whitehouse. "In his room, I think", replied the Third Officer. "He went below a few minutes ago". "Humph; hold on, will you, lad, while I go down and see him".

Eric Whitehouse descended the ladder and entered the Captain's cabin below the bridge. He knew the Captain had not been well, but he was not prepared for the sight which now confronted his startled gaze. Captain Peterkin was lying on the deck, writhing in agony, beads of sweat glistening on his face in the pale rays of the lamp. "That you, Whitehouse?" he faltered. "Guess that old quack was right after all!" "You should be in hospital, Sir," said Eric firmly. "I'll turn the ship around, and head her back". He rang for the Steward and, ignoring his Captain's feeble protests, hurried up to the bridge. "Hard-a-starboard, Third Mate", he ordered. Somewhat astonished, the Third Officer passed the order to the helmsman, and watched as it was executed. "The Old Man's very sick. We've got to get him to a hospital", offered the Mate by way of explanation. "Steer for Plumb Point. Oh, and get held of Sparks; I'll have to send a message to the Harbourmaster and the agent".

This was no easy, automatic choice, although Eric

Whitehouse could see no other option. In those days Kingston was a difficult port to enter at night, the tortuous channels being badly furnished with lighted navigation marks. The approach was so hazardous, in fact, that there was a specific injunction against entering Kingston at night, "under any circumstances", in the Company's Rule Book, a factor which Eric was painfully aware of, as well as the practical difficulties.

However, he was satisfied that this was the only course to pursue. A man's life was at stake, for he knew enough about appendicitis to realise that perforation would lead to peritonitis and death, if it were not treated surgically in time. He was sure that his employers would not question his action in these circumstances - provided of course that nothing went wrong. His mind refused to dwell on that possibility and he concentrated on his approach to the numerous reefs and shoals in the vicinity.

As it happened, all went well. Captain Peterkin reached hospital within a couple of hours, and an emergency operation set him well on the road to recovery and eventual repatriation.

Meanwhile, SCHOLAR continued her voyage to Vera Cruz and Tampico, Acting Captain Eric Whitehouse in command. On 27th September, while the ship was at Tampico, he was relieved by Captain Hansen who had been sent from Liverpool via New York and the US rail network to take command. For his 20 days as Acting Master, Eric Whitehouse was paid an extra £10/15/4d - a useful addition to his monthly stipend.

Captain A.G. Peterkin OBE, 1881-1959.

The voyage proceeded without further drama, and on 7th November the SCHOLAR docked in Liverpool. The gangway was shipped in place, and Eric Whitehouse was surprised to notice the bustling figure of Mrs. Peterkin, whom he knew slightly, among the first people to rush on board.

"Really; the dear lady should not have troubled herself to come down", murmured Eric, uneasily, anticipating effusive expressions of gratitude.

He was somewhat taken aback, therefore, when the lady, having sought him out in his cabin, launched into a verbal attack the like of which he had never heard before. The "dear lady" was beside herself!

"Miserable wretch!" was her first greeting. "What you did was despicable, leaving my husband in the evil hands of those foreign doctors!"

To say that Eric was dumbfounded would be putting it mildly. A confirmed bachelor, he was seldom at ease in the company of women, and he had never come across one like this...this termagant! So he said nothing, and let the tirade flow over him. He remembered the woman was a practising Christian Scientist, and although he knew less about Christian Science than appendicitis, he was aware that this sect of faith healers would have no truck with doctors or hospitals. But still...the man's life had been in danger. Dimly, at the back of his mind, the overriding fact was plain amid the high-pitched ranting. "My decision saved the life of this woman's husband!"

The diatribe went on. "My Alfred's body has been defiled, thanks to your meddling", she spat. "Vicious knives have pierced his flesh, and contaminated blood poured into his veins. And you call yourself his friend!"

It was too much. The unfortunate lady's faith had become an obsession, her piety the fanaticism of the bigot. At last, the malevolent stream of invective dried up, and the angry woman marched out of the room, leaving Eric to gather his scattered senses.

The lady, of course, was entitled to her beliefs, and if they included faith healing, then that was her prerogative. But she had not been there, at Kingston, to take responsibility. His was the responsibility, and his alone. A better theologian than Eric Whitehouse would have seen himself as the humble instrument of God's will, as were indeed the surgeons who performed that secular operation. True faith is one thing; fanatical prejudice another, and there can be no place for the latter in human relations.

Three days later, subdued, but as fit as a fiddle, Captain Peterkin relieved Captain Hansen, and rejoined his old ship. Eric Whitehouse was still there, and the pair made several more voyages together. Doubtless no direct reference was ever made to Mrs. Peterkin's intervention, but Eric was aware that his Captain silently acknowledged the debt he owed him. He never saw Mrs. Peterkin again. Nevertheless, he was not surprised to hear that, some time ago, the Peterkins had lost their only daughter through illness. No doctor was allowed near her, of course, but as the unfortunate child died of a brain tumour it is unlikely that she would have responded to medical help, anyway. Still, who knows? Perhaps surgical skill, fortified by the mother's faith and prayers, may well have given the child a fighting chance. The Peterkins had his deepest sympathy.[130]

206. AUDITOR 1924-1941 Steel steamship. Two decks and five holds. Two masts.
O.N. 147260 5,444g 3,427n 8,525d 410.0 x 52.3 x 33.15 feet. Cargo capacity: 469,850 cubic feet.
International Code KQTH (GKMJ after 1933).
T. 3-cyl. by Dunsmuir and Jackson Ltd., Govan; 24.5, 42.5, 72 x 54 inches, 12.5 knots.

17.4.1924: Launched by Charles Connell and Co. Ltd., Scotstoun (Yard No. 399) for the company. *11.6.1924:* Commenced sea trials but broke down and was towed back to the fitting-out berth. *18.6.1924:* Delivered at a cost of £101,239. Subsequently sailed from Liverpool for East Africa on her maiden voyage under Captain W.T. Owen. *23.2.1928:* Ran aground on the ebb tide in the approaches to Beira. Refloated on the next high tide, surveyed and pronounced seaworthy. *4.7.1941:* Torpedoed and sunk by the German submarine U 123 (Kapitänleutnant Reinhard Hardegen) 553 miles, 340 degrees from Sao Antao in position 25.53N, 28.23W. One of the lifeboats was destroyed in the explosion and one of the Lascar seamen was killed. The rest abandoned ship in the three remaining boats, and each one accomplished a remarkable voyage to safety in the Cape Verde Islands. At the time of the attack, AUDITOR was steaming independently, having dispersed from convoy OB 337 four days previously. She was on a voyage from London for Table Bay and Beira with 5,300 tons of general cargo including 10 aircraft.

Auditor at Capetown.   *[Ian Farquhar collection]*

Safe landfall - in triplicate[131]

After the AUDITOR had been torpedoed, and was clearly in imminent danger of sinking, the three serviceable lifeboats were launched smoothly and without difficulty as the crew abandoned ship. All the boats were sited amidships, and a number of seamen were trapped in the after part of the ship, which was going down by the stern. They were forced to jump into the sea, and swim to safety. Fortunately, the red lights clamped to their lifejackets, winking like fireflies in the darkness, rendered them relatively easy to locate, and most were picked up by the Chief Officer's boat. All three boats joined in the search, and those in number 1 heard the diesel engines of the U-boat also cruising the search area, but they saw nothing, and no attempt was made to contact the survivors, much to the relief of Captain Bennett, who had no wish to be a prisoner-of-war aboard a German submarine.

At daylight the boats came together for a conference. The roll was called, and revealed that 70 out of a total of 71 had survived the action; one Lascar seaman had been lost. The number of men in each boat was rather disproportionate, and the opportunity was taken to make a more equitable distribution, numbers 1 and 2 taking 23 men each, and No. 3 24. The provisions were checked, and found to consist of about nine gallons of water, one case of condensed milk, and large quantities of hard tack - a ship's biscuit with the consistency of concrete - to each boat. Fortunately, the weather was fine and clear, with a moderate northeasterly breeze and sea.

In charge of number 1 boat was the Master, Captain Edwin Bennett. With him were the Chief Engineer, D.C. Smith; the Chief Steward, R. Doyle; Chief Radio Officer, E. Walker: Second Radio Officer, G.V. Monk; the extra-Third Officer, H. Proctor; two other Europeans; and 15 Lascar seamen. The Chief Officer, H.T. Wells, was in charge of number 2 boat, and with him were the Third Officer, J.F. Tooth; five other Europeans, and 16 Lascars. No. 3 boat was in the care of the Second Officer, D.O. Percy, whose charge included eight other Europeans, and 15 Lascars.

Two of the boats were of timber construction, clinker built and inclined to leak, at least until the seams "took up". Number 3, however, was a US boat of steel construction evidently installed to replace the original boat which had either been damaged, or failed its survey. All were equipped with oars, masts, and sails, specifically the traditional standing lug and jib.

During the forenoon conference of Friday 4th July, Mr. Walker the Chief Radio Officer, assured the Master that he had successfully transmitted a distress signal several times on the emergency transmitter (since the mains supply had been lost). The message had been acknowledged by several ships and he was confident that it would be relayed. In the light of this information, Captain Bennett decided that they would have a better chance of rescue if they remained where they were, riding to sea anchors, rather than embarking on a hazardous boat voyage. At the convoy conference at Oban, which he had attended only a fortnight ago, the Naval Control Officer had advised his audience of shipmasters and radio officers to sit tight after being torpedoed, provided a distress message has been sent and acknowledged, since, "There is always a naval vessel within two days' steaming, so just wait for rescue".

Meanwhile, the officers discussed between themselves the other options open to them. There had been no time to collect the charts, books and instruments they now wished they had but George Monk chanced to find in his pocket the Shipping Diary he had bought in London six months ago. This contained several pages listing the co-ordinates of ports of the world, and with the aid of this invaluable little book the officers were able to assess their position relative to the various islands and land masses. The nearest land was in the Cape Verde Islands, some 560 miles south south east of their position; the islands were high and bold, conspicuous from seaward. If, however, they missed them, or got too far to leeward and were unable to beat up towards them against the prevailing north east trade wind, then their plight would be intensely magnified, with the prospect of a 1,300 mile journey through the tropics to the coast of Brazil as their only hope of survival.

After twenty-four hours of riding to sea-anchors, watching each other's boat bobbing up and down in the swell, officers and men became restive. They exhorted Captain Bennett to give the order to make sail and head for the Cape Verdes, but he urged them to be patient, that rescue was at hand. However, only too aware that meagre rations were dwindling, he conceded that, if no ships were in sight at

daybreak on Sunday 6th July, they would set sail. Another night was spent standing-to, burning flares at intervals; repeating the distress message on the portable lifeboat transmitter, but to no avail. The sun came up on Sunday morning, but failed to shine on anything that looked like a rescue ship. Another conference was held; the course decided upon. All boats were to proceed independently, sailing as best they could, and should one be picked up its crew would instigate a search for the others.

The sea anchors were hove inboard, the unwieldy lug sails hoisted, jibs set, and all made taut. The gaps between the boats widened, and a chorus of "Farewell" and Good Luck!" echoed across the waves as the sturdy little boats gathered way, close hauled on the port tack.

Incredibly, the scene took on the semblance of a race. Gradually, the Chief Officer's boat, number 2, drew ahead, while number 3, the Second Officer's boat fell far astern of the others. As dusk fell, his crew felt more than a little downcast to see their consorts well ahead, merging with the darkening horizon. By daylight on the Monday none of the boats were in sight of one another.

Don Percy and his crew set about seeking ways to enhance their chances. The all-steel boat rode high in the water, which had obvious advantages, but which caused the boat to make more leeway in a cross wind. The required true course was south south east, and to achieve this the coxswain had to steer a further two points at least to windward, on a compass course of south east. With the wind varying from north east to east north east, the coxswain found it impossible to hold the boat up to windward without luffing. To improve performance, two oars were lashed together, and seized to the after thwart to serve as a jury mast on which the yellow canvas hood was rigged as a sail. A piece of canvas cut from the boat cover served as an extra jib. The response was immediate. The boat surged forward, and leeway was much reduced.

The men's spirits rose and the boat averaged 80 miles per day over the next several days. Speed was estimated by dropping bits of wood over the bow, and timing the number of seconds until it floated past the stern, a distance of about 25 feet. The days passed; the frugal issues of food and water rations at dawn and dusk became a disciplined routine: half-a-dipper of water, a spoonful of condensed milk, and as much hard tack as a man could chew - which, without water or saliva, was very little indeed. There were times when the wind died away leaving the boat to drift aimlessly on the swell. Then the men would take the opportunity to have a refreshing dip over the side. There were other times when the trade wind blew with almost gale force and sail had to be reduced to the minimum required to maintain steerage way. But on the evening of Sunday 13th July, their tenth day in the boat, land was sighted on the starboard bow. All hands celebrated with an extra draught of drinking water.

The boat lay off the island all night and at dawn the men were confronted by the daunting prospect of sheer cliffs rising from the sea. Cautiously, they worked their way round the coast until they sighted a small beach backed by a cluster of dwellings, which turned out to be the village of Tarrafal del Monte, on the island of Sao Antao, the most northern of the Cape Verde Islands. A small flotilla of boats came out to meet them, bringing cans of water. It was clear that the fishermen were no strangers to this errand of mercy, a grim reminder of the times. The castaways' reception, and the generous hospitality of the islanders was, in Don Percy's words, "Beyond description", and after a willing volunteer had ridden a donkey some 20 miles to the nearest telegraph station, the outside world was notified.

At noon on 15th July, the Portuguese sloop BARTOLOMEU DIAS arrived to take the survivors to the main island of St. Vincent. It was only when they were greeted by the representative of Wilson's, agents to the Harrison Line, that the crew of number 3 boat realised that theirs was the first of AUDITOR'S boats to make a landfall, although last in the race after the first day. They waited anxiously for news of their shipmates.

They had another day at St. Vincent to wait. Number 2 boat, with Chief Officer H.T. Wells in charge, got away, as we have seen, to a good start and had established a substantial lead over the other two boats by nightfall of the first day. The men, of course, endured privations similar to those borne by their shipmates, with the added anxiety of having to bail out the water which seeped through the seams in the planking. The fact that morale remained high was due in no small measure to the inspiring leadership of one Lascar seaman, Officers' Boy Abdul

149

Rahman. The "Boy" rating is probably a misnomer in this case; he could have been of any age between 16 and 60, for Lascars were prepared to ship out in any capacity, so long as it provided regular employment to help sustain the heavy family responsibilities which all seamen from the sub-continent seemed to bear. Lascar seamen in those days were, perhaps, to the British Merchant Navy as the Ghurkas were to the British Army, an indispensable and reliable source of manpower. Abdul Rahman was a prime example.

According to Chief Officer Wells' report, Abdul Rahman "...inspired confidence in all of us... He was the first to volunteer for any job of work... He kept up the spirits (of his countrymen) by recounting stories and leading them at prayer. There is no doubt that his unfailing loyalty and energy kept up the morale of the natives and enabled all of us to come through our 13-day ordeal in very good order". It was this citation which led to Abdul Rahman being recommended for a British Empire Medal, Civil Division; and the announcement duly appeared in the London Gazette of Tuesday 16th December, 1942, "For good services in the S.S. AUDITOR in action with the enemy".

Also in number 2 boat was the man who was to become the leading survivor among all Harrison Line personnel. Senior Third Officer J.F. Tooth had already been among 58 survivors rescued from the PLANTER (216) torpedoed in the North Atlantic on 16th November 1940. He had now survived the AUDITOR'S confrontation with the enemy. Awaiting him in the future would be survival from the MERCHANT (233), mined and sunk off Yarmouth on Christmas Eve 1941; and finally, rescue from the sinking EMPIRE EXPLORER (254), torpedoed off Trinidad on 8th July 1942. It is hardly surprising that he spent the next two years doing relief work, but he was back at sea again in May 1944 in the EMPIRE RANGOON (257). John Tooth left Harrisons in September 1948 to enter Trinity House, and the London Pilot Service.

On the 13th day (16th July), the occupants of number 2 boat sighted the island of St. Vincent. They were then approached and picked up by a small Portuguese schooner, which carried them to Porto Grande, the capital, and to a hospitable welcome from the local townsfolk. They were also greeted by their jubilant shipmates, recently of number 3 boat, and also by the news that the Captain's boat had arrived safely that day at Sao Antao.

Captain Bennett and his crew in number 1 boat had also made good progress after the first day. They had their problems of course; at night the men suffered from cold, and by day from sunburn; and bailing continuously was an energy-sapping task, at least for the first few days. Rationing, especially the water ration, was an endless source of calculation and speculation. Radio Officer G.V. Monk records: "On Friday - the 8th day - the Master estimated that at dawn we had made some 300 miles since setting sail. It was cloudy, and during the morning there was a light rain shower. The inside cover of the radio transmitter was used to collect some of the spots of rain, after which it was licked dry. As thirst was our main problem, Captain Bennett increased our water ration to two half-dippers a day. On this basis our stocks should last for another seven days. If our present speed could be maintained, then one of the islands should be sighted before the water ration was exhausted. Ship's biscuits provided for lifeboat use were a disaster, being so dry and hard that no one could eat them. The only food we had that could be eaten was condensed milk, and the ration was increased to two spoonfuls a day."

On the Tuesday, the 12th day, as dawn broke, a grey smudge merging with grey cloud was discerned far away on the eastern horizon. Mr. Monk continues: "Could it be land? If so, then we were 40 miles or more off course. The effects of wind and current must have been greater than we had estimated. This smudge was watched by all of us for at least half-an-hour to see if there was any movement, like a cloud. It did not move, so it must be one of the islands. This gave us problems straight away."

The problems were only too evident. The land was right in the wind's eye, on a bearing of east north east, and to make good such a course meant frequent tacking on reaches as close to the wind as the boat could bear. The sea was rough, and there was quite a swell running. Inevitably the boat shipped a good deal of water, and all hands were kept hard at work either bailing, or going about on the other tack. On several occasions the heel of the mast broke and had to be hastily repaired, their only tools a knife and some cordage. All day, from dawn to dusk, they fought to reach the island which at sunset looked perceptibly larger, and was probably 20 miles nearer.

During the dark hours the battle continued with the beam from a lighthouse to steer by. Towards midnight the wind fell light as they came into the lee of the island. There they rested, and the exhausted men slept till dawn. It was Wednesday 16th July, and G.V. Monk describes the manner of their deliverance. "When dawn broke we could make out the layout of the island and it looked very menacing; the steep rocky cliffs came down to the sea with no place to land. As the sun rose behind the mountains it began to get very warm and the wind dropped completely. It was now time to get out the oars and row and, as the cliffs looked less steep to the

Mean tracks of *Auditor's* lifeboats.

"HISTORIAN"

3RD ENGINEER.

STEADY OLD TRIPLE EXPANSION
ENGINED VESSEL.

LONG LIFE FROM 1924 - 1960
AFTER BEING SOLD TO
THE GREEKS IN 1948.

SHE SURVIVED MANY ACCIDENTS
AFTE LEAVING TO JS IN 1948.

south, that was the way we headed. Every man took his turn at the oars but it was hot and very tiring work, particularly as we had not eaten anything substantial for almost 13 days. After rowing for three hours some colours appeared on the mountain side and these turned out to be small houses. At last here was some habitation. A little later we saw two boats making for us; they had brought two carafes of fresh water. How good it tasted! The boats, manned by fishermen, took our rope and towed us for the last two miles to the village of Tarrafal on the island of Sao Antao".

As were Don Percy and his crew two days before, the survivors in number 1 boat were treated with great kindness by the islanders. They were delighted to hear of the safe arrival of number 3 boat, and intrigued by its achievement in beating them by two whole days, when, at the beginning, she was looking like an also-ran. Nevertheless, the three boats had made it. Three outstanding voyages; and three crews remarkable for their courage and fortitude; for their skills in navigation and seamanship which, by Divine grace, had been the means of their salvation.

Next day, the inter-island water tanker arrived to pick up a cargo at the pipeline, and give the survivors passage to St. Vincent. At 18.00 they landed at Porto Grande to be greeted, not only by their own shipmates but by many more survivors from other U-boat victims, such as the CLAN MACDOUGALL (6,843/29) and the SILVERYEW (6,373/30). It is little realised what harbours of refuge these Cape Verde Islands provided for the human flotsam cast up during the Battle of the Atlantic.

Gradually, the AUDITOR'S men were provided with passages to the United Kingdom, some via Freetown, others via Bathurst, and a few via Lisbon. Unusually, Captain Bennett elected to take passage in a ship bound for Capetown, where he was given command of the Free French, Messageries Maritimes steamer, COMMANDANT DORISE (5529/17), which he brought home to England in June, 1942. After a month's leave, and a

month on dock duties, he was appointed Master of the RECORDER (225). Meanwhile George Monk and the Chief Steward of the AUDITOR, Mr. R. Doyle, were assigned to a group routed to Lisbon in a Portuguese liner, the SERPA PINTO, and it is here that the story must end on a tragic note. They left St. Vincent on 23rd August and, after a call at Madeira, arrived at Lisbon on 29th. Young Monk needed treatment for an eye infection and this was effectively dealt with at the English Hospital. A couple of weeks later he was offered a berth as Radio Officer in a small Danish vessel, the EBRO, for a voyage to the United Kingdom, and was glad to take it. Meanwhile, Mr. Doyle had been booked as a passenger aboard the MacAndrews steamer, CORTES (1,374/19). Both ships sailed on the evening of 15th September 1941, and arrived at Gibraltar two days later, just as a homeward bound convoy, HG 73, was leaving. A Naval Control Officer boarded, and hurriedly briefed the Master on the various convoy procedures before urging him to join the convoy which had just left. The CORTES was evidently given similar instructions, and later that evening both ships were in their assigned positions in Convoy HG 73.

That convoy was later subjected to a series of devastating U-boat attacks, and of the 25 ships which sailed from Gibraltar only 15, of which EBRO was one, reached ports in the United Kingdom. Among the victims was the CORTES, torpedoed on 26th. Mr. R. Doyle, the Chief Steward of the AUDITOR, who was travelling in her as a passenger, was picked up along with other survivors by another small ship in the convoy, the LAPWING (1,348/20). The submarine attacks, however, were incessant, and two hours later LAPWING herself was torpedoed, and sank rapidly. It was a case of third time unlucky for Mr. Doyle. This time there was no rescue ship; no lifeboat to give the chance of survival; no epic boat voyage; no unbridled joy in making a landfall. Just a lonely, wretched death in the dark Atlantic, a fate he shared with many in that ill-fated convoy.

207. HISTORIAN (3) 1924-1948 Steel steamship rigged as two-masted schooner. Two decks, five holds and deep tank.
O.N. 147290 5,074g 3,156n 8,030d 395.5 x 52.55 x 30.75 feet. Cargo capacity: 416,650 cubic feet.
International Code KRVQ (GKYF after 1933).
T 3-cyl. by David Rowan and Co.Ltd., Glasgow; 26, 43, 73 x 48 inches, 12.5 knots.

15.10.1924: Launched by Charles Connell and Co. Ltd., Scotstoun (Yard No. 400) for the company. *13.12.1924:* Delivered at a cost of £93,940. Subsequently sailed from Liverpool for Calcutta on her maiden voyage under Captain J.J. Egerton. *4.1925:* When inward bound to New Orleans from Savannah, Georgia, was in collision with the grounded tanker W.C. TEAGLE (9,552/17). A suit was subsequently filed against HISTORIAN for a claim of $100,000. *16.10.1939:* Stranded in the approaches to Cherbourg and refloated with the assistance of three tugs within half an hour. Proceeded to Southampton and dry docked, costs generated by the accident amounting to approximately £20,000. *23.4.1940:* In collision in the Irish Sea about 12 miles,

The long-lived *Historian.*   *[Roy Fenton collection]*

210 degrees from Chicken Rock, with the French troopship GENERAL METZINGER (9,312/06). Her bows were severely crumpled and she proceeded to Liverpool where her cargo was transhipped to WAYFARER. *5.5.1940:* Proceeded to Birkenhead to dry dock for a month. *12.7.1941:* In collision in convoy, in dense fog, in the North Atlantic with EMPIRE STEEL (8,138/41) and put back to Halifax for temporary repair. *9.3.1948:* Sold to G.A. Contomichalos Ltd. (Galbraith, Pembroke and Co. Ltd., managers), London and renamed MARLENE. *17.7.1948:* Struck a submerged object when entering Falmouth harbour with a cargo of iron ore. Beached at the entrance to St. Mawes creek as she was in danger of sinking. Subsequently refloated and beached again in Flushing Cove where the cargo of iron ore was discharged into lighters and the damage was inspected by divers. A gash was reported in the bottom shell plating extending 48 feet from number 1 double-bottom tank to number 2 port double-bottom tank. Steel plates were bolted over the gash. *1.9.1948:* Sailed with a tug escort for dry dock at Barry and permanent repair. *1949:* Sold to South African Lines Ltd., Capetown, South

Africa and renamed DAMARALAND. *1951:* Sold to Muzaffer Zorlu, Istanbul, Turkey and renamed SEMIRAMIS. *8.12.1951:* In collision with the collier CORFEN (1,867/44) off Saunders Ness in Greenwich Reach, River Thames. The port bows of both vessels were extensively damaged and although CORFEN was making water she was able to berth safely at Beckton. *1952:* Sold to Sanko Kisen K.K., Japan, and resold to Far Eastern and Panama Transport Corp. (Wheelock, Marden and Co. Ltd., managers), Panama and renamed SEMIRAMIS I. *29.5.1955:* Ran ashore on Landfall Island in the Andaman Islands in position 13.40N, 93.01E when on passage from Calcutta for Singapore with 7,000 tons of coal. Some days later, with the engine room flooded, she was abandoned by the crew who were picked up by CHOYSANG (1,889/44) and landed at Calcutta. Although declared a constructive total loss, she was refloated 13.1.1956 and following repairs was returned to service. *1960:* Sold to Japanese shipbreakers. *21.6.1960:* Arrived at Onomichi for breaking up. Subsequently sold to Kanbara Kisen K.K. and demolished at Tsuneishi.

Return to Halifax

The ships weighed anchor on the morning of 11th July 1941, and passed in orderly fashion from Bedford Basin, through the Narrows, to the open sea off Halifax, Nova Scotia. With plenty of sea room for manoeuvre, Convoy HX 138 took shape, 36 ships forming nine columns of four ships each. Taking their cue from the Commodore's signals, they headed eastwards like a well-trained battalion of troops, bound for the United Kingdom. For twenty-four hours all went well, then, soon after midday on 12th, the fine weather gave way to fog. The ships streamed their fog buoys, and sounded their whistles. Those ships in the rear could, of course, reduce speed a few revolutions and so lag behind, out of harm's way (discounting the U-boats for the time being), while those in the wing columns could steer a few degrees outwards to seek a similar, less hazardous position. Ships in central positions, however, had no option but to maintain their course and speed (which had been reduced when the fog came down) and keep a pretty sharp lookout. One such ship was HISTORIAN, third ship in the second column, still enshrouded in fog some nine hours later. All Captain W.J. Wearing and Third Officer George Sigsworth could do was keep a close eye on the fog buoy of the ship ahead, and try to read the whistle signals of the ships around them. A fog buoy, by the way, was rather like a sort of surf board towed astern at the end of a 100-fathom line, throwing up a fountain of water from a scoop at its rear end. It looked rather like the tell-tale wake of a submarine's periscope, and for this reason had, on occasion, been shot at by unwary, trigger-happy gunners!

Suddenly, out of the fog loomed the shadowy form of a vessel apparently crossing from starboard to port - and dangerously close. Urgent avoiding action was taken, but it was too late to avert a collision, and the tanker EMPIRE STEEL (8,138/41) came on to make violent contact with HISTORIAN's starboard bow. The shock of the impact drove the startled seaman on lookout on the EMPIRE STEEL's forecastle-head to leap aboard the HISTORIAN, while HISTORIAN's lookout, cowering behind the windlass, was sent sprawling. The two ships drew apart, and disappeared from each other's sight into the fog. Officers inspected the damage whilst their erstwhile companions steamed past, perilously close in some cases. If Captain Wearing and his officers had been unaware of the gradual disintegration of the convoy, they could be in no doubt of it now, for EMPIRE STEEL, the ship which had tried to cross their path in the second column, was number 72 on the convoy plan - second ship in the seventh column. The once orderly convoy had been reduced by the persistent fog to a surrealistic nightmare of jumbled ships.

Captain Wearing surveyed the broken and twisted steelwork in the forepart of his ship and decided the damage was too serious to justify continuing the voyage, so he turned the ship around, and headed back to Halifax, arriving without further mishaps on 14th July. However, a dry dock in Halifax would not be available for many weeks, and after making temporary repairs, the ship obtained special dispensation from the underwriters to proceed to New York to carry out permanent repairs, which the Salvage Association estimated would cost something in the region of $75,900. Meanwhile, EMPIRE STEEL, in somewhat better shape, pressed on with the convoy and docked at Swansea on 31st July.

HISTORIAN sailed from Halifax on 20th July, with the worst leaks patched up, and arrived safely at New York on 23rd. It was to be a lengthy visit. First of all, 2,800 tons of cargo had to be unloaded before the ship could enter the floating dry dock. When this was accomplished, a strike by tugboat hands delayed the ship another week. At last, on 18th August, the ship nosed her way into the dock, but at 18.00, with the water pumped out and the ship resting on the blocks, a foot or more of water still sluiced around the floor of the dock. The ship was still too heavy. So she was floated out and towed back to the berth where a further 700 tons of copper was discharged, and 200 tons of fresh water pumped out.

On 21st August the ship again entered the dry dock, and this time all went well. A week later she was back on the berth, the underwater repairs completed, ready to re-load the cargo they had put ashore. However, it was not until 19th September that the ship sailed from New York, bound for Halifax, to join up with the next homeward-bound convoy. HISTORIAN arrived at Liverpool on 6th October, nearly 10 weeks behind schedule, but intact.

---

208. MUSICIAN (2) 1924-1938 Steel steamship. Two decks and five holds. Two masts.
O.N. 140637 4,663g 2,886n 7,730d 384.9 x 52.0 x 29.41 feet. Cargo capacity: 398,174 cubic feet.
International Code KBSG (GCBT after 1933).
T. 3-cyl. by Rankin and Blackmore Ltd., Greenock; 27, 44, 73 x 48 inches, 11.33 knots.

4.6.1919: Launched by Lithgows Ltd., Port Glasgow (Yard No. 723 for Saint Line Ltd. (Rankin, Gilmour and Co. Ltd., managers), Liverpool) as SAINT BEDE. She had been laid down for the Shipping Controller as WAR MINK. *1.7.1919:* Ran trials. *26.9.1924:* Acquired by the company for £56,004. *18.2.1925:* Renamed MUSICIAN. *4.1929:* Fitted with a Clarke Chapman Pulverised Fuel System (see below). *23.5.1938:* Sold to African and Continental Steamship Co. Ltd., London for £23,500 and renamed AFRICAN EXPLORER. Employed running the blockade into Spanish ports during the Civil War. *19.10.1938:* Struck by a bomb during an air raid at Barcelona. The bomb pierced the ship's side and exploded in number 2 hold where the cargo of wheat helped mitigate the force of the explosion. Two winches were demolished, the navigation bridge smashed and three sailors injured. *10.2.1939:* Sustained further damage during an air raid at Cartagena. The crew made temporary repairs and she arrived Oran 9.3.1939 with fifteen Spanish refugees on board. She then proceeded to Marseilles for repair and refit but was laid up with the cessation of the Civil War. *1939:* Sold to Compania Genovese di Navigazione a Vapore S.A., Genoa, Italy, and towed to Genoa for repair. Renamed CAPO ROSA. *25.8.1941:* Taken over and interned by the Argentine Government. Subsequently sequestrated, allocated to Flota Mercante del Estado, Buenos Aires and renamed RIO DULCE. *23.5.1951:* Broke adrift from her moorings during a gale at Punta Arenas, striking the mole with her stern, and drifting on to a sandbank. Refloated quickly without assistance and anchored and although there was no bottom damage, the port quarter and deck plating were damaged as a result of contact with the mole. *1956:* Sold to La Austral S.A., Comercial, Industrial y Maritima, Buenos Aires, Argentina and renamed AUSTRAL. *1961:* Sold to Cantieri Riuniti del Golfo, Spezia for demolition. *6.1.1961:* Arrived at Spezia. The following day she dragged her anchors during a storm and collided with the Italian tanker ANDREA ZANCHI (10,606/43) causing some damage.

The Clarke Chapman Pulverised Fuel System

Although coal was still the most popular fuel at this time, the advantages of oil fuel were widely recognised, being cleaner and less labour intensive to operate. But it was still comparatively expensive. So why not put coal through a mill, reduce it to a powder, and inject it into the furnaces like oil, and so have the best of both energy resources? In 1928 the board of Thos. and Jas. Harrison Ltd. decided to put the system to the proof, and invited tenders from Clarke Chapman and Co. Ltd. of Newcastle-upon-Tyne and others, with a view to installing a pulverising system in the MUSICIAN.

Clarke Chapman's system was selected, and work began on 18th March 1929, while the ship was in Liverpool. It was necessary to shift a dynamo, and burn away part of the stokehold bulkhead to give access to the pulverising plant, also to modify the ship's hospital to accommodate an extra junior engineer. It was decided to convert just two of the ship's three single-ended boilers to pulverised fuel, thus enabling the stokehold crew to be reduced from 15 to 13. The work of conversion cost £7,720, and took over three weeks to complete, but the system was ready for use when the ship sailed for Kingston on 15th April.

The type of coal used was a sort of nutty slack obtained, on this occasion, from the Staffordshire coalfield. It was certainly much cheaper than the best Welsh or Yorkshire steaming coal normally supplied for firing ships out of Liverpool. Whatever coal is burned, however, there is always a residue after combustion in the form of soot, ash and clinkers. The pulverised coal was no exception, and the exhausted powder ejected after combustion tended to form a sticky slag on contact with cooler air, clogging the uptakes. Disposal of the dust raised by the pulverisers was a real problem in the confined space of the stokehold, and, together with the indescribable noise, constituted a source of stress and discomfort to the engineers and firemen working there.

On the ship's return to Liverpool on 1st July 1929 both pulveriser motors were sent to Newcastle-upon-Tyne for a complete overhaul; the funnel casing and main funnel were removed and landed on the North Wall of Herculaneum Dock for a thorough de-coke and modifications to the piping. The ventilation system to the stokehold was improved, but despite further trials and claims as to its cost-effectiveness, difficulties in getting suitable fuel at coaling stations around the world, the high cost of maintenance, and the obnoxious working conditions, led to the system being brought into disrepute, and finally abandoned in favour of more conventional means of firing boilers. See also under RECORDER (225), fitted for pulverised fuel as a new ship in 1930.[132]

Two views of *Musician* in the Mersey, the upper view as *Saint Bede*. The taller funnel is believed to have been fitted as a consequence of the trials with burning pulverised fuel.

[*Both J. and M. Clarkson*]

209. WANDERER (2) 1925-1949 Steel steamship. Two decks, five holds and deep tank. Two masts.
O.N. 147294 5,079g 3,152n 8,030d 395.5 x 52.55 x 30.75 feet. Cargo capacity: 435,600 cubic feet.
International Code KSFP (GLBM after 1933).
T. 3-cyl. by David Rowan and Co. Ltd., Glasgow; 26, 43, 73 x 48 inches, 12.5 knots.

A fine John McRoberts view of *Wanderer* in the Mersey on 14th August 1937. The absence of topmasts suggests she is also visiting
Manchester. *[J. and M. Clarkson]*

11.12.1924: Launched by Charles Connell and Co. Ltd.,
Scotstoun (Yard No. 401) for the company. *22.2.1925:*
Delivered at a cost of £94,004. Subsequently sailed from
Liverpool for Calcutta on her maiden voyage under Captain
R. Watson. *28.9.1935:* Driven ashore by a severe hurricane
at Punta del Dirril, Cienfuegos, southern Cuba, while
loading sugar. The hurricane caused damage estimated at
£800,000 to Cienfuegos alone, fifty people were killed and
some 450 injured. The town was placed under martial law to
prevent looting. The cargo of sugar and bunker coal was
discharged into lighters and an unsuccessful attempt made
at refloating 3.10.1935. Tugs were then despatched from
New Orleans and she was refloated 5.10.1935 seemingly
without damage. The cargo and bunkers were reloaded and
she resumed her voyage. *27.11.1935:* Dry docked in
Number 4 Herculaneum, Liverpool, and a large patch of
coral, measuring some 100 by 20 feet and two inches thick,
was found adhering to the bottom plating.[133] *5.1942:*
Participated in the Madagascar campaign. *7.4.1944:* When
proceeding up the Shatt al Arab River, at the head of the
Persian Gulf, the Pilot collapsed unconscious. As a result
she took the ground near Number 1 Red Buoy. After

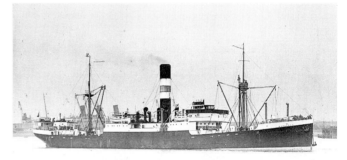

Wanderer with her full complement of topmasts off Gravesend on
20th April 1935. *[World Ship Photo Library collection]*

discharging ballast, she refloated within the hour, by which
time the Pilot had recovered and he piloted the vessel to a
safe anchorage at Khorramshahr. The soft mud of the river
bed prevented serious damage. *2.1949:* Sold to British Iron
and Steel Corporation for demolition, allocated to T.W. Ward
Ltd. *5.3.1949:* Arrived at Milford Haven.

The US Coast Guard photographed *Wanderer* entering a US port on 6th December 1943. *[Ian Farquhar collection]*

210. INANDA (2) 1925-1940/EMPIRE EXPLORER 1942 Steel steamship. Two decks, five holds and deep tank. Two masts. O.N. 147310 5,985g 3,746n 6,925d 407.0 x 52.25 x 31.27 feet. Cargo capacity: 324,400 cubic feet. Berths for 91 passengers *1942:* 5,345g 3,180n 7,207d.
International Code KSNF (GLMB after 1933).
Q. 4-cyl. by Wallsend Slipway and Engineering Co. Ltd., Wallsend; 26, 36, 52, 76 x 54 inches; 14 knots.

24.2.1925: Launched by Swan, Hunter and Wigham Richardson Ltd., Wallsend (Yard No.1259) for the company. *12.5.1925:* Delivered at a cost of £176,725. Subsequently sailed from London for the West Indies on her maiden voyage under Captain A.B. Nicholas. *14.4.1931:* Captain Nicholas died in London, while still on board. *3.2.1932:* Put into Swansea with 47 passengers on board to undertake repairs to a broken propeller. The work was undertaken at Palmers' Dry Dock and the passengers were accommodated in local hotels until the ship was ready to sail two days later. *13.8.1936:* The two Orsborne brothers, who had earlier absconded from Britain with the fishing vessel GIRL PAT, were placed in the custody of the Master, Captain Willis H. Gibbings, for transfer to authorities in London. The men gave no trouble and were handed over to police 2.9.1936 at Gravesend. *21.6.1940:* Sailed from London on the final voyage in the company's passenger service to the West Indies. *27.8.1940:* On return requisitioned by the Admiralty for service as an Ocean Boarding Vessel in company with her sister INKOSI (240). *7.9.1940:* Struck by bombs from German aircraft in a series of raids over three days whilst fitting out in Royal Albert Dock, London. Her accommodation was gutted, holds flooded and she settled on the bottom. Five West Indian ratings were killed and three injured, and the survivors were transferred to MAGICIAN (211) for subsequent repatriation to the West Indies.

4.10.1940: Refloated and taken over by the British Government. During the subsequent refit, the passenger decks were ripped out and she was rebuilt as a cargo vessel. *11.2.1942:* Registered in the ownership of the Ministry of War Transport, London (Thos. and Jas. Harrison Ltd., Liverpool, managers) as EMPIRE EXPLORER under the command of Captain E.B. Stephens. *8.7.1942:* Torpedoed by the German submarine U 575 (Kapitänleutnant Gunther Heydemann) when on passage from Demerara and Port of Spain, Trinidad, for Carlisle Bay, Barbados and the UK with a cargo of pitch, sugar and mail. After a second torpedo struck, the crew abandoned ship, whereupon a third torpedo was fired, the blast overturning two of the boats. The submarine then started shelling the vessel and this started a fire. *9.7.1942:* At about 04.00 sank in position 11.40N, 60.55W, about 307 degrees and 30 miles from Tobago North Point. A US aircraft subsequently dropped smoke-floats and morale was restored to the men in the water. Later a motor torpedo boat appeared and the distressed crew were picked from the water. Fourteen injured survivors were taken to hospital and only three of the crew of 71 were reported missing. In his report, Captain Stephens praised the exemplary behaviour of his crew, singling out Fourth Engineer Peter Hayes and Fifth Engineer Bernard London for special praise because of their outstanding devotion to duty.

Inanda on trials in the North Sea. Although built for Harrisons, she carried a traditional Rennie's name. *[Frank and Sons]*

Okay for some! Life in the INANDA in the thirties[134]

INANDA was one of the very popular single-class passenger vessels which sailed out of London in T. and J. Harrison's service to the West Indies during the years between the wars. She had replaced the old Rennie Line's INTABA (156) in 1925. Not only were the ships popular with passengers, many of whom travelled regularly in them, but also with the officers, engineers, and seamen who served in them. The reasons were not difficult to find - regular trips lasting six weeks, with a two-week sojourn in London between voyages, and 10 days leave every other voyage; excellent catering of a standard considerably higher than that to be found in the cargo ships; and a relaxed, congenial atmosphere on board with opportunities to strike up life-long friendships.

The fare for a single passage to Georgetown, or Trinidad was £32-£40, and about £75-£80 for the round voyage, including up to three nights in Georgetown's Park Hotel. These fares may seem cheap by today's prices, and even at that time they were considered quite reasonable. But to see them in perspective, compare, say a Second Officer's salary of £21 per month, or a Fourth Officer's £14, or a Quartermaster's £9.10s.0d.

Captain H.G. Skelly was Fourth Officer of the INANDA in the early 'thirties, and has recorded some of his impressions of that nostalgic period before the Depression spoiled everything. He writes of tea dances in the afternoon, and of dancing on deck under the stars (one can almost hear the muted sighing of saxophones); of well-dressed gamblers in the mini-casino set up in the smoke room; of treasure hunts, and fancy-dress parties.

"Food and conditions on board were excellent. Meals

155

consisted of many courses of well-cooked and enjoyable dishes. The junior officers had their own small table in the dining saloon. Senior officers had tables of their own, scattered amongst the passengers. On the ocean stretch senior officers and passengers dressed for dinner at 19.00 every night, but between the islands this convention was not enforced.

"On Sunday morning, church service was held in the Music Room at 10.00, and the Quartermaster tolled the bell on the forecastle head to call out the faithful. All the ladies wore hats, the Captain read the service, and a piano accompanied the singing of hymns. A plate was passed round in aid of the seamen's orphanage. All officers were expected to go to church, and did. It was all very well done. The usual deck games could be played after church, but not before. In the Music Room there

An adventure in futility

Captain Willis H. Gibbings, Master of the Harrison Line passenger liner INANDA, sat at his desk finishing off the obligatory arrival letter to his employers. His ship had just berthed at Booker's Wharf Number 1, Georgetown, Demerara, and passengers were preparing to go ashore to meet eager relatives waiting on the wooden wharf. The sunlit scene was as lively and colourful as nature and humanity could make it. A cheerful exchange of greetings passed between ship and shore as passengers waited impatiently for the gangway to be landed and secured. Near the sheds a string of passive donkey carts waited for their loads of baggage, while uniformed police and customs officers mingled suspiciously with the new arrivals. It was 12th August 1936.

As Captain Gibbings finished writing there was a subdued tap at his door. "Come in," he said. Evidently the gangway was in place at last, he thought, as the agent's clerk from Bookers brushed aside the curtain and entered the cabin. "Good morning, Captain; here's your mail", he announced, placing a slim wad of letters on the desk. "You'll be getting four gangs, starting at 1 o'clock." The Captain murmured a greeting, shook hands, and enquired the nature and quantity of the cargo to be loaded. This, and other matters being resolved, the agent's clerk prepared to take his leave. "Oh, by the way, Captain, we have two special passengers for you to take to London". "Special? What's special about them?" demanded the Captain, a note of suspicion in his voice. "Well, sir," replied the clerk hesitantly, "they are actually prisoners - criminals, in fact, going home to face trial". "Good heavens, man, what do they think I'm running? A prison ship?" Captain Gibbings was highly indignant. "No, no; of course not." The clerk's tone was conciliatory, but it had limited success. "No, not at all; but we do have an order from the Governor's office, and we have confirmed the arrangements with our principals - subject to your approval, of course", he added hastily. Captain Gibbings was not to be mollified, however, though he realised he did not have much choice in the matter. Great Scott! What sort of villains were these men? And what about the scores of women and children in his care? It seemed a good card to play, and he played it. "Oh, no, sir;" the clerk tried to be reassuring. "They are not violent types; they only stole a ship." "Stole a ship! And what about my ship?" "Well, sir, it was only a very small ship, a fishing boat, in fact; and these men have given no trouble since they were arrested!" "That's as maybe, young man, but I'm not accepting these - these miscreants until I've seen them for myself."

So Captain Gibbings stormed up to the gaol accompanied by the anxious clerk, and demanded to see his "special passengers". It was then that he learned that they were none other than the notorious Captain George Black Orsborne and his brother James, who had stolen a fishing vessel called the GIRL PAT. Captain Gibbings remembered seeing something in the papers about the mysterious disappearances and reappearances of this elusive little craft. He also remembered being in Georgetown a couple of months ago when, on 19th June, the Orsbornes and their crew had finally been arrested. The event had generated considerable excitement locally.

Looking at the desperadoes now, closely confined in their gloomy prison cell, Captain Gibbings decided that they did not appear to be very desperate, or aggressive types. He questioned them in uncompromising terms, and eventually one of them extended his arms, palms outwards, in a gesture of resignation.

"Look, Captain, we have no intention of stealing your ship - not even if it were the QUEEN MARY. All we want is a chance to get out of this god-forsaken hole, and get back to England, to face whatever is coming to us. We promise you there'll be no trouble." There was a hint of ingenuous sincerity

was a library for the passengers consisting of one hundred books, also a radio-gramophone type of instrument with loudspeaker leads to the upper deck to accompany the dancing. If anybody wanted more for their £35, they were very peculiar ... most were happy, and frequently said so.

Occasionally, kindly passengers would invite some of us out, perhaps to their homes, to a West End restaurant, or a theatre. Life took on an "Upstairs/Downstairs" flavour, and we had a little toe "Upstairs" now and again. It was very enjoyable.

Those ships gave me the happiest years of the 47 I spent at sea, and I, with many other Harrison Line personnel, remember them only with affection. They certainly were the nicest way to go to sea in those days, or indeed at any time. But they died with the war, and never came back."

in his voice, which the Captain, like many others before him found difficult to ignore. "Alright," he said grudgingly, turning to the prison officials. "Have them brought to the ship tomorrow; we sail on the p.m. tide."

Next day, the Orsbornes duly arrived alongside the gangway in a prison van, and embarked on the INANDA. On board, they were accommodated behind locked doors in the ship's hospital situated on the poop. Once the ship had sailed, however, the doors were left unlocked, but the brothers were forbidden to mingle or speak to the other passengers, who gazed at them curiously as they paced the tiny strip of deck outside their quarters.

This injunction, however, did not appear to apply to the ship's officers, some of whom struck up an acquaintanceship with the unwelcome passengers which could only be described as cordial. The engineers in particular made a point of dropping in for a yarn after making their inspection of the steering gear at the end of each watch. Gradually they pieced together the story - or as much of it as the Orsbornes were prepared to tell. Some of the gaps have been filled in from other sources, but this, as far as we know it, is the anticlimactic saga of the GIRL PAT.

The story began when the GIRL PAT sheltered in Dover harbour from bad weather in the North Sea. She arrived at Dover on Friday morning, 3rd April, and after berthing most of the crew, glad to get away from the narrow confines of the boat, went ashore. When they returned late that evening they found to their consternation that the boat had gone. She had put to sea with only four men on board; Skipper Dod Orsborne; H.F. Stone, the Mate; J.H. Harris, Deck Boy, and W.H. Stephen, Cook. It transpired that the Skipper's brother, Jim Orsborne, had stowed away on board.

The owners issued a writ of abandonment, and claimed payment of her value from the insurers. Actually, the boat had made for shelter in the Channel Islands where the men set about repainting and disguising her. Then, unseen and unreported, the boat set off to cross the Atlantic via the southern route, using a school atlas as an aid to navigation. She was reported first from Corcubion, Spain, then from Dakar, where she landed Henry Stone, the Mate, who had become seriously ill.

The glib skipper managed to obtain stores, fuel, and repairs for the boat's ailing engine, and skipped port without paying for any of it.

On 10th June she appeared at the French penal settlement of Devil's Island, where she was allowed to berth and to take on fuel and stores on no greater assurance than Dod Orsborne's promise to call at Cayenne, and pay for them! In case the Orsbornes' mysterious mission was to spring a prisoner from the island, armed guards kept a watchful eye on the boat and its occupants throughout their stay.

On 18th June a suspicious fishing vessel was reported near the entrance to the Demerara River. The Harbourmaster sent his launch out to investigate, but the unarmed launch was warned off by the crew, who appeared to be armed, in no uncertain terms. Eventually the armed Government steamer, POMEROON, was sent to apprehend the wanderer, and on 19th June she returned in triumph with the GIRL PAT in tow, her identity confirmed and her crew under police guard.[135]

It would appear that the errant Orsbornes enjoyed their voyage to England in the INANDA. They obviously got on well with the officers, and the latter, equally obviously, enjoyed their company despite their tattered reputations. To steal a fishing vessel from its rightful owner was like stealing a horse from a cowpuncher - and we all know what happened to horse-thieves. But why commit such an offence, and then brave the hazards of an Atlantic crossing, unless there was a profit motive? The

Orsbornes would talk about anything under the sun, and their tales were of the stuff of legends, but neither careful probing nor cunning insinuations on the part of their new-found friends could persuade the brothers to part with the secret of their mission. No answers were forthcoming, neither at that time, nor at any other. According to the Mate, Henry Stone, in a statement given at Dakar, Dod Orsborne had simply proposed to "proceed south and seek our fortune".

INANDA reached the London River on 2nd September, and the Orsbornes made their farewells. At Gravesend, a police launch swung smartly away from the jetty, and the brothers stepped aboard as it drew alongside. They waved with apparent cheerfulness to the sea of faces lining the ship's rails, their thoughts doubtless racing ahead to those next ports of call - Scotland Yard, the Old Bailey and Wormwood Scrubs.

Becoming notorious after the incident when she was stolen and taken to the West Indies, the fishing vessel *Girl Pat* went on show at various ports after she returned to the UK. Basil Feilden caught her at Liverpool. *[J. and M. Clarkson]*

211. MAGICIAN (2) 1925-1944 Steel steamship. Two decks, five holds and deep tank. Two masts.
O.N. 147314 5,105g 3,181n 8,065d 394.9 x 52.5 x 30.5 feet. Cargo capacity: 427,737 cubic feet.
International Code KSRJ (GLNR after 1933).
T. 3-cyl. by the New Waterway Shipbuilding Co., Schiedam, Holland; 26, 43, 73 x 48 inches, 11 knots.

5.5.1925: Launched by the New Waterway Shipbuilding Co., Schiedam, Holland (Yard No.129) for the company: their first vessel to be ordered outside the United Kingdom. *23.6.1925:* Delivered at a cost of £89,976. Subsequently sailed from London for South Africa on her maiden voyage under Captain P.O. Nicholas. *28.4.1933:* When outward bound for South Africa and some 1,600 miles northwest of Capetown, broke her low-pressure cylinder crank shaft. She was taken in tow by ACTOR (174) for a few days while her engineers endeavoured to carry out temporary repairs. When complete, the tow was cast off and, escorted by ACTOR, she set sail for Capetown under her own steam, arriving safely on 9.5.1933. *15.5.1936:* Sustained serious damage when rammed by the Spanish steamer MANUEL ARNUS (7,578/23) whilst berthed at Vera Cruz. She was able to proceed to Galveston for repairs. *23.3.1941:* Sailed from Halifax as Commodore ship for Convoy SC 26. In the absence of a Royal Naval officer qualified for the post, Captain D.H. Bryant had been appointed Commodore for the transatlantic voyage to the United Kingdom. *3.4.1941:* At midnight, when the convoy had reached position 58.20N, 28.30W, about 370 miles, 207 degrees from Reykjanes Lighthouse, Iceland, it was attacked by the German submarine U 46 (Kapitänleutnant Engelbert Endrass). The Canadian escort screen had long since returned to base, British escorts were not due for several days and the convoy was far beyond air cover from either side of the Atlantic. Only the Armed Merchant Cruiser HMS WORCESTERSHIRE remained as ocean escort, and she

was as vulnerable to U-boat attack as her charges. The German submarine was joined by others and considerable casualties were inflicted. At 04.20 the convoy was ordered to scatter by Commodore Bryant but at daybreak those vessels nearest to MAGICIAN reformed into four columns of two ships each. Later that day the destroyers HAVELOCK and HESPERUS arrived, to be followed by VETERAN and WOLVERINE. The remaining ships of the convoy finally arrived at their dispersal point in the North Channel 8.4.1941 and MAGICIAN docked at Liverpool the next day. Of the 22 ships that had left Halifax, eleven had been sunk and eleven arrived safely. *6.4.1942:* Attacked by Japanese aircraft at Vizagapatnam, India, but escaped damage. *4.1944:* When inward bound from the West Indies for London, joined a coastal convoy which was proceeding to Methil via the Pentland Firth. *14.4.1944:* Whilst rounding Duncansby Head in dense fog, Captain G.H. Howard missed sighting Buoy No.30, altered course to starboard too early and the vessel ran ashore on Craig Ewen Point, two miles north of Peterhead, on a falling tide. *4.5.1944:* Despite strenuous efforts at salvage, cracks started to appear in the hull and she seemed in danger of breaking up. *12.5.1944:* Moved 10 feet and slewed through 15 degrees but the weather then deteriorated. *17.5.1944:* When salvors boarded they found extensive hull damage and further attempts at refloating were abandoned. *21.5.1944:* All items of small gear were removed and formal notice of abandonment was given to the underwriters 22.5.1944. She was on a voyage from Trinidad to London with general cargo.

The Dutch-built *Magician* was Harrison's first ship ordered and completed outside the UK. *[Roy Fenton collection]*

212. WAYFARER (2) 1925-1944 Steel steamship. Two decks, five holds and deep tank. Two masts. O.N. 147324 5,068g 3,157n 8,030d 395.5 x 52.55 x 30.75 feet. Cargo capacity: 435,330 cubic feet. International Code KTCD (GLNT after 1933).
T. 3-cyl. by David Rowan and Co. Ltd., Glasgow; 26, 43, 73 x 48 inches, 12.5 knots.

4.6.1925: Launched by Charles Connell and Co. Ltd., Scotstoun (Yard No. 403) for the company. *26.8.1925:* Delivered at a cost of £93,964. Subsequently sailed from Liverpool for East Africa on her maiden voyage under Captain E.J. Sawyer. *22.5.1938:* A sudden explosion shook the engine room when in the vicinity of Bardsey Island, North Wales on passage from Cuba for Liverpool. A high-pressure cylinder had ruptured and two crew were scalded by the escaping steam. A tug was sent out from Liverpool and she was towed 27.5.1938 into the Mersey. *17.4.1939:* Struck the Dutch steamer VEERHAVEN (5,291/30) which was berthed alongside at Maceio, Brazil, causing some damage. *12.4.1944:* Berthed at Alexandra Dock, Bombay with a cargo of munitions from Liverpool. *14.4.1944:* The steamer FORT STIKINE (7,142/42), which was berthed in Victoria Dock and also loaded with ammunition, caught fire and exploded. The explosion flattened the whole area and thousands were killed or injured. Ten vessels were totally destroyed but WAYFARER was only slightly damaged by falling debris and she resumed her voyage following repairs. *19.8.1944:* Torpedoed and sunk by the German submarine U 862 (Korvettenkapitän Heinrich Timm) in position 14.30S, 42.20E, about 90 miles, 070 degrees from Mozambique. She sank in less than two minutes and only ten of the crew of 61 survived. She was returning to the United Kingdom with a cargo of Rhodesian copper loaded at Beira.

Wayfarer undergoing trials on the Clyde.

[W. Robertson and Co.]

WAYFARER's castaways

By mid-August 1944 it seemed to many that the war with Germany was all but over. The Axis were in retreat on all fronts. When the WAYFARER sailed from Beira on 16th August heavily laden with a close-weight cargo of copper and coal, she was far removed from any of the familiar battle zones. But vague reports of enemy submarine activity in the Mozambique Channel were sufficiently alarming to give rise to feelings of nervous apprehension.[136]

Routed independently to Aden, the ship steered zig-zag patterns during daylight as a precaution against submarine attack, but resumed a straight course after darkness fell. It was in darkness, however, that the attack came - at 21.30 on 19th August. A single torpedo struck the port side of the ship between the deep-tank and number 4 hold, rupturing the bulkhead, and flooding both compartments. The cargo of copper did the rest: WAYFARER went down stern first, and sank like a stone. Within a minute and a half she had completely disappeared, and men below decks never stood a chance. Loss of life was heavy; 51 out of a total crew of 61 were lost with the ship, among them Captain John Wales and all but three of his fourteen officers. Those who survived were either very alert and level-headed, or very lucky - perhaps both.

There had been no time to launch any boats, and few men had time to grab a lifejacket. Bosun Arthur Apps, a large, rotund man, getting on in years, slow in speech and manner, but of imperturbable character, was asleep in his cabin under the poop deck when he was awakened by the shock of the explosion. The speed of his reactions and rapid comprehension of a dire situation were remarkable on this occasion. Emerging on to the poop in 40 seconds, he found it already awash.

Promptly he made up his mind, and stepped over the side into the sea. He, and the gunner on watch, were the only men in that part of the ship to escape. Stolidly treading water only a few yards away, he had a sea-level view of the ship rearing skywards and sliding beneath the waves, a frightening vision of a steel hull hurtling past amid a cascade of fiery sparks from the funnel, and a roar of escaping steam. He was mildly surprised at the lack of suction which should have taken him down, too. He bobbed about in the water for a while, clinging to a wooden hatch-board, then spotted a damaged life-boat floating keel uppermost and swam across to it. A man whom he recognised as one of the firemen was sitting astride the keel, and he helped Apps aboard. Shortly afterwards they were joined by another fireman. They heard shouting, but could see no one in the enveloping darkness. The cries grew weaker, then gradually faded altogether.

Carpenter T. Allen was in the dining saloon having a smoke when the torpedo struck. He hesitated, wondering whether to go aft to his cabin to get his lifejacket, when a shipmate told him the after deck was already awash. Feeling the deck tilt under his feet, he rushed up the ladder to his boat-station on the lower-bridge - number 1 boat on the starboard side. At that moment Captain Wales came out of his cabin, and spoke briefly, saying, "There's no need to lower away yet". Surely, the most tragic of all notable last words. He then went back into his room, and immediately afterwards the ship really began to move, going down by the stern, her bow tilting towards the stars. Allen climbed desperately aboard number 1 boat, which was swung out ready for launching. Perhaps he had a vague notion that it would break adrift on impact with the water.

158

He clung to the gunwale, supporting his feet in the grab-lines becketed outside the boat. Gathering speed like an express leaving the station, the ship slid under, and Allen, still clinging to the boat, went down with her. He had no idea how far down he went, but at last, with lungs bursting, he let go, and fought his way towards the surface. As luck would have it, his flailing arms struck against a rope. He grabbed it. The rope, in fact, was attached to a timber griping spar which was darting for the surface much faster than he could swim. His head broke clear into the night air, and clinging to the spar he tried to look about him while he regained his breath. He saw nothing, except one or two flares of the type which ignite automatically on contact with the water. Then after a while he heard voices, and could just make out the outline of a raft a short distance away. He shouted, and swam towards it, then willing hands hauled him aboard where he lay prone on the gratings, gasping for breath, and coughing up salt water.

As he came round they saw, not far away, a darker shadow against the night sky, revealing the silhouette of the submarine whose stealthy assault had brought them to this sorry pass. She had surfaced probably to charge her batteries.

Was it Japanese? The men on the raft kept silent, acutely aware that Japanese submariners had a reputation for ruthless disposal of enemy survivors. Their dread of a hail of machine-gun bullets far outweighed their fear of the lonely ocean. Arthur Apps on his upturned boat was close enough to hear the crew speaking in German, but he and his companions also kept silent, until the U-boat finally got under way, and disappeared.

At daybreak, the survivors on the raft sighted the upturned boat supporting Arthur Apps and the two firemen. For an hour they laboured with the unwieldy oars, propelling their craft towards the lifeboat until they were close enough to throw a line aboard. Eventually the three men were able to clamber on to the raft, which was already quite crowded. They lashed the boat alongside, with a view to ransacking its provision lockers by diving underneath. However, the appearance of a sinister-looking dorsal fin gliding past was sufficient to deter them from that project, and the derelict boat was reluctantly cast adrift.

There were ten men on the raft, which consisted of a stoutly built timber framework enclosing several empty oil drums acting as buoyancy chambers. Such rafts were secured to the standing rigging on merchant ships at that time in such a way as to float clear if the ship were sunk. This particular raft had fulfilled its purpose magnificently. Besides Bosun Apps and Chippy Allen, the muster included Third Engineer J. W. Agar, Chief Steward J. Fitzpatrick, Purser R.B. Jones, Firemen D. Owens and G. Rowley, Cabin Boy J. Carroll, and two so-called "deck-hands" (a contemporary euphemism for gunners), J. Thompson and G. Berry. Ten men, ill-prepared and ill-equipped, against the Indian Ocean. By common consent they elected Bosun Apps as their leader; he was then 65 years old, with vast experience, and a fund of native common sense.

There were no navigators among the castaways; not that the raft was capable of being navigated in the strict sense of the word. Even so, they were aware that the continent of Africa lay not too far distant to the westwards, and, wielding that least efficient means of marine propulsion, the oar, they took turns to propel the raft in that direction, taking their cue from the rising sun which they placed astern. The weather was calm, and it was very hot during the day, so that their ill-clad bodies suffered from exposure. On the fourth day, the wind freshened from the east, so the Bosun stepped an oar to serve as a mast, and cut up and trimmed a sleeping bag to serve as a sail. Thereafter they made much better progress, holding the wind for six consecutive days. The raft, fortunately, was well provisioned, enabling the Bosun to issue two ounces of water to each man twice a day at dawn and dusk. During the course of the day each man also received two biscuits, two pieces of chocolate, and a spoonful of pemmican, a dried meat extract. It wasn't much, but it seemed to sustain them in reasonably good health.

On the seventh day since the sinking they sighted land, but another four days were to elapse before the raft grounded on the outer reef of an offshore island. The reef enclosed a lagoon, which separated the raft from the beach, presenting the men with the disappointing prospect of a long swim. Next morning, a party of strong swimmers left the raft and swam the three or four hundred yards to the beach. They returned before nightfall somewhat crestfallen, for as Robinson Crusoe islands

go, this was a washout. Not only did they fail to see any sign of human habitation, but they saw no wildlife, either. Nor was there much in the way of vegetation; no luscious tropical fruit, and the few coconut palms they saw were barren. Worst of all, they found no water.

Bosun Apps was not satisfied, however, and next day sent another, six-strong party of explorers to the beach, with instructions to explore further inland. Chippy Allen went with them, cutting his feet painfully on the razor-edged coral in the process. But this party of explorers was no more successful than the first, and spent a disconsolate night on shore to resume their search next day, 1st September. But all to no avail, and they were about to give up and return to the raft when one of them sighted a sail. A sail! Eagerly they watched it approach, skimming over the water like an angel from heaven! It was a native fishing boat with three ebony-skinned fishermen on board making a periodic visit to the island to set fish traps. On this occasion they were startled to find an unkempt reception committee, red-skinned and bearded, dancing and waving like lunatics. It was some time before the excited castaways could persuade the fishermen that it was safe to approach. By signs and gestures they managed to explain their predicament, and convey the idea that they needed help. At once the fishermen responded, and helped round up the rest of the crew, some of whom were still on the raft, and others scattered around the island.

Eventually, all ten boarded the fishermen's frail craft, and they set sail to traverse the coral-girt channels to the nearest habitation on the mainland. At dawn on 2nd September, a fortnight after their ship had been sunk, the weary but elated survivors came ashore at the village of Orlumbo, in Portuguese Mozambique, not far from the border with Tanganyika. A message was sent to the District Administrator at Palma, and that evening two cars arrived at the village to pick up the castaways and transport them to Palma, where the Portuguese authorities welcomed them with great kindness.

After a week or so, during which the men had been provided with food, clothing, accommodation, and medical care, the British authorities in Tanganyika, having authorised their repatriation, arranged to receive them at the border. The men crossed the Ruvuma River by canoe and landed at last on British soil, where an army truck was waiting to take them to Mikindani, then to Lindi where they boarded a Dutch coaster to Dar-es-Salaam. From there, a pair of naval patrol boats took them to Mombasa, where they boarded a troopship bound for Suez, and so to England. Sadly, Carpenter Allen recalled that their reception in Liverpool, chilly and formal, was in complete contrast to that which they had enjoyed in Palma.

Bosun Apps commented on the good behaviour and comradely spirit of the men placed in his charge. For his conduct and inspired leadership he was awarded a Bar to the British Empire Medal he already held.

Inevitably the question arises, where did the raft come ashore? The northern coast of Mozambique is littered with coral reefs and islands forming a protective barrier some five to fifteen miles off the mainland shore, any one of which could be eligible. The search is narrowed, however, by the fact that the castaways landed in a district administered from the town of Palma near the border with Tanganyika. The village of "Orlumbo", where the men came ashore, is probably the village of Olumbi, shown on Admiralty Chart No. 2938 some 13 miles south of Palma. Several islands girt the coast in this vicinity - Rongui, Queramimbi, Vamizi, Metundo, and Quifuqui. The first three are said to be thickly or densely wooded (which the castaways' island certainly was not); which leaves Metundo-Quifuqui, described as "inconspicuous" in the Admiralty Sailing Directions, and it also features a wide lagoon. So Ilha Metundo would appear to be the island most eligible for the raft's landfall.[137]

One other mystery remains. How could a raft drift in a north north westerly direction for some 220 miles against the accepted set of the Mozambique Current? For that is what happened, if the position ascribed to the sinking is acceptable. None of the castaways were navigators, and the U-boat's war diary has been lost. Consequently, the position of the sinking had to be estimated, probably by the naval authorities responsible for routing the ship. A tentative reconstruction does suggest that the estimate is reasonable. However, the current is at its weakest in July/August, and a steady south to southeast wind could well neutralise its influence. Nevertheless, it was a remarkable feature in a remarkable adventure.

213. COLONIAL (2) 1926-1941 Steel steamship. Two decks, five holds and deep tank. Two masts.
O.N. 147355 5,108g 3,129n 8,050d 396.05 x 52.6 x 30.75 feet. Cargo capacity: 426,420 cubic feet.
International Code KTRW (GCRL after 1933).
T. 3-cyl. by D. and W. Henderson and Co. Ltd., Glasgow; 26, 43, 73 x 48 inches, 12.5 knots.

19.12.1925: Launched by D. and W. Henderson and Co. Ltd., Glasgow (Yard No. 721) for the company. *19.2.1926:* Delivered at a cost of £101,620. Subsequently sailed from Glasgow for the West Indies on her maiden voyage under Captain R. Watson. *26.10.1927:* In collision with the Norwegian steamer STEINSTAD (2,476/12) at Cardenas,

Cuba. *26.5.1941:* Torpedoed and sunk by the German submarine U 107 (Kapitänleutnant Gunther Hessler) off the west coast of Africa in position 09.13N, 15.09W, about 120 miles, 291 degrees from Freetown. She was on passage from Liverpool for Freetown and Beira with general cargo. The crew was saved.

Colonial in the Mersey estuary.   *[J. and M. Clarkson]*

Life can be a drag
Cardenas Bay, Cuba, long before the revolution; ships in the anchorage loading bagged sugar in 100-kilo sacks; the sun beating down upon an industrious but tranquil scene. COLONIAL was riding gently to 30 fathoms of cable on her port anchor, while about 600 feet away on her starboard beam lay the Norwegian freighter, STEINSTAD. As darkness fell, the idyllic tropical scene faded, and storm clouds gathered on the northern horizon. At 19.00 the wind, which had hitherto been light to moderate from the east north east, suddenly backed north, and strengthened, with squalls and gusts of force 7. Cardenas Bay, open to the north, was in the grip of a "Norther".

At about 20.00 during a heavy rain squall, those on COLONIAL saw, or thought they saw, their neighbour STEINSTAD take a sheer towards them. Anxious to pay out more cable, as the conditions demanded, Captain W.G. Packe was now prevented from doing so by the close proximity of the STEINSTAD. Relentlessly, the gap between the two ships narrowed until at last they came into violent contact, COLONIAL's starboard side against the Norwegian's port bow. The damage sustained by both ships was substantial, and Harrisons initiated proceedings for damages against the owners of STEINSTAD, on the grounds of her giving COLONIAL a foul berth (she had come to an anchor after the arrival of the Harrison ship), for failing to take action to avoid collision, and for failing to keep a good lookout. The Norwegians refuted the

claim, and made a counter claim on similar grounds. The case was heard before Lord Merrivale, sitting with two nautical assessors in the Admiralty Division of the High Court, on 14th April 1930.

Movement is often relative, and relative motion sometimes creates strange illusions, especially at night. According to STEINSTAD'S witnesses, the COLONIAL, having been abeam, was now situated on the port bow, as might well be expected since the wind had backed some six points, and the ships were naturally wind-rode, there being no tide or current. As the wind freshened, STEINSTAD dropped her second anchor, and, as she was paying out cable, COLONIAL was observed to be dragging down on her. Frantically, STEINSTAD paid out shackle after shackle on both cables until 75 fathoms extended to the starboard anchor, and the port cable had reached the shackle bolted to the chain-locker bulkhead. It was as much as they could do, except yell helplessly at the advancing COLONIAL, dragging down on them until she collided with STEINSTAD'S port bow.

Unfortunately for Harrisons' case, this was the story, backed by corroborative evidence sworn by an independent witness summoned by the defendants' counsel, which was accepted by Lord Merrivale, who gave judgement in favour of STEINSTAD'S owners, with costs.[138]

Last voyage of the COLONIAL
The Liverpool section of Convoy OB 318 steamed from the Mersey on Friday 2nd May 1941. In the van was the Commodore, Rear Admiral Mackenzie RN (Retired), flying his flag in COLONIAL (Captain J.J. Devereux). North of Ireland the convoy linked up with the Clyde section, and eventually some 42 ships were formed into a square phalanx with a strong escort of destroyers and corvettes. Although COLONIAL was bound for Capetown, and many other ships for South Atlantic ports, it says much for the Navy's deep-seated anxiety and desire to confuse U-boat strategy that Control was constrained to route the convoy via far northern latitudes.

However, far from being confused, the U-boats on this occasion were able to concentrate a pack of no less than four in the vicinity of OB 318's dispersal position, that point in the North Atlantic where individual ships in the convoy would break off,

and go their separate ways. For four days between 7th and 10th May the pack attacked mercilessly and, despite the best efforts of the naval escort, sank six ships, and damaged two which eventually found a safe haven in Reykjavik, Iceland. On the credit side, U 110 was forced to the surface, boarded by seamen from the destroyer BULLDOG, and captured intact. Not only was the boat intact, but she was also taken with all her codes and the all-important Enigma cypher machine complete. Although U 110 sank while being towed to Iceland by HMS BULLDOG, this incident proved to be one of the most significant twists in the war at sea, for it gave British cypher experts the means of breaking German Naval codes, thus facilitating the twin tasks of hunting down U-boats, and protecting the convoys.

On 10th May, the convoy at last reached 60N, 35W, the dispersal point some 400 miles south west of Iceland. Gradually the ships parted company, the majority heading south-westwards towards ports in the Americas, the rest swinging south. COLONIAL was among the latter, intending to call at Freetown to land Rear-Admiral Mackenzie and his staff. For the next two weeks or so, all was peaceful, then, on the evening of 26th May, just as dusk was closing in, Captain Devereux saw the sky to the northeast illuminated by green and white flares. Convoy signals, perhaps - or submarines? The waters in the approaches to Freetown were reputed to be a real vipers' nest. Puzzled and apprehensive, Captain Devereux placed his crew on full alert. Half-an-hour later his apprehensions proved well-founded when a U-boat was sighted on the surface, off the starboard beam.

Unknown to COLONIAL's crew, the U-boat, which was the U 107, commanded by Kapitänleutnant Gunther Hessler, had already attacked with a single torpedo which had malfunctioned and missed its target. Hessler then resorted to machine gun fire, sweeping COLONIAL's decks with a prolonged burst of 20 mm shells to discourage the crew from manning the ancient 4-inch breech-loader he could see at the stern. But the gun's crew had already closed up and were rapidly training their weapon on the dimly discerned U-boat. Unfortunately, Captain Devereux had other bellicose ideas of his own and was already swinging his ship round on starboard helm to try to ram their tormentor, and consequently the gun could not be brought to bear. Meanwhile, the U-boat had no difficulty in evading COLONIAL's lumbering charge, and submerged out of sight.

COLONIAL resumed her course, zig-zagging desperately at full speed in an attempt to throw off pursuit. But Hessler had not given up. Forty-two minutes later, at 21.02, a torpedo found its mark in number 3 hold on the starboard side, quickly followed by a second torpedo in about the same place, each explosion throwing up tall columns of water and debris. Captain Devereux stopped engines, and gave the order to abandon ship, for COLONIAL was settling perceptibly, but not listing over. The two lifeboats on the starboard side, swung out ready for launching, had been blown away by the blast of the explosions, but the port boats were still intact. The sea was calm, and the boats were safely lowered to be held alongside while the crew climbed aboard. The Commodore and his staff of six yeomen and signalmen meanwhile had managed to evacuate the ship aboard a small raft. Before making for the boats Chief Radio Officer A. D. Gillespie had succeeded in sending out a distress message which was acknowledged by naval units in the area.

The boats sculled around in the darkness, fortuitously picking up two Lascars from the water. Then at about 22.00 they witnessed from a safe distance a third torpedo strike the ship in the vicinity of number 4 hold, where a consignment of nitro-glycerine was stowed. There was a spectacular explosion, and the ship disappeared almost immediately.

At daybreak, the two crowded boats and the raft drew together and took stock of their position and of the food and water available. Their deliberations were rudely interrupted when the boats were attacked by a school of sharks, which were eventually beaten off by vigorous application of oars and boathooks. After this singular and unnerving experience the survivors waited even more anxiously for rescue. On the late afternoon of the second day, some 20 hours after they had abandoned ship, they sighted the masts of a warship rising above their limited horizon. She bore down upon them rapidly, nets and ladders streamed over the side ready for the men to scramble aboard. She was a big ship; ostensibly HMS ANSON, the new King George V class battleship, and that was what the rescued seamen were led to believe. In point of fact, she was the old battleship CENTURION, built in 1913, used as a target ship between the wars, and now masquerading in disguise as the modern capital ship ANSON. Be that as it may, she had been on hand to rescue COLONIAL'S entire complement of 83 men, of whom only four were slightly injured (Captain J.J. Devereux, Chief Steward A. Barbier, and two Quartermasters, J. Douglas and M. Wing), and bear them all safely to Freetown.[139]

214. DIRECTOR (2) 1926-1944 Steel steamship. Two decks, five holds and deep tank. Two masts.
O.N. 147362 5,107g 3,128n 8,050d 395.7 x 52.6 x 30.75 feet. Cargo capacity 426,420 cubic feet.
International code: KTWP (GBFZ after 1933).
T. 3-cyl. by D. and W. Henderson and Co. Ltd., Glasgow; 26, 43, 73 x 48 inches; 12.5 knots.

12.2.1926: Launched by D. and W. Henderson and Co. Ltd., Glasgow (Yard No. 722) for the company. *8.3.1926:* Delivered at a cost of £101,507. Subsequently sailed from Liverpool to Brazil and West Indies on her maiden voyage under Captain W. Baird. *2.12.1943:* Damaged during the German bombing of Bari, and subsequent explosions which destroyed 17 merchant ships. Fortunate to escape destruction, as loaded with high octane fuel in cans. *15.7.1944:* Torpedoed and sunk by the Germany submarine U 198 (Oberleutnant Burkhard Heusinger van Waldegg) in position 24.30S, 35.44E, on passage Durban for Beira and Seychelles with general cargo. One man was lost but the 57 survivors reached the east coast of Africa in two lifeboats.

Director leaving Capetown.

[Ian Farquhar collection]

The holocaust that was Bari

As wartime voyages go, this one went auspiciously enough to begin with. After an uneventful transatlantic voyage, a dim prospect of New York, viewed through a summer heat haze from an anchorage off Coney Island. Then a coastal voyage via Delaware Bay and the Chesapeake Canal, to Baltimore, Maryland, arriving on 10th August 1943. During the next two weeks, the ship loaded a full cargo of military stores, munitions, and transport vehicles for the Eastern Mediterranean, sailing in convoy UGS 16 from Hampton Roads on 27th August. At Gibraltar the convoy split up and reformed for the voyage to Alexandria, DIRECTOR reaching Alexandria on 23rd September. After the ship had discharged her war cargo, the Master, Captain Bill Weatherall, was ordered to proceed to Haifa to load a full cargo of high octane petrol in jerricans, compact steel containers each holding about five gallons of fuel. The cargo, though fairly simple to stow, was a chancy one. No "leakers" could be accepted, and no smoking regulations were enforced both on board the ship, and on the quay alongside. There was no disguising the hazardous nature of the forthcoming voyage. Petrol, even in sturdy jerricans, is not a commodity to be treated lightly, and the prospect of carrying it to a front line port in Italy was enough to arouse misgivings in the stoutest heart. By this time the ship was rather shorthanded, Second Officer Humphrey Lloyd Jones and Cadet Edward J. Morgan having been left behind in an Alexandrian Hospital with some mysterious stomach complaint.

DIRECTOR sailed from Haifa on 11th November, calling at Alex to join a convoy escorted by a couple of corvettes. The weather became very stormy, and the convoy was delayed, but arrived off the port of Bari on 21st November in reasonably good order. The Italian pilot who boarded the ship was less than reassuring, however, when he informed the Captain that a minesweeper, HMS HEBE, had been blown up by a mine just outside the breakwater only a matter of hours before the convoy's arrival.

Nevertheless, the ships entered the harbour safely, and they were queued up on the North Breakwater, with two anchors down and mooring ropes out astern, to wait their turn for a vacant berth. DIRECTOR lay there for a week before moving to one of the berths in the inner harbour to begin unloading. Only then did the crew have an opportunity to go ashore to meet, with some curiosity, their former enemies. They found Italian citizens eager to welcome British soldiers and sailors into their shops and homes, only too glad to be rid of the hated Germans, whom they regarded as the authors of all their grief.

Early on Thursday 2nd December another large convoy entered the port direct from the United States, and the harbour became crowded once more with the newly arrived ships moored stern on to the North Breakwater. That afternoon a lone plane circled high above the town, too high to be recognisable, but most certainly German. Clearly this was another German reconnaissance plane checking on activity in Bari harbour. It found Bari like a well-stocked chicken coop waiting for the predatory fox.[140]

The raiders came over between 19.00 and 20.00. Opinions differ as to the strength of the attack varying between 105 Ju-88s[141] to a single bomber, whose pilot, returning from a raid over Yugoslavia and having two bombs remaining in his racks, dropped them with uncanny accuracy right on the ammunition ships in Bari harbour.[142] In view of the reconnaissance, however, the raid was almost certainly planned, and the truth lies probably somewhere between these estimates. An early success of the raiders was a direct hit on the US Liberty ship, JOHN L. MOTLEY. She had arrived that morning, laden with gasoline and explosives - a pernicious combination which would never be tolerated on a peacetime commercial voyage - and was one of the ships moored to the breakwater. The JOHN L. MOTLEY (7,176/43) and her cargo exploded with a roar and a flash that illuminated the entire harbour and town like day. It was not an instantaneous explosion - it seemed to go on for several minutes - and the ships in her vicinity just crumpled up, disintegrated, or burst into flames. This, of course, was not an isolated incident. Other ships and random targets in the town were also bombed, contributing to the general havoc.

Alongside in the inner harbour, a mere 1,200 yards from the conflagration on the North Breakwater, lay the DIRECTOR and her stable-mate DEFENDER (167). Their crews watched the inferno, appalled, acutely conscious of their own vulnerability. The initial blast had lifted all the DIRECTOR's hatchboards and tarpaulins from the hatches and blown them clean away. The open hatches gaped at the lurid sky from which, like a grotesque hailstorm, red-hot fragments of shattered ships rained down, some heavy enough to punch holes through the steel deck, others smashing the stacked jerricans of petrol in the holds. Amazingly, the crew, seeking what shelter they could in the ship's alleyways, and expecting to be blown to kingdom come in a ball of flame at any moment, suffered no casualties. A witness dimly recollects picking himself up from a corner of the alleyway, whither he and several others had been tossed by a blast, rubbing his bruises, and wondering if it were not time to take a walk ashore.[143] Just then a near-miss tore a great hole in the masonry of the quay alongside the ship, the blast knocking the men off their feet again. Cautiously inspecting the damage they found that the ship's starboard side had been stove-in in way of the stokehold, the ash hoist destroyed, and several plates, and a large number of rivets badly sprung, some near the waterline. Suddenly, the whine of bombs, the roar of planes, the rattle and boom of anti-aircraft guns subsided. The raid itself was over in a matter of minutes, but the explosions went on all night, as isolated pockets of ammunition in the blazing ships exploded, sometimes with a single shattering blast, in other cases like cascades of Roman candles of many colours. Some of the wrecked ships had managed to lower boats, their crews trying desperately to pull away from the breakwater, only to be overtaken by the flames as yet another ship blew up. Some crews sought refuge on the breakwater itself, sheltering in the purpose-built air raid shelters. For even the surface of the water was ablaze, as oil and gasoline from the sunken ships seeped to the surface and caught fire. It was fortunate that the offshore breeze prevented the flames from reaching the inner harbour and the town, but for the men marooned on the breakwater it was an ill wind indeed, for they were literally baked alive, trapped in their shelters. The survivors of a US ship, the JOHN BASCOM (7,176/43), about 50 of them, were gradually pushed right to the extreme eastern end of the breakwater as the conflagration advanced, and the flames were actually licking at them, leaving no alternative but a 20-foot drop into the Adriatic, when a rescue launch appeared on the seaward side to lift them to safety in the nick of time.

The explosions, the leaping flames and flying debris all combined with the blazing, oil-polluted water to form a magma poured from a crucible in Hell. But, unknown to the vast majority of victims and spectators of this infernal drama until many years after the war had ended, another satanic ingredient had been added to the brew. The deadly secret, known only to a very few, was that the American freighter JOHN HARVEY had been carrying, among her other cargoes of a volatile nature, 100 tons of mustard gas bombs. This consignment had been loaded and transported to Italy in pursuance of President Roosevelt's declared intention, supported by Prime Minister Churchill, that "any use of poison gas by any Axis power will be followed by the fullest retaliation upon munition centres, seaports, and other military objectives throughout the whole extent of the territory of such Axis country."

There was reason to believe at the time that the Germans, becoming more desperate as they were driven back on all fronts, might resort to chemical warfare. To lend substance to the President's words, stockpiles of the loathed weapons were positioned at various strategic centres for use in such an emergency. But its very existence must be kept strictly secret, and the lips of those who did know of its presence in Bari on that fateful night were sealed by orders. When the JOHN HARVEY blew up, the mustard was released into the harbour, some as gas but most of it mixed with the oil fuel scumming the surface of the water. Hundreds of seamen, forced to swim for safety, were thus immersed in the deadly fluid, in many cases absorbing it into lungs and eyes, and into their skin. Hospital staff, already overworked by the emergency, were puzzled by the ghastly blisters which afflicted many of their patients both internally and externally, and which did not conform to the symptoms normally associated with blast or burning, or the ingestion of oil fuel. Because of the secrecy surrounding the shipment doctors were not told, and so were unable to prescribe effective treatment. Many victims lingered a few days, suffering dreadfully, and died without knowing what had killed them. Those who had simply been exposed externally to the vesicant usually recovered, but only after long and painful illness. Thus the grim consequences of a violent act of war, exacerbated by the urge to counter the possibility of extreme measures, was further aggravated by the dictates of diplomacy.

As dawn broke on the stricken port, a dazed and subdued crew set about cleaning up the DIRECTOR. Means were contrived to cover the open hatches, but the reek of petrol swilling about in the bilges was everywhere. An injunction against smoking needed no urging; it was understood by everyone, and broken by no-one. The galley fires were not kindled that morning, and steps were taken to seal off the stokehold as effectively as possible. For orders had been issued by a dismayed Naval Control for every ship that could steam to leave the port and make for Port Augusta in Sicily. Of the 26 merchant ships which lay in Bari on the Thursday afternoon, only a bare half-dozen sailed that Friday morning. Seventeen gutted wrecks littered the harbour; and a few ships, though still afloat, had been disabled. Without waiting for tugs or pilot, DIRECTOR and her battered sisters pulled out of their berths, threaded their way gingerly between the wrecks, some of which were still burning, and headed for the open sea and its more familiar dangers.

DIRECTOR arrived at Port Augusta on 5th December, and lay there at anchor for a week, gas-freeing the holds and constructing an enormous cement box to contain the leaks in the stokehold. She returned to Bari on 14th, just twelve days after the raid, to unload the remainder of her essential cargo. It was said that 1,000 Allied servicemen died in the raid, or shortly afterwards, most of them merchant seamen. By then the bodies of many of these victims were rising to the surface of the harbour, bloated, mutilated, disfigured and barely recognisable as human. The stench of death, of scorched oil, of rancid desolation was like a miasma rising from the Pit; and there, cruising slowly upon those Stygian waters, was the latter-day ferry of Charon, a landing craft, manned by soldiers from a Pioneer battalion. Clad grotesquely in protective oilskins and wearing masks, they were painstakingly retrieving those sad remains from the harbour and taking them ashore, where more soldiers and teams from the military hospitals had the task of trying to establish their identity before transporting them to the mass graves. It was a horrid and melancholy scene, etched deeply for decades in the memories of those who were there.

Another five days went by while the remainder of the cargo was unloaded, after which it was no hardship at all to leave that ravaged port for ever. At Port Said the bomb damage was surveyed and it was ordained that DIRECTOR should return to England, and have repairs carried out in dry dock. It was almost with an air of light relief that the ship diverted to Burriana in Spain to pick up the orange crop on behalf of the Ministry of Food. It was a gesture which brought joy to the local Spaniards, and to the austerity-ridden markets of Britain it was a consignment of sunshine!

Last moments of DIRECTOR

DIRECTOR was on an ordinary commercial voyage from Durban to Beira when the final blow fell on Saturday 15th July 1944. In recent months, losses at sea had been comparatively light, and Harrisons had not lost a ship through enemy action since the CONTRACTOR (224) had been sunk in the Mediterranean nearly 12 months before. Captain W. Weatherall was still in command, and Chief Engineer Vivian Duff was still there, but all other officers from the previous voyage had moved elsewhere. The night of 14/15th July was very dark, but clear, with a moderate sea. Nothing was seen or heard of their assailant until the torpedo entered the port side of number 4 hold with a "dull thud" just before 01.00 on the 15th. The propeller shaft was fractured, and the ship brought up all standing as she began settling by the stern. The position was 24.30S, 35.44E, or about 30 miles east of Zavora Point in Portuguese East Africa. The explosion had brought down the main topmast, bringing with it the main aerial; shattered number 4 lifeboat; and blasted number 4 derricks out of their crutches, training them over the starboard side like the guns of a battleship.[144.]

The ship was sinking fast, and there was nought to do but abandon her while there was still time. The three remaining lifeboats were lowered and manned in good order, though number 1 had shipped a good deal of water. One man was slightly hurt when he fell through a crack in the deck, but he was hauled out and placed in a lifeboat. Two rafts had also been launched, and Captain Weatherall, after a final check all round, left the ship aboard one of them. Two minutes later, the ship reared spectacularly, and sank stern first beneath the waves. It was then 01.25.

A few minutes later the U-boat was seen to surface, and approach the little flotilla of survival craft. It closed one of the rafts and a German officer hailed it to enquire the whereabouts of the Captain. "Gone down with the ship", they told him. The officer then enquired the ship's name and destination, to which he was given truthful answers. The submarine by then was close to Captain Weatherall's raft, and again the officer made the same queries, to which Captain Weatherall gave similar replies, and remained incognito. The German then apologised politely for the inconvenience caused, and asked if there was anything he could do. "How about giving us a tow?" suggested Captain Weatherall. "I'm sorry; I cannot do that," replied the officer. "But don't worry; the RAF will be out looking for you in the morning!"

The rhythm of the diesels increased, and U 198 cruised on into the darkness. Meanwhile, the boats and rafts gathered together to compare notes, and plan their future. Number 3 boat had drifted too close to the sinking ship, and consequently, as the ship went down the boat was swept over to where the after deck had been. Then the main cross trees with

Master of the *Director* at Bari and at her demise, Captain W. Weatherall (1898-1974), photographed in 1957.

its cumbersome clusters of multi-sheave blocks, bore down on it, striking the gunwale, capsizing the boat and tossing its seven terrified occupants into the sea. Six of them, including Chief Officer Dudley Douglas-Kerr, managed to seize the grablines, and heave themselves on top of the upturned boat. The seventh man, Chief Radio Officer J. Tracy, however, disappeared and was lost, the only casualty of the sinking, although there is a possibility that he was picked up by the U-boat, and was lost in her four weeks later.

The waterlogged number 2 boat was laboriously baled out, restored to a seaworthy condition, and the survivors disposed evenly between that and number 1. Then the fresh water and stores in the rafts were distributed between the two boats. Captain Weatherall took charge of number 1 boat which held 29 men, and Douglas-Kerr number 2 boat with 28 men. They decided to proceed in company, and set sail on a westerly course at 11.30 on 15th July. The winds were light at first, with a slight sea, and a heavy south east swell. During the night the occupants of number 1 boat heard the diesel engines of a submarine, but saw nothing. At daybreak on 16th, number 2 boat was well astern, and later in the day, Captain Weatherall lowered his sail to wait for her. Eventually number 2 caught up and the Chief Officer reported all well.

During the night the wind freshened from the north east, raising a bit of a sea and an ugly cross-swell. Number 1 boat made good progress but the conditions were very uncomfortable, the boat shipping a great deal of water which was effectively controlled by the hand pump.

By next morning, the 17th, the wind had eased considerably, but of number 2 boat there was no sign. Eventually, the wind died altogether, and the men took to the oars, rowing and sailing as the conditions allowed. Although the crew had taken to the boats only 30 miles east of Zavora Point, the combination of north east winds and the south-westerly setting Mozambique Current ruled out any attempt to make a landfall there. Unfortunately for the castaways, the coast line in that region trends west south west - east north east. Consequently, the more progress they made towards the land across the set of the Mozambique Current, the further it eluded them.

At last, at 20.40 on Tuesday 18 July a light was seen on the port bow. Roman candles were fired, and distress flares lashed to oars waved high in the air. Eventually their frantic efforts to attract attention were rewarded when a searchlight stabbed the darkness. A vessel approached the boat and stopped close alongside. It was the Portuguese naval sloop GONCALVES ZARCO commanded by Capitao Zola da Silva. By 22.20 the DIRECTOR'S survivors were all on board the sloop, welcomed with every kindness. For although Portugal was neutral during this war, there is no doubt where her sympathies lay - with her oldest ally.

At the Portuguese Captain then informed his British colleague that they were in 25.38S, 33.38E, or 41 miles and 059 degrees from Cabo da Inhaca in the approaches to Lourenço Marques (now Maputo). Number 1 boat, it was established, had sailed 133 miles in 81 hours, on a course of 239 degrees. Ironically, the boat was no nearer the coast than when she set out. However, had they not been intercepted by the sloop they would certainly have sighted Cabo da Inhaca lighthouse on the following day.

At Captain Weatherall's request, the sloop began making a wide sweep in search of the Chief Officer's boat, but when nothing was sighted by 16.00 on 19th, the vessel was recalled to base. Fears for the safety of their shipmates began to grow.

Chief Officer Douglas-Kerr and his men were, in fact, in good heart. When weather conditions deteriorated on the night of 16th they rode comfortably to a sea anchor. Next day they resumed their course, but like their comrades in number 1 boat, had difficulty making a landfall against the cross current. In fact, they were set a point further south than their shipmates, making about four points leeway in all, so that they even missed Cabo

da Inhaca. Instead, they brought up off the entrance to the Kosi River, just two miles inside the border with Natal, on 20 July. Apparently they negotiated the hazardous bottleneck (of which the Africa Pilot Vol. III, Chapter 4, 92, says, "is always difficult and generally dangerous...landing should never be attempted from ordinary ships' boats.") and entered the smooth shallow lagoon of Kosi Bay. There they were sighted by a South African aircraft which dropped provisions, and reported their presence. Next day, the crew of number 2 boat were airlifted in two relays to Durban. For the record, they had sailed a distance of 211 miles in just over five days, on a course of 227 degrees, in their trusty lifeboat.

Meanwhile, Captain Weatherall and his men were making the journey from Lourenço Marques to Durban by train, a journey of over 40 hours. He ends his report with this comment on the crew's behaviour:

"All the Crew and Gunners behaved extremely well, and rendered every possible assistance throughout. There was no sign of panic whilst abandoning ship, nor was the slightest despondency shown by any of them while in the boats."

Both Captain Weatherall and Mr. Douglas-Kerr received the King's Commendation for their leadership qualities during the boat voyage.

215. COUNSELLOR (4) 1926-1940 Steel steamship. Two decks, five holds and deep tank. Two masts.
O.N. 149596 5,068g 3,158n 8,030d 395.5 x 52.55 x 30.75 feet. Cargo capacity: 435,020 cubic feet.
International code: KVHD (GMRL after 1933).
T. 3-cyl. by David Rowan and Co. Ltd., Glasgow; 26, 43, 73 x 48 inches, 12.5 knots.

18.5.1926: Launched by Charles Connell and Co. Ltd., Scotstoun (Yard No. 406) for the company. *31.8.1926:* Delivered at a cost of £94,983. Subsequently sailed from Glasgow for the West Indies on her maiden voyage under

Captain Arthur de Legh. *8.3.1940:* Sunk by magnetic mine in position 53.38N, 3.23W approaching Liverpool Bar Light Vessel from New Orleans and Halifax with cotton and general cargo. Crew of 67, nine injured but all saved.

Counsellor in the Mersey on 16th September 1934.   *[J. and M. Clarkson]*

Right on the doorstep
When COUNSELLOR left Halifax on 22nd February 1940, she sailed proudly at the head of Convoy HX 22, flying the pennant of Commodore Franklin, RN. The voyage home, escorted by the battleship REVENGE and a posse of destroyers, was uneventful. Somewhere southwest of Ireland the convoy divided, the Mersey section consisting of 18 ships, still under the command of Commodore Franklin and Captain Harold Coates of the COUNSELLOR, making its approach via St. George's Channel and the Irish Sea.[145]

The night of 7/8th March was very cold, with tendrils of fog and low cloud pleaching the topmasts and rigging. In the early hours of 8th, the convoy skirted the Anglesey coast and the sentinel rocks of the Skerries before forming single line ahead, COUNSELLOR leading.

By 06.00 the visibility had deteriorated, and speed was reduced. Moreover, there was no way of knowing the precise whereabouts of the swept channel leading to the Mersey Bar. From overhead came the sound of an approaching aircraft - friend? Or foe? Eighteen crews went to action stations, just in case.

Then in the pale light of dawn there appeared through wreathes of mist, the unmistakable shape of a Sunderland flying boat of Coastal Command, morse lamp winking, indicating the direction of the swept channel. Eighteen crews relaxed, and, as the column of ships headed towards the Bar, their spirits mounted.

At 08.50 the visibility had improved, and the Bar Lightship was in sight. Most of COUNSELLOR's officers were at breakfast, eagerly discussing the time of docking and the prospects for leave. Suddenly, the light-hearted conversation at the saloon table was shattered by a violent explosion. The ship heaved convulsively; the lights went out; and men rushed for daylight and the open air, their voices drowned by the roar of escaping steam.

A second explosion racked both the ship and the nerves of all on board. Captain Coates, nursing an injury, gave the order to abandon ship, and the boats were manned and lowered smartly - all except number 3 boat which hung, broken, from its davits. COUNSELLOR was in a sinking condition, her back riven by the force of that initial explosion. A destroyer, HMS WALPOLE, approached rapidly, and the men in the boats were quickly taken on board. An hour passed, and several officers and ratings boarded the sinking vessel with a naval officer. Their purpose was to assess the possibility of salvage, but the stricken vessel solved their problem by yielding to a final great shudder and settling on the bottom, giving the hopeful salvors but little time to scramble into the waiting boat. Later that day, COUNSELLOR's crew of 67 men, of whom nine were injured were landed at Princes Landing stage along with Commodore Franklin and his staff. It was not the sort of homecoming they would have wished - scuppered on their own doorstep!

216. PLANTER (1) 1927-1940 Steel steamship. Two decks, five holds and deep tank. Two masts.
O.N. 149645 5,887g 3,683n 9,150d 420.0 x 54.5 x 32.85 feet. Cargo capacity: 502,480 cubic feet.
International code: KWQD (GNJL after 1933).
T. 3-cyl. by David Rowan and Co. Ltd., Glasgow; 27, 46, 77 x 54 inches, 12.3 knots.

22.9.1927: Launched by Charles Connell and Co. Ltd., Scotstoun (Yard No. 408) for the company. *27.10.1927:* Delivered at a cost of £104,615. Subsequently sailed from Liverpool for the West Indies on her maiden voyage under Captain A.H. Brown. *16.11.1940:* Torpedoed and sunk by the German submarine U 137 (Kapitänleutnant Herbert Wohlfahrth) in position 55.38N, 8.28W. PLANTER was carrying Egyptian produce from Suez for Manchester, but straggling from convoy SL 53. There were 72 men on board of whom 13 were lost. The survivors were picked up by HMS CLARE.

A John McRoberts view of *Planter* passing New Brighton inward bound on 16th July 1935.   *[J. and M. Clarkson]*

Loss of the PLANTER, and the savage fate of JUMNA

Bound from the Cape to Manchester, PLANTER had joined Convoy SL 53 at Freetown on 27th October 1940 for the voyage to home waters. Beset with mechanical and boiler problems she had great difficulty keeping up with the convoy. On the evening of 16th November, while the convoy was rounding the north coast of Ireland, PLANTER had straggled far behind her consorts, limping along at her best speed, smoke belching from her tall funnel. The anxious lookouts did not see U 137 lurking in her wake. Kapitänleutnant Herbert Wohlfahrth had sighted the lame duck at 16.35, but realising his prey would not be going far, he delayed his attack until nightfall. At 19.15 he ran in for a surface attack, firing a torpedo which struck the fore part of the ship. At once she began to settle by the head, and within 20 minutes or so the sea was washing up against the bridge front. Wohlfahrth watched for a few minutes as the crew abandoned ship, then, when the PLANTER's distress call began flashing through the ether, he decided to retire.

Meanwhile, Captain D.H. Bryant of the PLANTER had ordered the crew to lower the four lifeboats, and the 72 men abandoned ship in good order. One man had been injured, however, but this had not prevented him from going back to his cabin to rescue his pet canaries before abandoning ship.[146] He was Chief Steward P. Dumbill who unfortunately died soon after his return home.

During the night the boats endeavoured to keep together, but one of them with 13 men on board drifted away and was never seen again. The castaways knew that land was not too far away. The attack had taken place in 55.38N 08.28 W, or a mere 23 miles, 341degrees from Tory Island lighthouse. From time to time they launched a red flare into the dark sky and, towards dawn, it was one of these flares which attracted the attention of HMS CLARE, a destroyer on escort duty with another eastbound convoy. She turned away to investigate, and soon sighted the PLANTER's boats. The survivors by then were feeling the effects of exposure, but their jubilation rang out clearly when the destroyer raced up in a welter of spray. Soon they were being hauled aboard by willing hands, wrapped in warm blankets, their spirits restored by hot beverages.

Next day, 18th November, the PLANTER's men were landed at Liverpool little the worse for their ordeal. Unhappily, that was not the end of the story. Of the 59 survivors, 43 were Lascars, Indian seamen who had been engaged at Calcutta in April. Not unnaturally they, too, expressed a desire to go home and arrangements were put in train to repatriate them in the

James Nourse steamer, JUMNA (6,078/29) as no Harrison vessel was scheduled to go to India in the near future.

Convoy OB 260 sailed from Liverpool on 16th December 1940. It was led by Commodore H.B. Maltby, RNR, flying his pennant in the steamer JUMNA, which was bound for Calcutta via Freetown and the Cape. On the night of 19th, the escorts broke off to meet an eastbound convoy from Halifax, HG 48, and the ships in OB 260 dispersed. Meanwhile, a fast troop convoy, WS 5A, had overtaken JUMNA and, on Christmas morning, had come under attack from the German heavy cruiser ADMIRAL HIPPER. The German was driven off, and her commander, Kapitän zur See Meisel, decided to break off operations, and make for the port of Brest. At 10.10 on 25th December the shape of a lone merchant ship was seen through the murk.

With facetious effrontery, HIPPER called up the freighter on the Morse lamp: "What ship? Have you seen any German raider?" The stranger immediately shied away, turning to port on to a northeasterly course, but flashed her name in reply. She was the James Nourse steamer, JUMNA.[147]

Over a quarter of an hour later JUMNA began calling on the distress frequency. The HIPPER's telegraphist was quick to intercept the message, which was apparently disjointed, and difficult to read. "From JUMNA...GSTM. Suspect vessel...probably raider..."

The rest was lost in the crash of the broadside from HIPPER's 8-inch guns. A minute later, at 10.28, she opened fire with her secondary armament, 4.1-inch shells combining with 8-inch to bring death and destruction to JUMNA in a merciless bombardment. Her radio was silenced by the first salvoes. Not content with this onslaught, HIPPER launched a pair of torpedoes into the blazing, lifeless hulk, completing its destruction. HIPPER's commander, if not in a panic, was nevertheless seriously worried about messages reaching the British cruisers which were doubtless still hunting him. Meisel attempted to vindicate his ruthless action: "I am keen to prevent the English ship from sending messages by immediately employing all weapons, and so get her under water as soon as possible before the enemy who may be following has a chance to arrive here. The steamer must not become a signpost for the enemy....".

JUMNA sank at 10.49 in position 44.51N, 25.47 W, or about 279 degrees and 727 miles from Cape Finisterre. There were no survivors. HIPPER resumed her flight, and arrived at her base in the port of Brest on 27th December.

217. RANCHER 1927-1949 Steel steamship. Two decks, five holds and deep tanks. Two masts. O.N. 149653 5,882g 3,696n 9,150d 420.0 x 54.5 x 32.85 feet. Cargo capacity 502,480 cubic feet. International code: KWTV (GNJP after 1933).
T. 3-cyl. by David Rowan and Co. Ltd., Glasgow; 27, 46, 77 x 54 inches, 12.5 knots.

22.11.1927: Launched at Charles Connell and Co. Ltd., Scotstound (Yard No. 409) for the company. *29.12.1927:* Delivered at a cost of £104,565. Subsequently sailed from Liverpool for Calcutta on her maiden voyage under Captain W.H. Gibbings. *5.1945:* Supported amphibious landings on the Arakan coast, Burma. *11.8.1949:* Sold to British Iron and Steel Corporation (BISCO) for demolition at Milford Haven.

Rancher at peace (top) and at war. In the photograph to the right, she is at anchor off a US port on 9th September 1942 with some particularly large pieces of deck cargo. She was the only Harrison ship to carry the name *Rancher.* *[J. and M. Clarkson and Ian Farquahar collection]*

218. OBSERVER 1928-1942 Steel steamship. Two decks, five holds and deep tank. Two masts. O.N. 149665 5,881g 3,695n 9,150d 420.0 x 54.5 x 32.85 feet. Cargo capacity 502,480 cubic feet. International code: LBHG (GNJM after 1933).
T. 3-cyl. by David Rowan and Co. Ltd., Glasgow; 27, 46, 77 x 54 inches, 12.5 knots.

24.1.1928: Launched by Charles Connell and Co. Ltd., Scotstoun (Yard No. 410) for the company. *29.2.1928:* Delivered at a cost of £106,077. Subsequently sailed from Liverpool for North Pacific ports via the West Indies and the Panama Canal on her maiden voyage under Captain F. Trinick. *6.10.1936:* Encountered CUSTODIAN (220) drifting in the Mediterranean with a broken tail-shaft and towed her

about 50 miles to Port Said. *16.12.1942:* Torpedoed and sunk by German submarine U 176 (Kapitänleutnant Reiner Dierksen) in position 5.30S, 31.00 W. The ship was on passage from Mersin and Table Bay for Trinidad and Baltimore with 3,000 tons of chrome ore. There were 15 survivors from a crew of 81.

Per ratem et fortitudinem ad Fortaleza[148]
When OBSERVER sailed from Capetown on 29th November 1942, bound for Baltimore via Trinidad, she was fully laden, mainly with chrome ore, 3,000 tons of which sat weightily on the tank tops of the two main hatches. Captain John Davidson had been instructed by Naval Control to hug the African coast to about 15S, then steer for Trinidad, zig-zagging on a west-north-westerly course. For there had been many reports of U-boat activity in the south equatorial regions of the Atlantic, and the zig-zag course was the independently routed ship's first line of defence against attack.

The days passed slowly, days of light winds and clear skies, the sort of weather cruise passengers dreamed of in the days before the war. But for Kapitänleutnant Reiner Dierksen,

who had spotted the OBSERVER's plume of smoke on the horizon at 10.30 on the morning of 16th December, this was a day strictly for business.

He at once put U 176 on a course to intercept. But it was after sunset before he had manoeuvred into a satisfactory attacking position. At about 18.30 he fired two torpedoes in quick succession, one of which found its billet in number 1 hold, the other somewhere between numbers 2 and 3 holds, on the starboard side. OBSERVER began sinking by the head immediately, the inrush of sea water and the dead weight of the ore cargo dragging her down. With no time to stop the main engine, the thrust of the churning screw helped push her under, and within half a minute of the first explosion she was gone, leaving only a skim of wreckage and a few struggling survivors on the surface of the placid ocean.

Carpenter S.G. Lewis had a narrow escape. "I tried to reach the boat deck, but on reaching the bottom of the ladder I saw that the fore part of the ship was completely submerged, with water reaching the ladder as I tried to climb. I was about half way up when the second torpedo struck the ship. This was a violent explosion, and the water swept up the ladder, washing me into the sea. When I came to the surface the ship had disappeared." After swimming around, clutching pieces of wreckage, Lewis spotted a raft some distance away. He swam towards it, but owing to exhaustion and a slight injury to his shoulder, he was unable to climb aboard, but the eight men already on the raft hauled him on board. He looked about him, recognised five Lascars and three Europeans. The latter were close friends: Quartermaster W. J. Smith, Gunner J. B. Wheelan, RN, and Merchant Seaman Gunner R. Montgomery.

A quarter of an hour after OBSERVER had disappeared, Dierksen brought his U-boat to the surface, and closed the raft. The nine men stared helplessly at the gaunt, sinister shape as it glided towards them, already shadowed in the gathering dusk. They nevertheless clearly saw the crew, smartly dressed in black trousers and white shirts, staring back at them with equal curiosity. High above, on the conning tower the Commander stared down and addressed them in impeccable English, but the Teutonic accent was unmistakeable. "What ship? Where bound?" he asked. They answered truthfully. "What company did your ship belong to? What cargo was she carrying? And the tonnage?" The questions came swiftly, all of which Q.M. Smith answered as best he could. However, the German commander expressed no interest in the men's plight. When they asked for food and water, and a course to steer for the nearest land, he paid no heed but swept away to be lost in the swiftly gathering darkness.

Some time later the men on the raft sighted a flickering light some distance away. They paddled towards it, and at 21.00 made contact with another raft, badly damaged, but still bearing five Lascars. Then another raft was seen, this one in much better condition, and the five Lascars were transferred to it, taking the stores with them to be evenly distributed later. Securing the two manned rafts together, they lay to for the rest of the night.

At dawn on 17th December they began searching the area and found a lone Indian seaman clinging to some wreckage. With some difficulty they manoeuvred the raft towards him and by 10.00 succeeded in hauling him aboard. There were now 15 survivors on the two rafts. They set about stepping a mast and improvising a sail, then with a pair of oars shipped on each raft, they pulled away from the scene, shaping a westerly course towards they knew not what. Quartermaster Smith took charge; only he had any idea of their position relative to the South American continent, and of what course to steer by sun and stars. A man of mature years, and resourceful by nature, his fellow countrymen at least felt they could put their trust in him. But not all the Lascars, unfortunately. To them a flash or two of gold braid would have perhaps been reassuring.

As it was, they had difficulty accepting the strict, but fair system of rationing imposed upon all, pleading for more water, and showing a marked unwillingness to take a turn with the oars. Their recalcitrant attitude is understandable only in the context of an underlying conviction that it wasn't their war, and they had no business to be in such a predicament. But whatever the reason, such tantrums had no place aboard a crowded raft alone on the ocean. Q.M. Smith therefore came to the reluctant conclusion that the two rafts should separate, and proceed independently. Consequently, seven dissident Lascars were assigned to one raft, the stores and fresh water evenly divided, and the lashing cast off. At 07.30 on 18th, the rafts drifted apart, and if any of the malcontents had second thoughts, it was now too late, though the rafts remained in sight of one another until the morning of 20th.

On Smith's raft the strict regimen of rowing and rationing was maintained on the basis of a 20-day ordeal. The Horlicks milk tablets seem to have been the mainstay of their diet; the biscuits were too hard and dry to eat without copious draughts of water, which of course was out of the question; and the pemmican was so salty they dared not eat it for fear of exacerbating their thirst.

At 11.00 on 20th the men were heartily cheered when a Catalina flying-boat circled overhead, and then flew off. Naturally, they fully expected to be rescued, if not within the hour, then before nightfall. The deflation to their spirits when nothing happened was sickening, nor was anything sighted on the following day.

At midnight on 22nd, a ship, brightly illuminated to declare her neutrality, passed them within a mile. They had no flares to attract attention, as they had all been ruined in contact with seawater. Again morale slumped, and Q.M. Smith could only revive their wilting spirits by repeating his assurance that rescue could not be far away.

A Feilden photograph of *Observer* entering the East Float, Birkenhead. Note the sailing ship behind. *[J. and M. Clarkson]*

On 23rd a heavy rain squall did much to restore their courage and optimism. For once they could drink copiously, and they were able to replenish their depleted water supplies substantially.

The decisive break came at 10.00 on 24th December, when they sighted a small fleet of fishing boats. The crew came to life at once, and pulled with all their might, striving to close the distance before the fishermen hauled in their nets and set off for home. But the raft had been sighted, and one of the boats cruised over to investigate, laid herself alongside and took the castaways on board.

Finding a common language was an insoluble problem, but the Brazilian fishermen, for such they were, needed no formal requests in Portuguese to lay on such essentials as drinking water and hot, brimming bowls of a fish stew. Thereafter, the survivors laid themselves down to sleep, while the fishermen resumed their labours while daylight lasted. At dusk they hauled in their nets for the last time that day, and set course to Fortaleza, a port in the Brazilian province of Ceará, some 30 miles distant. At 21.00 on Christmas Eve 1942, the eight survivors landed at Fortaleza (whose name is a Portuguese word for courage). Eight days had passed since

their ship had been sunk, and within that period their frail raft had carried them, gently aided by the South Equatorial Current, some 430 miles on a course of 284 degrees to the point where they had been rescued by the Brazilian fishermen.

The men were at once admitted to hospital to be treated for ailments due to exposure and salt-water boils, but nothing serious. There they were interviewed by the British Consul and an US naval officer from a nearby US naval base. Next day, patrol craft were sent out to search for the second raft, which was found in due course, and the seven Lascar survivors were brought into Fortaleza at 14.30 on Christmas Day. They were in a bad state, having run out of fresh water four days previously and had been subsisting on salt water ever since, risking madness and death. However, after a few days in hospital, sustained by good, nourishing food, all the survivors were restored to health, and by the end of the year were on their way to New York for embarkation to England.

Quartermaster Smith's contribution to the men's survival did not go unrecognised. On 16th May 1944, he was invested with the British Empire Medal for his inspired leadership; and his shipmate in adversity, Carpenter Lewis, received the King's Commendation.

219. LOGICIAN (2) 1928-1941 Steel steamship. Two decks, five holds and deep tank. Two masts.
O.N. 149678 5,993g 3,753n 9,210d 420.3 x 54.65 x 32.8 feet. Cargo capacity: 506,530 cubic feet.
International code: LBVG (GSLK after 1933).
T. 3-cyl. by Cammell, Laird and Co. Ltd., Birkenhead; 27, 46, 77 x 54 inches, 12.5 knots.

19.4.1928: Launched by Cammell Laird and Co. Ltd., Birkenhead (Yard No. 934) for the company. *15.6.1928:* Delivered at a cost of £109,001. Subsequently sailed from Liverpool for the West Indies and North Pacific ports on her maiden voyage under Captain W.H. Gibbings. *13.5.1941:* Bombed at Suda Bay, Crete and damaged by near misses.

15.5.1941: Struck by three bombs, badly damaged, disabled and on fire. *25.5.1941:* After discharging cargo, the hulk was anchored in the bay, and sunk by further bombing. Of the crew, five were killed, one missing, 20 became prisoners of war and 27 were saved after extraordinary adventures.

Logician preparing to lock in to Birkenhead Docks on 21st June 1931.   *[J. and M. Clarkson]*

Retreat from Crete[149]

The Harrison vessels LOGICIAN and DALESMAN (247) were part of a small convoy which sailed from Alexandria, bound for Crete, on 10th May 1941. The two ships were directed to Suda Bay, near Canea (Khania), the island's capital, and around 02.00 on the morning of Tuesday 13th May they dropped anchor in that large, natural harbour. At 18.00 that evening German and Italian bombers came over in force to attack shipping in the harbour. DALESMAN was sunk by a direct hit which exploded in the double bottom; LOGICIAN was slightly damaged by two near misses, but was able to go alongside later that evening, and for two clear days unloaded her precious cargo unmolested. The respite was short-lived, however, for enemy bombers came over again on the evening of 15th May. This time they made no mistake, and LOGICIAN was devastated by three direct hits in succession. She did not sink, but was completely disabled, and

several fires blazed in various parts of the ship. Four men were killed instantly, one died later ashore, and nine others were wounded.

The ship was a shambles, with bodies and wreckage strewn everywhere. The roar of escaping steam added to the frightening confusion, and made the verbal transmission of orders virtually impossible. Captain William Jones, fearing his ship to be lost, urged his crew down the gangway to the jetty, carrying the wounded with them. He himself chose to remain with his officers, while Chief Officer William Rennie supervised the men's disembarkation and rehabilitation ashore.

Meanwhile, the few men left on board fought the fires with buckets of water until they were joined by a naval fire-fighting party. Hoses were connected to a water supply provided by the Ellerman Wilson steamer VOLO (1,587/38), which came

168

alongside the LOGICIAN, and eventually the fires were extinguished. Chief Officer Rennie, who had lately joined in the fire fighting, again went ashore to see how the crew were making out. He found only 12, the rest having been dispersed, the wounded to hospital, others to various camps in the area. He then arranged for the 12 to be billeted at the nearby Royal Navy camp, and returned to the ship to report. He found Captain Jones determined to remain on board that night; Second Officer Jerry Penston volunteered to stay with him, while the rest found billets in the Navy camp. And so the scattered crew of the LOGICIAN settled down for the night, some in hospital beds, some stretched out on the unyielding earth of the camps; at least two slept in the gutted, deserted, blacked-out shell of the ship, and five lay still in the makeshift morgue.

Next morning, Friday 16th May, Rennie returned to the ship with his 12 men. Captain Jones expressed concern for the whereabouts and welfare of the rest of the crew, and the Chief Officer was despatched ashore again to find out. Somehow, through the good offices of a friendly Army officer, he acquired the use of a truck and a driver with whom he toured all the hospitals and camps in the area. He found the wounded being well cared for, took the names and addresses of next-of-kin, and then moved on to the temporary mortuary to seek out and identify among the rows of recent air raid victims the remains of his shipmates. It was a harrowing task which was to affect Bill Rennie deeply, for the bodies had been hastily laid out, few had been cleaned up, and some were not even whole. Sickened and disheartened, he at last found the bodies of his men, collected such personal items as were available from the Royal Army Medical Corp sergeant on duty, and added their names to his list before staggering out into the fresh air. Doggedly, he continued his tour of the camps but without success. (The men had in fact been transported to a camp near Canea). He then returned to the ship to find the scratch crew preparing to cast off before she was towed out to the anchorage. So LOGICIAN dropped her anchor for what was to prove to be the last time, and the remnants of her crew went ashore in the tug. Captain Jones was billeted in the RN camp, while the rest were trucked in another camp some four miles west of Canea, situated in an olive grove.

It soon became clear that, despite the many well-organised camps in the area - Army, Navy, even the Marines - no one had thought of setting up one for the Merchant Navy, and the merchant seamen had perforce to fend for themselves. Perhaps the staff planners assumed that M.N. survivors would kip with their cousins in the Royal Navy. And so they did for a brief while. But the R.N. camp was soon to become overcrowded, for the Navy suffered horrendous losses in Suda Bay and its vicinity, losing no less than three cruisers, four destroyers, two minesweepers, and seven patrol craft during the battle. On the other hand, the only merchantmen lost were DALESMAN, LOGICIAN, and a tanker, the ELEONORA MAERSK (10,684/36). However, merchant seamen are nothing if not resourceful and they quickly set about making the best of a bad situation. An Axis invasion was expected any day, and, advised by the local Brigade H.Q., the seamen began to organise patrols, and dig slit trenches. At least it gave them something to do - and somewhere to dive when the bombers came over, as they did with increasing frequency. During the afternoon of 18th May, the crew of the DALESMAN, led by Chief Officer Herbert Jones, joined LOGICIAN's men in the olive grove.

At dawn on 20th May the invasion of Crete began. The fighting was bitter and confused, the confusion augmented by a lamentable lack of communications equipment on the British side, preventing commanders from getting information about situations faced by their forward troops. Whilst all this was going on the Merchant Navy men felt about as much at home as might members of a local tennis club caught up in a Hell's Angels' Convention. Meanwhile, as the fighting drew perilously near the camp, orders came to evacuate it and fall back on Canea. Chief Officer Rennie mustered 32 of his men and marched them east to Canea, arriving there at about 11.00 on 20th. There they found shelter from the incessant air raids in the local police station by kind invitation of a New Zealand Headquarters Battalion. Next day, more seamen joined the party, so that it now numbered 50. Rennie realised they were something of a burden to the hard-pressed New Zealanders, and obtained permission to move to Tea Camp, at Suda Bay, near the Naval Camp. On 23rd they moved off in three sections led by himself, Second Officer Penston, and Third Officer Bill Ashton of the DALESMAN, arriving safely at Tea Camp a few hours later.

There they met up with Chief Officer Jones and his men, and the combined crews now mustered 74 men.

Anxious to see Captain Jones again, Rennie made out a revised list of names and took it that same evening to the Navy Camp where Captains Jones and Horne were still in residence. On the way he was badly shaken, but unwounded, by a bomb which exploded only 20 yards away, showering him with earth. He arrived at the Masters' tent more dead then alive; they welcomed him, cleaned him up, fed him, and sent him back to Tea Camp full of rumours of imminent evacuation by sea.

On 25th May the seamen moved into a gully nearer the R.N. camp, where, they believed, the feeding would be better, and so it was. Also, here, the officers could maintain contact with their respective Captains, and a system of liaison was evolved, with junior officers posted near the Captains' tent on a rota basis to advise the men in the gully should any dramatic change of fortune occur. Rennie himself strolled over twice a day to find out if there was "anything doing" - like evacuation.

Towards evening on 26th Rennie went across to see the Captains as usual, but Captain Jones was away attending to some matter in Suda. Rennie waited until dark, and then approached a naval officer with the imposing title of King's Harbourmaster, to enquire from him if there was "anything doing". The officer looked at him stonily, and said, "No; I'm sorry; there's nothing doing tonight; you'll just have to stay here with us and fight it out to the end - if you can call it a fight!"

Rennie was never to forget those words, nor the grim tone with which they were spoken. He returned to the gully in a thoughtful and rather depressed frame of mind. He slept fitfully, and was glad to rise next morning and set out on his usual visit to the Captains' tent. He was unprepared for the sight which greeted him. There was the camp, but it was deserted. There was not a soul in sight, though it was long past sunrise. The cold hand of despair gripped his heart, as his mind grappled for a cogent reason. There could be only one. Reluctantly, he realised that small naval craft must have crept inshore during the early hours of the morning and spirited them all away - including Captains Jones and Horne. Rennie felt the sickness of hopelessness bite into his gut, only gradually to be replaced by a cold anger. How could anyone do this? And where was the duty messenger? Young Miller, wasn't it? The DALESMAN's fifth Engineer? He, too, must have gone! Bitterly, Rennie returned to the gully to convey the appalling tidings to his men. There was an outcry, of course, but nothing could be done about it. Grimly, he mustered his men once more, and set off to hike to Retimo, some 20 miles to the eastward, where, a passing Army officer assured him evacuations by sea were already taking place.

Why? Why, indeed, had the crew been left behind? Why had their Captains apparently deserted them? Neither Bill Jones of the LOGICIAN nor "Paddy" Horne of the DALESMAN were of the type who would wilfully leave their subordinates in the lurch in a crisis. And this was not even a crisis, but an orderly evacuation. On reflection the explanation doubtless lay in the underlying confusion of battle and retreat. The rescue ships had come in stealthily in the dead of night, unseen and unannounced, while all but the sentries lay sleeping.

Once alerted, naval discipline took over; the officers and petty officers knew exactly what to do: rouse all the inmates of the camp as quietly as possible; organise them into parties of a score or so, and march them silently down to the beach - no talking; no arguments; just shut up, and get in line. No doubt the Captains' qualms were allayed by assurances that the men in the gully would be roused, too - but in the suppressed excitement no one quite got round to it...daylight was not far away...the ships had got to get away...now, stop arguing, and move along... The scenario is probably familiar to anyone who has ever been caught up in the turmoil of a battle which is going the wrong way, from Dunkirk to Singapore.

Meanwhile, the pace of the march was decidedly slower than formerly. Many of the men were weakened by dysentery and other gastric ailments. Rennie, bringing up the rear, often had to urge the men forward, assisted by their stronger shipmates. After about seven miles they came to a signal station which was just in the process of being evacuated by its naval staff. They informed Rennie that the Germans had cut the road to Retimo, and that future evacuation could only be contemplated from the south coast of the island, which was precipitous and boasted few harbours.

"Follow us", said the telegraphists. "We're heading over the mountains to Sfarkia". Rennie formed up his men and counted them: only 25. Some must be lagging far behind. There was no point in waiting. With heavy hearts they fell in behind the Navy men, and followed them, panting and labouring up the steep incline, across fields and over streams, up into the Levka (White) Mountains. Frequently harried by enemy aircraft, they halted at noon near a small village and rested until nightfall, when they resumed the long march. By now they had been joined by hundreds, perhaps thousands of retreating troops, all heading southwards, a long, disorganised column snaking through the mountain passes. Even then, the distant sound of gunfire assured them that a disciplined rearguard action was still being fought. Rennie urged his men to stick with the Naval party, believing that if anyone could get through to the evacuation beaches, they could. However, the distance to Sfarkia (Khora Sfakión) was variously estimated at anything between 25 and 40 miles. Without maps, they were simply following the men in front, and casually noting their direction in relation to the position of sun and stars. Grimly, Rennie wondered how many of his men would make it.

Motor transport frequently passed the slow-moving column on the narrow track, and when one of the drivers hailed Rennie and two companions, Second Officer Penston and Fourth Engineer Davies, offering them a lift, it was Rennie's turn to be confronted by a painful moral dilemma. Exhausted, weary, and close to despair, they accepted thankfully. Later, Rennie was to search his conscience unsparingly for taking a ride when most of his men were still trudging along on foot. At the time, his mind was too dulled by exhaustion to consider the niceties of moral debate. Later, he persuaded himself that he had done all he could for the men; they were in good hands with the naval party; he himself had been almost senseless with fatigue.

Nevertheless, he was very relieved on reaching the beaches to find that those who had been able to keep moving did eventually get away. Two who did not reach the beach in time were Cadet W. Dignan and Second Radio Officer H. Stephenson of the LOGICIAN. After a particularly vicious air attack on 27th May, the first day of the long march, they somehow lost touch with the Merchant Navy party. Some Cretan villagers told them that the main column was retreating south towards Sfarkia, so they, too, took the long trail over the Levka Mountains.

After several hours toiling up the mountain track they came to an isolated villa where an elderly lady, with fond memories of London long ago, gave them food and water. She urged them to take to the mountains and sit out the war.

"I will feed you and look after you", she said, her voice trembling with emotion. Regretfully, the two boys, for that was all they were, decided to press on and try to catch up with their shipmates. They thanked the old lady for her kindness and resumed their uphill journey, eventually reaching the cliffs overlooking Sfarkia - and they were still there when German troops moved in to take them prisoner.[150]

Meanwhile, Chief Officer Rennie and his companions dozed aboard the truck as it lurched and crawled along the track. At daylight on 28th they alighted at the village where Movement Control had set up its H.Q., several miles from the beach. They carried on along the track which soon came under air attack, forcing them to dive for cover among the rocks which littered the wayside. It was during one of these rock-seeking dives that Rennie stumbled, and sliced open his arm against a flinty rock. His mates bound it up, and they pressed on, hoping to find a field dressing station near the beach. Sure enough, there it was, in a nearby cave. As Rennie was receiving attention a captain, RN, accompanied by a brigadier, came in. They got talking, and that evening the naval officer sent them down to the beach accompanied by a lieutenant. There, naval vessels were already embarking troops, and Rennie and his companions joined the queue, patiently waiting to be ferried out to one of HM ships, already crowded with troops. Soon she was under way, and, after a swift passage, her elated passengers were landed at Alexandria at dusk on 29th May.

Epilogue

William Rennie, a native of Liverpool, was 39 when the events described above took place, and it is upon his records that the above account is largely based. He joined Harrison Line from Rankin Gilmour in January 1918. He became Chief Officer of the LOGICIAN in February 1941, and, after his experiences in Crete, arrived back in Liverpool in September 1941. After a few weeks leave he joined the WAYFARER (212) but reported sick during the voyage, and was hospitalised in Liverpool towards the end of the year. On his recovery he left the company and joined the Clyde Pilotage Service.

Captain William "Barmouth" Jones, on his arrival at Alexandria, was offered command of a Vichy prize, the Chargeurs Réunis steamer D'ENTRECASTEAUX, (7291/22) of Le Havre. Although the Ministry had placed the ship under the management of Ellerman's City Line, the managers had no master immediately available. Captain Jones accepted the post, and, for the time being at least, became an employee of Ellermans. On 7th November 1942, whilst on a voyage from Pernambuco to Trinidad, the ship was torpedoed and sunk by U 154 commanded by Korvettenkapitän Schuch. The incident took place in approximate position 15.15N, 56.54W, or about 260 miles due east from the island of Dominica. Captain Jones survived the sinking, and returned home, and back into Harrisons' employ, on 12th January 1943. He was later awarded an OBE.

220. CUSTODIAN (2) 1928-1950 Steel steamship. Two decks, five holds and deep tank. Two masts.
O.N. 149682 5,881g 3,695n 9,150d 420.0 x 54.5 x 32.85 feet. Cargo capacity 502,480 cubic feet.
International code: LCBN (GSMJ after 1933).
T. 3-cyl. by David Rowan and Co. Ltd., Glasgow; 27, 46, 77 x 54 inches.

31.5.1928: Launched by Charles Connell and Co. Ltd., Scotstoun (Yard No. 412) for the company. *5.7.1928:* Delivered at a cost of £109.561. Subsequently sailed from Liverpool for East Africa on her maiden voyage under Captain T. O'Connor. *5.10.1936:* Tail-shaft broke, shattering stern tube. *6.10.1936:* Towed by OBSERVER (218) to Port Said for repair. *18.7.1940:* Went to assistance of Argentine steamship HARPON (4,940/97) and towed her to Bermuda. *2.12.1945:* Serious bunker fire in New York, taking over two days to extinguish. *25.9.1950:* Sold to Indian National Steamship Co. Ltd., Calcutta and renamed SIVA RANJITA. *12.3.1952:* Start of persistent fires in bunkers and coal cargo from Calcutta. The vessel put into Aden and later Malta for assistance, finally sailing for Alicante with remnants of the cargo on 12.4.1952. *30.8.1958:* Demolition began at Calcutta by Pulsiram Bhagwandas.

Custodian standing off the Alfred Basin, Birkenhead.   *[World Ship Photo Library]*

Tactician preparing to dock.   [*J. and M. Clarkson*]

221. TACTICIAN (2) 1928-1950 Steel steamship. Two decks, five holds and deep tank. Two masts.
O.N. 149683 5,996g 3,754n 9,210d 420.3 x 54.65 x 32.8 feet. Cargo capacity 506,530 cubic feet.
International code: LCBT (GSMF after 1933).
T. 3-cyl. by Cammell Laird and Co. Ltd., Birkenhead; 27, 46, 77 x 54 inches, 12.5 knots.

22.5.1928: Launched by Cammell Laird and Co. Ltd., Birkenhead (Yard No. 935) for the company. *2.7.1928:* Delivered at a cost of £108,955. Subsequently sailed from Liverpool for Calcutta on her maiden voyage under Captain F. Trinick. *1945:* Like the RANCHER (217) she supported the Arakan campaign in Burma. *16.9.1950:* Sold to Deutsche Dampfshiffahrts-Gesellschaft "Hansa", Bremen, West Germany and renamed CROSTAFELS. *3.1951:* Converted to oil-burning. *5.9.1959:* Arrived at Osaka, Japan, for demolition by the Sumitomo Shoji K.K., which commenced 8.9.1959.

After her sale by Harrisons, *Tactician* spent nine years under the German flag as DDG Hansa's *Crostafels.*

171

222. DESIGNER 1928-1941 Steel steamship. Two decks, five holds and deep tank. Two masts.
O.N. 161062 5,945g 3,720n 9,223d 419.8 x 54.6 x 32.83 feet Cargo capacity 503,310 cubic feet.
International code LCJV (GSQK after 1933).
T. 3-cyl. by D. and W. Henderson and Co. Ltd., Glasgow; 27, 46, 77 x 54 inches, 12.5 knots.

3.7.1928: Launched by D. and W. Henderson and Co. Ltd., Glasgow (Yard No. 826) for the company. *7.9.1928:* Delivered at a cost of £109,689. Subsequently sailed from Liverpool to South Africa and Mauritius on her maiden voyage under Captain G. Packe. *9.7.1941:* Bound from the

Mersey for Capetown with military equipment and explosives, the vessel was torpedoed by the German submarine U 98 (Kapitänleutnant Robert Gysae) and sank just after midnight in approximate position 42.59N, 31.40W. There were 11 survivors from the crew of 78.

Designer in Canadian waters.   *[Ian Farquhar collection]*

Loss of the DESIGNER

Bound from the Mersey for Capetown with a cargo of military equipment and explosives, DESIGNER had recently dispersed from Convoy OB 341 and was proceeding independently when her column of funnel smoke was sighted by Kapitänleutnant Robert Gysae in U 98 during the afternoon of 8th July 1941. He kept the ship in sight and waited for darkness to fall before going in to attack on the surface. He fired two torpedoes at 23.55, one of which struck the ship in No. 2 hold.[151] She sank within six minutes, just after midnight, in position 42.59N, 31.40W, or about 354 degrees and 209 miles from the island of Flores in the Azores.

Out of 78 men on board, Captain D. McCallum and 66 of his men were lost. Several days later, the Portuguese schooner SANTA PRINCESA sighted an unusual object floating by. It was a railway tanker, lately an item among the DESIGNER'S deck cargo, which had evidently broken adrift and floated clear when the ship went down. Clinging to it

were seven survivors from the ill-fated ship, six Lascar crew, and the Royal Marine gunlayer. All were in bad shape after their ordeal, having had neither food nor water for several days. The gunner, in fact, had gone out of his mind, and never recovered. The men were cared for on board the schooner, and were eventually landed at Oporto, nearly 900 miles east of the DESIGNER's last position. It is known that at least one of the Lascar survivors, a humble topas, whose life's task was to sweep the decks and clean the toilets, continued to serve in Harrison ships. He was a happy little man who reminded Robin Williams, who sailed with him and to whom I am indebted for this part of the story, of Kipling's Gunga Din.

223. COMEDIAN (3) 1929-1950 Steel steamship. Two decks, five holds and deep tank. Two masts.
O.N. 161119 5,122g 3,162n 8,000d 395.5 x 52.55 x 30.75 feet Cargo capacity: 430,760 cubic feet.
International Code LDWF (GPTJ after 1933).
T. 3-cyl. by David Rowan and Co. Ltd., Glasgow; 26, 43, 73 x 48 inches, 12.5 knots.

20.8.1929: Launched by Charles Connell and Co. Ltd., Scotstoun (Yard No. 415) for the company. *15.10.1929:* Delivered at a cost of £94,991. Subsequently sailed from Liverpool for Kingston and Belize on her maiden voyage under Captain A. Cadogan. *10.2.1940:* In collision with the steamer KORANTON (6,695/20) when approaching Halifax, Nova Scotia 2.5 miles, 036 degrees from the Sambro Lightvessel. The collision occurred in fine and clear weather and both vessels were displaying navigation lights. Unfortunately, the KORANTON carried oil lamps and these were hard to distinguish. The situation was made more difficult by her confusing whistle signals. The stem of KORANTON sliced into COMEDIAN's starboard side, almost

at right angles, penetrating engine and boiler rooms. She sustained considerable damage, almost sinking and was towed into Halifax by the salvage tug FOUNDATION FRANKLIN (653/18) and remained there for four months undergoing repairs. *24.10.1950:* Sold to India Steamship Co. Ltd., Calcutta and renamed INDIAN IMPORTER. *4.1956:* Sold to Birch Steam Ship Co. Ltd. (Wheelock Marden and Co. Ltd., managers), Hong Kong and renamed SOUTH BIRCH. *17.10.1957:* Grounded in the Phnom Penh River, causing damage to her bilge keel. *1959:* Sold to the Hong Kong Chiap Hua Manufactory Co. Ltd., Hong Kong, for demolition and delivered 30.7.1959.

North Atlantic, Christmas 1942

The late Captain W. F. O'Neill commanded COMEDIAN for most of her war service, and has left a personal, poignant memoir describing a hard-hit Atlantic convoy, assailed by atrocious

weather and enemy U boats. The following account is based on Captain O'Neill's essay.[152]

The Convoy Conference had broken up in an

Comedian. [J. and M. Clarkson]

Photographed in the uniform of a third officer, Captain William F. O'Neill (above) had poignant memories of commanding *Comedian* in North Atlantic convoys.

atmosphere of optimistic good humour. The 40 or so shipmasters, accompanied by their senior radio officers, who had gathered together to be briefed on the broad strategy of the Atlantic crossing to Halifax, convoy formations, zig-zags, and the special codes and signals to be used, had listened patiently to their Royal Navy mentors. Afterwards, they had drifted away to seek out old friends, greet former acquaintances, and exchange news items of mutual interest. For it was surprising how frequently certain ships and their captains found themselves together in successive convoys. They were, in fact, like brothers in arms.

Captain O'Neill of the COMEDIAN was, incidentally, the envy of his many friends by virtue of his gold watch chain. Years earlier, when, as Chief Officer, he was weighing anchor one cold dark morning off Gravesend, he noticed in the beam of his torch something gleaming in the mud clinging to the first shackle. As it came up through the hawse-pipe, somewhat cleansed by the Bosun's hose, he raised a hand to stop the windlass. It was certainly not a twist of seizing-wire, but a gentleman's fashionable gold watch chain. He had worn it ever since. But it was not the gold watch-chain which his friends envied, but "Peggy" O'Neill's confounded luck!

And so they bade each other "Good-bye and Good Luck" as they returned to their respective ships to prepare for sailing on the next tide.

Convoy ON 153 sailed from Liverpool on 11th December 1942. The lifeboats, as was the custom, were swung out, fully provisioned, and triced to the boom ready for lowering. Individual seamen put together their "getaway bags" - a small bag or case containing perhaps a torch, socks, cigarettes, a bar of chocolate, the "judy's" photograph, and other small treasures - not much, just something to cling to should all else be lost.

As the convoy drew slowly away from the British Isles, the weather began to deteriorate ominously, rain pouring from leaden skies, and seas building up before a scouring sou'wester as the glass plummeted. The ships were in for a severe pounding - but not just from the weather. Already packs of U-boats were converging on the convoy, alerted by an efficient German intelligence. Anyone who might have been under the impression that bad weather was a deterrent to U-boat attack would be quickly disillusioned during the ensuing week. The convoy was already struggling to maintain cohesion, making barely five knots against the rising gale, when, on the night of 15th, two ships were torpedoed.

"One of the ships was very close to us", recalled Captain O'Neill. "In fact, I was looking at the ship when she was struck. There was a red flash and some smoke...it was all over in a matter of seconds... Words fail me to express the pity I felt for those poor unfortunate fellows plunged so suddenly to their doom in the teeth of a fierce gale. Any hope of getting boats away in those conditions was out of the question...the sea was fierce, with huge, white tops."

During that night and all next day the wind kept increasing in strength until it had reached hurricane force, with the barometer down to 27.96 inches (947 mb). The ship was swept fore and aft by massive combers, and the sea was white, as if it were boiling. The convoy was completely disorganised. Ships were virtually hove to, all faculties concentrated on maintaining steerage way and keeping head to wind. At 06.00 on 17th another ship was torpedoed, and at dusk the same day three more ships were sent to the bottom, one of them the destroyer commanded by the Senior Officer of the Escort, believed to be HMS FIREDRAKE.

"We sounded the alarm bells once more...all our men were ready...if the supreme moment should come, it would be a case of every man for himself... All were arrayed in full kit, with lifejackets, oilskins, seaboots...all were calm; we felt that our only hope would be to get a raft away then jump into the angry sea, hoping for the best. So this is the Battle of the Atlantic? Yet it must go on, or we all perish."

And of course, there was still the weather to contend with. "Huge seas like mountains, ships tossed about like corks...at times we were low down, as if in a valley; then we would climb up as if to the top of a mountain, bows high in the air. Then as we plunged down into the valley again our propeller would come clear of the water... You would think our racing engine was about to smash itself to pieces. Still onward we went, trying to get hurried meals and brief snatches of sleep in our wet clothes. But we had to see it through - there's no back door to the sea".

At 01.15 on 19th COMEDIAN shipped the "father and mother" of a sea, the legendary ninth wave. Number 4 lifeboat was swept away, taking with it the 8-inch spar of Oregon pine to which it was triced. As the sea swept aft it smashed in the weather door to the firemen's quarters under the poop and burst inside, half-drowning the inmates. The men tumbled out on deck, convinced the ship had been torpedoed, and were only reassured by the confident beat of the reciprocating engine, punctuated from time to time by the familiar rattle as the governor cut in.

Next day, at 19.20, an S.O.S. from yet another ship clamoured on the Radio Officer's headphones. It faded away as the ship disappeared unseen, whether a victim of U-boat attack, or the atrocious weather, was not known.

The ghastly conditions continued unabated until 23rd, when the weather improved. All round the horizon scattered ships drew closer together, shepherded by the Navy, until what was left of the convoy was once more a cohesive entity. Captain O'Neill paid tribute to his ship, and his crew:

"The old COMEDIAN behaved wonderfully, rising majestically to each huge wave... Have been along to congratulate the Cook and his staff for the wonderful way they carried on despite the heavy weather. I have nothing but admiration for the entire crew; all pulled their weight, though wet and weary."

Christmas Day dawned amid dull skies and misty rain. Over the ship's broadcast-receivers came a programme of Christmas music and carols from a station in Newfoundland.

More escorts joined the convoy from Canada and the United States. The weather improved as the day wore on, and the air of optimism returned. A Christmas message from King George VI to the men of the Merchant Navy and Fishing Fleets, assured the worn-out seamen that they were not forgotten:

"There is not one of us ashore who does not know the extent to which the safety of our common heritage of hearth and home depends on you. At this festival of peace in a world at war I send you every good wish, and pray...that you and the ships you serve in may return in safety to enjoy the blessings of the land and the fruits of your labours.

George R.I."

The irony was not lost upon Captain O'Neill, who thought sadly of all those hearty shipmasters he had met at the conference, and of those who had perished with their ships and crews in the icy turbulence of the North Atlantic, who would never see home again.

The surviving ships arrived at Halifax on 28th December without further loss. Captain O'Neill ended his soliloquy with the words: "Although I have served in both wars at sea, and in the employ of the Harrison Line, this was my worst experience".

Comedian in happier times: dressed overall on the Mersey, 25th May 1935.

[J. and M. Clarkson]

224. CONTRACTOR 1930-1943 Steel steamship. Two decks, five holds and deep tank. Two masts.
O.N. 162320 6,004g 3,755n 9,210d 420.3 x 54.65 x 32.8 feet Cargo capacity: 506,530 cubic feet.
International Code LGHP (GTNC after 1933).
T. 3-cyl. by Cammell Laird and Co.Ltd., Birkenhead; 27, 46, 77 x 54 inches, 12.5 knots.

11.6.1930: Launched by Cammell Laird and Co. Ltd., Birkenhead (Yard No. 968) for the company. *23.7.1930:* Delivered at a cost of £105,594. Subsequently sailed from London and Continental Ports for South Africa and Mauritius under Captain W.E. Harraden. *16.5.1932:* Played a useful part in the rescue of over 700 passengers and crew from the French liner GEORGES PHILIPPAR (17,359/31) which was on fire in the Gulf of Aden. *3.1933:* Rode out a typhoon in the Indian Ocean when on passage from Lourenço Marques for Mauritius with a cargo of coal. The voyage lasted fifteen days instead of the normal six, but she came through unscathed. Later, whilst at Rangoon, the ship's officers were able to help the victim of a ruthless attack. *8.9.1935:* In collision with the steamer CITY OF KIMBERLY (6,169/25) while transiting the Straits of Gibraltar on passage from Calcutta for London. She sustained damage to plates and frames in the starboard bow. *24.4.1940:* In collision with the Glasgow steamer GIRASOL (648/26) off the North Foreland when outward bound from London. GIRASOL was sliced almost in two but by keeping CONTRACTOR'S bow in the cavity created by the impact, the coaster's crew had time to

launch one of their boats before she sank in position 51.28.50N, 01.22.15E. *25.4.1940:* CONTRACTOR returned to Tilbury with substantial damage to her stem and bows. *29.11.1940:* Bombed and strafed by German aircraft and although slightly damaged, continued her voyage to Barbados. *11.3.1941:* Damaged during an air raid at Manchester following a brief period in dry dock. A near miss on the port side was close enough to start several plates. The engine room flooded and she rested on the bottom of the basin. The numerous holes were plugged and she was raised and returned to dry dock.[153] *1.1.1943:* Came under sustained air attack at Bone, Algeria, and the ship's spirited response undoubtedly contributed towards Captain W.B. Wilford's subsequent award of the OBE. Second Officer Alan Moreton received the MBE. *7.8.1943:* Torpedoed by the German submarine U 371 (Kapitänleutnant Waldemar Mehl) in position 37.15N, 07.21E, about 30 miles north west of Bone. 75 survivors were rescued by minesweepers but five men were killed, including the Captain and Chief Officer, and two later died in hospital. She was on passage from Gibraltar for Port Said with military stores and ammunition.

CONTRACTOR to the rescue
Fire at sea is a peril justly feared by seamen and one which they will go to extraordinary lengths to prevent if humanly possible. The anxiety and the horror is multiplied ten-fold when the ship concerned is a passenger liner. Such was the fate of the crack French motor vessel GEORGES PHILIPPAR of Messageries Maritimes, homeward bound from the Far East. At about 05.00 on 16th May 1932 a fire alarm sounding on the bridge indicated a fire in one of the first class staterooms. A fire party was sent below to investigate, but as they were dealing with it "hundreds of other fires" broke out in various places throughout the ship, and within half-an-hour the ship was a blazing inferno. The suspicion of sabotage cannot be ruled out, especially when a government inquiry revealed that most of the portable fire extinguishers available to passengers and crew had been

deliberately emptied. The radio officers just managed to transmit a single S.O.S. message at 05.54 before the advancing flames drove them from the wireless office.[154]

The message was received by several vessels in the vicinity, including the CONTRACTOR, homeward bound from Calcutta, and making up for Cape Guardafui (Ras Caseyr) on the Horn of Africa. CONTRACTOR, with Captain W.T. Owen in command, was one of the first ships on the scene, about five miles north of Guardafui. In the early morning light, the prospects for the passengers and crew aboard the liner looked very grave indeed. Leaping flames and billowing smoke prevented access to the lifeboats, some of which, though in the water, were empty, most of the passengers and crew being congregated at the ends of the ship, the only parts yet free of flames. Speedy relief from outside sources was clearly a matter of urgency.

A Russian motor tanker, SOVETSKAIA NEFT (8228/29), was already on the scene, with boats in the water, and soon they were joined by Brocklebank's steamer MAHSUD (7,540/17). With typical Harrison caution, Captain Owen stopped the CONTRACTOR about one mile from the blazing ship, and lowered two lifeboats. Neither of them had an engine, so the crews were faced with a long pull. The men pulled with a will at the heavy oars from the start, all but exhausting their strength before they were half way across. Anyone who has ever pulled a heavy ash lifeboat oar will know what back-breaking toil it is, stretching aching muscles which have lain dormant for years, and raising raw blisters on the palms of the

hands within minutes. The last half-mile was sheer torture but at last they reached the towering sides of the stricken liner, and scores of near-frenzied passengers tumbled from ropes and ladders or were hauled out of the water, until the boats could carry no more. Then began the daunting pull back to the CONTRACTOR. The crew, however, were by that time too exhausted to even lift an oar, but there was no lack of willing volunteers among the rescued Frenchmen ready to bend their backs to the oars. And so CONTRACTOR's rescue flotilla returned to the ship, where preparations to receive the survivors had been set in motion. In all, CONTRACTOR had rescued 128 persons, of whom 18 were injured: 66 civilian passengers, 15 military, 22 naval men, and 25 crew members - all of whom were landed safely at Aden next day, in the late afternoon.

Contractor at Liverpool.

[J. and M. Clarkson]

CONTRACTOR and the sampan lady[155]

In April 1933, CONTRACTOR was anchored in the Rangoon River loading a cargo of rice for London. It was a dark, still night, and the pungent odour of cooking fires on the lighters and sampans clustered around the ship hung heavily in the air. The cargo was almost completed, and the ship was due to sail next day. At about 22.00 Third Officer Robert Myles became aware of a commotion at the foot of the accommodation ladder. Glancing over the side, he saw two sampans, similar to those employed in ferrying people ashore from the ships in the stream, hitched to the bottom platform. The altercation was coming from the nearest, and Myles noted that its only occupant was a woman, a white woman, looking very wet and dishevelled, very angry and frightened. A Burmese Customs guard was apparently questioning her right to come aboard.

Instinctively aware that this was no way to treat a lady in obvious distress, the gallant Myles sent word to the Captain, descended the gangway, mollified the guard, and helped her on board. Captain Owen placed his cabin at her disposal to clean up and dry out. Some rather incongruous, but at least dry, masculine clothes were hurriedly found for her. Somewhat recovered, and fortified with a large brandy, she told her story.

The lady identified herself as a US doctor, travelling as a passenger aboard a British India steamer anchored further upstream. Wishing to go ashore that evening she had hired a sampan to carry her to the jetty. However, her choice of boatman was unfortunate, for no sooner had the sampan cleared the ship than the thug attacked her with intent either to rob or rape her - probably both. Her mind rebelled against the

hopelessness of the situation - alone in the boat with this monster, with no chance of rescue. She screamed, and struggled with all her might, so much so that she broke from his clutches, and fell overboard. Still undaunted, she grabbed the gunnel of the boat, and, perhaps preferring another confrontation with her assailant to a cold, watery grave, heaved herself out of the water. Her tormentor, doubtless thinking that his prey was about to be restored to him, probably gave her a helping hand, but he was evidently unprepared for the wildcat which leapt upon him, spitting, scratching, and kicking. Retreating backwards, he, too, fell over the side. The outraged young woman felt no compulsion to lend him a helping hand, and swinging on the steering oar, urged the craft into the current. But she had no idea of how to manage the native sampan, which was now adrift on the fast-flowing river and in danger of being swept out to sea. Quite by chance, however, it eventually brought up against another sampan which happened to be going out to the CONTRACTOR. The boatman hitched a line to it, and towed it to the ship's gangway.

Later, feeling much better, but loathe to leave CONTRACTOR's protection and hospitality, the lady was escorted ashore by a sympathetic policeman to make a statement before being conducted back to her ship. She said "Goodbye" to her hosts, and waved from the sternsheets of the police launch as it left the gangway. Bob Myles often found himself wondering what became of the "Sampan Lady", rescued from that boat which almost passed in the night.

Enemy attack - friendly fire[156]

Saturday 7th August 1943 was a fine sunny day in the Mediterranean, with light airs and a calm sea. Convoy GTX 6, bound from Gibraltar to Port Said, was comprised of ships loaded with military stores for the beleaguered armies of the Far East. The CONTRACTOR was leading the fourth column, steering a zigzag course to Admiralty Pattern No.10 at 8 knots. Suddenly, at 15.45, a violent explosion shook the ship and shattered the tranquillity of that placid afternoon. A tall column of water, laced with fumes and debris, shot up from the port side of No.2 hatch, scattering hatch-boards in all directions.

Three days out from Gibraltar, the ship's position was

given as 37.15N, 7.21E, or about 30 miles northwest of Bone (now Annaba), Algeria. Kapitänleutnant Waldemar Mehl, commanding U 371, had sighted the convoy an hour earlier following a hydrophone contact at about 11.00. He launched his attack with four torpedoes, but only the CONTRACTOR was hit. The U-boat then fled swiftly as the escort vessels closed in for a counter attack.

Meanwhile, everything that could go wrong seemed to be going wrong aboard the CONTRACTOR. The ship was settling rapidly by the head, listing to port, and still forging ahead. There was some delay in stopping the engines, as the telegraph had jammed and orders had to be transmitted vocally via the speaking tube. With the foredeck awash, Captain Andrew Brims gave the order to abandon ship, and the crew, mostly Lascars, ran to their boat stations. The boats were already swung out, secured by wire lashings to the griping spar, but otherwise ready to lower. Unfortunately, when the gripes of number 1 boat were released, the boat descended with a rush, dived into the sea, and became waterlogged. Someone had let go the falls, too.

Then, whilst the crew were lowering number 4 boat on the port side of the boat deck, the falls jammed and only by cutting through the 3-inch manila could the boat be released. The boat speedily completed its descent, striking a piece of wreckage with such force that the bottom strakes of planking were stove in. The boat filled rapidly to the gunwales. No attempt was made to launch number 2, which had been damaged by the explosion. However, number 3, on the starboard side had been lowered successfully, and was floating alongside, where members of the crew were climbing aboard.

Seeing that only one boat had been safely launched, Captain Brims and Second Officer Alan Moreton attempted to release the rafts, of which there were six. However, the forward pair, secured by patent slips to the foremast rigging were by now inaccessible; two rafts amidships jammed in the ways when the slips were released, and only the after starboard raft reached the water in the designated fashion. Meanwhile, Second Officer Moreton found himself in the water, swimming for the only lifeboat. He climbed aboard just as the after raft suddenly shot into the water. It missed the crowded lifeboat by a few feet, but as its painter tautened, it pressed the boat against the ship's side. With difficulty, both painters were released, but before the boat could get clear, the ship's stern reared up as she plunged for the sea bed, just ten minutes after the torpedo struck. Overcome by the turbulence, the boat capsized, throwing its 23 terrified occupants into the maelstrom. Seconds later, a loud, underwater explosion sent a column of water mushrooming above the swimmers, while violent shock waves beat against vulnerable bodies.

Meanwhile, more drama was taking place on the port side of the sinking vessel. Cadet David Bloom had jumped into the sea a few minutes earlier, and found himself in the midst of a small group of survivors swimming for their lives. He remembered forcibly advising Chief Steward Jack Lloyd to "get rid of all that dosh before you jump, or you'll go down like a stone!" For the pockets of Jack Lloyd's patrol jacket and trousers were bulging with the proceeds of the canteen cash sales - mostly silver and copper! But he must have heeded the young man's advice, for there he was, swimming alongside him. They paused to look up at the ship as her stern reared high in the air, her propellor still revolving slowly. They caught an agonised glimpse of Chief Officer John Sinclair clinging despairingly to the poop rail before the suction of the ship's violent passing dragged them down. After what seemed an age, they fought their way to the heaving, troubled surface, their lungs

seeming ready to burst. The convoy was fast disappearing into the distance, leaving them alone in a sea of wreckage. But not entirely alone; for bearing down towards the struggling survivors was the lean shape of a Royal Navy frigate with a bone in her teeth, and a long, black pennant streaming from her foremast - a sure sign that she was in ASDIC contact with a U-boat... The implications were all too clear to the horrified swimmers. David Bloom actually saw the pattern of depth charges leave the Y-launchers and hurtle skywards. One flew directly overhead, like a monstrous drop-kick at Twickenham, and plunged into the sea a mere thirty yards away. "On your backs!" someone yelled frantically, and most of the survivors within earshot obeyed. The explosion, when it came a few seconds later was like the kick of a demented mule. It lifted the men high out of the water...a tidal wave engulfed them and when it subsided they gazed fearfully about to see who was still swimming. Some lay still; but the frigate sped on, fulfilling its awesome duty.

But help was at hand, in the shape of four minesweepers, BYMS 11, 14, 24, and 209, which appeared on the scene and promptly began picking up the 75 shocked survivors, 15 of whom were injured. One of the minesweepers was diverted to Malta with the injured men, landing them at Valetta on 9th August. Those who had been in the close vicinity of the exploding depth charge were in a bad way. David Bloom and others who had had the wit to turn onto their backs received severe bruising to their backs and limbs, but were otherwise unhurt. Those who had remained swimming in a prone position had suffered severe internal injuries. At least two of them died, and Chief Engineer Arthur Jones never fully recovered, suffering abdominal pain for the rest of his days.

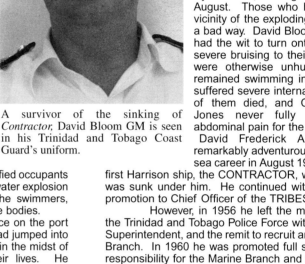

A survivor of the sinking of *Contractor,* David Bloom GM is seen in his Trinidad and Tobago Coast Guard's uniform.

David Frederick Alfred Bloom had a remarkably adventurous career. He began his sea career in August 1941, when he joined his first Harrison ship, the CONTRACTOR, which as we have seen was sunk under him. He continued with Harrisons, achieving promotion to Chief Officer of the TRIBESMAN in 1953.

However, in 1956 he left the merchant service to join the Trinidad and Tobago Police Force with the rank of Assistant Superintendent, and the remit to recruit and train a Police Marine Branch. In 1960 he was promoted full superintendent with the responsibility for the Marine Branch and the Port of Spain dock area. For his part in dealing with the potentially disastrous fire on board an islands schooner loaded with aviation fuel in the dock area he was awarded the George Medal.

When the islands of Trinidad and Tobago became independent, Superintendent Bloom's Marine Police became the nucleus of a Coast Guard Service. After a short period under the command of a seconded Royal Naval officer, and the abortion of the project to build a West Indian Federation with its own navy, Bloom, by now a Lieutenant Commander in the Trinidad and Tobago Defence Force, became the Coast Guard's Commandant. He retired as Captain, T. and T.C.G. in 1974.

225. RECORDER 1930-1950 Steel steamship. Two decks, five holds and deep tank. Two masts.
O.N. 162325 5,982g 3,732n 9,110d 420.3 x 54.65 x 32.8 feet. Cargo capacity: 508,242 cubic feet.
International Code: LGMC (GTPV after 1933).
T. 3-cyl. by Cammell Laird and Co. Ltd., Birkenhead; 27, 46, 77 x 54 inches, 12^1/$_2$ knots. Pulverised fuel system.

29.7.1930: Launched by Cammell Laird and Co. Ltd., Birkenhead (Yard No. 969) for the company. *19.9.1930:* Delivered at a cost of £117,894 and sailed from Liverpool to Kingston, Jamaica and Mexico on her maiden voyage under Captain J.J. Egerton. *1932:* The pulverised fuel system was not a success due to difficulties in obtaining suitable fuel and frequent breakdowns. The system was eventually withdrawn and replaced with a conventional coal-firing system. *5.3.1942:* Sailed from Port Sudan towing the gutted passenger ship GEORGIC (27,759/32) which had been heavily damaged in an air raid 14.7.1941 in Suez Bay.

19.5.1950: Sold to Audax Steamship Co. Ltd. (Chinese Maritime Trust Ltd., managers), Hong Kong and renamed AUDAX. *1951:* Sold to Pacific Union Marine Corporation (C.Y. Tung, manager), Panama, and renamed OCEAN STAR. *1952:* Sold to Hachiuma Kisen K.K., Nishinomiya, Japan and renamed OCEAN MARU. *1960:* Sold to Hokuyo Suisan K.K., Tokyo, Japan renamed SEIYO MARU and converted to a crab cannery. *1961:* Fitted with new engine. *1971:* Sold to Tung Ho Steel and Iron Co. Ltd., Taiwan, for demolition. *10.12.1971:* Work commenced at Kaohsiung.

Tow for a crippled trooper
On 14th July 1941 German aircraft, operating from Crete, carried out a heavy bombing raid on the Suez Bay area. The

Cunard-White Star liner GEORGIC (27,759/32), serving as a troopship and anchored off Port Tewfik, was bombed and set on

Seen here as steamer, *Recorder* was fitted with an oil engine after sale by Harrison, surviving until 1971.   *[Ian Farquhar collection]*

fire. The ship was gutted and the engine room flooded, but the crew managed to slip the cable and beach the ship. Despite the devastation, the burnt-out hulk was patched up and refloated on 27th October. It was decided to despatch her to the nearest available dry dock, at Karachi, for extensive repairs. Thus GEORGIC left Suez Bay on 2nd December 1941 towed by Cayzer, Irvine's CLAN CAMPBELL (7,255/37) and Ellerman's CITY OF SYDNEY (6,986/30). They reached Port Sudan on 14th December having taken 12 days to cover the distance of 710 miles. The crippled liner lay at Port Sudan for close on three months, patching up further leaks which had developed in transit, correcting a bad list, and awaiting another towing vessel to take her across the Arabian Sea.

Two months later the RECORDER, Captain W.B. Wilford in command, arrived at Port Sudan, and was promptly commissioned for the job, together with a small naval tug, the ST. SAMPSON (451/19). On 5th March 1942, the unlikely ensemble laboured awkwardly out of Port Sudan, gingerly skirting the off-lying reefs. RECORDER was towing ahead; ST. SAMPSON lying astern to steer; the hulk itself squatting stolidly between, devastated, but still majestic.

On the following day, the onset of a north west gale rendered the wallowing GEORGIC virtually unmanageable. The southerly course had to be abandoned, and the ships hove-to. For five hours RECORDER battled to bring her charge head to wind, and in the process the stern tug was damaged. Rapidly

filling with water, the little vessel slipped her tow rope, and drifted down wind. Shortly afterwards she foundered, the crew being picked up by the hospital ship DORSETSHIRE (9717/20) which was passing at the time.

For 12 hours, RECORDER and GEORGIC rode out the gale, then, as the winds abated, they cautiously swung back through 180 degrees to resume their course. Meanwhile, they were joined by another tug, the PAULINE MOLLER (422/18) and the British India steamer HARESFIELD (5,299/19), and together they guided their labouring charge past Abu Ail and the islands of the southern Red Sea, through the narrow Straits of Bab-el-Mandeb into the Gulf of Aden, and on to Karachi. The salvage crew responsible for the GEORGIC lived on board the RECORDER, and every few days boarded the liner from a motor launch in order to pump out the water which kept seeping through the liner's skin. It was fortunate that the weather in the Arabian Sea at this time of year remained calm and smooth.

On 31st March, 26 days out of Port Sudan, the ships arrived off Karachi, where GEORGIC was taken in hand by eight harbour tugs. RECORDER and her consorts, having traversed some 2,100 miles on passage, had completed one of the most successful salvage operations of the war. Captain Wilford was later invested with the OBE.

GEORGIC remained in a Karachi dry dock for a further nine months, carrying out repairs, and undergoing a thorough refit. She eventually returned to trooping in January 1943.[157]

226. DAKARIAN 1933-1939 Steel steamship. Three decks, five holds and deep tank. Two masts.
O.N. 145891 6,426g 4,065n 9,480d 400.3 x 52.5 x 37.83 feet. Cargo capacity: 467,023 cubic feet.
International Code: KLBJ (GFCY after 1933).
Q. 4-cyl. by D. and W. Henderson and Co. Ltd., Glasgow; 23½, 34, 49, 70 x 51 inches, 11½ knots.

10.11.1920: Launched by D. and W. Henderson and Co. Ltd., Glasgow (Yard No. 505) for Frederick Leyland and Co. Ltd., Liverpool as DAHOMIAN. She was completed as DAKARIAN. *4.11.1921:* Ran trials. *15.12.1933:* Acquired by the company for £22,421, the first of seven Leyland steamers to be acquired at a total cost of £203,358 along with certain rights and facilities in the Gulf of Mexico trade. The vessels had a substantial amount of refrigerated space when taken over by Harrison. This was subsequently removed from the after holds, increasing the cubic capacity by about 10% and the deadweight by about 2½%. *26.5.1939:* Sold to The Ben Line Steamers Ltd. (William Thomson and Co., managers), Leith for £15,206 and renamed BENVANNOCH. *1946:* Sold to Bank Line Ltd. (Andrew Weir and Co., managers), Glasgow and renamed BIRCHBANK. *1948:* Managers restyled Andrew Weir Shipping and Trading Co. Ltd. *1952:* Sold to Kato Sempaku K. K., Osaka, Japan and renamed SHUNKEI MARU. *1955:*

Sold to Osaka Shosen Kaisha, Osaka, Japan and renamed INDUS MARU. *1958:* Sold to Japanese shipbreakers who commenced demolition 23.11.1958 at Sakai.

First of seven ships bought from Leyland Line in the mid 1930s, *Dakarian* was not renamed by Harrison.   *[World Ship Photo Library collection]*

227. DORELIAN 1933-1936 Steel steamship. Three decks, five holds and deep tank. Two masts.
O.N. 147212 6,431g 4,069n 9,430d 400.4 x 52.4 x 37.8 feet. Cargo capacity: 460,176 cubic feet.
International Code: KPBJ (GJTL after 1933).
Q. 4-cyl. by D. and W. Henderson and Co. Ltd., Glasgow; 23½, 34, 49, 70 x 51 inches, 11½ knots.

4.4.1923: Launched by D. and W. Henderson and Co. Ltd., Glasgow (Yard No. 627M) for Frederick Leyland and Co. Ltd., Liverpool. *5.1923:* Completed. *20.12.1933:* Acquired by the company for £27,472. *16.1.1936:* Ran aground when entering the port of Barrow-in-Furness to lay up. Refloated and proceeded to a lay up berth where she remained for eight months. *7.9.1936:* Sold to Donaldson Line Ltd. (Donaldson Brothers Ltd., managers), Glasgow for £16,892. *27.6.1938:* Managers restyled Donaldson Brothers and Black Ltd. *2.1954:* Sold to British Iron and Steel Corporation (Salvage) Ltd. for £44,000 for demolition and allocated to W.H. Arnott, Young and Co. (Shipbreakers) Ltd., Dalmuir.

Dorelian. [*J. and M. Clarkson*]

228. DAVISIAN 1934-1940 Steel steamship. Three decks, five holds and deep tank. Two masts.
O.N. 147200 6,433g 4,065n 9,470d 400.3 x 52.5 x 37.83 feet. Cargo capacity: 467,658 cubic feet.
International Code: KNPV (GJSK after 1933).
Q. 4-cyl. by D. and W. Henderson and Co. Ltd., Glasgow; 23½, 34, 49, 70 x 51 inches, 11½ knots.

16.1.1923: Launched by D. and W. Henderson and Co. Ltd., Glasgow (Yard No. 511) for Frederick Leyland and Co. Ltd., Liverpool. *2.1923:* Completed. *29.2.1924:* Reported disabled with a broken propeller shaft when on passage from Boston to Liverpool. She was taken in tow by another Leyland ship, BELGIAN (5,287/19), and arrived 6.3.1924 at Horta, Azores. The tugs WITTE ZEE (465/14) and SEINE (308/08) were employed to tow her home, and she left Horta

15.3.1924 and arrived 27.3.1924 at Liverpool. *16.1.1934:* Acquired by the company for £27,503. *10.7.1940:* Attacked by the German commerce raider WIDDER about 410 miles, 047 degrees from Barbados North Point, and sank in position 18.00N, 54.30W. She was on passage from London and Cardiff for the West Indies with general cargo and patent fuel. Six men were injured, at least two seriously, one of whom died 17 days later.

Davisian photographed by Leslie Hansen, about 1936. [*National Museums and Galleries of Wales, Department of Industry, 234/447*]

Victims of the WIDDER[158]

It was Wednesday 10th July 1940, and Second Officer George Jolly had been watching the stranger ever since her masts had appeared above the horizon, three points before the port beam, at 13.45. DAVISIAN was approaching the chain of islands which girdle the eastern end of the Caribbean, on course for Barbados, and it was not unusual to see ships from time to time. George Jolly studied the intruder through his telescope, noting the details as she hove in sight on a rapidly converging course. Definitely a merchantman; painted grey with white upperworks; probably a neutral. Sure enough, there on the hull was painted the blue-and-gold emblem of Sweden. The tension relaxed, but the Second Officer continued his scrutiny, observing a single officer lounging on the bridge, and two men sunbathing on a "garden seat" on the poop. No maritime scene could have looked more innocent.

At 14.20 the serenity of the afternoon was rudely shattered by the report of a gun. That first salvo burst on the foredeck, injuring the bosun, and heralded a barrage of high explosive and shrapnel at a range of 3,000 yards rapidly closing as the stranger swept towards DAVISIAN, her false Swedish colours now partly concealed by the open flaps in her side, exposing the smoking 5.9-inch guns. From her triatic stay fluttered the International Code signal, "STOP. DO NOT USE YOUR WIRELESS" - a pointless command in the circumstances since the aerials had already been shot away.

Captain Tom Pearce had hastened to the bridge at the first sound of gunfire. The sight which met his gaze could not have been more unnerving. The decks were in a shambles, wounded men lay about dazed and in pain, the 4-inch gun on the poop had received a direct hit, wounding the gun-layer and several of his team. Resistance or escape was out of the question. Captain Pearce rang "Stop" on the engine-room telegraph, ordered George Jolly to acknowledge the signal, and Chief Officer Alec Smart to prepare the boats for lowering. He then set about methodically collecting various Admiralty code books and documents into a weighted bag which was promptly dumped over the side.

However, despite hoisting the red-and-white answering pennant acknowledging the raider's signals; despite a sudden cessation of the ship's propeller wash; despite the silence of the wireless transmitter; and despite the evidence of boats being cleared away, the raider still continued to fire over open sights at her helpless victim, the sharp crack of her heavy armament being joined by the chatter of machine guns. Seamen clearing the boats on one side were forced to the opposite side to escape the bombardment, and the boats themselves were quickly pitted with splinter-holes. Considering the ferocity of the attack, casualties were surprisingly light. At last, two boats were lowered safely with six wounded on board; the rest of the crew piled in and cast off. Only when the boats were seen pulling towards the raider did the shelling stop. As they drew near, sluggish and waterlogged, in danger of sinking despite frantic baling by willing hands, the men noticed with some curiosity the words painted on the stern "NARVIK STOCKHOLM". They wondered, even more curiously, what might be her real identity.

She was, in fact, "Schiff 21", the former Hamburg-Amerika liner NEUMARK (7851/30), requisitioned in 1939, and transformed into the commerce raider WIDDER. Known to the British Admiralty as "Ship D", she was armed with six 5.9-inch guns, two 4-inch, and several heavy machine guns. Two torpedo tubes, an Arado reconnaissance plane fitted with bomb racks, and a large consignment of mines completed her weaponry. Her commander was Kapitän-zur-see Helmuth von Ruckteschell.

The boats drew alongside, and a heavily accented voice ordered the Captain to come on board. Tom Pearce climbed the ladder and confronted an officer who questioned him about his ship. Somewhat impatiently, Captain Pearce pointed out that the boats alongside were close to sinking, and what did they propose to do about it? Rather reluctantly - it seemed - the order was passed for all hands to come on board, for it had been the German commander's intention to set them on a course for the West Indies, and leave them to it. The wounded were assisted on board by German sailors using hammocks and stretchers to pass them up the ship's side. Among the more serious casualties were Second Engineer J.L. McCulloch, Bosun J. Poynter, Storekeeper J. Davis, Gunner J. Plimmer, and Firemen T. Lavelle and A. Lloyd. When all were aboard the boats were cut adrift.

Then, despite protests, there followed the undignified process of stripping, bathing, delousing, and the fumigation of clothing - an unwarranted insult to the English; a hygienic necessity to the Germans, ever suspicious of the habits of foreigners. Meanwhile, Captain Pearce, Chief Officer Smart, and Chief Steward Cadogan, who had evidently been excused the cleansing ritual, had been ordered to accompany the boarding party, which was already embarking in a fast-looking launch, on a foraging expedition aboard the DAVISIAN.

The engine room stores were stripped of useful items, likewise the cabin stores and bonded locker. The three officers were ordered to collect as much as they could carry in the way of clothing and blankets. Then charges were laid at points along the hull, timed to detonate a few minutes after the launch was clear. They were midway between raider and victim when three explosions rent the air. Columns of water leapt skywards; then DAVISIAN heeled wearily over to port, and sank.

Captain Pearce and his officers returned to the raider to find that the prisoners had been sorted into their respective living quarters, and a meal of sorts was being served. They also met the officers and men of an earlier victim, the tanker BRITISH PETROL (6,891/25) sunk on 13th June.

Next morning, von Ruckteschell felt the time was opportune for a proclamation, which, issued through Captain Pearce, ran as follows. "Captain - The war between my ship and yours is over! From today you and your crew are my prisoners! You will be treated here on board in exactly the same way as any other sailor. You will get here the same food as my crew. If you will obey the orders given, so, according to the circumstances, you will not have it bad. However, for every disobedience there will be only one punishment, and that is - shooting! "Please will you inform your officers and your crew about what I told you. I am going to give it to you in writing, so that you can repeat it to them.

I am sorry that five (sic) men have been wounded. They are human beings and soldiers and I feel sorry for them. My doctors will do their best for them and I hope that they will get them through. Later on, as soon as everything is settled, I will give you the opportunity to see the wounded. None of my crew is allowed to have any conversation with your men...also, none of your crew will be allowed to talk to my men!

I repeat once more: there is only one punishment here on board, even for the slightest sort of disobedience: the one which I told you already. The First Officer will let you know the hours in which you will be allowed on deck. Every conversation between officers and crew is forbidden! If necessary I will give you the opportunity of speaking to your crew from time to time."

Later that morning, the interrogations which had begun the night before, were resumed. Apparently, during his interview, Chief Radio Officer K.E. Goddard gave himself the satisfaction of telling his captors, in detail, and with some relish, exactly what would happen to the Germans when their ship encountered a British cruiser. His little homily received a decidedly cool reception. Goddard was reported to von Ruckteschell, who was inclined to equate such insolence with the crime of disobedience. He was moved to utter another proclamation:

"Prisoners - Already I have noticed a difference between the two crews. Already I have had trouble with one of yours. It was not necessary for me to take you out of the water. I did it for your good because we Germans are conducting this war in our own fashion and in accordance with the wishes of our Führer. I do not expect from you who are my enemies, gratitude, but I will warn you again that for disobedience of my rules there is only one penalty - shooting!"

Radio Officer Goddard was not shot, however. Subsequent investigation persuaded the Commander that it was all a "misunderstanding". Goddard did not choose to argue.

Second Officer Jolly recorded that the prisoners' treatment aboard the raider was fair; that the food was plentiful, if the diet of sausage, gruel, black bread, synthetic tea and coffee was not entirely to their liking; but that exercise on deck was limited to a mere 20 minutes, morning and evening.

Three days after the DAVISIAN had been sunk, her crew were aroused from their morning lethargy by the sound of klaxons, and the rush of booted feet along the decks above. Sharp orders blared over the public address system, and a Sergeant-at-Arms appeared at the grille door to the prisoners' quarters and announced that an action was likely. He then supervised the mounting of a machine-gun trained on the door. The prisoners could only speculate as to its purpose, and the knowledge that the next compartment to theirs housed a consignment of mines did nothing to soothe their nerves. If this turned out to be Goddard's cruiser...! Apprehensively, they settled down as best they could to await developments.

One hour later came the crash of falling camouflage, and then the bombardment which lasted ten minutes. The victim this time was the British steamer KING JOHN (5,228/28). Besides her own crew, the ship also had on board that of a Panamanian ship, the SANTA MARGARITA (4,919/28), which had been torpedoed by a U-boat. They were described by the fastidious von Ruckteschell in his war diary as "Yugoslavs, Portuguese, Maltese and Spaniards...dirty and lousy people." [159]

Glumly, he must have wondered what to do with them, as they swelled the throng of 100 prisoners already on board. He was not long in doubt. The KING JOHN's lifeboats had escaped the bombardment, and were in excellent condition.

The prisoners were later herded up on deck in groups of 10 or 15, and ordered into the lifeboats lying alongside. Chief Officer Alex Smart was assigned to one boat with 24 men from the DAVISIAN's crew. Second Officer Jolly was assigned to another boat with 14 "Davisians" and 26 men from other ships. It became quite crowded. Masters and chief engineers were not given the chance to join the boat parties, but were detained aboard the raider along with the wounded and several boy ratings - among whom were T. Roscoe, Officers' Boy, and T. R. Brown, Deck Boy, from the DAVISIAN - whom the Commander considered too young to undertake the rigours of a boat voyage.

Extra provisions were put in each boat, including a German first aid kit and two bottles of ersatz rum. The officers were then given a bearing and distance - Guadeloupe; 218 degrees, 260 miles - and the painters cast off. Unfortunately, the wind which had been easterly now veered to the south east, making it impossible for the boats to steer the required course, and make due allowance for leeway. All they could do was sail as close to the wind as possible and hope to make some sort of

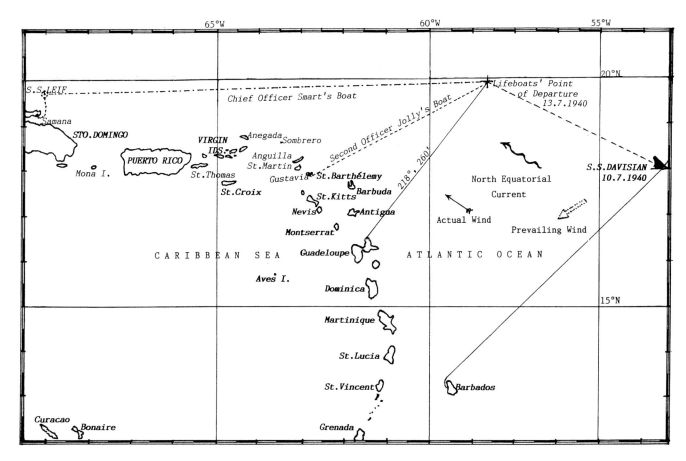

Mean track of boats following *Davisian's* sinking by the *Widder*.

landfall. Thus, sailing close hauled with wind and sea abeam made life very uncomfortable. In the Second Officer's overloaded boat all hands had to sit upright in the same position, and this coupled with the boat's lively motion, made sleep almost impossible. During the day they were exposed to the burning rays of the sun, but despite their ordeal, George Jolly records that the men behaved very well. On the third night a tropical rain squall swept over the boat, drenching the men with sweet water, an event which did a great deal to raise their morale. Mr. Jolly records, "The deluge sent everyone into the highest spirits. Songs and choruses rang out into the night and Mr. McGlynn (Third Engineer) with a yodelling song earned loud applause." The sheer abundance of water was, in fact, almost as intoxicating as, and certainly more palatable than, the German ersatz rum!

On the morning of the fourth day, they sighted land, which they approached cautiously on account of the off-lying reefs. They sighted a small port, but the prominent display of the French tricolour made them hesitate. Did the island owe allegiance to the Free French cause, or was it a den of Vichy sympathisers? Reluctant to venture forth upon another voyage into the unknown, they decided to take a chance, and pulled boldly into the little harbour of Gustavia on the island of St. Bartholemy. Their doubts, however, proved groundless. They were received with "the utmost kindness and generosity by a people who were themselves very poor". They were billeted in the local schoolhouse and slept on the floor, but after four days in an open boat they asked no other luxury. After three days, the men were picked up by a Royal Navy ship and transported to St. Kitts, where arrangements for their eventual repatriation were implemented.

The boat voyage had in fact lasted about 84 hours, during which they had sailed about 270 miles on an effective course of 243 degrees.

Alec Smart's boat had not been so fortunate, however. It, too, had been set well north of the desired southwesterly course, so far, in fact, that it missed the Leeward Island chain completely. After about 12 days, with the crew growing ever weaker and more dispirited, the boat was sighted from the Norwegian steamer LEIF (1,532/37), drifting off Cape Samana in the Dominican Republic, nearly 590 miles from their point of departure, having made an effective course of 269 degrees.

The Norwegians took them on board, and, in the words of LEIF's Captain Brynilsen, "we landed the survivors, more dead than alive, at the port of Samana', a few hours later."[160] It was reported in Lloyd's List of 24th July 1940 that a third boat-load of ex-prisoners from the WIDDER had landed on the British island of Anguilla.

Meanwhile, on board the WIDDER, the wounded fireman Lavelle was getting worse. His leg wound had become infected, and gangrene had set in. The leg was amputated; generous blood transfusions were administered, but all to no avail. On 27th July 1940, Lavelle died from his wounds, and at sunrise next day he was buried at sea with full honours. Nevertheless, von Ruckteschell could not resist the opportunity to deliver an extraordinary funeral oration, the sentiments of which would have earned him a nod of approval from Goebbels himself:

"Comrades, Sailors, - All medical skill and all carefulness could not prevent the loss of the life of this young man, whose mortal frame is lying in front of us. He died in consequence of the heavy wound which one of our shells inflicted on him. If the War shall have meaning, so it is necessary for us to look into his face with all awakedness, of which we are able to. We see, carved into his face, the great distress and the pains and the destructions and the suffering and the misery which the peoples are doing each other. And if this comrade, whom we are now giving the last honour, would not have done anything else in this world but that he has been waiting for this shell, in order to die here on board - so we will thank him for his sacrifice, because he taught us anew to long for the peace. His soul is free and returned to its Creator. On the rays of the morning sun, far beyond the horizon, which is encircling us, our loving thoughts and wishes are following him with all friendliness into his new empire. On this way, on which we are accompanying our comrade, we look into the divine sun and ask Her, the strength for peace and the will for peace to shine in our hearts. Then the death of our comrade will be a blessing for him and for us all. Yes, it is like that!"

Perhaps, in his Germanic way, von Ruckteschell meant well.

WIDDER, after sinking six more ships, and suffering almost perpetual engine trouble, reached Brest on 31st October. Captain Pearce and the other survivors of the DAVISIAN went into internment for the rest of the war.

229. DARIAN 1934-1939 Steel steamship. Three decks, five holds and deep tank. Two masts.
O.N. 145975 6,434g 4,065n 9,470d 400.4 x 52.5 x 37.83 feet. Cargo capacity: 467,658 cubic feet.
International Code: KMTN (GCJX after 1933).
Q. 4-cyl. by D. and W. Henderson and Co. Ltd., Glasgow; 23¹/₂, 34, 49, 70 x 51 inches, 11¹/₂knots.

8.8.1922: Launched by D. and W. Henderson and Co. Ltd., Glasgow (Yard No. 507) for Frederick Leyland and Co. Ltd., Liverpool. *9.1922:* Completed. *31.12.1928:* Grounded in the Savannah River in dense fog. Refloated the following day with the assistance of two tugs. *26.1.1934:* Acquired by the company for £25,482. *18.5.1939:* Sold to The Ben Line Steamers Ltd. (Wm. Thomson and Co., managers), Leith for £19,008 and renamed BENVRACKIE. *13.5.1941:*

Torpedoed and sunk by the German submarine U 105 (Kapitänleutnant Schewe), 547 miles 91 degrees from St. Paul's Rocks in position 00.49N, 20.15W, having been struck on the port side by two torpedoes. She sank in four minutes. She was on passage from London and Loch Ewe to Table Bay and Beira with general cargo. Seven European and six Chinese crew were lost. The survivors were picked up by the Bibby Line OXFORDSHIRE (8,646/1912).[161]

Darian photographed by Basil Feilden.   *[J. and M. Clarkson]*

230. DAYTONIAN 1934-1942 Steel steamship. Three decks, five holds and deep tank. Two masts.
O.N. 145984 6,434g 4,066n 9,470d 400.3 x 52.5 x 37.83 feet. Cargo capacity: 467,658 cubic feet.
International Code: KNBJ (GFKQ after 1933).
Q. 4-cyl. by D. and W. Henderson and Co. Ltd., Glasgow; 23¹/₂, 34, 49, 70 x 51; 11¹/₂ knots.

7.9.1922: Launched by D. and W. Henderson and Co. Ltd., Glasgow (Yard No. 508) for Frederick Leyland and Co. Ltd., Liverpool. *10.1922:* Completed. *15.12.1932:* The newly-constructed deepwater harbour at Cherbourg was unexpectedly inaugurated by DAYTONIAN when she discharged a cargo of bananas from Guadeloupe. The ship had been diverted from Le Havre, where dock workers were on strike. The operation was carried out successfully without the aid of tugs. *23.2.1934:* Acquired by the company for £25,439. *13.3.1942:* Torpedoed by the Italian submarine ENRICO TAZZOLI (Capitano di Corvetta Carlo Fecia di Cossato) about 140 miles, 073 degrees from Abaco in the Bahamas when on passage from Mobile to Halifax with general cargo. Two torpedoes struck the ship on the starboard side and Captain J.J. Egerton gave the order to abandon ship. The submarine then surfaced and opened fire and a third torpedo eventually sank DAYTONIAN in position 26.33N, 74.43W. One seaman was killed in the attack, but 57 survivors in four lifeboats were picked up the next day by the Dutch motor tanker ROTTERDAM (8,968/25) and were

Daytonian in Liverpool.   *[World Ship Photo Library]*

landed 15.3.1942 at Nassau. A homely footnote to the incident was supplied by Captain W.S. Eustance, who was then the Second Officer: "DAYTONIAN sank on an even keel, with flags flying, and a string of washing on the fore-deck".

231. ATLANTIAN 1934-1951 Steel steamship. Three decks, five holds and deep tank. Two masts. O.N. 149686 6,549g 4,016n 9,800d 414.6 x 54.6 x 37.0 feet. Cargo capacity: 465,110 cubic feet. International Code: LCFH (GSMD after 1933).
Caledon Shipbuilding and Engineering Co. Ltd., Dundee; 27, 39, 56, 80 x 54 inches, 11¾ knots.

17.5.1928: Launched by Caledon Shipbuilding and Engineering Co. Ltd., Dundee (Yard No. 316) for Frederick Leyland and Co. Ltd., Liverpool. *8.1928:* Completed. *4.4.1934:* Acquired by the company for £47,669. *7.2.1942:* Successfully fought a night engagement with a German submarine in the approaches to Halifax, Nova Scotia. In June, Second Officer C.A.V. Daly received the King's Commendation for his part in the action. *1.8.1951:* Sold to Wheelock, Marden and Co. Ltd., Hong Kong, and immediately resold to Miyachi Kisen K.K., Kobe, Japan, and renamed HAKUZAN MARU. *26.9.1956:* Driven ashore in a

storm on Koniya Seta Saki, off the island of Amami 0 Shima, southwest of Japan. The vessel had 106 passengers and 63 crew on board and the position was reported as serious. *30.9.1956:* Refloated with the assistance of the salvage vessel TATEGAMI MARU (596/36), and the passengers were transferred to KUROSHIO MARU (1,493/48). Damage to the bottom plates, bilge keels, rudder and propeller was subsequently found to be extensive. *1960:* Taken out of service and laid up. *1964:* Sold to Japanese shipbreakers at Sakai. *5.1964:* Work completed.

Atlantian.`   *[J. and M. Clarkson]*

Lay on the moon![162]

ATLANTIAN loaded a cargo of foodstuffs, cotton, steel billets, crated aircraft on deck, and, stuffed into the 'tween decks, 2,000 tons of TNT in Savannah, Georgia. She sailed on 2nd February 1942 for Halifax, Nova Scotia there to join an east-bound convoy.

After five days of gales and bitter cold, the weather moderated, and life on board returned to normal, or as normal as ever on an independently routed ship in wartime. Suddenly the lookout hailed "Ship close on the port bow, Sir!" A darkened shadow, its huge form silhouetted against the stars, rushed across the bow from port to starboard. Collision seemed inevitable, then equally suddenly, the stranger had gone, swallowed up by the darkness, and ATLANTIAN was left crossing her turbulent wake. The watch breathed again, and pulse rates subsided slowly. "Ships that pass in the night, indeed!"

Twenty minutes later, a distant explosion was heard. Heads turned in the direction whence it came. Had the stranger of recent memory been torpedoed? A flash near the eastern horizon, followed by a similar sharp report, and the shrill whine of a shell overhead suggested otherwise. The shell burst in the water alongside. Second Officer Daly came to his senses.

"It's a sub shelling us!" he yelled, fumbling in the darkness for the alarm switch which would summon all hands to action stations. "Hard a port, quartermaster". The ship swung away from her course, bringing the U-boat astern, but heading directly for the rocky shores of Nova Scotia only 20 miles away. He rang "Full ahead" on the telegraph just as Captain A. Brims came on to the bridge, leaving Daly free to assume his alternative role as Gunnery Officer. He sped aft to round up the gun's crew. He found them already closed up, with a round in the breach.

"Target green one-six-oh", he intoned. "Range two-eight hundred; deflection two right!" The orders were repeated calmly as the sight setters did their work. Apart from the occasional flash from its deck gun the target was not easy to see, but it was close to the path of moonlight.

"Lay on the moon, gunlayer: lay on the moon!" "On, sir! On-on-on!" "Independent rapid fire - open FIRE!"

The explosion of the charge rocked the poop, and the gas from the muzzle was hot and nauseous. The crew stood to its work manfully, loading, training, firing, sending an explosive steel missile hurtling towards the enemy submarine every 20 seconds. The range seemed shorter; shells burst ever closer to the ship. Strangely, no-one gave a thought for the 2,000 tons of TNT beneath their feet.

"Down four hundred!" the Bofors gun might have a go now. "Bofors gun - open fire over open sights!" The Maritime Royal Artillery section needed no second bidding. Live tracer hose-piped towards the target as the slender-barrelled Bofors, normally an anti-aircraft weapon, opened up at a rate of 80 rounds per minute. The battle raged for many minutes before Val Daly realized that enemy shells were no longer falling in their vicinity. The gun flashes and the target had also disappeared.

"Cease fire!" The sudden silence was tangible, almost a solid thing. "Smoke floats!" Half a dozen canisters were ejected astern, igniting astern, and providing a curtain of smoke behind which the ship could resume a less suicidal course.

Second Officer Daly congratulated his men on a fine performance. No hits were claimed, but no-one could be in any doubt that their spirited response to the surprise attack had at least scared their assailant away. The men grinned sheepishly, pleased and elated. One seaman-gunner could not resist a quip. "Lay on the moon!" he crooned. "Sounds like Vera Lynn's latest!" They all laughed, and the tension of the past half hour receded. Daly returned to the bridge and resumed his normal watchkeeping duties. Later that year he was to receive the King's Commendation in recognition of his work that night.

With the dawn came the welcome sight of the Sambro Lightvessel marking the approach to the swept channel leading to Halifax Harbour, and within hours ATLANTIAN was safely anchored in her allotted berth in the broad expanse of Bedford Basin.

232. DELILIAN 1934-1936 Steel steamship. Three decks, five holds and deep tank. Two masts.
O.N. 147207 6,423g 4,064n 9,430d 400.4 x 52.5 x 37.83 feet. Cargo capacity: 460,176 cubic feet.
International Code: KNSD (GJSQ after 1933).
Q. 4-cyl. by D. and W. Henderson and Co. Ltd., Glasgow; 23½, 34, 49, 70 x 51 inches, 11½ knots.

16.2.1923: Launched by D. and W. Henderson and Co. Ltd., Glasgow (Yard No. 512) for Frederick Leyland and Co. Ltd., Liverpool. *4.1923:* Completed. *1.5.1934:* Acquired by the company for £27,372. *5.2.1936:* Laid up at Barrow-in-Furness until 22.5.1936. *29.5.1936:* Sold to Donaldson Line Ltd. (Donaldson Brothers Ltd., managers), Glasgow for £16,892. *27.6.1938:* Managers restyled Donaldson Brothers and Black Ltd. *7.3.1941:* Torpedoed by the German submarine U 70 (Kapitänleutnant Otto Kreschmer) about 170 miles north of Rockall in position 60.28N, 13.38W and was extensively damaged. She was on passage from the Clyde to St. John, New Brunswick in Convoy OB 293. She was able to return to the Clyde under her own steam and was repaired and returned to service. *9.10.1951:* When inward bound

Delilian in the Mersey. *[J. and M. Clarkson]*

from Canadian ports to Newport, Monmouthshire with 7,105 tons of cargo, grounded on the North Middle Ground, four miles south of Newport pier head. Refloated on the next tide with the aid of tugs but she grounded again, one mile east of the scene of the original casualty. Two further attempts to refloat her failed until she was finally floated clear 10.10.1951 on the evening tide. *2.1954:* Sold to British Iron and Steel Corporation (Salvage) Ltd. for £44,000 for demolition and allocated to Smith and Houston Ltd. *2.2.1954:* Arrived at Port Glasgow to be broken up.

233. MERCHANT (3) 1934-1941 Steel steamship. Two decks, four holds and deep tank. Two masts.
O.N. 162411 4,572g 2,910n 7,960d 385.0 x 52.0 x 29.16 feet. Cargo capacity: 400,775 cubic feet.
International Code: GWWC.
T. 3-cyl. by Rankin and Blackmore Ltd., Greenock; 25, 42, 70 x 48 inches, 11 knots.

14.8.1934: Launched by Lithgows Ltd., Port Glasgow (Yard No. 841) for the company. The vessel had been acquired from the shipbuilder on the stocks and was the first launch from the yard for four years. *27.9.1934:* Delivered at a cost of £56,219 and sailed from Glasgow to the West Indies on her maiden voyage under Captain W. A. Hall.. *24.12.1941:* Struck a mine 10 miles east of Yarmouth in position 52.39N, 02.00E and abandoned by her crew the following day. She was sighted by aircraft in position 52.40N, 02.04E drifting, and is presumed to have sunk shortly afterwards. One rating was killed and two injured, the survivors being landed at Grimsby. She was on passage from London to Trinidad and Demerara with 3,000 tons of general cargo.

Merchant, launched at Port Glasgow (right) and on trials on the Clyde in September 1934 (below).

Explorer, photographed on the Thames (top) in original condition with tall funnel; in a US port during the Second World War (middle); and on the Mersey post-war with a shortened funnel (bottom). [*J. and M. Clarkson collection; Ian Farquhar collection; J. and M. Clarkson*]

234. EXPLORER (3) 1935-1957 Steel steamship. Two decks, five holds and deep tank. Two masts.
O.N. 164257 6,236g 3,842n 9,310d. 437.2 x 56.0 x 32.22 feet. Cargo capacity: 496,392 cubic feet
International Code: GYJX.
T. 3-cyl. by Wallsend Slipway and Engineering Co. Ltd., Wallsend; 28, 46, 81 x 54 inches, 13 knots.

2.4.1935: Launched by Swan, Hunter and Wigham Richardson Ltd., Wallsend (Yard No. 1497) for the company. *16.5.1935:* Delivered at a cost of £108,810 and later sailed from Liverpool to South and East Africa on her maiden voyage under Captain F. Trinick. *17.6.1941:* Ran ashore on Ringdove Rock, Isle of Tiree when on passage from Belfast to Glasgow. No explanation as to how she came to be so close to Tiree was given, but she was refloated without undue difficulty and proceeded to the Clyde for repair. *28.11.1941:* Left the Clyde to join one of the first convoys to North Russia via Iceland. *27.4.1942:* In collision with the Swedish KAAPAREN (3,386/30) whilst bound in convoy from Loch Ewe to Halifax. It was alleged that KAAPAREN suddenly reduced speed, forcing EXPLORER to starboard to avoid a collision, but KAAPAREN also swung to starboard into EXPLORER's side. Damage was extensive, but both vessels arrived safely 5.5.1942 at Halifax. In a subsequent court action, both vessels were found equally to blame. *6.2.1945:* In collision with FORT KOOTENAY (7,133/42) in the Thames Estuary close to the East Spile buoy, when on passage from Gravesend to Cardiff with a cargo of cement. The damage was such that return to Gravesend was essential and her cargo of cement was discharged into the Dutch BOSKOOP (5,620/27). Repairs took three months and she returned to service 7.5.1945 and was chartered to Royal Mail Line. *9.2.1952:* Reported disabled in position 05.10N, 50.12W, about 140 miles east of Devil's Island with a fractured tail shaft. The company's new steamer CROFTER (290) was loading at Demerara, homeward bound on her maiden voyage, and was called to assist. *11.2.1952:* The tow was connected and the two vessels arrived safely 17.2.1952 at Port of Spain, Trinidad. Repairs were put in hand and she sailed 18.3.1952. *29.3.1957:* Fire broke out in her cargo of cotton from New Orleans when berthed in Northwest Alexandra Dock, Liverpool. The fire was only extinguished by flooding the hold and about 652 tons of cargo were damaged. There was also considerable heat damage to fittings and furniture in the poop in addition to structural damage. *9.12.1957:* Sold for £122,500 to Panamanian Oriental Steam Ship Corporation, Panama (Whoolook Mardon and Co. Ltd., Hong Kong, managers), and renamed ELEANOR. *1959:* Sold to Hong Kong, Rolling Mills Ltd., for demolition. *21.9.1959:* Arrived at Hong Kong.

Top left: part of the chain-bridle, secured to the bitts, which was deployed from *Crofter's* port quarter, for towing *Explorer,* which can be seen in her wake. Top right: taken from *Crofter's* stern, this shows the bridle of cable shackled to the insurance wire. Bottom left: although the weather was fine throughout the tow, when the line was shortened on the approach to Port of Spain, *Explorer* took a wild sheer. Bottom middle: the cause of the salvage operation - the fracture of *Explorer's* tail shaft. Bottom right: Berthed at the old US naval base near Chaguaramas, Trinidad, *Explorer* has been trimmed by the head, exposing her stern frame. Supported by some flimsy staging, the contractor's men prepare to remove the damaged propellor to enable the fractured shaft to be removed. *[All: A.G. Nicholson]*

Aid to Russia

When Winston Churchill, in his broadcast to the nation on 22nd June 1941 (the day Hitler's armies invaded Russia) promised aid to Stalin, he little realised what a barrel of grief he was laying in store for the Royal and Merchant Navies. The convoys which began to move round the North Cape to the Russian arctic ports in August were to meet conditions of weather and enemy action more severe than anything experienced elsewhere in the whole of the war.

EXPLORER's call came in November, and on 25th she sailed from Liverpool with Captain E.G. Horne in command, bound for the Clyde to join a convoy sailing for the staging post of Reykjavik on 28th. The ships were deeply laden with war material that could ill be spared from Britain's own war effort, yet generously donated to an ally suffering tremendous losses on a front extending from the White Sea in the north to the Black Sea in the south. For most of the eight-day passage the weather was atrocious, inflicting considerable damage to ships and cargo. Aboard EXPLORER, an aircraft stowed on number 4 hatch was smashed by a heavy sea, and a number of tanks stowed in number 2 'tween deck broke loose from their lashings. They were resecured, but only "after much trouble".[163]

Pictured as a young third officer about 1908, Captain Ernest G. Horne OBE (1882-1954) was Master of *Explorer* during her voyage to North Russia in 1941.

The convoy arrived in Reykjavik on 6th December, where it was joined by a few more ships. Two days later the enlarged convoy set course for the North Cape on a voyage characterised by an almost continuous pall of darkness, for once north of Iceland the winter sun would not rise above the horizon again until spring.

Fortunately weather conditions were favourable, but when the ships turned into the White Sea on 19th, they ran into a thick carpet of pack ice. Few of the ships were strengthened sufficiently to plough through pack ice unaided. Consequently they had to wait nearly two days, a prey to marauding submarines, until the Russian icebreaker JOSEF STALIN arrived to clear a channel. And so they arrived, on 23rd December, at the ice-bound port of Molotovsk, EXPLORER being among the first to go alongside that same day.

The work of unloading the cargo was continuous in three eight-hour shifts, but nevertheless slow, due to interminable delays on the railways, the inexperience of the raw, low-quality troops used as labour, and the freezing conditions. Measures were needed to ensure that the ship and her crew could survive in temperatures which ranged from 20° to -20° Fahrenheit (-6.7° to -28.9° Celsius), below the range of any thermometers on board. The crew were provided with "adequate" Arctic clothing, though the fur-lined gloves tended to wear out quickly. Steam was maintained continuously on deck so that the windlass and winches could be kept running, and a half-inch steam pipe was led along the deck water main, though even this froze up at low temperatures. The valves to the flush-toilets were tied down to allow the free flow of water, and it was found that condensation in speaking tubes tended to freeze, cutting communications between such places as bridge and engine room. Remarkably, the ship's refrigerators maintained a steady temperature of 26°F (-3.3°C) for seven weeks, although the average ambient temperature was zero (-17.8°C). In the engine room the main condenser was kept circulating continuously, and the main engines were turned frequently, both in turning gear and by means of main steam.

On the night of 17th February 1942 the ship left Molotovsk bound for Murmansk, the icebreaker gain being called upon to clear a channel. EXPLORER arrived off the island of Kildin on 22nd, and anchored to await instructions. Meanwhile the crew took the oportunity to examine the fore-peak and number 1 hold, and to stop the leaks which had developed during her encounters with the ice.

At last, EXPLORER was called to take her place in the west-bound convoy QP 8, which sailed from Murmansk on 1st March. Its only adversary during this voyage to Iceland was the awful weather, for this was a comparatively peaceful period for the Russian convoys. In fact, out of 103 merchant ships which had made the passage since August, only one had been sunk. However, as the dark of winter gave way to spring, and then the all-night light of summer, German forces operating from bases in the north of Norway began to take a dreadful toll, culminating in the massacre of Convoy PQ 17 in July.

---

235. CRAFTSMAN (3) 1935-1941 Steel steamship. Three decks and six holds. Two goal-post masts.
O.N. 146553 7,896g 4,939n 11,335d 450.5 (471.5 o.l.) x 58.0 x 31.27 feet. Cargo capacity: 580,310 cubic feet.
International Code: KMBR (GFWL after 1933).
Two Brown-Curtiss steam turbines by John Brown and Co. Ltd., Clydebank, single reduction geared to a single screw, 14 knots.

21.6.1921: Launched by Furness Shipbuilding Co. Ltd., Haverton Hill-on-Tees (Yard No. 17) for Johnston Warren Lines, Liverpool as ROWANMORE. Transferred to Furness Withy and Co. Ltd., West Hartlepool and completed 5.1922 as FELICIANA. *15.5.1922:* During her maiden voyage from Southampton to Baltimore, broke down 715 miles west of Bishop Rock. *20.5.1922:* Limped into Queenstown for repair and 3.6.1922 resumed her voyage. *12.1922:* Transferred to Gulf Line Ltd., London and renamed LONDON MARINER. *1928:* Returned to Furness Withy and Co. Ltd. and employed on the services of Prince Line Ltd. Renamed IMPERIAL PRINCE. *10.9.1930:* Arrived in the River Blackwater and laid up off Tollesbury, Essex. She was to remain there for almost five years. *28.5.1935:* Acquired by the company for £46,152 and renamed CRAFTSMAN. *9.4.1941:* Intercepted and sunk by the German raider KORMORAN about 800 miles west of Dakar in position 00.32N, 23.37W.[164] Six of the crew were killed and Captain Ernest Halloway was severely injured. She was on passage from Rosyth to Izmit via Table Bay.

'More than biting time can sever'[165]

1. Memories awakened
In the spring of 1982 Captain W.G. Ellis, retired these ten years or more, received a phone call. The unexpected caller, having established Ellis's identity, revealed himself as a solicitor dealing with the last will and testament of the late Mrs. Mary Halloway, widow of the late Captain W.E. Halloway of 352 Aigburth Road, Liverpool. Having further established that Ellis knew the Halloways, though he had not seen Mrs. Halloway for years, he told him to expect a letter. Replacing the handset, long-dormant memories came flooding back.

He was lying face down on the steel deck, conscious of acute pain in his lumbar region, and of a tropic sun beating down remorselessly. He raised his head to look about him, and recognised familiar faces amongst the CRAFTSMAN's crew ranged along the rail under the watchful eyes of several armed sailors. He himself was one of several wounded men lying about in various attitudes of pain while white-coated sick bay attendants moved among them. To one side, Jock Carruthers, the Chief, lay still as an orderly struggled to stem the bleeding from his shattered legs. Ellis turned his head and focussed his gaze on the blackened, bloodstained figure which lay quietly beside him, patiently awaiting attention. He did not recognise the wretched figure at first, but something about the set of that bald head struck a chord. It was the Old Man! Captain Halloway was clearly in a bad way. During the brief action a direct hit on the concrete-protected wheelhouse had blasted his body and eyes. A splintered wooden upright had scored savagely down his belly, tearing the skin, and exposing the tidy, viscid coils of intestine. The doctors wrought with him tenderly, cutting away the tattered remnants of clothing, lifting him gently on to a stretcher, and bearing him away. Ellis tried to stand up, but the pain in his back was too excruciating. Then he, too, was picked up and carried away to the ship's well-equipped hospital. There,

Craftsman.   [J. and M. Clarkson]

the surgeons probed successfully for the piece of shrapnel in his back, and dressed the wound, so that he now felt a lot more comfortable. Resting in his cot, his mind turned to the cataclysmic events of the day which had brought them to this unhappy situation.

It was 9th April, 1941, and CRAFTSMAN was in the South Atlantic, outward bound from Rosyth to Capetown. The sea was calm, and empty - except for a ship fine on the starboard bow, apparently heading in the same direction. Gradually, CRAFTSMAN overtook the stranger; then, suddenly, as the ships were passing about a mile apart, a large Swastika-ensign burgeoned at the stern; and an array of guns appeared in the stranger's flank, belching flame and smoke. Soon CRAFTSMAN was blazing fiercely; five of the crew lay dead and several others, the Captain among them, were critically maimed in that opening burst of fire. The Chief Officer, Mr. Lewis, gave the order to abandon ship, and, assisted by the helmsman, managed to lift their blind and desperately wounded Captain into one of the two surviving lifeboats. Second Officer Ellis, dazed, and in considerable pain, found himself being assisted into the other boat by Third Engineer Dickie Proffitt.

As the boats pulled away from the blazing wreck, a smart motor launch approached, and a white-uniformed officer hailed them in English, ordering the boats' crews to pull towards the German ship. They complied reluctantly - where else could they go? - and so 43 survivors from the luckless CRAFTSMAN were picked up to become prisoners-of-war. Meanwhile, a demolition team had boarded the vessel to place explosive charges within the hull. The subsequent detonations provided a spectacular display, but the ship still sat stubbornly in the water until finally a precious torpedo was launched to give her the coup-de-grace. She sank slowly, and the Germans recorded the co-ordinates of her last resting place in position 0.32N, 23.37W, or 349 miles, 094 degrees from St. Paul's Rocks.

Some time later the prisoners learned that their aggressor was the German Handelsschutz-kreuzer (armed merchant cruiser) HSK VIII, commissioned in October 1940 as the KORMORAN. Built at the Deutsche Werft yard at Kiel just before the outbreak of war, she had been launched as the Hapag liner STEIERMARK (9,400/38), but was referred to officially by the Germans as SCHIFF 41, and was known to British naval intelligence simply as SHIP G. Finally equipped as a commerce raider, and with a rather confused identity, she had sailed from Gotenhafen on 3rd December 1940 to begin her predatory voyage. CRAFTSMAN was seventh in a long line of victims, and only three days after her demise the raider brought her tally to eight with the capture of a Greek steamer. Kapitän-zur-See Theodor Detmers, commander of the KORMORAN, was acutely conscious that his ship was again becoming over-burdened with prisoners (170 had been transferred to a supply ship in February). Besides, he was running low on stores, fuel and ammunition. It was time, therefore, to make for Point Andalusie, a pre-arranged rendezvous site in position 27S, 17W to meet up once again with his supply ships.

2. *Sea wolves' lair*

Arriving at Andalusie on 20th April, Detmers was mildly surprised to find a small fleet assembled there. Among them was KORMORAN's sister raider, ATLANTIS. There, also, was the tanker NORDMARK, and a blockade runner from the River Plate, the DRESDEN, as well as two submarines. Also present was the DUQUESA, a British refrigerated ship which had been captured by the pocket battleship ADMIRAL SCHEER in December.

Several launches were ferrying stores between the ships of that sequestered fleet, and Ellis, surveying the scene through the open port of the raider's hospital toilet, pondered what mayhem might be inflicted by a patrolling cruiser squadron, if it only knew where to look.

Meanwhile, prisoners were being transferred to the DRESDEN, but those who were wounded were sent to the NORDMARK, since she was equipped with a large, well-appointed hospital. DRESDEN was ordered by Berlin to head for Western France, and eventually reached the port of St. Jean de Luz. NORDMARK was to proceed, directly or indirectly, to Germany. Her captain, manifesting an air of supreme confidence, decided on the direct route - by running the gauntlet of the English Channel. With admirable skill, and a generous measure of good fortune, the ship evaded British patrols and safely reached German waters.

The prisoners in the hospital were called at sunrise one morning to see the white cliffs of Dover gleaming in the early May sunshine. Much to their disappointment, neither plane nor ship approached from the Kentish shore to investigate the intruder. It was an emotional moment for them; a sight they would never forget. Tragically, Jock Carruthers was not there to view this nostalgic prospect. He had died of his wounds some days earlier, and had been buried at sea. To Captain Halloway, whose sightless eyes would never see England again, it was a vision which could only be imagined - and recalled in memory. A commentary from Gordon Ellis only accentuated the precariousness of their present plight, and his own particular vulnerability. Yet he maintained his characteristic upright stance, and declined at any time to submit to self-pity.

Next day, NORDMARK berthed at Cuxhaven, at the mouth of the Elbe, and the prisoners were landed into the care of the local Gestapo. They were separated and housed in various locations. Captain Halloway was last seen being assisted into an ambulance, to be whisked off to some unknown hospital. Ellis watched him go, and wondered whether he would ever see the Old Man again. Meanwhile he was transferred to solitary confinement in a tiny attic room. He remained there for two months, during which he was interrogated by a succession of naval officers. He answered each of them in the same vein throughout his ordeal, establishing a story which they apparently came to accept, much to his surprise.

Yes; he had been the CRAFTSMAN's Second Officer. No; he did not know where the ship was bound. No; he did not know details of what her cargo consisted. For an intelligent officer of a British merchant ship, he did not know very much?

No; he was not a regular officer; he had in fact been a bank clerk - he was at sea just for the duration. A few weeks on a course in simple watch-keeping techniques, some elementary navigation and seamanship, and away as Third Mate. Promoted to Second Mate only a couple of months ago. Only the Captain and Chief Officer were privy to the ship's destination; only they took sights and had access to charts.

3. *The camps*

Eventually, the Germans wearied of the cross-examination game. Doubtless more promising prisoners were falling into their hands every day. So it was with a sense of relief that Ellis was transferred at last to a regular prisoner-of-war camp in a remote spot called Sandbostel, in eastern Germany. This turned out to be a camp within a camp; an enclave of Merchant Navy personnel within a vast camp of cosmopolitan prisoners, mostly Russians, who had recently started pouring in from the latest war zone - the Russian front.

Here, Ellis and his fellow prisoners settled down to the dull routine of prison camp life. Meanwhile, conditions in the main camp were becoming singularly unpleasant. Disease was rife, and an outbreak of cholera aroused considerable alarm among prisoners and guardians alike. The vile conditions were exacerbated by the Russians themselves, who took to concealing their dead in order to continue drawing the rations of the deceased. The days ran into weeks, the weeks into months, and then winter was upon them. It was about this time that the British and Allied seamen were transferred from Sandbostel to a special camp for merchant seamen, Marlag und Milag Nord, situated on Luneburg Heath, near Helmstedt. It housed some 3,000 prisoners, amongst whom were the survivors of the crews of no less than six Harrison ships.[166] It was here that Gordon Ellis teamed up with other Harrison line colleagues, characters like Herbert Jones and Bill Ashton. The camp was well organised, due in no small part to the efforts of the prisoners themselves. More prisoners were arriving at the camp every week, and one day, early in 1942, a fresh intake, transferred from a nearby prison hospital, appeared at the gates. Ellis, together with a few equally curious companions, was there to look them over. One seasoned inmate recognised an old shipmate among the newcomers, and greeted him with delight. Ellis smiled as he listened to their animated conversation.

Captain W.E. Halloway (1880-1952), Master of the *Craftsman*, was blinded when she was shelled and sunk by the raider *Kormoran*.

"Copped it in a Russian convoy...got knocked about a bit...hospital, in Norway and Germany...good treatment - but lousy conditions in that place down the road - no facilities for convalescents...why, there's one old chap...English skipper, I think he is...blind as a bat, and stumbling about the wards - completely lost."

They moved out of earshot, but Gordon's intuition had been aroused, and he followed them quickly into the reception hut. "Excuse me," he said, "but can you tell me more about that blind skipper you were talking about?"

The newcomer was pleased to oblige, and from his description it was a pound to a pinch of salt that the old man was Captain Halloway. Ellis remembered his old Captain as he had last seen him at Cuxhaven, patiently bearing his horrific injuries, and being lifted into an ambulance, lost in a painful, blind, and frightening world.

But the old boy had lived on. Ellis felt a sense of elation, and a deep concern for his indomitable Captain's welfare. He resolved, come what may, to get in touch with Captain Halloway (for there was now no doubt in his mind that it was he) and do all he could to lighten his burden.

He began by recounting his story to the Senior British Officer, asserting his belief that Captain Halloway was in the local hospital, and in need of help. The SBO readily agreed to approach the Camp Commandant on his behalf to ask permission to visit his old skipper.

Negotiations continued for several days, but at last the all-important pass was issued to the eager Ellis. On the following day, accompanied by a fully armed escort, he marched the few kilometres down the road to the hospital with a spring in his step. They reached the gates of the hospital, and the guard on duty briefly scanned his pass. They were let in, and at the desk Ellis enquired of the whereabouts of the blind British Captain. He was led along endless corridors and up steep flights of stairs to the ward. The windows were small, and barred. In the subdued light, he at once spotted the Old Man, standing upright beside his bed, grasping the head rail. At the sound of Ellis's deliberately muted greeting his head came up. "Ellis? Second Mate? Is that you?"

"It certainly is, Captain Halloway, and am I glad to see you!" He could have bitten his tongue at the involuntary lack of tact contained in this greeting. But the lapse went unnoticed, for Captain Halloway, despite the glassy stare imparted by a pair of artificial eyes, was clearly beaming with pleasure! His hand reached out, and Ellis gripped it firmly. He winced as the Captain clasped his shoulder with his other hand, as if loath to let go. How else could he express the joy which flowed through him at the sound of a familiar English voice? At last he was in contact with someone from his old, and well-remembered world. This first meeting was all too brief for both of them. An hour passed fleetingly, and then the guard was tapping Ellis's shoulder impatiently.

"I have to go now, Captain Halloway," said Ellis, regretfully. "But," he added more cheerfully, "I'll be back; and perhaps, before very long we'll get you out of this place, and I'll take you back to "Mersey Chambers""

"Mersey Chambers?", queried the Old Man. "Yes! At least, that's what we call that section of the camp inhabited by Harrison people. (Mersey Chambers was the building in Liverpool in which both Thos. and Jas. Harrison Ltd., and the Charente Steam-Ship Co. Ltd., have their head office). Oh, there's Freddie Hill, "Tiny" Hughes, Bert Creer and a dozen others, as well as the CRAFTSMAN's crowd - you would be better off there than in this place, and we'd look after you. I'll have to see what can be done".

On this hopeful note, they parted. Ellis continually pestered the camp authorities and eventually succeeded in persuading the hospital to discharge Captain Halloway and release him to the camp. Though he would never see again, the Old Man's general health was good, and he was able to walk about, so long as he took his time. Meanwhile, Ellis was determined to do all in his power to help the old boy overcome his chief disability, his blindness.

At last, one day, an army ambulance lurched through the camp gates to deliver the blind ship master to the general care of the Camp Commandant, and to the particular care of Gordon Ellis. In the ensuing months, Captain and Second Officer became close friends, each in his way dependent upon the other for the upkeep of morale; Captain Halloway for the eyes and guidance of his young and active subordinate; Ellis for the uplift which this new sense of purpose had given to his flagging spirits; and they both needed each other's companionship. Captain Halloway found he now had a trusted friend to read aloud to him, especially from the small stock of letters from home which had accumulated, the contents of which he was still largely ignorant. Fortunately, all seemed well on the home front. The house in South Liverpool had survived the blitz, and the cheerful thread of confidence which ran through the letters worked like a charm. With Ellis's help, Captain Halloway was at last able to reply in detail, brooking no amendments or grammatical turns of phrase to his forthright dictation. At the end, he appended his signature with a flourish, his hand guided to the appropriate space by the hand of his mentor.

Through the medium of the Red Cross, Ellis was able to contact that great institution for the blind, St. Dunstan's. One day, a large Red Cross parcel arrived for Captain Halloway. It contained a wealth of material designed to assist the rehabilitation of the blind, and to provide valuable guidance to those whose job it was to care for them. There was an elementary course in Braille, and an odd-looking watch with raised digits, sturdy, stubby fingers, and no protecting crystal. Ellis passed it over to the Old Man without comment. "Why, Ellis; it's a watch. And I can tell you what time it is - it's half-past three!"

Gordon would never forget how his old friend's face lit up with pleasure at this simple accomplishment. Together they studied the notes on Braille, and both became quite proficient in a comparatively short space of time. The days, which hitherto had dragged by so leadenly, now seemed to sail by on wings, as they do for all who seek to occupy themselves in worthwhile pursuits.

It could not last, however, and it eventually became clear that a separation was inevitable. Captain Halloway faced a succession of medical commissions and at first convinced them that his health was good and that he was coping well with his disability. He had no wish to be separated from his friends to be sent to an institution. But a day came when the medical commission came to the conclusion that a prison camp was no place for a blind person. The representative of the Protecting Power agreed, and it was ordained that Captain Ernest Halloway would have to leave the camp. No; Herr Ellis could not accompany him; there was an even chance that he might be repatriated in the next exchange of invalid prisoners-of-war. Captain Halloway felt little elation at this news, but when he recounted the outcome of the interview to his closest friend, Ellis was enthusiastic. He would miss the old boy, of course. But repatriation! That was marvellous - the dream of every prisoner-of-war! He persuaded his old friend that this was the best possible solution, and that they should plug it for all it was worth.

4. *The parting*

Thus it came about that after being some eighteen months in the camp, Captain Halloway's marching orders came through. There was no ambulance to take him to the station, just a motor-cycle combination. Captain Halloway somehow inserted his large frame into the inadequate sidecar; the rider kicked the starter, and away they went with a roar, in a cloud of dust and exhaust fumes. Ellis stood at the gate and watched him go.

Their hopes and aspirations were fully realised, for on 26th October 1943, Captain Halloway, along with several hundred other disabled prisoners-of-war, disembarked from the hospital ship ATLANTIS at his home port of Liverpool, and was there re-united with his family.

After the war, Gordon Ellis was a frequent visitor at the house in Aigburth Road where Captain Halloway lived with his wife, Mary. Many times she must have had to bear the re-telling of their mutual experiences during the difficult days of their captivity. And doubtless she bore it all with a woman's patience, and a secret smile, thankful that her man, though sorely wounded in body, was quite undaunted in spirit.

The years passed: Ellis got his own command, and the family moved to an outer district. The visits to Aigburth Road became less frequent, though a lively exchange of letters and cards continued. However, on 9th December 1962, Captain Halloway died at the age of 82.

Captain Ellis, who was at sea, regretted that he was unable to attend his old friend's funeral, and wrote a brief letter of condolence to Mary. That, he thought, sadly, was that - the end of a life; the end of an era. Except for the annual exchange of Christmas cards, the connection lapsed...that is, until today...

The promised letter duly arrived one morning. Gordon picked it up, noted the heavy-weight manila envelope; the first-class stamp post-marked Liverpool; the firm's title embossed on the flap; his name and address clearly delineated by a very superior typewriter. He slit the envelope carefully, and withdrew the expensively-headed sheet of notepaper.

"Dear Sir

...instructed to inform you ...under the terms of the last will and testament of the late Mrs. Mary Halloway, relict of the late Captain W.E. Halloway...the sum of £500...our cheque is enclosed...please sign and return the receipt... We remain, your obedient servants ..."

Gordon studied the letter and the cheque in silence. He was deeply touched. The Old Man's wife had remembered him, after twenty years! She had remembered his attempts to bring hope and succour to her husband at the time of his greatest need, and this was her way of saying, "We remember; thank you". It seemed to him likely that the couple had discussed the bequest in the closing weeks of old Halloway's lifetime: "Use it while you need it, dear, and later if you can see your way, don't forget Ellis". Gordon shook his head, profoundly moved by this unexpected gesture. Had he been in the habit of quoting the poets, he might have recalled the words of T.S. Eliot: "Friendship is more than biting time can sever..." Instead, he pulled himself together and walked slowly into the kitchen to tell his wife the whole remarkable story. Most of it she knew, of course - but not the sequel. "Hilda, my dear; do you remember the Halloways?"

236. COLLEGIAN (3) 1935-1947 Steel steamship. Three decks and six holds. Two goal-post masts.
O.N. 146693 7,886g 4,934n 11,335d. 450.4 (471.75 ol) x 58.0 x 31.27 feet. Cargo capacity: 574,200 cubic feet.
International Code: KNLT (GJPS after 1933).
Two Brown-Curtiss steam turbines by Richardsons, Westgarth and Co. Ltd., Middlesbrough, single reduction geared to a single screw, 14 knots.

Captain William Rowberry (1882-1954), Master of *Collegian* when shelled by *U 32*.

Collegian.   *[Zwaenepoel collection, World Ship Photo Library]*

18.8.1922: Launched by Furness Shipbuilding Co. Ltd., Haverton Hill-on-Tees (Yard No. 34) as NATALIANA. *1.1923:* Completed for Furness, Withy and Co. Ltd., London as LONDON COMMERCE. *5.1928:* Following a refit at Cobh employed on the services of Prince Line Ltd. Renamed ROYAL PRINCE. *1931:* Declared unsuitable for the Far East trade and sent to lay up in the River Blackwater off Tollesbury. *28.5.1935:* Acquired by the company for £44,118 and renamed COLLEGIAN. *22.9.1940:* Attacked by the German submarine U 32 in the North Atlantic in position 55.14N, 16.40W, about 320 miles west of Malin Head.[167] The first attack with torpedoes failed and the submarine surfaced

and renewed the attack with its deck gun, hitting COLLEGIAN three times without casualty. She returned fire and turned away, sending out distress signals. After two hours a patrolling aircraft was spotted and the submarine broke off the action and submerged. COLLEGIAN, under the command of Captain William Rowberry, was homeward bound from New Orleans with a cargo that included 800 tons of explosive. *12.1947:* Sold to British Iron and Steel Corporation for demolition and allocated to T. W. Ward Ltd. *1.1.1948:* Arrived at Milford Haven in tow. *5.1.1948:* Demolition commenced.

237. STATESMAN (4) 1935-1941 Steel steamship. Three decks and six holds. Two goal-post masts.
O.N. 147474 7,939g 4,947n 11,292d 450.4 (468.0 ol) x 58.0 x 31.27 feet. Cargo capacity: 561,390 cubic feet.
International Code KNVJ (GJQD after 1933).
Two Brown-Curtiss steam turbines by Richardsons, Westgarth and Co. Ltd., Middlesbrough, single reduction geared to a single screw; 14 knots.

21.12.1921: Launched by Furness Shipbuilding Co. Ltd., Haverton Hill-on-Tees (Yard No. 20) as AUSTRALIANA. *8.1923:* Completed for the Norfolk and North American Steam Ship Co. Ltd. (Furness, Withy and Co. Ltd., managers), London as LONDON SHIPPER. *14.1.1924:* When inward bound for Antwerp in the River Scheldt in collision with the Yugoslav steamer IZABRAN (4,307/12) which in turn collided with the British steamer CAMBRIAN PRINCESS (4,828/14). Damage to all three vessels was slight and confined to plates above the waterline. *12.1928:* Transferred to the services of Prince Line Ltd. Renamed BRITISH PRINCE. *1930:* Laid up in the River Blackwater off Tollesbury and remained there for almost five years. *15.2.1935:* The vessel was borrowed by the company at the instigation of the Chairman of Furness, Withy who was anxious to sell her and her sisters. Harrisons were asked to

take out the insurance for a voyage to South Africa. The voyage got off to an inauspicious start as on 4.3.1935 she collided with the Thames barge GWYNHELEN off Woolwich. The barge sank quickly but the crew were rescued. *23.5.1935:* Acquired by the company for £42,985 and renamed STATESMAN. *29.1.1937:* Suffered a serious fire in the cotton cargo in number 3 hold whilst berthed in Hornby Dock, Liverpool. The fire was only extinguished by flooding the hold and 1,200 bales of cotton were damaged or destroyed. *17.5.1941:* Bombed and sunk by German aircraft in position 56.44N, 13.45W, 232 miles, 290 degrees from Inishtrahull. Second Officer George Dewar was killed and the survivors were picked up from the lifeboats 12 hours later. She was on passage from New Orleans for Belfast and Liverpool with general cargo.

Statesman.

[Zwaenepoel collection, World Ship Photo Library]

Air strike, Atlantic[168]

At dawn on 17th May 1941, the STATESMAN, inward bound and sailing independently from New Orleans, was sighted by a Focke-Wulf Condor aircraft as she was entering the Northwest Approaches. The weather, was overcast with good visibility; wind west, force 3, with a moderate sea and heavy swell. The wheelhouse clock showed 06.20 as the lookouts spotted the 'plane on the starboard bow, sweeping in low to press home its initial attack. The gunners, already at their dawn stations, opened fire, as the aircraft, from an altitude of no more than 200 feet, released a single bomb. The crew watched, fascinated, as the bomb skipped towards them, bouncing over the waves like some lethal missile in a deadly game of ducks-and-drakes. The bomb struck the ship's starboard side in way of number 2 hold below the waterline. There was a dull explosion, and the ship's cargo of wood pulp spilled out into the sea. Then, as the plane swooped over the ship, the decks and bridge areas were raked with cannon and machine-gun fire.

STATESMAN retaliated as best she could with her 12-pounder and a pair of Hotchkiss machine guns mounted in the bridge-wings, but two Lewis guns jammed at the first burst. Her scant firepower proved inadequate, and STATESMAN endured two or three further attacks, suffering a further hit in the engine room. In the final attack, Second Officer George Dewar, still blazing away with the port Hotchkiss, was killed outright by machine gun fire.

The ship by this time was listing heavily to starboard, and 30 minutes after the attack began Captain

McCallum gave the order to abandon ship. With some difficulty the two port boats were lowered; 50 survivors clambered into them, and pulled clear of the sinking ship. Seeing the boats pulling away, the pilot of the Focke-Wulf made no further attacks, and flew off in a northeasterly direction.

Before taking to the boats, Radio Officer G. Cowin had managed to transmit an S.O.S. message, giving the ship's position. Some 200 miles east-south-east, Convoy OG 62 was in the vicinity of Tory Island when the signal was picked up. The Escort Commander in HMS BOADICEA responded by detaching the Canadian corvette HEPATICA with orders to search for survivors.

The message was also picked up by the outward bound Blue Star liner, TROJAN STAR (9,037/16), and she, too, proceeded with all speed towards the scene of the bomb attack.

Meanwhile, the STATESMAN's crew, adrift in their lifeboats continued to stand by their stricken ship. Shortly after the German plane's departure, an RAF Whitley reconnaissance plane flew overhead. As the survivors waved and cheered the pilot signalled that help was on its way. Greatly encouraged, the men hoped their ordeal would soon be over, and continued to sit tight. At 08.45 STATESMAN sank, and her crew watched grimly as the grey waters of the Atlantic closed over her, the disturbance of her going soon lost amid the restless waves.

The long day passed slowly, but at 17.00 TROJAN STAR hove in sight to revive flagging spirits like magic. She took on board all the survivors, and was then advised by a patrolling aircraft to remain in company with a passing tug towing a disabled merchantman under the protection of an escorting anti-submarine trawler, ST. APOLLO, until the arrival of a rescue ship. However, it was 21.00 before HEPATICA came up with the little flotilla. Arrangements were made to take off the survivors and convey them to Londonderry. This task, undertaken without a hitch in heavy swell conditions, was completed by 23.15. Then HEPATICA turned eastwards for Lough Foyle, while TROJAN STAR headed westwards to resume her interrupted voyage. At 16.00 on 18th May, HEPATICA entered Lough Foyle, and three hours later STATESMAN's survivors were disembarked at Londonderry. There, they were received "with the utmost kindness and appreciation", but nevertheless contemplating with great sadness the absence of their fallen shipmate, the gallant George Dewar.

238. POLITICIAN (2) 1935-1941 Steel steamship. Three decks and six holds. Two goal-post masts.
O.N. 147482 7,940g 5,032n 11,155d 450.4 (471.75 ol) x 58.1 x 31.27 feet. Cargo capacity: 559,250 cubic feet.
International Code: KPBH (GJQN after 1933).
Two Brown-Curtiss steam turbines by John Brown and Co. Ltd., Clydebank, single reduction geared to a single screw, 14 knots.

1923: Launched by Furness Shipbuilding Co.Ltd., Haverton Hill-on-Tees (Yard No. 19) as CANADIANA. *5.1923:* Completed for Neptune Steam Navigation Co. Ltd. (Furness, Withy and Co. Ltd., managers), London as LONDON MERCHANT. *1930:* Laid up in the River Blackwater off Tollesbury and remained there for almost five years.

28.5.1935: Acquired by the company for £45,355 and renamed POLITICIAN. *5.2.1941:* Struck rocks off Roshinish Point, on the island of Eriskay in the Hebrides, when on passage from Liverpool to Kingston and New Orleans. Subsequently refloated and beached, and partially broken up where she lay.

The star of Harrison's most famous accident, the *Politician,* is seen twice on the Mersey; in the lower view departing for Beira on 18th April 1936.
[Both: J. and M. Clarkson]

The legendary end of the POLITICIAN

So much has been written, discussed, and dramatised about the last voyage of the Harrison steamer POLITICIAN that any further outpourings could well be deemed superfluous. Even today, more than 60 years after the ship came to grief on the rocks off Eriskay, romantic speculation as to the precise nature and purpose of her voyage and cargo, and even financial speculation on the prospects of salvaging what is left, continues unabated. In fact, today, it is more difficult than ever to discern fact from fiction, reality from fantasy. Nevertheless, the following account based on contemporary and subsequent records, sets out to do just that.

On Monday 3rd February 1941, the POLITICIAN vacated her berth in Liverpool's Alexandra Dock and anchored in the Mersey for the night at 16.40. In those days the light buoys marking the Mersey channels were kept unlit as, from the air, they would be like a beckoning finger to enemy bombers bound for the port of Liverpool. So ships used the channels only in daylight. Shortly after 09.00 on 4th, the ship weighed anchor and put to sea, bound for Kingston and New Orleans. Her cargo consisted mainly of cotton goods,

general merchandise, stores for RAF and Army detachments in the West Indies, and 22,000 cases of Scotch whisky; in all, about 2,232 tons - by no means a full ship. In 1987 there was speculation in a national newspaper as to why such a valuable ship should have been sent across the Atlantic in wartime with such a frivolous cargo, the implication being that all ships should be employed carrying guns, tanks, and ammunition to the battle fronts.[169] The answer, in these days before US Lend-Lease aid, lay in the fact that Britain being a trading nation still had to earn the cash to pay for the war effort and there were still lucrative markets for fine cottons and whisky especially in the USA. Thus it was not uncommon to find ships loading export commercial cargoes from time to time.

The weather during the first twelve hours was fine enough, but after midnight the glass began falling rapidly heralding the approach of a depression. By 06.00 on Wednesday 5th it was blowing a full gale from the south, and the horizon was obscured by a curtain of heavy rain. The ship had been routed independently, without benefit of convoy, through the Minches, and at about 07.40 land was sighted where no land should have been, looming through the rain and darkness, 5 or 6 points in the starboard bow. It was obviously close-to, and the Chief Officer, Mr. R.A. Swain, ordered, "Hard-a-port", away, so he thought, from the menacing land. He also put the engine room telegraph lever to "Full astern", but, being a turbine-driven vessel, it is unlikely that the order would have been translated into action before the ship struck the rocks a few minutes later at 07.45.[170]

Due probably to a substantial trim by the stern, the forward section cleared the outcrop of rock, transferring the initial impact to a point somewhere abaft number 3 hold, tearing up the bottom plating from under the stokehold, engine room, number 4 and number 5 holds. The tank tops were also ruptured, and these compartments began flooding immediately. Soon, the engine room was untenable, and at 08.05, for the last time in POLITICIAN, Chief Engineer Ernie Mossman, rang "finished with engines", and ordered his men on deck. It was still blowing a gale, and at about this time both anchors were dropped on the sea bed to hold the fore part, which was still afloat, as steady as possible.

It is not possible today to determine what caused the grounding. There is evidence that POLITICIAN ran into a southbound convoy in the North Channel on the Tuesday night, demanding a number of violent helm actions to keep out of trouble. Perhaps this circumstance, coupled with a strong westerly set, was sufficient to force the ship west of her projected course, and in the prevailing weather conditions the lookouts failed to see either dimmed Skerryvore Light, or Barra Head. Be that as it may, when Chief Officer Swain did sight land close to, and broad on the starboard bow - it was probably the islet of Hartamul, or the hills above Ru Melvich on South Uist - his first instinct was to haul the ship away, to port. Sadly, his decision brought the ship, which had miraculously avoided the concealed rocks south and east of Eriskay, into the shoaling waters of Eriskay Sound, and inevitable disaster.

At 10.30 number 4 lifeboat was lowered with 26 men on board, but once it cleared the lee of the ship and encountered the full force of the gale it became virtually unmanageable, and was eventually washed ashore amid the boiling surf at the foot of the cliffs of Rudha Dubh, across the Sound on South Uist. To the tense watchers it seemed as though nothing could survive in that cauldron, but, miraculously, although the boat was smashed, the men survived, and remained huddled together for several hours before the Eriskay ferry was able to reach them, and return them to the comparative safety of the stranded ship.[171] At 16.45 the Barra Lifeboat arrived on the scene, and lifted the entire crew of 50 to Castlebay.

That night the weather moderated, and it is not unreasonable to suppose that some inquisitive local fishermen took the opportunity to take a look around the deserted ship so providentially dumped on their shores. It was inevitable that they would soon discover the cases of whisky - and the word spread like wildfire. With local stocks limited by wartime conditions to a few bottles a month, it was like manna from heaven! Indeed, encouraged by the local clergy, the Islanders were convinced that this windfall was a "gift from God", and had no qualms about taking as much as their small boats could carry in as many trips as they could accomplish during the hours of darkness. These forays were the first of many undertaken after dark when, for safety reasons, the cold, dead ship was deserted.

By Thursday morning the weather had moderated considerably, and the Barra Lifeboat set out from Castlebay carrying part of the crew back to the ship. The men loaded all

the personal baggage they could find into two of the remaining lifeboats, and returned with them to Castlebay, towed by the Barra lifeboat. Strong south easterly winds prevented any boatwork on the Friday morning, but during the afternoon the weather moderated sufficiently for a boarding party to check over the wreck. They found the forward holds still sound, but in numbers 4 and 5 holds and the engine room the water level was rising and falling with the tide. That afternoon the crew transferred by boat to Lochboisdale, on South Uist.

On Saturday 8th February, the Liverpool and Glasgow Salvage Association's tender RANGER arrived at Lochboisdale, and the POLITICIAN was boarded by a party of salvage experts led by a Commander Kay. Over the next three days further brief visits were made until a series of south easterly gales put a stop to further boatwork, and it was not until Saturday 15th February that divers were able to make an extensive survey of the hull. Next day, a steam pipe was led from RANGER and connected to serve POLITICIAN's winches. Mails and special items of cargo were off-loaded into the tender before she returned to base at dusk.[172]

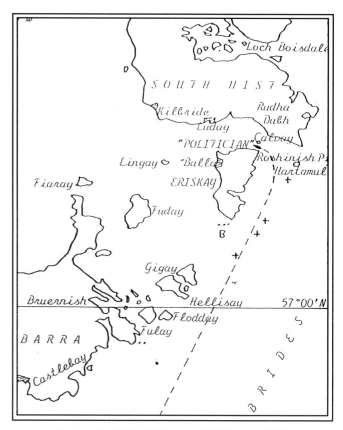

The last landfall of *Politician*, 5th February 1941

On Tuesday 18th February, the coaster CORTEEN (530/20) laid herself alongside number 2 hatch and began loading salvaged cargo during an operation which lasted over four days. On 22nd the coaster sailed for Glasgow fully loaded. Meanwhile, the salvors, having made their assessment, advised the owners that saving the ship was not a practical proposition. They intended to lift as much cargo as they could reach without diving, then withdraw from the case. As a result of this advice, Harrisons, on 24th February 1941, gave notice of abandonment of the vessel to the underwriters. The salvage of accessible cargo was finally completed on 12th March, when the Liverpool and Glasgow Salvage Association abandoned the project.

During this period, and beyond, the local populace, reinforced by raiding parties from Barra, Uist, and even Skye and Mull, continued their clandestine depredations, and succeeded in amassing large quantities of whisky which were either smuggled away, or cached in various parts of the island, to the frustrated annoyance of the authorities. Customs and Excise Officers in Portree and Glasgow huffed and puffed from behind their desks but did little to assist the harassed local Customs Officer, Charlie McColl, in the almost impossible task of nightly surveillance of the wreck. Nevertheless, despite the bitterness aroused by the alienation of lifelong friends, Charlie McColl resolutely did his duty. Aided by the constable from Lochboisdale he succeeded in arresting 36 islanders with their dubious salvage. Most were fined, but at least 16 received prison sentences ranging from four to six weeks. The local Home Guard was at one time called in to mount guard over the harbour, but the troopers, wholly recruited from Eriskay families, studiously looked the other way, while their Commanding Officer was, on occasion and with regret, put under "polite restraint" by the islanders. An official decision taken in October 1941 to blow up the remaining whisky cargo incensed the islanders, who universally condemned it as an act of vandalism. In the event the explosion was botched, only a few hundred bottles perishing.

In April 1941, the Salvage Association of London came to an arrangement with the British Iron and Steel Corporation (Salvage) Ltd. of Glasgow to carry out a second, sustained salvage operation, to recover as much cargo as possible, and perhaps even to refloat the vessel. In May the salvage vessel ASSISTANCE and a small fleet of coaster and lighters arrived at Lochboisdale. During the months which followed a great deal more cargo was lifted and forwarded to Glasgow, and on 20th September the salvors actually succeeded in refloating the POLITICIAN.

As the old ship lumbered clear of her rocky bed, she heeled alarmingly, manifesting an almost critical lack of stability. Nevertheless, she was taken in tow by the naval tug MARAUDER with the intent of seeking the sheltered waters of Loch Boisdale where the salvors could finish off their work, and prepare the ship for transport to a drydock on the Clyde. Unfortunately, the towing operation had scarcely begun when a radio message was received from the Admiralty ordering the tug to proceed with all speed to a ship in distress. The inert but so recently re-floated POLITICIAN was hurriedly beached on a sandy shore on the north side of the Sound, not far from her original position. MARAUDER then cast off and hastened away on her errand of mercy.[173]

It was a bitter moment for the salvage men, for they knew it might be weeks before the services of another tug could be obtained. Further inspections were carried out, and the surveyors became ever more concerned as they listed the toll of damage:

Bottom plates ripped open from engine-room bulkhead to stern frame;

Stern frame and rudder wrenched off;

Tail shaft, propeller, and stern tube resting on the sea bed.

One surveyor estimated that repairs would require four months in dry-dock, and cost about £100,000.[174]

But it was not to be. A series of gales from the southeast on 8th, 9th, and 10th November caused further damage which put paid to any faint hopes they might have had, and the ship was scuttled where she lay by flooding the forward holds which hitherto had remained intact. The ship was then abandoned until the spring of 1942 brought better weather.

The winter gales had taken their toll, however, and the ship was found with her back broken. The ship was separated into two halves, the forward section being towed to Kames Bay, Isle of Bute, and beached near Port Bannatyne, to be demolished by the Glasgow shipbreakers, W.H. Arnott Young and Co. The remains of the sunken after section were stripped of scrap metal where she lay, and were pared to the water line before the salvors finally abandoned the project in July 1944.

During the war the episode was not reported to the public, and the manifold rumours were confined to the highlands and islands of Western Scotland. At his home in neighbouring Barra the author Compton Mackenzie would have been fully briefed by his many friends, and very likely benefitted from the illicit haul. He acknowledged that his novel "Whisky Galore"[175] published in 1947 was based on the POLITICIAN incident, but in his book the ship was promoted to CABINET MINISTER, and the wreck took place on the fictitious island of Todday. The whimsical and hilarious events in the book, though freely elaborated, reflect incidents which actually happened. The book was followed by a film in 1948, and the two together elevated the tale from the level of local folklore to a national legend.

The year 1963 saw the publication of Arthur Swinson's "Scotch on the Rocks", claiming to be the "True Story of the 'Whisky Galore Ship'.[176] This book, however, written in journalistic and documentary style, lacks the magic of Mackenzie's prose, and the attempt at objective reporting is frequently marred by speculation and innuendo.

On Boxing Day 1982, BBC Scottish Television broadcast a competent documentary "A Drop in the Ocean", produced by Neil Fraser, an islander related to the hard-pressed Customs Officer Charlie McColl. Its interest lies in the recorded interviews with some of the surviving islanders who took part in the plundering of the ship, though some allowance must be made for a natural desire to elaborate for the benefit of the cameras, and the effect on waning memories of the lapse of some 40 years.

Five years later, in August 1987, the "Mail on Sunday" ran a series of articles on the POLITICIAN episode. The whole story was rehashed in the best popular Sunday paper manner, with a wealth of conjecture. A Mail-sponsored dive on the wreck recovered a few bottles of Scotch, but enthusiastic assertions about how it "rolled smooth and peaty over the tongue" must be taken with a pinch of salt, for how many corks, caps or stoppers would defy 40 years' immersion in salt water? Nevertheless, eight bottles auctioned at Christie's in Edinburgh on 11th November 1987 raised £4,020 - more, perhaps for their historic value than for their appeal to a discerning palate.

However, the newspaper's main, "exclusive" story was the disclosure that whisky was not the only desireable commodity in the POLITICIAN's cargo.[177] The ship was also carrying freshly minted Jamaican banknotes in large quantities. Certainly, the manifest includes an item under Bill of Lading No 61:

Eight cases currency notes Nos. 16/23
Marks: OHMS CA 1717/1
Commissioners of Currency, Kingston, Jamaica:
Measurement: 29 feet 4 inches

Shipped at Liverpool on behalf of the Crown Agents for the Colonies, by Greenshields, Cowie and Co. Ltd.

The measurement, of course, refers to the total cubic measurement of the consignment. It does not infer that each case measured 29 feet by 4 feet, as interpreted by the "Mail" reporter. Moreover, allegations that certain unnamed islanders had suddenly come into a fortune or acquired new boats were not backed by anything resembling firm evidence, and gloss over the practical difficulties of disposing of thousands of Jamaican banknotes. In any case, most of the cases were recovered by the salvors.[178]

In 1988 a public house was built on Eriskay by Allan MacDonald, a BBC producer. Aptly named "Am Politician", it was opened on 4th February 1988 amid much publicity. Barry McIlvean, Harrisons' Group Marketing Manager, who attended the opening ceremony at the invitation of Allan MacDonald, was moved to explain :

A 1904 photograph of *Politician's* master at the time of her stranding, Captain B. Worthington.

[Mowll and Morrison]

"A shipwreck hardly seems ideal publicity, and indeed the press were somewhat bemused by our willingness to assist with the project, but we took the view that, having involuntarily helped to put Eriskay on the map, we were inevitably involved and we did not believe that potential customers would draw any parallel between the fate of the POLITICIAN that stormy night in wartime conditions and our present-day services. It was not the wreck itself which made the POLITICIAN famous, but the nature of her cargo, and subsequent events."[179]

So far as the principal witnesses to the standing of the POLITICIAN were concerned, no stigma of blame was ever attached to them. They continued to serve the company with distinction, and Captain Worthington was subsequently appointed to command the ill-fated ARICA (252), after which he retired in 1943 at the age of 65. In due course Chief Officer Richard Swain was promoted to the rank of Master, and was given command of the CUSTODIAN (220) in October 1941. He retired in 1953. One factor still rankles, however. Most allegedly sensitive Government papers are released to the public after 30 years. According to certain press reports, this discretionary period has been extended to 75 years in the case of certain documents relating to the POLITICIAN. What can be the reason for such a drastic extension of the 30-year rule? This means that the full story of POLITICIAN's voyage, her cargo, and subsequent stranding and salvage attempts will not be known until the year 2016, by which time a fascinating legend may well have become an epic saga.

239. INVENTOR (3) 1935-1960 Steel steamship. Two decks, five holds and deep tank. Two masts. O.N. 164267 6,210g 3,840n 9,294d 437.9 (454.5 o.l.) x 56.0 x 32.2 feet. Cargo capacity: 495,490 cubic feet. International Code: GYMJ.
T. 3-cyl. by D. and W. Henderson and Co. Ltd., Glasgow; 28, 46, 81 x 54 inches, 13 knots.

3.7.1935: Launched by D. and W. Henderson and Co. Ltd., Glasgow (Yard No. 953) for the company. *9.9.1935:* Delivered at a cost of £109,083 and later sailed from Liverpool to South Africa on her maiden voyage under Captain O. Bostock. *3.6.1938:* In collision with the Estonian steamer MARET (3,025/10) in Gravesend Reach. *26.3.1943:* Attacked by torpedo-bombers off North Africa. *8.3.1947:* Struck by the Panamanian motor tanker OHIO (10,191/39) while berthed at number 289 Havendok, Antwerp. She sustained damage midships that cost B.Fr.8,000 to repair. *17.3.1947:* Broke adrift from the same berth, uprooting the mooring posts during a violent squall. Drifted across the dock and caused further superficial damage to OHIO which had broken adrift earlier and was anchored off the berth. *25.5.1957:* Sailed from Birkenhead on the company's final scheduled sailing to Calcutta with 7,485 tons of cargo (see below). *22.8.1960:* Sold to Etablissements Van Heyghen Frères S.A., Belgium for £55,000 for demolition. *29.8.1960:* Arrived at Ghent. *12.9.1960:* Demolition commenced.

Captain Oscar Bostock (1880-1947), *Inventor's* first Master.

Thames encounter

Inward bound from Bombay to London, INVENTOR was approaching Gravesend Reach shortly after midnight on 3rd June 1938. She slowed down, and eventually stopped engines, expecting to change pilots, and await the customary visit of Port Health and Customs officials. Fine on her port bow was the stern light of another vessel apparently going the same way. INVENTOR was still making about four knots through the water, and it was only when the stern light was a mere 300 feet away that those on INVENTOR's bridge realised that the strange ship was lying athwart the river. Simultaneously, three short blasts on her whistle warned them that her engines were going astern.[180]

Collision was imminent, and although INVENTOR used both helm and engines in a desperate effort to avoid contact, it was too late. The stranger's stern cannoned into INVENTOR's port side, just forward of the bridge, almost at right angles, causing massive damage to both vessels.

The stranger turned out to be an Estonian steamer, the MARET (3,025/10) bound from Archangel to London with a cargo of timber. She, too, had been overhauling another vessel, so slowed down and stopped. As she lost steerage way her head fell off to starboard, and to correct it the Pilot ordered port helm. At the wheel was a 15-year old boy who did not speak English. The outcome was that he overcompensated for the sheer, and sent the ship's head swinging rapidly to port, heading straight for the BLAIRATHOLL (3,319/25), a ship berthed at the Lower Moorings Buoys. The Pilot issued a stream of orders, but the Mate (who had been translating for the helmsman,) had been sent forward some minutes earlier to stand by, and the orders fell on untutored ears. The BLAIRATHOLL was looming

closer, and in desperation the Pilot ordered the Mate to let go the anchors, and rang full astern on the engines. These rapid manoeuvres, coupled with the action of the flood tide and a west south west breeze, caused the MARET to swing athwart the river, gathering sternway with every turn of the screw, right into the path of the INVENTOR whose navigation lights the Pilot could now see, coming up the Reach. By this time, everyone was powerless to avert the inevitable.

The case for claims and counter claims was heard in the Admiralty Division of the High Court before Sir Boyd Merriman and two assessors on 27/31 October 1938.[181] In his judgment, his Lordship attributed blame to both vessels, but not equally. The MARET, he found, was guilty of faulty seamanship, faulty signalling, and failing to keep a good lookout. INVENTOR, according to the Judge, showed a lack of caution in attempting to pass too close to a vessel she assumed she was overtaking, and failed to keep a good lookout in that those on board failed to appreciate that MARET was angled across the river. This latter point was underlined by the evidence of the skipper of a London County Council sludge vessel which was coming up astern of INVENTOR. He asserted that he had grasped the situation while still three cables distant, and acted accordingly.

The Judge consequently apportioned three-fifths of the blame to MARET, two-fifths to INVENTOR, and costs in similar proportions.

The long arm of the law

It was a simple, open-and-shut case of absence without leave. Fireman Gerard Mogan had felt the need for a day off, and took it, without permission, on Thursday 1st October 1942 whilst INVENTOR lay in dock at Southampton after a long and arduous voyage on Government charter. Mogan turned to next day, full of remorse, and prepared to take his punishment. In due course, he was summoned before the Master, Captain G.R. Windsor, who gave him a pithy lecture on reliability and attention to duty, before asking the culprit if he had anything to day. "Nothing to say, Sir", replied the contrite Mogan, and awaited his sentence.

Perhaps his apologetic demeanour mollified the Captain, who waived the fine, but ordained that he forfeit one day's pay, the sum of 7s. 5d. (about 37p.), and give an undertaking not to transgress again. The entire process was faithfully recorded in the log, and there, so far as Master and fireman were concerned, the matter ended, a fairly trivial but typical disciplinary procedure competently dealt with under Section 159 of the Merchant Shipping Act, 1894.

However, unknown to either party, the matter was far from over. Somehow, word of the incident reached the ears of a Ministry of War Transport official, probably when the log book was examined by the Superintendent of the Shipping Office a few days later when the crew paid off in Liverpool. The official, whose name was Roger Lewis, held the strict opinion that in wartime such cases could not be glossed over by mere forfeit of a day's pay, and should be dealt with in court, as a lesson to other potential absentees.

Mr. Lewis thereupon "laid an information" against Mogan before Liverpool City Magistrates on the grounds that the defaulter had committed a grave offence under Regulation 47A of the Defence (General) Regulations, 1939. Consequently, some weeks later, Mr. Mogan was astonished and not a little disturbed to be issued with a summons to appear before the

Magistrates to face the charge. Captain Windsor was equally astonished when required to attend as a witness.

However, Mogan's counsel submitted that his client's offence had already been properly dealt with by the Master of the ship, and that he had been punished by forfeiting a day's pay. He therefore could not, under English law, be punished again for the same offence. Counsel put it to the Magistrates that this was a case of "autrefois convict", a plea which they accepted, and promptly dismissed the case.

The persistent Mr. Lewis, however, was not to be thwarted, and appealed to the High Court against the Magistrates' decision.[182] The appeal was heard on 6th April 1943 before Mr. Justice Charles and Mr. Justice Stable, who upheld the appeal. They ordered the case to be referred back to Liverpool Magistrates, with a stern directive to hear the evidence and determine the case as it was presented, on the grounds that, (a) Action taken under the Merchant Shipping Acts was not a judicial action, but simply a domestic arrangement between Master and man in a form duly approved by the Board of Trade. (b) Although Section 44(5) of the Merchant Shipping Act, 1906 states that a seaman fined for an offence "shall not be otherwise punished under the Merchant Shipping Acts", it did not mean that he could not be charged under another instrument of the law. The appellant's case had been brought under the Defence (General) Regulations, 1939. (c) The plea of "autrefois convict" could not therefore apply, and should have been rejected.

So Mr. Mogan's transgression went back to the Liverpool Magistrate's Court for trial. Unfortunately, the outcome of this second hearing is not known, but the point made painfully clear to merchant seamen of all ranks was that they would have to abide by a new set of rules, if they wished to steer clear of the law - at least while hostilities continued.

Inventor on trials on the Clyde.

[W. Ralston]

Inventor was photographed by the US Coast Guard on 24th September 1942.

[Ian Farquhar collection]

Last voyages to Calcutta

On 25th May 1957 INVENTOR sailed from Birkenhead on the company's final scheduled sailing to Calcutta. This had been a traditional Harrison Line service which had found its origins in sailing ship days from 1865 onwards, and achieved formal recognition with the founding of the Calcutta Conference in 1875. She arrived on 17th July and sailed on 23rd August, but this was not in fact the final sailing from Calcutta, that distinction being reserved for TRIBESMAN (268) which sailed from there 19th September 1957. The trade and goodwill, nurtured by Harrisons over so many years, was henceforth transferred to Thos. and Jno. Brocklebank Ltd. The change was prompted by management's growing disillusion with the Calcutta trade as turn-round was extremely slow and ships were averaging less than two voyages a year, occupying cargo space that could be better employed on other routes.

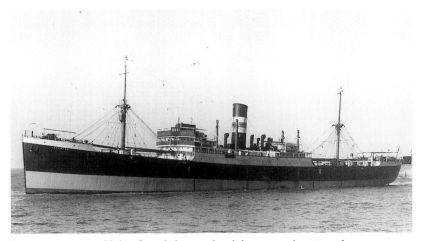

Inventor postwar, with her funnel shortened and the top at a jaunty angle.

[J. and M. Clarkson]

240. INKOSI (2) 1937-1940/EMPIRE CHIVALRY 1941-1946/PLANTER (2) 1946-1958 Steel steamship. Two decks and four holds. Two masts.
O.N. 164323 6,618g 4,055 6,940d 414.8 (430.0 o.1.) x 56.0 x 31.23 feet. Cargo capacity: 299,900 cubic feet. Berths for 82 passengers.
1941: 6,007g 3,616n 7,504d Cargo capacity: 395,570 cubic feet.
International Code: GZSS.
Q. 4-cyl. by Wallsend Slipway and Engineering Co.Ltd., Wallsend; 28, 41½, 59, 84 x 54 inches, 15 knots.

Captain John T. Ling OBE (1880-1964), first Master of *Inkosi.*

25.2.1937: Launched by Swan, Hunter and Wigham Richardson Ltd., Wallsend (Yard No. 1525) for the company. *3.6.1937:* Delivered at an approximate cost of £200,000 and later sailed from London to the West Indies on her maiden voyage under Captain J.T. Ling. *1.6.1940:* Sailed from London on her final voyage in the West Indies passenger service. *7.8.1940:* On her return requisitioned by the Admiralty for service as an Ocean Boarding Vessel. *7.9.1940:* Whilst fitting out at D Shed, Royal Albert Dock, London, bombed and damaged by German aircraft. Two bombs burst in the engine room, and, although they did not rupture the hull, the after bulkhead and ship's engines suffered severe damage. Another bomb penetrated the poop deck, ripping open the after peak bulkhead, the tunnel recess and the ship's side under the quarter below the waterline. Consequently water flooded forward into number 4 hold and into the engine room via the shaft tunnel then back through the torn bulkhead into number 3 hold. Efforts to close the tunnel watertight door using the remote controls proved impossible owing to distortions caused by the blast. *15.9.1940:* A naval salvage and diving team commenced work plugging leaks, sealing and shoring ruptured bulkheads and installing pumps to eliminate the flood water. Her stern

was resting on the mud in 32 feet of water, while her bow still floated at a draught of 14 feet. The engine was devastated. *8.10.1940:* Declared ready for docking. *14.10.1940:* Entered graving dock and formally taken over by the Ministry of War Transport. The refit was undertaken by R.H. Green and Silley Weir Ltd., and included the removal of passenger accommodation, decks and fittings. *27.12.1941:* Registered in the ownership of the Ministry of War Transport, London (Thos. and Jas. Harrison Ltd., Liverpool, managers) as EMPIRE CHIVALRY, under Captain A.H. Frew. *27.12.1941:* Sailed from Tilbury for Antigua. *26.4.1946:* Reacquired by the company for £61,753, registered at Liverpool and renamed PLANTER. *6.2.1954:* When outward bound from London for the West Indies, rounding Blackwall Point with tugs SUN XVI (233/46) and SUN III (197/09) on the port and starboard bow respectively, encountered the collier BRIXTON (1,635/46) inward bound from the Tyne. PLANTER overran the bend and the tow ropes on both tugs parted. With tide on her bow she took a sheer and fell into the path of BRIXTON. The SUN XVI, in grave danger of being crushed between the two ships took avoiding action and collided with SUN III, inflicting damage on both. Meanwhile PLANTER and BRIXTON collided and both were seriously damaged. BRIXTON was beached on Blackwall Point and 9.2.1954 was refloated. PLANTER returned to South West India Dock. Subsequently on 2.8.1955 in the Admiralty Division of the High Court, PLANTER was found wholly to blame for attempting to round Blackwall Point at too great a speed and sheering out of control into BRIXTON's water.[183] *24.9.1958:* Sold to Etablissements Van Heyghen Frères S.A., Belgium for £42,000 and towed to Ghent by the tug SEAMAN (369/24) for demolition.

Inkosi seen above on the Thames, and right after being rebuilt without passenger accommodation as *Empire Chivalry*, a photograph taken by the US Coast Guard on 27th March 1944. *[Right: Eric Johnson collection]*

196

Planter in post-war condition, having lost the topmasts she carried as *Empire Chivalry*.

241. TRIBESMAN (1) 1937-1940 Steel steamship. Two decks, five holds and deep tank. Two masts.
O.N. 164341 6,242g 3,777n 9,310d 437.3 (452.2 o.l.) x 56.0 x 32.18 feet. Cargo capacity: 500,577 cubic feet.
International Code: GCCR.
T. 3-cyl. by David Rowan and Co. Ltd., Glasgow; 28, 46, 81 x 54 inches,13 knots.

12.8.1937: Launched by Lithgows Ltd., Port Glasgow (Yard No. 900) for the company. *25.9.1937:* Delivered at an approximatecost of £180,000 and later sailed from Liverpool to the West Indies and Gulf of Mexico on her maiden voyage under Captain T.J. Lacey. *9.1939:* In Calcutta when the Second World War broke out, and fitted with a 4-inch gun, sited on the poop. *12.1940:* Intercepted, shelled and sunk by the German pocket battleship ADMIRAL SCHEER in the North Atlantic in position 15.00N, 35.00W, about 1,500 miles east of Dominica. She was on passage from Liverpool to Calcutta, via the Cape of Good Hope with general cargo. In addition to her normal complement, she was carrying 54 Lascar crew from EXPLORER (234) who were being repatriated. Despite a heavy bombardment there were apparently no casualties caused by the attack itself and three lifeboats and a jolly boat pulled away from the vessel. The crews of one lifeboat and the jolly boat were picked up by the raider, a total of 76 men. The other two boats with 59 men on board apparently made their escape in the darkness and were not seen again.

A proud *Tribesman* on trials. *[Glasgow University Archives GD320/10/1/106/1]*   *[World Ship Photo Library]*

The shoot[184]

The makeshift crew eyed the fearsome-looking weapon with suspicion; none more so than the Gunnery Officer, F.R. Hill, who, with frequent references to the handbook, was studiously attempting to drill the gun's crew into an aggressive defensive force (if that is not a contradiction in terms). The gun, a 4-inch, Japanese model of 1917 vintage, had been fitted on TRIBESMAN's poop only a week before, at Calcutta. Second Officer Hill had been given a hasty session of instruction at the naval barracks, and had emerged a somewhat bemused Gunnery Officer with instructions to carry out a practice shoot once clear of the Sandheads. The ship had sailed on 15th September 1939. Normally, a seasoned naval gunnery rating or Royal Marine was assigned to defensively equipped merchant ships, but this reassuring factor had apparently been overlooked in TRIBESMAN's case, and the inexperienced merchant seamen were left to work things out for themselves.

Game but apprehensive, sightsetters, layers, trainers and loaders took up their positions. Gingerly, the gun was loaded through the open breech block, first the four-inch shell, then the charge of cordite in its red sock. Meanwhile, the empty drum which had been dropped over the side for use as a target was fast disappearing out of sight as the gun's crew pursued its drill with great deliberation and not a little dissension. At last the piece was loaded and the breech closed with a satisfying "clunk". The Gunnery Officer called range and bearing in the approved formula, and the sight-setters fiddled with the little dials attached to the scope sights, one for the gun layer, and, on the other side, one for the trainer. Between them these gentlemen elevated the gun according to range, and trundled it round to the correct bearing, bringing the cross-wires of their scope-sights onto the target. When all was set the Gunnery Officer called "Shoot!" or perhaps, "Fire!", and the gun layer tugged at the firing lanyard.

That first salvo blasted the gun's crew's ears in spite of the plugs of cotton wool which had been inserted on the advice of the handbook. The blast shattered the docking-telegraph, and showered everyone with soot from the after-galley stove pipe. From the accommodation below, a motley crew of sailors and firemen emerged, streaming for the lifeboats, clutching little bundles of possessions, convinced the ship had been torpedoed. On the bridge, Captain T.J. Lacey peered nervously aft through his binoculars, counting heads, relieved to find they were still all there, and still attached to shoulders.

After everyone had calmed down, a second salvo was fired, whereupon the breech block was found to have jammed shut. However, a young engineer, who had fortuitously served his time in a Vickers Ordnance factory, was able to release the block. But by this time someone had noticed that the gun had developed a decided list to port, a circumstance which advised against any further shooting until the gun could be inspected by naval experts in Colombo.

The ship arrived at Colombo on 20th September, and Gunnery Officer Hill was whisked aboard a Brocklebank ship which was putting to sea that day for gunnery practice, equipped with a similar gun, but under naval supervision. All went well, but Mr. Hill noticed that the gun mountings were vastly superior to those in the TRIBESMAN. He reported this to the naval officer in charge, and invited him aboard to see for himself.

In due course the naval officer made his inspection, regarding the lop-sided gun with critical distaste. "A job for the Engineer O.C.", he remarked. The high-ranking Engineer Officer was even more critical, and his remarks on the professional capabilities of the ordnance fitters in Calcutta were both explosive and colourful. "Another round fired from the gun in this state would have sent it over the side taking half the crew with it", he stormed.

TRIBESMAN remained in Colombo for several days while the gun was properly mounted and its supports reinforced. On arrival at London, a Royal Marine, Gunner A. Austin was appointed to the ship. Twelve months later he, and the gun in his charge, were to acquit themselves well in a one-sided night action against the pocket battleship, ADMIRAL SCHEER.

Scheer terror

The attack came suddenly out of the tropical night. TRIBESMAN was bathed in brilliant light as a battery of probing searchlights turned night into day. Almost as suddenly came the thunder of gunfire and the shattering explosions of bursting shells. It was 21.00 in the evening of 1st December 1940, and the air of somnolent recreation which prevails aboard ship at that hour was savagely dissipated. The middle watchkeepers - always early to bed - tumbled out of their bunks pulling on clothes and lifejackets. Promising poker hands were discarded, and chessmen tumbled to the deck as players darted for the doors. On the bridge, Third Officer Philip Jones pulled the switch which sounded the alarm bells, adding a strident shrillness to the roar of escaping steam.

Third Radio Officer William Murray left his cabin and hastened towards the wireless room. Falling over debris, but keeping instinctively to that side of the ship which was in shadow, he reached the top of the ladder. Glancing aft, he had a fleeting glimpse of his friend, Gunner Austin, R.M., and his crew manning the 4-inch gun on the poop. Bathed in brilliant light, like a group of actors on stage reflecting flood and foot lights, they were putting up a good show. Blinded by the searchlights, unable to spot the fall of shot to establish the range, and ignorant of the nature of the target, they were, nevertheless, determined to have a go. When someone is hitting you, the instinct is to hit back, but had they known that the target was none other than the pocket battleship ADMIRAL SCHEER, capable of a broadside of six 11-inch and eight 5.9-inch guns, then perhaps even "Guns" would have been more circumspect about lobbing puny 4-inch shells in its direction.

Murray entered the wireless room where Second Radio Officer C.H. Pritchard, watched by his Chief, S.W. Lewis, was urgently tapping out the distress message: "RRR...GCCR...15N35W...", repeating it over and over again - until it was realised that the main aerial was down. Chief Lewis swiftly switched the apparatus to the emergency aerial, a move which must have alerted the enemy gunners, for Pritchard had no sooner resumed tapping than a near miss by a 5.9-inch shell demolished the little cabin and smashed most of the equipment. A direct hit would have finished off the three operators, too. As it was they were able to pull themselves out of the wreckage, dazed but unhurt, and make for their respective boat stations, after dumping the code books which Murray had collected in the special weighted bag.

On the way to his station on the bridge deck, Bill Murray nipped into his cabin to collect a few personal possessions. When he emerged the ship, still bathed in the baleful light of the searchlights, seemed deserted. Peering over the port side he saw the empty falls of his number 2 boat swinging listlessly as the ship rolled to the gentle swell. The boat itself had disappeared into the darkness. It was the same story at number 1 and number 4 boat stations - just empty falls. He found number 3 boat, on the starboard side of the boat deck, still suspended from its falls, but so badly damaged as to be clearly useless. There was not a soul to be seen. He peered aft through the rising smoke and steam. The gun was silent now, but still pointing truculently towards the raider standing off the port quarter, searchlights still blazing. And there, on the poop, he saw a group of figures clustered round the little jolly boat, that punt-like craft the sailors used when touching up the boot-topping.

The sense of lonely despair rising in his breast was quelled by a surge of hope, and young Murray hastened aft to join what was left of his shipmates. He found Second Officer Robert Sutcliffe in charge, who gave him a cheerful welcome.

"Hullo, Sparks; number 3 boat is 'kaput'. Come and join us", he said, motioning towards the rail below which the round, chubby face of Second Engineer Percy Williams was just disappearing as he descended the ladder. He was closely followed by the Fourth Engineer, C.F. Colquhoun, then it was Bill Murray's turn. He describes his experience thus:

"I glanced down from my high perch, endeavouring to see the boat, but could discern nothing and only sensed the black water rising and falling below me. Desperately...I hung on to the writhing ladder. It was as though we were descending into the abysmal pit of hell itself. Deeper we groped into the void, but progress was slow and the infernal ladder had no end. The lower we climbed, the more it twisted and jolted for it had no support from the ship's side due to our position near the stern. At last I saw the dinghy. The sea was not as calm as I had thought. Below me surged a boatload of upturned faces, most of them dusky, with bright eyes and glistening teeth. The next time the boat leaped up to meet me I dropped off the ladder into the sea of brown faces and floundered amid a jumble of seats, oars, arms, and legs... The Second Mate was the last to jump."[185]

With difficulty, the grossly overloaded little boat pushed off from the ship's side. It had been perforated by shrapnel, and constant baling was necessary to keep the gunnels a few inches above water. The officers contemplated the prospect of getting away in the darkness and perhaps joining up with the more seaworthy lifeboats in the morning. Second Officer Sutcliffe shook his head.

"No chance", he said simply, holding up the freshwater canister, riddled with shrapnel, from which the last drops of water were dripping "We would not last the night in this cockleshell, anyway".

Another light stabbed the darkness and the occupants of the dinghy could make out a smart motor launch rapidly approaching them.

An officer hailed them: "Row over to the cruiser," he shouted in excellent English. Slowly, with the sea lapping the gunnels of their frail craft, the survivors pulled towards the so-called cruiser, which, they now realised, looked more like a battleship - as, indeed, it was. Already there was a crowded lifeboat alongside disembarking its crew. They were snaking up the rope ladders which had been thrown over the warship's side. As the last man clambered on to the ladder, the boat was stove-in and cast adrift. Then it was the turn of the crowded dinghy to come alongside, and the crew climbed aboard, thankful to reach the solid security of the battleship's deck.

They were a forlorn-looking bunch, soaking wet, dispirited, staring defeat in the face. For now they were prisoners of war confronting an uncertain future, for they all knew what had happened to the ADMIRAL GRAF SPEE. Was there a similar fate in store for her sister, the ADMIRAL SCHEER? And could the prisoners again be so lucky?

It so happened that the 76 survivors, of whom 68 were Asians from Calcutta, eventually reached Germany, where all but one passed the remainder of the war in prison camps.[186]

At least two more boats carrying 59 survivors between them, left the doomed ship. In charge were Captain H.W.G. Philpott and Chief Officer Alexander Dewar respectively. Did they deliberately evade capture by the raider? Or did the searching launch simply fail to find them? We shall never know, for the boats disappeared that night, and neither they, nor their occupants, were ever seen or heard of again.

242. STRATEGIST (1) 1937-1957 Steel steamship. Two decks, five holds and deep tank. Two masts.
O.N. 164346 6,255g 3,788n 9,310d 437.3 (452.2 o.l.) x 56.0 x 32.18 feet. Cargo capacity: 500,577 cubic feet.
International Code: GCCF.
T. 3-cyl. by David Rowan and Co.Ltd., Glasgow; 28, 46, 81 x 54 inches, 13 knots.

30.9.1937: Launched by Lithgows Ltd., Port Glasgow (Yard No. 901) for the company. *24.11.1937:* Delivered at an approximate cost of £180,000 and later sailed from Liverpool to South Africa on her maiden voyage under Captain J. Lowe. *6.1940:* Transported 500 French soldiers, rescued from Dunkirk, from Avonmouth to Casablanca, returning to Gibraltar with 1,500 refugees who had been evacuated when the war started. *7.1940:* Embarked 800 Gibraltarian refugees to be transported to Britain; docked at Swansea early August. *12.1941:* The bridge-deck wings (normally used as coal bunkers) were stripped out at Liverpool and fitted with accommodation for 56 passengers, usually service personnel or the diplomatic corps. *3.1944:* Service in Italy, ferrying troops and stores between Naples and the Anzio beach-head led to Captain Peterkin's award of the OBE. *28.6.1955:* In collision in the Great Bitter Lake, Suez Canal, with the Norwegian tanker HERON (8,484/45). She sustained serious damage to her port bow plating and temporary repairs were effected at Port Said. *5.1956:* Caught up in a serious strike of dock workers at Kingston, Jamaica. On 13.5.1956 the Governor, Sir Hugh Foot, declared a state of emergency and troops were called in to discharge ships and armed police patrolled the docks. The strike collapsed 16.5.1956 and the port returned to normal working. *5.3.1957:* Sold to D.D.G. Hansa, Bremen, West Germany and renamed SCHONFELS. *25.4.1962:* When on passage from Rangoon to Antwerp, put into Bone, Algeria, with the two forward holds on fire. They were eventually extinguished, but 800 tons of cargo was found to be damaged and was discharged. *2.1963:* Sold to Leung Yau Co., Hong Kong, for demolition. *14.5.1963:* Arrived at Hong Kong. *27.5.1963:* Work commenced.

Strategist sailing from Capetown.

Transit of Venus
This is a true story, a story of love blighted by war, told with a simple directness which only serves to underline the sense of irretrievable loss suffered by the storyteller. His name is John, by the way. It began on board the Harrison steamer STRATEGIST, a vessel commanded throughout the war years on Government service by Captain A.G. Peterkin.

John was a cadet at that time, in his third year, and within a month or so of his nineteenth birthday. It was the summer of 1940, a chaotic and anxious time in many respects.[187]

Instead of being a bastion, the Rock of Gibraltar was looking very vulnerable, an obvious target for devastating fascist air attacks. It was decided to evacuate the women and children of Gibraltar to Britain or Canada. There were no cruise liners or passenger ferries to carry out this task; only cargo ships like the STRATEGIST were on hand to be pressed into this service. In Gibraltar Bay, she made hasty preparations to receive her contingent of refugees. Some makeshift cots and bunks were knocked together in the main 'tween-decks, but it had to be accepted that most of the refugees would have to sleep on dunnage laid on the steel deck. The day came when STRATEGIST left the anchorage to berth in the harbour and embark her several hundred passengers. John takes up the story:

"I shall never forget that day, as soldiers directed the women and children towards our gangway. Husbands and fathers shouted frenzied farewells as more troops with portable barricades strove to keep the gangway clear. Each refugee carried a bag or suitcase and a pitiful bundle of bedding. Up the gangway they came in an unending stream, some sobbing, some still calling back frantically to a loved one, the kids on the whole wide-eyed and interested. It was my job to give each person a lifebelt from the pile on deck, to direct them fore and aft to the holds, and try to get some idea of numbers. I remember one order from Captain Peterkin: "If you see any young woman soon to become a mum, tell the soldiers she must go ashore as we have no doctor on board!'"

Evidently Captain Peterkin who was so adept at setting broken bones, or stitching up gaping wounds did not fancy himself as a midwife. John could not see any problem. Surely, amongst all those women on board there would be some with at least elementary skills in midwifery? Anyway, when the first young woman to fit the bill arrived at the gangway accompanied by a young Red Cross nurse, John had no qualms about directing them to one of the grandly named "Staterooms", a small cabin on the starboard side. The Old Man observed this blatant disregard for his order, but shrugged, and retreated to his cabin, for, as John remarks, "he was really an old softie at heart". And perhaps the presence of a competent looking nurse was a mollifying factor.

The people were still coming aboard. John goes on: "Next up the gangway came a young nun in a grey habit leading some little girls by the hand. 'Where can these children go?' she asked. 'They are blind'. And that was when I gave away the Officers' Dining Saloon".

By this time it was well into the afternoon and becoming unbearably hot. Old tarpaulins were stretched over the derricks at the main hatches to serve as awnings. John's somewhat haphazard head count was hovering around 800, but the last group of people were now coming aboard. John continues:

"Leading the way was a girl of seventeen or so followed by three other girls, all wearing school uniform. I can still see her as she stepped off the gangway, and accepted her lifebelt from me. 'We would all like to be together', she said, 'and when my mother and brother arrive they will be the last of your passengers'. Five feet nothing, she was, with dark blonde hair, brown eyes, and very pretty. She looked cool and fresh then, and always did, even when things became rough. I was uncomfortably aware of my own uncouth appearance - hot, dirty, and sweaty - and felt rather foolish as I directed her party to number 2 hatch. 'Who are you?' enquired the cool young lady. 'I'm John, the Cadet,' I replied, a little breathlessly. Please, tell me - what is your name?' 'My name', she said simply, 'is Gardenia Morello', and she turned away in the direction I had indicated." John gazed after her. Yes, it was love at first sight for John and Gardenia! John and Gardenia - like Romeo and Juliet; Paris and Helen of Troy; Heloise and Peter Abelard. It has happened so often over the ages.

Later that day, the ship left the harbour and returned to the anchorage, where the passengers, putting aside their sorrows, co-operated fully with the crew in an effort to sort themselves out and establish some sort of order. At last a convoy was formed, and away went the ships, bound for Swansea. John, in his narrative, describes how the fears and difficulties of the voyage were faced and overcome. Although the dangers were very real, morale was high. One day a German Focke-Wulf Condor aircraft circled the convoy, and the refugees, anxious and apprehensive, were ushered below. But the plane did not attack. Was it scouting for U-boats, perhaps even now directing them towards the slow-moving convoy? It was during that night, and subsequent alarms, that John, mixing freely with the passengers, came to accept why the Old Man and the Mate kept strictly to themselves. The ship was equipped with only four lifeboats, a few rafts, and a number of old Carley floats discarded by the Navy. If the worst came to the worst, and the ship had to be abandoned, perhaps at night in heavy weather, only a minority could be saved. Some harsh decisions would have to be taken, and consequently it would not do for senior officers to become emotionally involved with any of their charges. So they remained aloof, and nursed their awful responsibilities in isolation.

John is understandably reticent about his relationship with Gardenia at this stage. We do not know what they talked about in stolen moments of seclusion - difficult, but not impossible to find on such a crowded ship - but we can guess. Together they roamed the decks, amusing the children, helping to minister to the sick, maintaining morale just by their very presence. For in spite of their efforts to conceal their feelings, their suppressed joy in each other's company bubbled free for all to see.

The days passed all too quickly (for some); the weather was good; and, by the grace of God the feared attack never came. Eventually, STRATEGIST docked safely at Swansea; the time for separation had arrived, and, as John recalls wistfully, "The moment of parting was sad indeed, and our good-byes were painful. All the refugees were going to the London area by bus, to be billeted somewhere near Earl's Court. We promised to visit them as soon as we could. Suddenly, they were all gone. The old STRATEGIST seemed like a dead ship that night."

In a war-torn world, however, a visit proved to be impossible, and a week or so later the ship sailed for the Middle East via the Cape of Good Hope loaded with equipment for the Eighth Army. It was a lengthy voyage, and mail was erratic and unreliable. John was disappointed, but not surprised, to receive no letters from Gardenia. In fact, nearly all the mail arrived on board when the ship docked in London four or five months later. There was but one from the girl, posted shortly after the ship had sailed, and several from his family. At the bottom of the pile was one in a strangely familiar hand which turned out to be from Arthur Jones, the STRATEGIST's former Third Officer, who had stayed ashore to sit for a Certificate. Its message was brief, but it might well have been a blow from a hammer.

"I am sorry to have to tell you, John, but your dear friend Gardenia has been killed in an air raid..." The bitter irony of the message bit deep into his soul. Uprooted from Gibraltar to seek safety from air raids; braving the perils of a sea voyage through U-boat infested waters, only to perish in the London blitz. Why, oh why billet refugees in London, anyway? Had not the capital already evacuated its own children "I cannot describe my feelings," says John. "Grief, certainly; outrage, yes; but I have no doubt that my senses were dulled by shock. I needed something more tangible than this kind, simple letter. I resolved to go up to London to seek out her family and friends, and there the awful truth was confirmed. Gardenia had gone out shopping, been caught in a daylight raid, and never returned."

Alas, poor John, his goddess of love and beauty, his Venus, had risen, not from the sea, but from the Rock; she had ascended briefly into his heart; crossed his meridian; and quietly descended below the horizon of his life. There would be other girls, of course, one of whom would become a well-loved and devoted wife; but in any man's life there is but one first love, one Gardenia.

Thirty-six years were to elapse before John found himself back in Gibraltar, this time as a mature and successful shipmaster, flown there with orders to join a ship. His visit to the agent's office to introduce himself and enquire about the ship's latest estimated time of arrival was full of surprises. The manager, a Mr. Victory, offered him coffee. "First visit to Gib?" he enquired politely. "I was here once, thirty-six years ago", replied John. "And would that have been a happy, or sad occasion?" persisted the agent. An

200

odd question, coming from a stranger. "Yes; it did indeed have its sorrows", replied John. Looking up, he saw the man's face wreathed in smiles, and realised that he knew him. "John, it's me - Lionel", said the agent, his hand outstretched. "Remember little Lionel? I was twelve years old when I sailed with you and Gardenia, and hundreds more aboard a ship called the STRATEGIST!"

John was bemused. He remembered, of course, but how had Lionel remembered? And why had he coupled Gardenia's name with his? Had they, so long ago, been so obvious - and oblivious - to all that even a young boy, now a grown man, had never forgotten them? He shook his head abruptly, as if to clear it of misty images, and returned Lionel's handshake with warmth and delight.

It turned out to be a memorable return to the front line Gibraltar of his youth, a visit cut all too short by the prompt arrival of his ship. The realisation that all his former charges still remembered him touched him to the quick, inducing an uncharacteristic sense of humility.

John ends his narrative on a wistful note: "It won't be long now before I say "Cheerio" to the sea, but I don't intend to give it up altogether. I shall have my own little boat to potter about in, and perhaps get away from under my dear wife's feet occasionally. So if ever you are in the Torbay area, and see a white-haired old-timer whose appearance strikes a chord in your memory, and who will very likely be pottering about in a boat, just check the boat's name. If it is named for a sub-tropical flower renowned for its beauty and fragrance, then you will be right - you will have remembered. "Welcome aboard!"

After her sale to D.D.G. Hansa, *Strategist* as *Schonfels* with a cut-down funnel.

243. SCIENTIST (2) 1938-1940 Steel steamship. Two decks, five holds and deep tank. Two masts.
O.N. 166247 6,199g 3,794n 9,000d 438.7 (453.0 o.l.) x 56.45 x 32.17 feet. Cargo capacity: 470,366 cubic feet. International Code: GNGR.
T. 3-cyl. with Bauer-Wach exhaust turbine by David Rowan and Co. Ltd., Glasgow; 29, 47, 81 x 54 inches, 14½ knots.

30.5.1938: Launched by Lithgows Ltd., Port Glasgow (Yard No. 911) for the company. *12.8.1938:* Delivered at a cost of £192,330 and later sailed from Liverpool to Kingston, Jamaica on her maiden voyage under Captain G.R. Windsor. *3.5.1940:* Sunk by the German raider ATLANTIS in the South Atlantic in position 19.20S, 04.15E, about 606 miles and 110 degrees from St. Helena. She was on passage from Durban to Freetown for convoy, loaded with general cargo, including chrome ore for the United Kingdom.

Scientist has steam to spare on her trials in 1938.   *[Glasgow University Archives GD320/10/1/115/2]*

Guests of the Kriegsmarine

Kapitän zur See Bernhard Rogge, commander of the German commerce-raider ATLANTIS, gazed round his ship. The converted Hansa Line cargo ship GOLDENFELS (7,862/37), she was now in disguise. Overside, the national colours of neutral Japan emblazoned the ship's black flanks. A Japanese ensign streamed from her stern, and the top quarter of her black funnel was painted red adorned with the white letter K, the symbol of the Kokusai Kisen Line of Tokyo. At bow and stern was inscribed the name, KASII MARU, supplemented by Japanese ideograms which might have meant anything, but which the German commander was sure no English sailors could decipher.

His keen but untested crew, three hundred strong, stood to their battle stations, tense and excited, as they awaited the arrival of the first victim of their cruise, a British cargo vessel which was steadily overtaking on the starboard quarter. "5,000 metres and closing", intoned Leutnant Kasch, the Gunnery Officer, who, from above the wheelhouse was using to good effect a range-finder cunningly camouflaged as a water tank.

The moment of truth could not be delayed much longer. Eventually, Rogge spoke the eagerly awaited orders: "Clear guns! Hoist battle ensign! Make signals!" In a flash, a flutter of bunting appeared on the triatic stay halyards, ordering the "Englander" to stop, and not use her radio; the red, white, and black Swastika ensign of the Third Reich swiftly replaced the Rising Sun of Japan; and flaps in the ship's side levered upwards, like so many suburban garage doors, to reveal the menace of the 5.9-inch guns. At Kasch's command, a smaller gun in the bow fired a shot across the freighter's bow.

Aboard the "Englander", the Harrison steamer SCIENTIST, homeward bound from Durban, surprise was complete. Second Officer Tom Anderson and the cadet on watch had been studying the strange Japanese vessel for some time, but, apart from a niggling doubt as to why the homely SCIENTIST should be overtaking such a powerful-looking vessel, their suspicions remained dormant. There had been no enemy activity in the South Atlantic since the unlamented demise of the ADMIRAL GRAF SPEE in December. Time enough to worry when the ship neared Freetown. It was 15.20 on Friday 3rd May 1940, and the

Seen here as a young third officer, Captain George Windsor (1880-1943) was Master of the *Scientist* throughout her brief career.

Goanese stewards were doing their rounds, bringing afternoon tea and tab-nabs to somnolent officers and engineers in their watch below. The sharp report of the raider's gun gave them a rude awakening. Captain George Windsor appeared on the bridge in shirtsleeves demanding to know who was "meddling with that damned gun?" He saw what appeared to be a neutral Japanese ship on the port bow, now swinging to cross ahead, and displaying a formidable armament. He at once came to grips with the situation.

"Hard-a-starboard, Quartermaster," he roared. "Double ring full ahead, Second Mate... Here, lad" - to the cadet - "tell Sparks he's got to get this message out". The Old Man scribbled on a pad with a steady hand: "QQQQ - G N G R - 19.20S, 04.15E" - "Challenged by unknown armed vessel", - and the boy raced down the ladder and along the deck to the wireless cabin situated on the boat deck. Radio Officer F.H. Compton's hand was already on the key, his equipment humming, and away into the ether went the all-important message, a cry for help and at the same time a warning to others. It is one of the ironies of war at sea that one may see nothing for days; suddenly one's patch of blue water is also occupied by the enemy; and when one's cry of distress is transmitted there is no one within 300 miles radius to hear it. For the message went out unheard and unheeded - except by an alert telegraphist on board the raider. He was on to the wavelength before three complete messages had been transmitted, and promptly jammed the signal with his own key.

"Enemy radio in action, sir!" he reported. Rogge swore as he watched his prey turning away. "Open fire!" he ordered. Leutnant Kasch needed no urging, and salvo after salvo crashed out. Several shells burst in the after holds of the target, igniting the cargo and sending flames leaping skywards. Another demolished the wireless cabin, leaving Radio Officer Compton severely wounded in head and arms. Despite his injuries Sparks

managed to retrieve his code books from the wreckage, transfer them to the specially weighted bag, and throw them overboard. His duty done, he staggered dazedly to his boat station. The bombardment ceased.

SCIENTIST, her after deck ablaze, had stopped and Captain Windsor ordered the boats away. He and Chief Officer Alec Watson busied themselves collecting sensitive books and papers which might have been useful to the enemy, and dumping them over the side. A group of walking wounded stood quietly beside the medicine locker patiently waiting for Chief Steward Harry Howarth to administer first aid. Harry shook his head over one Lascar with a gaping wound in his stomach. He was lifted gently into one of the boats, but died later aboard the raider.

Meanwhile, the boats were being lowered, and last minute thoughts took on a vital importance, though some were incongruous in the circumstances. "Tell the Chief Steward - he must bring the canteen accounts with him!" "Fetch me some tobacco out of the top drawer - oh! and my toothbrush!". "Please, Mr. Mate, have I got time to nip below for my bottom set?"

Quickly the boats were manned, and pushed away from the doomed ship's side, their crews eyeing the raider apprehensively as it bore down upon them with guns trained in their direction. Somewhat reassured by an amplified voice bidding them to pull alongside, they did so, staring up at the grinning faces of German sailors lining, the rail, most of them bearing arms. One or two, however, slipped nimbly over the rail and into the boats, and began strapping the wounded into hammocks and stretchers before hoisting them on deck, where they were taken to a well-equipped hospital. The rest clambered wearily up the ladders and into captivity.

Later, the prisoners looked back at the deserted ship. A witness recorded his feelings at the time:[188] "The SCIENTIST, looking very forlorn and blazing fiercely, lay on the raider's starboard beam about a mile away. An officer informed us that they intended to sink the ship by gunfire. Round after round slammed into the bridge and accommodation, starting more fires, but not once did the gunners succeed in hitting the waterline. It was getting dark, and the blazing SCIENTIST was a veritable beacon to any vessels cruising in the vicinity. With growing impatience the German commander decided to despatch the vessel quickly with a torpedo. A couple of minutes passed. Had the "tin-fish" missed its target? No chance; for suddenly a huge column of white water shot two hundred feet into the darkening sky, spouting upwards from a point just abaft amidships.

"I watched the destruction of my ship with mounting horror and disbelief. It was a nightmare. I willed myself to wake up, clenching my fists in my despair. But the pain caused by my nails digging into my palms was real - this nightmare was reality. The sense of loss became more personal. I thought of the prized hunting knife with the deersfoot handle, won in some boyish scouting expedition, lying in a drawer; the resplendent bridge-coat still hanging in the wardrobe; two months' work for my course tutor lying in another drawer, the family photographs standing on the chest; all gone, consumed in that awesome conflagration. I stole a sidelong glance at the faces of my companions and realised that they, too, were suffering in much the same way.

"The force of the explosion, and the drenching deluge of water seemed to dim the flames. The raider quickly gathered way; and so we left our ship silhouetted against the dark eastern horizon, the dull thunder of the explosion still reverberating in our ears". An hour or so later the prisoners were herded below and were pleasantly surprised to be ushered into a cosy, well prepared room.

The same witness recalls: "It was furnished with three long tables and benches, half-a-dozen basket chairs, and several lockers adorned the bulkhead. The deck was strewn with mats, and from the deck head several gaily shaded lamps were suspended. Leading off from the "living and dining room" were the "bedrooms" and washrooms...the bunks we found were quite comfortable, each one complete with straw mattress, pillow, blankets, and sheets".

Alec Watson, the Chief Officer, was anxious to ascertain how our Asian crew members had been accommodated. He was led away by a guard and returned some time later to report that they were in similar but more spacious quarters further aft, and seemed in good spirits.

Looking back, the writer can only marvel at the contrast presented by conditions in ATLANTIS with the very different conditions described by prisoners in other enemy ships. The German naval authorities had carried out the conversion of merchant ships to armed merchant cruisers efficiently, but the accommodation and care of prisoners was granted a low priority. In most cases, the arrangements were very haphazard, being left to the appointed commander, and inevitably leading to a great deal of discomfort, hardship, and ill-feeling. That things were vastly different aboard ATLANTIS can only be attributed to the efforts of Bernhard Rogge, whose humanity and active participation at the fitting-out stage ensured that ATLANTIS was capable of accommodating over 200 prisoners in a reasonable degree of comfort.

More unexpected surprises were revealed as time wore on. The Commander's A.D.C., Leutnant zur See Ulrich Mohr, was designated Prisoners' Liaison Officer. A tall, scholarly officer with a genial manner and a first class command of English, Leutnant Mohr went out of his way to win the trust of his country's enemies. The day after their capture a loudspeaker was installed in the prisoners' quarters, which broadcast music throughout the day, interspersed with news bulletins in English, not from Germany, but from the United States. Prisoners were served with the same food as the German crew, except the Asians. These the Germans allowed to employ their own cooks to prepare their traditional fare of rice, lamb, and curries. Indeed, the native "bandari's" curry and rice became a favourite dish with Kapitän Rogge and his officers. The German fare was plain, wholesome, and plentiful, though the black bread, ersatz coffee, blood sausage, and sauerkraut were not to everyone's taste. But the meats, vegetables, soups, dried fruit, and cheeses which frequently graced the tables in the "Gefangenem Raum" were greatly appreciated. Drinking water, sometimes laced with lime juice, seemed plentiful, but water for washing was strictly rationed. Soap, too, was scarce.

Exercise periods were at first limited to two hours each day, but restrictions were gradually relaxed and the hours extended to six and sometimes eight hours per day in fine weather. From the foregoing it will be appreciated that the word "Guest" in the title of this chapter is used advisedly, with no hint of irony.

On 10th June, six weeks later, ATLANTIS secured her second victim, the Norwegian motor vessel TIRRANNA (7,230/38). She survived the bombardment which led to her capture in a condition which could be made seaworthy. She also carried a valuable cargo of wheat, wool and canned goods, plus stores and mail for the Australian army in the Middle East.

On deck was a whole fleet of motor transport vehicles and field ambulances, while in her fuel tanks were 900 tons of priceless diesel oil. She was also the type of ship which could be readily adapted to carry a large number of passengers. She was thoroughly looted in the course of a week and was left in the charge of a prize crew while ATLANTIS continued her cruise. Two prizes and six weeks later ATLANTIS met up with TIRRANNA again, and transferred many of her by now numerous prisoners to her before sending her back to Germany with her valuable cargo. Among her non-combatant passengers were 180 Lascar seamen; all the Norwegians; British prisoners over 50 (except shipmasters); boys under 16; and those of the sick and wounded whom Dr. Reil considered could be better treated in Germany. Into some of these categories fell 25 men from the crew of the SCIENTIST: Chief Engineer Bob Scarrow; Third Engineer Dave Foulis; Chief Steward Harry Howarth; Quartermaster Dick Barrow; Mr. Chicken, the passenger from Durban, and 20 Lascars.

The same young witness remembers well the parting: "Nothing much was said; just a quick handclasp all round; a grin; the words, "Good luck", and they were off. We watched them climb down the pilot ladder clasping their pitiful bundles of possessions. They took their seats in the launch and waved cheerfully as the engine throbbed into life. On the boat deck someone called for three cheers; they were given and answered with a will. As we watched the boat rise and fall over the rolling swell a rich tenor voice began singing 'Auld Lang Syne'. It was taken up immediately, and the refrain kept up until the boat drew alongside TIRRANNA, and its occupants climbed aboard".

As TIRRANNA approached European waters Leutnant -zur-See Waldmann, the prize master, decided that, rather than make for his intended destination of St Nazaire, it would be safer if he made for a port in Southern, unoccupied France.[189] Making for the port of Arcachon, he anchored off Cape Ferret on 22nd September. The unco-operative Vichy French authorities passed him on to Bordeaux, and after an overnight passage anchored again off the mouth of the Gironde next morning. Waldmann was warned that the entrance to the river had been mined, and was told to wait for an escort of minesweepers. While cruising slowly off the entrance, she was sighted by HM Submarine TUNA. A large freighter standing off the Gironde, her decks crammed with army transport vehicles, was too important a target to miss, and TUNA's commander went in close for the kill. Two torpedoes struck the hapless TIRRANNA, and she quickly heeled over and sank, giving passengers and crew no time to work out their escape; the lucky ones were those cast, or who cast themselves, into the sea.

The minesweeper escorts for which TIRRANNA had waited all day arrived on the scene just in time to comb the wreckage for survivors. Sixty innocent passengers perished in this avoidable tragedy; men, women, and children. Of the SCIENTIST's contingent, Dave Foulis, Harry Howarth, and Dick Barrow survived to be interned in German prison camps for the duration of the war; Bob Scarrow and Mr. Chicken, the passenger from Durban, both lost their lives. TIRRANNA had been kept hanging around in dangerous waters for about 30 hours too long.

After parting company with the TIRRANNA on 4th August, ATLANTIS again moved north to cruise in the south tropical latitudes of the Indian Ocean. During the next six weeks or so she sank four more ships. The prisoner problem was again building, when the ancient Yugoslav tramp steamer DURMITOR (5,623/13) was captured on 22nd October. After she had been stripped of everything which could be of use to the raider, 260 prisoners, including all the remaining SCIENTIST men, were ferried across to her from ATLANTIS on 26th October.

28 days after parting company with ATLANTIS, and running seriously short of coal, the DURMITOR arrived off the coast of Italian Somaliland. With no response to his signal for a pilot, the prize master tried to approach the village he could see on the shoreline. He ran DURMITOR firmly onto the offshore reef barring the approaches. Grinding on the reef in the long Indian Ocean swell it was not long before the old tramp steamer began to show signs of breaking up. The order was given to abandon ship; all four of her boats were launched and used to ferry parties of prisoners ashore in steady succession. Our witness recalls: "I went ashore in the third wave (it is not surprising that rumours spread among many Italians that an Allied invasion was taking place!). By that time it was pitch dark. As we approached the beach through a heavy surf, we suddenly became aware that armed native soldiers were deployed facing our boat, and looking extremely nervous. One false move could have brought a fusillade of shots. We raised our arms, making it clear we had no weapons, and marched off to the village, called Warshiek, under guard, while volunteers stayed with the boat, and pulled back to the ship."

Next day, the prisoners were taken off to an Italian prison camp outside Mogadiscio. Their German gaolers accompanied them, but were kept in custody only until their credentials were checked by higher authority. They were then released, to commandeer a German merchant ship, the TANNENFELS (7,840/38), lying in Kismayu, in which they rejoined the ATLANTIS on 8th February 1941.

The war in East Africa was by now in its last stages, with defeat staring Italian forces in the face. On 25th February 1941 the camp was deserted by the Italian guards, and later in the day a South African patrol car liberated the compound and its inmates. Three days later HM cruiser CERES arrived offshore, to transport the prisoners down the coast to Mombasa.

HMS CERES got under way, and twenty-four hours later, on 1st March, they disembarked at Mombasa, no longer prisoners-of-war but distressed British seamen.[190] The many months of captivity were behind them. Even though life in the British transit camp was luxurious compared with Merca camp under Italian guards, the men fretted to be on the move again. In mid-April the troopship NEA HELLAS (16,991/22), formerly the Anchor Line's TUSCANIA, and commanded by Captain David W. Bone, the well-known author, arrived in Mombasa. Joyfully, the men packed up, bade hasty farewells to new-found friends and hastened down to Kilindini Docks to lay claim to a bunk in the six-berth cabins.

The ship called at Durban for bunkers, where the Navy was seeking crews for captured ships idling in the harbour. The response was enthusiastic. Most of SCIENTIST's officers volunteered, and left the trooper to man a captured Vichy French vessel which was reported to be "in good nick". Alec Watson, formerly Chief Officer of the SCIENTIST, was given command for the voyage to England. There now remained in the troopship only cadets, apprentices, elderly masters and chief engineers of the company which left Merca Camp. The ship made a further call at Capetown to embark a contingent of convalescent troops, before sailing in company with the aircraft carriers FURIOUS and ARGUS, bound for Gibraltar. The voyage passed without incident.

Their stay at Gibraltar was brief, but twenty-four hours after leaving the ship was forced to return by the news of BISMARCK's excursion into the North Atlantic. Eventually Captain Bone was informed that it was safe to proceed - at least, so far as the BISMARCK was concerned. And so it turned out to be. The NEA HELLAS entered the Firth of Clyde on 14th June, some of her passengers vaguely worried about what to do with the surplus docking bottles of Van der Hum and cakes of "Main Line" plug tobacco which had somehow been accumulated. They need not have worried, for HM Customs Officers in Glasgow had just come out on strike! Gleefully, they packed their contraband goods and made their way home.

When in July 1940 the Admiralty declared the SCIENTIST lost with all hands, certain loose ends had to be tied up. Allotments were stopped; the accounts of the missing seamen made up, and the money passed to the next-of-kin. Women who had been "widowed" nursed their grief and applied for the statutory pension. Some might have "married" again - I know of no specific case, but it was an obvious possibility. Parents received gently worded messages of condolence from Queen Elizabeth, but, despite the odds, there were many who never gave up hope. It was tacitly agreed that those at home suffered the greater ordeal, not knowing what had happened, or when to abandon hope. And, of course, all the raider's victims and their kin suffered similar strains.

Therefore, when "all well" messages began streaming in from Mombasa to be delivered to families all over Britain, there was unconfined joy, relief, and not a little consternation, throughout the land. Our witness quotes the family traditional version of this event: "Dad, who had a modest grocery business in Toxteth, and whose errand boys had either been absorbed into the forces, or evacuated, was out delivering groceries in Liverpool's suburbia when the momentous cable arrived. Mother at once discarded her apron, donned her best coat, pinned on her hat, and set off on foot and on tram in search of father, although she knew very well he would be home for his dinner in only a couple of hours. She ran him to earth in distant Childwall, just as he was completing his round, and triumphantly waved the auspicious cable in front of his nose, to the amusement of a curious and interested customer! Then she boarded a homeward tram, while Dad trundled his tricycle van back to base. The going, apparently, seemed downhill all the way".

When the euphoria had subsided a little some unpalatable situations had to be faced. "Widows" were obliged to refund to the state all the pension moneys they had received. Premiums (i.e. the sums payable to an employer by the parents or guardians of cadets and apprentices - £50 in those days), which had been refunded on "decease" had to be paid again. Company accountants later re-calculated balances of wages, some inevitably in the red after the spending spree in Mombasa, and "adjustments" had to be made. But, in the eyes of kith and kin these were but a small price to pay for the miracle of deliverance.

244. ADVISER (1) 1939-1960 Steel steamship. Two decks, five holds and deep tank. Two masts.

O.N. 166263 6,348g 3,886n 9,000d 445.5 (459.25 o.l.) x 56.5 x 32.17 feet. Cargo capacity: 482,532 cubic feet
International Code: GSSK.
T. 3-cyl. by David Rowan and Co. Ltd., Glasgow, with Bauer-Wach exhaust turbine; 29, 47, 81 x 54 inches, 14½ knots.

23.2.1939: Launched by Lithgows Ltd., Port Glasgow (Yard No. 917) for the company. *20.4.1939:* Delivered at a cost of £193,676. Later sailed from Antwerp and London to South Africa on her maiden voyage under Captain J.T. Ling. *9.1942:* Took part in the second phase of the Madagascar campaign. *15.11.1942:* Torpedoed by the German submarine U 178 in the Indian Ocean but managed to reach Durban where she was repaired. *10.1943:* The bridge deck wings were stripped out and fitted with accommodation for 56 passengers. *18.2.1959:* The body of her Captain, Stephen Richardson, was found floating in Princes Dock, Glasgow. *29.8.1960:* Sold to Jos. Boel and Fils, Belgium for £64,000 for demolition. *4.9.1960:* Arrived at Tamise in tow of the tug BREMEN (138/52).

Adviser on trials.   *[Glasgow Unuversity Archives GD320/10/1/120/1]*

Madagascar: second phase

The Madagascar campaign was conducted in two phases, the first of which, between May and July 1942, secured the northern ports. The second phase, starting in September and ending in November, secured the remaining ports, and eventually the whole island. Whereas WANDERER took part in both operations, ADVISER participated in the second phase only, and a lively description of the event has been recorded by Captain E.D. Ashdown, who was making his first voyage as a cadet at the time.[191]

The ADVISER sailed from Mombasa on 4th September 1942, loaded not only with war material, stores, and aviation fuel, but with two support landing craft (SLC) stowed on the after deck, and a contingent of about 70 King's African Riflemen (KARs) encamped on the foredeck. Captain Ashdown recalls: "After five days at sea in convoy, we saw many mastheads on the horizon one morning. Five convoys of merchant ships and most of the Eastern Fleet were massing. There were two convoys from Mombasa, and two from Durban, one of which included the old WANDERER, and one from Dar es Salaam. The fleet comprised two aircraft carriers, four battleships, a monitor, and a fair number of cruisers and lesser craft.

"We anchored close off Majunga (known as Mahajanga today) at about 23.00 that night. The intention was that all landing craft should attack at 03.00 next morning, 10th September. Soon after midnight, flights of aircraft from the carriers opened the invasion, destroying the airfield and other military targets. We could both see and hear the attack; we could see the bombs flashing as they fell, and the fires which they started.

"We put our first landing craft in the water without any trouble....the second unfortunately sat on the bulwark stag-horns. The carpenter did a rush job on it, which could not have been easy in the blackout." The purpose of the SLCs was to blast the opposition whilst the assault landing craft landed the troops. I was disgusted with one of the gunners who later joyfully described how he had seen a French soldier hiding in the bushes and had sent a stream of 0.5 inch bullets into the unfortunate man. I still don't know whether it was right or wrong." Daylight came, and Majunga was captured decisively. The supply ships moved into the harbour anchorage. The cross-channel ferry NORMANDY came alongside to collect the boom-defence, and the KARs were taken ashore to take up guard duties. We spent a few days discharging our supplies, including eight thousand gallons of aviation spirit. It broke our hearts when some Frenchman set fire to the lot - fortunately after it had been landed." Later, ADVISER, with her SLCs restowed, joined

An epic struggle[192]
Having played her part in the campaign to secure Madagascar from Japanese invasion, ADVISER returned to South Africa to resume her less dramatic but equally vital transport services. On 14th November the ship left Durban and headed south east into the Indian Ocean. In the early hours of the following morning, which was a Sunday, the vessel was torpedoed without warning, the undersea missile striking in number 1 hold and exploding with devastating effect. The hatch covers on number 1 flew skywards, followed by tons of black graphite, a large consignment of which had been stowed in that hatch. One bag landed in the crow's nest, prompting the lookout man to beat a hasty retreat by sliding down the forestay in the best windjammer tradition. The foredeck was a shambles of twisted beams and derricks, and the ship began sinking perceptibly by the head. Fortunately there were no casualties, though many had narrow escapes.

On the bridge, Second Officer Douglas-Kerr stopped the engines. Captain John T. Ling had not appeared immediately, and, becoming ever more anxious, Douglas-Kerr rushed below in search of him. He soon found him, trapped in his cabin, the force of the explosion having jammed the door. "Are you alright, Captain?" shouted Douglas-Kerr. "Of course I'm alright, Second Mate! But get me out of here, for God's sake," replied Captain Ling, more irritated than scared. He did not need to be told what had happened. Together they forced the door open, and hastened to the bridge. The ship had lost way, but the waves were lapping over the foredeck dangerously close to the gaping No. 1 hatch.

"Do you think the sub will hit us again, Sir?" inquired Douglas-Kerr apprehensively. The Captain shrugged. "I don't know," he said, "but it is more than likely. Check with Sparks; make sure he has sent out an S.O.S. with our position." (This was officially placed in position 32.03S, 33.52E, or about 200 miles southeast of Durban). Then addressing Chief Officer Eric Simmons who had appeared on the bridge, "Clear the boats, Mr. Mate, and stand by to abandon ship." The alarm bells rang out for boat stations, and the crew mustered in orderly fashion, some clutching a bag or a bundle. The Captain watched from the bridge. It was impossible to ascertain the extent of the damage in the darkness, and the sub might strike again. The only prudent thing to do was to leave her, at least for the time being. Captain Ling gave his officers their instructions as the four boats were lowered: "Stay together, and stay with the ship".

The few hours till daylight were uncomfortable, for the sea was choppy, and many of the men were sick. They could hear terrible noises coming from the stricken ship as steel members writhed and twisted against each other, emitting sounds like tormented cries of agony, while rivets cracked and flew like bullets. At last came the dawn, and Captain Ling brought his boat alongside for a closer look. But the ship was bending and sheering so badly he decided it would be unsafe to go aboard. His boat rejoined the little flotilla to wait and watch. Three hours later, the ship was no deeper in the water, so Captain Ling, the Chief Engineer, Carpenter, Radio Officer and a few volunteers boarded the wallowing ship. The furnaces, of course, were out, the boilers cold, but, using his emergency batteries, Sparks was able to renew contact with a shore station. The Carpenter took soundings, and apart from the flooded number 1 hold, found six feet of water in number 2 hold, and three feet in number 3. There were also several feet of water swilling about the engine-room and stokehold. Obviously the working of the weakened hull had started leaks in other compartments.

A sudden loud crack from somewhere forward plucked savagely at their taut nerves. A bulkhead collapsing, or another beam giving way? They did not wait to find out but tumbled

in the operation to capture Tamatave (Taomasina) on 18th September.

"Two destroyers raced up and down outside the reefs. They fired a few shells over the town and into the swamps beyond. They called up the signal station with a message to surrender or be shelled into submission. There was a fleet of landing craft off shore. The French hoisted a white flag, but their plan of defence was that no man was to lay down his rifle until he had fired two shots at the British enemy. Fortunately for them, few French soldiers obeyed orders, but there was little sign of hard feeling at Tamatave. "Perhaps we may not have played a major role in that episode of the war, but we did show the flag".

hastily into the waiting boat. All except Chief Engineer Douglas, torpedoed four times in the last war. He elected to remain since, as he put it, "Bloody lifeboats make me too bloody sick!"

Several hours passed; the eerie grinding and squealing of tortured steel had subsided a little, and although the sea still surged through the cavernous hole in her side, spouting from the hold ventilators like so many hydrants, the scant freeboard below the forecastle deck seemed no less than before.

Again the Master re-boarded his ship and this time the entire crew followed him. The Chief Engineer who had had time to conduct a personal survey, believed it was possible to raise steam, and save the ship. Volunteers were called for, and a squad was formed to descend into that black hole of a stokehold, knee-deep in rushing, jet black water, charged with the task of restoring some vestige of life into the dying ship. Furnaces were re-lit, and new warmth crept into the boilers. Four hours later there was sufficient head of steam to drive the pumps, and so dry out those leaky compartments swilling in water - including the engine-room and stokehold. But here a difficulty arose: the suction in the engine room bilge was blocked.

Third Engineer Archie Morrison volunteered to unblock it, although it was five feet under a noisome, turbid mixture of oil and water. For nearly three hours Morrison dived, groping desperately below the plates, feeling for the obstruction. Gradually, he cleared it; the pumps went into action; and soon the engine room became habitable again. Twelve hours after re-lighting the furnaces there was a head of steam capable of driving the main engines. The crew spent an uncomfortable, uneasy, and sleepless night aboard their crippled vessel, subsisting on scratch meals, and waiting for the dawn.

Meanwhile, help was on its way from Durban. A corvette and a naval tug had set sail, and by Monday morning aircraft were patrolling the vicinity on the lookout for U-boats. Also with the dawn came a gale warning, and the crew watched and waited anxiously as wind and sea arose to impose further strain on the shattered hull.

Towards noon, the corvette and tug were sighted. Together they approached ADVISER, their naval-type sirens whooping encouragement. Captain Ling asked for the towing spring to be sent aboard aft, in order to tow the ship stern first. To move ahead would only impose further unwarranted strain on the heavily stressed bulkheads in the fore part of the ship. Quickly, the towing spring was made fast, and the tug got underway, ADVISER using her engines to assist. After three hours the link parted under the strain of towing in a heavy swell, and worse, the line became entangled in ADVISER's propeller. It was freed eventually after much difficulty, and the ships got under way again, this time with ADVISER providing the motive power by going astern on her engines, while the tug lay out on the starboard quarter to provide steerage, and counter the transverse thrust of the screw. For a single-screw ship, navigating astern and left to her own devices, will simply turn round in circles, her rudder being comparatively useless.

Thus, rolling and pitching in the rough weather, the ship made but modest progress towards Durban, bucking the Agulhas current, and barely making three knots. However, on the Wednesday, ominous signs of further structural damage became apparent, as the foredeck started to buckle and plates began to fracture. Fortunately, the weather improved, and Captain Ling and his men were determined to carry on, resolution turning to obstinacy as they neared their goal. There were loud cheers when Cape Natal and The Bluff were sighted on Thursday morning, 19th, and by late afternoon a bewildered-looking pilot had climbed aboard. Then a couple of lusty harbour tugs came alongside, and nursed her tenderly, one each side, as ADVISER steamed stern first into the harbour, watched in astonishment by scattered groups of casual anglers idly casting their lines from the breakwater.

ADVISER had to wait several weeks for a vacant dry dock, in which she remained for nearly two months while gangs of boilermakers, platers and riveters rebuilt the devastated fore part of the ship. There was still much to be done after the ship left the dry dock, but eventually she loaded a cargo for home, and sailed on 19th August 1943, nine months after her

triumphant arrival. Finally, a momentous 18-months voyage came to an end when ADVISER reached Liverpool on 17th October.

At an investiture at Buckingham Palace on 9th January 1945, Captain J.T. Ling was awarded the OBE for his tenacity and steadfast concern for his ship. At the same time, Third Engineer J.A. Morrison, highly commended for his diving exploits in the darkened, watery abyss of the engine-room, received the MBE.

The riddle of Berth 6

At least, that is how the local papers described it, but most riddles have an answer: this one did not. It was still dark on the morning of Wednesday 18th February 1959 when the crew of the ADVISER began to stir; dark, and very cold. Fortunately, last night's fog had lifted, for this was sailing day, and ADVISER was due to sail at 06.00 for Liverpool to complete loading for the West Indies. On the bridge, officers were going through the familiar pre-departure checks, testing whistles, telegraphs and steering gear, and laying out the charts on the chartroom table. Down below, engineers were watching their gauges as the engines warmed through. The Clyde pilot came on board, and a pair of harbour tugs stationed themselves fore and aft, ready to swing the ship away from her berth at Plantation Quay, Glasgow. Even the Liverpool pilot was on board, having travelled up by train the day before. In fact, everyone was on board, each carrying out his alloted task and ready to go - everyone, that is, except the Master, Captain Stephen Richardson.[193] As the enormity of this unprecedented act of truancy dawned on officers and pilot alike, a hasty search was organised, but without result. Waiting on the quay was the agent's representative, huddled against the cold, anxious to see the ship away. He was briskly informed of the Captain's absence, and he in turn telephoned someone still abed to break the unwelcome tidings. After due deliberation it was decided to postpone the sailing and inform the police. Clyde Pilot and tugs were sent away, and the crew went to an early breakfast. However, by the time lunch had been served, with still no sign of the Captain, everyone had become seriously worried.

At 13.40, on board the police launch SEMPER VIGILO, cruising the upper reaches of the Clyde, Sergeant Robert Miller of the City of Glasgow Police, answered a call on the radio telephone. The despatcher's voice was terse, and matter-of-fact. "Sergeant, we have a report that a body has been found floating in Princes Dock. Go along and investigate". The launch turned, and surged towards Princes Dock. Recovering bodies from the Clyde was perhaps not an everyday occurrence, but Sergeant Miller was by no means unfamiliar with the dismal task. They found the body floating face down off Number 6 Berth in Princes Dock. It was partially clothed in shirt, vest, socks and underpants, but in Sergeant Miller's experience it was not unusual for victims of drowning to attempt to remove their heavy outer clothing.

Having heard on the morning bulletin that a man was missing from the ADVISER, he sent one of his constables along to the ship to find someone willing to come along and make a formal identification. Gently, awkwardly, the body was lifted onto

the quay to await an ambulance. Meanwhile, an officer from the ship turned up to confirm that the corpse was indeed that of Captain Steve Richardson.

At the Inquiry conflicting evidence was presented as to the Captain's intentions on the Tuesday night. He had just recovered from a bout of 'flu which had confined him to his cabin over the weekend, but his wife fully expected him to telephone her that evening. On the other hand, Chief Steward Peter Fitzpatrick, apparently the last person to see Captain Richardson alive, stated that when he looked in on him at 18.30, he informed the Chief Steward that he did not intend going ashore that evening as he had some correspondence to finish off. The Captain then appeared to be in good health and spirits.

Mr. Fitzpatrick later went ashore to telephone home from one of the public callboxes adjacent to Princes Dock, about five or ten minutes walk away. He returned at 21.45, and again called on the Captain. He was not in his cabin, however, nor had anyone seen him go ashore. The Chief Steward thought no more of it, and went to bed. So had the Captain gone ashore after all and somehow slipped and fallen into the Princes Dock? (It was not mentioned at the inquiry, but there is indirect evidence that it was foggy that night.) Or had he in fact fallen overboard from the ship, whence his body had drifted into the dock on tidal eddies and swirls? For Princes Dock is tidal; the entrance, about 400 metres downstream from Plantation Quay (which is a river berth), is wide open to the river. There was no evidence to point unequivocally to either hypothesis. The Police Surgeon, Dr. James Imrie, found no marks of violence on the body, and there was every indication that death had been caused by drowning. There was, however, a considerable amount of alcohol in the blood, compatible, suggested Dr. Imrie, with the ingestion of four large whiskies. It would be reasonable to suppose that this factor may have had a bearing as to how he came to fall in the water, but there was no evidence of this. There were no indications to suggest a heart attack, nor was there any sign of foul play. Suicide by such a method was most unlikely, and no note had been found. It had to be an accident.

An inquiry was held at Glasgow before Sheriff Gillies and a jury on 14th May 1959. Since there was no evidence to show how Captain Richardson came to be in the water, the jury was directed to bring in a formal verdict of "Found Drowned". And there the matter rested, a sad epitaph on the life of a respected shipmaster who had spent his life at sea, a shipmaster popular with his peers and subordinates alike, his untimely end bringing sorrow to them, and grief to his family.

A post-war view of *Adviser* with a modified funnel.

[*A. Duncan*]

245. BARRISTER (4) 1939-1943 Steel steamship. Two decks, five holds and deep tank. Two masts.
O.N. 166266 6,348g 3,886n 9,000d 445.5 (459.25 o.l.) x 56.5 x 32.17 feet. Cargo capacity: 482,532 cubic feet.
International Code: GTTF.
T. 3-cyl. by David Rowan and Co. Ltd., Glasgow, with Bauer-Wach exhaust turbine; 29, 47, 81 x 54 inches, 14½ knots.

6.4.1939: Launched by Lithgows Ltd., Port Glasgow (Yard No. 918) for the company. *15.6.1939:* Delivered at a cost of £193,219. Later sailed from west coast ports to South Africa on her maiden voyage under Captain H. Collins. *11.1942:* Supported troops in North African campaign, carrying supplies to Algiers. *4.1.1943:* Wrecked off Inishshark Island, County Galway when on passage from Algiers to the Clyde in ballast. The crew was saved, the majority picked up by HMCS KITCHENER and landed at Londonderry.

The unfortunate *Barrister* when new.

An Irish landfall
Christmas 1942 passed peacefully enough in Gibraltar Bay, where the BARRISTER had anchored to await the assembly of a convoy bound for the United Kingdom. Peacefully is used in a relative sense here, for the occasional audacious sortie of enemy frogmen operating from the Spanish port of Algeçiras to place limpet mines on ships in the anchorage was a continual source of menace. BARRISTER was homeward bound in ballast from Algiers, where she had unloaded a cargo of supplies for the troops in North Africa. Gradually, the convoy took shape, as more ships entered the Bay, and it sailed eventually on 27th December.

The weather during the next few days was consistently bad, with strong south west winds, driving rain, and poor visibility. By 3rd January 1943 the convoy was in the Western Approaches, and orders were given to split, the two outer columns to go northabout to the Clyde, and the two inner columns to pass south of Ireland into the Irish Sea. BARRISTER, bound for the Clyde, was in the former section. The bad weather still persisted, and visibility became worse, until it became very easy to lose track of the ship ahead. No ship had had sight of sun or stars for several days. Dead reckoning placed the BARRISTER some 10 miles west of the Irish Coast, and, only too aware that dead-reckoning positions are notoriously inaccurate, captain and officers were becoming very uneasy. However, they knew that some of the escort vessels were fitted with radar, a mysterious device whose qualities and limitations were virtually unknown to Merchant Navy officers in those days, but whose aura of secrecy and mystery inspired an unwarranted confidence. If a landfall was due, then the inshore escorts would be sure to locate it and warn the convoy in good time.

During the middle watch on 4th January, Second Officer Skelly found his next ahead, a US ship, to be an elusive station-keeper in the poor conditions. Surreptitiously, he eased the ship across to the next column to keep station on a large escort carrier whose bulk was more readily discernible. At 04.00 he handed the watch to Chief Officer Wells, and went below.

It is likely that during the next few hours, the convoy lost more of its cohesion, for when Third Officer Jack Bean came on watch a little before 08.00, there was no sign of any ship either ahead or astern, though vague shapes could be seen dimly to port and starboard. It was still pitch dark (clocks were kept on British Double Summer Time, i.e. nearly three hours ahead of true time in that longitude). The sky was heavily overcast, and a persistent drizzle enveloped everything. The wind had moderated a little, but there was a heavy swell running from the southwest. Chief Officer Wells and Captain Collins (who had been up and about at various times during the night) went below to freshen up. Then, a few minutes after 08.00 the lookout-man in the starboard wing of the bridge reported that he thought he could see something ahead.

A certain witness[194] who was on watch at the time, recorded an impression of what he saw: "Suddenly, out of the mist, and becoming more distinct with each leaden second, loomed the black silhouette of an enormous rocky crag, its conical peak towering above the fore-yard. At its base clouds of white spume rose high in the air as the Atlantic swells swept in. It could not have been more than half-a-mile away when first sighted. The Third Officer reacted swiftly.

"Hard-a-port! Two short blasts!" he yelled, casting an anguished glance aft to see whether our next astern was on our heels. There was nothing in sight. "Get the Old Man up here!" The ship's head was beginning to swing away from the dark menace of the cliff face, and it was only when we looked seaward again that we realised the ship was virtually surrounded by white water, the hallmark of rocky shoals. Captain Collins clambered up to the bridge just as the ship struck".

Second Officer Harold Skelly was still in his bunk, and he remembers how the impact lifted him bodily, not once, but twice, and he was quite sure the ship had been torpedoed. Already fully dressed he staggered out into the darkness and made his way to the bridge. There, he at once set about destroying the code books and signal logs which littered the chart room table; the Third Officer was igniting flares and rockets while a cadet sounded the ship's whistle to warn ships in the vicinity. Captain Collins leaned on the rail and stared ahead at the broken water in utter disbelief. Chief Officer Wells appeared looking very put out. He had been shaving and had nicked his chin when the impact threw him across the cabin. Then, at Captain Collins' request he went aft to organise the crew and prepare the boats for launching. Incongruously, a steward vigorously sounded the first gong for breakfast.

The ship was vibrating madly under full astern power, and the wash was sweeping forward, but the bow, held fast by the rocks did not budge. The stern of the ship, on the other hand, was undulating ominously to the swell. There was a crack like a rifle shot from somewhere below the bridge. Then another, quickly followed by a rattle like a burst of machine-gun fire. The rivets holding the ship's members together were bursting under the strain. Sadly, Captain Collins rang "Stop" on the telegraph and went to the engine-room voice pipe. He spoke to the Chief Engineer, who was down below. "Shut down, Chief, and bring your men up from there. Abandon ship!"

The first boat was launched just as the first grey wisps of dawn were appearing in the sky to the south east. The mist and drizzle had cleared and, as the light grew stronger, they could see with desperate clarity the extremity of their position. Close to starboard was the lofty island rock which had been sighted at the beginning of their ordeal, and which they later discovered was known as Inishshark. Another, larger island called Inishbofin lay further eastwards; and beyond, the soft green hills and craggy mountains of Connemara. The northern horizon was dotted with islands, and to the west the heaving expanse of the Atlantic Ocean. A corvette, one of the escorts, was standing off, available and ready to render assistance. The boat's coxswain was advised to head for the warship - there seemed little chance of finding a landing in that rock-strewn surf.

Two more boats were launched, and headed for the corvette which was later identified as HMCS KITCHENER (Commander Bill Evans, RCN). Meanwhile, the end of the BARRISTER was imminent. Amidships, the deck split asunder, and the two winches at number 3 hatch disappeared into the hold. By now, only the Master, Second Officer Skelly, Third Officer Bean, Cadet Eric Parry, Chief Steward Sid Owen, Chief Engineer Ernie Mossman, the Senior Radio Officer, and a few sailors remained on board. Some were still in the vicinity of the bridge, and had to leap smartly across the yawning gap amidships to reach the last remaining lifeboat. Some concern was felt because certain confidential documents still reposed in the Master's safe. However, the bridge accommodation was now inaccessible. The boat was launched, and the wreck abandoned to its fate.

The last survivors to leave were picked up by another escort vessel, HMS LANDGUARD,[195] whose commander was not at all pleased to learn that secret documents were still on board in the ship's safe. He insisted they must be retrieved. Captain Collins, whose responsibility they were, was an elderly man, obviously not up to scrambling about on a wreck. The commander fastened his gaze on Harold Skelly.

"Who? Me?!!", said Harold, somewhat shaken. "Yes, you, Mr. Skelly", replied the Commander implacably. "You are the next senior officer present, and you must endeavour to board that ship and retrieve or destroy those documents. It is your duty".

They stared over at the wreck. Tide and sea had risen, and waves were breaking over the fore part, still fast on the rocks. Second Officer Skelly politely declined the offer of a boat's crew that day. The commander relented in view of the conditions, and agreed to stand off until next morning. That afternoon, the ship's after section broke clear, drifted away, and eventually sank in deep water. When dawn broke on the 5th January, the sea was quieter, and LANDGUARD lowered a boat. Second Officer Skelly, together with the gunnery officer and six ratings, climbed aboard and set out cautiously for the wreck. They brought gelignite charges with them, intending to blow up the safe if the keys could not be found. They boarded the wreck with difficulty, the only practical means of access being via the port anchor. Dodging the seas which still broke on board occasionally, they reached the Captain's quarters. They were completely washed out, panelling stripped and furniture swept away through smashed doors. Fortunately, the safe was intact,

bolted to the steel frame, and, miraculously, the keys were found swilling about in a pool of water in a corner, together with Captain Collins' sextant.

The books and papers were taken from the safe, and hurriedly they left the wreck which was creaking and grinding alarmingly in its rocky bed. The improvement in the weather had brought out a small fleet of curious and expectant fishermen. It is doubtful whether rumours of the POLITICIAN (238) and her fabulous cargo of whisky, wrecked just two years earlier on the island of Eriskay in the Outer Hebrides, had yet reached this remote Irish outpost. If they had then these islanders must have been sorely grieved to find BARRISTER's remaining holds quite empty, except for sea water.

Meanwhile, the boarding party had returned triumphantly to the LANDGUARD, whose commander then decreed that three officers should go ashore to attend to the formalities which that august scrap merchant, the Receiver of Wrecks, would have in store for them. Mr. Skelly would be accompanied by Third Officer Bean and Cadet Parry, while Captain Collins and the other survivors would return to Liverpool in LANDGUARD. A fishing-boat was hailed alongside, and, after some inducement, her skipper agreed to take Mr. Skelly's party ashore. Before they left they were handed a pillow case stuffed with shag tobacco and matches, and £40 sterling "for contingency spending". Alexander Selkirk - the original Robinson Crusoe - fared far worse when he was marooned!

For several days the castaways remained on the island of Inishbofin until the weather moderated sufficiently for the officials to venture out from the mainland harbour of Ballynakill. Meanwhile they lived somewhat roughly in a large draughty house with a leaking roof, objects of considerable curiosity to the islanders, whose attitude nevertheless was plainly aloof. Eventually a boat arrived bearing representatives of the Galway Garda, the Army, Lloyds, and the inevitable Receiver of Wrecks from the Irish Customs and Excise. Second Officer Skelly signed over what was left of the wreck, which had by now almost entirely disappeared. The trio were then free to begin the long trek to Dublin, and so home, husbanding what remained of the £40, of which a full account had to be rendered to Mr. George Dean on on their return.[196]

Returning to those survivors picked up by HMCS KITCHENER, it is gratifying to recall how warmly they were welcomed. Despite the cramped and crowded conditions, every effort was made to make them as comfortable as possible. Hot food was passed around, and warm clothing provided for those who had come on board lightly clad. Of the total of 74 men who comprised the BARRISTER's crew, only one was injured - a DEMS gunner who had trapped his hand while releasing the forward davit-block in his pitching lifeboat. His wounds were expertly dressed as the corvette headed for Londonderry on the first stage of the journey home.

At 63, Captain Collins never went to sea again, though he continued to perform a useful role as a relief officer on the dock and on the Manchester Ship Canal until his retirement in 1950. Harold Skelly acquired his sextant (the one he had salvaged) for £5, since his own had been lost in the wreck. He used it throughout his sea-going career, becoming quite attached to it despite the memories it evoked of a calamitous Irish landfall, and that hair-raising venture aboard a severed, sea-swamped wreck off the Irish Coast.

246. SETTLER (2) 1939-1959 Steel steamship. Two decks, five holds and deep tank. Two masts.
O.N. 166273 6,202g 3,798n 8,800d 438.8 (452.75 o.l.) x 56.5 x 32.22 feet. Cargo capacity: 468,190 cubic feet. International Code: GTTX.
T. 3-cyl. by Barclay, Curle and Co. Ltd., Glasgow, with Bauer-Wach exhaust turbine; 29, 47, 81 x 54 inches, 14 knots.

2.5.1939: Launched by Charles Connell and Co. Ltd., Whiteinch (Yard No. 426) for the company. *6.7.1939:* Delivered at a cost of £183,543. Later sailed from London and Antwerp for South Africa on her maiden voyage under Captain E.G. Horne. *24.7.1941:* Attacked by enemy aircraft when bound in convoy from Malta to Gibraltar. Escaped with a succession of near misses, but a certain amount of damage was discovered six months later when inspected in dry dock. *1.1942:* The bridge deck wings were stripped out at Liverpool and fitted with accommodation for 56 passengers. *12.1942:* When bound from Capetown to Trinidad, and sailing independently, diverted to the assistance of a Catalina flying boat of the USAAF. This had been shot down by the German submarine U 176 off Brazil and the survivors were in a dinghy. The survivors were located and rescued some forty hours later. One, being injured, was only lifted aboard with great difficulty. The

survivors were landed safely 20.12.1942 at Georgetown, Demerara. *21.1.1944:* Involved in a complex collision situation in New York harbour (see below). *4.1945:* When berthed at Golfito on the Pacific coast of Costa Rica, it was learnt that the President was visiting the town and wished to come on board. Captain R.F. Phillips was uncertain as to the correct form of protocol for welcoming presidents, but was determined not to be found wanting. When the President arrived on the wharf, 21 blasts were ordered on the steam whistle, the final six sounding rather feeble due to rapidly declining boiler pressure. *2.10.1959:* Sold for £55,000 to Margalente Compania Naviera S.A., Monrovia, Liberia (Mavroleon Brothers Ltd., London, managers), and renamed MARGALENTE. Resold after one voyage to Leung Yan Trading Co., Hong Kong, for demolition. *11.12.1959:* Arrived at Hong Kong. *1.1.1960:* Demolition commenced.

A maritime pile-up[197]

On 21st January 1944 the anchorage off the New York Quarantine Station was packed with ships waiting for convoys. Among the many ships swinging anxiously to each tide was a group of four occupying the corners of a rhomboid shape measuring approximately $2^{1}/_{4}$ cables by $1^{3}/_{4}$. This group comprised the SETTLER, homeward bound with a cargo of sugar from Demerara and Trinidad; the SAMUEL DE CHAMPLAIN, (7,194/43) a US Liberty; the MARIT II (7,417/22), a Norwegian tanker, and the ROBERT FULTON, (7,176/42), another Liberty.

At 20.10 SETTLER swung to the ebb tide, and at 20.15 the Third Officer, Victor Harrison, who was on watch noticed that the CHAMPLAIN,

Settler in original condition.

[J. and M. Clarkson collection]

positioned about 360 yards away on the starboard bow, had her navigation lights on, and was under way. He watched her swing to starboard and realised with alarm that the ebb tide was carrying her down on the MARIT II. A collision was inevitable. The thought crossed his mind that the tanker may have a highly volatile cargo. Hastily, he called Captain Short to the bridge, and he, sensing trouble, ordered the crew to stations, and put the engines on stand by.

Meanwhile, in a vain attempt to clear the MARIT II, CHAMPLAIN came astern on her engines, and so threatened to fall foul of the SETTLER. Seeing the danger, her captain went full ahead - and again collided with the tanker. By this time he must have been running short of ideas, for without more ado he again came full astern, right across the ebb tide, and fell across SETTLER's bow, where Chief Officer Sid Diamond and the carpenter were frantically veering cable to give the other ship more sea room.

The pressure of the hapless CHAMPLAIN against the SETTLER's bow was too much for the latter's ground tackle, and she began to drag her anchor, falling down rapidly on the ROBERT FULTON, who seemed totally oblivious to the worsening situation. At 20.53 SETTLER dropped her second anchor, but even this did not prevent her from fouling the ROBERT FULTON four minutes later. By

21.17 CHAMPLAIN was clear, but still posing a threat to her infuriated neighbours. At 21.25 FULTON seemed to wake up to the confusion around her and suddenly went full astern on her engines, dragging her anchor forcibly out of the mud, and stretching the catenary of her chain until it slammed against SETTLER's most vulnerable parts, rattling the stern frame. At 21.29 she, too, was clear, and gradually the anchorage returned to normal, leaving the injured parties to check for damage.

SETTLER's visible damage consisted of dented plating, the poop rails smashed, and number 5 boat and davits damaged. It could have been much worse. Captain Short was, of course, concerned about damage to rudder and propeller which may have been caused by the FULTON's anchor cable, and engaged a diver to make an inspection. He was very much relieved when the diver reported that he could find no sign of damage in that area.

Captain Short was, understandably, incensed by the whole affair, and laid the blame squarely on the CHAMPLAIN whose very unseamanlike manoeuvres had started the whole chain of events. FULTON was also castigated for failing to keep an efficient anchor watch. One other unfortunate consequence was that SETTLER missed the convoy, and her sailing was delayed by one week.

A subtle alteration to her paintwork, and a shortened funnel, made a considerable difference to *Settler's* appearance.

247. DALESMAN (1) 1940-1941/EMPIRE WILY 1945-1946/DALESMAN (1) 1946-1959

O.N. 166295 6,343g 3,883n 9,000d 445.1 (459.6 o.l.) x 56.5 x 32.17 feet. Cargo capacity: 482,532 cubic feet.
International Code: GLWW (GQGL after 1945).
T. 3-cyl. by David Rowan and Co. Ltd., Glasgow, with Bauer-Wach exhaust turbine; 29, 47, 81 x 54 inches, 14½ knots.

26.3.1940: Launched by Lithgows Ltd., Port Glasgow (Yard No. 927) for the company. *10.7.1940:* Delivered at a cost of £186,000 and later sailed from Liverpool to the West Indies on her maiden voyage under Captain D. Flynn. *14.5.1941:* Bombed and sunk by German aircraft at Suda Bay, Crete. Struck by a single bomb which penetrated the main deck, 'tween deck, several tiers of the munitions cargo in number 4 lower hold and the tank top, before exploding against the bottom plating. The force of the explosion burst open the keel plates, flooding the after end of the ship, so that she settled on an even keel. The water was shallow and the upper decks remained clear and for three days efforts were made to salvage as much cargo as possible. Steam to work the winches was provided by a naval trawler which berthed alongside and connected a steam hose to the deck-line.

17.5.1941: Abandoned by her crew, 32 of whom, including all the officers and engineers, were subsequently taken prisoner. Twenty four, including the master, Captain, E.G. Horne, were able to escape. Subsequently raised by German forces, repaired and returned to service with Mittelmeer Reederei GmbH, Berlin as PLUTO. *1944:* Bombed and sunk during an Allied raid on Trieste. *1945:* Raised by the Royal Navy, repaired at Trieste and 10.1945: Returned to service with the Ministry of War Transport, London (Thos. and Jas. Harrison, Liverpool, managers) as EMPIRE WILY. *4.11.1946:* Reacquired by the company for £232,747. *15.11.1946:* Renamed DALESMAN. *11.9.1959:* Sold for £49,500 to Van Heyghen Frères S.A., Belgium for demolition. *15.9.1959:* Arrived at Ghent. *16.9.1959:* Demolition commenced.

Ships on trial continued to be photographed in wartime. This is *Dalesman,* completed in grey, in 1940.

[Glasgow University Archives GD320/10/1/126/4]

A quintet of Dalesmen

1. Cadet Dobson

John Halstead Dobson was born in Birkenhead in 1923, but in 1941, the year John joined Harrison Line, the family was living in Teignmouth, Devon. He was, in fact, still making his first voyage to sea in the DALESMAN when the ship was sunk at Suda Bay in May 1941. With the rest of the crew, he sought shelter amid the olive groves and scented gardens of Crete. He was also feeling extremely unwell at the time, suffering from a grumbling appendix.

During the invasion and subsequent evacuation of the island he, like so many of his shipmates and thousands of soldiers, was captured by the German paratroopers. It was while he was being marched into captivity near the head of a long column of fellow-prisoners that Cadet Dobson was seized with a sudden impulse to escape. With a ferocity improbable in such an amiable young man, he attacked the nearest guard, snatched his automatic rifle, and turned it on the other guards.

Whether he actually fired is not recorded, but apparently the guards' response was frozen by total surprise, for Dobson was able to reach cover and make a spectacular escape.[198] Shortly afterwards, he came across a New Zealand battery, and for several days he served voluntarily alongside the gunners as they covered the main retreat across the island to the south coast. Eventually he and his companions reached Sfarkia (Khora Sfakion) and were able to board one of the last evacuation vessels to leave the island, a landing craft crowded with troops.

As the ship headed out of the little port it soon became clear that no-one on board knew much about ships, and even

less about navigation. No-one, that is, except Cadet Dobson, still in the process of completing his rudely interrupted first voyage to sea. To him, therefore, devolved the task of navigating the ungainly craft across the Mediterranean to Egypt.

For several days they ploughed through sunlit seas, escaping the attentions of enemy bombers. In due course they made their landfall on the coast of Egypt, just inside the border with Libya, somewhere east of Sollum. It so happened that luck was still on their side, for they found themselves on the friendly side of a very fluid front line. A mile or two further west would have dropped them into the hands of Rommel's Afrika Korps.

Cadet Dobson's exploits did not go unrecognised. His initiative and courage were reported to Naval Headquarters, and the boy himself was interviewed, on his return to England in September, by Admiral Sir Percy Noble, Commander in Chief Western Approaches, at his headquarters in Liverpool. The outcome was that John Dobson's name appeared in the Supplement to the London Gazette of 4th August 1942, announcing his award of the British Empire Medal, Civil Division.

However, stirring events take their toll, even of the bravest, and John, like so many other casualties of war, was destined to suffer from the trauma of his experiences. The doctors called it war neurosis; known to the Americans as combat fatigue, and to First World War veterans as shell shock. Whatever its clinical definition, it incapacitated John as surely as a physically maiming, disabling war wound, forcing him to give up a promising sea-going career.

The second resurrection of *Dalesman*. Top: as *Pluto,* a name given to her after being raised at Suda Bay by the Germans, salvaged a second time but now by the Royal Navy at Trieste in 1945.

Middle: as *Empire Wily* repairs are almost complete in dry dock at Trieste during the winter of 1945.

Bottom: in service again as *Dalesman* after being reacquired by Harrisons from the British Government in November 1946.
[Middle: Pozzar & Figlio; Bottom: F.W. Hawks]

2. Ronald Russell

It would be difficult to find a more lowly rating aboard a British merchant ship than that of officers' boy. For such was Ronald Russell, aged 15, aboard the DALESMAN. Like many of his shipmates, he found himself camping in a Cretan olive grove a few days after his ship had been sunk. To a boy of his age it must have all seemed quite a lark. Things began to look more serious, however, when enemy planes began sweeping overhead, bombing and machine-gunning the camps, or casting out paratroops in clouds of billowing silk, and the retreat began. Like so many others, he found himself attached to an army unit, in his case a unit of the Royal Army Medical Corps, to which he apparently offered his services, despite suffering from some unspecified illness. His demeanour certainly impressed the unit's commander, who saw fit to mention him in despatches, the citation running thus: "To Whom it may Concern. Ronald Russell, Merchant Service, S.S. DALESMAN, aged 15 yrs. This boy, although ill, displayed the utmost gallantry under heavy Machine Gun fire from the air. Although exposed on the open ground he obeyed instructions to remain quiet in order not to give away the position of the Ammunition Lines and Petrol Dump to the low-flying aeroplanes which persistently attacked the site for over two hours. I consider his conduct most exemplary, and he showed great fortitude and courage for one so young. Signed: H. Freemantle, Captain, R.A.M.C., D.S.O., C.B.E., M.C."[199] Young Russell was later presented with a gold watch on behalf of the War Risks Association, "for utmost gallantry displayed while under heavy machine gun fire at Suda Bay, 28.5.41."

3. Bill Ashton

Third Officer William L. Ashton of the DALESMAN also sought refuge in the olive grove camp, along with his shipmates. There they found the survivors from the sunken LOGICIAN, and the two crews thenceforth endeavoured to keep together during the retreat, but were inevitably separated into small groups as they trekked across the island. However, most of them arrived at the evacuation port of Sfarkia in good order, but when Ashton and his companions came to board their alloted vessel they found it had broken down. There was no other, and there was nothing for it but to sit down and wait for the Germans to move in and capture them.[200]

They did not have long to wait, for next morning, they and hundreds more were rounded up and ordered to trek back across the mountains, back to Suda Bay. From there, Third Officer Ashton, Second Officer F.R. Hill, and Chief Officer Herbert Jones were flown to Athens on the first stage of their journey into captivity in Germany, together with many other officer prisoners. The plane was an old Junkers, but it was the last they were to see of modern transport facilities for quite a while. At Athens they were informed that they would have to walk some 300 miles to the railhead at Salonika "...because the English have destroyed all the bridges and railways".

About three hundred prisoners set off on the long trek, and occasionally they would get a lift from a passing train on those sections of line still open, but most of the time they walked. To anyone with any pretensions to a classical education it must have been a rewarding experience as they trekked across that ancient terrain, through the Pass of Thermopylae, into Thessaly, and round the foothills of Mount Olympus. But doubtless the men had more mundane factors to consider - like the whereabouts and adequacy of the next makeshift meal, or the urgent provision of new boots.

After a week's march they came to Salonika, footsore and weary, to be housed in an ancient Turkish barracks overrun with vermin, and surrounded by barbed wire. Ashton and his companions were appalled to see, hanging on the wire, the bullet-riddled bodies of British and Commonwealth servicemen - an ugly warning to anyone contemplating escape.

Several more days went by, after which the dispirited prisoners were marched to the station where a train of cattle trucks awaited them. They were crammed into the trucks, and the train-load of human misery moved off. For by this time most of the prisoners were ill, suffering from dysentery and enteritis, and conditions in the trucks quickly became indescribable. For one long week they rolled across Greece, Yugoslavia, Austria, and into Germany, until finally the train pulled into the station at Lubeck on the Baltic. The prisoners fell rather than jumped from the trucks, feeling more dead than alive, and badly in need of decent food and medical attention. But there was still more travelling to do. The servicemen were divided into groups to be despatched to different areas, Army, Air Force, and Navy. The merchant service seamen were grouped with the Royal Navy and despatched to Wilhelmshaven - fortunately by train, for they were in no fit state to walk. They remained at Wilhelmshaven for six weeks, during which time each man was interrogated by staff officers. The town also happened to be a prime target for the RAF at that time. The planes came over regularly to bomb the docks and the city, so it was almost with feelings of relief that the prisoners at last found themselves on the way to permanent camps in the German countryside, there to remain until the war in Europe ended in May 1945. (See also under CRAFTSMAN, 235, for further coverage of life in the German prisoner-of-war camps).

4. Bob Murray

Another of DALESMAN's crew caught up in the retreat from Crete was Robert Murray, a native of Garston, who had signed on as Messroom Steward. During the trek across the island he and his companions had been strafed more than once by low-flying aircraft. It was during one of these raids that Bob was wounded in the foot, not by a bullet, but by a chip of granite kicked up by the gunfire. Despite this handicap Bob reached Sfarkia only to find, like so many of his fellow fugitives, that he, too, had literally missed the boat.[201]

Consequently, he joined a column of prisoners winding its way over the mountains, hobbling painfully on his injured foot, until at last they found themselves back in Suda Bay. There a doctor examined his injuries, shrugged, and advised him to stand in the sea for a while. Proper medical treatment was evidently a very rare commodity at that time and place. Shortly afterwards, Bob and hundreds more boarded an Italian vessel, the ORION, which in due course brought them safely to Salonika in Greece. At least he was spared the long hike from Athens endured by so many of his compatriots.

Unlike the officers, ratings were required to work. At Salonika they loaded scrap for the foundries of Germany, and stacked timber. After several weeks they boarded a train, crammed like their comrades into old cattle trucks. For them the nightmare journey ended at a camp south of Munich, where the prisoners were cleaned up and deloused. Bob, like so many others, was suffering from dysentery, an affliction he attributed to drinking water from a contaminated stream during the trek back across the mountains. They rather belatedly found the source of the contamination as they toiled up the mountain track - the body of a dead German soldier lying in the water upstream.

Some attempt was made at this camp to re-kit the men and replace their ruined clothing. Bob recalls coming away dashingly attired in a pair of Yugoslav riding breeches, a French Kepi, a Czech military cloak, and a couple of odd shoes.

From Munich the captives were transported to Hamburg in a passenger train - much to their astonishment. Bob's foot was no better, and when they at last reached a permanent prisoner-of-war camp he was transferred to hospital to have several toes amputated. However, far from being dismayed by this calamity Bob put his native business sense to work, and was soon up to his neck in more than one camp racket.

Somehow, he got himself a job in the galley, or cookhouse, an influential position in any walk of life. One of his jobs involved a weekly trip into Bremen for stores - under guard of course, but that did not prevent a little judicious trading using Red Cross cigarettes as currency. Bartering with local farmers - galley slops for the pigs in exchange for new laid eggs was one of his lines, an enterprise from which many benefited. His entrepreneurial skills were simple but effective. For instance, a quarter-pound tin of coffee could get as many as 25 eggs from a farmer. Twelve eggs would buy another tin of coffee in the camp. Bob could not lose. It was a lesson in economics. Eggs, of course, were not the only commodity available in this thriving market. Fresh vegetables, potatoes, the occasional chicken, or bottle of Schnapps were among many desirable items.

Bob was also into the gambling business, his unlikely partner an ethnic Japanese gentleman from the Dingle, of all places. The main jeux des hasards were fantan, and a sort of homemade roulette. There were times when Bob, as banker, held thousands of German marks in his hands.

Then of course there was his distillery, a highly organised enterprise. Dried fruit, currants and sultanas from Red Cross parcels were essential to the fermentation process. These found their way into the vats of liquor concealed in the galley. The stuff was brewed on the stove and a pipe from the cooking pot led the vapour under the cold tap where it condensed and dripped into the waiting bottles. Bob's output was forty bottles a session - it was rough, mind-blowing stuff, flavoured sometimes with coffee ("Tia Maria") or fruit jellies - but there was a steady demand for it, even among the guards.

Came the day when the German storekeeper noted certain deficiencies and inconsistencies. Bob and his mate were sacked, and transferred to the job of pumping out the latrine sumps into large tanks, and trundling them out to the local farmers for spraying the fields. Here again, Bob maintained his touch, and invariably returned to camp laden with farm produce.

Perhaps it was fitting in the circumstances that Bob Murray should transfer his talents to the Harrison Line after his release, first as Cook, and later as Chief Steward.

5. Herbert Jones
Herbert Walter Jones was Chief Officer of the DALESMAN, and throughout the confusion, danger, and misery of Crete he had more or less kept his men together, and acted as their leader and spokesman. Those who failed to escape, however, soon became prisoners, and were separated into different groups for the journey to Germany.

Eventually, all were reunited in the Milag section of Marlag und Milag Nord, near Bremen. Around 1943, however, the camp, which housed about 3,000 merchant and naval seamen, was extended to include the growing number of Asiatic seamen-prisoners, particularly those from India.[202] Among them were 77 Lascars from the Harrison vessels SCIENTIST and TRIBESMAN. Their plight was complicated, to say the least.

Prisoners in a foreign land, amid an alien culture; unable to speak the language of their captors, nor they theirs; and outside the mainstream of European Red Cross activity, their problems in comparison with those of their European counterparts were doubled. The Germans, to give them their due, were scrupulously fair, meting out the same measure of treatment to them as to the European prisoners. Perhaps they were too rigid in their concept of fairness. Equal portions of German pork sausage, for instance, were meaningless to the largely Moslem seamen, to whom most of the fare was abhorrent. But communication was almost impossible - even the Germans who spoke English failed to understand the pidgin variety spoken by the Lascars, and soon lost patience.

Finally, the German authorities decided to appoint a Hindustani-speaking British officer to oversee the interests of their Indian prisoners. Among the hundreds of City, Clan, and Bank Line officers in the camp there were many who spoke, and even wrote, Hindustani. But of the volunteers who came forward, it was Herbert Jones of the Harrison Line who was chosen. He was given an assistant, Third Officer Bill Ashton, an office, and a title, Vertrauen Offizier (Confidence Officer), and together they moved into the Asian sector of Milag Nord.

Herbert Jones entered into his new duties with a fervour born of intense boredom. At last, he had a worthwhile job to do, and his day was filled listening to anxious petitions from Lascars who had not heard from their homes in India since their ships had left port. He was called upon to settle endless disputes which tended to develop rapidly in those barbed wire confines, disputes which often demanded the wisdom of Solomon to resolve. He was also their link with the Camp Commandant, and through Herbert's intervention many minor and major complaints were rectified. Arrangements were put in hand for them to cook their own traditional food based on an improved quota of rice. Through his efforts, Red Cross parcels began to arrive, often containing curry powder and spices instead of the cans of pork and beans, which the Europeans welcomed, but which the Asians reviled.

Herbert Jones and Bill Ashton spent many hours writing letters for the illiterate, of whom there were many, and also writing to embassy and Red Cross officials in an endeavour to trace missing relatives. Together they ran an impromptu school to teach their charges English, and organised a sick parade each day for those who wished to see the camp doctor. It was hard work of an administrative kind, but it had its compensations. Besides distracting their attention from the constrictions of prison camp life, they earned the respect of their charges, who clearly appreciated their efforts. The serangs ensured that the burra sahibs would want for nothing that was in their power to provide. A Goanese Christian steward called Manuel was delighted to prepare their food, and in fact became their batman, and there was always a topass on hand to do the cleaning.

In the spring of 1945, as the distant sound of artillery fire drew closer heralding the day of liberation, the rising tide of excitement was mingled with apprehension. At one stage the camp was situated between the opposing front lines, while shells and missiles hurtled overhead with a disconcerting shrillness. The camp's nominal neutrality was never violated, however, and the stillness which characterised the end of hostilities sent a wave of utter relief throughout all its inmates. There is, however, no hint of these emotions in the scraps of diary jotted down by Herbert Jones in those last hectic days of the war with Germany. His comments are laconic to the point of anticlimax:

"Saturday, 28th April 1945. 9.00 a.m. Camp relieved by Welsh Guards (The Desert Rats). With Brengun carrier named Sollum. Captain Flynn arrived.
Sunday, 29th April. 3.15 p.m. First contingent (94) left for home. 4.15 p.m. 5 Asiatics left for home. Gunfire close all day.
Monday, 30th April. 2.30 p.m. Second contingent, 50 men, ex TRIBESMAN; 7 ex GRACEFIELD; 5 ex DOMINGO DE LARRINAGA. "Minnie" still landing close. Woods not cleared of jerry yet. [This was the day Hitler committed suicide in his Berlin bunker].
Tuesday, 1st May. 2.00 p.m. Third contingent, 100. Took photos cemetery.
Wednesday, 2nd May. No transport. Deloused 100.
Thursday, 3rd May. 11.30 a.m. Fourth contingent left. 100 Indians.
Saturday, 5th May. No transport. Shifted down to Milag, Barracks 28 and 26. Took photos of Lager. [On this day, the surrender of German forces in North Germany, Denmark, and Holland, signed two days before at Montgomery's Headquarters on Luneburg Heath, came into effect.]
Monday, 7th May. 3.00 p.m. Transport for 50 men.
Tuesday, 8th May. 5.00 Transport for 75 men". [V.E. Day. The war against Germany was officially over.]
After the war, Herbert Jones' contribution to the welfare of Indian prisoners of war was acknowledged by the presentation of an MBE at an investiture on 20th November 1945. The decoration was accompanied by a Letter of Commendation for "meritorious conduct in a Prisoner of War Camp".

248. NOVELIST (1) 1940-1961 Steel steamship. Two decks, five holds and deep tank. Two masts.
O.N. 166296 6,133g 3,704n 9,134d. 423.4 (434.5 o.l.) x 54.5 x 32.6 feet. Cargo capacity: 487,997 cubic feet. International Code: GMLG.
T. 3-cyl. by J.G. Kincaid and Co. Ltd., Greenock; 27, 44, 77 x 54 inches, 11 knots.

4.6.1940: Launched by Harland and Wolff Ltd., Glasgow (Yard No. 1033G) for the company. *8.8.1940:* Delivered at a cost of £151,000. Later sailed from Glasgow for Galveston on her maiden voyage under Captain W.A. Hall. *11.3.1941:* Whilst loading war materials, including ammunition, at Manchester, hit by a large bomb in number 2 'tween deck during an air raid. The bomb started a serious fire in the cargo stowed above the ammunition, which was only extinguished by the courageous efforts of the crew, led by Chief Officer Bill Moore and Second Officer Charles Boam. Their action prompted a congratulatory letter from the Director of

Novelist in the Mersey, 9th August 1947.   *[J. and M. Clarkson]*

Sea Transport at the Ministry of Shipping. The damage was severe and all cargo was subsequently discharged into the company's COMEDIAN (223) and repairs were commenced. It was decided at the time to refit her as a catapult armed merchantman (CAM ship). This involved erecting a steel gantry in the fore part of the ship carrying a trackway some 80 or 90 feet long. Perched on the track was a trolley bearing a fighter aircraft, usually a Hawker Hurricane. To launch the fighter, the ship would be turned into the wind and a bank of rockets attached to the trolley would be fired, thus launching the aircraft. Its purpose then was to seek out and destroy German long-range reconnaissance aircraft which shadowed the Atlantic convoys, passing information to U-boats. The aircraft itself was expendable and, upon his return, the pilot would try to ditch close to an escort or rescue vessel. The blast of the rockets was found to have an alarming effect on the balance of magnetic compasses and NOVELIST thus became the first of the company's vessels to be fitted with a Sperry Gyro-compass. *8.1941:* Whilst crossing the Atlantic in Convoy HX 143 from Halifax encountered HMS PRINCE OF WALES. The battleship was returning home with the Prime Minister, Mr Winston Churchill, after his Atlantic Charter conference with President Roosevelt in Newfoundland. She passed between the extended columns of the convoy with Churchill clearly visible on the bridge.[203] *1.1.1943:* Damaged during a bombing raid whilst discharging Government stores at Bone, Algeria. *14.3.1952:* A serious fire broke out in the bunker coal when berthed at Beira. The fire was extinguished the following day after 700 tons of coal had been discharged and sold to local merchants. An inspection revealed number 3 forward bulkhead to be slightly buckled. *3.11.1960:* When outward bound from London to Demerara in collision with

Contentious Bone

NOVELIST arrived at the Algerian port of Bone (now known as Annaba) on 27th December 1942. She was loaded with a cargo of military supplies destined for the Allied armies operating in French North Africa. The port was subjected to frequent air attacks, and NOVELIST, recently equipped with the very effective, quick-firing Swedish Bofors A.A. gun manned by a detachment from the Maritime A.A. Regiment, and several Oerlikon 20-mm cannon, gave good account of herself. One of these was sited in the port wing of the bridge, and this weapon Captain A.J. Meek regarded as his own. Throughout the attacks he fought with a ferocious enthusiasm which belied his rather mild surname, and when later a flying splinter gashed his cheek, a bloodstained bandage completed the picture of a battle-hardened warrior.

It so happened that, on New Year's Day, HMS AJAX was berthed alongside NOVELIST when the port was hit by a particularly severe air attack. Wave after wave of bombers came over, singling out ships for individual attack, braving the flak which brought many down, two at least credited to NOVELIST's guns. Together, cruiser and freighter put up a furious barrage until AJAX was hit by a bomb near the base of the funnel. The bomb

Novelist after refit as a CAM ship and below with a Hawker Sea Hurricane mounted on the catapult.

NUDDEA (8,596/54) in the Thames off Tripcock Point, sustaining extensive damage to her stem and adjacent plating, and returned to London for repair. *18.5.1961:* Sold to Eastbound Tanker Corporation, Monrovia, Liberia (Rethymnis and Kulukundis Ltd., London, managers) for £74,000 and renamed PHOENIX under the Lebanese flag. Resold to Shiu Wing Co., Hong Kong, for demolition. *25.8.1961:* Arrived at Hong Kong. *15.9.1961:* Demolition commenced.

penetrated to the cruiser's thin outer skin, next to NOVELIST's port side, before exploding. The shell plating adjacent to NOVELIST's bunker space was split open, and soon both bunker space and engine room were flooded, and the ship settled on the bottom of the shallow harbour. AJAX, with her light draught, remained afloat, and was able to pull clear.

Meanwhile, the guns still blazed away until the last of the raiders flew off over the sea, some of them trailing smoke. Strenuous efforts were made over the next few days to repair the damage and plug the hole from the outside with the help of a Royal Navy salvage team, often under attack. Pumps were brought in from ashore, and eventually the flooded spaces were pumped dry, and the ship floated again. Numerous sprung rivets still sprayed water, however, and these had to be stopped before a cement box could be constructed over the ruptured steel work. It so happened that Second Officer Boam had the answer. One of his many hobbies was plasticine sculpture, and he had only recently completed a flattering likeness of himself. This startling effigy was now called upon to make the supreme sacrifice, and lumps of it were effectively remoulded to stop the weeping rivets while the enormous cement box was filled.

NOVELIST completed the discharge of her precious cargo of high-octane fuel, artillery, and stores, and sailed from Bone on 25th January 1943, in convoy. The voyage to Gibraltar was punctuated by air and submarine attacks, but was completed safely without loss. In the comparatively tranquil waters of Gibraltar Bay the opportunity was taken to reinforce the all-important cement box, but a spell of heavy weather on the homeward voyage put it under severe strain, starting the seams, and it was as much as the pumps could do to keep the ingress of water under control. However, the ship reached Liverpool safely on 16th February, and was eventually received on the welcoming blocks and shores of the Langton Graving Dock.[204]

These incidents, typical of many a merchant ship's war service, prompted a small spate of awards. The doughty Captain Meek was commended and awarded the OBE. Chief Engineer Bob Wilkins also received the OBE, while Second Engineer Joe Grierson was awarded an MBE. The names of six other officers and men, whose conduct during the action at Bone and its aftermath was no less significant, were put forward as deserving of honours, but these were declined with regret owing to rules limiting the number of awards granted. These, for the record, were Chief Officer Bill Moore, Second Officer Charles Boam, Third Officer William Brown, Third Engineer R. A. Catterall, Gunner C.E. Head, and Carpenter Rudolph Young.

249. TRADER (1) 1940-1961 Steel steamship. Two decks, five holds and deep tank. Two masts.
O.N. 166310 6,087g 3,726n 9,050d 420.5 (435.0 o.l.) x 54.6 x 32.6 feet. Cargo capacity: 486,380 cubic feet.
International Code: GNWX.
T. 3-cyl. by David Rowan and Co. Ltd., Glasgow; 27, 44$^{1}/_{2}$, 77 x 54 inches, 11$^{1}/_{2}$ knots.

18.10.1940: Launched by Charles Connell and Co. Ltd., Glasgow (Yard No. 430) for the company. *21.12.1940:* Delivered at a cost of £145,000. Later sailed from Liverpool to Jamaica on her maiden voyage under Captain E.G. Horne. *6.2.1943:* When anchored at the Tail of the Bank on the Clyde during a gale, her stern was hit by CITY OF WINDSOR (7,218/23) and she grounded near Kilcreggan. She was refloated the following day with the assistance of seven tugs. *29.4.1947:* While swinging in the basin, when moving from Number 7 Dock, Manchester, struck a floating crane causing damage to her navigating bridge and number 1 boat. Drawing clear of the crane, the tug's hawser parted and she

drifted towards the Trafford Road Swing Bridge. A disaster was averted by letting go both anchors but, as the ship brought up, her stern swung towards the bank striking the barge FAIRDALE and causing damage. The tugs were resecured and she was taken into dry dock. *23.12.1958:* Involved in two collisions in the River Mersey (see below). *24.5.1961:* Sold to Margalente Compania Naviera S.A., Panama (Mavroleon Brothers Ltd., London, managers), for £74,000 and renamed PEMPTO under the Lebanese flag. Resold to Hong Kong Rolling Mills Ltd., Hong Kong for demolition. *20.9.1961:* Arrived at Hong Kong. *6.10.1961:* Demolition commenced.

Trader goes to war, equipped with paravanes, liferafts in the shrouds and armed with a 4-inch gun.

A blighted Christmas

Inward bound to Liverpool from South Africa, Captain Tom Kent and the crew of the TRADER were agog with thoughts of Christmas at home, and happy to have made it in nice time. For it was 23rd December 1958, and spirits were running high with those hyper-feelings of emotion commonly known among seamen as the Channels. Men looked back to the time when they were last home for Christmas - some years ago, in most cases, when the kids were quite small, and still believed in Santa Claus. The 23rd - just nice time on the morrow to join the throngs of last-minute, Christmas Eve shoppers, and recapture that dimly-remembered spirit of Christmas. It was still dark that winter's morning as they approached the Bar with the pilot on board. Tom Kent looked up at the dull, heavy sky. Only one thing could frustrate their hopes and aspirations - the weather, which now had a decidedly foggy look about it. However, the channel buoys' lights were visible from the Bar, and Captain

Kent agreed with the pilot's advice to go upriver and anchor off the dock.

It was not a pleasant passage. The strain of picking out the elusive winking lights amid the wreaths of mist and drizzle which drifted across the channel was extremely trying. By the time they passed the Rock Light the weather was quite thick, and at 08.05 preparations were made to anchor the vessel off Seacombe Ferry Landing Stage.

As the ship crept up to her chosen anchorage a light was seen close ahead - the riding light of a vessel at anchor, a conclusion quickly confirmed by the frantic tolling of a bell. TRADER tried to take avoiding action, but the flood tide, running at nearly four knots, carried her on to the bow of the dimly seen vessel, which proved to be the Westminster Dredging Company's WD 51 (935/41). The collision, which occurred at 08.07 tore a hole in the TRADER's starboard side, just abaft the bridge, fortunately above the waterline. By 08.15 the ship was riding to her port anchor, and an hour later began swinging to the ebb tide. At 12.17, still in dense fog, an outward bound vessel was sighted close to. Unable to swing clear in time, she landed against TRADER's port bow, damaging her port lifeboat davits as she slid down river on the ebb. Before she disappeared into the fog, Tom Kent, fulminating with helpless rage in his silent wheelhouse, read her name: the BANNROSE (489/25) of Liverpool.

TRADER docked on the next tide, but whatever the rest of the crew did on Christmas Eve, it is safe to assume that Tom Kent spent it making verbal explanations and composing written reports and letters on those two untimely incidents which marred his Christmas that year.

Trader approaching Curacao post war.

250. WINNIPEG 1941 Steel twin-screw steamship. Two decks and shelter deck. Four masts and five holds.
O.N. 171465 8,379g 5,031n 8,150d 473.5 x 59.8 x 31.4 feet. Cargo capacity 532,000 cubic feet. 94 cabin passengers.
International code: BCVN (formerly FNRN, OSQM, OJUG).
Two T. 3-cyl. by Ateliers et Chantiers de France, Dunkirk driving twin screws; each 23, 38½, 64½ x 45 inches, 12 knots.

24.4.1918: Launched by Ateliers et Chantiers de France, Dunkirk (Yard No. 100) as JACQUES CARTIER. *10.1918:* Completed for Compagnie Générale Transatlantique, Paris and registered at Cherbourg. Traded to Mexico. *1929:* Renamed WINNIPEG and transferred to the Pacific Coast service: Le Havre, Panama, San Francisco and Vancouver. *1938:* Sold to Compagnie France Navigation S.A., Paris and renamed PAIMPOL. *1939:* Requisitioned by the French Government (Compagnie Générale Transatlantique, Paris, managers) and renamed WINNIPEG. *26.5.1941:* Seized by the Netherlands sloop VAN KINSBERGEN in position 15.05N, 60.39W and escorted to Port of Spain, Trinidad. *6.1941:* Owners became Ministry of War Transport, London (Thos. and Jas. Harrison, Liverpool, managers). *11.1941:* Managers became Canadian Pacific Steamship Co. Ltd., Liverpool and renamed WINNIPEG II. *22.10.1942:* Torpedoed and sunk by German Submarine U 443 (Oberleutnant zur See von Puttkamer) while in convoy ON 139, in position 49.51N, 27.58W, whilst on a voyage from Liverpool to St. John, New Brunswick. All 192 crew and passengers survived.

Winnipeg was briefly managed by Harrisons in 1941.

251. EMPIRE GAZELLE 1941-1946 Steel steamship. Two decks and five holds. Two masts.
O.N. 168209 4,828g, 2,989n, 7,630d 381.7 x 53.3 x 26.6 feet. Cargo capacity 412,000 cubic feet.
International Code: BCJJ.
T. 3-cyl. by Skinner and Eddy Corporation, Seattle, USA; 24, 40, 70 x 48 inches,10½ knots.

1919: Launched by Todd Dry Dock and Construction Corporation, Tacoma, USA (Yard No. 105) for United States Shipping Board, Washington as the HIGHO. *1.1920:* Completed. 1928: Managers became Barber Steamship Lines Inc., in West African service. *1937:* Owner became United States Maritime Commission. *7.1941:* Acquired by Ministry of War Transport, London (Thos. and Jas. Harrison, Liverpool, managers) and renamed EMPIRE GAZELLE. *3.8.1946:* Management ended. *11.1946:* Sold to S. T. Williamson, Hong Kong. *4.1947:* Transferred to Inch Steamship Co. Ltd. (Williamson and Co., Ltd., managers), Hong Kong and renamed INCHMAY. *5.1947 - 4.1949:* Chartered by Australian Shipping Board. *9.1951:* Transferred to Williamson and Co. Ltd., Hong Kong. *12.1953:* Sold to Nankai Kogyo Co. Ltd., Osaka. *2.1.1954:* Delivered to Nankai Kogyo K.K. and Okushoji Industries Ltd. for demolition. *5.1954:* Demolition completed.

Empire Gazelle, a US First World War steamer managed by Harrisons for the Ministry of War Transport. *[National Maritime Museum P22303]*

252. ARICA 1941-1942 Steel steamship. Two decks and five holds. Two masts.
O.N. 171464 5,431g 3,228n 8,760d 425.0 x 55.0 x 26.6 feet Cargo capacity 485,652 cubic feet.
International code BCTZ.
T. 3-cyl. by North East Marine Engineering Co. Ltd., Wallsend-onTyne; 28, 46½, 78 x 54 inches, 11.5 knots.

8.1921: Launched by Sunderland Shipbuilding Co. Ltd., (Yard No. 323) for Compagnie de Navigation d'Orbigny, La Rochelle, France as ZÉNON. *2.1934:* Sold to Compagnie Générale Transatlantique, Paris, France and renamed ARICA. *1.6.1941:* On passage Fort-de-France for Casablanca with 600 tons of sugar and rum, intercepted by the Netherlands sloop VAN KINSBERGEN, escorted to Port of Spain and taken over by Ministry of War Transport, London (Thos. and Jas. Harrison, Liverpool, managers). *6.11.1942:* Torpedoed and sunk by the German submarine U 160 (Kapitänleutnant Georg Lassen) in position 10.58N, 60.52W. She was on passage London and Trinidad for Demerara with general cargo and mail. There were 55 survivors from the crew of 67.

Arica in the ownership of Compagnie Générale Transatlantique. *[Ian Farquhar collection]*

The destruction of ARICA[205]

The convoy, variously classified as TAG 19 or T24, bound from Port of Spain to Demerara was not a very grand armada. Escorted by four trawlers, it consisted of eight ships deployed in four columns of two. ARICA, at that time commanded by Captain B. Worthington (formerly of the POLITICIAN, 238), was stationed at the rear end of the inshore column. They had sailed at 06.00 on the morning of 6th November 1942, and all had gone well until 14.20, by which time the convoy had reached a position eight miles north of Galera Point, at the eastern end of the island of Trinidad. The weather was fine and clear with excellent visibility, when a torpedo struck the ship amidships on the starboard side. Kapitänleutnant Georg Lassen, in command of the German submarine U 160, had sighted the convoy through his periscope about an hour earlier, and had successfully evaded the escorts to take up an attacking position on the inshore flank of the starboard column. He fired two torpedoes, waited, and when the shock wave of the explosion vibrated against the U-boat's hull, Lassen gave the order to dive.

For the escorting naval trawlers were surging in his direction like so many angry terriers. Depth charges burst all round the plunging submarine, shaking her severely, but causing no damage. Three hours later, U 160 ventured to periscope-depth, but Lassen could see nothing but an escort vessel some distance away, still dropping the occasional probing charge.

The fatal torpedo had shattered the ARICA, however, breaking her in two in the vicinity of the bulkhead between number 3 hold and the boiler room. Captain Worthington emerged from his cabin to find his ship a shambles, a nightmare of destruction: "The ship broke in half, and it was impossible to get from the bridge deck to the after end of the ship. Looking aft I could see the torn plating was turned outward, and the propeller was high in the air. The crew were accommodated in that part of the ship, and I saw some of the men jump into the water from the poop as it reared up. There was no possible chance of getting the lifeboats away and the rafts had jammed.

"I stepped off the lead grating [the Captain must have made his brief inspection from the little platform from which the hand-lead was swung when taking soundings] on to the forward portion of the ship as the water came up to my waist. The next thing I saw was the after end of the vessel as it reared up and sank only five minutes after being struck. I went back to my cabin to pick up my boots and jumped into the water with the rest of the crew. The bow of the ship was out of the water, remaining at an angle of 45 degrees. This part of the ship finally sank about three hours later."

The escorting trawler LADY ELSA appeared on the scene some two-and-a-half hours after the explosion, and picked up 55 survivors (of whom two were seriously injured) out of the crew of 67. They were landed at Port of Spain next day. Most of those who died, three of whom were engineers, were probably in the stokehold when the torpedo struck. They stood no chance.

253. EMPIRE CHIVALRY 1941-1946
See INKOSI, No. 240.

254. EMPIRE EXPLORER 1942
See INANDA, No. 210.

255. PROSPECTOR 1943-1961 Steel steamship. Two decks, five holds and deep tank. Two masts and a signal mast.
O.N. 168871 6,202g 3,663n 9,000d 420.3 (435.0 o.l.) x 54.65 x 32.6 feet. Cargo capacity: 479,258 cubic feet
International Code: GJMS.
T. 3-cyl. by David Rowan and Co. Ltd., Glasgow; 27, 43, 77 x 54 inches, 11½ knots.

Prospector on trials in 1943.   *[W. Ralston]*

14.10.1943: Launched by Lithgows Ltd., Port Glasgow (Yard No. 988) for the company. *19.12.1943:* Delivered at a cost of £249,292. Later sailed from Glasgow to Mombasa via Suez on her maiden voyage under Captain R.F. Herschell. *12.6.1953:* In collision with CHUSAN (24,515/50) off Dover. There were no casualties. *15.10.1955:* Whilst manoeuvring to embark the Cardiff Pilot in Barry Roads, lost her propeller. *22.12.1956:* Sailed from Tilbury for Port Sulphur, Louisiana in ballast. The weather was foggy, and shortly after leaving the dock she was in collision with the Liberian steamer SANTA ELENA (7,257/43) inward bound from Vancouver. PROSPECTOR sustained damage above the waterline and was towed back into Tilbury Dock. SANTA ELENA received damage to her starboard bow and was moored to a buoy off Gravesend. Following repairs, PROSPECTOR sailed again on 31.1.1957. *4.9.1961:* Sold to Margalante Compania Naviera S.A., Panama (Mavroleon Bros. Ltd., London, managers) for £77,000 and renamed EKTON. Resold to Nichimen Jitsugyo K.K. *25.3.1962:* Arrived at Yokosuka. *4.1962:* Demolition commenced.

Prospector post war, with a modified funnel, but still without topmasts and with a long signal mast.   *[F.W. Hawks]*

A close-up view of the damage to *Prospector's* bow taken at the Eastern Arm, Dover on 13th June 1953.   *[Lambert Weston and Son Ltd.]*

Collision in the Straits Of Dover

At 18.23 on 12 June 1953 the PROSPECTOR, deeply laden with a cargo of sugar from the West Indies, picked up her Trinity House pilot off Dungeness, and proceeded towards the Goodwins, and London. Some twenty minutes later the moderate visibility had deteriorated, so speed was reduced, extra lookouts were posted, and the steam whistle sounded as required by the regulations.

By 20.30 the weather was really thick; the ship was placed at the crossroads of some of the busiest sea lanes in the world, and Captain Harry Wells prudently instructed the pilot to anchor the ship as soon as possible, somewhere clear of the traffic lanes. Without radar, it was folly to proceed any further. Cautiously they moved ahead, listening intently to distant fog signals sounding from all directions, the twin blast of the South Goodwin's diaphone among them coming from somewhere on the port bow.

A deep bellow sounded from ahead, and speed was further reduced. It sounded again, rather nearer, and the engines were stopped. Again, the deep, sonorous tone was heard, this time close to, and a deepening shadow appeared out of the fog fine on the starboard bow, towering over the hapless PROSPECTOR, and heading straight for her.

The P. & O. liner CHUSAN, with a full complement of passengers, was outward bound from London, heading for the Mediterranean to begin a summer cruise. She had encountered fog soon after leaving the Thames channels, but since his ship was equipped with the latest radar her captain was confident that he could steer his vessel out of trouble. Unfortunately, the information provided on the radar screen either was not fully appreciated, or was tacitly ignored (for radar was still in its infancy, and its limitations not fully understood), and CHUSAN could not avoid PROSPECTOR when at last she loomed through the fog.

Meanwhile, Captain Wells had swung his ship to port, and levered the engine room telegraph to "Full Astern"; all to no avail. The immense bow of the liner, a feather of spray at the cutwater, seemed to surge on remorselessly, scything into PROSPECTOR's starboard bow like a knife into cheese, penetrating the protesting steelwork as far as the break of the forecastle head. The time was logged as 21.26. According to a Lloyd's surveyor, who inspected the damage in Dover Harbour, there was: "A V-shaped wound in way of the chain-locker and

number 1 hold, commencing about 7 feet abaft the stem and extending across the ship about 10 feet over a length of 30 feet at deck-level. It extended downwards through five strakes to about 15 feet under water. Number 1 lower hold was flooded, the 'tween deck awash, and there was a slight leak in the forepeak".

PROSPECTOR's engines continued to work astern and gradually, amid the rending of twisted steel, the two ships drew apart. At 21.28 the port anchor was let go in 26 fathoms, and the crew mustered at boat stations. Numbers 1, 2, and 3 lifeboats were swung out, ready for lowering but there was no premature move to abandon ship. Meanwhile, CHUSAN, with extensive damage to her stem and starboard bow above the waterline, stood by the more gravely injured PROSPECTOR until the arrival of the tug LADY BRASSEY (362/13) from Dover allowed her to leave the scene at 23.50 and return to Tilbury. There her damaged bow was patched up, and the liner resumed her delayed cruise three days late, on 15th June.

The collision had occurred in position 51.06.30N, 01.31E; or 096 degrees distant 5³/₄ miles from Dover East Pierhead. The ship remained at anchor until 09.45 on 13th, when two tugs, NAPIA (261/43) and SUN XV (183/25), arrived to assist her into Dover Harbour on top of the tide, and drawing 31 feet forward, 25 feet aft. No injuries had been suffered by the crew, but the damage was prodigious. Temporary repairs were effected to render the ship seaworthy, and on 21st June she made her way to Tilbury to discharge her cargo and make full repairs.

The claims and counter-claims were heard before Mr. Justice Willmer sitting in the Admiralty Division of the High Court on 6/9th December 1955. The Court found that both parties were at fault, the PROSPECTOR on three counts, (a) navigating in fog at an excessive speed - 8 knots, according to the assessors' calculations; (b) failing to stop her engines when the CHUSAN's fog signal was heard before the beam; and (c) altering course to port before visually sighting the liner. This latter observation conflicts with the statement in the Captain's report.

CHUSAN was found wanting in two respects, (a) proceeding at an excessive speed in fog, and (b) failing to keep a continuous and effective radar watch. In apportioning blame, the judge assessed PROSPECTOR to be 75% at fault, and CHUSAN 25%.

Prospector limps from Dover to the Thames following her collision with *Chusan*.

[*Roy Fenton collection*]

Contract or salvage: a moot question

PROSPECTOR's phosphor-bronze propeller simply dropped off its tail shaft at 17.11 on 15th October 1955, as the ship was approaching the pilot station in Barry Roads to embark the Cardiff pilot. The engines were working at full speed astern, when a heavy, muffled vibration was felt throughout the ship. The racing main engine was promptly halted. One minute later the Cardiff pilot climbed over the rail, and was somewhat surprised to be asked for the loan of his boat to enable Chief Engineer H. Bruce to make an inspection under the ship's cruiser stern, "as we think the prop's missing." The water was murky, and nothing could be seen below the surface, but when the engine was turned gingerly slow ahead, not a ripple disturbed the opaque surface. There was no longer any room for doubt - the ship had "cast her propeller".

At 17.15 the ship was anchored in 18 fathoms about two miles east north east of the Breaksea Lightvessel, and those structural parts adjacent to the stern frame were examined from the inside, but no damage or leaks were discovered. For the time being the ship was secure but nothing could be done to restore her motive power until she could be dry docked. However, Barry Roads is an exposed anchorage and the ship was secure only so long as the weather remained fine. It was arranged to dock the ship next morning; meanwhile, two tugs were contracted to stand by the ship all night as a precaution, and at 21.30 the Cardiff tugs LAVERNOCK (135/19) and FALCON (169/96) tied up alongside.

Next morning, the ship was towed by the overnight tugs to Cardiff Roads where they were joined by two more tugs for docking. An inspection by a diver when the ship was in her berth revealed that the propeller had shed itself cleanly, without damaging either rudder or stern frame. It must have sheered clean across the boss, for the tail shaft was still intact, and the conical locking nut still in place. The ship entered dry dock on 21st October, and eventually all was made good, enabling the ship to sail for London on 4th November.

Meanwhile, an interesting argument had developed between solicitors acting for the tug owner, and those acting for the shipowner. Was the employment of tugs in this case a normal "contract" job, or was there a legitimate case for salvage? The ship was never in any immediate danger, the owners were quick to point out. But had the weather turned nasty the risks were only too obvious. The Towage Contract, signed in 1938 and revised annually, called for the use of at least two tugs for docking at Cardiff, extra tugs to be provided if Master and Pilot deemed it advisable in the circumstances. An additional fee was payable if the ship were not under command, i.e. without means of propulsion or steering.

The tug owners insisted that the ship, having lost her propeller, was clearly "in distress", in which case normal rates could not apply under the terms of the contract which exempted cases of distress. Such cases clearly came under the rules governing salvage.

Unfortunately, the outcome of this case is not included in existing records, and it would have been interesting had it been tested in court. But it seems more likely that the issue was settled out of court by mutual agreement, on the basis of contract rates plus x% to cover the salvage element.

Prospector after her sale to Greek buyers and renaming *Ekton* in September 1961.

[*J. and M. Clarkson*]

220

256. GEOLOGIST (2) 1944-1955 Steel steamship. Two decks, five holds and deep tank. Two masts and a signal mast.
O.N. 168875 6,202g 3,663n 9,000d 420.3 (435.0 o.l.) x 54.65 x 32.6 feet. Cargo capacity: 479,258 cubic feet.
International Code: GJMR.
T. 3-cyl. by David Rowan and Co. Ltd., Glasgow; 27, 43, 77 x 54 inches, 11½ knots.

9.12.1943: Launched by Lithgows Ltd., Port Glasgow (Yard No. 989) for the company. *19.2.1944:* Delivered at a cost of £249,139. Later sailed from Glasgow to Alexandria on her maiden voyage under Captain D.H. Bryant. *13.7.1955:* Sank following a collision with the Liberian motorship SUNPRINCESS (5,168/43) off Corozal Point, Trinidad, in a position 10.49N, 61.40W. She was on passage from Glasgow to Maracaibo with general cargo. Twenty lives were lost from a crew of 42 making it the worst disaster to befall a Harrison ship in peacetime since the YEOMAN (124) was wrecked off the coast of Spain in 1904.

Geologist is seen (above) on the Clyde in 1944 with guns and torpedo nets, and (below) in peacetime colours on the Mersey on 12th June 1948.
[Lower: J. and M. Clarkson]

A tragedy of criminal folly[206]
When the GEOLOGIST left Barbados at 11.00 on the morning of 12th July 1955 there was no hint of impending tragedy in the sunlit air. The passage to Trinidad was one which GEOLOGIST and her predecessors had made a thousand times over the years. Schools of flying fish and porpoise disported themselves amid sunkissed waves breaking playfully before the gentle trade wind as the ship forged ahead at a steady twelve knots. The Barbadian crew, newly joined that morning, familiarised themselves with the ship and her equipment, unpacked their belongings and settled in, happy to be in employment for six to eight months. The day passed uneventfully, a routine day at sea in the tropics.

The visibility was crystal clear, and at about 20.30 that night the loom of Tobago North Point light was clearly visible 25 miles away. Captain A.E. Jackson adjusted the course for Chacachacare Island, 221 degrees true, anticipating a set of 3

221

A later view of *Geologist* than that on the previous page shows alterations to her funnel. *[Ian Farquhar collection]*

degrees due to the influence of the west-going Equatorial Current. At midnight, by which time the lofty Chacachacare Light was in sight bearing about 2 degrees on the starboard bow, Second Officer David Howard relieved Third Officer Meyer, and Captain Jackson retired to his cabin leaving orders to be called at 01.30, about one hour before the ship was due to reach Boca Grande.

Course and speed were maintained, and shortly after 01.00 the lights of a power-driven vessel appeared over the knife-edged horizon, first the white masthead lights, then a few minutes later a green starboard sidelight. The tiny cluster of lights bore about 10 degrees on the port bow.

Neither David Howard, nor the helmsman, nor the lookout survived the ensuing disaster, so we have no direct evidence to indicate with certainty what transpired on the bridge of the GEOLOGIST during that last fateful hour. Guided by the findings of the inquiry we can only speculate, and interpret the rules which should apply.

According to the Steering and Sailing Rules embodied in the International Regulations for the Prevention of Collisions at Sea then in force, Articles 19 and 21 ruled that the oncoming vessel on GEOLOGIST's port bow should give way; and that GEOLOGIST, on the other's starboard bow, should keep her course and speed, in other words, "stand on".

This is all very well, but any officer who has ever stood on the bridge of a stand-on ship will agree that the interval between sighting a crossing vessel on the port bow and actually seeing her turn to starboard to present her red sidelight can be an anxious time. To be in the "giving-way" ship, however, poses no problem. One is confident that one knows exactly what to do - alter course to starboard, and sooner rather than later. Standing-on, maintaining course and speed as the other ship draws ever closer, can be fraught with anxiety, and the relief when that menacing green light is seen turning to red is almost tangible. Such qualms are, of course, usually short-lived, but there are occasions when the agony can be long drawn-out, ending in some form of drastic action - or disaster.

For In such cases the Regulations gave the stand-on ship the discretion to take "such action as will best aid to avert collision". But such action could not

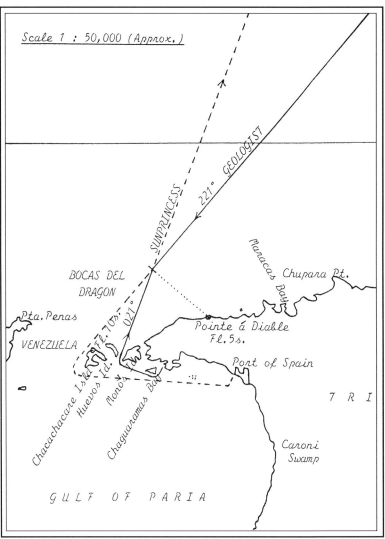

Relative tracks of *Geologist* and *Sunprincess* off Trinidad, 13th July 1955

222

be taken until that vessel "finds herself so close that collision cannot be avoided by the action of the giving-way vessel alone". The watchkeeper's dilemma was to know with certainty just when that point had been reached. Regulations promulgated much later, in 1972, addressed this point directly by allowing the stand-on vessel far greater latitude to take action as soon as it became apparent that "the vessel required to keep out of the way is not taking appropriate action in compliance with these Rules "- appropriate action" being defined in this case as "early and substantial action to keep well clear".

Such, then, was the type of situation which faced David Howard in the early hours of that Wednesday morning, a situation which was of the stuff of nightmares - a ship fine on his port bow, crossing on a steady bearing, which stubbornly refused to give way as required by the Rules. It is certain that GEOLOGIST maintained her course and speed until a very late moment, when young Howard (he was 22) judged that the moment had come when collision "could not be avoided by action of the giving-way vessel alone", and took the only course open to him at that stage - a vigorous turn to port. He sounded the appropriate signal, and took it. Unfortunately the officer on the other ship, the SUNPRINCESS (5,168/43), at that moment at last came to his senses, and did what he should have done at least 10 minutes earlier. He altered course to starboard. Thus, the two ships swung towards each other and a serious collision became unavoidable.

Captain Jackson, who had been called, reached the bridge a few seconds before the impact. He ordered the wheel hard-a-starboard in a vain attempt to swing the stern clear of the rapidly advancing stranger, but it was too late. The other ship's stem cleft deeply into GEOLOGIST's starboard side in way of number 4 hatch, almost at right angles, penetrating beyond the fore-and-aft centre line. The sea poured into the stricken ship, and GEOLOGIST began to sink rapidly by the stern. The crew made for the lifeboats, but there was no time to clear the chocks, swing the davits out and lower the boats before the water was lapping over the boat deck. Within five minutes of the impact those men who had not been carried down with the ship were struggling desperately in the water.

The matter-of-fact prose of witnesses' statements does not bring out the full horror of the nightmare which had suddenly enveloped them, but the frantic dilemma which confronted each survivor and victim can readily be imagined. To jump into the sea now, before it's too late? Or to try to launch a boat and perhaps be dragged down with the ship? The immediate crisis lasted only a few minutes - no time to call a meeting. Captain A.E. Jackson, making his way aft to the point of impact: "Before I got to the galley she started sinking suddenly and quickly. I was swept through the alleyway and over number 2 hatch, and was carried down with the ship. On coming to the surface I just got a last glimpse of the bow of the GEOLOGIST." Minutes later he reached the SUNPRINCESS and climbed a rope ladder to safety.

Second Engineer P.J. Murphy, after checking that the engine room had been evacuated, made his way to the port side of the boat deck where Third Officer D.M. Meyer and some seamen were trying to launch number 4 boat. "Suddenly, I was covered up by the water, and felt myself going down and down. My trousers were pulled off, and my lifejacket was pulled down, too. I managed to keep it on with my legs. When I came up, I was sick, and saw a West Indian holding on to me."

Murphy was later pulled into a lifeboat more dead than alive, but of the West Indian there was no sign. Cadet Andy Wills thought that the ship had run aground; he was rather an old hand in such matters having been in the NATURALIST (265) when that ship struck the Middle Mouse off Anglesey precisely twelve weeks earlier. He burst into the adjoining cabin where his mate, Cadet A.J. Anelay was still asleep. "Wake up, Smiler, we've done it again!" he shouted. By this time the ship was tilting alarmingly. Anelay told Wills to go and put on his lifejacket. Wills left him, grabbed his lifejacket and climbed up to the lower bridge to assist with the launching of number 1 boat. But before it could be cleared "....our ship started to go down fast. I heard loud crashes and noise and we all scrambled further forward. The sea then came up to the lifeboat and davits and everything crashed overboard. I looked away and shut my eyes and next thing I knew I was in the water." Andy Wills found a hatchboard to cling to and eventually he drifted alongside the SUNPRINCESS, where he followed his Captain up the Jacob's ladder which was hanging over the side.

Many more had similar experiences, the prevalent theme being the overwhelming nature of the disaster, and the swiftness with which it had come upon them. It is time to enquire what on earth had been going on aboard the Liberian-registered SUNPRINCESS. She had left Chaguaramas, Trinidad, at about 00.20 on 13th July, bound for Port Alfred, Quebec, with a cargo of bauxite. She cleared Boca de Huevos about 40 minutes later, when her Norwegian master, Captain Jacob Jacobsen, set a course of 021 degrees true, speed 14 knots. He then called the officer of the watch, Second Officer Stanley Mervyn Kemp, into the chartroom to indicate the position and course to be steered. At 01.20 Captain Jacobsen left the bridge in Kemp's charge, and retired to his cabin.

That was a mere 20 minutes before the collision, when the ships would be about nine miles apart, the navigation lights

Sunprincess.

[David Whiteside collection]

of one clearly visible to the other, for it was a very clear night. Yet Kemp paid no heed, slipped the steering gear into automatic, and his brain into neutral. There is no need to mince words. It is on record that Mervyn Kemp, holder of a British Master's Certificate of Competency, granted by the Ministry of War Transport in May 1944, was drunk, or, in the words selected by the Court of Inquiry, "under the influence of drink to such an extent as to be incapable of properly exercising his duty".

Moreover, he was the only person on watch during those fateful minutes leading up to the time of the collision. One seaman, also under the influence, apparently, had not even turned out for his watch; the other was aft, ostensibly streaming the log, but taking an inordinately long time over it. It is astonishing that the experienced Captain Jacobsen seemed totally unaware of the state of the watch on deck, and could retire unperturbed to his bunk twenty minutes before a disastrous collision destroyed a fine ship, cost so many men their lives, and ruined the lives of others.

Relentlessly, SUNPRINCESS stood on when she should have given way, and only in the closing minutes of a dire situation did a suddenly sobered Mervyn Kemp throw the steering gear out of automatic, seize the wheel, and swing the ship to starboard - an action which simply neutralized David Howard's last desperate move to avoid disaster. As GEOLOGIST sank, SUNPRINCESS stood off and eventually lowered a boat to search for survivors. Eleven of the stronger swimmers reached the ship's side, and hauled themselves aboard up the ladders which the crew had slung over. Eleven more survivors were picked up out of the water by the lifeboat, but twenty men perished.

SUNPRINCESS returned to Port of Spain with the 22 survivors and a gaping hole in her bow, a cratered mass of twisted steel which extended vertically from keel to sheerstrake, and horizontally from the stem to a point 30 feet further aft. Some sort of temporary repairs were patched together, and the ship resumed her voyage to Canada on 20th July. Some time later she entered dry dock in Lauzon, Quebec, where her ruined bow was rebuilt.

Meanwhile, a preliminary enquiry conducted by the Receiver of Wrecks had taken place in Port of Spain on 14th July. Then, and at a subsequent hearing on 19th, Second Officer Mervyn Kemp swore that he had seen the lights of GEOLOGIST at 01.20, about a point and a half on the starboard bow, and seven miles away by radar. He said he could see all the lights: two masthead lights, port and starboard sidelights. He then altered course 24 degrees to starboard, putting the other ship a few degrees on the port bow, and sounded a single blast on the whistle. Twenty minutes later, as the ships closed he saw GEOLOGIST go hard-a-port. He then went hard-a-starboard, but collision occurred at 01.42. He heard no whistle signals from GEOLOGIST.

This account was later proved to be a complete fabrication. Kemp, in fact, was so insensible as to what was going on that he was even unaware of which Boca, or channel, through which his ship had emerged from the Gulf of Paria. (There are four to choose from, formed by the chain of islands in the northern approaches). The course from the point of emergence to the point of collision naturally had some bearing on the case.

However, at the time, the two seamen on watch with Kemp bore out his story. It was only when one of them, Ordinary Seaman Oscar Rodney, a native of Georgetown, Demerara, retracted his Trinidad statement prior to the full Court of Inquiry in England, that the truth came out. Rodney's mate, Able Seaman Antonio Rodrigues had, in fact, been too drunk to take his watch, and had remained in his bunk while Ordinary Seaman Rodney steered the ship from the anchorage. Whilst at the wheel, Rodney noticed that "....the Second Officer was not doing anything other than stand about. The Master was not making any reference to him and it looked to me as if the Second Officer had been drinking. It seemed to me that the Master had no confidence in the Second Officer."

Later, according to Rodney's revised testimony, when SUNPRINCESS was back in Port of Spain, Kemp took him and Rodriques ashore, plied them with beer, and coached them in the story they must tell at the inquiry. The salient points of that story were to be that they had heard whistle signals from SUNPRINCESS before any from GEOLOGIST (Rodney, in fact, had heard her two-blast signal while he was aft); that he, Rodney, had seen nothing of the other ship before the collision (he had); that Rodrigues was on watch on the bridge (and not lying in a drunken stupor in his cabin); and that he had sent both men aft to stream the log. (He had sent only Rodney, who later succeeded in rousing Rodriques to give him a hand with the log).

Rodney went on to describe the launching of the lifeboats in the aftermath of the collision: "It was a state of confusion. I did not know how the davits worked and nobody else did, either. I started to cut the lashings and then I think it was the Chief Engineer who came up and knew how to work the davits and the boat was swung out quickly. The Second Mate appeared and got in... (he) just sat down as if in a daze and did not take charge of the boat, but an A.B., Duncan, told us what we had to do. We circled round and picked up eleven men." Rodney ends his revised statement thus: "When I was called to give evidence at the inquiry I told the story the Second Mate had told me to tell, and not what I have said today. What I have said today is the true story". He excused his lapse into perjury, "...because I felt I had some obligation to the ship, and Rodrigues had also asked me not to mention that he was drunk".

One of three stewardesses on board SUNPRINCESS, Florence Rosina Minus, was not called to give evidence in Trinidad. She remained with the ship, but in November she became ill and had to be landed in hospital at Barbados. On her recovery she was repatriated in the HILDEBRAND and arrived at Liverpool on 5th December 1955. From there she made her way home to Avonmouth, and told her husband all that had happened on the SUNPRINCESS. He advised her to get in touch with the Harrison Line in Liverpool, and so she telephoned on 8th December. The outcome was a statement, and a valuable voluntary witness at the Court of Inquiry.

Mrs. Minus gave evidence about the Second Officer's condition on the night SUNPRINCESS sailed from Chaguaramas. Her testimony included: "The Second Officer and Wireless Officer went ashore at Chaguaramas. They came back about 10.30 p.m. and the Second Officer had a half-bottle of rum in his pocket. Both he and the Wireless Officer had in my view had too much to drink when they came on board. I saw the Second Officer drinking from his bottle of rum after he came on board."

She saw him again at midnight, after the ship had sailed: "The Second Officer was then in a worse condition than when he came on board". Mrs. Minus remained on the boat deck for about an hour, until the ship had cleared the islands, then went below to the cabin she shared with another stewardess. Instead of turning in she decided to write a letter. About twenty minutes later she was thrown across the room by the impact of the collision. During the time she was in the cabin she testified that she heard no whistle signals or telegraph bells, all of which would have been clearly audible from within the cabin. She went out on deck, and saw "... half a ship sticking out of the water a few yards on our starboard side. The funnel was under the water, and then there was a big noise and the ship went down. I saw the Second Officer come from the wheelhouse round the bridge deck to look forward and he looked shocked." She then ran to the rail and assisted with the rescue of survivors struggling in the water to reach the ladders which had been flung over. As they climbed on deck she led them to the saloon where they were looked after.

The ship returned to Port of Spain at about 06.00 on 13th July, and shortly afterwards Mrs. Minus went to the Second Officer's cabin with a tray of coffee. There she found Kemp in great distress but apparently sober: "I am a murderer", he sobbed.

Next day, when the inquiry opened, "...the Second Officer was drinking very heavily. I remember one time taking half a bottle of rum from him in the Officers' Mess. He again said that he was a murderer." Later, during the voyage to Canada, Mrs. Minus stated that the Second Officer had told her "...that when he came out of the chartroom, 'it [the GEOLOGIST] was upon me'. It was generally said on the ship that the Second Officer was in the chartroom at the time of the collision".

The formal investigation was held in London from 10th to 15th May 1956, Mr. John Ronald Adams, Q.C., assisted by two nautical assessors, presiding. The court found that the loss of the GEOLOGIST was caused by "...the improper navigation of the SUNPRINCESS by her Second Officer, Stanley Mervyn Kemp," whose conduct and demeanour since the disaster had done nothing to further his case. Besides taking to the bottle at Port of Spain, "in order to obtain comfort or solace", he had made conflicting statements on oath, most of which had proved to be a tissue of lies, had committed perjury, and had even attempted to suborn witnesses. The court was satisfied that the circumstances of the case transcended simple negligence, and indicated its sense of outrage, not by mere suspension, but by outright cancellation of Kemp's Master's Certificate.

Perhaps Kemp was fortunate in one respect, for in recent years better men than he have had to face charges of manslaughter for their part in comparable marine disasters.

Those who died when GEOLOGIST was lost were:	
D.E.B. Howard, Second Officer.	Cleo Alleyne, Second Cook.
D.M. Meyer, Third Officer.	Rupert Innis, Messroom Steward.
P. Davies, Third Engineer.	Clarence Applewhaite, Officer's Boy.
L.A. Souter, Senior Purser.	Noel Cummins, Cabin Boy.
A.J. Anelay, Cadet.	Richard Smith, Donkeyman.
Lewis Sealy, Lamptrimmer.	George Wade, Donkeyman.
Theophilus Goddard, Able Seaman.	Austin Crawford, Storekeeper.
Seibert Broomes, Able Seaman.	Adolphous Goddard, Fireman.
George Phillips, Able Seaman.	Joseph Garner, Fireman.
James Elson, Chief Cook.	Samuel Rice, Fireman.

257. EMPIRE RANGOON 1944-1946 Steel motor vessel. Two decks and five holds. Two masts.
O.N. 168532 6,988g 3,871n 9,436d 425 x 56.0 x 36.75 feet. Cargo capacity 520,000 cubic feet.
International Code: GBWS.
6-cyl. 4SCSA Burmeister & Wain-type oil engine by Harland and Wolff Ltd., Belfast; 12 knots.

25.1.1944: Launched by Harland and Wolff Ltd., Belfast (Yard No. 1234) for the Ministry of War Transport, London as EMPIRE RANGOON. *30.5.1944:* Completed, placed under management of Thos. and Jas. Harrison Ltd., Liverpool and registered at London. *23.11.1946:* Sold to Reardon Smith Line Ltd. (Sir William Reardon Smith and Sons Ltd., managers), Cardiff while the ship was in Calcutta and later renamed HOMER CITY. *1960:* Sold to Grosvenor Shipping Co. Ltd., London (Mollers Ltd., Hong Kong, managers) and renamed GROSVENOR MARINER. *1966:* Sold to Tat On Shipping and Enterprises Co. Ltd. (Yick Fung Shipping and Enterprises Co. Ltd., managers), Hong Kong and renamed RED SEA, registered in London. *17.8.1971:* Driven ashore on Lantau Island, Hong Kong, during Typhoon Rose.

Empire Rangoon.   *[National Maritime Museum P22434]*

Subsequently refloated but sold to Yau Wing Metal Co. Ltd. *9.1971:* Demolition began.

258. EMPIRE CAPTAIN 1944-1946 Steel steamship. Three decks and six holds. Four masts.
O.N. 166217 9,875g 7,110n 11,975d 475.8 x 64.4 x 42.7 feet. Cargo capacity 720,000 cubic feet.
International Code: BFKF.
Two steam turbines double reduction geared to one shaft by C.A. Parsons Ltd., Newcastle-upon-Tyne; 15 knots.

25.2.1944: Launched by Caledon Shipbuilding and Engineering Co. Ltd., Dundee (Yard No. 404) for the Ministry of War Transport, London as EMPIRE CAPTAIN. *23.6.1944:* Completed, placed under management of Thos. and Jas. Harrison Ltd., Liverpool and registered at London. *15.5.1946:* Sold to Canadian Pacific Railway Co. (Canadian Pacific Steamship Ltd., Liverpool, managers) and later renamed BEAVERBURN. *3.1960:* Sold to E. G. Thomson Shipping Ltd. (Wm. Thomson and Co., managers), Leith and renamed BENNACHIE. *8.1964:* Sold to Atlantic Navigation Corporation Ltd., Monrovia, Liberia (W.H. Eddie Hsu, Taiwan, manager) and renamed SILVANA. *1969:* Transferred to Outerocean Navigation Corporation Ltd. (W. H. Eddie Hsu, manager), Taiwan. *6.4.1971:* Ming Kang Steel Enterprise Ltd. began demolition at Kaohsiung. *10.5.1971:* Demolition complete.

A fine portrait of the standard fast cargo liner *Empire Captain,* managed by Harrisons from 1944 to 1946.

259. EMPIRE LIFE 1945-1946 Steel steamship. Three decks and six holds. Four masts.
O.N. 166220 9,879g 7,054n 12,000d 475.8 x 64.4 x 40.0 feet. Cargo capacity 702,000 cubic feet.
International code: GBNW.
Two steam turbines double reduction geared to one shaft by Richardsons, Westgarth and Co. Ltd., Hartlepool; 15 knots.

12.1.1945: Launched by Caledon Shipbuilding and Engineering Co. Ltd., Dundee (Yard No. 407) for the Ministry of War Transport, London. *5.5.1945:* Completed, placed under management of Thos. and Jas. Harrison Ltd., Liverpool and registered at London. *2.4.1946:* Sold to Union-Castle Mail Steamship Co. Ltd., London and later renamed GOOD HOPE CASTLE. *17.7.1947:* Transferred to South African registry. *1959:* Sold to Hong Kong Salvage and Towage Co. Ltd., Hong Kong for demolition. *14.7.1959:* Arrived at Hong Kong. *9.1959:* Work began.

Good Hope Castle, managed by Harrisons from 1945 to 1946 as *Empire Life.*
[*Peter Newall collection*]

260. EMPIRE KENT 1945-1946 Steel motor vessel. One deck and shelter deck. Five holds. Two masts.
O.N. 180796 4,769g 2,735n 7,344d 408.5 x 56.6 x 21.3 feet. Cargo capacity 459,000 cubic feet.
International code: GRDS (DOVG prior to 1945).
7-cyl. 2SCSA oil engine by Fr. Krupp Germaniawerft AG., Kiel, Germany; 11 knots.

21.4.1939: Launched by Nordsee Werke, G.m.b.H., Emden, Germany (Yard No. 190) for Atlas Levante Linie, Bremen, Germany as LEVANTE. *7.1939:* Completed. *5.1945:* Captured by Allied forces at Oslo, Norway. *9.1945:* Taken over by Ministry of War Transport, London (Thos. and Jas. Harrison Ltd., Liverpool, managers), renamed EMPIRE KENT and registered at London. *24.7.1946:* Sold to Johnston Warren Lines Ltd. (Furness Withy and Co. Ltd., managers), Liverpool and renamed OAKMORE. *13.4.1967:* Arrived at Aviles, Spain having been sold to Desguaces y Salvamentos S.A. for demolition.

Empire Kent, as *Levante.*
[*Prof. Theodor F. Siersdorfer collection*]

261. EMPIRE SERVICE 1945-1946/SELECTOR 1946-1960 Steel steamship. Two decks and five holds. Two masts and a signal mast.
O.N. 169505 7,067g 4,802n 9,860d 432.7 (447.6 o.l.) x 56.2 x 36.9 feet. Cargo capacity: 531,110 cubic feet.
International Code: MARZ (BFGW prior to 1945).
T. 3-cyl. by Rankin and Blackmore Ltd., Greenock; 24½, 39, 70 x 48 inches, 11 knots.

Empire Service in the Clyde.   [*Glasgow University Archives GD320/10/1/141/1*]

20.5.1943: Launched by Lithgows Ltd., Port Glasgow (Yard No. 982) for the Ministry of War Transport, London (W.J. Tatem Ltd., Cardiff, managers) as EMPIRE SERVICE. *7.1943:* Completed. *5.4.1945:* Management transferred to Thos. and Jas. Harrison Ltd., Liverpool. *5.12.1945:* Acquired by the company for £165,740 and registered at Liverpool. *7.1946:* Renamed SELECTOR. *25.11.1947:* Shed a propeller blade in position 161 miles and 102 degrees from Valetta. *27.11.1947:* Put into Valetta but had to wait until 14.12.1947 before a dry dock became available. *18.12.1947:* Sailed after the spare was fitted. *1.4.1948:* Again shed a propeller blade off Zavora Point, Mozambique and the spare was fitted in dry dock at Durban. *23.9.1953:*

When inward bound to Liverpool from Belfast and swinging to port across the River Mersey, about four cables off Gladstone Lock, struck the steamer MANCHESTER TRADER (7,363/41) which was leaving the lock. The two ships met near the lock entrance and SELECTOR's stem struck the port bow of MANCHESTER TRADER almost at right angles, causing severe damage to hawse pipes and bow plating of both ships. *7.11.1960:* Sold to Margalante Compania Naviera S.A., Panama (Mavroleon Bros. Ltd., London, managers) for £52,000 and renamed MARGALANTE. *11.1961:* Sold to Kinoshita Sansho K.K., Japan for demolition. *9.5.1961:* Arrived at Hirao. *6.1961:* Demolition commenced.

Selector, ex-*Empire Service.* [A. Duncan]

262. EMPIRE ADDISON 1943-1945/PHILOSOPHER (2) 1945-1958 Steel steamship. Two decks and five holds. Two masts and a signal mast.
O.N. 168980 7,010g 4,973n 10,130d. 431.0 (446.0 o.l.) x 56.2 x 36.9 feet. Cargo capacity: 546,571 cubic feet.
International Code: BDPF (MAQV after 1945).
T. 3-cyl. by David Rowan and Co. Ltd., Glasgow; 23½, 37½, 68 x 48 inches, 11 knots.

30.12.1941: Launched by Lithgows Ltd., Port Glasgow (Yard No. 965) for the Ministry of War Transport, London (Charles Cravos and Co., Cardiff, managers) as EMPIRE ADDISON, registered at Greenock. *3.1942:* Completed. *11.8.1943:* Management transferred to Thos. and Jas. Harrison Ltd. *12.12.1945:* Acquired by the company for £138,156, registered at Liverpool and later renamed PHILOSOPHER. *15.1.1951:* When homeward bound from the United States, a serious crack in the main discharge pipe forced the vessel to return to Hampton Roads. The fault was repaired and she

sailed again 20.1.1951. *19.12.1952:* Bound from Antigua for London, forced to put into Falmouth, again with a cracked main discharge pipe. *1.12.1958:* Sold to Concordia Shipping Corporation, Monrovia, Liberia (Thrasyvoulos L. Boyazides, Athens) for £89,000 and renamed AIOLOS. *1962:* Sold to Parnassos Shipping Corporation, Beirut, Lebanon. *1963:* Sold to Hong Kong Chiap Hua Manufactory Co. (1947) Ltd., Hong Kong, for demolition. *16.1.1963:* Demolition commenced.

Philosopher, a standard Empire ship from the same Port Glasgow yard as *Selector,* above, but with major differences.

263. EMPIRE NEWTON 1944-1946/ARTISAN 1946-1959 Steel steamship. Two decks and five holds. Two masts and a signal mast.
O.N. 169006 7,037g 4,947n 10,380d 431.0 (446.5 o.l.) x 56.3 x 37.85 feet. Cargo capacity: 562,000 cubic feet.
International Code: BCRR (MAFK after 1946).
T. 3-cyl. by North Eastern Marine Engineering Co. (1938) Ltd., Sunderland; 24½, 39, 70 x 48 inches, 11 knots.

21.10.1941: Launched by Short Brothers Ltd., Sunderland (Yard No. 468) for the Ministry of War Transport, London (W.H. Cockerline and Co. Ltd., Hull, managers) as EMPIRE NEWTON, registered at Sunderland. *1.1942:* Completed. *15.5.1944:* Management transferred to Thos. and Jas.Harrison Ltd. *10.6.1944:* Sailed from London on the first of six voyages to the Normandy Beaches, carrying troops, stores and equipment. *24.1.1946:* Acquired by the company

for £139,398. *28.1.1946:* Renamed ARTISAN and registered at Liverpool. *23.9.1949:* Put into Dakar with a serious fire in her coal bunkers when on passage from Beira to Avonmouth. The fire was extinguished, without damage, the following day. *21.8.1959:* Sold to the British Iron and Steel Corporation for £42,000 for demolition and allocated to T.W. Ward Ltd., and arrived at Grays, Essex the same day.

Artisan in the Mersey.

264. PLANTER (2) 1946-1958
See EMPIRE CHIVALRY (253) and INKOSI (241).

265. EMPIRE TRUMPET 1944-1946/NATURALIST (2) 1946-1959 Steel steamship. Two decks and five holds. Two masts and a signal mast.
O.N. 168995 7,059g 4,805n 9,880d 432.7 (447.5 o.l.) x 56.2 x 36.9 feet. Cargo capacity: 531,110 cubic feet.
International Code: BFGT (MAPP after 1946).
T. 3-cyl. by David Rowan and Co. Ltd., Glasgow; 24½, 39, 70 x 48 inches,11 knots.

Naturalist.

9.3.1943: Launched by William Hamilton and Co. Ltd., Port Glasgow (Yard No. 458) for the Ministry of War Transport, London (Larrinaga Steam Ship Co. Ltd., Liverpool, managers) as EMPIRE TRUMPET, registered at Greenock. *4.1943:* Completed. *11.1943:* Chartered to the Government of South Africa. *13.4.1944:* Returned to commercial service.

14.12.1944: Management transferred to Thos. and Jas.Harrison Ltd. *18.10.1945:* When anchored in Mombasa Harbour, serious fires broke out in her cargo of cotton. At 09.00 the following day the decision was taken to flood the holds and the vessel grounded in shallow water. *21.10.1945:* Refloated, with fires extinguished and berthed at Number 2

Shed, Kilindini. There was considerable damage to ship and cargo caused by fire and water, and the crew's quarters were flooded. Repaired and returned to service. *9.7.1946:* Acquired by the company for £133,048, later registered at Liverpool and renamed NATURALIST. *19.12.1947:* Shed a propeller blade when on passage from Lourenço Marques to Beira, but reached port safely and discharged her cargo. Dispensation was obtained from Lloyd's to proceed to Durban with one blade missing from the four-bladed propeller, in order to dry dock for repairs. The spare propeller was stowed in number 5 'tween deck, the seat of the fire which had devastated the hold two years previously, and the Surveyor warned that the intense heat could well have had an adverse effect on the metal. However, the vessel coasted to Durban and eventually had the spare fitted in place 1.3.1948. *20.4.1955:* Struck the Middle Mouse, a rock off the coast of Anglesey, when on passage from Avonmouth to Liverpool (see below). *4.12.1956:* Fire broke

out in number 1 hold while lying at Brocklebank Dock, Liverpool, discharging cotton and other products from US Gulf and Mexican ports. The blaze was soon brought under control by the Bootle Fire Brigade, but approximately 300 bales of cotton were found to be damaged. *13.8.1959:* Sold to B. Ashworth and Co. (Overseas) Ltd., London for £53,000, on behalf of Iranian Lloyd Co. Ltd., Khorramshahr, Iran and renamed PERSIAN CYRUS. *1965:* Sold to Iranian Shipping Lines S.A., Khorramshahr, Iran, and renamed HAMADAN. *6.1966:* Reported renamed HELIAS but this name does not seem to have been registered. *7.1966:* Sold to P. Frangoulis and A. & I. Cliafas, Piraeus, Greece, and renamed KOULA F. *25.7.1966:* Ran aground on Qais Island in the approaches to the Straits of Hormuz, in a position 26.20N, 53.54E. Attempts at refloating by the Dutch salvage tug ORINOCO (670/64) were unsuccessful and she was abandoned as a constructive total loss. She was on passage from Bandar Shapur to Greece.

The NATURALIST and the Middle Mouse

"Sorry; wrong number!" How often have we offered this rueful apology to some unknown subscriber at the other end of the line after misdialling a simple telephone number? Probably the result of transposing a couple of digits? But it mattered little. Just a case of soothing an annoyed stranger, and redialling. But where the navigation of ships is concerned such an error can be disastrous, as demonstrated by the case of the NATURALIST in April 1955.

The ship sailed from Avonmouth early on 19th April bound for Liverpool. In command was Captain John Ivor Jones, RNR, son of "Peg-leg" Jones, who had been wounded in the GOVERNOR (168) in action with the MÖWE during the First World War. Ivor had returned to Harrisons in 1946 after a distinguished career in the Royal Navy commanding corvettes and destroyers during the Second World War. He had been decorated for his services, and was clearly seen by management as a future Marine Superintendent. His promotion to Master had been meteoric, judged by the custom of the day, but it was an open secret that Ivor Jones was destined for higher things - being groomed for stardom, as the smoke room pundits put it.

Ivor had served his time with Kaye, Son and Co., of London, and had joined Harrisons as Third Officer in 1937. Two years later, he was called up to serve in the Royal Naval Reserve. Sterling service in command of the corvette

HYACINTH earned him first a DSC and later, with the capture intact of the Italian submarine PERLA, a DSO. But with the coming of peace, Ivor realized he had to relearn the techniques of maritime commerce, the disciplines of cargo stowage, the mysteries of charter parties, and many other bread-and-butter skills seldom touched upon in the specialized pursuits of the Royal Navy. Thus he returned to the ranks, initially as Second Officer for about two years, then in April 1949, after a couple of months as Chief Officer, mainly on coastal and dock duties, he was appointed Assistant Marine Superintendent until a vacancy at the top ensured further promotion. However, two-and-a-half years later, in October 1951, it was decided that a future Superintendent would carry greater authority if he could assimilate some experience in command of the company's ships. Consequently, he went back to sea, first as Chief Officer of the EXPLORER (234) with Captain J.L. Curle. Some four months later, while the ship was at Port of Spain, Captain Harriman of the new WAYFARER (287) took ill, and was landed in hospital. Captain Curle took his place, leaving Ivor Jones in acting command of the EXPLORER. That was in February 1952, and on his return to Liverpool, his new rank was confirmed. Eventually, in November 1954, he became Master of the NATURALIST. There is no doubt that, whatever was planned for him, Ivor Jones would be sure to

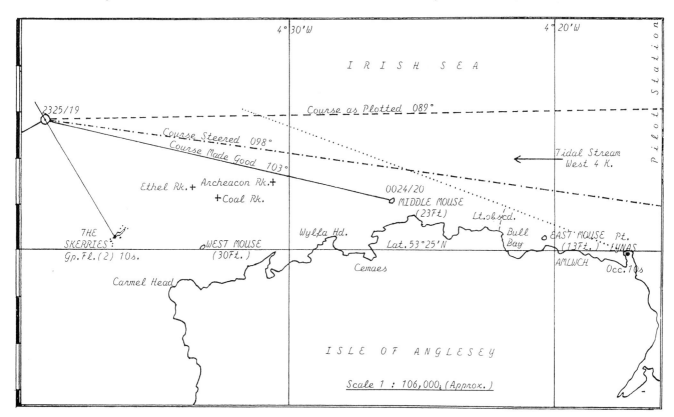

Naturalist: a misdirected approach to Lynas Pilot Station.

enter into it with that boyish enthusiasm and unmitigated zeal for efficiency which characterized all his endeavours. He was certainly a good shipmaster, promoting the company's interests in his tussles with agents or stevedores; firm but just in his dealings with the crew; and enduring the shortcomings of lesser mortals with patient resignation. This latter virtue was, however, often tested to the limit in his relations with old "Cheltenham" Davies, the Chief Engineer, whose casual, laid-back manner was anathema to Ivor's energetic thoroughness. This clash of personalities sometimes led to harsh words - especially when Ivor insisted on including the engine room in his twice-weekly round of inspections. For he ran a tight ship, conducting his inspections with scrupulous attention to detail, and insisting on correct dress both on and off duty. Most of his peers felt that he would prove to be an excellent Superintendent - a few felt they would rue the day... But with dreadful irony Ivor's prospects were destined to turn to ashes.

That fateful voyage round the land from Avonmouth was made in fine, clear weather. The ship passed the South Stack at about 22.15 on 19th April 1955, and an hour later was rounding the Skerries. At 23.25, with the Skerries light abeam bearing 148 degrees distant three miles, Captain Jones laid off the course for the pilot station off Point Lynas, about 12 miles to the east. He noted that the hidden dangers of Ethel Rock and Archdeacon Rock would be cleared by a good margin. Shifting the parallel rules, he read off the course indicated - 089 degrees - almost due east. With his pencil he jotted down the figures on the chart but, by some freakish quirk of the mind transposed them to 098 degrees! Underneath, he wrote down the compass error, 10 degrees west, applied it, and ordered Third Officer Dodds to steer 108 degrees (i.e., by standard magnetic compass).

Undoubtedly the Third Officer should have checked the course plotted, as is custom and practice, but the Old Man had given him a direct order and it was natural to carry it out right away. Then the compass error would have to be checked on the new heading with a bearing of a convenient star. All this took time, and by then it was getting near one bell (23.45), time to call the watch, write up the log, make the tea... Consequently, the vital check was never made.

Meanwhile, unsuspected by anyone, the ship was forging ahead 9 degrees off course. Worse, the deflection in the course angle had the effect of placing the four-knot, west-going tidal stream against the port bow, setting the ship down a further 5 degrees. It was a dark night, crystal clear, with every star showing in the celestial canopy overhead; the sea, darker than the sky, was calm and unruffled. However, Captain Jones must have been uneasy when the light on Point Lynas failed to appear when expected. He sent Second Officer Williams, who had just arrived on the bridge to take over the watch, up to the monkey island, where the standard compass was sited, to take a bearing of the Skerries light, still flashing with brilliant intensity on the starboard quarter.

Of course, the reason why Point Lynas light had not materialized was because the ship was still in the "blind" sector, where the light was obscured by the lie of the land. Meanwhile, the Second Officer's bearing, projected to the course line, put the ship due north of Lynas - which was ridiculous! Thoroughly alarmed, he went up the ladder to check the bearing again.

The impact, when it came at 00.24 on 20th, was violent. The 10,000-ton ship, moving at over 11 knots, careered full tilt into a solid rock rising some 23 feet above the surface of the sea. A witness recalls: "I was sound asleep at the time, and the force of the impact threw the ship on her side so violently that I was flung out of my bunk. Still half asleep but unhurt, I reached for my jacket and lurched out on deck. Outside, it was bedlam.[207]

The ship was still, immobile, but, mingling with the roar of steam escaping from the relief valves, was the screeching of a million demented sea birds. Overhead they swooped, weaving and diving amid the rigging, their wings,

ghostly pale, reflecting the light shining from the masthead lamps, their beaks agape, screaming their raucous protest at this sea monster which had driven them from their quiet roosting places on the rock. For there was the rock rising above the calm surface of the sea, shadowy, and obviously quite unmoved.

I ran up the ladders to the bridge, feeling the vibration as the engines began working astern. The roar of steam ceased abruptly, leaving only the angry shrieking of the sea birds to disturb the silence. Captain Jones was standing in the bridge wing.

'Where are we? What's happened?' I asked. 'That', replied Captain Jones dazedly, pointing towards the rock looming over the bow, 'That, Mr. Mate, I believe is the Middle Mouse!' I went to the chartroom, glanced at the chart...at the course line running almost due east...at the pencilled figures...and realised at once just what had happened". Three rocky islets stand off the northern shore of Anglesey, the East, West, and Middle Mouse, all of them 'blind', for none of them are lit, and the NATURALIST had hit the middle one. She was transfixed by her forefoot, held fast, and making no response to the engine's driving stern power. The ship's position was precarious, for the tide was still ebbing. Chief Officer, Carpenter, and Second Engineer Mike Merrifield checked the ship for damage, and found all compartments tight, except the forepeak and number 1 tank, which were flooded. Their thoughts reverted to the Old Man's lonely plight, and they felt a great sadness. Only old 'Cheltenham' introduced a sour note when he was heard to say, a hint of glee in his voice, 'Well, the old devil can't blame me for this one!'

Ivor Jones had no intention of blaming anyone - no-one except himself, for he had always been his own sternest critic. A vessel showing the white-over-red signal for a pilot boat was approaching cautiously. It was the Lynas cutter coming to find out what on earth a ship was doing in that position. An Aldis lamp flashed across the dark waters: "Do you require a pilot?" The question occasioned some rather hysterical mirth. "Affirmative", was the reply. When at last the large frame of Dick Lund, the Company's appropriated pilot, climbed over the rail, his bluff reassuring manner was like a tonic.

"The tide will start making in half-an-hour or so", he said confidently. "Then she'll float off". And so she did, and resumed her passage to Liverpool a little down by the head, but under her own steam. A few weeks later she was booked into Grayson's dry dock in Birkenhead where the damage to her forefoot was repaired.

Of course, there was quite a row. Captain Ivor Jones, Superintendent-elect, his career in ruins, and his hopes for the future dashed, resigned from the company for, as he said, he felt he could no longer command the confidence of the board. He left to study for an Extra Master's Certificate, with a view to becoming a surveyor for the Department of Trade. That did not work out, and eventually he found himself back at sea in the employ of Lamport and Holt Ltd., where he was soon commanding ships again.

However, the lesson is clear. No matter how confident and self-assured our superiors may appear to be, they, too, are prone to human failure in unguarded moments, and it costs nothing to run a discreet check over their calculations. Indeed, it could be vital, as this story shows.

Author's note. I saw Ivor Jones only once after his departure, and that was many years later, when I was pounding the dock. I was meeting a ship at Langton Lock one summer's evening, and when I arrived at the lock a Lamport and Holt ship was already lying there waiting for the level. A voice hailed me from the bridge. It was Ivor. He greeted me heartily, and we chatted in stentorian tones until the inner gates opened. He waved cheerfully as his ship passed through the lock, but shortly afterwards I read of his early death in the local newspaper.

266. EMPIRE WILY 1946
See DALESMAN (1) (No. 247).

267. DALESMAN (1) 1946-1959
See DALESMAN (1) (No. 247).

PART 5

THE INNOVATORY YEARS
1946 – 1977

The situation

For the second time in a mere three decades, much of Europe lay devastated by war. As the fighting ended the combatants began to realize that the enormous cost of restoration would be beyond the resources of nations whose coffers had been drained by the demands of war. Only the United States had cash to spare. Immediately after the war, the British Government negotiated a loan of $3,750 million to enable Britain to pay for the initial imports essential for the work of reconstruction, to rebuild her shattered cities, and renovate out-dated machinery. But Britain was not the only beneficiary of American affluence and generosity.

Unlike the situation in 1918, when the USA withdrew into isolation, virtually casting the nations of Europe - and herself - into recession, President Truman, with the support of Congress, decided it would be in the nation's best interests to help Europe to rehabilitate herself. In June 1947, the Marshall Plan was launched by General George Marshall, US Chief of Staff, in a speech at Harvard University. This was a relief plan of such open-handed generosity as to be almost visionary. Former enemies, as well as allies would be included, and even potential future enemies, the Soviet Union and her new array of satellite states, were invited, but declined to participate.

During the four years of its existence, Marshall Aid was funded to the sum of $13,150 million, of which Britain received the lion's share.[208] Of course, there was an element of self-interest. The Americans were hard-headed capitalists, and Europe seemed a good investment, not only in financial terms but in terms of security. A chaotic, impoverished Western Europe would not be able to withstand the growing Communist power in the east, and might well become Communist states - satellites of the Soviet Union which many Americans saw as the arch-enemy - leaving the USA isolated in an expanding Communist world. The purpose of the aid was to provide food, animal feeding stuffs, and fertilizers to ensure that Europeans were fed. Next came the purchase of industrial raw materials, machinery, vehicles, and fuel to get the wheels of industry turning again. Naturally, a large proportion of all these goods and materials - 69.7% - were purchased in the United States, which, in turn, was good for the US economy.

All this activity, of course, generated trade, most of it carried by sea, raising the demand for ships, and breathing new life into the shipyards. Thos. and Jas. Harrison Ltd., were equal to the challenge.

The response

In September 1939, the Harrison fleet had mustered 45 ships, totalling 275,580 gross tons, and serving at least ten regular trade routes. By late 1946 the fleet numbered 30 ships of 190,627 gross tons, and the old regular trade routes were in disarray, having to be restored in the face of strong competition. However, a comprehensive rebuilding and replacement programme was already under way. The standard ships - Empire and Liberty types - already in service were joined by TRIBESMAN and MERCHANT (Empire types), SCHOLAR, SENATOR, SCULPTOR, SPEAKER, STATESMAN, SUCCESSOR, HISTORIAN, and COLONIAL (Liberty types), so that by 1949, six Empires and ten Liberty ships formed the backbone of the fleet. The formidable rebuilding programme was also bearing fruit, and by the end of 1949 six fine modern ships had slid down the ways into the Clyde or the Wear to join their Harrison sisters on the Liverpool register, swelling the fleet to 40 vessels of 266,603 gross tons. This net increase is all the more remarkable when it is remembered that five elderly ships which had borne the brunt of war were disposed of during this immediate post-war period. By 1955

One of Harrisons' ten Liberties, *Scholar.*

[Ken Cunnington]

Harrison's first motor vessel, *Herdsman* of 1946. [*A. Duncan*]

the number of ships in the fleet had peaked at 43 (307,498 gross tons) but after that date there was a perceptible decline, slowly at first, but gathering momentum during the seventies.

However, post-war hopes and forecasts had no time for pessimism about the future. The rebuilding programme was pre-eminent, with striking ventures into new designs and means of propulsion. For the first time in their history Harrisons introduced motor ships into their fleet. Of course, during the War there had been brief flirtations with motor vessels managed for the Ministry of War Transport, such as the EMPIRE RANGOON (257) and EMPIRE KENT (260), equipped with oil engines built by Harland and Wolff and Krupps of Germany, respectively. But these were never home-spun members of the fleet, and there was no urge to purchase them after the war. Consequently, the HERDSMAN (269), launched in July 1946 from William Doxford's yard on the Wear, became Harrisons' first motor vessel, her five-cylinder Doxford diesel engine giving her a speed of 14 knots, and heralding a new generation of engineers with motor endorsements stamped on their steam-orientated certificates. With the diesel engine came the silent, powerful, electric

winches, which reduced the clatter of night work considerably, to the greater comfort of the crew.

Of course, steam was not abandoned all at once. Close on the heels of HERDSMAN came CRAFTSMAN (275) and LINGUIST (276), two steam ships built by Lithgows of Port Glasgow, and engined by David Rowan and Co. Ltd. In 1948, HERDSMAN was joined by two diesel sisters, INTERPRETER (278) and FACTOR (279), and the concept of motor ships, despite many initial setbacks, was firmly established in Harrison custom and practice. Their main attraction, of course, was fuel economy.

Despite being bigger, more powerful and faster than their pre-war counterparts, and although they boasted more spacious and more comfortable accommodation, the design of these new vessels remained conservative. They had two holds before the bridge, one between bridge and funnel, and two aft, all served by derricks (the heaviest only 15 tons S.W.L.) rigged to masts and samson posts, and were not dissimilar to the pre-war ADVISER class which had served the company so well.

However, changes were on the way. At this time the

The steamer *Craftsman* of 1947, on trials in the Firth of Clyde. [*Glasgow University Archives GD320/10/1/169/3*]

company was under the chairmanship of Sir T. Harrison Hughes, and its subsequent development was due largely to his vigorous administration. However, perhaps the greatest and most influential of the post-war innovators was Pat Wilson, who had joined the company in 1936 under the apprenticeship scheme which existed at that time. During the war he had served with the RAF and, after being demobbed in 1946, returned to Harrisons full of ideas and enthusiasm for modernising the company and its ships. After a refresher course, which included a voyage as Purser, he was given the post of Ship's Husband, a hoary old title whose origins are lost in the mists of antiquity. But the term means just what it says - he was there to take care of his ships, for better or worse. The Ship's Husband was involved at the design stage, and throughout the building, launching, and fitting out, ever watchful through the eyes of the technical staff for instances which might prove detrimental to ship or owners. If one of the ships got into trouble, it was the Ship's Husband who stood up in court to face the judge, the one to bear the brunt of corporate culpability, should it arise.

It was undoubtedly Pat Wilson who motivated the board to introduce most of those up-to-date features which characterised the post-war ships. No longer would it be necessary for a Harrison vessel to carry a portable "do-it-yourself" derrick on deck, to be rigged on the voyage for handling heavy lifts over 15 tons. Permanent 50-, 60-, or 70-ton derricks sited at the main hatches soon became standard equipment in the new ships. Then in 1960 the ADVENTURER (300) joined the fleet, the first British ship to be equipped with the German-patented Stülcken derrick, capable of lifting 180 tons, its ingenious rig enabling it to be used at either of the two main hatches.

Another of Pat Wilson's initiatives lay in the field of radio and electronics. For the first time, short-wave radio transmitters were installed in the ships, greatly increasing the range of communication, and in the wheelhouse appeared the extremely useful V.H.F. radio-telephone for local voice communication. These innovations culminated in the eighties with the introduction of INMARSAT, a satellite telecommunication system which brought each ship within a 'phone-call of the office, regardless of where in the world she might be.

Radar was another innovation of the fifties, and there is no doubting its eventual massive contribution to safety at sea. Harrisons, however, introduced the system to their ships rather later than most companies. This apparent reluctance was motivated by prudence rather than other considerations, and it certainly seemed in the early days that radar at sea was more of a menace than a safeguard. People in ships equipped with radar tended, so it seemed, to flout the old rules of proceeding with caution in fog, and failure to appreciate the quirks of relative motion as depicted on the radar screen sometimes led to the phrase, "radar-assisted collision" to appear in a number

Chairman Patrick Wilson B.E.M. (1916-1987) in a rare convivial mode.

A fine view of *Adventurer's* Stülcken derrick in action at Port Elizabeth. In the foreground is a South African Railway's bogie wagon waiting to take the load.

of well-publicised court cases. Only after a great deal of further research into the interpretation of radar information, and its processing by plotting, were Harrisons prepared to install expensive radar equipment in their ships. That was not until 1959, by which time all masters and officers had undergone an intensive course in radar navigation, and the introduction of true motion radar presented a more readily comprehensible picture on screen. A year or two later, the adoption in all ships of an automatic steering system linked electronically to the gyro-compass - another innovation in post-war ships - enabled the helmsman to be usefully employed on other duties, and ultimately to a reduction in crew numbers.

Propulsion machinery in Harrison ships

For 87 years Harrisons maintained faith in the steam engine, from the earliest simple two-cylinder engines developing 70 to 80 horse power fitted in GLADIATOR (37) and COGNAC (38) in 1860 to the impressive triple-expansion engines of nearly 700 nominal horse power, which powered CROFTER (290) and FORESTER (291) in 1951/52. It became customary to fit a Bauer-Wach low-pressure turbine to the later steam engines, a device which improved efficiency and increased power by over 20%. At the turn of the century, three of Harrisons' famous four masters - CUSTODIAN (120), MECHANICIAN (122) and WAYFARER (129) - were powered by two triple-expansion engines, rated at 700 nominal horse power, driving twin screws, while the passenger vessels built between the wars, INANDA (210) and INKOSI (240), were equipped with four-cylinder reciprocating engines. Meanwhile, EXPLORER (234) and INVENTOR (239) of 1935 were noted and admired for their innovative cam gear.

A diversion into steam turbines was initiated in the DRAMATIST (201) of 1920, but the idea did not catch on, and was not repeated until 1949, when the BIOGRAPHER (285) was built.

Almost exclusively from their inception, Harrison steamers had burned coal as fuel. Occasionally, when fuel oil became comparatively cheap, hasty conversions to oil fuel were carried out in some ships, only to be hastily re-converted to coal when the price of oil rocketed, as with GOVERNOR (187). Interesting but futile experiments in the use of pulverised coal as fuel were initiated in the MUSICIAN (208) and RECORDER (225) in the thirties, but were soon abandoned as the disadvantages quickly became obvious.

During the Second World War, Harrison Line managed a fleet of 16 ships on behalf of the Ministry of War Transport. These vessels came with a diversity of machinery to which Harrisons' engineers had to adapt. Little difficulty was experienced with the triple-expansion reciprocating steam engines, and the oil-burning Liberty ships, with their water-tube boilers, were particularly popular. But the technicalities of the turbine-driven EMPIRE CAPTAIN (258) and EMPIRE LIFE (259), and the motor ships EMPIRE RANGOON (257) and EMPIRE KENT (260), often presented difficulties of manning with engineer officers holding appropriate qualifications.

When the Board of T. and J. Harrison decided after the Second World War to include motor-ships in the post-war rebuilding programme, the difficulties of manning became more acute. So when HERDSMAN (269), INTERPRETER (278) and the Clyde-built FACTOR (279), all equipped with five-cylinder 67LB5 Doxford diesel oil engines, slid down the ways in 1947/48, finding senior engineers with appropriate qualifications to sail in them was still a problem. Fortunately, in a far-sighted move, many engineers had been seconded to other companies to obtain the sea-time and experience necessary to qualify to sit the examinations for a Board of Trade motor endorsement to their steam certificates, and many young men, invariably of junior rank in the steamers, soon found themselves elevated to Second, and even Chief Engineer, in a new motor ship. For the initial three were followed in 1951/55 by nine more motor ships from the Doxford yards.

A variant of the Doxford diesel oil engine new to Harrisons, the type 67LBD6 with six cylinders and opposed pistons, was installed in the next three motor vessels to be launched - ADMINISTRATOR (297), AUTHOR (298) and PLAINSMAN (299) - and similar engines were installed in the three heavy-lift ships, ADVENTURER (300), CUSTODIAN (302), and TACTICIAN (303), built 1960/61.

For the first time since 1925, Harrisons decided in 1960 to go abroad for the next series of new ships, and in 1961 EXPLORER (304) and DALESMAN (305) were launched at Amsterdam. In a further new departure, the hitherto ubiquitous Doxford oil engine was superseded by what some regard as the Rolls Royce of marine engines, that of Sulzer Brothers of Winterthur, Switzerland. The INVENTOR (306) was unique, equipped with an eight-cylinder Sulzer built under licence by Connells of Glasgow in 1964.

Thereafter, variety became the key to the theme, for the next series of ships, the DISCOVERER (307) class, built in Sweden in 1964/65, with seven-cylinder Gotaverken diesel oil engines installed, was followed in 1966 by two more Swedish-built ships, TRADER (312) and LINGUIST (313), fitted out with twin SEMT-Pielstick diesel engines. Then it was back to eight-cylinder Sulzer diesels for the MAGICIAN (314) and HISTORIAN (315), machinery built at Winterthur and actually installed at Sunderland by Doxfords. Two ships, MERCHANT (316) and SCHOLAR (317), were purchased from Cammell Lairds in 1969, and they too were equipped at Birkenhead with six-cylinder Sulzer engines built at Winterthur. Another purchase, the BENEFACTOR (318), was equipped with a seven-cylinder Sulzer diesel built and installed under licence by George Clarke and NEM Ltd. of Wallsend, although the ship itself was built by Doxfords at Sunderland.

Meanwhile, the super-heavy lift ship CRAFTSMAN (319) was also building at Sunderland, and was equipped with an eight-cylinder Sulzer diesel developing 16,000 brake horse power. Another feature of this vessel was her unmanned engine-room, all primary controls being located on the navigation bridge, and operated electronically by the navigating officers, whilst the ship's engineers monitored the multifarious connections, and carried out maintenance work.

In 1973, Harrison Line entered the bulk-cargo carrying trades, with the 16,317 tons gross WAYFARER (320) and her two sisters. Built in Japan, they, too, were fitted with six-cylinder Sulzer diesels built under licence by Sumitomo of Tamashima. These powerful units developed 12,000 brake horse power, giving a service speed of more than 15 knots. Two years later, two Panamax bulk-carriers were launched by Burmeister & Wain at Copenhagen. Their seven-cylinder B. & W. marine diesel engines developed 18,500 brake horse power to drive the 60,000 tonne deadweight vessels forward at 16 knots.

The first of three cellular container ships, ASTRONOMER (325), was launched from the Polish yard of Stocznia Gdansk in 1977. These vessels were each equipped with Cegielski-Sulzer 10-cylinder oil engines developing 29,000 brake horse power for a service speed of 20½ knots. Meanwhile, the container ship CITY OF DURBAN (327), jointly owned with Ellerman Lines, was building in Bremen, West Germany, joining the Ellerman-

Harrison Container Line in 1978. Her propulsion machinery consisted of two eight-cylinder MAN diesel engines each developing 25,680 brake horse power to drive twin screws for a service speed of 22 knots.

Of the final six vessels to join the Harrison Line fleet, five were built in Japan, and one in South Korea. All were bulk-carriers in the "handy" range (25,000-40,000 tonnes deadweight). Four were equipped with six-cylinder diesels, the remaining two with six-cylinder B.& W. diesels, all installed under licence by Far East shipbuilding and engineering companies.

Such a wide variety of engineering designs and systems must have presented the Superintendent Engineer and his staff with a succession of problems. Maintaining a stock of spare parts would have been a formidable task in itself, though doubtless the shipyards and engine builders could be relied upon to supply the bulk of them when needed. Nevertheless, the fact that the problems were confronted and solved reflects great credit on all those concerned with the management and maintenance of complex, modern machinery. Moreover, the range and scope of experience gained during this period proved invaluable when economic stresses and a rapidly diminishing fleet, ushered in the Harrison Care initiative.

Conditions at sea

During the immediate post-war years trade unionism flourished under Attlee's Labour government. This is not a political tract, and the writer does not propose to be drawn into political arguments. It may be argued that trade union power, by fostering restrictive practices and fomenting costly strikes, did much to retard industrial progress. But on the other hand it must be acknowledged that workforces throughout industry benefited from enlightened legislation and codes of practice initiated by the unions. As early as September 1944, while the war was still in progress, representatives of the merchant navies of twelve countries had held a conference in London and produced a charter outlining proposals for improving conditions at sea after the war.[209]

In retrospect, the demands of the charter do not seem unreasonable or excessive. The minimum wage for an able seaman would be £18 per month; for a third officer or fourth engineer, £22.10s.; for a chief engineer, £40.10s.; and for a ship master, £45. Each country would be required to set up a manpower pool of registered officers and seamen, funded by the state, the shipowners, and the maritime unions, and capable of paying the seamen a reasonable retainer between voyages. Hours of work would be regulated on the basis of a 56-hour week at sea, with only essential duties being carried out on Saturday afternoons and Sundays. Annual leave would be set at not less than 12 working days.

The pool of manpower, which had already existed throughout the war as an essential part of the war effort, became the Merchant Navy Establishment (M.N.E.), with offices in all major ports, financed by shipowners through the Shipping Federation. A seaman registered with the M.N.E. was sure of continuity of employment; and for the career officer there was also the option of a company contract, which had many advantages, and was renewable every two years.

The trades

The bright new order, with its emphasis on improved conditions, plus national insurance and company pension schemes - was to cost shipowners a great deal of money, money which had to be earned against increasing competition on the trade-routes of the world. After the war, Harrisons and many other established shipping companies returned to the old routes, regrouped their Conferences, and resumed liner trading. Some of these trades paid well - very well - whereas others involved considerable loss. One of the latter was the Calcutta trade, in pre-war days the jewel in Harrisons' crown, but latterly, especially after Indian independence, a thorn in the flesh of the body commercial.

Harrisons had been members of the UK-Calcutta Conference, outwards and homewards, since its inception in 1875 (other founder members were P&O, British India, Clan, City and Anchor Lines). Over the years other lines came in, including Brocklebanks in 1891, and a few parted company. Internal competition for cargoes was strong, but on the whole the Conference provided shippers and owners alike with a reliable, frequent, and profitable service, both ways, at fairly steady rates of freight. However, after the Second World War internal stresses and strains imposed by a newly independent and nationalistic Indian Government, and the obligatory affiliation of two Indian lines to both the UK and Continental Conferences, upset the rather cosy status quo, and boded ill for the future.

Cargoes for Harrisons dwindled, and ships began to encounter extraordinary delays, their round voyages reduced to only two per year instead of three, mortgaging valuable cargo space which could have been utilized more profitably elsewhere. By 1955, Harrisons had decided to leave the Calcutta Conference, selling their berthing rights, goodwill, and other interests in Calcutta and other ports in India, Pakistan, and Ceylon to Brocklebanks. These were valuable, but unquantifiable, commodities, and there was some perplexity on both sides as to what would constitute a "fair and proper price". In the end, Sir Harrison Hughes and Sir Denis Bates, Chairman of T. and J. Brocklebank, settled the matter "very agreeably and amicably" over lunch in the sum of £250,000.[210]

On 25th May 1957, the steamer INVENTOR (239), sailed from Vittoria Wharf, Birkenhead, with the last

PRESENT SERVICES

Liverpool to Port Said, Suez, Aden and Calcutta.

Liverpool to Brazil.

South Wales, Glasgow and Liverpool to Red Sea and East Africa.

South Wales, Glasgow and Liverpool to South Africa.

Liverpool and Manchester to West Indies, Venezuela, Curaçao, Colombia, Panama Canal Zone, Mexico and Belize.

London to Barbados, Trinidad and Demerara.

Middlesbrough, Continent and London to South Africa.

Glasgow to Barbados, Trinidad and Demerara.

Calcutta and Colombo to London, Liverpool, Dublin and Manchester.

Brazil to Liverpool.

East Africa and Red Sea to Avonmouth, Liverpool, Manchester, Glasgow, Dublin and Belfast.

South Africa to London, Avonmouth, Liverpool, Manchester, Glasgow, Dublin and Belfast.

West Indies to London, Liverpool and Glasgow.

U.S. Gulf Ports to Liverpool and Manchester.

LOADING BERTHS

LIVERPOOL:	East Side, Brunswick Dock
BIRKENHEAD:	East and West Float
LONDON:	West India Dock
GLASGOW:	Plantation Quay
MANCHESTER:	9 Shed, 8 Dock, Salford

35

From a brief history of the company published in 1953.

Harrison Line outward cargo to Calcutta. The final homeward sailing was taken by the steamer TRIBESMAN (268), which left Calcutta on 19th September 1957. Thus, after almost 90 years, Calcutta was dropped from Harrison Line schedules for good. Howrah Bridge, the Hooghly Bore, Garden Reach, the Jetties, Chowringhe, and Kidderpore Dock lapsed into the memories of those to whom, at one time, the "Calcutta run" had been a way of life.

Other trade routes were booming, however, notably those to the West Indies and Venezuela, where the oil companies were rapidly exploiting the oil fields and erecting refineries in Trinidad and Maracaibo. The demand for cotton for the Lancashire mills was rising to pre-war levels, and ports in the US Gulf were ready and eager to handle it and load it into the waiting ships. South Africa, and East Africa too, rich in minerals and raw materials, were anxious to receive imports of machinery and manufactured goods, providing full cargoes outwards and homewards. Competition in this trade, however, was fierce, not only from established maritime nations, but also from a growing Soviet merchant fleet, subsidised and operated by the State.

This had the effect of forcing freight rates below a level considered fair by traditional operators, but by adopting more efficient methods, Harrisons and others learned to live with it. Finally, the last link with yet another traditional trade was finally broken when Harrisons disposed of their berthing rights in the Charente brandy trade to Moss Hutchison and Co. Ltd. in 1955.

The dock

As the first post-war decade advanced, it became apparent that Harrisons' long-standing berth in East Brunswick Dock would soon become inadequate for the new generations of ships. Entry and exit via Brunswick Locks were restricted to an hour before high water for deeply laden ships, and the Mersey Docks and Harbour Board dredgers were finding it difficult and expensive to cope with the tons of silt deposited on the sill with every tide. A move to a less restricted berth was obviously in the best interests of both the M.D. & H.B. and Harrisons.

At a meeting of the Docks and Quays Committee of the M.D. & H.B. on 29th November 1961, Harrisons' application for an appropriated berth at South Canada Branch Dock No. 2 was approved, and was to become available after completion of the new Langton Lock project. It was agreed that a canteen at Canada 2 should be demolished to provide a site for the Dock Office, and a month later the canteen was duly demolished. However, at the next meeting on 21st February 1962, Harrisons decided that the site would be much more useful as a cargo working space and formally requested that a site at the eastern end of Canada 2 should be cleared to make room for a Dock Office. The clearance involved the demolition of several existing buildings, including a police storage depot, a medical centre, a traffic office, a fire station and a recreation centre, all of which had to be re-sited elsewhere. Nevertheless, the request was approved, and work began.[211]

The new Dock Office was designed by Donald Bradshaw of Liverpool, and was built by Holland, Hannen, and Cubitts of Bromborough.[212] Consisting of two storeys, it provided accommodation for superintendents and staff of the Marine, Engineering, Catering, and Cargo Departments dealing with the everyday requirements

for handling, repairing, storing, and loading of the company's vessels, several of which might be berthed in the dock, and at other berths along the line of docks, at any given time. Above the main building, a penthouse canteen and kitchen provided excellent lunches for the dock staff.

Moving from Brunswick Dock, Harrisons' citadel in the south end of Liverpool for over 90 years, was in itself quite a feat of logistics. Naturally, the normal processes of loading and discharging ships in East Brunswick had to continue uninterrupted right to the end, after which all the plant - including mobile cranes, trucks, spreaders, snotters, and slings - had to be on hand at South Canada 2 to continue those same processes. Then, of course, all the stores - paints, oils, cordage, canvas, derricks, blocks, shackles, and coils of wire - had to be transported by wagons, vans, and barges from their old home in the nondescript "Corner" to their new home at the western end of the South Quay of Canada 2, which became known affectionately and more exotically as "La Ponderosa", after a popular television western series showing at that time. This was followed by truckloads of office furniture and stacks of records, books, and stationery. It was a mammoth task performed with remarkable precision by the inimitable Shore Gang under the supervision of the Dock Superintendent himself, Mr. Charles Allister. Consequently, on 2nd December 1963 all was ready to receive the first ship on the newly appointed berth. She was the ADVENTURER (300) which came alongside to load for Kingston and Mexico, sailing on 7th December.

Diversification

During the 'sixties there was a trend among old-established shipping companies to divert some of their capital into enterprises other than shipping. The famous passenger carriers were among the first to follow this trend since their traditional services were declining as a result of the rapid growth of air passenger traffic during the post-war years. They diversified their interests by adapting to cruising, of course, and investing in hotels, property, insurance and financial services, even in airlines, on the well-established principle that, "If you can't beat 'em, join 'em". In the main, Harrisons clung loyally to shipping, but even they deemed it prudent to seek extra dividends in insurance and the home-furnishing industry. More substantial ventures, however, included the acquisition of Prentice, Service and Henderson Ltd., the Glasgow Shipping Agency, and S.C. Chambers Ltd., sale and purchase brokers of Liverpool.

It will be recalled that, in 1920, The Charente Steam-Ship Co. Ltd. (Thos. and Jas. Harrison Ltd., managers) acquired the remaining eight ships of the Crown Line from their owners, Prentice, Service and Henderson of Glasgow. Although P.S. and H. virtually ceased to be

Owned by a subsidiary company registered in Bermuda, *Author* was one of the finest ships Harrisons owned.

shipowners from that time (there was a brief single-ship venture during the early thirties which failed to prosper) they became prominent ship and freight agents for several companies, notably for all Charente vessels loading at Glasgow for the West Indies and Central America. Then in 1953 Harrisons, as managers of Charente, decided to place all agency and ship's husbandry matters in the hands of P.S. and H. for all services to and from the Clyde, including those East and South African services which had formerly been handled by Cayzer, Irvine and Co., and City Line, respectively. Finally, in October 1959, P.S. and H. became a private limited company, a wholly owned subsidiary of The Charente Steam-Ship Co. Ltd., and C.A.C. Booth of Harrisons was appointed Managing Director.[213] P.S. and H. subsequently became agents for Ben Line, United Arab, and Ellerman Harrison Container Line (EHCL). S.C. Chambers and Co. Ltd. of Liverpool had been Harrisons' sale and purchase brokers for many years. The company also had interests in other shipping activities, such as agency work, chartering, towage, and ship demolition. In 1971, Charente purchased a 40% interest in S.C. Chambers, and in 1985 acquired a controlling interest, with Denholms of Glasgow holding the remaining equity.[214]

The firm of Thomas Tweddle and Co. Ltd. had long been customs and consular agents to Liverpool shipowners and brokers trading to Spanish-speaking countries. Founded in 1835, the family firm's fortunes were based mainly on the preparation and translation of manifests and consular invoices, and operating a freight forwarding service. The firm had worked closely with Harrisons for many years, and in 1970 Harrisons acquired a 100% interest in the firm. In 1978 Tweddles moved from its offices in the Corn Exchange into Mersey Chambers, as if to foster even closer ties with its parent company.[215]

Another phenomenon of the fifties, the adoption of flags of convenience, was mainly a means of meeting foreign competition by avoiding costly, inflexible, and excessive seafarer manning and wage levels imposed by the seamen's and officers' organizations, whilst UK tax incentives for investment were drastically reduced. The device, naturally, was opposed by the trades union movement, which saw it as an attempt to undermine standards for workers, and the inevitable confrontations followed. For taxation reasons, Harrisons gave the system a brief trial in 1958 when the excellent new motor ships, ADMINISTRATOR (297) and AUTHOR (298) were delivered. A new company was formed, the Ruthin Steam Ship Co. Ltd., with offices registered in Hamilton, Bermuda, and to this company the two ships officially belonged. However, the ships continued to fly the Red Ensign, and were registered in Liverpool, and bare-boat chartered to Charente. This expedient was shortlived, however, and within a few years the ships reverted to the Charente Steam-Ship Co. Ltd.

But Harrisons' most important shift of policy, implemented towards the end of this period, involved a gradual drift away from the old liner trades into the dry bulk-carrying business, carrying cargoes all over the world, wherever a voyage - or time-charter - was offered, in other words, tramping. In 1973, three handy-sized identical bulk-carriers, each of 16,317 gross tons were launched at Shimizu, Japan, for delivery to the Charente Steam-Ship Co. Ltd. They were destined to operate in an international consortium known as Atlantic Bulkers Ltd. These ships were followed in 1975 by two gearless, Panamax bulk-carriers ordered from Burmeister & Wain's yards at Copenhagen. At 35,716 gross tons they were built to the maximum dimensions compatible with safe navigation in the Panama Canal.

At this time, purpose-built container ships were operating in strength on the former liner routes notably Europe/Australia, Europe/Far East and U.S.A. These, by their greater speed and an impressively reduced time of turn-round, were steadily infiltrating those services which had been built up over the years by operators of what became known as conventional ships. Harrisons considered many ways of meeting this form of competition, one of the earliest remedies being unitisation or palletization - the shipment of goods secured on standard pallets, often already slung to reduce the time spent in port. This, though effective, was not the answer, and Harrisons adopted containerisation, the first 20-foot standard containers being loaded aboard conventional ships as early as 1963. This procedure was never satisfactory, however, since the problems of loading them, winging them out in the 'tween deck, and securing them properly, inevitably led to damage and delays.

Harrison Line, of course, was not the only conventional carrier to be affected by the container revolution. Other British liner companies and many Continentals also had cause for concern, notably Hapag-Lloyd A.G., of Hamburg, and Koninklijke Nederlandsche Stoomboot Maatschappi B.V. (KNSM) of Amsterdam. These two companies, together with Harrisons, traded regularly to the Caribbean, and in 1973 they got together to form an organization known as RIOT (an anagram of TRIO) to study the prospects for co-operating in the establishment of a fast, joint liner service to and from the region. These early studies resulted in the formation of Caribbean Overseas Lines (CAROL), a close-knit consortium of like-minded shipowners who, singly, were almost powerless to face the competition from the USA and the Far East but, united, became a very powerful unit indeed.

Eighteen months later the trio was to be joined by the French Compagnie Général Maritime (CGM). A committee of marine and technical staff was formed to consider the latest and most practical forms of transport by sea. They included roll-on/roll-off systems (ideal for cross-channel or short-sea services, but unsuitable for long haul); lighters-aboard-ship (LASH), an ingenious system whereby loaded barges carrying several hundred tons of cargo were floated into a ship, the ship sealed, pumped out, and the barges secured until ready to be floated out at their destination. The practical difficulties were immense, and the idea never quite caught on. In the end, the new consortium settled for a purpose-built lift-on/lift-off container system. Six identical containerships were ordered from the Polish shipyard, Stocznia Gdanska, two of which were to be operated by Harrisons, two by the Germans, and one each by the French and Dutch.

The first sailing in the new service was taken by Hapag Lloyd's CARIBIA EXPRESS in December 1976, followed by Harrisons' ASTRONOMER (325) in February 1977. By 1978 the CAROL group was operating a weekly service from north west European ports and Britain to ports in the West Indies. Few of the latter were equipped to handle containers efficiently, and it would be many years before sophisticated container terminals could be built. Consequently, all CAROL ships carried a purpose-built gantry-crane capable of lifting 40 tonnes, and of moving from hatch to hatch, for use in ports where the appropriate equipment was not available.

A similar rationalizing process was introduced in the South African trade, and here Harrisons' share was much more restricted. The company joined forces in 1978 with Ellerman Lines to invest in a single container ship, the CITY OF DURBAN (327). Harrisons were to hold one-third of the equity, Ellermans two-thirds, an arrangement reminiscent of young Thomas Harrison's deal with Richard

Williamson over the brig TOM TOUGH (2) in 1836. Both companies would provide the personnel to man the ship on a rota system. Thus the Ellerman Harrison Container Line (EHCL) was born, destined, for a while at least, to operate in a wider consortium, Southern Africa Europe Container Service (SAECS), initially employing 11 vessels, and involving Safmarine, DAL, CGM, OCL, CMB, Lloyd Triestino, Messina, Nedlloyd, and EHCL.

One of the earliest manifestations of old rivals tending to combine together to form a common front in the face of overwhelming foreign competition appeared in 1966 with the founding of Associated Container Transportation Ltd. (ACT), a consortium of five British companies: Ben Line, Blue Star, Cunard, Ellerman, and the Charente Steam-Ship Company, whose combined trade routes spanned the globe from east to west. By so doing, they simply followed the example set a year earlier by Overseas Containers Ltd. (OCL), a consortium consisting of the combined resources of British and Commonwealth Shipping, Furness Withy, the Ocean Steamship Co., and P&O. From the earliest days, the two powerful consortia tended to co-operate by co-ordinating their services, and shunning a rivalry that could only have been mutually destructive.

In both cases, the emphasis was upon purpose-built container ships, and the investment in ships, plant, and thousands of isometric containers was colossal. Only people and organisations who believed in themselves and their ideas could contemplate enterprises of such magnitude.

Nevertheless, the die was cast, and the first ACT ship, ACT 1, sailed from Southampton on her maiden voyage to Australia on 22nd March 1969. By 1977 the five partners also had access to the Caribbean through CAROL's ASTRONOMER and ADVISER, and, in 1978, to South Africa through EHCL's CITY OF DURBAN.

Harrisons' container ship *Astronomer* in the English Channel.

We have already seen how the dissolution of empire and the growth of national shipping lines posed problems for the traditional carriers of the world's trade. India was not an isolated case; national lines, financed partly by development aid agencies, sprang up in Kenya, Ghana, Nigeria, and other former colonies.

Venezuela, Colombia and Mexico expanded their fleets, obliging Harrisons and others committed to the UNCTAD Code of Conduct for Liner Shipping Treaty to enter trade agreements with the national lines concerned, sharing space and freight, and assisting with the training of personnel including deck and engineer officers. Consequently, although there were increasing amounts of cargo moving during this period, the number of ships available to carry it was growing more rapidly than demand, and growing faster in the Far East and elsewhere than in Britain and Europe. Heavily subsidised shipbuilding and ship operations on the part of many developed as well as newly developing countries combined to threaten the economies of commercial liner shipping seriously. It was not all plain sailing, and management was continually on the lookout to exploit new services, and trim existing ones to a smooth and efficient level of operation.

Harrisons owned 22 of the 64 shares in *City of Durban* which ran for Ellerman Harrison Container Lines.   *[World Ship Photo Library]*

268. TRIBESMAN (2) 1946-1961 Steel steamship. Two decks and five holds. Two masts and a signal mast.

O.N. 180148 7,086g 4,889n 10,320d 429.8 (450.0 o.l.) x 56.3 x 37.85 feet. Cargo capacity: 528,147 cubic feet.
International Code: GBNZ.
T. 3-cyl. by Vickers Armstrongs Ltd., Barrow-in-Furness; 24½, 39, 70 x 48 inches, 11 knots.

29.10.1944: Launched by Shipbuilding Corporation Ltd. (Wear Branch), Sunderland (Yard No. 5) for the Ministry of War Transport, London (R. Chapman and Son, Newcastle-upon-Tyne, managers) as EMPIRE MANDALAY. Registered at Sunderland. *12.1944:* Completed. *26.11.1946:* Acquired by the company for £141,703 and registered at Liverpool. *4.12.1946:* Renamed TRIBESMAN. *19.9.1957:* Sailed from Calcutta taking the last Harrison Line homeward sailing from

that port after 87 years of regular trading. On 30.9.1957, she also made the last regular call at Colombo.[216] *15.5.1961:* Sold to Margalante Compania Naviera S.A., Panama (Mavroleon Brothers Ltd., London) for £65,000 and renamed DELTA under the Lebanese flag. Resold to Sigma Shipping Co. Ltd., Hong Kong for demolition and arrived 16.8.1961 at Hong Kong. *9.9.1961:* Demolition commenced

The war-built *Tribesman.*   *[Roy Fenton collection]*

269. HERDSMAN 1947-1965 Steel motor ship. Two decks and five holds. Two masts.

O.N. 181069 6,822g 4,020n 9,270d 442.8 (460.25 o.l.) x 60.0 x 32.5 feet. Cargo capacity: 517,534 cubic feet.
International Code: GPZX.
5-cyl. 2SCSA oil engine by William Doxford and Sons Ltd., Sunderland; 14 knots. First motor vessel in the fleet.

26.7.1946: Launched by William Doxford and Sons Ltd., Sunderland (Yard No. 739) for the company. *16.1.1947:* Delivered at a cost of £422,986 and later sailed from London and the Continent for South Africa on her maiden voyage under Captain W.A. Short. *7.6.1960:* Took her disabled sister INTERPRETER (278) in tow, and brought her safely to Dakar six days later. *21.7.1965:* Sold to Hwa Aun Company (Hong Kong) Ltd. (Chip Hwa Shipping and Trading Co. Ltd.), Hong Kong for £182,500 and renamed HOCK AUN. *1969:* Sold to Pacific International Lines (Pte.) Ltd., Singapore and renamed KOTA SELAMAT. *12.3.1969:* In collision with the Panamanian ferry DASMAN (1,359/31) off Port Sudan and sustained extensive damage to the hull abreast the mainmast. There were no casualties. *10.4.1969:* Sailed for Aqaba after completing temporary repairs. *1973:* Sold to Chinese shipbreakers. *9.11.1973:* Delivered at Whampoa.

Herdsman departs from Capetown.

270. SAMARINDA 1943-1947/STUDENT (3) 1947-1963 Steel steamship.[217] Two decks and five holds. Three masts.
O.N. 169672 7,252g 4,380n 10,510d 423.9 (441.5 o.l.) x 57.0 x 37.45 feet. Cargo capacity: 518,892 cubic feet.
International Code: GDZG (BFNZ prior to 1947).
T. 3-cyl. by Joshua Hendy Ironworks, Sunnyvale, California; 24½, 37, 70 x 48 inches; 11½ knots.

31.8.1943: Launched by California Shipbuilding Corporation, Los Angeles, California (Yard No. 249) for the United States War Shipping Administration, Washington as SAMSON OCCUM. Bareboat chartered to the Ministry of War Transport, London. *9.1943:* Completed as SAMARINDA. Thos. and Jas. Harrison Ltd. appointed managers. *30.9.1943:* Sailed from Los Angeles for Bombay via Hobart on her maiden voyage under Captain W.H. Slaughter. *29.4.1947:* Reverted to US flag and immediately purchased by the company for £139,183. Registered at Liverpool and renamed STUDENT. *1949:* Chief Officer R.W.C. Baldwin involuntarily went overboard at Beira (see below). *15.1.1963:* Sold to Parthenon Shipping Corporation, Monrovia, Liberia (Thrasybule Voyazides, Athens) for £40,500 and renamed PARTHENON.

Samarinda in Harrisons' colours.   *[John F. Hill collection]*

1964: Sold to Midsutra Shipping Ltd., London (Michel A. Araktingi, Beirut, Lebanon) and renamed AL AMIN under the Lebanese flag. *1966:* Sold to Ionia Shipping Co. Ltd., Panama (South East Asia Shipping and Trading Co. (George Zee), Hong Kong) and renamed FORTUNE SEA. *1967:* Sold to Chiu Ho Fa Steel and Iron Co., Kaohsiung. Prior to *25.4.1967:* Arrived at Kaohsiung for demolition.

Student.   *[J. & M. Clarkson]*

A comedy of anxious moments

It may have been mid-1949, or towards the tail-end of that year - the record is not at all precise - that the Liberty ship STUDENT lay anchored off the port of Beira in Portuguese Mozambique awaiting her turn to berth. In those days that could mean a delay of several weeks, weeks in which a diligent chief officer could marshal his crew to perform prodigies of maintenance. Ron Baldwin was one such chief officer, and one who was always prepared to lead by example. Thus, early on this particular morning he was to be found scaling patches of rust forming on the fish plate running along one of the main deck alleyways. In order to reach the target of his eager chipping hammer he had been obliged to stand on an old box which was imperfectly balanced in relation to the scupper. Consequently, it was no surprise to any student of the forces of equilibrium when, as he reached outboard, the box tilted, throwing him off balance and over the rail into the murky waters of the Rio Pungue.

Now Ron Baldwin (known affectionately as "Butch" to his many friends, a sobriquet inspired, I hasten to add, by his florid complexion, bull neck, brawny build and formidable strength) could not swim. Perhaps he belonged to that school of seafarers which resolutely declined to embrace the natatorial arts on the grounds that, if one did have the misfortune to fall overboard in mid-ocean, such skills only prolonged the agony without averting the inevitable.

Be that as it may, when Ron Baldwin surfaced he let out a mighty yell, expelling what air remained in his lungs before submerging for the second time. His bellow had been heard, however, the situation nicely judged, and men took up the ageless cry of "Man Overboard!"

Meanwhile, the Chief Officer's semi-submerged body was being carried aft on the swift-flowing tide. For a brief moment his streaming eyes cleared, and he saw before him the obdurate steel side of the ship, rising cliff-like from the muddy, brown stream, the pink boot-topping barnacle-studded, patchy with rust and green moss, and with not a hand-hold in sight.

As he went down for the third, and probably the last time, his flailing arms struck painfully against the stern frame with its complex arrangement of propeller and rudder. He hung on grimly, fighting for breath.

On the deck high above, the cries of "Man Overboard!" had reached the ears of Captain ("The Mighty Atom") William Pemberton. His reaction was swift, and predictable. "Call the Mate!" he cried. "But, Sir, it is the Mate!" was the anguished reply. Heads peering over the side had observed the Chief Officer's progress towards the stern, and another strangled yell from below had pin-pointed his precarious position as he clung to the stern frame.

Somewhat nonplussed, Captain Pemberton nevertheless took charge. "Fetch a ladder," he ordered. Unfortunately, this was easier said than done, for, owing to the depredations of local thieves, all moveable stores and equipment were locked away in port. Including the all-important rope ladder. The Bosun reported back to Captain Pemberton. "The ladder's in the forepeak, Sir, and it's locked!" "So! And where are the keys!?" "The Mate has them, Sir!"

All eyes locked on to the unfortunate Mr. Baldwin, and anxious enquiries confirmed the truth of this statement. Someone passed down a light heaving line, and with considerable difficulty, and at risk of being swept away, Butch managed to extract the bunch of keys from his sodden trousers pocket, and attach it to the heaving line. He watched anxiously as it was whisked away, and eventually, after what must have seemed an age, the ladder was shipped in position. Then, mustering what remained of even his considerable muscle-power, he climbed back to safety.

This incident, so fraught with anxiety, and with a clear potential for tragedy, had ended happily. But the story will live on in the rich folklore of the company's cautionary tales for many years to come.

271. SAMWIS 1943-1947/SPECIALIST (2) 1947-1964 Steel steamship. Two decks and five holds. Three masts.
O.N. 169686 7,263g 4,445n 10,547d 423.9 (441.5 o.l.) x 57.0 x 37.3 feet. Cargo capacity: 519,200 cubic feet.
International Code: GCYF (MYMW prior to 1947).
T. 3-cyl. by General Machinery Corporation, Hamilton, Ohio; 24½, 37, 70 x 48 inches, 11½ knots.

1943: Launched by Bethlehem-Fairfield Shipyard Inc., Baltimore, Maryland (Yard No. 2249) for the United States War Shipping Administration, Washington as EDWARD COOK. Bareboat chartered to the Ministry of War Transport, London. *10.1943:* Completed as SAMWIS. Thos. and Jas. Harrison Ltd. appointed managers. *27.10.1943:* Sailed from Baltimore for the Middle East and India on her maiden voyage under Captain A.H. Frew. *29.4.1947:* Reverted to US flag and immediately purchased by the company for £139,255. *20.6.1947:* Registered at Liverpool and renamed SPECIALIST. *20.8.1957:* In collision with the car ferry CATATUM in Maracaibo Harbour. Permanent repairs were later made at Willemstad, Curacao and consisted of three plates to repair and fair on the starboard side of number 3 hold. *21.1.1960:* Struck the German motor vessel STECKELHORN (2,526/53) while docking at Dunkirk. Damage to both vessels was slight. *4.2.1962:* Laid up at Barrow-in-Furness until 3.4.1962. *5.7.1962:* Laid up at Barrow-in-Furness until 29.8.1962. *25.5.1964:* Sold to Atlantic Maritime Carriers S.A., Panama (Harry Hadjipateras Brothers Ltd., London) for £80,000 and renamed MITERA

The Harrison-managed Liberty *Samwis* leaves a US port fully laden on 6th April 1944.

[John F. Hill collection]

under the Liberian flag. *12.12.1964:* Lost her propeller approximately 40 miles west of Borkum in position 53.32N, 05.31E, when on passage from Emden to Middlesbrough. Towed back to Emden by the Dutch salvage tug HOLLAND (548/52). *1967:* Transferred to the Greek flag. *1968:* Sold to Mollers Ltd., Hong Kong, for demolition. *8.11.1968:* Arrived at Junk Bay, Hong Kong.

Samwis when taken into Harrison ownership as *Specialist*.

[J. & M. Clarkson collection]

272. SCHOLAR (3) 1947-1964 Steel steamship. Two decks and five holds. Three masts.
O.N. 169905 7,280g 4,455n 10,494d 423.9 (441.5 o.l.) x 57.0 x 37.3 feet. Cargo capacity: 521,821 cubic feet.
International Code: GDCC (BTQT prior to 1947)
T. 3-cyl. by the Harrisburg Machinery Corporation, Harrisburg, Pennsylvania; 24½, 37, 70 x 48 inches, 11½ knots.

6.5.1944: Launched by New England Shipbuilding Corporation, South Portland, Maine (Yard No. 3022) for the United States War Shipping Administration, Washington as SAMIDWAY. Bareboat chartered to the Ministry of War Transport, London and Alfred Holt and Co., Liverpool appointed managers. *5.1944:* Completed. *29.4.1947:* Reverted to US flag and immediately purchased by the company for £139,217. *8.7.1947:* Registered at Liverpool and renamed SCHOLAR. *20.6.1953:* Roccuod fivo mon adrift in a dinghy in the English Channel. *8.2.1962:* Laid up at Barrow-in-Furness until 29.3.1962. *8.6.1964:* Sold to Karevena Marine Enterprises S.A., Panama ((J.C. Yemelos) (A. Lusi Ltd., London and later J.C. Carras and Sons (Shipbrokers) Ltd., London, agents) for £83,350 and renamed KOSTANTIS YEMELOS under the Greek flag. *1969:* Sold to Nichimen Co. Ltd., Japan, for demolition. *25.2.1969:* Delivered at Mihara. *5.3.1969:* Demolition commenced.

Samidway still with gun tubs at Cardiff on 6th June 1947. She was at the time managed by Alfred Holt and Co. for the Ministry of Transport, but later that month was purchased by Harrisons. *[Hansen Collection, National Museums and Galleries of Wales, Department of Industry. 1556/1651]*

Voices in the night [218]

It was around 02.00 on 20th June 1953, and SCHOLAR was outward bound from London to the West Indies, steering a mid-Channel course. By that time she had reached a position some 40 miles southwest of the Eddystone Rock, and Second Officer Jack Bobbin had just made himself another cup of coffee when he heard the voices. It was a fine night, clear, but quite dark under an overcast sky. He paused and listened. There it was again, a sort of half-human banshee wail heard faintly above the steady pulse-beat of the engines and the wash of the sea. Jack looked around uneasily - the "graveyard watch" is not so named without reason - and listened intently. The cry came again, like a wail of despair from the nether regions.

Nether? Like "lower"? He sprang to the bridge wing and gazed over the side at the black water, creamed with foam, sweeping past. At first he could see nothing more, but the cries came to his ears more clearly. Then, dimly, he saw it, tossing about crazily in the wash of the ship,

a small dinghy crowded with people shouting and waving. His presence of mind returned. He put the engine room telegraph to "Stand By"; released a lifebuoy with an automatic light attached, and called the Master, Captain Bob Myles.

The ship put about, slowed down, and headed for the pinpoint of light bobbing about in the waves. When they reached it they found the small dinghy hitched to the lifebuoy. Perched precariously in the little craft were five men, who were promptly taken on board. Four of them turned out to be Belgians, the other a German, and they revealed how their ship, the KRACK, a converted German E-boat bound for Tangier, had foundered somewhere between Plymouth Sound and the Eddystone Lighthouse. They had drifted a long way, and could not have lasted much longer in their tiny cockleshell of a boat. It had been their good fortune to be lying in the path of a passing ship whose officer of the watch had ears tuned to voices in the night.

It never rains but it pours [219]

When SCHOLAR was approaching the lock leading to Queen Alexandra Dock, Cardiff, on 17th January 1963 assisted by four tugs, the starboard tow rope parted. Another line was found and the ship was nosed into the lock, heaving lustily on the port bow rope which was hitched to a bollard. That rope then parted and deprived of all restraint (the head tugs had been cast off) the ship surged astern, and to counter this movement, the engines were put ahead. Unfortunately the tug on the starboard quarter was in the process of casting off, and her tow rope trailed rapidly into the threshing screw, effectively seizing up the ship's main engine. More ropes were sent ashore, and eventually the ship, now completely disabled, was at last secured in the lock. There a pair of docking tugs took over as the lock levelled. Two lines were passed to each tug, and the ship was eased into the dock, but with the wind freshening from the east they were unable to hold her, and all retreated hastily back to the lock. It was during this manoeuvre that the stern tug contrived to get both tow ropes wrapped around

Compared with other Harrison Liberties, *Scholar's* radio aerial is unusually prominent.
[J. & M. Clarkson]

her own propeller as the tug came astern. More tugs were procured and the ship was safely berthed at Empire Wharf, but not before yet another tow rope was carried away.

242

273. MERCHANT (4) 1947-1961 Steel steamship. Two decks and five holds. Two masts and a signal mast.
O.N. 169501 7,052g 4,876n 9,900d 432.7 (447.58 o.l.) x 56.2 x 37.0 feet. Cargo capacity: 529,654 cubic feet.
International Code: MAPF (BFGX prior to 1947).
T. 3-cyl. by David Rowan and Co. Ltd., Glasgow; 24¹/₂, 39, 70 x 48 inches, 11 knots.

Empire Miranda underway on the Clyde. Compared with the photograph of her as *Merchant* below, she has a miniscule wartime funnel.
[Glasgow University Archives GD320/10/1/142 and World Ship Photo Library]

18.3.1943: Launched by Lithgows Ltd., Port Glasgow (Yard No. 983) for the Ministry of War Transport, London (J. and J. Denholm Ltd., Glasgow, managers) as EMPIRE MIRANDA. Registered at Greenock. *4.1943:* Completed. *30.4.1947:* Acquired by the company for £194,768, registered at Liverpool and renamed MERCHANT. *26.6.1959:* Struck by the motor vessel PARAGUAY (7,555/44) while berthed in Liverpool Docks and damaged aft. Repaired and returned to service. *6.2.1961:* Sold to Margalante Compania Naviera S.A., Panama (Mavroleon Brothers Ltd., managers), for £53,000 and renamed TRITO under the Lebanese flag. Resold to Fourseas Enterprising Co., Hong Kong, for demolition. *26.5.1961:* Arrived at Hong Kong. *14.6.1961:* Demolition commenced.

243

274. SENATOR (4) 1947-1964 Steel steamship. Two decks and five holds. Three masts.
O.N. 169651 7,259g 4,449n, 10,439d 422.8 (441.5 o.l.) x 57.0 x 34.8 feet. Cargo capacity: 521,821 cubic feet.
International Code: BCYG (BKXN prior to 1947).
T. 3-cyl. by Iron Fireman Manufacturing Co., Portland, Oregon; 24½, 37, 70 x 48 inches, 11½ knots.

29.7.1943: Launched by Oregon Ship Building Corporation, Portland, Oregon (Yard No. 733) for the United States War Shipping Administration, Washington as ANTON M. HOLTER. Bareboat chartered to the Ministry of War Transport, London. *8.1943:* Completed as SAMBAY and Glen Line Ltd., London, appointed managers. *29.5.1947:* Reverted to US flag and immediately acquired by the company for £139,218. *20.6.1947:* Registered at Liverpool and renamed SENATOR. *19.11.1952:* When 40 miles west of Cape Villano on passage from Birkenhead to East Africa, a boiler explosion caused extensive damage to tubes and brickwork, but there were no casualties. She put into Corunna the same day. *24.11.1952:* Sailed from Corunna after completing repairs. *9.1956:* Departure from Barry was

delayed by the crew's refusal to sail. *9.11.1960 - 11.9.60:* Experienced an uneasy ride up the Manchester Ship Canal, sustaining contact damage no less than four times. Struck by the British BARON GARIOCH (8,337/58) on the starboard side while berthed at Runcorn Old Quay; touched on the port quarter by the Dutch coaster WULP (854/52); hit on the port side by the German motor vessel WIEDAU (1,866/54); and finally damaged her accommodation ladder entering Barton Lock. *5.6.1962 - 24.11.1962:* Laid up at Barrow-in-Furness. *8.6.1964:* Sold to Belvientos Compania Naviera S.A., Panama (Rethymnis and Kulukundis Ltd., London) for £82,500 and renamed AJAX under the Greek flag. *2.1968:* Sold to Nau-Tay Industries Co. Ltd., Taiwan for demolition. *29.4.1968:* Arrived at Kaohsiung. *1.5.1968:* Delivered

Senator is assisted into her berth at Capetown.

[A. Duncan]

The case of the reluctant seamen

During the early autumn of 1956, the Eastern Mediterranean was a hotbed of unrest, with a state of emergency in Cyprus, and the Suez Canal nationalized by Colonel Nasser of Egypt. To cope with these crises, the Government chartered a number of merchant ships, loaded them with military stores, and despatched them to Cyprus to augment the equipment already available to the troops out there. They, of course, had to be ready for anything - like, for instance, an assault on the Canal Zone.

On 6th September 1956 SENATOR, then lying in Amsterdam, was duly requisitioned, and ordered to Barry to load military stores and ammunition for Cyprus. This news was ill-received by the West Indian crew, who, when they had signed on at Liverpool on 31st August, had been given to understand that the ship was about to make a voyage to the United States - always a favourite excursion from their point of view. Besides, Cyprus was, in their opinion, a war zone, and, as their spokesman put it emphatically, "We have no wish to go there, man, to get shot!"[220]

The ship arrived at Barry on 9th September, but did not begin loading until 1st October. The time of departure was then fixed for 06.00 on 7th October. As loading progressed, the crew became more restless, and at last organised two deputations, one to put their case to the Master, Captain W.A. Pemberton, the other to confront the Superintendent of the Mercantile Marine Office. Simultaneously they announced their intention to refuse to sail the ship, and demanded a transfer for all hands.

In vain the Master and company officials, who had hastened to the scene by the earliest possible train out of Liverpool, pointed out that Cyprus was not a war zone in the strict sense of the word. There was a security operation in progress, and whatever trouble that might involve ashore, there was no threat whatsoever to merchant shipping. Their Articles of Agreement, signed only a month or so ago, was the normal document valid for two years between the latitudes of 75 degrees north and 60 degrees south. To breach such an agreement would be a serious offence; and, no, there certainly would be no extra cash inducements on offer.

But the men were unmoved by pleas, threats, or arguments. Sailing day dawned, and, one by one, the crew refused a direct order to go to stations and sail the ship. For a further day, Master and officials sought to change their minds. Finally, the law was invoked, and through a local solicitor Captain Pemberton made a complaint to the Barry magistrates: that his crew had refused to obey a lawful command as defined in the Merchant Shipping Act, 1894. The crew were then brought ashore under the court's jurisdiction, and were quickly replaced by another West Indian crew, whose members raised no objections whatsoever. Thus SENATOR sailed two days late, on 9th October.

When the original crew were paraded in court before the local justices there must have been some powerful advocacy in their favour, for the magistrates were persuaded that the men, indeed, had a valid point. The nature and character of the voyage was clearly different to what the men had envisaged when they signed on, and they were justified, in the circumstances, in refusing to obey the order to sail the ship. The case was dismissed.

One can almost hear the anguished cries of disbelief emanating from Mersey Chambers! However, solicitors for the Master appealed to the High Court, and the case was heard before Lord Chief Justice Goddard, Mr. Justice Hilberry, and Mr. Justice Donovan, primarily on 9th/10th May 1957, and again later on 4th October after queries had been submitted to and answered by the Barry magistrates. Eventually the court reached its decision and ruled that the magistrates were in error. Cyprus was not, as agreed throughout the industry, a war zone. The crew were entitled to differ, but such a minority difference of opinion was not sufficient grounds for a withdrawal of labour. The voyage was not "unusual" within the terms of the Agreement; the offences were found proved, and the case was remitted back to the justices with a direction to convict. This, however, was by now simply a matter of principle for the record, for the court was well aware that the respondents were all back in the West Indies by this time, and the sentences could not be enforced!

275. CRAFTSMAN (4) 1947-1967 Steel steamship. Two decks. Five holds and deep tank. Two masts.
O.N. 181101 6,726g 3,993n 9,160d 449.0 (464.1 o.l.) x 58.0 x 32.35 feet. Cargo capacity: 496,694 cubic feet.
International Code: GPZT.
T. 3-cyl. by David Rowan and Co. Ltd., Glasgow with Bauer-Wach exhaust turbine; 29, 47, 81 x 54 inches, 14½ knots.

22.5.1947: Launched by Lithgows Ltd.,
Port Glasgow (Yard No. 1020) for the
company. *18.9.1947:* Delivered at a cost
of £394,093 and later sailed from
Birkenhead for East Africa on her
maiden voyage under Captain W.F.
O'Neill. *8.3.1948:* In collision with the
British SAMPENN (7,219/43) in fog
about 150 miles west south west from
Ushant when on passage from Liverpool
to South Africa. There were no
casualties and CRAFTSMAN was able
to make for Falmouth under her own
steam, while SAMPENN continued her
voyage to Hull. *21.1.1965:* Involved in a
boycott of ships suspected of trading
with Cuba imposed by dock workers in
Venezuelan ports. As a result she
returned to Willemstad, Curacao and
discharged 2,000 tons of Venezuelan
cargo. *19.5.1967:* Sold to Sea Bird
Shipping Co. Ltd., Gibraltar (Mullion and
Co. Ltd., Hong Kong, managers) for
£76,000 and renamed SEA BIRD.
Resold to Taiwan shipbreakers.
8.11.1967: Arrived at Kaohsiung.

After taking delivery of their first motor vessel, Harrisons reverted to steam reciprocating engines for *Craftsman.*

Biscay encounter[221]

CRAFTSMAN sailed from Liverpool at 19.30 on 6th March 1948. She was loaded with 5,193 tons of general cargo destined for South African ports, but her first call was to be Dakar for bunkers.

Some 36 hours later the ship was clear of coastal and Channel shipping lanes, steering 200 degrees and heading across the Bay at 12 knots into a fresh head wind. At 08.30 on Monday 8th March, Captain W.F. O'Neill climbed to the bridge, sextant in hand, hoping for a snap sight of the sun which peered weakly at times from behind the drifting clouds. Finding the horizon to be a bit "mushy" he postponed his observations and went down to breakfast. A few minutes before 09.00, when the Second Officer came up to relieve the watch, the "mushy" horizon had crept closer to the ship greatly reducing the visibility. The Second Officer glanced at the young Third's anxious expression, rang the engine room telegraph to "Stand by", and tugged at the whistle lanyard.

"Better let the Old Man know what it's like", he advised his colleague, as the lad scampered down the ladder to breakfast. Captain O'Neill appeared a minute or two later, sniffed the breeze, and ordered, "Half ahead". As the fog came down in earnest, speed was reduced to "Slow ahead", and the urgent beat of the engines subsided to a mere murmur. During the silent period between raucous blasts from their own steam whistle, the officers listened intently.

Minutes later their attention was alerted. Faintly, from a point or so on the starboard bow, came the fog signal of a steamer under way. The engines were stopped, and, heading into wind and sea, the ship quickly lost way. For several more minutes the ship drifted, several pairs of eyes trying to pierce the fog. And then they saw it simultaneously, three points on the starboard bow, the white foam of a ship's bow wave advancing towards them through the grey water followed a second later by the loom of a ship, shapeless and shadowy in the fog at first, becoming more solidly menacing with each fleeting second.

Captain O'Neill reacted at once. "Hard-a-starboard; full astern", he ordered sharply. The Second Officer, momentarily mesmerised by the oncoming ship, like a rabbit in the headlamps' glare, jumped to obey, even remembering to sound the obligatory three short blasts on the whistle. The bridge structure began vibrating as the engines worked up to maximum revolutions astern. A boiling wash surged round the stern, racing forward. The log-line, which had been trailing limply from the end of the boom, began to drift ahead. The ship had sternway! But it was all to no avail. The SAMPENN - the name, writ large, was now clearly visible on her port bow - came on inexorably, her bluff stem ploughing into CRAFTSMAN's starboard bow like a bulldozer. There was a crash, the ship heeled crazily, and flame and sparks flickered ominously around

the point of impact.

Three-quarter inch steel plates from forecastle deck to below the waterline were swept back like a drawing-room curtain, severed steel frames folded into the drapes. The forecastle deck was uprooted; cargo in cases and drums tumbled into the sea, and the air was filled with the acrid fumes of chemicals released from ruptured containers.

It was a heart-stopping moment - and 09.18 by the chartroom clock, to be precise. At 09.20, twelve minutes after the first distant fog signal was heard, the ships drifted apart and engines were stopped. Clearly, CRAFTSMAN was the more gravely wounded, and, true to the tradition of the sea, Captain John Styrin of the SAMPENN stood by in case assistance was needed.

Aboard CRAFTSMAN, the initial shock had given way to urgent but orderly counter measures. A team of sailors under Chief Officer Les Williams and a phlegmatic bosun were running hoses along the foredeck, for the chances of a fire or explosion among the volatile chemicals stowed in number 1 'tween deck were substantial. Another team of sailors was preparing the boats for launching, for no one at that stage had any idea how long the ship might stay afloat. The carpenter was busily sounding tanks and bilges in the damaged sector, while a few others with no specific task in hand, went back to finish their interrupted breakfast.

The carpenter's report was encouraging. The forepeak, chain locker, and number 1 hold were flooded, but number 2 was bone-dry, indicating that the bulkhead was still secure. The Master held a brief discussion with his Chief Engineer, who confirmed there were no problems in his department.

"Right, Chief; give her revs. for seven knots and we'll head for Falmouth. It's over 200 miles, but we should get there by tomorrow evening. We don't want to overstress that bulkhead by going faster".

So CRAFTSMAN got under way, heading north easterly escorted by SAMPENN. News of the collision had been flashed to head office, and towards noon word was received from Harrisons advising that the salvage tug ZEALANDIA had set out from Falmouth to intercept and render assistance if required. Shortly afterwards, at about 13.50, Captain O'Neill released SAMPENN from escort duty, and that vessel headed up Channel bound for Hull. The rest of the day, and the night which followed, were replete with anxious moments. The crippled ship, lying more than eight feet by the head, was creeping along at no more than six or seven knots across the Channel sea lanes. The fog persisted, mainly in extensive patches, and sounding the regulation fog signal intermittently every two minutes ensured that no-one slept that

A crumpled *Craftsman*. Above: the damage inflicted by *Sampenn* on 8th March 1948 and below five weeks later, patched up in Carrick Roads for her return to Liverpool and permanent repairs.

night, nor the next day.

They were fortunate to get noon sights on 9th, which placed the ship 26 miles south by west of the Lizard, 40 miles from Falmouth, then the fog closed in again. Cross traffic was heavy, and further speed reductions were necessary as, with fingers crossed, they eased the ship out of one hazardous situation after another. In the circumstances, it was hardly surprising that the salvage tug never did meet the stricken vessel. Nor did they ever see anything of the Lizard; they simply probed their way north by means of soundings and the occasional radio direction-finding bearing. At last, at about 19.00, they were relieved to see the light on St. Anthony Head, which marked the entrance to Falmouth Harbour, stabbing through the gloom. At 20.30 the Pilot boarded and brought the ship safely to an anchorage. Next day, the ship was moored to a buoy in Carrick Roads. For five weeks CRAFTSMAN lay at her moorings in Carrick Roads while a firm of salvage operators, Risdon, Beazley and Co., fabricated an enormous patch with timber, metal rods, and concrete, simply to make the ship seaworthy for the voyage round to Liverpool.

She sailed on 16th April, and docked at Liverpool on 17th. Then the ADVISER (244) was brought alongside, and the cargo, long overdue in South Africa, was unloaded into ADVISER's empty holds. For the next three months or so, CRAFTSMAN lay in dry dock, rebuilding the badly mutilated bow in which 17 steel plates had to be renewed, and others faired.

Subsequently, a Ministry of Transport enquiry into the incident found SAMPENN 75% to blame, CRAFTSMAN 25%. It was a very serious accident, but it might well have been far worse.

276. LINGUIST (2) 1947-1966 Steel steamship. Two decks, five holds and deep tank. Two masts.
O.N. 182398 6,736g 3,993n 9,160d 449.0 (464.1 o.l.) x 58.0 x 32.35 feet. Cargo capacity: 496,694 cubic feet.
International Code: GQBC.
T. 3-cyl. by David Rowan and Co. Ltd., Glasgow, with Bauer-Wach exhaust turbine; 29, 47, 81 x 54 inches, 14½ knots.

19.8.1947: Launched by Lithgows Ltd., Port Glasgow (Yard No. 1021) for the company. *29.12.1947:* Delivered at a cost of £401,303 and later sailed from Birkenhead for South Africa on her maiden voyage under Captain A.H. Frew. *18.12.1965:* Collided at 04.30 with the Dutch tanker ALKMAAR (12,202/58) when inward bound from Demerara to Liverpool. The tanker was at anchor near the Bar Light vessel and both vessels sustained indents and localised superficial damage. *10.6.1966:* Sold to Transworld Carriers Inc., Monrovia, Liberia (Wah Kwong and Co. (Hong Kong) Ltd., Hong Kong, managers) for £86,000 and renamed JADE VENTURE. *26.6.1969:* Whilst anchoring off Shimizu, Japan, came into violent contact with the Japanese YUKEI MARU (3,904/68) sustaining damage to her boat deck plating, cabins and bulwarks in way of number 4 hatch on the starboard side. *1969:* Sold to Taiwan shipbreakers. *8.11.1969:* Arrived at Kaohsiung.

Funnel trouble
In days gone by Harrison ships had been noted for their tall, slender smoke-stacks, and in 1947 there were still quite a few of these around. However, when CRAFTSMAN and LINGUIST were delivered they each had a very short, rather squat sort of funnel, and this feature soon proved inadequate for dispersing the dense, oily smoke which, on occasion, belched forth coating the surrounding paintwork with a greasy, black film to the unending despair of many a ship-proud chief officer. In fact, one exasperated mate noted for his short-fuse (it was Tom Kent, of happy memory) went so far as to bring his ship home with her after section painted from truck to maindeck, and from boat-deck to ensign-staff, an unrelenting, gleaming, glossy black!
Predictably, this transformation was viewed with displeasure by management and superintendents alike. Nevertheless, in 1949, both ships had their funnel casings extended considerably, and even streamlined, which had a somewhat mitigating effect.

Linguist was a near-sister of *Craftsman*. The three views of the steamer show her, at the top, with her original cowl-topped short funnel, middle with a heightened funnel in August 1964, and bottom loading a tug in West India Dock, London in the early 1960s.

[Top and middle: J. & M. Clarkson]

277. SCULPTOR (4) 1948-1962 Steel steamship. Two decks and five holds. Three masts.
O.N. 169852 7,240g 4,441n 10,568d 423.3 (441.5 o.l.) x 57.1 x 37.3 feet. Cargo capacity: 519,026 cubic feet.
International Code: GCTW (MYRQ prior to 1947).
T. 3-cyl. by General Machinery Corporation, Hamilton, Ohio; 24½, 37, 70 x 48 inches, 11½ knots.

4.3.1944: Launched by Bethlehem Fairfield Shipyard Inc., Baltimore, Maryland (Yard No. 2336) for the United States War Shipping Administration, Washington as SAMCOLNE. Bareboat chartered to the Ministry of War Transport and Anchor Line Ltd., Glasgow, appointed managers. *3.1944:* Completed. *18.4.1947:* Reverted to US flag and immediately sold to Moller Line (U.K.) Ltd. (Mollers Ltd., managers), London and renamed MARY MOLLER. *25.3.1948:* Acquired by the company for £178,000, registered at Liverpool and renamed SCULPTOR. *3.2.1958:* When in position 36.15N, 35.09W, 340 miles off Fayal, on passage from New Orleans to Manchester, fire was reported in the cotton cargo in number 3 hold. The hatches and ventilators were sealed, steam injected into the affected compartments, and the

vessel made for Horta, Azores. She arrived late the following day and began fighting the fire with water, unloading the burning bales. *6.2.1958:* The fire was considered extinguished by which time 840 bales had been landed and a third of these were fire damaged. Despite a number of charred hatch-boards there was no structural damage to the vessel. *18.2.1958:* Eventually sailed from Horta. *15.2.1962:* Sold to Galaro Compania Naviera S.A., Panama (George Georgilis) (A. Lusi Ltd., London, managers) for £85,500 and renamed CAPE VENETICO under the Greek flag. *1965:* J.C. Carras and Sons (Shipbrokers) Ltd., London appointed managers. *1967:* Sold to Fuji Marden and Co. Ltd., Hong Kong, for demolition. *19.12.1967:* Arrived at Hong Kong. *2.1.1908.* Demolition

A fine portrait of a well-laden and well-cared for *Sculptor* sailing from Capetown.

Anchor away

On 29th June 1948, during the afternoon watch at sea in position 19.25S, 04.36E, when bound for Capetown, the Second Officer of SCULPTOR was disturbed to hear a sudden roar from forward. He realised that the port anchor was running out, of its own volition, at great speed. Before anyone could get forward to do anything the last shackle tore

away from the chain locker bulkhead, and the anchor, towing 150 fathoms of wrought iron cable, was plunging to the bottom of the South Atlantic Ocean. It was reported mysteriously that the brake was still "full on", but the claw secured to the cable had 'opened out'.[222]

278. INTERPRETER 1948-1967 Steel motor vessel. Two decks and five holds. Two masts.
O.N. 182429 6,815g 4,027n 9,270d 442.8 (460.7 o.l.) x 60.0 x 32.5 feet. Cargo capacity: 517,534 cubic feet.
International Code: GPZY.
5-cyl. 2SCSA oil engine by William Doxford and Sons Ltd., Sunderland; 14 knots.

14.11.1947: Launched by William Doxford and Sons Ltd., Sunderland (Yard No. 747) for the company. *11.4.1948:* Delivered at a cost of £447,997. When on passage for London to load for South Africa, one of her generators virtually disintegrated. As a result she was delayed in port until October while the generator was rebuilt. Subsequently sailed from Liverpool for Galveston on her belated maiden voyage under Captain H. Coates. *6.6.1955:* Grounded on Sandy Island, Antigua, in position 008 degrees, 2.3 cables from the lighthouse. *8.6.1955:* Refloated after discharging 320 tons of sugar. A divers' inspection showed slight bottom damage but no leaks. *15.6.1955:* Sailed. *21.1.1956:* Ran ashore off St. Josephs Island, Aransas Pass, Texas. Refloated the following day with the aid of two tugs. *23.1.1956:* Proceeded to Corpus Christi. A Seaworthy Certificate was granted after some temporary repairs. *29.1.1956:* Sailed for Brownsville, Texas. *6.1960:* Disabled when the main engine forward thrust bearing pads failed and subsequently towed to Dakar by HERDSMAN (269). *20.9.1961:* When bound from London to Hamburg anchored in dense fog near the Terschelling Bank Lightvessel. Whilst waiting for the fog to clear, struck by the Belgian BRUXELLES (6,529/53) sustaining severe damage. She

was obliged to put into Amsterdam where her cargo was unloaded into SCHOLAR (272) before entering the yard of Amsterdam Drydock Company for repairs. *20.10.1961:* Sailed for Middlesbrough upon completion of repairs. *18.8.1967:* Sold to Polina Armadora S.A., Panama (Hunter Shipping Co. Ltd., London, agents) for £165,000 and renamed TAXIARCHIS MICHAEL under the Greek flag. *22.10.1969:* When on passage from Rotterdam to China, put into Durban with extensive damage to the auxiliary boiler and main engine. Since the boiler would take eight weeks to repair, the matter was deferred. Meanwhile the top and bottom end bearings were re-metalled after a disastrous lubricating oil failure, damage which Lloyd's Agent in Durban alleged was due to crew negligence. *5.11.1969:* Sailed. *25.11.1969:* Arrived at Singapore, when the Captain claimed that heavy weather had damaged five winches by water contamination. Five winch brake-coils were renewed. The piston crown of number 4 main engine unit was fractured, and as no spare was available, the unit was blanked off for the voyage to Whampoa. *28.11.1969:* Sailed from Singapore. *12.12.1969:* Sold to Chinese shipbreakers at Whampoa after her cargo had been discharged.

248

The accident-prone *Interpreter* cautiously approaches Eastham Locks. Her topmast will have to be struck if she is proceeding up the Ship Canal to Manchester.   *[J.K. Byass]*

Grounds for dismay

"They should give that ship a set of wheels!" So spake an aggrieved Superintendent when news of INTERPRETER's second serious grounding incident in seven months reached head office. It was not unusual for ships to take the ground on occasion. In some mud berths it was almost normal to sit on the soft bottom at low water. But for a ship to run ashore at speed, unexpectedly and unaware was a serious departure from the norm, usually fraught with even more serious consequences.

The first instance occurred on 6th June 1955, off Antigua.[223] INTERPRETER, commanded by Captain Thomas Winstanley, had been loading sugar in St. John's Harbour, Antigua. The last empty lighter left the ship in the small hours, and at 01.30 the watch was roused to weigh anchor and get the ship under way bound for St. Kitts, a mere four hours steaming time away. Chief Officer R.E. Harvey had been about the decks most of the previous day and was due on watch at 04.00 so Captain Winstanley left him below, and instructed Second Officer R.B. Simmons to go forward with the anchor party, retaining a cadet on the bridge to keep the log book until the Second Officer had finished stowing and securing the anchor. This was quite a common practice on the "Island Run", and eminently sensible.

When the anchor came aweigh at 02.00 the ship was heading inshore, so had to be turned "short round" to starboard using engines and helm. It was then necessary to con the ship out of the harbour by eye, steering clear with Sandy Island to the south before heading for St. Kitts on a westerly course. Second Officer Simmons reached the bridge at 02.15, relieved the cadet and sent him below. He then went up to the standard compass on the monkey island to steady the ship on course in response to the Captain's order. By this time the ship was full away on passage, and Captain Winstanley was conning the ship round Sandy Island, giving helm orders to the quartermaster, who repeated them conscientiously.

The weather was generally fine and clear, but occasionally rain squalls blotted out the landmarks. Subsequently, Captain Winstanley would always blame those squalls for what happened next. Whatever the cause, he misjudged the distance offshore, brought his ship too close in, and at 02.25 ran her aground. The bump was scarcely palpable, (Chief Officer Harvey knew nothing about it until he was called by the watch at 03.45 - "One bell, Sir, and she's aground...!") but she was hard and fast on a coral reef, and no amount of desperate work with the main engines could dislodge her.

Frequent checks on bilge soundings confirmed that the ship was not making water, and that all compartments appeared to be sound. At daylight a kedge anchor with wire attached was carried about 400 feet astern and dropped in deep water. Later, the port bower was carried out, leading aft on the port side, and dropped in 28 feet of water. A check on the ship's position confirmed that she lay 2.3 cables on a bearing of 008 degrees from Sandy Island Lighthouse.

After consulting with the local agents, it was decided to lighten the ship by unloading some of her cargo and transferring it to the RIVERCREST (7,008/44). Next morning the lighters were alongside and three gangs of stevedores began unloading bags of sugar from hatches numbers 3, 4 and 5. By 17.20 only 320 tons had been discharged, about one eighth of what they were prepared to unload, but Captain Winstanley had a feeling that the ship was ready to move. High water was due at around 20.00, and at 19.53 a concerted heave on kedge and bower anchors, combined with some stern-thrust from the engines, succeeded in sliding the ship clear of the reef into deep water. She had been aground for almost 42 hours. An hour later INTERPRETER had returned to her old anchorage off Pillar Rock, and the Master and his officers steeled themselves for the inevitable inquiry which was bound to follow.

They had not long to wait. On Wednesday 8th June Captain Winstanley, his officers, and members of the crew on duty at the time of the stranding were summoned before an examining magistrate, and Harrison Line's representative in the West Indies, Colin Hutchison, arrived by air from Port of Spain. Meanwhile, Engineer Superintendent Nicholson accompanied by Captain T.E. Steel were flying out to Antigua from London. It was normal practice for an Engineer Superintendent to fly out to a ship in trouble, but the presence of a senior Master, who was currently the Marine Superintendent in London, was an ominous sign from Captain Winstanley's point of view, especially since Colin Hutchison had had instructions from Head Office to detain the ship at Antigua until their arrival.

Captain Winstanley' position was precarious. The dice were loaded heavily against him; the bond of trust between employer and employee had been broken, and the decision to relieve him of his command forthwith was inevitable. Hence the presence of Captain Steel, who assumed command of the INTERPRETER at Antigua on 14th June. Subsequently, on 18th, Captain Winstanley took a sad and lonely passage home aboard the French steamer, FORT CARILLON (4,887/53), to face a very uncertain future.

INTERPRETER's second stranding incident occurred about seven and a half months later, at which time the ship was under the command of Captain George J. Penston, and bound from New Orleans to Corpus Christi, Texas.[224] The night of 20th/21st January 1956 had been notable for a succession of heavy rain squalls accompanied by bouts of vivid lightning. However, the ship had been able to maintain her course and a speed of 14 knots since about 02.00 on the 21st. As dawn broke, the weather looked clear enough to seaward, but towards the land a tenuous horizon suggested the presence of fog. By that time, the lighthouse marking the entrance to Aransas Pass, the initial channel to Corpus Christi, should have been in sight, but no lights, landmarks, or buoys were to be seen. Unfortunately, the ship's echo sounder was out of order, and endeavours to check her position by means of radio direction-finder bearings had been frustrated by the thundery conditions. So the ship was approaching the coast blindly, and at 06.24 land was sighted, the low, hummocky sandhills prevalent on the Gulf Coast - but it was far too close for comfort. Like a startled horse, the ship shied away in response to an urgent helm order. But it was too late. A minute later the ship ran on to a shelving, sandy bank, and came to a shuddering halt.

Once again, desperate manoeuvres with the main engines failed to release the ship from the bank which held her. She had, after all, been travelling at 14 knots when she grounded and was consequently hard and fast. An hour later visibility had improved, revealing various landmarks, and enabling the officers to ascertain the ship's position. The tall tower of Aransas Pass lighthouse bore 237 degrees, distant 5½ miles. At 10.30 the ship radioed an appeal for tug assistance, and at 15.02 the tug W.A. WANSLEY, secured to the port quarter, was towing hard while the engines ran full astern. But there was still no movement. Eventually, they resorted to the expedient of carrying out anchors, and the tug obliged by carrying out the starboard anchor and dropping it in deep water. But a co-ordinated effort with tug, engines, and anchor ended with the ship's position unaltered, and the anchor hove home. During a later attempt the anchor held securely, but a link in the wrought iron cable snapped under the strain, and the anchor with two shackles (30 fathoms) of cable were temporarily lost.

A sisterly service rendered

Outward bound from Liverpool to Beira the white metal in the forward thrust pads on INTERPRETER's main engine ran out, due to a flaw in the lubrication system, and the thrust collar was badly scored. The ship was completely disabled, and there was nothing to do but let her drift while the engineers set about repairing the damage. Her position at the time was 02.44 N. 9.46 W, or about 157 miles, 231 degrees from Cape Palmas, Liberia, and it was 20.00 on a Saturday night, 4th June 1960. Fortunately, INTERPRETER's elder sister HERDSMAN (269), homeward bound from the Cape, was close at hand, and a message from Head Office directed HERDSMAN to the disabled ship's position. Her Master, Captain E.V. Dunn, was instructed to stand by, and assist if required.[225]

By 07.00 on Monday 6th June, HERDSMAN and INTERPRETER were in sight of one another. Repairs to the damaged thrust system were well in hand, and later that day INTERPRETER's engineers were ready for a trial run. After running for two hours at 70 rpm, the thrust bearings were opened up, only to reveal that the white metal pads were again wiped clean. The problem was obviously deep seated.

With approval from head office, the two masters on the spot decided INTERPRETER should be towed to Dakar, a distance of about 850 miles. The towing cable was set up, using the ships' anchor cables. Aboard HERDSMAN, the cable to the starboard anchor was broken at the first shackle, the anchor secured in the hawse pipe. Then a substantial length of cable was fleeted aft to be led through the fairleads. This was back-breaking work for the crew, labouring in the tropic heat, guiding the heavy links of cable along the foredeck, up and down ladders amidships, snaking along the after deck, up on to the poop, but they worked with a will, turning up the heavy cable round several sets of bitts to take the strain. Meanwhile, INTERPRETER had secured her port anchor, and unshackled the cable, whilst awaiting the series of messengers which would eventually carry the free end of her anchor cable to HERDSMAN - first a light line, then a 3-inch gantline, then the 3½-inch wire to which the cable was shackled and gradually paid out on the windlass to be hove up to HERDSMAN's stern, where

A second tug, the LAURA HADEN, was sent out to assist the stranded ship at 02.00 the following morning, but it was 13.30 on the afternoon of 22nd, after many a vain attempt, that the ship was finally refloated, and by 16.30 she was anchored off the Fairway Buoy. Holds and bilges, which of course had been sounded continuously since the mishap, remained dry, and a survey of the ship in Corpus Christi a couple of days later revealed surprisingly little damage considering the serious nature of the incident. Those areas affected by damage, such as buckled frames, floors and plating within the double bottom were reinforced to Lloyd's Surveyor's satisfaction with timber shores, and a Certificate of Seaworthiness issued. This would allow the vessel to continue loading and proceed with the voyage subject to dry docking and full repairs being carried out at Liverpool.

For Captain Penston the ensuing weeks were charged with anxiety, for he was acutely aware that his job and career were in grave jeopardy. At least he was spared the ignominy of being relieved of his command there and then, but he knew he would be subjected to searching enquiries regarding his actions that fateful January morning. If only the echo sounder had been functioning! He was also aware that the past nine months had seen too many serious incidents and tragedies. There was the NATURALIST's encounter with the Middle Mouse in April 1955; his own ship's grounding at Antigua in June; the tragic loss of the GEOLOGIST in July - and now this. He was afraid the firm would take a hard line, and he was right.

Sadly, for Captain George Penston was a good man, not one prone to those weaknesses of character which had been the downfall of lesser mortals but, having thus forfeited the confidence of his employers, Captain Penston, after 38 years, was dismissed from the company's service amid intense feelings of sorrow and regret in all quarters. Such was, and is, the loneliness of command, and (if I may borrow a phrase) it has never been said more truly than in the context of a master in command of his ship that "The buck stops here".

Two views from *Herdsman* as she begins to tow her disabled sister *Interpreter* on 6th June 1960. *Interpreter* flies signal balls indicating that she is not under command. Her deck cargo includes a diesel locomotive.   *[Noel Jones]*

the two cables were securely shackled together.

It was an operation which called for seamanship of a high order, needing a great deal of ingenious improvisation in the process. INTERPRETER paid out seven shackles (105 fathoms) of cable, relieving tackles were rigged, and on 7th June the ships headed for Dakar at a steady 6½ knots. The weather continued fine, and there were evidently no problems with the towing cable, for the ships arrived safely in Dakar Roads at 11.00 on Monday 13th June, disconnected the cable, and anchored. HERDSMAN sailed at 20.30 that evening to resume

her interrupted voyage to Liverpool, her sisterly helping hand ably completed.

On 15th, a pair of tugs took charge of INTERPRETER and laid her alongside the wharf, where a local engineering firm took the repairs in hand under the supervision of Superintendent Engineer "Tiny" Hughes, who had flown out from Liverpool for that purpose. By 25th all was ready for a rigorous sea trial, which was entirely successful. That evening, Lloyd's Surveyor issued a Certificate of Seaworthiness and the ship resumed her voyage to South Africa.

279. FACTOR 1948-1972 Steel motor ship. Two decks and five holds. Two masts.
O.N. 182418 6,533g 3,862n 9,230d 448.2 (463.83 o.l.) x 56.5 x 33.0 feet. Cargo capacity: 512,430 cubic feet.
International Code: GPZV.
5-cyl. 2SCSA Doxford-type oil engine by Barclay, Curle and Co. Ltd., Glasgow; 14¾ knots.

16.10.1947: Launched by Charles Connell and Co. Ltd., Scotstoun (Yard No. 456) for the company. *16.4.1948:* Delivered at a cost of £436,669 and later sailed from Birkenhead to South Africa on her maiden voyage under Captain J.M. Johnston. *26.7.1951:* Grounded heavily twice on a sand bar when approaching Boca Ceniza, Colombia. Soundings revealed that the vessel was making water in numbers 2, 3 and 4 holds and at Barranquilla all remaining cargo was discharged and transhipped in the United Fruit steamer CAPE AVINOF (5,124/45). Temporary repairs were effected and the damaged vessel was granted dispensation to sail. *4.8.1951:* Sailed for Galveston, the nearest suitable and available dry dock. Examination at the Todd Shipyard Corporation floating dock showed the damage to be extensive and, in all, 33 steel plates were renewed and 15 faired. Within the vessel eight tank-top plates were renewed along with 90 floors and frames. No satisfactory reason for the incident was found, the Master being exonerated of all blame, minor earthquakes having been known to distort the topography of the sea bed in the vicinity of the Magdalena Bar. *22.1.1962:* Trapped at Beira during Cyclone Daisy and damaged when drifting lighters were thrown against her. Temporary repairs

Factor in the English Channel (above) and in pristine condition leaving Capetown (below).

were effected. *27.1.1962:* Sailed for Durban to complete repairs. *6.1965:* Whilst loading at London the main engine suffered a major breakdown. The voyage was abandoned and cargo was transferred to WANDERER (288). *3.1972:* Sold to D. Alfonso Garcia y Cia., Spain for demolition for £55,125. *21.3.1972:* Arrived at Bilbao.

280. SPEAKER (2) 1948-1962 Steel steamship. Two decks and five holds. Three masts.
O.N. 169766 7,276g 4,452n 10,547d 422.8 (441.6 o.l.) x 57.0 x 37.3 feet. Cargo capacity: 519,064 cubic feet.
International Code: GCGT (MYPM prior to 1947).
T. 3-cyl. by General Machinery Corporation, Hamilton, Ohio; 24½, 37, 70 x 48 inches, 11½ knots.

9.12.1943: Launched by Bethlehem-Fairfield Shipyard Inc., Baltimore, Maryland (Yard No. 2290) for the United States War Shipping Administration, Washington as ROBERT WYCLIFFE. Bareboat chartered to the Ministry of War Transport, London. *12.1943:* Completed as SAMBALT. Cayzer, Irvine and Co Ltd, Glasgow, appointed managers. *1946:* David Alexander and Sons, Glasgow, appointed managers. *18.4.1947:* Reverted to US flag and immediately sold to Moller Line Ltd. (Moller Line (U.K.) Ltd, managers), London and renamed LILIAN MOLLER. *15.4.1948:* Purchased by the company for £175,000, registered at Liverpool and renamed SPEAKER. *1.3.1962:* Sold to Epos Marine Enterprises S.A., Panama (J.C. Yemelos) (A. Lusi Ltd., London, managers) for £85,000 and renamed BYZANTION under the Greek flag. *1965:* J.C. Carras and Sons (Shipbrokers) Ltd., London appointed managers.

6.4.1967: Grounded near Ras Gombo Lighthouse, Assab. *8.4.1967:* Refused assistance from the tug BRITONIA (568/63) which arrived on the scene at about 03.00. *9.4.1967:* Refloated unaided at 04.00 and, after being cleared by a surveyor at Assab, proceeded to Venice. However, the effort of getting off the reef had put a severe strain on the main engine, and when subsequently the vessel docked at Leghorn it was found that the main engine bearings, crosshead bearings, guide shoes and the main circulating pumps had all been wiped, fractured or damaged in some way, while the bottom plating had been set in, bilge keels torn away, the rudder twisted and the tail shaft distorted. *1969:* Sold to Koshin Sangyo K.K., Japan. *Prior to 20.1.1969:* Arrived at Onomichi. *5.5.1969:* Demolition commenced.

Although built to the same design, there were subtle differences in appearance between Harrisons' Liberties. *Speaker* had a particularly high crosstree on her mainmast. In this South African view she has a white topside strake.

281. STATESMAN (5) 1948-1962 Steel steamship. Two decks and five holds. Three masts.
O.N. 169849 7,254g 4,430n 10,568d 423.1 (441.6 o.l.) x 57.0 x 37.3 feet. Cargo capacity: 518,967 cubic feet.
International Code: GDJJ (MYRK prior to 1947).
T. 3-cyl. by General Machinery Corporation, Hamilton, Ohio; 24½, 37, 70 x 48 inches, 11½ knots.

In contrast to the upper photograph on this page, *Statesman* has a more conventional cross tree and all black topsides.

[World Ship Photo Library]

24.2.1944: Launched by Bethlehem-Fairfield Shipyard Inc., Baltimore, Maryland (Yard No. 2328) for the United States War Shipping Administration, Washington as SAMGAUDIE. Bareboat chartered to the Ministry of War Transport, London (T. and J. Brocklebank, Liverpool, managers). *3.1944:* Completed. *18.4.1947:* Reverted to US flag and immediately sold to Moller Line Ltd. (Mollers Ltd., managers), London. *11.7.1947.* Delivered and subsequently renamed NORAH MOLLER. *18.6.1948:* Acquired by the company for £175,000, registered at Liverpool and renamed STATESMAN. *20 3.1953:* Inward bound from Calcutta to London and two miles south of Dover in collision with the Greek steamship FLIGHT LIEUTENANT VASSILIADES RAF (7,232/43), which was bound from Hampton Roads to Bremen. Steel plates and frames in way of number 1 hold

and the forepeak of STATESMAN were torn away over a length of 40 feet; the sheerstrake in way of the engine room was holed, the foredeck plating distorted; and the starboard bulwarks set in. The Greek vessel was also seriously damaged, but in neither case was the ship damaged below the waterline, and no flooding took place. Both vessels proceeded unaided towards their respective destinations after the collision. *25.4.1962:* Sold to Aktina Compania Naviera S.A., Panama (J. Barzacos) (Pegasus Ocean Services Ltd., London, managers) for £86,000 and renamed AKTIS under the Lebanese flag. *3.11.1966:* Sustained severe damage to her starboard side plating due to pounding heavily against the quay at Madras during a cyclone. *1968:* Sold to Taiwan shipbreakers. *13.1.1968:* Arrived at Kaohsiung.

282. SUCCESSOR 1948-1963 Steel steamship. Two decks and five holds. Three masts.
O.N. 180037 7,249g 4,424n 10,568d 423.7 (446.0 o.l.) x 57.0 x 37.3 feet. Cargo capacity: 518,967 cubic feet.
International Code: GDJK (MYSC prior to 1947).
T. 3-cyl. by General Machinery Corporation, Hamilton, Ohio; 24½, 37, 70 x 48 inches, 11½ knots.

25.3.1944: Launched by Bethlehem-Fairfield Shipyard Inc., Baltimore, Maryland (Yard No. 2345) for the United States War Shipping Administration, Washington as SAMHOPE. Bareboat chartered to the Ministry of War Transport, London (Sir William Reardon Smith and Sons Ltd., Cardiff, managers). *18.4.1947:* Reverted to US flag and immediately sold to Moller Line Ltd. (Mollers Ltd., managers), London. *16.7.1947:* Delivered and subsequently renamed ROSALIE MOLLER. *6.10.1948:* Acquired by the company for £175,000, registered at Liverpool and renamed SUCCESSOR. *15.5.1951:* In collision with two vessels at New Orleans. *18.7.1962:* Sailed from Liverpool to lie up at Barrow-in-Furness until 5.1.1963. *7.4.1963:* Sold to Zela

Shipping Co. Ltd., London (K. Mouskas) (Thrasybule Voyazides, Athens, manager) for £44,000 and renamed ZELA M. Engine trouble delayed her first voyage. *23.4.1963:* Sailed from Liverpool for Cuba on her first voyage for her new owners. *1967:* Sold to Protaras Shipping Co. Ltd., Cyprus, Famagusta (K. Mouskas) (Transmarine Shipping Agencies Ltd., London, managers). *5.8.1968:* Grounded when entering the harbour at Ceuta. *8.8.1968:* Refloated at 14.00 with the aid of tugs. *1969:* Sold to Empresa Consolidada de Navigacion Mambisa, Havana, Cuba and renamed IGNACIO AGRAMONTE. *4.10.1974:* Left Cadiz for San Esteban de Pravia to be broken up by Sanchez, shipbreakers.

Successor in Dublin Bay during January 1951. The date suggests Harrisons' Liberties lost their white topside strake in the early 1950s.

[Pat Sweeney]

Mississippi blues
At 07.25 on 15th May 1951 the SUCCESSOR cleared St. Andrew Street Wharf in downtown New Orleans bound for Mobile to complete loading. The rains in the Mississippi Basin had been heavy that spring and the river was high, flowing majestically towards the Gulf of Mexico at a good six knots. A tugboat assisted SUCCESSOR to swing off the wharf, and remained fast on the port side to help the ship negotiate the sharp bend off Algiers Point, a mile or so downstream. Keeping over to the starboard side of the channel, their view partially obscured by jutting Algiers Point, both Captain Gabriel Holden and the pilot were a little put out to see, as the ship swept round the bend, the bulky silhouette of a large cargo ship heading towards them, apparently on their side of the river. Moreover, the ship was displaying the signal for a ship "not under command", and was being cosseted upriver by a pair of tugboats.[226]

The stranger may well have been in the wrong place at the wrong time, but the onus was on SUCCESSOR to take action to keep clear, a tricky proposition with a six-knot current under her stern. SUCCESSOR, responding to the pilot's order, took the only option, and swung to port towards midstream, the pilot tugging at the whistle lanyard to sound five urgent short blasts, the local emergency signal. The idea then was to apply starboard helm to clear the other ship, now identified as Lykes Lines' Victory type, TILLIE LYKES (7,855/45), and resume course downriver. Unfortunately, having got herself athwart the current, it was the devil's own job to get the ship back on course, even with the aid of the tug, still fast, but ill-sited to push her head round to starboard. The current was too strong, and she simply headed across river, crabbing downstream, and clipping the stem of TILLIE LYKES with her starboard

253

quarter as she crossed. Everyone, up to now, had had eyes only for the threat posed by the TILLIE LYKES, which led them to disregard the menace of the shipping alongside the wharves on the left bank of the river. When at last the pilot glanced ahead, he realized that the situation was irretrievable. Sounding five more short blasts, as much to relieve his own hapless frustration as to warn shipping, he turned to Captain Holden and in a rather breathless Southern drawl, passed him the con: "Waal, Cap, she's all yours!" A rather priceless remark in the circumstances.

Captain Holden, with his ship bearing down on the crowded Dumaine Street Wharf, gave the only two orders left to him - "Full astern; Let go forrard!" (referring to the anchors). At this point the tug skipper, perceiving a very real danger of being crushed against a ship alongside, hurriedly cast off. Meanwhile, away went the port anchor with a roar, and the brake firmly applied in an effort to force the ship's

head upstream, while the ship shuddered as the engines gathered stern power. But before either of these measures could fully take effect SUCCESSOR had rammed into the Guatemalan motor vessel, ANDREW JACKSON HIGGINS (2798/45), pushing her broadside into Dumaine Street Wharf and on into the shed, scattering longshoremen, wreaking havoc and confusion aggravated by a fractured water main which sprayed vulnerable cargo and panicky onlookers alike with spectacular effect.

At last SUCCESSOR, her anarchic dynamism spent, lay docilely off the wharf riding to her port anchor. The errant tugboat somewhat sheepishly returned and made fast. The anchor was weighed and, ignoring the pandemonium ashore, the ship returned to St. Andrew Street Wharf to face the questions of the port authorities and the lawyers, the inevitable writs, and, of course, to repair the damaged plates and bulwarks in starboard bow and quarter.

283. HISTORIAN (4) 1949-1962 Steel steamship. Two decks and five holds. Three masts.
O.N. 180496 7,262g 4,452n 10,521d 424.0 (441.6 o.l.) x 57.0 x 37.3 feet. Cargo capacity: 519,221 cubic feet.
International Code: GDJP (MYLP prior to 1947).
T. 3-cyl. by Worthington Pump and Machinery Corporation, Harrison, New Jersey; 24½, 37, 70 x 48 inches, 11½ knots.

31.8.1943: Launched by Bethlehem-Fairfield Shipyard Inc., Baltimore, Maryland (Yard No. 2223) for the United States War Shipping Administration, Washington as JAMES T. EARLE. Bareboat chartered to the Ministry of War Transport, London. *9.1943:* Completed as SAMAYE. Cayzer, Irvine and Co. Ltd., Glasgow, appointed managers. *21.4.1947:* Reverted to US flag and immediately sold to Queen Line Ltd. and Cadogan Steam Ship Co. Ltd. (Thomas Dunlop and Sons, managers), Glasgow and renamed QUEEN VICTORIA. *14.1.1949:* Acquired by the company for £165,000, registered at Liverpool and renamed HISTORIAN. *27.10.1952:* Whilst berthing alongside the jetty at Cardon, Venezuela, collided with the stern of the Royal Mail steamer LOMBARDY (3,537/21). The latter vessel sustained extensive damage to her stern plating and components; HISTORIAN had slight indents to her bow. *15.1.1954:* Encountered severe gales in the North Sea when bound from Rotterdam to London. The cargo stowed at the forward end of number 2 hold broke loose causing severe structural damage to the interior of the hold. *10.6.1958:* Whilst discharging sulphur from Port Sulphur, Louisiana in Alexandra Dock, Hull, the fire brigade was called to deal with a sulphur fire in number 3 hold. The fire was extinguished the following day and the dockers resumed discharging all

holds except number 3, where resumption depended on agreement of an appropriate award to the gang. *28.6.1962:* Sailed from Greenock to lie up at Barrow-in-Furness. *12.1962:* Returned to Liverpool from Barrow-in-Furness. *19.12.1962:* Sold to Jayanti Shipping Co. Ltd., New Delhi, India for £55,000 and renamed PARVATI JAYANTI. *6.9.1967:* Damaged by shellfire when three Israeli naval craft attacked installations at Suez and Port Tewfik. She was discharging chests of tea at a wharf in Suez. *22.2.1968:* Grounded at Azemmour, 50 miles from Casablanca, when on passage from Alexandria to Bombay with 4,000 tons of cotton. *23.2.1968:* Refloated without assistance, with bottom ruptured and all double-bottom tanks open to the sea. She proceeded to Casablanca where it was found that the tank tops had been set up under the main engine, misaligning the shaft, and 1,300 bales of cotton had been damaged by oil and water. The port authorities refused to allow discharge of the damaged bales and they remained on the vessel. Surveyors estimated that some 280 tons of steel would be required to repair the vessel's bottom and she was declared a constructive total loss. Sold to Desguaces y Salvamentos S.A., Spain. *14.4.1968:* Arrived at Aviles in tow of HERKULES and demolition commenced on the same day.

Harrisons seem to have worked through their supply of names beginning S for their Liberties, and a 1949 acquisition was named *Historian*. Here she butts through the Channel bound for London with two small containers on her afterdeck.

284. COLONIAL (3)/PLANTER (3) 1949-1962 Steel steamship. Two decks and five holds. Three masts.
O.N. 169976 7,285g 4,460n 10,521d 423.5 (441.5 o.l.) x 57.1 x 37.3 feet. Cargo capacity: 517,589 cubic feet.
International Code: GCVP (BKXQ prior to 1947).
T. 3-cyl. by Willamette Iron and Steel Corporation, Portland, Oregon; 24$\frac{1}{2}$, 37, 70 x 48 inches, 11$\frac{1}{2}$ knots.

Further evidence that Harrisons had a change of heart with painting their Liberties. *Colonial,* above, has the white strake, but when given the
more politically-correct name *Planter* in 1961 she was in plain black (below). *[Both: A. Duncan]*

22.7.1943: Launched by Permanente Metals Corporation
(Shipyard No.2), Richmond, California (Yard No.1713) for the
United States War Shipping Administration, Washington as
FRANK D. PHINNEY. Bareboat chartered to the Ministry of
War Transport, London. *7.1943:* Completed as SAMOVAR.
T. and J. Brocklebank, Liverpool, appointed managers.
28.4.1947: Reverted to US flag and immediately sold to
British and Burmese Steam Navigation Co. Ltd. (P.
Henderson and Co., managers), Glasgow. *21.5.1947:*
Delivered and subsequently renamed KANSI. *24.3.1949:*
Acquired by the company for £180,000, registered at
Liverpool and renamed COLONIAL. *6.1.1953:* An outbreak
of fire in number 5 'tween deck was extinguished by the
crew. The vessel was surveyed at Port Sudan and although
a substantial amount of cargo was damaged, there was no
structural damage to the vessel. *24.2.1961:* Renamed
PLANTER. (The former name was considered to allude to

repression. In view of changing political awareness and in
the interests of good public relations a change of name was
deemed necessary). *19.12.1962:* Sold to Jayanti Shipping
Co. Ltd., New Delhi, India for £55,000 and renamed GARGI
JAYANTI. *2.1.1963:* In common with many Indian national
vessels, she was manned by English officers and an Indian
crew. An engineer officer struck one of the seamen and
precipitated a near-mutiny. Fifty crew members refused to
co-operate with their English officers, who left the ship for
refuge in a nearby hotel. She was towed off her berth at
Rotterdam and the British Consul was called to mediate.
Peace was restored only after five officers and two seamen
had been replaced. *1967:* Sold to Pent Ocean Steamships
Private Ltd., Bombay, India and renamed SAMUDRA JYOTI.
1971: Sold to Indian Metal Traders Ltd., India for demolition.
12.1971: Delivered. *2.1972:* Arrived at Bombay and
demolition commenced.

285. BIOGRAPHER 1949-1964 Steel steamship. Two decks, five holds and two deep tanks. Two masts.
O.N. 183743 6,915g 4,123n 9,850d 449.3 (464.3 o.l.) x 58.0 x 33.0 feet. Cargo capacity: 564,377 cubic feet.
International Code: GQCB.
Two steam turbines by David Rowan and Co. Ltd., Glasgow, double-reduction geared to a single screw; 14¹/₂ knots.

18.3.1949: Launched by Lithgows Ltd., Port Glasgow (Yard No. 1029) for the company. *18.8.1949:* Delivered at a cost of £500,000 and later sailed from Glasgow and Birkenhead to South Africa on her maiden voyage under Captain R.F. Longster. *6.4.1960:* Landed nine survivors from the yacht TE VEGA at St. Johns, Antigua. The yacht, a schooner of 320 tons, had run aground at 21.00 on 5.4.1960 on a reef south of Nevis, where the crew had been picked up. The TE VEGA was later salvaged and dry docked at Martinique for repairs. *17.9.1964:* Sold to Tolmi Compania Naviera S.A., Panama (Ant. Angelicoussis and Dem. Efthimiou) (Pegasus Ocean Services Ltd., London, managers) for £100,000 and renamed TOLMI under the Liberian flag. *2.7.1966:* Boilers were surveyed

The turbine-steamer *Biographer* began life with a short, cowl-topped funnel (above, in the Mersey) but later gained a much more distinguished stack to better disperse soot and sparks (bottom).

[J. & M. Clarkson; World Ship Photo Library]

while the vessel was at Genoa. There had been a history of trouble, including a stop at Puerto Rico in February 1966 when it had been reported that flames were leaping from the backs of the boilers. The surveyor found the port and starboard boilers in a bad state of repair; walls and platforms had collapsed; steel panels and stiffeners were deformed, and the forced draught fans were burnt. Repairs were commenced. *23.7.1966:* Sailed upon completion of repairs. *1969:* Transferred to the Greek flag. *25.4.1969:* Reported stopped off Cape Agulhas during a voyage from Bangkok to Rotterdam with tapioca in bulk and bags with all three auxiliary diesels out of action. She subsequently proceeded slowly to Capetown. *1.5.1969:* Arrived in Capetown. Examination revealed that two of the auxiliaries were beyond repair. All had badly damaged crankshafts, crankcases and cylinder blocks which the surveyor could only attribute to crew negligence. Two replacement diesel engines were supplied and geared to existing generators. *25.4.1969:*

Sailed for Dakar on completion of repairs. *28.8.1969:* When in dry dock in Trieste it was found that the main thrust bearing was heavily damaged, due to lack of lubrication. Once again the crew was found culpable. Moreover, fragments of cast iron from the thrust bearing had been allowed to circulate in the lubricating system, and these had caused untold damage to all turbine bearings, gearings, and rotors. *12.5.1970:* Reported aground off Manki Point, Bangara River, India, in position 22.14 54N, 89.35 06E, when on passage from Chalna to Calcutta. She refloated on the next tide. *14.5.1970:* Arrived at Calcutta. *12.1973:* Reported to have broken down in the South China Sea, some 450 miles north east of Singapore. *9.12.1973:* Arrived at Singapore in the tow of the salvage tug SALVIPER (609/66). Found to be beyond economical repair and sold to Chien Chen Steel and Iron Works, Taiwan. *12.1.1974:* Arrived in tow at Kaohsiung. *2.5.1974:* Demolition commenced.

286. ASTRONOMER (4) 1951-1970 Steel motor ship. Two decks, five holds and deep tank. Two masts.
O.N. 183805 8,150g 4,525n 9,940d 444.1 (460.4 o.l.) x 59.4 x 37.86 feet. Cargo capacity: 603,659 cubic feet.
International Code: MLRP.
4-cyl. 2SCSA oil engine by William Doxford and Sons Ltd., Sunderland; 12 knots.

Escorted by a paddle tug believed to be *Corsair,* a brand new *Astronomer* proudly sets out from the Wear.

25.10.1950: Launched by William Doxford and Sons Ltd., Sunderland (Yard No. 785) for the company. *19.3.1951:* Delivered at a cost of £491,818 and later sailed from Liverpool to the West Indies and Spanish Main on her maiden voyage under Captain E. Whitehouse. *30.11.1954:* An unscheduled reversal of the main engine in heavy weather placed the vessel in grave danger (see below). *9.1956:* At 17.17 and in position 43.17N, 10.03W, (305 degrees, 42 miles from Cape Finisterre), when on passage from East Africa to the United Kingdom via the Cape and Las Palmas, suffered a total breakdown of the main engine. An immediate call for assistance was answered by the Dutch tug OOSTZEE (497/53). *16.9.1956:* At 08.40 she had a line on board and the ASTRONOMER was then towed across the Bay of Biscay. *9.9.1956:* Arrived at 10.30 at Falmouth. *29.9.1956:* Repaired and returned to service. *7.3.1963:* Commenced towing the company's GOVERNOR (292) towards Dakar following that vessel's main engine failure on 25.2.1963. She subsequently relinquished her charge to the Dutch ocean-going tug LOIRE (384/52) and resumed her voyage. *19.6.1963:* Narrowly averted a major disaster when

coming up-river to dock at Alfred Basin on the flood tide (see below). *6.1968:* Assigned dual tonnages (8,032 and 5,811g, and 4,372 and 3,041n) under the 1966 Load Line Act. Most ports levy dues based on registered tonnage, regardless of whether a ship is loaded or in ballast. The intention was that if a certain statutory mark known as the Tonnage Mark was submerged then ports would be expected to charge on the higher tonnage figure; conversely, if the mark was above the waterline then the lower figure would prevail. However, in practice, most port authorities chose to ignore this distinction, and invariably charged on the higher figure, or simply adjusted their rates to cover any shortfall. *7.7.1968:* Arrived at Kingston, Jamaica to be confronted with the consequences of a pilotage strike. *5.1970:* Sold to Karen Shipping Co. Ltd., Famagusta, Cyprus (B. and J. Tsakiroglou, London) for £222,500 and renamed ZAIRA. *6.7.1972:* Ran aground off Sibenik, Yugoslavia when inward bound from Belem, Brazil. *12.7.1972:* Refloated with tug assistance and brought into Sibenik. Sold for demolition to Cantieri Navali Santa Maria, Italy for £56,000. *28.7.1972:* Arrived at Spezia. *30.8.1972:* Demolition commenced.

The ship that ran backwards
It was one of the worst storms to strike the British Isles this century. It lasted almost a week, with scarcely a lull between wind shifts. The ASTRONOMER, homeward bound from the US Gulf with a cargo of cotton for Manchester, was riding it out with difficulty somewhere southwest of Ireland, and making little or no headway. It was late November 1954, and the weather was putrid, bitterly cold, with winds gusting to Storm Force 10 or 12 most of the time. Shipping around the coast was often in dire straits

The ASTRONOMER found herself battling to stay afloat in these atrocious conditions, her radio tuned to messages about the mayhem going on around her. Captain Eric Whitehouse was thankful to have a stout, well-found ship, tight in the seams, and with plenty of power at his disposal. 24 hours earlier he had read the signs, studied the forecasts, and decided to heave to, nursing his ship with wind and sea on the starboard bow. Everything had been secured; the Chief had fired the Riley boiler, shutting off the exhaust gas-heated Cochran boiler, necessary precautions in these extreme conditions. There was nothing more to be done, except ride it out.

Still, if anything should go wrong... His mind refused to pursue the thought. The situation had become extremely uncomfortable, and as the ship plunged into the wall-sided seas her propeller was frequently exposed, racing madly. That evening, the Chief Engineer, Harold Ingram, climbed the staircase to the bridge to check the telemotor and discuss the

latest weather reports with the Master. The wheelhouse was quite dark, the only light being a faint glow from the binnacle reflecting from the helmsman's face which hovered, disembodied, above the wheel.

Consequently the Chief had difficulty discerning the stocky figure of the Captain, who was leaning against the handrail which spanned the forepart. "Oh, it's you, Chief," growled Captain Whitehouse, whose eyes were better accustomed to the darkness. "It's another lousy, filthy night. You've heard the TRESILLIAN's gone? Capsized she did, poor devils. And this bitch is steering like an old cow!" Having thus voiced his opinion of the ship's behaviour to the unwarranted disparagement of distaff members of the animal kingdom, he lapsed into gloomy silence.

The Chief peered at the telemotor gear, and found nothing amiss. "Has to be the weather," he said. "I'll take a look aft and check the gear in the steering flat. What are the prospects, anyway?" "Not good, Chief; not good. The bottom's fallen out of the glass, and the Met. Office reckon we can expect gusts of 150 knots and 72-foot waves in this area. There's no sign of a break. And here we are, sou'west of the Fastnet, and supposed to be taking the pilot at Lynas three hours ago!" As if to underline his disgust, the ship plunged heavily, and shipped a big sea green over the weather rail. "Damn it! Keep her steady, quartermaster!" "Aye-aye, sir." The seaman wrestled with the wheel. "But she's not answering, sir..."

257

Making his way aft, the Chief entered the engine room where the Second Engineer was still on watch. All seemed as normal as could be expected in those conditions. The violent motion of the ship, and the bone-shaking rattle of the main engine each time the prop lifted out of the water, quickly muffled as the governor cut in, was disconcerting, but not unusual. Nevertheless, Harold Ingram could sense that all was not as it should be. The valves were lifting uniformly, the Second was calmly entering up his log; the donkeyman was casually dripping oil amid various moving parts. Yet all was not well. The tachometer needle wavered drunkenly between 30 and 80 rpm; the...then the aberration struck him, like the deliberate mistake in one of those puzzle pictures. *The shaft was revolving the wrong way!* Instead of going ahead, the main engine was going astern! Heaven only knew what the consequences would be in those conditions...no wonder the ship was not steering! The Chief bore down on his astonished subordinate. "The engine's going astern!" he shrieked above the din.

The Second's eyes swept the gauges and indicators. All was as it should be. "It can't be", he cried incredulously. "Look at the shaft, man!" yelled the Chief, struggling with the controls. The younger man's stomach contracted painfully as he realised the shaft was indeed rotating astern. Quickly, they stopped the engine and re-started it in the ahead mode. Almost at once the ship's crazy motion became easier. Somewhat calmer, and vastly relieved, the two engineers discussed the phenomenon, and came to the only logical conclusion, albeit one they had never before had to contemplate in all their long experience. At some stage, the ship's propeller, in one of its airborne phases, had slapped down with such force into a rising sea that it had been knocked into reverse, overcoming the torque of the shaft, and transferring the shock momentarily to the engine itself, which then took over and continued to turn the shaft in the opposite direction. Incredible, but apparently true.

The Chief wended his way up to the bridge to report. There he found Captain Whitehouse in a more cheerful frame of mind, but still down on the farm with his figures of speech. "Steering like a lamb now, Chief", he chuckled; "steering like a lamb! Wonder what got into the old bitch?" Chief Engineer Ingram at once proceeded to enlighten him, somewhat shaken, but not without a certain relish, as if he had just defused a bomb in the engine room.

The motor ship *Astronomer* leaving Capetown.

Touch and go on the Mersey
Inward bound from Swansea on a flood tide, expecting to dock in Alfred Basin, Birkenhead on 19th June 1963, ASTRONOMER was proceeding upriver in the wake of another steamer, the SOUTH AFRICAN TRANSPORTER, which was about three quarters of a mile ahead. It was about 08.45, and the Mersey Ferries and Wirral landing stages were crowded with commuters, all hurrying to their places of business in Liverpool. Suddenly, the busy, orderly scene became one of crisis and disarray. A whistle signal from SOUTH AFRICAN TRANSPORTER warned Captain Myles and Pilot Alan Ellis on ASTRONOMER's bridge that the ship ahead was about to turn to port, presumably to enter Sandon Dock on the Liverpool side. They watched her turn, and Pilot Ellis shaped a course to pass between her stern and the crowded Seacombe Ferry stage, where the ferry ROYAL IRIS was boarding her passengers.[227]

At the critical moment, however, SOUTH AFRICAN TRANSPORTER appeared to go astern into ASTRONOMER's path! Her bluff stern collided with ASTRONOMER's port bow, and again amidships. The impact slewed her head to starboard and, swept along by the incoming tide, the ship began to bear down on the Seacombe stage and ROYAL IRIS.

Strike action - and reaction
When ASTRONOMER had the misfortune to arrive at Kingston, Jamaica on 7th July 1968, in the midst of a pilotage strike, it was decided, with qualified approval from head office, that the ship should make a bold attempt to enter the port and berth without a pilot (and, incidentally, without tugs, which at that time were not available).

The situation was critical. If a collision were to occur, the ship would carry away the chain moorings holding the stage to the shore. Many of the crowding commuters would have been thrown into the river; and ROYAL IRIS placed in jeopardy. That these catastrophes did not occur was due to the prompt reaction to the crisis by those on board ASTRONOMER. Both anchors were let go and held firmly on the brakes until several tension-laden minutes later the ship brought up a mere 100 feet from the crowded landing-stage. A further indication of how close the ship was to disaster was the fact that her straining anchors fouled the landing stage moorings.

Meanwhile, the tugs which had been awaiting ASTRONOMER's arrival off the dock were now on the scene, holding the ship's stern up into the tideway, preventing her from swinging upstream and against the stage, with perhaps equally dire consequences. Gradually, order was restored. The ship, controlled by the tugs, slipped her cables, leaving the anchors to be retrieved later. Slowly, the ship drew clear of the ferry stage, and the agitated throng breathed again. But for several long, drawn out minutes it had been touch and go.

Now the channels leading into the harbour from Plumb Point are narrow and tortuous, culminating in a 150 degree turn round Port Royal Point, and the navigation is correspondingly difficult. From Port Royal, a long leg across Kingston Harbour, past Fort Augusta, led into the newly-dredged port area of Newport West. There the ship had to swing, turning short-round in quite a narrow space before berthing port side to at Western Terminals' Wharf. This was a tall order for any man, but Captain Stanley Bladon was never the man to shirk a challenge.

Indeed, he did extremely well to arrive off the berth without mishap. However, since this was Captain Bladon's first voyage in command, he had had little opportunity to assess his ship's manoeuvring qualities. He knew only too well that, in Liverpool, for instance, any aberrations from the norm would be speedily corrected by a heave or a push from one or more tugs - at least, most times. But here, at Kingston, Captain Bladon was very much on his own.[228]

It was about 07.00 when the ship arrived off the berth, which was crowded with four or five gangs of men, all gazing at the ship curiously as they waited for her to berth. All that remained to achieve this object was to turn short-round to starboard, and drop alongside. The manoeuvre was executed in the best textbook style - starboard anchor down; helm to starboard; engines alternately ahead and astern. The ship's head began to swing...but all too slowly...then stopped. Instead of turning the ship was forging ahead, perhaps in the grip of some unknown and unsuspected east-going current which was preventing her stern from canting. Full astern! Too late; ASTRONOMER's bow crunched into the timber-faced concrete wharf, splintering baulks of timber and demolishing blocks of masonry along 12 feet of wharf. The ship's stem was pushed back six feet, opening up an unsightly hole in the forepeak, which gaped back at the astonished, open-mouthed crowd on the quay. Quickly, lines were flung ashore, and ropes willingly man-handled on to mooring posts, enabling the ship to warp alongside. But the damage was extensive, and the ship could only be repaired in dry dock, the nearest suitable one being Todd's in Galveston. Temporary repairs were carried out to satisfy Lloyd's Surveyor at Kingston that the ship was fit to put to sea. ASTRONOMER then continued her voyage to Belize and Mexico before heading for Galveston, where she arrived on 9th August. It is difficult to assess the total bill for repairs, but around £42,000 was received from the underwriters.

Captain Bladon was exonerated, of course. Under pressure, the firm had taken a gamble which had not come off as planned. But if the horse does not win, it is no use blaming the jockey! Captain Bladon went on to pursue a distinguished career, and in the summer of 1982 took another ASTRONOMER (325) into the far South Atlantic, to work with the Royal Navy in the closing stages of the Falklands War, and for many months afterwards. He retired, greatly admired and respected by his many friends, in 1989.

287. WAYFARER (3) 1951-1971 Steel motor ship. Two decks, five holds and deep tank. Two masts.
O.N. 183811 8,150g 4,525n 9,940d 444.1 (460.4 o.l.) x 59.4 x 37.86 feet. Cargo capacity: 603,659 cubic feet.
International Code: GMNR.
4-cyl. 2SCSA oil engine by William Doxford and Sons Ltd., Sunderland; 12 knots.

9.1.1951: Launched by William Doxford and Sons Ltd., Sunderland (Yard No. 786) for the company. *2.7.1951:* Delivered at a cost of £492,119 and later sailed from Liverpool for Kingston and Mexico on her maiden voyage under Captain L.F. Harriman. *14.12.1966:* At 00.54 while passing 5½ miles off the Guajira Peninsula Colombia, in position 12.27.30N, 71.19.30W, was challenged by the Colombian gunboat CARLOS E. RESTREPO. Two shells were sent across the bow. Two further shots followed and at 09.58 the ship was stopped. At 10.17, after a verbal exchange, she was allowed to proceed. *10.9.1970:* Fire broke out in the cotton cargo in number 2 hold while the vessel was berthed at Liverpool. The blaze,

This view of *Wayfarer* emphasises the long forecastle introduced with *Astronomer.*
[World Ship Photo Library]

which was brought under control by midnight, was fought by 50 firemen. *23.7.1971:* Sold to Cassiopeian Shipping Co. Ltd., Famagusta, Cyprus (Canopus Shipping S.A., Athens (Andreas and George Kyrtatas), managers) and renamed MITERA ZAFIRA. *7.3.1973:* Caught fire and ran aground on rocks off Costinesti, Constantza Roads when on passage from Ashdod to Constantza with phosphate. Later abandoned by her crew. *20.6.1973:* Declared a constructive total loss.

A classic view of *Wayfarer* approaching Gladstone locks with the Wallasey waterfront in the background.   *[J. & M. Clarkson]*

288. WANDERER (3) 1951-1970 Steel motor ship. Two decks, five holds and deep tank. Two masts.
O.N. 183818 8,150g 4,525n 9,940d 444.1 (460.4 o.l.) x 59.4 x 37.86 feet. Cargo capacity: 603,659 cubic feet.
International Code: MMVR.
4-cyl. 2SCSA oil engine by William Doxford and Sons Ltd., Sunderland; 12 knots.

21.2.1951: Launched by William Doxford and Sons Ltd., Sunderland (Yard No. 790) for the company. *3.9.1951:* Delivered at a cost of £491,772 and later sailed from Antwerp and London to South Africa on her maiden voyage under Captain J.F.W. Wallis. *8.6.1956:* When bound from Trinidad to London was forced to put into Falmouth when a furnace in the Riley boiler collapsed. Repairs were carried out. *16.6.1956:* Resumed the voyage to London. *27.11.1964:* Suffered an engine breakdown in Lake Maracaibo while on passage from Maracaibo to Bachaquero, and as a result anchored 40 miles south of Maracaibo for two weeks. It transpired that the main engine thrust bearings pads were damaged due to fatigue of material. *11.12.1964:* Eventually arrived at Bachaquero. *15.12.1964:* Sailed for Barranquilla, Colombia. *2.10.1970:* Sold to Tricia Shipping Co. Ltd., Nicosia, Cyprus (Zannis Picoulis) (Hunter Shipping Co. Ltd., London, managers) for £275,000 and renamed CLEOPATRA. *1974:* Sold to Chung Lien Navigation Co. S.A., Panama (Great Pacific Navigation Co. Ltd., Taipei, managers) and renamed CHUNG THAI. *17.7.1974:* Whilst on passage from Kaohsiung to Yokohama with general cargo broke down in the vicinity of Okinawa. Two cylinders of the main engine had cracked, and water leaking from the cooling system into the engine room further complicated her predicament. Eventually she was towed into Naha by tugs and from there to Osaka for repair. *7.8.1974:* Arrived at Osaka where the engines were found to be beyond economical repair. Sold to Dongkuk Steel Mills Co. Ltd., South Korea. *9.9.1974:* Left in tow for Masan. *10.1974:* Demolition commenced.

Wanderer is seen above in almost-immaculate condition, and below looking somewhat tired after sale and renaming *Cleopatra*. Her red funnel band had been repainted blue, a bow crest had been painted on, and her masts painted buff.

[Ian Farquhar collection; J. & M. Clarkson collection]

289. ARBITRATOR (2) 1951-1970 Steel motor ship. Two decks, five holds and deep tank. Two masts.
O.N. 183823 8,150g 4,525n, 9,940d 444.1 (460.4 o.l.) x 59.4 x 37.86 feet. Cargo capacity: 603,659 cubic feet.
International Code: MMZR.
4-cyl. 2SCSA oil engine by William Doxford and Sons Ltd., Sunderland; 12 knots.

5.4.1951: Launched by William Doxford and Sons Ltd., Sunderland (Yard No. 791) for the company. *27.10.1951:* Delivered at a cost of £491,813 and later sailed from Liverpool to East Africa on her maiden voyage under Captain W. Moore. *16.3.1969:* Picked up six survivors from the Liberian VAINQUEUR (12,075/58) from the sea in the Gulf of Mexico and landed them at Beaumont, Texas. The VAINQUEUR, loaded with 20,000 tons of sugar, had foundered in position 27.21N, 90.30W (215 degrees, 122 miles from the South Pass Lighthouse) on 14.3.1969 following an engine room explosion. Twenty four survivors were picked up by USS HYMAN. *10.1970:* Sold to Dinaco Shipping Ltd., Famagusta, Cyprus (Methenitis Brothers Shipbrokers, Piraeus, managers) for £275,000 and renamed VASSILIKI METHENITIS. *1974:* Sold to Pyramid Lines (Pte.) Ltd. (Empress Shipping and Trading (Pte.) Ltd., Singapore, managers) and renamed YAN II. *1977:* Sold to Valibhoy and Sons, Pakistan for

Fourth member of the *Astronomer* class, *Arbitrator* in South African waters.

demolition. *21.5.1977:* Arrived at Karachi for delivery. *10.1977:* Work began at Gadani Beach.

260

290. CROFTER 1951-1971 Steel steamship. Two decks and five holds. Two masts.
O.N. 183830 8,377g 4,776n 10,520d 452.3 (468.0 o.l.) x 59.9 x 37.92 feet. Cargo capacity: 578,640 cubic feet. Equipped with 60-ton and 40-ton derricks serving numbers 2 and 4 holds respectively.
International Code: MNGX.
T. 3-cyl. by John Readhead and Sons Ltd., South Shields with Bauer-Wach exhaust turbine; 26½, 44, 74 x 48 inches, 12 knots.

In June 1953 whilst homeward bound from Demerara to London with a cargo of bagged sugar, *Crofter* was diverted to Spithead to represent Harrisons at the Coronation Review of the fleet. She is seen against a wonderful backdrop of cruisers, frigates and submarines.

16.8.1951: Launched by John Readhead and Sons Ltd., South Shields (Yard No. 568) for the company. *11.12.1951:* Delivered at a cost of £491,617 and later sailed from Liverpool to the West Indies on her maiden voyage under Captain S.H. Diamond. *10.2.1952:* Whilst loading sugar alongside at Georgetown, Demerara, received word that EXPLORER (234) was disabled by a fracture of the tail-end shaft. Sailed at 10.00 and found EXPLORER in the Atlantic the following day. A towing cable was in position by 22.00. *17.2.1952:* She delivered her tow at Port of Spain following a tow of some 800 miles. The effort of towing had taken its toll of the machinery of the brand new ship, and temporary repairs were effected. *24.2.1952:* Sailed for Grenada leaving her Demerara cargo for another vessel. *15.6.1953:* Participated in the Queen's Coronation Review of the Fleet at Spithead and Captain Diamond attended Her Majesty's cocktail party aboard the royal yacht SURPRISE. *12.11.1963:* Fire was discovered at 17.15 in number 5 'tween

deck when bound from Liverpool to Kingston in position 44.17N, 19.26W. The hatches and ventilators were sealed and steam injected into the compartments while the vessel headed for Punta Delgada. *13.11.1963:* She arrived off the port but bad weather prevented her from entering until 09.00 the following day, by which time the fire was believed to be extinguished. However, on inspection, the seat of the fire was found to be in consignments of coke and in drums of sodium hydrosulphite. The damage was estimated at £2.500. *8.1971:* Sold to Spica Shipping Co. Ltd., Famagusta, Cyprus (Canopus Shipping S.A., Athens (Andreas and George Kyrtatas), managers) for £95,000 and renamed AGHIOS GEORGIOS. *1976:* Sold to Ifestion S.A., Panama (Canopus Shipping S.A., Athens (Andreas and George Kyrtatas), managers) and renamed SAN GEORGIO II. *1977:* Sold to Spanish shipbreakers. *18.5.1977:* Left Bilbao bound for San Esteban de Pravia to be broken up.

Crofter was another case of a steamer needing to have her funnel lengthened to improve draft.   *[World Ship Photo Library]*

291. FORESTER 1952-1970 Steel steamship. Two decks and five holds. Two masts.
O.N. 185431 8,377g 4,776n 10,520d 452.3 (468.0 o.l.) x 59.9 x 37.92 feet. Cargo capacity: 578,640 cubic feet. Equipped with 60-ton and 40-ton derricks serving numbers 2 and 4 holds respectively.
International Code: MNMC.
T. 3-cyl. by John Readhead and Sons Ltd., South Shields with Bauer-Wach exhaust turbine; 26½, 44, 74 x 48 inches; 12 knots.

12.12.1951: Launched by John Readhead and Sons Ltd., South Shields (Yard No. 569) for the company. *5.1952:* Delivered at a cost of £532,486 and later sailed from Liverpool to the West Indies under Captain John Harnden. *5.10.1953:* When bound from Mauritius to the United Kingdom, the vessel put into Aden for bunkers. Shortly after leaving, she was forced to return due to a fault in the main engine. *10.10.1953:* She eventually sailed following repairs. *19.7.1965:* Stopped at sea for 12 hours in position 39.15N, 09.53W, about 20 miles west south west of the Burlings Lighthouse, Portugal to repair number 6 main bearing which was running hot. *30.12.1970:* Sold to Maldives Shipping Ltd., Male, Maldive Islands (Maldivian Nationals Trading Corporation (Ceylon) Ltd., Colombo, Ceylon, managers), for £155,000 and renamed MALDIVE AMBASSADOR. *11.3.1971:* Arrived at Maceio, Brazil with a severely damaged cast iron water box on the main condenser. A new box was cast by the makers and despatched to the vessel. *10.4.1971:* Sailed for Recife. *5.8.1972:* It was reported that the vessel had sprung a leak in number 1 hold during a period of very rough weather when on passage from Bangkok to Aden. Soundings were increasing daily despite continuous

Forester, Harrisons' last steamer. She and *Crofter* had the same hull as her immediate diesel-driven predecessors, but with funnels further forward to suit the arrangement of the boilers. The gantry abaft her superstructure distinguished *Forester* from *Crofter.* *[Ian Farquhar collection]*

pumping. At Aden a leak in the vessel's side was noted at strake 18 between frames 168 and 172. Later, after cargo had been unloaded, two holes were found, measuring about 1½ x 1 inch, joined by a crack 3 inches long. The leak was repaired. *12.8.1972:* Sailed for Mukalla but 3,596 bags of sugar had been damaged. *1973:* Sold through Mitsui and Co. to Mayachi Salvage Co. Japan for demolition. *30.10.1973:* Demolition commenced at Tadotsu.

292. GOVERNOR (4) 1952-1972 Steel motor ship. Three decks forward, two aft, five holds and deep tank. Two masts.
O.N. 185452 6,026g 3,128n 9,140d 447.4 (463.69 o.l.) x 59.4 x 37.86 feet. Cargo capacity: 587,340 cubic feet. Equipped with 70-ton and 60-ton derricks serving numbers 2 and 4 holds respectively.
International Code: GPSX.
4-cyl. 2SCSA oil engine by William Doxford and Sons Ltd., Sunderland; 14 knots.

The motor ship *Governor* in the Thames estuary in April 1970. She was the first of four ships which were a development of the *Astronomer* class. *[J. & M. Clarkson collection]*

8.5.1952: Launched by William Doxford and Sons Ltd., Sunderland (Yard No. 793) for the company. *23.12.1952:* Delivered at a cost of £660,188 and later sailed from London and the Continent for South Africa on her maiden voyage under

Captain H.W. Jones. *20.1.1954:* Tonnage openings in shelter deck permanently closed and vessel remeasured (8,202g 4,389n 9,770d). *25.2.1963:* Disabled south of Freetown by a serious fracture of the cylinder of number 1 unit.

For 10 days she drifted while the vessel's engineers struggled to restore mobility to the main engines. *7.3.1963:* The ASTRONOMER (286), outward bound from Birkenhead to the Cape, hove in sight, took her disabled sister in tow, and headed for Dakar. Three days later in position 06.35N, 14.58W, ASTRONOMER relinquished her charge in the care of the Dutch tug LOIRE (384/52) and resumed her voyage. *15.3.1963:* Reached Dakar completing the 500-mile tow. An act of General Average was declared, committing owners, shippers and all participants in the venture to contribute towards the costs generated by the mishap in proportion to their degree of interest. Her cargo was discharged, to be picked up later by the British steamer SYCAMORE HILL (7,126/44), chartered for the purpose. The cost of this phase of the operation was about £31,500, more than half the total claim of £58,000, of which the underwriters paid £38,000.[229]*6.4.1963:* Escorted by the Dutch tug OCEAAN (97/51), she sailed from Dakar having completed temporary repairs sufficient to sustain her for a voyage to Sunderland for full repair. *15.4.1963:* Handed over to the tug GELE ZEE (74/42) in the approaches to the English Channel. *18.4.1963:* Arrived at Sunderland. 5.7.1963: Shortly after clearing the Mona Passage whilst on a voyage from Liverpool to Kingston, she came across the disabled coastal vessel LADY ENID (106/43) in position 17.40N, 69.33W. A line was put aboard and the coaster was towed about 410 miles to Kingston. *1967:* Freeboard reduced 6 inches to conform with 1966 Load Line Convention (10,090d). *16.3.1969:* When bound for Liverpool after dry docking in Manchester, she was trapped in the Manchester Ship Canal after the Manchester Liner MANCHESTER COURAGE (11,899/69) had demolished the lock gate at Irlam. (The author was Master of GOVERNOR at the time.) *5.1972:* Sold to Pleiades Shipping Co. Ltd., Famagusta, Cyprus (Canopus Shipping S.A., Athens (Andreas and George Kyrtatas), managers) for £63,000 and renamed DIAMANDO. *1975:* Transferred to Celika Shipping Co. S.A., Panama (Canopus Shipping S.A., Athens (Andreas and George Kyrtatas), managers). *31.8.1977:* Reported laid up at Abidjan, Ivory Coast. *1979:* Sold to Spanish shipbreakers. *4.6.1979:* Arrived in tow at Santander.

The day the Ship Canal ran dry

We watched the Liner back out of Number 9 Dock with detached interest. Incidentally, reference to a "Liner" within the Port of Manchester, i.e., from Eastham Locks to Trafford Park, can have only one meaning - one of Manchester Liners Ltd., part of the Furness Withy Group, and the city's pride and joy. Inevitably, it seemed, Liners were privileged to take precedence anywhere on the Canal, at any time. Which was why the GOVERNOR was still lying at the dry dock jetty, waiting, although ready to sail for some time, for the MANCHESTER COURAGE to enter and clear Mode Wheel Lock, the lock which led from the dock system to the Ship Canal itself.[230]

It was 18.50 on 16th March 1969, and I was watching the manoeuvre from my dayroom window, while Pilot Bill Walker was keeping a professional eye on things from the wheelhouse above. The breeze was fresh from the east, and the two Canal Company tugs, MSC SABRE and SCEPTRE, seemed to be having difficulty holding the big ship up to windward as she headed towards the lock. In fact, she was clearly in danger of hitting the bullnose, that end of the lock wall which jutted out into the basin. One would have expected to see the screw churning astern at this crisis, but the dark, polluted water under her stern remained still. The silence of the evening was rudely broken by a harsh duet on air and pea-whistles as the pilot urged his tugs to push or pull the ship out of danger, but there was still no movement of the ship's own propeller. It would appear that she had some sort of engine trouble.

At last the tugs had her moving astern, but the ship still continued to fall down to leeward. Professional curiosity turned to alarm as it became apparent that MANCHESTER COURAGE was in grave danger of falling against the GOVERNOR! I made a hurried exit from my cabin to rouse officers and men to have fenders on hand, ready to cushion the anticipated blow. But they were already on their way, and in the wheelhouse I conferred with Pilot Walker, who was also showing signs of perturbation. Gradually the tugs began to win their battle and the ship began to draw away. As her bridge drew level with ours, the two pilots engaged in a lively and colourful conversation, expressing a mutual sense of grievance in pithy terms, and establishing the cause of the delay, which was indeed due to engine trouble. The pilot intended to place the ship alongside Salford Quay, opposite the berth at which GOVERNOR was lying, while the problem was sorted out. Any notions we may have entertained of slipping into the lock in the meantime were effectively snookered by the Liner's baulky position on Salford Quay. There was nothing for it but to wait patiently for an hour or so until the ship's engineers had completed their task.

When the time came there were no hitches and the Liner passed easily through the lock, and into the Barton stretch. GOVERNOR followed shortly afterwards entering Mode Wheel Lock at 21.15. However, when the ship was secured in the lock, Pilot Walker advised against immediate departure. "We'll wait until we know whether the sonofabitch has cleared the next lock," he growled, his natural Lancastrian caution amplified by recollection of the Liner's antics earlier in the evening. So we stayed in the lock until the telephone shrilled in the Lockmaster's office, and he emerged to tell us that, yes, Barton was all clear.

Our lock was lowered, and we pressed on through the next section, securing in Barton lock about 40 minutes later. Pilot Walker's wariness was not yet mollified, however, and the fact that the Liner had not yet cleared the much shorter Barton/Irlam section was in itself a sign that all was not well. So we played the waiting game again, determined to stay in high-level lock until Irlam was reported clear. The Lockmaster was not as co-operative as he might have been, but Pilot Walker could be very obstinate.

It was as well he was; and it must be said that, despite his instinctive fears, no-one was more surprised than he to hear some time later that Irlam lock was far from clear, and unlikely to be so for many weeks to come. For the unthinkable had happened. A major disaster had overtaken the MANCHESTER COURAGE. Briefly, she had charged through the lower lock gates, emptied the lock, and was now perched across the sill, wedged in by fallen masonry and other debris. The upper gates had not been closed - there had not been time - and they had been swept away in the rush of water, as the level of the two-mile Barton/Irlam section of the Canal fell 16 feet, and rapidly drained off into the Latchford section. Two Manchester Corporation sludge vessels, the MANCUNIUM and the PERCY DAWSON, both lying at the Corporation's berth serving the Davyhulme Sewage Works, were stranded in the mud, the former sustaining some damage.

If GOVERNOR had moved into the next stretch of water on cue, she too would have been lying high and dry, listing drunkenly in a noisome bed of Ship Canal mud and slime. Pilot Walker's instincts had been vindicated. Although the ship was now marooned in the upper reaches of the Canal, along with 16 other large vessels, she was still, at least, afloat. It was fortunate that Barton lower gates still held firm, in spite of the extra pressure.

We learned the cause of the accident later. MANCHESTER COURAGE was equipped with a variable-pitch propeller, a fairly recent innovation at the time. On going astern, the main engine continued to drive in the same direction, while the pitch of the propeller blades (i.e. the angle at which they were set on the boss) was hydraulically reversed, thus reversing the thrust. On this occasion, as the ship eased into Irlam Lock, the pilot ordered "slow astern" to take the way off the ship. The response was not forthcoming, so he ordered "half astern", then "full astern", thus compounding the fault, for he had no means of knowing that a valve in the hydraulic system had failed, and the propeller blades remained stubbornly in the "ahead" position.

It was not until 21st March 1969 that tugs were able to tow the MANCHESTER COURAGE clear of the shattered lock, and proceed to Gladstone Dock in Liverpool to discharge her export cargo. On 27th, she sailed for Middlesbrough to make good the damage to her hull, and thoroughly overhaul her hydraulic systems. On the same day, the debris in the lock was cleared and the small adjacent lock opened for coastal and barge traffic. Meanwhile, work on the main lock went ahead. New gates were installed, and on 18th April 1969, nearly five weeks after the disaster, the Manchester Ship Canal was fully operational once more.

293. DIPLOMAT (3) 1953-1972 Steel motor ship. Three decks forward, two aft, five holds and deep tank.
O.N. 185463 8,202g 4,523n 9,770d 447.4 (463.69 o.l.) x 59.4 x 37.86 feet. Cargo capacity: 589,990 cubic feet. Equipped with 70-ton and 60-ton derricks serving numbers 2 and 4 holds respectively.
International Code: MPTJ.
4-cyl. 2SCSA oil engine by William Doxford and Sons Ltd., Sunderland; 14 knots.

The motor ship *Diplomat* blows off steam from her auxiliary boiler whilst manoeuvring in Hamburg harbour.   *[Carl Schutze]*

9.7.1952: Launched by William Doxford and Sons Ltd., Sunderland (Yard No. 794) for the company. *8.3.1953:* Delivered at a cost of £664,854 and later sailed from London and the Continent for South Africa on her maiden voyage under Captain Lewis Jones. *18.2.1957:* In collision in the River Scheldt with the Norwegian motor tanker VANESSA (11,691/53) when inward bound from Middlesbrough to Antwerp. The incident occurred at 16.14 on a flood tide near Number 73 buoy in the Bat Channel. DIPLOMAT sustained damage to her port quarter from contact with VANESSA's port bow. At a subsequent judicial hearing the tanker was found wholly to blame for the accident. VANESSA was found to be on the wrong side of the channel. *2.1960:* An appeal brought by the owners of VANESSA was dismissed with costs to the plaintiffs.[231] *10.2.1962:* When coming astern off the berth at Lourenço Marques her engines failed to go ahead on completion of the manoeuvre, and consequently she struck the south bank of the river with her rudder. Both tiller-stops were broken as the quadrant ran off the rack and the rudder itself was twisted through 50 degrees. *2.3.1962:* Following temporary repairs she sailed for Durban escorted

by the tug J.R. MORE (805/61) and the company's INTERPRETER (278) into which her cargo was to be off loaded. *13.4.1962:* Following repairs in dry dock sailed for Lourenço Marques. The expenses in this case amounted to some £40,000. *16.11.1963:* Sailed from London but put back some hours later with serious engine trouble. She berthed at Tilbury and her cargo was later transferred to the Danish CRUSADER (3,338/57) which was on long-term charter to the company. Repairs were put in hand. *13.12.1963:* Engine trials took place in the North Sea. The results were unsatisfactory and after adjustments further trials took place a week later. *9.1.1964:* Finally sailed from the Thames. *12.1967:* Freeboard reduced 6 inches, tonnage becoming 10,090d. *16.10.1972:* Sold to Dioskouri Shipping Co. Ltd., Famagusta, Cyprus (Canopus Shipping S.A., Athens (Andreas and George Kyrtatas), managers) and renamed ANTONIOS. *1976:* Transferred to Tamassos Shipping Co. S.A., Panama (Canopus Shipping S.A., Athens (Andreas and George Kyrtatas), managers). *1980:* Sold to Mao Chen Iron and Steel Co. Ltd., Taiwan for demolition. *14.8.1980:* Work began at Kaohsiung.

294. JOURNALIST 1954-1973 Steel motor ship. Three decks forward, two aft, five holds and deep tank. Two masts.
O.N. 185487 8,366g 4,434n 9,670d 447.4 (463.83 o.l.) x 59.4 x 37.9 feet. Cargo capacity: 585,751 cubic feet. Equipped with 70-ton and 60-ton derricks serving numbers 2 and 4 holds respectively.
International Code: MSFQ.
4-cyl. 2SCSA oil engine by William Doxford and Sons Ltd., Sunderland; 14 knots.

20.1.1954: Launched by William Doxford and Sons Ltd., Sunderland (Yard No. 801) for the company. *3.6.1954:* Delivered at a cost of £743,628 and later sailed from Birkenhead for East Africa on her maiden voyage under Captain R.F. Phillips. *8.9.1960:* Commenced towing the Turnbull Scott motor ship PARKGATE (7,133/45), broken down off the Somali coast, to Mombasa.. *17.9.1960:* Arrived safely after a tow lasting 8 days, 20 hours, 49 minutes and 1,088 nautical miles at a speed of 5.11 knots - a good performance considering the adverse effects of the south west monsoon. *5.1973:* Sold to Neptune Shipping Co. Ltd., Famagusta, Cyprus (Canopus Shipping S.A., Athens (Andreas and George Kyrtatas), managers) for £212,000 and renamed AGHIA THALASSINI. *1976:* Transferred to Lamyra Compania Naviera S.A., Panama (Canopus Shipping S.A., Athens (Andreas and George Kyrtatas), managers). *1979:* Transferred to Greek flag. *1981:* Sold to unknown owners and renamed ELISSAR under the Lebanese flag. *1982:* Sold to Karim

Journalist in the Manchester Ship Canal.   *[J. & M. Clarkson]*

Shipbreaking Industries Ltd., Pakistan. *18.2.1982:* Arrived at Gadani Beach. *11.4.1982:* Work began.

264

Journalist in the Mersey. *[John and Marion Clarkson]*

"No cure - no pay"

As soon as the British motor ship PARKGATE (7,133/45) poked her prow into the boisterous Arabian Sea her troubles started. Flying light, with minimum ballast, she was not in ideal trim to buck the heavy seas, strong winds and adverse currents to be expected on passage from Khorramshahr, in the Shatt-al-Arab, to Port Elizabeth during the south west monsoon season. Subjected to constant pounding, and the wild racing of a propeller which sliced fresh air for half the time, the ship shuddered and shook from stem to stern, and certain structural weaknesses began to appear. The bulkhead between the deep-tank, which contained fuel oil, and number 2 hold began to leak at the seams. About 260 tons of oil were lost in this way. On 30th August 1960 her Captain reported faults in machinery and boilers, and a shortage of fuel. On 4th September, when parts of the scavenge pump disintegrated, the ship came to a halt wallowing in a heavy swell in position 02.20N, 51.14E, and out went an emergency signal on X X X priority, requesting a tow.

Built as the EMPIRE CALSHOT at Burntisland, Fife, in 1945, the ship had changed hands several times, and acquired several aliases (DERRYCUNIHY in 1946; ARGOBEAM in 1952) before becoming Turnbull Scott's PARKGATE in 1955. Now she was in dire trouble, broken down in heavy seas, veering away to leeward on the strong monsoon drift.

Several vessels acknowledged Captain Gibson's call for help but for various reasons were unable to render the assistance required. The message, after all, was prefixed X X X, which did not convey the same urgency or moral compulsion as an S O S. However, at 20.30 on 6th September, PARKGATE's repeated pleas were heard by Radio Officer W.F. Stirling aboard the JOURNALIST, which was on passage from Aden to Mombasa. By this time, PARKGATE was quoting a position 160 miles north east of her initial position, an indication of the strength of the current. Matters were becoming desperate. Supplies of food and water were running low. The message was passed to Captain Douglas Wolstenholme, who pondered it, estimated the disabled ship to be 200 miles east of his position, and replied, expressing a willingness to assist if no other vessel was on hand, subject to his owners' permission.[232] This was essential, for it would have been most imprudent to deviate from the declared voyage without re-insuring the ship - unless it was a matter of

life and death, as in an S O S situation. A much relieved PARKGATE replied: "Wish you obtain permission tow PARKGATE Mombasa basis Lloyds standard form of salvage agreement no cure no pay stop At present have no other contacts."

Captain Wolstenholme thereupon radioed Harrisons' Liverpool office, and shortly after midnight local time obtained clearance to proceed on his errand of mercy. At 00.51 on 7th September, JOURNALIST altered course towards PARKGATE's last reported position, nearly 200 miles away in an east north easterly direction, advising the anxious Captain Gibson that help was on its way.

Next morning, preparations for an ocean tow were put in hand under the supervision of Chief Officer John Mitchell. There was much to be done. The cable on the port anchor was broken at the ganger shackle, leaving a short, 45-foot length in the cable compressor. Next, some five or six shackles (about

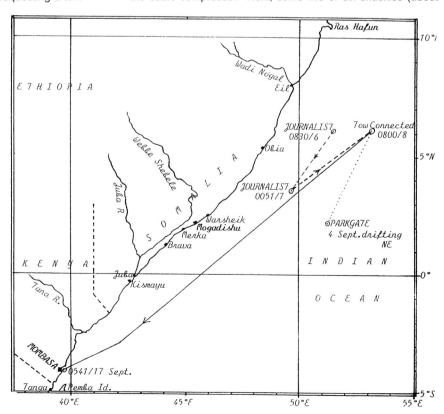

Positions of *Journalist* and *Parkgate*, September 1960.

265

500 feet) of cable were manhandled along the decks to the poop, timber channels being constructed wherever pipes and deck fittings appeared vulnerable to damage. The cable was then reconnected to the short ganger-length, thus making the anchor, which had been packed with timber between flukes and shell plating, the ultimate backstop absorbing any undue stresses. In the event, no such stresses occurred so far forward throughout the tow. Finally, the cable was straightened out, kinks eliminated, and some turns taken round the after bitts to absorb the slack, leaving the last link handy for joining the PARKGATE's cable.

Towards the end of the day, PARKGATE was sighted, and JOURNALIST later hove to, waiting for daylight before embarking on the tricky operation of joining cables. The ship's captains were in touch with each other in a rather lopsided way, Captain Wolstenholme using the radio telephone, Captain Gibson a Morse lamp, but they worked out a practical modus operandi, and established a mutual sense of understanding. As dawn broke, JOURNALIST steamed close to leeward of PARKGATE whose crew fired a rocket line across, making this all-important link at 06.07. JOURNALIST moved ahead, clear of the other ship's bow, and waited until the light-draughted ship fell to leeward, under the Harrison ship's stern, JOURNALIST using her engines to maintain a position relative to the helpless PARKGATE. Meanwhile, a series of lines passed between the two vessels, each one heavier than the last, until ultimately one of JOURNALIST's new 7-inch manilas was passed aboard PARKGATE. This was to carry that ship's starboard cable, already unshackled, ready to be secured to the 7-inch messenger. Foot by foot, and link by link, the heavy cable was hauled aboard JOURNALIST by the creaking, straining manila, coaxed through the fairlead and shackled firmly to JOURNALIST's cable. The towing-spring was complete. Whilst all this was going on the two ships danced a fantastic minuet together, bobbing and weaving, bowing and curtseying, in the relentless ocean swell. Second Officer John Dwyer, stationed at the poop telephone, intoned his estimate of the distance between the ships, providing Captain Wolstenholme with the vital information he needed to maintain station a mere 50 or 60 feet ahead of his partner, giving a touch ahead on the engines from time to time to keep out of trouble.

Once the link had been made, PARKGATE paid out seven shackles (630 feet) of cable, doubly secured it, and at 07.51 signalled that she was ready. JOURNALIST took the strain, and for a while the heavy bight of cable rose clear of the water, dripping in the sunlight, but by 08.15 on 8th September both ships were heading into the wind on course for Mombasa, over 1,000 miles away to the southwest. Once the disabled ship's initial inertia had been overcome, the bight descended

fathoms deep, acting as a "spring", or shock absorber.

Throughout the towing operation, deck and engineer officers were placed on double watches - four on and four off - while Captain Wolstenholme remained almost continuously on the bridge, watching the erratic behaviour of the tow, nursing the strain on the cable as best he could in the conditions which continued rough for several days.

By the early hours of the tenth day, the lights of Mombasa were in sight, and at 05.41 on 17th September two pilots boarded JOURNALIST a mile or so off the entrance to the harbour. It transpired that the harbour master was not prepared to bring in the crippled ship with harbour tugs. He did not think they would be able to hold her in the prevailing fresh southerly breeze. Was Captain Wolstenholme prepared to bring his tow through the entrance channel himself? This was not a welcome proposition, for the channel was narrow and winding, but, having come so far, Captain Wolstenholme was not inclined to cut his charge adrift at this stage. He discussed the problem with the pilots. They were quite confident. The tugs would be on hand to assist, of course; then the towing cable was shortened to about 450 feet to reduce sheer on the bends; the second pilot was despatched to the PARKGATE, and the cavalcade headed up for Ras Serani Lighthouse and the leading marks to the entrance channel. Once clear of the bends, the ships entered sheltered Kilindini harbour, where the tugs made fast to PARKGATE, and at 08.36 that ship dropped her port anchor. A minute later the towing cable, that umbilical cord which had for days been PARKGATE's only means of survival, was slipped with a roar and a triumphant splash, and at 09.04 JOURNALIST herself was brought up to her starboard anchor.

It had been a very satisfactory piece of work, and all hands had proved themselves worthy of congratulation. The tow had been undertaken in very unfavourable conditions, and both ships had arrived safely in harbour without damage. JOURNALIST and her crew had saved a valuable ship from possible loss, and a salvage award would surely follow. The amount of an award is normally settled by a special court, or by arbitration. Many factors are taken into consideration - the value of the ship saved and her cargo (unfortunately, PARKGATE was empty), the weather conditions, and the degree of effort and skill displayed by the salvors, and so on. In this particular case, the total award was £15,000, of which the owners received £10,000 - it was, after all, their ship which had done the job, and been delayed a week in the process - Captain Wolstenholme received £900; Chief Officer Mitchell £400, Second Officer Dwyer £155, and so on, each according to the measure of his responsibility. No one was left out; even the youngest boy ratings received £30, the equivalent of about $2\frac{1}{2}$ months' wages! The "cure" had been effective, and in this case the "pay" was assured.

Journalist tows the disabled steamer *Parkgate* into Mombasa.

295. BARRISTER (5) 1954-1974 Steel motor ship. Three decks forward, two aft, five holds and deep tank. Two masts. O.N. 185501 8,366g 4,434n 9,670d 447.4 (463.83 o.l.) x 59.4 x 37.9 feet. Cargo capacity: 585,751 cubic feet. Equipped with 70-ton and 60-ton derricks serving numbers 2 and 4 holds respectively.
International Code: MSFP.
4-cyl. 2SCSA oil engine by William Doxford and Sons Ltd., Sunderland; 14 knots.

1.6.1954: Launched by William Doxford and Sons Ltd., Sunderland (Yard No. 794) for the company. *28.9.1954:* Delivered at a cost of £742,315 and later sailed from Liverpool for the West Indies and Spanish Main on her maiden voyage under Captain D. Wolstenholme. *29.1.1958:* Berthed at Capetown when a serious fire engulfed the warehouses adjoining Duncan Dock and Victoria Basin. The vessel was not damaged, but cargo previously discharged was badly affected by water used to extinguish the fire. *21.3.1969:* Rudder damaged while canting off the berth at Market Street, New Orleans. *25.9.1974:* Sold to Empire Maritime Ltd., Monrovia, Liberia (Roussos Brothers, Piraeus, managers) for £500,000 and renamed GEORGE. *1976:* Transferred to Panormitis Marine Co. Ltd., Limassol, Cyprus (Roussos Brothers, Piraeus, managers) and renamed GEORGY. *19.2.1977:* Reported laid up at Piraeus. *1984:* Sold to Spanish shipbreakers. *6:1984:* Broken up at Castellon.

Fourth of the *Governor* class, *Barrister* (above) leaving Capetown homeward bound and deeply laden. She is seen again in the Manchester Ship Canal (below) on 29th September 1974, four days after her sale to Greek owners. She has been renamed *George,* re-registered in Monrovia and had her red funnel band painted out. Discharge had been completed at Manchester, and *George's* holds had to be partly flooded to bring her air draft down to below 70 feet clear the bridges. Her heavy-lift derrick had been raised by the time she reached Ellesmere Port. *[Paul Boot]*

Stern consequences[233]

Second Officer Trevor Platt glanced up from his work to see the enormous form of Zimmer framed in the doorway. "Alright, Zim, just give me three more minutes", he said. Carl Zimmerman eased his massive bulk into the small cabin, and lowered himself ponderously onto the settee which creaked in protest.

"Cap'n Simmons sent me down to see if the plan's ready," he drawled, "He's all set to go". Always the same, last minute rush! Mr. Platt was putting the finishing touches to an elaborate cargo plan which had to be completed, ready for airmailing to Liverpool, before the ship sailed, and, of course, a copy had to be deposited with the agents, Le Blanc-Parr Inc. This copy had particular significance because, from time immemorial, Alfred Le Blanc and his descendants at New Orleans had paid a modest fee to Second Mates for this service, the only agents known to do so, for it was somewhat in breach of company rules. But time had hallowed the practice, and the tradition still survived, despite the prevalent techniques of photocopying.

Consequently, Second Officer Platt was at pains to do a good job for his fee, and pressed on, adding up columns of figures fluently with profound concentration. However, at the back of his mind was the nagging thought that the mean draught was rather dubious - seven inches out, according to his calculations. The Old Man was aware of the discrepancy, and had had the ship sounded round that afternoon. They had found bottom at 28 feet forward, but shelving gradually to 23 feet aft. Without doubt the stern, where the marks indicated a ship's draught of 25' 11", was cosily wedged in the mud. But it was said to be mud of a soft, oozy consistency, and should, in Captain Simmons' opinion, present no obstacle to the ship's departure. This view was later corroborated by the Pilot, who evidently saw no reason to take any special measures to counter what was an extra-normal, if not abnormal, situation.

Trevor Platt gave his slide rule a final flick, inserted a figure, and got up in haste. "Just going to get the Old Man's signature," he said, and bounded up the staircase. He was back within two minutes. "There you are, Zim; all present and correct," he declared confidently, handing over the documents. Zimmerman got up with difficulty, discreetly dropped an envelope on the desk, and shook hands. "Take care, lad," he wheezed. "Have a good voyage, and come back soon." He squeezed through the doorway and lumbered aft in the direction of the gangway.

Carl Zimmerman, Le Blanc's runner, or leg-man, was an indispensable adjunct to the agency's operations. Liable to be called out at any time to meet or sail a ship, Zimmer also attended on board twice daily, his automatic, air-conditioned, all-American limousine on stand-by ready to take the Captain to the office, or sick men to the clinic. He knew where to contact shippers, ship chandlers, ship repair firms, and the various consulates, and was, in fact, a fount of all knowledge appertaining to New Orleans and its environs. He was also a good friend, and knew the ships and their people as well as anyone.

It was dark over the river, but the city glowed and pulsated with life, echoing with the rattle of streetcars, the wail of police sirens, and the beat of sundry jazz sessions on roisterous Bourbon Street. But for once, no one was interested, for the BARRISTER was homeward bound. The pilot, Captain Mike Estarlich, was already on board; the Crescent Towing and Salvage Company's tug E. LUCKENBACH was secured on the port side forward in the US fashion. Then, following Zimmer's departure, the crew lifted and secured the gangway before going to their harbour stations. It was 21.00 on Friday night, 21st March 1969, and up to now, but for the nagging doubt about the mud under the stern, everything had proceeded normally. But a veritable nightmare was about to begin.

It was the custom of the port, when a ship was leaving the wharf, to cast off the headropes, allowing the current acting against the bow to carry the ship's head round into the main stream, thus canting the stern perilously close to the wharf. In order to keep the stern clear of danger the pilot relied on the tug to give the ship headway, using the ship's engines with discretion when clear. But on this solitary occasion the plan did not work. Despite judicious use of the engines and the tug's best efforts, BARRISTER's stern remained stubbornly close to the pilings supporting Market Street Wharf, her unfettered head swinging ever more rapidly as the current tightened its grip. It was starkly obvious that the ship's extreme after parts were firmly trapped by the mud in which they were embedded.

By now the ship was lying at right angles to the wharf, and the pilot ordered the tug to hold the ship up against the stream while he summoned assistance. A second tug, the HUMRICK, positioned itself on the port side aft, but it was beyond the tugs' combined power to hold the ship, or wrestle her clear. An anchor was dropped, but BARRISTER continued to swing through almost 180 degrees, bringing her port side almost parallel with the wharf, with HUMRICK jammed dangerously between the ship's quarter and the wharf, her hawsers burst asunder.

Fortunately, the tug suffered no damage, but many of the wharf's timbers splintered like twigs. The arrival of a third tug, the VIKING, was the decisive factor which eventually succeeded in breaking the ship free of the glutinous suction exerted by the Mississippi mud, but as she broke clear, BARRISTER fouled the pipeline of the dredger TCHEFUNCTA working in the next berth, fortunately causing but little damage. The tugs were now able to work the ship out into mid-stream, but as she manoeuvred into the fairway control was lost, and the ship careered into a flotilla of barges moored close to the opposite bank, cannoning from one to the other, scraping and denting her sides, but mercifully failing to inflict severe damage on the immobile barges. The abrupt loss of control was an ominous indication that the ship's steering gear, subjected to intolerable stresses as the stern post twisted in the mud, had sustained serious damage.

At 02.24 on 22nd March, nearly five hours after the nightmare began, the tugs placed the ship alongside Perry Street Wharf where she was carefully examined. At first, no obvious damage could be found, but after a series of abortive trials later in the day it became lamentably clear that, although helm and indicators were functioning normally, something was seriously amiss with the rudder itself. There was no other course but to put the ship in dry dock, but this could not be contemplated in her present loaded condition. Consequently, several thousand tons of cargo had to be unloaded into barges until a tolerable weight level was achieved, and it was not until 28th March that BARRISTER was able to enter Todd's dry dock.

Exposed at last to the light of day, the rudder stock was found to be twisted through 31 degrees, deflecting the trailing edge of the rudder some three feet to port of the centre-line. Total costs, including dry docking, repairs to ship and wharf, handling cargo out of and back into the ship, amounted to more than $40,000, but in five days, BARRISTER was ready for sea again.

296. DEFENDER (2) 1955-1975 Steel motor ship. Three decks forward, two aft, five holds and deep tank. Two masts. O.N. 187116 8,367g) 4,432n, 9,570d 447.4 (463.83 o.l.) x 59.4 x 37.94 feet. Cargo capacity: 566,090 cubic feet. Equipped with 70-ton and 60-ton derricks serving numbers 2 and 4 holds respectively.
International Code: GTRT.
4-cyl. 2SCSA oil engine by William Doxford and Sons Ltd., Sunderland; 14 knots.

Towards the end of her career, *Defender* is outward bound in the Manchester Ship Canal, passing Ellesmere Port on 2nd October 1974.

[Paul Boot]

23.6.1955: Launched by William Doxford and Sons Ltd., Sunderland (Yard No. 809) for the company. *10.1955:* Delivered at a cost of £829,317 and later sailed from Liverpool for East Africa on her maiden voyage under Captain R.F. Phillips. *26.1.1957:* When outward bound from the Mersey ran aground on the revetment during a westerly gale but was subsequently refloated. *13.3.1964:* Struck by the motor ship PORT NEW PLYMOUTH (13,085/60) whilst in dock at Liverpool, sustaining considerable damage which put her in dry dock for repairs. *19.8.1966:* Put into Durban to carry out major repairs on the main engine. Because of the delay, Lourenço Marques and Beira cargoes were transhipped in the company's INVENTOR. The cost of the repairs was over £9,500. *7.5.1972:* Put into Falmouth with engine trouble and berthed at the County Wharf the following day. *20.5.1972:* Repairs were completed and

sailed for Mombasa. *23.10.1974:* When bound from Rotterdam for Capetown, reported that number 4 main bearings of the main engine had been wiped (i.e. the white metal had worn or melted away). The vessel put into Las Palmas where the bearing was remetalled and the shaft honed. *31.10.1974:* Sailed at 11.45 for Capetown. *7.1975:* Sold to Polimaris Maritime Corporation, Panama (Thenamaris Maritime Inc. Piraeus, Greece, managers) and renamed EUROMARINER under the Greek flag. *20.7.1977:* A major machinery breakdown caused by the entry of water into the lubricating system brought the vessel to a halt whilst on passage from Buenos Aires to Barranquilla. She was towed to Barranquilla, where the cost of repairs proved prohibitive and she was therefore sold to Colombian shipbreakers. *23.9.1977:* Arrived at Cartagena in tow and delivered to the shipbreakers.

"Over the wall's out...."[234]

It was after 20.00 on Saturday 26th January 1957, and the watch had just been relieved. On the bridge of the DEFENDER, outward bound from Birkenhead to East Africa via the Cape of Good Hope with a full cargo, the Master, Captain R.F. Phillips, and Company Pilot Dick Lund were engaged in desultory conversation as they gazed ahead through the wheelhouse windows. It was comparatively warm in the wheelhouse, but when they strolled from time to time into the open starboard wing they felt the full effect of the chill westerly wind which blustered across from the port bow, reaching gale force at times and kicking up a rough chop on the dark waters of the Mersey Estuary. It was a pitch black night, the sky overcast, but the visibility was excellent. Ahead, the Channel buoys could be seen winking cheerfully in a great arc towards the Bar Lightvessel on the horizon. Away on the port bow, the lights of an incoming coaster sparkled like jewels as she cut daringly across Askew Spit, for the tide was nearly full. Close ahead, the brilliant flash of the Crosby Light Float stabbed the darkness, while over to starboard the white stern light of an outward bound steamer glowed steadily. DEFENDER was rapidly overtaking this latter vessel, and as she drew closer those on the bridge could make out the characteristic top structure of a dredger silhouetted darkly against the lights of the Crosby shore. Probably the old, ungainly LEVIATHAN (8,877/09), whose atrocious handling qualities were a byword throughout the Mersey docks. Another light about three cables ahead would prove to be the stern light of the Company's STATESMAN, which had sailed on the same tide.

However, the immediate focus of attention was the large dredger, and the tactics of passing her at a safe distance to starboard, while at the same time passing the Crosby Light Float safely to port. It called for a steady, experienced eye, and a light touch on the wheel.

Third Officer Richard Carter jotted a few notes in the scrap log, and moved to the starboard wing of the bridge as DEFENDER glided past the lumbering dredger, deeply laden with her cargo of silt. He reckoned she was about 350 feet away, while a mere 70 feet away to port the Light Float was pitching and tossing in a choppy sea aggravated by the wash of passing vessels, for it was a busy tide. As the dredger's bows came abreast of DEFENDER's bridge, young Carter was astounded to see the dredger take a pronounced sheer to port, towards DEFENDER. His heart seemed to leap into his throat, choking him. But Pilot Lund had also seen the dredger's crass manoeuvre, and ordered the helm to starboard as the LEVIATHAN (for such it was) continued to close the gap. But for that timely helm order she would have struck DEFENDER somewhere between numbers 4 and 5 holds, with disastrous consequences. As it was, DEFENDER's stern pivoted clear, and LEVIATHAN plunged past. Bosun George Bennett, who was working aft, and had seen all, was badly shaken: "I cannot say how she missed us",

he stated. "She just slid across our stern end; I could have touched her, she was so close!".

But the emergency turn to starboard had to be corrected, and swiftly, for DEFENDER was now charging directly across the narrow channel. Engine and helm orders followed in quick succession, but the crunch they dreaded with fearful anticipation came at 20.14, and the ship shuddered to a halt, her screw churning madly astern, as if to warp time itself and put the clock back to a saner world. For the gravity of the situation was obvious to the Master and Pilot. DEFENDER was hard aground on the Taylor's Bank Revetment, somewhere between Gamma and C10 buoys. The tide was at its peak - if they could not get off now, low water in about six hours time would see the ship perched across the revetment like the plank of a see-saw. It did not require the expertise of a naval architect to imagine the formidable stresses to which a loaded ship would be subjected in such a position. But she would not budge. At 21.15 the New Brighton Lifeboat arrived alongside and stood by all night - just in case its services would be needed.

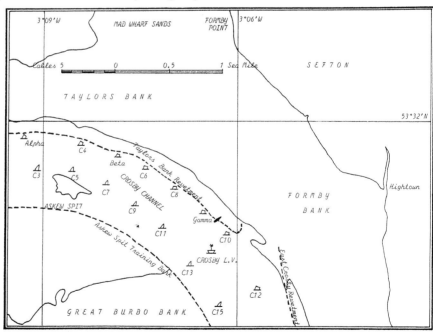

The Crosby Channel

Meanwhile, Captain Phillips had sent out a call for help, specifically tugs, knowing in his heart they could only arrive too late to be of use on this tide. Nevertheless, they had to try. The response was quite outstanding. Towards 22.00 a flotilla of five powerful tugs, HOLM COCK, GREBE COCK, PRAIRIE COCK, GAME COCK, and CROSBY, came storming along Crosby Channel to the aid of the stranded DEFENDER. One wonders how the towing company managed to assemble five crews so quickly at 21.00 on a Saturday night!

Quickly they made fast, and persevered in a valiant bid to drag DEFENDER clear, bursting several towropes in the process. However, towards midnight, when Chief

Engineer Harold Ingram pointed out that the propeller was now partially out of the water, threshing fresh air, it was reluctantly decided that further attempts would be futile before next high water. There was nothing for it but to wait, and suffer with the ship, as the water slowly drained away with the ebb tide.

The revetments, or training banks, had been progressively constructed in the main channels since 1909 (the year, incidentally, that LEVIATHAN came into service). Their purpose was to harness the scouring properties of the tides to maintain the depth of water in the Channels, and to inhibit the encroachments of sand and silt from the extensive banks which spread throughout the estuary. The brainchild of G.F. Lyster, Engineer-in-Chief to the Mersey Conservancy Commission, they were built mainly of limestone from Welsh quarries, or with clay from the excavations of the new docks works, faced with stone. Although the idea was a revolutionary one at the time, the passage of years has proved its worth.[235]

Soundings had been taken with frequent regularity since the stranding, and would continue to be taken throughout the night, both inside and outside the ship. To everyone's relief, and not a little astonishment, soundings inside the ship remained consistently normal, indicating that the integrity of the ship's hull, despite everything, had not been breached. DEFENDER had left Birkenhead on a mean draught of 24 feet 4 inches. Soon after the stranding, soundings taken outside the ship had indicated a depth of water of 30 feet forward, but only 21 feet in the vicinity of number 4 hold. It was then just on high water. But by 01.00 on the Sunday morning, with still about two hours to go to low water, the soundings had fallen to 24 feet forward, and a mere 6 feet abreast number 4. But still the ship remained dry and sound within.

The Taylor's Bank Revetment dries a few feet at low water, and it was just as well the night was dark enough to shroud the utterly desperate nature of the ship's predicament. At 05.40, the M.D. and H.B.'s tender SALVOR came alongside bringing a posse of Dock Board officials, Captain E.P. Simmons, Assistant Marine Superintendent to the Harrison Line, and Pat Wilson, the Ship's Husband. They were followed by the arrival of three more tugs, FIGHTING COCK, THISTLE COCK, and CANNING, and arrangements were made to refloat the ship as high water approached. There was also a radical change of plan, adopted on the advice of Captain Hill of the Dock Board's Marine Survey office.

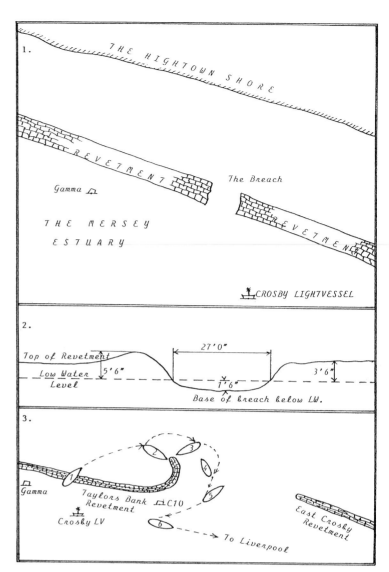

Defender breaches the revetment. The diagrams above, which are not to scale, are based on sketches by Captain D. Fraser and W. Keggin. Below: Assistant Marine Superintendent Captain Donald Fraser (in oilskin coat) gloomily contemplates the damage to the revetment on 16th March 1957.

Instead of trying to tow the ship astern into the main channel, an attempt would be made to move the ship ahead into the uncharted waters east of the revetment. Abreast C10 buoy, the end of the revetment curved inshore, like a horn, and Captain Hill was confident there would be sufficient water to enable the ship to "snub round the horn" into the main channel.

The tugs CROSBY and CANNING made fast forward, GAME COCK aft, and at 07.46 on Sunday 27th January, the ship's engines were set at full ahead, while the tugs strained away on their heavy towing springs. The response was immediate. The ship moved ahead, slowly at first, then faster, and the engines were slowed down. At 07.48 DEFENDER was clear of all obstructions and heading easterly towards the "horn" of the revetment. At 08.07, the ship took the ground again, this time with her bow wedged in the soft sand off the "horn". The tugs had to struggle to drag her clear, and all parted their lines in succession. But the incoming tide was helping the ship round, and at 09.06 she was moving astern under her own power, swinging into the

deep water of the Crosby Channel, and by 09.10 was heading upriver towards an anchorage off Gladstone Dock. Two hours later she entered the lock and at 12.55 was safely berthed in South West Gladstone No. 1 - her bilges still bone dry!

On 16th March, 1957, a group representing various interested parties left Liverpool Landing Stage in the tender SALVOR bound for the revetment off Crosby. The group included Captain D. Fraser, Captain E.P. Simmons, and W. Keggin of Harrisons; representatives of the Dock Board; and two photographers. Their brief was to conduct an examination of the revetment, and agree on the extent of the damage caused by DEFENDER's excursion over the wall. They found that the gap in the revetment between C10 and GAMMA buoys measured 27 feet across, and a mound of stones, rising two feet above the average level of the wall, was piled up on the western side of the breach. If any further proof were needed, traces of red bottom composition paint similar to that used on all Harrison ships, were found adhering to the stones. In the centre of the breach, the depth of water at low tide was 18 inches.

297. ADMINISTRATOR 1958-1978 Steel motor ship. Three decks forward, two aft, five holds. Three masts and a signal mast. O.N. 187193 8,714g 4,725n 11,455d (11,953d from 1968) 467.8 (488.8 o.l.) x 62.3 x 39.7 feet. Cargo capacity: 592,880 cubic feet. Equipped with two 70-ton derricks serving the main holds.
International Code: GXPN.
6-cyl. 2SCSA oil engine by William Doxford and Sons (Engineers) Ltd., Sunderland; 15½ knots.

Pictured on trials in the North Sea in August 1959, *Administrator* was the first of three sisters. They could be distinguished from earlier motor ships by their short forecastles.
[Turners (Photography) Ltd.]

20.3.1958: Launched by William Doxford and Sons (Shipbuilders) Ltd., Sunderland (Yard No. 826) for Ruthin Steamship Co. Ltd., Hamilton, Bermuda. (This was a wholly owned subsidiary of Charente Steam-Ship Co. Ltd. and the vessel was immediately bare-boat chartered to Charente at a rate of £13,500 per month.) *22.7.1958:* Delivered at a cost of £1,171,949 and later sailed from Liverpool to the West Indies and Spanish Main on her maiden voyage under Captain T.B. Littlechild. *25.2.1966:* Registered in the name of Charente Steam-Ship Co. Ltd. *6.2.1973:* The vessel was at the centre of a crippling strike at Liverpool, which brought the port and 29 vessels to a standstill. At its height 4,000 dockers were on strike for a week. It concerned the tight stowage of a cargo of cotton from Port Sudan which was being discharged from the vessel at Sandon Dock. Dockers were finding the bales difficult to move, and this was having a debilitating effect on their bonus pay. They walked off the ship, and the rest of the port demonstrated its solidarity by following suit. The men returned to work on 13.2.1973 while

a joint committee investigated the cause of the dispute and the manner of its resolution. *31.7.1978:* Sold to Stena Atlantic Line Ltd., Hamilton, Bermuda (Sten A. Olsson, Gothenburg, Sweden) for US$367,500 and renamed TYNE. *8.1978:* Resold to Oriental Maritime (Pte.) Ltd., Singapore and renamed ORIENTAL SEA. *1978:* Sold to Trans Overseas Ltd., Bangladesh for demolition. *29.12.1978:* Arrived at Chittagong.

Sanspareil
It was widely accepted that ADMINISTRATOR and her sisters AUTHOR and PLAINSMAN were the finest ships ever built by T. and J. Harrison for the general cargo trades. Somewhat larger and more powerful than their Doxford predecessors, they could carry almost 2,000 tons more cargo at a service speed of 15½ knots. When, in the early sixties, true-motion radar, automatic steering and air-conditioning were installed, they were 'sanspareil'.

Harrison cadets

A scheme for training boys straight from school to become deck officers seems to have started early in the last century. A summary of seagoing employees compiled in 1906 lists only seven cadets at a time when the fleet numbered 39 ships. Previously, boys were trained by serving as indentured apprentices, especially in sailing ships where six or eight boys were regularly assigned to the 'half deck'. Apparently, fewer legal formalities were required with cadets, but the parent or guardian was required to deposit a premium, usually £50, with the company, which was refunded with interest when the young man finished serving his time. Boys entered at 16 and, between the wars, were paid 10 shillings (50 pence) per month, which increased by annual increments to £2 in the fourth year. By the time he attained the age of 20 or 21, he was expected to have passed for his Second Mate's Certificate, when a job as Third or Fourth Mate was guaranteed. These photographs are from a company brochure aimed at recruiting cadets in post-war years when facilities and pay for cadets had improved enormously.

A cadet in a double-berth cabin.

The study room adjacent to the cadets' cabin.

The officers' lounge.

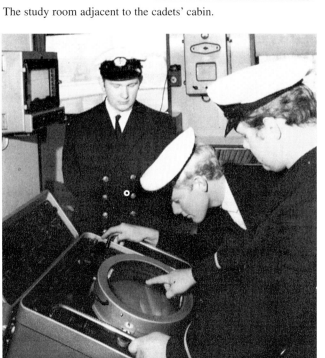

Radar instruction.

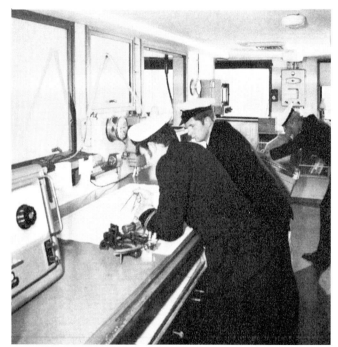

Chart work.

272

Cadets taking sights.

Training in helmsmanship.

Instruction in the rigging loft.

The three cadets seen right splicing a wire hawser.

Assembling a purchase block. The cadets are, from left to right: A. Gatiss; V.S. Richardson and J.H. Brierley.

298. AUTHOR (4) 1958-1978 Steel motor ship. Three decks forward, two aft and five holds. Three masts and a signal mast. O.N. 301282 8,715g 4,729n 11,455d (11,953 dwt after 8.1968) 467.8 (488.8 o.l.) x 62.3 x 39.7 feet. Cargo capacity: 534,010 cubic feet. Equipped with two 70-ton derricks serving the main holds.
International Code: GXSY.
6-cyl. 2SCSA oil engine by William Doxford and Sons (Engineers) Ltd., Sunderland; 15½ knots.

Author in the Mersey.   *[J. and M. Clarkson]*

4.6.1958: Launched by William Doxford and Sons (Shipbuilders) Ltd., Sunderland (Yard No. 827) for Ruthin Steamship Co. Ltd., Hamilton, Bermuda. (This was a wholly owned subsidiary of Charente Steam-Ship Co. Ltd. and the vessel was immediately bare-boat chartered to Charente at a rate of £7,000 per month.) 24.9.1958: Delivered at a cost of £1,164,226 and later sailed from Liverpool for the Spanish Main on her maiden voyage under Captain J.L. Curle. 5.11.1961: Fire broke out in a consignment of carbon black in number 1 lower hold when the vessel was moored at Number 5 Long Reach Dock, Houston. The hatch was sealed and carbon dioxide was injected into the compartment. The Houston Fire Brigade was called and further cylinders of carbon dioxide were injected. The hatch was then opened and two men wearing breathing apparatus descended into the hold and located the fire. They commenced the process of damping down, which involved the application of several high-pressure hoses, the jets of which destroyed those bags of carbon black which had not yet been destroyed by fire. The fire proved to be unduly stubborn, and at 17.00 the hold was again covered and sealed while further cylinders of carbon dioxide were injected. After 90 minutes, the hatches were opened again and the firemen were surprised to see the fire still smouldering and further damping down was commenced. A gang of longshoremen was at last able to get at what was left of the cargo, and discharge it to the quay. After the remains of the solid cargo had been unloaded the residue - which covered the tank top, spread up the vessel's sides, and choked the bilges - was removed by high-pressure hoses and a detergent mix. The consignment of 111 tons of carbon black was not replaced, instead the space was reserved for shipments of mahogany and wood pulp to be loaded at Pensacola and Panama City.[236] 31.5.1962: Sailed from Capetown for Avonmouth loaded full, and down to her marks with 10,261 tons of cargo. A record lift for a ship of her class and not surpassed until the advent of much

larger bulk carriers and container ships in the 1970s.[237] 25.2.1966: Registered in the name of Charente Steam-Ship Co. Ltd. 22.12.1966: When sailing in the Houston Ship Channel bound from Houston to New Orleans in collision with the US derrick-barge H.A. LINDSAY, towed by the tug PAN AMERICAN. The vessel was badly damaged and put into Galveston for repairs, which occupied 12 days. The total of insured claims exceeded £75,000. 21.7.1978: Sold to Stena Atlantic Line Ltd., Hamilton, Bermuda (Sten A. Olsson, Gothenburg, Sweden) for US$367,500 and renamed HUMBER. 30.7.1978: Entered Falmouth with engine trouble. 5.8.1978: Sailed for Kiel. 13.8.1978: A fire caused further damage in the engine room and the vessel was towed to Werft Nobiskrug GmbH, Rendsburg for repair. 11.10.1978: Reported stopped and disabled in the Red Sea due to a breakdown of the main engines. 18.10.1978: Eventually arrived off Karachi. 9.11.78: After berthing and discharging her cargo she was laid up awaiting repair. 1979: Sold to Muslim Rolling Mills Ltd. for demolition. 25.2.1979: Delivered at Gadani Beach. 18.6.1979: Demolition commenced.

Author outward bound passing Birkenhead shortly after her sale to Stena Atlantic Line Ltd. Her funnel has been painted black, but her new name *Humber* has not yet been applied.

[Paul Boot]

274

Violent encounter in the Houston Ship Channel[238]

AUTHOR sailed from Pier 2, Long Reach Docks, Houston, on 22nd December 1966 at 19.00, bound for New Orleans. She was flying light, having only 1,848 tons of cargo on board, and the evening was quite dark. There had been a time in the recent past when no Harrison shipmaster would have dreamt of hazarding his ship in the tortuous waters of the Houston Ship Channel after sunset. But times had changed, and the emphasis was on despatch insofar as (at the Master's discretion, of course) it was safe to proceed. Tonight the weather was fine, calm and clear; there was a moon; visibility was excellent, and the Channel was known to be well marked with buoys and range beacons. Consequently, Captain Robert Sutcliffe had no qualms about making his decision, and the ship sailed on schedule under the guiding hand of Houston Pilot J.B. Niday junior. The radar was switched on, but thanks to the excellent visibility, was not being closely monitored.

The difficult passage through the close confines of the upper reaches of the Channel passed without incident. As the ship approached Baytown, speed was reduced to a crawl to avoid disturbing the ships which were moored there. At 21.32, when AUTHOR had cleared the berths, speed was increased to full ahead. About one mile downstream was a fairly tight left-hand bend, and beyond the flat promontory could be seen the lights of a tug and tow approaching the bend from the other side. These were later identified as the tug PAN AMERICAN towing the derrick-barge H.A. LINDSAY. Otherwise, the channel appeared clear. However, shortly after 21.35, a small, dim white light, ostensibly the stern light of another vessel heading in the same direction, appeared ahead. AUTHOR was overtaking rapidly, and the pilot sounded a two-blast whistle signal to indicate that AUTHOR intended to overtake on the other vessel's port side. As the ships drew nearer, they could make out her

name, CHUCK HOBART, a tug secured astern of a pair of barges, pushing them along in the manner peculiar to tugs in US coastal waters. Suddenly, with the tug two or three cables ahead, it became clear to Captain Sutcliffe and the pilot that the HOBART's course was converging slightly with AUTHOR's track-line, raising the spectre of collision. Fuming, Pilot Niday sounded a single short blast, and at 21.38 pulled the ship's head round to overtake the tow on its starboard side. Perversely, as the vessels drew closer, HOBART took a sheer to starboard, crowding AUTHOR towards the bank. At 21.39, almost beside himself with frustration, the pilot swung the ship to port, narrowly missing HOBART's stern, sounding the emergency signal as AUTHOR swung inevitably into the path of the advancing PAN AMERICAN and her tow. A derrick barge loaded with massive sections of oil rig is an awesome sight at the best of times, but at night, on a collision course in a narrow, suddenly crowded channel, it would be positively terrifying.

At 21.40 AUTHOR's helm was swung hard-a-starboard; the engine room telegraph demanded full speed astern. The tug, PAN AMERICAN, swept clear, but there was no chance of avoiding the unwieldy barge and its menacing load. At 21.41 the vessels clashed like armoured jousting knights, the derrick barge slicing along AUTHOR's flank, cleaving it open. Unfortunately, one man on the barge was injured, but damage was restricted to plates above the waterline. Consequently, AUTHOR was able to proceed down channel to Galveston, where preparations were put in hand to repair the damage. The ship was delayed 15 days, and total claims on the underwriters amounted to about £75,000. When the ship sailed from Galveston on 7th January, bound for New Orleans, memories of the festive season must have been very dim indeed.

---

299. PLAINSMAN 1959-1979 Steel motor ship. Three decks forward, two aft and five holds. Three masts and a signal mast. O.N. 301313 8,732g 4,727n 11,455d (11,953d after 2.1970) 467.8 (488.8 o.l.) x 62.3 x 39.7 feet. Cargo capacity: 599,230 cubic feet. Equipped with two 70-ton derricks serving the main holds.
International Code: GDTA.
6-cyl. 2SCSA oil engine by William Doxford and Sons (Engineers) Ltd., Sunderland; 15½ knots.

4.11.1958: Keel laid. *21.5.1959:* Launched by William Doxford and Sons (Shipbuilders) Ltd., Sunderland (Yard No. 835) for the company. *20.8.1959:* Delivered at a cost of £1,177,666 and later sailed from Liverpool for Kingston, Jamaica and Mexico on her maiden voyage under Captain J.L. Curle. *27.10.1969:* Whilst berthed in the South East Canada Dock 2, Liverpool, fire broke out in the vessel's accommodation. The alarm was given at 20.00 and the fire was extinguished by the local fire brigade one hour later. This was the forerunner of several fires during the voyage. *19.6.1970:* Shortly after midnight a fire in the engine room was quickly extinguished whilst the vessel was in London. It was apparently caused by a flashback from the lower boiler. *27.4.1976:* A much more serious fire afflicted the vessel

while she was berthed at Number 9 Dock, Manchester. The accommodation was gutted, and the main switchboard was damaged. *18.5.1976:* Left Manchester in tow of two tugs and on reaching the Mersey was taken in tow by the ocean-going tug FAIRPLAY X (298/67). The vessel was then towed north-about to Swan, Hunter and Wigham Richardson Ltd., Wallsend for a major refit. She returned to service in July. *1.1979:* Sold to Motivo Compania Naviera S.A., Panama for US$615,000 and renamed EVLALIA. *1980:* Sold to Ierax Compania Naviera S.A., Panama (Canopus Shipping S.A., Athens (Andreas and George Kyrtatas) managers) under the Greek flag. *1985:* Sold to Nigdeliler A.S., Turkey, for demolition. *15.1.1985:* Arrived at Aliaga in tow from Piraeus where she had been laid up from 4.3.1982 to 11.1.1985.

Plainsman arriving at Liverpool on 24th May 1959. She was the last of the three ships of the *Administrator* class.   *[Paul Boot]*

275

A pyromaniac afloat

On 27th October 1969 PLAINSMAN was berthed on the south east berth of Number 2 Branch of the Canada Dock. The dockers had finished work for the day, and the duty officer, J.W. Henderson, had made his rounds and noted nothing unusual. However, towards 20.00 he was sure he could smell smoke, and left his cabin to investigate. He met the alarmed ship's carpenter, Mr. Sinclair, who was on his way up to report that the crew's quarters were on fire. Sure enough, dense smoke and fumes were billowing up from the lower alleyways, so much so that it was impossible to advance further to warn people who may have been trapped in their cabins. Fortunately, those which were occupied had already been evacuated. The Duty Officer sounded the alarm, and hastened to the nearest telephone to dial 999 to summon the fire brigade. It was by then 20.05.

Seven minutes later the fire brigade's appliance was alongside the ship, and the firemen quickly located the seat of the fire which was in the Petty Officers' messroom on the lower deck, port side. Hoses were run out on board, and firemen wearing breathing apparatus soon had two or three jets playing into the area. By 21.00 the fire was under control, and twenty minutes later the Chief Fire Officer was able to declare the fire extinguished.

There was a great deal of clearing up to do, and a great deal of damage to repair. The steelwork in the vicinity of the fire was buckled, and all fittings and furniture destroyed. Even the deck-head beams and pillars supporting the accommodation decks above were distorted. Electric wiring and switches were ruined, and throughout the accommodation a greasy black film covered everything.

How did it happen? There was no clear answer to this question, despite a searching internal enquiry. The two principal theories were (a) That some person or persons unknown had left the electrical grill switched on and, due to a fault, the cut-out switch had failed to operate; or (b) That a discarded cigarette had fallen into the crevices of a settee and ignited it. Whatever the cause, all were agreed that, however regrettable the incident, nothing more sinister than simple accident or human carelessness lay behind it.

Opinions were to change in the light of disturbingly similar outbreaks which were to occur a few months later. On 20th February 1970, whilst the ship was lying at Port of Spain, Trinidad, the donkeyman on duty raised the alarm at 02.05, when he saw smoke rising from the lower port alleyway in the crew's accommodation. The fire brigade was called, and Second Office B. Raper donned breathing apparatus. He descended into the smoke-filled alleyway and found that a settee in the Petty Officers' messroom was well alight, belching forth clouds of acrid smoke - a carbon copy of the recent fire in Liverpool, if ever there was one. It was promptly dealt with, and although damage was considerable, it was by no means as extensive as in the previous outbreak. Everyone marvelled at the coincidence which brought about two conflagrations in the same place on the same ship within the span of a few months.

The coincidence theory began to look decidedly thin, however, when, two nights later, the alarm bells again summoned the crew on deck at 01.05. Fire had broken out in the customs' room, an unoccupied cabin on the port side of the main deck. Again, thick volumes of smoke threatened any members of the crew who did not evacuate the accommodation promptly. A hose was rigged, and a jet of water soon played on the fire through a smashed porthole. The fire brigade arrived, but within half an hour the blaze was out. Again, damage to fittings and furniture was substantial.

Puzzled investigators looked in vain for a cause, and were still pondering the problem when the alarm was raised yet again at 04.20! Across the transverse alleyway from the burnt-out customs' room the cabin of one of the ship's stewards was well alight. Bleary-eyed crew members, many suffering from the

The owner's suite on *Plainsman* with bulkheads panelled in satin wood.

The officers' smokeroom, with bulkheads panelled in oak veneer.

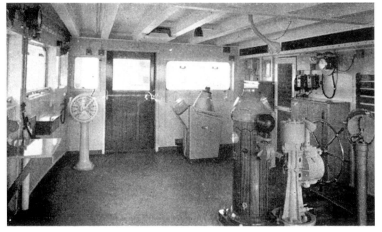

Plainsman's bridge.

276

effects of a drinking bout which had lasted until well into the small hours, staggered out on deck. Again, hoses were brought to bear, and by 05.00 only a pall of evil-smelling smoke remained, but again there was a great deal of damage.

This was all getting to be a bit too much for Captain Fred Scriven, who felt matters were getting out of hand. He called in the Trinidad C.I.D., convinced there was a fire raiser on board, and believing that a disaffected crew member was behind the series of fires. His crew that voyage harboured a bunch of delinquents, hard-drinking trouble-makers, and in the three weeks since the ship had left London no less than twelve entries in the logbook dealt with drink-related offences for which the appropriate fines and forfeitures had been levied. However, the police investigation was inconclusive.

They had their suspicions, but no evidence which would stand up in court. On 24th February, the day after the latest incident, the entire crew was discharged, nine of them with bad reports, or rather with reports ranging from the euphemistic "Good" (instead of "Very Good", and so, by implication, meaning "Bad"), to the noncommittal, but terminal, "D.R." - "Decline to Report". They were then driven to the airport and flown home, their berths on board PLAINSMAN occupied by a West Indian crew signed on locally. The Master had sufficient grounds for this action without laying charges of arson, for the men's conduct during the past three weeks had indeed been deplorable. Consequently, they were unlikely to find employment in another Harrison ship, or indeed, anywhere, for a long time to come. Captain Scriven and the remainder of his crew simply hoped that he had cast his net wide enough to snare the real culprit, whose vengeful, malicious nature had sought to endanger not only the ship, but the lives of his shipmates.[239]

300. ADVENTURER 1960-1979 Steel motor ship. Two decks and five holds. One mast.
O.N. 301316 8,971g 4,794n 10,900d (11,266 dwt after 1968). 469.7 (490.25 o.l.) x 65.25 x 37.9 feet. Cargo capacity: 610,270 cubic feet. Equipped with 180-ton Stülcken heavy-lift derrick.
International Code: GFCE.
6-cyl. 2SCSA oil engine by William Doxford and Sons (Engineers) Ltd., Sunderland; 15 knots.

Two views of *Adventurer:* with her pioneering design and Stülcken derrick, she was well named.

15.12.1958: Keel laid. *21.7.1959:* Launched by William Doxford and Sons (Shipbuilders) Ltd., Sunderland (Yard No. 834) for the company. *11.2.1960:* Delivered at a cost of £1,383,274 and later sailed from Liverpool for the West Indies and the Spanish Main on her maiden voyage under Captain L.J. Sharman, RD, RNR (Retired). *26.4.1963:* When lying at Assab, Ethiopia it was reported at 18.40 that number 5 hold was on fire. The vessel and cargo were to suffer considerable damage before the fire was extinguished some 28 hours later, and the risks associated with the incident were doubly enhanced by the presence of hazardous chemicals. *25.10.1979:* Sold to Prospel Maritime Ltd., (European Navigation Inc (S. Karnessis and D. Vlassakis), managers), Piraeus Greece, and renamed ELEFTHERIA. *1985:* Sold to Eleftheria Navigation Co. Ltd., Malta and resold to Haji Abdul Karim and Co., Pakistan, for demolition. *20.4.1985:*

Arrived at Karachi. *11.5.1985:* Work commenced at Gadani Beach.

A real adventurer

The ADVENTURER was fundamentally different from any Harrison vessel that had gone before. As a heavy-lift ship she was designed to carry very large bulky pieces both on deck and in the hold. To attain maximum efficient use of space, the uniformly shaped centre body of the vessel (numbers 3 and 4 holds) was always available for such cargo; while at the ends - numbers 1 and 2 holds forward, engine room space and number 5 hold aft - the compartments narrowed to a comparatively smaller capacity.

To compensate for the 920-ton weight of the main engines situated so far abaft the vessel's centre of gravity, number 2 hold was adapted for use as a deep tank in the light, ballasted condition.

By far the most outwardly striking feature was the heavy-lift derrick itself, forked at its peak, flanked by a pair of massive inclined samson-posts, and capable of lifting 180 tons. A quartet of powerful electric winches, their drums carrying endless fathoms of $4\frac{3}{4}$-inch steel wire, clustered round the derrick heel, controlled from four eyries perched half-way up the Samson posts. This was the justly celebrated Stülcken derrick, a German patent, installed and tested at Hamburg by Stülcken Sohn before the vessel went into service. At the time of its installation it was the largest of its kind afloat, and the only one of its type installed in a British ship - a genuine first for Harrisons. Two of the derrick's many good features were its versatility in use, capable of plumbing either number 3 or number 4 hold, and the speed with which it could be prepared - a mere 15 minutes compared with the hour or two it took to prepare conventional jumbo derricks.

Of necessity, most of the accommodation was situated aft, above the engine room. Normally, the navigating bridge would have been placed aft, too, but it was felt that the Stülcken complex,

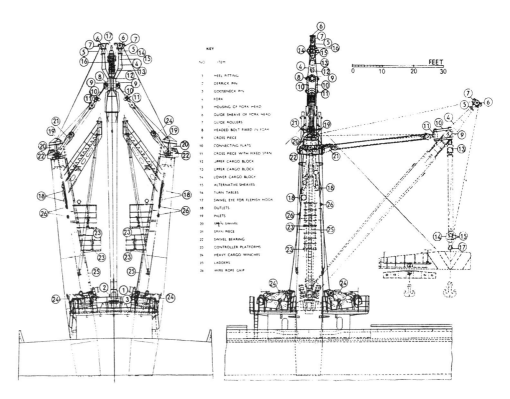

General arrangement of the Stülcken derrick on *Adventurer.*

intervening between bridge and horizon, would restrict the view of navigators unduly. Consequently, the bridge was constructed in the fore-part of the vessel, abaft number 2 hatch, the structure also providing accommodation for the Master and his team of deck officers. In practice, this truncated structure was as isolated as the Wolf Rock Lighthouse in heavy weather, but a small, well-stocked messroom, fitted with basic cooking facilities, and manned by the officers' steward rendered that isolation bearable in stormy conditions.

A conflagration of chemicals

The threat was a serious one, for, as the officers were acutely aware, number 5 hold and 'tween decks were loaded with all manner of hazardous chemicals. Anchored off Assab, Ethiopia on the evening of 26th April 1963 about 18.30 smoke was seen drifting from the ventilators at number 5 hold. The alarm was raised; the hatch sealed; and the contents of twenty carbon dioxide gas bottles injected promptly into the affected compartments. With no prospect of any help coming from the shore at that time, the crew was mobilised to shift about 100 drums of dangerous deck cargo - methanol and liquid chlorine - away from the hatch coamings to a place of comparative safety. Hoses were rigged with the object of cooling the deck, but they could not be used in the hold because of the presence of chemicals known to react violently with water. Meanwhile, injection of carbon dioxide had been hampered by a fractured pipe, which was quickly repaired by members of the engine room staff.

About an hour after the alarm was raised, the first of three muffled explosions was heard. Captain Sharman and Chief Officer Stan Bladon rightly, as it turned out, attributed these blasts to cylinders of Arcton gas stowed in the upper 'tween deck with some bales of cotton. The flames had evidently reached them. Further charges of carbon dioxide were injected, and the treatment repeated at intervals throughout the night, while hoses continued to drench the surrounding steelwork. Next morning, the decks and steel hatches were much cooler.

A section of hatch was opened, releasing a cloud of smoke, and a team of volunteers wearing breathing apparatus and led by the Chief Officer entered the still burning hold, dealing in passing with blazing bales and boxes with portable fire extinguishers. However, the main conflagration was confined to the forward part of the hatch, and seemed to be under control. Meanwhile, a gang of labourers from the shore had appeared, and were put to work unloading all the accessible cargo they could lay hands on, which included consignments of carbide and cyanide. Which was just as well, for at 10.00 the blaze flared up again, the smoke billowed forth, and the hatch was hastily evacuated, covered, and sealed. Another 20 bottles of carbon dioxide were injected, but at 12.25 another explosion, apparently the petrol tank of a Land Rover stowed in the lower 'tween deck, suggested that the fire was gaining ground. Supplies of carbon dioxide were running low by this time, and Captain Sharman decided that the only thing to do was to make a determined attack with water. Most of the water-hazardous cargo had been removed, but some still remained. He had to take the chance, but avoiding the area where it was known to be stowed as much as possible.

The hatch was re-opened, and five hoses poured water into the lower 'tween deck, drenching the blazing cargo, and sending up clouds of steam. After battling for an hour, the fire was under control, and the labourers were able to resume unloading. But it was 22.00 before the hold was clear, and cool enough to conduct a survey. The hatch coamings and adjacent deck plating had been distorted and buckled by the heat, wooden hatch-boards disintegrated to charred matchwood, and an unquantifiable amount of cargo had been destroyed or damaged. There was much clearing up to be done, and considerable amounts of damaged and volatile cargo had to be disposed of. Lack of any adequate facilities ashore led to this noxious detritus being jettisoned at sea, while on passage from Assab to Djibouti.

The cause of the fire was never conclusively established. When all the Assab cargo had been discharged from number 5, the hatch had been searched by three officers at about 15.00, and nothing untoward had been revealed. Yet three hours or so later, the hatch was ablaze. The possibility of arson could not be ruled out, of course, but the most likely cause lay in a consignment of active carbon stowed in the lower 'tween deck. This substance heated up rapidly in contact with moisture, and condensation dripping from above may have been sufficient to start a chain reaction. Another school of thought believed that spontaneous combustion in the consignment of cotton could have been the cause. But whatever the cause, the consequences had been bad enough (about £15,000 for repairs and General Average expenses; far more for lost cargo) and, but for a courageous and determined effort by the ship's crew to get on top of the situation, it could have been far worse.[240]

301. PLANTER (3) 1961-1962 (see COLONIAL (3) No.284)

302. CUSTODIAN (3) 1961-1979 Steel motor ship. Three decks forward, two aft and five holds. One mast.
O.N. 301366 8,847g 4,849n 10,920d (11,393d after 1971). 467.35 (489.0 o.l.) x 62.3 x 38.9 feet. Cargo capacity: 614,390 cubic feet. Equipped with 110-ton Stülcken heavy-lift derrick, serving numbers 3 and 4 holds.
International Code: GHKG.
6-cyl. 2SCSA oil engine by William Doxford and Sons (Engineers) Ltd., Sunderland; 16 knots.

The *Custodian* was a development of the *Adventurer* design.

18.3.1960: Keel laid. *5.10.1960:* Launched by William Doxford and Sons (Shipbuilders) Ltd., Sunderland (Yard No.844) for the company. *16.2.1961:* Delivered at a cost of £1,364,931 and later sailed from Birkenhead to East Africa on her maiden voyage under Captain A.H. Thompson. *26.4.1963:* When on passage from Birkenhead to Durban fire was discovered at 07.15 in number 1 lower 'tween deck. The hatch was sealed, and carbon dioxide gas introduced to smother the blaze. She altered course for Walvis Bay. *27.4.1963:* Arrived and began discharging cargo from the still burning hatch under the supervision of the local fire brigade. The seat of the fire was located in a consignment of activated carbon. *2.5.1963:* Resumed her voyage, calling at Capetown to replenish her depleted supply of carbon dioxide cylinders. *2.5.1967:* The main engine failed to go ahead when leaving the berth at Lobito, Angola. She had sternway and touched the bank with her stern before the anchors brought her up. Rudder and stock were damaged, being set over 14 degrees to starboard. Temporary repairs were carried out. *7.5.1967:* Left Lobito Bay escorted by EXPLORER (304). *11.5.1967:* Arrived at Capetown. *23.9.1975:* At about 13.30, Captain Eric Sherlock conned his vessel round Sandy Island in the approaches to St. John's Harbour, Antigua and swung onto the leading marks with Fort James in line with the cathedral bearing 110 degrees. At 13.37 speed was reduced, and the engines stopped at 13.39. The vessel, however, was carrying too much way and, to aggravate matters, when the "full astern" order came it was unaccountably delayed in execution. She overshot her chosen anchorage and ran aground on the sandy, shelving bottom of James Ground at 13.43. There she remained, hard and fast, until refloated at 16.39 with the aid of the tugs USHER and PATHFINDER. An inspection of the vessel's forefoot indicated no obvious damage. Meanwhile, the tug's claim for compensation was the subject of some haggling in the Agent's office. Lloyd's Salvage agreement had not been signed and the compensation was a matter for mutual agreement if expensive litigation was to be avoided. The sum anticipated was £1,250, reduced to £750 by negotiation. *30.8.1979:* Sold to Patmos Navigation Co. Ltd., Limassol, Cyprus (Thenamaris Maritime Inc., Piraeus, Greece,

managers) for US$850,000 and renamed SEA PEARL. *1981:* Sold to Cactus Shipping Co. Ltd., Limassol, Cyprus (Mighty Management S.A. (Vas. Maltezos), Piraeus, Greece, managers) and renamed MIGHTY PEARL. *1.1.1982:* When bound from St. Lawrence to St. John, New Brunswick smoke was seen rising from the main thrust bearing. She stopped briefly and then resumed her voyage at slow speed. When the thrust bearing was subsequently opened up it was found to be severely damaged, with the pads burnt out, and collar scored and torn. Attempts to turn the engine were abandoned when the turning-gear was lifted from its seating. The seizure was caused by a jammed thrust pad. These and other repairs were carried out at St. John. *27.1.1982:* Sailed for Kingston, Jamaica. *2.2.1982:* Reported aground on a reef, 500 yards southeast of Great Inagua Island, Bahamas in position 20.59N, 73.07W whilst on a voyage from Montreal to Kingston, Jamaica with general cargo including wood pulp and asbestos. There was reported to be 12 feet of water in the engine room and the vessel was abandoned. Although much of the cargo was salvaged, the ship and machinery were declared a total loss, and she was scuttled.

The last moments of *Mighty Pearl,* ex-*Custodian.*

[Laurence Dunn]

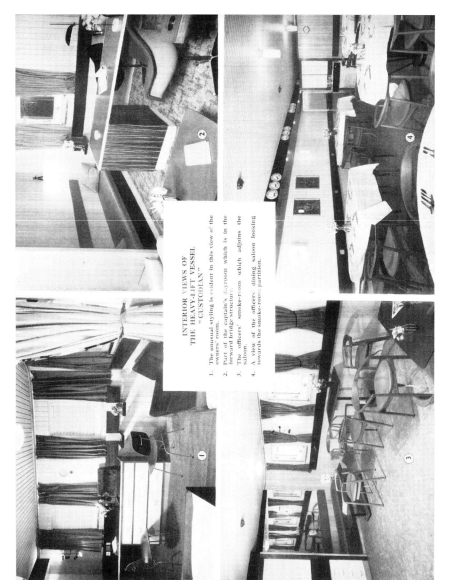

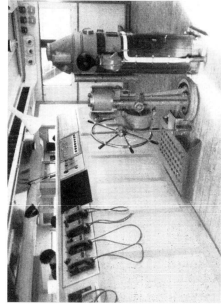

INTERIOR VIEWS OF
THE HEAVY-LIFT VESSEL
"CUSTODIAN."

1. The unusual styling is evident in this view of the owners' room.

2. Part of the captain's dayroom which is in the forward bridge structure.

3. The officers' smoke-room which adjoins the saloon.

4. A view of the officers' dining saloon looking towards the smoke-room partition.

Above: *Custodian's* 110-ton Stülcken derrick discharging a 100-ton transformer at Port Elizabeth. [*M.D.R. Jones*]

Near right lower: *Custodian's* chartroom with true-motion radar and echo sounder.

Far right lower: the wheelhouse.

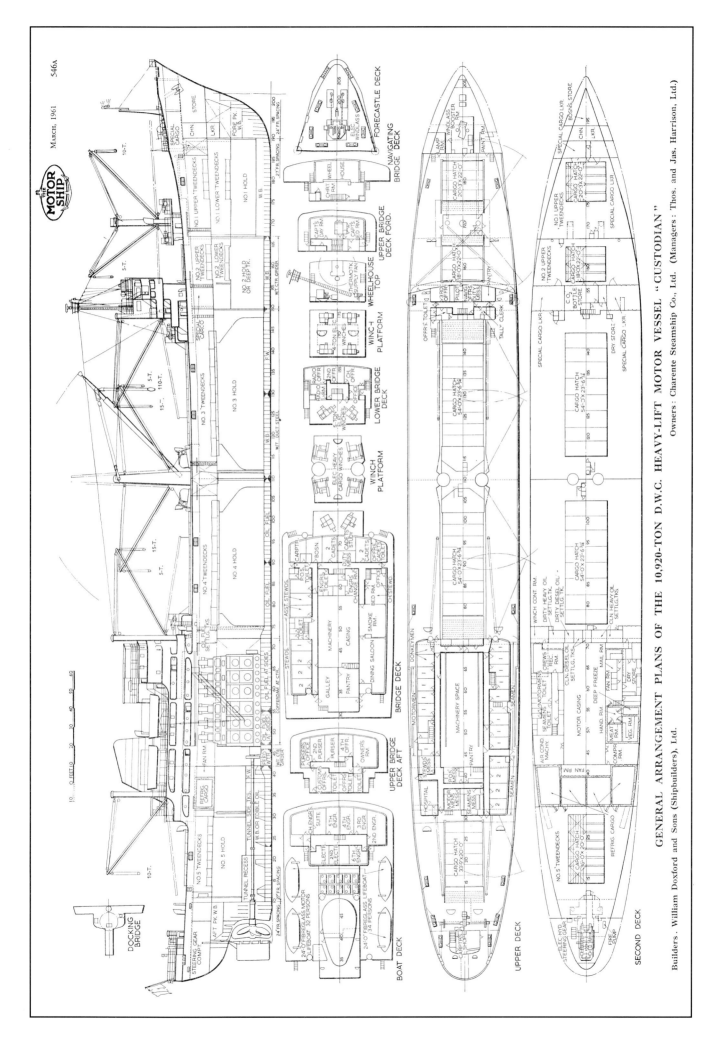

GENERAL ARRANGEMENT PLANS OF THE 10,920-TON D.W.C. HEAVY-LIFT MOTOR VESSEL "CUSTODIAN"

Owners: Charente Steamship Co., Ltd. (Managers: Thos. and Jas. Harrison, Ltd.)

Builders. William Doxford and Sons (Shipbuilders), Ltd.

The ship with the gammy rudder

Rule 6 (as it then was) of the company's Rule Book was sacrosanct. It dealt with the testing of essential equipment - telegraphs, whistles, steering gear, and, by implication, the main engines - before leaving a berth or anchorage. Not only was it a rule, but common prudence decreed that, in everyone's interest, it was the intelligent thing to do, and only the most unusual circumstances could be permitted to militate against its implementation. However, running the main engines, ahead and astern, while tied up alongside a congested quay, can be quite hazardous, no matter how gently the controls are handled. Moorings must be set up as tightly as possible, perhaps supplemented with extra hawsers. Ships in the adjacent berths ahead and astern have to be warned, and, finally, the harbour master's office must be advised, and permission sought to carry out the test. This often constituted a stumbling block. Some harbour masters, perhaps haunted by the memory of some disastrous mishap in the past, are very reluctant to grant, and are even adamant in refusing, permission. In such cases the ship is obliged to sail without the reassuring test, and in nine cases out of ten no harm comes of it. CUSTODIAN's, however, was the legendary tenth case.

On 2nd May 1967, prior to the ship's departure from Lobito, all the customary tests were carried out satisfactorily at 07.15 that morning, with the exception of the vital main engine test. Chief Engineer Alan Humphrey was concerned, for a considerable amount of maintenance work had been carried out on one of the units while the ship had been in port. But permission on this occasion was not forthcoming, the excuse offered being the unreliability of suspect bollards, i.e. the mooring posts on the quay. Alan Humphrey, therefore, was constrained to check and re-check the engine's systems and components while stationary, silently hoping that all would be well.

At around 08.30, with Pilot N. Montiero on board, and the tug CUBAL fast aft, the moorings were cast off, and the ship moved stern first off the berth. The first engine movement came at 08.33, "Slow astern", and for three minutes the ship gathered sternway as she swung in an arc to head for the harbour exit. At 08.36 the engines were stopped; it was time to halt the movement astern. But the telegraphed order at 08.37, "Slow ahead" was received down below in silence. At 08.38 the order was changed to "Half ahead". But there was still no response until 08.39 when the telegraph indicator lurched to "Stop", set

there by someone in the engine room. Clearly something was seriously amiss down below. The ship still carried considerable sternway, and was fast approaching the shallows. At 08.40 both anchors were dropped in an attempt to avert this danger, but the ship nevertheless touched the bank with her stern.

Down in the engine room engineers were feverishly trying to trace the cause of the trouble. The fault was found in the fuel injection system of number 1 unit. This was effectively by-passed, making it possible to operate the engines through the remaining five cylinders. The word was passed to the bridge, and at 09.02, with both anchors aweigh, the ship was able to move under her own power to a safe anchorage. By 09.18 the ship had brought up to her port anchor, but the brief manoeuvre had sufficed to show that all was not well with the steering gear. Divers were called, and in the crystal clear water of the harbour it was all too evident that the ship's rudder had been twisted through about 14 degrees to starboard.

The main engine fault was soon corrected, but the damaged rudder was a different question altogether. There were no facilities in Lobito capable of dealing with the problem. The nearest suitable docks were in the Cape, and somehow the ship had to get there, preferably under her own power. And so the gammy rudder evolved. On the advice of Lloyd's Surveyor, D. Ross Innes who had flown up from Capetown, the quadrant to which the rudder-head was geared was offset to counter the 14 degree deflection of the rudder, so that when the wheel was amidships, the rudder, too, was amidships.

The recommendations were carried out, and the ship put through successful sea trials. It was found that, although maximum port helm was limited to 20 degrees, and starboard to the normal 35 degrees, the ship was well under control throughout a range of speeds and manoeuvres. On the basis of this evidence, the Surveyor issued a provisional certificate of seaworthiness, recommending retention of class subject to further examination and repairs. As an extra form of insurance, the company's EXPLORER, which happened to be in the vicinity, was ordered to make contact and escort the handicapped vessel as far as Capetown. Eventually, the damaged rudder was fully repaired at Liverpool, but the final account, for temporary and permanent repairs, amounted to about £26,000, not all of which was refunded by the underwriters.[241]

---

303. TACTICIAN (3) 1961-1979 Steel motor ship. Three decks forward, two aft and five holds. One mast.
O.N. 303169 8,844g 4,844n 10,900d (11,372d after 1971) 467.35 (489.0 o.l.) x 62.3 x 38.9 feet. Cargo capacity: 614,390 cubic feet. Equipped with 110-ton Stülcken heavy-lift derrick, serving numbers 3 and 4 holds.
International Code: GHNL.
6-cyl. 2SCSA oil engine by William Doxford and Sons (Engineers) Ltd., Sunderland; 16 knots.

12.8.1960: Keel laid. *16.2.1961:* Launched by William Doxford and Sons (Shipbuilders) Ltd., Sunderland (Yard No. 845) for the company. *21.6.1961:* Delivered at a cost of £1,374,079 and later sailed from Liverpool for Kingston, Jamaica and Mexico on her maiden voyage under Captain W.S. Eustance. *31.10.1961:* Anchored off Belize when the port and town were devastated by Hurricane Hattie, one of the most destructive hurricanes of the decade. She had a narrow escape, but rode out the storm successfully, and was on hand next day to render assistance to the stricken citizens of Belize, most of whom were destitute. *23.1.1963:* Delayed at Belize by a dispute with the local customs officials about clearance. *5.5.1965:* Landed heavily in the approach to Latchford Lock in the Manchester Ship Canal sustaining damage which cost £6,000 to repair in a Glasgow dry dock. *22.9.1965:* Anchored in the designated explosives anchorage, Chapman's Reach, River Thames to load 90 tons of commercial explosives when outward bound from London to South Africa. At 16.00 fire broke out in a linen locker and quickly spread to adjoining storerooms. The Port of London Authority Control Centre at Gravesend was informed, and a PLA launch, eight tugs, and water-borne sections of Kent and Essex Fire Brigades converged on the ship. Meanwhile, the crew had achieved some measure of control with hoses, and by 20.45 the fire had been extinguished. The ship returned to Tilbury to repair the

damage and replace the stores which had been ruined by fire and water. *3.10.1965:* She eventually sailed and an act of General Average was invoked, total costs amounting to almost £30,000. *4.7.1968:* Fire broke out in the engine room when on passage from Nassau to Dublin. It was successfully dealt with by the crew, but the vessel was disabled by extensive damage to machinery and electrical installations. Consequently, she was towed into Ponta Delgada, Azores, by the Ellerman's Wilson motor ship RAPALLO (3,402/60). *6.8.1972:* An explosion and fire in the engine room brought the vessel to a halt, temporarily disabled, in the South Atlantic. Later, two engineer officers died from severe burns sustained in the blast despite expert medical assistance provided by the Russian tanker RICHARD SORGE (31,524/66). Temporary repairs were effected by the engine room staff. *7.8.1972:* She got under-way at 19.36 heading for Walvis Bay at slow speed. *5.2.1975:* Chief Engineer Malcolm Talt drowned at Beira. *7.1979:* Sold to Petralia Navigation Co. Ltd., Limassol, Cyprus (Thenamaris Maritime Inc., Piraeus, Greece, managers) for US$850,000 and renamed SEA LUCK. *1980:* Sold to Naviera Neptuno SA, Callao, Peru and renamed KERO. *7.1.1986:* Laid up at Callao, Peru. *5.1987:* Sold to Peruvian shipbreakers. *15.5.1987:* Arrived at General San Martin Bay for demolition.

Through the eye of the hurricane[242]

The hurricane season in the West Indies - July to October - is a period of subdued tension for seamen, ship operators, and, of course, local residents. The tension is subdued because ample warnings of the approach of a hurricane are a regular

feature of domestic as well as official broadcasts. So long as the disturbance is far away at sea, and not heading in our direction, it can be tacitly ignored - until, as so often happens, it changes course. Thus tension is seldom fully relaxed.

Despite constantly predicted movements, hurricanes cannot be expected to run on tramlines, and idiosyncratic track variations are the rule rather than the exception. A prime example was the West Indian hurricane of October 1961, designated Hattie.

On 29th October 1961 TACTICIAN was anchored at Stann Creek, a port in what was then British Honduras about 30 miles south of Belize City, quietly loading citrus products. The weather was fine and clear, with a light breeze and a blue sky. However, weather bulletins from Miami were full of information regarding another hurricane, already christened Hattie, which was located some 400 miles east of Belize, moving north, obviously on the point of recurving, and likely to strike Grand Cayman and Cuba.

Later that afternoon TACTICIAN weighed anchor and moved northwards to Belize to begin loading a cargo of lumber. Frequent weather reports still placed Hattie far to the east, still moving northwards well clear of the colony. Belizeans retired to bed that night with a certain sense of relief.

How different was the scene next day! The morning bulletin reported that Hattie had changed course in the night and was advancing rapidly, likely to cross the coast near the border with Yucatan in 24 hours. If this were true, Belize would escape the full force of the hurricane winds, but severe gales and the storm tide would be sure to disrupt the port area. Two red flags - the recognised storm signal - fluttered from the flagstaff at Government House, and over the signal station at Fort George. The Civil Defence Force was put on alert, schools closed, and residents who were free to leave town moved to the high ground in the hinterland.

By noon, a heavy swell was slamming against the outer reefs, and the fishermen's families on the Cays were evacuated. All cargo work came to a halt; barges were towed away upriver to find shelter inland; aboard TACTICIAN hatches were closed and secured, and derricks lowered.

A veteran able seaman, known to his mates as "Old Charlie", was horrified at the careless and cavalier attitude of some of the younger sailors, to whom the extra-curricular labour seemed an unnecessary chore for just another blow. "You wait," he said. "I've been through a hurricane. Years ago, when I was in the Navy back in the 'twenties." His eyes widened with fear at the recollection. "I've never forgotten it. You young lads don't know what you are in for!"

Captain Bill Eustance realised his ship was in an invidious position. Too late now to think of putting to sea and working his ship away from the track of the storm. His only option was to seek a more secure anchorage, and ride out the storm in whatever shelter the outer reefs might provide. At 14.30, amid reports that the hurricane now packed winds of up to 175 knots (200 mph), and was heading for the coast just north of Belize, TACTICIAN weighed anchor and proceeded south to a more secure anchorage off Grennells Cay with a Mr Locke, an experienced local pilot, on board.

W. Ledgard, at that time Third Engineer of the TACTICIAN, remembers Mr Locke well. "I have always admired the courage of this man," he said. "Knowing full well how devastating a hurricane can be, he was prepared to leave his family and take his chance aboard ship in the course of duty, just to place his local knowledge at the Captain's disposal. After the storm, when Captain Eustance called for volunteers to take the lifeboat ashore, he referred to Pilot Locke's selfless conduct and the boat was promptly manned, as if the men were eager to return him safely to his family."

At 16.00, when the ship brought up in her chosen anchorage, the wind was west north west force 5, but increasing steadily as the barometer fell. Ominously, as the evening progressed, the wind continued to blow from a west north west direction with a constancy which foretold that the storm centre was *not* going to pass somewhere north of Belize, but directly over TACTICIAN's precarious anchorage.

When midnight passed it was blowing a full gale, and although the sea was very rough the ship was maintaining her position, lying comfortably to six shackles of cable on the starboard anchor. All her deck lights were ablaze and all her systems were functioning. Between rain squalls the loom of the lights of Belize could be seen reflecting against the dark masses of cloud. Nothing as yet had happened to prepare the crew for what was to come, or shake their confidence in the ability of their splendid ship to ride it out. But Captain Eustance was well aware that the storm was only just beginning.

At about 01.00 on 31st October the ship began sheering unpleasantly, jerking at her cable like a fractious horse jouncing at its tether. A second anchor was dropped and the cables veered to five shackles on the port, eight on the starboard anchor. By this time the wind was piping to a pitch of incredible violence. The carpenter and Chief Officer Roy Simmons, who were on the forecastle head tending the anchors, were ordered aft to the shelter of the bridge-house accommodation, for they were in considerable danger of being lifted off their feet to be whisked away downwind into oblivion.

To ease the strain on the cables, the engines were run ahead from time to time, but the real battle had only just started. By 02.00, the wind was raging with greater force than ever, roaring and shrieking like an express train. But within the

Tactician, sister of *Custodian,* on trials in the North Sea in June 1961.   *[Turners (Photography) Ltd.]*

next half hour it was to double in fury, reaching a peak of violence far beyond the experience of anyone on board. The ship inevitably began dragging her anchors, swinging broadside on to the scouring wind. Over to starboard she heeled, the engine room clinometer swinging to 20 degrees as she yielded to that remorseless pressure. Leading away to windward, and fading rapidly into the drenched darkness, the anchor cables stretched like twin bars, as tenacious and as fragile as the fingers of a rock-climber who loses his foothold. For that was the situation - a veritable cliffhanger. TACTICIAN was hanging on by the links of her wrought iron cables, literally by a thread. If they had parted, nothing, not even her 8,000 horse-power engines, could have saved the ship from lurching to leeward, and driving ashore onto the reefs a mile or two away.

Visibility was down to a few yards, vision obliterated by torrential rain mingled with spray whipped from the wave tops, laden with sand and debris from the coral shores, driving in horizontal sheets, and blasting the paintwork from TACTICIAN's exposed flank. The radar was no longer functioning since the scanner refused to revolve in such conditions, and pointed fixedly into the wind's eye, like some sort of weathercock. Nor did the echo-sounder function. The aeration caused by the extreme turbulence ensured that no echoes from the sea bed ever returned to the transponder in the ship's keel.

The deck officers, cut off from their companions in the after part of the ship, kept anxious watch on the bridge, nursing the ship as best they could through her unprecedented ordeal. Down below, in the engine-room, engineers and electricians were fully occupied clearing weed and sand from vital injections, or tracing earths on the switchboard caused by water seeping into places where no water had ever penetrated before. At the main controls, Third Engineer Bill Ledgard, drenched by spray streaming from the vents overhead, braced himself against the list and fought the controls at the urgent behest of the bridge telegraph. At least three times the ship's propeller surged out of the water, causing the emergency governor to cut in. Each time it had to be reset manually under considerable difficulties, and the main engine restarted.

The rest of the crew, with little to do but hang on and wait, huddled together in the saloon or mess decks. They played cards, sang snatches of song, or prayed silently for deliverance. At this stage, Tom Pim recalls seeing "...dimly discerned through a streaming window, an apparition approaching the accommodation where most of the crew were sheltering. With considerable difficulty we eased open the steel door to admit the spectral figure, which now stood before us in the form of Second Officer Gordon Oxley. He had fought his way aft along the main deck, lurching into coamings and ventilators, clutching whatever solid fittings came to hand, and disregarding the flapping clothing torn from his back by the wind. He stood there, streaming with water, in nothing but his underpants, bleeding copiously from gashes in his legs and forehead, trying to muster all his dignity to deliver a verbal message of hope and confidence from the Captain. His mission accomplished, Gordon Oxley allowed us to dress his wounds, then fought his way back to the bridge."

Incredibly, one man slept through it all, a young steward who, next morning, knew nothing of the terrors of the night. At some time between 03.00 and 04.00 the barometer went into free fall until it reached its nadir of 27.3 inches of mercury (924.5 millibars) at 05.00. Shortly afterwards, with startling suddenness, the wind dropped to an uneasy calm, the seas subsided leaving only a sullen grey swell rolling in from the southeast, lit by a debilitated moon shining weakly through a break in the clouds. The sudden silence was uncanny. Men emerged on deck to look about them and marvel at the flocks of seabirds weaving and whirling overhead, some of them falling exhausted to the deck. For this was the legendary "eye of the hurricane", a phenomenon which only a select number of seamen have seen and lived to tell of it.

The opportunities presented by the eerie lull were not wasted. The cables were hove in and examined, and the ship re-moored. A suddenly restored radar system helped the navigators to plot their position despite the storm-induced clutter which blotched the screen. While it was still calm, Captain Eustance took the opportunity to make his way aft to see for himself how the crew were facing up to their ordeal. He found the men in good heart, but scared - and with good reason. The nightmarish conditions were quite outside their

experience, something they would remember and talk about for the rest of their lives. After a few well-chosen words of encouragement, Captain Eustance returned to the bridge. He was back just in time, for, with a roar like a train passing at speed through an underground station, the storm pounced once more upon the gallant ship and her defiant crew, the wind, as expected, blasting from the opposite direction. But it was 06.15. Though unseen, the sun was up, and things always look better in daylight, even that gloomy travesty of daylight which filters through the black maelstrom of a hurricane.

The terrors of the night were behind them; the glass was rising steadily; they felt that they and their ship had been through the crucible together and nothing more could ever daunt them. Even when the ship again dragged her anchors and listed over to leeward like an old square-rigger on a close-hauled tack, they knew the drill and nursed the ship through the worst repeated excesses of the storm, until, in the Captain's immortal words, "By 09.00 the wind had eased to hurricane force", in other words, from its pinnacle of 175 knots the wind had dropped to something just over 64 knots on the Beaufort Scale, and the ship lay easily to her anchors, head to wind. All hands breathed again, and the old familiar world began to drop into place once more when the young steward who had slept through it all appeared suddenly on the bridge with a tray of toasted bacon-and-egg sandwiches and hot coffee.

But there was still much that was unfamiliar. As the visibility improved the first signs of destruction came into view. The lordly palms which had crowned the cays and the mainland shore had all been decapitated, shorn of their foliage, leaving only bare poles, and many of these had been flattened. The sea was the colour of diluted milk, the normally clear waters holding in suspension thousands of tons of fine sand and coral particles, its surface strewn with debris and dead fish. The thoughts of all on board reverted to the town of Belize and its people. According to the forecasts, the storm tide was expected to top 15 feet, enough to inundate the entire city, creating unimaginable havoc.

At 13.00 the trusty anchors were hove home, and TACTICIAN made her way back to Belize, her crew fearful of what they might find. For the air was silent; the normally vociferous local broadcasting station was mute, and no response was received to the Radio Officer's repeated calls to the shore station. And so the ship came to an anchor in her usual berth off the port, and the motor-lifeboat was lowered into the still choppy sea of milk. Second Officer Gordon Oxley and a volunteer crew manned the boat, swarming down the lifelines since the rope ladder was useless in the high seas which were still running. Their instructions to contact the authorities and offer whatever assistance TACTICIAN was in a position to give. As they drew cautiously into the shattered landing they were confounded by the scenes of devastation which confronted them. Sunken wrecks littered the little harbour at the mouth of the river; buildings, their roofs torn away, leaned over at crazy angles; small boats and coasting schooners lay high and dry in the city streets among wrecked vehicles and uprooted trees, while a sea of mud lay everywhere.

Fort George still stood, but the signal mast which yesterday had bravely displayed the storm warnings, had been felled. Even Government House was in ruins, its communications centre destroyed.

When the boat returned later in the day the sea was still high, but Captain Eustance made a lee, enabling the crew to board TACTICIAN by means of the rope ladder "sideways on". Bill Ledgard, one of the boat's crew, recalls: "I will always remember the excellent meal provided for us by Tom Pim when we returned, looking and feeling like so many drowned rats, and the hot toddy to which the Captain treated us all was especially welcome!"

Apparently, communication was the first priority, and Gordon Oxley had returned to the ship bearing a sheaf of priority messages from the Governor, Sir Colin Thornley, for transmission to the outside world appealing for aid. Food and medical supplies were next on the agenda, and on the following day, 1st November, TACTICIAN's lifeboat again headed for the shore laden to the gunnels with cooking utensils, supplies of meat, rice, flour, tea, canned goods, and antibiotics, enough to set up a small field kitchen and clinic in the makeshift Red Cross centre. This operation was left in the capable hands of Chief Steward Tom Pim, ably assisted by Second Steward Ken Clapham, Pursers Coppell and Hartley, Cadet Hughes, and Third Engineer Bill Ledgard.

Suddenly, as if from nowhere, a troop of Boy Scouts and Girl Guides, somehow immaculately attired in smart uniforms, presented themselves for duty at the hard-pressed centre, the only local volunteers to offer help to TACTICIAN's relief team. Meanwhile, aboard the ship, Chief Cook "Taffy" Rowlands, working round the clock, baked scores of loaves for distribution next day.

In the ruined Port Office, Chief Officer Roy Simmons and Second Officer Oxley were in consultation with Harbour Master and Pilots, planning to lay temporary marks in the intricate channels leading from the sea to the stricken city, using empty oil drums as buoys to guide the relief ships in. Two US destroyers, CORRY and BRISTOL were standing off English Cay, 15 miles away, anxious to help, but unable to proceed because all navigational marks had been destroyed. Instead, they sent a pair of helicopters carrying medical supplies, a team of medics - and a TV camera crew. Thus Purser Hartley and Second Steward Ken Clapham found themselves starring on US television as they related their part in the emergency. Lack of navigational marks did not deter the British frigate, HMS TROUBRIDGE, however. Her navigator pressed on, feeling his way in, performing a feat of navigation inspired only by the urgency of the situation and perhaps by the fact that Belize was primarily a British responsibility. Packed with supplies from Kingston, several medical teams, and a contingent of Jamaican troops to help maintain order, she dropped anchor off the port at 08.30 on 2nd November.

That day, TACTICIAN's relief team resumed its labours, though supplies were running low. Out in the approaches, Third Officer Gwilym Jones, guided by Pilot Locke, continued the work of marking the channels and returned that afternoon, closely followed by the US warships. All available help was badly needed, for 15,000 people, nearly half the population, many of them injured, were roaming the ruined streets seeking food, and not too particular how they obtained it. Only the presence of a detachment from the security forces prevented the Red Cross Centre from being overwhelmed and looted.

According to the Governor's office, 70% of Belize had been destroyed, and 90% of Stann Creek. The season's citrus and banana crops had been wiped out, and hopes of recovery were dim. It was estimated that 340 people had lost their lives in the disaster. Concern had been expressed about the safety of the families of some of the employees of Belize Estates Co. Ltd. in view of the disorder which always threatened to break out. An appeal to Captain Eustance did not go unheeded, and consequently nine adults and two children embarked in TACTICIAN. Among them was the wife of Alan Peacock, a former purser with Harrison Line, and at that time a manager with B.E.C. He and his wife had spent the night of the storm in their devastated bungalow at Stann Creek, Alan shielding his wife as best he could from the debris which whirled about them, inflicting cuts and bruises in the process.

Later, as the ship was preparing to leave, and after climbing the ladder to see his wife safely on board, Alan Peacock suffered a seizure, and collapsed on the deck. Tom Pim recalls, "Quickly we carried him to a cabin. He was showing all the classic symptoms of a stroke: paralysis down one side; mouth twisted; an inability to speak. Ken Clapham and I worked on him for hours, bathing him alternately with hot and cold water, a treatment I vaguely remembered reading about in an old "Reader's Digest". It worked! Maybe he would have come round, anyway, but to us it worked, and Alan eventually made a complete recovery."

Meanwhile, the TACTICIAN, her duty done, and

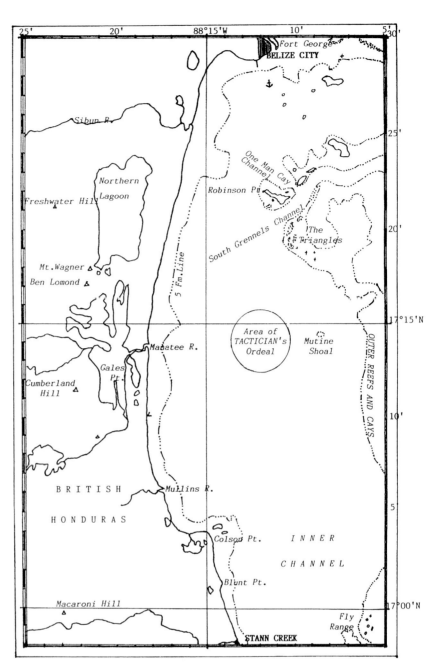

Tactician at Belize, 31st October 1961.

virtually stripped of supplies, had been released by the Governor and naval command to continue her voyage, and at 15.30 on 2nd November she sailed for Corpus Christi followed by the heartfelt good wishes of the Governor and people she had served. Her departure was succeeded next day by the arrival of the US aircraft carrier, ANTIETAM, which anchored off Stann Creek to land her substantial complement of relief and medical teams, thus bringing the international rescue effort to a peak, slowly but surely coaxing the country back to a state of something like normality. TACTICIAN's worthy efforts did not go unnoticed.

When the ship called at New Orleans she was given the marine equivalent of a ticker-tape reception. As she approached the city ships on the river and lining the wharves sounded their whistles and sirens in welcome; tugs and fire-tenders charged their hoses and directed them skywards to form iridescent sprays of fountain arcs; while representatives of press and radio gathered on the wharf to meet the ship as she docked - sure indications that the enthusiasm for public relations which sometimes motivated Alfred Le Blanc, the Harrison Line agent, had been at work. Then, some months later, recognition of TACTICIAN's achievements was acknowledged publicly in the Queen's Honours List with the award of the O.B.E. to her commander, Captain W.S. Eustance.

Belizean customs - and practice[243]

TACTICIAN visited Belize again in May 1962, and received a warm welcome, but her next visit eight months later was something less than warm. She arrived on 19th January 1963, in the midst of a bitter strike by port workers who were in dispute with their employers, the ubiquitous Belize Estates Co. Ltd. Those members of the crew who had been there during the hurricane doubtless anticipated another warm and generous welcome from people they had aided so ably, but a glance at the sullen expressions of the pickets was enough to dispel any such naive expectations. Memories can be very short when tempers are frayed. Captain Eustance was particularly hurt when a reception at the Governor's Residence, planned in his honour, was cancelled when leading politicians threatened to boycott it.

His orders were to the effect that, if the ship had not begun discharging within 24 hours, he was to proceed to Kingston and off-load the Belize cargo there. Except for some army supplies, which were unloaded by the troops themselves, the Belize cargo remained untouched. However, Captain Eustance had the option of moving to Stann Creek, 30 miles to the south, and there, much to everyone's surprise, found gangs and lighters ready to start work. All cargo marked for Stann Creek was discharged, and 286 tons of citrus products loaded for Liverpool. They even off-loaded some Belize cargo into lighters, planning to tow them to the strike-bound port.

But later on 21st everything came to a halt. The union activists had moved in and a noisy demonstration took place

Tactician's Master, Captain Eustance, in relaxed mood after his ordeal at Belize, meets Alfred Le Blanc, Harrison's agent at New Orleans.

on one of the lighters. Soon the gangs were on their way ashore, leaving the ship to weigh anchor at daybreak on 22nd and return to Belize towing two lighter loads of Belize cargo. The ship anchored in the harbour at about 13.00, and the lighters were towed away to be moored inshore under Customs' authority. Captain Eustance then went to the Custom House to obtain clearance for Kingston, hoping to sail that afternoon, since the strike was not settled. Clearance, however, was denied him. The strike-busting TACTICIAN had offended not only the union, but politicians and officialdom, too.

At 09.00 on 23rd January, Captain Eustance went ashore once more to note protest, and try again to obtain clearance. By this time, word of the TACTICIAN's manoeuvres had reached the ears of a popular and partisan press, and lurid stories of customs evasion were appearing under banner headlines which, if believed, could only be harmful to the company's reputation, and Captain Eustance's professional

integrity. It was whilst he was at the agent's office that Captain Eustance was handed a letter from the Comptroller of Customs. Dated 23rd January 1961, the letter accused the Master of the TACTICIAN of certain irregularities, such as proceeding to Stann Creek instead of New Orleans as declared on entry. This was humbug.

There was no Customs House at Stann Creek, and for all entry and clearance formalities Belize and Stann Creek were normally regarded as a single port. The next foreign port for which clearance was necessary was New Orleans. Besides, the agents had kept the Customs House informed of TACTICIAN's movements. The Comptroller also considered the unloading of Belize cargo into barges at Stann Creek a serious infringement of the regulations. Clearance was therefore withheld, for, as he said, "I shall have to satisfy myself that all your inward cargo has been duly accounted for."

Captain Eustance acknowledged the letter, and engaged the services of a lawyer. He was particularly incensed when the contents of the Comptroller's letter were broadcast on Belize Radio at noon that day.

On advice from Harrisons' solicitor, Captain Eustance instructed his lawyer to issue a writ against the Comptroller of Customs for unlawfully detaining his ship, claiming £1,000 per day for each day's delay. Nevertheless, throughout Thursday 24th, TACTICIAN continued to swing idly round her anchor, clearance still denied. That evening, the Union settled its dispute with B.E.C., and unloading began on the morning of 25th. When clearance was again applied for it was granted without further ado, and at daylight on 26th, having discharged all Belize cargo, TACTICIAN sailed from British Honduras. In his departure cable to Harrisons Captain Eustance revealed his frustration, ending ruefully, "...Many thanks for your help. Stop. Sorry our Hurricane turned to Winds of Change." In view of the pressures and mental strain to which Captain Eustance had been subjected, Harrisons were concerned about the state of his health. Consequently, Captain Ron Baldwin, resident Superintendent at Port of Spain, was instructed to meet the ship, see how matters stood, and report back. Meanwhile, the ship had been diverted to Vera Cruz, and it was there that Captain Baldwin met the TACTICIAN. He found Captain Eustance in good health, happy to discuss his problems in Belize, and reported accordingly. The court action was quietly withdrawn, and TACTICIAN's second stormy encounter with Belize was over.

Ordeal by fire[244]

On the night of 4th July 1968, aboard TACTICIAN, Dublin bound from Nassau in the Bahamas, at 21.50 P. Judge, donkeyman on the 8 to 12 watch, reported to Fourth Engineer D. Hughes that diesel oil was spraying from the fuel feed line to number 4 generator. It would have to be shut down at once, of course, but before this could be done, Mr. Hughes had first to start number 2 generator to absorb the load. As he was doing so, number 4 generator burst into flames, and a crisis suddenly became an emergency. For the fountain of oil was playing directly onto the red-hot generator exhaust manifold, and within a minute the oil had ignited. The presence of a ventilator nearby, and the proximity of the main turbo-blowers, produced a blow-torch effect which brushed aside Judge's prompt but vain application of a portable fire extinguisher. The alarm was sounded, but leaving Engineer Cadet Heppel to stand by the number 4 generator, Mr. Hughes leapt to the switchboard intending to put number 2 on load, and take off the blazing number 4, thus

hopefully avoiding a complete blackout and power failure. But, seeing smoke emanating from the main engine, he turned aside to the control platform to stop the ship.

Meanwhile, Cadet Heppel, cowering from the leaping flames as he waited in vain for Mr. Hughes' signal to switch off number 4, at last went to the switchboard himself, put number 2 on load, and threw out the switch to number 4. Unfortunately, something went amiss, and the engine room was plunged into darkness - except for the flare from the blazing generator.

Earlier, galvanised by the clamour of the emergency bell, the off-duty engineers had tumbled out and tried to get down below. Only Second Engineer John Beaton succeeded; the rest were beaten back by choking clouds of dense, black smoke. He arrived on the bottom platform just as the Fourth was closing valves to stop the main engine. The Second at once started the general service pump to charge the fire main, and tried to telephone the bridge, but without success, suggesting that the line was already damaged. He was coupling a fire hose to the hydrant when all the lights went out, to be replaced only by the dim, inadequate glow of the emergency system. By this time, smoke was making the control platform untenable, and he ordered the engine room to be evacuated via the last remaining escape route, the port middle platform exit. It was obvious that only a planned and orderly strategy, directed from outside, would succeed in extinguishing the blaze. Mr. Beaton then raced up to the boat deck to cut off all fuel to the engine room, using the remote controls.

Skylights and ventilators were sealed, and he waited for the signal from Chief Engineer Norman Thompson, who was checking that everyone was out of the engine room, before releasing the carbon dioxide. All were present - except the Fourth Engineer. Two engineers then volunteered to make their way down the tunnel escape shaft, then along the tunnel itself to the engine room to try and locate the missing man. The watertight door was raised to give them access and although they hailed Mr. Hughes repeatedly, they received no response. Eventually, driven back by the increasing heat and volumes of smoke, they retreated by the way they had come, and were immensely relieved to hear that, happily, the Fourth was safe. After stopping the main engines he had gone back to number 4 generator to try to cut off the fuel. Intense heat drove him back; smoke rasped his lungs, and it was all he could do to stagger painfully up the steel ladders to the main deck, finally emerging into the fresh air in a greatly distressed condition.

The young man had bravely played his part but, with only the cadet and the donkeyman to assist him, found he had too many jobs to do all at once. Fight the fire - shut off the fuel - retain light and power - change the jennies - start the fire pump - sound the alarm - inform the bridge - stop the ship - all matters of priority, yet it was impossible to do them all at once, or get them done coherently, in some sort of order. There was too little time. He stayed as long as was humanly possible and only retreated when there was dangerously little time to spare.

Meanwhile on the bridge, remotely situated at the forward end of the ship, there was some confusion as to what was going on. The first intimation that something was wrong was when the Kidde-Riche fire-alarm sounded in the wheelhouse. This was a cargo hold system activated by smoke, and the seat of the fire was indicated by a column of smoke emanating from one of many tubes installed in a glass-fronted cabinet in the wheel-house, each tube labelled with the name of the compartment it served. To ensure that the circuit was clear, each tube had a tiny ping-pong ball suspended above it, which danced in the current of air sucked through the system by a fan, making the cabinet look for all the world like a miniature shooting gallery. But on this occasion smoke was pouring from several tubes at once. For though the Kidde-Riche system was not connected to the engine room, smoke from the fire had drifted forward on the following wind, and had been sucked into the hold ventilators, triggering the alarm at several sensors at once. Consequently the officers had spent several precious minutes checking the holds before realising that the fire was aft, in the engine room. All this had happened in a very short space of time, for by 22.00 the engine room had been closed down and sealed, the roll-call checked, and carbon dioxide was already hissing into the blazing compartment.

At 22.05, Captain H.G. Skelly, master of the TACTICIAN, instructed Radio Officer Frank Lawton to send out an "Urgency" signal to all ships. Transmitted on 500 Kcs using battery power, it read: "XXX de GHNL CQ 0048Z 5 July TACTICIAN QTH Lat 41 30N Long 39 17W engine room on fire position serious ships in vicinity please stand by".

The message was picked up and relayed to Lands End Radio on short wave by the British tanker ASPRELLA (12,321/59). It was only about 02.00, British Summer Time, but the shore station notified Harrisons' designated duty man directly, in accordance with long-standing practice, and he alerted the management. Other ships were quick to respond, too. They included the German WESERMÜNDE (3,139/59) the US Coastguard Cutter HAMILTON, then on Ocean Weather Ship duty at Station DELTA; Ellerman Wilson's RAPALLO (3,402/60) the Polish ROMER (5,587/64); and the Italian passenger ship RAFFAELLO (45,933/65).

At dawn next day the rescue vessels began to close in. It was misty, which made it rather difficult for them to locate the disabled ship. WESERMÜNDE was first to arrive, and stood by at 05.00. At about the same time an aircraft from the Azores US airbase flew overhead, but was not seen on account of the fog. At 06.00, ROMER, RAFFAELLO and the other ships were released to resume their respective voyages. RAFFAELLO had been particularly helpful in relaying messages from TACTICIAN to England, Ponta Delgada, and to other ships and aircraft in the vicinity, when the power of her battery-charged transmissions began to wane. Around 07.00 the USCG cutter HAMILTON appeared through the veil of mist and at once sought permission to put a fire-fighting squad on board with their equipment. But by this time the carbon dioxide gas had done its work and the fire was out.

Nevertheless, Captain Skelly welcomed them aboard, knowing their expertise would be useful. In fact, shortly before the coastguards' arrival, Chief Engineer Thompson and Second Engineer Beaton, despite the heat, the smoke, and the carbon dioxide, had already made a preliminary inspection of the engine room protected by breathing apparatus. Their report had not been encouraging, but future decisions would have to wait until a further inspection could be carried out after the engine room had been ventilated and declared gas-free.

Meanwhile, WESERMÜNDE was released from stand by, and the next few hours were spent ventilating the scorched and smoke-blackened machinery space. At noon, several coastguards donned breathing apparatus and, using their sophisticated gas-detection instruments, were soon able to pronounce the engine room clear of gas.

A more thorough inspection confirmed the Chief Engineer's early doubts. The damage, mainly confined to the port side of the engine-room, was considerable, affecting generators, turbo-blowers, coolers, oil tanks, feed lines, purifiers, numerous gauges and hundreds of yards of electrical wiring, all militating against any notion of starting the main engines. Even if an attempt succeeded the risk of a renewed blaze, even an explosion, could not be ruled out. There were too many ruptured pipes; too much oil spread everywhere; and supplies of carbon dioxide were too depleted to deal with a renewed outbreak. It was clear that the ship would have to be towed to a port of refuge, the nearest being Ponta Delgada in the Azores, some 650 miles away.

Meanwhile, Harrisons, believing a tow would be the likely outcome, had entered into an agreement with the owners of RAPALLO, using Lloyd's Standard Form. Thus, later in the day, the Master of RAPALLO, who had earlier resumed course, having been released from the emergency along with the other ships, received a message from his owners instructing him to rendezvous with TACTICIAN and tow her to Ponta Delgada.

RAPALLO, bound from Barbados to Liverpool, was a comparatively small ship, being less than half TACTICIAN's tonnage, but was undoubtedly a handy-sized ship for the job.

Rapallo which towed *Tactician* into Ponta Delgada. *[J. and M. Clarkson collection]*

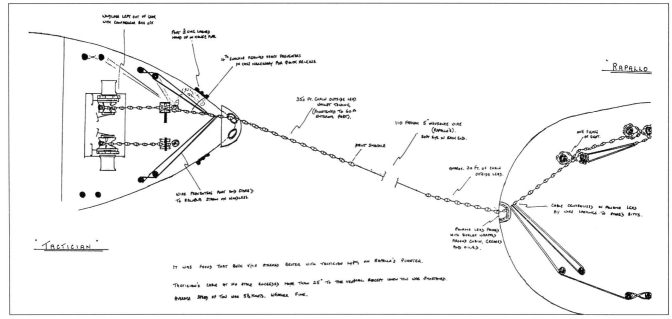

Towage of *Tactician* by *Rapallo,* July 1968.

She was still far to the west, however, and could not reach TACTICIAN before 21.30 ship's time, so arrangements to pick up the towing cables were deferred until daybreak on 6th July. Meanwhile, TACTICIAN's crew made preparations for the tow by securing the port anchor, and breaking out the cable. Down below, the engineers had succeeded in starting the least damaged generator, and were busy making temporary wiring repairs, and blanking off damaged pipes. When RAPALLO at last loomed up, the obliging US coastguards retired, and HAMILTON returned to her normal duties after an absence of over 24 hours.

At 06.45 a rocket fired from RAPALLO initiated the towing connection, linking the ships with a light line, the first of a series getting heavier and heavier until the RAPALLO's 5-inch insurance wire was passed. This heavy wire, 110 fathoms long, was shackled to TACTICIAN's cable at one end, and to RAPALLO's at the other, forging the link between the two ships. TACTICIAN then paid out four shackles (360 feet) of cable, and the towing-line was complete. Meanwhile, in the shaft tunnel, engineers were labouring to disconnect the tail-end shaft to reduce the drag of the propeller, leaving it free to revolve unimpeded as the ship moved ahead. By 13.45 all was ready, and the long tow began.

For the next five days TACTICIAN sauntered along at 5½ knots in RAPALLO's wake. The weather remained calm throughout, with light airs, and a low swell, ideal for the job in hand. No other assistance was needed, but at 19.25 on the second day of the tow the Greek tug NISOS CHIOS (555/43), based at Ponta Delgada, put in an appearance. Salvage tugs contribute greatly to the safety of life and the preservation of property at sea, but they have to make a living to justify their existence. So they are always on the lookout for ships in trouble, and tend to hang about like jackals waiting to take their wounded prey. It was not long before the airwaves were filled with reproaches from the skipper of the Greek tug. Despite Captain Skelly's courteous refusal of his services he persisted in his intention to "escort" TACTICIAN, and informed Captain Metham, the Master of the RAPALLO, that to continue to tow "without rescue" was "unjustifiable" to charterers and shippers, presumably inferring that, being an "urgency" incident, and not a life or death issue, RAPALLO was out of order in deviating to render assistance. But Captain Metham had had instructions from his owners, and that was good enough. The blustering NISOS CHIOS was left to her own devices, but she kept in touch, perhaps hoping that a sudden gale would deprive RAPALLO of her charge, and give the tug a chance to retrieve her.

But the weather remained fine under the influence of a slow-moving ridge of high pressure which persisted until the morning of the sixth day when RAPALLO and TACTICIAN arrived at Ponta Delgada. There was some delay waiting for other vessels to clear the harbour, but at 09.30 a pilot boarded each ship, and a launch brought the agent alongside,

accompanied by Engineer Superintendent George Baker, who had flown out from Liverpool. Shortly after midday the towing cable was shortened, the harbour tug CORPO SANTO was secured aft and, at 13.21 on Thursday 11th July, the cortege of ships entered port. An hour later TACTICIAN was safely berthed alongside the quay

During this period, the various departments in Mersey Chambers had not been idle. As we have seen, Engineer Superintendent Baker had been despatched promptly on a flight to the Azores; reports of damage, continuously coming in from the ship, were quickly analysed, and spare parts air freighted to the Azores; on the day before TACTICIAN made port, the company's DISCOVERER (307), outward bound to the West Indies, had called at Ponta Delgada to unload 95 cylinders of carbon dioxide gas to replenish TACTICIAN's depleted stock; and various agencies, ship chandlers and repairers, salvage associations, shippers, underwriters, and, of course Lloyd's had been notified and kept informed of TACTICIAN's progress and her needs.

On 17th July Mr. Baker was able to inform Harrisons that he and Captain Skelly were confident that TACTICIAN would be capable of returning to the British Isles, under her own power, and unescorted. Sea trials were planned for 19th, and at 08.00 that day the ship left her port of refuge. Gradually, speed was worked up to 12 knots, the engines turning comfortably on 88 rpm, and for the rest of the day the ship was put through a series of rigorous tests. At 20.45 Mr. Baker declared himself fully satisfied with the ship's performance, and at 21.00 she resumed her interrupted voyage to Dublin, maintaining an average speed of 12.7 knots, and arriving on 24th.

Though the incident did not result in any casualties, it prompted a searching in-house inquiry into the causes and consequences of the fire. For the ship had been in great danger, and it was necessary to find means of eliminating those factors which had led to, and accelerated, the blaze. Many recommendations were made, and many were adopted. For example, the initial oil spill had been caused by a small cock used for bleeding off pockets of air in the fuel system, which had worked loose and sprung from its socket. In future, all bleeder cocks on Allen diesel generators would be removed, and the holes plugged. Patent Minerva alarm systems would be installed in all engine rooms. Where possible, engine room watertight doors would be modified to render them capable of being operated locally. Radio telecommunications would be improved to give a voice-range of up to 2,500 miles. Because the recording of times was so important in emergency situations, synchronization of clocks would be achieved by installing a system whereby a master clock on the bridge would electronically govern a series of slave clocks throughout the ship. These and other recommendations were energetically put in motion. Certainly, no stones were to be left unturned in the task of ensuring that no such regrettable incident should ever occur again. Yet, four years later...

Tragedy kindles a lull in the cold war

There are few things more distressing at sea than the onset of serious illness or injury. The lack of facilities, and an indifferent level of medical expertise - though adequate for run-of-the-mill-ailments - are occupational hazards which not only place the unfortunate patient at risk, but fill those on the spot charged with the task of caring for him with a debilitating feeling of helplessness. First aid is an excellent, life-saving principle, and one does one's best at nursing, but unless a seriously ill patient can be brought swiftly to hospital he will have little chance. There is certainly no such recourse for most ships at sea.

The TACTICIAN was three days out of Capetown, bound for Dublin when, at about 22.15 on 5th August 1972 the Minerva fire alarm sounded harshly in the wheelhouse. This system, which covered the engine room, was extremely sensitive, and false alarms were of frequent occurrence. Nevertheless, the Captain, who could not fail to hear the alarm in his cabin, went up to the bridge to get a report.[245] Third Officer James Williams was speaking on the engine room telephone, while Chief Engineer Brian Chaloner, who happened to be making his nightly routine check on the telemotor steering gear, stood beside him. The report from the Engineer on watch was reassuring, and Captain and Chief left the bridge together.

However, five minutes later the telephone rang in the wheelhouse. This time, Fourth Engineer Tony Wood was not so confident. He spoke to the Chief who at once made his way aft, and down below. The steady beat of the engine had slowed noticeably already. Something was amiss; the Chief would make a report as soon as he could. At midnight the telephone shrilled, and the Chief reported that they had a scavenge fire on their hands, but it was under control, and soon all would be well.

But to those listening on the bridge the engine did not sound at all well. It was running very unevenly and noisily, "like a load of empty drums adrift in the 'tween decks", someone said, and showers of sparks were erupting from the funnel. On the bridge there was an atmosphere of uneasiness, of impending calamity.

At 01.05 on 6th August came the explosion, dull, muffled, but reverberating throughout the ship. A column of black smoke, blacker than the night, shot up through the open skylights. After a shocked pause, the 'phone rang again in the wheelhouse. The message was loud and clear, and distinctly chilling: "The engine room's on fire. For God's sake, someone please help us!"

Second Officer Doug Ellis sounded the general alarm, and, leaving him in charge of the bridge, the Captain hastened aft to see for himself the extent of the emergency. The ship was in complete darkness and without power, the only source of light being from hand torches. Smoke was pouring from vents and skylights, partly masking the evil flicker of flames far below. In the starboard main deck alleyway some sailors were trying to force open the steel door to the engine room, jammed tight by the blast which had distorted the frame. Someone on the other side was pleading to them to hurry. Eventually, yielding at last to the assault with crowbars and axes, the door flew open. The distraught figure of the junior engineer staggered out into the alleyway. He was alright, he said, but there were men down below in need of help.

Meanwhile, men with portable fire extinguishers were already tackling the blaze, which was centred on the after turbo-blower, while others searched for and found the injured men and assisted them up the steel ladders to the exit on the main deck. There were two victims, Chief Engineer Brian Chaloner and Third Engineer Michael Forde, both seriously injured, and clearly in extremis. They had taken the full force of the blast from the scavenge explosion and had fallen to the tank top plates where the rescuers had found them, the remnants of their clothing still alight. Their condition was pitiable. Where the skin was not blackened and pitted with tiny fragments of debris, it was an angry red and blistered. Hair and eyebrows had been scorched away, and their lungs had been seared by the heat, for they had difficulty breathing, but apart from a deep gash in the Third Engineer's arm there appeared to be no other injuries consistent with a fall. The woeful lack of adequate means of treatment was appalling. The application of burn sprays and dressings seemed but a puny response in face of the sheer magnitude of the task. Burns covered their entire bodies from head to foot, yet both men were conscious, spoke lucidly, and even joked about the state they were in. Both were in that deep trauma which seems to smother pain, and subsequent injections of morphine did much to keep extreme pain at bay.

But the situation cried out for expert medical care and attention. At about 01.30 an 'Urgency' message went out to all ships, requesting any vessel with a doctor on board to get in touch. It was repeated by the shore stations at Capetown and Walvis Bay, and acknowledged by several ships in the area. Only two had doctors on board, however, the South African passenger liner S.A. VAAL (30,212/61) and a Russian tanker, the RICHARD SORGE (31,524/66). The latter, by a long way, was the nearest, giving her ETA at TACTICIAN'S position as 06.00 that morning.

It was a long, distressful night. All that could be done to make the injured men comfortable was done. They were soon sleeping fitfully under the influence of morphine, but steadily weakening from the loss of vital fluids seeping through seared and blistered flesh.

Down below, the fire fighters had subdued the blaze, and gradually light and power had been restored to the ship's silent systems. Repairs to the main engine would take rather longer, but, in the opinion of Second Engineer Chris Barber, they were quite feasible using the ship's own resources. The damaged turbo-blower had to be blanked off, and the exhaust bend refitted to by-pass it. Number 6 scavenge-door had been blown off its studs, and this, too, had to be faired and refitted. At a later stage, Mr. Barber discovered that the after section of the camshaft covering numbers 5 and 6 cylinders was 25 degrees out of alignment. In his view, this could well have been the cause of the explosion - and not a result of it. Spent gases could well have been trapped, instead of being exhausted, building up pressure relentlessly with every turn of the engine. Engineers and electricians pressed on with their work. They were to carry on continuously, under Chris Barber's inspired leadership, for the next 40 hours before mobility could be restored to the ship's main engine. Later, after it was all over, he would say simply, "We had to see it through, if only for Mike and the Chief".

With the dawn came the big Soviet tanker, RICHARD SORGE, in response to the plea for medical assistance. She stood off a quarter of a mile away, and away went Chief Officer Fred Martin in TACTICIAN's motor lifeboat to welcome her. The boat returned quickly, bringing a young Medical Officer, Dr. Vyacheslav Starkov, and Chief Mate Victor Nemiaty who spoke some English and acted as interpreter. With them came a liberal supply of drugs, and a Russian/English dictionary which helped considerably in overcoming the language barrier.

Dr. Starkov was taken immediately to his patients, and after a careful examination he needed no English to express his obvious concern. The men needed intensive hospital care; he estimated the extent of their injuries as being third/fourth degree burns covering 70% to 80% of body surface, and the need for blood plasma was urgent. The doctor set up a drip for each patient and administered further injections of morphine, but in Mr. Chaloner's case it was already too late. He died at 10.00 on 6th August 1972, and his body was removed to the ship's hospital to be enshrouded in canvas ready for burial at sea.

Meanwhile, Radio Officer Frank Lawton had been searching traffic for a ship with a well-equipped hospital and supplies of blood plasma. Only one, the passenger ship S.A. VAAL could meet these requirements, but could not reach TACTICIAN's position before 22.00 on 7th. Frank Lawton next turned his attention to Capetown Radio. Could the South African Air Force perhaps drop the supplies so desperately needed? Capetown asked for details of the plasma required and soon after midday back came the reply: "...Have arranged for aircraft of SAAF to rendezvous with you at first light tomorrow morning."

This was a remarkable gesture of humanitarian goodwill, for the ship was more than 1,250 miles from the Cape at this time. A round trip of 2,500 miles over the ocean would test the capabilities of crew and aircraft to the limit. Both British and Russian observers were deeply impressed.

At 16.00 Third Officer Williams took the boat across to the RICHARD SORGE for further supplies of plasma, just about exhausting the Russian's limited stocks. When the boat returned, it brought with it three engineers and a young stewardess with nursing experience and a name like a ballerina - Tamara Nikiforova. The engineers volunteered to assist with the repairs, but what with language difficulties, and the unfamiliar complexities of a Doxford diesel engine compared to their own steam turbines, it was a forlorn task, and, though the gesture was warmly appreciated, they returned to their ship a couple of hours later.

Another long night wore on, punctuated by messages offering help and advice from many quarters. Doctor and nurse seemed tireless, tending their patient with constant care and inexhaustible patience. Soon after 02.00 on Monday 7th August a message from head office advised that the company's JOURNALIST (294), outward bound to the Cape, would rendezvous with TACTICIAN, render assistance if required, and escort her to a port of refuge. Then at about 02.40 the word came that a SAAF Shackleton aircraft had taken off from Capetown, her ETA 09.30. The doctor looked grave, and hoped it would not be too late to save Mr. Forde, for the last few c.c.s of available plasma had dripped into his poor ravaged body soon after midnight.

At 07.30 all members of the crew that could be spared were assembled on the foredeck to pay their last respects to Chief Engineer Brian Chaloner. A wooden hatch-board supported by a trestle was his bier; his shroud, a length of number 1 canvas weighted at the foot; his pall, a clean Red Ensign. It was a solemn and moving occasion as the Master read the short service approved by the Archbishop of Canterbury for the burial of the dead at sea:

"....We therefore commit his body to the deep in sure and certain hope of the Resurrection to eternal life, through our Lord Jesus Christ..."

Then two seamen gently raised the inboard end of the hatchboard and the canvas-encased body slid gently from under the ensign and into the sea, the splash of its going striking the ears like the knell of death. "...henceforth blessed are the dead which die in the Lord... for they rest from their labours..."

The log recorded the position of Brian Chaloner's last resting place 16.59S, 4.07E, or approximately 680 miles, 301 degrees from Walvis Bay.

Michael Forde's condition was deteriorating, but soon after 09.00 the steady hum of an aircraft's engines approaching galvanised hope. The lifeboat was launched, and took up station between the two ships. As the big Shackleton flew in the calm voice of the despatcher came over the R/T explaining procedure for the drop. She flew low passing between the ships four times, and on each pass a parachute bearing a canister splashed gently into the sea. The Master recalls, "I was watching the operation through my binoculars, enthralled by the precision with which the pilot guided his aircraft. I sensed rather than saw the figure at my elbow.

"It was the Purser/Catering Officer, Alan Peacock. 'Yes, what is it, Alan' I asked, alarmed by the expression on his face. 'It's Michael,' he faltered. 'He's gone. Died a few minutes ago. He heard the 'plane, sir. His eyes flickered open for a moment...and that was it'.

"The sense of failure, of anticlimax, was appalling. Mechanically I watched the plane turn south on its long return journey, dipping each wing in salute, the brave men of her crew doubtless congratulating themselves, with every justification, on a job well done. Had it all been for nothing? Our lifeboat was briskly gathering up parachutes and canisters, and lurching back through a choppy sea with its precious haul. Had their efforts, too, been all in vain?

"I made my way aft, and found Dr. Starkov and Nurse Nikiforova gathering up the pathetic remnants of their equipment. They both looked all in, and Tamara could not repress her tears. Dr. Starkov gestured to where Michael Forde lay in the narrow, coffin-like bed, his scarred features relaxed and peaceful as if in sleep. In halting English Dr. Starkov spoke, 'I am so sorry, Captain.' I shook him warmly by the hand, and thanked him and his nurse for their tireless efforts."

All political prejudice inspired by the Cold War had been swept aside, leaving only two men and a woman united by grief, and a very human sense of failure. Nevertheless, the Communist Russian had indeed proved to be a Good Samaritan.

The doctor insisted on remaining with the body for a further three hours, as required by Russian law. He then wrote out a death certificate for each case, but since he naturally wrote in the Cyrillic script it was necessary to make translations. This was achieved with the help of Chief Mate Nemiaty and his Russian/English dictionary.

At 13.35 the lifeboat set out on its final journey to the RICHARD SORGE, bearing the Russian party and messages of thanks to the Soviet captain for his assistance and unswerving determination to stand by the British ship for as long as was necessary. Following an exchange of courtesies on VHF radio, the Russian vessel resumed her interrupted voyage after a delay of 32 hours.

Meanwhile, in the engine room, Chris Barber and his team were nearing the end of their labours. A brief engine trial in the afternoon indicated that further adjustments were necessary, but by 19.30 TACTICIAN was ready to start her crippled main engine, and head towards Walvis Bay at slow speed.

TACTICIAN's escort, JOURNALIST, was in sight at daybreak next morning, Tuesday 8th August, and eventually she took up station on the quarter. But the crew of TACTICIAN still had yet another melancholy task to perform - the committal of Michael Forde's body to the deep. At about 10.00, with JOURNALIST in close company, the ship was stopped and the crew assembled for the second time to gather round the ensign-covered form of a former shipmate.

The difference on this occasion was that the Roman Catholic form of service was read. In the absence of a priest, Michael had died unshriven, a matter of some concern to followers of the faith, and some account of this factor was written into the service.

Michael Forde's body slipped into the sea in position 17.30S, 05.35E, or about 594 miles, 303 degrees from Walvis Bay. While the ship was stopped, the engineers made a quick examination of the camshaft, then she resumed her voyage. The weather remained fairly good, and at 10.00 on 11th August 1972, TACTICIAN berthed at Walvis Bay. Many and various were the delegations assigned to meet her, all eager to help, in their different ways, to restore the ship to normal, and comfort the bereaved. The company's representative in South Africa, Nigel Hollebone, was most concerned, and handled the inevitable interviews with lawyers requiring statements with skilful diplomacy. Engineer Superintendent E. Levison was there accompanied by several surveyors, and two engineer officers to fill the vacant posts. Agents, contractors, and the padre from the Missions to Seamen were quick to express their sympathy, and lay on those practical services which mean so much to the personnel of a disabled ship in port.

Quickly, repairs were put in hand, and promptly executed, so that by 14th August the ship was ready to resume her voyage to Dublin. Trouble and tragedy had indeed marred the serenity of the voyage, but had demonstrated once again that, despite differences of ideology, the bond of brotherhood which unites all seamen, yes, even in time of war when the battle is over, was as strong as ever. Russians and South Africans had combined to aid the crew of a British ship, and although their efforts ended in failure, yet will that sense of purpose and service which prompted those efforts never be forgotten by those who were privileged to witness it.

304. EXPLORER (4) 1961-1978 Steel motor ship. Two decks and four holds. Two masts and signal mast.
O.N. 301367 7,200g 3,750n 8,850d (9,037d after 1971) 414.15 (440.0 o.l.) x 59.7 x 36.15 feet. Cargo capacity: 462,761 cubic feet. Equipped with 70-ton conventional derrick serving number 2 hold.
International Code: GHHW.
5-cyl. 2SCSA oil engine by Sulzer Brothers Ltd., Winterthur, Switzerland; 16.5 knots.

19.3.1960: Keel laid. *22.10.1960:* Launched by Nederlandsche Dok-en-Scheepsbouw Maats., Amsterdam (Yard No. 490) for the company. *3.3.1961:* Delivered at a cost of £989,532 and later sailed from Liverpool for the West Indies and Demerara on her maiden voyage under Captain W. Moore. *12-14.11.1963:* Stood by the company vessel CROFTER (290) making for Ponta Delgada, Azores with a fire in number 5 hold. *29.7.1964:* While berthed at North Shed, South West India Dock, London fire broke out in the deck cargo stowed abreast number 1 hatchway. The local fire brigade extinguished the fire, which destroyed a number

of packages containing chloroform and bromide. *5.12.1964:* While anchored off Plymouth, Montserrat she dragged her anchors during a fierce squall, and drifted out to sea. A number of lighters were still secured alongside, and on returning to her berth two heavily laden lighters, MISS IRIS and MISS PATTY, were swamped and sank in deep water. They and their cargoes were declared a total loss. *21.9.1966:* Running suddenly into a bank of dense fog on the River Thames she lost way and dropped her anchor in Lower Hope Reach at 18.30. Coming up astern was the Swedish WERONA (499/58) which ran into EXPLORER's stern. Both vessels sustained damage, but WERONA continued her voyage to Gothenburg pending repairs to her stem and forecastle plating. *18.6.1967:* Ten days out of Capetown, an unwelcome stowaway was discovered on board, harboured by one of the seamen (see below). *11.12.1978:* Sold to Senator Maritime Inc. (Overlink Maritime Inc., managers), Monrovia, Liberia and renamed LINK TRUST under the Greek flag. *3.1.1979:* Passing through the Suez Canal on a voyage from Antwerp to Abadan, she ran aground at kilometre 62 due to a steering failure, and lost her starboard anchor while trying to avoid the bank. The vessel was refloated, and assisted to Ismailia by Suez Canal Authority tugs. The anchor was eventually recovered after resolving the Egyptian salvor's reluctance to accept Lloyd's Open Form (no cure, no pay). Underwater inspection revealed that the rudder stock was twisted through 20 degrees to starboard. The ship was carrying a full cargo of cement and the owners were not in favour of lightening ship

in order to dry dock. A compromise was reached with the approval of a Lloyd's surveyor and temporary repairs were conducted afloat. *16.1.1979:* Reached Suez. *21.2.1979:* Arrived safely at Abadan. *12.12.1980:* Ran aground at the entrance to the Calabar River, Nigeria when on passage from Antwerp to Calabar. *23.12.1980:* Refloated. *1981:* Sold to Corallina Maritime Inc., Monrovia, Liberia (Baru Seri, Incorporated, Piraeus, Greece, managers) and renamed BARU SPIRIT under the Greek flag. *1984:* Sold to Chinese shipbreakers. *11.6.1984:* Passed Suez en route from Sibenik. *1.8.1984:* Arrived at a mainland Chinese port prior to this date.

EXPLORER was the first vessel to be constructed overseas to Harrison's order since the MAGICIAN (211) was launched at Schiedam in 1925. She was also the first to be engined by Sulzer Brothers, believed by many to be the Rolls Royce of marine engine builders.

First of two ships with accommodation moved farther aft, *Explorer* passes Dungeness Lighthouse inward bound for London. The Dungeness Power Station is under construction.

A bird of passage

Occasionally, migrating birds alight uninvited on the decks of ships at sea, left behind by the flock through weakness or exhaustion. If they survive, they do not stay long, nor do they respond to well-meant fraternal gestures by the crew. Such birds of passage are welcome intruders into the humdrum routine of life aboard ship. Others, like the young female stowaway discovered aboard EXPLORER ten days out of Capetown, are not.

Ordinary Seaman Danny Reeves, a youth of 17 summers, was prone to spend most of his spare time in port frequenting the saloons and bars beyond the dock gates. It was in one such haunt in Capetown, known as the Navigators' Den, that Danny met Anna, and they were irresistibly attracted one to the other. They met on every possible occasion, and on the night prior to the ship's departure Danny brought Anna and two other girls on board the ship - strictly against regulations - for a farewell party. The watchman saw them come on board, and watched them go ashore at 23.30, noisily making their farewells.[246]

On the morning of 8th June 1967, the ship bustled with preparations for departure. Officers and engineers made the

customary tests, and carried out the obligatory search for stowaways; while the Purser/Catering Officer searched the accommodation and checked the crew. The tugs came alongside, and, within the hour, the ship sailed, bound for Avonmouth. Ten days passed without incident, then, shortly after midnight on 18th June, Third Officer H.R. Mason was approached by one of the seamen in his watch, David Owens, who confided that his mate, Danny Reeves, wished to speak to him. Reeves was sent for and, prompted by Owens, confessed that he was harbouring a stowaway in his cabin, a girl whom he had smuggled on board at Capetown. The astonished Third Officer accompanied Reeves to his cabin and there found the girl sitting tremulously on the settee. Mr. Mason escorted her up to the bridge deck and called the Master.

Captain Hugh Roberts was at once angry and alarmed. He realised what a furore would arise when the news broke, as surely it must. Shipmasters are vulnerable before the law in most countries for the misdemeanours and misconduct of their subordinates. Captain Roberts could see charges of abduction looming before him. The girl, who gave her full name as Anna Andrika Meyer, was clearly from a respectable family despite her predilection for dockland pubs. She would have been reported missing long since, and the police could even now be dragging Capetown docks for her body. The authorities must be notified at once - but not before he had informed his owners and received their instructions.

It was some consolation to learn that the girl was 18. At least he could not be charged with the even more heinous crime of abducting a minor. The two delinquents were closely questioned, and gradually the sorry story came out. After the watchman had seen the party pass down the gangway on to the quay, two of the girls made off, leaving Anna with Reeves in the shadow of the cranes. Later, instead of walking her to the gate, Reeves persuaded the young woman to return aboard the ship. They did not use the gangway. As the ship's rail was almost level with the quay they simply stepped on board unseen by the watchman. They repaired to Reeves' cabin, and Anna asked him to telephone a friend to come and fetch her. This he did - or said he did - but the fact remains that the friend never turned up.

Meanwhile, the two lovebirds fell asleep, she in the bunk, himself on the settee, and there they remained until the Purser/Catering Officer came round knocking on doors several hours later. When he peered into Reeves' cabin he ticked off the man's name, but saw nothing amiss, as the girl had been hastily concealed in a wardrobe.

For ten days her ladyship remained incognito, her presence unsuspected by any other member of the crew. She must have spent a miserable existence confined to the locked cabin, disappearing into the wardrobe when the Captain made his bi-weekly inspections. On these occasions, which must have put the culprits under great fear and trepidation, Reeves cunningly diverted the Captain's attention by showing him an injured hand which had recently been operated upon, inviting his opinion, and engaging his sympathy.

From time to time Reeves brought the girl food, but she was not a good sailor and suffered frequently from sea sickness. Reeves did his best to comfort her, and assured her that when they reached England he would take her to his home. But, on a long passage, discovery was inevitable, and when Reeves' watch mate, David Owens, caught the girl flitting out of the petty officers' bathroom, the game was up. Owens evidently possessed a mature sense of responsibility, for he persuaded Reeves to report Anna's presence to their watch officer, Mr. Mason. Anna was subsequently confined to a spare cabin near the bridge, and forbidden to have any further contact with Reeves, or attempt to leave her cabin without permission.

Eventually, on 24th June, the ship docked at Avonmouth to be met by a mixed posse of policemen, immigration officials, and gentlemen of the press who had somehow got hold of the story. There could be no happy ending, however. Anna was declared an illegal immigrant, and deported on the next available flight to South Africa, doubtless at Harrison's expense. Reeves was given a bad discharge and signed off in disgrace, to ruminate upon this sad conclusion to a foolish escapade. But at 17 one doubts whether the experience left any lasting emotional scars.

305. DALESMAN (2) 1961-1979 Steel motor ship. Two decks and four holds. Two masts and signal mast.
O.N. 303183 7,200g 3,754n 8,840d (9,027d after 1971) 414.15 (440.0 o.l.) x 59.7 x 36.15 feet. Cargo capacity: 462,761 cubic feet. Equipped with 70-ton conventional derrick serving number 2 hold.
International Code: GHMR.
5-cyl. 2SCSA oil engine by Sulzer Brothers Ltd., Winterthur, Switzerland; 16.5 knots.

31.10.1960: Keel laid. *15.6.1961:* Launched by Nederlandsche Dok-en-Scheepsbouw Maats., Amsterdam (Yard No. 506) for the company. *2.11.1961:* Delivered at a cost of £996,761 and later sailed from Liverpool for the West Indies and Spanish Main on her maiden voyage under Captain R.H.K. Ledger. *27.12.1962:* Loading homewards from the West Indies she encountered squally weather at Antigua. The lighter DAISY, loaded with 466 bags of sugar, foundered whilst lying alongside and became a total loss. *17.11.1965:* Fire was detected in number 2 hold, while the vessel was on passage from Liverpool to Kingston. Carbon dioxide was injected into the hold, and the ship headed for La Coruña, the nearest port of refuge. Fortunately, there was no structural damage. *1.12.1965:* Sailed for Kingston after completing small repairs, and reloading cargo which had been discharged during fire fighting. An act of General Average was declared, and claims amounted to £7,000. *29.3.1968:* Alerted by an "all ships" urgency signal to shipping in the western North Atlantic originating from the Indian motor ship STATE OF MYSORE (9,371/66) to look out for the Swedish auxiliary schooner LENNART (144/10) which was drifting disabled and short of supplies in position 17.30N, 50.15W, about 665 miles due east of Barbuda. The LENNART, bound from Varberg to the Leeward Islands, had lost her sails and use of her engine and the 10 people on board were in some distress. *30.3.1968:* LENNART located at 08.00 and DALEMAN was able to put a line aboard and took the vessel in tow for Dominica. At 15.00, in heavy seas, the tow rope parted, but DALESMAN stood by until midnight when the Dutch GEESTSTAR (1,927/60) arrived. Four of the crew were taken off and the US coastguard cutter SAGEBRUSH eventually towed the disabled craft to Antigua. *30.1.1979:* Sold to Tempo Shipping Co. Ltd., Monrovia, Liberia (Navibrokers Maritime Co. S.A. (P. Apostolou, D. B. and P. Doukas), Piraeus, Greece, managers) and renamed ADRIANOS under the Greek flag. *1980:* Sold to Oceanpride Marine Corporation, Monrovia, Liberia (Shipping and Commercial Corporation (M. Lambros), Piraeus, Greece, managers) and renamed IOANNIS under the Greek flag. *4.10.1982:* Laid up at Piraeus. *1984:* Sold to Chinese shipbreakers. *14.4.1984:* Arrived at Huangpu, near Canton for demolition.

Dalesman rounding to on the flood tide in the Mersey, ready for docking.

Elemental strife

It was a voyage to remember. Of the four cosmic elements, only earth was absent - air, fire, and water were present in abundance. Air took upon itself to blow with tumultuous force, whipping up the water of the sea to menacing heights, forcing the ship to heave to with much of her deck cargo adrift. Then came the fire, deep-seated and fierce, further to test the hearts of men.

DALESMAN sailed from Liverpool, bound for Kingston, on Saturday 13th November 1965. The ship ran into strong gales from the moment she rounded the Skerries, and punched her way south, and across the Bay of Biscay. During one period, the deck cargo - all hazardous goods - was torn from its lashings, and several leaking drums of acid had to be thrown overboard. For much of the time, about three days, the vessel was hove to in heavy seas, rolling and pitching, the crew longing for the break which would allow them to head southwards to sunnier latitudes.[247]

On 17th November the break still had not come, but a shift of wind to the northwest enabled the ship to head south. Then the element of fire added its contribution to the cosmic offensive. At 17.40, shortly after assuming the new course, the Kidde-Riche fire-detection system set the alarm bells ringing stridently in the wheelhouse. There was a fire in number 2 hold! Sure enough, a wisp of grey smoke could be seen filtering from the cowl ventilators to be whipped away by the wind.

There was only one drill in this crisis. While Chief Officer Tony Billington rounded up his men and led them forward to seal off the ventilators prior to injecting carbon dioxide gas, Captain Douglas Wolstenholme brought the ship round to a new course heading for La Coruña in Northern Spain, 400 miles east south east, and the nearest port of refuge.

Despite the continuing bad weather, the ship made good headway. From time to time more gas was admitted to the burning compartment, until stocks were exhausted. At 20.42 on Thursday 18th November the ship arrived off La Coruña, the fire dormant for the moment, but, like a wild animal scenting prey, sure to spring up fiercely at the first whiff of oxygen. The weather, however, was still too rough, and the port was closed. At daylight on 19th the pilot boarded, and brought the ship to an anchor in the harbour. That afternoon, in the presence of a surveyor, number 2 hatch was opened, and the crew set about clearing the cargo from the hatch square in an effort to locate the seat of the fire. Smoke was still seeping through the slab-hatches, and Chief Officer Billington donned a Bloman smoke-helmet and went down. For a while he disappeared from sight. When at last he reappeared he was able to demonstrate where the seat of the fire was located, and a pair of hoses were rigged to drench the area through spray nozzles.

Chief Officer Billington entered the hold repeatedly to readjust the hoses and direct them to the area where they would be most effective. But it was a stubborn conflagration, which was still smouldering sullenly when the ship was brought alongside on the Saturday afternoon. By this time the local fire brigade was standing by, but an hour or so later, after an inspection by the surveyor, the fire was pronounced to be out, and a gang of dockers began unloading the cargo to uncover the seat of the fire. It was revealed two days later. A great deal of cargo had been destroyed, including three cars, whose molten remains bore silent testimony to the intensity of the heat generated. Since the fire had been confined to the centre of the hold the ship sustained no structural damage, but several slab hatches were badly charred.

On 24th November dockers began restowing the undamaged cargo. The cause of the fire was never known, all the cargo in number 2 being non-hazardous consignments of general commodities. The crew were praised for their work in containing the fire and eventually killing it without resorting to outside help, and Chief Officer Billington in particular was highly commended for his courage and leadership qualities.

It is pleasant to record that these qualities did not go unrecognised by Lloyd's, as demonstrated by the award of the Society's Medal for Meritorious Services at a ceremony in London on 24th June 1966. Meanwhile a Certificate of Seaworthiness had been issued to the ship, and she sailed from La Coruña on 1st December to resume her voyage, hopefully to be called upon in future to do battle against no more than the customary pair of elements for which she had been very effectively designed.

306. INVENTOR (4) 1964-1981 Steel screw motor ship. Two decks and five holds. One signal mast.
O.N. 303892 9,171g 4,838n 10,495d (10,840d after 1969) 468.1 (493.04 o.l.) x 63.15 x 37.9 feet. Cargo capacity: 606,490 cubic feet. Equipped with 150-ton Stülcken derrick serving the two main holds.
International Code: GLRH.
8-cyl. 2SCSA oil engine by Sulzer Brothers Ltd., Winterthur, Switzerland; 17.75 knots.

Inventor, a further development of the *Adventurer* design.

4.1963: Keel laid. *22.8.1963:* Launched by Charles Connell and Co. Ltd., Scotstoun (Yard No. 502) for the company. *13.5.1964:* Delivered at a cost of £1,552,628 and later sailed from Birkenhead for East Africa on her maiden voyage under Captain C.S.S. Boam. *28.12.1965:* Disabled by a fracture occurring in the valve chest of the pump which supplied lubricating oil to the main engine. She was rounding the southernmost tip of Africa and the position was precarious. With engines out of commission indefinitely there was a danger that she could drift ashore. A call for tug assistance was put out giving position as 34.55S, 19.48E, 12.5 miles west south west of Cape Agulhas Lighthouse. The starboard anchor was paid out and the vessel was eventually

brought up in 17 fathoms and position was only maintained with very great difficulty. It held for some 42 hours while engineers laboured to repair the defective valve chest. *29.12.1965:* At 14.15 the tug DANIE HUGO (812/59) arrived from Capetown and stood by in case her anchor failed. By 21.00 repairs had been completed and she returned to Capetown under her own power.[248] *30.3.1981:* Sold to Penta World Private Ltd. (Ban Hock Ship Management (Pte.) Ltd., managers), Singapore for US$ 2,250,000 and renamed PENTA WORLD. *25.7.1982:* Laid up at Singapore. *1985:* Sold to Ging Ya Enterprise Co .Ltd., Taiwan, for demolition. *17.5.1985:* Arrived in tow at Kaohsiung.

A 12-month delay
Delivery of the INVENTOR was considerably later than anticipated. She was, in fact, nearly twelve months late, the intended delivery date being 30th June 1963. The reasons for the delay have been explained by P.H. Rosselli, who, as a junior director of the company in those days, had the job of overseeing the building of the ship.[249]

The first delay occurred at the tank-testing stage, when the performance of the model inferred that the speed of the ship would be about half a knot less than the contract called for. Consequently, the hull lines had to be redrawn, initiating a delay of three months. Then, after the ship was launched, one of the massive Stülcken posts was found to be cracked, due, it was alleged, to insufficient preheating of

the high tensile steel during the welding process. A further four months were lost while a replacement was fetched from Germany. At last the derrick was ready for testing, but, with the 165-ton load suspended ponderously from the creaking gear, a crack appeared in the other Stülcken post! A disaster was avoided, but a further four months was lost while the company awaited a further replacement.

However, speaking retrospectively, Peter Rosselli concluded, "Although the birthpangs of INVENTOR were difficult, to put it mildly, her subsequent career, both under our colours and thereafter, proved her to be a very good and well-built ship."

307. DISCOVERER (3) 1964-1977 Steel screw motor ship. Two decks and four holds. Two masts and one signal mast. O.N. 306476 6,162g 3,299n 7,725d (7,609d after 1968). 386.5 (407.17 o.l.) x 56.65 x 34.15 feet. Cargo capacity: 402,417 cubic feet. Equipped at the foremast with one conventional 30-ton derrick and a Stülcken-patent 10-ton derrick aft serving number 4 hold. The holds were also served by four conventional 10-ton derricks and four ASEA 5-ton cranes.
International Code: GMUC.
7-cyl. 2SCSA Gotaverken oil engine by A/B Lindholmens Varv., Gothenburg, Sweden; 16.25 knots.

The Swedish-built *Discoverer* brought a new look to the Harrison fleet. *[J. and M. Clarkson]*

7.6.1963: Keel laid. *21.11.1963:* Launched by A/B Lindholmens Varv., Gothenburg, Sweden (Yard No. 1083) for the company. *19.3.1964:* Delivered at a cost of £849,984 and later sailed from Liverpool for Kingston and Mexico on her maiden voyage under Captain Alan Moreton MBE. *28.8.1964:* An outbreak of fire was discovered among the bales of cotton in number 2 'tween deck at 02.15 when alongside at Manchester. Crew and dockers fought the fire until the arrival of the fire brigade. The fire was extinguished at 05.50 but had caused damage to steelwork on the port side and upper deck. An act of General Average was declared, claims amounting to £6,000. *13.7.1977:* Sold to China Ocean Shipping Co., Peking, People's Republic of China for US$2,225,000 and renamed JIN CHANG.

12.6.1979: In collision in the Gulf of Oman with the Korean bulk carrier OKPO PIONEER (9,471/69) when on passage from the Persian Gulf to Karachi. Although both vessels were seriously damaged they were able to reach Dubai where temporary repairs were effected. JIN CHANG had a gaping hole in her starboard side in way of number 4 hold which later took 50 tons of steel to rectify. The main, upper and lower 'tween decks were buckled as far as the hatch coaming, while propeller shaft and main engines were out of alignment. The OKPO PIONEER sustained damage to shell plates in the vicinity of the forecastle and fore peak tank, and the stem was holed. Her port anchor was lost overboard, and was later found damaged on board JIN CHANG. Temporary repairs were carried out at Bandar Shahpur and later completed at Singapore. *19.6.1979:* JIN CHANG transferred to Jebel Ali for permanent repairs. *14.8.1979:* Sailed for China. *1991:* Renamed SU YUAN. *1992:* Sold to J. Yang Shipping Co. Ltd., St.Vincent and the Grenadines (Jiang Tong Co. Ltd., Hong Kong, managers). *1994:* Disclassed by the Chinese Register and presumed broken up.

The DISCOVERER-class vessels were designed for the Caribbean and Gulf of Mexico trades and were considered comparatively small, fast and easy to manoeuvre.

Discoverer as the Chinese *Jin Chang,* the name being spelt *Jinchang* on her hull.
[J. and M. Clarkson]

308. STATESMAN (6) 1964-1977 Steel motor ship. Two decks and four holds. Two masts and one signal mast.
O.N. 306478 6,162g 3,296n 7,725d (7,609d after 1968) 386.5 (407.17 o.l.) x 56.65 x 34.15 feet. Cargo capacity: 402,417 cubic feet. Equipped at the foremast with one conventional 30-ton derrick and a Stülcken-patent 10-ton derrick aft serving number 4 hold. The holds were also served by four conventional 10-ton derricks and four ASEA 5-ton cranes.
International Code: GMUD.
7-cyl. 2SCSA Gotaverken oil engine by A/B Lindholmens Varv., Gothenburg, Sweden; 16.25 knots.

22.6.1963: Keel laid. *22.1.1964:* Launched by A/B Lindholmens Varv., Gothenburg, Sweden (Yard No. 1084) for the company. *29.5.1964:* Delivered at a cost of £844,959 and later sailed from London for the West Indies on her maiden voyage under Captain G.F. Penston. *4.11.1965:* Outward bound in dense fog from London for the West Indies, in collision with the Royal Mail motor ship DURANGO (9,801/44) off Thameshaven. Although only a glancing blow, side plating in way of number 2 hold was well set in, and six frames became detached. She returned to West India Dock for repairs. The bill for repairs came to about £14,000 and was settled by the underwriters.[250] *27.11.1965:* Sailed for Barbados. *16.2.1967:* Whilst anchored at the Tail-o'-the-Bank on the River Clyde was struck at 05.50 by CLAN MATHESON (7,553/57) and sustained extensive damage. The cost of repairs, about £6,300, was claimed from Cayzer, Irvine and Co. Ltd. *8.7.1977:* Sold to China Ocean Shipping

Co., Peking, People's Republic of China for US$2,225,000 and renamed JIAN CHANG. *11.11.1990:* Ran into heavy weather off the coast of Vietnam when bound from Singapore to Hainan. At 12.35 she sent out an "urgency" signal requesting immediate assistance "due to water entering the engine room" and presumably immobilising the ship. The British tanker BRITISH RENOWN (133,035/74) relayed the signal to Hong Kong, while the Danish container-ship LAURA MAERSK (43,325/80) and the British oil support vessel OIL HUSTLER (1,053/76) headed for her last reported position 15.00N, 110.09E, about 131 miles, 121 degrees from Da Nang. Subsequent messages reported that she was foundering and the crew was abandoning ship. Between them the two vessels rescued 37 survivors including the Master. Two bodies were seen floating in the water, but rough seas prevented their retrieval.

Statesman approaches Eastham.

[Tom Rayner]

309. PHILOSOPHER (3) 1964-1977 Steel motor ship. Two decks and four holds. Two masts and one signal mast. O.N. 306488 6,162g 3,296n 7,725d (7,609d after 1968). 386.5 (407.17 o.l.) x 56.65 x 34.15 feet. Cargo capacity: 402,417 cubic feet. Equipped at the foremast with one conventional 30-ton derrick and a Stülcken-patent 10-ton derrick aft serving number 4 hold. The holds were also served by four conventional 10-ton derricks and four ASEA 5-ton cranes. International Code: GNPU.

7-cyl. 2SCSA Gotaverken oil engine by A/B Lindholmens Varv., Gothenburg, Sweden; 16.25 knots.

The *Philosopher* demonstrates her speed and manoeuvrability on trials prior to delivery on 1st September 1964.

25.11.1963: Keel laid. *18.3.1964:* Launched by A/B Lindholmens Varv., Gothenburg, Sweden (Yard No. 1089) for the company. *1.9.1964:* Delivered at a cost of £825,259 and later sailed from London for the West Indies on her maiden voyage under Captain G.W. McGuiness. *28.4.1967:* When lying alongside at Georgetown, Demerara rested on the mud at low tide, setting in several bottom plates and causing damage to the value of £5,000. This was unusual, for vessels often lay safely aground at Demerara, and in this instance she must have had the misfortune to find a hard patch. *31.5.1975:* Fire broke out in a cargo of cotton in number 3 hold whilst berthed at Santo Tomas de Castilla, Guatemala. Some 300 bales were destroyed and another 200 damaged by smoke and water before the blaze was extinguished. *16.12.1975:* Shortly after departing from Willemstad, Curacao following a call for bunkers on a voyage from Colombia to

Philosopher at anchor. *[J. and M. Clarkson]*

Manchester, her cargo of cotton in number 4 hold was found to be on fire. The hold was flooded with carbon dioxide and the vessel returned to Willemstad. The fire proved to be particularly stubborn and it was only when high-expansion foam generators were air freighted from the United States that it was finally subdued. The success of this system encouraged the board to equip all their vessels with high-expansion foam generators and ample supplies of foam compound. *8.7.1977:* Sold to China Ocean Shipping Co., Peking, People's Republic of China for US$2,225,000 and renamed YONG CHANG. *21.8.1979:* Struck heavily by the South Korean bulk carrier HAE DUCK No.1 (9,469/69) whilst lying alongside at Kelang, Malaysia discharging

general cargo. She sustained severe damage in way of number 4 hold on the starboard side and a considerable quantity of perishable cargo was destroyed. Temporary repairs effected at Kelang. *8.9.1979:* Arrived at Singapore under tow for permanent repair. *24.9.1982:* In collision with the Japanese tug SEIKO MARU (199/70) about 2.7 miles south east of Yokohama. The tug sank with the loss of one life. YONG CHANG, with 1,500 tons of general cargo on board, was proceeding from Yokohama to seek shelter from Typhoon Ken in Tokyo Bay and sustained bow damage and flooding as a result of the collision. *1990:* Sold to Treveni Shipbreakers. *13.11.1990:* Arrived at Alang.

310. NATURALIST (3) 1965-1977 Steel motor ship. Two decks and four holds. Two masts and one signal mast.
O.N. 308649 6,162g 3,217n 7,725d (7,484d after 1968) 386.5 (407.17 o.l.) x 56.65 x 34.15 feet Cargo capacity: 402,001 cubic feet. Equipped at the foremast with one conventional 30-ton derrick and a Stülcken-patent 10-ton derrick aft serving number 4 hold. The holds were also served by four conventional 10-ton derricks and four ASEA 5-ton cranes.
International Code: GRSU.
7-cyl. 2SCSA Gotaverken oil engine by A/B Lindholmens Varv., Gothenburg, Sweden; 16.25 knots.

10.11.1964: Keel laid. *2.3.1965:* Launched by A/B Lindholmens Varv., Gothenburg, Sweden (Yard No.1091) for the company. *16.9.1965:* Delivered at a cost of £843,745 and later sailed from Liverpool for Kingston and Mexico on her maiden voyage under Captain Alan Moreton MBE.

26.8.1977: Sold to China Ocean Shipping Co., Peking, People's Republic of China for US$2,370,000 and renamed YI CHANG. *12.1991:* Sold to Chinese shipbreakers. *1992:* Broken up in Guangdong Province.

Naturalist.   *[J.K. Byass]*

311. NOVELIST (2) 1965-1977 Steel motor ship. Two decks and four holds. Two masts and one signal mast.
O.N. 308650 6,162g 3,200n 7,725d 386.5 (407.17 o.l.) x 56.65 x 34.15 feet. Cargo capacity: 368,267 cubic feet. Equipped at the foremast with one conventional 30-ton derrick and a Stülcken-patent 10-ton derrick aft serving number 4 hold. The holds were also served by four conventional 10-ton derricks and four ASEA 5-ton cranes.
International Code: GRTA.
7-cyl. 2SCSA Gotaverken oil engine by A/B Lindholmens Varv., Gothenburg, Sweden; 16.25 knots.

18.1.1965: Keel laid. *6.5.1965:* Launched by A/B Lindholmens Varv., Gothenburg, Sweden (Yard No.1092) for the company. *22.10.1965:* Delivered at a cost of £803,238 and later sailed from London for the West Indies on her maiden voyage under Captain T.W. Kent. *28.10.1977:* Sold

to China Ocean Shipping Co., Peking, People's Republic of China for US$2,370,000 and renamed WU CHANG. *1995:* Owners became Fujian Shipping and Enterprises Co. Ltd., Hong Kong, but remained registered in Fujian, People's Republic of China. *10.2003:* Still listed in Lloyd's Register.

Novelist docking at Liverpool.   *[J.K. Byass]*

312. TRADER (2) 1966-1980 Steel motor ship. Two decks and four holds. One signal/radar mast.
O.N. 308671 6,448g 3,292n 7,925d 396.5 (418.15 o.l.) x 59.1 x 32.25 feet. Cargo capacity: 412,045 cubic feet. Equipped with 70-ton Stülcken derrick serving numbers 2 and 3 holds. The holds were also served by two ASEA 10-ton and two 5-ton cranes and six 5-ton derricks.
International Code: GSRH.
Two 8-cyl. 4SCSA Pielstick vee-type oil engines by A/B Lindholmens Varv., Gothenburg, Sweden, single-reduction geared to a single screw; 16.25 knots.

9.12.1965: Keel laid. *23.4.1966:* Launched by A/B Lindholmens Varv., Gothenburg, Sweden (Yard No.1097) for the company. *15.9.1966:* Delivered at a cost of £1,248,070 and later sailed from Liverpool for Kingston and Mexico on her maiden voyage under Captain W.E. Hinde. *22.5.1967:* Assisted in the rescue and salvage of the British yacht BRAEMAR off Land's End. *22.12.11975:* Her cargo of pipes and heavy vehicles shifted in bad weather. *24.12.1975:* Put into Halifax, Nova Scotia, as a port of refuge. *20.3.1980:* Sold to Hong Leong-Seatran Lines Pte. Ltd., Singapore (Seatran Shipping Co. Ltd., Bangkok, Thailand, managers) for U.S.$1,437,000 and renamed BANGPRA-IN. *1983:* Sold to Thai Mercantile Marine Ltd., Bangkok, Thailand and renamed PICHIT SAMUT. *1986:* Sold to Thailand Demolition Co. Ltd., Thailand for demolition. *11.1.1986:* Arrived at Rayong.

TRADER and her sister LINGUIST were the first British-registered vessels to be powered by twin S.E.M.T.-Pielstick oil engines geared to a single shaft. The innovatory Pielstick system, originally a French design, was more compact and of lighter weight than conventional diesel engines of similar power. Consequently, the propulsion machinery could be sited at the extreme after end of the vessel without having recourse to elaborate ballast techniques to compensate for excessive trim, thus leaving broader sections of the hull available for cargo. Another space/weight saving factor was the elimination of boilers, since the engines were designed to run on oil of 250 seconds viscosity and/or diesel oil, which did not need preheating in the double-bottom tanks.

Two photographs of *Trader* on trials, including an unusual view from directly overhead. Slightly larger than her Swedish predecessors, she was of a new design with a Stülcken derrick and accommodation right aft.

Drama off Land's End

In the spring of 1967 Sir Francis Chichester, in his yacht, GIPSY MOTH IV, was expected back in Plymouth after a momentous single-handed voyage around the world. Among the reporters and TV crews hovering in helicopters or tossing about off the Cornish coast in a motley fleet of craft, eager to be first to sight GIPSY MOTH's mainsail and record the triumphant homecoming, was the British yacht BRAEMAR, chartered by Independent Television News (ITN), which had selected a cruising area between Lizard Head and Bishop's Rock. The crew's only incentive to brave the acute discomfort and misery brought about by the onslaught of persistent south west gales was the tenuous prospect of a few dramatic close-ups of Sir Francis and his weather-stained yacht as he made his landfall. However, this worthy mission was all but forgotten when BRAEMAR started making water in the engine room. At 05.18 on 22nd May Land's End Radio received and relayed a distress call from BRAEMAR, who gave her position as 49.26N, 6.21W, or about 27 miles south of Bishop's Rock. The call was acknowledged by several ships in the vicinity, but TRADER, 16 miles to the westward, happened to be nearest. She informed Land's End that she expected to reach BRAEMAR's position at 06.45. On her arrival, preparations were made to take the little vessel in tow, a difficult and sometimes dangerous task in the gale force wind and heavy seas.[251]

Nevertheless, by 09.00 the towing line was connected, and TRADER set off on a north easterly course towards Falmouth, some 70 miles distant, her charge lurching in her wake. The sea seemed determined to take its toll, however. The incessant jerking and chafing as the yacht wallowed before the heavy following sea proved too much for the towing gear, and soon after midday the tow-rope parted, leaving the hapless craft gyrating wildly in the trough of the waves. All TRADER's efforts to reconnect the tow-rope were frustrated by the conditions, but by 13.00 the St. Mary's Lifeboat, GUY AND CLARE HUNTER, had appeared on the scene, which had now shifted to a point 19 miles south by west of Wolf Rock. By 13.30 the lifeboatmen had secured a line to the waterlogged vessel, and set off towards Newlyn, a mere 30 miles away, bearing north north east. Nevertheless, it took over 24 hours for the lifeboat to reach her destination with her charge. Conditions were so bad that on more than one occasion the coxswain believed he would have to abandon the sluggish craft. At dusk on 22nd, in difficult circumstances, he took off 16 of the 19 persons on board the casualty, and hove to for the night. Early next morning course was resumed and at 14.30 on 23rd May the lifeboat, with her semi-submerged tow, reached the haven of Newlyn.

It had been a fruitless and harrowing experience for the men from ITN, and their commentaries on this occasion must have been something to listen to.

Rogue cargo 1

The securing of cargo in holds and 'tween decks is a vital task which often taxes the ingenuity of chief officers and other responsible officials to the limit. It is not a task to be undertaken lightly, and can only be effectively carried out after substantial outlay in hundreds of fathoms of lashing wire, scores of bottle-screws, and yards of heavy timber for chocking and shoring. Many cargoes readily chock themselves, others are more difficult, and some - at least from this aspect - may be described as rogue cargoes, especially when all fails, and they break adrift in heavy weather. Then they become about as manageable and as dangerous as a herd of stampeding elephants.

It was with a cargo of such potential that TRADER sailed from Houston, Texas, on 16th December 1975. It was a large consignment of bulky oil-well material and steel pipes. The pipes, 10 inches in diameter, and lengths varying from 36 feet to 48 feet, were stowed in numbers 2 and 4 holds in a regular, fore-and-aft pattern, strips of dunnage separating each tier. Three body-and-soul lashings of doubled 2-inch wire, set up with bottle-screws, parcelled up the finished stow. In the wings, where the run of the ship left unwanted gaps between the

Trader fully loaded and outward bound in the Mersey.

pipe-stow and the skin, vertical baulks of timber were shored off to the ship's side frames to hold the stow in place. This exacting work was carried out by the Houston longshoremen, who could turn their hands to most things. Besides, Texas waterfront unions insisted that it was their work, anyway. However, they worked under the supervision of the ship's Chief Officer, and invariably carried out whatever demands he made on them, without question. And, undoubtedly, the finished product looked neat, workmanlike, and secure.[252]

A floor of dunnage was laid over the pipe stow, and a number of heavy lifts weighing up to 20 tons were landed thereon, and wire lashed to whatever lashing-points were available. Few were ideal; most were makeshift, such as drainage-holes in stringer plates, lightening holes in beam knees, and any perforation in the steelwork which would take a 2-inch wire. When finished it looked rather like a monstrous spider's web. Captain Geoff Lovell and Chief Officer Richard Bourne were under no illusions as to the weather they were likely to encounter on the voyage home, and spared no pains to make the job as tight and secure as possible.

For the few days after the ship had sailed, the crew diligently tended the lashings, taking up slack on the wires caused by vibration of the ship at sea, and hardening up the timber shores, getting ready for the bad weather which would surely come. Their forecasts were correct. By 21st the ship was being buffeted by a south-easterly gale, and during breakfast on 22nd, by which time the ship had reached a point about 400 miles south of Halifax, a particularly heavy sea swept on board, sending her lurching over to port. Instead of righting herself, however, the ship seemed to hang there, rolling sluggishly, while from the holds came the ominous rumbling and banging noises which could only mean that the cargo had broken adrift, and was battering away at the ship's side. Captain Lovell at once put the ship onto a northerly course to ease the violent motion, while Chief Officer Bourne led his sailors into the holds.

They were confronted by a daunting sight. In both holds, Caterpillar tractors, oil-well drills, castings, and freight containers lay in untidy heaps in the port-wing, or slithered and rolled about with the ship's motion, from time to time ramming the ship's side with a deafening clamour. The once so tidy stow of pipes was an amorphous mass, with pipes sticking out at random like needles from a tangled skein of steel knitting. All the wire lashings had given way, mostly due to bottle-screw failure. The sturdy shores had collapsed and been smashed like so much matchwood.

There was nothing the crew could do to restow the cargo; all they could do was secure it in situ, to prevent further movement and damage. Crawling about on the unstable mass at great risk to life and limb, they passed wires across the ridged and furrowed floor of pipes, secured the lumbering pieces of steel, hog-tying them as and where they lay. Captain Lovell, meanwhile, had decided there was nothing for it but to make for the nearest port of refuge - Halifax - where every facility for the discharging and restowing of that rogue cargo would be available.

The ship sidled into Halifax harbour in the small hours of 24th December, and work began on Boxing Day. This time, after the jumbled cargo had been landed, sorted, and restowed, the pipe-stow was kept clear; all heavy and bulky items were stowed on their own ground in 'tween decks and on the weather deck where ample and more suitable lashing points were available. A great deal of the cargo had been damaged, unfortunately, and the ship, too, had suffered. Frames had been hammered over, twisted and distorted; welded joints had been cracked, the shell plating dented; pipe casings and ladders had been destroyed; the timber spar-ceiling shattered.

Temporary repairs were made good, and a Certificate of Seaworthiness issued, allowing the ship to proceed. She sailed on 29th December, and arrived at Liverpool on 7th January 1976 without further mishap.

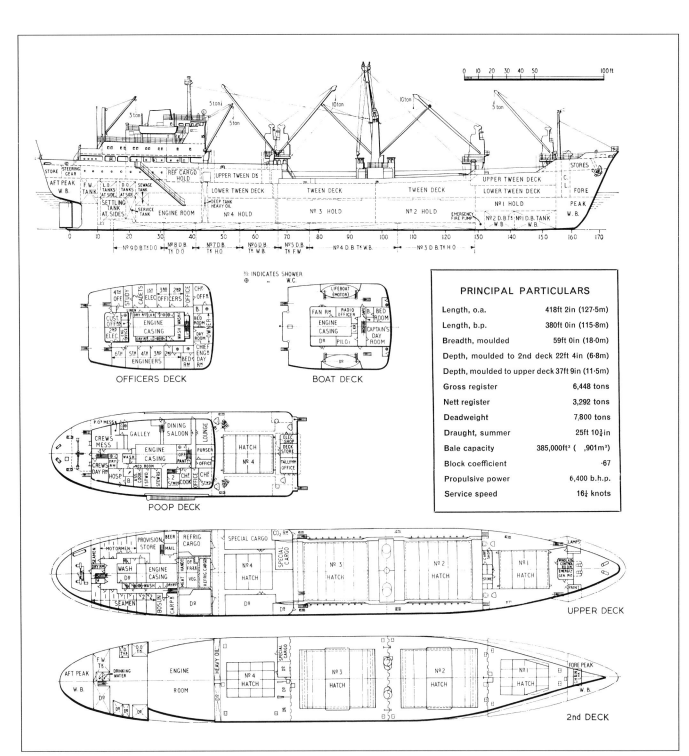

PRINCIPAL PARTICULARS

Length, o.a.	418ft 2in (127·5m)
Length, b.p.	380ft 0in (115·8m)
Breadth, moulded	59ft 0in (18·0m)
Depth, moulded to 2nd deck	22ft 4in (6·8m)
Depth, moulded to upper deck	37ft 9in (11·5m)
Gross register	6,448 tons
Nett register	3,292 tons
Deadweight	7,800 tons
Draught, summer	25ft 10¾in
Bale capacity	385,000ft³ (,901m³)
Block coefficient	·67
Propulsive power	6,400 b.h.p.
Service speed	16¼ knots

OFFICERS DECK

BOAT DECK

POOP DECK

UPPER DECK

2nd DECK

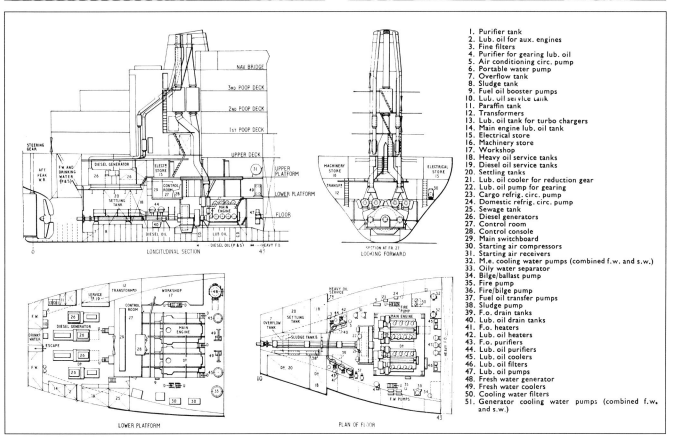

1. Purifier tank
2. Lub. oil for aux. engines
3. Fine filters
4. Purifier for gearing lub. oil
5. Air conditioning circ. pump
6. Portable water pump
7. Overflow tank
8. Sludge tank
9. Fuel oil booster pumps
10. Lub. oil service tank
11. Paraffin tank
12. Transformers
13. Lub. oil tank for turbo chargers
14. Main engine lub. oil tank
15. Electrical store
16. Machinery store
17. Workshop
18. Heavy oil service tanks
19. Diesel oil service tanks
20. Settling tanks
21. Lub. oil cooler for reduction gear
22. Lub. oil pump for gearing
23. Cargo refrig. circ. pump
24. Domestic refrig. circ. pump
25. Sewage tank
26. Diesel generators
27. Control room
28. Control console
29. Main switchboard
30. Starting air compressors
31. Starting air receivers
32. M.e. cooling water pumps (combined f.w. and s.w.)
33. Oily water separator
34. Bilge/ballast pump
35. Fire pump
36. Fire/bilge pump
37. Fuel oil transfer pumps
38. Sludge pump
39. F.o. drain tanks
40. Lub. oil drain tanks
41. F.o. heaters
42. Lub. oil heaters
43. F.o. purifiers
44. Lub. oil purifiers
45. Lub. oil coolers
46. Lub. oil filters
47. Lub. oil pumps
48. Fresh water generator
49. Fresh water coolers
50. Cooling water filters
51. Generator cooling water pumps (combined f.w. and s.w.)

Trader was designed for the great variety of merchandise carried in Harrison's Caribbean trade, and for rapid loading and discharge. The general arrangement drawing opposite shows her particularly large hatches, and the photographs below it show the special 'tween deck hatch covers. Resting on rolling hatch beams, the covers were divided into three. The centre section folded athwartships (left hand view) and the forward and aft sections folding longitudinally (right hand view). The aim of this arrangement was to achieve precisely the 'tween deck area required on a particular voyage.

This page clockwise from top left: the galley; a seaman's single-berth cabin; the engine room layout; the machinery control room; reduction gearing; a view across the cylinder tops.

301

313. LINGUIST (3) 1966-1980 Steel motor ship. Two decks and four holds. One signal/radar mast.
O.N. 308686 6,448g 3,292n 7,925d 396.5 (418.15 o.l.) x 59.1 x 32.25 feet. Cargo capacity: 412,045 cubic feet. Equipped with 70-ton Stülcken derrick serving numbers 2 and 3 holds. The holds were also served by two ASEA 10-ton and two 5-ton cranes and six 5-ton derricks.
International Code: GTSA.
Two 8-cyl. 4SCSA Pielstick vee-oil engines by A/B Lindholmens Varv., Gothenburg, Sweden, single reduction geared to a single screw; 16.25 knots.

7.3.1966: Keel laid. *22.6.1966:* Launched by A/B Lindholmens Varv., Gothenburg, Sweden (Yard No.1098) for the company. *15.12.1966:* Delivered at a cost of £1,245,535 and later sailed from Liverpool for the West Indies on her maiden voyage under Captain A. Moreton MBE. *18.10.1972:* Fire broke out in number 2 hold while the vessel was lying at City Docks, Houston. She sustained no structural damage, but about 30 bales of cotton linters were badly charred and off-loaded. *18.12.1978:* Briefly ashore in the Crosby Channel in the approaches to Liverpool. *1.2.1979:* When bound from Liverpool to Houston, pieces of heavy cargo stowed in no.3 'tween deck broke adrift, putting the ship in some danger. *18.4.1980:* Sold for to Hong Leong-Seatran Lines Pte. Ltd., Singapore (Seatran Shipping Co.

Ltd., Bangkok, Thailand, managers) for US$1,437,500 and renamed BANG PLEE 12. *1981:* Sold to Naviera Universal S.A., Lima, Peru and renamed UNISOL. *7.12.1983:* Loading bagged cement, rolls of paper and foodstuffs at Chandler, Canada for Matarani, when high winds and heavy swell rolling in from the sea caused her to break adrift from her moorings. Swept ashore about half a mile from her berth in position 48.20N, 64.40W, and began breaking up on the rocks. 34 crew members and a pilot who happened to be on board were air-lifted to safety by a Canadian Armed Forces helicopter. Shortly afterwards the ship broke her back, releasing hundreds of tons of fuel oil into the sea and causing pollution on a wide scale.[253]

The sister to *Trader, Linguist* leaving Liverpool on 24th November 1979. *[Paul Boot]*

Fog on the river
Inward bound from Belfast on 18th December 1978, LINGUIST approached the Liverpool pilot cutter, on station off the Bar Lightbuoy, just after 07.30, and the pilot boarded at 07.43. Weather and visibility were excellent - even the light on Great Orme, 21 miles away, was visible - and LINGUIST headed for the Queen's Channel at full speed, expecting to dock at Langton at 09.00. It was a nuisance that the ship's radar, which had served well crossing the Irish Sea, had developed a fault, and the Radio Officer was working diligently to bring it back into service. Not that it was essential in pilotage waters - provided the weather remained clear...[254]

At 08.18 LINGUIST passed the starboard hand Channel Buoy C5, and those on the bridge became uneasily aware that the shore lights, still bright in the grey light of dawn, were fading rapidly...and then were suddenly blotted out. A low-lying bank of dense fog was drifting swiftly across the channel ahead of them. All at once, as the moist, grey blanket enveloped the ship, the morning's mood of optimism deteriorated to one of gloom. Speed was immediately reduced from 13 knots to about 6½ knots, but pilot and navigators, blinded both visually and electronically (for Sparks was still tinkering with the defunct radar) were painfully aware that their ship, swept along by a flood tide, was careering up a narrow channel whose marks had been

obliterated. At C5 Buoy the Crosby Channel sweeps through a graceful arc to starboard into the river itself, and instinctively the pilot put the ship into the turn, hoping to bring the ship to an anchor, but preferably not in the bend...

At 08.25 officers on the bridge and in the engine-room felt a slight shudder, and the ship heeled to starboard. They realised at once that the ship was aground - but where? They would have to report their predicament to Port Radar, and meanwhile try to wrest the ship off the bank back into deep water. Fog is an insidious phenomenon. Not only does it obscure all that is familiar to the senses, but it disorientates mentally and physically, and one cannot help feeling literally lost. The following is an extract from the transcript of the VHF conversation between LINGUIST and Port Radar after the grounding.
08.35 m.v. LINGUIST... Have you got us on radar by C3? [i.e. to LINGUIST's starboard ('right') side of the Channel.]
08.36 Port Radar... Can't see you by C - did you say C3?
LINGUIST. Yes. Where do you think we are?
Port Radar. Well, I've got an echo over the other side of the Channel, almost outside the wreck buoys. I can't see you; only the big echo there.
LINGUIST. Yes; where do you think we are? We're in dense fog now.

302

Port Radar. Yes; I think you are going out of the Channel. Stand by a second.

0838 Port Radar. I appear to have you going outside the Channel between C6 and C8 [buoys]. [i.e., on the port ('wrong') side of the Channel]. If that is you, you'll have to come to starboard immediately to clear. I'll tell the duty officer to put a fix on you.

LINGUIST Yes; do that, please.

08.43 Port Radar. Is your radar inoperable?

LINGUIST. No, it's operating now. Would you have us between C7 and C9? [i.e., hopefully, still on the starboard side of the channel].

Port Radar. No, I have been trying to pick out which one is you and it obviously must be you between C6 and C8. [i.e., on the opposite side.].[255]

Clearly (if the word can be used in this context), in the few minutes since entering the fog bank, LINGUIST, with the flood tide on her starboard quarter, had inadvertently crossed over to the opposite side of the channel and grounded on

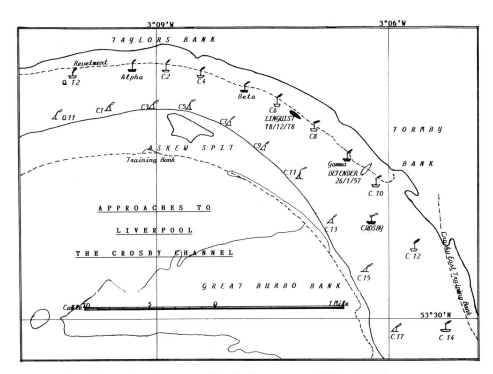

The positions where *Linguist* and *Defender* encountered Taylor's Bank revetment.

the Taylor's Bank revetment, less than a mile, incidentally, from the spot where the DEFENDER had grounded that wild January night nearly 22 years before.

The DEFENDER's mishap and narrow escape must have been very much in the minds of the anxious pilot and navigators aboard LINGUIST. Would they, too, be so lucky? Several factors stood in the ship's favour. It seems she grounded broadside on to the sandy bank fronting the training wall at a comparatively low speed; internal soundings established that the watertight integrity of the ship had not been breached; and the rising tide offered every prospect of floating clear sooner rather than later. Now that Port Radar had fixed the ship's position (confirmed by her own radar which was now functioning) plans could be made to retrieve the situation.

Thus, at 09.14, still in dense fog, the ship came

astern, floated clear, and dropped her starboard anchor. At once the flood tide began swinging the ship's stern upstream, until eventually she lay head out with her starboard side against the training wall. It was at this moment that the LINGUIST became temporarily disabled due to an excess of sand entering and clogging the intakes into the machinery cooling systems, and until they were cleared the ship was without power. However, by 10.00, power was restored, and the ship was manoeuvred clear of the bank to anchor in deep water. During the next hour, visibility improved, but before proceeding to dock, the Master decided to return to more open waters off the Bar to carry out technical trials of engines and steering gear. The trials proved satisfactory, and the vessel re-entered the channel once more to resume her delayed docking programme without further mishap.

Rogue cargo 2

The LINGUIST was about 650 miles south of Cape Race, Newfoundland, riding out a severe storm, when part of the ship's cargo of containers and heavy items of machinery broke adrift in number 3 'tween deck as lashings and shores yielded to the ship's violent motion, and gave way. The ship had sailed from Liverpool on 10th February 1979, bound for Houston, Texas, and although the weather had been bad for most of the time it reached its frightening climax at 10.30 on 21st February, when all hell was let loose. The ship was promptly hove to, head on, to wind and sea, but by that time no fewer than nine heavy lifts of between 20 and 25 tonnes were charging freely around the 'tween deck threatening the lives and limbs of anyone who got in the way. With the mindless ferocity of stampeding buffaloes they battered away at the remaining cargo and each other, ramming the unprotected ship's side as if to seek the freedom of the open sea. Valiantly, members of the crew descended into the hold to try and secure the hurtling monsters, and succeeded several times in passing wires round individual pieces. But invariably, before they could be set up taut a sudden, violent lurch would part them and send the sailors scampering for safety.[256]

The situation was desperate, and called for desperate measures. After some urgent discussion Captain Dennis Riley decided to transfer oil, and give the ship a 10 degree list to starboard. This would at least have the effect of concentrating the errant cargo to one side. More controversially, he sounded the Chief Engineer's views on welding the heavy pieces to the steel deck.

Chief Engineer Reg Bishop agreed that it was the only recourse left to them and, with the help of Second

Engineer R. Cornforth, began assembling his equipment. It was not a decision to be taken lightly. The risk of starting a fire in the cargo-filled hold was very high, but the risk of breaching the ship's side if nothing was done was even higher. Captain Riley made his decision; stringent fire precautions were taken, and Chief and Second set about their work with a will. One wonders how long it had been since they had last used a welding torch. Probably not since they served their time, for it is not a trade practised every day by ships' engineers.

Nevertheless, the operation was highly successful. With their late antagonists effectively hobbled, the exhausted sailors found new heart, and set up further lashings, working non-stop until midnight, when Captain Riley felt sufficiently confident to turn the ship onto her proper course to resume her voyage, still leaning rather drunkenly to starboard.

LINGUIST arrived at Houston on 1st March without further incident, and was met on the dock by Captain J.B. Mitchell, the Marine Superintendent, who had flown out to inspect the damage, and enquire into the causes of the near-disaster. As is often the case, they were several and diverse. A strike of lorry drivers had affected delivery to the ship's side thus restricting the planning of suitable space; by the late seventies most handy cargoes (one recalls the thousands of bags of nuts and bolts endemic to most shipments out of the United Kingdom) used in former times to fill broken stowage and make a tight stow, were now being shipped in containers; instead, reliance was being placed on shores, which were all too easily displaced, due to vibration, or shrinkage, or both.

303

314. MAGICIAN (3) 1968-1981 Steel motor ship. Two decks and five holds.
O.N. 334250 8,454g 4,710n 11,100d 468.7 (494.0 o.l.) x 63.2 x 37.9 feet. Cargo capacity: 601,961 cubic feet. Equipped with 150-ton Stülcken serving the two main holds, along with four 5-ton conventional derricks. In addition there were two ASEA 10-ton and three 5-ton cranes and 10-ton Stülcken derrick at number 5 hatch.
International Code: GYPQ.
8-cyl. 2SCSA oil engine by Sulzer Brothers Ltd., Winterthur, Switzerland; 17.3 knots.

15.3.1968: Launched by Doxford and Sunderland Shipbuilding and Engineering Co. Ltd., Sunderland (Yard No. 884) for the company. *2.10.1968:* Delivered at a cost of £1,436,040 and later sailed from Liverpool for Kingston and Mexico on her maiden voyage under Captain G.W. Sigsworth. *9.9.1974:* Ran into heavy weather east of Bermuda when on passage from Houston to Manchester and cargo in number 3 'tween deck was found to be adrift. Investigation was hampered by oil fumes and the space could only be entered wearing breathing apparatus. The space contained three heavy pieces of machinery, 12 standard containers, and some pieces of structural steel. All except one item of machinery had broken adrift, causing extensive damage. Some of the containers held drums of lubricating oil and oil additives and many were crushed, spilling their contents so that containers and heavy lifts were covered in oil. The ship was hove to easing her motion and the following day the hatches were opened and the holds ventilated. The cargo was re-secured as far as possible and the voyage was resumed. *15.9.1974:* Arrived at Manchester without further incident, but the damage to cargo and containers was extensive. *13.1.1977:* Another similar incident occurred when the vessel was on passage from Beira to Capetown. Again, the location was number 3 'tween deck where 14 standard containers loaded with pallets of bagged asbestos were stowed. The stowage was inspected daily, the final inspection being the day before her arrival at Capetown. Heavy weather made any further inspection impossible and it was only when the hatch was opened that the full extent of the havoc wrought was realised. All the boxes except one had broken adrift, and were scattered throughout the 'tween deck with their contents shed overall. Only two of the boxes were suitable to be used again; the rest were written off. *12.5.1981:* Sold to Admiral Shipping Co. (Pte.) Ltd. (Madam Dolly Seah), Singapore for US$3,000,000 and renamed CHERRY CRYSTAL. *21.10.1982:* Arrived at Le Havre to load barley but shortly afterwards the crew came out on strike, claiming that their wages were 18 months in arrears. *8.12.1982:* The ship was arrested on security of $300,000 until the matter was later settled. *11.12.1982:* Ship released. *1985:* Sold to Indian shipbreakers. *19.6.1985:* Arrived at Alang.

Harrisons returned to British builders for *Magician* (seen here on trials prior to delivery on 2nd October 1968) and *Historian*.

[Turners (Photography) Ltd.]

The main cylinder heads in *Magician*.

315. HISTORIAN (5) 1968-1981 Steel motor ship. Two decks and five holds.
O.N. 334255 8,454g 4,710n 11,100d 468.7 (494.0 o.l.) x 63.2 x 37.9 feet. Cargo capacity: 601,961 cubic feet. Equipped with 150-ton Stülcken serving the two main hatches, along with four 5-ton conventional derricks. In addition there were two ASEA 10-ton and three 5-ton cranes and 10-ton Stülcken derrick at number 5 hatch.
International Code: GYRD.
8-cyl. 2SCSA oil engine by Sulzer Brothers Ltd., Winterthur, Switzerland; 17.3 knots.

Historian approaches Eastham on 28th April 1979 with her Stülcken derrick, but not her radar mast, lowered to transit the Manchester Ship Canal.
[J. and M. Clarkson]

11.6.1968: Launched by Doxford and Sunderland Shipbuilding and Engineering Co. Ltd., Sunderland (Yard No. 885) for the company. *29.11.1968:* Delivered at a cost of £1,424,020 and later sailed from Birkenhead for East Africa on her maiden voyage under Captain R.P. Jones. *7.4.1971:* While discharging pipework from number 4 hatch at Vera Cruz, Mexico a sling parted and a section of pipework fell to the tank top, piercing number 5 fuel oil tank, and spilling oil into the hold. The local Lloyd's Surveyor recommended that the vessel proceed to Galveston for repairs, leaving the hatch open to prevent the accumulation of gas. *10.4.1971:* Arrived at Galveston. *29.9.1972:* Fire broke out in number 3 hold whilst berthed at Huskisson Dock, Liverpool after a voyage from East Africa. Firemen successfully fought the blaze using high-expansion foam. *4.9.1974:* Sailed from the Spithead anchorage and returned the following day with engine trouble. *8.9.1974:* Sailed for Maracaibo after completing repairs. *31.10.1979:* When on passage from Dar es Salaam to Avonmouth via the Suez Canal, a sudden emergency arose when the packing and ring of the stern gland, where the propeller shaft protrudes from the body of the ship, failed completely, flooding the shaft tunnel. Only prompt manipulation of the connecting watertight door kept water out of the engine room. The rush of water was beyond the capacity of the bilge pump and this was supplemented by the ballast pump. *1.11.1979:* Arrived at Gibraltar to repack the gland and agreement was obtained to carry out the work afloat. The voyage was resumed the following day. *18.5.1981:* Sold to Bunga Shipping Co. (Pte.) Ltd. (Madam Dolly Seah), Singapore for US$3,000,000 and renamed CHERRY ORIENT. *1985:* Sold to K.S. Steel Ltd., Chittagong for demolition. *22.5.1985:* Arrived at Chittagong. *19.8.1985:* Work began at Fouzderhat.

Left the bridge layout and right the lower engine room platform on *Magician*-class ships.

In 1969 Harrisons acquired two cargo liners from Cunard, made redundant by containerisation of North Atlantic services. This is a slightly tired-looking *Merchant.*

316. MERCHANT (5) 1969-1979 Steel motor ship. Two decks and four holds. Four masts and signal mast.
O.N. 306495 5,837g 2,829n 7,662d (8,131d after 1970) 436.4 (457.0 o.l.) x 60.1 x 37.5 feet. Cargo capacity: 461,900 cubic feet. Equipped with four 5-ton derricks, twelve 10-ton derricks and one 25-ton derrick serving number 2 hatch.
International Code: GNHT.
6-cyl. 2SCSA oil engine by Sulzer Brothers Ltd., Winterthur, Switzerland; 17.5 knots.

17.10.1963: Keel laid. *25.8.1964:* Launched by Cammell Laird and Co. (Shipbuilders and Engineers) Ltd., Birkenhead (Yard No.1314) for North Western Line (Mersey) Ltd. (Cammell Laird and Co. (Shipbuilders and Engineers) Ltd.), Liverpool as SCYTHIA. *4.12.1964:* Delivered and immediately long-term chartered to Cunard Line for their London to New York service. *9.12.1969:* Acquired by the company for £910,379 and renamed MERCHANT. *1979:* Laid up at Leith. *6.7.1979:* Sold to Totnes Shipping Corporation, Monrovia, Liberia (Manta Shipping Co. Ltd. of Liberia, Piraeus, Greece, managers) for US$900,000 and

renamed SISAL TRADER under the Greek flag. *13.1.1984:* Arrested for non-payment of debts and crew wages at Dzaoudzi, Ile Mayotte in the Comoro Group. Subsequently abandoned by her crew. *12.4.1984:* Driven aground by the cyclone Kamisy. *16.4.1984:* Refloated by a French naval tug, but found to be making water through ruptures in the bottom plating. Subsequently taken in tow by the tug BISON 1. *3.5.1984:* Arrived at Mombasa and moored at buoys. *1.1986:* Reported sold to Murri International Salvage Co. *30.9.1986:* Sailed in tow of the tug BARBARA for Pakistan and demolition at Gadani Beach.

Scholar in US waters.   *[J.K. Byass]*

317. SCHOLAR (4) 1969-1979 Steel motor ship. Two decks and four holds. Four masts and signal mast.
O.N. 306499 5,837g 2,844n 7,662d (8,131d after 1970) 436.4 (457.0 o.l.) x 60.1 x 37.5 feet. Cargo capacity: 461,900 cubic feet. Equipped with four 5-ton derricks, twelve 10-ton derricks and one 25-ton derrick serving number 2 hatch. International Code: GNVA.
6-cyl. 2SCSA oil engine by Sulzer Brothers Ltd., Winterthur, Switzerland; 17.5 knots.

25.11.1963: Keel laid. *22.10.1964:* Launched by Cammell Laird and Co. (Shipbuilders and Engineers) Ltd., Birkenhead (Yard No.1315) for North Western Line (Mersey) Ltd. (Cammell Laird and Co. (Shipbuilders and Engineers) Ltd.), Liverpool as SAMARIA. *11.2.1965:* Delivered and immediately long-term chartered to Cunard Line for their London to New York service. *23.12.1969:* Acquired by the company for £910,686 and renamed SCHOLAR. *1.1979:*

Laid up at Manchester. *18.7.1979:* Sold to Brora Shipping Corporation, Monrovia, Liberia (Manta Shipping Co. Ltd. of Liberia, Piraeus, Greece, managers) for US$900,000 and renamed STEEL TRADER under the Greek flag. *26.8.1980:* Arrived off Khorramshahr and 20.9.1980 trapped in the Shatt-el-Arab in the anchorage at the outbreak of the Iran-Iraq War. Hit several times by shellfire in ensuing months and abandoned by her crew.

318. BENEFACTOR (2) 1971-1982 Steel motor ship. Two decks and five holds. Three bipod masts and signal mast.
O.N. 339949 11,299g 6,508n 17,028d 157.43 (164.44 o.l.) x 21.38 x 13.0 metres. Cargo capacity: 24,186 cubic metres. Equipped with six 10-ton derricks, ten 9-ton derricks, one 50-ton and one 25-ton derrick serving number 3 and number 4 hatch respectively.
International Code: GOTQ.

Bought from Greek owners whilst fitting out at Sunderland, *Benefactor* was Harrisons biggest general cargo ship. She is seen in Table Bay.

2.9.1970: Launched by Doxford and Sunderland Ltd., Sunderland (Yard No. 894) for Maroccidente Compania Naviera S.A., Greece as ION and purchased for £2,735,178 by the company while fitting out and renamed BENEFACTOR. *5.1.1971:* Delivered and later sailed from London for South Africa on her maiden voyage under Captain W.G. Jackson. *10.4.1974:* Whilst swinging in the turning basin at Walvis Bay prior to sailing for Avonmouth, it was alleged that her rudder touched an underwater obstruction which twisted the rudder stock 36 degrees over to port. However, subsequent surveys using inadequate equipment in inclement conditions failed to find conclusive evidence of any obstruction or uncharted shoal. An action brought against South African Railways and Harbours in the South African courts was equally inconclusive. Temporary repairs to re-align the rudder and enable the vessel to continue her voyage occupied ten days, and the final bill amounted to £45,000. *17.9.1976:* In collision with the fishing vessel ELLY GERDA (TH50) of Teignmouth, Devon. The incident occurred as she was approaching the channel between Land's End and the Isles of Scilly in position 49.43N, 06.09W, on the final stage of a voyage from Walvis Bay to Avonmouth. *21.6.1978:* Time-chartered to Continental Lines S.A., Antwerp for a voyage to Karachi and Bombay at a rate of $4,900 per day. The scope for a

conventional 'tween decker on the company's African and Caribbean services had almost ended, these ships being overtaken by the container revolution, and BENEFACTOR and a number of her consorts were placed on the charter market. This was the first of many such charters undertaken during the next four years. *26.8.1979:* Sustained damage when she came into contact with the breakwater while entering Madras due to a steering gear failure. Three plates on the sheer strake, and one below sheer on the port side, were set in, and 30 feet of deck plating buckled and even fractured in places. Temporary repairs were carried out in Madras. Permanent repairs were deferred to the next dry docking. *16.4.1982:* At the conclusion of a charter to Safmarine, re-delivered at Capetown and sold almost immediately to Seltaka Shipping Co. S.A., Panama (Naviera Interoceangas S.A., Valparaiso, Chile) (Wallem Shipmanagement Ltd., Hong Kong, managers) for US$ 4,325,000 and renamed SOUTHERN LADY. *1987:* Sold to Gladiator Shipping Ltd., Valletta, Malta (Haltree Enterprises Ltd., London, managers) and renamed LADY. *1991:* Sold to Tong Shun Shipping (Panama) Inc., Panama (Wah Tak Marine Engineering Co. Ltd., Hong Kong, managers) and renamed TONG SHUN. Sold to Indian breakers. *29.1.1998:* Arrived at Alang.

319. CRAFTSMAN (5) 1972-1981 Steel motor ship. Two decks and five holds. One signal mast.
O.N. 357405 10,219g 5,169n 13,035d 153.98 (162.0 o.l.) x 22.43 x 12.54 metres. Cargo capacity: 47,703 cubic metres.
Equipped with two 250-ton Stülcken derricks, one 10-ton and two 5-ton cranes; two 10-ton and six 5-ton conventional derricks and one 10-ton luffing derrick serving number 5 hold.
International Code: MUEV.
8-cyl. 2SCSA oil engine by Sulzer Brothers Ltd., Winterthur, Switzerland; 18 knots.

23.6.1971: Launched by Doxford and Sunderland Ltd., Deptford, Sunderland (Yard No. 900) for the company. *28.2.1972:* Delivered (after a delay of nearly five months due to a strike at the shipyard) at a cost of £2,387,803 and later sailed from London and Continental ports for South Africa via Bonny, Nigeria on her maiden voyage under Captain Ronald Bell. *3.1978:* On passage to South Africa, a considerable amount of cargo was damaged by fire in number 1 hold and by flooding in number 4 hold, obliging the vessel to make for Monrovia as a port of refuge. *8.3.1978:* Arrived Monrovia. *16.11.1981:* After completing her final voyage to Venezuela, she was sold as she lay at Curacao to Ierax Shipping S.A., Panama (Forum (Shipping) S.A. (St. Katsounis), Piraeus, Greece, managers) for US$3,500,000 and renamed FORUM CRAFTSMAN under the Greek flag. *2.9.1982:* Commissioned to tow the Greek motor ship DESPOULA K (8,497/60) from Monrovia to Yugoslavia. After progressing only 14 miles, the towline parted in heavy seas, and DESPOULA K was driven ashore in position 06.30N, 10.57W and became a total loss. *1983:* Managers restyled Forum Maritime S.A. *26.7.1983:* While anchored in the Outer Roads off Santos, Brazil, struck by the Panamanian motor ship EDITA (4,961/72). The superstructure of EDITA on her starboard side came in contact with FORUM CRAFTSMAN's starboard bow. Permanent repairs were carried out at Flushing and consisted of the renewal of the starboard forecastle deck, bulwark plating and stays, the cropping and renewal of three soft nose plates, five shell plates and associated internals in

way of the forecastle space and forepeak tank. *9.12.1983:* Repairs completed. *1985:* Owners became Marigold Navigation Co. Ltd., Limassol, Cyprus (Forum Maritime S.A., Piraeus, managers). *1988:* Managers became Veritas Marine Consultants Ltd., London and renamed REGAL CRUSADER. *1988:* Owners became Tapee Navigation Co. Ltd., Limassol, Cyprus (Veritas Marine Consultants Ltd., London, managers). *1992:* Sold to Navalway Shipping Ltd., Nicosia, Cyprus (Ilios Shipping Co. S.A. (C.P. Eliopoulos), Piraeus, Greece, managers) and renamed CHRISTINA J. *8.1994:* Sold to Thai shipbreakers and broken up at Bangkok.

CRAFTSMAN was the first Harrison vessel to have an engine room designed to be unmanned for sixteen hours per day, all propulsion controls being governed electronically directly from the bridge conning position. She was also, in her day, the only vessel on the British register capable of lifting loads of up to 500 tons (508 tonnes). The two Stülcken derricks were each operated by four 110 h.p. winches, and each derrick manipulated by a remote control in the hands of a single winchman. To handle lifts in excess of 250 tons the derricks were capable of being operated simultaneously, with each derrick hooked to the lift. Inevitably, placing a load of 500 tons 22 feet from the ship's side, by means of a pair of 84 feet derricks would cause a ship to heel alarmingly. To counteract the list, heeling tanks were built into the wings of numbers 3 and 4 lower holds, and the counter-ballasting operation was controlled from the bridge.

Seen against a background of Thames-side cement works, *Craftsman* was the last of the Harrison's heavy-lift ships, with two Stülcken derricks capable of a combined lift of 500 tons. The tug *Burma* escorts her.

A voyage to forget
Bound for South Africa, CRAFTSMAN sailed from Dunkerque, the last of several British and Continental loading ports, late on Saturday 25th February 1978.[257] In her capacious holds she carried many heavy lifts as well as general cargo, while on the open deck were several parcels of low flash-point, hazardous goods, and a 150-ton separator stowed athwart number 4 hatch. The latter was a massive, cigar-shaped piece of machinery,

open to the weather at one end, a factor which occasioned Captain Rennison Shipley considerable anxiety. For if a heavy sea, moving a couple of hundred tons of salt water at a velocity of perhaps 50 feet per second, were to sweep into that gaping maw, it could generate a momentum sufficient to wrench the piece from its lashings, and over the side, with consequences too grave to contemplate. Of course, this item was situated on deck in full view of the bridge. Its presence could inevitably excite concern, but at least it could be nursed and protected, its lashings checked frequently, and, if necessary, the ship's course could be trimmed to keep the heaviest seas on the opposite bow.

But as so often is the case, it is the forces unseen which do the damage, and such forces were already at work. Out of sight and almost out of mind, at the bottom of number 4 hold, several railway wheel and axle units were loose, and starting to create havoc. The weather had been bad from the start. On the Sunday afternoon, in a Force 9 gale, several small items of deck cargo had been torn from their lashings. It was in the act of re-securing them that the Bosun and Carpenter were struck by a sea, flung against the windlass, and quite badly injured. Even Captain Shipley was not immune to the sea's caprices, for a couple of nights later he was flung from his bed to the deck, gashing his ankle painfully against an outflung drawer.

However, by the fifth day the weather had moderated sufficiently to enable Chief Officer Michael Hudson to carry out an inspection of the holds and the cargo therein. All seemed secure until he climbed down into number 4 hold. There he found a substantial quantity of water swilling across the tank top, reducing bags of malt, polymer granules, and bicarbonate of soda to a noisome sludge, while the heavy lifts still stood like half-tide rocks, their lashings mercifully still intact. In the creaking depths of the hold he could hear, amid the swirling wash of the water, the splash of a hose jet. Obviously the source of the flooding. However, it was not a hose sending that jet of water into the hold, but a three-inch gash in the steel bulkhead of the lower port wing ballast tank, a tank which he knew contained about 250 tons of water. Mr. Hudson lost no time in reporting the matter, and a check of the gauges suggested that the tank had lost about 80 tons of ballast. The tank was pumped out as quickly as the pumps could deal with it and, of course, its companion tank on the starboard side, to maintain trim.

Further inspection of the damage revealed one of the axle units, still lashed in place with its hub flush against the timber sparring which protected the tank side, had been the punch which had broached the tank. The hammer had been a second axle unit which had broken adrift from its lashings and had found sufficient space to roll to and fro, striking the stationary axle forcibly against the tank side. With the irresistible, monotonous patience of a steam-hammer it had splintered the sparring, loosened the lashings and attacked the steelwork, eventually creating the mischievous consequences which now confronted the dismayed officers.

Working up to their knees in water, the crew set about re-securing the axles. Attempts to pump out the free water through the bilge lines were frustrated by frequent pump stoppages due to granules of polymer and other debris clogging valves and filters.

A few days later the ship entered the calmer waters of the tropics, the crew still trying to clear up the mess, the injured still nursing their wounds, and the engine room staff still coaxing the pumps to extract the flood water from number 4 hold. Then at 19.30 on Monday 6th March,

the Kidde-Riche smoke detector in the wheelhouse was noisily activated. Without any shadow of doubt it pointed to a fire blazing away in number 1 upper 'tween deck. Their attention firmly focussed on this new danger, officers and men set about dealing with the outbreak. All vents were sealed, and carbon dioxide gas injected into the compartment. Knowing only too well what volatile substances were invariably stowed in that space, Captain Shipley turned his ship about and set course for Monrovia, Liberia, which, 500 miles to the north north west, was the nearest port of refuge where expert assistance could be expected. However, in the event, and by injecting two cylinders of carbon dioxide gas every hour or so after the original application of ten cylinders, and by cooling decks and hatches with hoses, the temperature of the hold dropped from 55 to 25 degrees centigrade overnight. The ship arrived off Monrovia at about 22.00 on 7th March and berthed at Number 3 Wharf at midday on 8th, to be met by a posse of port officials and company superintendents. The hold was still cool and quiescent, and a further outbreak seemed unlikely, so at 12.50 the hatch was opened to disperse the carbon dioxide, at the same time revealing a disturbing vista of charred and smoke-ruined cargo. More back-breaking hours of clearing up followed, and investigators found evidence that the fire had probably been started spontaneously after a drum containing cod liver oil had sprung a leak, and dripped onto a hessian bale of yarn.

Mopping up (water was still present down number 4), re-charging carbon dioxide cylinders, and restowing cargo was completed by 16.00 on 11th March. Shortly afterwards the ship sailed for Capetown, her decks piled high with rubbish and debris brought up from the ravaged cargo spaces, destined to be dumped at sea (for these were still the days of environmental licentiousness) far from any shore line. Thus far, it had not been a voyage to remember with any sense of satisfaction. There was one crumb of comfort, however. Lloyd's Agents and Surveyors do not often feel impelled to distribute bouquets, but on this occasion the surveyor assigned to the vessel felt bound to comment, under dateline Monrovia, 9th March 1978, "Efficient handling of the fire by Master and ship's crew greatly reduced the damage to cargo and vessel".[258]

Both *Craftsman's* Stülckens are needed to lift a 275-tonne tanker mooring buoy in Rotterdam on 4th May 1972.
[C. Kramer]

320. WAYFARER (4) 1973-1986 Steel motor bulk carrier. One deck and six holds. One radar/signal mast.
O.N. 360126 16,317g 10,473n 27,569d 169.42 (174.1 o.l.) x 22.91 x 14.75 metres. Cargo capacity: 36,118 cubic metres.
Equipped with five 8-tonne cranes fitted with grabs.
International Code: GRHB.
6-cyl. 2SCSA Sulzer-type oil engine by Sumitomo Shipbuilding and Machinery Co. Ltd., Tamashima, Japan; 15.25 knots.

13.1.1973: Launched by Nippon Kokan K.K., Shimizu, Japan (Yard No. 319) for the company. *5.4.1973:* Delivered at a cost of £3,088,672, bare-boat chartered to the Atlantic Bulkers Consortium, and later sailed from Shimizu for Nauru and Kwinana on her maiden voyage under Captain Rennison Shipley. *27.12.1978:* When on passage from the Great Lakes for Italy with a cargo of corn, forced to put into Gibraltar Bay to investigate a serious leak in number 6 hold. By the time she arrived, the hold was flooded and divers found a vertical crack measuring 80 by 0.75cms in a steel plate on the port side in way of number 6 hold. The fissure was situated about two metres below the summer load line, and had probably been caused by some rough handling while negotiating the locks in the St. Lawrence Seaway. Wooden wedges were driven into the crack to reduce the flow and later in the Naval Dockyard a plate was welded over the crack. *28.12.1978:* Sailed for Naples where most of the cargo was discharged. *18.2.1979:* Returned to Gibraltar with some 3,000 tons of wet grain still on board; cargo which the consignees had refused to accept. The cargo was discharged into lighters at the detached mole and taken out to sea and dumped: a lengthy and dirty operation. *5.3.1979:* Sailed for Dakar. *18.7.1980:* Whilst on passage from Richards Bay, South Africa to Taiwan she came across a boat of Vietnamese boat people whom they rescued and eventually landed at Manila. *2.9.1982:* Arriving at Poro Point, San Fernando in the Philippines at the end of a voyage from Nikiski, Alaska, she took a sheer as she approached the berth and part demolished the pier. *9.1986:* Sold to Springwave Marine Co. Ltd., Nicosia, Cyprus for US$ 950,000 and renamed WAVE. *9.1987:* Sold to Ave Shipping Corporation, Panama (Thome Ship Management Pte. Ltd., Singapore, managers) for US$2,500,000 and renamed AVE. 1992: Managers became Roymar Ship Management Inc, New York. *1995:* Renamed CHEROKEE BELLE. *1996:* Sold to Springtide Holdings Ltd., Panama (Samios Shipping Co. S.A. (Athanasios Samios), Piraeus, Greece, managers) and renamed COSTATHEA. *1999:* Sold to Burnside Trading Corporation, Panama and renamed MIRTIDIOTISSA. *1999:* Sold to Indian breakers. *25.11.1999:* Arrived at Alang.

Harrison's first bulk carrier, *Wayfarer.*

[Russell Priest]

Harrisons' bulk carriers

WAYFARER, the first of three sister ships built at the same Japanese yard, heralded a radical change in company policy. An apparently permanent decline in the conventional liner trades had long been foreseen, and a determined bid to enter a charter market dominated by bulk carriers was at least a partial remedy. The other part, of course, was the decision to build cellular container ships to compete in the liner trades, but these would come later.

To achieve maximum benefit from their investment in this novel project, Harrisons were pleased to join a consortium known as Atlantic Bulkers. The consortium comprised about a dozen ships belonging to various owners, such as Bowrings (two ships), Brostroms (two ships), Denholms (two ships) and Ocean (three ships). Harrisons' contribution would also be three ships by the end of the year. The consortium was operated by Denholm Coates, who arranged charters for individual ships, mainly through the Baltic Exchange in London.

Ships personnel quickly found themselves pitched into a different world. No friendly agents interposed between Masters and shippers - it was always strictly business; seldom, if ever, did the vessels enter a British port. Crews, on average, did a four-month stint before being relieved at some far distant port, becoming in the process almost as inured to flying as they were to sailing. Consequently, departments in Mersey Chambers charged with managing officer and crew matters, became almost synonymous with travel agents, their knowledge of flight data, passports, visas and World Health Organisation regulations ever expanding as time went on.

The boat people

The end of the Vietnam War in 1973, and the abrupt departure of the Americans, left the communist regime in Hanoi in the ascendancy. By 1974, the Paris Peace Agreement, under which free elections in both Vietnams were to be held, was scrapped, and soon South Vietnamese forces were trying to resist heavy troop infiltrations from the North. By May 1975, however, the communists were in control of the whole of Vietnam. The regime was an oppressive one, and by the end of the year some 230,000 South Vietnamese refugees had fled the country, most over neighbouring borders, but many by boat to seek refuge in Malaysia, Hong Kong, or the Philippines. Henceforth, year after year during the favourable summer months, waves of disillusioned and oppressed Vietnamese, sometimes entire families, took to the sea in flotillas of unseaworthy boats to seek a better life

Thus it was hardly surprising that, during the afternoon watch of Friday 18th July 1980, Second Officer William Butcher sighted a small boat away on the port bow.[259] The WAYFARER was ploughing through the South China Sea at the time, deeply laden with a cargo of coal from Richards Bay to Kaohsiung. Through his binoculars the Second Officer could see that the boat was crowded with people, and had very little freeboard. He called the Captain, who at once came on the bridge, and altered course towards the boat for a closer look. Captain Sydney Marlowe knew all about the boat people. How they relied on passing ships to be picked up, and how difficult it was to get rid of them at ports in the area. But Captain Marlowe, like many other British shipmasters before and after him, was not one to pass by on the other side. If these people needed help, he would worry about the consequences later. So he took the way off the ship, and made a lee for the boat to come alongside. The thought crossed his mind that they might be pirates - a growing menace in the region - but looking down and seeing the anxious, expectant expressions on the upturned faces of so many women and children, that possibility seemed remote. However, to diminish the risk only two persons were allowed to come on board, a man and a woman. In halting English they explained that they needed food and water, and were confident of reaching land if the Captain would supply their needs, and escort them for a few hours. Captain Marlowe was aware that the island of Lubang in the Philippines Group lay only 80 miles to the eastward, and the boat must have travelled almost 600 miles already.

The required provisions were passed down to the boat, and both vessels headed east in company. It soon became apparent, however, that the boat could barely make three knots, and seemed lower than ever in the water. They called her alongside again and Second Officer Butcher went down the ladder to make an inspection. He was disturbed to find many of the seams leaking like a sieve, and several inches of water sluicing around the bottom boards. In view of this circumstance, and the fact that a Pacific Typhoon called Joe was reported to be a few hundred miles east of the Philippines heading their way, Captain Marlowe decided there was no alternative but to take the refugees on board.

They needed no second invitation. The adults boarded by way of the rope ladder which hung over the side, while babes and children were hoisted aboard in an empty oil drum. Reaching the deck they stood together in a forlorn group, dishevelled and unkempt, clutching their sparse belongings, many of the children fearful and crying. The latter were quickly pacified by liberal doses of ice cream produced by Catering Officer Norman Coppell, while the officers took stock. There were 43 souls, all told - 19 men, 9 women, and 15 children. Considering they had been cooped up in a 25-foot boat for the past seven days subsisting on meagre rations, they were in pretty good shape. The women and children were accommodated in the smoke room, the men in the recreation room, while meals were taken together al fresco on the boat deck. Access to unlimited washing facilities, showers, baths for the children, and a fully equipped laundry, did much to boost morale. The women in particular were quick to restore appearances, manifesting themselves some hours later wearing bright, print dresses, clean, and elegantly coiffured, to the amusement of their menfolk and the open admiration of the WAYFARER's crew.

During their stay, the children were kept amused in the swimming pool, or on hastily devised swings, whilst in the evenings film shows were laid on for all. After a while, the officers came to realise that sadly some of the children were

Sheer bad luck?

In August 1982 WAYFARER loaded 24,000 tonnes of urea in bulk at the Alaskan port of Nikisi. She sailed soon after 18.00 on Friday 13th August, which, to some seamen at least, boded no good for the future. After a call at Yokohama for bunkers, the vessel reached her destination, Poro Point, near San Fernando in the Philippines, some 20 days later, at about 15.00 on Thursday 2nd September. Half an hour later the pilot boarded. He gave his name as Capitan Querido, a name which appeared to give him such cause for jocular pride, that he translated it - Captain Lover - for the benefit of his English listeners. Nevertheless, he seemed a competent pilot, a man who exuded confidence, and Captain Harry Traynor was content to hand him the conn, with a few comments on the ship's handling capabilities and, of course, the draught - 10.5 metres.[260] The pilot guided the ship between the outer reefs, and headed towards the berth on the south side of the bay. Shipside's Wharf was a finger-like jetty, 80 feet wide, and extending 800 feet in a north easterly direction into the bay. At least, it was supposed to be 800 feet. What Captain Traynor did not know, and the pilot did not seek to enlighten him, was that, over the years, it had been eroded nearly 100 feet by the effects of typhoons and a succession of accidents.

The ship lined up on the pier, approaching in such a manner as to lay her port side against the western side of the wharf. There was a tug on the opposite side of the pier, but it was making no move, and the pilot apparently had no use for it. The approach was good, but there does seem to be some substance in the allegation that the ship was carrying too much way. Consequently, when the ship suddenly and inexplicably sheered to port there was neither the time nor the space in which to retrieve the situation. A crowd of people on the jetty turned and fled in panic as the ship's aspect changed and they realised she was heading straight towards them. The impact, scarcely felt by those on board, came at 15.52, and the ship ploughed into the head of the jetty, burying her bows in the timber structure for a hundred feet or more. A further hundred feet was displaced, pushed out of alignment by the sheer mass

unaccompanied, having been thrust aboard the boat by desperate, anguished parents in an extraordinary gamble to give them the opportunity for a better life.

Meanwhile, the communication networks had been busily transmitting the news of the rescue to a slightly cynical management in Liverpool. Far removed from the drama, penalty and deviation clauses looming in the charter party shadowed their natural concern for the refugees. Nevertheless, and despite the onset of the weekend, wheels were set in motion. The International Organisation for the Rehabilitation of Refugees was notified, and that body in turn contacted the Philippines Government. The outcome was that WAYFARER was granted permission to proceed to Manila to land her passengers, and Captain Marlowe, much to his relief, received an encouraging message from Harrisons expressing approval of his actions. Subsequently, WAYFARER anchored in Manila Bay at 22.30 on the Sunday night, but plans to disembark the refugees on the morrow were disrupted by the tempestuous arrival of Typhoon Joe, whose centre passed about 70 miles north of the capital. Nevertheless, very strong winds were experienced in Manila Bay. Two ships were driven ashore during the night, but WAYFARER rode it out without incident. On Tuesday 22nd the officials boarded: immigration, customs, the High Commissioner for Refugees, and the British Consul. The Vietnamese had but time for one more meal before the launch arrived to ferry them ashore, and on to a camp at Bataan where they were likely to remain until settled, i.e. until accepted by some nation prepared to offer them citizenship.

As the refugees filed down the gangway to the waiting launch they each took their leave of the Captain who had undoubtedly saved them from a watery grave. Mr. Vo, the Vietnamese coxswain, shook hands and presented Captain Marlowe with the only possession in his gift - the barely adequate car compass with which he had navigated the South China Sea. The compass is now kept in the museum at Mersey Chambers, a silent symbol of the despair and hope which drove a brave group of people to a desperate venture. The launch drew away, and brown hands waved cheerfully as the refugees moved into the next phase of an uncertain future. It seemed inevitable that they would look back upon that brief interlude aboard WAYFARER as a blissful but unlikely dream in the midst of an ongoing nightmare.

of 32,000 tonnes moving with ponderous force. Fortunately, no one was injured, and the ship was undamaged. By this time, of course, the engines were going astern, and an anchor had been dropped, and these measures certainly helped to mitigate the damage, which nevertheless, was substantial. The pier consisted of a wooden deck supported by piles of Oregon pine, reinforced above sea level by diagonal braces. Adequate, but by no means elaborate. Yet the claim made against the ship, originally almost US$2M, was out of all proportion. It was of course disputed, but the final claim, in the region of US$1M was still a great deal of money.

When it was all over, and the ship had pulled clear to berth alongside what remained of the wharf, the question on everyone's lips was, what made the ship sheer to port against full starboard helm with the engines going ahead, and continue to do so against the transverse thrust of the screw when the engines were going astern? No questions had been raised at the inquiry to cast doubt on the efficiency of the steering gear, or the competence of the helmsman. A maverick current acting against the starboard bow, perhaps? If so, it was a phenomenon contrary to anything experienced by the harbour authorities. Besides only a very strong current could have deflected the ship's head so much against the action of the rudder while the ship (as all agreed) was carrying substantial steerage way. A gust of wind, then? Weather conditions were calm throughout, with a light breeze from ahead. An underwater obstruction? This seems to be the most feasible explanation. The pier had admittedly been cropped. Clusters of old piles were still sticking up out of the water beyond the head of the jetty. Was it not possible that similar clusters of wrecked piles lurked below the surface? Could not WAYFARER's bow have been deflected by such an obstacle resisting the combined power of rudder and engines to cant her clear? WAYFARER, one of the largest and deepest ships to use the pier, was drawing 10.5 metres. It was possible that smaller, shallower vessels had passed clear, so that the obstruction had hitherto escaped detection. It is perhaps unfortunate that this hypothesis does not seem to have been fully explored at the time.

321. WANDERER (4) 1973-1987 Steel motor bulk carrier. One deck and six holds. One radar/signal mast.
O.N. 360137 16,317g 10,482n 27,569d 169.42 (174.1 o.l.) x 22.91 x 14.75 metres. Cargo capacity: 36,118 cubic metres.
Equipped with five 8-tonne cranes fitted with grabs.
International Code: GRHA.
6-cyl. 2SCSA Sulzer-type oil engine by Sumitomo Shipbuilding and Machinery Co. Ltd., Tamashima, Japan; 15.25 knots.

6.4.1973: Launched by Nippon Kokan K.K., Shimizu, Japan (Yard No.320) for the company. *6.1973:* Delivered at a cost of £3,014,552, bare-boat chartered to the Atlantic Bulkers Consortium, and later sailed from Shimizu for Gladstone, New South Wales on her maiden voyage under Captain M.D.R. Jones. *21-22.11.1977:* During a period of severe weather in the Mediterranean, sustained severe damage to her port side plating while ranging heavily alongside her berth at Algiers. At least six mooring ropes parted and her accommodation ladder was smashed. She was in port to discharge a cargo of grain from San Pedro, Argentina. *19.7.1979:* Struck and damaged the breakwater at Kashima, Japan sustaining severe damage to her stem and bulbous bow. *27.2.1981:* Grounded on the submerged breakwater in the approaches to Port Said while on a voyage from New

York to Bombay with a cargo of scrap metal. Damage was minimal and the vessel was granted a certificate of seaworthiness to continue the voyage. *28.2.1981:* Refloated. *7.5.1987:* Sold to Golden Sunrise Marinera S.A., Panama (Lygnos Brothers Shipping Inc, New Jersey, managers) and renamed SOTIRAS. *1989:* Sold to Solsea K/S (Johannes Solstad), Skudeneshavn, Norway and renamed SOLSEA. *1993:* Sold to Ocean Spirit Maritime Inc., Panama (Parthenon Agencies Inc., Piraeus, Greece) and renamed OCEAN SPIRIT. *1999:* Sold to Ocean Waves Inc., Panama and renamed OCEAN WAVE. *8.10.1999:* Stranded and abandoned on approach to Mongla port pilot station with 14,500 tonnes of bagged cement. Subsequently broke up and sank.

Wanderer on trials in Suraga Bay, June 1973.

The bulker and the breakwater

Kashima is a new and rather artificial port on the east side of Honshu, the main island of Japan. The WANDERER arrived off the port on 13th July 1979, and picked up her pilot one mile off the South Breakwater at 16.08. She had no difficulty negotiating the dog's leg fairway, and less than an hour later she was berthed at the Zeno Grain Silo to discharge her cargo of 18,000 tonnes of sorghum from Australia.[261]

On 19th July, her cargo discharged, and tanks fully ballasted, WANDERER prepared to take her departure. She was, of course, flying light with a draught of 13 feet 3 inches (4.04 metres) and 22 feet 4 inches (6.81 metres) forward and aft, respectively. Thus her propeller was barely submerged, the protruding, bulbous part of her bow scarcely awash; and a formidable expanse of bow plating was exposed to whatever wind prevailed. However, in the sheltered berth where the silo was located it was raining, but there seemed to be very little wind. Nevertheless, the forecast indicated strong northerly winds locally associated with an area of low pressure 100 miles east of Kashima. But to Captain C.D. Riley there appeared to be nothing his ship could not handle. Soon after 14.00 the pilot, who introduced himself as Mr. Hikasa, came on board. He discussed the weather with the Captain, who found his English a little difficult to comprehend. Still, he gathered there would be no problem getting her berth with the aid of two tugs, and swinging into the channel. He was rather taken aback, however, when the pilot asked to be disembarked off the Signal Station, just a mile down the channel. Mr. Hikasa explained in his laboured English that the weather outside was too rough for

boatwork. Captain Riley looked askance at the elderly little man, silently acknowledged his frailty, and agreed, after being assured that there were no navigational hazards of an unusual nature existing in the fairway, and that a tug would guide him out.

Superficially, there was nothing unusual in this request. It happens, for instance, at Durban quite frequently, and also Tampico, and at many other ports throughout the world. The master is faced with the choice of either complying, or waiting for the weather to moderate, with all the pressures such a course would undoubtedly bring to bear. Invariably, except on occasions when the weather is so bad that even the pilot advises against leaving the berth, the Master exercises his professional judgment, accepts responsibility, and accedes to the pilot's request. In the vast majority of cases it is quite a straightforward operation, simply a case of dropping the pilot, increasing speed, and maintaining course until the breakwaters are cleared and the ship enters the open sea. But this case proved to be anything but straightforward.

As WANDERER backed out of the inner harbour and swung round into the Central Fairway, the wind had freshened from the north north east. At 15.16 the tugs were cast off, and the pilot shaped a course 055 degrees towards the signal station, disembarking onto one of the tugs at 15.24, while the other tug took station ahead of WANDERER. As the signal station was on the north side of the fairway, so WANDERER was technically on the wrong side of the channel. To reach her own side, Captain Riley was obliged to steer 080 degrees, in the tug's wake. Three-quarters of a mile east of the signal station, the Central Fairway turns into the Kashima Fairway, orientated along an axis of 003 degrees, thus demanding a minimum turn of 52 degrees. But as WANDERER was heading 80 degrees the turn required became 77 degrees, thus making the manoeuvre that much more difficult, and with little time and space in which to execute it. To make matters worse, the wind was now blowing from the north at Force 6/7, exerting extreme pressure against the ship's towering port bow which resisted the action of her rudder like a gigantic foresail. Four minutes after dropping the pilot, barely time to gather steerage way after slowing down, WANDERER went into the turn. Sluggishly the lubber's line crept round the compass card, then stopped. Clearly, she was not going to make it. Rapidly, the wall of the South Breakwater loomed nearer. Captain Riley hit the telegraph handle to "Full Astern", and again, to warn the engineers that this was an emergency. He also ordered the Chief Officer to let go the port anchor. The time was 15.30. By now the WANDERER was crabbing down the fairway, the transverse thrust of the screw uniting with the wind on her bow to swing her at right angles to the breakwater, but still with enough headway to close it, and eventually to strike it, quite gently, at 15.32. Gently, it may have been but the proud, bulbous bow crumpled on impact, yet managed to gouge a great lump of concrete out of the breakwater. With water cascading from the ruptured forepeak tank, she backed off, narrowly missing a small coaster at anchor, but failing to avoid fouling her anchor on the coaster's cable, thus further complicating a complex situation. Soon, four tugs, hastily summoned by VHF and urgent whistle signals, gathered round and gradually restored some semblance of control, holding the ships in position while the anchor was laboriously cleared. At 15.47 old Mr. Hikasa, the pilot who had left the ship so prematurely barely twenty minutes ago, boarded her once again. The manner of his greeting is not recorded, but an hour later, the fouled anchor having been cleared, he had brought the ship back to her old berth at Zeno Silo.

After inspecting the damage, Lloyd's Surveyor granted the ship permission to proceed to Yokohama to dry dock for repairs. The vessel sailed at 18.00 on 20th July, and arrived off the Asano Dry Dock 15 hours later. Although the impact had not been unduly severe, damage to at least one of the massive concrete caissons which formed the breakwater had been substantial, the estimated cost of repairs being in the region of 33 million yen, or about £66,500.

Gratuitous advice

Bound from New York to Bombay with 21,250 tonnes of scrap metal, WANDERER anchored three miles north of Port Said Fairway Buoy on 27th February 1981 to await instructions, and her turn to transit the Suez Canal. Entry into the Canal is strictly regulated by the authorities. Ships do not enter singly as and when they please, but assemble in waiting anchorages until the appointed hour, by which time a sizeable convoy of ships has gathered. Eventually, instructions are issued, and the ships get under way, following each other in single line ahead according to strict procedure, into the channel, and thence through Port Said harbour into the Canal. A similar system operated at the southern end, in Suez Bay, and the two north and southbound convoys are timed to meet in the Great Bitter Lake, where there is plenty of room for manoeuvre. It does not always work out as simply as that, but when it works, it is a good system.

At 17.30 that evening, Captain J.M. Proctor of the WANDERER received instructions via the VHF to weigh anchor, head towards the Fairway Buoy, enter the channel, and proceed to number 2 Buoy to pick up a pilot.[262] There was a time, long since passed, when pilots boarded at the Fairway Buoy but nowadays ships are expected to make their way up to within a mile of the port to embark their pilots in the shelter of the breakwater.

It was 18.00 by the time the ship was under way. The sun had set, and the lights of Port Said, nearly ten miles away, provided a luminous background against which it was difficult to pick out and identify the many navigation beacons and buoys which marked the approach. Captain Proctor had noted that, since his last visit, the northern approach to the channel had been bent to the westward, ostensibly with a view to widening it. Several new buoys had been laid to mark the new bend in the channel, but to complicate matters a second deep water channel was being dredged a mile or so east of the old channel, and it, too, was marked with lighted buoys, many with similar characteristics.

It was a fine, clear evening, with a light easterly

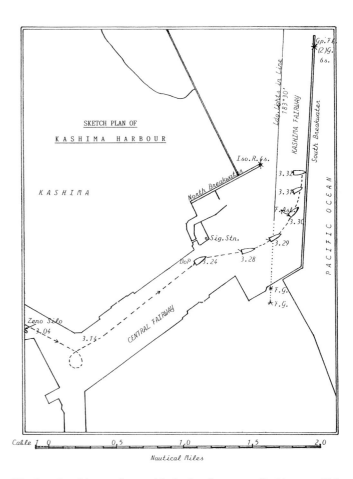

Wanderer's mishaps: above with the breakwater at Kashima on 19th July 1979, and below in the approaches to Port Said 27th February 1981.

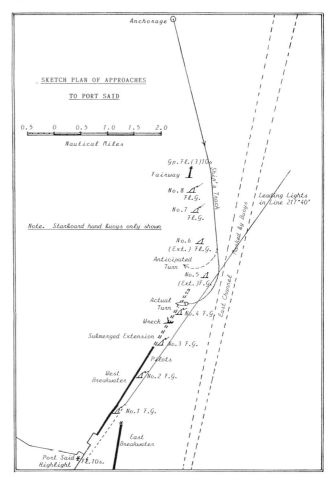

breeze, as Captain Proctor made his approach with caution, passing the Fairway Buoy at 18.20. WANDERER, incidentally, was to be the leading ship in the next southbound convoy. Number 8 and number 7 green-flashing buoys were passed to starboard in succession, by which time the Master expected to be able to pick out the range lights leading into Port Said harbour, but they were indiscernible against the increasing glare of the bright, city lights. His mood of caution intensified. Another buoy bobbed down the starboard side. He almost missed seeing it, for it was unlit. It was number 6. A buoy showing a fixed red light appeared to port, and WANDERER turned to starboard to enter the old channel on a heading of 217 degrees, her Captain still trying to pick out the leading lights as well as the buoys.

At this point a small, fast vessel, quickly identified as the pilot launch on traffic duty, took a hand in the navigation by remote control. Flashing a bright searchlight disconcertingly to attract attention, the launch approached rapidly from astern, the raucous tones of her skipper coming over the VHF, urging WANDERER to go "hard-a-starboard", and to follow him down channel. The launch swept by to starboard, and narrowly rounded WANDERER's bows on to her port side. Again, the heavily accented voice came over the radio: "Go hard to port, Captain, and follow me!"

This was easier said than done, for WANDERER was now passing close to another green buoy on her starboard side, which the Captain believed to be number 5. A precipitous swing to port would have caused the ship's stern to ride over the buoy with disastrous consequences. But something had to be done; there was no mistaking the urgency in that disembodied, glottal voice shouting instructions. The ship must be out of position. Captain Procter made up his mind; he would continue the swing to starboard, out of the channel (there was plenty of water between buoys 5 and 6), complete a full circle, and start again. By now, the voice on the radio was calling excitedly for "Full astern, Captain; Full astern!" for the buoy the Captain believed was number 5 was, in fact, number 4. Number 5 buoy had been passed unseen, for its light, like that of number 6, had been extinguished. Consequently, WANDERER was further up channel than her Captain supposed, and instead of turning into fairly deep water as he expected, the ship turned on to the submerged extension of the West Breakwater. It was 18.37.

There is little doubt that, given time, Captain Procter would have established the ship's position and made an impeccable approach. But the hectoring advice emanating gratuitously from the VHF loudspeaker had disturbed his composure, and so his ship meandered into trouble.

There was no dramatic impact. The ship simply stopped turning and came to a halt, heading north north west. Only in the engine room did they feel a slight bump, and Chief Officer E.P. Oddy on the forecastle head heard a crumpling noise coming from below. But the ship was well and truly stuck, defying all initial efforts to wrench free. Internal soundings indicated that her hull was still intact, which was encouraging. Shortly after 19.00 an Egyptian pilot boarded from a launch, and an hour later the first of several tugs came out, followed by the Harbourmaster himself. After a great deal of pushing and pulling the ship still remained immovable, and at midnight, when an outward bound convoy began emerging from the Canal, all operations were suspended for the night. Nor did the presence of an ancient wreck in close proximity on the breakwater do anything to inspire confidence.

Meanwhile, the ship had transferred oil from forward to aft, and filled a couple of after ballast tanks to trim the ship by the stern and raise the bow. Next morning the tugs returned accompanied by the large, twin-screw salvage tug ANTAR. Another outward convoy was passing and it was almost noon before the three tugs were harnessed in position and efforts to free the vessel could be resumed. ANTAR proved to be the decisive factor, and at 14.12 the ship slid clear. Not without incident, however. ANTAR's towing wire at one stage fouled the lantern of number 4 red lightbuoy, smashing the glass. The towing wire of another tug carried away, one end flailing back aboard WANDERER, fortunately without injuring anyone, and falling into the sea to foul the propeller. Eventually the ship was towed to the anchorage where next day, 1st March, a diving team made an inspection and cleared the wire from the propeller. According to the team's report, only a few innocuous indents marred the ship's forefoot, and Lloyd's Surveyor was content to issue a Certificate of Seaworthiness, the ship to remain as classed.

At 17.30 on 4th March, WANDERER again weighed anchor to approach the channel for the second time. On this occasion, all went well, and observers were pleased to note that, this time, all the buoys, with the notable exception of number 6, were lit.

322. WARRIOR (4) 1973-1988 Steel motor bulk carrier. One deck and six holds. One radar/signal mast.
O.N. 360158 16,317g, 10,482n, 27,569d 169.42 (174.1 o.l.) x 22.91 x 14.75 metres. Cargo capacity: 36,118 cubic metres. Equipped with five 8-tonne cranes fitted with grabs.
International Code: GTIN.
6-cyl. 2SCSA Sulzer-type oil engine by Sumitomo Shipbuilding and Machinery Co. Ltd., Tamashima, Japan; 15.25 knots.

21.9.1973: Launched by Nippon Kokan K.K., Shimizu, Japan (Yard No. 324) for the company. *21.12.1973:* Delivered at a cost of £2,849,155, bare-boat chartered to the Atlantic Bulkers Consortium, and later sailed from Shimizu to Nauru and Newcastle, New South Wales on her maiden voyage under Captain M.D.R. Jones. *9.11.1978:* Chief Officer fatally injured at Itapai. *24.8.1980:* Took the ground at Caleta Patillos, Chile while loading a cargo of rock salt for Baltimore. The vessel sustained serious damage to her forward bottom plating, and fell heavily against the loading plant causing further extensive damage. *1.8.1982:* Arrived off the island of Nauru to load a cargo of phosphates for Western Australian ports. However, it was blowing hard from the west and she was unable to berth. The bad weather persisted, week after week, and she continued to drift aimlessly off the island until 19.10.1982, sixty-nine days later. The monotony was only relieved by the rather dramatic rescue of a lone yachtsman, adrift in the wastes of the Pacific Ocean in his disabled boat. *4.10.1988:* Having completed discharge in the port of Xingang, China, sold to Navycoral Marine Ltd., Nicosia, Cyprus (Prosperity Bay Shipping Co. Ltd.(G.M. Lignos), Piraeus, Greece, managers) and renamed OURANIA L. *1991:* Sold to Compatriot Shipping Co. Ltd., Nicosia, Cyprus (Norfolk Shiptrading S.A, (G. Th. Sigalas), Piraeus, Greece, managers) and renamed OURIOS. Sold to Chinese breakers. *23.1.1999:* Arrived Xinhui.

Launch of *Warrior* at Shimizu, 21st September 1973.

Warrior.   *[J.K. Byass]*

"Whiplash"

On 9th September 1978 WARRIOR was berthed at Itajai, Brazil, starboard side to the quay, loading a cargo of bagged sugar for the Persian Gulf. During the course of the work it became necessary to warp the ship 150 metres astern, and arrangements were made to carry out this routine manoeuvre at 07.00 on 9th September. Neither pilot, nor tugs, nor even the ship's engines would be required, the means of propulsion being provided by ropes carried along the quay and led to the ship's winches.

At the appointed time, Chief Officer Bernard Illingworth mustered his men on the forecastle head and began singling up the moorings prior to slacking away as the Second Officer and his gang, stationed aft, hauled on their lines, coaxing the ship to move astern. To assist with the sternway, a rope backspring was led aft from the forecastle and heaved taut on the windlass drum-end.

When all was ready, the appropriate ropes were put under tension or slacked away, and the ship began to move. However, at 07.05, by which time the ship had moved astern about 30 feet, a loud report from forward alerted Captain Steele to the fact that one of the ropes had parted under the strain. He expected to see a replacement rope passed ashore pretty quickly, and when this did not happen he tried with some asperity to contact the Chief Officer by means of his portable VHF radio, for the bow was canting slowly but surely off the quay. He got no reply, however, and then became aware that one of the sailors was running along the foredeck shouting, shouting for help.

It had, in fact, been the rope backspring which had parted, an 8-inch polypropylene rope, apparently one of indifferent quality, although better ropes were available. One of the properties of polypropylene fibre is its elasticity, a desirable quality in a mooring rope, but one that can be highly dangerous should it break under stress. For the resultant whiplash effect can inflict severe, even fatal, injuries on anyone so unfortunate as to be in the way.

Bernard Illingworth, who had been standing near the break of the forecastle head, was one such victim. The rupture had occurred at or near a point where the rope was led round the bitts to the windlass, and the severed end had whipped back to strike the Chief Officer's right calf, inflicting a severe wound and rupturing several large blood vessels.[263]

With commendable presence of mind, one of the West African sailors, Thomas Davies, whipped off his jacket and wrapped it around the wound in an effort to stem the copious bleeding. Shortly afterwards, Captain Steele, and Catering Officer J. van Pelt arrived on the forecastle head and applied a tourniquet. Meanwhile, the ship had drifted far off the quay, and steps had to be taken to bring her alongside. Someone on the quay summoned an ambulance; the gangway was lowered, and within minutes Bernard Illingworth was on his way to hospital. Sadly, however, the loss of blood and subsequent shock to the system had been fatally severe, and Bernard Illingworth was declared dead on arrival. At the request of his relatives, his remains were buried in the local cemetery. He was 52.

"A good and safe port...... Always safely afloat"

The time-honoured words of the Charter Party seem plain enough. But there are subtle shades of meaning even in such sound words as "safe" and "safely". For example, if a car is driven along a safe, clear road, when suddenly, for whatever reason, it swerves into the ditch alongside, does it mean that the road itself is unsafe? "Certainly", retorts the unfortunate driver, "there should be a safety zone between the road and the ditch!" "Ridiculous", say the highway police. "Just careless driving". Granted that casting shore-based analogies into marine settings is liable to subscribe only to the confusion of the problem, there are parallels in the situation in which the WARRIOR found herself in the little Chilean port of Caleta Patillos on 24th August 1980. The main difference was that the motorist's road was clearly marked with white lines and traffic signs, and the driver was aware that deviation from it would lead to trouble. If, however, he did finish up in the ditch, the verdict could only be mechanical failure or careless driving.

A ship, however, is much more cumbersome and difficult to manage than a car. Moreover, in WARRIOR's case, the "road" was singularly bereft of any means of demarcation, a situation calling loudly for the generous provision of a "safety zone" to absorb the effects of minor deviations. The fact that there was virtually no such "safety zone", or marginal allowance for error, created a great deal of grief and financial loss for her people.

The WARRIOR at the time was on charter to the Compania Sud Americana de Vapores of Valparaiso, hired to load a cargo of 26,000 tonnes of rock salt and carry it to Baltimore. As a port, Caleta Patillos had little to offer. There was nothing there, except rock, sand and salt, and the only available chart was totally inadequate. A cluster of huts and a rather ramshackle gantry, hopper, and belt arrangement geared to load the salt into the ships, appeared to be the only man-made structures. But there was no wharf alongside which a ship could lie comfortably. Instead, the ship had to manoeuvre herself by means of ropes led to five buoys, gingerly hauling back and forth to bring the chute of the fixed loading gantry over each hatch in turn, manoeuvring each hold at least twice under the loading arm. A sixth buoy, which would have taken a starboard breast rope, had been withdrawn in favour of the

315

ship's starboard anchor. The drift between ship and buoys was in some cases so great that 200-metre mooring ropes were not long enough, and had to be extended by joining two ropes together. In all, a minimum of 12 ropes were required to secure the ship.[264]

WARRIOR arrived off the port in the small hours of Thursday 21st August, and stood off until daylight. As the sun climbed above the backdrop of mountain ranges, Captain Harry Traynor, Master of the WARRIOR, eyed a daunting panorama with some misgiving. He could see the loading berth, open to the sea, and the low swell breaking on a rocky and inhospitable shore. The loading gantry seemed very close to the surf. Still, his reference books and the Charter Party guaranteed a safe draught of 12 metres - not a minimum depth of 12 metres, but a "safe draught", which implied at least a metre or two of under keel clearance.

The pilot, Señor Hindrichsen, came out to the ship shortly after 08.00, not in a tug, as Captain Traynor had been led to believe from his reading, but from a launch. There were, in fact, no tugs in the port. The nearest was in Iquique, thirty miles to the north, whence the pilot himself had come by road. Captain Traynor voiced his misgivings, but the pilot assured him that bigger ships than the WARRIOR had loaded at Caleta Patillos without any trouble at all. He explained the berthing procedure in general terms, from dropping the starboard anchor to running the lines to the five buoys ("also a headrope ashore, if you wish"), and the precise positioning of the ship with the loading chute over the appropriate hold. The ship would be in a position heading 228 degrees, with the lighthouse on Caleta Point bearing about 2 degrees on the port bow.

The ship was in position at 09.30. Captain Traynor was still rather uneasy and called his officers together to discuss the procedures outlined by the Pilot. Señor Hindrichsen then left the ship to drive back to his home in Iquique. All things considered, Captain Traynor decided it would be prudent to keep the main engines on stand-by, and took an early opportunity to sound round the vessel. He was somewhat reassured to find the depths all round to be in excess of 13.5 metres.

The work of loading the ship began, and the lumpy rock salt roared into the waiting holds in steady succession, in accordance with a carefully prepared plan. Excessive trim by the head or stern had to be avoided at all costs to keep within the 12-metre parameter. Ten times during the next 60 hours WARRIOR warped to and fro between the buoys. As cargo poured in, ballast was pumped out, again within the dictates of the prepared plan. Ten times the crew went to stations at all hours of the day or night, to tend the moorings and re-position the ship for another hatch. Ten times the operation went ahead without any hitches whatsoever.

Towards midnight on 23rd August the final tranche had been loaded into number 1 hold. It was time to make one more shift to bring number 6 under the chute to complete the whole consignment. Of course, the ship by now was lying much deeper in the water, and it was with some anxiety that Chief Officer John Northam boarded the launch to read the draught before shifting, for he knew there was still 400 tonnes of ballast in the forepeak tank, still in the process of being pumped out. He was relieved therefore to find that, although about 2 metres by the head, the forward draught read 11¾ metres - still within the "safe draught" criterion. The ship was still on line to finish at an even keel draught of 11 metres.

Thus assured, the crew were ordered to stations for the eleventh time, the Captain on the bridge, Chief Officer forward, and Third Officer George Stewart aft, all equipped with personal VHF radios. The drill was routine by now. The Third Officer slacked away on his stern ropes; the Chief Officer took his headropes to the windlass, and hauled in. The ship began to move slowly ahead.

Later, the pilot would insist that, during his discourse with Captain Traynor on the day the ship arrived, he had explained that, rather than maintain a constant heading of 228 degrees when shifting to bring the after hatches under the chute, the ship's head should be allowed to veer on to about 235 degrees, thus bringing the lighthouse to nearly a point on the port bow. This was on account of shoaling extending seawards with the trend of the coastline. Captain Traynor was equally adamant that no such advice had been offered, other than the minimum heading of 228 degrees.

Be that as it may, 35 minutes after midnight on 24th August, a rare commotion sounded from forward, variously described in witnesses' statements as a "gentle booming noise," up to a "loud screeching noise of tearing metal", a sound which signified without any shadow of doubt, that the ship's bow had taken the ground, probably on a hard, rocky outcrop. Apparently, as the ship moved forward, her bow had meandered inshore - not much; just a few degrees. Perhaps there was too much weight on the inshore breast-line, or perhaps not enough weight on the starboard anchor. Whatever the cause, it was sufficient to deflect the ship's bow beyond the unmarked limits of the "safe berth".

Attempts to refloat the vessel by hauling on the starboard cable failed, for the anchor just tripped along the rocky bottom with no sign of taking a secure grip. The headropes, too, were ineffective, and a few kicks astern on the main engines were equally futile. Inboard soundings confirmed the grave suspicion that the forepeak and number 1 double-bottom tanks were breached, and open to the sea. To compensate, number 6 wing tanks were flooded, oil was transferred from forward to aft; and the crew under Second Officer Brian Birch were detailed to begin jettisoning cargo from numbers 1 and 2 holds, all in an endeavour to lighten the forward draught. But the ship remained stubbornly transfixed to the unyielding rocks.

Meanwhile, an urgent radio message had summoned the pilot and a pair of tugs from distant Iquique. The pilot arrived on board four hours later, at about 05.00, but the tugs never did materialise. By this time, the ship was lifting and falling to a gentle ground swell, pounding on the rocks with her forefoot, and canting down towards the concrete dolphin supporting the loading gantry. Fenders were put out, but at 05.10 the ship slammed against the dolphin, splintering the fenders, and causing substantial damage both to the structure and to her own side plating. Again the engines were run astern, the offshore ropes hove taut, but another 40 anxious minutes were to tick away before the ship at last tore herself clear, narrowly avoiding a foul-up with number 5 after mooring buoy. The ship was afloat, but with her forefoot ripped wide open, and drawing about 45 feet forward and 35 feet aft. With difficulty, she cleared the berth

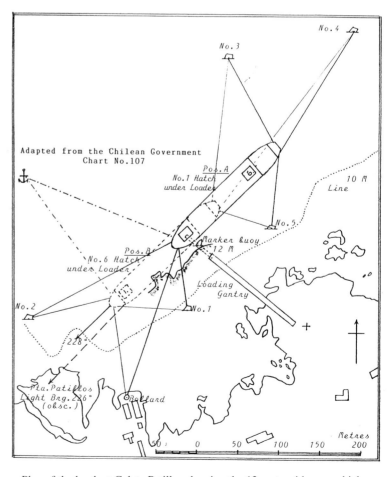

Plan of the berth at Caleta Patillos showing the 12-metre ridge on which *Warrior* almost foundered.

unaided, and moved to a safe anchorage well offshore.

Subsequent surveys, albeit unofficial, suggested that the 12-metre contour of soundings extended much closer to the berth than was indicated on the best Chilean chart that could be procured. A minor yaw of half-a-point was sufficient to bring WARRIOR's forefoot into fateful contact with the rocky sea bed.

After a week in the anchorage, unloading number 1 hold into number 2 hold, Lloyd's Surveyor gave permission for the ship to proceed to the Chilean port of Talcahuano, where a dry dock was available. WARRIOR reached Talcahuano on 4th September, after a rough and thoroughly nerve-wracking passage floating on number 1 tank tops, and docked on 8th September. Repairs were put in hand at once, but it was not until 20th October 1980 that she was ready to put to sea again.

Naturally, the owners accused the charterers of failing to provide a safe berth, according to the terms of the Charter Party. They in turn claimed the berth was perfectly safe, and blamed imprudent seamanship. Millions of dollars in claims were at stake, and expert consultants commuted to and from Caleta Patillos to assess causes and effects and build up their cases for claim and counter-claim. Not until 1986 was the matter settled - and then out of court, to avoid exorbitant arbitration fees. After a great deal of argument the principals agreed to assume equal shares of the total liability covering damage to ship and plant, and loss of hire and earnings, an arrangement which cost each side (or their underwriters) nearly one million pounds.

Warrior at an Australian port.   *[Russell Priest]*

The WARRIOR and the YANKEE CUTTER

The island of Nauru, once called Pleasant Island, but no longer entitled to that fair name once it became no more than a gigantic phosphate quarry, is situated half a degree south of the Equator in the western part of the South Pacific Ocean. On 30th August 1982, a sharp-eyed harbourmaster sighted the white sails of a yacht drifting past the north point of the island about five miles away. A barely audible and unintelligible conversation on VHF radio was the only contact, but there was no sign or suggestion that the unknown yacht was in need of assistance. However, the wind got up during the night, reaching storm force by morning, and when further attempts to contact the yacht proved futile, an uneasy harbourmaster warned all vessels in the vicinity to keep a sharp look-out.

There were several ships standing off the island, all awaiting their turn to berth under the phosphate loading plant. Among them was the WARRIOR, Captain Ron Bell in command, whose ship had been lying off the island since 11th August.[265] There was, of course, no secure anchorage off the steep-to island, and the ship simply drifted at a respectful distance, using the engines from time to time to keep them operational and the ship out of trouble. The crew rapidly became bored by the oppressive inactivity, and when the harbourmaster's warning came through they livened up considerably, the prospect of some worthwhile quest exercising their minds. Preparations were elaborate. Working from the last known position, and by feeding estimates of drift and leeway into the satellite computer, they were able to establish an optimum search area.

Confidently WARRIOR headed south for the search area. No sooner had she reached it and started on the first leg of the search pattern than, "Hey, presto!" there was the little craft, right ahead, wallowing in the swell. She had been found 65 miles southeast of the island.

Establishing contact by VHF as he approached, Captain Bell gathered that the yacht, YANKEE CUTTER, was indeed in dire straits. Her sails had been blown out during the overnight storm; her auxiliary engine had seized up; the transom was cracked and the rudder broken; the skylights were leaking, and the fresh water tanks had been contaminated by sea water. The yachtsman, who seemed very weak, asked Captain Bell to tow him to Nauru. With some misgivings, for the sea was still running high, the Captain agreed. A line was passed aboard,

but scarcely had the ship taken the strain than it parted.

Manoeuvring the WARRIOR once more to make a lee for the boat, Captain Bell urged her skipper to come aboard, and abandon the yacht. With manifest reluctance the skipper agreed, but insisted on collecting his personal belongings. A sailor went down the ladder to assist him, obligingly bending parcels and packages on to the lines as they were thrown down to him. The process had scarcely begun when abruptly, at 15.20 on 31st August, the YANKEE CUTTER sank, leaving both men floundering in the water. A dozen willing hands reached out to rescue them and haul them on board. Eventually, the owner of the yacht, feeling better after some rest and good food, was able to tell his story.

Marvin Jeldon Perry was, and doubtless still is, a US citizen from Wilmington, Delaware. He was 43 years old and had been working in Ponape in the Caroline Islands for the past two years. He had always been keen on boats, and it was his ambition, one day, to sail a boat single-handed around the world. He had no deep-sea experience, and no qualifications, but that, apparently, was no deterrent. In 1980 he bought the YANKEE CUTTER, a ten-year-old, ferro-concrete sloop, 50-feet long, and of 25 tons burthen, with an auxiliary diesel engine firing on only three of its four cylinders. After two years of tinkering with the boat and its equipment it was still not ready for his ambitious project. It would have to go to a boat yard, the nearest, most suitable, being at Madang, New Guinea, 1,000 miles to the southwest.

Perry set sail at the end of July, but when, after a silence of several weeks, there was no sign of him, his friends became alarmed, and initiated an air search along his supposed route. But contrary winds and currents had conspired to divert YANKEE CUTTER at right angles to the course her skipper wished to steer. Instead of south west, his course made good was south east, which, about 30 days and 650 miles later had brought the boat in sight of Nauru, and into the object lens of the harbourmaster's telescope. Thanks to his rather belated warning, a large slice of luck, and Captain Bell's professionalism, the adventure ended happily. Mr. Perry lived to sail again, though it is doubtful whether he ever contemplated a second circumnavigation of the globe. Besides, YANKEE CUTTER had not been insured.

323. STRATEGIST (2) 1975-1983 Steel motor Panamax bulk carrier. One deck and seven self-trimming holds. Two masts. O.N. 364416 35,716g 25,385n 60,920d 217.87 (224.4 o.l.) x 32.29 x 18.04 metres. Cargo capacity: 79,903 cubic metres. International Code: GUVL.
7-cyl. 2SCSA oil engine by A/S Burmeister & Wain's Motor-og Mfbk. af 1971, Copenhagen; 16 knots.

25.7.1975: Launched by A/S Burmeister & Wain's Skibsbyggeri, Copenhagen, Denmark (Yard No. 863) for the company. *5.11.1975:* Delivered at a cost of £9,225,060 and later sailed from Copenhagen and Gdansk for Taranto with coal, then on to South Africa, on charter to Bocimar, Antwerp to load a cargo of iron ore for Teesport under Captain Tom Wilson. *6.1.1976:* Berthed at Redcar Wharf, Teesport. The rare appearance of one of the company's bulk carriers in a home port prompted the management to organise a coach party of office staff from Liverpool to Redcar to pay her a visit. This privilege was as unexpected as it was appreciated by all who took part. *15.7.1983:* Sold to Bridgeworth Ltd., Hong Kong (British and Commonwealth Shipping Co. Ltd., London) (Wallem Shipmanagement Ltd., Hong Kong, managers), Hong Kong and renamed BARNWORTH. *1986:* Sold to Apiliotis Maritime Corporation, Monrovia, Liberia (Embiricos Shipping Agency Ltd. (E.G.E. Embiricos and C. Patsalides), London, managers) and renamed APILIOTIS under the Greek flag. *1991:* Sold to Agios Minas Shipping Co., Monrovia, Liberia (Aeolos Management S.A., Piraeus, Greece, managers) and renamed AGIOS MINAS. *1993:* Transferred to E.N.E. Agios Minas Ltd., Athens (Aeolos Management S.A., Piraeus, managers). *9.2003:* Delivered to shipbreakers at Aliaga. *13.9.2003:* Beached.

The Panamax bulk carrier *Strategist*.

324. SPECIALIST (3) 1975-1983 Steel motor Panamax bulk carrier. One deck and seven self-trimming holds. Two masts. O.N. 364418 35,716g 25,385n 60,920d 217.87 (224.4 o.l.) x 32.29 x 18.04 metres. Cargo capacity: 79,903 cubic metres. International Code: GUVU.
7-cyl. 2SCSA oil engine by A/S Burmeister & Wain's Motor og Mfbk. af 1971, Copenhagen; 16 knots.

31.10.1975: Launched by A/S Burmeister & Wain's Skibsbyggeri, Copenhagen, Denmark (Yard No. 865) for the company. *19.12.1975:* Delivered at a cost of £9,030,080 and later sailed from Copenhagen in ballast for Belle Chasse on the Mississippi River under Captain H.S. Bladon. *17.4.1977:* Able Seaman George Bryan drowned while the vessel lay alongside Cargill's Grain Elevator, Norfolk, Virginia. *30.8.1978:* Took the ground at Rio Grande, Brazil. *2.9.1978:* Refloated. *5.9.1978:* Following the grounding incident she anchored further south in the widest part of the estuary between numbers 12 and 14 buoys to resume loading. In the morning the visibility varied from moderate to poor, down to 3 cables at times. At 08.00 the Third Officer called the Captain to the bridge reporting a radar echo at a range of 1.5 miles, approaching from astern (she was then on a northerly heading). At a range of three cables the inward bound vessel, later identified as the Greek KINGSNORTH (15,568/64) was sighted shaping a course to pass on the starboard side. Apart from the fact that inward ships had hitherto passed on the port side there was nothing alarming in the approach. However, as her bow drew level with SPECIALIST's bridge she appeared to be set down by the south-going current, and struck a blow in the vicinity of number 3 hatch. About 25 feet of deck rails were bent back and twisted, and several sheer strake plates were set in together with internals. Repairs were deferred until re-delivery in Hamburg. *4.3.1983:* Sold to Corinth Bay Shipping Co. Ltd., Monrovia, Liberia (Thenamaris Maritime Inc. (Athanasios Martinos), Piraeus, Greece, managers) and renamed ELENI II under the Greek flag. *5.1988:* Sold to Gretchen W. Ltd., Monrovia, Liberia (Denholm Ship Management (Hong Kong) Ltd., Hong Kong, managers) and renamed GRETCHEN W. *1992:* Sold to Black Stallion Ltd., Hong Kong (Pacific Carriers Ltd., Singapore). *1994:* Sold to Cotswold Navigation Ltd., Valletta, Malta (Chartworld Shipping Corporation, managers) and renamed AIFANOURIOS. *1999:* Sold to Indian breakers. *25.12.1999:* Arrived at Alang for demolition.

318

The new *Specialist* leaving Copenhagen.

[Burmeister & Wain]

A case for arbitration

In August 1978 SPECIALIST, under the command of Captain John W. Cubbin, was on hire on a time charter basis to Cremer of West Germany for a voyage from the River Plate area to Hamburg with a cargo of soya beans. The ship loaded nearly 40,000 tonnes at the Argentinian ports of Rosario and Buenos Aires, and had been ordered into Rio Grande, Brazil, to top off with a further 10,000 tonnes. Berthing alongside the Cotrijui Grain Elevator invariably meant joining a queue and, while waiting for a berth, ships usually began loading from barges and floating elevators while anchored in the stream. Nevertheless, SPECIALIST had to wait four days even for this service. It was not a good place for a large, deeply laden bulk carrier to anchor. Limitations of depth, and of area in which to swing, were critical, and to those in charge life could never be relaxing in such circumstances.

Consequently, when SPECIALIST arrived on 24th August 1978 and anchored off the Grain Terminal in 15.5 metres of water, full watches were maintained and the engines kept at a moment's readiness.[266] Cargo began arriving alongside on 28th August, and the ship commenced loading. All this time, the ship had maintained her position, heading into a steady north wind, Force 4. The outgoing current was quite strong, flowing at about three knots by the doppler log, and for this reason a good scope of cable, seven shackles, stretched from the starboard hawse pipe to the anchor.

On 29th August, the weather became changeable, with flurries of rain which interrupted the cargo work, and that afternoon the moderate northerly wind gave way to a strong southerly, which gradually halted the outgoing current, and then reversed it.

SPECIALIST began to swing, drifting over her anchor, until she lay athwart the fairway, her stern to the east. By 22.00 the process was complete; the ship had swung through the full semicircle, and was now heading south, holding nicely, but with only a metre or so between keel and river bed. A set of anchor bearings fixed the ship's bridge 700 metres north of its former position.

Depths in the Barra do Rio Grande are influenced much more by wind force and direction than the weak tidal streams. Southerly winds raise the level of the water in the harbour and adjacent lagoons, while northerly winds lower the water level. So depths are seldom consistent, and predictions are hedged with uncertainty.

At daylight on 30th August, soundings were taken round the ship and, although she was still afloat, Captain Cubbin was uncomfortably aware that the depth of water in this new position was insufficient to resume loading. He therefore made arrangements with the harbourmaster to move his ship to a more accommodating anchorage. At around 10.00 he noticed that the ship was no longer yawing gently through the customary few degrees. She was stock still, and had developed a slight list to starboard. He hoped the move, when it did come, would not be too late.

But it was 15.00 before pilot and tugs arrived. And only when they came to get under way; when the cable-lifter on the powerful windlass failed to bring the ship up to her anchor; and when the tugs churned the water to no avail; only then did it become obvious that the ship was aground. More tugs were called to the ship, but neither their combined pull, nor the ship's mighty engines, could budge the SPECIALIST from her unseemly predicament.

The first intimation that one of the company's big ships was in trouble reached Harrisons' Liverpool office in a telephone call from Hull, of all places, on 31st August. For a while, no-one could understand what the caller was talking about, but in the end it all became clear. The mystery caller was a Captain A.J. Oakley, Managing Director of the salvage firm, United Towing (Marine Services) Ltd. of Hull. One of his colleagues happened, by chance, to be in Rio Grande, when he heard that a big bulker was aground in the fairway. His salvaging instincts aroused, he at once put through a call to his office in Hull. Captain Oakley told him to make himself and his expertise known to the master of the stranded ship while he himself contacted her owners. The situation explained, Captain Oakley was told politely that, although there was no objection to his representative, Captain D.E. Pearce, calling on the Master of the SPECIALIST, it was profoundly hoped that his services would not be required.

Shortly afterwards, a telex message from the ship, transmitted that morning and delayed several hours, came in, giving full details. It emerged during the crisis that communications with Rio Grande were very difficult and largely intermittent, with long, anxious periods of silence punctuated by bursts of interlocution, whether by telephone or telex.

On Friday morning 1st September, Captain Oakley telephoned to say that he and a colleague were about to set off for Liverpool, hoping for an interview with the management. "Management" that day was pretty thin on the ground. Due to holidays and other engagements, only one director was in the office, and he was not available at the material time. The Marine Superintendent was on holiday, leaving only his assistant, the Ships' Husband, the Manager of the Claims Department, and the assistant to the Operations Manager, on hand to meet the delegation from United Towing.[267] They were joined later by representatives of the P. and I. Club and the Liverpool and Glasgow Salvage Association, old friends of the firm whose advice in such matters was greatly respected.

They discussed the prospects of refloating SPECIALIST, and, somewhat reluctantly, United Towing's confident assumption of a salvage action. Captain Pearce came through on the 'phone again. The situation had changed dramatically. A shift of wind back to north had begun emptying the lagoon like a cistern. The water level had fallen by a metre overnight. Company spokesmen and salvors alike were only too aware of the stresses and strains to which a loaded ship perched on a sandbank would be subjected following a drop in water level. The company's representatives looked anxious; Captain Oakley and his colleague left the office looking smug.

At that moment the telex link with the charterer's agents came to life, confirming, if any confirmation were needed, that Captain Cubbin was deeply concerned over the crisis which had overtaken his ship, and was seeking permission to begin lightening the cargo into barges, as the water level was still falling. The flickering vision of mounting disaster in the minds of the managers came into sharp focus.

The ship was perched on a ridge of sand; the water level was falling remorselessly; a ruptured fuel tank would cause widespread pollution; there was no telling when the water would rise again. It was Friday afternoon, and the pressure was on. The telex link was still open, but once it was closed there was no guarantee that it could be re-opened. Consequently, the decision was taken there and then to advise the Master to accept Captain Pearce's services on the basis of Lloyd's Salvage Agreement. Thus, at 12.25 local time on 1st September, Captains Cubbin and Pearce signed the Agreement. It was a decision which was to provoke some severe criticism, once the ship was safely afloat, but events need not have turned out so felicitously.

Meanwhile, on the Salvage Master's instructions, the ship was ballasted down to hold her position firmly on the sandbank while the lightening operation was in progress. Otherwise, the ship would drift further on to the bank. Lighters, elevators, and gangs were ordered but it was Saturday morning before work began. Several hours later, and with a perversity which could only be interpreted by Murphy's Law in the light of the decisions taken, the wind backed south, and the water began to rise. By the end of the day 1,750 tonnes of cargo had been discharged, and, taking all factors into consideration, the port authorities prevailed upon the salvors that it was time to attempt to refloat the vessel. Five tugs clustered round the stranded ship; water ballast was rapidly released, and at 18.12 on 2nd September, SPECIALIST was afloat once more, and on her way to a safer anchorage. Except for a seized hydraulic pump on the windlass, and some fractured steam pipes in the duct keel, (a pertinent reminder of the hogging stresses borne), she was none the worse for her ordeal.

Everyone was vastly relieved, but after the relief came the haggling. United Towing's invoice for services rendered - £45,600 - seemed rather high, considering the relative ease with which the ship had been refloated. Of course, their expertise had helped, but surely the operating costs of an ocean-going tug, diverted in mid-Atlantic, and still a week's steaming from Rio Grande when SPECIALIST floated, could not be termed a legitimate expense contributing to the salvage? This, and other unworthy items were hotly disputed, and so the matter was referred to the arbitrator who would determine the salvage award. This is a judicial process, binding on both sides, and designed to determine impartially the size of an award, after taking into account all the relevant circumstances.

The arbitration was heard in chambers on 21st February 1980 before Mr. Justice Gordon Wilmer. It was fully expected that United Towing's claim for expenses would be well-watered down, and that the award would be a nominal figure, but the actual outcome seems to be veiled in secrecy, as no hints occur in the otherwise voluminous records of the case.

Specialist.

Harrison ships in colour
Selected by Paul Boot

Merchant (273) inward bound on the Manchester Ship Canal near Runcorn.   [*Eddie Jackson*]

The Liberty-type *Colonial* (284) passes Runcorn. The old Runcorn-Widnes transporter bridge can be seen and its replacement under construction.
[*Eddie Jackson*]

Linguist (276) in Liverpool Docks during 1965.   *[Malcolm Donnelly]*

Craftsman (275) in Liverpool. *[Malcolm Donnelly]*

Tolmi, formerly the *Biographer* (285), in 1972. *[World Ship Photo Library 35447]*

Factor (279).   [World Ship Photo Library 36114]

Interpreter (278) in September 1966.   [World Ship Photo Library 9992]

Crofter (290) sails from Eastham in June 1967.   *[Eddie Jackson]*

Wanderer (321) docking at Liverpool in September 1967.   *[Eddie Jackson]*

Forester (291) on a Harrison berth in the West Float, Birkenhead on 19th April 1969.   *[Paul Boot]*

Forester (291) seen again in Canada Dock, Liverpool on 20th February 1971, just after her sale and renaming *Maldive Ambassador*. The wording on the stern might suggest not all ships are female!   *[Paul Boot]*

Diplomat (293) approaching the locks at Avonmouth on a glorious spring morning in 1972.

[J. Wiltshire, courtesy Nigel Jones]

Governor (292) arriving at a South African port. [World Ship Photo Library 36118]

Inward bound against the familiar Mersey backdrop of the Clarence Power Station chimneys, Journalist (294) passes Seacombe on 6th June 1972.
[Paul Boot]

Barrister (295) on 17th October 1970. [Gould collection, World Ship Photo Library 10201]

Defender (296) in No. 2 Branch, Canada Dock, Liverpool.
[Eddie Jackson]

Administrator (297) sails from Eastham. [Eddie Jackson]

A rather dishevelled-looking *Author* (298) approaches Eastham on 10th May 1978. [Paul Boot]

In pristine condition, probably after dry docking, *Plainsman* (299) is eased through Birkenhead Docks on 30th November 1974.   *[Paul Boot]*

The last conventional cargo liner built to a Harrison design, *Dalesman* (305) is inward bound at Eastham in April 1965.   *[Eddie Jackson]*

Tactician (303) passes Eastham, inward bound in May 1968.

[*Eddie Jackson*]

Inventor (306) in Alfred Basin, Birkenhead during May 1964, shortly after delivery. The Liberty *Successor* is berthed behind her.

[*Eddie Jackson*]

The former *Craftsman* (319), now *Forum Craftsman*, on the Nieuwe Waterweg, 7th July 1983.

[*World Ship Photo Library 36116*]

Adventurer (300) berthed in the East Float, Birkenhead in July 1965.

[*Eddie Jackson*]

Custodian (302) approaching Eastham in June 1965.

[*Eddie Jackson*]

Passing New Brighton on 31st May 1971, *Naturalist* (310) is clearly bound for the Manchester Ship Canal as her topmasts have already been struck.

[*Paul Boot*]

Linguist (313) sailing from Liverpool on 24th November 1979.

[*Nigel Bowker*]

Discoverer (307) inward bound in the Eastham Channel in September 1964. [*Eddie Jackson*]

Philosopher (309) on the Clyde, 4th June 1967. [*World Ship Photo Library 36133*]

[Paul Boot]

Without tugs because of a strike, *Trader* (312) heads cautiously for Eastham Locks on 26th July 1978.

Magician (314) arriving at Liverpool on 8th March 1975.   *[Paul Boot]*

Merchant (316) sails from Eastham, 27th May 1978.   *[Paul Boot]*

Scholar (317) off Woolwich on 15th August 1970.   *[World Ship Photo Library 36141]*

Benefactor (318) arriving at Liverpool, 23rd June 1980.   *[Nigel Bowker]*

Harrison charters

Despite their sizeable fleet, Harrisons were frequently obliged to augment their resources to maintain their services, taking ships on both time and voyage charter. Illustrated is a selection of ships on charter in Harrison colours during the early 1970s.

An unusual charter in 1973 was Lamport and Holt's *Raphael* (7,852/53), seen loading at Birkenhead. *[Paul Boot]*

Houlder's *Westbury* (8,414/60) in Huskisson Dock during February 1974 discharging bulk sugar for Tate and Lyle's Liverpool sugar refinery. *[Paul Boot]*

In 1971 *Nurjehan* (8,380/71) was time chartered for two years from Hain-Nourse Ltd. and renamed *Advocate*. Surprisingly, it was the only time this name was used by Harrisons. *[Paul Boot]*

Foreign-flag vessels were sometimes taken on charter, but were often of British origin. *Pleias* (10,736/60) was formerly *Silverleaf*. *[Paul Boot]*

Seen on a stormy October afternoon in 1970, *Petra Skou* (4,427/54) was one of several Ove Skou vessels to carry Harrisons' colours. *[Paul Boot]*

PART 6

THE EBBING TIDE
1977 – 2002

Changing times

By the beginning of 1977 the Charente fleet, which had been declining slowly since 1956 when it comprised 43 ships totalling 307,000 gross tons, had been reduced to 27 ships, of 294,000 tons.[268] Of these, seven were specialised heavy-lift ships, five were bulk carriers, and 15 were dry cargo vessels of conventional type. They were all motor ships with oil engines of various makes and types - Doxford, Sulzer, Gotaverken, Pielstick, and Burmeister & Wain. The year 1977 was a watershed in the company's fortunes. That year saw the addition of two modern cellular container ships to the fleet, and the departure of five conventional ships, all of them to the People's Republic of China. Thereafter, the decline in the number of ships was rapid (the decline in tonnage less so), leading inevitably to redundancies among the sea staff, and staff reductions ashore. For it was confidently asserted that one container ship was capable of moving more tonnage in one year than six conventional ships, thanks to greater capacity, faster speed, and a quicker turnround in port, the latter made possible by the unit system of stowage, and the rapid loading and unloading processes intrinsic to the box concept. This claim was to be more than justified, and it soon became obvious that the days of conventional break-bulk cargo ships were numbered. But in addition to the human cost in lost jobs, there was a heavy financial price to pay.

The capital cost of the new ships and their containers was extremely high; the expense of setting up modern facilities ashore in ports at home and abroad was equally daunting. Such massive outlays of capital could only be contemplated by operators in a given trade banding together to form a consortium, and pooling their resources. Even then, opportunities to mitigate handling costs were severely constrained by the dock workers' unions in most traditional ports insisting on maintaining manning levels similar to those which prevailed on conventional ships. At that time, when the provisions of the National Dock Labour scheme still held sway, dockers could only volunteer to become redundant; compulsory redundancy was contrary to the terms of the scheme. Thus, if an employer of dock labour was forced out of business, the men on his payroll were simply transferred to another employer, usually the Mersey Docks and Harbour Board, or the Port of London Authority, or similar corporate body, whether the employers liked it or

not. By contrast, trade flowing through less orthodox but more accommodating container-oriented ports, such as Felixstowe and Sheerness, increased rapidly, and ship operators vied with each other to contract for regular berthing facilities in these new, non-affiliated ports to the detriment and rapid decline of the old.

Two years later, by the winter of 1979, Harrisons' fleet had been reduced to 15 ships totalling 290,000 gross tons, and the first redundancy programme was well underway. Ironically, the first half of the decade had been characterised by an acute shortage of deck and engineer officers. On numerous occasions, senior cadets were signed on as uncertificated third officers, and it was sometimes necessary for a loaded ship to leave the dock and anchor in the Mersey while superintendents, aided on occasion by the local police, scoured the countryside for junior officers on holiday, almost begging them to return to Liverpool to complete the manning requirements, and so enable the ship to sail. The reasons for this shortfall were threefold: fewer recruits were coming forward to seek a career at sea, despite the comparatively high salaries on offer which allowed officers to marry earlier. Subsequently, the men found it difficult to resist the siren voices of young wives determined to persuade their husbands to "come ashore and settle down". Finally, the conditions generated by relatively full employment ashore, which reduced the risks of cutting ties with the sea, encouraged young men to swallow the anchor and seek new land-based careers.

A similar shortfall prevailed among petty officers and ratings, but the effect was less noticeable due to the ready availability of West Indian and other non-domiciled crews. Meanwhile, the cost of training an officer or engineer cadet was estimated to be in the region of £10,000 and, with newly qualified officers leaving after two or three years, the rapid turnover was a serious and constant drain on resources.[269]

To counter this trend, shipowners had introduced a stream of incentives to encourage young men to pursue a career at sea. Salary scales were improved, with enhanced increments for years of service. The post-war concession of "two beers per man per day" had been swept aside by the introduction of fully equipped bars, installed in saloon and mess deck by enterprising brewers, and supplied with draught beer, wines, and spirits at duty free prices. In most cases, the bars were well run by appointed committees and,

Adviser (326) on the cover of a Harrison Line brochure from the 1980s.

if the house rules were obeyed, they developed into beneficial institutions, but in cases where such criteria failed to apply, they became sources of fierce contention, often leading to closure. Film projectors and film libraries were provided at a cost to the firm of about £60,000 per annum,[270] until they were eventually supplanted by video recorders in the eighties. Since 1969, and for the first time since the days of sail, wives had been encouraged to accompany their husbands on foreign voyages. At first, this privilege applied only to masters and senior officers, but it was soon extended to include all officers, and later, petty officers. It quickly became apparent that many wives could not leave small children at home, and so provision was made for young children to accompany their parents. There were limits, of course, and often these were drawn by statute, specifically by the number of persons the lifeboats were certified to carry. Voyage leave entitlements had also been increased until a rate of one day's leave for every two days spent on articles was reached. Extra leave for studying, for compassionate and family matters, and for sickness had also been negotiated, all of which increased the demand for further recruitment to meet these commitments. The circle of inducements was complete.

Redundancy and severance

In 1976 some 45 cadets were inducted into the company's service. In that year, recruitment was still considered by the industry to be a priority, and the Sealife Project was launched by the shipowners' trade association, the General Council of British Shipping, in co-operation with individual companies and the seafarers' unions, to investigate how to make life at sea more attractive to young people. Committees were set up on board certain ships and ashore, and many suggestions were put forward, from low-interest home loans (it wasn't easy to get a mortgage at that time) to more luxurious carpets in cabins, and language courses. But it was really a pointless exercise, for already the spectre of redundancy was abroad.

Precipitated, to some extent, by conditions prevailing after the transport drivers' strike in January 1979, when there were no liner sailings from Liverpool between 22nd December 1978 and 9th February 1979, company after company began trimming its costs by reducing its workforce. To the Harrison Line Board the prospect of having to dispense with the services of loyal staff was a bitter pill to swallow, and they resisted the inevitable for as long as possible. But they operated in a harsh, competitive world, and overheads had to be cut in order to survive. The blow fell in the summer of 1979, when 118 officers, 20% of the entire strength at that time, received notices of redundancy. Many had seen the blow coming. They had witnessed the inexorable depletion of the fleet, and could see no possibility of replacement tonnage on such a scale. They had heard of the cutbacks in Cunard, Clan Line, Ellerman, and others during the previous two years. Yet, when the axe fell, the shock was devastating, particularly for men in the middle age groups who had served the company for twenty years or more. Aged 40-plus, it would not be at all easy for them to find new employment. Many did, however, but mostly in ships of foreign nationality, in the burgeoning fleets of the Far and Middle East. A few of the older hands retired willingly, happy to accept early retirement with extra severance pay. Few could see it at the time, but the terms of redundancy were quite generous, severance pay in most cases amounting approximately to two weeks' pay for each year of service. It came as no surprise when more ships had to be sold to meet the enormous cost of the redundancy scheme.

Harrison Care

The effect of fewer ships following changing trading patterns - which seldom included Liverpool - led to redundancies in the shore-based labour force. In 1978, the Superintendent Engineer, E. Levison, supervised a shore-based staff consisting of nine assistant superintendents, eight shoregang fitters, four electricians, nine foremen, and 30 scalers.[271] Hitherto, this workforce had been fully employed attending to repairs and maintenance aboard ships as they came into Liverpool, but in the changed circumstances either new work would have to be found for them, or they would have to go. Consequently, in September 1979, an organisation financed and supported by the company, and known as Harrison Care, was born. This was the name under which the abilities and skills of Harrisons' engineering work force were marketed in and around Merseyside. They were prepared to go anywhere, and do anything compatible with their training and experience.

The superintendents had amassed a great deal of knowledge relating to shipbuilding and shipyard practice, and work was found for them supervising the building of new ships for foreign companies, mostly in the Far East, but occasionally in Europe. Other shipowners, including Harrisons' partners in the CAROL organisation, found work locally for the shore gang. Unfortunately, after a promising start, the shore gang had to be reduced by half as the work available on Merseyside declined further in step with the recession which continued to affect the industry. Meanwhile, the marine engineering skills of the shore-gang fitters were scaled down to encompass the intricacies of automobile engines, enabling them, after an intensive course in car maintenance at Ford's Dagenham plant, to service the company's fleet of cars and vans.[272] A further indication of the lengths to which Harrison Care was prepared to go in search of employment was the appointment, on one occasion, of a superintendent to supervise the installation of machinery in a butter factory in North Wales, built to order of the Milk Marketing Board.[273] By 1986, however, the work force had been reduced by redundancies and natural wastage, and Harrison Care, having served its purpose usefully and well, was disbanded.

Meanwhile, the attrition among the sea staff continued relentlessly. In July 1980 a further 42 officers were laid off, and on September 30th Harrisons closed down their stevedoring operations at Canada Dock, and the Dock Office, with its staff of riggers, shipwrights, and labourers, became redundant. Then for a couple of years, natural wastage was allowed to take its toll. However, in December 1982, ten senior members of the superintendents' staffs were made redundant, followed in March 1983 by 84 ships' officers, a figure which represented 30% of the existing sea staff.

Union intransigence.

Early in 1981, in the midst of recession, of ship sales, of increasing foreign competition, of declining freight rates, and of desperate rearguard actions against the inevitable onset of redundancies, the attrition process was accelerated by a disastrous strike instigated by the National Union of Seamen in support of their annual pay claim. The employers offered 9.5%, and when this was rejected they raised their offer to 10.5%. This was put to a ballot, with the Union hierarchy recommending rejection. The offer was rejected, but by a very small majority. In a gesture which smacked of desperation, the employers submitted an offer of 12%, an increase which the industry realised it could not afford without delving into precious reserves. This attempt to buy peace failed to move an obdurate union executive, however, which voted for industrial action. To call an all-out strike would, under the Thatcher Government's new

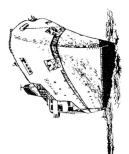

By bringing together a specialised group of small long standing businesses in the Port of Liverpool, skills in all aspects of ship repair, under expert supervision, are now collectively offered to you under the name of HARRISON CARE. With the organisation now available you can contact one centre and be assured that all your repairs and requirements will be co-ordinated to give you rapid and expert service at sensible cost. We are able to serve you 24 hours per day 7 days a week.

IN BRIEF WE OFFER:

Drydock facility
243.66m x 28.42m

Repairs and overhauls to:

Main engines.
Auxiliary machinery.
Turbo blowers.
Scavenge cleaning.
Boilers.
Hydraulic and pneumatic systems
Cargo and domestic refrigeration.
Bearings remetalled and machined.
Metal spraying-shaft build up.
Castings in bronze and aluminium.

Fuel injection service and spares:

Doxford	Bryce
British Polar	Simms
Sulzer	Pielstick
B & W	C.A.V.

Machine Shop:

Turning up to 21 in. dia.
Boring up to 28 in. dia x 3' long.
Facing up to 4' dia.
Milling-12 in. x 55 in. table
Drilling from 0.008 in. upwards
Grinding-universal and surface.
Honing-internal and external.

Diesel service and spares:

Ruston	M.A.K.
Paxman	Rolls Royce
Dorman	Deutz
English Electric	A.B.C.

Electrical and electronic

A.C. and D.C. motor rewinds—24 hour service.
Alternators and generators overhauled and repaired.
Control gear repairs and replacements.
Instrument repairs and supply.
Dynamic balancing of rotary machinery-armatures, shafts, fans etc., max. length 8', max. dia. 4', max. weight 2,000 lb.
Electrical installation repairs onboard.

Steelwork repairs

Deck fittings.
Derricks.
Ship side rails.
Bulwarks.
Medium size shell and internal damages.
Steel fabrications.
Boiler retubing.
Machinery guards.
Cab structures.

Cargo gear:

Repair and supply blocks, shackles etc.
Testing facilities.

General

Scaling, blasting and painting.
Gas freeing and tank cleaning.
Divers' services and underwater cleaning.
Plumbing and pipe fabrication.
Woodwork.

Repairs to:

Hatch covers.
Deck Machinery.
Winches.
Windlasses.
Cargo and engine room cranes.
Lifeboat lifting gear.
Marine air tools.

Supply and manufacture:

Spares for winches, windlasses cranes and hatch covers.
Shafts and bearings.
Cast iron and gun metal globe and gate valves.
Ball and roller bearings.
Brake friction materials-discs, pads and strip.
Perspex glazing for cabs.

Harrison Care

Thos & Jas Harrison Ltd
Mersey Chambers
Covent Garden, Liverpool L2 8UF.

Tel: 051-236 5611
Telex 628404

Names of contacts outside normal business hours

H.M.K. Jeffrey	**M.W. Merrifield**
051-342 1519	0704 25713
R.J. Carter	**J. Beaton**
07048 75784	051724 5718

HARRISON CARE
FOR YOUR SHIP REPAIR

A leaflet advertising the skills of Harrison's engineering work force.

industrial legislation, require a ballot of all members, a move the union would not contemplate in view of the narrow margin by which the previous ballot had been decided. Instead, with Machiavellian cunning, the NUS called for a series of "selective stoppages". The effect on British shipping was damaging; for Harrisons it was little short of disastrous. On 17th January, the new container ship, AUTHOR, sailed into Rotterdam on her maiden voyage, ready to deliver to Compagnie Générale Maritime, on long-term charter. Instead, the ship was marooned there for eight weeks. Her sister-ship, ADVISER, languished in Amsterdam, while EHCL's CITY OF DURBAN idled away two months in Hamburg. In foreign ports all over the world other selected ships came to a halt, many of the crews responding reluctantly to the dictates of the union. Losses in cancelled charters, off-hire charges, lay-up expenses, and lost income were devastating. When the strike ended in March the effects were dramatic, though predictable. The number of British ships put up for sale trebled; the number of officers and ratings reporting availability to the Merchant Navy Establishment (i.e. seeking jobs) went up from about 1,850 in December 1980 to 3,650 by the following March. The premier British line, P&O, disposed of 100 officers, sold four ships to foreign owners and chartered them back immediately on grounds of economy. Meanwhile, Charente sold INVENTOR, MAGICIAN, and HISTORIAN as a direct result of the losses and lack of confidence inflicted by the strike, three prime ships which could have expected to soldier on for several more years in the liner or tramp trades.[274]

It would be wrong to assume that the action of the NUS and the MNAOA (waiting in the wings to exploit the Seamen's Union's so-called success) was the sole cause of the British Merchant Navy's decline, but the unseemly action at a critical time turned a dignified retreat into something like a rout.

A similar malaise hung over the port of Liverpool during this period, for in the six months from May to October 1981, eight CAROL vessels were prevented from loading at Seaforth due to labour disputes. Liverpool's reputation among the CAROL partners had never been high due to poor productivity and a disreputable strike record. Even at the best of times, the Seaforth base was only marginally better than Port of Spain which had actually been dropped from the scheduled ports of call. It seemed at one time that Liverpool would suffer a similar fate, and only persistent lobbying by Harrison Line management persuaded their reluctant European partners to keep the port in the schedule.

In December 1983, a further development of the redundancy process gave 14 senior sea-going officers the option of either being made redundant or transferring to the off-shore personnel agency, Denholm (Bermuda) Ltd., part of the world-wide, Glasgow-based Denholm Shipping and Ship Management Group. The purpose of the agency was to provide full crews to vessels as and when required by shipowners. Officers who transferred would find their salaries considerably enhanced, and certain tax concessions available. But their tenure of employment was less secure, and such matters as insurance and pension contributions became their own personal responsibility. They were, to all intents and purposes, self-employed, to be drafted to any ship at the behest of the agency. However, whenever possible, senior Charente staff were assigned to Harrison-operated vessels, and so the link was maintained for a few more years.

On 2nd April 1982 Argentinian forces invaded the Falkland Islands, and within days an expeditionary force was despatched south to eject the invaders. Harrison vessels were not involved in these initial stages, but when, at the end of May, ASTRONOMER arrived at Felixstowe in the course of a regular CAROL voyage, her crew was greeted by the news that their ship was to be STUFT - the unlovely term used by the M.o.D. requisition officers to describe "Ships Taken Up From Trade" - and employed in support of the Falklands Task Force. ASTRONOMER's valued contribution to Operation Corporate and beyond is recounted elsewhere, but the episode shed a brilliant ray of sunshine on an otherwise drab and depressing maritime panorama.

Consortia and slot-sharing

But what was being done to brighten the economic gloom which had so beset the shipping industry in recent years? There was certainly no help forthcoming from the Government, which, despite the obvious lessons propounded by the Falklands War, seemed intent on damaging recovery in the interests of market forces. Soviet and East European ships, subsidised by the state, carried freight at absurdly low rates; while newly-fledged third-world fleets, subsidised by United Nations agencies, insisted on carrying their own exports in their own ships - not an unreasonable stipulation, perhaps, provided they were carried at commercial rates. The British shipping industry

Author (328).

[*J. and M. Clarkson collection*]

did not ask for subsidies, but in the circumstances tax concessions would not be altogether contrary to the Government's market principles. All the General Council of British Shipping asked was for a level playing field on which to compete fairly.[275] Instead, the 1984 budget removed what meagre fiscal concessions were then available to the industry by abolishing the 100% capital allowances on newbuildings, together with free depreciation. Another casualty of that budget was the 30-day rule, whereby individuals who spent more than thirty working days out of the country could claim against tax. This hit merchant seamen hard, and increased pressure on employers for ever higher wages to meet the depletion in income.

Thus, left to themselves to find the means of survival, companies flagged out more ships, sold others, and whittled down their work forces. They also banded together to form consortia, operating together in trades where once they had operated as commercial rivals. The CAROL organisation, of which Harrison Line was a prominent member, has already been mentioned, but problems were to be found even in that proud enterprise. Of major concern was Port of Spain, Trinidad, whose abysmal performance as a port had a devastating effect on the tight schedules vessels had to maintain to remain competitive. There was also increasing concern regarding the Harbour Authority's ability to maintain sufficient water in the approach channel. Thus, despite Port of Spain being, at that time, the most important port on the CAROL route in the Caribbean, it came as no surprise when it was dropped from the mainstream CAROL schedule. Thus, when the ADVISER sailed from Port of Spain on 7th June 1978, almost seven years would elapse before calls could be resumed. In the interim, Trinidad cargo was transhipped from Ponce, Puerto Rico, in small feeder vessels, until direct calls were resumed with the arrival of the AUTHOR on 2nd March 1985.

It was becoming increasingly clear to management that it was more economical to charter-in foreign ships than to operate ships under the Red Ensign. Better still, why not hire space on ships chartered-in by a consortium of which one is a member? This theory was put into practice when the organisation known as SAGUMEX (South Atlantic, Gulf & Mexico Line) was inaugurated in July 1980. In a similar set-up to CAROL, the members of the consortium included Harrison Line, Hapag Lloyd, C.G.M., and the Dutch company, I.C.T. Initially, the ships were provided by Hapag-Lloyd and I.C.T., and later by Compagnie Générale Maritime. Harrisons simply rented space, although in the following year the AUTHOR, on charter to C.G.M. and re-named CGM PROVENCE, took her place in the schedule.

The service was geared to operate weekly sailings from Rotterdam, Bremerhaven, Le Havre and Greenock to the US ports of Miami, New Orleans and Houston. The Mexican sector of the service was delayed for about a year waiting for the installation of facilities at the port of Vera Cruz. In the meantime, Mexican cargo was transhipped by means of a feeder vessel operating from Houston. Harrison's slot share was initially defined as 45 slots westbound and five slots eastbound, and marketing efforts were directed entirely towards the British sector of the trade, leaving Continental traffic to the European partners.[276]

Harrisons' conventional liner service to the US and Mexican ports in the Gulf had been for some years in the doldrums. A succession of poor returns, bureaucratic interference in the free flow of trade by the US Federal Commission, and a deep, seemingly unending, recession in the Mexican economy were all factors leading to the demise of this traditional service. Moreover, a lack of discipline in the Mexican trade had spawned a free-for-all, leading to incredibly low freight rates. Therefore, with the advent of SAGUMEX, the service was finally suspended after over 100 years trading going back to the end of the American Civil War. With it went the long and mutually beneficial relationship between Harrison Line and their ships' officers with the Phillips brothers, Peter and Tom, and three generations of Le Blancs, Harrison Line agents in the Gulf since the beginning. For, when Harrisons' application to trade to Florida and US Gulf ports within the consortium was successfully blocked by local interests, the connection was irrevocably broken.

Swiftly on the heels of SAGUMEX came another chartering consortium known as BEACON (Britain East Africa Container Line). Members originally included Union Castle, P&O, British & Commonwealth, Harrison, and Ellerman Lines, but a few months after the service began, with the sailing of the SLOMAN MIRA from Felixstowe on 11th February 1981, the rights of the first

The chartered *Sloman Mira* made the first BEACON sailing from Felixstowe in 1981.

three partners in the consortium were absorbed by Overseas Container Lines. BEACON began by operating a fortnightly service from Hull, Felixstowe, Antwerp, Marseilles, Genoa, and Leghorn to Port Sudan, Djibouti, Mombasa, Tanga and Dar es Salaam, using small, geared container vessels of about 400 to 600 TEUs* capacity, on time charter. A three-weekly service by conventional ships from the United Kingdom operated in conjunction with the container ships, at least for the first six months. In December 1981, a Harrison name appeared in the BEACON schedules BARRISTER. It was the custom for the chartered-in ships to be managed by one or other of the partners, and BARRISTER, a new German vessel

The *Barrister* was managed by Harrison Line during her two year charter to BEACON.

with a capacity of 1,150 TEUs and formerly known as CARMEN, was assigned to Harrison management. Thus, for the duration of a two-year charter, although her hull was green, her funnel was painted in the familiar Harrison Line colours, and she bore a traditional name.[277]

Later, when calls at Mauritius were included, it was found that the voyage became over-extended for little return. To counter this anomaly, Harrisons allied themselves with the French lines in a continental consortium known as CAPRICORNE, serving islands in the Indian Ocean, and arranged to take space on a slot-charter basis with fortnightly sailings from Felixstowe, commencing with the C.G.M., vessel DEGAS on 25th May 1982. This arrangement relieved the BEACON service of a considerable burden.[278]

An extension of the CAROL container service to the mainland shores of South and Central America had long been seen as a natural corollary to that service, so much so that the concept was originally referred to as CAROL Phase II. In the end, a new consortium, to be known as Euro-

Caribe, was formed, its component firms being, as with CAROL, Hapag Lloyd, Nedlloyd, C.G.M., and Harrison Line. The service would involve fortnightly sailings from Hamburg, Amsterdam, Le Havre, and Greenock, to La Guaira, Puerto Cabello, Cartagena, and Puerto Limon; while Liverpool would continue to be served by a break-bulk, Hapag Lloyd ship on a monthly basis. Three container vessels, each with a capacity of about 500 TEUs, were chartered-in by Euro-Caribe, the partners dividing the space or slots in accordance with an agreed formula. The service was inaugurated by the GUATEMALA, when she was delivered at Hamburg on 9th November 1982 to begin loading for a voyage scheduled to last 42 days. Her sisters, the HONDURAS and the COSTA RICA, the latter managed by Harrison Line, followed in succession.[279]

* TEU = Twenty-foot Equivalent Unit, the international standard of measurement for container ships. Thus a 40-foot container would be considered as two TEUs in estimating a ship's capacity.

The *Guatemala* was chartered by the Euro-Caribe consortium.

Flagging out

Chartering-in and hiring space, or slots, were just two of many tactical manoeuvres in the battle to cut costs and maintain competitiveness; another was flagging out. Harrisons had tried this gambit before, in the late fifties, when the subsidiary Ruthin Steamship Company of Bermuda was established but the idea was abandoned after a few years. However, by the eighties the need was more pressing. Therefore, in an attempt to escape the fiscal bonds of the Inland Revenue, and the costly demands of the unions, the Harrison Line board began to take an interest in the advantages of Hong Kong registry. The outcome was Blairdale Shipping Ltd. of Hong Kong, and the subsequent negotiations between Charente, Harrisons, Blairdale, Denholms and Charles Connell, owner of two 30,000-tonne geared bulk carriers, were complex and extremely discreet. The conclusion of the transactions in March 1982 gave Harrison Line a substantial interest in the company and the ships, which were managed by Denholms and promptly chartered-out to Charente, in a move reminiscent of P&O's manoeuvre of the previous year. One of the ships, the LANTAU TRADER, was assigned to the Atlantic Bulker consortium (in which Harrisons' three W-class bulkers were already operating), while the other, the LAMMA FOREST, was assigned to Scanscot, a Swedish-based consortium.

These ships were manned by Hong Kong Chinese crews and Asian junior officers, but the Master, Chief Officer, Chief and Second Engineers were assigned by Charente. About a month later, on 16th April, the last of Harrison's conventional, break-bulk 'tween deckers, the BENEFACTOR, was sold to a Panamanian registered company.

The mid-nineteen eighties witnessed the continued erosion of the British merchant fleet on a scale greater, if less dramatic, than the nation's enemies were able to attain in either 1917, or 1942. Even Ellerman family shareholders concluded that there were better ways of making money than running a shipping company. In 1983 they went in search of a buyer for their world-famous shipping group, and finding one in the finance and property organization of J. and F. Barclay. Meanwhile Booker Brothers, for many years a friendly trading rival of Thos. and Jas. Harrison in the West Indies, sold all its ships. For twelve months Bookers continued shipping cargo in chartered ships, then ceased trading altogether. In May 1984, the oldest, and perhaps the best known of family shipping firms, Bibby Brothers, transferred four of its six vessels to the Hong Kong register, and transposed all its officers to an off-shore agreement. In October that year Seawinds Inc. of Hong Kong, the San Francisco-based company in which Harrisons had invested 18 months earlier, and to which the ADVISER had been chartered as the ASIA WINDS, got into financial difficulties, leaving ASIA WINDS out on a limb in Singapore.

For Harrisons, however, 1984 was not all doom and gloom, for that year saw the founding of Crossfish Ltd., a Hong Kong company established by Harrisons to retain two 35,000 tonne bulk carriers, delivered from Shimizu in the spring of that year. The PISCES PIONEER and PISCES PLANTER were assigned immediately to Charente management, but manned by Denholm (I.O.M.) Ltd., on an off-shore basis.

In July 1985, the CITY OF DURBAN and other former Ellerman vessels were transferred to the Isle of Man

In the colours of Crossfish Ltd., the *Pisces Pioneer* in the English Channel, December 1985.

register; while in August the Reardon Smith Line of Cardiff went into voluntary liquidation. Early in 1986, British Petroleum made 1,690 men redundant and transferred 30 of its proud fleet of British tankers off-shore, while the old Blue Funnel line faded into history when Ocean Transport and Trading Ltd. sold its last ship in January. In August 1986, Shell flagged out 27 of its tankers to the Isle of Man register, and it was not surprising that, by the end of the year, British-owned flagged-out tonnage exceeded that of the home-registered fleet, while the number of British registered seafarers had slipped from 58,000 in 1981 to 35,000 in five years.

Harrison Line was not immune from this cheerless process, and continued to dispose of ships and men as the British share of the market diminished, until by 1988 only two of Harrison's remaining seven ships sailed under the UK flag, the AUTHOR and the CGM PROVENCE (ex-ADVISER). In December 1988 the board decided to transfer these two ships to the Isle of Man register, and at the same time offer the remaining 75 officers still on the Charente books either early retirement, a transfer to Denholm (I.O.M.) Ltd., or redundancy.

When the news broke there was an angry but pointless reaction, and for a brief interval the ships concerned, the AUTHOR in Liverpool and the CGM PROVENCE in Felixstowe, were delayed while union representatives argued and pleaded for a reprieve. But this time the deck was stacked against both parties; there was no way the company alone could man two ships on an economical basis, and the decision was irrevocable.[280]

The final break occurred in January 1989 when, for the first time in its long history, The Charente Steam-Ship Company was reduced to two vessels (one of which was owned by Barclays' Bank), both registered in Douglas, I.O.M., and no sea-going staff whatsoever.

Extrinsic investments

Despite, or perhaps because of, the difficulties besetting the shipping industry, Harrison Line, or Charente, continued to hedge its interests by investing in various projects, some related to shipping and others quite diverse. Most have been mentioned elsewhere,[281] like Bidston Shipping Ltd., Harrison Care, and Seawinds Inc., but in October 1985, Harrisons acquired 100% of the Liverpool chart specialists and agents to the Hydrographic Office, Dubois, Phillips and McCallum Ltd. The company's portfolio of non-shipping related investments was catholic in its diversity, embracing such elements of manufacturing industry as domestic appliances, garden furniture, blood analysis equipment, North Sea oil, and insurance.

In 1988 Harrisons made an investment in a chemical tanker, MULTITANK CATANIA (1,599/83), one of 15 similar vessels operated and managed by C.F. Ahrenkiel in an organisation known as Multitank Incorporated. At about the same time a similar investment was made in a liquefied gas carrier, ELBEGAS (5,958/83) also managed by C.F. Ahrenkiel, but outside the Multitank pool. Harrisons' interest in these vessels amounts to a quarter share in each, a portion which stirs vague, nostalgic memories of a young Thomas Harrison buying his first quarter share in the brig JANE from his patron, Richard Williamson, in 1836. But it is difficult to visualise either of these two specialised vessels as true Harrison ships. The MULTITANK CATANIA is registered in Elsfleth, Germany, while ELBEGAS, initially registered in the Faroes as the NORGE, is now registered in Panama; and both, naturally, carry foreign crews. As shareholders, Harrisons have a say in overall policy, but day-to-day management is Ahrenkiel's responsibility. The ships simply represent an investment, interesting and profitable no

doubt, but about as relevant to the Harrison Line's psyche as, say, an investment in British Gas.

On 11th January 1990, for the first time since the beginning of the Second World War, a Harrison vessel sailed from the United Kingdom to the West Indies with regular, fare-paying passengers on board. The accommodation of the container ship AUTHOR had been modified in luxurious style to accommodate six passengers, and even with a fare structure in the region of £3,000 for the 55-day round voyage, the new service was soon fully subscribed for twelve months ahead. A year later, her sister-ship ADVISER, newly returned to the CAROL consortium after eight years in the charter jungle, was similarly modified.

Government moves

By 1989 there were signs that the Government was at last taking a belated interest in the depressed state of British shipping, the depletion of the merchant fleet, and the gradual disappearance of British seamen from the maritime scene. It was suddenly realised that, in times of crisis, it might be comparatively easy to charter-in foreign tonnage, perhaps not so easy to persuade alien crews to risk their necks in someone else's quarrel.

So the concept of a Merchant Navy Reserve (the M.N.R., forsooth!) was evolved within the Department of Transport. A pool of several thousand experienced seafarers no longer working at sea would be established on a voluntary basis. In a time of national emergency the men would be liable to be called up, just like reservists in the Army, Navy, and Air Force. In the meantime, all would be entitled to receive a modest annual bounty of £150. An enabling statute, the Merchant Navy Reserve Regulations, came into effect on 27th May 1989.[282]

The other Government gesture was the introduction in April 1989 of a bill to abolish the National Dock Labour Scheme which, since 1947, had frustrated employers' efforts within the ports and docks to rationalise the system. The scheme gave dock workers immunity from enforced redundancy, employers a lasting headache, and shippers an expensive, inefficient service in the docks industry. No other industry had ever granted its workers such preferential treatment, and the Scheme was quite out of touch with the modern industrial climate. Still, it was a ferocious nettle for any government to grasp, but one which gave Mrs. Thatcher no qualms, and the bill became law in June 1989. Of course there was an uproar, leading to futile but damaging strikes in many of the 63 ports to which the old Scheme had applied. But there were other ports, most of them quite unaffected by either the Scheme or the strikes, and to these ports cargo and ships were resolutely diverted at considerable expenditure of time, energy, and funds. It was later estimated that, insofar as the CAROL and Euro-Caribe partners were concerned, the financial cost of transferring cargo and re-routing ships over a three-month period was about £250,000, a sum which was apparently almost cheerfully paid, and said to be "well worth it".[283]

This unexpected change of fortune was welcomed by shippers, shipowners and port authorities throughout the land, but still the 1989 budget proposals had not revealed any of the fiscal concessions so long awaited by the shipping industry, those tax rebates which would have contributed so much to the financial well-being of the industry, and encouraged owners to invest, and build new ships. Once again the pleas and well-reasoned arguments of the General Council of British Shipping had been ignored by the Chancellor, and the rot was set to continue. Later in the year, the General Council submitted yet another memorandum setting out the industry's aims and aspirations, and highlighting the areas where Government

Top: Part of Harrison's portfolio of investments was a part-ownership of the liquefied gas tanker *Elbegas*.

Middle: Harrisons also invested in the chemical tanker *Multitank Catania*.
    [D. Whiteside collection]

Bottom: the chartered-in *Arbitrator*.
    [D. Whiteside collection]

intervention would be most helpful.

The paper concluded: "The General Council of British Shipping therefore calls on the Government to give the British Shipping Industry the positive policy support which is available to shipowners elsewhere. The availability for five years of a 100% First Year Allowance, minor improvements to the rules for roll-over relief for balancing charges and to the Business Expansion Scheme, and the elimination of National Insurance and Seafarers' income tax liabilities* would give British Shipping Companies and British Seamen the opportunity to reverse the recent decline and make their full contribution to the country's economy and national interest, in peace and in war."[284]

Though studiously rational, and backed by statistical

evidence which could not be refuted, this paper had no better success than its predecessors, despite the appearance in office of a new Chancellor. The prospect of a level playing field on which to compete was as remote as ever.

*To meet fierce worldwide competition from low-cost foreign fleets, several European Governments had taken steps to ease the tax burdens on their shipping companies and seafarers. In Sweden, for example, the Government returns to shipowners all tax and insurance contributions paid by Swedish seafarers; in Denmark, income tax and social security payments by seafarers have been abolished; while highly favourable rates exist in Greece, Germany, and the Netherlands.

FLEET LIST Part 6

325. ASTRONOMER (5) 1977-1986 Steel motor container ship. One deck, four holds, each split into six compartments. O.N. 364436 27,868g 15,348n 23,120d 199.42 (204.0 o.l.) x 30.85 x 18.8 metres. Cargo capacity: 1,412 TEUs. Two masts and one 40 tonne Liebherr gantry crane.
International code: GVOC.
10-cyl. 2SCSA Sulzer-type oil engine by H. Cegielski, Poznan, Poland; 20.5 knots. Bow thrusters.

Astronomer above and below right at Liverpool soon after her sale to Hong Kong owners in 1986. She has been renamed *Admiralty Island*, but is still in the grey she wore as a fleet auxiliary.
[Below: Ambuscade Marine Photography, courtesy David Whiteside]

6.7.1976: Launched by Stocznia Gdanska im Lenina, Gdansk, Poland (Yard No. B463/101) for the company. *20.1.1977:* Delivered at a cost of £9,665,336. Later sailed from north west European ports and Liverpool for the Caribbean and Central America on her maiden voyage under Captain Tom Wilson. *28.5.1982:* Chartered by the Admiralty. Converted into a helicopter support and repair vessel at Devonport. *8.6.1982:* Sailed south to take part in the recovery of the Falkland Islands. *3.12.1982:* Returned to Devonport to be decommissioned. *25.4.1983:* Arrived at Cammell Laird's Shipyard, Birkenhead, to be converted into a Royal Fleet Auxiliary, an experimental helicopter support ship, introducing the ARAPAHO/SCAD system of container ship conversion. *16.11.1983:* Renamed RELIANT. *3.12.1983:* Conversion completed. *1.1984:* Support ship to British UN forces in Lebanon. *11.2.1984:* Airlifted 514 civilians to safety from West Beirut. *11.1984:* Returned to Falklands station. *25.7.1986:* Arrived at Birkenhead for reconversion to mercantile service but was bought by Ministry of Defence. *27.10.1986:* Sold to Parramatta Shipping Co. S.A., Panama (Miltrend Shipping Co. Ltd., Hong Kong, managers) (Hong Kong Islands Line Ltd., Hong Kong) and renamed ADMIRALTY ISLAND. *4.1989:*

Renamed WEALTHY RIVER. *1990:* Transferred to Unison Maritime S.A., Panama (China Merchants Steam Navigation International Ship Trade Co. Ltd., Taipei, Taiwan). *1994.* Owners became Rubimonte Maritime Inc., Panama (Cosco Container Lines, Beijing, People's Republic of China). *7.9.1998:* Arrived at Alang to be broken up.

ASTRONOMER joins the South Atlantic Task Force

The Harrison Line container ship ASTRONOMER, inward bound from the West Indies, was approaching the chops of the Channel when news of the rocket attack on the ATLANTIC CONVEYOR in the South Atlantic came over the radio. The crew were at once deeply concerned. "She's a Liverpool ship, isn't she?" said one. "Yes; and with a Liverpool crew. Ian North, the Master, is a local man." Only later did it emerge that Captain North and eleven of his crew had died when the Exocet missile struck his ship.[285] With her went nine helicopters and many hundreds of tons of vital stores and equipment. In material terms, the loss of the ATLANTIC CONVEYOR was the most serious single casualty suffered by the Task Force during the entire Falklands War. To the Ministry of Defence and General Staff her replacement was a matter of urgency.

On the day after the ship sank, MoD officials contacted Harrison's Liverpool office to enquire the whereabouts and availability of the ASTRONOMER. They were informed that the ship was due to dock at Felixstowe that very evening, 28th May 1982. The men from the Ministry promised to meet her to assess her potential as a helicopter carrier. ASTRONOMER was due for a crew change at Felixstowe, and anticipating the likely outcome of the MoD inspection, the opportunity was taken to engage a crew consisting entirely of volunteers, having first briefed them on the possible nature of the next voyage. Despite acute awareness of the fate of the ATLANTIC CONVEYOR and other ships in the Task Force there was no lack of men willing to come forward.

No sooner had the ship docked than the requisition men came on board. In no time at all they decided that she was just the ship they were looking for, and so she became STUFT - ship taken up from trade. Her CAROL schedule was immediately cancelled, causing consternation in the CAROL Co-ordinating Office in Hounslow, and all her containers, whether full or empty, were to be discharged there and then. Captain Derek Skillander handed his ship over to Stan Bladon with mixed feelings. "I can't imagine what you're being let in for this trip," he said ruefully. Captain Bladon, imperturbable as ever, simply drew on his pipe and grinned. "At least it'll be a change," he said. "Now, let's go over this check list."

At dawn on 30th May, ASTRONOMER canted out of her berth at Felixstowe and coasted round to Devonport to be converted into a helicopter support ship, arriving next day.[286] Then for six days, 500 dockyard fitters swarmed over the ship, apparently determined to tear her apart, and when she emerged a third of her foredeck had been transformed into a hangar and heli-pad. Portakabins were installed on deck to accommodate the additional personnel, and extra cooking facilities were introduced to meet the demand. Replenishment at sea gear for the transfer of fuel at sea; satellite communication equipment, and a pair of Oerlikon anti-aircraft guns were also installed. The latter were of a type familiar to Second World War veterans with long memories, but the "chaff-chukkers" were not, since their purpose was to confuse the radar on modern incoming missiles and deflect them from their target. To the merchant seamen it was a comforting armoury. An amazing variety of stores and equipment came on board in containers to be stowed below, and on 7th June ASTRONOMER left her berth in Number 10 Dock to anchor in Plymouth Sound to receive her quota of helicopters. On board were the 34 Merchant Navy types who comprised the ship's crew; 53 Royal Navy, 21 Royal Air Force, and 8 "Pongoes", or Army types, a total of 116 men.

Captain Bladon was soon left in no doubt as to the extent of his new and weighty responsibilities. As the first helicopter, a Wessex 5, hovered expectantly alongside the anchored ship, Captain Bladon looked on with interest, for it was a novel experience for him. There was a slight cough, and a voice from beside him said, "Permission, sir, for the helicopter to land?" It was the F.D.O.A. (Flight Deck Officer's Assistant - this awful jargon was another thing the "Merchies" would have to get used to). The Captain was nonplussed. "Permission? Surely the pilot and that chap on deck (this was the F.D.O. himself) are

better qualified than I to say when the chopper can land?" "Well, sir", replied the F.D.O.A. respectfully, "In the Navy only the commander of the carrier can grant permission to land and take off." "In that case, permission granted", murmured the Captain.

His next lesson was on replenishment at sea (RAS). At 07.00 on 8th June ASTRONOMER kept a rendezvous with the RFA tanker, BLACK ROVER, off Portland Bill. Then, while steaming at 10 knots on parallel courses, 200 feet apart, two fuel pipes and a fresh water pipe bridged the gap, linking the two ships in a life-giving umbilical connection. It required a nice sense of timing, careful steering, and a delicate adjustment of engine revolutions to eliminate any risk of a nasty spill off England's south coast. Fortunately, the weather was calm with a smooth sea, circumstances which greatly facilitated the operation. Meanwhile, from the yardarm flew an enormous red flag, indicating the type of operation which was in progress. What was significant was the legend emblazoned in black lettering on the red ground: "MV ASTRONOMER", and beneath it, "HMS INCREDIBLE".

Captain H.S. Bladon, Master of *Astronomer* in the South Atlantic.

It transpired that the young servicemen on board were so impressed by the standards of accommodation and feeding on the "Merchie", and grateful for their incredible luck in being assigned to "the best carrier in the fleet", that they re-christened her. It was a name which would grow in lustre throughout her service with the Task Force, thanks in large measure to the efforts of Alf Eady, the Catering Officer, and his team of cooks and stewards.

The RAS operation was completed in just over an hour, and the ship drifted in Lyme Bay awaiting the last of her litter of helicopters. In all, six Wessex 5s, four Scouts, and three Chinooks completed ASTRONOMER's air arm. By 14.00 all were safely secured and the ship began her long voyage south.

The first few days were fully occupied settling into a purposeful routine, punctuated by a series of essential drills embracing all those contingencies which might have to be faced in the war zone - damage control, fire party musters, gunnery practice, care of casualties, man overboard (i.e. ditched pilots) procedures, and, naturally, abandon ship. In lighter vein, there was much friendly rivalry between the representative services in competitive board games, general knowledge quizzes, and the ubiquitous horse racing game. All this activity helped boost morale, and keep boredom at bay.

Meanwhile, the war in the Falklands, towards which they were heading, was approaching its final bloody stages. ASTRONOMER had left British waters on 8th June, the day RFA SIR GALAHAD, with 300 Welsh Guardsmen on board, was bombed off Fitzroy, near Bluff Cove. Despite this setback, British troops began their final three-pronged advance towards Port Stanley on the 12th June. There was some fierce hand-to-hand fighting and casualties on both sides, but the outcome was never in doubt. HMS GLAMORGAN, out at sea, was struck by a shore-based Exocet. Thirteen men were killed, and the ship was badly damaged, but she was able to continue her task. By 14th June it was all over. British forces surrounded Port Stanley, the Argentinians had suffered heavy losses, and at 21.00 their Commander, Major General Menendez, signed a formal document of surrender.

All these events were, of course, closely monitored via BBC radio on board ASTRONOMER, and when the cease fire was announced feelings of profound relief swept through the ship. The crew were all volunteers; they had offered their services in the full knowledge of the price they might have to pay, and the fact that the shooting war came to an end before they even reached the war zone should not detract one jot from their gallant spirit of endeavour. Besides, they had a shrewd idea there would still be plenty of work to do.

ASTRONOMER arrived at Ascension Island at 18.00 on 16th June, two days after hostilities ceased. Bunkers were taken from the tanker ALVEGA, and next morning more urgently needed stores were loaded, "vertrepping" (to vertrep = to supply by "vertical replenishment", i.e. by helicopter) them aboard from helicopters. Amongst the mountain of stores were some ten tons of mail for all service units and 66 ships in the war zone, all

RFA *Reliant,* formerly *Astronomer:* photographs which demonstrates why warships and auxiliaries are painted grey.

[*Crown Copyright/MOD 0596-33; 83/2364-6]*

Astronomer "vertrepping."

of which had to be carefully sorted in the next week or so.

On 18th June, as the ship sailed away from Ascension, she was approached by a strange, sinister-looking ship, quickly identified by the naval officers as a Soviet Primorye-class A.G.I. surveillance vessel. She came in close, and it did not take long for the watch on deck to realise just what had excited the Russians' curiosity.

Back in Lyme Bay, where the ship had loaded her helicopters, the three Chinooks - large twin-rotored machines - had their rotors removed prior to stowing them away stern first in the hangar. Too big to be entirely enclosed, their nose and cabin parts projected on deck. To protect them from the weather they were draped in green canvas covers in such a way that Captain Bladon, eyeing them from the bridge, remarked that they looked for all the world like "three Yogi Bears from some 'It's a Knockout' extravaganza". The innocent remark was overheard, and touched off an artistic response among the RAF servicemen whose job it was to take care of these monsters. With liberal applications of paint they lovingly added eyes, nose, and mouth to the featureless "faces", and even fitted each with a pair of Wellington boots. Perhaps Yogi got a little confused with Paddington, but the result was three fabulous Disneyland creatures, apparently guarding the entrance to the hangar. It is little wonder the Russians came in closer for further incredulous, eyes-rubbing scrutiny!

The days passed quickly, and the weather grew colder and more blustery. Although the war was officially over, the Navy insisted that precautions be maintained, even to the extent of steaming at night without lights and without radar. On 26th June a stirring sight met the concentrated gaze of the lookouts. The fleet flagship, HMS HERMES with her attendant frigates and destroyers, some fifteen ships in all, were in sight deployed in review order. ASTRONOMER was ordered to take station in the fleet formation and, as the weather was calm, the gantry crane was put to good use bringing the mail up on deck. Word soon got around, and in no time at all, ASTRONOMER quickly resembled, in Captain Bladon's apt phrase, "a jam-pot in summertime", as Wessex, Lynx, Sea King, and Scout helicopters buzzed on and off, like so many wasps, as they vertrepped the mail to the waiting ships. With them went also 40 tons of spare parts for HERMES' Sea Harriers, a long awaited bounty. Having successfully completed this, her first important assignment with the Task Force, ASTRONOMER was given permission to detach from the fleet, and proceed to Port Stanley. Adjusting speed to arrive at daybreak, the ship entered Port William Sound at dawn on Sunday 27th June, and anchored north of West Tussac Island.

During the next three months ASTRONOMER carried out all manner of tasks, and with such panache that her rightful claim to the honorary nickname of HMS INCREDIBLE was never in doubt. The ship's hangar became a hospital for ailing helicopters which flopped aboard like ducks winged in flight, and, after a few days in intensive care, took off once more with renewed vigour. The ship also became established as a unique

R and R (rest and recuperation) centre, a sort of convalescent home for weary troopers camped out in the freezing wilderness. With her comfortable beds, unlimited hot water showers, and five-star catering, ASTRONOMER became the sort of earthly paradise that tired and hungry soldiers dreamed about, and commanding officers made a point of sending their men, a few at a time, to ASTRONOMER for a day or two's R and R to boost morale, and help them face the rigours of the Falklands winter in inadequate camps and billets ashore.

It was frequently necessary for the ship to put to sea in order to operate the desalination plant to produce fresh water. On these occasions, SNOFI (Senior Naval Officer, Falkland Islands) took the opportunity to promote the vessel to coastal surveillance ship, thus relieving one of the naval vessels which continuously patrolled the waters of the Exclusion Zone. It was during one such patrol that ASTRONOMER intercepted the Russian tanker RIJEKA and escorted her into international waters. On another occasion she guided a Polish trawler through the minefields to Port Stanley to land a sick seaman. In another incident, the gyro compasses aboard the RFA SIR BEDIVERE failed, and ASTRONOMER escorted her to Port San Carlos. At the end of one patrol, the ship had no sooner dropped anchor in Berkely Sound when she was instructed to pick up a Lynx gearbox from the FORT GRANGE at San Carlos. This assignment did indeed raise a few cost-conscious eyebrows

To send a 28,000-ton ship 80 miles just to pick up a 2,000 lb parcel did seem a bit extravagant, but this, along with countless similar jobs, large and small, were promptly dealt with. It was with pleasure, therefore, that Captain Bladon proudly accepted the coveted BZ Plaque from the hands of Rear Admiral Reffell aboard HMS BRISTOL, for ASTRONOMER's patrol work. "BZ" is the Royal Navy's signal for "Well Done".

ASTRONOMER'S empty containers found many uses ashore. Some became lock-up stowages for munitions and spare parts; others became living quarters for the troops or offices for the administrators. Six palatial 40-foot units were deployed in the hills around the harbour to accommodate the Rapier missile air-defence crews. At the end of August the 1,000th helicopter landed on ASTRONOMER's flight deck to refuel. The pilot of the Sea King, who was from HMS INVINCIBLE, was surprised and delighted to receive a bottle of Task Force beer to mark the event! No, it was not Prince Andrew. However, the Prince was recognised on another occasion when a Sea King from INVINCIBLE touched down to refuel, but he did not leave the cockpit and took off shortly afterwards.

On 15th September 1982, ASTRONOMER's relief crew arrived, and disembarked from the former North Sea ferry NORLAND at Port Stanley. Captain Bladon handed over his well-seasoned charge to Captain Brian Jones, who was somewhat perplexed to see the changes wrought upon the ASTRONOMER he remembered, and to hear the incomprehensible naval gibberish on the tongues of former shipmates. It was, of course, a passing phase. They soon got used to it, and quickly slotted into the unfamiliar routine like old hands. Meanwhile, Captain Bladon and his crew were on their way to Ascension "pigging it" in the crowded NORLAND. From Ascension they took off in a noisy, vibrating, and comfortless RAF Hercules, only the thought of going home making the flight bearable. Captain Bladon was heard to remark drily that he was not surprised that "paratroopers jump willingly from these things!"

A 14-hour flight via Dakar brought them to RAF Brize Norton in Wiltshire, where, on 28th September, they landed to a rapturous welcome from a coach-load of wives and relatives. Sir Thomas and Lady Pilkington were there with Mr. and Mrs. Peter Rosselli and Captain Michael Jones, to greet them. In the VIP reception area, each member of the crew was welcomed in turn, and received a specially engraved tankard as a memento of yet another brief but significant chapter written by a Harrison ship in the nation's service.

ASTRONOMER soldiered on in the Falklands for another two months before her services could be relinquished. Eventually she set sail for home waters in November, and arrived at Devonport on 3rd December to be de-commissioned, a shining example of the Merchant Navy's role in wartime. It was the C. in C., Admiral Sir John Fieldhouse, who remarked, "I cannot say too often or too clearly how important has been the Merchant Navy's contribution to our efforts. Without the ships taken up from trade, the operation could not have been undertaken - and I hope this message is clearly understood by the British Nation".[287]

326. ADVISER (2) 1977-1993 Steel motor container ship. One deck.
O.N. 378035 27,868g, 15,343n, 23,120d 199.42 (204.0 o.l.) x 30.85 x 18.8 metres. Cargo capacity: 1,412 TEUs. Four holds each split into six compartments. Two masts and a Liebherr 40-tonne gantry crane.
10-cyl. 2SCSA. Sulzer-type oil engine by H. Cegielski, Poznan, Poland; 20.5 knots. Bow thruster.

Adviser could be distinguished from sister *Astronomer* by the 'wings' fitted to the funnel.

28.10.1976: Keel laid. *8.4.1977:* Launched by Stocznia Gdanska in Lenina, Gdansk, Poland (Yard No. B463/102) for the company. *23.9.1977:* Delivered at a cost of £9,617,881, registered at Liverpool and subsequently sailed for the Caribbean and Central America (the CAROL Service) on her maiden voyage under Captain H.S. Bladon. *2.2.1982:* Made first scheduled call at Felixstowe. *25.7.1982:* Laid up at Amsterdam. *21.3.1983:* Chartered long term to Seawinds Inc., Hong Kong and renamed ASIA WINDS under Captain E. J. Maxwell. *10.1984:* Seawinds Inc. became bankrupt, ending the charter. *16.11.1984:* Dry docked at Singapore; name reverted to ADVISER. *12.1984:* Chartered to CGM to operate in the SAGUMEX service between North West Europe and the Gulf of Mexico. *2.2.1985:* Renamed CGM PROVENCE. *17.9.1985:* Draught increased by one metre giving new deadweight tonnage 27,893 with increased cargo capacity of 1,520 TEUs. *19.4.1988:* Completed 1,000,000

miles since completion. Total time since delivery: 92,696 hours; total steaming time: 52,877 hours. Average speed: 18.91 knots. Number of port visits: 976. Average number of ports per annum: 92. Average time in port (excluding lay-up and dry docking): 21.98 hours. Total tonnes loaded: 1,892,120.[288] *3.3.1989:* Transferred to Douglas, Isle of Man register. *25.1.1990:* Rescued the crew of the US tug MARION MORAN (284/1982) while on passage Savannah for Le Havre. *15.5.1990:* CGM charter completed. Renamed ADVISER and re-entered CAROL service. *2.1991:* Modified to carry six fare-paying passengers. *22.6.1993:* Sold to Toddle Shipping Inc., Monrovia, Liberia (Costamare Shipping Co. S.A. (V.K. Constantakopoulos), Athens, Greece) under the Greek flag. Chartered to Laser Line of Stockholm and renamed LASER STREAM. *1996:* Renamed CAP VILANO. *12.2000:* Renamed MSC NAMIBIA. *9.2003:* Still in service.

"Prompt, professional action"
On Thursday 25th January 1990, in her guise as CGM PROVENCE, the container ship ADVISER was homeward bound from Savannah, Georgia, to Le Havre in the final stages of yet another voyage for SAGUMEX.[289] In the spacious wheelhouse the VHF radio was, as usual, tuned to the international distress frequency, Channel 16. Nevertheless, it came as something of a surprise, out there in mid-ocean, a thousand miles east of the State of New Jersey, when at 06.25 the speaker crackled into life: "MAYDAY MAYDAY MAYDAY. American tug MARION MORAN. Fire in engine room. Assistance required immediately. Position Latitude 40.04N. Longitude 48.12W. MAYDAY MAYDAY MAYDAY."
It did not take long for the bridge staff to deduce that the origin of the call was a mere twenty miles or so astern.

Chartered to Compagnie Generale Maritime for the SAGUMEX service, *Adviser* became *CGM Provence*.

Three minutes after the call came through CGM PROVENCE was turning through 180 degrees, her lofty radar scanner searching beyond the visible horizon for the tiny target. Captain R.J. Smith went on the air to assure the imperilled crew that help was on the way, and would be on the scene in little over an hour. A few more minutes went by as eyes tried to pierce the darkness of the western horizon. Then another message, stark in its urgency, came through on Channel 16: "MARION MORAN to CGM PROVENCE. Fire raging out of control. Crew taking to liferaft".

Fifteen, twenty minutes went by. Suddenly, the grey gloom ahead was riven by a festoon of light from a bursting flare, and there, on the radar screen, eleven miles ahead, was the tell-tale blip. PROVENCE was right on course. Soon, the blessed daylight was spreading from the east, and within minutes the tug was sighted, a plume of black smoke rising from somewhere amidships. Nearby, bobbing about on the gentle swell, was the crowded liferaft.

The weather was quiet as the ship manoeuvred into position, and there was no difficulty getting the men aboard up the pilot ladder. There were nine survivors, none of whom was injured, and all were thankful to accept PROVENCEal hospitality. The empty life raft was hoisted aboard; US,

Canadian, and British Coastguards were informed of the rescue; the tug skipper spoke reassuringly to his anxious owners; and CGM PROVENCE resumed course for Le Havre. The still burning tug boat, which had been returning to New York after delivering a barge to Southampton, was left behind to be picked up by a salvage tug from Halifax, chartered for the purpose by her owners.

The entire operation, from receipt of the first MAYDAY call to resumption of course and speed, had occupied just over two hours. The castaways could only have been impressed by the service.

A few days later, Sir Thomas Pilkington, Chairman of Thos. and Jas. Harrison Ltd., received a letter dated 26th January from his counterpart in the Moran Towing Corporation of Greenwich, Connecticut, Thomas E. Moran. After recapitulating the events of the previous day, the letter ended: "We at Moran along with the crew of the MARION MORAN would like to take this opportunity to express our deepest gratitude to the Captain and crew of m.v. CGM PROVENCE for their prompt, professional action."

They did indeed act in the finest traditions of the sea, and deserve congratulations on a job very well done".

327. CITY OF DURBAN 1978-1998 Steel twin-screw motor container ship. One deck and seven cellular holds. O.N. 377502 53,790g, 34,895n, 47,269d. 248.2 (258.5 o.l.) x 32.26 x 24.15 metres. Container capacity: 2,436 TEUs (886 refrigerated).
International code: GXIC.
Two 8-cyl. 2SCSA oil engines by Maschinenbau Augsburg-Nürnberg (MAN), Augsburg, West Germany; 22 knots. Two bow thrusters.

16.9.1977: Launched by A. G. Weser G.m.b.H., Bremen, West Germany (Yard No. 1401) for Ellerman Harrison Container Lines (EHCL). *6.12.1978:* Delivered, registered in London, owned Ellermans 42/64 shares, Harrison 22/64 shares, and managed by Ellermans. Harrison's 22 shares cost £14,169,740. Manning divided between staff of the two firms. Subsequently sailed from Northwest Europe for Capetown on her maiden voyage in the South African and European Container Services (SAECS). *10.1982:* Damaged entering a lock at Le Havre. *2.1983:* Chartered to Overseas Container Lines (OCL) and renamed PORTLAND BAY. *12.1983:* Reverted to EHCL and CITY OF DURBAN. *7.1985:* Chartered to Associated Container Transportation

(ACT), renamed ACT 8 and transferred to Isle of Man register. *1.1991:* Reverted to EHCL and renamed CITY OF DURBAN. *11.10.1991:* Ellermans' shares sold to P&O Containers Ltd., who took over management. *22.7.1996:* Chartered to P&O Container Lines, renamed PEGASUS BAY and operated in Europe/Australasia service. *31.7.1998:* Harrison sold remaining EHCL shares to P&O Nedlloyd Ltd. who became owners with P&O Nedlloyd B.V. as managers. Thus Harrison's involvement in the South African trade came to an end after some 96 years. *14.11.2002:* Arrived at Zhenjiang, Jiangsu Province, Peoiple's Republic of China to be broken up by Jiangyin Changjiang Shipbreaking Factory.

City of Durban was built for Ellerman Harrison Container Lines, her colours reflecting Ellerman's majority shareholding.

328. AUTHOR (5) 1981-1995 Steel motor container ship. One deck.
O.N. 389169 28,031g, 14,787n, 22,858d. 193.12 (214.02 o.l.) x 30.82 x 18.83 metres. Container capacity: 1,412 TEUs. Four holds each split into six compartments. Two masts and one 40-tonne Liebherr gantry crane.
International code: GBSA.

15.1.1980: Keel laid. *14.6.1980:* Launched by Stozcnia Gdanska im Lenina, Gdansk, Poland (Yard No. B463/103) for the company. *5.1.1981:* Delivered at a cost of £13,038.489 to Barclays Mercantile Industrial Finance Ltd., under Harrison Line management, registered at Liverpool, and chartered to CGM. After six weeks' delay due to a seamen's strike she sailed on her maiden voyage in the SAGUMEX service from Europe to the Gulf of Mexico under Captain R.J. Smith. *7.1981:* Completed CGM charter, chartered to Ben Line and renamed BENARMIN. *1.1982:* Completed charter and name reverted to AUTHOR. *6.1982:* Replaced ASTRONOMER in the CAROL consortium when that ship was taken up by the Ministry of Defence. *2.3.1985:* Arrived at Port of Spain to resume CAROL visits which had been suspended since June 1978 due to inefficient working of the port, labour unrest and silting of the approach channel.[290] *23.1.1986:* Draught increased by one metre giving new deadweight tonnage of 27,631. *25.4.1986:* Held hostage at

Port au Prince by rebellious port workers for four days.[291] *2.1989:* Registry transferred to Douglas, Isle of Man. *11.5.1993:* Sailed from Liverpool for Ponce, Puerto Rico under Captain G.A. Walter. That was the final sailing of a Harrison Line vessel from Liverpool. The consortium's centre of operations became Felixstowe on 1st July 1993. *19.5.1995:* Sold to Ambassador Shipping Ltd., Cayman Islands (Safman Shipping Ltd., Douglas, managers) (South African Marine Corporation Ltd., Capetown, South Africa). Time-chartered to Harrison Line to resume trading under her old name in the New Caribbean Service (NCS). *23.2.1999:* End of charter. Renamed SCL INFANTA by The Maersk Co. Ltd., who had recently taken over her owners. *8.2000:* Sold to Anco Holdings S.A. (Target Marine S.A., managers), Piraeus, Greece and renamed SAFMARINE INFANTA under the Marshall Islands flag. *2002:* Renamed MSC CORSICA. *9.2003:* Still in service.

The final container ship delivered to Harrison Line, *Author.*   *[Russell Priest]*

329. LAMMA FOREST 1982-1990 Steel motor bulk carrier. One deck and five holds.
O.N. 377268 18,604g, 11,256n, 29,566d. 160.00 (170.62 o.l.) x 27.21 x 14.10 metres. Cargo capacity: 39,508 cubic metres.
One 25-tonne and three 15-tonne cranes.
6-cyl. 2SCSA. Sulzer-type oil engine by Mitsubishi Heavy Industries Ltd. Hiroshima, Japan; 15 knots.
International code: GWIB (VRLT after 3.1982).

Lamma Forest on 25th November 1988. Owned by Blairdale Shipping Ltd. the bulker was under the technical management of Harrisons.

[World Ship Photo Library]

11.1.1977: Launched by Mitsubishi Heavy Industries Ltd. Hiroshima, Japan (Yard No. 274) for H. Clarkson and Co. Ltd., London (Denholm Ship Management Ltd., Glasgow, managers) as CLARKSPEY. *4.1977:* Delivered. *1978:* Renamed STAR BAY for the duration of a charter. *1981:* Renamed CLARKSPEY and registered at Hong Kong. *3.1982:* Sold to Blairdale Shipping, Ltd., London, a subsidiary of Denholms, for £5,734,341, renamed LAMMA FOREST and registered in Hong Kong. The ship continued to be managed by Denholm Ship Management (Overseas) Ltd. Technical management was the responsibility of Thos. and Jas. Harrison Ltd., who operated the ship commercially in the SCANSCOT consortium. *7.1985:* Arrested briefly at Providence, Rhode Island, due to alleged non-payment of a fuel bill following a dispute over the poor quality of fuel supplied at Tampa. *5.1986:* After discharging a cargo of

bagged rice at Dakar, arrested at the request of the cargo owners "against possible cargo claims". The ship had been about to sail, but the legal formalities took three days to unravel. This was apparently a quaint local custom where bagged cargoes were concerned - a draconian measure probably born out of bitter experience.[292] *6.3.1988:* Whilst on passage from Muscat to Richards Bay, Captain Frank Steele suddenly became very ill and died at sea, aged 60. *2.8.1990:* Whilst at Yokohama sold to the Peoples' Republic of China (Bureau of Maritime Transport Administration), renamed XUE FENG LING and allocated to the Guangzhou (Canton) Branch. *1993:* Owners became Guangzhou Maritime Transport (Group) Co., Guangzhou. *1997:* Owners became China Shipping International Intermodal Co. Ltd., Shanghai. *4.2003:* Still in existence.

330. LANTAU TRADER 1982-1995 Steel motor bulk carrier. One deck and six holds.
O.N. 384333 17,396g, 10,880n, 28,873d 170.0 (180.8 ol.) x 23.11 x 14.51 metres. Cargo capacity: 37,183 cubic metres. Five 15-tonne cranes.
International code: GWOX (VRCD after 3.1982).

15.7.1977: Launched by Hakodate Dock Co. Ltd., Hakodate, Japan (Yard No. 058) for Graig Shipping Co. Ltd. (Idwal Williams and Co. Ltd., managers), Cardiff as GRAIGLWYD. *9.1979:* Delivered. *3.1982:* Sold to Blairdale Shipping Ltd., London (Denholm Shipmanagement (Overseas) Ltd., Hong Kong, managers) for £5,681,788, registered in Hong Kong and renamed LANTAU TRADER. Technical management remained with Thos. and Jas. Harrison Ltd., who operated the ship in the Atlantic Bulkers Consortium. *12.1987:* During a ballast passage from Immingham to St. John, New Brunswick, very heavy weather was encountered. The

violent working of the ship caused fractures at the base of the bulkhead between the ballast hold and adjacent hold, and also in the tank top to number 4 double-bottom fuel tank, contaminating the diesel oil. Repairs were carried out at St. John in sub-zero temperatures and blizzards, with all the problems attendant upon such conditions.[293] *6.12.1995:* Sold to the Freshwater Bay Shipping Ltd., Cyprus (Oceanbulk Maritime SA (Petros Pappas), Athens, Greece, managers), and renamed STRANGE ATTRACTOR under the Cyprus flag. *9.2003:* Still in service.

Lantau Trader. *[Russell Priest]*

A diagnosis of appendicitis
When bound from Durban to Kinuura, Japan in July 1987 LANTAU TRADER was within a few days of her destination when Captain James Brierly began to suffer acute pain in his abdomen. The usual palliatives brought no relief, so he dipped apprehensively into the pages of "The Ship Captain's Medical Guide". There he found his own tentative diagnosis of appendicitis all too blatantly confirmed, complete with illustrations. Still another day to go to reach port! In great pain, Jim Brierly wondered if he could last that long. At Kinuura a Japanese doctor was already waiting to come on board. He found a very sick patient indeed, and was concerned that the abscess was due to burst at any moment, if it had not done so already. He lost no time in transporting the Captain to hospital, where surgeons at once performed an emergency operation. This prompt response

undoubtedly saved Jim Brierley's life, a fact he will never forget, despite the complications which set in, and which led to further operations. It took time, but eventually he recovered fully from his painful experience, to treasure fond memories of the care he received in that Japanese hospital. He wrote fervently to "...thank everyone in the Handa City Hospital for the wonderful treatment I received'...also Mr. Yamada (the agent), who could not have done more, and Mike Merrifield (Assistant Superintendent Engineer) who was in Japan on business; he cheered me up no end. Finally, to the little Japanese nurse who tucked me up each night and whispered, "Oyasumi Nasai"; and to the one who woke me up with "Ohayo Gozai Masu", I can only say, "Diolch yn Fawr lawn....."[294]

331. PISCES PIONEER 1984-1998 Steel motor bulk carrier. One deck and five holds.
O.N. 706815 21,309g, 13,027n, 35,310d 167.01 (177.5 ol.) x 29.51 x 14.81 metres. Cargo capacity: 47,019 cubic metres. Four 16-tonne cranes.
International code: ZEOD (MWQE-5 after 11.9.1996).
6-cyl. 2SCSA Sulzer-type oil engine by Sumitomo Heavy Industries Ltd., Tamashima, Japan; 15 knots.

1.7.1983: Launched by Nippon Kokan Kabushiki, Shimizu, Japan (Yard No. S406) for Crossfish Ltd., Hong Kong (Charente Steam-Ship Co. Ltd., Thos. and Jas. Harrison Ltd., Liverpool, managers) and registered in Hong Kong. *28.2.1984:* Completed at a cost of $14,407,356. Managed by the company in the bulk trades, manned by Denholm Ship Management (Overseas) Ltd. and registered in Hong Kong. Maiden voyage to Brisbane, Australia chartered by Sammi Lines to carry grain to Taiwan. *8.1986:* Whilst anchored off Ulsan, South Korea, waiting to enter dry dock, the approach of a typhoon forced the ship to put to sea to seek a safer quadrant of the storm, which passed directly over Ulsan, causing extensive damage to installations, including the dry dock. *9.1996:* Transferred to the Isle of Man register and registered at Douglas. *9.9.1998:* Sold to Financial Shipping Enterprise Ltd., Valletta, Malta (OTM Schiff Management A.G., Lugano, Switzerland, managers) and renamed S. PIONEER. *9.2003:* Still in service.

Pisces Pioneer, first of four bulkers delivered to Crossfish Ltd.

Crossfish

Unlike the Blairdale venture (LAMMA FOREST (329) and LANTAU TRADER (330) which had been purchased second-hand through an Atlantic Bulker/Denholm connection), PISCES PIONEER and PISCES PLANTER were to be the basis of a wholly Charente enterprise. For reasons of economy and fiscal discretion it was decided to register these new ships also in Hong Kong. To achieve this it would be necessary to establish a separate holding company in that city to which the ships could be assigned on the Hong Kong Register. Searches in Hong Kong for an off-the-shelf company produced a limited selection of titles on offer for the board to consider. Few were at all evocative of the nautical or shipping world, with the exception of one - Crossfish Ltd. - the word "fish" being associated with water and the sea, "Cross" with the cross-trading patterns of world-wide shipping lines, and so it was decided. Next came the question of funnel and flag insignia. The Chairman called for suggestions. It so happened that he was wearing that day a club tie of attractive design which featured a leaping dolphin as its primary motif. It was one which had been universally admired. "Of course!" exclaimed one of the younger directors. "Crossfish - a pair of dolphins back to back!" There was a murmur of approval. "They're not speaking - cross, you see," he added in an undertone. Finally, whilst there was an unanimous desire to preserve the traditional Harrison nomenclature of trades and professions, there was also a need to maintain, at least for the time being, some degree of anonymity. It was not considered prudent to advertise too early that these ships were, in fact, Harrison ships. Consequently, although the names PIONEER and PLANTER were promptly chosen, they were preceded by the generic word PISCES, the Latin plural of fish, a word of zodiacal significance (and coincidentally the Chairman's birth sign), to shield, if not conceal, the owners' true identity.

332. PISCES PLANTER 1984-1999 Steel motor bulk carrier. One deck and five holds.
O.N. 706816 21,309g, 13,027n, 35,310d 167.01 (177.5 ol.) x 29.51 x 14.81 metres. Cargo capacity: 47,019 cubic metres. Four 16-tonne cranes.
International code: ZEOE (MWQF-5 after 20.9.1996).
6-cyl. 2SCSA Sulzer-type oil engine by Sumitomo Heavy Industries Ltd., Tamashima, Japan; 15 knots.

17.10.1983: Launched by Nippon Kokan Kabushiki, Shimizu, Japan (Yard No. S407) for Crossfish Ltd., Hong Kong (Charente Steam-Ship Co. Ltd., Thos. and Jas. Harrison Ltd., Liverpool, managers) and registered in Hong Kong. *15.3.1984:* Completed at a cost of $14,977,488. Operated in the bulk trades by Thos. and Jas. Harrison Ltd., manned by Denholm Ship Management, Ltd. Maiden voyage to Brisbane, Australia, chartered by Sammi Lines to load sorghums for Kobe, Japan. *20.9.1996:* Registry transferred to Douglas, Isle of Man owned by Crossfish (U.K.) Ltd. *16.12.1999:* Sold to the Lentport Shipping Co. Ltd. (Maryville Maritime Inc., managers), Nicosia, Cyprus, renamed MAIROULI II and registered at Limassol. *3.2002:* Sold to Ythan Ltd. (Eastwind Shipmanagement Pte. Ltd., Singapore, managers) and renamed YTHAN under the Marshall Islands flag. *9.2003:* Still in service.

Pisces Planter. [*Russell Priest*]

333. PISCES EXPLORER 1994-2002 Steel motor bulk-carrier. One deck and five holds.
O.N. HK 0200; after 1996 727834 22,992g, 12,715n, 38,584d. 180.02 (189.97 ol) x 28.45 x 15.52 metres. Cargo capacity: 48,364 cubic metres grain, 46,426 cubic metres bale. Four 25-tonne deck cranes.
International Code: VRUP7. After 1996: MWQD-5.
6-cyl. 2SCSA Mitsui-B. & W. type 6L6OMCE oil engine by Mitsui Engineering and Shipbuilding Co. Ltd., Tamano, Japan; 9,200 BHP, 14 knots.

1985: Launched by Koyo Dockyard Co. Ltd., Mihara, Onomichi, Japan (Yard No. 1067) for Puma Shipping Corporation, Panama (Tokudo Shosen K.K., Tokyo, Japan) as YURI. *6.1985:* Owners became Prosperidad Shipping Inc. Manila, Philippines (J. R. Teihicson and Management Co. Ltd., Hong Kong), and renamed STAR ESPERANZA. *1987:* Transferred to Dakila Shipping Corporation, Manila (J. R. Teihicson and Management Co. Ltd., Hong Kong). *1989:* Renamed ESPERANZA. *1991:* Sold to Albar Shipping and

Trading Corporation, Makati, Philippines. *12.8.1994:* Acquired by Crossfish Ltd. (Denholm Ship Management (Overseas) Ltd.,) Hong Kong for approximately £9,000,000, renamed PISCES EXPLORER and registered in Hong Kong. Operated in bulk trades by Thos. and Jas. Harrison Ltd., Liverpool. *27.8.1996:* Transferred to the Isle of Man register. *27.2.2002:* Sold to San Moritz Maritime Ltd. S.A., Panama (Leros Brothers, Piraeus, Greece) and renamed CONQUEROR under the Maltese flag. *9.2003:* Still in service.

The Crossfish funnel colours are apparent in this photograph of *Pisces Explorer.*

355

334. PISCES TRADER 1996-2002 Steel motor bulk-carrier. One deck and five holds.
O.N. 727818 24,609g, 13,564n, 41,824d. 176.0 (183.78 ol) x 30.53 x 15.95 metres. Cargo capacity: 51,174 cubic metres grain, 48,615 cubic metres bale, 836 TEUs. Four 25-tonne deck-cranes.
International code: MWPM2.
5-cyl. 2SCSA Hyundai-B. & W. type 5L60 MC oil engine by Hyundai Heavy Industries Co. Ltd., Ulsan, South Korea; 9,800 BHP, 14 knots.

1986: Launched by Hyundai Heavy Industries Co. Ltd., Ulsan, South Korea (Yard No. 400) for the Unity Shipping Corporation (Efploia Shipping Co. S.A. (Pantelis C. Lemos), Piraeus, Greece as OINOUSSIAN UNITY. *9.1986:* Delivered. 1990: Sold to the Yasinovataya Shipping Co. Ltd., Limassol, Cyprus (Black Sea Shipping Co., Odessa, USSR) and renamed YASINOVATAYA. *1992:* Sold to Bareli Shipping, Inc. (Torvald Klaveness and Co., A/S, managers), Oslo, Norway and renamed BARELI. *23.5.1996:* Acquired by Crossfish (UK) Ltd., (Denholms Ship Management I.O.M., managers) for $15,000,000, renamed PISCES TRADER and registered at Douglas, I.O.M., being operated in bulk trades by Thos. and Jas. Harrison Ltd., under contract to Denholms. *6.3.2002:* Sold to European Integrity Maritime S.A., Panama (Stavros Roussos Management and Chartering S.A., Piraeus, Greece) and renamed WORLD TRADER 1. *9.2003:* Still in service.

Two views of *Pisces Trader.*   *[Upper: Russell Priest]*

Above: Mersey Chambers, Liverpool

In 1882 T. and J. Harrison Ltd. moved from 18 Chapel Street to Mersey Chambers, a new building otherwise known as 4/8 Old Churchyard. It underwent many refurbishments over the years, and during one upheaval in 1978/79 a small museum and archive was established on the top floor. The building escaped bombing during the Second World War, and was evacuated and sold in November 2002.

Right: Charente House, London

15 Devonshire Square, or Charente House as it was known during Harrison's occupation, was completed in 1898 to house a firm of solicitors. 'Building News' recorded that architect Howard Hatfield Clark had used red bricks and Monk's Park stone. Harrisons sold the building in July 2000 having occupied it for 22 years.

EPILOGUE - THE FINAL CHAPTER

On a bleak March day in the year 2001 I stood in a vast echoing room contemplating a sad expanse of litter, the desolate residue of a traumatic exodus. The room was in Mersey Chambers, headquarters of the erstwhile flourishing shipping company of Thos. and Jas. Harrison Ltd. It was not just any old room - it had been the nerve centre of a thriving business, the dynamic Outward Freight Department. This was the place where cargoes had been booked, classified, sorted by mark, ported out, and assigned to ships. It had once been a hive of industry housing a legion of bustling clerks, computer operators, visiting clients and canvassers; where shipping notes and bills of lading jostled with customs forms and manifests. This room on the ground floor stretched the whole width of the building, with managerial outposts on the outer walls, and despite several metamorphoses in recent years it had always hummed with life and expectancy. But now the desks were empty except for heaps of empty files and unwanted scraps of stationery, while the few remaining computer terminals stood lifeless, their screens blank. Doubtless their memories still lingered on hard drives, forgotten and unwanted. I stood there, appalled at the contrast between the situation as it then was, and the situation as it had been in former, happier times. But worse was to come.

In October of the previous year the last of the liner trades, managed by Thos. and Jas. Harrison Ltd. on behalf of the Charente Steamship Company, had been relinquished, and all rights and privileges transferred to P&O Nedlloyd. Outstanding commitments had been finally wound up, and the staff disbanded. Certainly, Charente still flourished as parent of the Charente Group of Companies, comprising shipping and forwarding enterprises, warehousing, trucking and logistics, marine instrumentation and chart distribution. Maritime expertise within the group still survived in the shape of two bulk carriers belonging to a subsidiary, Crossfish (UK) Ltd. But the Harrison Line, after 147 years of vibrant existence, was no more.

As noted earlier in this work, the year 1977 had seen a distinct change in the company's post-war fortunes. It is true that the number of ships, and hence the number of sea-going personnel, had been declining over the past two decades, but because replacement units were so much larger the gross tonnage of the fleet remained fairly consistent at around 300,000 tons. On the world scene, purpose-built cellular container-ships were rapidly rendering conventional cargo carriers obsolete, and in 1977 the Harrison Line joined the container revolution with the delivery from Gdansk, Poland, of two container ships capable of lifting 1,400 TEUs Inevitably, their arrival hastened the run-down of the company's conventional tonnage, and triggered a spate of redundancies.

However, confidence among surviving staff remained buoyant. After all, the company's fortunes had waxed and waned frequently during the past hundred years or so, and recovery had followed recession as sure as day follows night. The company's first bread-and-butter trade - the shipment of wines and brandy from the Charente region of France - had come to an end in 1935; the bold venture to North American Pacific Ports, inaugurated in 1911, had been discontinued in 1933; and the last sailing from Liverpool to ports in Brazil was made by the HISTORIAN on 12th January 1940, after 74 years. Similarly, the Second World War called a halt to the popular West Indian passenger service when the INANDA and INKOSI were both commandeered for naval service in the summer of 1940.

None of these trades were resumed after the war,

and in 1957 the latest important bastion fell when the TRIBESMAN sailed from Calcutta for the last time on 19th September, ending a 90-year old tradition. These were all disappointing setbacks, certainly, but there was still a resilience in the air that enabled redundant ships and men to be absorbed into expanding trades, creating an impression that the firm of T. and J. Harrison would always ride out commercial and economic storms, and survive.

Even the great economic depression of the early thirties, desperate though it seemed, was instinctively assumed to be a temporary recession that could only get better. And so it did. Men were laid-off, certainly, but most were kept on in jobs of lower grade, or in dock work, or in ship-keeping duties on board ships laid up in creeks and estuaries around the British coast. Consequently, when the global economic situation improved, the ships were brought out of mothballs, fully manned, ready and waiting to ply the trade routes of the world, and, a few years later, confront the grim challenges of the Second World War.

But during the nineteen eighties no such optimism prevailed. Few could see any sign of relief - those who thought they could saw only a mirage. Long-established shipping companies, with Harrisons in the van, fought an unequal struggle to survive against restrictive practices, flag discrimination, new national shipping lines financed through United Nations agencies, and tigerish, often unfair competition from Soviet Bloc and Far Eastern shipping lines.

The Conference System, which had sustained British Shipping since the beginning of the Twentieth Century, was discredited, its cosy practices overruled by court after court in favour of ships of the emerging nations. Crippling strikes by seamen and dock workers, doubtless worried to distraction by the loss of jobs in their industries, seriously undermined the financial structures of struggling companies, hastening their fall. The passenger trades became victims of cheap jet air travel, and thousands of ships' stewards became redundant. The delivery of each container ship ensured the swift disposal of at least six conventional cargo ships, along with their crews, whilst more and more raw materials were being shipped in bulk carriers in much bigger consignments. The rate of attrition was appalling, and many famous flags and funnels disappeared from the shipping scene as firms sold out to bigger conglomerates, or diversified into strange and novel shore-based industries.

Harrison Line was not immune from these destructive forces - how could it be? Gradually, that which men termed its niche operation in the various trades was overwhelmed. World tonnage of shipping was rising, despite the omens; yet cargoes were becoming more scarce, leading to an imbalance which inevitably depressed freight rates. Even a full ship could barely meet her expenses for the voyage, let alone pay a dividend to shareholders. Unsubsidised by government, taxed to the hilt, bled white by strikes and uneconomic freight rates, Harrison Line was forced to dispose of its ships. A system then evolved whereby space in foreign tonnage was chartered, or a certain number of boxes allocated, to accommodate the firm's tonnage share in the consortium, and thus cater for those valued clients who still insisted that Harrisons "care for their cargo". It was expensive, but doubtless more economical than building, manning, and running a ship.

But even this final desperate rearguard action was not enough to bring profitability back to the trades, and in July 1998 Harrisons sold their one-third share in the CITY

OF DURBAN to P&O Containers Ltd., thus bringing to an end their involvement in SAECS, and the South African trade generally after more than a hundred years. In October 1999 it was the turn of interests in the Red Sea and East African trades, which, after 90 years, were disposed of to P&O Nedlloyd. In that same year, the company extricated itself from the loss-making Mexican service. There now remained only the West Indies, Central America, and Spanish Main operation, as represented by its share in the New CAROL Service consortium (NCS). The decision to withdraw was made with extreme reluctance, but in October 2000 P&O Nedlloyd announced their acquisition of the remaining liner trading business interests of Thos. and Jas. Harrison Ltd. Thus the old firm lost its raison d'être and ceased to exist. All hopes now rested on the success of the cargo-forwarding, warehousing and transport enterprises in which depleted resources had been courageously invested by Charente in the acquisition of the transport firms of Henry Tyrer and Co. Ltd., Martin Bencher International, and Gardner Freight. These were combined with the cargo-forwarding businesses of Thomas Tweddle and Co. Ltd., and Prentice Service and Henderson, which had long been part of the Charente Group, the whole now being joined together, in January 2000, under the overall banner of Harrison Logistics.

The early weeks and months were characterised by a mood of optimistic enthusiasm. The network spread rapidly throughout the United Kingdom, Europe, and beyond, using air, rail, road, and sea transport; but the all-important profits, without which no enterprise can prosper, no matter how ambitious or inspired, failed to materialise. Sadly, this bold venture did not succeed in achieving its potential, nor in fulfilling the dreams of its creators, and in January 2002, Harrison Logistics went into voluntary liquidation. Inevitably, scores of jobs were lost; Mersey Chambers, which for more than 120 years had resounded to the clamour of shipping and commercial enterprise, its many departments jostling each other for space, was now but an empty shell, its voids replete with nought but memories.

When I began researching this work some twelve or more years ago, I hoped - and indeed, assumed - that it would close on an upbeat note, with expressions of confidence in the old firm's prosperity. Alas, for Harrison Line that is no longer a valid option, and the task is simply one of picking up the pieces. For the record, those precious pieces are now enshrined in that group of companies known as Charente Ltd, formerly the Charente Steamship Company Ltd., which continues to flourish in diverse fields of a commercial and nautical stamp, carving a secure niche in a highly competitive world. Thus, in bringing my labours to a close, I choose to reflect with warmth on those halcyon post-war decades during which I was privileged to serve the Company at the peak of its activity, and to pray that its surviving entity, Charente Ltd., may secure a meaningful and prosperous future.

Graeme Cubbin
Greasby, Wirral
September 2003

Inanda of 1925 (210), surrounded by lighters and Thames barges. *[Laurence Dunn]*

FLAGS AND FUNNELS

Illustrated are flags, funnels and insignia used by Harrisons, their predecessors, subsidiaries and partnerships (date of introduction in brackets); and by the major companies from whom they acquired ships (date of acquisition in brackets).

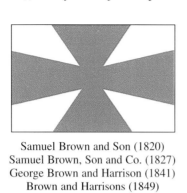

Samuel Brown and Son (1820)
Samuel Brown, Son and Co. (1827)
George Brown and Harrison (1841)
Brown and Harrisons (1849)
Harrison Logistics (1999)

Thos. and Jas. Harrison (c. 1866)
Charente Steam-Ship Co. Ltd. (1884)

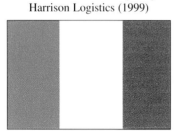

Richard Williamson and Son
(1813)

 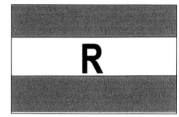

Star Navigation Co. Ltd.
Rathbone Brothers
(Four ships acquired, 1889)

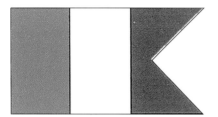

Richard Williamson and Son
(1813)

 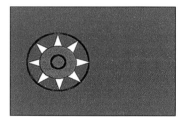

Aberdeen Direct Line
John T. Rennie and Sons
(Seven ships acquired, 1911)

Thos. and Jas. Harrison (1853)

Saint Line
Rankin, Gilmour Ltd.
(Twelve ships acquired, 1918)

 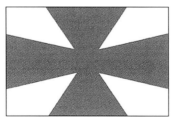

Thos. and Jas. Harrison (1860) -
early steamers

 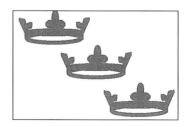

Crown Line
Prentice, Service and Henderson Ltd.
(Eight ships acquired, 1920)

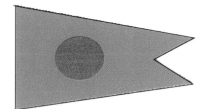

Scruttons, Sons and Co. Ltd.
(Five ships acquired, 1920)

Associated Container Transportation (ACT)
The white and blue were interchangeable

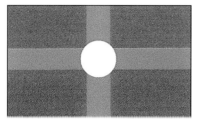

Frederick Leyland and Co. Ltd.
(Seven ships acquired, 1934)

Ellerman Harrison Container Line (EHCL)
The white and blue were interchangeable

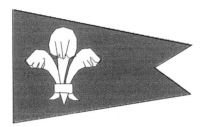

Prince Line
Furness, Withy Ltd.
(Four ships acquired, 1935)

Blairdale Shipping
Co. Ltd.

Black-hulled vessels

Green-hulled vessels

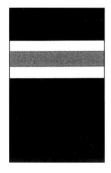

Ruthin Steamship Co. Ltd. (1958)
Thos. and Jas. Harrison Ltd.

Crossfish Shipping (Hong Kong) Ltd.
(1984)
Crossfish (UK) Ltd. (1996)

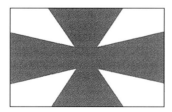

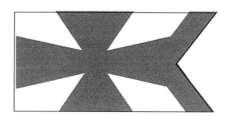

Senior Master (Commodore's) flag. The style varied according to the individual's taste.

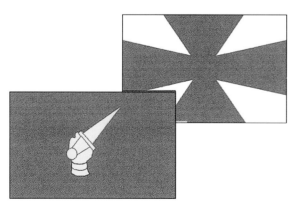

Bibby Harrison Management Services Ltd. (BHNS) (1997)

The classic Harrison Line funnel

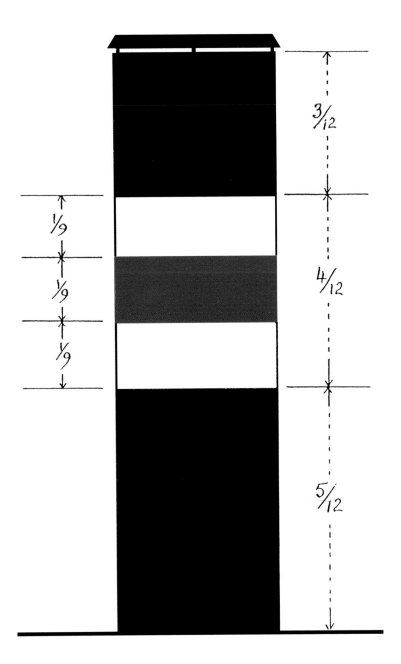

NOTES ON THE TEXT

1. Neal, Frank *An Analysis of Shipping Registers*, unpublished, c. 1966.
2. Ibid.
3. Ibid.
4. Williamson; Jean-Marie *An Introduction to the Memoirs of his Great-great-grandfather, Richard-Pierre Williamson*. Published privately in French and English at Nantes, May 1991.
5. Ibid.
6. Ibid.
7. Williamson, Richard-Pierre *Names of Ships I Have Commanded and Ports that I Have Been at, 1834-1858*. Subsequently referred to as R-PW's notes.
8. R-PW's notes
9. Liverpool Customs Registers, 227/1836; 108/1834.
10. R-PW's notes
11. From an article in *Shipbuilding and Shipping Record,* Volume LXVII, No. 12, 21st March 1946. Richard Harrison died in 1862.
12. Ibid.
13. Harrison, Edward Hodgson Unpublished personal notebook.
14. Orchard, B. Guinness *Liverpool's Legion of Honour,* 1893.
15. Ibid.
16. R-PW's notes
17. Ibid.
18. Stapleton, M. *Cambridge Guide to English Literature*, Cambridge University Press, 1983.
19. Bulfinch, Thomas *Myths of Greece and Rome*, Allen Lane, 1979.
20. Deduced from the calculations on page 28 of Edward Hodgson Harrison's contemporary notebook:
    1855 8/64 "Ad. Grenfell" Cost £500.00.00
    Returns:
1856	£8. 7. 6.
1857 -	
1858	£366. 8. 2.
	£374.15. 8.
Balance Loss Without Int.	£125. 4. 4.
	£500. 0. 0.
    However, this conclusion is flatly contradicted by Hyde, Francis E. in *Liverpool and the Mersey* (David and Charles, Newton Abbot, 1971), who on page 52 asserts that "the voyage of the Harrison ship ADMIRAL GRENFELL to the China Coast ... made a net profit to her Owners on this voyage alone of £20,000."
21. *The Marine Observer*, April 1974.
22. Voyage Books, Harrison Line Archives.
23. Haws, Duncan *Merchant Fleets, Volume 15 - Thos. and Jas. Harrison;* T.C.L. Publications, Hereford, 1988.
24. From a description in *Shipping Wonders of the World*, edited by Clarence Winchester (Fleetway House, 1937).
25. Letter dated March 1960 and signed "Thos. and Jas. Harrison". Harrison Line Archives.
26. From the Dudley Collection, Dudley to Seward No. 9, The Huntington Library, San Marino, California.
27. Voyage Book BC3. Harrison Line Archives.
28. Typescripts of press reports. Harrison Line Archives.
29. Hyde, Francis E. *Shipping Enterprise and Management; Harrisons of Liverpool, 1830-1939*, Liverpool University Press, 1967, page 18.
30. Williamson; Jean-Marie. *An Introduction to the Memoirs of his Great-great-grandfather, Richard-Pierre Williamson*. Published privately in French and English at Nantes, May 1991, and family papers.
31. Ibid.
32. *American Civil War Blockade Runners*, a loose-leaf notebook attributed to Wardle, A.C. in the Liverpool Nautical Research Society archives.
33. United States Navy *Civil War Naval Chronology 1861-1865,* Washington, USA, 1971.
34. Ibid. Part VI, page 315.
35. Ibid. Part VI, page 208.
36. Nepveux, Ethel S. *George Alfred Trenholm and the Company that Went to War, 1861-1865,* Published privately, Charleston, South Carolina, 1973. Mrs. Nepveux is a descendant of G. A. Trenholm.
37. *American Civil War Blockade Runners*, a loose-leaf notebook attributed to Wardle, A.C. in the Liverpool Nautical Research Society archives.
38. Harrison Line Archives.
39. Ibid.
40. Ibid.
41. Ibid. From a press report pasted in Voyage Report BC6, Harrison Line Archives
42. Ibid. Typescript of press report.
43. Bulfinch, Thomas *Myths of Greece and Rome*, Allen Lane, 1979.
44. This seems an incredible feat. The distance from Cuxhaven to Liverpool is over 900 miles (north about) and one suspects an error in the recorded dates.
45. From a letter to Alfred Le Blanc from Frederick J. Harrison, 26th October 1886.
46. From correspondence in Harrison Line Archives.
47. Attributed to R.J. Burnett of Agencias Mundais Ltda., Belem, in a letter to D.A. Peate of Booth Line, Liverpool.
48. Typescript of press report. Harrison Line Archives.
49. From the *Liverpool Courier*, August 1866; quoted by Ritchie-Noakes, Nancy *Liverpool's Historic Waterfront*, H.M.S.O., 1984.
50. 7 Geo.2, c.15.
51. Articles of Association of The Charente Steam-Ship Co. Ltd., 1884. Harrison Line Archives.
52. Letter to J. W. Hughes from James Harrison, 12th November 1887. Harrison Line Archives.
53. Lewis, F.M. and Gnosspelius, J. *An Outline History of the Grange Hotel, Holmefield Road, Aigburth*, The Gateacre Society, Liverpool, 1989.
54. From an obituary notice in the *Times*, 1934, reprinted in the *Malvernian.*
55. Correspondence: F. J. Harrison, Lucas E. Moore, Alfred Le Blanc. Harrison Line Archives.
56. Harrison-Rathbone correspondence. Harrison Line Archives.
57. Hyde, Francis E. *Shipping Enterprise and Management; Harrisons of Liverpool, 1830-1939*, Liverpool University Press, Liverpool, 1967, page 84.
58. *Harrison Line Newsletter* No. 48, page 5.
59. Hyde, op cit, page 127.
60. Hyde, op cit, page 106.
61. The inquiry was held in Dale Street Police Court, Liverpool on 9th April 1897, the Deputy Stipendiary Magistrate, Mr. Kinghorn, presiding. He was assisted by two nautical assessors, Captains Anderson and Brooks.
62. Based on reports in the *Times* 23rd, 24th March and 10th April 1897.
63. From a Superintendent Engineer's notebook, Harrison Line Archives.
64. Based on a report of the inquiry in the *Times,* 4th May 1898.
65. *Lloyd's Register Wreck Returns,* 1922.
66. Harrison/Rathbone correspondence. Harrison Line Archives.
67. Based on a report in the New Orleans *Times Democrat,* 21st November 1892; and on the late John Corbishley's private papers.
68. *Lloyd's Register Wreck Returns,* 1922.
69. Lecky, S.T.S. *Wrinkles in Practical Navigation* 15th Edition, George Philip, 1910, page 35.
70. Foreign Documents Section of the Ministry of Defence, London. Details provided by R.M. Coppock.
71. Ibid.
72. Movement Book (MB) No. 3. Harrison Line Archives.
73. Ibid. MB 9.
74. Coppock, op. cit.
75. Haws, Duncan *Merchant Fleets, Volume 15 - Thos. and Jas. Harrison;* T.C.L. Publications, Hereford, 1988, page 59.
76. Based mainly on a court report in the *Times,* 19th March 1904, with additional material from the Harrison Line Archives.
77. Coppock, op. cit., and Hurd, Archibald *The Merchant Navy*, Vol. II John Murray, 1924.
78. Coppock, op. cit.
79. Account based on a report by Robert W. Wilkins, OBE, who was Fourth Engineer on board COMEDIAN in 1915. His story, written in 1959 from contemporary notes, is now in the Harrison Line Archives. Background material from official histories of the Gallipoli campaign.
80. From an account by Captain F. R. Hill. Harrison Line Archives.
81. From the recollections of F.T. Rochell, Assistant Superintendent Engineer, with additional material supplied by Captain R.F. Longster.
82. *Lloyd's List Law Reports*, Volume 12, page 129
83. From an account by Captain J. J. Devereux. Harrison Line Archives.
84. H.M.S.O. *British Vessels Lost at Sea, 1914-1918*. Reprinted by Patrick Stephens, Cambridge, 1977.
85. *Liverpool Daily Post*, 22nd February 1908.
86. Casualties as noted in the diary of Commander Michael Barne R.N. of HMS MAJESTIC.
87. Coppock, op. cit.
88. Hurd, Archibald *The Merchant Navy*, John Murray, 1924.
89. Coppock, op. cit.
90. *Lloyd's Register Wreck Returns*, 1927, 1928.
91. Noted by Captain H.G. Skelly. Harrison Line Archives.
92. Hurd, Archibald *The Merchant Navy*, John Murray, 1924.
93. Details attributed to Joseph Anderson.
94. Coppock, op. cit. and H.M.S.O. *British Vessels Lost at Sea, 1914-1918*. Reprinted by Patrick Stephens, Cambridge, 1977.
95. Haws op. cit.
96. Murray, Marischal *Ships and South Africa*, Oxford University Press, 1933
97. *Lloyd's List Law Reports*, 1920, volume 4.
98. Chatterton, E. Keble *Q-Ships and their Story*, Sidgwick and Jackson, 1923; and Richie, Carson I.A. *Q-Ships*, Terence Dalton, 1985.
99. *International Code of Signals.* The Revised (1931) International Code came into force during 1933. One of its objectives was to harmonise ship call signs by nationality: for instance, G or M to be the initial letter of a four-flag hoist for British ships; J for Japanese; D for German. To avoid confusion during the transition period it was ordained that when using the new, Revised Code, a "weft" or waft" was to be hoisted, i.e. the answering pennant with its tail tied to the halyard. From *Shipping Wonders of the World*, Winchester, Clarence ed., Fleetway House, 1937, page 798.
100. From the official German history of cruiser operations in MOD Archives. (Coppock, op. cit.)
101. Based on the diary of the Captain R.F. Phillips, Third Officer of INGOMA in 1916. Harrison Line Archives.
102. *Harrison Line Newsletter* No. 7, February 1975.
103. From the recollections of the Captain L.F. Harriman, Third Officer of DISCOVERER in 1917. Harrison Line Archives.
104. Braine, Eric Carter *Recollections*. Typescript in Harrison Line Archives.
105. Ibid.
106. Lloyd, Trevor "The Post War Slump", in *Purnell's History of the 20th Century*, B.P.C. Publishing Ltd., 1968, chapter 34.

107. Ibid.
108. Roberts. J.M. "Shock Waves of the Crash" in *Purnell's History of the 20th Century,* B.P.C. Publishing Ltd., 1968, chapter 45
109. Carter Braine, E. op. cit.
110. Hyde, Francis E. *Shipping Enterprise and Management, 1830-1939: Harrisons of Liverpool,* Liverpool University Press, Liverpool, 1967, chapter 7.
111. Braine, Carter E. op. cit.
112. Ibid.
113. Beazley, J. *A Personal Diary of Events During the Last Voyage of the HUNTSMAN.* Typescript in Harrison Line Archives.
114. Braine, Eric Carter, op. cit.
115. H.M.S.O. *British Vessels Lost at Sea, 1939-45,* Reprinted by Patrick Stephens Ltd., Cambridge, 2nd Edition 1983.
116. Joseph Anderson, Engineer, DEFENDER. Harrison Line Archives.
117. From correspondence and reports by Captain W.A. Short, kindly loaned by his son, Michael Charles.
118. Infield, Glen B. *Disaster at Bari,* Robert Hale, London, 1974.
119. Foreign Documents Section of the M.o.D. London. Details provided from German sources by R.M. Coppock.
120. Ibid.
121. Captain H.G. Skelly, Harrison Line Archives.
122. Munro, D.J. *Convoys, Blockades, and Mystery Towers;* Sampson Low, Marston.
123. Robert W.M. Wilkins O.B.E., Chief Engineer. Harrison Line Archives.
124. *Lloyd's List Law Reports,* 1921, Volume 9, page 355
125. Report of Captain W. B. Wilford, Harrison Line Archives. Also Maher T. in *Sea Breezes,* Volume XXII, page 34.
126. *Lloyd's Lists Law Report* 1940, Volume 68, page 21. Mr. Justice Langton apportioned four-fifths of the blame to MANCHESTER REGIMENT, one-fifth to OROPESA.
127. *Lloyd's List Law Reports,* 1924, Volume 20, page 78.
128. Rowe; Roy H. "Slow Boat to Europe", *Harrison Line Newsletter* No. 33, December 1981.
129. Report by Captain A. P. Brown. Harrison Line Archives
130. Based on the story confided by Captain E. Whitehouse to Captain W.G. Ellis, who recounted it to the author.
131. Account based on reports submitted by Donald Percy and G. V. Monk, officers in the AUDITOR. Harrison Line Archive. Also Chief Officer H.T. Wells' official report, P.R.O. ref. ADM 199/2137, page 283.
132. From technical reports and engineers' diaries. Harrison Line Archives.
133. Captain A. P. Brown. Harrison Line Archives.
134. Skelly H.G., "Looking Back, etc.", *Harrison Line Newsletter,* No. 40, September 1983.
135. The story of the GIRL PAT has been based on an account written by. W. Williams, who was Second Engineer of the INANDA in 1936. It has been supplemented by material in *Lloyd's List.*
136. This account has been compiled from Arthur Apps' official report to the Admiralty (Trade Division), P.R.O., ref: ADM 199/2137, page 128, and an article by T. Allen, published in 1984 in the Marine Society's *Sea Pie,* and reproduced with the permission in *Harrison Line Newsletter* No. 47, June 1985.
137. *The Africa Pilot,* Vol. III, and Admiralty Charts Nos. 2110 and 2938 were consulted in compiling this analysis.
138. *Lloyd's List Law Reports,* 1930, Volume 36.
139. This account has been compiled using material from Captain J.J. Devereux's official report to the Admiralty (Trade Division), P.R.O., ref: ADM 199/2137, page 128, and information in Slader, John *The Red Duster at War,* William Kimber, 1988, page 137.
140. This account based on the author's own experiences, supplemented by material from Infield, Glen B. *Disaster at Bari;* Robert Hale, 1974. and Sieff, Marcus *Don't Ask the Price,* Weidenfeld and Nicholson, 1986.
141. Infield, Glen B. op cit.
142. Sieff, Marcus op cit.
143. The "certain witness" referred to is the author, who was serving as Third (Acting Second) Officer of the DIRECTOR at the time.
144. This account is based on Captain Weatherall's report to the Admiralty (Trade Division), P.R.O. ref: ADM 199/2147, page 191, dated 21st September 1944.
145. This account is based on a memorandum written by the ship's Chief Officer, Captain Bill Moore, and now held in the Harrison Line archives.
146. From an article in *Illustrated,* 7th December 1940. Harrison Line Archives.
147. The facts relating to the sinking of the JUMNA are taken from the war-diary of the ADMIRAL HIPPER, through the courtesy of R.M. Coppock of the Foreign Documents section of the Ministry of Defence, London, and G.A. Cooke, of St. Anselm's College, Birkenhead, who translated the original German
148. This account is based on Carpenter S. G. Lewis's official report to the Admiralty (Trade Division), P.R.O. ref: ADM 199/2143, page 257, dated 23rd February 1943.
149. This account is based mainly on a report to the company from Chief Officer William Rennie, dated Alexandria, 2nd June 1941.
150. From a letter dated 20th October 1988 to the author from W. Dignan, who was serving as a cadet in the LOGICIAN in 1941.
151. Coppock op. cit.
152. From the personal notes and correspondence of Captain W.F. O'Neill. Harrison Line Archives.
153. Based on an account written by Captain A.P. Brown. Harrison Line Archives.
154. Macdougall, Philip *Mysteries on the High Seas,* David and Charles, Newton Abbot, 1984, chapter 10, and *Lloyd's List Casualty Reports.*
155. From an account related by Captain R. Myles, who was Third Officer of the CONTRACTOR at the time. Harrison Line Archives.
156. This account is based on Second Officer Alan Moreton's report to the Admiralty (Trade Division), P.R.O., ref: ADM 199/2145, page 306, dated 21st September 1943. Additional material from David Bloom.
157. From Slader, John *The Red Duster at War,* William Kimber, 1988, page 153; also an article by McNeill, D. in *Merseymart,* 2nd June 1988.
158. This account is based on reports to the company from Captain A.E.T. Pearce and Second Officer G.F. Jolly. Harrison Line Archives.
159. Woodward, David *The Secret Raiders,* William Kimber, 1955, chapter 3.
160. The story of the LEIF appeared in a national newspaper in 1940. The cutting is not dated, but was probably from the *Times.*
161. Slader, op cit.
162. Based on Captain C.A.V. Daly's account of the action. Harrison Line Archives.
163. This account is based mainly on Captain Horne's report. Harrison Line Archives.
164. This is the position recorded in the war diary of Kapitan Detmers of the KORMORAN.
165. This saga was related to the author by Captain W. G. Ellis, and appeared in *Harrison Line Newsletter* No. 55, December 1987.
166. The Harrison ships referred to were as follows:
SCIENTIST sunk by ATLANTIS 3rd May 1940.
DAVISIAN sunk by WIDDER 10th July 1940.
TRIBESMAN sunk by ADMIRAL SCHEER 1st December 1940.
CRAFTSMAN sunk by KORMORAN 9th April 1941.
DALESMAN sunk at Crete 15th May 1941.
LOGICIAN sunk at Crete 25th May 1941.
167. H.M.S.O. *British Vessels Lost at Sea 1939-45,* op cit.
168. The account of the loss of the STATESMAN and subsequent rescue of survivors has been compiled from reports submitted to the Admiralty by Captain J. McCallum and Lieutenant C.W. Copelin of HMCS HEPATICA. These reports are held at the Public Records Office, Kew under references ADM 199/2137, page 76, and ADM 199/1179, pages 170/172, respectively. The author is grateful to G.V. Monk for bringing them to his attention.
169. The *Mail on Sunday* 9/16th August 1987.
170. Times, etc, have been taken from the POLITICIAN's deck log. This is the edited version of the log, which in wartime contained no references to positions, courses, or landmarks sighted. These would be confined to the secret log, which is no longer extant, and may even have been kept on a slate and subsequently erased. Harrison Line Archives.
171. MacInnes, Duncan in *Scots Magazine,* September 1983, and also from log book entries.
172. Details of surveys and salvage operations were found in the Salvage Association's *Statement of Facts,* and summarized reports.
173. Extract from survey report, Glasgow, 12th January 1942.
174. Ibid.
175. Mackenzie, Compton *Whisky Galore,* 1947.
176. Swinson, Arthur *Scotch on the Rocks,* Peter Davies, London, 1963.
177. *The Mail on Sunday,* op cit.
178. Extract from H. M. Customs & Excise *Manifest and Out-turn of Cargo.* Harrison Line Archives.
179. McIlvean, B.D. *Harrison Line Newsletter* No. 56, March 1988.
180. Details of this incident are taken from the description in *Lloyd's List Law Reports,* 1938, volume 62, page 101.
181. Ibid.
182. *Lloyd's List Law Reports,* 1943, volume 75.
183. *Lloyd's List Law Reports,* 1955, volume 1, page 279.
184. Based on an account written by Captain F.R. Hill. Harrison Line Archives
185. Murray, William *Atlantic Rendezvous,* Nautical Publishing Co., Lymington, 1970, chapter 6.
186. The single exception was William Murray, Third Radio Officer of the TRIBESMAN, who escaped. He tells his story in his book *Atlantic Rendezvous* (op. cit.), from which this account of the loss of the TRIBESMAN has been adapted.
187. Adapted from Cubbin, J.W. "Return to Gibraltar - A True Story", *Harrison Line Newsletter* No. 16, June 1977.
188. The "witness" referred to was the author who at 16 was making his first voyage to sea as a Cadet in the SCIENTIST.
189. Many years passed before the writer learned what had happened to the TIRRANNA. This version is based on accounts appearing in Rogge, Bernhard *Under Ten Flags,* Weidenfeld and Nicholson, 1957 and Mohr, Ulrich, and Sellwood, A.V. *ATLANTIS: The Story of a Germany Surface Raider,* Werner Laurie, 1955.
190. A seaman detached from his ship abroad through sickness or shipwreck was designated, under the Merchant Shipping Acts, a Distressed British Seaman until his repatriation could be accomplished.
191. Ashdown, E.D. "A Forgotten Campaign", *Harrison Line Newsletter* No. 22, December 1978.
192. This account is based on an article which first appeared in *Writtle News* February 1986 (Writtle, in Essex, being Captain Ling's birthplace). It was reproduced by kind permission in *Harrison Line Newsletter* No. 51, August 1986.
193. From a transcript of the Court of Inquiry proceedings convened under the Fatal Accidents Inquiry (Scotland) Acts, 1895, 1906, on 14th May 1959.
194. The "certain witness" referred to was the author who was serving in BARRISTER as a cadet at that time. Further material was provided by

Captain H. G. Skelly, BARRISTER's Second Officer. The substance of the narrative appeared in an article by the author in *Harrison Line Newsletter* No. 42, March 1984.

195. HMS LANDGUARD was a converted yacht requisitioned by the Admiralty for escort duty. The owner was said to be a certain Mr. Wrigley, well-known purveyor of chewing gum. In 1943 the First Lieutenant was Lt. Curphey R.N.R., the son of Captain C. B. Curphey who had died in Beira just before the outbreak of war, while in command of the STRATEGIST.

196. George Dean; Manager of Harrisons' Stores Department, and self-appointed monitor of officers' salaries and expenses.

197. Based on Captain W.A. Short's report to the company's legal representative, dated New York, 26th January 1944. Harrison Line Archives.

198. Cadet Dobson's experiences are recorded in papers and correspondence in Harrison Line Archives.

199. A copy of Captain Freemantle's report and papers relating to Russell's award are kept in Harrison Line Archives.

200. This account is based on the recollections of Captain W. L. Ashton, Third Officer of the DALESMAN as set out in the transcript of a recorded interview with Tony Lane of Liverpool University.

201. This account is based on the recollections of R. Murray, Messroom Steward of the DALESMAN as set out in the transcript of a recorded interview with Tony Lane of Liverpool University.

202. Several files of documents, copies of letters, etc., from Milag und Marlag Nord are held in the Herbert Jones collection, Harrison Line Archives.

203. From the recollections of the late Captain W. Moore. Harrison Line Archives.

204. Ibid.

205. Quoted from Captain Worthington's report to the Admiralty, (Trade Division), P.R.O. Ref: ADM 199/2137, page 59.

206. This account is based on the statements of material witnesses and the findings of a Formal Investigation, as recorded in *Report of the Court No. 7992*, published by H.M.S.O., in July 1956.

207. That "certain witness" was again the author, who was Chief Officer of the NATURALIST at the time.

208. Of the major participating countries, Great Britain received $3,176 million in Marshall Aid; France $2,706m; Italy $1,474m; West Germany $1,389m; and Holland $1,079m.

209. *Daily Mail*, 28th September 1944.

210. Brocklebank Mss. Correspondence of Sir Denis Bates, 1947-60. Merseyside Maritime Museum.

211. Minutes of the Docks and Quays Committee, Mersey Docks and Harbour Board Mss. Merseyside Maritime Museum Record Centre.

212. *Journal of Commerce*, 3rd December 1963.

213. The facts relating to P. S. and H. are taken from an article in *Harrison Line Newsletter*, No. 38, March 1983.

214. From an article attributed to Seaford, M.A. in *Harrison Line Newsletter* No. 55, December 1987.

215. Mitchell, T.A. *Harrison Line Newsletter* No. 35, May 1982, page 19.

216. From the Voyage Books in Harrison Line Archives.

217. EC2-S-C1 Liberty type. The type reference signifies: E = emergency war programme; C = cargo ship; 2 = length 400-500 feet; S = steam propulsion; C1 = the design, of which there were three

218. From the report compiled by Assistant Marine Superintendent Jack Bean. Harrison Line Archives, ref. J1/6.

219. From a story related by Captain R. Myles, Harrison Line Archives.

220. *Lloyd's List Law Reports*, 1957, Volume 1, page 261.

221. This account of the CRAFTSMAN/SAMPENN collision is based on contemporary documents, and the recollections of the author who was Second Officer of the CRAFTSMAN at the time.

222. Report in Harrison Line Archives

223. From official reports and witnesses' statements, Harrison Line Archives.

224. Ibid.

225. From official reports, cables, and log extracts, Harrison Line Archives.

226. Based on *Lloyd's Weekly Casualty Reports* and the recollections of the author, who was Second Officer of the SUCCESSOR at the time.

227. From company records and reports. Harrison Line Archives, ref. H2/1.

228. Ibid. Ref. J1/8.

229. Ibid..

230. This account of the incident is based on company reports, *Lloyd's Weekly Casualty Reports*, and the author's own notes as Master of the GOVERNOR at the time. Harrison Line Archives, ref. Q2/4.

231. For a detailed analysis of the case, see *Lloyd's List Law Reports*, 1959, Volume 2, page 179.

232. This account of JOURNALIST's salvage work is based on Captain Wolstenholme's report, and interviews with some of the participants, supplemented by information from Lloyd's publications. Harrison Line Archives, ref. P1/1.

233. This account is based on official reports in Harrison Line Archives, supplemented by information from Lloyd's publications. Harrison Line Archives, ref. N2/1.

234. Account based on official reports, witnesses's statements, and local newspaper reports. Harrison Line Archives.

235. Details from Mountfield, Stuart *Western Gateway*, Liverpool University Press, Liverpool, 1965.

236. From official reports, and the recollections of the author who was Chief Officer of the AUTHOR at the time.

237. Ibid.

238. Based on Captain Sutcliffe's Statement of Facts to the Authorities. Harrison Line Archives, ref. H2/6.

239. Based on official reports and statements of witnesses. Harrison Line Archives.

240. Based on Captain Sharman's report and other documents. Harrison Line Archives, ref. M1/3.

241. Based on official reports, and the minutes of an in-house inquiry dated 21st July 1967. Harrison Line Archives, ref. N1/6.

242. Based on Captain Eustance's letters and reports, and an article by him in *Harrison Line Newsletter* No. 20, May 1978, page 6, with additional material provided by S.T. Pim and W. Ledgard. Harrison Line Archives, ref. J1.

243. From correspondence and cables relevant to the incident now in Harrison Line Archives.

244. From reports and log entries covering the incident (Harrison Line Archives, ref. M2/1) with additional material supplied by John Beaton

245. From the author's official reports, and his recollections as Master of the TACTICIAN at the time.

246. From Captain Roberts' report and statements made by the culprits. Harrison Line Archives, ref. Fg. 1/19.

247. From reports and extracts of log. Harrison Line Archives.

248. From Captain Boam's reports and cables. Harrison Line Archives, ref. 01/3.

249. Extracted from Rosselli, P.H. "The Birthpangs of mv INVENTOR", *Harrison Line Newsletter* No. 49, December 1985.

250. From the Master's report. Harrison Line Archives, Ref. H2/4.

251. Based on reports in *Lloyd's Weekly Casualty Reports,* and Harrison Line Archives, ref. P1/2.

252. From the Master's report, cargo plans, etc. Harrison Line Archives

253. From the reports in *Lloyd's List*, 9th December 1983.

254. From the Master's report. Harrison Line Archives.

255. From the Mersey Docks and Harbour Board transcript of a recording of the VHF conversation between LINGUIST and Port Radar.

256. Based on the Master's report and the findings of the Marine Superintendent's enquiry.

257. This account is based on reports and statements made by master and officers of the CRAFTSMAN. Harrison Line Archives.

258. *Lloyd's Weekly Casualty Returns*, Volume 231, No. 11, page 299.

259. This account is adapted from Captain S. Marlowe's narrative in *Harrison Line Newsletter* No. 29, page 12; and Harrison Line Archives ref. E1/27.

260. This account is based on reports and statements by the master and officers of the WAYFARER and others. Harrison Line Archives.

261. This account is based on reports and statements by the Master, Officers, and crew of the WANDERER. Harrison Line Archives.

262. Ibid.

263. From reports and correspondence in Harrison Line Archives.

264. From Captain Traynor's report, statements of witnesses, and consultants' analyses, Harrison Line Archives.

265. From Captain Bell's account of the incident, as described in *Harrison Line Newsletter* No. 37, page 16.

266. Based on the reports of salvors and others, and an account of the arbitration proceedings, now in Harrison Line Archives.

267. The Assistant Marine Superintendent referred to is the author.

268. Refer to Appendix 2 for the state of the fleet at the end of each year, 1884-2002.

269. Rosselli, P.H. *Harrison Sealife Project,* November 1977, page 3.

270. Ibid; page 6.

271. Charente Steamship Co. Ltd., Chairman's Report to Shareholders and Employees, 1979; page 6. Harrison Line Archives.

272. Ibid, 1981; page 6.

273. Ibid, 1985; page 7.

274. The facts relating to the seamen's strike of 1981 have been extracted mainly from the Charente Steamship Co. Ltd. Chairman's Report, 1980, dated March 1981.

275. General Council of British Shipping *A Level Playing Field for Merchant Shipping* 1989.

276. Warwick, E.S.R. *Harrison Line Newsletter,* No. 28, page 9.

277. Hickling, J.M. *Harrison Line Newsletter,* No. 31, page 11.

278. Dickens, T.H. *Harrison Line Newsletter,* No. 36, page 9.

279. Dawson, J.B. *Harrison Line Newsletter,* Nos. 35-37.

280. *Lloyd's List,* 14th December 1988.

281. A brief account of these ventures is included in Part 5.

282. From a pamphlet issued by the Ministry of Transport in May 1989, and reprinted in *Harrison Line Newsletter,* No. 60, page 13.

283. Charente Steam-Ship Co. Ltd., Chairman's Report, 1989

284. General Council of British Shipping *The Way Ahead,* December 1989.

285. Eddy, P. and Linklater, M. *The Falklands War;* William Collins, Glasgow, and Times Newspapers, London, 1982.

286. From "Harrison Line and The Falklands", a supplement to *Harrison Line Newsletter* No. 37, and featuring Captain Bladon's report on his voyage in the ASTRONOMER.

287. Admiral Sir John Fieldhouse (C-in-C, Operational Headquarters, Northwood), quoted in the Supplement to *Harrison Line Newsletter,* No. 37.

288. Quoted in *Harrison Line Newsletter,* No. 57, page 5.

289. Details from telex messages, and an article by Captain R.J. Smith in *Harrison Line Newsletter,* No. 62, page 7.

290. Dawson, J.B. *Harrison Line Newsletter,* No. 47, page 13.

291. Ibid. No. 51, page 15.

292. Arkell, J.D. *Harrison Line Newsletter,* No. 51, page 13.

293. Arkell, J.D. *Harrison Line Newsletter,* No. 56, page 12.

294. Captain James Brierley, in *Harrison Line Newsletter,* No. 58, page 4. The Japanese and Welsh quotations simply mean, "Goodnight"; "Good morning"; and "Thank you very much indeed!" respectively.

HARRISON SHIPS
An alphabetical list of owned and managed vessels

Notes and abbreviations

A number appearing after the name of a ship indicates the number of times that name has been used.

Rig, or means of propulsion:

Bg = brig	Bt = brigantine	Bq = barque
Sc = schooner	S = full-rigged ship	Sn = snow
ss = screw steamer	mv = motor vessel	

Superscripts:
1. Purchased from Rathbone Brothers, 1889.
2. Purchased from J.T. Rennie, 1911.
3. Purchased from Rankin Gilmour, 1918.
4. Purchased from Prentice, Service and Henderson, 1920.
5. Purchased from Scruttons Ltd., 1920.
6. Purchased from Leyland Line, 1934.
7. Purchased from Prince Line, 1935.
8. Managed and manned on behalf of Ministry of War Transport during Second World War; many being acquired by Harrisons post war.

SHIP'S NAME	NO. IN FLEET LIST		YEARS IN FLEET	RIG	SHIP'S NAME	NO. IN FLEET LIST		YEARS IN FLEET	RIG
ACTOR	1	91	1885-05	ss	ARBITRATOR	1	66	1872-76	ss
ACTOR	2	174	1917-39	ss	ARBITRATOR	2	289	1951-70	mv
ADMINISTRATOR		297	1958-78	mv	ARCHITECT	1	83	1880-97	ss
ADMIRAL GRENFELL		28	1854-58	Bq	ARCHITECT	2	161	1912-33	ss
ADVENTURER		300	1960-79	mv	ARICA[8]		252	1941-42	ss
ADVISER	1	244	1939-60	ss	ARTISAN[8]		263	1946-59	ss
ADVISER	2	326	1977-93	mv	ARTIST	1	44	1864-86	S
ALHAMBRA		49	1866-71	ss	ARTIST	2	144	1909-17	ss
ALICE		50	1866-86	ss	ASTRONOMER	1	35	1860-83	S
AMAZON		46	1865-72	ss	ASTRONOMER	2	90	1884-03	ss
AMBASSADOR		67	1872-76	ss	ASTRONOMER	3	173	1917-40	ss
AMERICA		15	1849-54	Sn	ASTRONOMER	4	286	1951-70	mv
ANLABY		16	1849-50	Sc	ASTRONOMER	5	325	1977-86	mv

Architect (161) in a US port.

[*Mike McGarvey, courtesy Chris Mills*]

Auditor (206) docking at Liverpool, 13th June 1936.

[*J. and M. Clarkson*]

Author (175) passing through Knutsford Road Swing Bridge on the Manchester Ship Canal. [*Nigel Farrell collection*]

SHIP'S NAME		NO. IN FLEET LIST	YEARS IN FLEET	RIG
ATALANTA		57	1870-73	ss
ATLANTIAN[6]		231	1934-51	ss
AUDITOR		206	1924-41	ss
AUTHOR	1	82	1880-90	ss
AUTHOR	2	137	1905-16	ss
AUTHOR[3]	3	175	1917-35	ss
AUTHOR	4	298	1958-78	mv
AUTHOR	5	328	1981-95	mv
BARRISTER	1	109	1893-14	ss
BARRISTER	2	169	1915-17	ss
BARRISTER[3]	3	183	1918-18	ss
BARRISTER	4	245	1939-43	ss
BARRISTER	5	295	1954-74	mv
BELLONA		58	1870-75	ss
BENEFACTOR	1	158	1912-35	ss
BENEFACTOR	2	318	1971-82	mv
BIOGRAPHER		285	1949-64	ss
BOTANIST	1	41	1863-81	Bq
BOTANIST	2	157	1912-20	ss
CANDIDATE	1	139	1906-15	ss
CANDIDATE[4]	2	191	1920-28	ss
CAPELLA[1]	1	100	1889-89	ss
CAPELLA	2	104	1890-10	ss
CASTILLA		54	1869-70	ss
CELLA		60	1870-74	ss
CENTURION	1	141	1908-15	ss
CENTURION[4]	2	195	1920-25	ss
CHANCELLOR	1	70	1873-86	ss
CHANCELLOR	2	106	1891-01	ss
CHANCELLOR	3	125	1902-15	ss
CHANCELLOR[4]	4	192	1920-39	ss
CHARENTE		40	1862-63	ss
CHARLES SOUCHAY		8	1845-61	Sc
CHRYSOLITE		52	1867-86	ss
CITY OF BRUSSELS		62	1870-71	ss

The short-lived second *Chancellor* (106). [*Ian Rae collection*]

367

Civilian (126). The name was only used once.

[Nigel Farrell collection]

Counsellor (131).   *[Nigel Farrell collection]*

Custodian (120) at Galveston.

[Paul Verkin, courtesy Nigel Farrell]

SHIP'S NAME		NO. IN FLEET LIST	YEARS IN FLEET	RIG
CITY OF DURBAN		327	1978-98	mv
CITY OF LINCOLN		13	1848-50	S
CIVILIAN		126	1902-17	ss
COGNAC	1	38	1860-98	ss
COGNAC	2	127	1902-35	ss
COLLEGIAN	1	119	1899-17	ss
COLLEGIAN[4]	2	190	1920-33	ss
COLLEGIAN[7]	3	236	1935-47	ss
COLONIAL	1	130	1903-25	ss
COLONIAL	2	213	1926-41	ss
COLONIAL	3	284	1949-61	ss
COLUMBIA		26	1854-59	S
COMEDIAN	1	128	1903-17	ss
COMEDIAN[4]	2	194	1920-25	ss
COMEDIAN	3	223	1929-50	ss
COMMANDER		79	1877-84	ss
COMMODORE	1	140	1906-15	ss
COMMODORE[4]	2	189	1920-25	ss
CONTRACTOR		224	1930-43	ss
CORDOVA		59	1870-80	ss
COUNSELLOR	1	78	1877-93	ss
COUNSELLOR	2	131	1903-16	ss
COUNSELLOR[4]	3	188	1920-25	ss
COUNSELLOR	4	215	1926-40	ss
CRAFTSMAN	1	116	1897-19	ss
CRAFTSMAN[4]	2	193	1920-33	ss
CRAFTSMAN[7]	3	235	1935-41	ss
CRAFTSMAN	4	275	1947-67	ss
CRAFTSMAN	5	319	1972-81	mv
CRESCENT		3	1837-62	Sc
CROFTER		290	1951-71	ss
CUSTODIAN	1	120	1900-23	ss
CUSTODIAN	2	220	1928-50	ss
CUSTODIAN	3	302	1961-79	mv
DAKARIAN[6]		226	1933-39	ss
DALESMAN	1	247	1940-41/46-59	ss
DALESMAN	2	305	1961-79	mv
DARIAN[6]		229	1934-39	ss
DARING		29	1855-61	Bg
DAUNTLESS		12	1846-50	S

Craftsman (275).   *[Roy Fenton collection]*

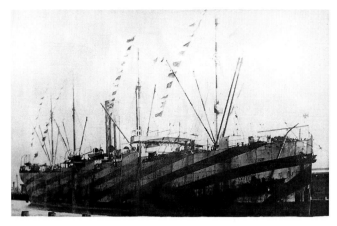

Custodian (120) in dazzle paint during the First World War.

[*Nigel Farrell collection*]

SHIP'S NAME	NO. IN FLEET LIST	YEARS IN FLEET	RIG
DAVISIAN[6]		228	1934-40	ss
DAYTONIAN[6]		230	1934-42	ss
DEFENDER	1	167	1915-52	ss
DEFENDER	2	296	1955-75	mv
DELILIAN[6]		232	1934-36	ss
DESIGNER		222	1928-41	ss
DEVONPORT		25	1853-54	S
DICTATOR	1	107	1891-15	ss
DICTATOR[3]	2	176	1918-32	ss
DIPLOMAT	1	160	1912-14	ss
DIPLOMAT	2	202	1921-40	ss
DIPLOMAT	3	293	1953-72	mv
DIRECTOR	1	132	1903-25	ss
DIRECTOR	2	214	1926-44	ss
DISCOVERER	1	76	1877-93	ss
DISCOVERER	2	163	1913-35	ss
DISCOVERER	3	307	1964-77	mv
DORELIAN[6]		227	1933-36	ss
DRAGON		39	1862-66	ss
DRAMATIST	1	164	1914-16	ss
DRAMATIST	2	201	1920-49	ss
EDITOR		92	1885-97	ss
EDWARD BOUSTEAD		23	1852-64	Bq
ELECTRICIAN	1	95	1887-05	ss
ELECTRICIAN[3]	2	180	1918-32	ss
EMPIRE ADDISON[8]		262	1943-45	ss
EMPIRE CAPTAIN[8]		258	1944-46	ss
EMPIRE CHIVALRY[8]		253	1941-46	ss
EMPIRE EXPLORER[8]		254	1942-42	ss

Custodian (220) as the *Siva Ranjita*.   [*Peter Newall collection*]

A member of the ex-Leyland Line 'D' class in wartime colours.

[*Ambrose Greenway collection*]

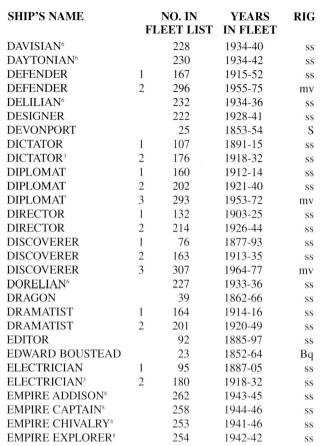

Dictator (107) at Calcutta.   [*Peter Newall collection*]

Euromariner ex-*Defender* (296).   [*J. and M. Clarkson*]

Engineer (143). [Ambrose Greenway collection]

Gladiator (185), ex *Saint Quentin* of Rankin, Gilmour. [Peter Newall collection]

SHIP'S NAME		NO. IN FLEET LIST	YEARS IN FLEET	RIG	SHIP'S NAME		NO. IN FLEET LIST	YEARS IN FLEET	RIG
EMPIRE GAZELLE[8]		251	1941-46	ss	GEM		21	1851-54	Sn
EMPIRE KENT[8]		260	1945-46	mv	GEOLOGIST	1	34	1859-72	S
EMPIRE LIFE[8]		259	1945-46	ss	GEOLOGIST	2	256	1944-55	ss
EMPIRE NEWTON[8]		263	1944-46	ss	GLADIATOR	1	37	1860-61;64-78	ss
EMPIRE RANGOON[8]		257	1944-46	mv	GLADIATOR	2	135	1904-15	ss
EMPIRE SERVICE[8]		261	1945-46	ss	GLADIATOR[3]	3	185	1918-32	ss
EMPIRE TRUMPET		265	1944-46	ss	GOOD INTENT		11	1846-58	Bt
EMPIRE WILY[8]		266	1946-46	ss	GOVERNOR	1	86	1881-00	ss
ENGINEER	1	88	1882-99	ss	GOVERNOR	2	168	1915-17	ss
ENGINEER	2	143	1908-20	ss	GOVERNOR	3	187	1918-50	ss
EUPHEMIA		4	1838-40	Bg	GOVERNOR	4	292	1952-72	mv
EXPLORER	1	77	1877-06	ss	GREYHOUND		43	1864-71	S
EXPLORER	2	148	1910-32	ss	HEBE		19	1851-60	Sc
EXPLORER	3	234	1935-57	ss	HERDSMAN		269	1947-65	mv
EXPLORER	4	304	1961-78	mv	HERO		14	1849-58	Bg
FACTOR		279	1948-72	mv	HISTORIAN	1	56	1870-91	ss
FIRE QUEEN		48	1866-79	ss	HISTORIAN	2	114	1896-21	ss
FORESTER		291	1952-70	ss	HISTORIAN	3	207	1924-48	ss
FRANKFORT		47	1865-74	ss	HISTORIAN	4	283	1949-62	ss

An interior view of the first *Inkosi* (154). [Peter Newall collection]

The second *Inkosi* (240). [Ian Rae collection]

SHIP'S NAME		NO. IN FLEET LIST	YEARS IN FLEET	RIG	SHIP'S NAME		NO. IN FLEET LIST	YEARS IN FLEET	RIG
HISTORIAN	5	315	1968-81	mv	INVENTOR	1	81	1878-05	ss
HUNTSMAN	1	133	1904-17	ss	INVENTOR	2	147	1910-32	ss
HUNTSMAN	2	203	1921-39	ss	INVENTOR	3	239	1935-60	ss
INANDA²	1	155	1911-20	ss	INVENTOR	4	306	1964-81	mv
INANDA	2	210	1925-40	ss	INVINCIBLE		22	1852-54	Sc
INGELI²		151	1911-14	ss	INYATI²		150	1911-12	ss
INGOMA		162	1913-37	ss	JANE		1	1836-49	Bg
INKONKA²		153	1911-19	ss	JARNAC		105	1890-22	ss
INKOSI²	1	154	1911-18	ss	JOURNALIST		294	1954-73	mv
INKOSI	2	240	1937-40	ss	JURIST		65	1872-73	ss
INSIZWA²		152	1911-13	ss	KING ARTHUR		63	1871-78	S
INSTRUCTOR³		177	1918-18	ss	LAMMA FOREST		329	1982-90	mv
INTABA²		156	1911-27	ss	LANCASHIRE		24	1853-64	S
INTERPRETER		278	1948-67	mv	LANTAU TRADER		330	1982-95	mv
INTOMBI		159	1912-32	ss	LAUREL		18	1850-60	Bg

Kota Salamat ex *Herdsman* (269) at Bangkok on 11th March 1973.
[Ambrose Greenway collection]

Interpreter (278) in the English Channel.

Inventor (239) in the River Scheldt.
[World Ship Photo Library]

Logician (219).   [Nigel Farrell collection]

Magician (115).   [Nigel Farrell collection]

Merchant (142) off Penarth.
                    [Wehrley, courtesy Ambrose Greenway]

SHIP'S NAME	NO. IN FLEET LIST	YEARS IN FLEET	RIG
LEGISLATOR	1	68	1873-87	ss
LEGISLATOR	2	96	1888-98	ss
LINGUIST	1	74	1874-79	S
LINGUIST	2	276	1947-66	ss
LINGUIST	3	313	1966-80	mv
LOGICIAN	1	111	1894-23	ss
LOGICIAN	2	219	1928-41	ss
MAFIA		171	1915-21	ss
MAGICIAN	1	115	1896-22	ss
MAGICIAN	2	211	1925-44	ss
MAGICIAN	3	314	1968-81	mv
MARINER		84	1881-96	ss
MATADOR	1	134	1904-17	ss
MATADOR[3]	2	182	1918-32	ss
MAZEPPA		17	1849-60	Bg
MECHANICIAN		122	1900-18	ss
MEDIATOR		75	1876-84	ss
MERCHANT	1	85	1881-97	ss
MERCHANT	2	142	1908-29	ss
MERCHANT	3	233	1934-41	ss
MERCHANT	4	273	1947-61	ss
MERCHANT	5	316	1969-79	mv
MIRA		102	1889-09	ss
MONARCHY		20	1851-75	S
MUSICIAN	1	112	1894-23	ss
MUSICIAN	2	208	1924-38	ss
NATURALIST	1	42	1863-79	S
NATURALIST[8]	2	265	1946-59	ss
NATURALIST	3	310	1965-77	mv
NAVIGATOR	1	94	1886-10	ss
NAVIGATOR	2	165	1914-32	ss
NOVELIST	1	248	1940-61	ss
NOVELIST	2	311	1965-77	mv
OBERON		69	1872-79	ss
OBSERVER		218	1928-42	ss
OLINDA		45	1865-72	ss
ORATOR	1	80	1878-89	ss

Olinda (45) at Bristol in the colours of the Moss Steamship Co. Ltd.
                                          [J. and M. Clarkson]

Philosopher (262). [Roy Fenton collection]

Politician (118). [Ian Rae collection]

SHIP'S NAME		NO. IN FLEET LIST	YEARS IN FLEET	RIG	SHIP'S NAME		NO. IN FLEET LIST	YEARS IN FLEET	RIG
ORATOR	2	138	1905-17	ss	PLANTER	1	216	1927-40	ss
ORATOR[3]	3	178	1918-32	ss	PLANTER	2	264	1946-58	ss
ORION		103	1889-09	ss	PLANTER	3	301	1961-62	ss
ORKNEY LASS		27	1854-57	Bq	POLITICIAN	1	118	1899-22	ss
PALLAS[1]		99	1889-94	ss	POLITICIAN[7]	2	238	1935-41	ss
PANTHEON		51	1867-69	ss	PRINCE OF ORANGE		31	1855-58	Bq
PATRICIAN	1	123	1901-14	ss	PROFESSOR	1	87	1881-95	ss
PATRICIAN[3]	2	184	1918-38	ss	PROFESSOR	2	145	1910-30	ss
PEMBA		170	1915-21	ss	PROSPECTOR		255	1943-61	ss
PEVERIL OF THE PEAK		36	1860-69	S	RANCHER		217	1927-49	ss
PHILOSOPHER	1	33	1857-79	S	RECORDER		225	1930-50	ss
PHILOSOPHER[8]	2	262	1945-58	ss	REDBREAST		10	1846-57	Sc
PHILOSOPHER	3	309	1964-77	mv	ROBERT PRESTON		7	1845-58	Bg
PISCES EXPLORER		333	1994-2002	mv	SAMARINDA		270	1943-47	ss
PISCES PIONEER		331	1984-98	mv	SAMWIS		271	1943-47	ss
PISCES PLANTER		332	1984-99	mv	SAPPHIRE		53	1867-70	ss
PISCES TRADER		334	1996-2002	mv	SCHOLAR	1	93	1886-03	ss
PLAINSMAN		299	1959-79	mv	SCHOLAR	2	205	1922-40	ss

Ocean Maru ex *Recorder* (225).   [*Peter Newall collection*]

Sculptor (277).   [*Roy Fenton collection*]

Cattle as deck cargo on *Senator* (110).   [*Nigel Farrell collection*]

SHIP'S NAME	NO. IN FLEET LIST	YEARS IN FLEET	RIG
SCHOLAR	3	272	1947-64	ss
SCHOLAR	4	317	1969-79	mv
SCIENTIST[5]	1	197	1920-25	ss
SCIENTIST	2	243	1938-40	ss
SCULPTOR	1	89	1882-89	ss
SCULPTOR	2	149	1911-17	ss
SCULPTOR[3]	3	186	1918-18	ss
SCULPTOR	4	277	1948-62	ss
SELECTOR[8]		261	1945-60	ss
SENATOR	1	73	1874-89	S
SENATOR	2	110	1893-14	ss
SENATOR	3	172	1917-38	ss
SENATOR	4	274	1947-64	ss
SETTLER[5]	1	198	1920-28	ss
SETTLER	2	246	1939-59	ss
SIR COLIN CAMPBELL		5	1839-45	Bg
SONGSTER[5]		199	1920-26	ss

The short-lived *Spectator* (166) of 1914, sunk in 1917.　　　　　　　　　　　　*[Nigel Farrell collection]*

Traveller (97) above and after sale to the Limerick Steam Ship Co. Ltd as *Inishboffin*, below.　　　*[Both: Terry Conlan collection]*

SPECTATOR	1	166	1914-17	ss
SPECTATOR[3]	2	179	1918-27	ss
STATESMAN	1	55	1869-91	ss
STATESMAN	2	113	1895-16	ss
STATESMAN[3]	3	181	1918-32	ss
STATESMAN[7]	4	237	1935-41	ss
STATESMAN	5	281	1948-62	ss
STATESMAN	6	308	1964-77	mv
STRATEGIST	1	242	1937-57	ss
STRATEGIST	2	323	1975-83	mv
STUDENT	1	64	1871-77	ss
STUDENT	2	146	1910-30	ss
STUDENT[8]	3	270	1947-63	ss
SUCCESSOR		282	1948-63	ss
TACTICIAN	1	121	1900-22	ss
TACTICIAN	2	221	1928-50	ss
TACTICIAN	3	303	1961-79	mv
TEMPLAR		6	1842-55	S
TIMANDRA		32	1856-61	S
TOM TOUGH		2	1836-45	Bg
TRADER	1	249	1940-61	ss
TRADER	2	312	1966-80	mv

SHIP'S NAME		NO. IN FLEET LIST	YEARS IN FLEET	RIG
SPEAKER[5]	1	196	1920-26	ss
SPEAKER	2	280	1948-62	ss
SPECIALIST[5]	1	200	1920-36	ss
SPECIALIST[8]	2	271	1947-64	ss
SPECIALIST	3	324	1975-83	mv

SHIP'S NAME	NO. IN FLEET LIST		YEARS IN FLEET	RIG	SHIP'S NAME	NO. IN FLEET LIST		YEARS IN FLEET	RIG
TRAVELLER	1	97	1888-19	ss	WARRIOR	1	61	1870-72	ss
TRAVELLER	2	204	1922-42	ss	WARRIOR	2	72	1874-88	ss
TRIBESMAN	1	241	1937-40	ss	WARRIOR	3	136	1905-27	ss
TRIBESMAN	2	268	1946-61	ss	WARRIOR	4	322	1973-88	mv
URGENT		9	1845-48	S	WAYFARER	1	129	1903-23	ss
VANGUARD		71	1873-81	ss	WAYFARER	2	212	1925-44	ss
VEGA[1]		98	1889-90	ss	WAYFARER	3	287	1951-71	mv
VESTA[1]		101	1889-98	ss	WAYFARER	4	320	1973-86	mv
WANDERER	1	108	1891-22	ss	WEST DERBY		30	1855-76	S
WANDERER	2	209	1925-49	ss	WINNIPEG[8]		250	1941-41	ss
WANDERER	3	288	1951-70	mv	WORKMAN		117	1898-12	ss
WANDERER	4	321	1973-87	mv	YEOMAN		124	1901-04	ss

Wanderer (288).   *[Roy Fenton collection]*

Wayfarer (287) photographed by John MacRoberts.   *[J. and M. Clarkson]*

APPENDIX 1: THE GREAT AGE OF HARRISON SAIL, 1865-1885

A careful study of the voyages undertaken by the ship-rigged sailing vessels which flew the Harrison flag during this epoch, for which certain fragmentary records are still extant, cannot fail to evoke mental pictures of an heroic age which carry overtones of almost Homeric grandeur. Let me hasten to add that it is not my intention in this brief appendix to indulge my frugal talents in the creation of a latter-day Odyssey or Iliad. Nevertheless, the story of those fine old sailing ships should not be overlooked.

Screw-driven steamers were well established upon all the oceans of the world by this time, although fleets of swift and beautiful clipper ships were meeting the challenge with considerable vigour and notable success. The opening of the Suez Canal in 1869, however, coupled with the successful development of the more efficient compound steam engine, gave steamers an unassailable advantage on voyages to India and the Far East. The commercial appeal of the proud and graceful clippers gradually declined and builders and owners in sail sought to design and develop a new type of sailing vessel capable of competing successfully with the steamers.

The result was the windjammer, a word evoking scorn and derision at first, a pejorative term which quickly became a proud and honoured title. The windjammers were large iron or steel-built vessels fitted with three, four, sometimes five masts, and either ship or barque-rigged. Their massive hulls lifted up to five times more cargo than their dainty predecessors, and they were capable of carrying large bulk cargoes over the longest ocean distances at minimum expense.

They were built, not primarily for speed like the clippers, but to carry great loads and withstand the worst weather in the world. The vast expanse of sail carried on their towering masts was awe-inspiring, and in later ships braces and halliards of steel wire-rope could be led to steam-driven winches and capstans, thus reducing manpower requirements. Instead of a crew of 50 or 60 men normally shipped aboard the clippers, these sailing leviathans required only 25 to 30 men.

Some idea of the magnitude of the decline in the demand for sailing ships during the latter half of the 19th century can be gleaned from Table 1.1 which shows the annual average net tonnage of merchant ships launched from British shipyards for British, Colonial and foreign owners. Meanwhile, the proportion

of sail to steam tonnage on the U.K. Register declined from 20:1 in 1850 to 4:1 in 1870, in an expanding industry.*

Harrison sailing ships were among the early participants in this rearguard action and made some very respectable passages over the oceanic trade routes. Of course, the brothers Harrison and their partners had operated sailing vessels ever since they began in business, mainly small brigs and schooners restricted for the most part to short Continental voyages to the Charente, Baltic and Mediterranean areas. Nevertheless, there were occasional sorties further afield before 1860; to Brazil in the brig JANE (1) as early as 1838, to India in the ship TEMPLAR (6) in 1847 and notably to the Americas and the Far East in the barque ADMIRAL GRENFELL (28), an enterprise distinguished by her subsequent circumnavigation of the globe under the intrepid Captain Richard-Pierre Williamson in 1856-1858. It was upon the evidence of these long voyages that the partners became convinced that lucrative trading need not be restricted to the Charente and the brandy trade. Consequently, India came to be chosen as a regular source of trade, beginning with the ship BOTANIST (41) in 1863. A similar approach was made in the direction of China in the MONARCHY (20), and to Australia in the PHILOSOPHER (33) in 1865, but it was the Indian trade which developed and prospered (see Table 1.2).

Table 1.1: Annual average net tonnage of merchant ships launched from British shipyards

Period	Sail	Steam	Total
1858-59	153,909 (68.5%)	70,740 (31.5%)	224,647
1870-74	104,840 (22.6%)	358,669 (77.4%)	463,509

*Statistical Tables and Charts relating to British and Foreign Trade and Industry, 1854-1908, and Accounts and Papers CII (1909), LX (1913); quoted by Gerald S. Graham in his paper, "The Ascendancy of the Sailing Ship, 1850-85"; Economic History Review Vol. 9, 1956-57, page 74.

Table 1.2: Harrison sailing ships - general trading patterns 1865-1885

No.	Vessel	India Burma	North America east coast	Caribbean South America east	Australia & New Zealand	South & East Africa	Far East	North America west coast	South America west coast	Total
20	MONARCHY	3	6	6	1	1	1	-	-	13
30	WEST DERBY	5	6	6	-	-	2	-	-	19
33	PHILOSOPHER	14	5	3	2	2	-	-	-	26
34	PEVERIL OF THE PEAK	5	-	-	-	-	1	-	-	6
35	GEOLOGIST	6	-	1	-	-	2	-	-	9
36	ASTRONOMER	13	6	-	2	-	-	2	-	23
41	BOTANIST	12	7	1	-	1	-	-	-	25
42	NATURALIST	12	7	1	-	1	-	-	-	21
43	GREYHOUND	2	-	1	1	-	-	-	1	5
44	ARTIST	16	9	6	-	-	1	1	-	33
63	KING ARTHUR	7	3	5	-	2	-	-	-	17
73	SENATOR	11	6	2	1	-	-	1	-	21
74	LINGUIST	4	1	2	1	-	-	-	-	8
Total		110	54	31	10	7	7	5	2	226
% of total		48.7	23.9	13.7	4.4	3.1	3.1	2.2	0.9	100

The route to India via the Cape of Good Hope steered by a sailing ship in the 1860s was by no means a direct one. Every advantage had to be taken of the prevailing favourable winds and every opportunity seized to minimise the influence of adverse conditions.

This essential policy led to wide detours from the so-called direct route, normally the shortest route followed by steam vessels. Thus, the distance of 11,600 miles from Liverpool to Calcutta via the Cape of Good Hope normally covered by a steamer, would expand to about 13,700 miles for a sailing vessel (this figure does not, of course, include the many miles covered on tacking reaches). It was not surprising, therefore, for a ship to set sail and not be seen or heard of again for three, sometimes four, months. The waiting time between estimated time of arrival and a report was an anxious period, and must have seemed interminable. Full advantage was taken of an ad hoc reporting system developed between ships which passed within sight of one another, whereby each agreed to report the other's position and course on arrival at her destination.

From there, the information was telegraphed to the ship's owners and passed on to the press. Such reports were most welcome in head office and home alike, but they were few and far between. The ocean is a vast place - even more so in a world without modern communications - and it was not unusual for a ship to make an entire voyage without seeing so much as another sail close enough to hail or signal.

Leaving the Irish Sea, or the Channel, on her voyage to India, the ship would prudently make as much westing as possible, beating against the westerlies, fighting for every mile, in order to avoid the notorious indrafts into the Bay of Biscay which threatened the ship with the risk of being embayed. At last, from a position somewhere south west of Ireland, the Master could shape a course south south west to pass westward of Madeira and the Cape Verde Islands, almost reaching as far west as the thirtieth meridian, scudding along before the north east trade wind with all sails set. Having passed the Cape Verdes, he would head south, his ship passing within 300 miles of the coast of Brazil. In these latitudes the ship could be becalmed, spending many days waiting for that fitful breeze which would carry the ship into the south east trade belt. Then more beating southwards assisted by the Brazil Current, until the influence of the westerlies was felt well beyond Capricorn and the ship could head south easterly towards that point where the Greenwich meridian meets the fortieth parallel. From there she would be buffeted by the boisterous winds of the Roaring Forties as she forged her way eastwards past the Cape of Good Hope.

Having weathered the violent storms and phenomenal seas experienced in that region, the ship entered the Indian Ocean, still maintaining that easterly course until she reached longitude 60 east. She would then steer north easterly, beating across the south east trade belt, before heading north up the Bay of Bengal towards the Sandheads of the Hooghly delta. It would depend on the time of year just what disagreeable conditions would confront the ship on this final leg of the voyage: strong adverse winds during the north east monsoon season (October to April), or driving rain and poor visibility during the south west monsoon (May to September).

Outward bound to Calcutta the more prevalent cargoes included coal (ironically good steaming coal for coaling stations established to service the steamer opposition), railway iron, or salt, the latter usually for owner's account for it could be sold readily in Calcutta for a good profit. Her cargo discharged, the ship might wait weeks for a suitable cargo to load, perhaps tea to London, or rice to Mauritius, or coolies to Demerara, but the most frequent assignment usually turned out to be a voyage to New York with a mixed cargo of jute, hides, linseed and saltpetre.

The passage to New York involved less of a detour - 12,900 miles as against 12,250 "steamer" miles. To make for a port of call on these long oceanic voyages was almost unheard of and only happened in the direst circumstances, perhaps to repair damage after being dismasted in a cyclone, or in the case of the coolie ships, a call at St. Helena on the insistence of the Commissioner's Agent, to land sick emigrants, or obtain fresh food and water. But the normal practice was to press on regardless of privation and so avoid expensive and unnecessary port dues.

Cargoes in New York were usually readily available consisting mainly of wheat, tallow, tobacco, cotton and lumber; and the passage to Liverpool in the prevailing westerly winds was the most direct and swiftest of all. The round voyage, Liverpool - Calcutta - New York - Liverpool would typically last anything from ten to twelve months depending on weather and the availability of cargoes. The turnround would perhaps be achieved in three weeks, then outward bound again, almost invariably with the same master, officers and apprentices. Members of the crew would also ship out again - if they were still around. Most of them, however, would have spent their hard-earned pay in a few days of hedonistic living and shipped out again in the next available vessel. It was the only life they knew.

Table 1.3 indicates some of the better passages, and some not so good, made by Harrison ships on this fairly regular run.

Most shipmasters in those days stayed with their ship for many years: Alexander Ross in the PHILOSOPHER for eight years; Michael Clarke in the GEOLOGIST for seven years; John Sergent in the ARTIST for a record 18 years, while George Jeffrey and W. Ball shared the SENATOR throughout her 15 years of service in the company. Making a profitable voyage in the shortest possible time, with a minimum of damage to ship and cargo, called for a high degree of skill and sound judgement in all things nautical and indeed in all things commercial, on the part of these men. It was the Master, alone, who made the decisions on what cargo to load in distant ports abroad, on what courses to steer when the ship was at sea, what way-points to make for and how much sail to carry in deteriorating conditions. He had to understand and appreciate the seasonal nuances of the winds; his judgement of just how much stress his ship's hull and standing rigging could safely endure was crucial. He carried an awesome responsibility. A change of Master could radically alter a vessel's performance for better or worse, as the following, probably invidious, comparison demonstrates in Table 1.4.

Table 1.3: Some passages on a staple Harrison sailing ship voyage

Passage	Liverpool to Calcutta ~ 13,700 nm.				Calcutta to New York ~12,900 nm.				New York to Liverpool ~3,100 nm			
	Fstst.	Av. Spd.	Slst	Av. Spd.	Fstst.	Av. Spd.	Slst	Av. Spd.	Fstst.	Av. Spd.	Slst	Av. Spd.
	days	kn	days	kn	days	kn	days	kn	days	kn	days	kn
PHILOSOPHER	92*	6.20	143	3.99	109	4.93	119	4.52	19	6.80	28	4.61
ASTRONOMER	91*	6.27	136	4.20	110	4.89	138	3.89	22	5.87	29	4.45
BOTANIST	99	5.77	119	4.80	120	4.48	134	4.01	20	6.46	26	4.97
NATURALIST	105	5.44	136	4.20	97	5.54	119	4.52	21	6.15	27	4.78
ARTIST	100	5.71	133	4.29	118	4.56	132	4.07	19	6.80	32	4.04
SENATOR	96	5.95	106	5.38	93	5.78	149	3.61	17	7.60	22	5.87
Overall average	115.5 days				121.44 days				23.9 days			
Sample size	57 passages				27 passages				31 passages			

* These two outstanding passages were achieved during the south west monsoon season and it is possible that the ships' Captains, Alex. Ross and James Edgar, respectively, elected to take the more intricate, alternative route through the Mozambique Channel, thus shortening the distance considerably.

Table 1.4: NATURALIST - UK to Calcutta, a tale of four shipmasters

Year	Master	Voyage	Days on passage	Mean days	%age difference related to norm over 12 voyages
1865	Arthur Hyde	Liverpool to Calcutta	132	140.0	+ 15.4%
1866	Arthur Hyde	London to Calcutta	152		
1868	Arthur Hyde	Liverpool to Calcutta	136		
1869	C.H. Gregory	Liverpool to Calcutta	115	119.0	- 1.9%
1870	C.H. Gregory	Liverpool to Calcutta	121		
1871	C.H. Gregory	Liverpool to Calcutta	119		
1872	C.H. Gregory	Liverpool to Calcutta	121		
1873	J. Thomas	Liverpool to Calcutta	108	112.7	- 7.1%
1874	J. Thomas	Liverpool to Calcutta	108		
1875	J. Thomas	Liverpool to Calcutta	122		
1876	Captain Nelson	Barrow to Calcutta	117	111.0	- 8.5%
1877	Captain Nelson	Liverpool to Calcutta	105		
		Total (12 voyages)	**1,456**	**121.3**	-

Harrison sailing vessels ranged far and wide during this period, pursuing voyages to the Far East, Australia and round the Horn to the west coast ports of South and North America. A number of examples are listed in Table 1.5.

Table 1.5: Some typical world-wide voyages by Harrison sailing ships 1865-1885

No.	Vessel	From	To	No. of days	Master	Year	Cargo n/s = not specified.
20	MONARCHY	Cardiff	Woosung	164	Arthur Day	1865	Coal?
		Foochow	Bremerhaven	169	Arthur Day	1866	n/s
30	WEST DERBY	Akyab	Liverpool	138	John Sergeant	1866	Rice
		Mauritius	London	142	J. Wilkinson	1870	Rum, sugar
33	PHILOSOPHER	London	Sydney, NSW	96	Alex. Ross	1865	General
		Sydney, NSW	London	114	Alex. Ross	1866	n/s
		Portsmouth	Melbourne	105	Alex. Ross	1869	General
34	PEVERIL OF THE PEAK	Liverpool	Madras	107	W. Loftus	1865	Salt?
		Akyab	Falmouth	141	W. Loftus	1866	Rice
35	GEOLOGIST	London	Hong Kong	155	Michael Clarke	1869	n/s
		Bassein	Queenstown	136	Michael Clarke	1870	Rice
36	ASTRONOMER	London	Adelaide	111	Arthur Day	1879	n/s
		San Francisco	Liverpool	156	Arthur Day	1881	Flour, lumber
41	BOTANIST	London	Sydney, NSW	104	James Edgar	1865	General
		Sydney, NSW	London	121	James Edgar	1866	n/s
		Cardiff	Valparaiso	106	J. Black	1880	Coal
		San Francisco	Queenstown	163		1881	Wheat
42	NATURALIST	Colombo	London	159	Arthur Hyde	1867	n/s
43	GREYHOUND	London	Port Lyttelton	105	I.G. Wright	1865	n/s
		Callao	Rio de Janeiro	60	I.G. Wright	1865	Guano
44	ARTIST	Liverpool	San Francisco	141	John Sergeant	1881	Coal
		Cardiff	Singapore	161	J. Everett	1884	Coal
		Rangoon	Liverpool	180	J. Everett	1885	Rice
63	KING ARTHUR	New York	Calcutta	84	Rickwood	1872	Jute, etc.
		Calcutta	Dundee	109	Rickwood	1874	Jute
73	SENATOR	Liverpool	Melbourne	87	George Jeffrey	1877	General
		Newport, Mon.	San Francisco	154	W. Ball	1884	Railway iron
		San Francisco	Liverpool	130	W. Ball	1884	Wheat, flour
74	LINGUIST	Calcutta	Demerara	95	Charles Curry	1875	Seed, coolies
		Liverpool	Melbourne	91	Charles Curry	1877	General

It should perhaps be noted that the record for the longest sea passage of this era was held by Captain J. Everett of the ARTIST, who left Rangoon on 6th July 1885 and arrived at Liverpool 180 days later on 2nd January 1886, to complete her last voyage for Harrisons. Six long months at sea! During this time she was spoken only once, by the barque LINDA, off Cape Colony in position 35.25 south by 33.07 east, on 24th September 1885. She also touched briefly at Ascension Island on 21st October. ARTIST was loaded with 1,825 tons of rice to owner's account for this voyage, a commodity purchased in Rangoon at 4s. 11d. per quarter and sold in Liverpool at 8s. 1d. per quarter, which probably made it all seem well worthwhile. Ten per cent of the profit of £23,116. 13s. 4d. was assigned to freight charges.

However, despite the enterprise, the courage and the sheer hard work which made these voyages possible, the Harrisons and their associates, the Hughes brothers, now visualised a future in steam and in the development of regular advertised services operated by sturdy, reliable screw steamers.

The year 1879 can be seen as a watershed in the fortunes of the Harrisons, for that was a black and disastrous year by any standards, thanks to a series of calamitous ship losses unprecedented before the First World War. The tale of tragedy began on 1st January with the news that the ship KING ARTHUR (63), had run ashore in Bannow Bay, County Wexford, on New Year's Eve, to become a total loss. Worse was to follow, for on the night of 10th January the latest addition to the sailing fleet, the ship

LINGUIST (74), foundered and sank in St. George's Channel with the loss of 15 lives. Some months later it was becoming increasingly clear to a distraught head office that the NATURALIST (42) which had left Calcutta on 2nd February 1879 and had not been reported since, was long overdue. She would have been expected in Liverpool in June, or July at the latest, but more months of agonised uncertainty had to be endured before the ship was officially posted as missing at Lloyds, on 22nd October 1879. Meanwhile, a few weeks earlier, the telegraph lines from Calcutta had been humming with news of the disaster which had befallen the PHILOSOPHER (33). On 26th September, three days after leaving Calcutta, the ship was wrecked on the Orissa Coast, near the town of Puri. Half the crew perished in that tragedy and it would hardly be surprising if confidence in sail began to wane, especially in the hearts of the younger generation of Harrisons.

Gradually, their interests in the remaining sailing ships were sold off; The Charente Steam-Ship Company Limited was incorporated in 1884 and only ARTIST and SENATOR, last of the windjammers, remained as outsiders. At last, the ARTIST, at 22 years one of the longest-serving of all Harrison's sailing vessels,* was sold in 1886. Three years later in 1889, and one year after the death of the senior partner, the SENATOR was sold, still destined to make some outstanding passages under her new owners before ending her days as a hulk in a creek up the Amazon.

So ended a remarkable era in the annals of the company, an era which must be rich in untold tales, far more than I have been able to record here. The complete saga has yet to be told.

* CRESCENT served 25 years; MONARCHY 24 years; ASTRONOMER 23 years; PHILOSOPHER 22 years; and WEST DERBY 21 years.

APPENDIX 2: ACQUISITION AND DISPOSAL OF VESSELS, 1884-2002

| Year | Fleet additions | | | Losses and sales | | | Fleet totals at 31 December | | | Avg. cost £/ton | Remarks |
	No	Gross tons	Purchase price £	No	Gross tons	Purchase price £	Total vessels	Total gross tons	Total purch. price £		
1884							22	39,771	512,000	12.87	CSS Co incorporated
1885	2	3,324	41,770	0	0	0	24	43,095	553,770	12.57	
1886	2	4,206	50,725	3	3,635	66,532	23	43,666	537,963	12.06	
1887	1	2,924	34,460	1	2,126	38,000	23	44,464	534,423	11.79	
1888	2	6,039	67,050	1	1,231	26,477	24	49,272	574,996	11.10	
1889	6	19,033	218,000	3	6,101	82,400	27	62,204	710,596	11.45	Star Line purchased (4)
1890	2	3,733	48,000	2	4,457	45,039	27	61,480	713,557	12.86	
1891	3	12,955	162,110	2	3,681	72,788	28	70,754	802,879	12.51	
1892	0	0	0	0	0	0	28	70,754	802,879		
1893	2	9,439	116,364	2	4,435	77,900	28	75,758	841,343	12.33	
1894	2	9,654	103,875	1	3,175	50,000	29	82,237	895,218	10.76	
1895	1	6,322	68,294	1	2,593	21,500	29	85,966	942,012	10.80	
1896	2	11,922	123,206	1	1,443	46,000	30	96,445	1,019,218	10.33	
1897	1	6,196	70,580	3	5,010	73,365	28	97,631	1,016,433	11.39	
1898	1	6,116	75,000	3	6,542	71,850	26	97,205	1,019,583	12.26	
1899	2	14,451	162,000	1	2,667	45,282	27	108,989	1,136,301	11.21	
1900	3	25,539	310,233	1	2,623	43,500	29	131,905	1,403,034	12.15	
1901	2	14,853	221,595	1	4,753	60,000	30	142,005	1,564,629	14.92	
1902	3	12,459	147,573	0	0	0	33	154,464	1,712,202	11.84	
1903	5	29,333	361,119	2	4,710	73,750	36	179,087	1,999,571	12.31	
1904	3	14,219	162,282	1	7,379	107,374	38	185,927	2,054,479	11.41	
1905	3	10,544	124,086	3	6,864	95,365	38	189,607	2,083,200	11.77	
1906	2	9,042	118,633	1	2,011	27,500	39	196,638	2,174,333	13.12	
1907		0	0	0	0	0	39	196,638	2,174,333		
1908	3	15,510	171,787	0	0	0	42	212,148	2,346,120	11.08	
1909	1	3,570	39,600	2	6,380	83,000	41	209,338	2,302,720	11.09	
1910	4	22,448	238,287	2	5,686	67,725	43	226,100	2,473,282	10.62	
1911	8	28,201	274,047	0	0	0	51	254,301	2,747,329	9.72	Rennie Line purchase (7)
1912	5	30,119	362,089	2	8,632	85,060	54	275,788	3,024,358	12.02	
1913	2	11,095	184,066	1	2,984	19,552	55	283,899	3,188,872	16.59	
1914	3	13,021	198,396	5	27,456	333,975	53	269,464	3,053,293	15.24	Outbreak WW1
1915	5	18,345	267,000	6	27,007	309,624	52	260,802	3,010,669	14.55	
1916	0	0	0	4	20,185	251,115	48	240,617	2,759,554		
1917	4	24,029	495,002	11	54,075	683,904	41	210,571	2,570,652	20.60	
1918	12	61,579	1,796,090	5	26,868	588,707	48	245,282	3,778,035	29.17	Saint Line purchased (12)
1919	0	0	0	3	12,668	134,151	45	232,614	3,643,884		
1920	14	64,743	2,801,868	3	17,661	191,115	56	279,696	6,254,637	43.28	Crown Line purchased (8)
1921	2	16,436	793,448	3	7,921	80,824	55	288,211	6,967,261	48.28	Scruttons purchased (5)
1922	2	7,903	376,010	5	24,264	302,351	52	271,850	7,040,920	47.58	
1923	0	0	0	4	28,467	320,579	48	243,383	6,720,341		
1924	3	15,181	251,183	0	0	0	51	258,564	6,971,524	16.55	
1925	4	21,237	454,669	7	27,509	812,483	48	252,292	6,613,710	21.41	

| Year | Fleet additions | | | Losses and sales | | | Fleet totals at 31 December | | | Avg. cost £/ton | Remarks |
	No	Gross tons	Purchase price £	No	Gross tons	Purchase price £	Total vessels	Total gross tons	Total purch. price		
1926	3	15,283	298,120	2	8,079	350,841	49	259,496	6,560,989	19.51	
1927	2	11,769	209,180	3	12,897	235,695	48	258,368	6,534,474	17.77	
1928	5	29,696	543,283	2	9,100	407,246	51	278,964	6,670,511	18.29	
1929	1	5,122	94,991	1	3,682	43,450	51	280,404	6,722,052	18.55	
1930	2	11,986	223,488	2	7,161	79,361	51	285,229	6,866,179	18.65	
1931	0	0	0	0	0	0	51	285,229	6,866,179		
1932	0	0	0	10	53,832	1,161,229	41	231,397	5,704,950		
1933	2	12,857	49,893	3	20,663	653,226	40	223,591	5,101,617	3.88	
1934	6	36,845	209,684	0	0	0	46	260,436	5,311,301	5.69	7 Leyland ships purchased.
1935	6	44,106	396,503	4	17,330	344,812	48	287,212	5,362,992	8.99	4 Furness ships purchased
1936	0	0	0	3	17,141	274,437	45	270,071	5,088,555		
1937	3	19,115	560,000	1	5,686	103,888	47	283,500	5,544,667	29.30	
1938	1	6,199	192,330	3	14,075	313,601	45	275,624	5,423,396	31.03	
1939	3	18,898	570,438	5	31,745	810,912	43	262,777	5,182,922	30.19	
1940	3	18,563	482,000	10	63,293	1,703,231	36	218,047	3,961,691	25.97	
1941	0	0	0	9	57,180	798,260	27	160,867	3,163,431		4 MOWT ships excluded
1942	0	0	0	3	16,278	222,071	24	144,589	2,941,360		1 MOWT ship excluded
1943	1	6,202	249,292	2	12,352	298,813	23	138,439	2,891,839	40.20	3 MOWT ships excluded
1944	1	6,202	249,139	3	15,282	285,457	21	129,359	2,855,521	40.17	4 MOWT ships excluded
1945	2	14,077	303,896	0	0	0	23	143,436	3,159,417	21.59	3 MOWT ships excluded
1946	5	33,532	708,649	0	0	0	28	176,968	3,868,066	21.13	1 MOWT ship excluded
1947	8	56,357	1,970,023	1	7,886	44,118	35	225,439	5,793,971	34.96	
1948	6	42,367	1,623,666	1	5,074	93,940	40	262,732	7,323,697	38.32	
1949	3	21,462	845,000	3	16,767	500,437	40	267,427	7,668,260	39.37	
1950	0	0	0	5	29,133	560,585	35	238,294	7,107,675		
1951	5	40,977	2,459,139	1	6,549	47,669	39	272,722	9,519,145	60.01	
1952	2	16,579	1,192,674	1	8,078	118,307	40	281,223	10,593,512	71.94	
1953	1	8,202	664,854	0	0	0	41	289,425	11,258,366	81.06	
1954	2	16,732	1,485,943	0	0	0	43	306,157	12,744,309	88.81	
1955	1	8,367	829,317	1	6,202	249,139	43	308,322	13,324,487	99.12	
1956	0	0	0	0	0	0	43	308,322	13,324,487		
1957	0	0	0	2	12,490	288,810	41	295,832	13,035,677		
1958	2	17,429	2,336,175	2	13,017	199,909	41	300,244	15,171,943	134.04	
1959	1	8,732	1,177,666	4	26,641	688,736	38	282,335	15,660,873	134.87	
1960	1	8,971	1,383,274	3	19,625	468,499	36	271,681	16,575,648	154.19	
1961	5	39,376	4,905,293	6	39,845	1,061,763	35	271,212	20,419,178	124.58	
1962	0	0	0	5	36,317	879,000	30	234,895	19,540,178		
1963	0	0	0	2	14,468	317,183	28	220,427	19,222,995		
1964	4	27,657	4,072,830	4	28,717	917,690	28	219,367	22,378,135	147.26	
1965	2	12,324	1,646,983	1	6,822	422,986	29	224,869	23,602,132	133.64	
1966	2	12,896	2,493,605	1	6,736	401,303	30	231,029	25,694,434	193.36	
1967	0	0	0	2	13,541	842,090	28	217,488	24,852,344		
1968	2	16,908	2,860,060	0	0	0	30	234,396	27,712,404	169.15	
1969	2	15,212	1,821,065	0	0	0	32	249,608	29,533,469	119.71	
1970	0	0	0	4	32,827	2,007,889	28	216,781	27,525,580		
1971	1	11,299	2,735,178	2	16,527	983,736	27	211,553	29,277,022	242.07	
1972	1	10,219	2,387,803	3	22,936	1,788,711	25	198,836	29,876,114	233.66	
1973	3	48,951	8,952,379	1	8,366	743,628	27	239,421	38,084,865	182.88	Blairdale bulkers
1974	0	0	0	1	8,366	742,315	26	231,055	37,342,550		
1975	2	71,432	18,255,140	1	8,367	829,317	27	294,120	54,768,373	255.56	
1976	0	0	0	0	0	0	27	294,120	54,768,373		
1977	2	55,736	19,283,217	5	30,810	4,167,185	24	319,046	69,884,405	345.97	2 container ships.
1978	1	53,790	14,169,740	3	24,629	3,325,707	22	348,207	80,728,438	263.43	⅓ of City of Durban
1979	0	0	0	7	57,806	8,117,766	15	290,401	72,610,672		
1980	0	0	0	2	12,896	2,493,605	13	277,505	70,117,067		

	Fleet additions			Losses and sales			Fleet totals at 31 December			Avg. cost £/ton	
Year	No	Gross tons	Purchase price £	No	Gross tons	Purchase price £	Total vessels	Total gross tons	Total purch. price		Remarks
1981	1	28,032	13,038,489	4	36,298	6,800,491	10	269,239	76,355,065	465.13	
1982	2	36,000	11,416,129	1	11,299	2,735,178	11	293,940	85,036,016	317.11	
1983	0	0	0	2	71,432	18,255,140	9	222,508	66,780,876		
1984	2	42,618	18,365,528	0	0	0	11	265,126	85,146,404	430.93	
1985	0	0	0	0	0	0	11	265,126	85,146,404		
1986	0	0	0	2	44,185	12,754,008	9	220,941	72,392,396		
1987	0	0	0	1	16,317	3,014,552	8	204,624	69,377,844		
1988	0	0	0	1	16,317	2,849,155	7	188,307	66,528,689		
1989	0	0	0	0	0	0	7	188,307	66,528,689		
1990	0	0	0	1	18,604	5,734,341	6	169,703	60,794,348		
1991	0	0	0	0	0	0	6	169,703	60,794,348		
1992	0	0	0	0	0	0	6	169,703	60,794,348		
1993	0	0	0	1	27,868	9,617,881	5	141,835	51,176,467		
1994	1	22,992	9,000,000	0	0	0	6	164,827	60,176,467	391.44	
1995	0	0	0	2	45,428	18,720,277	4	119,399	41,456,190		
1996	1	24,609	9,400,000	0	0	0	5	144,008	50,856,190	381.97	
1997	0	0	0	0	0	0	5	144,008	50,856,190		
1998	0	0	0	2	75,099	23,174,338	3	68,909	27,681,852		
1999	0	0	0	1	21,309	9,360,930	2	47,600	18,320,922		
2000	0	0	0	0	0	0	2	47,600	18,320,922		
2001	0	0	0	0	0	0	2	47,600	18,320,922		
2002	0	0	0	2	47,600	18,320,922	0	0	0		
Totals:	234	1,652,398	177,602,553	256	1,692,169	178,114,553				107.4	

APPENDIX 3: HARRISON VESSELS LOST
DURING THE FIRST WORLD WAR

Ship	gt	Attack date	Type	Approx.position.		Casualties POW	injd.	died	Enemy vessel, position
DIPLOMAT (1)	7,615	13.9.14	Raider	17.55 N	86.45 E	0	0	0	EMDEN, 480m NE of Madras
CANDIDATE (1)	4,521	06.5.15	U-boat/G	51.47 N	06.27 W	0	0	0	U 20, 16m SExS Saltees, Ireland
CENTURION (1)	5,945	06.5.15	U-boat/T	51.51 N	06.23 W	0	0	0	U 20, 15m S of Barrels, Ireland
GLADIATOR (2)	3,359	19.8.15	U-boat/T	50.59 N	06.47 W	0	0	0	U 27, 68m NxW of Bishop Rock
DICTATOR (1)	4,116	05.9.15	U-boat/G	49.36 N	08.48 W	0	0	0	U 20, 112m SxE½ E of Fastnet
CHANCELLOR (3)	4,545	23.9.15	U-boat/G	50.00 N	09.10 W	0	0	0	U 41, 86m SxE of Fastnet.
COMMODORE (1)	4521	02.12.15	U-boat/T	35.15 N	17.28 E	0	6	1	U 33, 145m ExS¼S of Malta.
AUTHOR (2)	3,490	13.1.16	Raider	39.05 N	13.56 W	56	0	0	MOEWE, 225m W ½ N of Lisbon
COUNSELLOR (2)	4,958	14.9.16	Mine	51.28 N	09.03 W	0	0	0	5m SW of Galley Head
STATESMAN (2)	6,322	03.11.16	U-boat/T	35.50 N	18.41 E	0	0	6	UB 43, 200m E of Malta
DRAMATIST (1)	5,415	18.12.16	Raider	33.12 N	37.40 W	50	0	0	MOEWE, 500m SW of Azores
ARTIST (2)	3,570	27.1.17	U-boat/T	51.37 N	07.14 W	0	0	35	U 55, 58m W½S of Smalls.
HUNTSMAN (1)	7,460	25.2.17	U-boat/T	53.04 N	13.38 W	0	0	2	U 50, 180m NWxW of Fastnet
GOVERNOR (2)	5,524	14.3.17	Raider	50.35 N	34.12 W	33	10	4	MOEWE, 930m W¼S of Fastnet
SCULPTOR (2)	3,845	18.4.17	U-boat/T	52.30 N	12.18 W	0	0	1	U 53, 120m NWxW of Fastnet
COMEDIAN (1)	4,889	29.4.17	U-boat/T	48.05 N	09.48 W	1	0	3	U 93, 170m SWxW of Bishop Rock
BARRISTER (2)	3,679	11.5.17	U-boat/T	51.54 N	07.43 W	0	0	0	U 49, 7m S of Mine Head, Waterford
ORATOR (2)	3,563	08.6.17	U-boat/T	51.56 N	11.41 W	0	0	5	U 96, 84m WNW of Fastnet
MATADOR (1)	3,400	03.7.17	U-boat/T	51.57 N	12.33 W	0	0	2	UC 31, 115m WxN½N of Fastnet
SPECTATOR (1)	3,808	19.8.17	U-boat/T	51.24 N	08.47 W	0	0	0	UC 33, 11m SE of Galley Head.
CIVILIAN	7,100	06.10.17	U-boat/T	31.27 N	29.52 E	0	0	2	UC 74, 15m N of Alexandria
COLLEGIAN (1)	7,237	20.10.17	U-boat/T	32.28 N	28.51 E	0	0	0	UB 48, 100m NWxN¼N of Alexandria
MECHANICIAN	9,044	20.1.18	U-boat/T	50.34 N	01.30 W	0	0	13	UB 35, 8m W of St. Catherines, IOW
INKOSI (1)	3,576	28.3.18	U-boat/T	54.32 N	04.30 W	0	0	3	U 96, 14m SExE½E of Mull of Galloway.
SCULPTOR (3)	4,874	17.5.18	U-boat/T	36.15 N	01.46 W	0	1	7	U 39, 60m NWxW¼W of Oran
INSTRUCTOR	4,422	14.7.18	Collision	43.50 N	34.50 W	0	0	16	Collision with US Transport AMERICA, 790m ExS of Cape Race
BARRISTER (3)	4,952	19.9.18	U-boat/T	54.04 N	05.05 W	0	0	30	UB 64, 9m W½N of Chicken Rock, IOM
Totals:	135,750					140	17	130	

APPENDIX 4: ANALYSIS OF SECOND WORLD WAR SERVICE AND CASUALTIES IN HARRISON VESSELS

1. The Second World War, from its outbreak on 3rd September 1939 to the surrender of Japanese forces on 14th August 1945, lasted a total of 2,173 days. During this period, 64 steam-vessels, owned or operated by Harrison Line and manned by Harrison-employed personnel, were deployed at sea at various times. Twenty-seven of these vessels were sunk by enemy action, and four were lost as a result of marine peril. Seventeen vessels survived the war at sea from beginning to end, and of these, only three were ever damaged by enemy action.

2. By summation of the number of days served by each vessel, and multiplying by the number of crew members, an estimate of the number of man-days served during the war is obtained.

Total ship days	69,162;
Total man days	4,618,242 (average crew 66.77)

3. The total number of man-days divided by the war's duration of 2,173 days gives the average overall total of the number of men employed at sea in Harrison vessels, viz:

$$4,618,242 \div 2,173 = 2,215 \text{ men}$$

Similarly, the average overall deployment of vessels throughout the war was,

$$69,162 \div 2,173 = 32 \text{ ships}$$

Incidentally, a small number of women are included in the crew estimates, notably as stewardesses in the INANDA and INKOSI in the early months of the war, and also in ADVISER, SETTLER and STRATEGIST after their conversion to carry 60 passengers. None, however, were numbered among the casualties.

4. Casualty figures

(a) Table 4.1 lists casualties on vessels lost during the war, taken from Harrison Line records.

(b) If these figures are applied to the actual 27 ships in which the casualties occurred, a seaman's chances of escaping unscathed were little better than 50/50. The actual number of men on board the 27 ships when they were sunk was 1,717 - a comparatively low figure due to the fact that INANDA and INKOSI were sunk in dock undergoing a refit, with only a scratch crew on board.

Killed	422 =	24.6% of men on board (1,717).
Injured	37 =	2.1% of men on board
POW - early release	170 =	9.9% of men on board
POW - duration	202 =	11.8% of men on board
Total	831 =	48.4% of men on board

(c) From the foregoing, it might be assumed that 408 men, or 19.2% of seafarers, had a comparatively quiet war. This assumption, however, would be misleading even if one ignores the crews of the four ships lost by marine peril (in which there were no casualties). Many ships saw plenty of action in convoy, but were lucky to escape when many did not. Many were attacked by aircraft while in port; some of these sustained damage and suffered casualties which are not included in the figures for ships lost.

5. The number of men employed in a ship's crew tended to vary considerably from voyage to voyage. A Lascar crew could be as much as 50% larger than a "white" crew, and these were often switched indiscriminately, often on alternate voyages. Moreover, a Lascar crew, due for repatriation to India, could double the normal complement to as many as 134 men, as in the case of the TRIBESMAN (241) when she was sunk. On the other hand, in home ports, particularly during a refit, the crew might be reduced to a fifth of its normal strength. Then, as time went on, crews would be supplemented by four, six, or as many as twelve, marine gunners seconded from the Maritime Division of the Royal Artillery as anti-aircraft armament increased in power and sophistication. Therefore, estimating an average crew for each ship in the fleet throughout the war is a daunting task. The writer's estimates in Table 4.2 are based on entries in the Crew Books of the period, an exercise which has been conducted as precisely as possible. Even so, he would be the first to concede that the margin for error is a broad one, but would also maintain that the overall average figure extracted (about 67 men per vessel per voyage) is not unreasonable in the circumstances.

6. Behind these prosaic but revealing statistics lies a long history of sacrifice which the nation can ill afford to forget. They apply to only one British shipping company, and the figures should be multiplied by a factor of 60 or 70 to reach a comparable estimate for the Merchant Navy as a whole.

After surviving one, or even more attacks, merchant seamen regularly went back to sea. Of course, they and their families needed the money, but the call of duty was stronger. No man wanted to experience the loss of his ship by having it blown up from under him, leaving him to fight a puny struggle for survival against the forces of nature, yet the idea of staying at home while still mentally and physically fit was unthinkable. True, most seamen preferred the familiar dangers of a life at sea to the unknown and often imaginary horrors of life in the Army. And the pay was certainly better. Still, Jack was essentially a civilian, albeit a belligerent one when roused, or in his cups, but he was always deeply sceptical about guns and explosives, no matter how ready he might be to settle more mundane disputes with his fists.

7. The analysis of casualties described above may perhaps be seen in better perspective when compared with those listed in Table 4.5.

Table 4.1: Casualties on vessels lost during the war, taken from Harrison Line records

Fate	Number	Percentage of total work force (2,125).
Killed	422	19.9%
Injured	37	1.7%
POW released early	170	8.0%
POW for duration	202	9.5%
Total	**831**	**39.1%**

(8 vessels suffered casualties in excess of 85%; 9 had less than 5%).

Table 4.2: Summary of fleet war service, 3rd September 1939 to 14th August 1945

Vessel	Days in war service	Average crew	Man days	Fate and remarks
ADVISER (1)	2,173	72	156,456	Survived torpedo attack and the war.
ARICA	449	63	28,287	MOWT Sunk by enemy action - submarine.
ASTRONOMER (3)	274	55	15,070	Sunk by enemy action - submarine
ATLANTIAN	2,173	68	147,764	Survived the war.
AUDITOR	671	73	48,983	Sunk by enemy action - submarine
BARRISTER (4)	1,218	59	71,862	Wrecked, West of Ireland.
CHANCELLOR (4)	91	45	4,095	Foundered after collision.
COLLEGIAN (3)	2,173	60	130,380	Survived submarine attack and the war.
COLONIAL (2)	632	54	34,128	Sunk by enemy action - submarine.
COMEDIAN (3)	2,173	63	136,899	Survived collision and the war.
CONTRACTOR	1,435	76	109,060	Sunk by enemy action - submarine
COUNSELLOR (4)	188	57	10,716	Sunk by enemy action - mine.
CRAFTSMAN (3)	585	52	30,420	Sunk by enemy action - raider.
CUSTODIAN (2)	2,173	64	139,072	Survived the war.
DALESMAN (1)	309	56	17,304	Sunk by enemy action - bombed.
DAVISIAN	312	48	14,976	Sunk by enemy action - raider.
DAYTONIAN	923	57	52,611	Sunk by enemy action - submarine.
DEFENDER (1)	2,173	66	143,418	Survived the War.
DESIGNER	676	78	52,728	Sunk by enemy action - submarine.
DIPLOMAT (2)	452	53	23,956	Sunk by enemy action - submarine.
DIRECTOR (2)	1,776	70	124,320	Sunk by enemy action - submarine.
DRAMATIST (2)	2,173	60	130,380	Survived the war.
EMPIRE ADDISON	735	68	49,980	MOWT Survived the war.
EMPIRE CAPTAIN	418	90	37,620	MOWT Survived the war.
EMPIRE CHIVALRY	1,355	64	86,720	MOWT Survived the war.
EMPIRE EXPLORER	148	73	10,804	MOWT Sunk by enemy action - submarine.
EMPIRE GAZELLE	1,478	50	73,900	MOWT Survived the war.
EMPIRE LIFE	102	80	8,160	MOWT Survived the war.
EMPIRE NEWTON	456	73	33,288	MOWT Survived the war.
EMPIRE RANGOON	442	76	33,592	MOWT Survived the war.
EMPIRE SERVICE	132	60	7,920	MOWT Survived the war.
EMPIRE TRUMPET	242	56	13,552	MOWT Survived the war.
EXPLORER (3)	2,173	68	147,764	Survived the war.
GEOLOGIST (2)	543	72	39,096	Survived the war.
GOVERNOR (3)	2,173	65	141,245	Survived the war.
HISTORIAN (3)	2,173	63	136,899	Survived the war.
HUNTSMAN (2)	38	82	3,116	Sunk by enemy action - raider.
INANDA (2)	371	98	36,358	Sunk by enemy action - bombed.
INKOSI (2)	371	78	28,938	Sunk by enemy action - bombed
INVENTOR (3)	2,173	70	152,110	Survived the war.
LOGICIAN (2)	622	56	34,832	Sunk by enemy action - bombed
MAGICIAN (2)	1,686	80	134,880	Wrecked, Peterhead.
MERCHANT (3)	844	45	37,980	Sunk by enemy action - mined
NOVELIST (1)	1,833	76	139,308	Survived the war.
OBSERVER	1,201	80	96,080	Sunk by enemy action - submarine.
PLANTER (1)	441	73	32,193	Sunk by enemy action - submarine.
POLITICIAN (2)	522	50	26,100	Wrecked, Eriskay.
PROSPECTOR	605	54	32,670	Survived the war.
RANCHER	2,173	80	173,840	Survived the war.
RECORDER	2,173	60	130,380	Survived the war.
SAMARINDA	655	52	34,060	MOWT Survived the war.
SAMWIS	670	52	34,840	MOWT Survived the war.
SCHOLAR (2)	385	43	16,555	Sunk by enemy action - submarine.
SCIENTIST (2)	244	79	19,276	Sunk by enemy action - raider.
SETTLER (2)	2,173	80	173,840	Survived the war.
STATESMAN (4)	623	51	31,773	Sunk by enemy action - bombed.
STRATEGIST (1)	2,173	80	173,840	Survived the war.
TACTICIAN (2)	2,173	70	152,110	Survived the war.
TRADER (1)	1,698	76	129,048	Survived the war.
TRAVELLER (2)	877	52	45,604	Sunk by enemy action - submarine.
TRIBESMAN (1)	456	116	52,896	Sunk by enemy action - raider.
WANDERER (2)	2,173	60	130,380	Survived the war.
WAYFARER (2)	1,993	60	119,580	Sunk by enemy action - submarine.
WINNIPEG	41	50	2,050	MOWT Sunk later.
Total	**69,162**	**66.77**	**4,618,242**	

Notes

War service is calculated for the period between 3rd September 1939 and 14th August 1945, i.e 2,173 days or 313.3 weeks.

Average length of war service for the 64 ships listed above: 69,162 ÷ 64 = 1,081 days

Average number of Harrison ships deployed during war: 69,162 ÷ 2,173 = 31.83 ships

Average number of men employed on Harrison ships during war: 31.83 x 66.77 = 2,125 men

17 vessels served throughout the war and survived.

Table 4.3: Vessels lost and casualties during the Second World War

Vessel	GT	Attack Ddate	Type	Saved Unin-jured	Injured	Taken Prisoner Early Release	Taken Prisoner For Duration	Killed/ Died in Action	Total Died Later		Remarks
Through enemy action											
HUNTSMAN	8,196	10.10.39	R	-	-	82	-	-	-	82	4 released from GRAF SPEE 78 released from ALTMARK
COUNSELLOR	5,068	8.3.40	M	58	9	-	-	-	-	67	
SCIENTIST	6,199	3.5.40	R	-	-	47	24	1	4	76	47 released from Mogadishu
ASTRONOMER	8,681	2.6.40	S	39	11		-	4		54	
DAVISIAN	6,433	10.7.40	R	-	-	40	8	1	1	50	40 released in Lifeboat
INANDA	5,985	7.9.40	B	33	4	-	-	5	-	42	Stand-by crew
INKOSI	6,618	7.9.40	B	26	1	-	-		-	27	Stand-by crew
SCHOLAR	3,940	21.9.40	S	41	4	-	-		-	45	
PLANTER	5,887	16.11.40	S	15	-	-	-	13	44	72	43 Lascars lost in JUMNA on repatriation voyage
DIPLOMAT	8,240	27.11.40	S	43			-	14	-	57	
TRIBESMAN	6,242	1.12.40	R	-	-	-	76	59	-	135	54 Lascars on board ex-EXPLORER, repatriation
CRAFTSMAN	7,896	9.4.41	R		-	1	42	5	1	49	
STATESMAN	7,939	17.5.41	B	50	1	-	-	1	-	52	
LOGICIAN	5,993	25.5.41	B	27	-	-	21	5	-	53	9 POWs injured
COLONIAL	5,108	26.5.41	S	73	3	-	-	-	-	76	
DALESMAN	6,343	14.5.41	B	24	1	-	31	-	1	57	
AUDITOR	5,444	4.7.41	S	69	-	-	-	1	1	71	
DESIGNER	5,945	9.7.41	S	11	-	-	-	65	3	79	
MERCHANT	4,572	24.12.41	M	42	2	-	-	1	-	45	
TRAVELLER	3,963	26.1.42	S	-	-	-	-	52	-	52	
DAYTONIAN	6,434	13.3.42	S	57	-	-	-	1	-	58	
EMPIRE EXPLORER	5,345	9.7.42	S	68	-	-	-	3	-	71	
ARICA	5,379	6.11.42	S	52	1	-	-	12	-	65	
OBSERVER	5,881	16.12.42	S	15	-	-	-	66	-	81	
CONTRACTOR	6,004	7.8.43	S	76	-	-	-	5	2	83	
DIRECTOR	5,107	14.7.44	S	57	-	-	-	1	-	58	
WAYFARER	5,068	19.8.44	S	10	-	-	-	51	-	61	
Total	163,910			886	37	170	202	366	57	1,718	
					924		372	423			
Marine causes											
POLITICIAN	7,940	5.2.41	W	50	-	-	-	-	-	50	
CHANCELLOR	4,607	2.12.39	C	42	-	-	-	-	-	42	
BARRISTER	6,348	4.1.43	W	74		-		-	-	74	
MAGICIAN	5,105	22.5.44	W	80		-		-	-	80	
Total	24,000			246	-		-		-	246	
Grand total	187,910			1,169		372			423	1,964	
				59.5%		19%			21.5%		

KEY:- B = Bombed by aircraft   R = Raider   S = Submarine   C = Sunk in collision   M = Mine   W = Wrecked

The deep-laden four-masted *Diplomat* (202) ready to sail from the Mersey.

[J. and M. Clarkson]

Table 4.4: Fatal casualties 1939-1945 by ship and rank

Vessel	Masters	Chief Engrs.	Officer Cadets	Engrs.	Chief St'ds	Radio Off'rs	Surg	Pursers	Passengers	Euro. Ratings	Lascars	West Indians	Total
HUNTSMAN	-	-	-	-	-	-	-	-	-	-	-	-	-
COUNSELLOR	-	-	-	-	-	-	-	-	-	-	-	-	-
SCIENTIST	-	1	-	-	-	-	-	-	1	-	3	-	5
ASTRONOMER	-	-	-	-	-	-	-	-	-	4	-	-	4
DAVISIAN		-	1	-	-	-	-	-	-	1	-	-	2
INANDA	-	-	-	-	-	-	-	-	-	-	-	5	5
INKOSI	-	-	-	-	-	-	-	-	-	-	-	-	-
SCHOLAR	-	-	-	-	-	-	-	-	-	-	-	-	-
PLANTER	-	1	-	-	1	1	-	-	1	2	51	-	57
DIPLOMAT	-	-	-	-	1	-	-	-	1	12	-	-	14
TRIBESMAN	1	1	3	-	1	2	1	-	-	5	45	-	59
CRAFTSMAN	-	1	1	1	-	-	-	-	-	3	-	-	6
STATESMAN	-	-	1	-	-	-	-	-	-	-	-	-	1
LOGICIAN	-		-	-	-	-	-	-	-	5	-	-	5
COLONIAL		-	-	-	-	-	-	-	-	-	-	-	-
DALESMAN		-	-	-	1	-	-	-	-	-	-	-	1
AUDITOR	-	-	-	-	1	-	-	-	-	-	1	-	2
DESIGNER	1	1	6	3	1	3	-	-	-	10	42	-	67
MERCHANT	-	-	-	-	-	-	-	-	-	1	-	-	1
TRAVELLER	1	1	5	3	1	3	-	1	-	9	-	28	52
DAYTONIAN	-	-	-	-	-	-	-	-	-	1	-	-	1
EMP. EXPLORER	-	-	-	-	-	-	-	-	-	-	-	3	3
ARICA	-		-	3	-	-	-	-	-	1	-	8	12
OBSERVER	1	1	6	3	1	3	-	-	-	12	39	-	66
CONTRACTOR	1	-	1	-	-	-	-	-	-	2	3	-	7
DIRECTOR	-	-	-	-	1	-	-	-	-	-	-	-	1
WAYFARER	1	1	5	2	-	3	-	-	1	38	-	-	51
TOTAL	6	8	28	16	8	16	1	1	4	106	184	44	422

Table 4.5: Fatal casualties suffered by the armed forces of the main belligerents during the Second World War
Source: Dupuy RE and TN The Encyclopaedia of Military History, Janes, 1986

Nation	Forces mobilised	Fatal casualties	Percentage
UK	6,200,000	397,762	6.4%
USA	14,900,000	292,100	2.0%
USSR	20,000,000	7,500,000	37.5%
France	6,000,000	210,671	3.5%
Australia	575,111	33,826	5.9%
Germany	12,500,000	2,850,000	22.8%
Italy	4,500,000	77,500	1.7%
Japan	7,400,000	1,506,000	20.4%
British Merchant Navy	130,000	29,996	23.1%
Harrison Line	2,125	422	19.9%

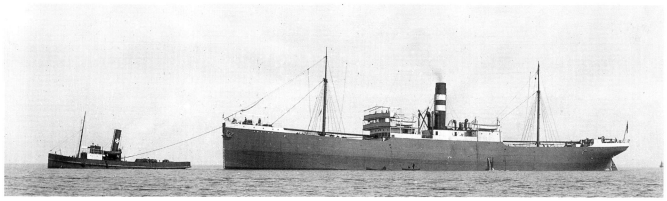

Orator (138).

[*K.O.Donoghue collection*]

APPENDIX 5: A ROLL OF HONOUR OF THOSE WHO LOST THEIR LIVES AT SEA IN HARRISON VESSELS, 1939-1945

Name	Rank	Ship
ABBOT, H.	Able seaman	WAYFARER
ACKERLEY, A.E.	Third officer	TRAVELLER
AINSWORTH, J.	Ordinary seaman	WAYFARER
ALLEN, E.*	Fireman	INANDA
ANDERSON, F.W.*	Fireman	TRAVELLER
ANDREWS, A.E.G.	Chief steward	TRIBESMAN
ASHBOURNE, R.	Able seaman	WAYFARER
ASHBY, V.*	Fireman	ARICA
ATKINS, Garfield*	Able seaman	TRAVELLER
BANCROFT, D.T.*	Fireman	TRAVELLER
BANCROFT, M.*	Fireman	TRAVELLER
BARRETT, J.J.	Assistant steward.	DESIGNER
BARVEY, L.W.	Deck hand	OBSERVER
BERQUEST, J.	Greaser	WAYFARER
BIGGS, W.A.	Quartermaster	TRIBESMAN
BIRTWHISTLE, J.	Fourth officer	DESIGNER
BLACKETT, M.*	Able seaman	TRAVELLER
BRAND, D.	Fireman	ASTRONOMER
BREHEIST, J.A.	Chief steward	DIPLOMAT
BRIMS, Andrew	Master	CONTRACTOR
BULPETT, W.	Quartermaster	OBSERVER
CAMPBELL, H.	Quartermaster	PLANTER
CAMPBELL, J.	Fireman	LOGICIAN
CANHAM, D.A.	Third radio officer	WAYFARER
CARRUTHERS, R.S.	Chief engineer	CRAFTSMAN
CATTERALL, R.A.	Second engineer	WAYFARER
CAVE, Archibald*	Fireman	TRAVELLER
CAVE, W.R.	Lamp trimmer	WAYFARER
CHICKEN, C.	Passenger	SCIENTIST
CLARKE, C.*	Greaser	ARICA
CLARKE, Vernon*	Able seaman	TRAVELLER
CONNOR, F.	Fireman	LOGICIAN
CONNOR, H	Messroom steward	WAYFARER
COOK, D.	Assistant engineer	CRAFTSMAN
CORRIE, P.A.B.	Second radio officer	DESIGNER
COURT, C.	Able seaman	WAYFARER
COWARD, E.M.	First radio officer	TRAVELLER
COWELL, J.R.	Second officer	TRAVELLER
CURTIS, H.	Sailor	DESIGNER
DAVIDSON, J.	Master	OBSERVER
DAVIES, Henry*	Lamp trimmer	TRAVELLER
DAVIES, T.	Third officer	OBSERVER
DAVIES, T.	First radio officer	WAYFARER
DEANE, P.	Officer's boy	TRAVELLER
DEVANEY, J.	Carpenter	TRAVELLER
DEWAR, A.McD.	Chief officer	TRIBESMAN
DEWAR, G.	Second.officer	STATESMAN
DICKINSON, A.M.	Third radio officer	OBSERVER
DOLLAH, J.	Able seaman	WAYFARER
DONNELLY, E.	Quartermaster	TRIBESMAN
DOYLE, R.	Chief steward	AUDITOR
DUMBILL, P.	Chief steward	PLANTER
DUNN, G.B.	Messroom steward	TRAVELLER
DUNN, M.L.	Fireman	CRAFTSMAN
DUNPHY, T.O.	First radio officer	PLANTER
DUNSTAN, L.S.	Third radio officer	DESIGNER
EBSARY, J.	Ordinary seaman	WAYFARER
EDNEY, W.J.	Deck hand	OBSERVER
EDWARDS, R.	Carpenter	TRIBESMAN
ELLIS, R.M.	Chief engineer	PLANTER
EVANS, A.E.	Deck hand	WAYFARER
EVANS, F.	Deck hand	OBSERVER
EVANS, W.J.	Able seaman	DIPLOMAT
EXON, R.W.	Third engineer	TRAVELLER

Name	Rank	Ship
FARLEY, H.	Deck hand	WAYFARER
FARRAND, H.	Deck hand	OBSERVER
FARRELL, G.	Quartermaster	DESIGNER
FERNS, F.J.	ER storekeeper	CRAFTSMAN
FITZSIMMONS, H.M.	Master	TRAVELLER
FOSTER, W.	Able seaman	CRAFTSMAN
FORBES, J.S.	First radio officer	DESIGNER
FOULDE, N.	Fourth engineer	WAYFARER
FOULIS, J.	Ordinary seaman	DIPLOMAT
FOWLER, Sydney*	Fireman	TRAVELLER
FRITH, T.	Fourth Engineer	OBSERVER
FROST, Leslie	Second officer	WAYFARER
GIBBONS, P.	Fireman	DIPLOMAT
GIBSON, B.	Fourth Engineer	ARICA
GILL, W.*	Fireman	EMPIRE EXPLORER
GILLIN, J.	Able seaman	WAYFARER
GOLDHAM, A.	Able seaman	WAYFARER
GOSLING, Cardinal*	Fireman	TRAVELLER
GRAFTON, S.M.	Ordinary seaman	WAYFARER
GRAVES, E.*	Fireman	ARICA
GRICE, R.F.	Fireman	DIPLOMAT
HAMBLIN, Egbert*	Bosun	TRAVELLER
HAMBLIN, McDonald*	Ordinary seaman	TRAVELLER
HANCOCK, T.A.	Fireman	WAYFARER
HANDLEY, T.	Fireman	DIPLOMAT
HARDING, Alfred*	Cook	TRAVELLER
HARRIS, T.E.	Chief engineer	TRIBESMAN
HAYCOCKS, John	Second officer	DESIGNER
HEFFERMAN, J.	Fireman	WAYFARER
HOLDER, E.*	Fireman	ARICA
HOLDER, E.*	Fireman	EMP. EXPLORER
HOLDSWORTH, W.	Surgeon	TRIBESMAN
HOPKINSON, R.	Galley boy	WAYFARER
HUGHES, T.W.	Second radio officer	WAYFARER
JENKINS, R.	Fireman	WAYFARER
JOHNSON, J.	Carpenter	PLANTER
JOHNSTON, R.W.	Chief engineer	OBSERVER
JONES, E.	First radio officer	OBSERVER
JONES, P.B.	Third officer	TRIBESMAN
JONES, T.	Able seaman	DAYTONIAN
JOSSE, K.	Deck boy	LOGICIAN
KANE, F.	Third radio officer	TRAVELLER
KIBBLE, A.H.	Cadet	TRIBESMAN
KIMMIETT, M	Assistant steward	TRIBESMAN
KING, Leonard*		TRAVELLER
KING, Wycliffe*	Fireman	TRAVELLER
KIRWAN, P.J.	Second radio officer	TRAVELLER
LAVELLE, T.	Fireman	DAVISIAN
LAW, E.S.	Cadet	DESIGNER
LAYNE, Cheeseman*	Greaser	TRAVELLER
LEE, T.	Donkeyman	DIPLOMAT
LENNON, J.	Quartermaster	DESIGNER
LEWIS, S.W.	First radio officer	TRIBESMAN
LEYLAND, S.H.	Chief officer	OBSERVER
LICORISH, Lionel*	Able seaman	TRAVELLER
MACDONALD, A.J.		CONTRACTOR
MACKEY, I.	Cadet	TRAVELLER
McCAFFNEY, E.	Able seaman	WAYFARER
McCALLUM, D.A.	Master	DESIGNER
McCARTNEY, R.	Fireman	DIPLOMAT
McCOY, H.	Donkeyman	WAYFARER

Name	Rank	Ship
McCULLOCH, J.L.	Second engineer	DAVISIAN
McCUTCHEON, J.	Fireman	WAYFARER
McKAY, W.	Deck hand	OBSERVER
McKENZIE, K.	DBS	WAYFARER
McMAHON, W.	Quartermaster	DESIGNER
McNAMARA, T.	Deck hand	DESIGNER
McNICHOLAS, J.P.	Fireman	WAYFARER
MAGNIER, J.	Quartermaster	OBSERVER
MALABAR, A.	Third engineer	ARICA
MALONE, J.	Fireman	WAYFARER
METCALF, E.J.	Second cook	WAYFARER
METCALF, H.E.	Chief cook	WAYFARER
MOFFAT, L.J.	Cadet	WAYFARER
MONTGOMERY, W.#	Chief steward	DALESMAN
MOODY H.	Deck hand	DESIGNER
MOONEY, M.F.	Quartermaster	DESIGNER
MORGAN, W. *	Steward's boy	TRAVELLER
MORRIS, C.*	Fireman	ARICA
MORRIS, J.*	Fireman	ARICA
MORRIS, J.H.	Purser	TRAVELLER
MUGFORD, T.M.	Sailor	OBSERVER
MURRAY, H.*	Fireman	INANDA
MUSGROVE, W.E.	Deck hand	DESIGNER
NISBET, A.J.	Deck hand	DESIGNER
O'BRIEN, J.	Donkeyman	MERCHANT
O'CONNELL, G.*	Fireman	TRAVELLER
O'NEALE, C.*	Greaser	EMP. EXPLORER
O'PREY, H.	Fireman	DIPLOMAT
OTHER, W.	Second steward.	WAYFARER
PARFITT, S.*	Fireman	ARICA
PEARSON, J.	Second radio officer	OBSERVER
PHILLIPS, M.S.	Chief engineer	DESIGNER
PHILPOT, H.W.G.	Master	TRIBESMAN
PINK, W.E.	Cadet	WAYFARER
POLLOCK, J.	Fourth engineer	DESIGNER
POOLER, Adalbert*	Able seaman	TRAVELLER
POTTER, F.W.	Fireman	WAYFARER
POWELL, J.M.	Deck hand	WAYFARER
PRESCOD, Rubing*	Fireman	TRAVELLER
PRITCHARD, C.M.	Second radio officer	TRIBESMAN
PUCKETT, W.A.	Second steward.	TRAVELLER
QUINE, G.L.	Chief engineer	TRAVELLER
QUILLAN, W.	Donkeyman	WAYFARER
RAWLINSON, J.	Officer's boy	LOGICIAN
RAY, J.	Deck hand	OBSERVER
REES, K.	Fireman	LOGICIAN
REID, A.	Quartermaster	OBSERVER
REYNOLDS, J.T.	Deck hand	OBSERVER
RICHARDS, J.H.	Cadet	CRAFTSMAN
RICHARDS, R.I.	Second engineer	DESIGNER
RILEY, D.S.*	Fireman	TRAVELLER
ROACH, Evan*	Second cook	TRAVELLER
ROBERTS, D.D.	Cadet	OBSERVER
ROBERTS, H.	Chief cook	DIPLOMAT
ROBERTS, J.	Second officer	OBSERVER
ROBERTS, J.H.	Chief officer	TRAVELLER
ROBERTS, R	ER storekeeper	WAYFARER
ROBERTS, S.M.	Extra third officer	OBSERVER
ROCKLIFF, F.E.	Deck Hand	DESIGNER
ROGERS, A.E.	Chief officer	WAYFARER
ROLSTONE, F.*	Able seaman	TRAVELLER
ROSS, G.	Fireman	ASTRONOMER
RUDLING, E.M.	Sailor	TRAVELLER
SALKELD, F.	Carpenter	ARICA
SCARROW, R.B.	Chief engineer	SCIENTIST
SCOTT, W.E.*	Fireman	INANDA
SERGEANT, E.	Third engineer	DESIGNER
SERGEANT, W.	Third engineer	OBSERVER
SHEEHY, P.	Able seaman	DIPLOMAT
SHERIDAN, J.	Fourth engineer	TRAVELLER
SHERIDAN, T.	Fireman	WAYFARER
SHUTTLEWORTH, F.	Chief steward.	DESIGNER
SIMPSON, L.	Ordinary seaman	WAYFARER
SIMPSON, L.	Deck hand	OBSERVER
SINCLAIR, J.C.	Chief officer	CONTRACTOR
SMITH, J.E.	Cadet	TRAVELLER
SMITH, St.Clair*	Able seaman	TRAVELLER
SMITH, St.Elmo*	Ordinary seaman	TRAVELLER
SOBERS, Stanley*	Fireman	TRAVELLER
SOUTHWORTH, H.	Second engineer	OBSERVER
STEVENSON, J.	Chief engineer	WAYFARER
STEVENTON, F.	Third officer	DESIGNER
STOKES, T.	Chief steward.	TRAVELLER
SULLIVAN, J.	Able seaman	WAYFARER
SWIFT, R.D.	Officer's boy	WAYFARER
TALBOT, J.S.	Cadet	DESIGNER
TAYLOR, F.	Quartermaster	TRIBESMAN
TAYLOR, G.H.	Deck hand	WAYFARER
THARRETT, F.	Fireman	WAYFARER
THOMAS, R.	Cadet	OBSERVER
THOMPSON, Hilary*	Fireman	TRAVELLER
TOUGH, A.	Fireman	ASTRONOMER
TRACEY, J.	First radio officer	DIRECTOR
TROTMAN, J.*	Able seaman	ARICA
VARTY, J.	Second engineer	TRAVELLER
WAISON, A.McD.*	Fireman	TRAVELLER
WALES, J.	Master	WAYFARER
WALMSLEY, F.	Second engineer	ARICA
WALTER, S.	Fireman	WAYFARER
WALTERS, L.	Deck hand	TRAVELLER
WANDELL, J.	Deck hand	WAYFARER
WARREN, J.T.	Third officer	WAYFARER
WATTERSON, G.	Able seaman	DIPLOMAT
WEIR, J.	Ordinary seaman	TRAVELLER
WILKINSON, C.J.	Chief steward	OBSERVER
WILLIAMS, R.	Able seaman	DIPLOMAT
WILLIS, G.	Deck hand	TRAVELLER
WOOD, A.J.	Chief officer	DESIGNER
WOODWARD, W.		CONTRACTOR
YOUNGER, R.P.	Cadet	DESIGNER

* West Indian crew member
# Died in prisoner-of-war camp

To this list should be added the names of 189 unknown seafarers which, for one reason or another, are not in any available records.

3 Asian seamen		SCIENTIST
1 British seaman		ASTRONOMER
2 West Indian seamen		INANDA
1 British seaman		PLANTER
8 Asian seamen		PLANTER
43 Asian seamen lost while being repatriated in Nourse Line's JUMNA		PLANTER
1 French passenger		DIPLOMAT
45 Asian seamen		TRIBESMAN
1 Asian seaman		AUDITOR
42 Asian seamen		DESIGNER
39 Asian seamen		OBSERVER
3 Asian seamen		CONTRACTOR

APPENDIX 6: AWARDS FOR MERITORIOUS CONDUCT AND SERVICE AT SEA TO HARRISON LINE PERSONNEL 1939 - 1945

Name	Rank	Ship	Award	Citation	Date of investiture
ALLAN, W. Hay	Chief Officer	DIRECTOR	King's Commendation	For Meritorious Service in M.N.	16.10.45
APPS, Arthur	Bosun	WAYFARER	B.E.M. and Bar	For Meritorious Service in M.N.	8.1.44 8.5.45
BENNETT, E.	Master	AUDITOR	O.B.E.	For Meritorious Servicein M.N.	1941
BRAMHILL, W.F.	Third Officer	MERCHANT	King's Commendation	For Meritorious Conduct in Action.	9.7.41
COVENTRY, W.	Donkeyman	DIRECTOR	B.E.M.	For Meritorious Service in M.N.	3.1.45
CUBBIN, John W.	Chief Engineer	-	O.B.E.	For Meritorious Service in M.N.	24. 6.46.
DALY, C.A.V.	Second Officer	ATLANTIAN	King's Commendation	For Meritorious Conduct in Action	19.6.42
DOBSON, J.H.	Cadet	DALESMAN	B.E.M.	For Meritorious Conduct in Action.	4.8.42
DOUGLAS-KERR, D.	Second Officer	DIRECTOR	King's Commendation	For Meritorious Service in M.N.	9.1.45.
DUFF, N. Vivian	Chief Engineer	DIRECTOR	King's Commendation	For Meritorious Service in M.N.	16.10.45.
GRIERSON, J.W.	Second Engineer	NOVELIST	M.B.E.	For Meritorious Servicein M.N.	15.6.45.
HATTON, G.	Quartermaster	TACTICIAN	B.E.M.	For Meritorious Servicein M.N.	3.1.45
HEATON, A.A.	Chief Officer	-	King's Commendation	For Meritorious Service in M.N.	1943.
HOWARTH, H H	Able Seaman	ADVISER	B.E.M.	For Meritorious Service in M.N.	9.1.46
JONES, H.W.	Chief Officer	DALESMAN	M.B.E. King's Commendation	For Meritorious Service in M.N. and in P.O.W. Camps	20.6.45 11.45.
JONES, J.I.	Lieut. (3rd Off.)		D.S.O. D.S.C. & Bar Twice Mentioned in Despatches.	R.N.R. at Greece and Crete For Distinguished Service while serving in HMS HYACINTH For capture intact of Italian submarine PERLA	1941. 26.11.42
JONES, T.J.	Able Seaman	EMPIRE TRUMPET	B.E.M.	For Meritorious Service in M.N.	8.1.44.
JONES, William	Master	LOGICIAN	O.B.E.	For Meritorious Service in M.N.	1942.
LACEY, T.J.	Master	DEFENDER	O.B.E.	For Meritorious Service in M.N.	26.6.45
LANGTON, W.J.	Chief Steward	DEFENDER	B.E.M.	For Meritorious Service in M.N.	9.1.46.
LEWIS, S.G.	Carpenter	OBSERVER	King's Commendation	For Meritorious Conduct in Action.	16.5.44.
LING, J.T.	Master	ADVISER	O.B.E.	For Meritorious Service in M.N.	9.1.45.
LONGSTAFF, G.	Bosun	CUSTODIAN	B.E.M	For Meritorious Service in M.N.	9.1.46.
MEEK, A.J.	Master	NOVELIST	O.B.E. and King's Commendation	For Meritorious Service in M.N.	9.1.46, 23.7.46.
MORETON, Alan	Second Officer	CONTRACTOR	M.B.E.	For Meritorious Service in M.N.	27.4.43.
MORRISON, J.A.	Third Engineer	ADVISER	M.B.E	For Meritorious Service in M.N.	9.1.45
MOSSMAN, E.H.	Chief Engineer		O.B.E.	For Meritorious Service in M.N.	9.1.46
NEWSOM, J.W	Chief Engineer		O.B.E	For Meritorious Service in M.N.	1943
PERCY, D.O.	Second Officer	AUDITOR	King's Commendation	For Meritorious Conduct in Action	15.9.42.
PETERKIN, A.G.	Master		O.B.E.,	For Meritorious Service in M.N.	3.1.45
ROBERTS, A.T.	A.B	DEFENDER	King's Commendation	For Meritorious Conduct in M.N	26.6.45.
ROHMAN, Abdul	Officer's Boy	AUDITOR	B.E.M.	For Meritorious Conduct in Action.	15.4.42
RUSSELL, R.	Officers' Boy (Aged 15).	DALESMAN	War Risks Association's Gold Watch.	For Gallantry at Crete.	1941
SHORT, W.A.	Master		O.B.E.	For Meritorious Service in M.N.	15.6.45.
SMART, A.	Chief Officer	DAVISIAN	King's Commendation	For Meritorious Conduct in Action.	29.4.41.
SMITH, J.	Bosun	WANDERER	B.E.M.	For Meritorious Service in M.N	9.1.46.
SMITH, W.J	Quartermaster	OBSERVER	B.E.M.	For Meritorious Service in M.N.	16.5.44.
SWAIN, R.	Master	INVENTOR	King's Commendation	For Meritorious Service in M.N.	1943.
TRAYNOR, P	Fireman		B.E.M	For Meritorious Service in M.N.	3. 1.45.
WEATHERALL, W.	Master	DIRECTOR	King's Commendation (Twice)	For Meritorious Service in M.N.	9.1.45. 16.10.45.
WELLS, H.T.	Chief Officer	AUDITOR	King's Commendation	For Meritorious Conduct in Action.	15.9.42.
WILFORD, W.B	Master	RECORDER	O.B.E	For Meritorious Service in M.N.	27.4.43.
WILKINS, R.W.M.	Chief Engineer		O.B.E.	For Meritorious Service in M.N.	10.6.44

Abbreviations

B.E.M. British Empire Medal
D.S.C. Distinguished Service Cross
D.S.O. Distinguished Service Order
M.B.E. Member of the Order of the British Empire
M.N. Merchant Navy
O.B.E. Officer of the Order of the British Empire
R.N.R. Royal Naval Reserve

Since the award of Meritorious Conduct and Gallantry medals was strictly limited, many who deserved such recognition were often inevitably excluded. Such names, as submitted by the company, are remembered here:

Allen, S.	Bosun	Jones, W. A.	Second Engineer	Nowlan, H.	Fireman
Biles, S.T.B.	Bosun	Kane, A.J.	Second Engineer	Paton, H.	Second Engineer
Boam, C.S.S.	Second Officer	Keig, J.	Able Seaman	Penston, G.H.	Chief Officer
Brown, W.J.	Third Officer	Kelly, T.A.	Chief Engineer	Price, S.	Second Engineer
Catterall, R.A.	Third Engineer	King, W.	Deckhand	Rowan, F.E.	E.R.S.
Coates, H.	Master	Lake, J.	Able Seaman	Sabin, E.	Cadet
Craig, H.	Chief Steward	Ledger, R.H.K.	Second Officer	Savage, G.A.	Donkeyman
Dempsey, T.	Donkeyman	McCormick, N.S.	Second Officer	Sawle, W.L.	Master
Frew, A.	Master	McKee, J.	Fireman	Sharp, A.G.	Chief Engineer
Harvey, G.	Second Officer	Magan, P.J.	Donkeyman	Stephens, E.B.	Master
Head, C.E.E.	Deckhand	Mainey, H.	Chief Steward	Watts, C.V.	Second Officer
Horne, E.G.	Master	Malcolm, J.	Deckhand	Williams, R.L.	Chief Officer
Jones, D.V.	Second Officer	Milburn, G.H.	Chief Steward	Young, R.	Carpenter
Jones, W.	Fireman	Moore, W.	Master		

INDEX OF SHIPS

All ships mentioned are listed. Names in capitals are those carried whilst in Harrisons' ownership of management, with the fleet list number being given in brackets. Page numbers of fleet list entries are in bold type.

INDEX OF PERSONS

Partners, shareholders, employees, and associates of Harrisons are listed, and other individuals mentioned in the history and anecdotes, but not owners and managers of ships before or after their time in the Harrison fleet.

The chartered German container ship *Actor* (23,986/98) is believed to have been the last vessel to carry Harrison colours.

[W. Paul Clegg]

A final look at a Harrison ship on Merseyside, the second *Naturalist* (265) in Liverpool Docks.　　　*[S.H. Bulgin]*